CHEFS AND CRITICS ALIKE LOVE
JOY OF COOKING

"This book is number one on my list . . . *the* one
book of all cookbooks that I would have
on my shelf—if I could have but one."
—Julia Child

"The finest basic cookbook available.
A masterpiece of clarity."
—Craig Claiborne

"The classic work, which covers the entire gamut of
kitchen procedures and is easy to use."
—James Beard

"The best-loved, most important cookbook to
come out of the United States."
—Cecily Brownstone

VOLUME II
APPETIZERS, DESSERTS AND BAKED GOODS

Joy
OF
COOKING

Irma S. Rombauer

Marion Rombauer Becker

Illustrated by Ginnie Hofmann
and Ikki Matsumoto

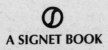

A SIGNET BOOK

SIGNET
Published by the Penguin Group
Penguin Putnam Inc., 375 Hudson Street,
New York, New York 10014, U.S.A.
Penguin Books Ltd, 27 Wrights Lane,
London W8 5TZ, England
Penguin Books Australia Ltd, Ringwood,
Victoria, Australia
Penguin Books Canada Ltd, 10 Alcorn Avenue,
Toronto, Ontario, Canada M4V 3B2
Penguin Books (N.Z.) Ltd, 182–190 Wairau Road,
Auckland 10, New Zealand

Penguin Books Ltd, Registered Offices:
Harmondsworth, Middlesex, England

Published by Signet, an imprint of Dutton Signet,
a member of Penguin Putnam Inc.

Published by arrangement with Scribner, an imprint of Simon and Schuster,
Inc. Originally published by the Bobbs-Merrill Company, Inc.

First Signet Printing, November, 1997
10 9 8 7 6 5 4 3

Ⓡ REGISTERED TRADEMARK — MARCA REGISTRADA

Printed in the United States of America

To friends of the **Joy** who over the years through their countless letters and words of appreciation have made us feel that our efforts are worthwhile.

"That which thy fathers have bequeathed to thee, earn it anew if thou wouldst possess it."
—GOETHE: *Faust*

ACKNOWLEDGMENTS

Joy has always been a family affair. Written by my mother, Irma Starkloff Rombauer, a St. Louisan, it was tested and illustrated by me, with technical assistance from my mother's secretary, Mary Whyte Hartrich. It was privately printed in 1931 and distributed from the home. The responses Joy evoked were collected and published on its thirtieth birthday in a celebratory account entitled Little Acorn. Now over forty, Joy continues to be a family affair, revealing more than ever the awareness we all share in the growing preciousness of food.

Since his retirement from architectural practice, my husband, John, has given constant and unstinting effort toward Joy's enrichment. My sons—Ethan, with his Cordon Bleu and camping experiences, and Mark, with his interest in natural foods—have reinforced Joy in many ways, as has my own sensitivity over the years to a oneness with the environment, culminating in the highly satisfying experience of writing Wild Wealth with ecologists Frances Jones Poetker and Paul Bigelow Sears.

As the scope of Joy has increased, so have other generous sources of proffered knowledge—too many and too specialized to mention in detail. Ever-ready understanding has continued to come from Jane Brueggeman, our valued co-worker for thirty years; from our competent home economics consultants Lolita Harper and Lydia Cooley; from our legal literary aide, Harriet Pilpel; from our guide to the New York cooking world, Cecily Brownstone; and from our kitchen mainstay, Isabell Coleman. More recently we have received thorough testing help from Joan Woerndle Becker, devoted editorial advice from Marian Judell Israel, and perfectionist secretarial assistance from Nancy Swats. Throughout the years Leo Gobin, now president of Bobbs-Merrill, has guarded for us great freedom in our work, and Eugene Rachlis, the editor-in-chief, has lent a sympathetic ear. Thanks also to Gladys Moore, our copy editor, for unending patience; to William Bokermann for the excellent book design; and to John van Biezen for his care in the physical production of this edition. We are sure our readers are as grateful as we are to Ginnie Hofmann and Ikki Matsumoto, whose drawings so skillfully enhance our text.

But **Joy**, we hope, will always remain essentially a family affair, as well as an enterprise in which its authors owe no obligation to anyone but themselves and you.

—MARION ROMBAUER BECKER

CONTENTS

FOREWORD

We present you first with the front-door key to this book. Whenever we emphasize an important principle, we insert a pointer to success ▶. We use other graphic symbols, too—❀, ▲, ( ), ◗, 人, 目, ★—described on the next page to alert you quickly to foods appropriate for certain occasions or prepared by certain methods. Among the symbols is the parenthesis, which indicates that an ingredient is optional. Its use may enhance, but its omission will not prejudice the success of a recipe. ▶ Note, too, the special meanings of the following terms as we use them. Any meat, fish, or cereal, unless otherwise specified, is raw, not cooked. Eggs are the 2-ounce size; milk means fresh whole milk; butter is sweet and unsalted; chocolate means bitter baking chocolate; flour denotes the unbleached all-purpose variety; spices are ground, not whole; condensed canned soup or milk is to be used undiluted. In response to many requests from users of the **Joy** who ask "What are your favorites?" we have indicated some by adding to a few recipe titles the word "Cockaigne," which in medieval times signified "a mythical land of peace and plenty" and which we chose as the name for our country home. Where a recipe bears a classic title, you can be assured that it contains the essential ingredients or methods that created its name in the first place. And for rapidity of preparation we have grouped in Brunch, Lunch and Supper Dishes many quickly made recipes based on cooked and canned food.

There is a back-door key, too—the Index. This will open up for you and lead you to such action terms as simmer, casserole, braise, and sauté; such descriptive ones as printanière, bonne femme, rémoulade, allemande, and meunière; and to national culinary enthusiasms such as couscous, Devonshire cream, strudel, zabaglione, rijsttafel and gazpacho.

Other features of this book which we ask you to investigate include the chapter on Heat, which gives you many clues to maintaining the nutrients in the food you are cooking. Know Your Ingredients reveals vital characteristics of the materials you commonly combine, how and why they react as they do, how to measure them and, when feasible, how to substitute one for another. Then, in the paragraphs marked "About," you will find information relating to those food categories, including the amounts to buy.

But, even more important, we hope that in answering your question "What shall we have for dinner?" you will find in Foods We Eat a stimulus to combine foods wisely. Using this information, you may say with Thomas Jefferson, "No knowledge can be more satisfactory to a man than that of his own frame, its parts, their functions and actions." Choose from our offerings what suits your person, your lifestyle, your pleasure; and join us in the joy of cooking.

—M.R.B.

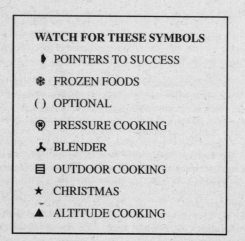

WATCH FOR THESE SYMBOLS

❧ POINTERS TO SUCCESS

❀ FROZEN FOODS

( ) OPTIONAL

❂ PRESSURE COOKING

⋏ BLENDER

▤ OUTDOOR COOKING

★ CHRISTMAS

▲ ALTITUDE COOKING

ENTERTAINING

When you are entertaining, try not to feel that something unusual is expected of you as a hostess. It isn't. Just be yourself. Even eminent and distinguished persons are only human. Like the rest of us, they shrink from ostentation; and nothing is more disconcerting to a guest than the impression that his coming is causing a household commotion. Confine all noticeable efforts for his comfort and refreshment to the period that precedes his arrival. Satisfy yourself that you have anticipated every possible emergency—the howling child, the last-minute search for cuff links, your husband's exuberance, your helper's ineptness, your own qualms. Then relax and enjoy your guests.

If, at the last minute, something does happen to upset your well-laid plans, rise to the occasion. The mishap may be the making of your party. Capitalize on it, but not too heavily. Remember that 'way back in Roman times the poet Horace observed, "A host is like a general: it takes a mishap to reveal his genius."

We are frequently asked what is the ideal number for a dinner party. Estimates vary. On the absurd side, we are reminded of the response made to this question by a less-than-gregarious nineteenth-century gourmet: "Myself and the headwaiter"; and of Aubrey Menen's Ceylonese grandmother, who regarded the act of eating as so vulgar that she practiced it only when alone, in complete seclusion. Seriously speaking, there is no ideal answer to the question. Some of the reasons will become apparent in the discussion that follows. Yet there is probably a workable minimum; and unless the guests are very close friends, that minimum much exceeds two. Back in the living room afterward, first-time acquaintances must be able to exercise options and establish small centers of mutual interest; and we suggest that this can only be engineered with any degree of success among groups of at least eight. Twelve is an even happier number.

The procedures below represent simple, dignified current practice in table service. If you plan to serve cocktails or nonalcoholic beverages before a meal, have glasses ready on a tray. With the apéritif, you may pass some form of cracker, canapé or hors d'oeuvre. If you and your guests are discriminating diners, you will keep this pickup light. Too generous quantities of food and drink beforehand will bring jaded palates to the dinner on which you have expended such effort. Should you have the kind of guests who enjoy a long cocktail period and varied hors d'oeuvre, be sure to season your dinner food more highly than usual. You may politely shorten the cocktail preliminaries, which have a bad habit these days of going on indefinitely, by serving a delicious hot or cold consommé or soup, either near the bar area or from a tureen on a cart.

Never forget that your family is really the most important assembly you ever entertain. Whether for them or for friends ▶ always check the freshness of the air, the temperature of the dining area, and the proper heat or chill for plates, food and drinks—especially hot ones. If warming oven space is limited, use the heat cycle of your dishwasher; or, if you entertain often, you may wish to install an infrared heating unit which can be raised or lowered above a heatproof counter. Be sure that each diner has plenty of elbow room, about 30 inches from the center of one plate service to the center of the next.

Formal meals, given in beautifully appointed homes, served by competent, well-trained servants—who can be artists in their own right—are a great treat. We cannot expect to have ideal conditions at all times in the average home. However, no matter what the degree of informality, always be sure that the table is attractive and immaculately clean—and always maintain, as nearly as possible, an even rhythm of service.

TABLE DÉCOR

As to the table itself, a top that is heat- and stain-resistant lends itself to the greatest ease of service and upkeep. You can expose as much or as little of its surface as you like. If you have a tabletop of natural hardwood, you must protect it against heat at all times with pads or trivets.

For versatility and effective contrast, keep your basic flatware and dishes simple in form and not too pronounced in pattern or color. Then you can combine them, without fear of clashing, with varied linens, fruits and flowers and—most importantly—varied foods. You will find that changes in décor and accessories stimulate the appetite as much as changes in seasoning.

It is pleasant to vary table presentations by serving soup not only in cups and bowls, but from a tureen; or by making use of a crescent-shaped salad plate designed to fit at the side of a round dinner plate and so give the table a less crowded feeling. Individual serving dishes for vegetables may be replaced by an outsized platter holding several kinds of vegetables attractively garnished.

Also, small raw vegetables and fruits may be subtituted for garnishes of parsley and cress to give meat platters a festive air. Instead of using pairs of matching dessert dishes, try contrasting bowls of glass or bright pottery. For a rustic effect, serve a hearty menu on your everyday dishes and use light linens and wooden salad bowls with a centerpiece of wooden scoops filled with pears and hazelnuts in the husk.

For a more elegant effect, serve a dainty meal on porcelain and crystal dishes, against a polished board decorated with fragile glasses and flowers. See sketch below.

Whatever your decorative scheme, flower arrangements should be low or lacy. Tall arrangements that obstruct the view discourage across-the-table conversation. There is nothing more distracting than dodging a floral centerpiece while trying to establish an intimate relationship among your guests. For the same reason, candles should be placed strategically. On a formal buffet or tea table, which is viewed from above, the decorations may be as tall as you wish. In fact, food or lower accents that are elevated on epergnes or stemmed dishes add a note of drama.

Lacking an antique epergne, you can still expand the impact of flowers and fruit on a framework structured from tumblers, tinware or silverware, as shown in the chapter heading. Leaves and bloom clusters, vines and fruits bind these disparate elements and disguise or expose their origins. There, as suggested by my friend and one of my coauthors of *Wild Wealth*, Frances Jones Poetker, is an opulent arrangement made on a bare structure she suggested of a reversed wide bowl surmounted by a flat plate on which a stemmed compote is centered—and centered on that, in turn, a stemmed glass.

Several harmonious small containers of flowers or fruit—similar or varied—can be effectively grouped around a central element or scattered along the length of a table to replace a single focal point such as the one described above. One of these small units could be long-needled pine tufts bracing snowdrops; or clematis, as illustrated in the semiformal luncheon service, at left.

A piece of sculpture scaled to your table makes a charming base for a centerpiece. Surround it with an ivy ring and vary the décor from time to time with other greenery or any elements that suggest borders or garlands. If the sculpture is slightly raised on a base, it can be enjoyed to great advantage. Whatever you use, don't overcrowd the table. One of the most important things to remember is that ♦ no matter what the decoration, it should be suited in color and scale to the foods served to enhance it. Don't make your efforts so stagey that your guests' reactions will be, "She went to a lot of trouble." Make them say, rather, "She had a lot of fun doing it!"

Consider, too, the colors of the flowers, food and linens available to you, and plan your menu accordingly. Beets or beet soup may be just the strengthening note you want on a cold day;

grapefruit and avocado may bring that chill delicacy of palette you need for a torrid summer lunch. The sources at your command are really legion.

Cramped dining quarters can be eased by unconventional service distribution—a bar in the study, soup on the patio or on a traveling tea cart, a long, narrow buffet to facilitate traffic flow. But whether the party is large or intimate, you can stretch your normal equipment with unconventional use of trays, baskets, pumpkin soup tureens, watermelon fruit bowls, or ice punch bowls, 57.

TABLE SETTING

There are certain time-honored positions for tableware and equipment that result from the way food is eaten and served. So keep in mind these basic placements. ◗ Forks to the left except the very small fish fork, which goes to the right. ◗ Spoons, including iced-tea spoons, and knives to the right, with the sharp edge of the knife toward the plate. There is, of course, a practical reason for placing the knife at the diner's right, since right-handed persons, who predominate, commonly wield the knife with their favored hand, and do so early in the meal. Generally, having cut his food, the diner lays down his knife and transfers his fork to the right hand. Formal dining makes an exception to this rule; and with left-handed or ambidextrous persons the transfer seems superfluous to us, on any occasion. ◗ Place flatware that is to be used first farthest from the plate. It is also better form never to have more than three pieces of flatware at either side. Bring in any other needed table utensils on a small tray as the course is served. The server is always careful to handle tableware by the handles

only, including carving and serving spoons and forks, which are placed to the right of the serving dish.

If you look at some of the place settings illustrated, you can, with a few exceptions, practically predict the menu. Let's consider the semiformal luncheon setting, 3. Line up the bases of the handles about one inch from the edge of the table. Some people still consider it important to supply a knife at luncheon, even if that knife is not needed for the actual cutting of meat. Others omit the knife if a typical luncheon casserole is passed or is served in individual containers. For a formal luncheon, a butter plate is placed to the left on a level with the waterglass. The butter knife is usually located as shown, and a butter ball or curl, 201, is already in place before the guests are seated. Later, the butter plate is removed simultaneously with the salad plate. Both are taken from the left side. The butter plate is picked up with the left hand, the salad plate with the right.

At semiformal luncheons, you may have the dessert spoon and fork in place above the plate, as sketched on 3. This indicates that no finger bowl will be supplied. Or you may, as in the dinner service, bring the dessert silver to the table with the finger bowl, as sketched on 9.

Water and wine glasses are already in place as sketched on 3. The water is poured in the former to about two-thirds capacity; the wineglasses are left empty. ◗ Glasses are filled from the right and are never lifted by the server when pouring. Goblet types are always handled by the stem in presentation, replacement or removal by the diner or server; tumbler types are always held well below the rim.

When it is time to serve coffee, empty cups and saucers are placed to the right. There is a spoon on the saucer, behind the cup and parallel to the cup handle, which is turned to the diner's right. After all the cups are placed, they are filled by the server, and afterward sugar and cream are offered from a small tray from the left. But the entire coffee service may be offered, even for luncheon, in the living room, after the dessert.

Individual ashtrays and cigarettes may be placed on the table. Fortunately, a host or hostess is not required to press his conviction that smoking is injurious to either health or gastronomy. But if you are a strong-willed hostess, you may prefer to have the ashtrays and cigarettes placed on the table just after the dessert is served.

At informal dinner parties, place cards may be omitted and the hostess may indicate where guests are to sit. When the diners number six, ten or fourteen, the host is at one end of the table, the hostess at the other. If the guests number eight or twelve and you want to alternate men and women guests, place the host at one end and the hostess to the left of the other end.

The honor guest, if a woman, is seated to the right of the host; if a man, to the left of the hostess. At a formal meal, a dish is presented, but ◗ not served, to the hostess first. Food is actually offered first to the woman guest of honor. The other women are then all served. Finally, the men are served, beginning with the guest of honor. If there is no special guest of honor, you may want to reverse the direction of service every other course, so that the same people are not always served last.

While it is not the best form, some people prefer to have the hostess served first. She knows the menu, and by the way she serves herself she

sets the pattern for the other guests. This is a special help if the guest of honor is from another country. In America it is customary for guests to wait until everyone is served and the hostess begins to eat. In Europe, however, where each course is usually served complete on one plate, it is permissible to start eating as soon as one is served.

◗ Plates are usually removed from the right and placed or passed from the left. Service and dinner plates are frequently of different patterns. For the purpose of clarity in the illustrations following, service plates are sketched with a solid banding, plates on which cold food is being served are shown with a thin double-banded edge, and plates for hot food are unadorned.

FORMAL ENTERTAINMENT

Most of us moderns look with amazement, not to say dismay, at the menus of traditionally formal dinners. Such meals are a vanishing breed, like the whale—but, like the whale, some manage to survive. They begin with both clear and thick soups. Then comes an alternation of **entrées** and **relevés**, each with its accompanying vegetables. The relevés are lighter in quality and fewer in number than the hefty joints and whole fish which make up the entrées; but by current standards many of them amply qualify as main dishes in their own right.

However, in the parlance of the haute cuisine, the term "entrée" had a quite different significance. Classic entrées commonly occurred immediately after the main entrée as we now define it, and consisted of timbales, seafoods and variety meats, served in rich pastes and with delicate sauces—tidbits distinguished for their elegance.

A **salad** takes next place in this stately procession and is usually made of a seasoned cooked vegetable such as asparagus, with greens doing garnish duty only. After this, the diner may choose from a variety of cheeses.

Entremets—hot or cold sweets—succeed the cheese course; and these are topped off, in turn, by both hot and cold fruits. Thus, in outline—if "outline" can be regarded as *le mot juste*—a dinner in the grand manner; except, of course, to add that each course is accompanied by a choice and sympathetic wine.

We marvel at the degree of sophistication required to appreciate so studied and complex a service—to say nothing of the culinary skills needed to present the menu in proper style. But, more critically, we ask, "Where do the guests stow away all that food?" Granted that a truly formal dinner lasts for hours and that each portion may be a dainty one, the total intake is still bound to be formidable. Such an array is seldom encountered in this casual and girth-conscious era. But a semiformal dinner with traces of classic service still graces the privileged household.

When the guests come into the dining room, the table is all in readiness. ♦ Again the setting forecasts the menu through the first three courses. If more silver is required, it is always brought in separately later. The water glasses are about two-thirds full; the wineglasses, though empty, stand in place, see illustrations opposite.

At formal and semiformal dinners, butter plates are seldom used. Melba toast or crackers are served with the appetizer or soup, and hard rolls without butter later, with the roast.

The setting indicates a seafood cocktail, a soup, a meat course, 8, a salad course, water and two wines. Water and wine are poured from the right. The glasses may stay in place throughout the meal, but it is preferable to remove each wineglass after use. A third wineglass may be strung out on a line with the others or placed to form a triangle slightly forward toward the guest and just above the soup spoon. However, if more than three wines are to be served, fresh glasses replace the used glasses as the latter are removed.

Once the guests are seated, the server's steady but unobtrusive labor begins ♦ There is a plate, filled or unfilled, before each guest throughout the meal. The server usually removes a plate from the right and replaces it immediately with another from the left, so that the courses follow one another in unbroken succession. At such a dinner, second helpings are seldom offered.

When a platter is presented, it is offered from the left to the guest by the server, who holds it on a folded napkin on the palm of his left hand, and may steady it with the right. The server should always make sure that the handles of the serving tools are directed toward the diner.

The passing of crackers, breads and relishes, the refilling of water glasses, and the pouring of wines take place during, not between, the appropriate courses. When the party is less formal, the host may prefer to pour the wines himself from a decanter or from a bottle. If the wine is chilled, he will wrap it in a napkin, and hold a napkin in the left hand to catch any drip from the bottle. The hostess on such occasions may pass relishes to the guest at her right, and the guests may continue to pass them on to one another. Also, relishes may be arranged at strategic places on the table, but must be removed with the soup. However, even with these slight assists, the work of the server is one that calls for nicely calculated timing. It is easy to see why ♦ one server should not be called on to take care of more than six or eight guests—at the most—if smooth going is expected.

Let us go back to our dinner, which begins—as forecast by the setting sketched below—with a seafood cocktail, and goes on to the soup. The seafood, served in a specially iced glass, is in place when the guests enter the dining room.

After the seafood has been eaten, the empty seafood cocktail glasses are removed—leaving the service plate intact. The soup plate is placed on it—served from the left. Crackers and relishes are presented.

The service plate is now removed,

along with the empty soup plate, from the right. If a platter of hot food is to be passed, an empty hot plate is placed before the guest—from the left.

However, if the meat course is to be carved and served in the dining

room, the soup plate only is removed, leaving the service plate before the guest. The meat platter is put before the host, who carves enough meat for all the guests before any further serving takes place. The server, who has replaced the host's service plate with a hot one, stands to the left of the host, holding an extra hot plate on a napkin. When the host has filled the individual plate before him, the server removes it and replaces it with the empty hot plate he has been holding. Then, after taking the service place in front of the guest of honor from the right, the server gives him the filled hot plate from the left, returns to the host via the buffet for the next hot plate, and waits to replace the plate being filled by the host for another guest.

When all guests have been attended to, the server passes the gravy and then the vegetables—with a serving spoon and fork face down on the platter and the handles directed toward the guest. The hot breads come next. During this course, the server replenishes water and wine.

The menu we have been serving has consisted of three courses: seafood cocktail, soup, meat-and-vegetable. A salad and dessert course will follow; but first let us consider a different menu—one that omits the cocktail and introduces a fish course.

Obviously, a different setting of flatware is in order for this alternate menu. The illustration will show you that it consists of soup, first. After that, there is a fish course, followed by meat, salad and so on. You will notice that there are one water and two wine glasses. Because no seafood cocktail is included, the napkin is placed on the service plate, with a place card on top. For this setting, individual salts are placed to the left of the glasses, and a small dish of mixed nuts is centered above the service plate. No other food is on the table when the guests are seated.

For this second menu, plates of soup are passed from the left and

placed directly on the service plates—after guests have removed napkins and place cards.

After the soup has been relished, the soup plate and service plate are removed together from the right and the fish course, arranged in the pantry on individual plates, is presented next from the left. If sherry accompanied the soup, the sherry glass is removed at this time.

After the server has removed the empty fish plate from the right, a hot plate is put before the guest from the left, as shown next.

The meat course follows—either carved by the host, or previously arranged in the pantry. A vegetable placed on a narrow so-called bone plate shown to the left of the meat plate may follow. With such vegetables as asparagus and artichokes, or salads with vinegar dressings, no wines are served.

A handsomely arranged fruit compote, passed during the meat course, can be used as an alternate to a salad. If a compote is substituted for a salad, a spoon is put on the right of the setting, instead of a salad fork on the left, as illustrated.

The next illustration shows a separate salad set-up after the meat course

is removed. After the salad course is removed, the table is denuded for a

short time. Any unused flatware, salts and peppers and relishes are taken away. The table is crumbed. The server uses a folded napkin and brushes the crumbs lightly onto a plate or a crumb tray.

Now, the dessert setting with the finger bowl and doily is placed in front of each guest.

The finger bowl, partially filled with water, may have a scented geranium leaf, a fragrant herb or flower, or a thin slice of lemon floating in it. Each guest places the fork and spoon to either side of the plate and then puts the doily, with finger bowl on it, to the upper left side of his place setting—opposite the water glass.

An exception to this finger bowl procedure is made when fruit is to be served after dessert. In this case, the dessert plate complete with flatware

is placed in front of each guest. After the dessert has been passed and eaten, the dessert plate is removed. Next comes a fruit plate with doily, finger bowl, fruit knife and fork.

Should coffee be served at the table, empty demitasse cups and saucers are, at this time, placed to the right of the diners. Demitasse spoons are on the saucers, behind the cup and parallel to the handle. Coffee is poured from the right and cream and sugar passed on a small tray from the left. Liqueur may be served with the coffee or passed on a tray later, in the living room.

Women's liberation works both ways. A host or hostess may still welcome a lull of 15 minutes or more after dinner, during which the sexes are segregated and free to develop conversational topics of special and specific interest. The traditional— and entirely suitable—time for such a break is between dessert and coffee. The men may remain in the dining room to converse over glasses of port or brandy; or the entire company, after the English custom, may first share a savory, 542. The hostess may then retire to the drawing room with the ladies and later pour coffee for her reassembled guests there. By this time, good food, wine and conviviality have usually broken down the minor social inhibitions, and the coffee service may be completely informal.

INFORMAL ENTERTAINMENT

Your chances for a successful informal dinner party are much greater if you key your efforts to your own belongings and service rather than struggling to meet the exacting demands of the kind of dinner just described. ◗ Plan a menu that will make advance preparation and last-minute serving feasible. Offer fewer courses and put several kinds of food on one platter. But please do not let your guests sit, trying to make conversation, with a rapidly congealing slice of meat before them, waiting with embarrassment for a seemingly shipwrecked gravy boat to follow.

There are actually two kinds of informal company meals—and by informal we mean those which can be successfully carried off by a hostess acting more or less alone. The first is a small sitdown affair; and when we say small we mean one limited to eight guests—six is a more confidence-inspiring number. Such a dinner flourishes not on spur-of-the-moment activity but on careful forethought and now and then some nimble footwork. Main dishes should be limited to two or three: a casserole, for instance, an aspic and a pôtde-crème. Many such dishes that can be prepared in advance will be found in the chapters on Lunch, Brunch and Supper Dishes; Salads; and Frozen Desserts. Five minutes before your guests are expected, everything should be organized and in readiness: hors d'oeuvre and cocktails—which may be simple—on a conveniently available side table, plates warming in the oven, and dining table completely set, needing only that last-minute ceremonial touch—the lighting of the candles.

One of the hostess's more important roles is a deliberately unobtrusive one. After she sees to it that serving dishes and implements are in place on the table, she sets the first main dish and a stack of heated plates in front of the host, whose responsibility it becomes to fill them and pass them along to the guests. She then promptly takes her own seat at table, determined not only to remain graciously installed there until the time comes for main-dish replenishment or for bringing on another course, but to be generally at ease throughout the rest of the meal.

When the guests have finished the first course, serving initiatives are largely hers. She gathers the plates left over from the first course, removes them from the dining area, and reappears with whatever serving dishes and implements are needed for the next course. These she sets at her own place at table; she seats herself again and serves each guest in turn, repeating the host's previous procedure. The main objective here is to ensure that guests and hosts remain at table: nothing disrupts a little sit-down dinner so much as the inclination of anyone present to execute a series of disappearing acts and U-turns.

The hostess's continuing presence

may be further assured by arranging to serve the wine in a decanter, which can be passed from hand to hand during the meal, like the relishes and the bread. The bread, incidentally, may be of the crusty-loaf variety cut into thick slices and buttered, then warmed in the same oven used to heat the dinner plates.

For removing relishes and odd items, a small tray is handy. "Crumbing" may be dispensed with. But do resist the messy and quite intolerable practice of stacking plates as you remove them from the table.

While we deplore the kind of pinch-hitting that often turns the maidless dinner into a volunteer free-for-all, we do not in the least reject an unobtrusive dependable assist from the host, or from a close friend of the hostess who knows her way around the house and is cooperatively disposed. The host may help by carrying out such far-flung responsibilities as mixing salads and drinks, greeting the guests and taking care of their wraps, inquiring about and distributing "seconds," and in general seeing to it that the company is kept promptly and well supplied. The help that a close friend can proffer is less thoroughgoing and less well defined: it may vary from filling water glasses to clearing the table. Whatever its extent, it should stop short of officiousness. A hostess who wants to keep her sanity should resolutely resist the invasion of her kitchen by a guest who is inspired to "keep her company" while she makes her final preparations for the meal.

In order for food to reach the table at the right temperature, it is wise to use such aids as covered dishes—in which case, remember to allow a place to put hot lids; double dishes with provision underneath for ice or hot water; and a samovar arrangement for hot drinks.

For both service and removal, a cart may facilitate matters, unless there are children trained to lend unobtrusive help. Impromptu deputization of your guests may invite chaos and should be avoided except in extreme emergencies or in deliberate plans such as those described in participatory menus, 30.

BUFFET SERVICE

Obviously, from the hostess's standpoint, buffet service is the most satisfactory way to take care of large groups informally. However, under no circumstances should you expect your guests to eat without enough chairs or table space for all.

Plan a menu from foods that hold well, keeping hot foods above 140° and cold foods below 40°. The best way to keep an attractive buffet looking that way is to concentrate on individual portions. These can be replenished easily, thus preserving the looks of the table. For instance, rather than a large aspic, use individual fancy molds—even if released from paper cups. Use sea shells or vegetable cups, (I, 53), as individual containers for seafood or other mixtures. You may cut turkey, ham and salmon into individual portions. Also

see About Stuffed Vegetables, (I, 284), and Cases for Food, (I, 236). For garnishes see (I, 53 and 54).

Types of food especially suitable for buffet service are a risotto or jambalaya, a goulash, a seafood Newburg, moussaka, empanadas, a cheese tray. Meats served **en croûte**, (I, 556), and as **chaud-froid**, (I, 428), make dramatic features of buffet service. Both types of preparation keep buffet food from drying out. Avoid soups and other sloshy food that may prove hazardous for diners in motion.

If the servings are not individual, cater generously, as guests are apt to take larger portions at buffets. Layouts below and on 12 show typical buffet settings. The first one represents a dinner at which the host or hostess serves the guests, who then proceed to tables which are already set. The menu includes duck with orange cups, wild rice, podded peas and a green salad. The serving platters are later removed and replaced by the dessert; or individual desserts may be served at table.

Note again that height in candles or flowers is often a distinct asset in buffet service, as is the use of tiered dishes.

The drawing on 12 shows a buffet at which the guests serve themselves and proceed to sit at small tables. If there are no tables, individual trays

may be used. For tray service, plan food that does not call for the use of a knife.

Shown are a meat or fish casserole dish; artichokes vinaigrette filled with masked hard-cooked eggs with herbs; relishes and rolls. A dessert may be on the table at the beginning of the service. If the serving table seems too crowded, place the water and hot drinks on another serving surface.

TEA SERVICE

The institution of afternoon tea is going out of fashion—menaced on the one hand by the cocktail party and on the other by the "coffee break," which in America is beginning to assume the proportions of a compound fracture. We still find tea or coffee in the afternoon—whether of the formal or the informal type—a revivifying event, even if an occasional one. When it is informal, the hostess does the honors alone. However, when the tea is formal, friends of the hostess sit at each end of the table and consider it a privilege to pour.

The drawing on 14 shows a handsome, formal tea set-up with a coffee service at one end. Tea may be served at the other. It is wise to instruct a supplier to keep in frequent touch with the pourers to anticipate their need for additional hot water, coffee or cups. It is also canny to have additional platters

ready to replace those at the table that have become rather ragged-looking. Medium-sized rather than large platters are easier to keep in trim.

CASUAL ENTERTAINING FOR ONE OR FOR MANY

Tray meals can be a delightful stimulant if they include a surprise element in the form of a lovely pitcher, a small flower arrangement or some seasonal delicacy. Make sure, especially if the recipient is an invalid, that all needed utensils are present, that the food is hot or cold as required, sufficient in amount and fresh and dainty looking.

A cookout, whether a mere wienie roast or a luau, can be—although it seldom is anymore—one of the least complicated ways to entertain. Unless your equipment is equal to that of a well-appointed kitchen and you can assure your guests of comparably controlled cooking, we suggest that you choose menus that are really enhanced by outdoor cooking procedures, (I, 108).

Have enough covered dishes on hand to protect food from flies. Give your guests a tray or a traylike plate if there are no regular places set or normal seating arrangements. And prepare an alternate plan of accommodation in case of bad weather.

We recall an informal party that was really too big for our quarters and whose pattern might provide a substitute for a weather-beleaguered barbecue. The guests arrived to find no evidence of entertaining, only a most gorgeous arrangement of colchicum, those vibrant fall blooms that resemble vast, reticulated crocuses. After drinks were served and hors d'oeuvre passed, the host circulated a cart with soup tureen and cups. In its wake followed tray baskets containing white paper bags, each fitted out with individual chicken salad, olives, endive filled with avocado, cocktail tomatoes, cress and cheese sandwiches, bunches of luscious grapes and foil-wrapped brownies. Coffee was served, again from the circulating cart.

In order to get an informal after-supper party rolling, young hostesses are often so eager to present the fruits of their labors that refreshments are served too early for the comfort of the guests, most of whom have rather recently dined. Instead of hustling in solid food and alcoholic or carbonated drinks, it might be pleasant to open the proceedings with a tisane, (I, 31).

Here are a few parting reminders as we wind up this chapter on entertaining. In cooking for more people than you are normally accustomed to, allow yourself enough extra time both for preparing the food and for heating or cooling it. Please read the comments on the enlarging of recipes, 283. Be sure that your mixing and cooking equipment is scaled to take care of your group, and ▶ most important of all, that you have the refrigerator space to protect chilled dishes and the heated surfaces to maintain the temperature of the hot ones. Don't hesitate to improvise steam tables or iced trays. Utilize insulated picnic boxes or buckets either way, and wheelbarrows or tubs for the cracked ice on which to keep platters chilled.

If you often entertain casually, it may be worthwhile to make—as one of our friends did—a large rectangular galvanized deep tray on which the dishes of a whole cold buffet can be kept chilled. Or try confecting an epergne-like form such as that shown on 53 for chilling seafoods, hors d'oeuvre or fruit.

For camping trips or boating parties, consider the safety factor when choosing the menu. No matter what the outing ▶ don't transport perishable foods in hot weather in the even hotter trunk of a car.

Not all types of entertaining—formal or casual or in-between—can be detailed here. But, whatever the occasion, assemble your tried skills in menu planning so as to reflect the distinctive character of your home. Flavor the occasion with your own personality. And keep handy somewhere, for emergency use, that cool dictum attributed to Colonel Chiswell Langhorne of Virginia: "Etiquette is for people who have no breeding; fashion for those who have no taste."

COOKING FOR
LARGE PARTIES

Most of the recipes in this book make 4 to 6 servings and will double satisfactorily for 8 to 12. But at times all of us are called on to produce meals for larger groups, and it is then that we must be on our guard. For unexpected surprises are apt to pop up just when we want everything to go particularly well. No matter how rich or how simple the menu, remember, first, that for special occasions it is preferable to cook from recipes with which you are familiar. Secondly, cook in several moderate-sized batches, rather than in one big chunk, because, mysterious as it sounds—but true, even for the experts—quantity cooking is not just a matter of indefinite multiplication, 283. If you overexpand, too, you may run into a number of other problems.

Take into account the longer time needed in preparation—not only for paring and washing of vegetables or drying salad greens, but for heating up large quantities. Even more important, you may be confronted with a sudden pinch of refrigerator space—discovering that the shelves are needed for properly chilling large aspics or puddings just when they should be doubling to keep other sizable quantities of food at safe temperatures. ▶ This warning is of great importance if you are serving stuffed fowl, creamed foods, ground meat, mayonnaise, cream puffs, custards or custard pies: these foods spoil readily without showing any evidence of hazard. Before completing the menu for larger groups, assess equipment for mixing, cooking, refrigerating and serving.

If the meal is a hot one, plan to use recipes involving both the oven and top burners. Increase your limited heating surfaces by supplementing them with electric skillets, steam tables or hot trays to hold food in good serving condition above 140°. But do check the electric capacity of your system.

If serving individual casseroles, see that you have enough oven space; or, if the casseroles are large, that they will fit. In fact, stage a dress rehearsal—from the cooking equipment requirement right through to the way the service dishes and table gear will be placed. Then, satisfied that the mechanical requirements are met, schedule the actual work on the menu so that enough can be done in advance to relieve the sink and the work surfaces of last-minute crowding and mess.

Stick not only to those dishes you are confident you can handle without worry, but to those that make sense for the time you can spare for them. If one dish is going to require much last-minute hand work and fiddling, balance it against others that can be preassembled or are easy to serve: casseroles, baked or scalloped dishes,

gelatins or frozen foods. See Menus for further suggestions, 16.

One of the hardest things in mass cooking is to give the food that personalized and cherished look that is achieved in intimate dinners. Do not hesitate to serve simple foods for company. Choose seasonal ingredients and cook them skillfully. Then wind up with a home-baked cake or pastry—nothing is more delicious or more appreciated. Guests are really captives, so build a menu, in any case, that is not too restrictive. If you decide on octopus pasta, be sure you know the guests are adventurous enough or have sophisticated enough palates to enjoy it—or that they know you well enough to be able to ask for an egg instead.

MENUS

When to eat what is a matter of ever-changing habit and custom. Think of an epicure's diet in pre-Communist China: the constant nibbling of small rich confections, interspersed with light, irregularly spaced meals. Think of the enormous breakfast, late dinner and bedtime repasts of early nineteenth-century England, with a little sherry and biscuit served at lunchtime to guarantee survival. And, if you imagine for a moment that we have triumphantly freed ourselves from the excesses of the Groaning Board, think of the multitude of strange hors d'oeuvre that are downed during a typical big cocktail party in the Age of Anxiety.

Present-day nutritionists are divided, the majority sticking to three square meals a day, while others advocate scrapping this custom in favor of a sort of Chinese dietary of intermittent snacks.

◗ For the sheer amounts of food that, according to statistics, hold the average American body and soul together, see 609. More importantly, check Foods We Eat, (I, 1). Whichever menu practice we decide to follow, there is in the combining of foods a perennial fascination; and we can still on all occasions respond sympathetically to Brillat-Savarin's aphorism: *"Menu malfait, dîner perdu."*

Below are some suggestions for assembling meals. They are suggestions only. Your tastes, girth, circumstances, market, mood—and, we hope, imagination—will modify them considerably. ◗ For further service suggestions, please read the previous chapter on Entertaining. Note also that individual recipes frequently carry recommendations for congenial or time-honored accompaniments.

◗ If the party is to include more people than you usually cook for, see 23 for important suggestions both for the safe handling of food and ease of preparation, and do check the availability of cooking and serving equipment and sufficiency of heating power.

BREAKFAST AND BRUNCH SUGGESTIONS

Breakfast can be the most exciting meal of the day, whether it is shared with those you love, or served in seclusion with time to contemplate ways to make the day meaningful. Or it can be delayed into that charming social hour called brunch. Whatever the setting, proteins are better utilized if they are eaten at breakfast time than at any other time of day, and nutritionists advise that one-third of our daily protein intake be allotted to this meal. If tea, coffee, hot chocolate or milk, all favorite breakfast beverages, fail to appeal to you with the menus below, try a tisane, (I, 31). Remember that hot chocolate and milk will add both calories and protein.

———

Banana slices and
orange sections, 125
Scrambled Eggs, (I, 215),
and Bacon, (I, 615)
Hot Whole Wheat
Biscuits, 350,
and honey

———

Papaya, 131, garnished with lime
French Omelet, (I, 222)
Bacon in Muffins, 345

———

Sliced fresh peaches, 131,
on hot cereal, (I, 177),
with milk and brown sugar

———

Chilled Tomato and Clam Juice, (I, 36)
Bagels, 324, and Cream Cheese, 71
Eggs with Smoked Salmon, (I, 215)

———

Orange and grapefruit sections, 125
Boiled Smoked Tongue, (I, 651),
and Scrambled Eggs, (I, 215)
Brioches, 320

———

Prunes in Wine, 135
Broiled Stuffed Mushrooms

Cockaigne, (I, 329),
garnished with watercress, (I, 45)
Toasted Cheese Bread, 304

———

Orange and Lime Juice, (I, 36)
Pecan Waffles, 150,
with Brown-Sugar
Butter Sauce, 570,
and Rich Cream Cheese, 195

———

Chilled fresh pears, 132
Eggs Poached in Wine, (I, 214)
Toasted Panettone, 327

———

Poached plums, 111
Buttered Hominy Grits, (I, 179)
Eggs Baked in Bacon Rings, (I, 218)
Broiled grapefruit, 127, with sherry
Grilled Kippers, (I, 492), on toast
with Scrambled Eggs, (I, 215)

———

Pork Scrapple or Goetta, (I, 637)
Hot Applesauce, 118, or
hot Poached Rhubarb, 137
Quick Drop Biscuits, 349

———

Eggs Poached in Tomato Soup, (I, 214)
Baked Winter Squash, (I, 364)
Melba Toast, 355,
and Bel Paese Cheese, 543

———

Dry cereal: wheat or
bran biscuit topped with
Baked Custard, 508, or Yogurt, 189,
and Sugared Strawberries, 122

———

Broiled Pineapple Rings, 112
Souffléed Omelet, (I, 223), with cheese
Whole-Grain Muffins, 345

———

Chilled Concord grapes, 128
Sautéed Sausage Meat
Patties, (I, 636),
topped with Poached Eggs, (I, 213)
Croissants, 322,
and Orange Marmalade, 673

———

Fresh black raspberries, 124
Creamed Chipped Beef, (I, 252),
on Toasted Oat Bread
Cockaigne, 310

———

Baked Fresh Fruit Compote, 111
French Toast Waffles, 152,
with Maple Syrup, 230
Canadian Bacon, (I, 616)

———

Blueberries, 122,
with sweet cream
Sautéed Ham and Eggs, (I, 614)
Quick Sour Cream Coffee
Cake, 339
Paradise Jelly, 665

———

Fresh Pineapple Cup, 135
Broiled Fresh Scrod, (I, 488),
with lemon garnish
Fried Cornmeal Mush, (I, 180)

———

Macedoine of Pears and
Melon Balls in Port, 107
Oyster and Chicken Croquettes, 163
Brioches, 320,
and Five-Fruits
Jam Cockaigne, 668

———

Pared rounds of honeydew melon
filled with red raspberries, 131
Ham and Potato Cakes, (I, 249)
Shirred Eggs, (I, 217)

———

Sliced mango, 129
Sautéed Chicken Livers
on Toast, (I, 639),
with Grilled Tomato Slices, (I, 367)

———

Cranberry Juice, (I, 37)
Corned Beef Hash
and Potatoes, (I, 254)
with Poached Eggs, (I, 213)

———

Canteloupe Melon Baskets, 131
Broiled Veal Kidneys, (I, 648)
Whole-Grain Toast, 309
Lime Marmalade, 673

———

Ripe or Poached Cherries, 124
Baked Brains and Eggs, (I, 646)
No-Knead Yeast Coffee Cake, 327

———

LUNCHEON SUGGESTIONS

Although various luncheon menus are listed below, you may turn to Brunch, Lunch and Supper Dishes, (I, 236); Pastas, (I, 199); and Eggs, (I, 211), where you will also find many combination dishes that need only a simple salad or bread to form a complete meal. If speed is your object, remember, too, that many fish and ground meat dishes are quickly prepared from scratch. Also, if attractive presentation is your goal, remember that tomatoes, avocados or cucumbers are handy ever-ready containers for meat and fish salads, (I, 65–68), and that small eggplant, squash and cucumbers make attractive cases for sauced meat and fish fillings. To make, see Vegetables, (I, 284).

LUNCHEONS WITH MEATS

If you are tight on time, turn to meat salads, (I, 68), or Sandwiches, (I, 267), for quick solutions to the problem. But if you are turning lunch into a luncheon—with leisure to prepare and to enjoy—consider some of the menus below.

———

Jellied Ham Mousse, (I, 86)
Fresh Corn Pudding
Cockaigne, (I, 316)
Sliced fresh cucumbers, (I, 58)
and basil
Brownies Cockaigne, 457

———

Tomato Aspic Ring II, (I, 78),
filled with Chicken Salad, (I, 68),
with Curry Mayonnaise, (I, 422)
Corn Dodgers Cockaigne, 342
Lemon and Orange Ice, 558

———

Sausage and Millet Casserole, (I, 251)
Celeriac Salad, (I, 57)
Apples Cockaigne, 118

———

Chicken Soufflé II, (I, 228),
with Suprême Sauce, (I, 388),
and cress garnish
Sautéed Okra, (I, 333)
Filled Pineapple, 134
Pecan Drop Cookies, 463

———

Turkey Divan, (I, 259), on toast
Flambéed Peaches, 112
Curled Nut Wafers, 486,
filled with chocolate cream cheese

———

Pot-au-Feu, (I, 131)
Melba Cheese Rounds, 354
Chicory-Beetroot Salad, (I, 49)
Plum Cake Cockaigne, 393

———

Club sandwiches, (I, 275)
Fennel Sticks, (I, 323),
and Bread and Butter Pickles, 679
Poached Cherries, 124,
with Yogurt, 189

———

Clear Watercress Soup, (I, 133)
Tripe à la Mode, (I, 653)
Boiled New Potatoes, (I, 344),
with parsley
Blender Fruit Whip, 526

———

Pineapple Tidbits, 134
Lamb Patties, (I, 620)
Broccoli Timbale, (I, 230)
Cloverleaf Rolls, 315
Floating Island, 510

———

Ham Noodles, (I, 202)
Watercress Salad, (I, 45),
with raw mushrooms
Quick Cherry Crunch, 395

———

Garnished English Mixed Grill, (I, 595)
Tomato Pudding Cockaigne, (I, 368)
Asparagus Salad, (I, 55)
Hard Rolls, 323
Baked Fruit Compote, 111, using
rhubarb

———

Cold Sliced Roast Beef, (I, 565)
Tomato Stuffed, (I, 63),
with Russian Salad, (I, 54)
Sourdough Rye Bread, 311,
and cheese
Flan with Fruit, 385

———

LUNCHEONS WITH FISH

Although Lent no longer controls the spring dietary as in ages past, and church strictures against meat have relaxed, appreciation of their protein and unsaturated fat values and the sheer deliciousness of truly fresh seafoods have brought about a resurgence in their consumption.

———

Shrimp Pilaf, (I, 194)
Tossed Green Salad, (I, 46),
with Chutney Dressing, (I, 416)
Bread Sticks, 307
Banana Pineapple Sherbet, 560

———

Frog Legs Forestière, (I, 504),
garnished with Green Peas
and fresh mint, (I, 338)
Melon Salad, (I, 72)
Corn Zephyrs Cockaigne, 342
Cream Meringue Tart
Cockaigne, 438

———

Onion Soup, (I, 133)
Omelet, (I, 222), filled with seafood
Seedless Grape and Celery Ring, (I, 83)
Angel Cake, 405,
with Lemon Filling, 451

———

Bouillabaisse, (I, 161),
with French Bread, 306
Black olives, 94, and Finocchio, (I, 323)
Spiked Melon, 131

———

Cream of Asparagus Soup, (I, 150)
Paella,
Escarole Salad, (I, 44)
Crème Caramel, 509

———

Jellied Tomato Bouillon, (I, 137)
Scallop Kebabs, (I, 450)
Sautéed Summer Squash, (I, 362)
Deep-Fried Parsley, (I, 338)
Date Spice Cake, 421

———

Crab Louis, (I, 65),
garnished with avocado slices, (I, 71)
Parker House Rolls, 315
Lemon and Orange Ice, 558,
with a cherry liqueur

———

Clam Broth, (I, 157),
Cheese Popovers, 348
Butterfly Shrimp, (I, 464)
Cooked Celery Salad, (I, 57),
with Boiled Salad Dressing, (I, 424)
Chocolate Charlotte, 530

———

Jambalaya with Fish, (I, 196)
Oakleaf lettuce, (I, 43),
with Thousand Island
Dressing, (I, 421)
Melba Toast, 355
Orange Chiffon Pie, 389

———

Leek-Potato Soup, (I, 154)
Fillets of Sole Florentine, (I, 501)
Corn Sticks, 341
Spiked Honeydew Melon, 131

———

Tomato Bouillon, (I, 131)
Fish Fillets Baked in
Seafood Sauce Marguéry, (I, 478)
Baked Green Rice, (I, 191)
Crêpes, 144, with Tutti-Frutti
Cockaigne, 674

———

Stuffed French Pancakes, 144,
with Creamed Oysters, (I, 442)
Celery, 93,
and olives, 94
Chilled fresh figs, 128
Nut Bars, 459

———

Quick Cucumber Soup
Cockaigne, (I, 167)
Crab or Lobster Salad, (I, 65),
with Herb Mayonnaise, (I, 420)
Chilled green grapes, 128
Quick Coffee Cake, 339

Mushrooms Stuffed with
Clams, (I, 330)
Purée of Peas, (I, 339)
Bibb lettuce salad, (I, 43),
with Green Goddess Dressing, (I, 420)
Overnight Rolls, 317
Caramel Custard, 509,
with Sauce Cockaigne, 564

Waffles, 150,
with Seafood à la King, (I, 259)
French Tomato Salad, (I, 62)
Frozen Lemon Surprise, 558
Pecan Puffs, 465

Sautéed Shad Roe, (I, 498)
Glazed Celery, (I, 312)
Podded Peas, (I, 339)
Corn Zephyrs Cockaigne, 342
Frozen Orange Surprise, 558,
with Marzipan leaf decorations, 581

Consommé Madrilène, (I, 130)
Artichokes Stuffed with Crab Meat
Salad, (I, 55)
Buttermilk Crackling Corn Bread,
341
Pineapple Snow, 527

Quick Tomato-Corn Chowder, (I, 167)
Cucumbers Stuffed, (I, 59),
with Tuna or Shrimp Salad, (I, 67)
Seeded Crackers, 354
Lemon Meringue Pie, 387

Smelts, (I, 499)
Buttered Peas and Carrots, (I, 339)
Scalloped Potatoes, (I, 345)
Poached Apricots, 111
Sand Tarts, 472

Scallops Mornay, (I, 451)
Corn Creole, (I, 317)
Blender Coleslaw, (I, 51),
with Mayonnaise, (I, 418)
Bran Muffins, 346
Coffee Cream Tarts, 387

Seafood à la King, (I, 259)
Grilled Tomatoes, (I, 367)
Watercress, (I, 45),
with Sour Cream Dressing, (I, 425)
Rhubarb Pie, 380

Poached Quenelles, (I, 187)
with Newburg Sauce, (I, 413)
Green Peas and Mushrooms, (I, 339)
Wilted Cucumbers, (I, 58)
Cloverleaf Rolls, 315
Velvet Spice Cake, 420

Chilled Cream of Spinach
Soup, (I, 155)
Shrimp Sandwiches with Cheese
Sauce, (I, 276)
Avocado and Fruit Salad, (I, 71),
with Curry Dressing for Fruit Salad,
(I, 425)
Rich Roll Cookies, 472

Tomatoes Stuffed, (I, 63),
with Crab Salad, (I, 65)
Pepper Slices, (I, 60),
filled with Cream Cheese Spread, 71
Whole-Grain Bread, 309
Orange Fruit Soup, 114

Gazpacho, (I, 133 or 165)
Fillets of Fish Florentine
with Shrimp and Mushrooms, (I, 479)
French Bread, 306
Seedless grapes, 128,
and assorted cheese, 542

————

Lobster or Seafood Curry, (I, 460),
in a Rice Ring, (I, 189),
served with Chutney, 685
Celery and spinach, (I, 45),
with French Dressing, (I, 413)
Pears in Liqueur, 133

————

LUNCHEONS WITH EGGS AND CHEESE

Called by some "meatless" menus,
those below are comparable nutritionally to meals which include meat
and fish. Strict vegetarians exclude
egg and dairy products. Since the
structuring of such restricted diets,
(I, 5), needs constant care and skill to
maintain sufficient proteins and accessory factors, they are not included
in these cursory suggestions.

————

Eggs in Aspic Cockaigne, (I, 82),
on watercress, (I, 45)
Brioche Loaf Cockaigne, 306
Macédoine of Fresh Fruit, 107
Molasses Crisps Cockaigne, 480

————

Ratatouille Provençale, (I, 321)
Cannelloni, (I, 204),
with cheese filling, (I, 208)
Dandelion Salad, (I, 46),
with oil and vinegar, (I, 47)
Wine Gelatin, 525,
with Custard Sauce, 565

————

Bean Soup with Vegetables, (I, 142)
Puffed Bread Blocks, 353

Tossed Green Salad, (I, 46)
Prune Whip, 526

————

Bulgarian Cold Cucumber
Soup, (I, 152)
Curried Eggs, (I, 218)
Refrigerator Bran Rolls, 327
Fresh Cherry Pie, 377

————

Cheese Custard Pie, (I, 244)
Tomato Aspic, (I, 77),
on mixed salad greens, (I, 46)
Strawberries with Kirsch, 122, on
Meringues, 375

————

Quick Spinach Soup, (I, 168),
with Tofu, 192
Creamed Eggs and Asparagus
Cockaigne, (I, 218)
Ambrosia, 107
Anise Drop Cookies, 466

————

Soupe Paysanne, (I, 139)
Cheese Soufflé Cockaigne, (I, 226)
French Bread, 306
Citrus Fruit Salad, (I, 72),
with French Dressing, (I, 415)
Devil's Food Cake Cockaigne, 417

————

Quick Consommé Fondue
Cockaigne, (I, 165)
Cold Stuffed Tomatoes II
with Eggs and Anchovies, (I, 63)
Swedish Rye Bread, 311,
with assorted cheeses, 542
Angel Cup Cakes, 446

————

Cheese Casserole, (I, 242)
Waldorf Salad, (I, 70),
on watercress, (I, 45)
Apricot Whip, 526

————

Quick Onion Soup, (I, 168)
Deviled Eggs in Sauce, (I, 220)
Rye Rolls, 320
Green Bean Salad, (I, 56),
with French Dressing, (I, 413)
Florentines, 465

———

ONE-PLATE LUNCHEONS

This is the most convenient way to
serve food easily to a large number of
people, especially if the menu is
planned for what in England is called
a "fork" luncheon. If hot and cold
foods are to be served on the same
plate, be sure that the hot is in a
ramekin and the cold in a container
that will not be affected by a heated
plate.

———

Beef Stroganoff, (I, 571)
Rice Ring or Mold, (I, 189)
Grilled Tomatoes, (I, 367),
with watercress garnish, (I, 45)

———

Small Eggplant Stuffed
with Lamb or Ham, (I, 322)
Molded Vegetable
Gelatin Salad, (I, 76),
with Boiled Salad Dressing, (I, 424)

———

Ham Timbales, (I, 232), or Ham
Croquettes, 161,
with Mushroom Sauce, (I, 395)
Molded Pineapple Ring, (I, 85)
Popovers, 347

———

Quick Chicken Pot Pie, (I, 239)
Romaine or cos salad, (I, 44),
with Lorenzo Dressing, (I, 415)

———

Fish Paupiettes, (I, 479),
with Oyster Sauce, (I, 386)
Podded Peas, (I, 339)
Hard Rolls, 323

———

Blanquette de Veau, (I, 590), on
Boiled Noodles, (I, 200)
Panned or Sicilian Spinach, (I, 359)

———

Stuffed Eggs on Rosettes
with Savory Sauce, (I, 219)
Asparagus Tip and
Green Pepper Salad, (I, 55),
with bib lettuce, (I, 43)

———

Honeydew or canteloupe melon, 130,
filled with creamed cottage
cheese, 195,
garnished with
seedless green grapes, 128
Quick Nut Bread, 334

———

DINNER FOR FAMILY
OR FRIENDS

We have preferred not to sort these
into family and company categories,
but to leave the choice to you. First,
our families can be our best company; second, almost any menu can
be for guests, depending on who's
coming to dinner and what you do
particularly well. The most important
quality of a "company" dinner should
be the excitement of the unusual—
for them. This need by no means be a
matter of fancy versus plain, nor a
selection as far out as that of the
Franklin Roosevelts when they enter-
tained the King and Queen of England at Hyde Park with hot dogs as
the unforgettable pièce de résistance.
At a recent spectacular dinner in

Lyons for the top-flight chefs of France, hosted by one of them, the multicourse menu included among its openers wild strawberries and Caspian caviar—foods appropriate enough for these jaded palates. But the main and surprise course consisted of six magnificent American prime ribs of beef grilled on the spit before a natural charcoal fire and served with baked Idaho potatoes.

Don't forget that with any of the following meals a salad of seasonal greens is not amiss. Serve it as many Europeans do—the mixed greens in a large bowl, ready to be dressed, with a double cruet such as that shown on (I, 42) standing by—to which the Italians have given the inimitable name of *nuora e suocera*—mother-and-daughter-in-law.

Prosciutto and Fruit, 87
Lasagne, (I, 203)
Tossed salad, (I, 46),
with French Dressing, (I, 413)
Zabaglione, 511

German Meatballs, (I, 621)
Noodle Rings III, (I, 201)
Tomato Aspic, (I, 77)
Linzertorte, 433

Small Tomatoes filled with
Coleslaw de Luxe, (I, 50)
Roast Cornish Hen, (I, 534),
with Rice Dressing, (I, 435)
Braised Leeks, (I, 325)
Hard Rolls, 323
Strawberry Bombe, 555

Crown Roast of Lamb, (I, 593),
with Tangerine-Rice
Dressing Cockaigne, (I, 436)
Steamed Zucchini, (I, 361)
Belgian endive, (I, 44),
Vinaigrette, (I, 413)
Sour Cream Apple Cake Soufflé
Cockaigne, 519

Stuffed Veal Roast, (I, 586)
Green Bean Casserole, (I, 292)
Cold Beet Cups, (I, 56)
Rice Flour Muffins, 346
Profiteroles, 372

Fillet of Beef, (I, 566),
with Marchand de Vin Sauce, (I, 392)
Potatoes Anna, (I, 348)
Stuffed Baked Artichokes, (I, 289)
Peach Ice with Cassis, 557

Tiny Broiled Sausages, 96
Sautéed Mushrooms, (I, 328)
Summer Squash
Casserole Cockaigne, (I, 364)
Prunes in Wine, 135
Molasses Nut Wafers, 464

Sweetbreads on Skewers with
Mushrooms, (I, 643)
Braised Celery, (I, 312)
Sliced tomatoes, (I, 62),
with French Dressing, (I, 413)
Cheese Straws, 363
Coffee Chocolate Custard, 509

Liver Lyonnaise, (I, 639)
Shoestring Potatoes, (I, 351)
Sweet-Sour Beans, (I, 293)
Blueberries, 122, and cream

Shrimp Casserole
with Snail Butter, (I, 463)
Pheasant in Game Sauce, (I, 541)
Wild Rice Ring, (I, 198)
with Spinach, (I, 358)
Strawberries Romanoff, 122

———

Braised Lamb Shanks, (I, 597) with
vegetables Boiled Noodles, (I, 200)
Cucumber Salad, (I, 58)
Jelly Tot Cookies, 481

———

Veal Roast, (I, 585)
Kohlrabi, (I, 325)
Wilted Greens, (I, 49)
Riced Potatoes, (I, 344)
Mocha Gelatin, 524

———

Onion Soup, (I, 133)
Roast Wild Duck, (I, 538)
Oranges in Syrup, 126
Chestnut Dressing, (I, 433),
with sausage
Celeri-Rave Rémoulade, (I, 57)
Almond Torte Cockaigne, 430

———

Baked Ham, (I, 612)
Green Soybeans, (I, 293)
Crusty Soft-Center
Spoon Bread, 343
Applesauce, 118,
with crushed pineapple and ginger

———

Baked Green Rice, (I, 191)
Scallops Meunière, (I, 450)
Belgian endive, (I, 44),
with French Dressing, (I, 413)
Champagne Sherbet, 561
Pecan Wafers, 464

———

Broiled Steak, (I, 568),
with watercress garnish

———

Never-Fail French Fries, (I, 351)
Cauliflower, (I, 311),
with Polonaise Sauce, (I, 399)
Applesauce Cake, 421

———

Cold Sliced Roast Beef, (I, 565)
Peppers, (I, 340),
stuffed with Corn Creole, (I, 317)
Popovers, 347
Persimmon Pudding, 538

———

Chicken Broth with Egg, (I, 131)
Lamb Kebabs, (I, 595)
Baked Kasha with Almonds, (I, 181)
Bibb lettuce salad, (I, 43),
with Yogurt Dressing, (I, 426)
Baklava, 601

———

Romanian Noodle
and Pork Casserole, (I, 202)
Coleslaw, (I, 49)
Uncooked Cranberry Relish, 123
Gingersnaps, 466

———

Fresh Cod à la Portugaise, (I, 487)
Corn Pudding Cockaigne, (I, 316)
Deep-Fried Zucchini, (I, 363)
Fresh peaches, 131, in Marsala

———

Tarama, 98, on lettuce
Moussaka, (I, 624)
Roasted chestnuts, 86
Dried figs, 128
Vin Brûlé, 55

———

Artichokes Vinaigrette, (I, 287)
Coq au Vin, (I, 519)
Boiled New Potatoes, (I, 344)
Boston lettuce salad, (I, 43),
Beignets, 159,
with Sauce Cockaigne, 564

———

Cold Borsch, (I, 140)
Broiled Salmon Steak, (I, 496)
Potatoes with parsley, (I, 344)
Broccoli, (I, 302),
with Polonaise Sauce, (I, 399)
Lemon Soufflé, 518

Gänseklein, (I, 533)
Apples Stuffed
with Sauerkraut, 118
Nockerln, (I, 183)
Rote Grütze, 532

Beef Goulash, (I, 582)
Spätzle, (I, 186)
Lettuce and
watercress, (I, 43–44, 45)
Lemon Sponge Custard, 512

Cucumber Aspic, (I, 77),
on tomato slices, (I, 62)
Couscous, (I, 599)
Pomegranate, 136,
with Yogurt, 189

Belgian Beef Stew, (I, 577)
Mashed Potatoes, (I, 344)
Brussels sprouts, (I, 303),
with lemon juice and nutmeg
Belgian endive salad, (I, 44)
Strawberry Bavarian Cream, 528

Winter Melon Soup, (I, 155)
Chinese Egg Rolls, (I, 237)
Stir-Fried Chicken
Breasts, (I, 527),
with almonds
Sweet and Sour Pork, (I, 607)
Boiled Rice, (I, 189)
Oriental Bean Sprout Salad, (I, 49)
Litchi nuts, 129

New England Clam Chowder, (I, 163)
Swordfish Steaks, (I, 501)
Corn on the Cob, (I, 316)
Creamed Onions, (I, 334)
Cranberry Sherbet, 561

Iced Poached Shrimp in Shell, (I, 462),
with Quick Pink Chaud-Froid, (I, 428)
Fish Fillets Sautéed Palm
Beach, (I, 485)
Tiny New Potatoes, Sautéed, (I, 344)
Steamed Asparagus, (I, 290),
with buttered bread crumbs
Baked Bananas II, 120

Meatless Dolmas, (I, 626)
Persian Chicken, (I, 520),
and Flat Bread, 313
Young spinach leaves, (I, 358),
with Yogurt Dressing, (I, 426)
French Pancakes, 143
Currant Jelly, 664

Avocado Slices, (I, 71),
with French Dressing, (I, 413)
Turkey Casserole Mole, (I, 524),
with Tortillas, 343
Orange and Onion Salad, (I, 73)
Crème Frite, 515

Braised Oxtails, (I, 656)
Noodles, (I, 200)
Carrots Vichy, (I, 310)
Cold Green Beans à la Grecque, (I, 285)
Date Spice Cake, 421

Roast Duckling, (I, 531)
Apple Dressing, (I, 434)
Polenta, (I, 180)
Peas and Mushrooms, (I, 339)
Ginger Crisp, 395

Potage St. Germain
with Croutons, (I, 144)
Veal Scallopini, (I, 586),
with Marsala and mushrooms
Risotto alla Milanese, (I, 193)
Sicilian or Panned Spinach, (I, 359)
Fresh tangerines, 126

———

Shrimp Tempura, (I, 464)
Sukiyaki, (I, 571),
with Boiled Rice, (I, 189)
Curried Fruit Fondue, 113

———

Chestnut Soup, (I, 151)
Rabbit à la Mode, (I, 662),
with Gnocchi, (I, 185)
Creamed Lettuce, (I, 326)
Compote of Greengage Plums, 111

———

Baked Pork Chops, (I, 605)
Sweet Potato Puffs, (I, 356)
Creamed Spinach, (I, 359)
Gingerbread, 425

———

Boeuf Bouilli, (I, 576),
with Horseradish Sauce, (I, 386)
Boiled New Parsley Potatoes, (I, 344)
Mulled Cucumbers, (I, 319)
Raspberry Trifle, 436

AFTERNOON TEA SUGGESTIONS

The essentials of this gracious interlude are embodied in the comment of a kindergartner who volunteered to us, "Mommy's having friends over this afternoon and we're serving tea and 'sordid' cookies." Assorted small sandwiches, as well, go with this cozy type of sociability, and even a

delicious cake like Poppy Seed Custard Cake, 437, served with tea, coffee or hot chocolate. "High" tea, that old British custom more like a late-day brunch, fortifies the urbanite before the theater or a very late dinner; for the country-dweller it is often the last meal of the day. Formal afternoon teas haven't changed much in character since Brillat-Savarin dubbed them "an extraordinary form of entertainment—offered," he added, "to people who have already dined well and therefore feel neither thirst nor hunger, so that its purpose is solely of passing the time and its foundation is no more than a display of dainties." Be that as it may, we all still enjoy teas at special times.

———

Dry sherry
Seeded Crackers, 354
Creamed Seafood, (I, 260),
in Timbale Cases, 160
Orange Tea Rolls, 323
Almond Torte Cockaigne, 430,
with Sauce Cockaigne, 564
Individual Babas au Rhum, 437
Chocolate Eclairs, 371
Glazed Mint Leaves, 602

———

Dubonnet
Salted Almonds, 85
Eggs in Aspic Cockaigne, (I, 82)
Small Choux-Paste Shells, 370,
filled with Chicken Salad, (I, 68)
Sandwiches of Cream
Cheese Spread, 71,
and Persimmon Purée, 133
Lemon and Orange Ice, 558
Madeleines, 447
Molasses Crisps Cockaigne, 480
Bourbon Balls, 595
Glazed Fresh Fruits, 602

———

Claret Cup, 59
Flower Canapés, 66
Crêpes, 144,
with Creamed Oysters, (I, 442)
Rolled Cress Sandwiches, 65
Dobos Torte, 431
Pecan Slices, 459
Candied Citrus Peel, 604

———

May Wine, 60
Fish Quenelles, (I, 187)
Toasted Mushroom Canapés, 75
Cucumber Lilies, 93
Peach Ice Cream, 549
Macaroons, 469
Small Mohrenköpfe, 436
Turkish Fruit Paste, 598

———

COCKTAIL AND BUFFET SUGGESTIONS

Today the cocktail party is the favored mode of repaying social obligations. In some areas, when you are invited for cocktails, it may be strictly a prelude to dinner. Elsewhere the custom is to provide a sturdier assortment that carries you into the later hours of the evening. In the first type of party, choose delicate, rich, spicy morsels that are drink-inducers and appetite-stimulators, see Hors d'Oeuvre, 81, and Canapés, 63, and note particularly the illustrations in these chapters and in Salads, (I, 42), for decorative ways to present them. The other kind of gathering calls for some blander types of food, which may include large joints or fowl and salads, and turns into a light buffet. In either case, your menu should include foods such as butter, cheese, nuts and rich dips that absorb the impact of the alcohol, with raw vegetable tidbits as a foil. Often a hot soup or a few nonalcoholic drinks are welcomed by nondrinkers.

Seafood in Creole Sauce, (I, 261)
Seviche, 99, in avocado halves, (I, 70)
Cold Fillet of Beef, (I, 566)
Mushroom Ring Mold
with Sweetbreads, (I, 234)
Cold Fried Chicken, (I, 517)
Manicotti, (I, 204)

———

Lobster or Seafood Curry, (I, 460)
Beef Kebabs, (I, 573)
Jellied Chicken Mousse, (I, 86)
Veal Terrine, (I, 632)
Spiced Beef, (I, 579)
Lasagne, (I, 203)

———

Mousseline of Shellfish, (I, 89)
Cold Baked Ham, (I, 612)
Tongue in Aspic, (I, 651)
Beef Stew Gaston, (I, 573)
Sliced turkey, (I, 515)
Cannelloni, (I, 204)

———

Cold Glazed Salmon, (I, 496)
Standing Rib Roast of Beef, (I, 565)
Souffléed Liver Pâté
Cockaigne, (I, 632)
Shrimp in the shell, (I, 462)
Chicken à la Campagne, (I, 524)
Fondue, (I, 243)

———

Swedish Smorgasbord, 84

FORMAL MENUS

There are Occasions—with a capital O—when nothing but perfection will do. The menus in this section are all in what we might call the champagne class. Incidentally, don't overlook the Champagne Fountain, 48, as a preliminary, on a day when an outpouring of joy and congratulations is in order. For other appropriate wines, see chart

on 49. Celery, olives and hard rolls are
the usual accompaniments of such
menus and may be placed on the table
before the guests are seated. In this
day and age when the pink-cheeked
domestic is on the endangered species
list, all but the most formal meals may,
with advance planning, be served buffet style. And you need not sacrifice
a premeditated seating arrangement—
or even the use of place-cards if you
are a true-blue perfectionist. Follow
the meal, if you like, with coffee and
assorted liqueurs.

LUNCHEON

Quick Clam and
Chicken Broth, (I, 169)
Cheese Straws, 363
Fish Soufflé with Lobster, (I, 229)
Broiled Lamb Chops, (I, 594),
garnished with
Stuffed Baked Artichokes, (I, 289)
Tomato Olive Casserole, (I, 368)
Bibb, watercress and
endive salad, (I, 43),
with Avocado Dressing, (I, 416)
Assorted cheeses, 542
Cabinet Pudding, 527

DINNER

Consommé, (I, 130),
with Royale, (I, 135)
Bread Sticks, 307
Lobster Parfait, (I, 460)
Broiled Fillet Steak, (I, 568)
with Béarnaise Sauce, (I, 412)
Soufflé or Puffed Potatoes, (I, 350)
Creamed Spinach, (I, 359)
Belgian endive, (I, 44),
Vinaigrette, (I, 413)
Lemon Sponge Custard, 512

HOLIDAY DINNERS

Clear Soup, (I, 130),
and Marrow Balls, (I, 174)
Christmas Canapés, 66
Hearts of Finocchio, (I, 323)
Goose, (I, 532),
stuffed with Sweet Potatoes
and Apple, (I, 437)
Turnip Cups, (I, 372),
filled with peas, (I, 338)
Corn Zephyrs Cockaigne, 342
Fresh Cherry Pie, 377

Oysters Rockefeller, (I, 444)
Roast Stuffed Turkey, (I, 515),
with Chestnut Dressing, (I, 433)
Glazed Onions, (I, 335)
Brussels sprouts, (I, 303),
with Hollandaise Sauce, (I, 410)
Filled Pimientos or
Christmas Salad, (I, 60),
on watercress, (I, 45)
Mince Pie, 380

Hot Consommé, (I, 130)
Roast Suckling Pig, (I, 602),
with Onion Dressing, (I, 433)
Duchess Potatoes, (I, 353)
Red cabbage, (I, 307)
Escarole and romaine, (I, 44), with
Thousand Island Dressing, (I, 421)
Hazelnut Soufflé, 518

Mushroom Broth I, (I, 132)
Pâté de Foie de Volaille, (I, 631)
Rib Roast of Beef, (I, 565),
Stuffed Baked Potatoes, (I, 347)
Green beans, (I, 291),
with Amandine Garnish, 221
Tossed Salad, (I, 46),
with Roquefort Dressing, (I, 415)
White Fruit Cake, 427
Pulled Mints, 589

WEDDING BUFFET

Hot Consommé Brunoise, (I, 130)
Mushrooms à la Schoener, (I, 329)
Rolled Sandwiches,
Cress and Cucumber, 65
Pastry Cheese Balls, 90
Galantine of Turkey, (I, 529)
Lobster Newburg, (I, 460),
in Patty Shells, 369
Bibb lettuce salad, (I, 43),
with Sour Cream Dressing, (I, 425)
Stuffed Endive, 93,
and olives
Macedoine of Fruits with Kirsch, 107
Wedding Cake, 403
Petits Fours, 447
Spiced Nuts, 594
Peppermint Cream Wafers, 579

─────

HUNT BREAKFAST

Bloody Marys, 42
Hot Buttered Rum, 55
Café Brûlot or Diable, (I, 28)
Blended Fruit Juice, (I, 37)
Baked fresh fruit, 111
Steak-and-Kidney Pie, (I, 583)
Pheasant in Game Sauce, (I, 541)
Baked Bacon, (I, 615)
Pan-Broiled Sausage, (I, 636)
Scrambled Eggs, (I, 215)
Grilled Tomatoes, (I, 367)
Prunes and Chestnuts in Wine, 136
Toasted English Muffins, 323
Croissants, 322
Red Red Strawberry Jam, 667
Orange Marmalade, 673
Scandinavian Pastry, 330

─────

SUGGESTIONS FOR PARTICIPATORY MENUS

Many guests offer to be where the action is, and the hostess, in conventional gatherings, is often hard pressed to find more to suggest than the last-minute pouring of the ice water. The setups listed below can utilize willing manpower to good effect either in helping serve or in doing some at-table cooking, and in exploiting the guests' special talents to add to the conviviality.

I. Have a soup tureen filled with a hearty protein-rich lentil soup, (I, 143), with Sausage Balls, (I, 173); or a clear soup, (I, 130–133), with Farina Balls Cockaigne, (I, 184); an assortment of salad makings and dressings or a large salad plate as illustrated on (I, 52), from which guests can select their choice. Have nearby an assortment of pastries and cheeses.

II. With guest chefs in charge, have two chafing dishes or skillet setups such as those illustrated on 141 for omelet- or crêpe-making. Read About Omelets, (I, 221), for suggestions, and have on hand an assortment of fillings such as creamed seafood, (I, 260), or poultry, (I, 257); a piquant cheese or mushroom sauce, (I, 385 or 395); a large tossed salad, (I, 46), with generous vegetable components; and an Almond Torte Cockaigne, 430, with fresh strawberries and whipped cream or Sauce Cockaigne, 564, or Hot Fudge Sauce, 567.

III. Have all the makings for open-faced sandwiches similar to those described and illustrated on (I, 268), with a "sampler" tray as your buffet decoration, flanked by baskets of assorted fresh fruits that can serve as dessert.

IV. Prepare the ingredients for one of the following recipes which give guests a choice of combinations:

Rijsttafel, (I, 197); Chinese Firepot, (I, 577); Boeuf Fondu Bourguignonne, (I, 570).

V. And for teens, set up a hamburger stand serving the less usual hamburgers, (I, 616–619), with varied buns and fixings, and a platter of iced raw vegetables. For dessert, serve assorted ice cream in cones, or sundaes or malts, (I, 33).

PICNIC SUGGESTIONS

Picnics are fun; but picnic food is subject to hazards not all of which are ants and sand. Transport perishables in the coolest part of your car, covering them against the sun. If you use a cold box, pack it with well-prechilled foods. If you have no cold box or insulated plastic bags, carry frozen juices. Use them en route to cool such perishables as mayonnaise and deviled eggs. Or fill a plastic bag with ice cubes and put it in a coffee can to improvise a chilling unit that will last out transportation time. Or insulate the sandwich boxes with damp newspapers. ◗ Do not repack in your cold box or carry over to a second picnic meal during the day any foods that spoil easily. ◗ Should you use dry ice, be sure the container and the car windows are partially open to allow the gas to escape. To mix picnic salads conveniently, see (I, 47).

Most important of all, if it's a basket picnic ◗ plan the kind of food that holds well and is easily served, so everyone can enjoy every minute of the outing. If it's to be a cookout, please read About Outdoor Cooking and Pit Cooking, (I, 108 and 109). All **Joy** recipes marked ▤ are suitable for outdoor preparation. Check also Clambake, (I, 447), and Fish Baked in Clay, (I, 477).

Sandwiches, salads, fruits and cookies are naturals for picnics. Consult these sections; or for slightly fancier combinations, see the menus below.

Grilled Frankfurters, (I, 250)
Potatoes baked in embers
Bread and Butter Pickles, 679
Buttermilk Rolls, 316
Cheddar cheese, 542
Gingerbread, 425
Pears and grapes, 132, 128

Lamb Kebabs, (I, 595)
Flatbread, 313
Tossed Salad, (I, 46), with
Thousand Island Dressing, (I, 421)
Pound Cake, 415
Blue plums, 135

Cold Fried Chicken, (I, 517)
Potato Salad Niçoise, (I, 61)
Oat Bread Cockaigne, 310
Marble Cake, 410
Watermelon, 130

Fried Fish, (I, 484)
Grilled or Roasted Corn, (I, 316)
Coleslaw, (I, 49)
Quick Oatmeal Cookies, 468
Peaches, 131

Hot or Cold Barbecued
Ribs, (I, 608)
Carrot and celery sticks, (I, 310)
Black olives, 94
Dill Batter Loaf, 305
Gold Layer Cake, 413
with Caramel Icing, 494
Apples, 115

Baked Ham, (I, 612)
Nut Creams Rolled in Chives, 89
Picnic Tossed Salad, (I, 47)
Rye Rolls, 320
Brownies Cockaigne, 457
Bananas, 120

BACKPACKING MENU SUGGESTIONS

If you intend to travel by shank's mare far from civilization, you should be interested in food and equipment that are light in weight and low in bulk. Choose food that cooks in little or no time to conserve fuel, whether it be fuel hauled on your back or that provided by nature on the spot. For ways to build fires, see (I, 109). But in case of inclement weather, it is wise to carry a solid-fuel stove. Solid fuel, a variety of hexamethylene tetramine, can be purchased in bulk from a chemical supply house in granules or in tablets at outfitters'. This fuel is practical only for emergencies or for traveling light.

Pretest your meals at home first; what tastes good at home will be excellent fare on the trail. Menu planning and prepackaging are essential for fast and foolproof trail cooking. Each meal for each person should be prepackaged with seasonings in polyethylene bags with excess air removed, sealed with heat or rubber bands. One day's meals, along with that day's munchies and extra beverage mixes, vitamin pills and sundries should be placed in a large marked bag. Try to provide at least one course in each meal—or a large part of the main course—in a form that can be eaten without cooking, in case of a weather or fuel emergency or some other disaster. Always include

the welcome extra munch items in a separate bag. If you are in very dry country where water is likely to be in short supply, remember that proteins require fairly large amounts of water to be utilized by the body, so increase carbohydrates in the expedition diet. In cold weather you will notice a craving for foods heavy in fats. Also during cold weather you may wish to serve soups more often and coffee or tea less. Dried fruits, nuts, chocolate bars and the conglomeration of raisins, nuts and chocolate drops known to climbers as "gorp" make good desserts and trail munchies. See Fruit-Nut Pemmican, 109, for a nourishing mixture with honey. If you plan your initial meals around sandwiches and later ones around tinned fish, freeze-dried meats, jerked meat—see beef Jerky, 633—instant rice, instant potatoes, vegetable flakes and Japanese-style quick-cooking noodles, you will have more time to enjoy the outdoors. At high altitudes, be certain that all foods are easy to digest and blander than usual, for altitude sickness seems to be more prevalent when the expedition diet is highly spiced or difficult to digest.

Pick outdoor cooking utensils that can also serve for storage of water

or food. Shown on 32 are the GI canteen and GI stainless steel cup—aluminum cups burn the lips—as well as a square aluminum storage box for pot and frypan, and the French army cook kit. Some campers prefer the shallow Sierra cup. Basic outdoor cooking tools are a sharp hunting knife and stainless steel soup spoon. One person can easily scrape by on two canteens and two canteen cups—one cup for beverages and the other to cook the main course in.

After meals, be sure to carefully scrape clean and rinse all cooking and eating utensils and then dunk them first in soapy boiling water and then in clear boiling rinse water; or if water or fuel is scarce, scorch the insides and food-bearing surfaces over an open flame. Remember that even a mild case of dysentery can be disabling far from civilization. Wilderness water supplies should be treated with suspicion. If you have the slightest doubt as to the water's purity, boil it for at least five minutes, or treat it with halazone or iodine tablets according to the instructions which come with them.

DRINKS

The chapter on Beverages (I, 24) has to do with nonalcoholic drinks. This one takes up the subject of liquor, from cocktails to what the host or hostess offers late in the evening, either to give the dinner party a new lease on life or—hopefully in the rarest emergencies—to mark the passage of time and allow it to dawn on at least some members of an ill-chosen guest list that leave-taking might be an act of extreme unction.

Because when to serve what drinks is as important as any other aspect of menu building, and because to so many hostesses the intricacies of mixing drinks are pretty much a total mystery, this section of the text remains explicit and detailed. Always in the back of our minds, spurring us on, is the memory of a cartoon which depicted a group of guests sitting around a living room, strickenly regarding their cocktail glasses, while the hostess, one of those inimitable Hokinson types, all embonpoint, cheer, and fluttering organdy, triumphantly announces, "A very dear friend gave me some wonderful old Scotch and I just happened to find a bottle of papaya juice in the refrigerator!"

COCKTAILS AND OTHER BEFORE-DINNER DRINKS

The cocktail is probably an American invention, and most certainly a typically American kind of drink. What-

ever mixtures you put together—and part of the fascination of cocktail making is the degree of inventiveness it seems to encourage—hold fast to a few general principles. ♦ The most important of these is to keep the quantity of the basic ingredients—gin, whisky, rum, etc.—up to about 60% of the total drink, never below half. ♦ Remember, as a corollary, that cocktails are before-meal drinks—appetizers. For this reason they should be neither oversweet nor overloaded with cream and egg, in order to avoid spoiling the appetite instead of stimulating it.

Illustrated on 34 are some of the tools included in basic bar equipment. To the left of the ice bucket and tongs are a strainer, jigger, and muddler; next left, the only corkscrew we know that doesn't induce complete frustration; above it is an ingenious substitute which raises the air pressure inside the bottle by means of a hand-operated tube-and-piston device, and so gently pushes out the cork—a real boon if the cork is in crumbly condition. Next to these are a combination bottle-cap remover and can puncturer and, at far left, a lemon peeler guaranteed to get only the colored part of the rind. To the right of the ice bucket we show a martini pitcher and bar spoon, a heavy glass cocktail shaker, and, at the far right, a bitters bottle with a dropper-type top. Not illustrated here are an ice crusher or a heavy canvas bag and wooden mallet for converting cubes to crushed ice; a blender, (I, 375), indispensable for preparing frozen summer concoctions, and the squeezer, ice pick and sharp knife your equipment probably includes if you mix drinks in your kitchen.

A simple Sugar Syrup is a useful ingredient when making drinks. Boil for 5 minutes 1 part water to 2 parts sugar, or half as much water as sugar. Keep the syrup in a bottle, refrigerated, and use it as needed.

In addition to various liquors, it is advisable for the home bartender to have on hand a stock of: bitters, carbonated water, tonic water, bitter lemon, dry ginger ale, cola and tomato juice; lemons, oranges, limes, olives and cherries. For garnishes, see (I, 34). See also the chapters on Canapés and Hors d'Oeuvre, 63 and 81, for suitable accompaniments for cocktails—besides a steady head.

Note the two types of cocktail glasses illustrated on the left below. Both are so designed that the heat of the hand is not transferred to the contents of the glass. These hold about 3 ounces each. The old-fashioned glass featured next holds about 6 ounces and retains its chill by reason of a heavy base. This type of container is increasingly used these days by people who prefer their martinis "on the rocks" instead of "up"—that is, in the rather more fussy and more precise cocktail-glass type of presentation. The next drawing shows a typical "sour" glass. It holds about 4 ounces. Champagne cocktails are often served in such a glass, rather than in the more traditional sauce-bowl stem glass at the end of the line, the better to retain bubbles. The little glass in between is for straight whisky.

♦ Mix only one round at a time. Your stock as a bartender will never go up on the strength of your "dividend"

drinks. The cocktails that follow are some fundamental ones, listed according to their basic ingredients. ▶ Each recipe, unless otherwise noted, makes about 4 drinks. When cracked—not crushed—ice is indicated, use about ³/₄ cup. ▶ All "shaken" cocktails should be shaken and strained into the glasses just before serving.

ABOUT MEASUREMENTS FOR DRINKS

1 dash	= 6 drops
3 teaspoons	= ¹/₂ ounce
1 pony	= 1 ounce
1 jigger	= 1¹/₂ ounces
1 large jigger	= 2 ounces
1 standard whisky glass	= 2 ounces
1 pint	= 16 fluid ounces
1 fifth	= 25.6 fluid ounces
1 quart	= 32 fluid ounces

ABOUT GIN AND GIN COCKTAILS

Gin is a spirit—that is, a distilled liquor. Much of its distinctive flavor comes from the juniper berry. Victorian novelists tended to assume that only the lower classes—footmen, scullery maids and the like—had a taste for gin; just as they implied that rum was an equally vulgar tipple and might be relegated to the common seaman. The "bathtub" concoctions of the Roaring Twenties did nothing to enhance gin's repute. Recent generations, however, have recognized the fact that this liquor, regardless of its shady past and its possibilities as a straight drink, is probably the best mixing base ever invented.

Of the three general gin types, Geneva and Holland are somewhat bitter and highly aromatic. They ap-

peal to a small minority and should be taken "neat." By far the most popular kind of gin is the dry London type, which can be found in all liquor dispensaries. More perhaps than is the case with most other liquors, the quality of commercial gin varies: its cost is a rough measure of its worth. Certain brands of gin, which we happen to prefer, are aged for a time in sherry casks, a process which imparts a golden color.

ALEXANDER

Shake with ³/₄ cup cracked ice:
  1 jigger sweet cream
  1¹/₂ jiggers crème de cacao
  5 jiggers gin
Strain into chilled glasses.

BRONX

Shake, using ³/₄ cup cracked ice:
  1 jigger dry vermouth
  1 jigger sweet vermouth
  1 jigger orange juice
  5 jiggers gin
Strain into chilled glasses. Add a twist of orange peel to each glass.

GIMLET

Shake, using ³/₄ cup cracked ice:
  1 tablespoon Sugar Syrup, 35
  2 large jiggers lime juice
  5 jiggers gin
Strain into chilled glasses.
Substituting orange juice for ¹/₂ the lime juice changes a Gimlet into an **Orange Blossom**. Vodka is becoming increasingly popular as a base for both.

GIN BITTER

1 Serving
With bourbon or rye whisky this becomes a **Whisky Bitter**.

Half-fill an old-fashioned glass with cracked ice. Shake, using ³/₄ cup cracked ice:

- **2 jiggers gin**
- **2 dashes angostura or orange bitters**

Pour into glass. Top with twist of orange peel or a thin slice of cucumber, unpeeled.

GIN OR WHISKY SOUR

This recipe becomes a **Whisky, Rum** or **Brandy Sour** if the base is changed. Shake, using ³/₄ cup cracked ice:

- **1 jigger Sugar Syrup, 35**
- **2 jiggers lemon or lime juice**
- **5 jiggers gin or whisky**

Strain into chilled glasses.

MARTINI

With a small onion in each glass, this cocktail becomes a **Gibson**. Try also a hazelnut and name it yourself. Changing the base makes a **Vodka Martini**. How the "Gibson" got its name, incidentally, makes an engaging if perhaps apocryphal story. As a skillful and popular American diplomat, Hugh Gibson found himself obliged to attend a stupefying number of cocktail parties. What impressed his fellow corpsmen was his apparently unlimited capacity for dry martinis, although they considered rather peculiar his insistence that his own glass contain a pickled onion instead of the protocol-hallowed olive. What they did not know, of course, was that by prearrangement with cooperative waiters Gibson's glass, pickled onion intact for ready identification, was brought in at each fresh round replenished simply with cold clear water. True martinis follow.

I. Stir well, using ³/₄ cup cracked ice:

- **1 to 2 jiggers dry vermouth**
- **6 to 7 jiggers gin**

Twist over the top:

- **Lemon peel**

or add:

- **A small seeded olive**

II. A formula we happen to prefer, and which would be more nearly recognizable by Signor Martini who—presumably—invented this world-renowned concoction three-quarters of a century or so ago. Stir well, using ³/₄ cup cracked ice:

- **1 jigger dry vermouth**
- **1 jigger sweet vermouth**
- **6 jiggers gin**

Add to each drink:

- **1 dash orange bitters**

Serve with olive in bottom of glass.

PINK LADY

Shake, using ³/₄ cup cracked ice:

- **¹/₂ jigger grenadine**
- **1 jigger lemon or lime juice**
- **1 jigger apple brandy**
- **2 egg whites**
- **4¹/₂ jiggers gin**

Strain into chilled glasses.

WHITE LADY

Shake, using ³/₄ cup cracked ice:

- **1¹/₂ jiggers lemon juice**
- **1 jigger Cointreau**
- **2 egg whites**
- **4¹/₂ jiggers gin**

Strain into chilled glasses.

ABOUT WHISKY AND WHISKY COCKTAILS

There are, as everyone knows, several kinds of whisky; but two in particular, bourbon and Scotch, far outrank all others in popularity. Bourbon is of American—that is, United States—manufacture, distilled chiefly from corn. Scotch—as might be expected—is made in Scotland, of barley. Its characteristic taste is achieved by smoking the barley malt on a porous floor, over peat fires, before distillation.

Government regulations have required that before a manufacturer can label his whisky "bourbon," the mash from which it is made must be at least 51% corn. But no restrictions are put on the kinds of grain which make up the remainder. The freedom of choice which results, plus the distillers' option of using a "sweet" or a "sour" mash, gives bourbons their distinctive "body," aroma and flavor. These qualities are often impaired if it becomes necessary to overdilute a given whisky in compliance with federal requirements that overall proof not exceed 110. Proof simply designates alcoholic content: a 100-proof liquor has 50% alcohol, 200-proof 100%, and so on.

In addition, if the mash is less than 80% corn, the whisky can be labeled "straight" bourbon, even if blended, as long as the components are distilled more or less at the same time and come from the same distillery. Otherwise, the bourbon must be labeled "blended." If, in any case, another kind of spirit is used than whisky itself, the resulting product cannot be called bourbon at all, but simply "blended whisky," or "whisky—a blend."

A word as to "bond." Bonded bourbon, like other high-class bourbons, is at least 4 years old, sometimes older, and then so acknowledged on the bottle. Bonding is also a guarantee of the whisky's "straightness" and its proof. Otherwise, "bottled in bond" has no qualitative connotations whatever. We suggest, however, that in selecting bourbons you choose from among straight and bonded brands only.

An American whisky that has a limited but steady popularity is rye, based on a mash that is predominantly made up of that cereal rather than corn. It also comes in various degrees of quality, including "bondage," and can be used interchangeably with bourbon in most formulas. "Tennessee" is another nonbourbon whisky, but most tasters can detect little difference between it and various bourbon types.

A few years ago the government relaxed some of the rather arbitrary standards it had applied to the manufacture of domestic whisky. The result has been a proliferation of "light" whiskies. These are usually aged in used barrels to reduce "hardness." They are paler in color and "drier," to suit the prevailing taste, by reason of their dilution with neutral spirits; and at once smoother and somewhat less flavorsome than traditional bourbons. Light whiskies range in color from crystal clear to a brown somewhere between that of old-fashioned bourbons and Scotch.

Coming back to Scotch whiskies, almost all are blended, several varieties being expertly combined before bottling; and they are always blended "straight"—that is, without the admixture of neutral spirits, i.e., alcohol. As with bourbons, Scotches are not acceptable unless at least 4 years old.

Which is "better," bourbon or Scotch? This is a little like asking whether a peach or a pear is better. It depends, like the appreciation of a good many other kinds of liquor, on one's personal taste. It can certainly be said that in concocting mixed drinks—cocktails, old-fashioneds, sours, etc.—bourbon is immeasurably superior to Scotch, the smoky taste of which tends to balk successful mergers.

Incidentally, a fifth kind of whisky, Irish, which makes a rather offbeat choice—except in Irish Coffee, (I, 29)—is manufactured in both smoky and nonsmoky types. It benefits by at least 7 years of aging.

MANHATTAN

Scotch may replace the bourbon or rye in this formula and the one following, in which case the cocktail is called a **Rob Roy**. When a dash of Drambuie is added, a **Rob Roy** becomes a **Bobbie Burns**. Try substituting Peychaud bitters as a variation.

I. Stir well with ice cubes:
>   1 to 2 jiggers dry vermouth
>   6 to 7 jiggers bourbon or rye

Add to each drink:
>   1 dash angostura bitters
>   A twist of lemon peel

II. A more nostalgic version.
Stir well with ice cubes:
>   1 jigger dry vermouth
>   1 jigger sweet vermouth
>   6 jiggers bourbon or rye

Add to each drink:
>   1 dash angostura bitters
>   (maraschino cherry)

OLD-FASHIONED

>   **1 Serving**

Put into an old-fashioned glass and stir:
>   ¹/₂ teaspoon Sugar Syrup, 35
>   2 dashes angostura bitters
>   1 teaspoon water

Add:
>   2 ice cubes

Fill glass to within ¹/₂ inch of top with:
>   **Bourbon or rye**

Stir. Decorate with a twist of lemon peel, a thin slice of orange and a maraschino cherry. Serve with a muddler.

The above formula, like that for the Mint Julep, 53, is a rock-bottom affair. Some like their old-fashioned on the fancy side, adding a squeeze of lemon juice, a dash of curaçao, kirsch or maraschino liqueur or a spear of fresh pineapple; or substituting a fresh ripe strawberry for the time-honored cherry. Try also, if you care to, a Scotch old-fashioned.

SAZERAC

Stir with ice cubes:
>   **4 teaspoons Sugar Syrup, 35**
>   **4 dashes Peychaud bitters**
>   **4 dashes anisette or Pernod**
>   **7 jiggers bourbon or rye**

Pour into chilled glasses. Add a twist of lemon peel to each glass.

ABOUT RUM AND RUM COCKTAILS

Another spirit, this, as blithe and potent as whisky and gin and, next to gin, perhaps the most versatile of "mixers." Rum is distilled from sugar cane—or, rather, molasses. Generally the rum available to the American consumer is of two fairly sharply differentiated types: Puerto Rican, or light-bodied, and Jamaican, a heavier-bodied, darker and quite dissimilar-tasting product. Only the light type and of the highest quality should be used for cocktails: that marked "white label" for dry drinks, "gold label" for sweeter ones. Save the heavier, more pungent types of rum for long drinks, punches, nogs, colas and shakes.

Some people like the taste and look of a frosted glass and consider it the final fine touch to cocktails of the rum type.

❧ To frost a cocktail glass: cool the glass and swab the rim with a section of lemon or lime from which the juice is flowing freely. Swirl the glass to remove excess moisture, then dip the rim to a depth of ¼ inch in powdered or confectioners' sugar. Lift the glass and tap it gently upside down to remove any excess sugar. To frost a julep glass, see 53.

BÉNÉDICTINE

Shake with ¾ cup cracked ice:
  1½ jiggers lime juice
  1½ jiggers Bénédictine
  5½ jiggers rum
Strain into chilled glasses.

CUBANA

Shake with ¾ cup cracked ice:
  ½ jigger Sugar Syrup, 35
  1½ jiggers lime juice
  2 jiggers apricot brandy
  4 jiggers rum
Strain into chilled glasses.

DAIQUIRI

With grenadine substituted for sugar syrup, this cocktail becomes a **Pink Daiquiri** or **Daiquiri Grenadine**. Stir well with ¾ cup cracked ice:
  ½ jigger Sugar Syrup, 35
  1½ jiggers lime juice
  6 jiggers rum
Strain into chilled glasses.

☘ BLENDER FROZEN DAIQUIRI

Spectacular and delicious frozen cocktails may be made by using an electric blender. In the Daiquiri recipe, for instance, by increasing the amount of crushed ice to between 2 and 3 cups, substituting 2 table-spoons confectioners' sugar for each jigger of syrup and blending the ingredients until they reach a snowy consistency, you will achieve a hot-weather triumph. Serve it in champagne glasses. This is a formula that can be interestingly varied. For a group, try using more ice, more rum and, instead of the lime juice and sugar, a chunk of frozen concentrated limeade fresh out of the can.

EL PRESIDENTE

Shake with ¾ cup cracked ice:
  1½ jiggers dry vermouth
  1½ jiggers lemon juice
  2 dashes grenadine
  2 dashes curaçao
  5 jiggers rum
Strain into chilled glasses and decorate with a twist of orange peel.

KNICKERBOCKER

Shake with ¾ cup cracked ice:
  ½ jigger raspberry syrup
  ½ jigger pineapple syrup
  1½ jiggers lemon juice
  5½ jiggers rum
Strain into chilled glasses and serve with a twist of orange peel.

MAI TAI

Shake well:
  1 jigger orgeat syrup
  1½ jiggers curaçao
  1½ jiggers dark rum
  1 jigger light rum
  3 jiggers lime or lemon juice
  ½ teaspoon powdered ginger
Half-fill outsized old-fashioned glasses, add finely crushed ice, garnish with pineapple sticks and serve with straws. It will be observed that a Mai Tai comes close to the rococo limit for a cocktail. Substituting Southern Com-

fort for the rum will push this drink over the line and into the warm-weather after-dinner period.

ABOUT BRANDY AND BRANDY COCKTAILS

Here is a spirit distilled from fruit, most commonly from grapes. Except for apple brandy, known in America as **applejack** and in France as **Calvados**, virtually no brandy is produced in America. Most alleged fruit brandies made in this country are cordials, not true distillates. In the formulas which follow, references always apply to grape brandy, although experimentation with a superior grade of applejack is encouraged. Incidentally, the name "cognac" does not by any means apply to all grape brandies—only to the top-level French product.

Aging is of great importance in the quality of this liquor, but, due to a variety of circumstances, most brandies sold over American counters neither boast of nor confess to their true age. The only sure signs, in order of increasing seniority, are these: Three-Star, V.O., V.S.O., V.S.O.P., and V.V.S.O.P. While we firmly adhere to the belief that "the better the liquor, the better the drink," no one in his right mind and of sound palate should use brandies more venerable than V.O. for any purpose other than reverential sipping.

Brandy cocktails, too, may be served in frosted glasses, see 40, with grenadine substituted for the lemon juice in preparing the glass for frosting.

CHAMPAGNE COCKTAIL

1 Serving
Pour into a large champagne glass:
½ **teaspoon Sugar Syrup, 35**
½ **jigger chilled brandy**
Fill glass almost to top with:
Chilled dry champagne
Add:
2 **dashes yellow Chartreuse**
2 **dashes orange bitters**

CURAÇAO COCKTAIL

Shake well with ¾ cup cracked ice:
1½ **jiggers curaçao**
½ **jigger lemon juice**
6 **jiggers brandy**
Add to each drink:
1 **dash angostura bitters**
Strain into chilled glasses and add a twist of lemon peel.

SCARLET O'HARA

Shake well with ¾ cup cracked ice:
4 **jiggers Southern Comfort**
3 **jiggers cranberry juice**
1 **jigger lime juice**
Strain into chilled glasses and serve with a twist of lime peel.

SIDECAR

The use of apple brandy changes a Sidecar into a **Jack Rose**. Shake with ¾ cup cracked ice:
½ **jigger Cointreau**
1½ **jiggers lemon juice**
6 **jiggers brandy**
Strain into chilled glasses and serve with a twist of lemon peel.

STINGER

Shake with ¾ cup finely crushed ice:
1½ **jiggers white crème de menthe**
6 **jiggers brandy**
(½ **jigger lime juice**)
Strain into chilled glasses.

ABOUT VODKA, AQUAVIT, TEQUILA AND THEIR COCKTAILS

The spirits mentioned above just about complete the roster of those normally obtainable in the American market. They are strikingly different in character. Vodka and aquavit look—deceptively, we hasten to add—like branch water. But whereas vodka is almost tasteless while going down and almost odorless afterwards, aquavit has a strong aroma of caraway. It follows that while vodka is often used instead of gin or whisky in mixed drinks—particularly sours—aquavit is almost invariably drunk straight and very cold. Occasionally, it is combined with tomato juice as a cocktail. Tequila, which a friend of ours has dubbed "the Gulp of Mexico," appeals to a very limited number of aficionados. Try it before you buy it.

MARGARITA

Stir well with ³/₄ cup cracked ice:

    5 **jiggers tequila**
    2¹/₂ **jiggers lime or lemon juice**
    ¹/₂ **jigger Triple Sec**

Pour into glasses, the rims of which have been rubbed with citrus rind and then spun in salt.

TOVARICH

Shake well with ³/₄ cup cracked ice:

    3¹/₂ **jiggers vodka**
    2¹/₂ **jiggers kümmel**
    2 **jiggers lime juice**

Strain into chilled glasses draped with a small sprig of parsley.

BLOODY MARY

This and the cocktail that follows are noticeably less aggressive than the usual run. In fact, they are widely recommended for the morning after, as well as the night before. When gin takes the place of vodka, we have a **Ruddy Mary**.

Shake well or blend with ³/₄ cup crushed ice:

    3 **jiggers vodka or aquavit**
    6 **jiggers or 1 cup chilled tomato juice**
    1 **teaspoon lemon juice**
    1 **teaspoon Worcestershire sauce**
    2 **drops hot pepper sauce**
    ¹/₄ **teaspoon celery salt**
    ¹/₄ **teaspoon salt**
    Pinch garlic salt

Serve without straining in whisky sour glasses.

SCREWDRIVER

Shake well with ³/₄ cup cracked ice:

    2 **jiggers vodka**
    6 **jiggers very fresh orange juice**

Strain into chilled glasses decorated with a small slice of orange. If the orange juice is bland, this drink benefits from a small quantity of sweetened lemon juice to taste.

ABOUT WINE

All this talk about the wine explosion in America goes with our conviction that the Revolution is here with a bang. And high time, too, that we blew up the wall of snobbery shutting out the Common People from the sanctum haunted by such characters of fact and legend as Dumas père, who declared that certain wines should only be drunk kneeling, with head bared; the French general who ordered his troops to present arms each time they marched past his favorite vineyard; and the Feinschmecker in the

New Yorker story who could remark with perfect aplomb to a fellow diner sharing first sips of a new vintage: "Ah, an obscene little wine!"

The obvious reason for the explosion is the number of traveling Americans exposed to the boons of the Old World, where wine is a staple like bread. Another sign of the times is the spectacular progress in the development of better and better wines on this side of the Atlantic. We rejoiced when one of the last bastions of snobbery came tumbling down in the spring of 1974. Two top French gastronomic critics began with a kind word for a certain wine available by the half gallon in our supermarkets. This was no news: all the cognoscenti have been in agreement that our wines in this class far outrank their Old World counterpart, the workingman's *vin ordinaire*. But then these two experts dropped their bombshell: A certain scarce vintage-marked California varietal was the rival of one of the finest French Bordeaux!

So as the Grape Revolution gains ground, we join the cause, gently proclaim the appreciation of wine as one of the Rights of Man, and make a few primer remarks that may serve as a preamble for those learning to develop an individual taste. To those far ahead of us, we cite Rabelais: *"Fays ce que vouldras"*—which, from fifteenth-century French to twentieth-century English, means "Do your own thing"—still the best advice about wine drinking. For the whole point of wine, as our ancestors well knew, is that it should be enjoyed—whether you pour it from a raffia-skirted chianti bottle like the one illustrated in the chapter heading; or the hand-blown flacon with the built-in ice chamber, on its left; or the crystal and silver walrus reminiscent of the many animal-shaped vessels of antiquity and after; or the more familiar Burgundy bottle at ease in its willow cradle.

Whatever pomp and trappings surround it, wine is basically the product of the grape and the airborne yeast that turns the sugar of the grape juice into alcohol. Wine is alive. Unlike soft drinks—or hard liquor—it can't be bottled up by its makers and forgotten. From the time the grape is picked until the wine is poured, it is responding to its surroundings with an almost feminine waywardness. Consider, for instance, the process called "racking"—transferring the clear young wine from one barrel to another: to produce the happiest results, this must be done when the moon is full, the wind from the north, and the weather clear.

The color of wine is due not to the color of the grape but to the length of time the skins remain with the juice. White wines may be made from red or black as well as from white grapes, but for white wine the skins are removed at the earliest possible moment. For the rosés—"pink" in French—red or black grapes are used, and the skins remain one to three days. For red wine, the skins remain for varyingly longer periods.

How to describe wine has always been a problem. **Dry** in wine parlance—not sour—is the opposite of sweet; all table wines—those of lower alcoholic content we drink with our meals as distinguished from the fortified types—are dry in varying degrees. All of this has more to do, of course, with taste than with quality. For body the best definition is substance. A full-bodied wine is not necessarily higher in alcohol, but it gives an impression of weight rather than lightness, and a sort of afterglow we associate with alcoholic drinks. Full body is far from always being a virtue. One wine can have flavor and alcoholic content similar to another's, yet be relatively more light-bodied and "delicate." You may like one or the other—or you may like both, though with different foods. When delicacy and body exist together, the balance is there that is one of the requisite qualities of a fine wine. The professional wine-tasters' accolade of "great" is reserved for the rarest combination of traits, for great wines, like great men and women, are few and far between.

As with man, age in wine can be a merit but often is not. Every wine has a youth, a prime and an old age. All table wines improve more in the bottle than in the cask, but some of them for only six or eight months, while others—especially among the reds— if properly stored, go on improving for years and years. Most wine, however, is as good when a year old as it will ever be, and will go downhill after its third birthday. Wines that should be consumed by the time they are three years old, and certainly by five, include most of the lesser reds in the world, most whites, and all the rosés. These include, in short, most of the wines that most of us will be drinking most of the time.

If wine, like art, is a matter of taste, we owe it to ourselves to become as discriminating as we can. Voltaire put it more graphically: "Beauty to the toad is the she-toad." How, then, do you go about training your palate? You taste all you can; you read all you can—or can stand to; and, when you get that far, you cultivate someone who knows wine and knows you—it could be your friendly wine seller. Sooner or later you will probably want to sample one

of the fine, aged wines of the Old World to understand the meaning of the standards of excellence.

Many countries of the world produce good wines, and everywhere the quality depends on four factors; soil, grape type, man and climate. The last is, naturally, what enters most into the custom of marking on the bottle a wine's vintage; that is, the date of the specific harvest. The more unpredictable the summer weather in a particular part of the world, the more important is the vintage labeling; where summers are invariably hot, vintage ratings are of little or no importance. And, for a number of reasons, vintage years taken out of context can mislead. Even in colder and variable climates, a year designated poor does not exclude the possibility of fine wines in some vineyards where microclimates may have protected the crop. Charted vintage ratings on the whole represent a consensus on how good the wines are going to be at their peak—which may be in five years, maybe in ten, or maybe in two. Putting such subtleties aside, there are nevertheless years to remember, and in one 10-year period in France and Germany there were many, though not necessarily in both countries at one time: '66, '69, '70, '71, '72, '73. Memorable wine years are coming thicker and faster than ever before—a fact due not only to climate but also, in part, to the increase of knowledge and skill among growers.

One can't stay for very long on the subjects of food and wine—those pleasures of life on which, with love included, the French are often considered authorities—without lapsing into their tongue and opening the atlas to France. For more than half the world's fine wines come from there, and in America and elsewhere some

French regional names like Burgundy and Chablis have been appropriated as broad terms for wine classification. French precision has developed a legal system of controlled place-names—*appellation contrôlée*—that guarantees not only the place of origin but the quality of a wine. The more specific the locale indicated on the label, the higher the quality. The system closes in like a series of concentric circles. For example, all the wines produced within a wide radius of the city of Bordeaux or blended with wines of the same general area can call themselves Bordeaux. Within that section are the smaller areas—townships such as St. Emilion or Graves—within which the legal requirements are higher. Wines grown within the district and meeting the standards have the right to use the specific district name, and the buyer can expect certain distinctive characteristics of wines grown there. Then comes a series of still smaller place names—specific parishes or communes within which the minimum requirements for quality are still more stringent.

Wine bottled at the *château* or *domaine* where it is grown, and not blended with wines from elsewhere, is labeled *Mise en bouteilles au château,* and often bears the name of the grower himself. A specific vineyard and its product may be marked as a certain *cru*—or growth—which implies that the wine is among the élite of its kind. One needn't add that the more specific the label, the more expensive the wine. As on all imported-wine labels, the French bottle often carries the name of the shipper or dealer first; the contents represent his choice or his blend.

The Bordeaux region in the southwest is by far the major wine-producing section of France, and the *cabernet sauvignon* is the most important grape type for Bordeaux wines—whose English synonym is claret. Despite its fame, the old province of Burgundy, southeast of Paris, produces only about 2% of the wines of France. But there are as many place "appellations" as there are separate and distinct wines, and the system reaches its logical conclusion when it zeroes in on the tiny parcels that produce the superb wines of the Côte d'Or—some of them only a few acres. This "Golden Slope" of scrubby hills has long produced the unparalleled wines that have given Burgundy its international name. The Burgundy grape types are chiefly *pinot noir* and *Chardonnay,* and all the wines carry the name of their village. The vineyards of the Beaujolais district produce a lighter and fruitier red wine from the *Gamay* grape; this wine, unlike the classic Burgundies, has to be drunk very young. The red wines of the Rhone Valley, considered sidekicks of the Burgundies, are grown in a sunnier region.

Moving northeast on the map of France, we come to Alsace, that ancient border province whose wines, like the names of its inhabitants, have a strong German accent. Its vineyards, among the world's loveliest, produce mostly white wines that, like those produced across the Rhine, are known for their pleasant lightness. They are usually named after the grape from which they are made, and sometimes carry the village name as well. Across the border in Germany, all the wines of consequence—many of them outstanding—are white and of varying degrees of sweetness. As in France there are two main districts, Rhine and Moselle, and two chief grape types, *Riesling* and *Sylvaner.*

There are nongeographic names such as Liebfraumilch and Moselblüm-chen that include all qualities. The German labeling system, prior to 1971, was a monument to the thoroughness of the Teutonic mind, and, after a pointer or two, we will leave you on your own in its orderly thicket.

The less favorable northern climate with its unpredictable doses of sunshine made the vintage year on German wines very important. The names on the labels reflected how much sun was available and how man manipulated the degree of sweetness: Spätlese—wine from ripened grapes picked after the main vintage is over; Auslese—from very ripe grapes in perfect bunches, some of them afflicted by the cultivated illness that the French call "noble rot"; Beerenauslese—only the finest, ripest grapes, picked out one by one; Trockenbeerenauslese—an echt-German term meaning piled together like a ten-car collision on the Autobahn, but here, grapes picked individually and left on the vine until practically raisined. Today, one need only look for the terms Qualitätswein or Qualitätswein mit Prädikat to assure a fine German wine.

When we've talked about wines from the hand-embroidered-handkerchief plots of Burgundy and those that come in minuscule amounts from German grapes chosen lovingly one by one, we have arrived—but where? In those very rarefied reaches we had wanted to avoid. It's time we headed home. For meantime, back at the ranch, things are happening to brighten the horizon for every wine amateur.

In California—whence comes 85% of our domestic wines—and in the East, too, the new watchword is **varietals**. This refers to wines named after the grape variety from which they are made—as against the **generics,** those tagged with the old misappropriated European regional names—like California claret or New York State Burgundy—and which are often available as jug wines. Varietal grapes—among many others are *cabernet sauvignon, pinot noir, Chardonnay, Riesling*—are more expensive and have a smaller yield per acre than those used in the generics, and are more complex in taste and aroma. Dedicated growers are planting more of the top grape varieties in the microclimates that suit them. Law requires only 51% of the name grape in a varietal bottle, but with more prime grapes available, more wineries are using from 75% to 100% varietals, blending for consistent flavor and other qualities rather than for economic reasons alone. And the red wines that need aging are being held longer. In short, wine-making in America is developing some overtones of the Old Country, where wines of individually distinctive character have been gradually differentiated over the centuries by nuances of geography, method and aging. It's a heartening trend.

The one great havoc that all but "did in" the European wines was wrought last century by a devastating plant louse, phylloxera. The phylloxera story is a curious series of vines-across-the-seas exchanges that hasn't ended yet. It began when the louse was transported to Europe by accident on some American vine cuttings exported for experimentation. Vines native to the eastern United States had apparently always been host to the louse, to which they had grown resistant, thanks to their tough, heavy roots. But in Europe, the more tender

Vitis vinifera, from which almost all the good wines of the world are made, was almost fatally vulnerable. The remedy *in extremis* was for us to send over our resistant stocks, on which the agonizing vinifera—"the wine-bearer"—was grafted. Practically all the wines of Europe now come from these vines grafted on American roots—and so do most American wines. The moral of the tale: Cast your vines on the water and they come back varietals.

But, strictly speaking, the only really American wines are from New York State—from such varieties as the Delaware and the Elvira—and, in much smaller amounts, from Ohio, where the grape type is the Catawba that had its heyday on the Rhinelandish Cincinnati hillsides in the 1890s. These varieties are from that entirely different breed, the native *labrusca* that could face up to the depredations of the plant louse and the North American winters. The sturdy *labrusca* harks back to the wild "fox" grapes that Viking explorers found growing in such profusion on these shores that they named their discovery Vineland. But non-foxy varietals are also now grown in these New York and Ohio vineyards, and white wines of the Riesling and Chardonnay types have met with increasing favor.

Our American champagnes—as well as their stepsisters the sparkling wines—come from vineyards both east and west. Whether or not they are in any way relatives of their French namesake is the question asked by some experts about all American wines of legitimate or illegitimate lineage. In any case, champagne the world over keeps its aura of felicitation. One of its French discoverers exclaimed that it tasted like stars, while Art Buchwald says he likes it because it tastes as though his foot's asleep. In buying imported champagne, the brand is—for once—more important than the vineyard, for virtually all champagne is a blend. By law, French champagne must be made by the laborious and expensive process of bottle-fermenting and must come from the Champagne country to the east of Paris. In America, any sparkling wine—even red—can legally call itself champagne if it's bottle-fermented and clearly labeled with its geographical origin—New York State, California or American. Sweetness in all champagne is produced by artificial "dosage" with small percentages of sugar. Beginning with the driest, the degrees are brut, extra-dry, and dry or sec. Champagne and sparkling wines come with a wired-down cork that has to be eased out gently—→ the bottle thoroughly chilled, to 35° to 40°, and held away from you and anyone else nearby. Devotees of champagne find it a good accompaniment to any meal, including breakfast. For those events in life which call for celebration with a gala, nothing equals a champagne fountain.

A single pouring from a jeroboam takes care of 34 glasses placed in fountain form. Shown, 48, is a glorious fountain for 31. For smaller parties, 11 glasses will work. Whether you pour champagne or punch, the effect is memorable. Better practice first, though, with tap water!

In the non-table-wine category come the sherries; their Italian cousins the Marsalas; the ports and the Madeiras—all again bearing Old World generic names from the towns of Jerez in Spain, Marsala in Sicily, Oporto in Portugal, and the Portuguese island of Madeira. These are "made" rather than natural wines: that is, they are fortified with alcohol while young to stop fermentation and preserve sweetness. In sherries, any sweetness and color is added, and neither is in any degree accidental. The drier sherries, like the drier Marsalas, are often used in cooking. They are distinguished by their nut-like flavor and make excellent apéritifs, as does a rare dry Madeira. They may be served chilled or at room temperature, as you prefer—here again controversy has raged. The darker, heavily sweetened sherries, including cream sherry, are, like the ports and most of the Madeiras, best enjoyed at the dessert end of a meal—or alone. Their relatives the fortified apéritif wines, sold under proprietary names such as Byrrh, Pernod, Dubonnet and Cinzano, are—except for some of the vermouths—really too sweet to be appetite stimulators, but they fill their niche as late-afternoon socializers.

The chart following is a bare-bones outline of suggestions as to what goes with what. It reflects the experience of generations in combining those traditional good marriages of food and wine. Their principles were sound and may still be followed, but one should leave some leeway for infidelity. For example, the purist dictum that wine served at a meal be preceded by the product of the grape—not the grain—will no doubt be more honored in the breach; it limits happy-hour intake to dry sherry or Madeira, dry white wine or champagne, or dry vermouth. The rest is common sense. If more than one wine is being served, white goes better before red. Sweet wines should be reserved for dessert. As a rule, the heavier the food, the heavier the wine: neither should overpower the other. And some foods fight with wine like cat and dog, so beware of any showdowns with vinegary salads, fishy hors d'oeuvre, onions, garlic, curries and strongly flavored sauces.

While the rosés do not usually compare with the reds or whites as dinner companions, they can be useful in bringing together the various flavors of a cold buffet, a barbecue, a picnic or a sandwich at lunch—or perhaps at dinner on a hot summer night, whatever the menu. Which brings us to the matter of temperature. The whites and rosés are served chilled; as for the reds, let the climate, the quality of the wine, and your own preference be your guide. If it bothers you to be told you can

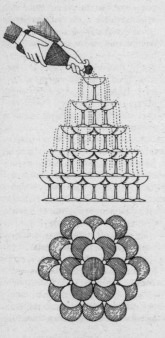

KEY

RED   WHITE   ROSÉ   CHAMPAGNE   SWEET WINE

Veal, lamb, pork and poultry

Beef and game

All kinds of foods   Desserts

serve red wine only at room temperature, think of the European peasant and cool it: he drinks his *vin ordinaire*—red or white—cooled in the brook in the summer and at the prevailing temperature in the winter. You might follow his style for an everyday wine. But for the Sunday red chosen for its special character, chilling could be a dirty trick. Bear in mind, too, that the "room temperature" rule came before central heating, and 72° is the top limit.

A few hints about serving and storing, and we will leave you with your corkscrew and your friends. The old custom of pouring a small amount of wine into the host's glass first—a sensible gesture that allowed him to check its quality—is less often observed today. In formal serving, wine is poured from the diner's right—where the glass is. The bottle should at all times be handled as little as possible. Wine bottles should be stored horizontally so that the wine covers the cork. If they are "laid away," the storage space should have some ventilation and as even a temperature as possible, with 45° and

70° as permissible extremes. A fine red wine should be stood upright to settle for a few hours and the cork removed for a time before serving. For how long? Again there is controversy. So, we repeat, put hidebound rules aside, and above all, enjoy!

Above are shown various types of glasses. From left to right: first is a versatile 6-ounce glass suitable for all types of wine. It is usually filled about halfway, as shown; for dessert wines, a little more than a third. Next in order are a traditional Rhinewine röhmer; a tall tulip glass for champagne—preferable to the saucer type, as it keeps the drink cold and preserves the fizz; a bubble glass for sparkling Burgundy; a pipe-stem sherry glass; a balloon brandy snifter; a liqueur glass. All are shown filled to the proper levels at the initial pouring. All except the brandy glass are held by the stem for drinking. The brandy glass is held cradled in the hand to warm the liquor and release its aroma. Some people even like their brandy warmed, see illustration for Café Brûlot, (I, 28).

The average serving of dinner wine or champagne is 3 to 3½ fluid ounces; of cocktail or dessert wine, 2 to 2½ ounces. The chart below gives volumes and servings:

SIZE	OUNCES	DINNER WINE AND CHAMPAGNE SERVINGS	COCKTAIL AND DESSERT WINE SERVINGS
Fifth—			
⁴/₅ qt.	25.6	8	8–12
Tenth—			
⁴/₅ pt.	12.8	4	4–6
Split	6.4	2	
Quart	32	10	10–14
Pint	16	5	5–7
½ Gallon	64	20	20–30
Gallon	128	40	40–60

ABOUT LIQUEURS AND CORDIALS

A common characteristic of almost all liqueurs and cordials is their sweetness. This quality relegates them as straight drinks to the after-dinner hour, along with a second demitasse. With some, such as kümmel, curaçao, Cointreau, Grand Marnier, anisette, crème de menthe or crème de cacao, a single flavor predominates. In others—Chartreuse, Bénédictine, Vieille Cure, Drambuie, for example—the flavor is more intricate. Those of still a third category are used almost entirely as components of mixed drinks. Of these

the following are perhaps the best known: falernum and orgeat, both with an almond flavor; kirsch/wild cherry; maraschino/cherry; crème de cassis/currant; grenadine/pomegranate. However, do not overlook the "mixing" potential of other liqueurs: a few drops, experimentally added, have touched off many a brave new cocktail. By themselves, serve liqueurs at room temperature or a little below, and in small quantities.

ABOUT BEER AND ALE

The storied nut-brown ale of old was a prosaic drink—cloudy, yeasty and unstable. The sparkling brews of today are the result of complex technological advances during the past century and a half. Those we now enjoy are brewed from barley malt and hops, chiefly, and vary in alcoholic content from around 3 to a little over 4% by weight. They are basically of 3 types, depending in large part on the degree of heat in processing: the light-bodied—"champagne"—and medium-bodied types, both greatly preferred by American consumers, and a heavy type. The last tends to be more substantial, more flavorsome, more bitter than the first two. Except for "Bock," virtually all the heavy-bodied beers currently distributed in this country are imported from Germany, Holland and Scandinavia and are usually labeled "Dark." Bock, the domestic manufacture of which seems to be dwindling, is a fairly heavy-bodied variant brewed in winter for spring sale—an "Easter beer."

Whether you purchase beer in bottles or in cans—and we have detected no difference in quality—never forget that despite pasteurization it is still full of living organisms, subject to deterioration and shock. So, if you wish to savor beer at its height, look at the date to make sure it won't be over 2 months old when it is served. Keep it stored in a dark place. Chill it slowly before serving and once cold do not allow it to warm up again and be rechilled. Never allow it to freeze.

Like the wine connoisseur, the beer expert is most particular about the temperatures at which he serves his brew. Forty degrees is favored as producing the fullest flavor, a not too great contrast between the temperature of the drink and that of the taste buds.

A slightly higher serving temperature is suggested for ale. This drink is made from the same ingredients as beer, except for the strain of the yeast. It is fermented rapidly and at room temperature rather than at the almost freezing temperatures modern beer demands, in its long, slow and intricately controlled processing.

Here are the traditional beer and ale glasses and mugs: a sentimental-looking stein, a Pilsner glass for light beer and an ale glass and mug. The true enthusiast is probably happiest drinking from an opaque container. It does not allow him to see the small imperfections in the appearance of the beer, which are visible when it is served in improperly washed glasses. Grease is the natural enemy of beer, for it kills the foam. So wash glasses with detergent, not with soap. The glasses should never be dried, but allowed to drain on a soft cloth.

Glasses may be chilled, but in any case they should be rinsed in cold water just before using and the beer poured into a tilted wet glass.

You may like a high or a low collar. The usual size is one-fourth the height of the glass or mug. A bottle of beer, despite popular superstition, is not so caloric as the average cocktail, but since it lacks the disembodied quality of table wines it is usually served with snacks and suppers.

ABOUT MIXED DRINKS

In the foregoing pages of this chapter we have dealt with our material on the "basic ingredient" principle and have attempted a chronological résumé of the drinks, simple or compound, which are likely to precede, go along with or follow meals—from the ceremonious to the completely informal. The following sections describe a number of between-meal or special-occasion drinks of such variety as to defy systematic listing—at least as far as their components are concerned.

Glasses and cups for mixed drinks vary greatly in size and shape. Collins glasses and lemonade and highball glasses, shown on 52, are similar in shape and vary in content from 8 to 16 ounces. The one illustrated is a 12-ouncer.

Silver cups with a handle, so that the frost remains undistributed, are highly favored for such drinks as mint juleps. Some persons dislike drinks served in metal, but if straws are used no metallic taste is noticeable. Juleps without straws should be served in very thin glassware. To frost the glasses, see 53.

Tom and Jerry mugs, shown next, hold about 8 ounces; punch glasses or cups, 3 or 4 ounces. These are frequently made of porcelain, an advantage when serving mulled or flaming drinks.

ABOUT TALL DRINKS

King-size drinks are commonly served in glasses holding 8 ounces or more. When mixers such as carbonated water—seltzer, club soda, Vichy, etc.—or ginger ale are used, refrigerate them if possible before adding them to the drink. To make decorative ice cubes for tall drinks, see (I, 35).

HIGHBALLS AND RICKEYS

Individual Servings
Use bourbon, Scotch, rye, or gin.
Into a 6-oz. glass, put 2 large ice cubes and add:

1 jigger of liquor chosen
Fill the glass with:

Carbonated water
Stir lightly with bar spoon and serve. For a rickey, add before the carbonated water:

Juice of ¹/₂ large lime
With dry liquors, you may add:

¹/₂ teaspoon Sugar Syrup, 35
A luxurious rickey can be concocted by adding a teaspoon or so of liqueur to the lime juice. Interesting effects in the tall-drink categories above are possible by further varying the basic ingredient. Try an applejack highball or one made with Dubonnet. The three following drinks are classic results of using one's imagination

freely in this area: **Vermouth Cassis,** with a base consisting of 1 pony crème de cassis and 1 jigger dry vermouth; **Horse's Neck** or **Cooler,** with a long spiral of lemon peel draped over the edge of the glass and ginger ale substituted for carbonated water; and **Spritzer,** with half Rhine wine and half carbonated water.

TOM COLLINS

1 Serving
Collinses, like rickeys, are a large family. But this one is the granddaddy of all the rest.
Combine in a 14- or 16-oz. glass with 4 ice cubes:

1 tablespoon Sugar Syrup, 35
Juice of medium-sized lemon
2 jiggers gin
Fill glass with:

Carbonated water
Stir and serve immediately.

GIN FIZZ

1 Serving
Fizzes may be made with whisky, rum or brandy as a base.
Combine in a bar glass:

1 tablespoon Sugar Syrup, 35
Juice of medium-sized lemon or lime
1¹/₂ jiggers gin
Shake well with ¹/₂ cup crushed ice and strain into prechilled 8-oz. glass. Fill with:

Carbonated water
Stir and serve.
A **Silver Fizz** is made by beating into the above Gin Fizz ingredients:

1 egg white

MINT JULEP

1 Serving

This drink can be superlative. And it is well, at this point, to remember that, as Voltaire put it, "The good is the enemy of the best." Use only the best bourbon; tender, terminal mint leaves for bruising; and very finely crushed or shaved ice. Chill a 14- or 16-oz. glass or silver mug in refrigerator.
Combine in a bar glass:

> **2 teaspoons Sugar Syrup, 35**
> **6 medium-sized mint leaves**
> **(1 dash angostura bitters)**

Bruise leaves gently with muddler and blend all ingredients by stirring together. Pour into bar glass:

> **1 large jigger bourbon**
> **whisky**

Stir again. Remove serving glass from refrigerator, pack it with ice and strain into it the above mixture. With a bar spoon, churn ice up and down. Add more ice to within 3/4 inch of top. Add:

> **1 pony whisky**

Repeat churning process until glass begins to frost. Wash and partially dry:

> **A long sprig of fresh mint**

and dip it in:

> **Powdered sugar**

Decorate glass with the sugared mint sprig. Insert long straws and serve.

When making a number of mint juleps, a less nerve-racking way to frost the glasses is to omit prechilling them. After churning, instead of waiting for them to frost in the open, place them in the refrigerator for 30 minutes. ▶ Be careful throughout this whole process not to grasp glasses with bare hands.

The stand illustrated, with its tiers of ice and carrying ring, makes a julep server par excellence. If the number of glasses required is not enough to fill all the shelf space, use the ones at the top for hors d'oeuvre. A deep tray, packed with finely crushed ice, will make an acceptable substitute for the julep stand.

CUBA LIBRE

1 Serving

Combine in bar glass:

> **Juice of 1 lime**
> **1/2 squeezed lime**
> **1 large jigger rum**

Put ingredients into 12- or 14-oz. glass. Add 3 large ice cubes. Fill with:

> **Cola**

Stir and serve.

MAPLED RUM

1 Serving

Combine in 10-oz. glass:

> **Juice of 1 lemon or lime**
> **1 tablespoon pure maple**
> **syrup**
> **1 jigger rum**
> **2 dashes grenadine**

Fill glass with finely crushed ice and churn up and down with bar spoon. Have ice within 3/4 inch of top. Add:

> **1 pony rum**

Churn again, insert straws and decorate before serving with:

> **Pineapple stick**
> **Slice of orange**
> **Cherry**

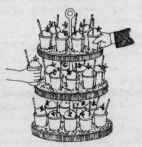

TONIC

1 Serving

Into a 12-oz. glass place 3 ice cubes and add:

1 large jigger gin or vodka

Fill glass with:

Quinine water or bitter lemon
(Lime or lemon juice to taste)

ABOUT PLUGGED FRUIT

We had no luck when, much younger, we plugged a watermelon and cautiously tried to impregnate it with rum. We never quite solved the problem of distribution. Later we discovered we had been too impatient. Time does the trick—about 8 hours. For those fortunate ones who can easily come by an abundance of other kinds of fruit, we give the following formulas for a couple of picturesque and delightfully refreshing drinks. Shown below are watermelon, coconut and pineapple.

COCONUT EXTRAVAGANZA

1 Serving

This rather beguiling specialty, as well as the one which follows, is only feasible if you have at hand a fairly plen-tiful supply of the featured container. To hold a coconut upright for serving, see at left. Cut or saw off the top of:

A coconut

This should produce a hole about 2¹/₂ inches in diameter. Drain and reserve the milk and add to it that of a second coconut. Pour into the hollow:

1 large jigger light rum
3 teaspoons apricot liqueur or Cointreau
3 teaspoons coconut cream, 244
The coconut milk

Add ³/₄ cup finely crushed ice, stir, insert straws and serve.

PINEAPPLE TROPIC

1 Serving

Slice off the top of:

A ripe pineapple

Hollow out a cavity about the size of a highball glass. Pour into it:

1 large jigger light rum
3 teaspoons Bénédictine

Fill cavity with finely crushed ice; stir well, bruising the inside of the pineapple, and garnish with:

Fresh fruit

Serve lidded, or cut a notch in the lid to insert the straw.

SHORT DRINKS

"Some like it hot, some like it cold." The drinks which follow are of both varieties, in that order.

GROG

1 Serving

In a 8-oz. mug, stir together:

1 teaspoon Sugar Syrup, 35
1 tablespoon strained lemon juice
1 jigger dark rum

Fill mug with:

Very hot tea or water
Garnish with a twist of:
Lemon peel
Try this drink using maple syrup instead of sugar syrup. Dust top with a little:

**Ground nutmeg or
cinnamon**

HOT BUTTERED RUM

1 Serving

Place in a hot tumbler:
1 teaspoon powdered sugar
Add:
¼ cup boiling water
¼ cup rum
1 tablespoon butter
Fill glass with boiling water. Stir well. Sprinkle on top:
Freshly grated nutmeg
This is an old-time New England idea of an individual portion. It may be modified. Curious, isn't it, that the Puritans made drinks like this one, which has been said to make a man see double and feel single.

TODDY

1 Serving

In a 8-oz. mug, place:
1 teaspoon Sugar Syrup, 35
1 stick cinnamon
**1 jigger whisky, rum or
brandy**
Fill mug with:
Very hot water
Impale over edge of mug:
½ lemon slice
studded with:
3 cloves

★ HOT TOM AND JERRY

4 Servings

Beat to a stiff froth:
3 egg whites

Beat separately until light in color:
3 egg yolks
Beat into yolks gradually:
3 tablespoons powdered sugar
**½ teaspoon each ground
allspice, cinnamon and
cloves**
Fold yolks into white and pour 2 tablespoons of this mixture into each of four 8-oz. china mugs. Add to each mug:
½ jigger lukewarm brandy
1 jigger lukewarm dark rum
Fill mugs with very hot water, milk, or coffee. Stir well and sprinkle the tops with:
Grated nutmeg

★ VIN BRÛLÉ

4 Servings

This winter-evening cheer, outdoors or in, offers a bonus before and after. When touched with a match, it bursts briefly into a tall blue flame—worth extinguishing the lights for. And the French say this grateful potion is better than aspirin to ward off the grip of a cold as well as the night chill.
Place in a saucepan, covered, over high heat:
1 bottle dry red wine
4 sticks cinnamon
Peel of 1 orange
3 or 4 tablespoons sugar
When the mixture comes to a boil, uncover and ignite. When the flame has died down, remove mixture from heat and ladle at once into mugs.

★ EGGNOG

1 Serving

If you are preparing this drink for an invalid, see note on uncooked eggs on 523.
In a small bowl, beat until light:
1 egg yolk

Beat in slowly:

    1 tablespoon sugar

    ¹/₄ cup cream

    ¹/₈ to ¹/₄ cup rum, brandy or whisky

    A few grains salt

Whip separately until stiff:

    1 egg white

Fold white lightly into other ingredients. Transfer mixture to punch glass. For eggnog in quantity, see About Party Drinks, following.

FLIP

                          1 Serving

Shake in bar glass with cracked ice:

    1 whole egg

    1 teaspoon sugar

    1 jigger sherry, brandy or port

Strain into 6-oz. glass. Sprinkle over top:

    Grated nutmeg

SANGRIA

                          6 Servings

An adaptation of a favorite Spanish summer thirst-quencher, to be served iced from a pitcher.

Mix:

    ³/₄ cup brandy

    ¹/₂ cup Cointreau

    4 cups red wine

    Juice of 3 lemons

    Sugar to taste

Add:

    2 thinly sliced oranges

    1 thinly sliced lemon

    ³/₄ cup seeded sweet cherries

    1 cup sliced fresh or canned peaches

SYLLABUB OR MILK PUNCH

                          2 Servings

Beat together in bar glass:

    1 tablespoon Sugar Syrup, 35

    1 jigger top milk

    1 large jigger heavy cream

    ¹/₂ cup sherry, port, Madeira or bourbon whisky

Serve at once in punch glasses.

ABOUT PARTY DRINKS

Most of the formulas in this section are of the punchbowl variety. In each instance, the ▶ quantity of liquid will amount to approximately 5 quarts and will serve about 20 persons—each one having two 4-oz. cups. When the word "bottle" is used, it means a fifth of a gallon or 25 ounces.

Fruit juices used in the concoction of party drinks should preferably be fresh; but frozen, unsweetened concentrates are quite acceptable, as long as you dilute them only about half as much as the directions on the container prescribe. Canned and bottled juices vary in quality—the best, in our opinion, being pineapple, apricot, cranberry, raspberry and grape. Ideally, punch mixes should be allowed to blend for an hour or so and, if served cold, chilled in the refrigerator before carbonated water or ice is added. With cold punches, be on the alert for dilution. Ice only two-thirds of the liquid at the outset and add the remainder just before the guests come back for seconds. Speaking of ice, avoid small pieces. At the very least, remove the cube grid from your ice trays and freeze a full unit. However, the two chilling devices illustrated are a lot more fun.

Before taking leave of cold party drinks, we want to remind you that any of the "sour" type cocktails—those made of an alcoholic base plus fruit juice—may serve as the foundation for delectable punches and cups. See Cocktails, 34–42.

DECORATIVE ICE MOLDS

Set aside in a bowl the amount of water to be frozen. Stir it well 4 or 5 times during a 10- or 15-minute period to break up and expel the air bubbles with which newly drawn tap water is impregnated. Otherwise, the

ice mold you build will be cloudy instead of crystal clear.

Have at hand such decorative ingredients as whole limes, lemons, oranges, slices of citrus fruit, large fresh cherries or strawberries, clusters of grapes, sprigs of mint, sweet woodruff, lemon thyme or other herbs and a few handsome fresh grape or bay leaves, etc.

Select a decorative metal mold of the tubular or ring type. Avoid vessels which are so deep as to induce top-heaviness in your final product and risk its turning turtle later.

Begin operations by partially freezing a layer of water in the container—proceeding much as you would in making a fancy gelatin salad, 234. In this case, of course, successive hardenings are frozen instead of being chilled. On the first slushlike layer, arrange a wreath of fruit and greenery. Cover the decoration carefully with a second layer of very cold water, returning the mold to the freezer, so that with renewed freezing the decoration is completely surrounded by clear ice. Repeat this procedure if the depth of the mold permits. Allow the contents to become thoroughly frozen. When the refrigerated drink has been transferred to the punch

bowl, reverse the ice mold container, wrap a hot wet towel around the metal until the ice is disengaged, and float it in this position on the drink.

To make decorative ice cubes for individual drinks, see (I, 35).

ICE PUNCH BOWLS

Next, we show a punch bowl which is ice itself—particularly useful if you wish to dilute a cold drink as little as possible. Place in the kitchen sink a 50-pound cube of ice. Choose a round metal bowl of at least 3-quart capacity. Chip out a small depression in the center of the ice block and set

the bowl over it. Fill the bowl with boiling water, being careful not to spill any on the ice beneath. As the heat of the bowl melts the ice, stir the water; and as the water cools, empty and refill the bowl, each time bailing out the depression in the ice, until the desired volume is displaced. Now, set the ice block where you wish to dispense the drink, moving it onto a waterproof tray or a leakproof square of heavy-duty aluminum foil. The foil square should be a couple of inches larger than the block, with the edges turned up about 1¹/2 inches all around to form a channel. Any crudities can be masked by greenery or flowers. The "ice bowl" may, of course, be utilized equally well for serving sherbets and mixing cocktails.

A subtle flavor can be imparted to punches by steeping in the basic mix, during the lagering period, slices of peeled seeded cucumber, then removing them before the drink is further processed. Sometimes a few dashes of bitters will confer "the old one-two" on an otherwise flabby punch. However you serve party drinks, go easy on decorative heavy fruit trimmings in the bowl itself.

PLANTER'S PUNCH

The difficulty with this drink, we have discovered, is that—in the ideal form we now present it—it has become complicated for single-drink construction. Accordingly, we have moved it to this part of the chapter: first, because it really should be shared with others; second, because we hope, having done so, you may go to the trouble of putting together, on occasion, an improvised approximation just for yourself.
Mix in a large pitcher or bowl:

   2 cups dark Jamaica rum
   2 cups curaçao
   8 cups light rum
   6-oz. can frozen pineapple
      juice concentrate
   6-oz. can frozen orange juice
      concentrate
   6-oz. can frozen limeade
      concentrate
   10 oz. frozen lemonade
      concentrate

Test for sweetness, using, if desired, remaining:

   (2 oz. lemonade)

Fill tall glasses three-fourths full with crushed ice. Pour punch mixture to within ³/4 inch of top. Decorate with pineapple chunk, slice of orange, strawberry or maraschino cherry. Serve with straws. The above formula makes a little more than a gallon and, being hefty to start with, should make 20 servings.

FISH HOUSE PUNCH

Mix in punch bowl:

   1 cup Sugar Syrup, 35
   1 cup lemon juice
   1 bottle dark rum
   1 bottle light rum
   1 bottle brandy
   7 cups water
   ¹/2 cup peach brandy

If peach liqueur is used instead of peach brandy, the amount of syrup should be reduced to taste. Some recipes for this famous punch use strong tea instead of water.

BOWLE

A German favorite that may be made with any of a variety of fruits.
Slice and place in a large bowl one of the following fruits:

   6 ripe unpeeled peaches or
   8 ripe unpeeled
      apricots or 1 sliced
      pineapple or
   1 quart strawberries

Sprinkle over the fruit:

   1 cup powdered sugar

Pour over mixture:

   1¹/2 cups Madeira or sherry

Allow to stand 4 hours or longer. Stir, then pour over a block of ice in a bowl. Add:

   4 bottles dry white wine

CHAMPAGNE PUNCH

Most punches are traditionally mixed with plain rather than carbonated water. When carbonated water is a component, the drink becomes a **cup**. Champagne Punch, sacred to weddings, occupies middle ground.

Peel, slice, crush and place in a large bowl:

3 ripe pineapples

Cover pineapple and juice with:

1 lb. powdered sugar

Let mixture stand, covered, for 1 hour. Add:

2 cups lemon juice
1/2 cup curaçao
1/2 cup maraschino
2 cups brandy
2 cups light rum

Stir and let stand for 4 hours. Place in a punch bowl with a block of ice. Stir to blend and chill. Just before serving, add:

4 bottles chilled champagne

WHISKY OR BRANDY CUP

Slice, place in a large bowl and crush:

2 cups fresh pineapple

Add:

1 quart fresh strawberries

Sprinkle over the fruit:

3/4 lb. powdered sugar

Pour over mixture:

2 cups dark rum

Allow mixture to stand, covered, for 4 hours. Add:

2 cups lemon juice
1 1/2 cups orange juice
1 cup grenadine
2 bottles bourbon or brandy

Place in punch bowl with block of ice. Stir to blend and chill. Just before serving, add:

2 quarts chilled carbonated
water or
dry ginger ale

If you like a predominant rum flavor, substitute for the fruit-steeping ingredient above:

1 1/2 cups brandy

and for the basic ingredient:

2 bottles light rum

In this as in other punch bowl drinks, it is wise to test the mix for flavor and sweetness before adding the diluent.

RUM CASSIS CUP

Mix in a punch bowl:

2 1/2 bottles light rum
2 1/2 cups dry vermouth
2 1/2 cups crème de cassis

Add block of ice. Pour over the ice:

2 quarts carbonated water

CLARET CUP

Slice, place in large bowl and crush:

1 cup fresh pineapple

Peel, halve and add:

4 ripe peaches
1/2 cup brandy

Sprinkle over mixture:

1 cup powdered sugar

Let stand for 4 hours. Add:

1 cup lemon juice
2 cups orange juice
1/2 cup maraschino
1/2 cup curaçao
2 bottles claret or other red
wine

Chill the mixture for 1 hour; remove peaches and pour over a block of ice in a punch bowl. Stir and add:

2 quarts carbonated water

RHINE WINE CUP

Mix in punch bowl:

1 cup Sugar Syrup, 35
2 cups lemon juice
1 cup brandy
2 cups dry sherry
1 cup strong tea
3 bottles Rhine wine or other
dry white wine
2 cups thinly sliced, peeled,
seeded cucumbers

After 20 minutes, remove cucumber. Add a large block of ice and pour over it:

1 quart carbonated water

MAY WINE

Another German drink, dedicated to springtime and featuring fresh waldmeister or sweet woodruff, 279, which, incidentally, may be grown in a shady corner of your backyard. Place in a bowl:

12 sprigs young waldmeister
1¼ cups powdered sugar
1 bottle Moselle or other dry white wine
(1 cup brandy)

Cover this mixture for 30 minutes, ▶ no longer. Remove the waldmeister. Stir contents of bowl thoroughly and pour over a block of ice in a punch bowl. Add:

3 bottles Moselle
1 quart carbonated water or champagne

Thinly sliced oranges, sticks of pineapple and, most appropriately of all, sprigs of waldmeister may be used to decorate the "Maitrank."

★ EGGNOG IN QUANTITY

I. A rich and extravagant version that is correspondingly good. Some people like to add a little more spirit to the following recipes, remembering Mark Twain's observation that "too much of anything is bad, but too much whisky is just enough." See note on uncooked eggs, 523. Beat separately until light in color:

12 egg yolks
Beat in gradually:
1 lb. confectioners' sugar
Add very slowly, beating constantly:

2 cups dark rum, brandy, bourbon rye

These liquors may each form the basic ingredient of the nog or may be combined to taste. Let mixture stand covered for 1 hour to dispel the "eggy" taste. Add, beating constantly:

2 to 4 cups of liquor chosen
2 quarts whipping cream
(1 cup peach brandy)

Refrigerate covered for 3 hours. Beat until stiff ▶ but not dry:

8 to 12 egg whites
Fold them lightly into the other ingredients. Serve the eggnog sprinkled with:
Freshly grated nutmeg

II. Less powerful, less fluffy than the preceding nog, and a boon to the creamless householder. Beat until light in color:

12 eggs
Beat in gradually:
1 lb. confectioners' sugar
½ teaspoon salt
¼ cup vanilla
Stir in:
8 cups evaporated milk
diluted with:
3 cups water
Stir in:
4 cups dark rum, brandy, bourbon or rye

Cover the nog closely and let it ripen in the refrigerator for 24 hours. Stir again and serve sprinkled with:
Freshly grated nutmeg

★ TOM AND JERRY IN QUANTITY

See note on uncooked eggs, 523. Beat until stiff ▶ but not dry, cover and set aside:

1 dozen egg whites
Beat separately until light in color:
1 dozen egg yolks

Into the yolks, beat gradually:

> **³/4 cup powdered sugar**
> **2 teaspoons each ground allspice, cinnamon and cloves**

Fold seasoned yolks into whites. Into each of twenty 8-ounce china mugs, place 2 tablespoons egg mixture and:

> **¹/2 jigger lukewarm brandy**
> **1 jigger lukewarm dark rum**

Fill each mug with:

> **Very hot water, milk or coffee**

Stir vigorously until drink foams. Dust top with:

> **Grated nutmeg**

★ GLOGG

> **Twenty 6-Ounce Servings**

Heat separately in stainless steel pans ♦ but do not boil:

> **2 quarts claret**
> **2 quarts aquavit**

Place in the hot claret:

> **Peel of 1 orange**

and also a silver tea ball holding:

> **Seeds from 4 cardamom pods**
> **12 whole cloves**

In a silver punch bowl, place:

> **16 lumps sugar**

Pour over it 2 cups of the heated aquavit and ignite it. While it is still burning, pour in, so as to extinguish the flame, the rest of the aquavit and the hot wine. Meanwhile place in individual heated mugs:

> **3 or 4 whole blanched almonds**
> **3 or 4 seeded raisins**

Fill the mugs with the hot mixture and serve at once.

★ MULLED WINE OR NEGUS IN QUANTITY

Make a syrup by boiling for 5 minutes:

> **2¹/2 cups sugar**

> **1¹/4 cups water**
> **4 dozen whole cloves**
> **6 sticks cinnamon**
> **3 crushed nutmegs**
> **Peel of 3 lemons, 2 oranges**

Strain syrup. Add to it:

> **4 cups hot lemon or lime juice**

Heat well ♦ but do not boil, and add:

> **4 bottles red wine or Madeira, port or sherry**

Serve very hot with slices of:

> **Lemon and pineapple**

★ WASSAIL

The best time to "come a-wassailing" is, of course, Christmas week.
Core and bake, 117:

> **1 dozen apples**

Combine in a saucepan and boil for 5 minutes:

> **1 cup water**
> **4 cups sugar**
> **1 tablespoon grated nutmeg**
> **2 teaspoons ground ginger**
> **¹/2 teaspoon ground mace**
> **6 whole cloves**
> **6 allspice berries**
> **1 stick cinnamon**

Beat until stiff ♦ but not dry:

> **1 dozen egg whites**

Beat separately until light in color:

> **1 dozen egg yolks**

Fold whites into yolks, using large bowl. Strain sugar and spice mixture into eggs, combining quickly. Bring almost to boiling point separately:

> **4 bottles sherry or Madeira**
> **2 cups brandy**

Incorporate the hot wine with the spice and egg mixture, beginning slowly and stirring briskly with each addition. Toward the end of this process, add the brandy. Now, just before serving and while the mixture is still foaming, add the baked apples.

Wassail can also be made with a combination of beer and wine, preferably sherry, in which case the proportion should be roughly 4 of beer to 1 of sherry.

CANAPÉS AND TEA
SANDWICHES

In contrast to hors d'oeuvre, which follow in the next chapter, canapés have their own built-in bread or pastry component and often resemble very small tea sandwiches. Since the making is similar, they are discussed here together. For additional fillings in sandwiches served as luncheon entrées and for heartier large sandwiches, see (I, 267).

Illustrated above on the long leaftray is a varied assortment. Beginning at the handle end are, first, several two-tiered sandwiches, the top layer of which is doughnut-shaped, so that the filling is partially revealed. Next come those perennial favorites—watercress sandwiches—rolled in the thinnest of buttered bread; followed by some two-toned triangles and open-faced cucumber disks garnished with tiny shrimp and seafood-filled barquettes; crabmeat sandwiches garnished with parsley; and, finally, strips of toasted bread filled with mushrooms. Although a set piece like this laden big leaf creates a sensation when initially presented, it loses effect if some of its contents manage to survive the first round. For this reason it is often better practice to serve on smaller platters which can be quickly replenished. This is especially true for heated or toasted items, as shown on the right in an attractive heatproof ceramic dish with a handle for easy passing.

The upper tiers of the extended oriental box are filled with mayapple blossoms and ivy for double duty as a centerpiece. In the other trays are small cream puff shells, 370, filled with pâté, and filled sandwiches rolled like snails, 69.

Because a gay and festive presentation of canapés and tea sandwiches is so desirable, we suggest ways in which breads and pastries can be made to look their best, by methods either fast and furious or more leisurely and elaborate.

It is often easier to make small sandwiches in quantity ◗ by working with a whole loaf rather than with individual slices. A number of methods of cutting and combining different breads are illustrated. In several instances the crusts have been removed and the bread cut horizontally. It is possible to get six or seven long slices from the loaf and then spread the entire surface before stacking and shaping. A variety of forms cut economically from a single big sandwich base is sketched on 65. Parti-colored sandwiches can be produced by combining white, whole wheat, rye and brown bread.

Rolled sandwiches may be made quickly from long thin slices. A number of other shapes are illustrated on 63. Lower left are two-layer sandwiches, the top layer of which is doughnut-shaped to allow the color of the filling to show through. On 65, lower right, successive thin bread or sausage slices are shown bound with a filling and cut in pie-shaped wedges, 96.

When making sandwiches of any kind in quantity ▶ time is saved by setting up an assembly line and using mass-production techniques. Line up bread slices in rows. Place dabs of seasoned butters or mayonnaise on one row, filling on the next. Then do the final spreading by bringing the fillings and butters well out to the edges. Put hard butter or mayonnaise twice through a grinder with other ingredients and use a coarse blade. For closed sandwiches, do all the assembling, stacking, cutting and packaging in turn. For open-faced sandwiches, cut garnishes just before serving and keep them from drying out by placing them in plastic bags. After the base is spread, complete the garnishing of one type, then of another, before arranging for presentation.

PREPARING AND KEEPING SANDWICHES

▶ A few preliminary steps help toward serving sandwiches in prime condition. Have ready foil; moistened, wrung-out cloths; transparent self-sealing tissue, or plastic bags. Refrigerate double sandwiches, wrapped, without delay.

Open-faced sandwiches, if made of materials heavy in fat, may be quick-frozen and can then be wrapped without damage to their decorations or surfaces. Store in boxes to keep them free from the weight of other foods. Also place them away from freezer coils or fast-freeze area. For more details, see 657. ▶ It is often preferable to freeze the fillings alone and make up these fancy sandwiches shortly before serving.

When preparing in advance sandwiches that include watery materials like lettuce not suitable for freezing, be sure that any moist or juicy filling is put on bread well spread with a firm layer of butter or heavy mayonnaise, so that the bread will not get soggy. If tomato or cucumber slices are used, see that they are cut and allowed to drain well on a rack before putting them in the sandwiches.

To avoid excessively dry bread in preparing canapés on toast, proceed as follows for open-faced types: toast bread on one side under broiler; apply spread or topping to toasted side; and return to oven until topping is warmed through. For double-toasted sandwiches, toast under broiler one side only of each slice; spread topping between toasted sides; return to oven to toast the top untoasted surface; and serve—toasted side up. For toasted canapés which must be prepared more than a few minutes in advance, use Melba toast, 355, and heat briefly in a moderate oven just before serving.

BREAD FOR SANDWICHES

The number of sandwiches to a loaf of bread is hard to gauge because of shape variations, but from a 1-pound loaf of sandwich bread you can expect at least 20 slices. Allow about 1 pound butter for 3 to 4 pounds of sandwich loaf. Do not have the loaf presliced, but slice it thin yourself. The number of sandwiches to allow for each guest is even harder to judge, although 8 to 10 small snacks, either sandwiches or canapés, are not too much to count per person.

◗ To avoid raggedy sandwiches, use a finely textured bread. Otherwise, try chilling or freezing ordinary bread before cutting. This procedure makes for more practical handling throughout, particularly in preparing rolled shapes, which should be very thin and made of very fresh bread. Other sandwiches are easier to make if the bread is one day old. Cut fresh or frozen bread with a very sharp hot knife. Remember, though, that all bread which has been frozen dries out quickly after thawing and that precautions should be taken to keep the sandwiches as moist as possible. Have spreads at about 70° to protect bread from pulling or tearing. If the spread happens to be an aspic, keep it

in place by applying to the bread a very thin preliminary coating of mayonnaise.

SANDWICH SHAPES

It is surprising how a few fancy sandwiches with attractive garnishes, (I, 268), will help to perk up a platter. A combination of open and closed sandwiches gives variety to the tray. Sometimes medium-sized oblong trays filled with alternating rows of similarly cut but contrastingly spread openfaced sandwiches—placed closely together—make a quick and pleasant change from large platters more sparsely arranged with fancy sandwiches. Rolled sandwiches with sprigs of cress or parsley projecting—placed like the spokes of a wheel—make a charming border for a platter.

ROLLED SANDWICHES

Freeze:

Fresh unsliced sandwich bread

Remove crusts and slice as thin as possible with a hot sharp knife. Spread the bread with:

A softened filling

We particularly enjoy as a filling:

(Cream cheese mixed with cucumber and onion juice)

Be sure the filling goes out to the edges, so the roll will be well sealed. When the bread is completely thawed, roll the sandwiches. Tuck into the ends, but allow to protrude:

Cress or parsley sprigs

◗ Wrap firmly and refrigerate, so the sandwiches will hold their cylindrical shape when served.

RIBBON SANDWICHES

Cut the crusts from:

**White bread
Dark bread**

Spread the slices with:

**Butter or Cream Cheese
Spreads, 70, 71**

Place 3 to 5 slices of bread alternately in stacks. Cut them into bars, squares or triangles, see illustration, on 65.

FLOWER CANAPÉS

If you have an herb garden, many enchanting sandwiches can be made from the small-scaled leaves and blossoms. Or in winter, cut:

**Small rounds or squares
of bread**

Flatten with a rolling pin before spreading with:

Soft cream cheese

Place across each sandwich a very narrow:

**Strip of green pepper or
stem of chive or parsley**

This represents a stem. Place at the top to form the flower:

**A slice of stuffed olive or a
fancy cut of carrot or
radish**

Cut into lengthwise slices to form leaves:

Small sweet-sour pickles

Place the pickle slices opposite each other on the green pepper stem.

★ CHRISTMAS CANAPÉS

I. Cut into 2-inch rounds:

Thin bread slices

Spread the rounds with:

A cream cheese mixture, 71

Cut into tiny rounds, about $1/8$-inch:

**Maraschino cherries,
pimiento, cranberries—or
use tiny red decorettes**

Chop until fine:

Parsley

Make a narrow ring of the parsley around each piece of bread. Dot it at intervals with the red rounds to suggest a holly wreath.

II. Or, use:

A sprig of parsley

shaped like a tree and dot it with the small red "balls" described above.

ZOO SANDWICHES

For very young children's parties, make closed double or triple sandwiches in animal shapes using fancy cookie cutters. Triple-layered sandwiches can be made to stand upright on the plate as shown below.

SANDWICH LOAVES

These can even be a meal by themselves—an excellent luncheon dish with coffee and a dessert, and, when made in individual sizes, real charmers. As a decorative center for a birthday buffet, use one large loaf, as shown above; or make an individual loaf for each guest, seen above on the right, and group the loaves around a pile of gaily wrapped gifts.

I. Cut the crusts from:

**A loaf of unsliced white or
whole wheat bread**

Cut the loaf into 3 or 4 lengthwise slices. Butter the inner sides of

the slices and spread them with a
layer of:

**Chicken, shrimp, ham, egg
or salmon salad**

a layer of:

**Drained crushed pineapple
and cream cheese**

a layer of:

**Drained sliced tomatoes,
lettuce or watercress**

or any appetizing combination of
salad or sandwich ingredients. If it
suits your filling, add some:

**Anchovy paste or curry
powder**

to the cream cheese. Be sure to cut
the bread thin enough and spread the
fillings thick enough to keep the
bread from dominating. Wrap the loaf
firmly in a moist towel, chill well,
unwrap and place on a platter. Cover
with:

**Softened cream cheese,
smooth cottage cheese, or
Mayonnaise Collée, (I, 427)**

Individual slices cut from the finished loaf are shown above.

II. This holds well if prepared in advance. Cut the top and bottom from:

**An unsliced large round
rye loaf**

and reserve them as the base and lid
for a crust container. Using as much
of the bread as possible, carefully cut
out in one piece a straight-sided
cylinder from the soft center, leaving
a crust ring. Then slice this cylinder
of bread horizontally into 6 thin
slices. Coat the tops of the second,
fourth and sixth slices with butter and
with not too moist:

Seasoned fillings

Cover the spread slices with the first,
third and fifth slices. Keeping the
shape of the large cylinder orderly,
cut it into narrow wedges. Now, carefully place the cut cylinder on the bot-

tom crust and surround with the crust
ring. Insert picks around the outer
edge of the crust bottom to impale
the crust ring and keep it from slid-
ing. Cover with the top crust as a lid.
Wrap and refrigerate until ready to
serve.

BREAD OR OTHER BASES FOR
CANAPÉS

Use coarse ryes, whole wheats and
cheese breads from the Yeast and
Quick Bread section, 296, and suggestions from Uses for Ready-Baked
Breads, 353. There are good cracker
suggestions in Soups, (I, 172), and
suggestions for various pastries in
Pies, 357–374.

Or use small versions of luncheon
sandwiches, (I, 267); Ravioli, (I, 204);
Bouchées, 369; or Tarts or Barquettes,
below. Don't forget the many available "ethnic" bases, like tortillas or
crisp thin Japanese rice crackers.

TARTS AND TARTLETS FOR
CANAPÉS

I. Preheat oven to 425°.
Prepare:

**Biscuit Dough, 348, or
Pie Dough, 360**

Roll or pat it until it is about 1/8 inch
thick. Cut it into 3-inch squares.
Place in the center of each square one
of the fillings listed under:

**Fillings for Pastry
Canapés, 70**

Moisten the corners of the dough
lightly with water. Fold up the sides
of the dough and pinch the corners to
make a tart shape. Bake tarts about
10 minutes.

II. Or, fill the tart with:

**A thin slice of cheese,
1 1/2 × 2 inches**

Top this with:

> ¹/₂ slice tomato

Season the tomato with:

> A grating of pepper
> A little salt
> (A sprinkling of brown
> sugar)

Sprinkle the top with:

> Cooked diced bacon

Bake as in **I,** above.

III. Fill with:

> Hot spicy puréed spinach

Lay on it:

> A smoked oyster

Brush with:

> A little White
> Sauce I, (I, 383)

to which has been added:

> Grated Swiss cheese

Bake as in **I,** above.

RICH COCKTAIL TART OR QUICHE

A physician in our family once took to task a scandalously obese patient. "But, doctor," said the patient plaintively, "one must offer the stomach something from time to time." This is a favorite offering in our family. Preheat oven to 400°.
Prepare any unsweetened:

> Pie Dough, 360

Shape into tiny tarts and bake about 5 minutes. Remove from oven. ◗ Lower heat to 325°. Fill each tart with 1 tablespoon of the following mixture:

> 1 beaten egg
> ³/₄ cup cream
> 2 teaspoons grated Parmesan
> cheese
> (2 tablespoons sautéed
> mushrooms or crab meat)
> ¹/₂ teaspoon salt
> A small pinch coriander

Bake the tarts 15 minutes or until the quiche has set. Keep them hot and toasty in an electric skillet. For other Quiche recipes, see (I, 244).

BARQUETTES FOR CANAPÉS

I. Preheat oven to 425°.
Prepare:

> Biscuit Dough, 348, or
> Pie Dough, 360

Roll until it is about ¹/₈ inch thick. Since barquettes are shaped like a scow or flat-bottomed boat, but with pointed ends, use either a barquette mold or something similarly shaped to form the pastry. Place in the barquettes a:

> Filling for Pastry Canapés,
> 70, suitable for heating

Bake 10 to 12 minutes.

II. Line the bottoms of the baked barquette shells with a coating of:

> Mayonnaise

Make a pattern of:

> Chilled caviar
> Pearl onions

Coat the top with:

> Aspic Glaze, (I, 427)

The aspic should be based on fish or chicken stock. Flavor with:

> Lemon

Refrigerate several hours before serving.

STUFFED CHOUX, PUFF PASTE OR PÂTE SHELLS

I. Bake:

> 1-inch Choux Paste Shells,
> 370, or Bouchées, 369

Split them on one side. Fill with one of the softer fillings, see:

> Fillings for Pastry
> Canapés, 70

Reheat the puffs in a 425° oven.

II. Put into the base of a small cream puff shell a layer of:

Sweetened whipped cream
Lightly insert with the pointed end up:
A flawless ripe strawberry

III. Or, fill the puffs with:
Soft cream cheese
A dab of bright jelly

TURNOVERS, RISSOLES OR FRIED PIES

These triangular or crescent-shaped pastries make attractive canapés. If baked, they are **turnovers**. If deep-fat-fried, you may apply the homely title of **fried pies** or the more exotic one of **rissoles** or **empañadas**.
Roll to the thickness of ⅛ inch any:
Pie Crust, 360
Cut it into 2½-inch rounds or squares. Place in the center of each round any of the:
Fillings for Pastry Canapés, 70
Brush the edges of the rounds lightly with water. Fold the dough over into crescents. Be sure to seal the pastries very firmly if you are deep-fat frying, so that none of the filling escapes into and ruins the frying fat. Fry in deep fat heated to 365° until golden. For turnovers the tops of the pastries may be brushed with:
(1 egg yolk, diluted with 2 tablespoons cream)
Bake in a 400° oven until brown. Serve them around a large garnish of:
Fried Parsley, (I, 338), or chervil

CANAPÉ SNAILS

If the approval of guests is to be taken as a criterion of excellence, this is the prize-winning canapé. It reminds us of a fellow guest who hesitated to help himself, saying, "Well, I shouldn't—I've had two already." Which remark was capped by his hostess's brisk and crushing reply: "You've had six, but who's counting?"
Preheat oven to 425°.
Cut into very thin oblongs any:
Pie Crust, 360, or crustless soft bread
The bread will be easier to cut if wrapped in foil and chilled thoroughly. Spread the oblongs with:
Fillings for Pastry Canapés, 70
Roll them like a jelly roll. Chill; cut in ½-inch slices and bake on a greased pan until light brown.

TACOS

This popular Mexican snack is called by many names in different parts of the country. Tacos are toasted tortillas cut into thirds and filled with hot or mildly seasoned ingredients. This mix is fairly mild. Sauté until golden brown:
1 finely chopped onion
in:
2 tablespoons butter
Add and simmer about 3 minutes:
½ cup tomato juice
3 peeled minced green chilis
1 cup shredded cooked chicken or cooked pork sausage meat
⅛ teaspoon thyme
1 teaspoon salt
Dash of cayenne
Set this filling aside. Now fry in deep fat heated to 380° until golden:
About 18 Tortillas, 343
Remove them from the fat and drain. Cut into thirds. Place 1 teaspoon of the above filling on each piece. Fold in half, secure with a pick and bake until almost crisp in a 450° oven.

GLAZED CANAPÉS AND SANDWICHES

Small glazed canapés are very showy for cocktail service and in larger sizes make a lovely luncheon plate when garnished with a salad. ▶ But they must be kept refrigerated, as they have a natural tendency to turn soggy.
Use:

Choux Paste Shells, 370, tartlets or fancy-shaped thin toasts

Coat these canapé bases first with:

Mayonnaise

Then spread them with:

Well-seasoned fish paste, turkey, drained tomato slices, ham strips or asparagus tips

You may sprinkle with:

(Chopped dill)

or any combination suitable for open-faced sandwiches. Cover with a ¼-inch to ⅜-inch layer of:

Well-seasoned Aspic Glaze, (I, 427)

using 1⅓ cups stock or vegetable juice, 1 tablespoon gelatin and 1 tablespoon lemon juice. Place the canapés on a rack. The aspic should be jelled to the thickness of heavy cream partially beaten. Allow it to coat the surface of the tart or envelop the canapé. Refrigerate at once and let the gelatin set 1 to 2 hours. Then serve as soon as possible.

FILLINGS FOR PASTRY CANAPÉS

Place in the center of the preceding pastry cases 1 teaspoon or more of one of the following ingredients.

Cheese Spreads, 71
Anchovy paste and soft cream cheese

Well-seasoned or marinated oysters
Mushrooms, heavily creamed and seasoned
Chicken or other croquette mixtures, highly seasoned
Chicken, lobster, crab or fish salad
Caviar and soft cream cheese
Liver sausage or braunschweiger, seasoned with catsup
Cooked sausage meat, seasoned with mustard
Sliced link sausages and stuffed olives
Deviled ham, cream cheese and catsup
Minced cooked clams or crab meat
Cooked calf brains with Hollandaise Sauce, (I, 410)
Curried shrimp or poultry
Thin slices of ham, smoked tongue or smoked sausage and cheese

BUTTER SPREADS

There are many ways of preparing flavorsome, quick sandwich spreads with a butter base. Beat the butter until soft. Add other ingredients gradually. Chill the butter mixture until it is of spreadable consistency or shape it attractively. For Butter Shapes, see 201.
Use one of the simple suggestions in this recipe or in the more elaborate Seasoned Butters, (I, 397).
Beat until soft:

¼ cup butter

Add to the butter slowly one or more of the following:

½ teaspoon lemon juice
½ teaspoon Worcestershire sauce or ½ teaspoon dry mustard

½ teaspoon grated onion or
    minced garlic
(⅛ teaspoon lemon rind)

Additions to the butter mixture may
be chosen from these fresh herbs and
other ingredients—either chopped or
made into a paste by using your mortar and pestle:

2 tablespoons parsley
2 tablespoons chives
1 tablespoon dill or fennel
1 tablespoon mixed herbs:
    basil, tarragon, burnet and
    chervil
2 tablespoons watercress
1 tablespoon nasturtium
    leaves
¼ cup soft or grated cheese:
    Parmesan or Romano
1 tablespoon anchovy or
    other fish paste
1 tablespoon horseradish
1 tablespoon olive paste
2 tablespoons Catsup, 686, or
    Chili Sauce, 686
1 tablespoon chutney
¼ teaspoon curry powder
    Season to taste

🕯 SEAFOOD BUTTER

For a more economical form, see
(I, 399).

Put through a sieve or blender, or chop:

1 cup cooked shrimp, lobster,
    lobster coral, fish roe, etc.
¼ lb. butter
1 teaspoon or more lemon
    juice
    A fresh grating of white
    pepper

Mold and chill to serve on an hors
d'oeuvre platter or use as a spread.

DRIED HERBS IN WINE FOR
BUTTER SPREADS

Combine:

2 tablespoons crushed dried

herbs: thyme, basil,
    tarragon, chervil
½ cup dry white wine or
    lemon juice

Permit the herbs to soak for 2 hours
or more. Follow the recipe for Butter
Spreads, opposite, adding the herb
mixture to taste. Keep the rest to use
combined with melted butter as a
dressing for vegetables.

🕯 BLENDER MUSHROOM
BUTTER

Sauté until golden brown:

½ lb. sliced mushrooms

In:

¼ cup butter

Put the mushrooms and butter into an
electric blender and add:

½ cup soft butter
¼ teaspoon pepper
¼ teaspoon salt
3 tablespoons dry sherry or
    brandy

Blend until smooth.

NUT BUTTERS

I. Cream until soft enough to stir:

½ cup butter

Stir in:

1 cup finely ground pecans or
    walnuts
2 tablespoons Worcestershire
    sauce

II. 🕯 In electric blender combine:

1 to 2 tablespoons salad oil
1 cup salted peanuts, cashews
    or pecans

CREAM CHEESE SPREADS

What would we do without cream
cheese?—the perfect emergency
binder for one of the many taste-
provokers listed below.

Rub a bowl with:
    (Garlic)
Mash until soft and combine:
    **1 package cream cheese:
       3 oz.**
    **1 tablespoon cream or
       cultured sour cream**
Add one or more of the following:
    ¹/₂ teaspoon onion juice
    **1 teaspoon chopped onion or
       chives**
    **1 tablespoon lemon or
       lime juice**
    **1 tablespoon finely chopped
       Fines Herbes, 253**
    **1 tablespoon finely chopped
       parsley**
    **1 tablespoon finely chopped
       celery or green pepper**
    **¹/₄ cup chopped ripe or
       pimiento-stuffed olives**
    1 tablespoon horseradish
    **3 tablespoons chopped crisp
       bacon, minced chipped beef
       or ground cooked ham**
    **¹/₂ tablespoon anchovy or
       fish paste**
    **¹/₂ cup shredded salted
       almonds or other nuts**
    1 tablespoon caviar
    **1 tablespoon chopped fresh
       marigold petals**
Season with:
    **Salt, paprika or red pepper,
    if needed**
For a tea canapé, use a:
    Bar-le-Duc mixture, 544

CUCUMBER CREAM CHEESE SPREAD

Mash with a fork:
    **2 packages cream cheese:
       6 oz.**
Into a fine sieve or cheesecloth bag, grate:
    1 medium-sized cucumber
    1 onion

Press out the juice and combine with the cream cheese. Add:
    Salt to taste
    ¹/₈ teaspoon hot pepper sauce
Add to spreading consistency:
    Mayonnaise

CHEESE PUFF CANAPÉS

Preheat broiler.
Beat until very stiff:
    2 egg whites
Fold in:
    **1 cup shredded American
       cheese**
    **1 teaspoon Worcestershire
       sauce**
    ¹/₂ teaspoon paprika
    ¹/₂ teaspoon dry mustard
Toast on one side:
    **Small rounds of bread or
    crackers**
Spread the untoasted side with the cheese mixture. Place the canapés under a broiler for about 6 minutes, until the cheese is well puffed and brown.

ROQUEFORT SPREAD

This delicious spread keeps well and improves with age—better when 1 week old than when newly made.
Combine to a paste:
    ¹/₂ lb. Roquefort cheese
    **2 packages soft cream
       cheese: 6 oz. or use an 8-oz.
       package**
    2 tablespoons soft butter
    (1 small grated onion)
    **1 tablespoon Worcestershire
       sauce**
    2 tablespoons dry sherry
    Salt as needed
Keep the spread in a closely covered jar in the refrigerator. May be spread on crisp potato chips, crackers or toast rounds. Decorate with:
    Radish slices and capers

PUFFED ROQUEFORT STICKS

Preheat broiler.
Remove crusts from:

> 4 slices bread several
> days old

Cut each slice into 4 strips and coat with:

> Butter

Prepare:

> 3/4 cup White Sauce II, (I, 383)

Combine with:

> 2 oz. Roquefort cheese
> 1 beaten egg
> Season to taste

Spread the sauce on the bread and run under the broiler about 5 minutes. Serve at once.

CHEESE SPREADS FOR TOASTED SANDWICHES OR CHEESE DREAMS

I. This practical sandwich spread will keep refrigerated a week or more. Scald in a double boiler:

> 1/2 cup milk

Add:

> 1 beaten egg
> 1/4 teaspoon dry mustard
> 1/2 teaspoon salt
> 3/4 lb. diced American cheese

Cook these ingredients ▶ over, not in, boiling water 15 minutes. Stir constantly. When ready to use, spread the mixture between:

> Rounds of bread

Place on each side of the canapés or sandwiches a generous dab of:

> Butter

Toast in a 350° oven or under a broiler until crisp.

II. ⚡ This filling is more quickly made, but not so bland as the preceding one. Combine and stir to a smooth paste or blend in the electric blender:

> 2 cups soft shredded sharp
> cheese
> 1/2 teaspoon salt
> A few grains cayenne
> 1 teaspoon prepared mustard
> 3 tablespoons cream or 1 to
> 2 tablespoons soft butter

Cut the crusts from:

> Thin slices of white bread

Spread and roll the slices. Toast as in **I.** Serve the rolls very hot.

BACON AND CHEESE CANAPÉS

Preheat broiler.
Toast on one side:

> Rounds of bread

Spread the untoasted side thickly with a mixture of:

> 2 cups shredded sharp cheese
> 2 slices minced crisp bacon
> 1/4 teaspoon dry mustard
> A few grains cayenne
> 1 tablespoon Worcestershire
> sauce

Broil the canapés until cheese is melted.

CHUTNEY AND CHEESE CANAPÉS

Preheat broiler.
Cover:

> Round crackers or toast

with:

> Chutney, 685
> A thin slice of American
> cheese

Broil the crackers to melt the cheese.

TOASTED CHEESE LOGS OR ROLLS

Preheat oven to 350°.
Trim the crusts from:

> Thin slices of bread

Place on each slice, not quite covering it:

A thin slice of cheese

or, place on each slice of bread:

An oblong block of cheese

Spread the cheese lightly with:

Anchovy paste, prepared mustard or horseradish

Gather up 2 opposite corners and fasten them with a pick, or roll the bread. Brush the outsides of the logs with:

Melted butter

Toast them in the oven until light brown. Serve piping hot on picks.

SWEET TEA SPREADS

For those of us equipped with a "sweet tooth," it is always a welcome sight to behold on the canapé tray something less acid, spicy or tart than the usual fare. And for less venturesome nibblers, don't forget Nut Butters, 71, and Cinnamon Toast, 355.

I. Moisten:

Cream cheese

with:

Cream

Add:

Chopped ginger or dried apricots
Chopped almonds

This makes a great partner for:

Brown or whole wheat bread

II. Spread on small toasts:

Bar-le-Duc, 544

III. Combine:

1 package soft cream cheese: 3 oz.
Grated rind of 1 orange or 2 tablespoons orange or ginger marmalade
¼ teaspoon salt

⅛ teaspoon paprika

Spread:

Thin slices of bread

with:

Mayonnaise or butter

Cover with the cheese and:

Toasted chopped pecan meats

IV. Combine:

Equal parts soft butter and honey

V. Spread toast with:

Butter
Apple butter

Sprinkle with:

Grated cheese

Run under the broiler until the cheese is toasted.

HARD-COOKED EGG SPREADS

I. Combine and mix to a paste with a fork:

2 hard-cooked eggs
1 tablespoon or more cultured sour cream
¼ teaspoon salt
⅛ teaspoon paprika
1 tablespoon chopped chives
(1 teaspoon lemon juice)

Garnish the canapé with a row of:

(Sliced stuffed olives)

II. Combine:

4 chopped hard-cooked eggs
1 cup chopped pecan meats
2 dozen chopped stuffed olives
Well-seasoned mayonnaise

III. Combine:

Chopped hard-cooked eggs
Minced anchovies
Minced celery

Moisten these ingredients with:

Mayonnaise

IV. Marinate 30 minutes:
>**Shrimp or crab meat**

in:
>**French dressing or
>lemon juice**

Drain, chop and combine, by making into a paste, with:
>**Mayonnaise
>A dash Worcestershire
>sauce
>Hard-cooked eggs**

V. Combine:
>**Finely chopped hard-
>cooked eggs
>A liver pâté, (I, 631–632)**

ROLLED ASPARAGUS CANAPÉS OR SANDWICHES

Cut the crusts from:
>**Thin slices of bread**

Spread them thinly with:
>**Butter and mayonnaise**

Sprinkle lightly with:
>**Chopped chives**

Place on each slice a well-drained:
>**Asparagus tip**

Roll the canapés. Wrap the rolls in foil until ready to serve. These sandwiches may be toasted.

MUSHROOM CANAPÉS

Sauté:
>**Mushrooms, (I, 328)**

Mince the mushrooms. Prepare:
>**White Sauce II, (I, 383)**

Make half as much sauce as mushrooms. Season with:
>**Salt and paprika
>Freshly grated nutmeg**

Combine sauce and mushrooms. When cold, add a little:
>**Whipped cream**

Heap these ingredients on:
>**Small rounds of bread or
>toast**

Garnish the canapés with:
>**Paprika and parsley**

Serve immediately or run under the broiler.

ONION AND PARSLEY CANAPÉS

Parsley tends to neutralize onion odors. Use it profusely in this decorative sandwich and preserve group charisma.

Make a filling of:
>**1 grated onion
>1 cup stiff mayonnaise
>1/4 teaspoon Worcestershire
>sauce
>A few drops hot pepper
>sauce
>1/8 teaspoon turmeric**

Put the filling between small rounds of:
>**Brioche-type bread**

or a bread that will not become soggy. Spread the outside edges of the sandwich with:
>**Mayonnaise**

and roll these edges in:
>**Finely chopped parsley**

BLACK RADISH CANAPÉS

Peel and mince:
>**2 black radishes**

Combine with:
>**1 small minced onion
>2 tablespoons cultured sour
>cream or yogurt
>1 tablespoon lemon juice
>1/8 teaspoon salt**

Just before serving, spread on thin slices of:
>**Pumpernickel**

TOMATO OR CUCUMBER SANDWICHES

Very attractive for a spring tea party. To keep these sandwiches from becoming soggy, drain the sliced tomatoes and cucumbers well in advance of use.

Cut:

Small rounds of bread

Spread them lightly with:

Butter

Place on each round, covering it completely:

Small round of peeled sliced tomato or
a large round of pared sliced cucumber or both

or you may hollow out the cucumber before slicing and fill each hollow slice with:

(A tiny shrimp)

Decorate each sandwich with a generous:

Dab of mayonnaise

Garnish the mayonnaise with a tiny sprig of:

Lemon thyme

CAVIAR AND ONION CANAPÉS

I. Sauté in butter:

Rounds of thin toast

Combine and spread on the toast equal parts of:

Caviar
Finely chopped onion

Season with:

Lemon juice

Garnish the edges of the canapés with:

Riced hard-cooked egg yolks

Top with:

(Tiny shrimp or prawns)

II. Sauté:

Chopped onions

in:

Butter

Make a mound of the chopped onions on a round of:

Pumpernickel

In the scooped-out center, put some:

Cultured sour cream

and a dab of:

Caviar

CAVIAR AND CUCUMBER CANAPÉS

Dip:

Slices of cucumber

in:

French Dressing, (I, 413)

Drain them. Prepare:

Small rounds of buttered toast

Peel, then slice crosswise:

Mild onions

Separate the slices into rings. Place a ring on each round of toast, so that it will form a curb. Place a slice of cucumber in each ring. Cover the cucumber with:

Small mounds of caviar, seasoned with lemon and onion juice or chives

Garnish the canapés with:

Capers
Riced hard-cooked egg

SMOKED TONGUE CANAPÉS

Cut thin slices of:

Smoked tongue

to fit squares of:

Melba or rye toast

Spread toast with:

Bercy Butter, (I, 398)

Place on it one of the tongue slices and cap with a dab of:

Freshly grated horseradish

DEVILED OR POTTED CHICKEN SPREAD

About 2½ Cups

Grind together 3 times, using a fine blade:

2 cups cooked chicken
¼ cup boiled or baked ham
⅛ teaspoon nutmeg

A pinch of white pepper
1/2 teaspoon salt
3 tablespoons butter
1 tablespoon lemon juice or
1/2 teaspoon lemon zest, 252

You may further press this through a fine wire sieve or knead gently before storing, covered and refrigerated. It will keep longer if the top is coated with Clarified Butter, (I, 396). When serving, garnish with:

Chopped fresh herbs

DEVILED OR POTTED HAM SPREAD

About 3 Cups

Preheat oven to 350°.
Grind 3 times with a fine blade:
1 lb. lean ham
1/4 lb. ham fat
Season with:
A pinch of cayenne
1/8 teaspoon each mace,
nutmeg and pepper

Put the mixture in a buttered 5 × 9-inch bread pan. Cover with foil. Bake about 45 minutes. When cool, cover top with Clarified Butter, (I, 396), and store refrigerated. Remove butter before serving.

CHICKEN OR HAM SALAD SPREAD

Chop until fine:
1 cup cooked chicken or ham
Add:
2 tablespoons finely chopped
celery
1/4 cup chopped blanched
almonds or other
nutmeats
(1/4 cup chopped pineapple or
1/2 cup finely chopped green
olives)

Combine these ingredients with sufficient:

Highly seasoned
mayonnaise
to make a paste that will spread easily.

SMALL PIZZA CANAPÉS

Preheat broiler.
Serve sectioned pizzas, 313, as canapés. If you are in a hurry, substitute for pizza dough:
Biscuits or small English
muffins
Tear either in two horizontally and toast the flat sides under the broiler; spread on the reverse a mixture of:
1 1/2 teaspoons Chili
Sauce, 686
Strips of sharp cheddar or
grated Mozzarella
or Gruyère cheese
1/8 teaspoon oregano
Top with an:
Anchovy fillet
and drizzle over all:
A little olive oil
Toast 5 inches below broiler element until the cheese is thoroughly melted.

FOIE GRAS AND LIVER CANAPÉS

You may serve pâté in a crust, sliced, as a canapé, (I, 629); cut it into rondelles on toast; or incorporate it into Brioches, 320. Bouchées, 369, pastry, barquettes or turnovers. See (I, 629–632) for a number of versions of liver pastes, soufflés and pâtés—simple and complex.

LIVER SAUSAGE CANAPÉS

I. Combine and mix to a paste:
1/4 lb. liver sausage
1 or more tablespoons cream
(1 tablespoon brandy)
Fold in lightly:

¼ cup or more chopped
    watercress
Serve on rye bread or toast.

II. Make a paste of:
    ½ cup liver sausage
    2 tablespoons tomato paste
       (A few drops
       Worcestershire sauce)
Spread on thinly cut crustless bread,
then roll and toast.

CLAM PUFFS

Try also some of the dips on 101 as
ingredients in this recipe.
Preheat broiler.
Combine:
    1 package cream cheese:
       3 oz.
    2 tablespoons whipping
       cream
    1 cup minced clams
    ¼ teaspoon mustard
    1 tablespoon Worcestershire
       sauce
    ¼ teaspoon salt
    ½ teaspoon grated onion or
       onion juice
Heap the mixture on toast rounds and
run under broiler.

CRAB OR LOBSTER PUFF
BALLS

Serve these only if you have time to
whip the cream and fill the puff shells
at the last minute. The charm of this
canapé lies in the bland creaminess
of the filling and the dry crunchi-
ness of the casing.
Shred or dice:
    Cooked crab or lobster
    meat
Combine lightly 2 parts of the chilled
seafood with:
    1 part stiffly whipped
       seasoned cream

Put the mixture into:
    Small cream puff shells,
    370
Sprinkle the tops with:
    Chopped parsley and basil
Serve open or put puff lid on top after
filling. Good hot or cold, but serve
promptly—and we mean at once.

SHRIMP PUFFS

24 Puffs

Preheat broiler.
Chop:
    12 cooked shrimp
Whip until stiff:
    1 egg white
Fold in:
    ¼ cup shredded cheese
    ⅛ teaspoon salt
    ⅛ teaspoon paprika
       A few grains red pepper
    ½ cup mayonnaise
and the shrimp. Heap these ingredients lightly onto crackers or rounds
of toast. Broil the puffs until light
brown. Serve hot.

LOBSTER CANAPÉS

Combine:
    Chopped cooked lobster
    meat
    Chopped hard-cooked
    eggs
    Chopped cucumbers
    Well-seasoned mayonnaise
Serve on:
    Barquettes, 68

CREAMED SEAFOOD CANAPÉS

A little messy, but definitely in the
class of what the French call amuse-
geules or, freely translated, palate-
teasers.
Preheat broiler.
Combine:

½ lb. cooked oysters, lobster,
crab or tuna meat
½ lb. Sautéed Mushrooms,
(I, 328)
1 cup rich White Sauce II,
(I, 383)
1 tablespoon finely chopped
green pepper
1 tablespoon chopped
pimiento
¼ teaspoon curry powder or
1 teaspoon Worcestershire
sauce
3 tablespoons dry white wine
Salt and pepper
Heap the mixture on rounds of:
Toast
which may be spread with:
Anchovy paste
Sprinkle the tops with:
Au Gratin II, 221
Broil the canapés until slightly brown.
Serve at once.

MARINATED HERRING AND ONIONS ON TOAST

Drain:
Marinated herring
Place fillets on:
Squares or rounds of toast
Cover with:
Thin slices of Bermuda
onion
Sprinkle with:
Chopped parsley or
watercress
Serve promptly.

ANGELS ON HORSEBACK

May also be served as a savory,
see 542.
Preheat oven to 400°.
Toast lightly and butter:
Small rounds of bread
Wrap:
Large drained oysters

with:
Very thin pieces of bacon
You may lightly spread the inner surface of the bacon with:
(Anchovy paste)
Secure with picks and place the
canapés in a pan. Bake about 3 minutes or long enough to crisp the bacon. Drain well. Remove the picks
and serve on the toast.

SMOKED SALMON CANAPÉS

If the salmon you are served is pale
pink and not salty, it has been truly
smoked; but if it is a strong red in
color and very salty, smoke salt extract, 250, has been used in the processing. Salmon for canapés should
be sliced across the grain as thinly as
possible. It is delicious when served
garnished with cucumber or egg. The
thin slices make an ideal lining for
tarts or barquettes.

I. Place on crackers or squares of
toast very thin slices of:
Smoked salmon
Dust with:
Freshly ground pepper
Sprinkle with:
Lemon juice
Serve at room temperature.

II. Or, top with a slice of:
Stuffed olive
Brush the canapés with:
Mustard or Aspic
Glaze, (I, 427)

III. Or, top the salmon with:
Guacamole, 91
and serve on toasted bread rounds.

IV. Or, garnish with a mixture of:
Hard-cooked egg yolk,
grated onion and capers

SARDINE CANAPÉ ROLLS

Preheat oven to 400°.
Mash with a fork:
> 12 **skinless, boneless sardines**

Add:
> ½ **teaspoon Worcestershire sauce**
> ½ **teaspoon Tomato Catsup, 686**
> 1 **tablespoon finely cut celery or onion**
> 1 **tablespoon chopped stuffed olives**

Moisten these ingredients until they are of spreading consistency with:
> **Mayonnaise or French Dressing, (I, 418 or 413)**

Season with:
> **Salt and pepper**

Cut the crusts from:
> **Thin slices of white bread**

Spread the sardine mixture on the bread. Roll the slices and secure them with picks. Toast the canapés until lightly browned and serve very hot.

HORS D'OEUVRE

Hors d'oeuvre and canapés are types of food served with drinks. The canapé, 63, sits invitingly on its own little couch of crouton or pastry tidbit, while the hors d'oeuvre is a free agent, so to speak, gregarious and ready to meet up with whatever bread or cracker is presented separately.

If hors d'oeuvre and canapés are served at a cocktail party, they become an end in themselves, and so may be more varied and substantial than when they are designed as appetizers. The illustration above shows an assemblage of such hors d'oeuvre. What a fillip to festivity when you get out an heirloom caviar server like the one above, or the compartmented dishes you triumphantly bid on at last month's antiques auction, and fill them with smoked salmon curls, toasted nuts, olives, cheese-stuffed celery or green pepper slices, marinated mushrooms and buttered radishes! Hot hors d'oeuvre are represented by the candle-warmed dish of quenelles, (I, 186), and you may lighten the effect of more formal containers by including on the buffet table a handsome big Savoy cabbage—a "centerpiece" all in itself—scooped out, 83, to hold a shellfish dip, 103, and festooned with small shrimp. When you add a few canapés of your choice, and put within easy reach some of the delightful breadstuffs now commercially available, you will already have gone a long way toward confounding that jaded circuit-goer who characterized the cocktail party as "a fête worse than death."

When intended for appetizers, many hors d'oeuvre are rich in fat or are combined with an oil or butter base to buffer the impact of alcohol on the system. If, during preprandial drinking, the appetizer intake is too extensive, any true enjoyment of the meal itself is destroyed. The palate is too heavily coated, too overstimulated by spices and dulled by alcohol. For these reasons and on most occasions, don't hesitate to simplify your appetizer list; nuts, olives, and a few interesting spreads usually suffice. A very hot, light soup between hors d'oeuvre and dinner is often a help in clearing the palate for the more delicate and subtle flavors of the meal.

While hors d'oeuvre, freely translated, means "outside the main works," and while we approve of serving imaginative combinations, it is important to remember that, unlike the opera overture, the hors d'oeuvre course should not forecast any of the joys that are to follow. Should you serve—either in the living room or a table—caviar in pickled beets or anchovy eggs on tomatoes, forget the very existence of beet and tomato when planning the dinner. This is not a superfluous caution, for one encounters many such carelessly repetitious meals. ♦ Choose for living room service bite-sized self-contained canapés or hors d'oeuvre, unless you are furnishing plates. Serve hot hors d'oeuvre fresh from the oven. If they are the type that will "hold," use a hibachi, (I, 110), a chafing dish, or an electrically heated tray. ♦ Cold hors d'oeuvre may be transferred directly from refrigerator to serving point, or set first on chilled platters over cracked ice. Cheeses should be presented at a temperature around 70°. ♦ Allow 6 to 8 hors d'oeuvre per person.

Here are a few types of food which are particularly appropriate for the hors d'oeuvre course: caviar, 97, pâtés and terrines, (I, 629); Vegetables à la Grecque, (I, 285); Stuffed Artichokes, (I, 55); Stuffed Brussels Sprouts and Beets, 92 and 91, and Cherry Tomatoes, 93; and Marinated Mushrooms, 94. You may also use spreads and dips, 101; deviled, pickled, truffled or chopped eggs, 90; skewered or bacon-wrapped tidbits, 87; sauced smoked seafood; quenelles, (I, 186); and timbales, (I, 229); choice hot and cold sausages; glazed or jelled foods; nuts,

olives or cheeses. From the Salad chapter, choose individual aspics; a filled ring of aspic, (I, 77); one of the mousses, (I, 86); or an Italian, Viennese or Russian salad. From the Vegetable chapter, choose Ratatouille, (I, 321).

WAYS TO SERVE HORS D'OEUVRE AND CANAPÉS

Food often looks more dramatic if some of it can be presented on several levels. Sometimes, unfortunately, this technique can be exhibited in quite alarming ways. Look at the complex, inedible architectural underpinnings by which the glories of ancient chefs used to be supported—and still are today, on celebratory occasions—in some large hotels and restaurants. Artificial coloring, fussy detailing, slick surfaces abound. Don't torture and mortify buffet food. Instead, play up its gustatory highlights and allow its subtle natural colors and textures to glow. And set off hors d'oeuvre with plenty of attractively cut vegetables and garnishes of fresh herbs and greens, (I, 53).

Keep in mind, too, what the hors d'oeuvre platter will look like as it begins to be demolished: it is often more sensible to arrange several small plates which are easily replaced or replenished than one big one which may be difficult to restore to its pristine glory.

Illustrated on 83 are a few effortless constructions designed to give the hors d'oeuvre platter a focus of interest. Simplest are a big red apple cut off at the bottom for stability; stud it with delicacies on picks for a small impromptu children's party; or, for an outdoor grill, use a big potato. The grapefruit "pincushion" will look more attractive if it consists of a three-quarter round, as shown, instead of a mere half. Larger and more ambitious are the pair of pineapple halves at center; the shrimp-studded eggplant pictured on (I, 438); and the cabbage-container on 81. While Savoy cabbages make perhaps the most elegant receptacles, red cabbages harmonize colorfully with foods like stuffed beets and slices of pâté. Even plain, everyday cabbages can be made interesting if you can persuade your greengrocer to let you have one from which the outer leaves have not been hacked, or if you can get one intact straight out of the garden. Curl the leaves back carefully, so as not to bruise them. Into the center of these and other cabbages you may cut a cavity into which you can insert a sauce bowl, deep enough so the curled leaf edges will conceal its rim.

Just by the adroit placement of food on an hors d'oeuvre platter, you can bring about height variations and attractive color relationships. On an oblong plate, for instance, try centering some dainty triangular toasts or breads, peaks up like a long mountain range. Place small well-drained marinated shrimp along the base of the range on either side, and accent the watercress-garnished edge of the platter with French endive or celery filled with Guacamole, 91, and smoked salmon wrapped around individual marinated asparagus tips.

If platters need not be passed, you may also achieve height contrasts by placing cold hors d'oeuvre on crushed ice on a layered tray similar to that shown on 63, or on a simple épergne. If you use a silver or metal tray ▶ you may want to protect it from food acids by an undergarnish of lettuce, grape leaves, croutons or diced aspic, (I, 77).

We saw a chef friend rapidly arrange a tray almost entirely from stored foods—a gala quickie you can reproduce when a merry mob descends on you with short or no warning. Garnish a large platter with lettuce. For the center, make a large mound of Russian Salad, (I, 54), using canned drained vegetables; or one of shrimp salad; or a Spiced Cabbage Mound, 92. Garnish it with slices of tomato as a base for hard-cooked egg slices and top with a tiny tip cluster of tarragon, thyme or parsley. Or cut the eggs and tomatoes into wedges and border the mound by placing the wedges against it, with the yolk side against the salad, see 90.

Other possibilities—depending on the state of your larder—are a mound of creamed cottage cheese decorated with tender stalks of burnet pressed into the mound to resemble coarse fern fronds and accented with borage blossoms; a double spiral of overlapping radish disks, the interstices filled in with chopped chives. The platter may be garnished at each end with lemon slices and a cluster of canned white asparagus tips bound together with onion or lemon rings, or green pepper cups holding caviar or a Liver Sausage Pâté, 77. Another expedient is to open a fresh crock of cheddar or Liptauer cheese and press it into instant service as the principal feature; or prepare a filled Edam or Gouda, 88. Even the contents of a can of good white-meat tuna, coated with mayonnaise and attractively garnished with ripe olives or capers, looks good when surrounded by canned drained artichoke hearts or hearts of palm and filled in with shrimp or mussels. These may be sprinkled with a vinaigrette, sour cream and chili sauce, or mayonnaise; or you may place a few small bowls of sauces on the platter. Don't forget an occasional garnish of anchovy or pimiento strip. And remember that a plate of interesting breads and crackers is a most attractive foil and accessory.

ABOUT ANTIPASTO

Antipasto—or "what comes before the pasta course"—can be a snack with drinks or the base of an entire luncheon. This ever-present constituent of Italian menus is an assortment of hard sausages; prosciutto with melon or figs; fish, such as anchovies, sardines and Mediterranean tuna; pickled onions, beets, peppers, artichokes, cauliflower and mushrooms; highly seasoned garbanzos; and cold eggplant in tomato purée. It also includes fresh tomatoes, fennel, (I, 323), cheeses—the hard types, as well as Mozzarella and ricotta—fine crusty breads, and deep-fat-fried fish, meat, fowl or game, which goes under the name of Fritto Misto, 154, when encased in a light batter.

Some suggestions for antipasto are listed below. Serve them on platters or make them up on individual plates.

**Tomato slices cut
lengthwise
Vegetables à la
Grecque, (I, 285)
Anchovies
Seviche, 99
Smoked Salmon Rolls, 99
Rollmops, 100
Pickled Oysters, 100
Marinated Mushrooms, 94
Stuffed Celery, 93**

**Pickled Beets and
Caviar, 97
Ratatouille, (I, 321)
Sardines
Slices of salami
Hard-Cooked Eggs, (I, 212)
Masked Eggs, (I, 219)
Garlic Olives, 94
Cucumber and green
pepper sticks
Stuffed Leeks, 93
Black Radishes, 93
Artichoke Hearts à la
Grecque, (I, 285)**

ABOUT SMORGASBORD

This Scandinavian spread has been so thoroughly adapted in this country to the casual cocktail hour that some of us have lost sight of its original importance. Smorgasbord in its home territory is a square meal in itself, not the prelude to one. Its mainstays of meat and fish—and the aquavit which washes them down—are climatic imperatives when subarctic weather hovers for months outside the door. Like all native dishes, it closely reflects a country's ecology and its people's way of life.

The foods of which a smorgasbord is traditionally composed are sufficiently dissimilar to require at least three plates and silver services per person, so that the flavors of one course do not disturb those of the next. Typical of those first presented are herring, hot and cold, smoked eel, salmon or shellfish—all served with small boiled potatoes, seasoned with dill—and at least three kinds of bread with small mountains of butter balls. In fact, it is its bread and butter that gives this kind of meal its name.

With the first change of plate come cheeses, deviled eggs, pancakes and omelets with lingonberries, sausages, marinated and pickled vegetables, and aspics.

With the next, hot foods are in order, such as meatballs, ham with apples, goose with prunes, tongue and baked beans. Although many of these foods are prepared in advance, their true charm lies in the freshness of their garnish and arrangement. Do not leave the platters with their cut meats exposed too long on the buffet table.

To assemble a smorgasbord from some of the recipes in this book, see Herring, (I, 491), Swedish Rye Bread, 311, salmon hors d'oeuvre, 99, Cold Glazed Salmon, (I, 496), Swedish Meatballs, (I, 621), Crêpes with Lingonberries, 143, and shrimp dishes.

CRACKERS AND BREADS TO SERVE WITH HORS D'OEUVRE

Bought crackers and breads can be dressed up into delightful additions to the hors d'oeuvre table with the cut of a knife, a few aromatic seeds, a bit of cheese and an oven. See fancy Breads and Crackers for Soup, (I, 172), and bread and cracker recipes on 353–356.

You may also bake small Biscuits, 348, Beaten Biscuits, 351, Corn Dodgers, 342, and Corn Zephyrs Cockaigne, 342. Bake Grissini, 307, or some good rye, cheese or French breads. Make Potato Chips, (I, 352), and don't forget Cheese Straws, 363, and unsweetened pastries in variety, 357 to 363.

NUTS AS HORS D'OEUVRE

These can be roasted or shallow-fried.

I. Preheat oven to 300°.
To roast, put in a greased shallow pan:
Blanched or unblanched nuts, 236: almonds, pecans, peanuts, pistachios or cashews
Bake until golden, 15 to 20 minutes.
Sprinkle during baking with:
(Melted butter)
seasoned lightly with:
(Celery salt, onion salt, cayenne, chili powder or paprika)

II. Have ready:
Blanched or unblanched nuts, 236
For every cup of nuts, allow:
1/2 cup vegetable oil
Cook the nuts in oil heated to 365° until golden. Test so as not to overcook—pecans and Spanish peanuts will need about 2 minutes. Drain nuts on paper toweling. After salting, store tightly covered.

CURRIED NUTS

Combine in a skillet:
1/4 cup olive oil
1 tablespoon curry powder
1 tablespoon Worcestershire sauce
1/8 teaspoon cayenne
When this mixture is very hot, add:
2 cups nuts
Stir until well coated. Line a baking pan with brown paper, pour in the nuts and bake at 300° about 10 minutes or until crisp.

SKEWERED CHESTNUTS

Prepare:
Boiled Chestnuts I, (I, 313)
by boiling in milk. Omit the vinegar. When the chestnuts are cooked until soft enough to penetrate with a fork, roll them in a mixture of:
Au Gratin III, 221

Place on a greased baking dish and run under a hot broiler for a few moments. Dust with:

Chopped parsley

Serve at once on picks.

☰ ROASTED CHESTNUTS

Preheat oven to 425°.

♦ Prick the shells of:

Chestnuts

with a fork before putting them in the oven for 15 to 20 minutes—or they may explode. More hazardous, but more fun, is to roast the chestnuts in a pan such as that shown below, on a cold winter's evening, on the coals of an open hearth. A childhood game was for each of us to cheer on our own chestnut to pop first.

TOASTED SEEDS

Separate the fiber from:

Melon, pumpkin, squash, sunflower or watermelon seeds

Cover with:

Salted water

Bring to a boil and ♦ simmer 2 hours. Drain and dry on brown paper. Then:

I. Fry as for Nuts as Hors d'Oeuvre II, 85.

II. Spread the seeds in a shallow pan. Coat with:

Vegetable oil
(Salt)

Bake in a 250° oven until golden brown. Stir from time to time.

PUFFED CEREALS FOR COCKTAILS

Melt in a skillet, over low heat:

3/4 cup butter

Add:

(1 clove garlic, pressed)

Stir in lightly:

12 cups crisp small cereals
1 1/2 teaspoons curry powder
1 teaspoon celery salt
1 tablespoon Worcestershire sauce
(1 cup pumpkin seeds or nuts)

Mix gently until the cereal has absorbed the seasoned butter. Drain on paper toweling and serve at once.

SEASONED POPCORN OR POPPED WILD RICE

Prepare:

Popcorn, 596, or wild rice as for popcorn

Season with:

Melted butter
(Squeeze of garlic or onion juice)
(Grated sharp cheese)

STUFFED DRIED FRUIT APPETIZERS

Highly decorative surroundings for Glazed Cocktail Ribs, 95.

Prepare well in advance, as described in Prunes in Wine, 135:

Dried apricots, dates or prunes

Drain the fruit and reserve the liquor for sauces, gravies, etc. Place in each cavity 1 or 2 of the following:

A walnut or other nutmeat
A canned water chestnut

A sautèed chicken liver
Chutney
Cheddar or Roquefort
cheese

The fruit may be served cold or hot.
You may also wrap each piece with:
A narrow strip of bacon

Secure with a pick and bake in a 375°
oven until the bacon is crisp.

COLD SKEWERED TIDBITS

Altnerate on cocktail picks:
Small onions with pieces of
cocktail sausages and
gherkins
Squares of cheese with
pickle slices, stuffed olives
or small onions
Slices of raw carrot and
blocks of tongue or ham
Shrimp, lightly flavored
with mustard and pieces of
celery, or Celeri-Rave
Rémoulade, (I, 57)
Squares of cheese and slices
of green onion, topped with
a ripe olive
Chilled balls of cream
cheese, sprinkled with
paprika or mixed with
chopped olives and
anchovy or smoked herring
or salmon sections
Pieces of ham and
watermelon pickle
Cubes of smoked turkey
and honeydew melon

PROSCIUTTO AND FRUIT

On small picks alternately interlace:
Prosciutto or Virginia ham
slices
around:
Melon balls
Pineapple, pear or peach
chunks

Fresh figs
The fruit may be marinated in:
(Port wine)
At the very tip of the pick, impale a
clustered tip of:
Mint leaves

▤ HOT SKEWERED TIDBITS OR
TIDBITS EN BROCHETTE

Hors d'oeuvre en brochette may be
broiled with or without wraps. Attractive skewer combinations of the
unwrapped kind include: bacon and
blanched sections of onion; scallops,
mussels, shrimps or oysters with
bacon and firm miniature tomatoes;
chicken livers or pieces of calf liver
or kidney alternating with cocktail
sausages and mushrooms; diced eggplant or squash, blanched small
onions, cherry tomatoes and bacon;
shrimp or diced lobster, diced cucumber and stuffed olives; pieces of fish,
sections of blanched celery and bacon; sections of sausage and pickled
onions; bacon and small chunks of
unpeeled apple. See also Skewered
Chestnuts, 85.
Any of the following may be surrounded by:
Thin strips of bacon
or ham
secured to them with picks, impaled
on skewers, and broiled until the bacon is crisp:
Pineapple chunks
Spiced cored crab apples
Prunes stuffed with
almonds
Watermelon pickles
Dates stuffed with
pineapple
Skinned firm grapefruit
sections
Large stuffed olives
Pickled onions
Smoked oysters or mussels

Raw scallops or oysters
Cooked shrimp
Sautéed chicken livers

RUMAKI

Cut into bite-sized pieces:
Chicken livers
Sprinkle with:
(Soy sauce)
Prepare an equal number of:
**¼-inch canned water
chestnut slices**
Marinate the chestnuts in:
(Port wine)
Wrap a piece of liver and one of water chestnut together in:
½-inch-wide slice of bacon
Secure with a wooden pick or small metal skewer and broil slowly until the bacon is crisp. Serve hot.

FILLED EDAM CHEESE

Fine for a buffet meal. Hollow:
**A small Edam or Gouda
cheese**
Crumble the removed part. Combine it with:
**2 teaspoons or more
Worcestershire sauce or
red wine**
**1 tablespoon prepared
mustard**
A few grains cayenne
**1 or 2 tablespoons fresh or
dried minced herbs**
Or, to preserve its lovely characteristic flavor, blend just enough:
Whipping cream
with the cheese to make it easy to spread. Refill the cheese shell. Serve it surrounded by toasted crackers.

EDAM NUGGETS

About 16
Combine:

1 cup shredded Edam cheese
**2 tablespoons finely chopped
celery**
⅛ teaspoon dry mustard
2 tablespoons cream or ale
Make into small balls and roll in:
Finely chopped parsley

VICKSBURG CHEESE ROLL OR BALL

Blend with a fork until smooth:
⅓ Roquefort cheese
⅓ cheddar cheese
⅓ soft cream cheese
Sprinkle thickly a large piece of waxed paper with:
Paprika
Roll the cheese mixture into a sausage shape, then on the paper until it has a generous coating of paprika. You can cut it into slices later. You may also shape the mixture into a large ball, which can be rolled in:
**(Chopped nuts or finely
chopped dried beef)**
Place in refrigerator to chill.

NUT CHEESE BALLS

About 16
Work to a paste:
**1 cup Roquefort cheese, or
part Roquefort and part
cream cheese**
2 tablespoons butter
**1 teaspoon Worcestershire
sauce or 1 tablespoon
brandy**
1 teaspoon paprika
A few grains cayenne
Shape into 1-inch balls. Roll them in:
½ cup ground nutmeats
**Chopped herbs or
watercress**
Chill. This is also effective made into one large cheese ball.

TOMATO ASPIC WITH TASTY CENTERS

8 servings

I. Prepare:

Tomato Aspic, (I, 77)

When it is about to set, pour into wet individual molds or ice cube molds and fill them to one-third of their capacity. Combine and roll into balls:

1 package soft cream cheese: 3 oz.
1 tablespoon anchovy paste
2 drops Worcestershire sauce

Drop a ball into each mold and cover it with aspic. Chill the aspic until firm. Unmold on lettuce leaves. Serve with:

Mayonnaise

II. Use for the filling:

Any small pieces of well-seasoned cooked meat, fowl or fish

ANCHOVY CHEESE OR KLEINER LIPTAUER

See also Liptauer Cheese, 544.
Work until smooth:

2 packages cream cheese: 6 oz.

Work in:

3 tablespoons soft butter
2 minced anchovies
1½ tablespoons grated onion or 1 minced shallot
1½ teaspoons chopped capers
½ teaspoon caraway seed
¾ teaspoon paprika
2 drops Worcestershire sauce
Salt as needed

Shape the mixture into small patties. Chill thoroughly.

NUT CREAMS

Roll into ¾-inch balls:

Soft cream cheese

(Squeeze of garlic or lemon juice)

Flatten balls slightly between:

2 salted English walnuts or pecans

CHEESE CARROTS

Grate:

Yellow cheese

Moisten with:

Cream or salad dressing

until it is of a good consistency to handle.
Shape into small carrots. In the blunt end, place:

A sprig of parsley

DEEP-FAT-FRIED HORS D'OEUVRE

If you can lick the service problem and offer this type of hors d'oeuvre while hot and just out of the fryer, nothing is more delicious. Consider the other suggestions in this chapter, as well as Tempura, (I, 464), and Fritto Misto, 154.

CHEESE BALLS FLORENTINE

About 30

♦ Please read about Deep-Fat Frying, (I, 94).
Measure by packing closely:

1 cup well-drained cooked spinach

Put it through a purée strainer or chop it in the ⚙ blender until fine.
Stir in:

2 beaten eggs
1½ cups fine dry bread crumbs
1 tablespoon grated onion
½ cup shredded cheese
1 teaspoon salt
1 tablespoon lemon juice

Shape this mixture into 1½-inch balls. Coat with a Bound Breading,

220. Fry in deep fat heated to 375°
until brown and crisp. Drain on paper
toweling. Serve with:

**Thickened Tomato Sauce,
(I, 400), or
Hollandaise Sauce, (I, 410)**

FRIED CHEESE DREAMS

About 36

▶ Please read about Deep-Fat Frying, (I, 94).
Mix:

**¹/₂ lb. shredded Swiss cheese
3 well-beaten eggs
1 teaspoon double-acting
  baking powder
1 tablespoon sherry
¹/₈ teaspoon paprika**

Put some flour in a narrow glass or
cup. Drop a tablespoon of the mixture into the flour and swirl until it is
coated with flour. Fry in deep fat
heated to 375° until golden brown.

PASTRY CHEESE BALLS

About 36

Preheat oven to 450°.
Prepare dough for:

Cheese Straws, 363

Pinch off pieces of dough and form
into ³/₄-inch balls. Chill for 2 hours, if
possible, and bake about 10 minutes.
Serve hot or cold.

ABOUT EGGS AS HORS D'OEUVRE

Perhaps no other single food plays
such a varied role in hors d'oeuvre as
eggs do. You find them plain hard-
cooked as a bland foil for the many
spicy items surrounding them; deviled
in the most complex ways, with anchovies, curry, capers, caviar; truffled
and En Gelée, (I, 81), or pickled. They
are particularly useful cut into
fancy shapes as garnishes for other
hors d'oeuvre—or with the whites
and yolks chopped very finely.

Overlap slices of hard-cooked egg
as shown in the clay casserole, left, at
the top on the right, or pink the
whites with an hors d'oeuvre cutter—second from the top on the left.
Garnish egg slices with caviar, olive,
small shrimp, herbs or rolled anchovy
fillets shown bottom left and on the
far right in the second row. Deviled
or plain hard-cooked eggs may be
similarly garnished, and the deviled
ones may be further decorated by
using a pastry tube filled with the
softened yolk. On the bottom right
are 3 cuts for deviled egg cups. Pictured lower left center is a molded
salad garnished with sliced egg sections in a pinwheel and wreathed with
parsley or chervil. Another mold to the
right shows a center of sieved egg yolk
and sections of white forming a casual
chrysanthemum motif. To make the
border on the top left, alternate wedges
of tomato and hard-cooked egg.

GARNISHED ASPARAGUS SPEARS

Marinate:

**Canned white asparagus
tips**

in:

French Dressing, (I, 413)

Wrap around the base of each spear:
**Thinly sliced ham,
smoked salmon or
prosciutto**
Serve chilled.

AVOCADO SPREAD OR GUACAMOLE

★ A holiday touch here is a bit of pimiento or a slice of stuffed olive for garnish. Guacamole makes a great celery stuffer.

I. Peel:
1 or 2 ripe avocados
Mash the pulp with a fork. Add:
**Onion juice and lemon
juice
Salt
(Tomato pulp—a very
small amount)**
Heap this on small crackers or toast. Garnish with:
**Paprika and parsley or a
touch of peeled, seeded,
chopped green chili
peppers**

II. Have ready a combination of:
**1 peeled, seeded, chopped
ripe tomato
1 finely chopped scallion with
2 inches of the green
(1/2 seeded, chopped green
pepper)
1/2 teaspoon chili powder
1 teaspoon olive oil
1 tablespoon lemon or lime
juice
1/2 teaspoon coriander
Salt and pepper**
Add to the above, just before spreading:
**2 peeled mashed ripe
avocados**

AVOCADO AND CHUTNEY

Peel just before serving and slice lengthwise into 4 to 6 thick slices:
Avocado
Fill the hollow at the base of each slice with:
Chutney, 685

MARINATED BEANS

Drain:
**2 cups canned garbanzo
beans or freshly cooked
haricots blancs**
Prepare the following marinade and soak the beans in it 4 hours:
**2 tablespoons lemon juice
2 tablespoons red wine
vinegar
1/2 cup olive oil
Garlic clove
Various herbs**
Drain and serve chilled.

STUFFED BEETS COCKAIGNE

I. Prepare, leaving them whole, very small and shapely:
Cooked or canned beets
If small beets are not available, shape large ones with a melon scoop. Hollow the beets slightly. Fill the hollows with:
Caviar
sprinkled with a very little:
Lemon juice
Garnish with:
**A sprig of parsley or lemon
thyme**

II. Fill the beet cups with:
**Frozen Horseradish
Sauce, (I, 408)**

III. Or fill them with a combination of:
Chopped hard-cooked eggs

Mayonnaise
**Herbs, preferably chives
and tarragon**

IV. You may also fill them with:
**Chopped vinaigretted
cucumbers**
and garnish with:
Anchovy

STUFFED BRUSSELS SPROUTS

Drain well:
**Cooked or canned Brussels
sprouts**
Cut a small hollow in each one, preferably from the top. Drop into each hollow:
**1/2 teaspoon French
Dressing, (I, 413)**
Chill them. Fill with any:
**Sandwich spread or salad
mixture**
Use liver sausage and tomato paste, cream cheese and chives or anchovy, adding the chopped center portion of the sprouts to the spread. Garnish with:
**A sprig of parsley, savory,
basil, etc.**
Serve several as a salad or use as hors d'oeuvre.

SPICED CABBAGE MOUND

A decorative platter for a buffet or first course. Shred:
White cabbage
Dress it with equal parts of:
**Mayonnaise
Chili Sauce, 686**
Arrange it in a mound. Cover the top with:
Marinated shrimp
Surround the mound with:
**Deviled eggs, topped with
caviar**

MARINATED RAW VEGETABLES OR CRUDITÉS VINAIGRETTE

Slice julienne, (I, 280), and arrange in groups on a large platter a combination of some of the following:
**Raw sweet green peppers,
carrots, zucchini, turnips,
Florence fennel, cucumber,
celery, green and red
cabbage, very fresh large
mushrooms**
Coat each pile with:
**Herbed French
Dressing, (I, 414)**
Serve chilled.

MARINATED CARROTS

Slice as thin as soup noodles:
Carrots
Marinate the slices in:
**Lemon or orange juice
A little sugar**
Serve well chilled.

RADISH HORS D'OEUVRE

I. Dip whole or strips of:
White or red radishes
in:
Whipped cream
seasoned with:
**Salt
Vinegar**

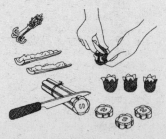

II. Or serve red radishes cut in rose shapes, illustrated 92, filled with:

> **Anchovy Butter or other Seasoned Butters, (I, 397)**

III. Remove the rind from solid black radishes and slice thinly across the grain. Soak them covered in a little salted water about 15 minutes. Drain. Marinate in a mixture of:

> **Oil**
> **Vinegar**
> **White pepper**

Serve chilled.

CELERY CURLS

Separate, then wash the inner smaller:

> **Stalks of celery**

Trim leaves. Cut several long gashes in each rib. Soak in ice water until crisp and curled, as sketched above, and serve on a tray with buttered radish roses, see II, above.

STUFFED CELERY, FINOCCHIO, FRENCH ENDIVE OR BAMBOO SHOOTS

I. Combine:

> **1 tablespoon butter**
> **1 tablespoon Roquefort cheese**
> **1 package cream cheese: 3oz.**
> **Salt**
> **(1 teaspoon caraway, dill or celery seed)**

Place this mixture in:

> **Dwarf celery or finocchio ribs, the leaves of French endive, or separated canned bamboo shoots**

If you want them to look very elegant, force the cheese mixture through a large pastry tube onto small individual ribs or endive. Sprinkle with:

> **Paprika**

Chill.

II. Fill vegetable with:

> **Guacamole, 91**

III. Or with:

> **Caviar and cultured sour cream, with a little lemon juice**

STUFFED CHERRY TOMATOES

Cut off tops and with a melon scoop hollow out:

> **Large cherry tomatoes**

Fill with crab meat or any salad mixture or sandwich spread.

STUFFED LEEKS

18 to 24 Pieces

Cut into 1½-inch cross sections the white portions of:

> **3 large cooked leeks**

When chilled, cut the cross sections in two, lengthwise. Stuff the leeks with **Shrimp or Shad Roe Salad, (I, 67).** Coat the top with more:

> **(Mayonnaise)**

or garnish with a tiny sprig of:

> **(Fresh lemon thyme)**

CUCUMBER LILY

Have ready:

> **Thin slices unpeeled cucumber**
> **3-inch carrot sticks**

Gently fold the cucumber slice around the base of the carrot stick. Fold a second slice around the stick from the other side. These form the lily petals, with a carrot stamen in the center. Fasten with a pick, being careful to catch all four lapped edges of the cucumber as well as piercing the carrot stick. Wrap flowers lightly in a moistened paper towel and refrigerate until ready to use as garnish for the hors d'oeuvre or salad tray.

MARINATED MUSHROOMS

Be sure to include in your repertoire Stuffed Mushrooms, (I, 329–330). Marinate 1 hour or more:

Small button-type mushrooms or thinly sliced large mushrooms
French Dressing, (I, 413)
(Dash herb vinegar)
Chopped chives or onion juice
Chopped parsley

Serve on:

Lettuce or watercress

or on picks.

ABOUT OLIVES

While the grading and typing of olives is taken very seriously by the processors, what should matter most to the cook is that size does not necessarily have anything to do with quality. You don't have to be a connoisseur to know that the big, woody dull-green queen olives can't compare in flavor or in texture with the small, succulent, yellowish Manzanilla fines.

Try various types in making up your hors d'oeuvre tray. The green ones, picked unripe, are treated with a potassium or ash solution and then pickled in brine. Since they have not been heat-treated, a film sometimes forms after the bottle is opened. If this happens, you may float olive oil on the surface of the liquid in the bottle before storing again, or rinse the olives in cold water, drain, place in a clean jar and re-cover with a solution of 1 teaspoon salt and 1 tablespoon white vinegar to a cup of water. Black olives are picked ripe, put in a boiling brine and sold dried, pickled or in oil. To reduce the saltiness of dried or pickled olives, store them in olive oil that you can later use for dressing.

There are many stuffings for olives: a sliver of almond or pimiento, a slice of anchovy, smoked salmon, prosciutto, etc. For a real treat, put in a little foie gras and close with a pistachio nut.

GARLIC OLIVES

Drain the liquid from:

Green or ripe olives

Add:

12 peeled cloves garlic

Cover with:

Olive oil

Let stand 24 hours or more under refrigeration. Drain. Remove the garlic and use the oil for salad dressing. You may dust the olives with:

Chopped parsley

PASTRY-WRAPPED OLIVES

About 4 Dozen

Preheat oven to 400°.
Prepare the dough for:

Cheese Straws, 363

Wrap individually with about 1 teaspoon of this dough, depending on size of fruit:

50 stuffed olives

so as to cover each fruit completely. Arrange the covered olives on ungreased baking sheets. Bake until dough is golden.

✻ If you want to reserve these nuggets for later use, freeze until firm, then place at once in plastic bags. Do not defrost before baking about 15 minutes and serving promptly.

MARINATED ONIONS

Skin, then slice:
Bermuda onions
Soak 30 minutes in:
**Brine: ⅔ cup water to
1 tablespoon salt**
Drain. Soak 30 minutes in:
Vinegar
Drain, then chill. They are then ready
to be served side by side with celery,
radishes, olives, etc.

PEPPER HORS D'OEUVRE

Remove skins from:
Sweet green or red peppers
by roasting under a broiler until soft
and pliable. Also remove top and bottom, core and seeds. Marinate 15
minutes in:
**Olive oil
Lemon juice**
Slice the peppers vertically into
thirds. On each strip, put:
**1 tablespoon Tuna Salad,
(I, 67), or anchovies with
capers**
seasoned with the marinade and:
Chopped parsley
Form the strips into small sausage-
like rolls and hold closed with a pick.

STUFFED SNOW PEA PODS

Scrub:
Snow pea pods
Blanch the pods in boiling water for
30 seconds. Drain, rinse in cold water
and drain well again. Refrigerate
covered. Just before serving, cut off
the stem end of the pod diagonally.
Fill a pastry bag with:
**Vicksburg Cheese, 88, and
very finely chopped nuts**
or:
**Finely chopped filling for
Crab Puff Balls, 78**
thinned down with:

Whipping cream
to a consistency that passes easily
through the bag without splitting the
pod. Allow about 1 teaspoon of filling for every pod.

MARROW HORS D'OEUVRE

Bake:
Beef marrowbones, (I, 591)
Serve the marrow with long spoons.
It is delicious.

GLAZED COCKTAIL RIBS

Allow 2 to 3 Ribs per Person
Preheat oven to 350°.
Cut into 1-rib sections:
**2 racks of spareribs,
about 5 lb.**
Season with:
Salt and pepper
Place in a pan. Roast about 40 minutes. Drain the fat. Reduce oven heat
to 300°. During the next 35 minutes
of cooking, brush the ribs frequently
and lightly with a marinade of:
**3 tablespoons catsup or Chili
Sauce, 686
4 tablespoons honey or
molasses
1 tablespoon grated fresh
gingerroot
2 crushed garlic cloves
4 tablespoons soy sauce
2 tablespoons sherry**
When crisp and well glazed, serve
at once.

STEAK TARTARE OR CANNIBAL BALLS

Forty-Eight 1-inch Balls
We always tender this recipe with
some misgiving because of the risks
run in eating uncooked meat and eggs.
Cannibal balls are a mini-version of the
classic **Steak Tartare** or **Cannibal
Mound:** a clump of raw beef with a

shallow indentation on top into which a raw egg yolk is broken, garnished with chopped onion, caviar or anchovy, and capers. The amounts indicated here will serve six persons. Both for the cocktail hors d'oeuvre below and for steak tartare the meat is prepared just before serving as follows:

Scrape with the back of a knife, turning the meat several times until only the fibers remain, or grind at home using a medium blade:

3 lb. top sirloin

If you grind, the fibrous muscle will periodically choke the grinder, allowing only the velvety portion of the meat to get through. Whether you scrape or grind, you will end with about 2 pounds of meat. Mix with the meat:

2 egg yolks
¹/₂ cup very finely minced Bermuda onion

Reserve about one-fourth of the meat and arrange the rest in 48 shapes similar to Jelly Tots, see illustration on 481. Into each depression put:

1 caper
¹/₈ teaspoon caviar: 2¹/₂ oz. in all; or ¹/₂ mashed anchovy

Close the tops of the balls with the reserved meat.
Dip them in:

2 unbeaten egg whites

Roll them in:

³/₄ cup very finely chopped parsley

Arrange on a platter surrounded by small:

Sandwiches of buttered pumpernickel

Garnish the platter with radish roses, 92, and sprigs of parsley.

MEATBALL HORS D'OEUVRE

Prepare:

Tiny meatballs, hamburgers, nutburgers,

Königsberg Klops, (I, 621), or small-sized Dolmas, (I, 626)

Season them well. Serve very hot on picks or between small biscuits.

TONGUE, CHIPPED BEEF OR BOLOGNA CORNUCOPIAS

Prepare one of the following spreads:

Seasoned creamed cheese, 71
Hard-Cooked Egg Spread, 74
Piccalilli, 681
Cultured sour cream and horseradish

Spread the mixture on very thin slices of:

Smoked boiled tongue, chipped beef or bologna

Roll into cornucopias. Or stack 6 slices, wrap them in waxed paper, chill and cut into 6 or more pie-shaped wedges.

TINY BROILED SAUSAGES

Heat on a hibachi or broil:

Very small sausages

Serve them hot on picks with:

Cold Mustard Sauce, (I, 409)

or grouped on skewers, flambéed in:

Jamaica rum

SHERRIED CHICKEN BITS

Stew and place while still warm in a large jar:

Breasts of fat stewing hens

Leave the meat on the bone and cover with:

Sherry

Cover the jar closely and refrigerate 10 days before using. Skin, bone and cut the meat into bite-sized pieces. Serve cold on picks between:

Salted walnut meats

ABOUT CHICKEN AND GOOSE LIVERS AS HORS D'OEUVRE

Both these delicacies may be cut to bite size and briefly sautéed; overcooking, as usual, is disastrous. The centers should remain pink. Simply seasoned with salt, the livers may be served on picks, or they may be wrapped in thin slices of bacon and run under the broiler until the bacon is crisp. See Rumaki, 88. You may prefer a liver pâté, (I, 631 and 632), and use it for stuffing olives, artichoke hearts or mushroom caps; or roll it up like small cheroots in the thinnest slices of prosciutto. Use liver pastes also in individual molds, glazed with port or an aspic, (I, 427). For pâté surrounded by pâte, see Foie Gras Canapés, 77.

CHOPPED GOOSE OR CHICKEN LIVERS

Drop into boiling seasoned water and simmer until barely done:

   1 lb. chicken or goose livers

Drain and cool them. Cook until hard, shell, chop and add:

   2 eggs

Chop coarsely, then sauté:

   2 medium-sized onions

in:

   2 tablespoons butter

Chop or blend these ingredients to a finé paste.

   Season to taste

adding:

   (2 tablespoons chopped parsley)
   (1 oz. cognac or brandy)

SMOKED TURKEY OR PHEASANT HORS D'OEUVRE

Roll:

   Thin slices of smoked turkey or pheasant

around:

   Large pitted green olives

Serve on small picks.

ABOUT CAVIAR AND OTHER ROES

A lady was once moved to ask plaintively why caviar is so expensive; to which a helpful maître d' replied: "After all, madam, it is a year's work for a sturgeon." The best caviar is the roe of the sturgeon, and the most sought-after caviar comes from Iran and Russia as **Beluga** and **Oscietre**. A third type, smaller because taken from a smaller Caspian sturgeon, is called **Sevruga** and is the kind usually obtainable in this country. None of these is either fishy in taste, or

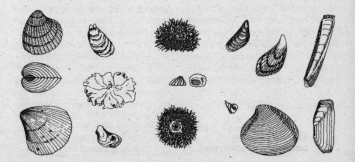

briny—as only 2% salt by weight is added as a preservative before trans-shipment to America. The eggs should be shiny, translucent, gray and large grained. ♦ As imported fresh caviar spoils in a few hours in temperatures of 40° or above, always serve it on ice. Its high oil content keeps it from freezing.

To serve individual portions attractively, heat the back of a metal spoon, press it into an ice cube, and fill the depression with the caviar—using a plastic spoon. ♦ Never allow the caviar itself to touch metal or to be served on it. If you spread it on canapés or in barquettes, see 68, or stuff beets with it, 91, be careful not to bruise the eggs. The classic accompaniments are lemon wedges, parsley, black bread, pumpernickel or not-too-dry toast. Although hard-cooked egg whites and yolks and onions—all very finely minced and separately arranged—are more frequently used as a garnish, connoisseurs consider them less suitable than the simpler lemon and parsley. Other favored ways to serve caviar are in blinis with sour cream, 147, or simply mixed half and half with sour cream. Caviar should be accompanied by either slightly chilled white wines or—preferably—champagne or vodka.

Other types of caviar are the roes of salmon, carp, cod, herring, lumpfish, pike, tuna and gray mullet. Those of cod, salmon, carp, pike and tuna are red or pink, and all are more gelatinous than sturgeon roes. To cook roes, see (I, 497). For a sauce made of roe, see Caviar Butter, (I, 398), and the recipe just below. To preserve caviar, see 634.

TARAMA

About 2½ Cups

This coral-pink roe mixture is served throughout Greece as a salad dressing. We use it most often as a dip, or to give added color and flavor to other hors d'oeuvre.
Prepare:

1 cup Riced Potatoes, (I, 344)

Keep them hot and toss promptly with:

2 tablespoons olive oil

Let this mixture cool. Beat in a mixer:

**½ cup smoked salmon or
carp roe**

1 tablespoon chopped onion

Combine with the potato and:

3 tablespoons lemon juice

Add slowly as for Mayonnaise, (I, 418):

⅓ to ½ cup olive oil

The whole mixture should thicken to the consistency of a heavy cream sauce; no more. You may incorporate:

**(1 tablespoon finely chopped
parsley)**

**(A small amount of tomato
purée)**

Season to taste

and refrigerate until ready to serve.

ABOUT SEASIDE TIDBITS

When you go collecting at the shore, you can often find edible treats. Those sketched on 97 can be eaten raw as hors d'oeuvre. Reading from top to bottom on left are **Nuttall's Cockle** and at the base the **Giant Atlantic Cockle,** with a side view between of the heart shape that gives them their name. Next are the **Eastern** and the native **Pacific Oyster,** with a bit of **Laver,** one of the large edible purple seaweeds, centered between them. The bristly **Sea Urchin** follows, shown at top as it hugs the rocks, and at the bottom revealing the unprotected edible contents. ♦ Always be certain to wear leather gloves when handling urchins. To prepare for eating raw or for cooking, free the tangerinelike sections from the gut. Cook as for Poached Eggs II, (I, 213). The flavor is much like that of brains. If eaten raw with a spoon, both roe and milt—the creatures are bisexual—are highly prized. In Japan the flesh is served as a fermented paste. In Latin America it frequently finds its way into an omelet. Between the urchins is the keyhole **Limpet.** You eat the foot, shown shaded, and discard the visceral hump. Second at top right is the **California Mussel** and beside it the **Common Mussel**—more about these on (I, 445). Below them is the **Periwinkle,** which can be extracted with a pin or a fine crochet hook. Below the "winkle" is a **Clam,** and top and bottom at extreme right are the long **Atlantic Jack Knife** and the shorter **Pacific Razor Clam;** more about these on (I, 445). For other sea tidbits try small shellfish, (I, 438), in spicy sauces. Serve hot or cold. ◗ Due to red tides, mollusks may be poisonous during the summer months. Be sure to check local conditions.

SEVICHE

Raw fish marinated in lime juice is very popular as an hors d'oeuvre in South America and Japan. If you are squeamish ◗ or if you are not sure your fish comes from unpolluted waters, you may prefer—as Europeans often do—to poach the fish lightly and pour over it a hot marinade of olive oil and vinegar, rather than relying merely on the acidulous action of lime juice. The poached and marinated fish is refrigerated covered 24 hours and served cold. This dish is called **escabèche.**
For seviche, skin, remove bones and dice the meat of:

    2 lb. very fresh firm-fleshed raw sole, pompano or red snapper

Or you may dice:

    (2 lb. raw lobster, crab meat or scallops)

Marinate in a glass dish, covered, and refrigerate 3 to 4 hours, entirely immersed in:

    2 cups lime juice
    1/2 cup finely chopped onions
    1/4 cup chopped green chilis
    1 cup chopped, peeled and seeded tomatoes
    2 teaspoons salt
    A few grains of cayenne
    1/8 teaspoon oregano

Serve on picks in small scallop shells with:

    Corn Dodgers Cockaigne, 342, or Tortillas, 343

and a garnish of:

    Hot chili peppers

FISH BALLS

Prepare very small:

    Codfish Balls, (I, 487), or Gefilte Fish Balls, (I, 482)

Serve them hot on picks with:

    Tartare Sauce, (I, 421)

ANCHOVY, EEL OR SMOKED SALMON ROLLS

I. Cut into 1/2-inch strips:

    Smoked salmon, eel or anchovies

Roll the strips around small:

    Sweet-sour or other gherkins or thin strips of cucumber

Secure and serve the rolls with picks.

II. Cut into very thin slices:

    Smoked salmon

Spread on the slices:

    Cream cheese seasoned with cucumbers, horseradish, chopped chives, parsley or caviar

Roll the strips. Secure and serve them on picks.

HERRING OR SARDINE HORS D'OEUVRE

Have all ingredients very cold.
Place on plates:

Lettuce leaves

Build up into a small cone:

Finely shredded coleslaw

Pour over the cone:

Cultured sour cream

The cream may be thinned with a few tablespoons of the liquor from the pickled herring. Top the cone with:

Small pieces of pickled herring, sardine or anchovy

ROLLMOPS

On a:

Herring fillet

Place a layer of:

Capers
Chopped shallots
Chopped gherkins
A little prepared mustard

Roll the fillet and fasten with a wooden pick. Place the rolled herrings in jars and cover well with:

Wine vinegar

to which you have added:

Slivers of lemon peel
Mustard seed
Sliced onion
Peppercorns

Allow the rollmops to steep for 10 days in the refrigerator. Drain and serve cold, lightly brushed with:

Olive oil

COLD OYSTER OR MUSSEL HORS D'OEUVRE

Prepare:

Sour Cream Dip, below

Coat with this sauce:

18 oysters or mussels in the half shell

Decorate tops with:

Red caviar

Serve on a bowl of ice.

PICKLED OYSTERS

Combine in the top of a double boiler:

1 quart oysters
1 quart oyster liquor

If needed, supplement the liquor with canned clam juice. Heat until the oysters are plump. Drain and wipe them. Reserve the liquor and simmer it 15 minutes with:

1 tablespoon peppercorns
1 tablespoon whole allspice
1 thinly sliced lemon
2 tablespoons vinegar
Dash of hot pepper sauce
Season to taste

Pour the sauce over the oysters and refrigerate at least 24 hours before serving.

PICKLED SHRIMP

For your most fiery guests.
Cover:

5 lb. shelled, deveined shrimp

with:

Flat draft beer or
2/3 vinegar and 1/3 water

Add:

1 tablespoon bruised peppercorns
1/4 cup salt
3 bay leaves
1 teaspoon hot pepper sauce or 1/8 teaspoon cayenne pepper
1/4 cup chopped celery tops

Bring to a boil and simmer 15 minutes. Remove from the heat and let shrimp stand in the liquor at least 1 hour in the refrigerator. Drain and place on a platter of crushed ice on artichoke leaves.

ASPIC-GLAZED SHRIMP

Clean and devein, (I, 461):

1½ lb. boiled shrimp

Cut them lengthwise down the center, as shown on (I, 461). Prepare:

Aspic Glaze, (I, 427)

Chill the glaze until it begins to set. Spear the shrimp on picks. Dip them into the glaze. When partly set, dip again. Chill well and serve cold.

⊟ BROILED SHRIMP COCKAIGNE

Without cutting into the meat, shell, clean and devein, leaving the tails on, (I, 461):

2 lb. jumbo shrimp

Marinate the shrimp in the refrigerator for several hours in:

1 pressed clove garlic
1 cup olive oil
½ cup sauterne wine
Juice of ½ lemon
3 tablespoons parsley and basil, chopped together
1 teaspoon salt
¼ teaspoon pepper

Grill or broil the shrimp about 10 minutes, being careful not to scorch them. Serve at once with:

Lemon Butter, (I, 397)

flavored with:

1 large pressed clove of garlic

or for a touch of the Orient use:

Chinese Low-Calorie Dressing Cockaigne, (I, 417)

FRIED SHRIMP BALLS

Mix and shape into balls:

1¼ lb. shelled, deveined, minced shrimp
6 finely chopped canned water chestnuts
1 piece ginger, finely chopped
1 small onion, chopped
1 egg white
1 teaspoon cornstarch
3 teaspoons wine
1 teaspoon sesame or other vegetable oil
Dash of pepper

Fry in deep fat heated to about 365° until golden brown.

ABOUT DIPS

Dangerously close to overimmersion, perhaps, dipped dainties are still the most popular types of hors d'oeuvre, and the easiest to prepare. They are versatile, too: entirely acceptable not only just before dinner, but as afternoon and late-evening snacks. Don't forget to use for dipping some of the spreads listed in Canapés; Welsh Rarebit, (I, 240); Cheese Fondue, (I, 242); Guacamole, 91; or the sauce which accompanies Bagna Cauda, 102. Make them juicier ◗ but still on the firm side, with a little cream, lemon juice or mayonnaise; and choose additional seasonings to your own taste. When serving ◗ it is wise to set the dip container over crushed ice.

FOOD DIPPERS

Crackers or strips of pumpernickel or rye toast
Potato or corn chips
Small wheat biscuits
Toast sticks
Fried oysters
Cooked seafood chunks
Chilled vegetables
Meatballs and small sausages

SOUR CREAM DIPS

I. Combine:

2 cups thick cultured sour cream

2 tablespoons chopped parsley

2 tablespoons chopped chives

1 teaspoon dried herbs

1/8 teaspoon curry powder

1/2 teaspoon salt

1/4 teaspoon paprika

II. Combine:

1 cup cultured sour cream

1 or more tablespoons horseradish

1/2 teaspoon salt

1/4 teaspoon paprika

CHEESE DIPS

The mania for cheese dips, cold, has replaced that for cheese dips, hot—without which no party used to be complete.

Try serving the following dips in a hollowed-out:

Round loaf of dark rye bread

Slice off the top of the loaf; then with a curved serrated knife remove the soft inner part of the loaf, leaving about 1 inch of thickness at sides and bottom. Use the removed bread later as chunks for dipping. ◗ Fill the hollow loaf with the dip just before serving.

I. Combine:

3/4 lb. cheddar cheese

1/4 lb. Roquefort cheese

2 tablespoons butter

1/2 teaspoon Worcestershire sauce

1/2 teaspoon prepared mustard

1/4 teaspoon salt

1/2 pressed clove of garlic

and melt over heat with:

1 cup beer

II. Beat until smooth:

2 packages cream cheese: 6 oz.

1 1/2 tablespoons mayonnaise

1 tablespoon cream

1/4 teaspoon salt

1 teaspoon grated onion or chives

1 teaspoon Worcestershire sauce

LONG-LIVED CHEESE SPREAD OR DIP

About 1 1/2 Cups

This concoction, if refrigerated, keeps for a week or so and makes excellent toasted cheese sandwiches or a sauce. Thin it as needed with a little milk in a double boiler.

Cut into small pieces and stir over very low heat, or over—not in—boiling water until melted:

1/2 lb. cheese

We find a soft cheese or a processed one preferable for this recipe. Add:

1 cup evaporated milk

3/4 teaspoon salt

3/4 teaspoon dry mustard

1/4 teaspoon curry powder

1/2 teaspoon caraway seeds

Remove from heat and stir in:

1 beaten egg

Stir and cook the cheese mixture very slowly until the egg thickens a bit. Remove from heat. Pour into a dish. Cool it slowly, beating as it cools, to keep a crust from forming. Cover and chill.

BAGNA CAUDA

Place in a heavy fondue pot, shown on (I, 243):

1/2 cup butter

1/2 cup olive oil

8 mashed anchovy fillets

2 cloves garlic, pressed

and simmer about 5 minutes, stirring occasionally. Add:

¹/₂ teaspoon freshly ground black pepper

Have ready a platter of bite-sized young vegetables, thinly sliced if the vegetables are fibrous, and peeled or seeded if necessary. Suitable are:

Carrots, Florence fennel, Belgian endive or celery, young artichoke hearts, cherry tomatoes, green peppers and zucchini

Let the guests dip their choices into the warm sauce on fondue forks.

ORIENTAL DIP

Good with raw mushrooms and raw cauliflower. Combine:

¹/₂ cup finely chopped green onions
¹/₂ teaspoon fresh coriander
¹/₄ cup chopped parsley
2 tablespoons chopped fresh ginger
1 tablespoon soy sauce
2 tablespoons chopped canned water chestnuts
1 cup cultured sour cream
2 tablespoons mayonnaise

HUMMUS

About 3¹/₂ Cups

Combine in a 🔨 blender:

2 cups strained cooked chick-peas
²/₃ cup Tahin, 241
³/₄ cup lemon juice
2 pressed cloves garlic
¹/₄ cup seeded black olives
1 teaspoon salt

After removing this mixture from blender, add:

3 tablespoons finely chopped parsley

Serve as a dip with:

Rye toast fingers
Strips of unleavened bread

CAVIAR DIP

Whip:

¹/₂ cup whipping cream

Fold in:

2 to 3 tablespoons caviar
1 to 2 tablespoons finely chopped onion

Place in the center of a dish and garnish with:

Sliced hard-cooked eggs and small rounds of toast

CLAM DIP

Drain:

1 cup minced clams

Combine with:

1 package soft cream cheese: 3 oz.
1 tablespoon Worcestershire sauce
¹/₈ teaspoon mustard
Salt, as needed
1 tablespoon, more or less, onion juice
¹/₄ cup whipping cream

CRAB MEAT OR TUNA DIP

Flake:

1 cup cooked crab meat or tuna

Stir in:

2 tablespoons mayonnaise
1 to 2 tablespoons tomato paste, catsup, or Chili Sauce, 686
Juice of 1 lemon
Seasoning, as needed
(Chopped celery or olives)

SHRIMP DIP

Combine:

1 can cooked cleaned
   shrimp: 5 oz.
1 cup creamed fine-curd
   cottage cheese
3 tablespoons Chili
   Sauce, 686

$\frac{1}{2}$ teaspoon onion juice
2 teaspoons lemon juice
1 to 2 tablespoons cream, if
   needed for consistency

FRUITS

"It was not a watermelon that Eve took," observed Mark Twain. "We know it because she repented." There is something about "a piece of fruit"—no matter which—so tidy, shapely, self-contained and full of promise as to appeal to the larcenous instincts in all Eve's children.

Shown above, in addition to Twain's irresistible watermelon, are such staples of the world's diet as bananas and dates—and in more northerly climes, the pear; a papaya, whole and halved, next to a compote of kiwi. A spray of litchi and a Japanese persimmon contrast with the sweet-sour carambola, shown whole and in starry cross-section.

Today's menu-builder often takes herself too seriously and tops off an impressive edifice with a disastrously rich dessert, forgetting that fresh fruit, with perhaps a cheese, would be a far happier conclusion of the meal for all concerned. Well worth exploiting, too, are the virtues of fruit—in either cup, compote, salad or sherbet form—as a "lightener" during as well as after a big meal.

If fruits lack flavor, serve them or prepare them with candied peels, ginger, zest or spices; or add a little lemon or lime juice to cooked fruits and fruit fillings. Vary the flavor of a particular fruit by steeping it in the juices of other fruits or in wine, or by blending it with others in a purée. You may glaze poached fruit with contrasting fruit jellies, especially those of apple and quince, which are high in pectin; or combine canned, frozen and fresh fruits—cold or slightly heated—in what the French call a **compôte composée**. Try presenting your "composed compote" in a giant lidded snifter, laced with brandy or liqueur, and serve it to your guests in smaller individual snifters.

Serve Fruit with Custards, 507, or Creams, 449; Fruit Brûlé, 113, or Flambé, 112. For dried or preserved fruits used as garnishes, see About Candied and Glazed Fruits, 602. For fresh fruit combinations, see 106, and also consult the Salad chapter, (I, 42–90). For frozen and canned fruits, see 646 and 618. Recipes involving fruit used as an ingredient in desserts will be found in the Dessert chapter, 507–544.

ABOUT FRESH FRUITS

Pomologists have been working tirelessly—never more than now—to hybridize the most popular domestic fruits in order to lengthen the harvest season early and late; to produce plants more resistant to disease and adverse climate; and to improve shipping and keeping characteristics. In fact, much of this effort has been carried forward with little regard for retaining juiciness and flavor. Furthermore, crossbreeding within varieties has proceeded so rapidly, and the new cultivars have been so casually styled, that among apples, for example, 20 or 30 descendants may be traced to McIntosh and Winesap, but never through their names, which reveal not the slightest hint of their ancestry. In view of so confusing a situation, it is often advisable to sample fruit before buying it—a precaution that is a little difficult to arrange for in the average supermarket.

Should you undertake to grow your own fruit, choose catalog stock expressly labeled "for the home garden." Such fruit has been developed with an eye to immediate consumption, and so comprises varieties more delicate in flavor and texture than those commercially propagated.

Most ripe fresh fruit may be stored under refrigeration at temperatures between 35° and 40°. Most fruit varieties, too, including tangerines, benefit from the protection of a sealed plastic bag—exceptions being other citrus fruits, melons and pineapples. Mature bananas will keep chilled for a day or two.

Be wary of "fruit specials." Such produce may include pieces that are below standard in either quality or size and could prove to be no bargains at all. U. S. Government standards are of necessity variable, but you can judge for yourself as to size: ♦ the smaller the number of fruits per box or basket, obviously, the larger the individual fruit.

Not all varieties of fruit ripen satisfactorily after plucking. Those which do are apricots, avocados, bananas, melons, mangoes, medlars, nectarines, pawpaws, peaches, pears, persimmons, sapodillas, tamarinds, strawberries to a limited extent, and pineapples; none of these grow sweeter, however. If purchased underripe, these fruits should be stored at room temperature in a dark place. Keep each variety in a partly closed paper bag, the individual pieces—except for strawberries, bananas and melons—separated by loose wraps of paper toweling. Examine them twice daily, keep from bruising and, as soon as ripened, chill in the refrigerator before serving.

There is a persistent but mistaken belief that all fruits abound in vitamin C. Many do, notably the citrus family; but in others, like apples, pineapples, pears, figs and bananas, the C content is conspicuously low. Virtually all fresh fruits lose their flavor rapidly when soaked in water, so always ♦ wash them quickly in gently flowing water just before using and dry at once. If peaches, plums, apricots and cherries are cooked with the seeds in, be careful ♦ that the inner kernel of the pit which looks nutlike is not eaten. Eight to ten such kernels, if chewed, can release enough hydrogen cyanide to prove fatal.

ANTI-BROWNING SOLUTION FOR FRESH FRUITS

Solutions that prevent the browning of fruits and certain vegetables on ex-

posure to air are used in both canning
and freezing and can be successfully
applied to fresh fruits peeled slightly
in advance of serving. For fresh fruits
we like to use Acidulated Water II,
167, or to combine pared fruits with
citrus fruits to prevent darkening.

FRUIT CUPS

Sweetened fresh fruit may be served
in attractive small bowls or glass
cups, in melon baskets, see 131, or in
a Caramel Cornflake Ring, 439. ▶ To
frost containers, see 40. Use seedless
grapes, citrus sections, and watermelon and green and yellow melons
cut into balls with a French potato
cutter, see (I, 54).
Chill and prepare for serving:
Fresh fruit
Five minutes before serving, sprinkle
lightly with:
Confectioners' sugar
Immediately before serving, flavor
with:

> **Lime juice, lemon juice,
> sherry, a liqueur, or lightly
> sweetened fruit juice**

Garnish with:

> **Glazed Mint Leaves, 602,
> or sweet woodruff**

AMBROSIA

4 Servings

A versatile old favorite, especially
popular in the South.
Peel carefully, removing all membrane:

> **2 large Valencia or navel
> oranges**

Peel and cut into thin slices:

> **3 ripe bananas**

Pineapple is sometimes added, or
other fruits: seeded grapes, apples,
etc. Combine and stir:

¼ **cup confectioners' sugar**
1½ **cups shredded coconut**
Arrange alternate layers of oranges
and bananas in individual serving
dishes or in a bowl. Sprinkle each
layer with part of the coconut mixture, reserving some for the top. Pour
over the fruit:

> **A little orange juice**

Chill well before serving. Instead of
the coconut topping, try a garnish of:

> **(Crushed mint, a cherry or
> a strawberry)**

MACÉDOINE OF FRESH FRUITS

The following fruit and wine or
liqueur combinations should be made
with ripe, perfect, pared, seeded and
sliced seasonal fruits. Favorites for
this dessert are strawberries, raspberries, peeled seedless green grapes,
peaches, apricots, kiwi slices, orange
and grapefruit sections, melon balls,
cherries and nectarines. Be sure to
prick the fruits to allow the marinade
to soak in. If you use raw apples or
pears, marinate the slices for several
hours in wine or liqueur or they will
be too hard in texture. Some good
marinating combinations are:

> **Brandy with oranges or
> with cherries and clove-
> studded peaches
> Port with melon balls
> Kirsch with strawberries
> Grand Marnier with peeled
> seedless grapes**

A macédoine is usually served cold,
but you may flambé it, see 112, if
the fruit is at room temperature—and
if you add extra liqueur, slightly
warmed.
Place in layers in a crystal bowl:

> **Prepared fruit, see above**

Sprinkle each layer with:

> **Confectioners' sugar**

Stir the fruit gently until the sugar is almost dissolved, then add for each quart of fruit:

>**2 to 4 tablespoons brandy, kirsch, Grand Marnier or Southern Comfort**

Serve very cold over:

>**Vanilla ice cream, 547**

or with:

>**Cake**

FRUIT FOOLS

>**4 Servings**

Long ago the word "fool" was used as a term of endearment. We have an old-fashioned fondness for the recipes in which fruit is combined with cream.

I. With Fresh Fruit

Prepare:

>**Raspberries or strawberries**

Add to taste:

>**Confectioners' sugar**

Let the mixture stand 10 minutes. Combine it with an equal amount of:

>**Whipping cream**

flavored with:

>**(3 tablespoons kirsch, port or Madeira wine)**

Chill well before serving.

II. With Cooked Fruit

Whip until stiff:

>**$1/2$ cup sweetened whipping cream**

Fold in:

>**1 cup applesauce, rhubarb, berry, apricot, currant or other fruit purée**
>
>**$1^1/2$ teaspoons grated lemon rind or $1/4$ teaspoon almond extract**

Place the mixture in the bowl from which it is to be served. Chill thoroughly. Sprinkle the top with:

>**Crumbled Macaroons, 469**

or serve with:

>**Ladyfingers, 448**

ABOUT RAISINS AND OTHER DRIED FRUITS

The high caloric and nutritive values of dried fruits can be readily grasped if you realize that it takes $5^1/2$ pounds of fresh apricots to yield 1 pound when dried. When fruits are dried without cooking, their subsequent contact with the air—as well as the enzymatic activity that takes place within them—tends to darken the pulp. A sulfur dioxide solution is often used to lessen darkening. If you are interested in drying your own fruits, see 637.

Dates, figs, apples, peaches, pears, plums, apricots, currants and grapes are among the fruits most often dried. They must all be ◗ stored tightly covered in a cool, dark place. Under most household shelf conditions, they are likely to deteriorate in a matter of months. This is especially true of the increasingly numerous dried fruits that are treated and tightly packaged so as to remain plump and soft. All varieties must be watched for the insect infestation that develops in them with age.

Raisins, which of course are simply dried grapes, divide into **seedless,** those which grow without seeds; and **seeded,** which have had the seeds removed. As their flavors are quite different, it is wise to use the types called for in the recipes—without interchanging. White raisins, often called **muscats,** are especially treated to retain their lovely color.

Currants and raisins both profit, unless they are very fresh, by plumping, especially when used in short-cooking recipes. This can be done by soaking them in the liquid in which they are to be cooked—such as the liquid called for in cakes—for 10 to 15 minutes before use. Raisins and currants may also be plumped by washing briefly, draining, spreading on a flat pan and then heating, closely covered, in a 350° oven until they puff up and are no longer much wrinkled.

In cooking dried fruits, do not soak them first unless the processor so directs on the package. The less water used, the more natural sugars will be retained within the fruit. If you must soak fruit such as dried apples, cover with boiling water and soak until tender. Use this water in further preparation. Allow 1 pound dried for 3¹/₂ to 4 pounds fresh apples and proceed as for any apple recipe.

Small dried fruits are often messy to cut or chop. If they are sticky, flour them, ◗ using for this purpose, when baking, a portion of the flour called for in the recipe. They may also be more easily cut if the scissors or the knife blade is heated. Handle the knife as for chopping nuts. But if you are chopping in quantity, you may want to use a meat grinder instead. ◗ Heat the grinder very thoroughly in boiling water before feeding in the fruit.

Candied and preserved fruits are sometimes substituted for dried fruits. If large amounts of candied fruits are used, allow for their extra sugar content. With preserved fruits, compensate for both sugar and liquid.

Fine-quality dried dessert fruits are an elegant note on the cheese platter, especially dried Malaga grapes. Should any of the fruits have become unpleasantly dried out, steam them lightly—sprinkled with wine or water—in the top of a double boiler ◗ over—not in—bo_ ng water; or prepare them for stuffing by steaming

10 to 15 minutes in a colander ◗ over boiling water, until tender enough to pit. Stuff with a hazelnut or with fillings suggested under confections, 600.

FRUIT-NUT PEMMICAN

This quite palatable albeit gooey substance is the modern outdoorsman's version of the old suet–parched corn–fruit concoction that sustained both Indians and frontiersmen in earlier times. Grind in a meat grinder, using the coarse plate:

¹/₃ **cup each: raisins, dried apricots, dried apples, pecans, toasted soybeans and Spanish peanuts**

Combine with:

2 tablespoons honey

These ingredients may be changed to fit individual preferences. For a tasty variation, use pecans as the only nuts. Package for the trail in wide-mouth plastic bottles or plastic bags.

ABOUT COOKED FRUITS

A good reason for serving fruits uncooked is to retain fully their high vitamin content. But if we do cook them, we can minimize the loss of vitamins and natural sugars by using as little water as possible and by cooking briefly. Fruits may be poached, puréed, baked, broiled, sautéed or pickled, see Spiced Syrup, 110.

Fruits should always be poached rather than stewed. ◗ Drop them into a boiling liquid, ◗ reduce the heat at once and simmer until barely tender. Remove from the heat and drain them immediately, so they will not continue to cook in the pan and get mushy. Soft, juicy fruits, like ripe peaches, are best poached by putting them for a few moments into heavy boiling syrup and then plunging the pan into a larger pan of cold water to arrest the cooking. Apples and other hard fruits should be poached in simmering water. Watch closely to guard against overcooking. If necessary, add sugar, but only after poaching. A baked fruit compote or a mixture of cooked fruits makes a refreshing addition to a meat course, provided that fruit juices have not been used in basting the meat. Always pare fruit with a ♦ stainless steel knife to avoid discoloration.

SYRUPS FOR FRUITS

I. Thin Syrup
For apples, grapes and rhubarb.
Combine and heat:

> 1 cup sugar
> 3 cups water
> 1/16 teaspoon salt

II. Medium Syrup
For apricots, cherries, grapefruit, pears and prunes.
Combine and heat:

> 1 cup sugar
> 2 cups water
> 1/8 teaspoon salt

III. Heavy Syrup
For berries, figs, peaches and plums.
Combine and heat:

> 1 cup sugar
> 1 cup water
> 1/8 teaspoon salt

SPICED SYRUP FOR FRESH FRUITS

> **Enough for 1 to 1 1/2 Pints Fruit**
Tie in a cheesecloth bag:

> 1 1/2 teaspoons each whole cloves, whole allspice
> 1 stick cinnamon

Add and boil 5 minutes:

> 1 1/2 cups white or brown sugar or 2 cups honey
> 1 cup cider vinegar
> 1 cup water

Remove the spice bag and discard. Drop whole, sliced, pared or unpared fruit into the boiling syrup. Cool and serve.

SPICED SYRUP FOR CANNED FRUITS

Drain and reserve the syrup from:

> **Canned peaches, apricots, pears or pineapple**

Measure the syrup and ♦ simmer until slightly reduced with:

> 1/4 to 1/2 as much wine vinegar

Allow for every 2 cups of juice and vinegar:

> 1 stick cinnamon
> 1/2 teaspoon cloves without heads
> (2 or 3 small pieces gingerroot)

After simmering about 10 minutes, add fruit. Remove pan from heat and let fruit cool in the liquid. Strain out the spices and serve hot or cold with meat.

POACHED OR "STEWED" PARED FRUIT

Please read About Cooked Fruits, 109.
Boil 3 minutes:

> **A Syrup for Fruit, above**

Drop into the boiling syrup about:

> 1 quart peeled or pared fruit

♦ Reduce the heat at once. Simmer gently until tender. You may season the syrup with any of the following:

> (Spices)
> (Crème de menthe)
> (Wine)
> (Stick cinnamon)
> (Slice of lemon)

Drain fruit and reduce syrup. Pour syrup over fruit and chill before serving.

POACHED OR "STEWED" THIN-SKINNED FRUIT

By adding the sugar late in the cooking as suggested here, you will need less of it to sweeten the same quantity of fruit than if you had used it from the start. This method will also keep the skin soft.

Boil:

2 cups water

Prepare and add:

1 quart unpared fruit: peaches, pears, apricots or nectarines

Reduce heat at once. Simmer fruit until nearly tender. Add:

1/2 to 3/4 cup sugar

During the last few minutes of cooking, add:

(A vanilla bean, 261)

POACHED OR "STEWED" THICK-SKINNED FRUIT

Use whole or cut into halves and if necessary remove the seeds from:

4 cups thick-skinned fruit: plums, blueberries or cherries

You may prick the fruit before dropping it into:

1 to 1 1/2 cups boiling water

Reduce heat at once. Simmer until nearly tender. Add:

1/2 to 1 cup sugar

Cook a few minutes longer. ◗ After cooking blueberries, to which lemon juice is a good addition, shake the container to avoid clumping.

BAKED FRESH FRUIT COMPOTE

4 Servings

Use this also as a garnish for custard or blanc-mange.

Preheat oven to 350°.

Pare:

8 small peaches, apples or pears

Place them whole or in thick slices in a baking dish. Combine, heat but do not boil, stir and pour over them:

2/3 cup red wine or water
2/3 cup sugar
1/2 stick cinnamon
4 whole cloves
1/8 teaspoon salt
1/2 thinly sliced seeded lemon or lime

Bake the fruit either covered or uncovered until tender when tested with a fork. If cooked uncovered ◗ it must be basted every 10 minutes. For more rapid and even cooking, some people prefer to turn the fruit over after the first two bastings.

ADDITIONS TO BAKED FRUITS

I. To be served as a meat garnish. After baking, fill centers of fruits with:

Mint, currant or cranberry jelly, or a mixture of pearl onions, shredded candied ginger and seasoned cream cheese

II. As dessert. Fill centers with:

A mixture of Roquefort or blue cheese, cream cheese and chopped almonds, pecans, hickory nuts or walnuts

ABOUT PURÉED FRUITS

Puréed fruits are most delicate if cooked covered over gentle heat. ◗

We do not recommend pressure-cooking of any fresh fruits. Apples, rhubarb and cranberries, especially, tend to sputter and obstruct the vent. They are almost explosive unless every vestige of steam is expelled before removal of the cover. ♦ If you want to purée canned fruit, you should know that, after draining, a No. 2½ can will yield 1¼ to 1½ cups.

GARNISHES FOR PURÉED FRUITS

Serve puréed fruit hot or cold with one of the following toppings:

> **Grated lemon rind or cinnamon**
> **Whipping cream and nutmeg**
> **Chopped Glazed Chestnuts, 605, and marmalade**
> 6 **crushed dry macaroons to 1 cup whipped cream**
> **Cultured sour cream or yogurt with sugar, rum and nuts**
> **Bread or cake crumbs browned in butter with chopped slivered almonds**
> **Freshly chopped mint**

BROILED FRUITS

Drain:

> **Poached or canned peaches, pears or pineapple rings**

Place peaches or pears, hollow side up, in a shallow pan. Place on the centers:

> **A dab of butter**

Plug up the pineapple hole with:

> **A preserved cherry**

Sprinkle each piece of fruit lightly with:

> **Salt and cinnamon**

Broil under moderate heat until light brown. You may garnish the fruits with:

> **(Cranberry or other jelly)**

FRESH FRUIT KEBABS

8 Servings

Serve with meat course or as a dessert. Marinate about 30 minutes:

> 6 **canned peach halves— drained and cut in half**
> 3 **thickly sliced bananas**
> 2 **apples, cut in sections**
> 1 **cubed fresh pineapple**
> 3 **sectioned grapefruits**

in a mixture of:

> 1 **cup grapefruit juice**
> ½ **cup honey**
> 2 **tablespoons Cointreau**
> (1 **teaspoon chopped mint**)

Broil on skewers about 5 minutes, basting often with the marinade.

FLAMBÉED FRUITS

For best results, use at least 2 ounces of alcoholic liquor, and remember that ♦ unless the temperature of the fruit is at least 75°, you may not get any effect at all. Heat the fruit ♦ mildly in a ♦ covered chafing dish or electric skillet. ♦ Warm the liquor, too, but do not boil it. Sprinkle the fruit lightly with sugar and, after pouring the warm liquor over the warm fruit, re-cover the pan for a moment before lighting. Stand back!

The following recipe makes 6 servings as a sauce, but only 3 if used as a main dessert dish. Caramelize, 232, lightly over low heat:

> 3 **tablespoons sugar**

Add:

> 3 **tablespoons butter**

or, if you are lazy, melt the butter first and substitute brown sugar, stirring until dissolved. Cook over very low

heat for 4 to 5 minutes. Add 2 of the
following:

> **3 split bananas, mangoes,
> peaches or pears or
> 3 slices pineapple**

Simmer until tender, basting occasionally. Since the banana will cook more rapidly than the rest of the fruit, it should be added later. Flambé the fruit with:

> **2 oz. brandy, dark rum or
> liqueur**

FRUIT BRÛLÉ

4 to 5 Servings

This recipe is most often made with seedless green grapes but lends itself equally well to strawberries, raspberries and peaches.
Fill the bottom of a 9-inch ovenproof baker or glass pie pan with an even layer of one of the above-mentioned:

> **Fruits**

Cover the fruit with:

> **1 cup cultured sour cream**

mixed with:

> **1 teaspoon vanilla**

Cover and refrigerate until thoroughly chilled.
Preheat broiler.
Just before serving, dust the cream evenly with:

> **About 1 cup light brown
> sugar**

so that none of the cream shows through. Place the filled pan over a pan of equal size filled with:

> **Cracked ice**

Put the stacked pans under the hot broiler until the sugar caramelizes, 232. This is a moment for watchfulness, as the sugar must fuse but not scorch. Serve at once.

SAUTÉED FRUITS

6 Servings

Core and slice or cut into rings:

> **6 tart, well-flavored apples;
> or peaches, apricots, or
> pineapple slices**

Melt in a skillet over high heat:

> **2 tablespoons butter or
> bacon drippings**

When the fat is hot to the point of fragrance stir in the fruit. Cover until the fruit steams. Sprinkle with:

> **½ cup white or brown sugar**
> **⅛ teaspoon salt**

Cook uncovered over gentle heat until tender. Add, if needed:

> **(Butter or drippings)**

Serve with a meat course or with:

> **Bacon**

To serve with meat, you may begin making this dish by placing a layer of finely sliced onions, about 1 cup, in the butter. Cook slowly in the fat 5 minutes. Season with salt and paprika. Add the fruit and proceed as directed.

CURRIED FRUIT FONDUE

8 Servings

Fruit in season may be dipped into or served in a two-way hot sauce—hot with both spice and cooking.
Combine and simmer covered ½ hour:

> **1 cup chicken broth**
> **1 cup dry white wine**
> **1 tablespoon curry powder**

Add:

> **1 tablespoon quick-cooking
> tapioca**

soaked in:

> **3 tablespoons water**

Stir the sauce until thickened. Add:

> **1 cup freshly grated coconut**
> **1 cup slivered, toasted
> almonds**
> **½ cup white raisins**

While the sauce is cooking, cut into cubes or finger-sized sections a combination of:

About 4 cups fresh fruit: pineapple, mangoes, papayas, bananas and melons

Keep the sauce hot in a chafing dish. Dip the fruits in the fondue; or pour sauce over individual fruit portions just before serving. For other fruit fondue sauces, see 563–565.

ABOUT FRUITS FOR MEATS AND ENTRÉES

Fruit Compotes, 111, Fruit Kebabs, 112, Sautéed Fruits, 113, or pickled or spiced fruits served with meat are delights we may have a tendency to neglect. Consider using as occasional decorative fruit garnishes:

Apple Rings, 116
Glazed Stuffed Apricots, 602
Kumquats
Orange slices with cranberry or other jelly
Cranberries

FRUIT SOUPS

In Scandinavia, fruit soups are served as a dessert, but in Germany they constitute a chilled summertime prelude to the entrée. Mix fresh and dried fruits; use one variety or a combination, cooked until they can be puréed easily. If served at the beginning of the meal, go easy on the sugar. Fruit soups are also refreshing when made from frozen fruits, in winter, as a dessert. Rote Grütze II, 532, will serve in the dessert capacity, or use the cherry, orange or rose hip recipe following.

I. CHERRY SOUP

4 Cups

Prepare:

1 lb. stoned sour cherries

Place in an enamel pan and cover with:

2 cups water
1 cup red wine

Cook until the fruit is soft, about 10 minutes. Add and stir until dissolved:

¼ cup sugar
½ teaspoon grated orange rind

Blend or sieve the fruit and thicken the juice with:

1 teaspoon arrowroot

mixed with a little of the cooled syrup. Return the mixture to the soup and cook about 2 minutes. Serve hot or cold. Garnish with:

Unsweetened whipped cream, croutons or Dumplings, (I, 182)

II. ORANGE SOUP

6 Servings

Scrub and remove the orange-colored peel in shreds from:

1 Valencia or navel orange

Add these peelings to a syrup of:

1 cup sugar
½ cup currant jelly
¼ cup water

Simmer about 15 minutes. Meanwhile, section the peeled orange, 125, and also:

5 more peeled Valencia or navel oranges

♦ Cool the syrup to about 85°. Pour it over the orange sections. Add:

2 tablespoons brandy

Refrigerate, covered, about 12 hours, before serving with:

A crisp thin refrigerator cookie, 479, or a curled cookie, 483

Also good with:

Cinnamon toast

ROSE HIP SOUP

Crush in a stainless steel or enamel
pot:

2 cups fresh rose hips
▶ but be sure the bushes from which
they are gathered were not sprayed.
Cover with:

1 quart water
Bring to a boil, then simmer, covered, about 45 minutes. Strain
through a sieve lined with several
thicknesses of cheesecloth. Add
enough:

**Fruit juice: raspberry,
peach, orange**
to make about 1 quart liquid in
all. Mix:

1 tablespoon arrowroot
with a small quantity of the liquid and:

⅓ cup honey
Simmer and stir until the mixture begins to thicken. Chill well and serve
garnished with:

**Whipped cream
Slivered Spiced Nuts, 594**

INDIVIDUAL FRUITS

Already familiar and now seasonably
obtainable in most American markets
are the fruits shown below: the fresh
fig with its renowned leaf; a decorative spray of kumquats; a mango,
shown cut to reveal its large fiber-
covered seed. Next is a pomegranate;
then the ugly duckling of the apple
family, the quince; and finally the
prickly pear.

ABOUT APPLES

A predecessor of ours, Amelia Sim-
mons, in her pioneering *American
Cookery*—circa 1845—had this to
say: "If every boy in America planted
an apple tree (except in our com-
pactest cities) in some useless corner,
and tended it carefully, the net saving
would in time extinguish the public
debt." A century or so later it is becoming evident that a solid layer of
applesauce a half-mile thick would
not suffice to "extinguish the public
debt." And we are even beginning to
wonder, in these days of office visits
only, just how politic we were more
recently to invent the adage about the
apple a day and the doctor.

Although apples are in the market
the year around, they are not at their
peak from January to June. There is
probably no flavor superior to that
of the Greenings or Transparents that
fleetingly initiate the harvest. If you
plan canning or freezing, do try to get
the first picking for prompt preservation of this unusual tart flavor.

So-called dessert apples—firm,
long-keeping types always eaten
uncooked—include Yellow and Red
Delicious and Newtown Pippin. We
find most varieties of Delicious too
dry and their somewhat corky aftertaste faintly unpleasant.

All-purpose apple varieties—good
for eating, for salads and for most
cooking—are Northern Spy, Spitzen-
burg, Baldwin, Jonathan, Stayman,
Winesap, Wealthy, McIntosh, Gra-
venstein, Grimes Golden, Melrose,

Russet, and Rhode Island Green-ing—which cooks best of all. Wealthys and McIntoshes are not good bakers. ◗ Best for this purpose are Spitzenburgs, Northern Spys, Cortlands, York Imperials, Staymans, Winesaps, Baldwins and Rome Beau-tys, unless the latter are overripe. In that condition they become mealy.

Mealiness in apples, to which larger varieties are more prone, may also denote too long or improper storage. Browning near the core means that the fruit has been stored at too low a temperature.

If you wonder why the apple in commercial pies has a firmer texture than yours, it is due to added cal-cium. An apple of poor flavor can be improved in cooking by the addition of lemon juice, but remember that nothing can really compensate for natural tartness. After paring, should apples seem dry, simmer their cores and skins, reduce the liquid and use it to moisten them during cooking.

If you receive a windfall from a friend's orchard and want to reserve some of it, let it stand in a cool, shady place for 24 hours. Inspect for blem-ishes. Wrap each fruit in paper and store in slotted boxes in a cool, dark, airy place.

For apple recipes, see below and the Index.

APPLE RINGS

Wash, core and cut crosswise into slices:
    3 large, perfect cooking
        apples
Heat in a skillet:
    3 tablespoons bacon fat or
        butter
Place in it a single layer of apple rings. Sprinkle lightly with:
    Confectioners' sugar

Add to the skillet:
    2 tablespoons water
Cover the skillet and ◗ simmer the apples until tender. Remove cover and brown rings on both sides. Serve hot, the centers filled with:
    Bright red jelly
or dust the rings with:
    Cinnamon

GLAZED APPLES

                    6 Servings
Recommended only for tart apples. If the only ones at hand are listless, try the next recipe below instead.
Preheat oven to 350°.
Pare, core and slice thinly:
    4 cups tart apples
Place them in a 6 × 9-inch pan. Pour over them:
    3 tablespoons melted butter
Bake 15 to 30 minutes, or until tender. Remove from oven and dust with:
    ¾ to 1 cup white or brown
        sugar
    (2 to 3 tablespoons dark rum)
Run under a broiler, leaving the oven door ajar, until the sugar and rum glaze the surface. ◗ Watch carefully. Serve at once.

HONEY APPLES

An excellent way to use a dull-flavored apple. Heat in a small porce-lain or stainless steel pan:
    1 cup honey
    ½ cup vinegar
Pare, core and slice thinly:
    2 cups apples
Drop the apples a few at a time into the simmering, bubbling honey mix-ture. Skim them out when transpar-ent. Serve chilled or hot as a relish with pork, as a tart filling, or as a dessert with cream.

SAUTÉED APPLES AND BACON

4 Servings

A fine breakfast or luncheon dish.
Pare and core:

Tart cooking apples

Cut them into cubes. There should be about 4 cups. Sauté in a heavy skillet:

8 slices bacon

Remove the bacon when crisp. Keep it hot. Leave about 2 tablespoons of fat in the skillet. Add:

2 tablespoons vegetable oil

Add the apples. Sauté uncovered over high heat until translucent. Sprinkle with:

2 tablespoons white or brown sugar

Place apples on a hot platter. Surround them with the bacon. Serve garnished with:

Parsley

BAKED APPLES

I.
4 Servings

Preheat oven to 375°.
Wash and remove core to ¹/₂ inch of bottoms of:

4 large tart apples

Combine:

**¹/₄ cup white or brown sugar
(1 teaspoon cinnamon)**

If the apples are bland, add:

(¹/₈ teaspoon grated lemon rind)

Fill the centers with this. Dot the filled cores with:

Butter

Put the apples into an 8 × 8-inch pan with:

**³/₄ cup boiling water
(2 tablespoons sugar)**

Bake about 30 minutes—or until tender but not mushy. Remove from the oven and baste the apples several times with the pan juices. Should the juices be thin, remove the apples to a serving dish and reduce the pan juices before glazing the apples with them. Serve hot or chilled.

II.
6 Servings

Obviously a richer dish than that produced by the above recipe.
Preheat oven to 425°.
Pare and core:

6 large baking apples

Fill the cores with a mixture of:

**¹/₂ cup chopped blanched almonds or pecans
¹/₂ cup sugar
2 tablespoons raisins, chopped figs or prunes, or mincemeat
(1 egg white)**

Make another mixture of:

**¹/₂ cup fine bread crumbs
2 tablespoons sugar
1 teaspoon cinnamon or ¹/₂ teaspoon powdered ginger**

Coat the apples with:

6 tablespoons melted butter

Roll them in the bread crumbs. Bake the apples in individual buttered bakers about 25 minutes. Serve hot, covered with:

Caramelized Sugar, 232

or cold with:

Cream

BAKED APPLES FILLED WITH SAUSAGE MEAT

6 Servings

A three-star winter dish.
Preheat oven to 375°.
Wash:

6 large tart baking apples

Cut a slice from the tops. Scoop out the cores and pulp, leaving shells ³/₄ inch thick. Cut the pulp from the cores and chop it. Combine it with:

1 cup well-seasoned sausage meat or small sliced sausage links

Sprinkle the shells with:

(2 tablespoons brown sugar)

Fill them heaping full with the sausage mixture. Bake in a baking dish until tender. Serve with a mound of:

**Boiled Rice, (I, 189), or
Boiled Noodles, (I, 200)**

APPLES STUFFED WITH SAUERKRAUT

4 Servings

Preheat oven to 375°.

Pare the tops of:

4 large baking apples

Remove the pulp and discard the core, leaving a 1/2-inch shell. Chop the pulp and add to it:

**2 cups drained canned or
cooked sauerkraut**
1/8 teaspoon pepper
**1/4 teaspoon caraway seeds
Salt, as needed**

Fill the shells. Place them in a baking dish with 1/4 cup water or dry wine. Bake until tender. Baste frequently with pan juices.

APPLES COCKAIGNE

4 to 5 Servings

Wash, core and pare down to about 1 to 1 1/2 inches from the top:

**4 or 5 medium-sized baking
apples**

Place them in a heavy 8-inch pan with a mixture of:

2 1/2 cups water
1 cup sugar
**2 tablespoons red-hots or
cinnamon drops**

The red-hots give the apples a spicy tang and a beautiful color. The fruit should be submerged to a level just below the upper edge of the peel. Simmer about 20 minutes, or until the steeped portion of the apples gives slightly at the pressure of a spoon. Turn them over and simmer about 3 minutes longer. Remove the fruit carefully from the syrup and place on a rack in a broiler pan. Preheat the broiler.

Reduce the syrup to about 1 cup. Ladle a tablespoon of syrup over each apple. Broil the apples about 3 minutes, at least 5 inches from heat source. Repeat the ladling and broil 2 minutes longer. Baste with remaining syrup. Place the apples in individual dishes and spoon the syrup from the bottom of the baking pan into the cored centers. Serve warm or cold, with or without:

Cream

APPLESAUCE

◗ Please read About Puréed Fruits, 111.

I.   About 1 Quart

Wash, cut into quarters and core:

**2 1/2 lb. apples: preferably Early
Transparents, Northern
Spys or Russets**

Place them in a saucepan and partly cover with water. Old apples require more water than new ones. ◗ Simmer the apples until tender. Put them through a food mill or ricer, or ⅄ blend, skin and all. Return the strained apple pulp to the saucepan. Add enough:

Sugar

to make it palatable. Cook gently about 3 minutes.

Add to tasteless apples:

Lemon juice or Zest, 252

Canned applesauce may be seasoned in the same way. Sprinkle it, if desired, with:

(Cinnamon)

Serve hot or cold. If hot, add:

1 or 2 teaspoons butter

If cold, add:

1/2 teaspoon vanilla or a few
     drops almond extract
When served with pork, you may
add:
     (1 or 2 tablespoons
        horseradish)

II. Combine:
     2 cups applesauce as cooked
        above
with:
     1 cup puréed apricots or
        raspberries
or with:
     1 cup crushed pineapple
     1 teaspoon finely crushed
        preserved ginger
or with:
     2 cups Cranberry Sauce, 123
sprinkled with:
     Grated orange rind

ABOUT APRICOTS

Fresh apricots have a beautiful blush
and should be firm in texture. If they
appear wilted or shriveled, they lack
flavor and will decay quickly. Apricots may be eaten raw or cooked in a
very light syrup and served flambéed
in Meringues, 375.

As a purée made from the dried
fruit—a modification of the recipe
below—the apricot is a frequent addition in the European cuisine. Especially, in a more or less cooked-down
or glazed state, it enlivens a whole
galaxy of filled cakes, open tarts,
torten and frozen desserts.

COOKED DRIED APRICOTS

                              10 Servings
Place in a heavy pan:
     1 lb. dried apricots
     3 cups water
Simmer the fruit about 35 minutes.
Add:

     1/2 to 1 cup sugar
Heat until the sugar is dissolved,
about 5 minutes longer. You may
purée the fruit.

ABOUT AVOCADOS

A native of America, this valuable
fruit harbors no less than 11 vitamins.
Two varieties are usually available,
depending on the season: a smooth
green-skinned type, and a much
darker one with pebbled skin. Like
the banana, the avocado is never allowed to mature on the tree. Buy it
slightly underripe and ripen it at 70°,
hastening the process, if you like, by
enclosing it in a paper bag. Test an
avocado not by poking it with a finger, but by applying gentle pressure
with the entire hand. When the fruit
yields slightly it is ready to eat.

The flesh of the avocado discolors
rapidly when exposed, and becomes
bitter if cooked. To forestall browning, sprinkle with citrus juice. When
combining avocado with cooked foods
▶ add it at the last moment, away
from heat, to keep it from turning bitter. If using only half an avocado,
keep the unused part unpeeled, with
the seed still embedded in it; wrap it
in foil and store at a temperature between 40° and 70°. For salad combinations and ways to cut avocado,
see (I, 70).

BAKED AVOCADOS STUFFED
WITH CREAMED FOOD

Cut into halves:
     Avocados
Place in each half:
     1 tablespoon Garlic Vinegar,
        179
Let stand 30 minutes. Discard vinegar. Fill them with well-seasoned, hot
creamed:

**Cooked crab, lobster,
shrimp, chicken, or ham**

Use one-fourth as much sauce as filling. Place the avocados on waxed or buttered paper.

Preheat oven to 375°.

Cover the tops with:

**Grated cheese, buttered
crumbs or cornflakes**

Bake until ▶ just heated through.

ABOUT BANANAS

Bananas have been called "the humblest fruit": nobody takes them quite seriously. Yet in this country they happen to be the fruit most frequently eaten—not surprisingly, for they are by and large the most easily digestible and the least expensive. Indeed, for nutritive value they probably rank as the cheapest of all foods, including milk—despite their low protein content.

Bananas, when ready to eat, vary in size and in skin color, which ranges from a pale creamy yellow to russet red. Cook all bananas called **plantains, (I, 342)**. Commercial varieties, always picked unripe, are matured by special moist processing, before reaching the point of sale. They should not be eaten until further ripened by holding them at 70° in a closed paper bag until yellow in color. Once cut, they darken rapidly unless sprinkled with citrus juice. As a rule use slightly underripe bananas for cooking, except in Quick Banana Bread, 335.

For decades we were warned, to music, "never, never" to refrigerate bananas. We find, however, that although the skins darken ominously, the interiors remain palatable even after 2 or 3 days of refrigeration. Bananas may also be successfully frozen if, after partially thawing in the refrig-

erator, they are used immediately. In fact, there are a number of ways in which we may prepare frozen bananas and enjoy them even without thawing. One is simply to cut them into chips, spread the chips out on a piece of foil, wrap them securely, freeze, and munch them as occasional snacks. Or mash up the pulp, if ripe, with a palatable mixture of lemon juice, honey and cinnamon before freezing. Another freezing process—which really turns the youngsters on—is conversion into Chocolate-Dipped Bananas, opposite.

🗎 BAKED BANANAS

I. Preheat oven to 375°.

Bananas may be baked in their skins in an oven or on an outdoor grill about 20 minutes. On opening, sprinkle with:

**Lemon juice
Salt or confectioners' sugar**

II.   **2 Servings**

A candied version.

Preheat oven to 375°.

In a small saucepan, melt together and boil about 5 minutes:

**½ cup dark brown sugar
¼ cup water**

Peel, slice in half the long way and then once laterally and place in a buttered shallow dish:

**1½ to 2 slightly underripe
bananas**

Sprinkle with:

Salt

Add to the cooled syrup:

Juice of ½ lemon or 1 lime

Pour the syrup over the bananas and bake about 30 minutes, turning the fruit after the first 15 minutes. Serve on hot dessert plates, sprinkled with:

**Rum
Chopped candied ginger**

BANANAS IN BLANKETS

Prime as a breakfast dish or served with a meat course.
Preheat broiler.
Peel and cut into lengthwise halves:
Firm ripe bananas
Place between the halves:
Canned pineapple sticks
Wrap the bananas with:
Slices of bacon
Broil in a pan, turning frequently until the bacon is crisp.

CARIBBEAN BANANA

For each serving, melt in a skillet:
1 tablespoon butter
Peel and split lengthwise:
A moderately ripe banana
Simmer the banana gently in the butter, first on one side, then on the other.
Baste with:
**2 tablespoons Sauce Cockaigne, 564
(A dash of lime juice)**
Serve on a hot plate, flambé, 112, with:
Rum
and garnish with:
(A candied kumquat and a sprig of lemon thyme)
or, after flambéing the bananas, garnish with:
Vanilla ice cream

❀ CHOCOLATE-DIPPED BANANAS

12 Sticks

Peel and cut in half crosswise:
6 perfect ripe bananas
Insert firmly in the flat end of each half a wooden meat skewer about 6 inches long—or, better still, a tongue-depressor. Store the bananas in the freezer, on a sheet of foil, at least 1 hour.

Prepare:
Quick Chocolate Fondue Sauce II, 568
making up half the recipe. Pour the coating from the double boiler while still warm into a small shallow pan. Remove bananas from freezer and dip them one by one into the chocolate, twirling to assure complete coverage. Serve at once; or return to freezer in a plastic bag for later use.

ABOUT BERRIES

Good color, firm flesh and plumpness in berries denote prime condition. Remember, in preserving, 662, that the less ripe berries contain more pectin. Store ripe berries immediately in the refrigerator, covered, unwashed and unstemmed. Do not crowd or press.

For an attractive way to serve berries out of doors, make some berry cones. We saw them first in the shadows of the rain forest in Puerto Rico, where we were greeted beside a waterfall by children with wild berries

in leaf cones held in punctured box tops. Glorify your box top with foil.

FRESH SELF-GARNISHED BERRIES

Clean:
1 quart berries
Reserve two-thirds and chill. Rub the

remaining third through a sieve or ⅄ blend if using strawberries. Sweeten the pulp and juice with:

Powdered sugar

and stir until well dissolved. Serve the whole berries chilled and garnished with the sweetened pulp.

BERRIES COCKAIGNE

Serve:

Unhulled berries

Arrange them on the plate around mounds of:

Brown sugar or shaved maple sugar

Pass a dish of:

Cultured sour cream, yogurt or whipped cream

ABOUT STRAWBERRIES

It is hard to reconcile so luscious a fruit with its absurdly arid name—a fruit so constantly in demand that growers' catalogs offer not infrequently a choice among twenty-five or thirty varieties, and which has now become a fresh "fruit for all seasons." Most varieties are a ruddy red, and most very large cultivated fruit is less flavorsome than that of medium size. No one, however, has really experienced paradise on earth until he has plucked and eaten a clutch of tiny fully ripe wild strawberries, warmed by mountain sunshine.

FRESH STRAWBERRY VARIATIONS

Serve sliced strawberries in fruit cocktail glasses with one of the following variations.

Simmer 10 minutes equal parts of:

Orange juice

Strawberry juice

with:

¼ as much sugar or as much as is palatable

Chill the syrup. Season well with:

(Sherry or kirsch)

Or cover:

Chilled strawberries

with:

Chilled pineapple juice

Add, if needed:

Confectioners' sugar

Or, sprinkle berries lightly with:

Lemon juice

Confectioners' sugar

Decorate fruit with:

Mint leaves

STRAWBERRIES ROMANOFF

Prepare:

2 quarts sugared strawberries

Whip slightly:

1 pint ice cream

Fold into the ice cream:

1 cup whipped cream

Add:

6 tablespoons Cointreau

Blend the cream and the strawberries together ▶ very lightly with a spoon. Serve immediately.

ABOUT BLUEBERRIES AND HUCKLEBERRIES

If the seeds are small it's blueberries you have. If they are many and large, it's huckleberries. The difference is why the blueberry is preferred, both for eating out of hand and for cooking. Pick before the dew is off:

Blueberries or huckleberries

To cook, see Poached Thick-Skinned Fruit, 111.

CRANBERRY SAUCE AND CRANBERRY JELLY

Pioneer New England sea captains knew the value of the vitamin C content of cranberries as a preventive against scurvy. Color differences in the fresh fruit have to do with the variety, not relative age.

Wash and pick over:

4 cups cranberries: 1 lb.

Place them in a saucepan. Cover with:

2 cups boiling water

As soon as the water begins to boil again, cover the saucepan with a lid. Boil the berries 3 or 4 minutes or until the skins burst. Put them through a strainer or ricer. Stir into the purée:

2 cups sugar

Place over heat and bring to a rolling boil. If you want cranberry sauce, remove from heat at once. If you want to mold cranberry jelly, boil about 5 minutes, skim, then pour into a wet mold. The cooking periods indicated are right for firm berries. Very ripe berries require a few minutes longer.

SPICED CRANBERRY JELLY

Prepare:

Cranberry Jelly, above

adding to the water:

2 inches stick cinnamon
2 whole cloves
1/4 teaspoon salt

WHOLE CRANBERRY OR ROSELLE SAUCE

1. Place in a saucepan and stir until the sugar is dissolved:

2 cups water
2 cups sugar

Boil the syrup 5 minutes. Pick over, wash and add:

4 cups cranberries: 1 lb.

Simmer the berries in the syrup ♦ uncovered, very gently without stirring, until the berries are translucent, about 5 minutes. Skim off any foam. Add:

(2 teaspoons grated orange rind)

Pour the berries into 1 large or several individual molds which have been rinsed in cold water. Chill until firm. Unmold to serve.

II. A pleasant substitute for cranberries in this recipe makes use of the tropical **roselle**. Cut off the red part and discard the green pod of:

2 cups well-washed roselles

♦ Simmer, uncovered, about 10 minutes in:

1 cup water

Mix and add:

1 1/2 cups sugar
2 tablespoons cornstarch

Cook about 5 minutes longer or until the cornstarch cannot be tasted. Serve cool with meat or dessert.

UNCOOKED CRANBERRY RELISH

To be served like a compote.
Grind:

4 cups cranberries: 1 lb.

Remove the seeds, then grind:

1 whole orange

You may prefer to use only the yellow portion of the orange skin, as the white is often bitter. Stir into the cranberries the orange and:

2 cups sugar

Place these ingredients in covered jars and refrigerate. Let them ripen 2 days before using. Serve the relish with meat or fowl or with a hot bread.

ABOUT RASPBERRIES

With the exception of mulberries, all the fruits under this heading belong to one species—*Rubus*—and have similar characteristics. **Raspberries** proper come in four colors: red, amber, purple and black. **Dewberries** are simply cultivars of the **blackberry; loganberries** and **boysenberries** are, in all probability, crosses between the dewberry and the tarter and more distinctively flavored red raspberry. Rarely encountered in this country is a small acid-tasting red raspberry of oriental origin usually called **wineberry**. The **mulberry**, despite its close resemblance to members of the *Rubus* family, is not in the least related. As everyone knows, the leaves of the white-fruited tree make up the traditional diet of the silkworm. Purple-fruited mulberry trees are best suited, in our opinion, for varying the diets—and flexing the muscles—of marauding schoolboys.

ABOUT CURRANTS AND GOOSEBERRIES

Both of these fruits are almost invariably cooked and are nearly always used as jelly or preserves. In their dried state, currants taste delicious when used in sweet breads: see About Raisins and Other Dried Fruits, 108. Black currants, small and bitter in the wild state, have been improved during the past quarter-century and now appear with more and more frequency at market, along with the usual red and white varieties. Currants and gooseberries, being of the same species, hybridize; and the cross has produced some interesting new cultivars. For those who like "dessert" gooseberries, look for large, completely ripe fruit with a slight tawny blush. To cook gooseberries, see Poached Thick-Skinned Fruit, 111. Even the homely **elderberry**—a fruit which should not be used in its

uncooked state—has been taken in hand recently by the experts, who promise continuing selectivity, systematic cultivation, larger size and better flavor.

ABOUT CHERRIES

Mark Twain claimed that women, if given enough time and hairpins, could build a battleship. Hairpins, also mighty useful as cherry-pitters, are growing scarce. You may prefer to substitute a fresh, strong pen point inserted in a clean holder—although these accessories, too, we regret to report, are harder and harder to come across, as is a cherry-pitter like the one shown on 607.

The best sour or "pie" cherries derive from the **Morello** strain. **Montmorency** is the one most frequently available in the United States. Cultivated sweet cherries are either very deep red in color, or pale yellow flushed with red; favored varieties are **Black Tartarian** and **Napoleon,** respectively. Included in this fruit category—by courteous extension—is the **Surinam cherry:** not a cherry at all but a Brazilian fruit which resembles it and is now grown rather extensively in California and Florida. It makes a spicy and delicious jelly.

POACHED CHERRIES

I. For preparing a compote of sour cherries, see Poached Thick-Skinned Fruit, 111.

II. Cook until tender but still shapely, see Poached Thick-Skinned Fruit, 111:
    Pitted sweet cherries
For each pound cherries, have ready:
    1/2 **cup currant jelly**
melted in:
    1/4 **cup kirsch or other liqueur**

Drain the cherries. Reserve the juice for pudding sauce or use it in basting meats or in baking. Shake the drained cherries in the jelly mixture until well coated. Chill and serve.

ABOUT CITRUS FRUITS

Citrus fruits are so delightful in and of themselves that it almost seems a shame to dissect them into their nutritional components. But it must be pointed out that they are a potent source of vitamin C, as well as furnishing several other dietary essentials.

When they appear at market, citrus fruits are usually equipped with a thin coating of wax to protect them during distribution. The wax is harmless, but it is undesirable if you are grating the skin and may be removed by lightly scrubbing with detergent and water. ◗ In grating, do not take off more than the highly colored outer coating: the white skin beneath may be bitter. To extract citrus juice easily, first roll the fruit on a hard surface, exerting pressure.

To section a small or average-sized citrus fruit, hold it over a bowl to catch all the juices, and use a sharp knife to remove the rind, including the pulpy white skin. Pare it around and around like an apple so that the cells are exposed. Loosen the sections by cutting between the fruit and the membrane. Lift out each segment in one piece, as shown, and remove any seeds.

To section larger fruits like grapefruit, remove the outer skin, pull into halves, and split the membrane as shown. Pull the membrane down and around the outer edge to the base of the section. Let the released membrane hang loose. With your thumb, separate the section from the remaining membrane. The segment may break, but virtually none of the juice is lost. You may prefer the method shown for smaller citrus, opposite.

ABOUT LEMONS AND LIMES

Both of these fruits are quite indispensable, but for obvious reasons we discuss them more fully under Ingredients, 252. In buying lemons, choose yellow-colored ones. If tinged with green, they are not properly "cured." In choosing limes, the dark green ones are usually stronger in acid and preferable to the yellowish types. Many uses for lemon and lime juice and rind are indicated in individual recipes. For their use in beverages, see (I, 34); for use to arrest discoloration of fresh fruits and vegetables, see 647; as decoration and garnish, see 252.

ABOUT ORANGES

For many of us the day begins with oranges, which we often casually classify as "juicers" or "eaters"—more accurately as varieties of **Valencia** on the one hand and **navel** on the other. In our household—and strictly en famille—if we have fruit of interesting flavor in either category, we often cut it in half right across the middle and section each half into thirds or fourths, then proceed to eat the slices at table, as if we were handling those of a Lilliputian watermelon. This untidy approach is encouraged by the recent proliferation of seedless oranges of all types. And it lets us ingest the fibrous parts of the valuable pulp as well as its juice. For the same reason, when we ream oranges for juice, we prefer not to use a fine strainer.

Highly desirable for table use is the **blood orange,** with dark red meat. For special uses no variety can equal the **Seville** or **bitter orange,** although it is not often available. Bitter oranges make superb components of marmalade and lend piquancy to meat and fish dishes and to various drinks.

An orange variant is the **tangerine** or **mandarin**. A **calamondin** is a strain of tangerine; and **Murcott** and **Temple** oranges result from an orange and tangerine cross. The **kumquat,** which has become as definitely associated with Christmas holidays as plum pudding, closely resembles the tangerine, but is actually in its botanical classification not a citrus fruit at all, though a close relative. Just the opposite applies to **citron**—a true citrus derivative which doesn't taste like one, at least in the processed form we find it packaged at market. See Candied Citrus Peel, 604.

The skins of ripe oranges often remain greenish in color. Growers and packers bring them closer to the conventionally acceptable warm yellow in two ways. One is by the use of ethylene gas, which breaks down the chlorophyll component present in the skin. Ethylene, incidentally, has also become a highly useful agent in controlling the maturization of a number of other fruits, especially apples and bananas. The second coloring device is simply a skin-dye, carefully restricted as to its chemical makeup by the USDA, prohibited in some citrus-growing states, and in any case applied to the fruit for a limited period during the year. All oranges so treated must bear the stamp "color added."

A word about frozen orange juice: why it all tastes alike, and why it doesn't taste anything like fresh orange juice. The juice to be frozen may come from several varieties. It is boiled to a high viscosity in a vacuum, separated into several component batches, reassembled, flavored—at which time fresh juice may be added—and at long last frozen solid. Finally, note that something labeled "orange drink" under federal regulations need contain no natural orange at all.

ORANGES IN SYRUP

8 Servings

Wash:

6 large well-flavored navel oranges

Peel the fruit, leaving no white showing, and cut the peel from three of the oranges into slices about $1/4$ inch thick. Boil these peels 3 minutes in:

1 cup water

Strain and discard the water. Combine:

1 cup sugar

$1/3$ cup water

When boiling and clear, add the orange peel. Cook about 5 minutes over low heat. Arrange the orange slices in a dessert bowl. Pour the peels and sauce over the oranges and chill at least 2 hours.

KUMQUAT COMPOTE

Calamondins and kumquats may be eaten raw without paring, and make beautiful garnishes. They may also become a dessert or may accompany a meat dish, as below.
Parboil, unpeeled, 5 minutes:

Kumquats

Drain and cool. Slice the top off each. Remove seeds and fill each fruit with:

1/2 to 1 teaspoon sugar

Stand upright in a shallow buttered pan. Bake about 15 minutes in a preheated 350° oven, basting frequently with:

Pineapple juice

For Preserved Kumquats, see 604.

ABOUT GRAPEFRUIT

The main types are whitish or pink-fleshed, with a few varieties ruby-red. Late in the season, the skin may change in tint from yellowish to greenish, a sign of real maturity and high sugar content. But beware of late-season grapefruit if it seems unduly light in weight or if the skins are puffy, for the flesh may then be dry. Offbeat and piquant grapefruit hybrids are the **tangelo** and the aptly named **ugli**—both crosses with the ever-promiscuous tangerine. ◗ Always chill grapefruit at once. It will not ripen after picking and keeps better at lower temperatures.

SWEETENED GRAPEFRUIT

4 Servings

Peel, section, see 125, and chill:

2 large grapefruit

Place the fruit in glass compotes. Fifteen minutes before serving, sprinkle lightly with:

Confectioners' sugar or honey

Immediately before serving, add to each compote:

(1 tablespoon Cointreau)

or fill each compote one-fourth full of:

Chilled orange juice

GRAPEFRUIT CUPS

I. Chill:

Grapefruit

Cut into halves. Loosen the pulp from the peel with a sharp-toothed, curved grapefruit knife, see (I, 327), or remove the seeds and cut out the tough fibrous center with a grapefruit corer. Five minutes before serving, sprinkle the grapefruit with:

Confectioners' sugar

Add to each half immediately before serving:

1 tablespoon curaçao or a Crystallized Mint Leaf, 602

II. Preheat broiler.
Prepare:

Grapefruit Cups, above

When grapefruit is very ripe it is inadvisable to loosen the pulp from the peel, as it makes the fruit too juicy. Sprinkle each half with:

1 tablespoon or more sugar

Place the fruit under the broiler until heated through. Remove and pour over each half:

1 tablespoon dry sherry

Serve the fruit at once.

ABOUT DATES

In desert regions the date palm was traditionally put to almost total use— for food and fibers. It dominated a culture as exclusively as the bison did among the Plains Indians in the New World—shaping, regulating and limiting a life-style. Date varieties now cultivated in the United

States—**Medjool, Deglet Noor** and **Khadrawy**—are all, as their names indicate, of Arabic origin. About half the fruit consists of sugar, which accounts for the grayish crystallization that frequently shows up on both fresh and dried dates. It also explains why eating only a few brings on a surfeit; and why, served as a garnish for a fruit dessert tray, see 600, they are often stuffed with cream cheese and nuts, with a fondant made piquant with almond paste and spices, or with a tangy marmalade. ❀ Dates freeze successfully and, refrigerated, may be kept for an extended period. For other uses of dates, see Index.

ABOUT FIGS

When Cato advocated the conquest of Carthage, he used as his crowning argument the advantage of acquiring fruits as glorious as the North African figs, specimens of which he pulled from his toga as exhibits in the Roman Senate. These fruits have become so popular in America that many varieties—purplish, brownish and greenish—are grown in profusion. Even when shipped, they must be tree-ripened.

Fresh figs are very different from the dried ones we get from Smyrna and our South. They are ripe when soft to the touch and overripe when sour in odor, indicating a fermentation of the juice. For figs with prosciutto, see 87; for dried fig confections, see 600.

STUFFED FRESH FIGS

Fill stemmed fresh:
    Figs
with:
    **Cultured sour cream and
    grated orange peel**
or with:
    Ham Salad Spread, 77

POACHED FIGS

Wash and remove the stems from:
    1 lb. dried figs
Add:
    Cold water to cover well
1½ **tablespoons lemon juice**
    A piece of lemon rind
    **(A large piece of
    gingerroot)**
Stew the figs, covered, until they are soft. Drain and sweeten the juice with:
    Sugar: about 1 cup
Simmer the syrup until thick. Add:
    1 tablespoon lemon juice
Replace the figs in the syrup. Cool. Add:
    (1 tablespoon dry sherry)
Chill and serve with:
    Cream

ABOUT GRAPES

Table grapes—as distinguished from wine grapes—can be grouped into three classes. Of these the *labruscan,* or slip-skin types, all of which have at least some trace of native American "blood," and the *vinifera* are most important. The distinction between the two is best pointed up by citing Concord as the *labruscan* with which we are most familiar and Tokay as the prototype of *vinifera.*

Tokay types—we are temped to call them "non-slip" varieties—grow only in California, and in a rather limited area. Their flesh is solid, and their shipping and keeping qualities are so outstanding that those in commercial production are available all winter long. A new variety of **Tokay** is **Flame Tokay,** a very beautiful purplish-red. **Malaga** ripens several weeks earlier than the true Tokays. Among the "white" *vinifera* are **Olivette,** with—as the name indicates—oval berries, and **Thompson Seedless**. **Ribier** heads the "black" *vinifera*, which are actually a very deep blue.

In contrast to *vinifera*, all *labruscans* are more perishable and for this reason seasonal, their availability being limited more or less to the four months between July 1 and the end of October. A seedless **Concord** has been developed—look for it and many other hybrids ranging in color from palest green or yellow through red to darkest purple. Most widely distributed, perhaps, and in order of ripening are **Ontario, Early Giant, Interlaken Seedless, Delaware, Caco, Catawba, Fredonia, Van Buren, Worden, Niagara, Kenka** and **Steuben**.

Table grapes of a third and much smaller class are the spicy **muscadines** from the American South—technically *Vitis rotundifolia*—of which **scuppernong** is an ancestor, and **Golden Muscat,** one of the finest new hybrids. Here again, as in all other categories of grape, seedless varieties have been recently developed that will modestly revolutionize grape cookery, especially—we speak with feeling—pie-making. From the muscadines come the seedless packaged **raisins**. Only three varieties in this country are used in the production of raisins: Thompson Seedless, Muscat, and **Black Corinth**. All canned grapes are seedless.

In buying grapes, choose clusters with green stems, plump berries and full color. "Whites" will taste better if they have acquired a slightly tawny blush. See grape recipes in Salads, (I, 72); Desserts, 507; and Pies, 380. To frost grapes, see 602.

GUAVAS

When ripe, guavas vary in color from white to dark red and in size from that of a walnut to that of an apple. They may be served puréed, baked or fresh, alone or in combination with other fruits such as bananas or pineapple. They have an exceptionally high vitamin content. Sprinkle:

Peeled and sliced guavas

lightly with:

Sugar

Chill and serve with:

Cream

or bake in a 350° oven about 30 minutes and then serve with the cream. See also Apple Cake Cockaigne, 393, and prepare guava jelly with cream cheese, as for Bar-le-Duc, 544.

LITCHIS

A little like jellied incense, these most oriental of fruits are protected by an exquisitely fragile shell, as shown on 105. The fresh fruit is white; when dried it becomes much smaller and turns dark brown. Serve 3 to 5 nuts on a green leaf, or use them to garnish a fruit bowl. Litchis are also available canned, but the flavor is not so hauntingly aromatic.

MANGOES

These delicious flattish oval fruits are about 8 inches long, of a yellowish-green color and sometimes flecked with red or black. When chilled and eaten raw, they are as good as any peach-pineapple-apricot mousse you can concoct—rich and sweet but never cloying. If unchilled, they sometimes have the faintest savor of turpentine. The seed, which extends the length of the fruit, makes eating somewhat awkward, and special holders, not unlike those which bring corncobs under control, may be used. Pare, slice and serve mangoes on vanilla ice cream. Sauté ripe fruits. Use them when just mature in chutneys and when unripe for poaching or baking. If you want to freeze mangoes, see Frozen Puréed Fruits, 649.

MEDLARS

In the South of Europe and in southern United States these 2-inch fruits, which resemble crab apples, are eaten fresh-plucked. In England, quite far north in their range, they are always overtaken by frost and look shabby indeed, although their flavor is desirable, especially for jellies.

ABOUT MELONS

Melons are being developed into so many delicious strains that it is difficult to list them all by name. A distinction is usually made between **muskmelons** and **winter melons**. The skins of the former are variously netted, the reticulations being raised and of a paler color. Muskmelons are aromatic even before being opened—and short-lived. In America—but not abroad—the **cantaloupe** is in this group, the name being reserved here for a smallish, very heavily and regularly netted melon with pale orange colored flesh. The flesh of a new hybrid named **Ogen,** however, developed in Israel, is green.

Winter melons are usually smooth-skinned, sometimes striated, and lack netting; they have little or no aroma and keep over a much longer period. Some of the best-known varieties are **Casaba, Persian, Crenshaw** and **honeydew**. **Watermelons** are rather a race apart: their size and their festive red interior suggest merry group

eating; the small round ones of recent introduction never quite generate the meltingly sweet succulence of the old-time giants.

Melons are usually eaten raw. The varieties can be served singly or in combination. Try a palette ranging from the pale greens of the honeydews, through the golden peach tones of the cantaloupes, to the blue-reds of the watermelon. They can be served from one end of a meal to the other in many attractive ways.

In order for it to be genuinely sweet—and this is one's perennial hope as he bites into each fresh specimen—the fruit must have matured on the vine. If it did, you will see that the scar at the stem end is slightly sunken and well calloused. The more fragrant the melon, the sweeter it will be. A watermelon, if truly ripe, will respond by giving up a thin green shaving if scraped with a fingernail.

If you want to store melons for several days, keep them at between 50° and 70°, away from sunlight; and chill just before serving. To protect other food in your refrigerator from taking on a melon taste, seal the fruit in plastic or foil. Melons respond favorably to lime or lemon juice or a sprinkling of powdered ginger, and can be cut into highly decorative shapes. For an aspic-filled melon, see (I, 85). For fancy melon cuts see below.

MELON BASKETS OR FRUIT CUPS

8 Large Servings

Cut into halves or make into baskets, as shown above:

4 cantaloupes or other melons

Remove the seeds. Scallop the edges. Chill the fruit. Combine the following ingredients:

2 cups peeled, sliced seeded or seedless oranges
2 cups peeled, sliced fresh peaches
2 cups diced pineapple: fresh or canned
1 cup sliced bananas
(1 cup sugar, dissolved in the various fruit juices)

Chill thoroughly. Just before serving, fill the melon cups with the fruit. Pour over each cup:

(1 tablespoon Cointreau or rum)

Top with:

(Lemon and Orange Ice, 558, or Sherbet, 559)

MELON ROUNDS FILLED WITH RASPBERRIES OR STRAWBERRIES

Cut into 1- to 2-inch crosswise slices:

Chilled pared honeydew melons or cantaloupe

Allow 1 slice for each person. Remove seeds. Fill the centers with:

Chilled, sugared raspberries or strawberries

Serve on individual plates with:

Lime or lemon wedges
(A sprinkling of ginger)

SPIKED MELON

Cut a plug in the upper side of a:

Melon

Dig out seeds with a long-handled spoon. Pour in:

³/₄ to 1 cup port wine

Chill melon in ice in the refrigerator at least 8 hours. Slice and serve with rind removed and use the marinating wine as a dressing.

PAWPAWS

These smoky-tasting native fruits should be picked—and eaten—after the first heavy frost. Wrap them individually in tissue paper and store in a cool place until soft. A taste for them, we feel, is an acquired one.

PAPAYAS

Papayas grow up to 20 inches in length. When fully ripened, the flesh develops orangey tones and the greenish rind turns soft and yellow. They are eaten like melons. Their milky juice, when chilled, makes a pleasant drink, and their black seeds, which contain pepsin, are used for garnish, eaten raw or used as for capers. Many of us know this plant only by its derivative papain, the tenderizer made from the enzymes of its leaves, (I, 550).

Use underripe fruits for cooking. Process them as for summer squash types, (I, 360). If serving papayas raw, chill and sprinkle with lime or lemon juice. See sketch in the chapter heading, 105.

ABOUT PEACHES AND NECTARINES

As fruits so often curiously do—but queens seldom if ever—the "queen of fruits" leads a double life. The mostly yellow-fleshed **freestones** are favorites at table and for canning and drying; **clingstones,** with white flesh and somewhat sharper flavor, make excellent "poachers."

Choose firm but well-colored fruit without the flattened brownish bruises which betray areas of decaying flesh underneath. If plucked green, peaches will not ripen. They merely soften and wither, gaining nothing in flavor. ▶ Discard peach seeds, as their almondlike kernels are high in deadly prussic acid.

Although their smooth skin and their flavor strongly suggest a cross between peach and plum, **nectarines** are in fact simply a variety of peach, resulting from what botanists call "bud variation."

FILLED PEACHES

8 Servings

Peel, halve and pit:
    4 chilled peaches
Place them in a bowl. Combine and stir:
    2 cups chilled berries
    6 tablespoons sugar
    1¹/₂ tablespoons lemon juice
Pour the berries over the peaches. Serve with:
    Sweetened Whipped Cream, 449

STUFFED PEACHES

8 Servings

Preheat oven to 350°.
Peel, halve and pit:
    4 peaches, or use 8 canned halves
Chop until fine:
    ¹/₃ cup blanched toasted almonds
    1 tablespoon glazed orange peel
Blend thoroughly with:
    ¹/₄ cup confectioners' sugar
Fill the fruit with the above mixture

and place in a baking pan. Sprinkle with:
    ¹/₂ cup dry sherry
    ¹/₄ cup confectioners' sugar
and if canned peaches are used:
    (A little lemon juice)
Bake 10 minutes and serve warm.

ABOUT PEARS

All types of pears seem to keep congenial company with cheese. Follow the season, beginning with the **Bartletts,** of which **Max Red Bartlett** is an interesting all-red-skinned variety. **Seckels** are apt to come next: tiny, sugar-sweet and unprepossessing-looking, but much in demand, along with the **Kiefers,** for cooking and pickling. The Bartletts, highly flavored but perishable, have vanished by November—except for the **Winter Bartletts**—but they are succeeded by a dazzling array of hardier fall varieties, some of which can still be purchased far into the winter months: the ruddy **comices,** the green-skinned **Anjous,** the **Winter Nellises,** and the russet **Boscs,** among others.

Pears are picked when they are approaching maturity but haven't reached full ripeness. They may then be ripened at 60° to 65°. If you plan to cook them, make sure to use them while they are still firm. To store for eating, wrap the fruit in paper and put them away in a slotted box in a cool place. If pears or peaches that look sound have become brown inside, they have been held too long at a too-low temperature.

STUFFED PEARS

4 Servings

Preheat oven to 350°.
Pare, core and halve:

4 firm pears

Mix together and stuff into the hollows:

¼ cup white raisins
2 tablespoons chopped walnuts
2 tablespoons sugar
1 tablespoon lemon juice

Place the pears in a baking dish with:

2 tablespoons water

Pour over them:

½ cup light corn syrup

Cover and bake until tender, about 30 minutes. You may baste during the cooking with:

(Pineapple juice and brown sugar)

or remove the cover and sprinkle the fruit lightly with:

(Granulated sugar)
(A light dusting of cinnamon)

then place under the broiler until golden brown and serve immediately.

PEARS IN LIQUEUR

4 Servings

Pare, quarter, core and prick lightly:

4 pears

Combine:

1 cup chilled orange juice
1 tablespoon confectioners' sugar
2 tablespoons curaçao or kirsch

Cover the pears with the juice. Chill until ready to serve.

PERSIMMONS

Be sure, in the recipes, to distinguish between our native *Diospyros virginiana* and Kaki, the oriental type, the latter seen on 105. Ours are small, full of seeds and ▶ inedible until after frost. In fact, we wonder how we sur-

vived the many we consumed as children, because the skins resist digestion and can form waddy balls, as obstructive as hair-balls in animals.

Both native and oriental persimmons sometimes tend to be puckery, even when ripe—depending on variety. The orientals lose their astringency if stored for 2 to 4 days in a plastic bag with a ripe apple. The natives do not always prove so amenable. Eat as fresh fruit, in salads or puréed, fresh or frozen, combined in ice creams, custards or sherbets.

ABOUT PINEAPPLES

So beloved was this fruit that on many southern mansions it was carved above the door as a symbol of hospitality. In fact, the first fruits grown in England in a nobleman's "stovehouse" were graciously rented to his friends for their table decorations.

A small compact crown usually denotes the finest type of fruit. As neither skin nor fruit color indicates ripeness, a dull solid sound when the finger is snapped against the side of the fruit, along with protruding "eyes" and a delicious aroma, is perhaps the most reliable test for ripeness.

Store at 70° away from sunlight. Pineapple lends itself magnificently to all kinds of combinations, but watch for one thing: ▶ be sure to cook fresh pineapple before combining it with any gelatin mixture, see (I, 75). For pineapples as decorative containers for other foods, see 83, (I, 69) and 134.

To prepare pineapple slices, trim the sharp points of the tuft. Grasp the tuft firmly and pare the skin with wide downward strokes. Then further remove the "eyes" by grooving the pineapple diagonally. Cut off the tuft.

The fruit may then be sliced cross-wise or in wedges or flat thin slices from top to bottom. Trim out the core if it is tough.

PINEAPPLE TIDBITS

I.   **8 Servings**
This dish is alluring in appearance, but must be made with very ripe pineapple. Trim two-thirds from the leafy top of:

    1 chilled ripe pineapple

Cut the fruit into 8 lengthwise wedges. Cut off the core and place each part so that it will resemble a boat, as sketched. Pare the skin in 1 piece, leaving it in place, and cut the pulp downward into 5 or 6 slices, retaining the boat shape as shown at right, top right. Serve each boat on an individual plate, with a small mound of:

    Confectioners' sugar

Add:

    5 or 6 large unhulled
    strawberries for each
    serving

II. A Texas girl taught us to prepare a pineapple this way. Divide a chilled pineapple into small sections by cutting it down to the core, diagonally, with a sharp knife as seen at right, top left. Impale each section with a pick and let the guests serve themselves.

III. Pineapple can make an attractive edible centerpiece. Cut off the top and bottom of a ripe pineapple and reserve them. Insert a long sharp knife about 1/2 inch from the outer edge so the fruit is entirely loosened but the pineapple as a whole retains its shape. Leaving the fruit in this cylindrical shell, cut it in about 12 long pie-shaped wedges. Set it back on its base and use the top for a lid as shown on right below. Let guests remove the long spears with a two-pronged fork.

FILLED PINEAPPLE

For a more elaborate version, see (I, 69).

Cut in half, hollow out and chill:

    A fresh pineapple

Cube the cut-out pineapple and some:

    Slices of melon

Fill the chilled pineapple shells with the cubed fruit and add:

    A few raspberries

Sprinkle with:

    Chopped mint leaves
    (2 tablespoons liqueur)

FRESH PINEAPPLE CUP

6 Servings

Pare, core and dice:
    1 fresh pineapple
Chill it. Boil for 1 minute:
    1 cup sugar
    ¹/₃ cup water
Chill this syrup. Add:
    ¹/₂ cup chilled orange juice
    3 tablespoons lime juice
Place the pineapple in glasses and
pour the syrup mixture over it.

GRILLED PINEAPPLE

4 Servings

Drain:
    8 pineapple spears
Wrap around them:
    8 slices bacon
Fasten the slices with picks and broil
the bacon under moderate heat.

ABOUT PLUMS

As with many fruits under centuries-
old cultivation, plum varieties from the
Old World still predominate—with
modern improvements. These **European plums** are green- or yellow-
fleshed. They include the **greengage,**
or **Reine Claude,** from which, by an
incredibly complicated procedure, au-
thentic sugar plums are still produced
in Portugal; the **blue plum;** the **yellow
egg plum;** the darker **Lombards** and
Italians; as well as a host of larger
more recent introductions. A European variety with special characteristics is the **Damson,** very dark, tart
and thick-skinned. It is not, like the
others, suitable for table use or for
canning and drying, but it makes
superb conserves, 670.

The earliest native varieties of the
American plum, such as the **red
plum,** the **wild goose,** the **Pacific** and

the **beach plum,** are now, after decades of neglect, in the hands of
breeders who have introduced some
interesting variants and combinations. American plums are smaller
than the European favorites; their
flesh is yellow to pale orange; and
they are by and large best suited
to jam, desserts, and sweet sauces.
Similar uses are recommended for
the less often encountered **Oriental**
or **Japanese plum,** whose fruits are
even more ruddy in color, and spicier.
A non-plum with plumlike characteristics, available now and then at market, is the tropical **Carissa,** or **Natal
plum**. ♦ To cook plums, see Poached
or Stewed Thick-Skinned Fruit, 111.

Prunes are simply small purplish-
black freestone plums sufficiently
high in sugar content and firm
enough to battle successfully the twin
hazards of drying out and of interior
decay.

STEWED PRUNES

8 Servings

♦ If the label calls for soaking, please
read About Raisins and Other Dried
Fruits, 108. Otherwise, cover with
cold water:
    1 lb. dried prunes
Bring to the boiling point. ♦ Reduce
the heat and simmer gently about 20
minutes. Add:
    (¹/₄ cup or more sugar)
Cook about 10 minutes longer. You
may add to the prunes, during this
second cooking period:
    (¹/₂ sliced lemon)
    (1 stick cinnamon)

PRUNES IN WINE

4 Servings

Cook by the above method until
almost tender:

¹/₂ lb. dried prunes
Add:
   3 tablespoons sugar
Cook 5 minutes longer. Remove from heat and add:
   **¹/₂ cup or more dry sherry or
   ¹/₂ to ³/₄ cup port
   (6 very thin slices lemon)**
Place in a covered jar. Chill thoroughly. Shortly before serving, the prunes may be pitted and filled with:
   **Halves of walnuts or
   blanched almonds**

PRUNES AND CHESTNUTS

                                4 to 6 Servings
Drain and place in a casserole:
   **1¹/₂ cups canned chestnuts
   ³/₄ cup pitted stewed or
   canned prunes**
Combine, heat and pour over the above:
   **1 tablespoon butter
   ¹/₄ teaspoon salt
   (1 tablespoon sugar)
   ¹/₂ cup dry white wine**
Heat thoroughly and serve with ham or fowl.

PICKLED PRUNES

Keep this delightful compote on hand, for it makes a decorative meat garnish and may be drained and pitted and used in Stuffings, (I, 430). Place in a heavy pan:
   **3 cups water
   1 cup cider vinegar
   2 cups brown sugar
   2 cups dried prunes
   1 teaspoon whole cloves, with
   heads removed
   1 teaspoon whole allspice
   1¹/₂ sticks cinnamon**
◗ Simmer about 45 minutes or until fruit is plump. Place the prunes in a jar. Straining out the spices, pour the

liquor over the prunes to cover. Keep refrigerated.

POMEGRANATES

By eating a single seed of the pomegranate offered her by the wily Pluto, Proserpine was obliged to return periodically to the infernal regions, leaving earth for six months in the cheerless embrace of winter. We have always wondered—since our own first encounter with the crimson cells enclosing seed and luscious pulp—how Proserpine managed to eat only one. These jewel-like morsels make a most beautiful garnish. Use them in French dressing, or roll them in small cream cheese balls. Or, if you live where the fruit is available ripe and in abundance, you may feel it is sacrilegious to eat them any way but plain—or chilled, with yogurt. If you use them for jelly, do not bruise the seed kernels, for then an unpleasant flavor develops. See illustration on 115.

PRICKLY PEARS

A cactus also known as **Indian** or **Barbary fig** or **tuna,** the so-called prickly pear, illustrated on 115, is now as much at home on the shores of the Mediterranean as in its native America. The red and yellow fruits, which are eaten raw, have sharp spines which can be removed by singeing before peeling.

BAKED QUINCES

                                4 Servings
These hard uncooperative-looking fruits, illustrated on 115, turn pink when cooked and make delicious preserves and confections. See Index. Preheat oven to 350°.

Wash:

4 large whole quinces

Rub with:

Butter

and bake about 45 minutes until almost tender. Core and hollow out about two-thirds of the remaining fruit and mix this pulp with:

1/3 **cup fine bread crumbs**
1/4 **cup chopped nuts**
1/4 **cup brown sugar**
Grating of lemon rind
Salt

Return mixture to the partially hollow rind and bake about 15 minutes longer or until tender. Serve hot or cold.

RHUBARB

Only by the wildest stretch of the imagination can rhubarb be included in this chapter, but its tart flavor and its customary uses make it a reasonable facsimile, when cooked, of fruit. Hothouse-grown rhubarb is tenderer and sweeter and needs no peeling. If the hardier type is used, the reddish young shoots are preferred. Should the stalks be tough, peel them back like celery and remove the coarsest strings before cooking. In any case, use as little water as possible. ▶ Never cook the leaves, as they are heavy in poisonous oxalic acid.

POACHED RHUBARB

4 Servings

Wash and cut, without peeling, into 1-inch pieces:

1 lb. rhubarb

Place in heavy pan. Sprinkle lightly with water. Simmer over medium heat until segments can be easily pierced with fork. Add and stir:

1/2 **to** 3/4 **cup sugar**

Continuing poaching until rhubarb is soft. Dot with:

(**Butter**)
(**Cinnamon or powdered ginger**)

BAKED RHUBARB AND JAM

Preheat oven to 350°.

To give color to rhubarb and keep it whole, have ready:

1/4 **cup seedless red jam**
1/2 **cup sugar**

Coat a small baking dish with one-third of the jam. Cut into 2-inch slices:

1 lb. rhubarb

Lay the slices in the jam base in close patterns and sprinkle with half the sugar and:

(1/2 **teaspoon powdered ginger**)

Add another layer of rhubarb and cover with the rest of the jam and sugar. Bake covered for about 15 minutes.

TROPICAL EXOTICS

The fruits listed below are occasionally or more often available at "ethnic" groceries or plain ordinary fruiterers with a well-traveled or novelty-struck clientele. Illustrated on 138 are passion fruit, far left; cherimoyas, next left; the fruit and the great cut leaves of monstera, right, close to the trim mangosteen, shown whole and in cross section. Rounding out the picture are akee, below center, and tamarind.

ACEROLA

The size and habitat of this tart fruit are indicated by its aliases: **Barbados** and **West Indian cherry**. Acerolas contain much greater quantities of ascorbic acid, even when cooked, than do fresh citrus fruits.

AKEE

Blighia sapida, named after the infamous Captain Bligh, is one of the most strikingly beautiful and delicious of fruits; however, ♦ unless it has ripened to the point of voluntary opening, it is a deadly poison. No overly ripe, fallen, discolored or unripe fruit dare be eaten, and the greatest care must be used to ♦ remove all seeds before cooking, as these are always poisonous. When picked ripe, hulled and completely seeded, the akee may be eaten raw or cooked. Parboiled it may be used hot or cold, customarily with a main dinner course. See illustration, below.

PURÉED AKEE

3 Servings

Remove the white pods from:

6 firm unbruised open akees

♦ Discard every seed. Place the pods in:

Boiling water

to cover. ♦ Reduce the heat at once and simmer gently until soft. Strain and mash them until coarsely crushed. Season with:

Salt and pepper

(Grated Parmesan cheese)

(Toasted chopped cashews)

CARAMBOLA

Yellow, translucent, juicy and refreshing, this lobed fruit, shown in the chapter heading, may be eaten unpeeled and the seeds disregarded. It is a versatile addition to a southern menu. Serve it raw as a vegetable or salad. When fully ripe it is delicious as a dessert.

CERIMAN

Shown below, this fruit is known to most of us as **monstera,** a desirable house plant with great cut and holey leaves. Unless we are in subtropical climates, we seldom see the 8- to 10-inch cylindrical pine-conelike fruit with its pineapple-banana flavor. A single fruit ripens over a 3- to 4-day period, and the lower sections, which break apart first at the base of the stem, should be eaten only as the shell ripens to a yellow color. To keep the top sections unbruised until ripened, place the fruit, stem end up, in a jar and pluck as the segments ripen.

CHERIMOYA

The nineteenth-century traveler Humboldt, who left his scientific imprint over South America and Mexico, declared that this fruit, shown below, is worth a trip across the Atlantic. It must be tree-ripened but still firm when picked and should be handled carefully so as to avoid bruising. Sometimes called **sherbet fruit,** the cherimoya shows on its light green skin jacquarded engravings or

longish bumps. Discard the hard black seeds which occur at random in the pulp. Eat raw or use to make drinks and sherbets. Other less widely known fruits of the *Annona* or custard apple family are the **sweetsop** or **sugar-apple,** and the **soursop,** which has an acidulous taste.

DURIAN

Fruits of this famous tree, native to Southeast Asia, weigh up to 20 pounds and have been described as "smelling like Hell, and tasting like Heaven." They are highly favored by certain wild animals; and tales abound of Malays who gather durians, only to be gathered up in turn by elephants. The large seeds are roasted and eaten like nuts.

FEIJOA

Often called **pineapple guava**—a sobriquet which aptly reflects the feijoa's delicious and complex flavor—this fruit is dark green, about 2 inches long, with a white interior; it is used chiefly for jellies and preserves.

GENIP

Sometimes called **Spanish limes** because of their taste only, these 1-inch round Caribbean fruits are eaten fresh, like grapes.

KIWI

Also known as **Chinese gooseberry,** this fruit comes from New Zealand. The hairy, soberly brown exterior of kiwis does not prepare one in the least for their vivid green translucency when sectioned, or the lovely intricacies of pattern the seeds reveal when the fruit is sliced as shown in the chapter heading, 105. Kiwis are not only highly decorative but may be

served with a little lime juice as a table fruit; or peeled, poached and garnished with lemon juice and kirsch. Remove the hairs by hand-friction.

LOQUATS

These olive-sized fruits, yellow and loosely clustered, mature in the springtime. New cultivars have a larger ratio of flesh to seeds, and so are beginning to lift the loquat out of the mere garnish and jelly-making categories. They may be eaten fresh or stewed. When cooked, their flavor is rather similar to that of poached plums.

MANGOSTEENS

This 2- to 3-inch-diameter fruit has a most exquisite milky juice. Its sections—5 to 6 in number—may be easily scooped out and eaten with a spoon, see illustration, opposite.

PASSION FRUITS

Sometimes called the **purple granadilla,** this tropical American fruit, shown opposite, is egg-sized and is at its best when a little overripe and wrinkled-looking. As the sweet aromatic pulp is inseparable from the seeds, passion fruit is used mainly as a table ornament or for its quite delicious juice.

SAPODILLAS

Sapodilla is the tree whose sap produces **chicle gum**. The fruit has a rather grainy but entirely edible flesh, with somewhat the texture of moist brown sugar. The seeds must be removed, after which the raw pulp may be eaten fresh or used in puddings and other desserts. A sprinkling of lemon juice helps. A close relative, the **sapote,** has similar traits and makes an excellent sherbet.

TAMARINDS

The 2- to 6-inch pods of this graceful tree are shown on 138. When fresh and tender, they can be either cooked with rice and fish or sucked raw for their spicy pulp with its date-apricot flavor. This spicy pulp is also preserved for use in curries and chutneys, as well as a medicinal drink. If you wish to preserve tamarinds, remove the seeds and pack the pulp into a jar with alternate layers of sugar. Refrigerate.

GRIDDLE CAKES AND FRITTER VARIATIONS

Perhaps no foods lend themselves to more occasions than those in this chapter, which can be served as hors d'oeuvre; as breakfast, luncheon or supper treats; or as desserts. What's more, they are an ideal way to glamorize leftovers. Many people like to cook these delicacies at table, using auxiliary heat so that they reach the diner in peak condition. Waffle irons, 150; electric skillets, (I, 91); or a double crêpe pan set, shown in the heading, left rear, where the crêpes can be both cooked and sauced, are all tableside conveniences; while in the kitchen, both iron and soapstone griddles have their adherents. The soapstone, which needs no greasing, is shown in the left foreground, filled with small-sized so-called silver-dollar pancakes from the batter in the pitcher upper left. Above and below it are elderberry and hemerocallis blossoms, both delicious when deep-fat-fried in batters, 154. In the right foreground is a rosette iron on which several shapes can be inserted; a honey dipper and a pancake turner. At the right rear are honey and molasses dispensers, jellies and nuts on a lazy-susan stand near liqueurs for flambéing, (I, 108).

ABOUT PANCAKES, GRIDDLE CAKES OR BATTER CAKES

No matter what your source of heat—a hot rock or an electric skillet; no matter how fancy the name—blintzes, crêpes or Nockerln—all these confections are easily mixed and made from simple batters.

There are three equally important things to control in producing pancakes and waffles: the consistency of your batter, the surface of your griddle or pan, and the evenness of its heat. Mix the liquid ingredients quickly into the dry ingredients. ◗ Don't overbeat. Give just enough quick strokes to barely moisten the dry ingredients. ◗ Ignore the lumps. Superior results are gained if most pancake doughs are mixed and ◗ rested, covered, refrigerated, 3 to 6 hours or longer before cooking. This resting period does not apply to recipes which include separately beaten egg whites, or to yeast-raised cakes that have the word "raised" in the title. Variation in moisture content of flours, 209, makes it wise to test the batter by cooking one trial cake first. Adjust the batter, ▶ if too thick, by diluting it with a little water, ▶ if too thin, by adding a little flour. You may also use a pancake dough for waffles provided you ▶ add for each recipe at least 2 extra tablespoons of butter or oil to keep the dough from sticking.

If your griddle is a modern one or is of soapstone, you may not need to use any type of fat. Nor should you need to grease any seasoned pan surface if you have at least two tablespoons of butter for every cup of liquid in the recipe. If you are using a skillet or crêpe pan, you may grease it lightly and continue to do so between batches. ▶ Before cooking, test the griddle by letting a few drops of cold water fall on it. If the water bounces and sputters, the griddle is ready to use. If the water just sits and boils, the griddle is not hot enough. If the water vanishes, the griddle is too hot. See illustration at right.

▶ To assure a well-rounded cake, don't drop the batter from on high but let it pour from the tip of a spoon. Make the cakes large or small. It will be two to three minutes before the cakes are ready to turn. When bubbles appear on the upper surfaces, but before they break, lift the cakes with a spatula to see how well they have browned. ▶ Turn the cakes only once and continue cooking them until the second side is done. Cooking this side takes only about half as long, and the second side never browns as evenly. Serve the cakes at once. If this is not possible, keep them on a

toweled baking sheet—well separated by the tea towel—in a 200° oven. Or fold for yourself a sort of cloth file in which to store them. ▶ Never stack one on the other without the protection of cloth—for the steam they produce will make the cakes flabby.

▲ In high altitudes, use about one-fourth less baking powder or soda than indicated in the following recipes.

Several egg dishes approximate pancakes, see Eggs Fooyoung, (I, 224), and Frittata, (I, 225).

Pancakes are delicious stuffed, rolled or glazed with a sauce and run under the broiler. Try filling with prunes and cinnamon or with creamed seafood, (I, 260). The batter may be seasoned with sautéed chopped onions and, when cooked, filled with seafood, creamed sweetbreads or chicken. Or you may incorporate in the batters finely chopped nuts and candied fruits or currants; or wheat germ, soy flour or flaked bran. To do this, let the cereal or fruit rest in the liquid called for in the recipe about half an hour before making up the batter. For additional garnishes and sauces, see Dessert Sauces, 563.

PANCAKES, GRIDDLE CAKES OR BATTER CAKES

About Fourteen 4-Inch Cakes

Sift before measuring:

1 1/2 cups all-purpose flour

Resift with:

1 teaspoon salt
3 tablespoons sugar
1 3/4 teaspoons double-acting baking powder

Combine:

1 or 2 slightly beaten whole eggs
3 tablespoons melted butter
1 to 1 1/4 cups milk

Mix the liquid ingredients quickly into the dry ingredients. ♦ To test griddle and cook, see About Griddle Cakes, 141. Serve the cakes with:

(Sausages and syrup)

WHOLE-GRAIN GRIDDLE CAKES

About Fourteen 4-Inch Cakes

Sift before measuring:

1/2 cup all-purpose flour

Resift with:

1/2 teaspoon salt
1/2 teaspoon double-acting baking powder
3/4 teaspoon baking soda

Stir in:

1 cup finely milled whole wheat flour

Combine and beat:

2 tablespoons sugar, honey or molasses
1 egg
2 cups buttermilk or yogurt
2 tablespoons melted butter or bacon drippings

♦ To test griddle and cook, see About Griddle Cakes, 141.

WHOLE-GRAIN AND SOY GRIDDLE CAKES

Prepare:

Whole-Grain Griddle Cakes, left

Substitute for the all-purpose flour:

1/4 cup soy flour
1/4 cup cornmeal
1 cup finely milled whole-grain flour

FRENCH PANCAKES OR CRÊPES

Fourteen to Sixteen 5-Inch Cakes

Sift:

3/4 cup all-purpose flour

Resift with:

1/2 teaspoon salt
1 teaspoon double-acting baking powder
2 tablespoons powdered sugar

Beat:

2 eggs

Add and beat:

2/3 cup milk
1/3 cup water
1/2 teaspoon vanilla or 1/2 teaspoon grated lemon rind

Make a well in the sifted ingredients. Pour in the liquid ingredients. Combine them with a few swift strokes. Ignore the lumps; they will take care of themselves. You may rest the batter refrigerated 3 to 6 hours. Heat a 5-inch skillet. Grease it with a few drops of oil. Add a small quantity of batter. Tip the skillet and let the batter spread over the bottom. Cook the pancake over moderate heat. When it is brown underneath, reverse it and brown the other side. Use a few drops of oil for each pancake. Spread the cake with:

Jelly

Roll it and sprinkle with:

Confectioners' sugar

STUFFED FRENCH PANCAKES OR CRÊPES

I. With Seafood

Prepare but omit the sugar:

French Pancakes, 143

Prepare:

Creamed Oysters, (I, 442)

or cream any available canned or frozen seafood. Spread the pancakes with the creamed mixture. Roll them. Cover with the remaining sauce. Sprinkle with:

(Grated cheese)

Brown lightly under a broiler.

II. With Meat or Vegetables

Follow the above recipe, filling the pancakes with:

Hash with gravy, or creamed vegetables, chicken, ham, chipped beef or other precooked meat

The cream sauce may be made from a condensed cream soup.

III. Roll in the pancakes:

Precooked pork sausages

Serve very hot with:

Applesauce

GÂTEAU CRÊPE

10-Inch Skillet

Prepare batter for:

French Pancakes, 143

Make four or five large pancakes. Cool them.

Stack and spread between the layers:

Lemon, Orange or Lime Sauce, 563, or Lemon or Orange Filling, 451

You may spread over the top layer:

Caramelized sugar, see Clear Caramel Glaze, 505

or simply sprinkle the top with:

Powdered sugar

FRUIT PANCAKES

Four Large (9-Inch) Cakes

Prepare batter for:

French Pancakes, 143

Prepare and have ready:

1 cup or more thinly sliced, lightly sugared, sautéed apples, peaches, bananas or blueberries

Also have ready two 9-inch skillets.
Melt in each:

2 teaspoons butter

2 teaspoons shortening

When the fat is hot, pour one-fourth the batter into each skillet. Turn the cakes when they are lightly browned and cook the other side. Place one of the cakes on a hot platter. Sprinkle over it half of the still-warm fruit. When the other cake is browned on the second side, slide it over the fruit. Cook the other two griddle cakes for the remaining warm fruit. Serve hot, dusted with:

Powdered sugar

or a mixture of:

$^1/_2$ teaspoon cinnamon

$^1/_2$ cup sugar

BLINTZES OR COTTAGE CHEESE PANCAKES

4 Servings

Prepare:

French Pancakes, 143

Use a 5-inch skillet. Cook very thin cakes on one side only, until the top is bubbly. Place them on a damp tea towel, cooked side down. Prepare the following filling.

Mix well:

1$^1/_2$ cups smooth, rather dry cottage cheese: 12 oz.

1 egg yolk

1 teaspoon soft butter

1 teaspoon vanilla or grated lemon rind

Place about 2 tablespoons of filling on the center of each cake. Roll the edges up and over from either side. At this point the blintzes may be cooked at once; or, if you are not ready to serve them, they may be placed seam side down in a closely covered dish and chilled for several hours. Melt in a large skillet:

 1/2 **tablespoon oil**
 1/2 **tablespoon butter**

Place several blintzes in it, seam side down. Fry them to a golden brown, turning them once. Repeat, adding more oil or butter to the skillet, as needed, until all are done. Serve them hot, sprinkled with:

 Sugar and cinnamon

You may pass:

 (Cultured sour cream)

CRÊPES SUZETTE

 4 Servings

At an early age the famous Franco-American cook, Henri Charpentier, invented Crêpes Suzette—a glorified French pancake.

One day when he was composing a complicated crêpe sauce for his patron, Albert, Prince of Wales, the cordials accidentally caught fire, and the poor boy thought both he and his sauce were ruined. Quickly he plunged the crêpes into the boiling liquid, added more of the cordials and let the sauce flame again. The dish was a triumph. Below is an approximation of Henri's crêpe batter and sauce.

Combine and stir until the ingredients are the consistency of thin cream:

 3 eggs
 2 tablespoons all-purpose flour
 1 tablespoon water
 1 tablespoon milk

 A pinch of salt

We recommend keeping this batter 3 hours to overnight, covered and refrigerated. Place in a 5-inch crêpe pan:

 1 tablespoon butter

When this bubbles, pour in enough batter to cover the bottom with a thin coating. Keep the pan moving, for this is a delicate substance. A minute of cooking and the job is three-fourths done. Turn the cake and keep turning it until it is well browned. Fold it twice so it will be triangular in shape. The cakes may be stacked with a cloth between them and reheated in sauce much later. Although they may be frozen and reheated, we do not feel that freezing improves them.

BUTTER SAUCE FOR CRÊPES SUZETTE

This may be made in advance and kept for months refrigerated. Cut into very thin strips a piece of:

 Lemon rind, 3/4 inch square
 Orange rind, 3/4 inch square

using only the colored portion of the rind. Add:

 1 teaspoon Vanilla Sugar, 229

Or substitute a few drops of vanilla and 1 teaspoon sugar. Let these ingredients stand closely covered 12 hours or more. Melt in a large skillet:

 1/2 **cup butter**

When it starts to bubble, add:

 1 pony maraschino
 1 pony curaçao
 1 pony kirsch

Put a lighted match to the sauce. As the flame dies down, add the lemon and orange mixture. Place the sauce in a cool place until ready to use, if you wish. Make the crêpes. You may place in each crêpe before rolling:

 (1 tablespoon Hard Sauce, 572)

Plunge the cakes into boiling sauce. Turn them. Again, add:

1 pony each maraschino, curaçao and kirsch

Put a lighted match to the sauce. Let it flame. Serve the cakes at once. The final performance—plunging the folded crêpes into the hot sauce, adding and burning the liquor—is done at table just before serving the crêpes on a hot plate.

PFANNKUCHEN OR GERMAN PANCAKES

1 Large Pancake—2 Servings

Henriette Davides, the German counterpart of the fabulous English Mrs. Beeton, says that the heat under this pancake must be neither "too weak nor too strong," that it is advisable to put "enough butter in the skillet, but not too much," and that the best results are obtained in making this simple great pancake with not more than 4 eggs. Henriette's recipes make mouth-watering reading. But on Henriette's terms, only a strongly intuitive person with a madly active imagination has a chance of success. Firming up Henriette's rule, will you try our version of this famous pancake?

Combine and stir until smooth:

4 beaten egg yolks
2 tablespoons cornstarch
¼ cup lukewarm milk
¼ cup lukewarm water
¾ teaspoon salt
1 tablespoon sugar
    Grated rind of 1 lemon

Beat until very stiff:

4 to 5 egg whites

Fold them into the yolk mixture. Melt in a heavy 10-inch skillet:

2 tablespoons butter

When the skillet is hot, pour in the pancake batter. Cook it over low to medium heat, partly covered with a lid, for about 5 minutes. Or the batter may be cooked until it begins to set and then be placed briefly in a preheated 400° oven until it is puffed and firm. Cooking time in all is about 7 minutes. It should puff up well, but it may fall. So serve it at once with:

Confectioners' sugar and cinnamon or lemon juice; covered with jam or jelly and rolled; or with wine, fruit or rum sauce

AUSTRIAN PANCAKES OR NOCKERLN

6 Cakes

In Salzburg, when we were last there, few visitors failed to indulge in one or more of these souffléed globular puffs between the delights of the annual Musical Festival. Make them immediately before serving.

Preheat oven to 225°.

Beat until very light:

4 egg yolks

Beat in:

¼ cup cake flour

Whip until stiff:

6 to 8 egg whites

and add gradually while continuing to beat:

½ to ¾ cup sugar
½ teaspoon vanilla

Fold the yolk mixture lightly into the egg whites. Melt in a 9-inch skillet:

2 to 3 tablespoons butter

The butter should coat the bottom and sides of the pan and be bubbling when the soufflé mixture is put into it. Heap the soufflé into the hot skillet in 6 even mounds and cook until the undersides color lightly. Place the skillet in the oven and bake until the puffs are golden, about 8 to 10 minutes. The center should remain soft. If you are serving the Nockerln without fruit or sauce, sprinkle them with:

Confectioners' sugar

◗ Serve at once on heated plates.

RUSSIAN RAISED PANCAKES OR BLINI

About Twenty-Four 2-Inch Cakes

Dissolve:

    1 cake compressed yeast

in:

    2 cups scalded milk which has cooled to 85°

Stir in until well blended:

    1½ cups sifted all-purpose flour

    1 tablespoon sugar

Cover the bowl and set this sponge to rise in a warm place about 1½ hours. Beat until well blended:

    3 egg yolks

    1 tablespoon melted butter

Stir in:

    ½ cup sifted all-purpose flour

    1 teaspoon salt

Beat these ingredients into the sponge and let it rise again about 1½ hours or until almost doubled in bulk. Whip until stiff, but not dry:

    3 egg whites

Fold them into the batter. After 10 minutes, cook the batter, a very small quantity at a time, in a greased skillet or on a griddle. See About Griddle Cakes, 141. Turn to brown lightly on the other side. Serve each blini rolled and filled with:

    1 tablespoon caviar

and garnished with:

    Cultured sour cream

BUTTERMILK PANCAKES

About Ten 4-Inch Cakes

Sift before measuring:

    1 cup cake flour

Resift with:

    1 teaspoon sugar

    ½ teaspoon salt

    ¾ teaspoon double-acting baking powder

    ½ teaspoon baking soda

Beat until light:

    1 egg

Add:

    1 cup buttermilk

    1 to 2 tablespoons melted butter

Combine the sifted and the liquid ingredients with a few swift strokes. To test griddle and cook, see About Griddle Cakes, 141.

CORNMEAL PANCAKES

About Twelve 4-Inch Cakes

Measure and place in a bowl:

    1 cup white or yellow cornmeal

    1 teaspoon salt

    1 to 2 tablespoons honey, syrup or sugar

Stir in slowly:

    1 cup boiling water

Cover these ingredients and let stand 10 minutes.

Beat:

    1 egg

    ½ cup milk

    2 tablespoons melted butter

Add these ingredients to the corn-meal mixture.

Sift before measuring:

    ½ cup all-purpose flour

Resift with:

    2 teaspoons double-acting baking powder

Stir the sifted ingredients into the batter with a few swift strokes. To test griddle and cook, see About Griddle Cakes, 141.

▤ CRISP CORN FLAPJACKS

About 20 Thin 2-Inch Cakes

If you make up this traditional camp treat without the eggs, the pancakes become lacy.

Place in a bowl:

1¹/₃ cups white cornmeal
1¹/₄ teaspoons salt
¹/₂ teaspoon baking soda
¹/₄ cup sifted all-purpose flour

Cut into this with a pastry blender:

¹/₄ cup butter

Combine and beat:

2 cups buttermilk
(1 to 2 eggs)

Stir the liquid into the sifted ingredients with a few swift strokes. Make the cakes small for easier turning. The batter settles readily, so beat it between spoonings. To test griddle, cook and serve, see About Griddle Cakes, 141.

JOHNNYCAKES

About 2 Dozen 4-Inch Cakes

Heat in a double boiler ◗ over—not in—boiling water:

1 cup stone-ground cornmeal
¹/₂ teaspoon salt

To avoid lumping, stir constantly and scald the cornmeal by adding in a thin stream:

1¹/₄ cups boiling water

Continue to stir about 10 minutes more, then add:

2 tablespoons butter
1¹/₄ to 1¹/₂ cups milk

to make the batter easy to drop, a tablespoon at a time, onto a greased hot griddle. Cook over low heat about 10 minutes, or until the underside is golden brown. Turn and cook until the other side is golden brown. Serve with:

Maple syrup and butter

HOMINY CAKES

5 Servings

Drain:

2¹/₂ cups cooked or canned hominy

Combine it with:

2 tablespoons flour
1 egg
Salt and pepper

Form these ingredients into flat cakes. Sauté them until they are brown in:

Butter or drippings

Serve them hot—plain or with:

Honey or syrup

RICE-CORNMEAL GRIDDLE CAKES

Twelve 4-Inch Cakes

Sift before measuring:

¹/₂ cup all-purpose flour

Resift with:

1 teaspoon salt
¹/₂ teaspoon baking soda
1 tablespoon sugar

Add:

¹/₂ cup stone-ground cornmeal
1 cup cold boiled rice

Combine, beat, then stir into the sifted ingredients with a few swift strokes:

2 cups buttermilk
2 egg yolks
2 tablespoons melted, cooled shortening

◗ Beat until stiff, but not dry:

2 egg whites

Fold into the batter. To test griddle and cook, see About Griddle Cakes, 141.

RICE FLOUR GRIDDLE CAKES

About Eighteen 4-Inch Cakes

Mix, then sift:

2 cups rice flour

GRIDDLE CAKES AND FRITTER VARIATIONS 149

4½ teaspoons double-acting
    baking powder
2 teaspoons maple sugar
2 teaspoons salt

Beat the mixture while adding:

2 cups milk

Add and barely blend:

1 beaten egg
1 tablespoon melted butter

To cook and serve, see About Griddle
Cakes, 141.

OATMEAL GRIDDLE CAKES

About Twelve 4-Inch Cakes

Sift before measuring:

½ cup all-purpose flour

Resift with:

1 teaspoon double-acting
    baking powder
½ teaspoon salt

Beat:

1 egg

Stir in:

1½ cups cooked oatmeal
½ cup evaporated milk
¼ cup water
2 tablespoons melted butter
    or bacon drippings

Stir this mixture into the sifted ingredients. To cook and serve, see About
Griddle Cakes, 141.

BUCKWHEAT CAKES

About Forty 3-Inch Cakes

Mix together thoroughly:

1 cup buckwheat flour

1 cup sifted all-purpose flour
    or whole wheat flour
2 teaspoons double-acting
    baking powder
1 teaspoon baking soda
2 teaspoons sugar
1 teaspoon salt

You may substitute 2 teaspoons molasses for the sugar. If so, add it to the
buttermilk, below. Stir into the flour
mixture:

2 beaten egg yolks
¼ cup melted butter
2 cups buttermilk

Whip until ▶ stiff, but not dry:

2 egg whites

Fold them into the batter until it is
blended only. Cook on a greased hot
griddle, see About Griddle Cakes, 141.

RAISED BUCKWHEAT CAKES

About Eighteen 2½-Inch Cakes

Scald, then cool to 105° to 115°:

2 cups milk

Add and stir until dissolved:

1 package active dry yeast

Add and stir to a smooth batter:

1¼ cups buckwheat flour
½ cup all-purpose flour or ¼
    cup flour and ¼ cup
    cornmeal
1 teaspoon salt

Cover the batter with a cloth and
place in refrigerator overnight. In the
morning, stir in:

1 tablespoon molasses
½ teaspoon baking soda

dissolved in ¼ cup
lukewarm water
1 egg or ¼ cup melted
shortening

Let stand at room temperature 30
minutes. To cook, see About Griddle
Cakes, 141. Serve with:

Maple syrup

ABOUT WAFFLES

You don't have to be told how good
these are with syrup, honey, marmalade or stewed fruit. But you may
not realize what attractive cases they
make for serving creamed foods,
shown center on 149, and for leftovers
and ice creams. You can even cook
raw bacon placed directly on the batter, as shown on 149, and have it come
out crisp and nut brown. But be sure to
treat your iron with care. Manufacturer's directions should be followed
exactly in seasoning a new electric
waffle iron. Once conditioned ♦ the
grids are neither greased nor washed.
You may brush the iron out to remove any crumbs. ♦ The iron itself is
never immersed in water. After use,
merely wipe down the outside with a
cloth well wrung out in hot water.

Heat a waffle iron until the indica-
tor shows it is ready to use. If it has
been properly conditioned, it will
need no greasing, as most waffle batters are heavy in butter. Have the batter ready in a pitcher. Cover the grid
surface about two-thirds, as sketched
on the left on 149. Close the lid and
wait about 4 minutes. When the waffle
is ready, all steam will have stopped
emerging from the crack of the iron.
If you try to lift the top of the
iron and the top shows resistance, it
probably means the waffle is not
quite done. Cook slightly longer and
try again.

The richer the waffle dough, the
crisper the waffle becomes. With the
butter flavor baked in, there is then
no reason for ladling butter on top of
the waffle. We also suggest ♦ beating
egg whites separately for a superbly
light result. Since waffles are made
from a batter ♦ keep them tender by
not overbeating or overmixing the
dough.

▲ In high altitudes, use about one-
fourth less baking powder or soda
than indicated in our recipes.

WAFFLES

6 Waffles

♦ If used with savory foods, omit the
sugar.
Sift before measuring:

1¾ cups cake flour

Resift with:

2 teaspoons double-acting
baking powder
½ teaspoon salt
1 tablespoon sugar

Beat well:

3 egg yolks

Add:

2 to 7 tablespoons melted
butter or vegetable oil
1½ cups milk

Make a hole in the center of the sifted
ingredients. Pour in the liquid ingredients. Combine them with a few
swift strokes. The batter should have
a pebbled look, similar to a muffin
batter. At this time, superb as these
waffles are "as is," you may want
to include for variety one of the
following:

(½ cup fresh fruit or berries)
(¼ cup raisins or puréed dried
fruit)
(¼ cup finely chopped nuts or
coconut)
(¼ cup grated semisweet
chocolate)
(½ cup shredded sharp cheese)

(1 cup finely diced cooked
  ham)
◗ Beat until stiff, but not dry:
   3 egg whites
Fold them into the batter until they
are barely blended. To cook, see
About Waffles, above. Good served
with:

   Maple syrup or Honey
   Sauce, 571, or sweetened
   fruit or a dessert sauce, 563

GOLDEN YAM OR SQUASH
WAFFLES

                         6 Waffles
Prepare:
   1/2 cup boiled mashed yams,
     (I, 355), or winter squash,
     (I, 364)
Add:
   3 well-beaten eggs
   1 1/2 cups milk
   2 tablespoons melted butter
     or shortening
Sift together and add to the yam
mixture:
   1 cup sifted all-purpose flour
   1/2 teaspoon salt
   2 teaspoons double-acting
     baking powder
   2 tablespoons sugar
   (1/8 teaspoon cinnamon or
     nutmeg)
◗ Stir only enough to moisten. To
cook, see About Waffles, 150. Serve
with:

   Honey and butter or Sauce
   Cockaigne, 564
The sauce makes this a dessert
waffle.

BUTTERMILK WAFFLES

                         6 Waffles
Sift before measuring:
   2 cups all-purpose flour
Resift with:

   1/4 teaspoon baking soda
   1 1/2 teaspoons double-acting
     baking powder
   1 tablespoon sugar
   1/2 teaspoon salt
Beat in a separate bowl until light:
   2 egg yolks
Add and beat:
   1 3/4 cups buttermilk
   6 tablespoons melted butter
Combine the liquid and the dry ingredients with a few swift strokes. ◗
Beat until stiff, but not dry:
   2 egg whites
Fold them into the batter. To cook,
see About Waffles, 150.

SOUR CREAM WAFFLES

                     About 4 Waffles
Sift before measuring:
   1 cup cake flour
Resift with:
   1 1/4 teaspoons double-acting
     baking powder
   1/8 teaspoon salt
   1 teaspoon sugar
   1 teaspoon baking soda
Beat in a separate bowl until light:
   3 egg yolks
Add:
   2 cups thick cultured sour
     cream
Combine the liquid and the dry ingredients with a few swift strokes. ◗
Beat until stiff, but not dry:
   3 egg whites
Fold them into the batter. To cook,
see About Waffles, 150.

BACON-CORNMEAL WAFFLES

                         6 Waffles
Don't worry about too much grease
from the bacon, as this is all absorbed
in the cooking.
Beat slightly:
   2 eggs

Add:
1³/₄ cups milk
Sift:
**1 cup cake flour or ⁷/₈ cup
all-purpose flour
2¹/₂ teaspoons double-acting
baking powder
1 tablespoon sugar
¹/₂ teaspoon salt**
Add:
**1 cup yellow stone-ground
cornmeal**
Combine these ingredients with the eggs and milk in a few quick strokes.
Add:
**¹/₄ cup melted bacon fat or
other shortening**
Cut into halves or quarters:
6 to 12 very thin slices bacon
Place pieces of bacon on each waffle iron section after pouring the batter, see illustration, 149. To cook, see About Waffles, 150.

CHOCOLATE WAFFLES

6 Waffles

Delectable with ice cream.
Sift before measuring:
1¹/₂ cups cake flour
Resift with:
**2 teaspoons double-acting
baking powder
¹/₄ teaspoon salt
(¹/₄ teaspoon cinnamon)
(¹/₄ teaspoon nutmeg)**
Cream:
¹/₂ cup butter
with:
1 cup sugar
Beat in, one at a time:
2 eggs
Add:
1 teaspoon vanilla
Melt, ♦ cool and add:
2 oz. unsweetened chocolate
Add the sifted ingredients in about three parts, alternately with:

¹/₂ cup milk
To cook, see About Waffles, 150.

FRENCH TOAST WAFFLES

Combine:
**1 beaten egg
¹/₄ cup milk
2 tablespoons melted butter
¹/₈ teaspoon salt**
Cut into pieces to fit a waffle iron:
Sliced bread
Coat the bread well in the batter. Toast it in a hot waffle iron.

ABOUT FRITTERED FOODS

The term fritter is rather confusingly used to cover three quite different types of food. We think of a true fritter as a delicately flavored batter, heavy in egg and deep-fat-fried. While they are not called fritters, crullers and doughnuts, 157–160, are very closely related to them—the crullers usually richer in fat, the doughnuts heavier in flour. The success of these batters depends on the care and skill with which they are mixed and fried, so please read About Deep-Fat Frying, (I, 94).

♦ Don't confuse the texture of any of the aforementioned fritters with certain pan- or shallow-fried mixtures like corn fritters, (I, 318). The term fritter may also apply to bits of meat, fish, vegetable or fruit dipped in a batter and dried before deep-fat frying. In this last type, the fritter batter acts as a protective coating. Other examples of fritterlike foods are Deep-Fat-Fried Vegetables, (I, 282), and Croquettes, 161.

Variations of this completely encased food are rosettes, illustrated in the chapter heading, 141, and timbale cases or *cassolettes* in which the deep-fat-fried casing is a free-standing af-

fair, so shaped that it may be filled. ◗
Be sure to choose fillings that are
rather on the stable side with these
types, and put them in just before
serving, so the fritterlike casing will
stay crisp.

Either cooked or uncooked foods
may be fried in batter, although uncooked meats are more satisfactory if
minced. ◗ But veal, pork and pork
products should always be cooked,
and brains and sweetbreads must be
parboiled before deep frying. To prepare frittered vegetables, use almost
any leftover or raw vegetables.
Seafood and sliced, firm tomatoes are
also delectable served this way.

To cook fritters, please read About
Deep-Fat Frying, (I, 94). One at a
time ◗ slide the fritters into the heated
fat at the side of the kettle. If using a
spoon, first dip it into the hot fat before picking up the fritter. Time depends on the size of the fritter. If
slightly smaller than doughnut size,
precooked food requires only 2 to 3
minutes at about 365° to 375°. Uncooked food in larger units is better at
350° to 360° and will need from 5 to
7 minutes. This allows more time for
thorough cooking of the interior.

▲ Batters for deep-fat-fried fritters
and doughnuts must be adjusted and
the temperature of the fat usually
must be lowered when cooking at
high altitudes.

ABOUT FRITTER BATTERS

These are really much like simple
pancake mixtures, but they ◗ must
have the consistency that makes them
stick to the food to be fried. As in all
recipes involving flour, measurements can only be approximate. If the
surface of the food you are frying is
as dry as possible, the dough will adhere if it follows this easy test: ◗ Take

a generous spoonful of batter and
hold it above the mixing bowl. Instead of running from the spoon in a
broad shining band, a consistency
that the French call *au ruban,* the batter should start to run for about a 1½-
inch length, then drop in successive
long triangular "splats." When the
batter is this consistency ◗ beat it until very smooth. ◗ Cover it refrigerated at least two hours. It may even
be stored overnight. This resting period allows a fermentation which
breaks down any rubberiness of the
batter—a process that is further activated if beer or wine forms part of
the liquid used.

◗ If you do not have time to let the
batter rest, mix it to smoothness with
as few strokes as possible so as not to
build up the gluten in the flour. Batters heavy in egg yolk resist fat penetration during frying. Use whole eggs
if you wish, but if you separate them
and plan to rest the batter, fold in the
whites beaten ◗ stiff, but not dry, at
the last minute before coating
the food.

ABOUT FRUIT FRITTERS

Fritter batter for fruit, like any other
batter, profits by resting at least 2
hours after mixing. ◗ Please read
About Fritter Batters, above.

It is very important that fruit used
in these desserts be ripe but not
mushy. Keep fruit slices about ½
inch thick. Use apples—cored and
cut crosswise—pineapple and orange
wedges, halves of canned or stewed
apricots, or bananas cut in 3 or 4 diagonal pieces. In season, even try
fuzzy white elderberry blossoms,
141. Dusted with powdered sugar
and sprinkled with kirsch, they are
dreamy.

The fruit is often marinated in

advance in a little wine, kirsch, rum or brandy. This marinade may also be used in the batter, but in this case you must marinate and drain prior to mixing the batter and adjust the amount of liquid to that called for in the recipe. Even beer can be used as a liquid. Both beer and wine help to break down the gluten and make a tender batter. After marination of about 2 hours, be sure to ◗ drain the fruit well and dust it with confectioners' sugar just before immersing it in the batter. To cook, please read about Fritter Batter for Fruit, below. Either dust fritters with sugar or serve with a sauce.

If a variety of fruits are served in this way, they are called a **Fritto Misto**.

FRITTER BATTER FOR FRUIT

About 8 to 10 Servings

This batter can be used either to encase about 2 cups diced fruit or to hold the same amount of small fruits and berries that are mixed directly and gently into it. See About Fruit Fritters, above.

I. Beat together:

> 2 egg yolks
> 2/3 cup milk or the liquid from the fruit marinade
> 1 tablespoon melted butter

Sift before measuring:

> 1 cup all-purpose flour

Resift with:

> 1/4 teaspoon salt
> 1 tablespoon sugar

Combine liquid and dry ingredients. If you have the time, rest the dough at least 2 hours, covered and refrigerated. Then beat this mixture well, until smooth. Otherwise, stir until just blended. Just before using the batter, whip ◗ until stiff, but not dry:

> 2 egg whites

Fold them into the batter. Dip into the batter or mix with it the well-drained sugared fruit. To cook, have deep fat heated to 375°. The fritters will take from 3 to 5 minutes to brown. Drain them on paper toweling. Dust with:

> **Confectioners' sugar**

II. Prepare:

> **Fritter Batter for Vegetables, opposite**

omitting the pepper and adding:

> 1 to 2 tablespoons sugar

Follow directions given in I, above.

III. Mix together and beat until smooth:

> 1 1/4 cups sifted all-purpose flour
> 1 cup white wine
> 1 tablespoon sugar
> 1/2 teaspoon grated lemon rind
> 1/4 teaspoon salt

Rest the batter refrigerated and covered 3 to 12 hours. Just before using ◗ whip until stiff, but not dry, and fold in:

> 1 egg white

Follow directions given in I, above.

BLOOMS IN BATTER

There is a chichi revival of the age-old custom of eating flowers. If you are an organic gardener and if you know your flowers, all is well. A lily of the valley which always looks good enough to eat is very poisonous, and the sprays used on roses are lethal not only to pests but to you. From sprayed gardens, save petals for fragrance only—not eating. Wash and drain well any kind of blooms and leaves you use for garnish.

◗ To make fritters of blossoms, please read About Fritter Batters, 153. Pick with the dew on them and dry well:

Unsprayed elderberry,
squash, pumpkin, lilac,
yucca or hemerocallis
blooms

Dip them in:

Fritter Batter for Fruit II,
opposite

Fry them in deep fat heated to 350°.

UNSWEETENED CHOUX PASTE FRITTERS

Prepare:

Choux Paste, 370

Omit the sugar. Add:

(¼ cup grated Parmesan
cheese)

(½ teaspoon prepared
mustard)

Shape dough with greased spoons or a small greased self-releasing ice cream scoop. Fry in 370° deep fat about 6 minutes.

FRITTER OR TEMPURA BATTER FOR VEGETABLES, MEAT AND FISH

Enough to Coat About 2 Cups
Food

♦ Please read About Fritter Batters, 153.

Put in a bowl and mix well:

1⅓ cups all-purpose flour or
rice flour

1 teaspoon salt

¼ teaspoon pepper

1 tablespoon melted butter or
vegetable oil

2 beaten egg yolks

Add gradually, stirring constantly:

¾ cup flat beer

Allow the batter to rest covered and refrigerated 3 to 12 hours. Just before using, you may add:

(2 stiffly beaten egg whites)

PURÉED VEGETABLE FRITTERS

3 Servings

♦ Please read About Frittered Foods, 152.

Beat until light:

1 egg

Add and beat well:

1 cup mashed or puréed
cooked carrots, parsnips or
butter beans

Stir in:

¼ teaspoon salt

1½ tablespoons melted butter

1½ tablespoons all-purpose
flour

6 tablespoons milk

1 teaspoon Worcestershire
sauce or 2½ teaspoons
onion juice

½ teaspoon dried herb, or
2 tablespoons chopped
parsley

Spread these ingredients on a greased platter. When they are chilled, shape into 1-inch balls. Flour and roll the balls in:

Bound Breading, 220

Fry the balls in deep fat heated to 365°.

EGGPLANT FRITTERS

6 Servings

♦ Please read About Frittered Foods, 152.

Pare and slice:

A small-sized eggplant

Cook until tender in:

Boiling water to cover

1 teaspoon vinegar

Drain the eggplant. Mash it. Beat in:

1 egg

½ teaspoon salt

3 tablespoons all-purpose
flour

½ teaspoon double-acting
baking powder

Drop the batter from a spoon into deep fat heated to 365°.

RICE FRITTERS

About 10 Fritters

♦ Please read About Frittered Foods, 152.

Combine:

    2 cups Boiled Rice, (I, 189)

    2 tablespoons all-purpose flour

    1 tablespoon finely chopped parsley

    1/2 teaspoon paprika

    1/2 teaspoon salt

    (1 teaspoon onion juice)

    (1/2 cup grated sharp cheese)

Beat and add:

    2 egg yolks

    2 tablespoons milk

Beat until stiff:

    2 egg whites

and fold into the rice mixture. Drop into deep fat heated to 365° and cook until golden. Serve with:

    Mushroom Wine Sauce, (I, 392), or a tomato sauce

CALF BRAIN FRITTERS

3 Servings

♦ Please read About Frittered Foods, 152.

Prepare and blanch:

    1 set calf brains, (I, 645)

Dry them between towels. Pull them into small pieces. Sift:

    1 cup all-purpose flour

    1 teaspoon double-acting baking powder

    1/4 teaspoon salt

Beat until light and add to flour mixture:

    2 egg yolks

Beat in:

    1 tablespoon melted butter

    1 teaspoon grated lemon rind

    A grating of nutmeg

    1/2 cup milk

    (1 tablespoon wine or brandy)

Beat until stiff ♦ but not dry:

    2 egg whites

Fold them into the batter with the brains. Drop the batter from a spoon into deep fat heated to 365°. Serve when golden.

COOKED MEAT FRITTERS

Prepare and deep-fry as for:

    Calf Brain Fritters, at left

substituting for the brains about:

    1 1/2 cups chopped cooked meat

Add to the meat, if desired:

    (2 tablespoons chopped parsley)

    (1 tablespoon lemon juice or 1 teaspoon Worcestershire sauce)

Serve the fritters with:

    A tomato sauce or Horseradish Sauce, (I, 386)

CORN AND HAM FRITTERS

6 Servings

♦ Please read About Frittered Foods, 152.

Beat until light:

    2 egg yolks

Add and combine with a few swift strokes:

    1/2 cup milk

    1 1/3 cups sifted all-purpose flour

    2 teaspoons double-acting baking powder

    3/4 teaspoon salt

    1/4 teaspoon paprika

Fold in:

    2 tablespoons minced parsley or onion

    1/4 cup drained cream-style corn

    3/4 cup cooked minced ham

    2 stiffly beaten egg whites

Drop the batter from a spoon into deep fat heated to 365° and cook until golden brown.

ABOUT DOUGHNUTS, CRULLERS AND BEIGNETS

Crullers are richer than doughnuts, and beignets richer than both. For tender cakes ◗ have all ingredients at about 70°, so the dough can be mixed quickly. This prevents the development of gluten in the flour, which would tend to toughen the batter. Keep the mix just firm enough to be easy to handle. Chill the dough slightly to shape it, before cutting, so that the board won't have to be too heavily floured. Roll or pat the dough to about 1/2-inch thickness. ◗ Cut with a well-floured double cutter, or 2 sizes of biscuit cutters. ◗ If you allow the dough to dry 10 or 12 minutes on a very lightly floured board or paper toweling, the doughnuts will absorb less fat while frying. The richer and sweeter the dough, the more fat they absorb.

◗ Please read About Deep-Fat Frying, (I, 94). For delicate flavor, the frying fat must be impeccable. Bring the fat to 375° unless otherwise stated. Then, one at a time ◗ slide the doughnuts into the fat at the side of the kettle. They will keep their shapes if you transfer them to the fat with a pancake turner which has already been dipped into the kettle.

Each cake takes 2 to 3 minutes to a side to cook, depending on size. ◗ Never crowd the frying kettle. You can develop a machinelike precision by adding one at a time at about 15-second intervals. Turn each as soon as it browns on one side. It will usually rise at this point. When done, remove with a fork or tongs and place on paper toweling to drain. Replace it immediately with an uncooked cake to keep the fat at an even temperature.

When the cakes cool, dust with powdered, spiced or flavored sugar.

For an easy method, use a paper bag as shown on 220. Or glaze them with Milk or Lemon Glaze, 504. Beignets may also be served hot with a sauce.

▲ Yeast-based doughnuts require no adjustment for high altitudes. For quick leavened doughnuts, reduce the baking powder or soda by one-fourth. ◗ But do not reduce soda beyond 1/2 teaspoon for each cup if sour milk or sour cream is used.

SWEET MILK DOUGHNUTS

About 36 Doughnuts

◗ Please read About Doughnuts, above.

Beat:

    2 eggs

Add slowly, beating constantly:

    1 cup sugar

Stir in:

    1 cup milk
    5 tablespoons melted shortening

Sift before measuring:

    4 cups all-purpose flour

Resift with:

    4 teaspoons double-acting baking powder
    1/2 teaspoon cinnamon or 1 teaspoon grated lemon rind
    1/2 teaspoon salt
    (1/4 teaspoon nutmeg)

Mix moist and dry ingredients. Fry in deep fat heated to 375° until golden brown.

SOUR CREAM DOUGHNUTS

About 36 Doughnuts

◗ Please read About Doughnuts, above.

Beat well:

    3 eggs

Add slowly, beating constantly:

    1 1/4 cups sugar

Stir in:

1 cup cultured sour cream

Sift before measuring:

4 cups all-purpose flour

Resift with:

1 teaspoon baking soda

2 teaspoons double-acting baking powder

1/2 teaspoon cinnamon or nutmeg

1/2 teaspoon salt

Stir the sifted ingredients and the egg mixture until blended. Fry in deep fat heated to 375° until golden brown.

YEAST DOUGHNUTS

About 48 Doughnuts

♦ Please read About Doughnuts, 157.

Prepare dough for:

Buttermilk-Potato Rolls, 318, or

No-Knead Yeast Coffee Cake, 327

After dough has risen to double its bulk, place on a lightly floured board and pat or roll to 1/2-inch thickness. Cut into rings or into strips 1/2 × 31/2 inches. Twist the strips gently. You may bring the ends together to form twisted wreaths. Allow the twists to rise ♦ uncovered about 30 minutes. Fry in deep fat heated to 375° until golden brown. While still warm, shake in a bag filled with:

Sugar or sugar and cinnamon

BUTTERMILK-POTATO DOUGHNUTS

About 36 Doughnuts

♦ Please read About Doughnuts, 157.

Prepare:

1 cup freshly riced boiled potatoes

Beat well:

2 eggs

Add very slowly, beating constantly:

2/3 cup sugar

Stir in the potatoes and:

1 cup buttermilk

2 tablespoons melted butter

Sift before measuring:

4 cups all-purpose flour

Resift with:

2 teaspoons double-acting baking powder

1 teaspoon baking soda

2/3 teaspoon salt

1/4 teaspoon nutmeg or 1/4 teaspoon cinnamon

Stir in the sifted ingredients and the potato mixture until they are blended. Chill the dough until it is easy to handle and cut. Fry in deep fat heated to 375° until golden brown.

DOUGHNUT VARIATIONS

I. Berlin or Jelly Doughnuts

Prepare Yeast Doughnuts, above. Cut the dough into 1/4-inch-thick 21/2-inch rounds instead of rings. Place on one round:

1 heaping teaspoon jelly or preserves

Brush the edges of the round with:

Egg white

Cap it with another round. Press the edges together. Repeat the process. After allowing the doughnuts to rise, fry them as directed in About Doughnuts, 157.

II. Orange Doughnuts

Prepare any of the recipes for Doughnuts. Substitute for 1/4 cup of the milk:

The grated rind of 1 orange and 1/4 cup orange juice

III. Chocolate Doughnuts

Prepare any one of the recipes for Doughnuts, adding:

5 tablespoons flour

Melt:

1½ oz. unsweetened
chocolate

Add it to the melted shortening plus:

¼ cup additional sugar

1½ teaspoons vanilla

IV. Pecan or Date Doughnuts

Prepare any recipe for Doughnuts.
Add:

½ cup broken nutmeats or
diced pitted dates

V. Drop Doughnuts

While devoid of the characteristic
hole, these are lighter in texture. Prepare any recipe for doughnuts not requiring yeast, using ¼ to ½ cup less
flour. Slide a tablespoon of dough at a
time into the hot fat.

**BEIGNETS OR FRENCH
FRITTERS**

I.   **4 to 6 Servings**

These are light as air. ▶ Please read
About Doughnuts, 157.

Combine in a saucepan and boil and
stir over low heat about 5 minutes:

6 tablespoons water

1 tablespoon butter

6 tablespoons all-purpose
flour

Remove the pan from the heat. Beat
in one at a time:

4 eggs

Beat the batter about 3 minutes after
each addition. Add:

1 teaspoon vanilla

Drop the batter from a teaspoon into
deep fat heated to 365°. Cook until
golden. Drain. Dust with:

Confectioners' sugar

Serve at once with:

Lemon Sauce, 563, or
Gooseberry
Preserves, 672

II. Prepare dough for:

Cream Puff Shells, 370

Add:

(½ teaspoon grated lemon or
orange rind)

but instead of baking, drop a teaspoon of dough at a time into deep fat
heated to 365°. As soon as they are
cooked enough on one side, they will
automatically turn themselves over.
Remove when brown on both sides.
Drain and sprinkle with:

Powdered sugar

Serve with:

Vanilla Sauce, 571, or
Sauce Cockaigne, 564

CRULLERS

This recipe makes a lot—it is hard to
gauge the exact amount! ▶ Please
read About Doughnuts, 157.

Beat until light:

4 eggs

Add gradually:

⅔ cup sugar

Blend until mixture is creamy. Add:

¾ teaspoon grated
lemon rind

⅓ cup melted shortening

⅓ cup milk

Sift before measuring:

3½ cups all-purpose flour

Resift with:

1½ teaspoons cream of tartar

½ teaspoon soda

¼ teaspoon salt

(½ teaspoon nutmeg or
¼ teaspoon cardamom)

Stir the sifted ingredients into the egg
mixture. Roll the dough to the thickness of ¼ inch. With a pie jagger,
cut it into strips of about ½ × 2½
inches. To make a fancier shape, twist
the strips slightly. Fry in deep fat
heated to 365° until golden brown.
Drain and sprinkle with:

Confectioners' sugar

RICE CRULLERS OR CALAS

4 or 5 Servings
♦ Please read About Doughnuts, 157.
Mix together:

  **2 cups cold Boiled Rice,
    (I, 189)
  3 beaten eggs
  1/2 cup sugar
  1/2 teaspoon vanilla
  1/2 teaspoon nutmeg or grated
    lemon rind
  2 1/4 teaspoons double-acting
    baking powder**

And add only enough flour to bind
the batter. You may need:

  1/2 to 1 cup all-purpose flour

Drop the batter from a teaspoon into
deep fat heated to 365°. Fry the cakes
until they are golden brown—about 7
minutes. Drain on paper toweling.
Sprinkle with:

  Confectioners' sugar

Serve with:

  Tart jelly

ROSETTES

**About Thirty-Six
2 1/2-Inch Rosettes**
Rosettes are shaped with a small iron
made for the purpose and shown in the
chapter heading, 141. Onion or
garlic salt, paprika and other seasonings enliven the rosettes when used as
a base for creamed chicken or sweetbreads. For dessert, add the sugar and
vanilla and serve with a sweet sauce
or stewed fruit or alone with coffee.
♦ Please read About Deep-Fat Frying, (I, 94).
Beat until blended:

  **2 eggs
  1/4 teaspoon salt
  (1 tablespoon sugar)
  (1 teaspoon vanilla)**

Stir alternately into the egg mixture:

  **1 1/4 cups sifted all-purpose
    flour**

and:

  1 cup milk

Beat until smooth. If you are using a
thin 3/4-inch-high rosette mold, the
frying fat need be only about 2 1/2
inches deep. When using taller
molds, increase the depth of the fat.
Heat the fat to between 325° and
350°. Prepare the iron by dipping first
in the hot fat; then dip in the batter,
but do not let it run over the top of
the iron, for then it is difficult to remove the rosette when cooked. Hold
the batter-coated iron over the fat a
moment before completely immersing 20 to 35 seconds. Remove the
rosette with a fork. Reheat the iron in
the deep fat and repeat the process.
Drain the rosettes on paper toweling
and, if served as a dessert, dust with:

  Confectioners' sugar

TIMBALE CASES FOR FOOD

Select a timbale iron that is fluted,
like the one shown in the chapter
heading, 141. It is easier to handle
than a plain one.
♦ Please read About Deep-Fat Frying, (I, 94).
Sift:

  **3/4 cup all-purpose flour
  1/2 teaspoon salt**

Combine and beat:

  **1 egg
  1/2 cup milk**

Combine the liquid and the sifted ingredients with a few swift strokes.
Add:

  **1 teaspoon olive oil or melted
    butter**

Let the batter stand for 1 hour to
avoid bubbles which disfigure the
cases. For a crisper, thinner case,
rest the batter 2 hours or longer, covered and refrigerated. To fry timbale
cases, prepare the iron by immersing
its head in deep fat. Heat the deep fat

to 365°—hot enough to brown a cube of bread in 1 minute. Wipe the iron with a cloth wrapped around a fork. Plunge the iron into the batter, within ³/₄ inch of the top. Remove it. Allow the batter to dry slightly on the iron. Fry the timbale in the hot fat until it is golden brown, about 1 to 1¹/₂ minutes. Remove it from the iron and drain it on a paper towel. Repeat the process.

ABOUT CROQUETTES

Well made, these are literally crunchy on the outside, as their name implies, but should retain a creamy interior texture whether they are of a sweet or a savory type. Because their cooking time is short—3 to 4 minutes—the recipes nearly always call for already cooked minced foods. With seafoods such as oysters and mussels and with brains and sweetbreads, parboiling is called for. ◗ Beef, pork and pork products should always be precooked. ◗ Use about ³/₄ cup of heavy White Sauce III, (I, 383), or Brown Sauce, (I, 391), to 2 cups of cooked ground or minced solids, meat or fish and vegetables. ◗ The solids should never be watery—always well drained. You may add to the hot sauce 1 to 2 egg yolks and let them thicken slightly off the heat. Add enough sauce to the solids so they are well bound. There is a good deal of leeway in this relationship, provided—after chilling—the mixture can be handled. Spread it in a greased pan to about 1-inch thickness. You may also brush the top of the mixture lightly with butter or cover with waxed paper to avoid crusting. Chill at least 2 hours or freeze for 1 hour. When cool, it is best to cut the chilled mixture into squares or bars, not larger than 1¹/₂ × 2¹/₂ inches. Have ready a flour-covered paper. Put

the coquette shapes, one at a time, on it and shape into a cylinder or round by manipulating the paper. Then coat thoroughly with a Bound Breading, 220. ◗ Let the coated croquettes dry on a rack at least 1 hour. ◗ Or if the mixture is a very soft one, dry for 10 minutes, after breading, and recoat with a bound breading again. This time allow a full hour for the drying period. ◗ Should the outer coating not be all-enveloping and very dry when it meets the hot fat, the coquette mixture may leak into the fat and cause boiling over. ◗ Please read About Deep-Fat Frying, (I, 94). Immerse the croquettes, a few at a time, in a basket in deep fat heated to 365°. They will be golden in 2 to 4 minutes, unless otherwise indicated. Drain on paper toweling. You may hold them briefly on a rack in a 350° oven before serving. ◗ To reheat croquettes, once they have cooled, use a 400° oven.

CROQUETTES OF MEAT, FISH, FOWL OR VEGETABLES

About 12 Croquettes

◗ Please read About Croquettes, above.
Prepare:

White Sauce III, (I, 383)

When the sauce is smooth and hot, remove from heat and add:

    1 to 2 egg yolks

allowing them to thicken slightly. Add to the sauce until it binds:

    2 cups minced solid food: cooked meat, fish, fowl or vegetables

    2 teaspoons grated onion or onion juice

    2 tablespoons chopped parsley

Return the pan to very low heat and season the food well with a choice of one of the following:

    (Salt, pepper or paprika)

(Freshly grated nutmeg or
celery salt)
(2 teaspoons lemon juice)
(1 teaspoon Worcestershire
sauce)
(1/2 teaspoon hot pepper
sauce)
(2 teaspoons sherry)
(1/2 teaspoon dried or 1
tablespoon fresh herbs)
(1/2 teaspoon curry powder)

Cool and shape as directed above
and, in shaping, place in the center of
each croquette either:

(A sautéed mushroom)
(A piece of cooked chicken
liver)
(A pimiento-stuffed olive)

Bread, dry and deep-fat-fry the croquettes as directed. Drain on paper
toweling. You may serve the croquettes with one of the following if
suitable to your croquette mixture:

(Onion Sauce, (I, 387),
Mushroom Sauce, (I, 395),
Piquant Sauce, (I, 393), a
tomato sauce, or leftover
gravy)

CHEESE CROQUETTES
COCKAIGNE

12 Croquettes

♦ Please read About Croquettes, 161.
Melt:

1/4 cup butter

Stir in:

5 tablespoons all-purpose
flour

Stir in gradually until thickened:

1 cup milk
1/3 cup cream

Stir in, over low heat:

1/2 lb. shredded Swiss cheese

Cool slightly. Stir in:

3 beaten egg yolks
3/4 teaspoon salt
1/8 teaspoon paprika

Pour the custard into a well-greased
pan, about 6 × 9 inches. Chill well.
When ready to use, immerse pan for a
moment in hot water, reverse it and
turn the custard onto a flat surface. Cut
into shapes. Bread and dry twice as directed. Fry in deep fat heated to 365°.
Drain on paper toweling. Serve with:

Mexican Tomato Sauce,
(I, 401)

HAM AND CORN CROQUETTES

8 Croquettes

♦ Please read About Croquettes, 161.
Combine and mix well:

1 1/4 cups cream-style corn
2 tablespoons finely chopped
green pepper
1 cup ground or minced
cooked ham
1 beaten egg
1/2 cup dry bread crumbs

Chill, shape, bread, dry and deep-fat-
fry as directed. Drain on paper toweling. Serve the croquettes with:

A tomato sauce

MUSHROOM CROQUETTES

About 6 Croquettes

♦ Please read About Croquettes, 161.
Prepare:

1/2 cup White Sauce III, (I, 383)

Remove it from the heat. Add:

1/2 teaspoon Worcestershire
sauce
1/8 teaspoon curry powder
1 slightly beaten egg
2 tablespoons cracker
crumbs
1 cup chopped mushrooms
1/2 teaspoon salt
1/4 teaspoon paprika

Chill, shape, bread, dry and deep-fat-
fry the croquettes as directed. Drain
on paper toweling. Serve at once.

SWEET RICE CROQUETTES

About 12 Croquettes

◗ Please read About Croquettes, 161.
Combine:

> 1 cup chopped walnuts or
>   butternuts
> 1/2 cup toasted white bread
>   crumbs
> 2 cups cold cooked rice
> 1 teaspoon sugar
> 1/2 teaspoon salt
> 1 beaten egg
> 1 teaspoon grated lemon rind
>   or vanilla

Chill, shape, bread, dry and deep-fat-fry as directed. Drain on paper toweling. Serve with:

> **Tart jelly**

CHICKEN OR VEAL CROQUETTES

◗ Please read About Croquettes, 161.
Try adding poached sweetbreads or brains.
Combine:

> 1 1/2 cups finely minced
>   cooked chicken or
>   veal

with:

> 1/2 cup chopped sautéed
>   mushrooms, minced celery
>   or minced nuts

Add, until these ingredients are well bound:

> **About 3/4 cup hot Velouté
> Sauce, (I, 387)**

Chill, shape, bread, dry and deep-fat-fry the croquettes as directed. Drain on paper toweling. Serve with:

> **Mushroom Wine Sauce,
> (I, 392), or
> Poulette Sauce, (I, 390)**

OYSTER AND CHICKEN CROQUETTES

About 12 Croquettes

◗ Please read About Croquettes, 161.
The addition of whole oysters in a chicken croquette mixture is interesting. Heat in their liquor until they are plump:

> 1 pint oysters

Drain but reserve the liquor. Dry them.
Melt:

> 2 tablespoons butter

Sauté slowly in the butter until golden:

> (3 tablespoons minced onion)

Stir in, until blended:

> 1/4 cup flour

Slowly add:

> 1 cup oyster liquor and
>   Chicken Stock, 172
>   Season to taste

and add:

> A few grains cayenne
> A few grains nutmeg

Stir in:

> 1/2 cup minced cooked chicken

Reduce the heat and add:

> 3 beaten egg yolks
> 1 tablespoon minced parsley

Allow mixture to thicken. Whip until stiff and fold into the chicken mixture:

> 1/2 cup whipping cream

Spread the mixture on a platter. Chill. Dip the oysters one at a time in the chicken mixture until they are well coated. Shape, bread, dry and fry the croquettes in deep fat as directed. Drain on paper toweling. Serve garnished with:

> **Lemon slices
> Parsley or watercress**

SALMON CROQUETTES

About 12 Croquettes

Please read About Croquettes, 161.
Mix:

2 cups flaked cooked or
    canned salmon
2 cups mashed potatoes
1½ teaspoons salt or anchovy
    paste
⅛ teaspoon pepper
1 beaten egg

1 tablespoon minced
    parsley
1 teaspoon lemon juice or
    Worcestershire sauce

Chill, shape, bread, dry and fry the cro-
-quettes in deep fat as directed. Drain
on paper toweling before serving.

KNOW YOUR INGREDIENTS

What a wealth of materials we have to work with! Staples like milks and stocks, oils, beans, sprouts, honeys, gelatins, leavens, cheese and eggs, nuts, seeds, herbs, and exotics like chocolates and spices. Where do these supplies fit into your kitchen maneuvers? What qualities make them interchangeable? Which must you compensate for?

Oddly enough, many of the most basic cooking materials—those that go into ninety-nine out of a hundred recipes—are so familiar, or rather so constantly used, that their character-istics are taken for granted even by experienced cooks. And, by beginners, their peculiarities are often simply ignored. Yet success in cooking depends largely on one's becoming fully aware of how both common and uncommon ingredients react. Here and now we put them all—from water to weather—under the magnifying glass and point out just what it is that they contribute to the cooking process. With the knowledge gained in this chapter and the chapter on Heat, plus the information keyed by symbol and reference into our recipes at the point of use, we assure you a continuous and steady development from would-be to sure-fire cook.

ABOUT WATER

One of our family jokes involved an 1890 debutante cousin from Indianapolis who, when asked where her hometown got its water, replied: "Out of a faucet." Many of us have come to assume that there is a kind of nationwide standardization in tap water. As long as it runs clear, plentiful, hot and cold, and reasonably pleasant to the taste, few of us bother our heads further about its purity than did our pretty Victorian cousin. Yet there is a growing awareness that a galaxy of pollutants such as viruses, nitrates, heavy metals, pesticides, and asbestos and other carcinogens can and must be removed from our water supplies, just as purifying plants were set up earlier to control the bacteria that produced cholera, typhoid and dysentery. Both the quality and the composition of water remain essential to community health. And they are not irrelevant to the results we achieve in our kitchens.

In this book, when the word ◗ water appears in the recipes, we assume it has a 60° to 80° temperature. ◗ If hotter or colder water is needed, it is specified.

◗ Soft water is best for most cooking processes, although very soft water will make yeast doughs soggy and sticky. ◗ Hard water and some artificially softened waters affect flavor. They may toughen legumes and fruits and shrivel pickles. They markedly alter the color of vegetables in the cabbage family and turn onions, cauliflower, potatoes and rice yellow. If your water is hard, cooking these vegetables à blanc, (I, 555), is a superior method of preparation. Hard water retards fermentation of yeast, although it strengthens the gluten in flour. Alkaline waters, however, have a solvent effect on gluten, as well as diminishing its gas-retaining properties—and, consequently, the size of the loaf.

Water hardness is due to various combinations of salts, and there are a number of ways by which it may be reduced. Passing hard water through a tank containing counteractive chemicals may be helpful, but most of these systems principally exchange sodium for calcium compounds and are more effective in treating water used in dishwashing than water used in cooking. If the salts happen to consist of bicarbonates of calcium and magnesium, simply boiling the water for 20 or 30 minutes will cause them to precipitate. But if the water originally held in solution large amounts of sulfates, boiling it will increase hardness rather than reduce it, because the sulfates are concentrated by evaporation. ◗ Certain types of hard water

must be avoided by people who are on low-sodium or salt-free diets.

Sodium chloride, or common salt, may occur in inland as well as ocean waters. The Public Health Service's drinking water standards recommend that not more than .025% salt be permitted in a public drinking water supply. Should you be interested in finding out what type of water you have, call your local waterworks or health department if you live in a town, or your county agent if you live in the country.

Most old recipes recommend long soaking of food in water. But we know that fruits, salad greens and vegetables should be washed as quickly as possible. Soaking leaches out water-soluble vitamins. ◗ And, because of this leaching action, it is a good plan to utilize soaking and cooking waters, unless they have bitter or off-flavors or unless discarding is specified in a given recipe.

Occasionally recipes indicate ◗ water by weight, in which case use 1 tablespoon for $1/2$ ounce, 1 cup for 8 ounces, 2 cups for 1 pound.

▲ The boiling temperature of water at sea level—212°—is increased in direct proportion to the number of particles dissolved in it. The amount of salt added in cooking is not enough to change the normal sea-level boiling point. With the addition of sugar, however, the boiling point is lowered appreciably. For boiling at high altitudes, see (I, 92).

WATER PURIFICATION

In using or storing water, be sure of two things: that the source from which you get it is uncontaminated, and that the vessels you store it in are sterile. The color of water has nothing to do with its purity. As disease germs are more often derived from animal than from vegetable matter, a brown swamp water may be purer than a blue lake water. ◗ If water has been exposed to radioactive fallout, do not use it. Water from wells and springs, if protected from surface contamination, should be safe from this hazard. For water storage in shelters, use plastic bottles or glass ones that are surrounded by and separated from each other by excelsior or packing. Inspect the stored water periodically and replace any that is cloudy. Allow for each person, for drinking, a minimum of 7 gallons for each 2-week period; and for personal cleanliness, another 7 gallons.

If you are in doubt as to the purity of water, treat it in one of the following ways:

I. Boil water vigorously 3 minutes. Boiled water tastes flat but can be improved in flavor if aerated by pouring it a number of times from one clean vessel to another.

II. Use water purification tablets in the dosage recommended on the label.

III. Add to ◗ clear water, allowing 8 drops per gallon, any household bleach that contains hypochlorite in 5.25% solution. The label should give you this information. ◗ If the water is cloudy, increase to 16 drops per gallon. ◗ In either case, stir and allow the water to stand 30 minutes after adding the hypochlorite. ◗ The water should have a distinct chlorine taste and odor. This is a sign of safety, and if you do not detect it by smell, add another dose of the hypochlorite and wait 15 minutes. If the chlorine odor is still not present, the hypochlorite may have weakened through age, and the water is not safe for storage or drinking.

IV. Add to clear water, allowing 12 drops per gallon, 2% tincture of iodine. Stir thoroughly before storing. ◗ To cloudy water, allow 24 drops for each gallon. Stir thoroughly before storing or drinking. This method is not recommended for persons with thyroid disturbances.

ACIDULATED WATER

I. To 1 quart water, add 1 tablespoon vinegar.

II. To 1 quart water, add 2 tablespoons vinegar or 3 tablespoons lemon juice (1 teaspoon salt).

III. To 1 quart water, add 1/2 cup wine.

IV. Also see Anti-Browning Solutions for Canning, 618, and for Freezing, 647.

ABOUT STOCKS

Antique dealers may respond hopefully to dusty bits in attics, but true cooks palpitate over even more curious oddments: mushroom and tomato skins, fowl carcasses, tender celery leaves, fish heads, knucklebones and chicken feet. These are just a few of the treasures for the stockpot—that magic source from which comes the telling character of the cuisine. The juices made and saved from meat and vegetable cookery are so important that in France they are called bases or **fonds.** You will note in the recipes for gravies, aspics, soups or sauces the insistent call for stocks. While these need not always be heavily reduced ones ◗ do experiment by tasting the wonderful difference when these liquids replace water. ◗ When stocks are specified in long-cooking recipes, they are always meat stocks, as vegetable and fish stocks deteriorate in flavor if simmered longer than 30 minutes.

You will want to store separately, refrigerated, and use very sparingly certain strongly flavored waters like cabbage, carrot, turnip and bean or those from starchy vegetables, if the stock is to be a clear one. And you will certainly reserve any light-fleshed fish and shellfish residues for use in fish dishes exclusively. Fish and vegetable stocks with vegetable oils are important in **au maigre** cooking, on those days when religious observance calls for meatless meals, as contrasted with **au gras** or meat—and meat-fat-based—cooking.

Like us, you may look askance at the liquids in which modern hams and tongues have been cooked, because of the chemicals now used in curing. If you use cooking waters from salt meat, even a preliminary blanching, (I, 106), may not reduce salt content sufficiently to allow its use in sauces. You will never, of course, want to use the cooking water from an "old" ham. But whether you are a purist who uses only beef-based stock with beef, and chicken with chicken, or whether you experiment with more complex combinations, for both nutrient values and taste dividends ♦ do make and save stocks.

MEAT STOCK MAKING

While we urge you to utilize the kitchen oddments described under Quick Household Stock, 173, we become daily more aware that the neatly packaged meats and vegetables most of us get at the supermarket give us a decreasing minimum of trimmings. The rabbits, old pheasants and hens that make for such picturesque reading in ancient stock recipes—fairly

thrusting the hunter and farmer laden with earthy bounty straight into the kitchen—have given way to a well-picked-over turkey carcass and a specially purchased **soup bunch** including celery stalks and leaves, carrots, green onions and parsley. But even these are worthwhile.

♦ Stock making is an exception to almost every other kind of cooking. Instead of calling for things young and tender ♦ remember that mature vegetables and meat from aged animals will be most flavorsome. Remember, too, that instead of making every effort to keep juices within the materials you are cooking, you want to extract and trap every vestige of flavor from them—in liquid form. So ♦ soaking in cold water and starting to cook in cold water—both of which methods draw juices—are the first steps to your goal; but have the ingredients to be cooked and the water at the same temperature at the onset of cooking. ♦ Bones are disjointed or crushed; meat is trimmed of excess fat and cut up; and vegetables, after cleaning, may even be ⚖ blended.

♦ In making dark stocks, browning a portion of the meat or roasting it until brown, but not scorched, will add flavor, but before proceeding, pour off any grease that develops. ♦ For a sturdy meat stock, allow only 2 cups of water to every cup of lean meat and bone. They may be used in about equal weights. When this much meat is used, only a few vegetables are needed to give flavor to the soup.

Bones, especially marrowbones and ones with gelatinous extractives, play a very important role in stock. But if a too large proportion of them is used, the stock becomes gluey and should be reserved for use in gravies and sauces. Raw and cooked bones should not be mixed if a clear stock is desired. Nor, for clear stock, should any starchy or very greasy foods be added to the stockpot. Starchy foods also tend to make the stock sour rapidly.

Essential to retaining the flavor of the extracted juices most is ▶ a steady low heat for the simmering of the brew. You may laugh at the following primitive suggestion. But it is our answer to the thinness of modern pots and the passing of that precious source of household heat, "the back of the stove," now found only in special equipment. ▶ If you do not have an asbestos pad to produce an evenly transmitted heat, get two or three bricks—depending on the size of your pot and the size of the heating area. Put them on your burner, set at low heat and place your soup pot on them, as shown in the sketch opposite. You need then have no worries about boiling over or about disturbing the long, steady simmering rhythm. Or, for a similar effect, use a double boiler. When choosing a heavy stockpot, avoid aluminum, as it may affect the clarity of the stock.

As the stock heats, quite a heavy scum rises to the surface. ▶ If a clear soup is wanted, it is imperative to skim this foamy albuminous material before the first half hour of cooking. After the last skimming, wipe the edge of the stockpot at the level of the soup. Some nutritionists advise against skimming stocks to be used for brown sauces.

Add whatever seasoning vegetables are called for and simmer the stock ▶ partially covered, with the lid at an angle, until you are sure you have extracted all the goodness from the ingredients—at least 2 hours, and as long as 12 if raw bones are used. To keep the stock clear, drain it, not by pouring, but by ladling. Or use a

stockpot with a spigot. Then strain the stock through 2 layers of cheesecloth that have been wrung out in water. Cool it ▶ uncovered. To cool quickly, place the stock in a tall container and partially immerse in cold water. Store it ▶ tightly covered and refrigerated. The grease will rise in a solid mass which is also a protective coating. Do not remove this until you are ready to reheat the stock for serving or use. For more about this coating, see About Drippings, 204.

Stocks keep 3 to 4 days refrigerated; for a longer period if frozen. The best practice is to bring them to a boil at the end of this period and cool partially before re-storing. It is also good practice to bring them to a boil if adding other pot liquors to them.

SEASONINGS FOR STOCKS AND SOUPS

These all-important ingredients ▶ should be added sparingly, about half an hour after the soup begins to simmer and the scum has been removed. The seasoning should be corrected again just before the soup is served.

▶ Never salt heavily at the beginning of stock making. The great reduction both in original cooking and in subsequent cooking—if the stock is used as an ingredient—makes it almost impossible to judge the amount you will need. And a little extra salt can so easily ruin your results. If stocks are stored, the salt and seasoning are apt to intensify, and if any wine is used in dishes made from stock, the salt flavor will be increased.

The discreet use of either fresh or dried herbs and spices is important. Use whole spices—peppercorns, allspice, cinnamon and coriander—and celery seeds and bay leaf, but not too much. Add mace, paprika and cayenne in the stingiest pinches. Be sure to use a Bouquet Garni, 253. For a quick soup, try a Chiffonade, 251. An onion stuck with two or three cloves is de rigueur, and, if available, add one or two leeks.

CLARIFYING STOCK

If you have followed carefully the directions in Meat Stock Making, 168, your product should be clear enough for most uses. But for extra-sparkling aspic, jellied consommé, or chaud-froid you may wish to clarify stock in one of two ways. Both are designed to remove cloudiness; the second method also strengthens flavor. ◗ Be sure the stock to be clarified has well degreased, and never let it boil.

I. Allow to each quart of broth 1 slightly beaten egg white and 1 crumpled shell. If the stock to be clarified has not been fully cooled and is still lukewarm, also add a few ice cubes for each quart. Stir the eggs and the ice into the soup well. Bring the soup very, very slowly ◗ without stirring, just to a simmer. As the soup heats, the egg brings to the top a heavy, crusty foam more than an inch thick. Do not skim this, but push it very gently away from one side of the pan. Through this small opening, you can watch the movement of the simmering—to make sure no true boiling takes place. Continue simmering 10 to 15 minutes. Move the pot carefully from the heat source

and let it stand 10 minutes to 1 hour. Wring out a cloth in hot water and suspend it, like a jelly bag, above a large pan. Again push the scummy crust to one side and ladle the soup carefully, straining it through the cloth. Cool ◗ uncovered. Store ◗ covered tightly and refrigerated.

II. This method of clarification produces a double-strength stock for consommé. Add to each quart of degreased stock 3 to 4 ounces of lean ground beef and 1 egg white and crumpled shell, and to the pot several uncooked fowl carcasses; and, if the stock is beef, fresh tomato skins. Some cooks also use a few vegetables. Beat these additions into the stock. Then ◗ very slowly bring the pot just to a simmer.

If the stock has boiled at any time during the process just described, the clarification is ruined. It will be necessary to start over again, proceeding as follows. After what should have been the simmering period in the second method, remove the pot from the heat and skim it. Allow the stock to cool to about 70°. Again add an egg white and a crumpled eggshell for each quart of stock. Then continue as for the first method above. Simmer up to 2 hours. Then remove the pot from the heat source and let it rest an hour or more. Ladle and strain it, as previously described. Cool ◗ uncovered. Store ◗ tightly covered and refrigerated.

REDUCING STOCKS OR GLAZES

Glazes are meat stocks cooked down very slowly, uncovered, until they have solidified and have formed a glutinous substance that will coat a spoon. Reduction usually involves condensing to about half the original amount of liquid. See Glazes and Glaçage, (I, 426). When we have the patience to make them, these overpoweringly strong stocks from meat and fowl are most valuable for seasoning and finishing. They ❀ freeze very well, too.

BROWN STOCK

I.
About 2 Quarts
◗ Please read About Stocks, 167.
Cut into pieces and brown in a 350° oven:

    6 lb. lean shin bones and
        marrow bones

Place them in a large stockpot with:

    4 quarts cold water

Bring slowly to a boil. ◗ Reduce heat and simmer, uncovered, about 30 minutes. Remove scum, see 170, and add:

    8 black peppercorns
    6 whole cloves
    1 bay leaf
    1 teaspoon thyme
    3 sprigs parsley
    1 large diced carrot
    3 ribs celery, diced
    1 cup drained canned or
        fresh tomatoes
    1 diced medium-sized onion
    1 diced small white turnip

Bring to a boil and then simmer, partly covered, at least 6 hours. Strain the stock. Cool uncovered, and refrigerate covered.

II.
About 3½ Cups
While Brown Stock I is more strongly flavored and clearer, do not scorn stocks made from cooked meats and bones. ◗ Please read About Stocks, 167.
Cut the meat from the bone. Place in a heavy stockpot:

    2 cups cooked lean meat and
        bones
    4 to 5 cups cold water

Bring the stock just to the boiling point, turn down the heat, and simmer, uncovered, 30 minutes. Remove the scum. Add:

    ¼ teaspoon salt
    1 cup chopped vegetables:
        carrots, turnips, celery,
        parsley, etc.
    1 small onion
    1 cup tomatoes
    ½ teaspoon sugar
    4 peppercorns
    ¼ teaspoon celery salt

Continue to simmer, partly covered, about 2 hours. Strain the stock and chill it. Remove the fat, reheat and season to taste before using.

LIGHT STOCK WITH VEAL

About 2 Quarts
◗ Please read About Stocks, 167.
Blanch 5 minutes, using method II, (I, 106):

    4 lb. veal knuckles or 3 lb.
        veal knuckles and 1 lb. beef

Drain, discard water, and add meat and bones to:

    4 quarts cold water

Bring slowly to a boil. ◗ Reduce the heat at once and simmer, uncovered, about ½ hour. Remove scum. Add:

    8 white peppercorns
    1 bay leaf
    1 teaspoon thyme
    6 whole cloves
    6 sprigs parsley
    1 diced medium-sized onion
    3 ribs celery, diced
    1 diced medium-sized carrot

Continue to simmer, partly covered, 2½ to 3 hours or until reduced by about half. Strain stock and ◗ cool uncovered. Refrigerate covered.

LIGHT STOCK FROM POULTRY

I. From Poultry Parts
About 2 Quarts
◗ Please read about soup stocks, 167.
Blanch 5 minutes, using method II,
(I, 106):

**4 lb. poultry backs, necks,
wings and feet**

Drain, discard water and bring the
poultry slowly to a boil in:

4 quarts cold water

◗ Reduce the heat at once and simmer, uncovered, about 30 minutes.
Add:

**8 white peppercorns
1 bay leaf
1 teaspoon thyme
6 whole cloves
6 sprigs parsley
1 diced medium-sized
     onion
3 ribs celery, diced
1 medium-sized diced carrot**

Remove the scum and continue to
simmer, partly covered, about 3
hours or until reduced by half. Strain
stock. Cool uncovered, and refrigerate covered.

II. From Chicken Feet
A jellied, not too flavorful, but economical base. Cover with boiling
water:

Chicken feet

Blanch them about 3 minutes. Drain.
Strip away the skin and discard.
Chop off the nails. Place the feet in a
pan and cover with:

Cold water

Bring to a boil and ◗ reduce heat at
once. Simmer, uncovered, about 30
minutes. Remove scum. Add:

Vegetables

as suggested under Fowl Stock I, below. Continue to simmer about 1½
hours, or use a ◉ pressure cooker, following directions in Quick Household

Stock, 173. Strain the stock and cool
uncovered. Refrigerate covered.

FOWL, RABBIT OR GAME
STOCK OR FUMET

When cold, this stock should solidify
sufficiently to make a good aspic
without additional gelatin.

I.   About 9 or 10 Cups
Put into a heavy pot:

**4 or 5 lb. cut-up fowl or
     rabbit
3 quarts cold water**

Bring to a boil and ◗ reduce heat at
once. Simmer uncovered, about 30
minutes. Remove scum. Add:

**5 celery ribs with leaves
½ bay leaf
½ cup chopped onions
½ cup chopped carrots
6 sprigs parsley**

Continue to simmer the stock for
about 2½ hours, partly covered.
Strain and season to taste. Cool uncovered, and refrigerate covered. Degrease before serving.

II.   1½ to 2½ Pints
The housewife frequently meets up
with the leavings of a party bird from
which a good stock can be made. Try
this simpler soup when you have leftover cooked chicken, duck or turkey.
Break into small pieces:

**1 cooked chicken, duck or
     turkey carcass**

Cover with:

4 to 6 cups water

The amount of liquid will depend on
the size or number of carcasses you
use. Bring slowly to a boil and ◗ reduce heat at once. Simmer, uncovered, about ½ hour. Remove scum.
Add:

**1 cup chopped celery with
     tender leaves**

1 large onion, sliced
¹/₂ cup chopped carrots
    Lettuce leaves
¹/₂ bay leaf
3 or 4 peppercorns
    Parsley
    A Bouquet Garni, 253

Continue to simmer, partly covered, 1 to 1¹/₂ hours. Strain and cool uncovered. Refrigerate covered. Degrease before serving.

○ QUICK HOUSEHOLD STOCK

A careful selection of refrigerator oddments can often produce enough valid ingredients to make up a flavorful stock to use as a reinforcer for soups—canned, dried and frozen—and in gravies and sauces. If cooked and uncooked meats are combined, a darker, cloudier stock results. Put into a pressure cooker and use in all:

1 cup nonfat meat, bone and
    vegetables, cooked and
    uncooked
1 to 1¹/₂ cups cold water

Use the smaller amount of water if you are short on meat. For vegetables, see Vegetable Stock Making, 174. ◗ Do not fill the pressure cooker more than half full. If raw meat and bone are included, add:

(2 tablespoons vinegar)

and cook the raw ingredients first for 10 minutes at 15 pounds pressure. ◗ Reduce pressure and add the cooked meats and the vegetables and cook about 10 minutes longer at 15 pounds pressure. Reduce pressure. Strain the stock and cool uncovered. Refrigerate covered.

FUMET OR FISH STOCK

About 3 Cups

Most useful for cooking *au maigre*. Combine the fumet with vegetables

and cream as a base for soup or use it in sauces or aspics. It will keep for several days, covered, in the refrigerator, or for several weeks frozen.

I. Place in a pan:

2¹/₂ cups cold water
¹/₂ cup chopped onions or
    shallots
¹/₄ cup chopped carrots
¹/₂ cup chopped celery
6 white peppercorns
3 or 4 cloves
    A Bouquet Garni, 253
    A twist of lemon rind
¹/₂ cup dry white wine or 2
    tablespoons lemon juice
1 to 1¹/₂ lb. washed lean fish
    bones, tails, skins,
    trimmings, and heads with
    the gills removed

The fish heads are particularly flavorful, but ◗ avoid trimmings from strong-flavored fish like mackerel, skate or mullet. Use salmon only for salmon sauce. Shells from crab, shrimp and lobster are delicious additions. Heat until the liquid begins to ◗ simmer, and continue simmering, uncovered, no longer than 15 minutes—or a bitter flavor may develop. Skim the surface to remove scum and foam. Add, at the last minute:

Any extra oyster or clam
    juices

Strain the stock and use in soups or sauces. To clarify fish fumet for aspic, proceed as for the first method of stock clarification, 170.

II. An emergency fish stock.
Combine and simmer, uncovered, until liquid is reduced to 2¹/₂ cups:

1 cup water
1 cup dry vermouth
1 cup bottled clam juice
2 diced celery ribs
1 diced small onion

 3 sprigs parsley
Strain before using.
 Season to taste

VEGETABLE STOCK MAKING

In making vegetable stock, your goal is to draw all the flavor out of the vegetable. Use 1 1/2 to 2 times as much water as vegetable. Prepare vegetables as you would for eating—wash, scrape or pare, as needed, and remove bruised or bad portions. Onions are the exception: the skins may be left on to give color to the stock.

◗ For quicker cooking and greater extraction, you may 𝕬 blend the vegetables before cooking. But it is very important to taste the vegetable liquors you reserve. They vary tremendously, depending on the age of the vegetable and whether the leaves are dark outer ones or light inner ones. Green celery tops, for instance, can become bitter through long cooking in a stock, while the tender yellowish leaves do not. Often, too, celery is so heavily sprayed with chemicals that the outer leaves and tops taste strongly enough of these absorbed flavors to carry over into foods. Nutritionists recommend the outer leaves of vegetables because of their greater vitamin content. Eat these raw in salads, where the bitterness is not accented, as it is in soups or stocks.

Also balance the amounts and kinds of vegetables with other stock flavors. The cooking liquors from white turnips, cabbage, cauliflower, broccoli and potatoes, used with discretion, may be a real asset to a borsch but a real calamity in chicken broth. We find water from peas or pea pods, except in pea soups, a deadening influence. Carrots and parsnips tend to oversweeten the pot. Tomatoes, unless just the skins are used, can make a consommé too acid and yet be just the touch you want in a vegetable soup or a sauce. Some vegetable juices, like those from leeks, watercress and asparagus, seem ever welcome. ◗ Use any of these liquids, whether from fresh, canned or frozen vegetables, if they taste good.

You may also purée leftover cooked vegetables as thickeners for soup.

There are several ways to bring up the flavor of soup vegetables. One is to sauté them gently in butter, see Consommé Brunoise, (I, 130). Another is to cook them in meat stocks.

Unlike the above ◗ when you add vegetables to soup as a garnish, the trick is not to soften them to the point where their cells break down and they release their juices, but to keep them full of flavor. However, if the vegetables you are using as a garnish are strong, like peppers or onions, blanch them first.

VEGETABLE STOCK

 About 1 Quart
Sauté:
 1/2 **cup finely chopped onions**
in:
 2 **tablespoons fat**
Add:
    A dash of white pepper
    A dash of cayenne
 1/2 **teaspoon salt**
    A Bouquet Garni, 253
 1/4 **cup each carrots, turnips, parsnips**
 2 **cups diced celery ribs and yellow leaves**
(1 **cup shredded lettuce)**
    (Mushroom or tomato skins)

Add enough:

Cold water

to cover. Bring to a boil, ◗ cover partially with a lid and simmer about 1½ hours or until the vegetables are very tender. Strain and chill. Degrease before using, if necessary. If you prefer a more colorful stock, add a small amount of:

Caramelized Sugar, 232

STOCK REINFORCERS

I. BEEF JUICE

This is another rich stock item. To make it, see Beef Tea, (I, 132).

II. BOUILLON AND CONSOMMÉ

These are both a great help. You may prefer canned bouillon—which is less sweet than canned consommé. Bouillon cubes and beef extracts, each diluted in ½ cup boiling liquid, are also useful.

III. CANNED, FROZEN AND DRIED SOUPS

Alone or combined with household stocks, these can produce very sophisticated results. Suggestions for their use appear in detail under Soups, Sauces, Aspics and Gravies.

IV. MILK AND CREAM

As a diluent, milk or cream is always preferable to plain water.

ABOUT COURT BOUILLON

Court bouillons are seasoned liquids which, as their name implies, are cooked only a short time. Their composition varies. They may simply be Acidulated Water, 167, acidulated water reinforced with braised or fresh vegetables, or even a hot marinade with oil.

They are not actual broths or stocks in themselves, but rather prototypes that may develop into them. Sometimes they are used only as a blanching or cooking medium. Then they are discarded, as in the cooking of vegetables, where their purpose is to preserve color in the vegetable or leach out undesirable flavors from it. Sometimes they are a liquid storage medium for food processed in them, as in Vegetables à la Grecque, (I, 285). Or they may be used as a hot marinade in which fish is soaked before cooking. And sometimes, as in the cooking of delicately flavored fish, they become—after the fish is drained from them—a Fumet or Fish Stock, 173.

COURT BOUILLON FOR FISH

2 Quarts

Use this for any fish that is to be poached or "boiled." For court bouillon for trout, see Truite au Bleu or Blue Trout, (I, 502).

Trim and clean:

3 lb. fish

and rub with:

Lemon juice

Meanwhile, in a large pan, bring to a boil:

2 quarts water

Add:

½ bay leaf
¼ cup chopped carrots
½ cup chopped celery
1 small onion stuck with 2 cloves
½ cup vinegar or 1 cup dry white wine
1 teaspoon salt
(Parsley or a Bouquet Garni, 253)

When the mixture is boiling, plunge the fish in and ♦ at once reduce the heat. Simmer the fish ♦ uncovered, 30 minutes or until tender. Drain and serve. You may keep and use this court bouillon for several days for poaching fish, but it should not be used in other soups, sauces and gravies, as is a fumet or fish stock.

COURT BOUILLON BLANC

For use in maintaining good color in variety meats and vegetables.

I. Allow to every:

    1 **quart boiling water**
    2 **tablespoons lemon juice**

Blend until smooth and add to the above:

    2 **tablespoons water**
    1 **tablespoon flour**
    (3 **tablespoons chopped suet**)

Add:

    Celery, carrot, leek, or an onion stuck with cloves

II. Or add the vegetables to a boiling mixture of:

    1/2 **water, seasoned with herbs**
    1/2 **milk**

Reduce to a simmer at once. The milk may curdle slightly, but this will not affect the food adversely.

ABOUT WINE AND SPIRITS FOR COOKING

There is no doubt that the occasional addition of wine—or of spirits and cordials—gives food a welcome new dimension. If yours is a wine-drinking household, you have probably always enjoyed cooking with "the butts." If wine is a stranger to your table, you may be hesitant about breaking open a new bottle for experimentation. When you do decide to take the plunge ♦ remember that the wine you choose need not be a very old or expensive one, but that it should at least be good enough to be drunk with relish for its own sake.

What kind of wine to use? The specific answer depends on the kind of food it is combined with; consult the list below. Start your purchasing with a dry white and a full-bodied red, and before you know it you will have developed a palate and a palette and will be well on the way to some strikingly colorful effects in a new medium. In general, however, keep wine away from very tart or very piquantly seasoned foods, unless you are using it as a Marinade, 180.

How much wine to use? That true sophisticate, Joseph Wechsberg, has observed: "*La cuisine alcoolisée* has no justification in serious cooking." ♦ Never add so much as to overbalance or drown out the characteristic flavor of the food itself. ♦ Count the wine as a part of any given sum total of liquid ingredients, not as an extra. A recipe for pot roast with wine may call for the addition of as much as a cup per pound. When you use it in such dishes, be sure it is warmed before adding, so as not to interrupt simmering. In meat or fowl recipes calling for both wine and salt pork, watch for too great saltiness. Season to taste ♦ at the end of cooking.

Fortified wine, 48, such as sherry and Madeira, is frequently used in dishes where a definite wine flavor is desirable; for example, to combat a too-fishy taste. Two tablespoons of fortified wine are equal in flavoring strength to about 1/2 cup of dry red or white table wine. Wines may be reduced to increase their flavoring power and to avoid overdilution in sauce-making; 1 cup of wine will reduce to about 1/4 cup in 10 minutes of uncovered cooking. In aspic recipes, each cup of liquid indicated may be replaced by 1 1/2 tablespoons fortified or 2 to 2 1/2 tablespoons ordinary wine, and the wine should be added after the gelatin is dissolved.

When to add wine? This question is a hotly disputed one. If a wine sauce is heated, it loses not only its alcoholic content but, if cooked too long, its flavor. Fortified wines are usually added shortly before serving. Add wine to a sauce only during those periods when the dish can be covered, whether marinating, cooking, storing or chilling. While you may boil wine to reduce it ◗ never raise the heat to above a simmer when cooking food in wine. If you aim at mellow penetration or at tenderizing, the time to add wine is at the onset of cooking. ◗ To avoid curdling or separation, wine should always be added beforehand in any recipes which include milk, cream, butter or eggs. The wine should be reduced slightly and the ingredients just mentioned as likely to curdle should be added off the heat. If the dish cannot be served at once, it may be kept warm in a double boiler ◗ over—not in—boiling water.

To achieve a pronounced wine flavor, swirl reduced wine into food at the very end of the cooking process, after it has been removed from the heat. One of our favorite practices is to add wine to a pan in which meat has been cooking, deglazing (I, 381) the pan juices and so building up a pleasant substitute for roux based gravy.

Spirits, liqueurs and cordials are most frequently used in flavoring desserts. Whiskey is becoming increasingly popular, but, except for desserts, do not use bourbon, as it is too sweet. A spectacular use of spirits in cooking is flambéing—sometimes done at midpoint in preparation and sometimes as a final flourish in the dining room. ◗ Flambéing is sure-fire only if the liquor to be ignited, as well as the food, is previously warmed, see (I, 108). To flambé fruits, see 112.

Exceptions not only prove the rule—they sometimes improve it. We list below certain time-tested combinations in wine cookery; but we encourage defiance and initiative.

For Soups: Cream sherry or semi-sweet white wines.

For Fish, Poultry and Eggs: Dry white wines; except, for Coq au Vin, dry red.

For Red Meat: Dry red wines or rosés.

For Pork, Veal, Lamb or Game: Red or white wines or rosés.

For Aspics and Wine Jellies: Any type—but red wines tend to lose their color. Brandy complements an aspic of game.

For Sauces: Dry or semisweet Bordeaux or Burgundy, champagne, Riesling, vermouth; see individual sauce recipes.

For Desserts: Sweet sherry, port, Madeira, Marsala, Tokay, muscatel, rum, liqueurs, cordials.

Beer and cider, as well as wine, have their own virtues in cooking, especially if the beer is flat and the cider hard, as their fermentative qualities help tenderize meats, doughs and batters. You will find them indicated in recipes where their use is appropriate.

ABOUT VINEGAR

Whether a vinegar is sharp, rich or mellow makes a tremendous difference in cooking. ◗ All vinegars are corrosive—with a 4% to 6% acidity—so be sure to mix pickled, vinaigretted or marinated foods in glass, enamel or stainless vessels. Keep away from copper, zinc, aluminum, and galvanized or iron ware. Be sure to store in glass with cork or noncorrodible tops.

Vinegars divide roughly into the following types:

DISTILLED WHITE VINEGAR

Based on dilute distilled alcohol fermented to a 4% acetic acid count. It is used in pickling when the pickle must remain light in color.

CIDER AND MALT-BASED VINEGARS

These are full-bodied and usually run between 5% and 6% acetic acid. Cider vinegar results from the fermentation of the juice of apples. Malt vinegars are the fermentations of an infusion of barley malt or cereals whose starch has been converted by malt.

WINE VINEGARS

These have about a 5% acetic acid content.

We have often admired the lovely, light quality of dressings based on Italian wine vinegar. A friend told us his secret lies in fermenting a homemade unpasteurized red wine, but not allowing it to reach the point of bitterness. If you don't want to bother with this process, a substitute is to dilute sharp vinegars with red or white wine. Wine vinegars "mother," forming a strange, wispy residue at the base of the bottle. As they are of uncertain strengths, they are not recommended for pickling. If you plan to make spiced vinegars in quantity for gifts, please profit by our experience and mix in small batches: spices are tricky, see 257.

HERB VINEGARS

Make these with any of the above vinegars. Use individual herbs like tarragon or burnet or develop your favorite herb combinations—allowing not more than 3 tablespoons fresh herb leaves per quart of vinegar. If garlic is used, crush it and leave it in the jar only 24 hours. The reason for not overloading the vinegar with vegetable matter is that its preservative strength may not be great enough to prevent botulism, 613. After 2 to 4 weeks of steeping, filter the vinegar, rebottle it in sterilized containers and keep tightly corked.

FRESH HERB VINEGAR

A quantity recipe that serves well for making gifts. Heat slowly to just below the boiling point:

> **3 gallons cider or white wine vinegar**

Combine:

> **2 dozen peppercorns**
> **1 dozen sliced shallots**
> **3/4 cup tarragon**
> **8 sprigs rosemary**
> **8 sprigs thyme**
> **4 branches winter savory**
> **1 sprig chervil**
> **1 well-cleaned, unpeeled, sliced celeriac root**
> **1/2 cup parsley**
> **1 sliced parsley root**

Bottle these ingredients. After 2 weeks, strain the vinegar through cheesecloth. Place in sterile bottles and cork tightly.

SPICED VINEGAR

An excellent, if deceptive, mixture. It tastes like a delicious blend of herbs, but it is flavored with spices whole or ground.

Combine, stir and heat slowly until just under the boiling point:

1/4 cup whole cloves
1/4 cup allspice
2 tablespoons mace
3 tablespoons celery seed
1/4 cup mustard seed
6 tablespoons whole black pepper
3 tablespoons turmeric
1/4 cup fresh or dried gingerroot
1 1/2 gallons cider vinegar
2 cups sugar

Place these ingredients in a covered noncorrodible container. Slice and add for 24 hours:

4 or more cloves garlic

Remove the garlic. Allow the other ingredients to steep 3 weeks. If ground spices are used, filter the vinegar before storing; otherwise strain and pour into sterile glass bottles. Cork tightly.

GARLIC VINEGAR

Heat to just below the boiling point:
1 cup vinegar
Cut into halves and add for 24 hours, then remove:
4 cloves garlic
Place the vinegar in a sterile glass bottle. Cork tightly. Use it in dressings or sauces.

QUICK HERB VINEGAR

About 1 Cup

Combine:
1 cup well-flavored vinegar: wine or cider
1 teaspoon dried crushed herbs: basil, tarragon, etc.

You may use this at once with salad oil. You may add 1/2 clove of garlic and fish it out within 24 hours. Shortly before serving, add:

2 tablespoons chopped parsley
1 tablespoon chopped chives

TARRAGON OR BURNET VINEGAR

About 2 Cups

Wash, then dry well:
1 1/2 tablespoons fresh tarragon or burnet leaves
Bruise them slightly and add them to:
2 cups warmed cider vinegar
2 whole cloves
1 skinned, halved clove garlic

Place these ingredients in a covered jar. After 24 hours, remove the garlic. After 2 weeks, strain and store the vinegar in sterile, well-corked bottles. This makes a strong infusion that may be diluted later with more vinegar.

RED RASPBERRY VINEGAR COCKAIGNE

Would you believe this makes a marvelously refreshing summer drink served over crushed ice? See (I, 40).
Put into a large enamel or stainless steel pan:
2 quarts ripe red raspberries
Cover them with:
1 quart cider vinegar
Let stand covered in a cool place about 48 hours. Then strain. Use this liquid to cover another:
2 quarts ripe red raspberries
Again, let stand 48 hours, then strain and measure the liquid into an enamel or stainless steel pan. Add an equal quantity, or slightly less, of:
Sugar
Bring to a boil and ♦ simmer 10 minutes. Skim and cool. Store in well-corked sterile bottles.

CHILI VINEGAR

You can make a really fiery French dressing with this. See also Chilis Preserved in Sherry, 683.

Steep:

1 oz. chilis

in:

1 pint vinegar

for 10 days. Shake daily. Then strain and bottle in sterilized containers.

GINGER VINEGAR

Combine:

1 cup cider vinegar
4 one-inch pieces dried
**   gingerroot**
2 tablespoons sugar

Strain after 1 week and bottle.

ABOUT MARINADES

Never underestimate the power of a marinade. These aromatic tenderizing liquids are easily abused. Every marinade contains varied amounts of seasonings, sometimes oil, and always an acid, ♦ so any marinade container should be of glazed ceramic, glass or an impervious metal like stainless steel. Less marinade is needed to cover if the meat is placed in a container just large enough to hold it. Use a wooden spoon to stir or turn the meat occasionally during the process.

Marinades are a means of spreading flavor by immersion. The soaking period may vary from only a few minutes to many hours. Stronger, spicier marinades may be devised to make bland food more interesting. But perhaps the most important function of a marinade is to tenderize tough foods. Sometimes marinades contain as one of their ingredients extract of papaya, a tenderizing agent.

Marinades may be cooked or un-cooked. The cooked ones more effectively impart their flavors to food, and are preferable if the soaking is to exceed 12 hours. The liquid should be cooked in advance and thoroughly chilled before the food is immersed. The amount of vinegar should be reduced slightly if meat is to be marinated longer than 24 hours.

The effects of marinating are hastened by higher temperatures, but so is the danger of bacterial activity. ♦ Refrigerate any foods in their marinade if the immersion period indicated is 1 hour or more.

Both cooked and uncooked marinades may be used in finishing sauces. So do not discard a marinade before deciding whether you want to incorporate it in your sauce. Poivrade Sauce, (I, 393), for venison is an example. And dishes such as Hasenpfeffer, (I, 662), and Sauerbraten, (I, 574), are cooked in the marinade, which is then converted into a proper sauce just before serving.

Allow about $1/2$ cup of marinade for every pound of food to be processed. Cubed meat is soaked just 2 to 3 hours; a whole 5- to 10-pound piece, overnight. Longer marination may be too pungent and may kill the flavor of the meat. Marinating 12 hours or more cuts the cooking time by one-third. In an emergency, try mixing oil and vinegar with packaged dried salad seasonings to achieve a quickly prepared marinade for meats or vegetables.

MARINADES FOR VEGETABLES

Marinated vegetables are usually served cold as hors d'oeuvre or salads. Suitable for the short-term marinating of vegetables are:

French Dressing, (I, 413),
seasoned with herbs

Ravigote Sauce, (I, 389)

See also Vegetables à la Grecque, (I, 285).

FISH OR LAMB MARINADE

Enough for 1 Pound Lamb Kebabs

I. Combine:

> 2 tablespoons lemon juice
> 1/4 cup olive oil
> 1 teaspoon salt
> 1/8 teaspoon pepper

Marinate the meat refrigerated and covered for 2 to 3 hours. Turn frequently.

II. Combine:

> 1/2 teaspoon turmeric
> 1/2 teaspoon powdered ginger
> 1 small pressed clove garlic
> 2 to 3 tablespoons lemon juice
> 1/2 teaspoon grated lemon rind

Toss the meat in this mixture, coating it thoroughly. Cover and refrigerate 2 hours.

III. Combine:

> 1/4 cup pineapple juice
> 2 teaspoons soy sauce
> 2 teaspoons lemon juice
> 1 minced clove garlic

Marinate the meat covered and refrigerated for 2 hours. Turn it frequently.

LAMB OR GAME MARINADE

About 2 Cups

For marinated leg of lamb. Combine:

> 1 cup dry red wine
> 1/4 cup lemon juice
> 1/2 cup olive oil
> 3 to 4 juniper berries or 2 or 3 sprigs rosemary
> A sprig of parsley
> A sprig of thyme

> 2 bay leaves
> 1 to 2 crushed cloves garlic
> A pinch of nutmeg
> 1 tablespoon sugar
> 1 teaspoon salt
> A dash of hot pepper sauce

Marinate 24 hours, covered and refrigerated.

YOGURT OR BUTTERMILK MARINADE

About 2 Cups

This marinade can subsequently be incorporated into a sauce.
Add to:

> 2 cups yogurt or buttermilk
> 2 pressed cloves garlic

Season to taste with:

> Salt and pepper or curry powder or cinnamon or ginger or cardamom

APRICOT OR SASSATIES MARINADE

Enough for 3 Pounds of Meat

Cook and purée:

> 1/2 lb. Dried Apricots, 119

Sauté until golden:

> 3 large sliced onions
> 1 minced clove garlic

in:

> 2 tablespoons butter

Add and cook for a minute longer:

> 1 tablespoon curry powder

Then add the apricot purée with:

> 1 tablespoon sugar
> 1/2 teaspoon salt
> 3 tablespoons vinegar
> A few grains cayenne
> 2 tablespoons lemon or lime juice

Bring to a boil, then remove from heat and cool before pouring over raw meat.

COOKED MARINADE FOR GAME

About 8 Cups

This is a cooked marinade that can be stored in the refrigerator and used as needed for venison, mutton or hare. Sauté a combination of:

    1 cup chopped celery
    1 cup chopped carrots
    1 cup chopped onions

in:

    1½ cups vegetable oil

until the onions are golden. Then add:

    3 cups vinegar
    2 cups water
    ½ cup coarsely chopped
        parsley
    3 bay leaves
    1 tablespoon thyme
    1 tablespoon basil
    1 tablespoon cloves
    1 tablespoon allspice berries
        A pinch of mace
    1 tablespoon crushed
        peppercorns
    6 crushed cloves garlic

Simmer for 1 hour. Strain and cool.

BEER MARINADE FOR BEEF OR PORK

I.   **2 Cups**

Combine:

    1½ cups flat beer
    ½ cup vegetable oil

stirring the oil in slowly. Then add:

    1 clove garlic
    2 tablespoons lemon juice
    1 tablespoon sugar
    1 teaspoon salt
    3 cloves

II.   **2 Cups**

More pungent.
Combine:

    1½ cups flat beer
    ½ teaspoon salt

    1 tablespoon dry mustard
    1 teaspoon ground ginger
    3 tablespoons soy sauce
    ⅛ teaspoon hot pepper
        sauce
    2 tablespoons sugar or
        honey
    4 tablespoons marmalade
    2 minced cloves garlic

PORK MARINADE

**Enough for 1 Pound of
Pork Chops**

Combine:

    4 tablespoons Chili Sauce,
        686
    3 tablespoons lemon juice
    1 tablespoon grated onion
    ¼ teaspoon dry mustard
    2 teaspoons Worcestershire
        Sauce, 688
    ½ teaspoon salt
    ¼ teaspoon paprika

MARINADE FOR CHICKEN

¾ Cup

Use for chicken to be broiled or grilled.
Combine:

    ¼ cup vegetable oil
    ½ cup dry white wine
    1 minced clove garlic
    1 finely chopped medium-
        sized onion
    ½ teaspoon celery salt
    ½ teaspoon salt
    ½ teaspoon coarsely ground
        black pepper
    ¼ teaspoon dried thyme,
        tarragon or rosemary

Mix well. Chill several hours in covered jar or dish. Shake well, then pour over the chicken pieces. Chill about 3 hours, turning pieces at least once. Baste during cooking with any excess marinade.

TERIYAKI MARINADE FOR CHICKEN AND STEAK

About 2¹/₂ Cups

For Shrimp Teriyaki, see (I, 463).
Combine and mix well:

- ¹/₂ **cup vegetable oil**
- 1 **cup soy sauce**
- 3 **tablespoons brown sugar**
- 3 **mashed cloves garlic**
- 1 **tablespoon grated fresh gingerroot**
- 2 **tablespoons sherry**

Marinate the meat 4 to 12 hours, refrigerated. Baste with the marinade during cooking.

ABOUT MILK AND CREAMS

"Drink your milk" has been a time-worn admonition at many an American family table, for the high food value of milk is an accepted fact. But nowadays many of our children almost automatically pour "down the hatch" considerably more than the 1¹/₂ to 2 pints they need daily—and thus cancel their appetite for other equally nourishing foods. Beware, incidentally, of assuming that chocolate milk is the nutritional equivalent of whole milk, see (I, 32).

Most adults, including the middle-aged and their seniors, are well aware of the value of milk in their diet and manage to ingest their daily pint, if not as a drink, in soups, sauces or puddings. Expectant mothers should have at least 3 glasses of milk a day and nursing mothers 4. Sometimes adults may prefer to substitute cheeses. But if they do, they must be sure to get adequate B vitamins in the rest of their diet, for in cheese-making, more B vitamins are lost in the whey than can be subsequently re-created in the final product.

Milk is as perishable as it is valuable. Everything possible should be done ◗ to keep it constantly refrigerated at about 40°; ◗ to protect it from sunlight, which robs it quickly of vitamin B content; and ◗ not to hold milks of any type longer than 3 days, refrigerated. Milks vary in color, even when the animals from which they are taken have all been pastured in the same fields, on the same fodder. The milk of Jersey cows will be yellower than that of Holsteins; Holstein milk, in turn, will be yellower than the almost chalk-white milks of ewes and goats. Yellow coloring reveals the presence of a provitamin A factor called carotene, which some humans can convert better than others into vitamin A, which is almost colorless.

◗ In this book the word milk means pasteurized, fluid, whole milk unless otherwise specified. Such milk contains about 87% water, 4% milkfat, 3% protein, 5% lactose or carbohydrate, and 1% ash, plus minerals and vitamins. Examine labels for the milk components you want or need, and be sure you are not getting "non-milks," 188.

PASTEURIZATION OF MILK AND CREAM

Milks sold in interstate commerce must by law be pasteurized, and most communities have enacted the same regulation for milk sold within their limits. Some people oppose pasteurization because of certain changes that occur in the milk as a result, such as losses of vitamin C and enzymatic changes affecting fermentation. But pasteurization, a mild, carefully controlled heating process, effectively halts many dreaded milk-borne diseases that the sanitary handling and certification of raw milk—no matter how scrupulously carried out—cannot always achieve.

Raw milk or cream may be pasteurized at home. Arrange empty, sterile, heatproof glass jars on a rack in a deep kettle. Allow an inch or two of headroom when you pour the raw milk or cream into the jars. Fill the kettle with water until it comes above the fill line of the milk in the jars. ♦ Put a sterile dairy thermometer in one of the jars. ♦ Heat the water and, when the thermometer registers 145°, hold the heat at that temperature 30 minutes. ♦ Cool the water rapidly until the milk is between 50° and 40°. ♦ Refrigerate, covered, at once.

If pasteurized milk develops an "off" or bitter flavor, it has been held too long after processing. Unpleasant flavor may also appear in milk when cows eat wild garlic or other strongly scented herbage. "Cowy" or cardboardy tastes are also due to improper feeding, and a fishy taste may be the result of processing in the presence of copper.

SCALDING MILK

Scalding is employed more often to hasten or improve a food process than to destroy bacteria. To a chemist, scalding is that point at which milk begins to come up to a light froth, just as it boils, around 212°. In practice, we rely on the age-old visual test for scalding, and in this book milk is scalded ♦ when tiny bubbles form around the edge of the pan and the milk reaches about 180°. Heating may be either over direct heat or in the top of a double boiler ♦ over—not in—boiling water. Before heating milk for scalding, it is a help in later cleaning to rinse out the pan with cold water.

ABOUT SWEET MILK

Milk is sold in many forms, some with added vitamins—especially D—to make its calcium and phosphorus more available to the body. For calorie count, see (I, 19). Much milk is "standardized," which simply means that it comes from a milk pool covering a wide area and has cream or skim milk added to make it conform to the prevailing legally required balance between these two elements. Each of the following labels indicates the legally defined composition of the respective type of milk.

WHOLE MILK

A fresh, fluid milk typically contains at least 3.25% milkfat, and at least 8.25% protein, lactose and minerals. A cream line forms above the milk when the fat particles rise. The cream is plainly evident if the milk remains undisturbed for some time.

HOMOGENIZED MILK

Also a fresh, fluid milk, with the same percentage of ingredients as whole milk. However, it has no cream line, as during preparation the fat particles are broken up so finely that they remain uniformly dispersed throughout. Its finer curd is more easily digested than that of whole milk. Processors appreciate homogenization because it allows them to mix older and newer milks without the telltale evidence of curdling which characterizes milks beginning to stale.

In cooking, fresh homogenized milk gives a different texture from that produced by whole milk: Sauces may be stiffer and fat separation greater; cornstarch puddings more granular. Soups, gravies, cooked cereals, scalloped potatoes and custards tend to curdle. These texture changes are not present, however, when homogenized milks are evaporated.

SKIM, NONFAT AND LOW-FAT MILK

Skim and nonfat milks have only 1/2% or less of milkfat but all the protein and mineral value of whole milk. However, these milks are deprived of the valuable fat-soluble vitamins A, D, E and K. In "fortified" skim and low-fat milks, nonfat dry milk solids and vitamins A and D are added. Other examples of partly skimmed fortified milks are the 1% or 2% milks. The percentages refer to the small amount of fat retained to keep flavor and texture similar to those of whole milk.

EVAPORATED MILK

A canned whole milk freed of 60% of its moisture content and containing not less than 7.5% milkfat. Reconstitute by adding 1/2 cup water to the same quantity of evaporated milk and use to replace 1 cup fresh whole milk in any recipes except those calling for rennet. Because it can be preserved during times of excess production, it is sometimes less expensive than whole milk. It has a slightly caramelized taste due to the processing. The cans, which come in 51/3-ounce and 13-ounce sizes, should be inverted every few weeks in storage to keep solids from settling. ♦ Do not hold condensed milk over 6 months before using. Once opened, the milk should be stored and treated as fresh milk. To make it flow easily from the can, punch two holes near the rim at opposite sides of the top. ♦ To whip, see Whipped Cream Substitute III, 187.

SWEETENED CONDENSED MILK

This process, used as early as Civil War days, reduces by about half the water content of milk and adds sugar. It contains not less than 8.5% milkfat. The 14-ounce can contains the equivalent of 2 1/2 cups milk and 8 tablespoons sugar. It too settles during storage. The can should be inverted about every 2 weeks and ♦ held not longer than 6 months before using. Once opened, the can should be refrigerated. Because of the high sugar content, the milk will keep somewhat longer after opening than will evaporated milk.

DRY MILK SOLIDS

These are pasteurized milk particles, air-dried to eliminate all but about 5% moisture. In whole dry milk form they contain not less than 26% milkfat, and in nonfat dry milk form about 1.5% milkfat. Milk solids should always be stored in a cool place. Once opened, it is best to refrigerate them in a lightproof, airtight container. Discard them if they acquire any rancid, tallowy, scorched or soapy flavor.

♦ Be aware that some markets are selling reconstituted milk on the same shelves with fresh milk, so read the labels carefully.

♦ To reconstitute whole or skim dry milk solids, follow package instructions; or use 3 to 4 tablespoons powdered milk to 1 cup of water—which will be slightly more than a cup of fresh whole or skim milk in volume, and its equivalent in nutrition. For the best flavor, reconstitute at least 2 hours in advance of use and refrigerate.

Dry milk solids are useful in enriching the diet, but they need special handling. They scorch easily, requiring lower cooking and baking temperatures. To avoid scorching gravies and sauces made with dry milk, use a double boiler or very low heat. In preparing sauces, do not add more than 3 tablespoons of milk solids to each cup of liquid. To avoid lumping, mix the milk solids first with the flour and then with the melted fat, off the heat, and then add the warm, but not hot, liquid gradually.

In cooked cereals, add 3 tablespoons dry milk solids to each 1/2 cup of the dry cereal—before cooking—then use the same amount of water or milk called for in the regular recipe.

For cocoas, custards and puddings, add 3 tablespoons dry milk solids for each cup of liquid called for in the recipe.

To substitute reconstituted dry skim milk in recipes requiring fresh whole milk, add about 2 teaspoons butter for each cup reconstituted dry skim milk.

In baking, mix dry milk solids with the flour ingredients, see Cornell Triple-Rich Formula, 301, but be careful never to add more than 1/4 cup of milk solids for each cup of flour, or the dough will have poor rising properties and the crumb will be too dense.

To whip nonfat dry milk, see Whipped Cream Substitutes, IV, 187.

ABOUT SWEET CREAMS

Cream is that fatty part of whole milk that slowly rises to the surface on standing. The longer the milk stands, the richer it gets—up to a point, as described below.

The following terms are used throughout this book:

HALF-AND-HALF OR CEREAL CREAM

A mixture of milk and cream, frequently homogenized, containing 10 1/2% to 18% milkfat, and often suggested as a drink in fattening diets.

LIGHT CREAM, COFFEE OR
TABLE CREAM

Contains between 18% and 30% milkfat, which may be skimmed off after whole milk has stood 12 hours or longer.

WHIPPING CREAM

This is skimmed from milk that has been standing 24 hours or longer. **Light whipping cream** has 30 to 36% milkfat. Cream containing 36% to 40% milkfat is referred to as **heavy cream**.

WHIPPED CREAM

Whipping cream must be at least a day old; it expands to twice its volume by the incorporation of air. To get the right texture, bowl, beaters and cream should all be ♦ chilled in a refrigerator at least 2 hours before whipping, so that the milkfat stays firm during whipping rather than becoming oily from the friction involved. ♦ In warm weather beat over ice, see illustration, (I, 187). If the cream is warmer than 45°, it may, on beating, quickly turn to butter. ♦ Never overwhip.

♦ To beat cream with an electric beater, turn to medium-high speed until the chilled cream begins to thicken, then lower the speed and watch like a hawk. ♦ Do not try to whip cream in a blender. We like our cream whipped just to the point where it falls in large globs and soft peaks, but still carries a gloss. This is a state almost comparable to the ▶ stiff, but not dry, of beaten egg white, 207. It is possible to use it in this desirably delicate state only if it is prepared the last split second before serving. If whipped cream is to be held for 24 hours or so, it sometimes is suggested that a small amount of gelatin be incorporated for stiffening, but we have never found this technique to be an advantage.

It does help, if the cream is to be flavored, to mix in a small quantity of confectioners' sugar, as the cornstarch in the sugar forms a stabilizer. For interesting ways to flavor whipped cream, see 449.

If whipped cream is to be used decoratively, bring it to the point where the cream molecules are about to become buttery. Should the cream really threaten to turn to butter, whip in 2 or more tablespoons of cream or evaporated milk and continue to beat. Cream at this stage may also be forced through a pastry tube for decorating. ▶ To freeze small decorative garnishes, shape them on foil. Freeze them uncovered on the foil, wrap when firm, and return to the freezer for future use.

CRÈME CHANTILLY

The French equivalent of our Sweetened Whipped Creams, 449. Unsweetened, it is called **Fleurette**. For Crème Fraîche, see 191.

WHIPPED CREAM SUBSTITUTES

First, let us say there are really no very satisfactory substitutes for whipped cream, but the following makeshifts are sometimes used. It is often wise to add vanilla, 1 teaspoon per cup, or one of the other flavors suggested in Sweetened Whipped Creams, 449–450, to mask the inferior flavor and texture of these substitutes.

I. If you allow light cream to stand refrigerated for 48 hours and skim it, the skimmed portion will sometimes—not always—whip. Handle as for whipped cream, above.

II. About 2 Cups

Soak:

> 1 or 1 1/2 teaspoons gelatin

depending on heaviness of cream desired, in:

> 2 tablespoons cold water or fruit juice

When it is clear, dissolve it well in:

> 1/2 cup scalded light cream

Add:

> 1 cup light cream
> 1 tablespoon confectioners' sugar

Refrigerate. Stir from time to time. During the early part of the 4 to 6 hours needed to chill properly, add:

> 1/2 teaspoon vanilla

Then beat as for whipped cream, about 5 to 7 minutes.

III. Evaporated milk whips to 3 times its volume. Chill for 12 hours:

> 1 can evaporated milk

For each 13-ounce can, add:

> 3 tablespoons lemon juice

Whip until stiff.

IV. About 1 3/4 Cups

Dissolve:

> 1/2 cup nonfat dry milk

in:

> 1/3 cup cold water

Chill. Whip until mixture stands in soft peaks. Add:

> 1 tablespoon lemon juice

Whip again until peaks are soft. Beat in lightly:

> 2 to 4 tablespoons sugar

Refrigerate until served.

FILLED MILK

There are innumerable varieties of this imitation milk sold under a plethora of trade names. Ninety-seven percent of these products are made of skim or nonfat dry milk products or of soy products, 192. The remainder are composed of either vegetable or coconut oil or a combination of the two. Filled milk has approximately the same texture and caloric value as whole milk, but is not its nutrient equivalent.

MILK AND CREAM SUBSTITUTIONS

Sometimes it is convenient to substitute milk for cream. But if the substitution is made for baking, a different texture will result—unless the fat content of the cream is compensated for. ♦ To substitute for 1 cup light cream, use 7/8 cup milk and 3 tablespoons butter. To substitute for 1 cup whipping cream, use 3/4 cup milk and 1/3 cup butter. This substitution, of course, will not whip.

SWEET AND SOUR MILK
SUBSTITUTIONS

If recipes for baking specify sour or buttermilk and only sweet milk is available, you may proceed as follows: interchange sweet milk and baking powder with sour milk and soda. ♦ Use the same amount of liquid as is called for in the recipe. ♦ To sour sweet milk, have it at 70°. Place in the bottom of a measuring cup:

    **1 tablespoon lemon juice or
    distilled white vinegar**

Then fill the cup with:

    **Fresh sweet milk or the
    equivalent amount of
    reconstituted evaporated or
    dried whole milk solids**

Stir and let the mixture stand about 5 minutes to clabber. **Clabber,** much like cultured buttermilk or yogurt, is milk that has soured to the stage of a firm curd but not to a separation of the whey. ♦ If the leaven is baking powder or soda, be sure that it is added to the dry, not the liquid, ingredients. Make the following adjustments: for every teaspoon baking powder indicated in the recipe, use 1/4 teaspoon baking soda plus 1/2 cup sour milk or buttermilk, or 1/4 teaspoon baking soda and 1/2 tablespoon vinegar or lemon juice plus enough sweet milk to make 1/2 cup. For other substitutions, see 292.

ABOUT SOUR AND FERMENTED MILKS AND CREAMS

The longevity of certain groups of Arabs, Bulgars and other eastern peoples is often attributed to their diet of sour and fermented milks. The friendly bacteria in these milks settle in the intestines, where they break down the milk sugar into lactic acid, and where some are reported to manufacture B vitamins and to stimulate beneficial growth in the intestinal flora.

Known by many names—**yogurt** from ewe's milk, **kumiss** from mare's milk, **kefir** from camel's milk—they are often today made from cow's milk inoculated with various bacilli that create differences in acidity, flavor and content. The best known are the rather acid *Lactobacillus bulgaricus* used in yogurt and *L. acidophilus*. When yeast cells are also present—as in kumiss and kefir—fermentation takes place, producing a mild alcoholic content as well. Starters for these milk products are available at drug and health food stores. They come with full directions for their use and often produce more stable results than inoculation with the already made up yogurt or kefir, which will have been exposed to airborne contaminants or whose bacillus count may have been weakened through pasteurization.

Soured milks and creams also play an important part in cooking. The presence of lactic acid gives them all a tenderer curd, and this in turn makes for a tenderer crumb in baking and a smoother texture in sauces. In sauces, too, they contribute a slightly acid flavor that is highly prized. In cooking ▶ be sure to add these milks and creams at the very last and off the heat or over very low heat, or they will curdle. Stir constantly but gently. And in bread making, don't scald; just heat until warm. In any sour cream recipes, use salt sparingly, as salting also tends to cause curdling. None of these soured milks freezes well.

Milks and creams may be allowed to sour naturally, but yogurt and today's commercial buttermilk are processed by means of specially introduced bacterial cultures. In this book, for reasons of safety, we recommend souring or fermenting only milks and creams that have been pasteurized—and for best results use only the freshest of such products.

BUTTERMILK

Originally this was the residue left after butter making. Today it is usually made from pasteurized skim milk and contains about 8.5% milk solids other than fat. A culture is added to develop flavor and to produce a heavier consistency than that of the skim milk from which it is made. Buttermilk differs nutritionally from skim milk mainly in its greater amount of lactic acid. As its protein

precipitate is in the form of a fine curd, it is also more quickly digested than skim milk. Commercial buttermilk frequently has added cream or butter particles. Try making buttermilk yourself.

Combine:

1 quart 70° to 80° skim milk
¹/₂ cup 70° cultured buttermilk
¹/₈ teaspoon salt

Stir well and cover. Let stand at 70° until clabbered. Stir until smooth. Refrigerate before serving. Store as for fresh milk. In recipes calling for sour milk, you may substitute buttermilk.

SOUR MILK

This is whole or skim milk that is allowed to sour naturally. ▶ It is good only if it results from unpasteurized or unscalded milk, because pasteurized or scalded milk will not sour, but simply spoil. Therefore, recipes which formerly called for sour milk now call for buttermilk. Or you may sour sweet milk still another way, see Sweet and Sour Milk Substitutions, 188.

YOGURT

Eastern yogurts are made with milk reduced by about one-third. Ours have the same milkfat percentage as the milk used. To make **yogurt cheese,** a substitute for sour cream, drip yogurt through cheesecloth in refrigerator 8 hours.

Like yeast, the activator in yogurt is a living organism sensitive to temperatures. For consistent results, test the milk with a cooking thermometer. Use milk from skim to half-and-half richness. Yogurt has the added idiosyncrasy that it doesn't care to be jostled while growing, so place all your equipment where you can leave it undisturbed. If you use one of the many electric devices for quick yogurt making, follow the directions carefully.

We make yogurt successfully, using either an insulated picnic cooler or an oven preheated to 100°. Have ready and keep warm a large sterile crock or enough sterile glass jars to receive the amount of milk you are preparing.

For the first batch, you will need a starter. Buy a jar of yogurt, get a small quantity from a friend, or buy a package of yogurt culture from a health food store. Heat a pint of milk to 180° or almost boiling. Cool it to between 105° and 110°. Stir into this milk very thoroughly a package of the culture or 2 to 3 tablespoons 70° yogurt. Do not allow the milk to register less than 106° when it is in the jars. Then place them in the warmed oven or insulated cooler. Cover the jars at once. The milk with the added yogurt should reach a custardy consistency in 3 to 4 hours; the milk with the yogurt culture may take 7 to 8 hours, depending on the weather. Check every half hour. Refrigerate when ready. Reserve from this first batch a small quantity to use for another batch. Preferably, yogurt should be not older than 5 days when used as a starter. Yogurt in general will keep 6 to 7 days.

You may wonder why so little starter is used and think that a little more will produce a better result. It won't. The bacillus, if crowded, gives a sour, watery product. But if the culture has sufficient *Lebensraum,* it will be rich, mild and creamy. If your yogurt does not coagulate within 8 hours, it may be because the temperature of the milk was too high and the culture was destroyed; or because your culture was

a poor one; or there were antibiotics in the milk. Always remember ♦ don't eat every drop of your recent batch. Keep 2 to 3 tablespoons to form the starter for the next one.

If you wish to incorporate fruit when making yogurt, have the warm sweetened crushed fruit in the bottom of the jars before adding the milk and yogurt. When using yogurt in cooking, ♦ fold it gently into the other ingredients, as beating breaks down its texture.

CULTURED OR DAIRY SOUR CREAM

Many uses for this smooth semiplastic cultured cream are suggested in this book. If your dairy does not carry it, try making it yourself. Place in a quart glass jar:

**1 cup pasteurized 20% or
   light cream**

♦ The cream must be at least this heavy and may be heavier—the heavier the better for the texture of the end product. Add:

**5 teaspoons cultured
   buttermilk**

The commercial type which is 1% acid and has carefully controlled bacteria is suggested rather than the less acid and less controlled homemade buttermilk. Cover the jar and shake these ingredients vigorously. Stir in:

**1 cup pasteurized 20% or
   light cream**

Cover the jar and allow this mixture to stand at 75° to 80° for 24 hours. The sour cream may then be used at once, although storage under refrigeration for another 24 hours makes a finer product. It does not freeze well. ♦ Add sour cream at the end of cooking processes over low heat and stir gently to avoid curdling. ♦ Do not overstir.

SOUR CREAM SUBSTITUTES

A low-calorie substitute to be used only in uncooked dressings or for garnish.

I. Mix for 2 or 3 seconds in a blender:

    1 tablespoon lime or lemon juice
    ¹/₃ cup buttermilk
    1 cup smooth cottage cheese

II. Mix:

    1 cup 70° evaporated milk

with:

    1 tablespoon vinegar

Allow the mixture to stand until it clabbers and thickens.

DEVONSHIRE OR CLOTTED CREAM

One of those regional specialties calling for certified unpasteurized cream. In winter, let fresh cream stand 12 hours; in summer, about 6 hours, in a heatproof dish. Then put the cream on to heat—the lower the heat, the better. It must never boil, as this will coagulate the albumen and ruin everything. When small rings or undulations form on the surface, the cream is sufficiently scalded. Remove at once from heat and store in a cold place at least 12 hours. Then skim the thick, clotted cream and serve it very cold as a garnish for berries.

CRÈME FRAÎCHE

A raw 30% cream which in France is allowed to mature until its flavor is nutty rather than acid. It tolerates higher temperatures in cooking than sour cream before it curdles. For a substitute, mix:

    1 cup whipping cream

    1 teaspoon cultured buttermilk

Heat to 85°. Let stand at a temperature between 60° and 85° until thickened. Stir gently and refrigerate until ready to use.

IMITATION MILK AND CREAM

Concocted in the laboratory of corn-syrup solids, vegetable fat, sodium caseinate or soybean protein, sugar, salt, chemical thickeners, colors, artificial flavors and water. The USDA is now working on a standard for this product. Read the labels with awareness.

ABOUT VEGETABLE AND NUT MILKS

These are all valuable nutritionally, but not comparable to animal milks, as their protein is of lower biologic value and their vitamin content is different.

NUT AND COCONUT MILKS

Almond and walnut milks have long been known to Europe's peasants. Our own Indians used hickory and pecan milk. These rather fragilely flavored milks, as well as coconut milk, are a great delicacy in sauces and puddings. ◗ They are as perishable as cow's milk and in storage and cooking should be treated like Coconut Milk, 244.

As nuts vary in weight, look up the measurement equivalent for almonds and blanch the nuts, if necessary. Then substitute accordingly in the following recipe. These milks are often used to substitute for milk in desserts, with sugar added. If using for sauces other than dessert sauces, you may combine them with stock as your liquid base.

ALMOND MILK

I. Blanch, 237:

⅔ **cup almonds**

Drain and discard the liquid. Cool the nuts. Remove skins. Pound the nuts in a mortar with:

¼ **cup sugar**

(1 tablespoon orange water)

If necessary, add from time to time a tablespoon or so of ice water to keep the nuts from becoming oily. When this mixture is quite smooth, stir in:

2 cups cold water

Cover and refrigerate about 2 hours. Strain the liquid through a cloth-lined sieve and refrigerate until ready to use.

II. 🔏 For a hurry-up version, use the above ingredients, but first blend the nuts with:

2 tablespoons water

(2 tablespoons orange water)

Proceed as above. Strain through a cloth-lined sieve. Refrigerate.

SOY MILK

About 4½ Cups

This milk can be substituted cup for cup for cooking and baking but should not be thought of as nutritionally equal to human milk or other animal milk. If used as a mainstay in infant feeding, it must be fortified. In Asia, drinks combined with soy milk are used to lure the populace from the consumption of nonnutrient cola drinks.

Soak 12 hours in:

Water to cover

½ **lb. dried soybeans:**

1¼ **cups**

After soaking, drain and rinse. 🔏 Purée beans in a blender with:

3 cups water

until the smooth consistency of whipped cream. In a 2-gallon heavy pot, have ready:

1 cup hot water

Add the blended soybean mixture and bring to a boil, stirring gently with a wooden spoon to avoid scorching. When foam suddenly rises, remove the pot from the heat. Have ready a large colander lined with a generous square of sterilized thin cotton muslin. Set the lined colander over a large bowl in the sink and pour the mixture into the colander. Tighten the cloth around the bean pulp—the *okara*—and press out as much milk as possible with the back of a spoon and, when cool enough, by wringing with the hands. Sprinkle over the pulp in the opened cloth:

¾ **cup warm water**

Press again and set aside the pulp, which is a nutritious filler used in Oriental dishes. Pour the milk into the cleaned 2-gallon pot and bring to a boil. ◗ Reduce the heat to low-medium and cook 10 minutes, stirring constantly to prevent sticking. ◗ The boiling is necessary to destroy the anti-nutritional factor trypsin. Cool the milk slightly and refrigerate before serving. ◗ But if you plan to make bean curd, use the milk at once while still hot, see following recipe.

TOFU OR SOYBEAN CURD

About 1½ Cups

Bean curd, a valuable complete-protein product of delicate cheeselike consistency, must be processed from the freshly made hot soy milk opposite. Have ready two 1-quart plastic freezer boxes of the type that nest. Perforate the bottom and lower portion of one with holes about ¼ inch in diameter as though on a 1-inch grid. For a solidifier, combine:

1 cup water

1½ **teaspoons epsom salts**

or calcium sulfate; or use

2²/₃ tablespoons lemon
juice, or 2¹/₄ tablespoons
cider vinegar

Heat to boiling point, then remove
from the heat:

4 cups soy milk, opposite
6 cups water

Add one-third cup of the solidifier
solution. Stir gently and completely.
Gently stir in another one-third cup
of solidifier, and cover the pot for 3
minutes to await the forming of the
curds. Sprinkle the remaining solution over the milk and gently stir the
surface. Cover for 3 minutes, or for 6
minutes if using epsom salts or calcium sulfate. If curds do not form
during this period, add:

(A little more dissolved
solidifier)

Line the perforated quart container
with a generous square of moist thin
muslin and place the container in the
sink. Gently ladle in the soy curd
mixture and fold the ends of the cloth
over the top. Partly fill the other plastic container with water to use as a 1-
pound weight. Let set 10 to 15
minutes or until the whey no longer
is expressed. The whey can be saved
for stock. Submerge in cold water the
perforated container with the wrapped
curd. ◗ Very gently unwrap the curd
under water and let it sit undisturbed
for 3 to 5 minutes to firm up. It is
highly perishable; store it refrigerated in water for only a few days. Use
squares of drained Tofu as a soup
garnish, in salads, or as a dressing,
(I, 429). For other suggestions, see
The Book of Tofu, by William Shurt-
leff and Akiko Aoyagi.

SOYBEAN PASTE OR
EXTENDER

This is used to stretch meat loaves and
patties. Thoroughly drain cooked soybeans, (I, 291), and when free from
moisture, rice or press through a colander. Store covered and refrigerated.
Season when adding to other foods.

ALTERNATE OR
ENGINEERED FOODS

These are defined by the USDA as
foods so processed that they improve
nutrition, reduce cost, provide ease of
preparation and improve stability.
They include **Textured Vegetable
Proteins,** a processor's answer to
prayer, a backpacker's delight and a
shopper's caveat. They are usually
extractions of soy, wheat or cottonseed, although rape and yellow mustard seed and peanuts, field peas and
beans, onions and oil seeds are all being experimented with. TVPs, as they
are called, can be tailored in many
forms, shapes, colors, textures and
tastes. Those micronutrients naturally
found in meat but lacking in TVPs
and considered critical are added to
TVPs to meet government specifications. Dehydrated TVPs are shelf-
stable. As spun protein they must be
kept frozen or refrigerated. In this so-
called analog form they are about
16% to 20% protein, 12% to 18% fat,
and 55% to 60% moisture.

Available separately or already
combined with foods, Textured Vegetable Proteins are used to replace
meat in patties up to 40%. In canned
and prepared foods they sometimes
replace meat altogether. In poultry
and seafood combinations they usually substitute for about 30% of the
flesh, in sausage products up to 30%
of the lean meat; and although they
are there, you may be unable to detect them in some salad dressings,
pizzas, jerky, dips, sandwich spreads,
cheeses, sour creams, yogurts and
bakery goods. Since they absorb and

retain moisture from the food with which they are combined and exude no fat during cooking, Textured Vegetable Proteins are shrinkproof.

Two other USDA-approved alternate foods are macaroni enriched with fortified protein, a blend of corn, soy and wheat with a fivefold increase over the protein in macaroni; and formulated grain-fruit products which provide both cereal and fruit-juice components and are recommended to be eaten with milk to round out the protein.

Other engineered foods which have been distributed worldwide are a corn-soya-milk blend—**CSM**—of 64% gelatinized cornmeal, 24% soya flour, 5% nonfat dry milk, and a 2% premix of minerals and vitamins. Enough oil may be added to bring the minimum required fat level up to 6%. CSM has a protein minimum of 20% and a PER or protein efficiency rate nearly equal to the 2.5 of casein. **WSB** is a wheat-soy blend with nutritional values equal to CSM. Some of these cereal milks are combined with whey.

ABOUT CHEESE

We heartily agree with Clifton Fadiman, who called cheese "milk's leap to immortality." A bit of cheese as garnish, topping or dessert not only enlivens the taste but often adds those necessary aminos which round out the protein content to make a dish nutritionally satisfying as well. Like eggs, cheeses are very heat-sensitive, and individual recipes reflect their special needs. But unlike eggs, many cheeses depend for their flavor and cooking quality on skillful aging.

In some climates certain hard cheeses are cellared for years like wines, but the American housewife

seldom has the kind of storage facilities to keep cheeses *à point*. Soft cheeses, like mozzarella and Petit Gervais, are best eaten the day they are made. Like wine, cheese is a substance constantly in the process of change. Cheeses do not freeze well, and refrigerate only on a short-term basis. They should be bought in small lots, brought to their peak of ripeness, and served promptly. There are special cheese-keepers with a cloche cover and a platform elevated above a vinegar-holding base. Another device for short-term preservation is to wrap cheese in cloths which have been wrung out in vinegar. Sometimes storing cheese in covered glass or enameled containers helps; and the separate wrapping of each variety of cheese under refrigeration is essential. The most drastic method—at which true turophiles wince—is to buy canned cheese; or to pot natural cheese in crocks, 543, with a sufficient addition of wine, brandy or kirsch to arrest enzymatic action.

MAKING UNRIPENED SOFT CHEESES

Time was when milk was allowed to rest in a warm place until clabbered, when the curds and whey were separated by draining through a cloth bag. When the curds were firm to the touch, they were refrigerated for several hours, after which they could be beaten with additional cream until smooth to make a cottage cheese or **Schmierkäse**.

Today, for safety reasons, the recipes that follow are given for ◗ pasteurized milk. But, because the milk is pasteurized, ◗ Cultured Buttermilk, 189, or Rennet, 236, must be added to all the recipes to activate the curdling process. In making these cheeses, use stainless steel, enamel or glazed crockery vessels. Have ready: a dairy thermometer, a long wooden spoon, a large pan, a rack, and a muslin sack or Chinese cap strainer, (I, 375), for dripping the cheese. A long stainless knife is needed for cutting the curd. If you make these soft cheeses often, make yourself a curd cutter of a stainless wire looped into an elongated "U" with the arms from 1 to 2 inches apart, and deep enough to fit the pan in which you develop the curd. Make up the recipes as described. When the curd is ready, cut through it with your curd cutter, lengthwise and crosswise of the pan as shown on 197. Then cut from the bottom of the pan horizontally at 1-inch intervals to form cheese curd cubes. Process as described in the recipe. ◗ Store these cheeses refrigerated. Do not keep more than 4 or 5 days. Serve garnished with:

> **Chopped chives, burnet,
> basil or tarragon
> Chopped olives or nuts**

Use as a base for hors d'oeuvre and dips and to fill tomato cases. Or use them in:

> **Cottage Cheese
> Dessert, 544
> Coeur à la Crème, 543**

COTTAGE CHEESE

About 1½ Pounds

Commercially available today is a confusing variety of cottage cheese. If called **creamed,** they have been recombined so as to have the approximate fat value of whole milk. If called **bakers'** or **hoop** cheese, they are, like cottage cheese, made of skimmed milk but are more acid because the curd is not washed. If called **farmer's** cheese, they may

have been made with whole milk, but the curd has been pressed sufficiently so the cheese may be sliced.
◗ Please read about Making Unripened Soft Cheeses, 194.
Have at 70° to 72°:

> **1 gallon pasteurized fresh
> skim milk**

If whole milk is used, the cream is lost in the whey. Stir in:

> **½ cup fresh cultured
> Buttermilk, 189**

Let this mixture stand at 70° to 75° temperature until clabbered, 12 to 14 hours. Cube the curd, as described previously. Let rest 10 minutes. Add:

> **2 quarts 98° to 100° water**

Set the pan on a rack in a larger pan of water and heat until the curd reaches 98° to 100°. Hold at this temperature, ◗ not higher, 30 minutes to 1 hour, stirring gently every 5 minutes—or the curd will toughen. Do not break the curd. As the whey is forced out, the curds will settle. ◗ To test for doneness, squeeze them. They should break clean between the fingers and, when pressed, should not leave a semifluid milky residue. Pour the curds and whey ◗ gently into a scalded sack or Chinese cap strainer. Rough handling can cause as much as a 20% loss in bulk. Rinse the curds with:

> **(Cold water)**

to minimize the acid flavor. Let drain in a cool place until whey ceases to drip; but the surface of the cheese should not become dry-looking. The cheese may then be combined with:

> **(Whipping cream)**

To serve or store, see Making Unripened Soft Cheeses, opposite.

RICH CREAM CHEESE

About 1½ Pounds

◗ Please read about Making Unripened Soft Cheeses, opposite.

Combine:

1 gallon fresh pasteurized whole milk
¹/₂ cup fresh cultured Buttermilk, 189

Dissolve thoroughly in:

¹/₄ cup cold water
¹/₄ to ¹/₂ household rennet tablet—available at dairy supply houses

and mix with the milk, which should be at 85°. ◗ Stir gently 10 minutes and begin to watch for any thickening. ◗ Stop stirring the moment you sense the thickening. Put the filled bowl you are using into a large one of warm water and maintain the milk at 80° to 85° until whey covers the surface and the curds break clean from the sides of the bowl when it is tipped. Cut into 1-inch curds as described above. Now put the curds and whey into a colander and, when nearly drained, press out any remaining whey. Reserve and chill the whey until you can skim off butterlike cream, and work it back into the curds. When the cheese is firm, add:

1¹/₂ teaspoons salt
(Additional seasoning)
(Additional cream)

To serve or store, see Unripened Soft Cheeses, 194.

MAKING SEMIHARD AND HARD CHEESES

There are many variations, but the harder and more frequently you press the cheese during processing, the firmer the cheese will become. Except for a cheese press, which can be improvised as described below, hard cheeses can be made with regular sterile household equipment suggested in making soft cheeses, 194. The process described below is for about 1¹/₂ pounds of cheese. If you

plan aging the cheese, you may want to make larger wheels to keep it from drying out.

Pour into a large stainless or enamel pan:

1 gallon milk: certified raw or homogenized, or goat's or ewe's milk

Add and stir in well:

3 tablespoons cultured Buttermilk, 189

If you have used goat's or ewe's milk, you may need to double the amount of buttermilk. Cover and let stand at 70° temperature at least 4 but not longer than 12 hours. If you care to color the cheese, use:

(A coloring tablet based on malt—available at dairy supply houses)

Dissolve the tablet well in:

2 tablespoons water

Now place the pan of prepared milk in a larger pan of hot water and slowly bring up the heat until the temperature of the milk is 86° F. If you are coloring the cheese, stir in the liquid color thoroughly at this time. While the milk is reaching the required temperature, prepare a coagulant by thoroughly dissolving:

1 household rennet tablet— available at dairy supply houses

in:

2 tablespoons cold water

Then allow the milk to reach 88° to 90° before stirring in the rennet solution. Continue stirring about 1 minute. Remove the pan from the hot water and allow the mixture to rest covered 30 minutes to 1 hour. If you have used certified raw milk or homogenized milk, it should coagulate during this period. If, however, you have used milk solids, it may be necessary to leave the pan immersed in the hot water, maintaining the 88° to

90° temperature of the milk. In either case, to test for the proper degree of coagulation, insert your well-washed finger in the curd at an angle as if to lift some out. If the curd breaks clean over your finger, it is ready for cutting.

Cut the curd lengthwise and crosswise at ¹/₂-inch intervals, as shown at right, using a long stainless steel curd cutter or a stainless knife. Then cut diagonally at a 45° angle as shown. These repeated cuts will divide the curd into small, even bits. If these cuts have been carefully made from the top to the bottom of the pan, there should be no large lumps when you start to work the curd with your hand. Should there be some, however, cut them with the curd cutter rather than smashing them between your fingers. Then for 15 minutes work the curd with one well-washed hand, in long slow movements around the edge and up through the curd from bottom to top, letting the portion you bring to the surface gently recede into the mass. The curds will begin to shrink in size as they separate from the yellowish whey. Cook the curd a second time by returning the pan to its hot water bath and bringing the developing curds and whey to 102° over a 20- to 30-minute period. Hold at 102° for 30 to 40 minutes longer. During this time stir gently with a long wooden spoon every 3 to 5 minutes. The curd is ready for firming when it forms a loose mass in your hand. The individual curds will be of wheat-grain size and the entire mass will look like eggs scrambled over too high heat. To firm the curd, remove the pan from the hot water and let the curds-and-whey mixture stand, covered, 1 hour. During this period, stir every 5 to 10 minutes.

To drain the curd, line a colander with several thicknesses of cheesecloth that are large enough so the ends hang well over the sides of the colander. Pour the curds and whey into the lined colander, and drain off the whey by lifting the curds in the cloth and rolling the mass from one side of the cloth to the other. Now set the drained curd, still in the cloth, in the colander again. You may work into it with your well-washed hand about:

(5 teaspoons salt)

Then form the curd into a ball within the cloth and squeeze out as much whey as possible. Knot the cheesecloth around the ball to form a bag you can hang from your sink faucet, and let the cheese drain another 20 minutes. Just before pressing, you may add flavoring such as:

**2 tablespoons caraway seed
or preserved chopped
peppers**

Now prepare to press the cheese. As pressing is a drippy business, confine your activities to the sink area. If you have no press, improvise one by cutting a 7- to 8-inch-deep rim from a plastic container about 4 to 5 inches in diameter. Place it on a plate, as shown below. This will form your mold. Line it with a 15-inch square of boiled muslin. After heaping the curds into the lined mold, fold the muslin over the top so all the curds are wrapped. You will also need two 1-inch-thick oak disks, just smaller in diameter than the mold, and bricks for weighting them down. First, put on one disk and weight it down with the bricks. As the whey rises and runs or is poured off and the curds contract, you may add the second disk under the bricks to allow pressure to continue.

During the next 20 minutes, increase the pressure by adding weight gradually with extra bricks. Be careful to add weight only to the point at which whey, and not curds, escapes. Then let the cheese rest in the press 12 to 24 hours in a cool place. Remove the cheese from the press, unfold the muslin and allow the cheese, again in a cool place, to air, unwrapped, on a rack from 12 to 36 hours. For an alternate way to make a mold and weight it, see 193.

This so-called new cheese is bland in flavor and suitable for cheese spread recipes, 71, and for some dessert cheeses, 542. To age this "new" cheese and allow it to develop its full flavor, dip it, when the exterior is absolutely dry, into a thin coat of melted paraffin, 663, to seal off the air and prevent mold. Refrigerate where the temperature drops no lower than 35°; or in the vegetable crisper of your refrigerator, where the temperature is about 40°. Temperatures above 55° cause the cheese to spoil. Date the wrapping with a masking-tape label. Flavor will de-

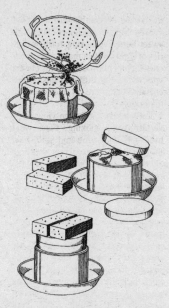

velop within 2 weeks to 2 months or longer. ◗ If you have used unpasteurized or uncertified milk, age the cheese at least 6 months before serving. If any surface mold has formed, wipe it off; or if it has penetrated the cheese, cut it out. Mold-ripened cheese like Roquefort and blue which show a mold pattern throughout are specially impregnated with a bacillus during aging and are beyond the skills of most household operations. **Cheddaring** of cheese calls for still another cooking operation and elaborate cutting and layering of the cheese, as well as aging up to 3 years for a sharp cheddar.

ABOUT FATS IN COOKING

Nothing reveals the quality of a cuisine so unmistakably as the fat on which it is based. Bacon arouses memories of our South, olive oil evokes Mediterranean cooking, and sweet butter will bring forth memories of fine meals in many places. Not only flavors but food textures change with the use of different fats, whose characteristics are as individual as their tastes.

Let's take a bird's-eye view of fat versatility in cooking. Fats, when used with discretion and skill, have the power to force flavor in foods and to envelop gluten strands and "shorten" them into a more tender structure. Fats also form the emulsifying agent in gravies and mayonnaise and can act as a preservative in coating some foods like Stocks, 169, and Terrines, (I, 629). And butter gives the most beautiful browning in breads and pastries.

Fats for cooking, of course, include both solid fats and liquid oils. ◗ Fats are solid at about 70°. ◗ Oils remain liquid at these temperatures, although they may become solidified when refrigerated. It is fashionable today to scorn fats for their calories and to fear "saturated" fats for their cholesterol. Examples of highly saturated fats are butter and the commercially hydrogenated shortenings. ◗ Other fats, like vegetable and nut oils, are polyunsaturated. Peanut and olive oils, called monounsaturated, are almost neutral in their effect. For more about the properties of fat, see (I, 8).

MEASURING BULK FATS

We suggest measuring bulk fats by the displacement method. If you want $1/2$ cup fat, fill the measuring cup half full of water. Put in fat until the water reaches the 1-cup calibration mark. Drain the cup of water. The amount of fat remaining in the container will then, of course, equal $1/2$ cup.

Some people prefer to use a set of measuring cups, especially for solid shortenings. These hold respectively $1/4$, $1/3$, $1/2$ and 1 whole cup. ◗ But if you use them, push the solid shortening down well into the bottom of these measures or a considerable space may be left, which will make your measurement inaccurate.

ABOUT BUTTER

◗ Most of the recipes in this book call for **sweet butter**—first-grade butter made from sweet cream with no added salt. Sometimes amounts vary in a single recipe. In such instances, the lesser amount will give you a palatable result, while the larger quantity may produce a superlative one.

If you wonder why the lovely, pale, delicately fragrant, waxy curl on your Paris breakfast tray is so good, here is one reason. The Brittany cows are fed and milked so the butter making can be coordinated with the first possible transportation to Paris, where it is served at once. So use butter promptly.

All butter is made from fresh or soured cream and by law must have a fat content of 80%. The remaining 20% is largely water, with some milk solids. Small amounts of salt are sometimes added for flavor or for preservative action. **Salt butter** may be purchased or made at home from sweet or soured cream and keeps longer than sweet butter. Without the addition of color, most butter would be very pale rather than the warm "butter yellow" to which we are accustomed.

Processed butter, often sold in bulk, is made by rechurning less desirable butter with fresh milk to remove unwanted odors or flavors.

The word "creamery" which sometimes appears on both sweet and salt butter packages is a hangover from the days when cream went to a place called a creamery to be processed. The word now carries no standard or type significance—it's just meant to be reassuring!

2 cups   ¹/₂ cup or 8 tablespoons

◗ All butter should be stored in the refrigerator and kept covered to prevent absorption of other food flavors. Two weeks is considered the maximum storage time for refrigerated butter.

❀ Freeze butter for no more than 6 months at 0° temperature. If no refrigeration is available, butter is best wrapped and kept in brine, 249, in a cool place.

◗ One pound of butter equals 2 cups, and when the pound is wrapped in quarters, each stick equals 8 tablespoons or ¹/₂ cup. See sketch above.

◗ To substitute butter for other fats, see 288. While these substitutions are satisfactory in cooking, flavor and nutritional factors are not necessarily similar. For seasoned butters, see (I, 396); for nut butters, see 71 and 240. For Clarified or Drawn Butter, see (I, 396).

CHURNED SWEET BUTTER

Butter is only as good as the cream from which it is made. Clean whole milk is kept cool and covered during separation, which takes about 24 hours by gravity. Skim the cream and pasteurize it, 183, stirring frequently to deter "skin" formation. Cool the cream at once to 50° or less and keep it at about 55° during the entire buttermaking process. Start to churn after 3 to 24 hours of chilling. Most of us have inadvertently turned small quantities of cream into butter in an electric beater or ⚙ blender, see below. We may even have imitated churning by flipping a jar of cream rhythmically in a figure-8 motion. For larger quantities, use a churn and keep the cream between 55° and 60°. A higher temperature will produce a greasy consistency; a lower one, a brittle, tallowy one. A gallon of cream should yield about 3 pounds of butter.

Using at least 30% cream, fill a sterile churn one-third to one-half full. Depending on the quantity you are churning, the butter should "make" within 15 to 40 minutes. We used to visit a neighbor while she churned and were amazed at how much slower the process was in threatening or stormy weather. The cream usually stays foamy during the first half of churning. By and by it will look like cornmeal mush. At this point, proceed cautiously. It then grows to corn-kernel size. Now, stop churning. Drain off and measure the buttermilk. Wash the butter twice, with as much 50° and 70° pure water as you have buttermilk.

If you salt the butter, use ²/₃ to 1 tablespoon salt to 1 pound butter, folding the salt into the butter with a wet paddle. Mold it in a form or fashion it into rolls, using a damp cloth.

Wrap it in parchment or foil. To store, see About Butter, 199.

♣ BLENDER SWEET BUTTER

Chill the blender. Blend at high speed about 15 seconds:

1 cup light Whipping Cream, 186

or until the cream coats the blades. Add:

½ cup ice water

Continue to blend at high speed until the butter rises to the surface. Strain off the butter. Press out any additional moisture; mold and chill. Keep the liquid residue to add to soup; it is not rich enough to substitute for buttermilk.

GELATIN-EXPANDED BUTTER

For dieters and frugal housewives, there are two types of expanded butter. Whipped butter, a commercial product, has had air or some inert gas incorporated to increase volume and ease of spreading. The other type is increased by the addition of gelatin.

About 2 Pounds

Soak until dissolved:

¼ cup gelatin

in:

2 cups milk

Heat the milk and gelatin in a double boiler ♦ over, not in, boiling water. Cut into pieces and put into a deep bowl to soften:

1 lb. butter

Warm the butter bowl over hot water. Whip the gelatin mixture gradually into the butter. Add to taste:

(Salt)

Should milk bubbles appear, continue beating until they go away. Pour the butter into molds and chill well before serving.

ABOUT BUTTER SHAPES

Such a delicious staple deserves attractive presentation. Try using a butter curler, shown in use on 202 on the right. It is our favorite because the light ⅛-inch-thick shells are such decorative assets and of just the right texture for spreading. Dip the curler into warm water before pulling it lightly over firm butter. If the butter is too cold, the curls will crack. Put the curls at once into cold water and store in the refrigerator until ready to drain and serve. The same procedure will keep intact the butter balls and molds described below.

Butter for molding is first cut into ½-inch-thick slices. It is most easily molded with a plunger, as shown lower center; or, if formed into balls, with a pair of corrugated wooden paddles, shown lower left. Use the paddles so their striations form a crisscross pattern. Then treat as for butter curls, above. Both types of utensil must be conditioned for use by pouring over them a generous stream of boiling water, then submerging them in ice water. For an easier if less elegant way to make butter balls, try melon ballers, which come in various sizes. Dip ballers first into hot water. Scoop out the butter ball and drop it into a dish of ice water. Serve the balls piled on a rack over ice in a sliding-domed covered dish, shown top left. Another attractive way to serve butter is in small clay crocks. Our favorite, second on the left, is one that fits into a base that holds ice water. You may decorate evenly cut squares of butter with tiny herb leaves or flowers, lightly pressed into the surface.

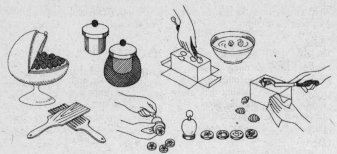

ABOUT VEGETABLE SHORTENINGS

Frequently these have a polyunsaturated-oil base—soybean, corn, cottonseed, peanut—refined, deodorized and
▶ hydrogenated. This process, which adds hydrogen, solidifies the polyunsaturated vegetable oils, absorbing the oxygen in their free fatty acids and converting them to saturated fats. Often these oils also have some added animal fats or saturated vegetable fats such as coconut.

There may also be minute additions of emulsifiers and mono- and diglyceride fats. These and the air incorporated into them make these bland shortenings technically superior for baking: they add a greater volume than that achieved with other solid fats like butter, and they create a softer, spongier texture. If color has been added to any of these products, the label so states.

▶ Vegetable shortening may be stored covered in a tin at 70° over long periods.

▶ To substitute solid shortening for butter, replace measure for measure, as the water in the butter compensates for the air in the shortening.
▶ But, if substituting weight for weight, use 15% to 20% less shortening than butter.

ABOUT MARGARINES

Margarines, like butter, must by law contain 80% fat—the rest being water, milk solids and salt. Almost all margarines are enriched also with added vitamins and color, to try to make them comparable to butter. Margarines today are usually emulsions of milk and refined vegetable oils, some of which may be hydrogenated. Also, some may have added animal fats. Read the label for this information.

▶ Margarines, because of their similar moisture content, may be substituted for butter, weight for weight or measure for measure. They produce textures somewhat different from butter in both cooking and baking and lack the desirable butter flavor. They are perishable and must be kept covered, under refrigeration.

ABOUT OILS

Vegetable oils are pressed from various seeds, fruits and nuts. Nutrients are best retained by cold press processes. Among the oil sources are corn, cottonseed, olive, soybean, sesame, safflower, sunflower and peanut. There are also such nut oils as walnut, hickory and beechnut, which are better used for salad dressings than for cooking, as they break down under high heat.

After being pressed, the oils are refined, bleached and deodorized so thoroughly that, except for olive, the end products are rarely distinguishable one from the other by flavor or odor; but in cooking they differ greatly in their smoking points. Safflower, soybean, cottonseed and corn oil have higher smoking points than peanut and sesame oils. Soybean oil is not recommended for deep-fat frying, as it foams. Olive oil, the lowest, ranges around 400°.

Most oils for salad are further treated to remove cloudiness at refrigerator temperatures. Oils should not be held too long at 70° even if tightly closed and in dark bottles. Most of them remain in a liquid state under refrigeration. Olive oil, which becomes semisolid when refrigerated, should be allowed to stand at 70° to return to a liquid condition before using.

Olive oils are like wines in the way their flavors are affected by the soils in which they are grown. Greek, Spanish, Italian—try them all to find your favorite. Olive oil is cheaper by the gallon, but, as it is susceptible to rancidity—especially the cold-press type—when exposed to light and air, decant it into smaller containers. Use one and keep the other resealed bottles in a cool, dark place. For further discussion of the value of oils in the diet, see (I, 8).

As oils are 100% fat, they ▶ must be reduced by 15% to 20% when substituted for butter, either by weight or by measure. However, there are additional complications when substituting them for solid fats, especially in baking, see 429. So in this book ▶ when oil is used in baking recipes, it is specifically indicated and the

proper amounts and procedures are given.

ABOUT LARD

Lard, which is fat rendered from pork, is a softer, oilier fat than butter, margarine or the other solid shortenings. **Leaf lard**—whether bought or home-rendered—is a definitely superior type. It comes from the layered fat around the kidneys, rather than from trimmings and incidental fatty areas. Due to the more crystalline structure of this lard, it cuts into flour to create a flakier texture in biscuits and crusts, although this same crystalline character handicaps it for cake baking. This is less true for those lards which have been hydrogenated, refined and emulsified. Ordinary lards are offered in bulk or package form. ▶ All lards should be stored in covered containers in a cool place, preferably the refrigerator.

▶ To substitute lard for butter in cooking, use 15% to 20% less lard.

ABOUT POULTRY FATS

Fats from chicken, turkeys, ducks and geese, whether home or commercially rendered, are highly regarded for dietary reasons. When rendered from the leaf or cavity fat, they are firm, bland and light in color. From sources such as skimmed broth and other cooking, they are likely to be soft, grainy and darker in color. ▶ Store them covered in the refrigerator.

▶ To substitute, use $3/4$ cup clarified poultry fat to 1 cup butter.

ABOUT PORK FAT

This is used in both fresh and salted form. Salt pork, which comes from the flank, is used to line Pâtés, (I, 629);

for Lardoons, (I, 551); and for Barding, (I, 511). Fresh pork fat, especially the kidney fat, is used as an ingredient in farces and sausages and in pâté mixtures. ♦ To remove excess salt from salt pork, see below.

ABOUT DRIPPINGS

These are fats that are rendered in the process of cooking fat meats. When making gravies, they are all desirable in reinforcing the flavors of the meats from which they come, although lamb and mutton should be used with great discretion. Bacon and pork fats are often stored separately for use in corn breads and meat pie crusts and for flavoring other dishes where salt pork may be called for. Other fats may be mixed together for storage. ♦ All these fats should be clarified, as described below, before storage in the refrigerator, to improve their keeping qualities. The natural desire to keep a container handy at the back of the stove to receive and reuse these drippings needs to be curbed. Exposed to varying degrees of warmth, these are subject to quick spoilage.

♦ To substitute drippings for butter, use 15% to 20% less drippings.

RENDERING OR TRYING OUT FATS

Trying out or rendering solid fats such as chicken, duck, suet and lard improves the keeping quality by removing all connective tissue, possible impurities and moisture. Dice the fat and heat it ♦ very slowly in a heavy pan with a small quantity of water. You may speed up this process by pressing the fat with the back of a slotted spoon or a potato masher. When the fat is liquid and still fairly

warm, strain it through cheesecloth and store it ♦ refrigerated. The browned connective tissues in the strainer—known as **cracklings**—may be kept for flavoring.

CLARIFYING FATS

To clarify fats that have been used in frying and to rid them of burned food particles and other impurities ♦ heat them slowly. You may add to the fat during this heating 4 to 5 slices of potato per cup of fat to help absorb unwanted flavors. When the potato is quite brown, strain the fat while still warm through cheesecloth. ♦ Store refrigerated. To clarify butter, see (I, 396).

REMOVING EXCESS SALT FROM FATS

To remove excess salt from bacon or salt pork, parblanch it before use for larding, (I, 550), or in delicate braises and ragoûts. Put it in a heavy pan. Cover it with ♦ cold water. Bring the water slowly to a boil and ♦ simmer uncovered 3 to 10 minutes. Allow the longer time if the dice are as big as $1 \times 1 \times \frac{1}{2}$ inch. Drain and use.

To remove salt from cooking butter, heat it slowly to avoid browning it. Skim it. Allow it to cool in the pan and remove the fat cake. Any sediment and moisture should be in the bottom of the pan. Butter so clarified is used in a number of ways, especially to seal off potted meats and in cooking where a slower browning is wanted, as for boned chicken.

ABOUT EGGS

Nothing stimulates the practiced cook's imagination or the nutritionist's enthusiasm like a good fresh egg, for eggs contain all the balanced nutrients from which a complete organism develops.

Eggs can transform cake doughs by providing a structural framework for leaven, can thicken custards and make them smooth, can tenderize timbales and produce fine-grained ice creams. They bind gravies and mayonnaise, clarify or enrich soups, glaze rolls, insulate pie doughs against sogginess, create glorious meringues and soufflés, and make ideal luncheon and emergency fare.

Because fresh eggs do all these things better than old eggs and because there is no comparison in taste and texture between the two, ◗ always buy the very best quality you can find. It doesn't matter if their yolks are light or dark or if their shells are white or brown—as long as the shells are not shiny. While there is no test, except tasting, for good flavor, ◗ the relative freshness of eggs may be determined by placing them in a bowl of cold water. Those that float are not usable. Unshelled onto a plate as shown at right ◗ a truly fresh egg has a yolk that domes up and stays up, and a thick and translucent white, containing a ropelike strand of material called chalaza which anchors the yoke in place. This is usable, as is the small dark fleck which indicates that the egg has been fertilized. Remove the fleck only if using the egg in a light-colored sauce or confection.

Strange as it may seem after stressing the purchase of fresh eggs, we now tack on an amendment. ◗ Do not use eggs fresher than three days old for hard-cooked eggs or for beating and baking. If you do, hard-cooked eggs will turn greenish and become difficult to peel, and cakes may fail to

rise properly because the eggs will not beat to the proper volume.

◗ Never use a doubtful egg with any odor or discoloration, especially one that is cracked: here is where salmonella can develop, see (I, 550).

Eggs should really be bought and measured by weight, but tradition is against this sensible approach. ◗ We assume in this book that you are using 2-ounce eggs. These are known in the trade as "large." They should carry a Grade A stamp as well as the date of grading. If in doubt about size, weigh or measure them. The yolk of a 2-ounce egg is just about 1 tablespoon plus a teaspoon; the white, about 2 tablespoons. For more equivalents, see 290 and 291. To realize how great a difference egg size has on volume, notice below that two large eggs give you about half a cup, but it takes three medium eggs to fill that same half-cup. When you decrease a recipe and want to use only part of an egg, beat the egg slightly and measure about 1 1/2 tablespoons for half an egg and about 1 tablespoon for one-third.

Don't expect the same texture or flavor from eggs of other fowl—from lark to ostrich; one of the latter, by the way, will serve 24 for brunch. In using off-beat eggs be very sure of freshness.

✳ To freeze and thaw eggs, see 654. To preserve eggs, see 634.

DRIED EGGS

When fresh eggs are not available, dried eggs are a convenience, but they are not an economy. Because of bacterial dangers, they must always be used in recipes that call for thorough cooking, unless a large percentage of acid is indicated. Packaged dried eggs should be stored at 70° and, if opened, should be refrigerated in a tightly lidded glass container. To reconstitute the equivalent of 3 fresh eggs, sift 1/2 cup dried whole egg powder over 1/2 cup water. Whip until smooth. To substitute for 1 egg, use 2 1/2 tablespoons sifted dry egg powder to 2 1/2 tablespoons water. Beat until smooth. ▶ Use either of these mixtures within five minutes after combining. You may prefer to add the egg powder to the dry ingredients, and the water to the rest of the liquid called for in the recipe.

COOKING EGGS

It is possible, on a hot summer day, "they" say, to fry an egg on the sidewalk. We do not recommend this particular extravagance; we mention it to remind you that eggs cook quickly over any kind of heat—beginning to thicken at 144°.

Sometimes, even when eggs are cooking in a double boiler ▶ over—not in—boiling water, the heat of the pan will cause them to curdle. Be doubly careful then ▶ with all egg dishes, not to use excessive heat and not to prolong the cooking period. Should you suspect you have done either of these things, dump the egg mixture at once into a cold dish and beat vigorously, or add a tablespoon of chilled cream. You may thus save the mixture from curdling.

Only prior precautions, however, will produce smooth baked custard dishes. For, once the protein of the egg has shrunk, it can no longer hold moisture in suspension, and the results are bound to be watery. If you are combining eggs with a hot mixture, condition them first by adding a small quantity of the hot mixture to the beaten eggs. Then add the eggs to the remaining hot mixture. Often, too, at this point in egg cookery—if you are preparing a soufflé base or thickening soup or a sauce with yolks—there is enough stored heat in the pan to do the necessary cooking.

If you are going to cook an egg yolk and sugar mixture, beat the eggs, add the sugar, and continue to beat until the mixture runs in a broad ribbon from the side of the spoon. When this condition has been reached, the eggs will cook without graining. In preparing soft-cooked eggs, the use of an egg-timer, shown 205, is a safeguard against overcooking.

Now, armed with two more secrets, you can expect real magic from the rich, complete and tasty protein that is tidily packed inside an eggshell. For more details about the nutritive value of eggs, see (I, 4). In baking and in making omelets and scrambled eggs, remember that eggs will give better texture and volume if they are about 65° to 75° at the outset. Also remember that because egg yolk is almost one-third fat, you can count on some slight thickening action as eggs cool in a pudding or sauce.

BEATING EGGS

▶ To beat whole eggs to their greatest volume, have them at 65° to 75°. Before adding them to batters and doughs, beat whole eggs and yolks vigorously—unless otherwise directed in the recipe—until they are light in color and texture.

For some recipes, whole eggs and yolks profit by as much as 5 minutes or more of beating in the electric mixer and will increase up to six times their original volume.

To describe the beating of egg whites is almost as cheeky as advising how to lead a happy life. But, because the success of a dish may rest entirely on this operation, we go into it in some detail. To get the greatest volume ◗ see that the egg whites are 65° to 75° and properly separated. We have already referred to the bride who couldn't boil an egg. But there are plenty of housewives who can't even break one. Here's how. Have 3 bowls ready, as sketched. Holding an egg in one hand, tap the center of the side of the egg lightly, yet sharply, on the edge of one of the bowls—making an even, crosswise break. Then take the egg in both hands with the break on the upper side. Hold it over the center of a small bowl and tip it so that the wider end is down. Hold the edges of the break with the thumbs. Widen the break by pulling the edges apart until the eggshell is broken into halves. As you do this, some of the egg white flows into the bowl underneath. The yolk and the rest of the egg white will remain in the lower half of the shell. Now pour the remaining egg back and forth from one half-shell to the other, let-

ting some more of the white flow into the bowl each time until only the yolk remains in the shell. During this shifting process, you will be able to tell quickly, with each egg in turn, if there is any discoloration or off-odor. You can discard the dubious egg before it is put with the yolks on the left or with the whites in the large bowl on the right.

Should the yolk shatter during breaking, you can try to remove particles from the white by inserting the corner of a paper towel moistened in cold water and making the yolk adhere to it. Should you fail to clear the yolk entirely from the white, keep that egg for another use, because the slightest fat from the yolk will lessen the volume of the beaten whites and perceptibly change the texture.

◗ Choose a large deep bowl in which to beat, shaped as sketched on the right, below. Be sure it is not aluminum, which will gray the eggs; or plastic, which in spite of careful washing may retain a slight film of grease, deterring volume development. The French dote on copper. But if cream of tartar is used to give a more stable and tender foam, the acid present will turn the eggs greenish in a copper bowl.

In recipes for meringues and in some cakes, a portion of the sugar, about 1 teaspoon per egg, is beaten into the egg whites when they are foamy. Although this reduces volume

slightly and means a longer beating period, it does give a much more up-standing foam.

The lightness of the beating stroke, plus the thinness of the wire whisk used, also make an appreciable difference in building up the air capacity of egg-white cells. ♦ Choose as a beater a long many-thin-wired whisk, as shown. ♦ Be sure that bowl, beater and scraper are absolutely free of grease, but if made of plastic the equipment may not be greaseproof. To clean them, use a detergent or a combination of lemon juice and vinegar. Rinse and dry carefully.

If you are going to use the whites in baking, have the oven preheated. Start beating only when all other ingredients are mixed and ready. Be prepared to give about 300 strokes in 2 minutes to beat 2 egg whites. You can expect $2^{1}/_{2}$ to 4 times the volume you start with. Begin slowly and lightly with a very relaxed wrist motion and beat steadily until the egg whites lose their yellowish translucency. They will become foamy. Then gradually increase the beating tempo. Beat without stopping ♦ until the whites are both airy and glossy and stand in peaks that are firm, but still soft and elastic, see 207.

From start to finish, there should be no stopping until that state is reached that is best described as ♦ stiff, but not dry. Another test for readiness is the rate of flow when the bowl is tipped. Some cooks use the inverted bowl test in which the whites cling dramatically to the bottom of the upside-down bowl. Usually, when this is possible, the eggs have been beaten a trifle too long and are as a consequence too dry. Although they may have greater volume, their cells will not stretch to capacity in baking without breaking

down. If using an electric mixer, follow the manufacturer's directions. We do not recommend the use of a blender for beating egg whites.

Folding in egg whites should always be a manual operation rather than a mechanical one, since it is essential again to retain as much air in the whites as possible. ♦ Work both quickly and gently. Add the heavier mixture to the lighter one. Then combine the two substances with two separate movements. Various special tools, like wire "incorporators" and spatulas, have been suggested for this process, but nothing can compare for efficiency with the human hand. First use a sharp, clean action, as though cutting a cake. Then, with a lifting motion, envelop the whites by bringing the heavier substance up from the bottom of the bowl. Repeat these slicing and lifting motions alternately, turning the bowl as you work, trying meanwhile not to break down the air in the beaten whites.

STORING EGGS

The storage of eggs is not difficult if you follow a few simple rules. ♦ Whether from nest or market ♦ eggs should not be washed until ready for use, as they are covered with a soluble film which protects the porous shell against bacterial entry. ♦ If there is no special storage area for them, place eggs still in their carton in the refrigerator. ♦ Raw eggs in the shell and foods containing eggs—like mayonnaise and custards in which the eggs are raw or only slightly cooked—should be kept covered, under refrigeration, and away from strong-smelling foods, as they absorb odors easily.

To store egg whites in the refrigerator, cover them closely and do not keep them longer than 4 days. Then ◗ use them only in recipes that call for cooking. To store unbroken egg yolks, cover them first with water, which you then drain off before using. Cover the storage dish before refrigerating. Yolks may be stored uncooked up to 4 days, or for a few days longer if poached in water until firm. Then ◗ they should only be used in recipes that call for cooking. If poached, sieve the eggs with a pinch of salt and use in sauces or as a garnish for vegetables. For other uses of extra whites or yolks, see 295.

Before we leave this subject, we pull out of our hat a conjurer's trick. Should you have any doubts about which eggs in your refrigerator are hard-cooked and which are not, a quick test is to twirl them on their pointed ends. The hard-cooked eggs will spin like a top: the others will simply topple over.

And a hint about washing egg-soiled dishes. Start with cold water, which releases rather than glues on the protein. Rub egg-stained silver with salt if polish is not handy.

ABOUT FLOURS

We have become so accustomed to our highly bleached white flours that we forget that earlier cooks knew only whole-kernel flours. These were not the so-called whole wheat of our commercial world, but the whole grain, which includes the germ. Even the fine manchet flour of tradition contained some germ. But many flours in general use today completely lack it. As Dr. A. J. Carlson, a leading investigator on foods and nutrition, says so graphically, "When rats and gray squirrels are given corn in abundance, they eat the germ and

leave the rest. People leave the germ and eat the rest." This nutritious and tasty entity, the germ, is usually removed in modern milling, because flours made with it are harder both to mill and to keep. After the removal of the outer coats and germ, our flours may be "enriched," but the term is misleading. ◗ Enriched flour contains only some of the many ingredients known to have been removed from it in milling. You may further fortify your enriched all-purpose flour by combining it with some of the flours described below which may have as much as sixteen times the protein value of wheat along with other important substances lacking in the wheat and rye flours we commonly use. If you are interested in these cereal components, see *Composition of Foods*, published by the USDA.

Flours must meet rigid government specifications and, when manufactured, must contain not more than 15% moisture. But they often acquire more in careless storage. Keep flour in clean, airtight containers and store in a cool place. Flours tend to dry out in high altitudes or during the winter months. Varying moisture content affects the way flours "handle." So some recipes for breads and pastries may read "2½ to 2¾ cups flour." If they do, ◗ measure the smaller amount of flour first, then add enough of, or even more than, the remaining flour until the dough is no longer sticky and begins to clean the sides of the bowl. Moisture also affects volume, and therefore we recommend sifting white flours for cakes and cookies. But neither white flours nor coarser flours nor cornmeal need be sifted in bread making.

In our miraculously mechanical but standardized economy, the average housewife, oddly enough, usually finds at hand only two kinds of white flour, both the results of highly milled or "patent" processing. These two easily available flours, called "all-purpose" and "cake," are used as their names imply. ◗ The single word "flour" in **Joy** recipes always means all-purpose unbleached wheat flour. For various ways to use flours as thickeners, see (I, 378–379). For Browned Flour, see (I, 379).

MEASURING FLOURS

It is particularly important that flour is not packed in measuring. Spoon the flour lightly into the cup so that it overflows the rim. Then level it off gently with a knife, as shown below.

◗ In baking, sifting-before-measuring is essential. There is a very easy way to do this neatly and quickly. Keep two 12-inch squares of stiff paper, foil or plastic on hand. Sift the flour onto the first square, as shown opposite, left. Rest your sifter on the second. Pick up the first sheet and curve it into a slide from which the flour can funnel itself into the measuring cup, which should be a dry measure shape, center. For very accurate measuring, cups designed for 1/4, 1/3 and 1/2, as shown lower center, are also desirable. When the measure is filled, level the flour by running a knife across the top of the cup; see below. ◗ Never try to level the flour

contents by shaking the cup, as this just repacks the sifted flour. Now you are ready to resift the flour with the other dry ingredients. Between siftings, move the sifter to the empty sheet and funnel the dry ingredients of the other sheet into the sifter top, as you did in measuring the flour in the center illustration.

Forgive us if we repeat, but always remember the important fact that ◗ flour can vary more than 20% in its ability to absorb moisture, depending on the type of wheat from which it was milled, its processing, and the amount of moisture absorbed during storage. For this reason, even the most accurate measurement may not always result in unqualified success, and sometimes adjustments must be made, on a purely experimental basis. Read about Flour Substitutions, 291.

ABOUT WHEAT FLOURS

Most grains are similar in their structure to the wheat kernel sketched in enlarged cross section opposite. The outer or bran layers contain, with the germ—indicated by the darker swirl on the right—most of the grain's vitamins and minerals. The germ, which is only 2% of the entire kernel, contains the highest grade protein and all of the fat. The endosperm indicated on the left is largely starch, with some protein—different from but complementary to the protein of the germ. The outer coatings and the germ—small though they are compared with the whole kernel in this enlarged drawing—are of unchallenged importance in content and irreplaceable in flavor.

Older and slower methods of milling—such as stone grinding, which distributes the germ oil evenly

and keeps the grain cooler during processing—prevent rancidity. High-speed steel milling produces greater heat and less even oil distribution, necessitating the removal of the germ to ensure longer shelf life. After buying very freshly ground unbleached flour, let it age about six weeks for best gluten development. However, try to use all flours containing gluten within 2 months of purchase, even though stored in the refrigerator or freezer, for gluten loses its strength with advancing age.

ALL-PURPOSE FLOUR

This is a blend of hard and soft wheat flours. The presence of more and tougher gluten in the hard wheat constituent results in a rather elastic and porous product. ◗ All-purpose flour, bleached or unbleached, can be used interchangeably, but unbleached has higher nutritional value. Some of the flours sold in our South as all-purpose are closer to cake flour in texture. In using them with yeast,

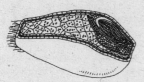

give them only one rising period—to not quite double the volume—and then let the dough rise to normal, as indicated by the finger test sketched on 297. You may substitute for 1 cup of all-purpose flour 1 1/8 cups of cake flour.

CAKE FLOUR

This is made of soft wheats, and their delicate, less expansive gluten bakes to a crumblier texture. Although you will not get the same result, in emergencies you may ◗ substitute 1 cup minus 2 tablespoons sifted all-purpose flour for 1 cup cake flour.

BREAD FLOUR

Although not easily come by, this flour is highly desirable for bread making, as its high proportion of gluten indicates a greater protein content. The gluten also gives elasticity to dough and allows it to expand and hold the gas liberated by the yeast. Bread flour feels more granular or gritty when rubbed between the fingers.

PRESIFTED FLOURS

These are ground to a point of pulverization and, whether resifted or not, give a different texture to baking. Some of them also have a larger

percentage of hard durum wheat, and although the manufacturers may suggest them to replace cake flour, the greater gluten content may tend to toughen cakes. If you use them for cakes, be sure to use 1 tablespoon less per cup than our recipes call for. ◗ We also suggest resifting.

PASTRY FLOUR

Soft, finely milled, low-gluten flour—often available in the South, where it is used for quick breads and pastries.

SELF-RISING FLOUR AND PHOSPHATED FLOURS

These contain the right amounts of leavens and salt for baking. Many people do not like to use them because, during delays in merchandising or storing, the leavens are apt to lose their potency. If used in pastry, these flours give a spongy, rather than flaky, texture. They should be used only for crusts where a low fat content is the objective and the fat in the recipe has been reduced. They are not recommended for making bread, but if you must use them, omit the salt called for in the recipe.

INSTANT FLOUR

A specialty flour used in the making of gravies and sauces. ◗ Never substitute for all-purpose flour.

SEMOLINA

A creamy-colored, granular, protein-rich durum wheat flour used commercially for all types of pasta. It is not your fault if homemade pastas and noodles fail to hold their shape no matter how carefully you have prepared and cooked them. The trouble lies in the lower gluten content of all-purpose flour on which housewives frequently depend.

FARINA

Also a creamy-colored, granular, protein-rich meal made from hard wheat other than durum, with the bran and most of the germ removed.

WHOLE-GRAIN, WHOLE WHEAT OR GRAHAM FLOUR

These and some commercial whole wheats retain their original vitamins, mineral salts, fats and other still unknown components—whether coarsely or finely milled. Scientists are aware of about twenty of these substances, even if they have so far failed to isolate them all or to produce them synthetically.

◗ You may substitute 1 cup of very finely milled whole-grain flours for 1 cup of all-purpose flour. For coarsely ground whole-grain flour, substitute 1 cup plus 2 tablespoons for 1 cup of all-purpose flour. This should be stirred lightly rather than sifted before measuring.

Yeast breads made from whole wheat flours do not have to be kneaded. They can be mixed and allowed to rise just once in the pan. However, if kneading is omitted, the texture will be coarser and denser.

BRAN FLOUR

This flour often gives a dry result unless you soften the bran by allowing the wet bread mixture, minus the yeast or baking powder, to stand for 8 hours or so. Bran flours are usually mixed with some all-purpose flour.

CRACKED WHEAT

Cut rather than ground, this flour gives up little of its starch as a binder. Therefore, it must be mixed with all-purpose or whole wheat flour in baking. We also prefer cooking it as for Coarse Cereals, (I, 178), before adding it to the flour mixture.

GLUTEN FLOUR

This is a starch-free, high-protein flour made by washing the starch from hard wheat flour. The residue is then dried and ground. See Gluten Bread, 312. ♦ For 1 cup all-purpose flour, substitute 13 tablespoons gluten flour. Other flours lacking in gluten such as rye, soya and rice can be used in proportionately greater quantity if gluten flour instead of the usual all-purpose flour is added to them.

Gluten is found in its most complete form in wheat. Scientists think—but are not sure—that 2 substances, glutenin and gliadin, occurring separately in the wheat, interact to form gluten. Gluten can never develop except in the presence of moisture and when the grain is agitated, as in kneading. ♦ To prepare gluten from gluten flour, knead into a stiff dough:

4 cups whole-grain or unbleached flour
1¹/₂ to 3 cups lukewarm water

Roll it into a ball and submerge it in water for 2 hours. Then, still keeping the dough ball under water, work the starch out of it by kneading. At intervals, pour off the starchy water. Replace the water you pour off and continue to knead, repeating this operation until the water is almost clear. The gluten is then ready to cook. ♦ Form the starch-free dough into a loaf and cut it into ¹/₂-inch slices. Put

into a 3-quart pan for which you have a tight lid:

¹/₄ cup vegetable oil

You may flavor the gluten at this point by sautéing until clear and golden:

1 finely sliced medium-sized onion

Put the gluten slices into the pan and cover with:

Boiling water

Simmer, closely covered, for 1 hour and drain. Store refrigerated and closely covered. The gluten slices can then be further cooked by dipping them in egg and potato or rice flour and browning them slowly in an oiled pan. Or cover with undiluted tomato, mushroom or celery soup and place in a preheated 350° oven about 20 minutes or until thoroughly heated.

WHEAT-GERM FLOUR

This must be refrigerated after opening. It may be ♦ substituted by using ¹/₃ cup of powdered wheat germ and ²/₃ cup of all-purpose flour for 1 cup of all-purpose flour. Be sure that the wheat germ, either powdered or whole, is very slightly toasted before combining it with the dough.

TRITICALE FLOUR

A nutritious sweet-tasting flour originally obtained from intergenetic hybridization by crossing durum wheat, hard red winter wheat and rye. Although the flour is higher in protein than all-purpose wheat flour, it is low in gluten and should be mixed with higher gluten flours for bread making. Use the grain as sprouts, 241, or cook as for Coarse Cereals, (I, 178).

ABOUT NONWHEAT FLOURS

Some of the following nonwheat flours can be used alone. But in any bread recipe that fails to call for wheat flour at least in part, you must expect a marked difference in texture, as wheat gluten has a unique elastic quality. This protein gluten factor in wheat is activated when the flour is both moistened and handled, at which time the gluten is said to "develop." The flour is then able to absorb as much as 200 times its weight in moisture. In discussing nonwheat flours, some of which are richer in overall protein content than wheat, we give the closest substitutions we have been able to find, but ♦ we advise, if possible, using at least 1 cup wheat flour for every 2 cups other flour, or a very heavy dough results. For increased protein content, we suggest the use of Cornell Triple-Rich Formula, 301. ♦ Coarse flours need not be sifted before measuring. They do need more leavening than wheat types. ♦ Allow 2 1/2 teaspoons baking powder for every cup of coarse flour.

CORN FLOUR

Yellow or white corn may be milled into corn flour, or the flour may be a by-product in the making of cornmeal. Use in baking, mixed with other flours.

CORNSTARCH

A refined starch obtained from the endosperm of corn, this is a very valuable thickener. ♦ Substitute 1 tablespoon cornstarch for 2 tablespoons all-purpose flour.

The new waxy starches made from certain varieties of corn are revolutionizing frozen sauces and fillings by their great stabilizing powers, ♦ but they are not to be used in baking. For thickening ♦ substitute 1 tablespoon waxy corn flour for 1 tablespoon all-purpose flour.

There is nothing more discouraging than the lumps any cornstarch can form or the raw taste it produces if it is badly handled or insufficiently cooked. Here are the things we have learned that help us to handle it more easily:

♦ Use a double boiler.

In recipes calling for sugar, avoid lumping by mixing cornstarch, sugar and salt together just before adding gradually to the ♦ cold liquid.

In recipes without sugar, make a paste of 1 tablespoon of cornstarch to 1 cup of the liquid called for in the recipe. Introduce this paste gradually into the ♦ hot, but not boiling, liquid.

Cornstarch, along with tapioca and arrowroot, is recommended for thickening very acid fruits because it does not lose its thickening power as quickly as flour does in the presence of acid. But if it is ♦ overcooked, it loses its thickening power very quickly, regardless of the presence of acid. These facts account for the countless letters we get on pie fillings. In the extra special care cooks lavish on fillings, they are apt to overcook, ♦ or overbeat them after cooking. Be very careful to check the cooking stages described later on.

Other causes for breakdown of thickening may come from a too high percentage of sugar in the recipe and, strangely, even from using too much cornstarch.

Also, tests have shown that ♦ the material from which the double boiler is made has a direct result on the thickening quality and the success of unmolding cornstarch puddings. Stainless steel and enamel are superior to heatproof glass or heavy crockery.

But to get on with the cooking. Once the cornstarch is properly added to the liquid, dispersed either in sugar or in a cold paste, it goes through 2 main cooking periods, 3 if the eggs are added. To keep the temperature right for the timing given here, use an enamel or stainless steel pan. Fill the base of the double boiler so that the water just dampens the bottom of the liner. ▶ Bring the water to a bubbling boil before starting the timing. During the first period of about 8 to 12 minutes ▶ constant, gentle stirring is necessary to blend the mixture free from lumps and to hold the starch particles in suspension until gelatinization takes place and the mixture thickens. In this time, it should have reached at least 185°, the temperature that is essential for proper unmolding.

Then follows the second period of about 10 minutes when the mixture is ▶ covered and cooked undisturbed to complete gelatinization. Maintain the 185° temperature.

A third period, of about 2 minutes, follows the addition of the eggs. This adding procedure is just like any other when eggs or egg yolks must meet hot liquid. The eggs are well beaten first. A portion of the hot mixture is added to the eggs very gradually. This is returned to the original mass, which has temporarily ▶ been removed from the heat. ▶ The stirring is less constant and extremely gentle during the next 2 minutes. The pudding should thicken much more in cooling. Have ready molds rinsed out in cold water. Stir the mixture very gently into them—releasing steam which would condense and thin the mixture. Cool for about 30 minutes at room temperature. For successful unmolding, store individual

molds 1 to 2 hours in refrigerator; larger molds, 6 to 12 hours.

▲ At altitudes of 5000 feet or higher, maximum gelatinization of cornstarch cannot be achieved in a double boiler. Use direct heat.

CORNMEAL

When stone-ground, cornmeal not only retains the germ but has a superior flavor. Yellow cornmeal has more vitamin A potential than has white cornmeal, but there is little difference in their nutritional or baking properties. Cornmeals can be used alone in Corn Dodgers Cockaigne, 342, or mixed with other flours in quick and yeast corn breads. To avoid graininess in corn breads, mix cornmeal and the liquid in the recipe, bring to a boil, and cool before mixing with the other ingredients.

RICE FLOUR

This makes a close but delicately textured cake in recipes heavy in egg. For recipes using rice flour, see Index. ▶ Substitute 1 cup minus 2 tablespoons rice flour for 1 cup all-purpose flour. But be sure, in baking, not to choose a waxy type of rice flour, also known as **mochika** or **sweet flour**. Instead, use these **waxy rice flours** in making sauces. They have remarkable stabilizing powers which prevent the separation of frozen gravies and sauces when reheated. They are also much less likely to lump.

RYE FLOUR

When used in most of the commercial rye breads, this flour is usually combined with a varying proportion of wheat flour. This is because the rye flour gluten factor provides stickiness but lacks elasticity. Breads made largely with rye flour are moist and compact and usually call for a sourdough leavener, 224. ♦ Substitute 1¼ cups rye flour for 1 cup all-purpose flour.

RYE MEAL

This is simply coarsely ground whole-rye flour. ♦ Substitute 1 cup rye meal for 1 cup all-purpose flour. See Rye Flour, above.

SOY FLOUR

This flour has both a high protein and a high fat content. However, some soy flour is made of beans from which the fat has been largely expressed, when it is known as **soybean low-fat flour**. It may be made from very lightly toasted beans or from raw beans, when it is known as **soybean flour**. Because of the fat, it is not mixed with the dry ingredients but is creamed with the shortening or blended with the liquids. Stir before measuring and substitute ♦ 2 tablespoons of soy flour plus ⅞ cup of all-purpose flour for 1 cup of all-purpose flour. but if you like the flavor, use up to 20% of the weight of the flour in the recipe. Soy flour causes heavy browning in the crust, so reduce baking temperature about 25°.

SOY MEAL

This coarse meal should be soaked with 2 parts boiling water until all moisture is absorbed. Keep in the refrigerator and use as an extender for meats.

POTATO FLOUR OR POTATO STARCH

Made from cooked potatoes that have been dried and ground, this flour is used chiefly in soups, gravies, breads and cakes, in combination with other flours, or alone in Sponge Cakes, 406. To avoid lumping, blend it with sugar before mixing—or cream it with the shortening before adding a liquid. In bread recipes, it gives a moist, slow-staling loaf. ♦ To use as a thickener, substitute 1 tablespoon potato flour for 2 tablespoons all-purpose flour; in baking, ⅝ cup potato flour for 1 cup all-purpose flour.

SORGHUM FLOUR

Also called **milo maize,** this flour is often used to thicken soups.

TAPIOCA AND SAGO

These are similar in their uses. Tapioca is processed from the Brazilian cassava root and sago from certain Indian palms. Cassava is poisonous until heated to release the hydrocyanic acid. Sago and the so-called pearl tapioca must both be soaked for at least 1 hour before using. Soak ¼ cup of the pearls in ½ cup water, which should be completely absorbed; if it isn't, the pearls are too old to use. If you have already embarked on mixing the recipe, you can substitute rice in equal parts for pearl tapioca. ♦ To substitute so-called minute or granular for pearl tapioca, allow 1½ to 2 tablespoons of this finer form for 4 tablespoons of the soaked pearl. As a thickener, substitute 1 tablespoon quick-cooking tapioca for 1 tablespoon flour.

TAPIOCA FLOUR

Like the waxy rice and corn flours, above, these are popular for sauces and fruit fillings that are to be frozen. These sauces reconstitute without breaking down and becoming watery as do flour-thickened sauces after frozen storage.

◗ To use in freezing, substitute 1 tablespoon tapioca flour for $2^{1}/2$ tablespoons all-purpose flour to 1 cup liquid. ◗ In nonfrozen sauces, substitute $1^{1}/2$ teaspoons tapioca flour for 1 tablespoon all-purpose flour.

Tapioca flour is popular for making very clear glazes. Cook the tapioca and fruit juice or water only to the boiling point. ◗ Beware of overcooking, as the tapioca will become stringy. ◗ Never boil. When the first bubbles begin to break through the surface, remove the pan from the heat at once. The mixture will look thin and milky. Let it stand 2 or 3 minutes. Stir. Wait 2 or 3 minutes longer and stir again. If the recipe calls for butter, stir it in at this time. After 10 minutes more of undisturbed cooling, the glaze should be thick enough to apply to the food you are glazing.

ARROWROOT FLOUR OR STARCH

This is another popular base for cream sauces and clear and delicate glazes. It cooks by the same method as cornstarch, but ◗ substitutes in the amount of $1^{1}/2$ teaspoons arrowroot to 1 tablespoon flour. To ensure an attractive consistency when arrowroot glaze is to be used on cold acid fruits, dissolve $1^{1}/2$ teaspoons gelatin in 1 tablespoon cold water and add it to the hot glaze. Spoon the cooled, thickened glaze over the chilled fruit and keep cold until you serve.

BARLEY FLOUR

◗ To substitute, use $1/2$ cup barley flour for each cup of all-purpose flour.

BUCKWHEAT FLOUR

This flour of high biologic value is best used in the proportion of $1/4$ cup buckwheat to $3/4$ cup other flour for good texture.

COTTONSEED FLOUR

With at least four times the protein value of wheat, this flour is often used to enrich breads. ◗ Substitute 2 tablespoons cottonseed flour plus $7/8$ cup all-purpose flour for 1 cup all-purpose flour.

PEANUT FLOUR

Contains at least sixteen times the protein value of wheat. It may be ◗ substituted by using 2 tablespoons peanut flour plus $7/8$ cup all-purpose flour for 1 cup all-purpose flour.

OAT FLOUR AND OATMEAL

These are ground to different consistencies to combine with wheat flours up to one-third. Oatmeal is better in baking if soaked in boiling water with the shortening and cooled before the yeast or other leaven is added.

ROLLED OATS

These are separate flakes formed by rolling the groats with hulls removed, and steaming them. The thinness of the flake determines regular or quick-cooking oats. They are popular for adding flavor to cookies. Steel-cut oats are obtained by passing the groats or kernels through special cutting machines. ◗ Substitute $1^{1}/3$ cups rolled oat flakes for 1 cup all-purpose flour. To combine with wheat flours for breads, use $1/3$ cup oat flakes for each cup flour.

BEAN FLOUR

◗ Substitute 4 to 5 cups bean flour for 1 cup all-purpose flour.

NUT MEAL

These finely ground dry nuts are used as a flour substitute in many Torten, 430.

CAROB FLOUR OR POWDER

A chocolate-flavored powder milled from the carob-tree pod, which is also known as Saint-John's-bread. A nutritious substitute for chocolate for the allergic, low in fat and delicious in its own right.

◗ To substitute for flour, allow 1/8 to 1/4 cup carob powder plus 7/8 to 3/4 cup flour for every cup of flour. ◗ To substitute for chocolate, 3 tablespoons of carob flour plus 2 tablespoons liquid equals 1 ounce unsweetened chocolate. Use less sugar, as it is naturally sweet.

WHEAT-FLOUR ALLERGY SUBSTITUTE

This can be kept on hand for use in gravies and some quick breads, pancakes and biscuits. Sift together 6 times, 1/2 cup cornstarch and 1/2 cup of any of the following: rye flour, potato flour or rice flour. If you use this combination for baking, you will need 2 teaspoons baking powder for each cup of the flour mixture. ◗ If using cornstarch or rice flour in baking, be sure to avoid the waxy types.

COOKED CEREAL SUBSTITUTE

This may be ◗ substituted 1 cup cooked cereal for 1/4 cup flour. But you must also cut the fluid in the recipe by 1 cup for each cup of cooked cereal used. To mix, stir the cooked cereal into the remaining fluid before combining with the other ingredients.

ABOUT CRUMBS

In reading recipes, note what kind of bread crumbs are called for. The results are very different, depending on whether they are dry, fresh, browned or buttered.

Finely crushed cracker crumbs or cornflakes, corn or potato chip crumbs are sometimes used in place of bread crumbs in breading and in au gratins, see below.

DRY CRUMBS

These are made from dry bread, zwieback or cake. If these materials are not sufficiently dry, crisp them on a baking sheet in a 200° oven before making the crumbs. Do not let the crumbs color. If only a few are being made, grind them in a rotary hand grater, as sketched on 238, or in a ⅄ blender. If making them in large quantities, put them through a meat grinder with a medium chopping blade. Tie a bag tightly over the mouth of the grinder to catch them all.

◗ Measure dry bread crumbs as you would sugar, 227. Store dry bread crumbs in a cool, dry place, not too tightly lidded, or they may mold.

SOFT BREAD CRUMBS

To prepare these, use two- to four-day-old bread. You may crumb it very lightly with your fingers. But a safer way to retain the light texture desired in such crumbs is to pull the bread apart with a fork—using a gingerly motion, as sketched opposite. Do not crush the bread with the hand that is holding it.

◗ To measure soft bread crumbs, pile them lightly into a cup. Do not pack them down unless the recipe calls for soaking these fresh crumbs in water, milk or stock and pressing the moisture out before using, when they naturally compact. Use at once.

BROWNED OR BUTTERED BREAD CRUMBS

To prepare these, use dry bread crumbs, as described. Allow for each cup dry bread crumbs ¹/₂ teaspoon salt and brown them slowly in ¹/₃ cup butter. Use at once. You may enliven them with bits of chopped minced bacon, chopped nutmeats or grated cheese and paprika.

CROUTONS

These dry or fried seasoned fresh bread morsels come in all sizes. As coarse crumbs, they are an attractive garnish for noodles, dumplings or Spätzle. In small dice, they add glamour to pea and other soups. Use croutons in tiny dice and mound them around game, or, as larger toasts, under game or a chop. They can be spread with a pâté or be used as a spongy surface for the natural juices. In large size, they can also be placed under a dripping rack during the roasting of meats to catch and hold the juices.

I. Dice bread, fresh or dry, and sauté it in butter until it is an even brown. Or butter slices of bread, cut them into dice and brown them in a 375° oven.

II. When 2 cups croutons have been sautéed or browned in the oven, drop them while still hot into a bag containing:

>   1 **teaspoon salt**
>   1 **teaspoon paprika**
>   2 **to 4 tablespoons ground Parmesan cheese or very finely minced fresh herbs**

Close the bag. Shake it until the croutons are evenly coated. Add them to hot soup.

III. Use for soup, noodles or Caesar salad. Cut into ¹/₂-inch cubes:

>   **Bread**

Sauté the cubes in:

>   **Hot butter or olive oil**

You may rub the skillet with garlic or add grated onion to the butter. Stir them gently or shake the skillet until they are coated. Sprinkle with:

>   **Grated cheese or herbs**

FLOURING, BREADING AND CRUMBING FOODS

When **dredging** or lightly covering food with flour or crumbs or with a more elaborately bound coating, the main thing to remember is this: you want a thin, even and unbroken covering that will adhere. The food should be about 70° and should be ◗ dry. If the food is floury to begin with or is made with a thickened sauce, the flouring may be omitted. But for fish fillets, shrimp, meat, or anything with a moist surface, it is essential to dry it first and then flour it.

◗ To prepare a simple breading,

have ready finely sifted crumbs, flour or cornmeal. Cornmeal gives the firmest coating. If the food is not fragile, simply put a small quantity of the seasoned coating material in a paper or plastic bag with the food you want to cover, and shake. You will find this method gives a very even, quick and economical coating. Or prepare the following Seasoned Flour or Crumbs.

SEASONED FLOUR OR CRUMBS FOR BREADING

I. Mix:

1 cup all-purpose flour, finely sifted dry bread crumbs or finely crushed cornflakes
1 teaspoon salt
1/4 teaspoon pepper or 1/2 teaspoon paprika
(1/8 teaspoon ginger or nutmeg)

II. Mix:

1 cup finely sifted dry bread crumbs or crushed cornflakes or crackers

3 tablespoons grated Parmesan cheese
1/2 teaspoon dried herbs, choosing from: savory, chervil, chives, basil or tarragon; or 1/16 teaspoon rosemary

BOUND BREADING OR COATING À L'ANGLAISE

Enough to Coat 8 Croquettes

To prepare a more adhesive bound breading—or coating à l'anglaise—begin by wiping the food dry. Then dip the dry food into a shallow bowl of seasoned flour. Have ready, aside from the flour, two other bowls. In the first bowl, put a mixture of:

1 slightly beaten egg
2 to 3 teaspoons water or milk
(2 teaspoons oil)

Stir these ingredients together with 10 or 12 mild strokes. ◖ Do not let the egg get bubbly, as this makes the coating uneven. In the other bowl, have ready:

3/4 cup sifted seasoned dry bread crumbs

As each piece of food is floured, toss it lightly from one palm to the other, patting it gently all over and encouraging any excess flour to fall off, as sketched on the left. Then slide the flour-coated food through the egg mixture, making sure the entire surface is contacted, as shown at center. Allow any excess moisture to drip off. Then place the food in the crumb-lined bowl. See that the crumbs adhere evenly to all the edges of the food as well as to its larger surfaces. If you see any vacant places, sprinkle a few crumbs on them. Pat on any excess crumbs that might fall off and brown too rapidly, thus discoloring the frying fat. Handle the food very gently, so that the coating will not be cracked. ◗ Place on a rack to dry for about 20 minutes before frying. ◗ Do not chill this food before frying, as this will tend to make it absorb an undue amount of fat.

AU GRATIN

Au gratin is a term that in America is usually associated with cheese. But the term may merely refer to a light but thorough coating of fine fresh or dry bread crumbs or even crushed cornflakes, cracker crumbs or finely ground nuts placed on top of scalloped or sauced dishes. These are then browned in the oven or under the broiler to form a crisp golden crust. A sprinkling of paprika helps to induce browning. Such dishes are usually combinations of cooked shellfish, fish, meats, vegetables or eggs, bound by a white or brown sauce and served in the dish in which they were cooked. If the sauce is heavy in fat, it is wise to place the scalloped dish in a pan of hot water before running it under a broiler. Or you may set the casserole or baking dish on a piece of foil, shiny side down to deflect the heat. Or just set the casserole on a baking tin.

◗ To make the following au gratin mixtures quickly, put the ingredients in a ⟑ blender in the proportion and amount you need.

I. Place:
   Dry bread crumbs

in a thorough, but light, covering over the sauced food. Bake in a 350° to 375° oven. Or place the dish under a preheated broiler 3 inches below the source of heat until a crisp, golden brown crust forms.

II. Place:
   Dry bread crumbs and dots of butter
   (Paprika—about
   1/2 teaspoon per cup)
to make a thorough but light covering over the food, before baking it in a 350° oven. Or run the dish under a preheated broiler 5 inches from the source of heat, to produce a crisp golden crust.

III. Completely cover the food to be au gratined with:
   Dry bread crumbs, dots of butter and grated cheese
   (Paprika—about
   1/2 teaspoon per cup)
Place the dish under a preheated broiler, 5 inches below the source of heat, to form a glazed golden crust. The finished result should be neither powdery nor rubbery but "fondant." It will be more "fondant" if you use natural-aged American or cheddar cheese, and drier if you use Parmesan or Romano.

ALMOND OR AMANDINE GARNISH

                    A Scant 1/2 Cup
This garnish is a classic. It glorifies the most commonplace dish.
Melt:
   1/4 cup butter
Stir and sauté in it over low heat, to avoid scorching, until lightly browned:
   1/4 cup blanched shredded almonds

Salt, as needed

As a variation on almonds as a vegetable garnish, try:

(Roasted pumpkin, squash or sesame seeds)

ABOUT LEAVENS

We are all so accustomed to light breads and cakes that we seldom question the part that leavens play.

Where does this rising power lie? First, the steam converted from the moisture, in any baking, may account for a third to four-fifths of the expansion of the dough. The greater amount is characteristic of popovers and cakes rich in egg white. So, to encourage the generation of this easily lost asset, ▶ preheat your oven.

We usually think of leavens as resulting from baking powders, 225, sour milk and soda, 226, and yeast—all of which expand with the steam to form gas as a major force. But we tend to forget the importance of the mechanical incorporation of air from which the rest of the rising power comes. To give a boost to the chemical reactions, be sure you know how to cream fat and sugar, 399; how to fold and mix batters, 399; how to beat eggs, 206; and, especially, how to beat egg whites to that state called "stiff, but not dry," 208. And who would ever guess that fresh-fallen snow—or even old snow from below the surface—makes an excellent substitute for eggs as a riser in puddings and pancakes—because of the snow's ammonia content?

ABOUT YEAST

Yeasts are living organisms with 3200 billion cells to the pound—and not one is exactly like another. They feed on sugars and produce alcohol and carbon dioxide—the "riser" we are after. But you may prefer, as we do, to accept a Mexican attitude toward yeast doughs. They call them almas, or souls, because they seem so spirited.

When flour is mixed with water to form a dough, which is then kept in a warm place, the wild yeast coming from the air and in the flour will start working and form a sourdough. There are enzymes in the flour to convert the wheat starch into the sugar on which the yeast feeds, making alcohol and carbon dioxide. Organic acids and other fragrant compounds are also created to give the sour effect. Sourdoughs, discussed on 224, are products of this primitive bacterial ferment. They are so primitive that they are recorded in Egyptian history in 4000 B.C. This leavened bread has been called the first "convenience" food, as its yeast content gives it excellent keeping quality.

The different yeasts, compressed and dried, activate at different temperatures, see 223. These temperatures and the amount of food available limit the life span of the yeast. Its force, therefore, can be easily computed. One-half ounce raises 4 cups of flour in 1 1/2 to 2 hours. One ounce raises 28 cups of flour in about 7 hours. For speedier raising, an excess of yeast is often added. But this is not necessary, and it often affects flavor and gives a porous texture. Small quantities of sugar also speed yeast activity, but too much will inhibit it. You may have noticed that it takes very sweet doughs longer to rise. As salt also inhibits yeast, ▶ never use salted water for dissolving yeast. In very hot weather, after the yeast is dissolved and added to the flour, salt may be added in small quantities to control too rapid fermentation.

Yeast dough is allowed to rise and fall a number of times during dough-making to improve the texture, but if allowed to overexpand, it can use up its energy. In this case, there is little rising power left for the baking period, when it is most needed.

For different methods of incorporating yeast in doughs, read about Mixing Bread Dough, 297. The liquids added to yeast, either alone or in combination, are water, which brings out the wheat flavor and makes a crisp crust; or skim milk, which not only adds to the nutritive value but also gives a softer crumb. The fat in whole and homogenized milk tends to coat the yeast and prevent its proper softening. Potato water may also be used, but it hastens the action of the yeast and gives a somewhat coarser, moister texture to dough. Both milk and potato water somewhat increase the keeping quality of bread.

To produce the best yeast bread, you must give the dough time to rise slowly; the entire process takes about 4 or 5 hours before baking. If you use 1 cake of yeast to 1 1/2 cups of liquid and if the temperature is right, you can count on about 2 hours or more for the first rising; 1 or more for the second; and 1 hour for rising in the pans. You may increase the yeast content in any recipe and reduce your rising time considerably. Some successful quick recipes are given, but if you are going to the effort of using yeast, you might as well work for the superlative result which comes from the slower process.

COMPRESSED YEAST

This living organism is dependent on definite temperature ranges. It begins to activate at about 50° ♦ and is at its best between 78° and 82°. It begins to die around 120° and is useless for baking after 143°. We prefer using this moist cake weighing about 3/5 ounce. But it must be kept refrigerated. Although compressed yeast comes in larger sizes, when 1 cake is specified in this book it means the 3/5-ounce size. If bought fresh, it will keep about 2 weeks. Frozen, it will keep for 2 months. Take out only what is needed and let it defrost overnight in the refrigerator. When at its best it is a light grayish-tan in color. It crumbles readily, breaks with a clean edge and smells pleasantly aromatic. When old, it becomes brownish in color. To test for freshness, cream a small quantity of yeast with an equal amount of sugar. It should become liquid at once. You may let crumbled, compressed yeast dissolve in warm water or warm pasteurized skim milk at 80° to 90° for about 5 minutes before combining with the other ingredients called for in the recipes.

ACTIVE DRY YEAST

This granular form of yeast comes in airtight, moisture-proof packages measuring 1 scant tablespoon or in 4-ounce vacuum-packed jars. It is often preferred for its better keeping qualities. It comes dated and, if kept in a cool place, will hold for several months—and somewhat longer in a refrigerator. Greater heat and more moisture are needed to activate it than for compressed yeast. ♦ Use more water to dissolve it; but ♦ decrease by that amount the liquid called for in the recipe and ♦ heat the dissolving water to between 105° and 115°. To dissolve it readily, sprinkle the powdered yeast on the surface of the water. Or it may be mixed with the dry ingredients in the mixer method, 298, and activated by using 120° to 130° liquid. Since this yeast does not contain excess starch, it will not bubble when placed in water. For growth, add small quantities of flour and sugar.

♦ To substitute dry granular yeast for compressed yeast, use 1 package or 1 scant tablespoon active dry yeast granules for a ³/₅-ounce cake of compressed yeast.

DEBITTERED BREWERS' OR
NUTRITIONAL YEAST

Another form of dry yeast—but one without leavening power—which adds nutritive value to foods. It may be added to breads in the proportion of 1 to 3 teaspoons to 1 cup of flour without affecting flavor or texture adversely.

ABOUT SOURDOUGH

This term brings to mind at once the hardbitten pioneer whose sharing of the bread "starter" was a true act of friendship. Of course, the best French breads and many other famous doughs are also based on flour and water mixtures fermented in various ways to trap natural yeast. In kitchens where yeast baking has been going on for centuries, these organisms are plentiful in the air, and success is quickly assured, see II, opposite. But in an uninitiated streamlined kitchen, we recommend beginning a sourdough with a commercial yeast, especially in winter, see I, right.

Remember, the sourdough starter is just as fragile as the yeast and must

be cosseted along. For a good method of fermenting and maintaining an 80° to 90° temperature during fermentation, see Potato Salt-Rising Bread, 308. Keep the starter away from drafts or too high heat. ♦ Two cups of this foamy mixture are substituted for 1 cake or package of yeast and the dissolving liquid. After you have made your starter, you can continue to use it for about 3 days at room temperature without reworking it and for about a week if it is refrigerated, then allowed to rest at 70° at least 1 hour before using. Try to use the sourdough at least once a week; you may freeze the starter if it is not to be used for several weeks. ♦ Allow at least 24 hours for the frozen starter to become active again at room temperature before using.

Keep at least 1¹/₂ to 2 cups starter on hand, covered loosely to allow escape of the gas which accumulates. If an alcoholic liquid forms on top, pour it off. To replenish, see opposite.

Expect the sourdough to have an odor very like salt-rising bread. Should it develop any abnormal coloration, discard it. To avoid spoilage, wash the starter crock about once a week with a detergent and warm water. Rinse well and dry carefully before returning the starter to the crock. Try the sourdough recipes listed in the Index if you are adventurous, persistent and leisurely.

SOURDOUGH STARTER

I. For kitchens lacking yeast spores in the air. Combine in a large widemouthed crockery or glass jar:

    1 package active dry yeast
    2 cups lukewarm
      water: 85°
    2 cups all-purpose flour
Stir with a ♦ wooden spoon—never

use any metal. Let stand uncovered at 80° to 90° for 4 to 7 days, or until it bubbles and emits a good sour odor. During this period, stir down once a day; if a crust develops, stir it down also. Use at once or refrigerate until ready to do so.

To replenish, discard all but 1 cup of the starter, because any excess, unless reactivated, may become rancid. Add the cupful to:

1 cup all-purpose flour
1 cup lukewarm water

Let stand overnight until fermented and bubbling, then use or refrigerate.

II. For kitchens laden with yeast spores from previous bread making, follow the directions in I, above, omitting the yeast, and using:

1 cup lukewarm milk
1 cup all-purpose flour
1/2 cup sugar

To replenish, add these 3 ingredients in these amounts to 1 cup starter.

ABOUT BAKING POWDERS AND BAKING SODA

When confronted with the questions growing out of the use of the various baking powders now on the market, the puzzled layman is apt to sigh for the good old days when this product was rather haphazardly mixed at home. ◗ Just in case you run out of baking powder mix—for each teaspoon of baking powder called for in the recipe—1/2 teaspoon cream of tartar, 1/8 teaspoon bicarbonate of soda and 1/8 teaspoon salt. After adding the above ingredients, do not delay putting the batter into the oven. ◗ And don't try to store this mixture, as it has poor keeping qualities. If you doubt the effectiveness of any baking powder ◗ test by mixing 1 teaspoon of baking powder with 1/3 cup of hot

water. Use the baking powder only if it bubbles enthusiastically.

There are three major kinds of baking powders, and you will find the ◗ type carefully specified on the label. For substitutions, see 288. In all of them there must be an acid and an alkaline material reacting with each other in the presence of moisture to form a gas—carbon dioxide—which takes the form of tiny bubbles in the dough or batter. In baking, these quickly expand the batter, which is then set by the heat to make a light-textured crumb. Before measuring any of these leavens, stir and break up any lumps, and use a dry measuring spoon.

▲ Because of the decrease in barometric pressure at high altitudes, the carbon dioxide gas expands more quickly and thus has greater leavening action. For this reason, the amount of baking powder should be decreased if you are using a recipe designed for low altitudes. You may select recipes designed especially for high altitudes if you wish; see 442.

▲ In high altitudes, baking soda is decreased as for baking powder, above; but in recipes using sour milk, where its neutralizing power is needed, never reduce soda beyond 1/2 teaspoon for every cup of sour milk or cream called for in the recipe.

TARTRATE BAKING POWDERS

In these, the soda is combined with tartaric acid or a combination of cream of tartar and tartaric acid. They are the quickest in reaction time, giving off carbon dioxide the moment they are combined with liquid. Therefore, if you are using this kind, be sure ◗ to mix the batter quickly and ◗ have the oven preheated so that too much gas does not escape from the dough before the cells can become heat-hardened in their expanded form. Especially ▶ avoid using tartrate powder for doughs and batters that are to be stored in the refrigerator or frozen before baking.

PHOSPHATE BAKING POWDERS

These use calcium acid phosphate or sodium acid pyrophosphate, or a combination of these, as the acid ingredient. They are somewhat slower in reaction but give up the greater part of their carbon dioxide in the cold dough. The remainder may be released when the mixture is baked.

DOUBLE-ACTING OR S.A.S. BAKING POWDERS

Often referred to as ▶ combination, or double-acting, baking powders, these are the baking powders we specify consistently in this book. They use sodium aluminum sulfate and calcium acid phosphate as the acid ingredients. They too start work in the cold dough, but the great rising impact does not begin until the dough contacts the heat from the hot oven.

SODIUM BICARBONATE OR BAKING SODA

Used alone, baking soda has no leavening properties. But used in combination with some acid ingredients such as sour milk or molasses, it gives one of the very tenderest crumbs. The proportion of baking soda to sour milk or buttermilk is usually 1 teaspoon soda to 1 cup sour milk. For more details about soda and sour milk or cream reactions, see 188. The reaction of the soda with the acid is essentially the same as that which takes place when the two ingredients in baking powder meet

moisture, so always mix the baking soda with the dry ingredients first.

The acidity of chocolate, honey or corn syrup is not strong enough to be the only source of acid, so some recipes with these acid ingredients may call for both baking powder and baking soda. If they do, use about 1/2 teaspoon baking soda and 1/2 teaspoon baking powder for each 2 cups flour. The small amount of soda is desirable for neutralizing the acid ingredients in the recipe, while the main leavening action is left to the baking powder. The amounts of baking powder per cup of flour suggested above are for low altitudes, see About Baking Soda, 225. To substitute baking soda for baking powder, see Substitutions, 288.

AMMONIUM BICARBONATE

This forerunner of our modern and more stable leaveners is also known as powdered baking ammonia, carbonate of ammonia, and **hartshorn**. Used for years in Europe to produce long-lasting crisp cookies, it must be pounded to a fine powder and then sifted with the dry ingredients or dissolved in a warm liquid such as water, rum or wine.

Substitute it for the baking powder and baking soda called for in cookie and cake recipes. Buy only small amounts from the drugstore, as it quickly evaporates if not very tightly contained.

ABOUT SOLID SUGARS

Most of our cooking is done with sugars made from beets or from cane. Both are so similar in their cooking reactions and taste that only the label gives us the clue to their source. But the various grinds of solid sugars affect not only their comparative volumes but their sweetening powers as well. Liquid sweeteners—again, according to type—react very differently in cooking combinations. Whichever type you use, more is needed to sweeten iced dishes or drinks.

Among other things, sugars, like fats, give tenderness to doughs. In small amounts, they hasten working of yeast. However, too much sugar at this early juncture will inhibit yeast activity. Sugar in bread, rolls and muffins produces a golden brown crust. Small pinches added to some vegetables bring up their flavor.

Sugars, whether solid or liquid, are not interchangeable. For a quick comparison of sugar weights and volumes, see 282. Many baking recipes call for the sifting of sugar before measuring. In America, where we are spoiled in having free-flowing, unlumpy granulated and powdered sugars, this initial sifting before measuring is usually ignored. But it is important to measure these and other sugars, except brown sugar, 228, by filling the measuring cup with a scoop or spoon to overflowing, taking care not to shake down the contents to even it, then leveling off the top with a knife, as shown for flour on 210. ◗ In substituting liquid for dry sweeteners, an adjustment in other liquid ingredients must be made, especially in baking, as discussed in About Liquid Sugars, 229.

GRANULATED SUGAR

◗ In this book when the word sugar appears, the recipe calls for granulated sugar—beet or cane both being 99.5% pure sucrose. However, do not expect the same baking results if using a granulated sugar now on the market which is a combination of sucrose and dextrose. Its moisture-attracting characteristics will make baked goods softer—a disaster in some products. As we buy granulated sugar in America, it can be used for almost every purpose, even for meringues. The English granulated is too coarse for this, and their **castor sugar,** closer to our powdered, is used instead. ◗ One pound of granulated sugar equals approximately 2 cups.

LUMP OR LOAF SUGARS

These are granulated sugars molded or cut into convenient rectangular sizes for use in hot drinks. Rock Candy Crystals, 591, make an interesting stand-in for lump sugar and, when separated or crushed, a sparkling garnish for iced cakes.

SUPERFINE OR BERRY SUGAR

This finer grind of granulated sugar is still coarse enough so that the individual crystals are easily discernible. It is best used in meringues and for sweetening fruits and drinks. If it becomes lumpy, try rolling the sugar in a plastic bag with a rolling pin. ◗ It can be substituted cup for cup for granulated sugar.

CONFECTIONERS' OR POWDERED SUGAR

These two terms refer to the same product, known in the East as confectioners' and in the West as powdered sugar. In its finest form—10X—it may at a quick glance be mistaken for cake flour. Confectioners' sugar is the counterpart of the European or English **icing sugar.** In order to lessen lumping, it comes with a small quantity of cornstarch added. But when it does lump, sieve it, as shown below. Measure confectioners' sugar as you would flour, 210. Since the cornstarch tends to give so-called un-cooked icings a raw flavor, it is wise, before spreading this kind of mix-ture, to let it heat about 10 minutes ◗ over boiling water, see 496. The dense texture of confectioners' sugar also gives a different crumb to cakes in which it is used. ◗ Do not try to substitute it for granulated sugar in baking. However, in other uses, sub-stitute 1¾ cups confectioners' for 1 cup granulated.

BROWN OR BARBADOS SUGAR

This is a moister beet or cane sugar which comes light or dark—the latter more strongly flavored with mo-lasses. As both types harden and lump easily, keep them in tightly cov-ered containers or in a tightly closed plastic bag in a cool, moist place. If sugar should become lumpy, sprinkle it very lightly with a few drops of water and heat in a low oven for a few moments or put it through a strainer as shown below, forcing the lumps out with a spoon. ◗ In this book the term brown sugar means the light form. If a stronger flavor is wanted, the term dark brown sugar appears.

Different forms of granulated brown sugar now appearing on the market may not be as sweet, so be sure you

know what you are buying and fol-low directions on the package.

◗ To substitute brown sugar for granulated sugar, use 1 cup firmly packed brown sugar for each cup granulated sugar. Always, in measur-ing brown sugar, pack it firmly into a measuring cup and level it by press-ing with the palm of the hand. Then unmold it, sand-castlewise, as shown.

RAW AND TURBINADO SUGARS

Raw sugar is processed from cane, and the USDA notes that it is "unfit for direct use as a food ingredient be-cause of the impurities it ordinarily contains." Turbinado is a partially refined, coarse, beige-toned crystal containing the molasses portion of the sugar. It is closest in character to the yellow or brownish **Demerara sugar** often called for in English recipes. ◗ Substitute cup for cup for granulated sugar, but be aware of its heavier molasses flavor.

CORN SUGAR

A crystallized dextrose-glucose ob-tained by hydrolizing cornstarch with acid.

FRUIT SUGARS

Fructose, the natural sugar in fruits, has the same caloric value as cane sugar, but because its sweetening power is 1.7 to 1 of sugar, use only about two-thirds as much.

MAPLE SUGAR

Evaporation of maple sap or syrup gives this sugar its distinctively strong, sweet taste, but, because of its high cost, it is often reserved just for flavoring. As it dissolves slowly, grate or sliver it before combining it with other ingredients. ♦ In substituting, allow about ¹/₂ cup for each cup of granulated sugar.

ABOUT SEASONED SUGARS

Keep these on hand for quick flavoring.

CINNAMON SUGAR

Mix 1 cup sugar with every 2 tablespoons cinnamon. Use for toast, coffee cake and yogurt toppings.

CITRUS FRUIT FLAVORED SUGARS

Extremely useful in custards and desserts. Mix 1 to 2 tablespoons grated citrus fruit rind for every cup of sugar. Store covered in a cool place.

VANILLA SUGAR

Make this by keeping 1 to 2 vanilla beans closed up in a canister with 2 cups of sugar. Or you may crush the beans with a few tablespoons of sugar before adding to the sugar you are storing. Then, you may strain the sugar before using, replace it with new sugar, and use until the beans lose their flavoring power.

ABOUT LIQUID SUGARS

There are a number of factors to contend with in substituting liquid for solid sweeteners: their sweetening powers vary greatly; their greater moisture content has to be taken into account; those that have an acid factor need neutralizing by the addition of baking soda. To measure liquid sugars, you may want to grease your measuring container first. Then pour or spoon these sticky substances into the measure, just to the level mark. Scrape out all the contents. ♦ Never dip a measuring cup into the honey or syrup container, for the added amount clinging to the outside may make your dough too sweet or too liquid.

CORN SYRUP

Corn syrup is dextrose and glucose and is generally used in canning and jelly-making. ♦ In this book the term corn syrup applies to the light type. If called for, the stronger-tasting dark is specified. ♦ For the same amount of sweetening power, you must substitute 2 cups corn syrup for 1 cup sugar. In cooking, for best results ♦ never use corn syrup to replace more than half the amount of sugar called for in a recipe. In baking, you are taking a chance in substituting corn syrup. But if you must, for each 2 cups of sugar in the recipe, reduce the liquid called for—other than syrup— by ¹/₄ cup. For example: suppose you are baking a cake that calls for 2 cups of sugar. "Maximum syrup tolerance" here would be 1 cup sugar, 2 cups syrup. And for each 2 cups of sugar originally called for, you would reduce the other liquid ingredients by ¹/₄ cup.

HONEY

This valuable ingredient has long been treasured because of its preservative qualities due to its high sugar content and an antimold enzyme. It is cherished by cooks for the remarkable keeping qualities, chewy texture and the browner color it gives to cakes, cookies and bread doughs. It is composed chiefly of levulose and dextrose. Its high liquid quality causes great variability in handling, and German cooks of old often refused to use it until it had aged for about a year. Variations in honey today are due in part to adulteration with additional glucose. Pasteurization, used to destroy the yeasts that may cause the honey to ferment, also reduces its nutrient value.

The varying flavors of thyme honey from Hymetos in Greece, of tupelo from Florida, and of orange blossom from California are easily distinguished, but honeys from the same plant taste markedly different when the plant is grown on different soils and in different climates. Very dark honeys may be disagreeably strong.

Honey is sold in two basic forms: comb and extracted. However, the extracted honey is in either liquid or crystallized form, and the latter may be labeled "creamed," "candied," "fondant" or "spread."

Warm the honey or add it to the other liquids called for to make mixing more uniform. To measure honey, oil the measuring cup or spoon so the honey will slip off easily, or measure the shortening first, then the honey in the same utensil.

◗ As honey has greater sweetening power than sugar, we prefer to substitute 1 cup honey for $1\frac{1}{4}$ cups sugar and to reduce the liquid in the recipe by $\frac{1}{4}$ cup. However, too much honey in a recipe may cause too brown a product. To neutralize the acidity of honey—unless sour milk or sour cream is called for in the recipe—add a mere pinch of baking soda. If honey is substituted in jams, jellies or candies, a higher degree of heat must be used in cooking. In candies, more persistent beating is needed and careful storage required against absorption of atmospheric moisture.

Honey is best stored covered in a dry place at room temperature. If it becomes crystalized, it can easily be reliquified by setting the jar on a trivet in a pan of ◗ warm water until the crystals are melted.

◗ Children under a year old should not be given honey, a suspected source of infant botulism.

MAPLE SYRUP

If so labeled, pure maple syrup must weigh not less than 11 pounds to the gallon. Largely sucrose with some invert sugar, the best grades are light in color. It is often stored covered at room temperature, but after it is opened it must be stored in the refrigerator to inhibit mold growth. If a mold develops, strain and bring the syrup to a rolling boil before rebottling. Should the syrup crystallize, set the jar in hot water; the syrup will quickly become liquid and smooth again.

◗ To substitute for sugar in cooking, generally use only $\frac{3}{4}$ cup maple syrup to each cup of sugar. ◗ To substitute maple syrup for sugar in baking, use these same proportions, but reduce the other liquid called for in the recipe by about 3 tablespoons for every cup of syrup substituted. One pint maple syrup has the same sweetening power as 1 pound maple sugar.

MAKING MAPLE SYRUP

Maple, that choicest of all syrups, is yours for the taking, with no harm to the trees that produce it. Collecting, however, is simpler than processing, for you will get only about one part syrup out of about forty to fifty parts of sap. The sugar maple, *Acer saccharum*, gives the sweetest sap. *Acer negrum* and *rubrum*, lower both in sugar and in yield, are also tapped, as are butternut, box elder, and some of the birches. The best months are late February, March and early April, when night temperatures are 20° and daytime 45°. Trees with diameters 10 to 30 inches at breast height can be hung with from one to four buckets. The taps can be on any area of the trunk from 2 to 5 feet from ground level, but if made late in the season should be on the north side. With a 7/16-inch bit, bore a hole diagonally upward 2 to 3 inches. Insert a sap spout with a bucket hook attached, as shown at right. Hammer the spout in gently but firmly so as not to split the bark, which will cause a leaky tap hole. If your bucket has a rim, make a small incision in the bucket beneath the rim so the bucket will be almost flush against the tree. Or use a special plastic collecting bag.

Within 12 hours you should find clear transparent sap in the bucket. Empty the buckets every day, strain the sap through a fine mesh strainer into sterile containers, and store under refrigeration until you have collected enough to boil. During cold weather you will probably not be bothered with microbial development at tap holes or in buckets. Should a mucouslike formation appear, scald or wipe both taps and buckets with a chlorine solution. Sap runs clear and usable until buds begin to swell, when an unpleasant odor and slight discoloration will warn you that the season is over.

When you have collected enough sap, it is advisable to start boiling it in shallow pans out of doors, as the boiling-off process produces quantities of sticky vapor. At first there is no danger of scorching the syrup, because of its great water content, but there is danger of its boiling over.

As the sap begins to thicken, you can move it to a more controlled heat source and cook it down in any heavy kettle whose capacity is three times the volume of the sap you are reducing. Maple sap, like water, boils at 212°. It becomes syrup at 219°. ▲ Adjust the temperature, therefore, at higher altitudes, depending on the boiling point of water at your altitude.

To make **maple cream,** boil to 225° to 227°; to make **maple sugar,** bring to 230° to 233°. Beat until it starts to thicken, then pour into molds. Before storing maple syrup and while it is still hot, filter it through a cloth-lined colander to rid it of sugar sand, a malate of lime. If sealed at 180°, the syrup will remain sterile for a year or more unrefrigerated.

MOLASSES

Rich in iron, molasses also improves the keeping qualities of breads and cakes. Molasses in this book means unsulfured or light molasses unless otherwise specified. There are 3 major types of molasses:

1. The best is unsulfured molasses deliberately made from the juice of sun-ripened cane which has grown from 12 to 15 months. 2. Sulfured

molasses is a by-product of sugar making; the sulfur fumes used in the manufacturing of sugar are retained as sulfur in the molasses. Light molasses results from the first boiling of the cane. So-called dark molasses is a product of the second boiling. 3. Blackstrap molasses is a waste product. It is a rather unpalatable residue of a third boiling in which more sugar crystals are extracted but in which minerals such as iron remain.

Since molasses is not so sweet as sugar, use 1 cup molasses for $3/4$ cup granulated sugar. The molasses should replace no more than $1/2$ the amount of sugar called for in the recipe. Add $1/2$ teaspoon baking soda for each cup molasses added, and omit or use half the baking powder called for. Make sure also to reduce the other liquid in the recipe by 5 tablespoons for each cup of molasses used.

CANE SYRUP

A concentrated sap of sugar cane, this is substituted as for Molasses, above.

TREACLE, GOLDEN OR REFINER'S SYRUP

Golden syrup, a residual molasses, is clarified and decolorized, which makes it mild in flavor. Treacle is darker and heavier. Neither substitutes properly for molasses.

SORGHUM

Thinner and sourer in flavor than cane molasses, sorghum is substituted as for Molasses, above.

CARAMELIZED SUGAR

A marvelous flavoring which can be made in several ways. While its cara-

mel flavor is strong, its sweetening power is reduced by about one-half.

I. For Hard Glazes

Heat in any ♦ very heavy, nonferrous pan over ♦ very low heat:

1 cup granulated sugar

Stir constantly with a long-handled spoon for 8 to 10 minutes until the sugar is melted and straw-colored. Remove the pan from the heat. Add:

$1/4$ cup very hot water

♦ very slowly and carefully, for a quick addition might cause explosive action. This safeguard against the spurting of the hot liquid will also help make the syrup smooth. To make the syrup heavier, return the pan to low heat for another 8 to 10 minutes, continuing to stir, until the sugar mixture is the color of maple syrup. Toward the end of this process, to prevent its becoming too dark, you may remove the pan from the heat and let the caramelization reach a bubbling state from the stored heat of the pan. Store the syrup covered on a shelf for future use. The syrup hardens on standing but, if stored in a heatproof jar, is easily remelted by heating the jar gently in hot water. Should the sugar burn, use it for coloring, see below.

II. For a Croquant or Brown Nougat

Follow as in I, above, but at the beginning of the recipe, combine with the sugar:

1 tablespoon water

Proceed as directed.

III. For Coloring

If stored covered on a shelf, caramelized sugar will keep indefinitely. This can be used to replace the more highly seasoned commercial gravy colorings. The intense heat under which it is processed destroys all sweetening power.

Melt in a ♦ very heavy nonferrous pan over low heat:

1 cup sugar

Stir constantly until it is burned smoke-colored to black. ♦ Remove from the heat and be sure to let it cool. ♦ Quick addition of water to intensely hot sugar which is well over 300° can be explosive and very dangerous. Then, as in caramelizing above, add ♦ almost drop by drop:

1 cup hot water

After the water is added, stir over low heat until the burnt sugar becomes a thin dark liquid.

SYNTHETIC OR NON-NUTRITIVE SWEETENERS

There is some reason to question the systemic effect of all noncaloric sweeteners. ♦ Any of these sugar substitutes should be used on doctor's orders only and, in cooking or baking, according to manufacturers' directions. The FDA allows the saccharin-based substitutes to be sold without restrictions, but cyclamates alone or in combination with saccharin must be labeled as drugs. The saccharin types should not be cooked, as they produce a bitter flavor. Cyclamates can be heated, and in some cooked foods their sweetening power actually increases. But they do not give the same texture in baking as do true sugars and therefore should be used only in recipes specially developed for them. For amounts to be used in substitutions for sugars, see 294.

ABOUT GELATIN

To get the most nourishment out of gelatin, which is not a complete protein, see (I, 4). Meat, fish, eggs, nuts or milk may be added to enrich its value. To get the most allure ♦ never use too much. The result is rubbery and unpleasant. The finished gelatin should be quivery—not rigid—when jostled. It is sympathetic to almost all foods ♦ except fresh or frozen pineapple, which contains a substance that inhibits jelling. Cooked pineapple presents no problem.

Gelatin is full of tricks. It can turn liquids into solids to produce gala dessert and salad molds. It makes sophisticated chaud-froid and ingenuous marshmallows. It also makes a showcase for leftovers and keeps delicate meats and fish in prime condition for buffet service. Chopped and used as a garnish, (I, 77), or cut into fancy shapes, clear gelatins add sparkle to many dishes. Gelatin also gives a smoother texture to frozen desserts, to jellies and cold soups. It thickens cold sauces and glazes, (I, 426), and, in sponge and whipped desserts, doubles the volume.

♦ Gelatin dishes must, of course, be refrigerated until ready to use. And, in buffets, they are best presented on chilled trays or platters set over crushed ice. While gelatin must be kept cold, it should ♦ never be frozen unless the fat content of the recipe is very high—as in certain ice creams.

Gelatin's power to displace moisture is due to its "bloom," or strength. In household gelatins this is rated at 150 and means that the contents of 1 package of unflavored gelatin or about 1 tablespoon can turn about 2 cups of liquid into a solid. Gelatin often comes ready to use in granules, but the most delicate fish and meat aspics are made with stocks reduced from bones, skin and fish heads. It also comes in sheets. For equivalents, see 291.

High sugar concentrations retard gelatinization and reduce thickening power. Unless a recipe is exceedingly acid, 1 tablespoon of gelatin to 2 cups of liquid should produce a consistency firm enough to unmold after 2 hours of chilling—if the gelatin is a clear one. But it must get 4 hours of chilling if the gelatin has fruits, vegetables or nuts added to it. Also, allow proportionately more jelling time for large, as opposed to individual, molds. If you prefer a less firm texture, use 1 tablespoon of gelatin to 2¼ to 2½ cups liquid. These gelatins will not mold but are delightful when served in cups or in coupes. If you are ▶ doubling a gelatin recipe that originally called for 2 cups of liquid, use only 3¾ cups in the doubled recipe.

For basic gelatin aspic recipes, see (I, 76–86). For Gelatin Desserts, see 521–530. For an aspic glaze for hors d'oeuvre or open sandwiches, see (I, 427). For interesting molds and gelatin combinations to fill them, see (I, 76).

MIXING GELATIN

I. Sprinkle 1 tablespoon of gelatin granules over the surface of ¼ cup cold water and ▶ without stirring let it soak about 3 minutes until it has absorbed the moisture and is translucent. Have ready just at the boiling point 1¾ to 2 cups stock, fruit juice, milk, wine or water. Combine with the soaked gelatin and stir until dissolved.

You may allow the dissolved gelatin to cool at room temperature over a bowl of cracked ice, or in the refrigerator—but not in the freezer, as a gummy look is apt to develop, and

the surface cracks miserably. It is interesting that gelatins that are slow to jell are also slow to break down when they are removed from the refrigerator, but any gelatin will begin to weep if exposed too long to high temperatures.

II. If you do not want to subject the liquid in the recipe to high heat or reduce its flavor and vitamin content, use a double boiler and sprinkle 1 tablespoon gelatin over ¼ cup cold water. Dissolve this mixture ▶ over—not in—boiling water. Add to the dissolved gelatin 1¾ to 2 cups 75° liquid and stir well.

III. If you are in a hurry and are making a gelatin that calls for 1 cup water and 1 cup stock or fruit juice, you can prepare the gelatin as in I above, boiling your cup of stock or fruit juice and then stirring about 8 large or 10 small ice cubes into the hot liquid to cool it. Stir the cubes constantly 2 to 3 minutes. Remove the unmelted ice. Let the mixture stand 3 to 5 minutes. Incorporate the fruit or other solids called for, and mold.

IV. For an even faster gelatin with frozen fruit, see Blender Fruit Whip, 526.

MAKING FANCY GELATIN MOLDS

▶ To prepare molds for clear gelatins, rinse them well in cold water, as shown opposite. Another method is to coat the mold with vegetable oil, but we do not recommend this for clear gelatin, because a blurred surface results. After filling an undecorated mold, run a knife through the mixture to release any air bubbles that might be trapped in it. Then refrigerate until ready to unmold.

Before starting to make fancy designs in gelatin, have ready well-drained and chilled foods. Allow about 1¼ cups of solids for each cup of gelatin or aspic. Just as the gelatin thickens to about the consistency of uncooked egg white, put a small amount in a chilled mold or dish with sloping sides which has been rinsed in cold water. Roll and tip the mold in such a way that a thin layer of gelatin coats its inside surface. Refrigerate the mold to set the gelatin.

Now impale bits of food on a skewer or toothpick. Dip them one by one into the gelatin and place them

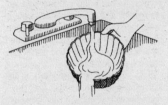

just where you want them on the hardened layer in the mold, to form the design. When the decorations for one layer are in place, fill the spaces between with more gelatin. Return the mold to the refrigerator until this has set, and proceed with this method until the mold is filled.

When using a fish-shaped or other fancy mold, accent the lines of the design with slivers of egg white, cucumber or peppers, if for a salad; with citron, cherries, crystallized rinds or fruits, if for a dessert.

An easier way to make layered molds is to choose nuts, fruits and vegetables of different weights and porosity. Put them in a very slightly jelled mixture and let them find their own levels. The floaters are apple

cubes, banana slices, fresh grapefruit sections or pear slices, fresh strawberry halves, broken nutmeats and marshmallows. The sinkers are fresh orange slices, fresh grapes, cooked prunes, and the following canned fruits: apricots, Royal Anne cherries, peaches, pears, pineapple, plums and raspberries. If you are making gelatins to serve in champagne coupes, you can decorate the tops with grape halves. Even though they are technically sinkers, you can wait until the gelatin is almost set and hold each grape for just a second until it makes enough contact not to turn wrong side up.

Another way to make fancy molds is to combine layers of clear and whipped or sponge gelatins, see About Gelatin Puddings, 522.

♦ To unmold aspics or gelatin puddings, have ready a chilled plate large enough to allow for a garnish. You may moisten the dish slightly. This will prevent the gelatin from sticking, and enable you to center the mold more easily. You may first use a thin knife at several points on the edge to release the vacuum. Then reverse the mold onto the plate. If necessary, place a warm damp cloth over the mold for a few seconds, as shown on 236. If the food is still not released, shake the mold lightly, bracing it against the serving dish. Some people dip the mold into hot water for just a second. We find this risky with delicate gelatins, as the heat must not go above 115°.

OTHER GELATINOUS THICKENERS

AGAR

This dried seaweed looks like transparent soup noodles. Its gel strength

is not easily destroyed by heat or acid. For aspics or jelled desserts, allow 1 teaspoon agar for each cup of liquid to be jelled. Soften by first soaking in ¼ cup cold liquid, then dissolving in ¾ cup hot liquid. To avoid a weedy flavor, be sure the agar you buy is highly purified. If used as a salad garnish, soak 2 hours, changing the water 2 or 3 times. Cut into 2-inch lengths before serving.

IRISH MOSS OR CARRAGEENAN

Another seaweed which also needs to be well purified if a weedy odor is to be avoided. It is used as an emulsifier, stabilizer and thickener in a variety of foods. Allow from 6 to 10 grams powder per cup of liquid, depending on how stiff a gel you want. Prepare as for agar, above. It needs to be heated to 140° to dissolve, and becomes thin in the presence of acid.

GUM TRAGACANTH

Used in some icings to give pliability, and in salad dressings to add body. Use from 1 to 4 grams of powder for each cup liquid, depending on the thickness desired.

RENNET

Dioscorides said that rennet had the power to join things that were dispersed and to disperse things that came together. No chemist these days dares match such a claim! Rennet, an extract from the lining of the first stomach of calves, is the coagulant in cheese making, 194. See Rennet Pudding or Junket, 530.

ABOUT NUTS

Whether they are seeds, like pecans and walnuts; fruits, like lichees; or tubers, like peanuts—nuts contain concentrated protein and fats. Except for chestnuts, 238, they contain very little starch. But it is for their essential oils, which carry the flavor, and for the textural contrast that we treasure them so much. The reason they are so often listed as an optional ingredient in our recipes is merely that the recipes will carry without them—and with so much less cost and calorie value. Except for green almonds and pickled green walnuts, nearly all nuts are eaten when ripe.

The best way to store nuts is to keep them in their shells. This protects them from light, heat, moisture and exposure to air—factors which tend to cause rancidity in the shelled product. The difference in the keeping time for shelled pecans, for instance, may range from 2 months at about 70° to as long as 1 year in a freezer. So, if nuts are already shelled, store them tightly covered in a cool, dark, dry place or in a freezer. Unsalted nuts have longer storage life than do salted ones, which tend to rancidity. Refrigerate after opening. Some nuts, like pecans and Brazil nuts, are more easily shelled if boiling water is poured over them and they are allowed to stand in it 15 to 20 minutes. Be sure to discard any kernels that are moldy, shriveled or dry, as they may prove bitter or rancid.

As a rough rule, a pound of nuts in

the shell yields about ¹/₂ pound shelled. For more detailed yields, see 293.

BLANCHING NUTS

In addition to the tough outer shell, some nuts have a thin inner lining or skin that may need removing. If so, just before using, pour boiling water over the shelled nuts. For large quantities, you may have to let them stand, but only for about 1 minute at the most. ♦ The briefer the length of time, the better. Drain. Pour cold water over them to arrest further heating and drain again. Pinch or rub off the skins.

For peanuts, filberts and pistachio nuts, you may prefer to roast in a 350° oven 10 to 20 minutes and then rub off the skins.

ROASTING OR TOASTING NUTS

This both crisps them and brings up the flavor. Unless otherwise specified, place them blanched or unblanched in a 300° oven and turn frequently to avoid scorching. ♦ To avoid loss of flavor and toughening, do not overtoast, as nuts tend to darken and become crisper as they cool.

SALTING NUTS

♦ Coat a bowl with egg white, butter or olive oil, add the nuts and shake them until they are coated. If you salt before cooking, allow not more than ¹/₂ teaspoon salt to one cup of nuts. Spread the nuts on cookie tins and heat in a 250° oven. Roast about 10 to 15 minutes, stirring frequently to achieve even browning. A more rapid way is to heat in a heavy iron skillet 2 tablespoons oil for every cup of nuts. Add nuts and stir constantly about 3 minutes. Drain on paper toweling. Salt and serve.

CHOPPING NUTS

If rather large pieces are needed, simply break nuts like pecans and walnuts with the fingers. For finer pieces, use a knife or a chopping bowl and chopper, see (I, 430). Or chop as shown below. ♦ It is easier if the nuts are moist and warm and if the knife is a sharp French one. Group the nuts in a circle with a diameter of about the length of the blade. Grasp the knife on the top at both hilt and blade ends as shown. Rock the blade briskly from point to hilt, gradually turning the knife toward you in a semicircle. Gather the chopped bits together and repeat the rocking until the bits are as fine as you want them.

Almonds may be chopped in a ⅄ blender. ♦ Process no more than ¹/₂ cup at a time for 30 seconds at highest speed.

GRINDING NUTS

♦ Use a special type of grinder—one that shreds or grates them sharply to keep them dry, rather than a type that will crush them and release their oils. Do small quantities in a rotary grinder, as sketched on 238. Light, dry, fluffy particles result, which become a binder in Torten, 430.

Sometimes, however, for butters and pastes, a a meat grinder or a ⅄ blender is used. We do not otherwise recommend a blender for grinding nuts, as it tends to make the nuts too

oily—except for almonds, which should be done in small quantities.

Peanut butter is so popular that it has overshadowed the use of other nut butters. Try grinding almonds,

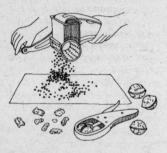

pecans or walnuts into butter. These are so rich they need no additional oil. Use for every cup of nuts 1/3 teaspoon salt.

ALMONDS AND ALMOND OIL

Grown in Europe, Asia, Australia, South Africa and California, almonds are available in the shell or shelled and toasted with skins on or blanched with skins removed. Untoasted are best for baking, as toasted ones may become too brown. Look for a plump, smooth kernel, and buy in the shell for economy and freshness. Relatively high in balanced protein for a vegetable source, they are high in fat compared to beans. Almonds may be ground to make torten, marzipan, and almond paste, or slivered for toppings. As a garnish, see Amandine, 221. They may also be eaten while green and soft with cheese and wine. Almond oil is used like other vegetable oils, 202. It has a yellow-white appearance and is odorless, with a mild nutty flavor.

BITTER ALMONDS AND BITTER ALMOND OIL

Used as a flavoring and called for in some classic European recipes such as Orgeat syrup, bitter almonds are not available in the United States in concentrated form because they contain the poison prussic acid.

BEECHNUTS

A real treat—but just try to beat the squirrels to this harvest.

BRAZIL NUTS

The more delicate types do not ship well, and we must rely on a rather coarse, tough variety that does. To slice these large kernels, cover the shelled nuts with cold water and bring slowly to a boil. Simmer 5 minutes. Drain. Slice lengthwise or make curls with a vegetable slicer. You may toast the slices at 350° for about 12 minutes.

CASHEW NUTS

Cashews have an edible, fleshy fruit covering which can be eaten raw without harm. But between the outside shell and the kernel is a very irritating toxic oil related to poison ivy, which must be removed or destroyed by heat. Make cashew butter as for Peanut Butter, 240. For baking, use the untoasted cashew.

CHESTNUTS: MARRONS AND OTHER VARIETIES

The chestnuts in **Joy** recipes are not to be confused with the poisonous kind found in ornamental allées, or with the edible crisp Chinese water chestnuts, we usually know only in canned form and in oriental dishes, see below.

Chestnuts are frequently used as stuffing for fowl and traditionally combined with Brussels sprouts and red cabbage. One of our more knowing European friends insists that if navy beans are substituted for chestnuts in desserts strongly laced with coffee or almond paste, one cannot tell the difference.

To shell chestnuts, make two crosscut gashes on their flat side with a sharp pointed knife. The outer shell may come off when you do this, but the inner skin will still protect the kernel. To remove both the inner and outer coverings, place the nuts in a pan over high heat, dropping oil or butter over them—1 teaspoon to 1 pound of nuts. Shake them until coated, then place in a moderate oven until the shells and inner brown skin can be easily removed. This brown inside skin is bitter and must be peeled off while still warm.

Or, if you are using the chestnuts in a recipe calling for boiled chestnuts, they may be covered with boiling water, simmered 15 to 25 minutes and drained, after which the shells and skins may be removed. The meats may be tender enough to be put through a purée strainer. If not, again cover with boiling water and cook until tender. To boil, bake or steam chestnuts, see (I, 313). To roast, see 86.

To reconstitute dried chestnuts, soak overnight in water to cover. Rinse and pick over. Simmer until they are tender and puffed up. ◗ Substitute them for cooked fresh chestnuts, cup for cup.

Allow about 1 1/2 pounds in the shell for 1 pound shelled chestnuts. Thirty-five to 40 whole, fairly large chestnuts make about 2 1/2 cups peeled. For the numerous uses of chestnuts, see Index.

The European blight that has almost destroyed *Castanea sativus* and its opulent hybrids such as the marron de Lyon, with its simple large kernel, has somehow spared the good Italian chestnuts that are still regularly imported to our American markets. And on our own American soil some blight-impervious oriental varieties are coming into their own: *crenata* from Japan and *mollissima* from China—not to mention the ever-sturdy little native chinquapin.

All chestnuts need long doses of tender loving care. In China they are roasted in hot sand which is continuously stirred, producing a constant moderate heat on all sides. For the French method, which is also slow but produces delicious chestnuts, see Steamed Chestnuts, (I, 314).

WATER CHESTNUTS

There are two types—both of which are crispy and delicious. In one type, the shell grows together into a horn at one end. The other is bulbous. Use water chestnuts in Hors d'Oeuvre, 85–86, and Vegetables, (I, 372–373).

FILBERTS AND HAZELNUTS

Varieties less rich than pecan, these are almost identical in their sophisticated flavor. Filberts are the more subtle European versions of our native hazelnuts.

HICKORIES AND BUTTERNUTS

Rich natives, like pecans, and they never need blanching.

MACADAMIA NUTS

Use these exotic, nutritious 1-inch-round nuts roasted or unroasted, in recipes calling for nuts; as cocktail snacks or as substitutes for Chinese chestnuts. As these nuts are hard to crack, try wrapping each one in heavy cloth and hammering it on a very hard surface. To roast, spread shelled nuts in a shallow pan and heat in a 250° oven 12 to 15 minutes, stirring often. Salt lightly and store in an airtight refrigerated container.

PINE OR INDIAN NUTS

Known also as piñon in Spain or pignolia in Italy—where the variety is richer. These are good in Dolmas, (I, 626), and in Pesto, 251.

PISTACHIO NUTS

These nuts, loved for their green color and haunting flavor, are often used in farces or pâtés. To skin, spread on baking sheets and heat at 400° for 4 minutes. Cool and slip off skins.

ENGLISH AND AMERICAN WALNUTS
AND PECANS

Walnuts are highly polyunsaturated. Blanching for 3 minutes rids them of an acid which some people find indigestible. Then dry and toast as indicated above. The English or Persian walnut and the American or black walnut are perhaps the most familiar. Hull at once after harvesting. Pecans are probably the heaviest in fat of all our natives, with sometimes as much as three-fourths of their bulk in fat.

PEANUTS

These underground legumes—also called ground-nuts or, in their larger form, goobers—are high in valuable, if incomplete, proteins. If the heart is left in, they make a real contribution to the diet. The small Spanish types will grow in the northern states. All peanuts are best eaten right after roasting, before they get limp. If roasting them in the shell at home, keep the oven at 300° and roast 30 to 45 minutes, or 20 to 30 minutes if shelled. Turn them constantly to avoid scorching. Check for doneness by removing skins. The inner skins, heavy in thiamin, are pleasantly flavored. But little is gained by home roasting, as a steam process used commercially for roasting peanuts in the shell gives superior results. ♦ Discard any peanuts that are moldy.

♣ PEANUT BUTTER

Federal regulations require commercial peanut butter to contain 90% shelled roasted ground peanuts, with additions of no more than 10% of salt, sweeteners and oil. However smooth and satisfying commercial peanut butters may seem, they are often made without the germ of the nut. This valuable portion—as in grains—contains minerals, vitamins and proteins, yet it is literally fed to the birds. The commercial objection to the germ is twofold: (1) It gives the butter a somewhat bitter flavor, and (2), as with whole grains, the heat of processing and the heat in storage may cause the finished product to grow rancid. ♣ If you are smart, you will make your own full-bodied peanut butter in an electric blender. Use:

**Fresh roasted or salted
peanuts**

It is wise to start with a bland oil:

Safflower or vegetable oil

Allow 1½ to 2 tablespoons oil to 1 cup peanuts. If nuts are unsalted, add salt to taste:

**About ½ teaspoon salt
per cup**

ABOUT SEEDS, GRAINS, BEANS AND PEAS

♦ Be certain to use only seeds which have not been fumigated or treated with pesticides or fungicides. **Sunflower, pumpkin, buckwheat, barley** and **squash seeds** should be hulled before eating or using in recipes. All of these are flavorful and nutritionally valuable. To roast, see the general rule under Nuts, 237. However, to roast **soybeans,** soak 1/4 cup beans overnight, refrigerated, in 1 cup water. Drain and dry thoroughly. Roast in a shallow pan about 2 hours in a 200° oven, then put pan under broiler to brown the soybeans. Use as is or season and mix with oil.

Poppy seeds come from *Papaver somniferum,* but the seed has no narcotic properties. The most desirable is grown in Holland and is a slate-blue color. The seed is best when roasted or steamed and crushed before use in cooking—so its full flavor is released. If it is one of your favorite flavors, it is worth getting a special hand-mill for grinding it. Use it in baked items and try it on noodles.

Sesame or benne seeds are a favorite topping for breads, cookies and vegetables. Their nutty flavor is strongest when the unhulled seeds are lightly toasted about 20 minutes in a 350° oven and stirred frequently. If hulled, the seeds are white. Crushed, they may be made into an oily paste, called Tahin, see at right. Crushed sesame, together with cooked chick-peas, also forms the base for Hummus, 103. Sesame oil from the seeds is desirable in salads. For other seeds, see About Spices, 257, and Herbs, 262.

⅄ TAHIN

A Mideast seed butter of yogurtlike consistency, used to dress salads or as a base for sweets.
Combine in a blender:

    4 tablespoons ground sesame seeds

    1 teaspoon sesame oil

    1 tablespoon lemon or lime juice

    1/2 teaspoon salt

Add slowly while blending:

    About 1/2 cup water

Remove from the blender and stir in if you wish:

    (1 to 2 pressed garlic cloves)

SPROUTING GRAINS, BEANS AND PEAS

Sprouting seeds not only are one of the wonders of this world but probably produce by far the most nutritively valuable addition to the diet in relation to their cost. One-quarter cup of grain or beans expands into one pint of sprouts with rich protein content. The sprouting action greatly increases the already rich vitamin content. Soybeans, however, are the only seeds in which the protein is complete, (I, 4).

Use or buy seeds, preferably organically grown, ♦ that have not been chemically pretreated for agricultural purposes. Remove any damaged or moldy seeds. For about a one-pint yield, wash and soak overnight in:

    1 cup water

    1/4 cup seeds: alfalfa, red clover, fenugreek, mustard, radish, sesame, sunflower; any grains, beans or peas

♦ Avoid potato and tomato seeds, which, when sprouting, are poisonous, and fava and lima beans, which are extremely toxic when used raw. Next morning, drain, reserving the liquid for stock. Place the seeds in a one-quart wide-mouthed glass jar securely closed with nylon mesh or cheesecloth so that air can reach the seeds. If the jar is stored on its side the seeds can be shaken to spread over a larger area, which is desirable. Place the jar in a dark, warm cupboard or in an opaque bag so that light is excluded but air is still available. If this method is used, it is important to rinse and drain the seeds three times daily and to invert the jar to let it drain thoroughly after each rinsing. If you cannot rinse three times daily, place the seeds in a well-soaked new clay flower pot. The newness is important to discourage fungal development. The drain hole should be stopped up with a cotton wad or a cork. Place the pot in a saucer of water that you keep filled all during the process of sprouting. Place the pot in its saucer, loosely covered with a plate, in a dark, warm place. Whichever method you use, watch closely and discard if molding. Sprouts should develop in 3 to 5 days, although mung and soybeans may take 6 to 8 days.

A general rule is to serve the sprouted seeds when the sprout is at least as long as the seed, although sunflower and sesame are served when the sprout first appears. Chickpeas, flax, lentils and soybeans can be used with about half-inch sprouts, and mung bean sprouts can be more than 2 inches. If not served at once, refrigerate sprouted seeds in a covered colander or a loosely covered container. Do not hold more than a day or two. They can be frozen, but considerable nutritive value is lost. You may also add them to stir-fried dishes or to soups and stews just before serving, but for best nutritional results serve them raw, hulls and all,

as a garnish or in salads or sandwich fillings. If you care to remove the hulls, stir the sprouts in a bowl of cold water until the husks rise and may be skimmed off. A famous tea sandwich combining sprouts of "cress"—not watercress but garden cress, *Lepidium sativum*—with sprouts of mustard, *Brassica nigra* or *Sinapsis alba,* takes advantage of an age-old English custom of producing fresh greens on a minuscule scale all year around in the kitchen. The sprouts, so tiny-leaved as to be reminiscent of doll houses, can be germinated between blotters or in a wrung-out piece of flannel or Turkish toweling in from 10 to 14 days. To have them ready simultaneously, sow the mustard 4 days later than the cress, as it germinates more rapidly. When sprouted, leave the sprouts on the germinating surface. Keep them moist and exposed to light until the two small leaves are green and about $1/8$ inch long. Serve scattered on very thin, lightly sweet-buttered rounds of bread.

ABOUT CHOCOLATE AND COCOA

Both of these delights come from the evergreen trees of the genus *Theobroma,* "Food of the Gods." The manufacture of the two is identical up to the moment when the chocolate liquor is extracted from the nibs, or hulled beans, and molded into solid cakes. At this point, part of the "butter" is removed from some of the cakes, which become cocoa, and added to others, which, in turn, become the bitter chocolate we know as cooking or baking chocolate.

Cocoa butter is remarkable for the fact that, under normal storage conditions, it will keep for years without becoming rancid. There are many pharmaceutical demands for it, and in inferior chocolate it is sometimes replaced by other fat.

Ideal storage temperature for chocolate is 78°. The bloom that turns chocolate grayish after it has been stored at high temperatures is harmless—merely the fat content coming to the surface.

Semisweet chocolate, available in 8-ounce cakes or in bits or pieces, is good for candy dipping because of its sheen when melted. It is also good for icings, sauces and fillings. The best sweet chocolate is made by combining the melted bitter cake with 35% cocoa butter, finely milled sugar and such additions as vanilla and milk—depending on the type of chocolate desired. German's chocolate, which is conditioned against heat, refers not to the country but to a very canny person of that name who early realized there was a greater profit if the sugar was already added to the chocolate when it was sold. Milk chocolate—best known as candy bar chocolate—may be used for icings, pies and puddings.

An entire square of chocolate equals 1 ounce. Two-thirds cup of semisweet chocolate is 6 ounces by weight—or 10²/3 tablespoons by volume. But in any semisweet chocolate, you have about 60% bitter chocolate and 40% sugar. Should you want to substitute semisweet for bitter, make the adjustment in the recipe, using less sugar, more chocolate and a dash of vanilla.

◗ For exact substitution and equivalents of chocolate and cocoa, see 289. In some quick-cooking recipes, this substitution may not be successful, as the sugar doesn't crystallize properly with the chocolate. If semisweet chocolate stiffens when melted—in sauces, for instance—add a small amount of butter and stir well until smooth.

It is easy to substitute cocoa for chocolate in sauces: just add 1 tablespoon butter to 3 tablespoons cocoa for each ounce of chocolate. But in baking it is wiser to choose recipes written either for cocoa or for chocolate, as the cocoa has a flourlike quality that must be compensated for if chocolate is substituted, or the cake will become doughy. In cakes and cookies, soda is often used to give chocolate a ruddy tone. A few drops of vinegar serve the same purpose.

◗ All chocolate scorches easily, so melt it slowly over hot water. Do not use boiling water, as even a small amount of steam may harden or stiffen the chocolate. If this should happen, add for each ounce of chocolate 1/2 teaspoon or more of vegetable shortening—not butter—to reliquify the chocolate. If you don't like to clean the pot, float the chocolate on a small foil "boat" and discard the foil after use. Or place wrapped squares, folded edges up, in the top of a double boiler ◗ over—not in—hot water for 10 to 12 minutes. Cool chocolate to about 80° before adding it to cake, cookie or pudding mixtures.

To grate chocolate, chill it and try shaving or grating it in a rotary grinder, 238. Have a big bowl ready to receive it—or you may be annoyed by its flighty dynamism.

To make chocolate curls for decorating parfaits or cream pies, hold a wrapped square of chocolate in the hand to warm it slightly. Unwrap and shave chocolate with long thin strokes, using a vegetable peeler or a small sharp knife.

Cocoa is pulverized from the dry cocoa cakes, which, after processing, still contain from 10% fat for regular cocoa up to 22% to 24% fat for breakfast cocoa. The so-called Dutch type maintains the heavier fat content, and the small quantity of alkali introduced during the processing to neutralize the acids produces a slightly different flavor. Instant cocoa, which usually contains 80% sugar, is precooked and has an emulsifier added to make it dissolve readily in either a hot or a cold liquid.

For details about cocoa and chocolate as beverages, see (I, 32). For Dipping Chocolate, see 582.

So-called **white chocolate** contains no chocolate at all but is prepared from vegetable fats, coloring and flavors. Should you be allergic to chocolate, try carob, 289, which tastes almost like chocolate, although not so strongly flavored.

ABOUT COCONUTS

If you live in coconut country, you know the delight of using the flower sap as well as the green and the mature fruit of this graceful palm. In cooking, you may substitute its "milk," "cream" and "butter" for dairy products. However, be aware that this exchange is not an equal one nutritionally, because the coconut is much lower in protein. ◖ Coconut products are very sensitive to high heat. For this reason they are added to hot sauces at the last minute or are cooked over hot water. They are especially treasured in preparing curries and delicate fish and fruit dishes.

The first thing to do with a coconut, of course, is to get at it. Lacking power tools, you drop the large fruit onto a rocklike substance. If it doesn't crack open enough so that the husk pulls away, use your trusty axe. Out comes a fiber-covered nut. Shake it. A sloshing noise means that the nut

is fresh and that you can count on some watery liquid erroneously referred to as milk. If the husked coconut is green, the top can be lopped off with a large, heavy knife or a machete. The liquid within is clear, and the greenish jellylike pulp makes ideal food for small children and invalids. To open the harder shell of the mature nut, pierce the three shiny black dots which form a monkey face at the peak. Use a strong ice pick, and hammer it in. Reserve the drained liquid under refrigeration and be certain to use within 24 hours, or freeze it. Tap the nut briskly all over with a hammer. It usually splits lengthwise, and these halves can be used as containers for serving hot or cold food. See illustrations, opposite.

You may also open the shell with heat, but then the shell is useless for serving food. To do so, place the undrained husked coconut in a preheated 325° oven 15 to 20 minutes. ◖ Do not overcook, as this destroys the flavor. Remove from the oven and cool until the nut can be handled. Wrap it in a heavy cloth to prevent any pieces from flying off. Then crack it with hammer taps. ◖ Have a bowl ready to catch the milky liquid.

Coconut milk and cream, very rich in fat, are made from the grated, mature, stiff white meat of the nut. The grating is sometimes done while the meat is still in the shell. Note the illustration opposite of a grater given to us by a friend from India which simplifies preparing coconut for cakes, garnishes or Coconut Dulcie, 571. Or you may leave the thin brown skin on and use it to protect the fingers as you hand-grate. Use a vegetable parer to remove the skin. If the skin is removed, you may cut the meat into small chunks and chop in the ⅃ blender, no more than ½ cup at a time. Add ¼ cup hot water to make coconut milk; hot milk to make coconut cream. Then strain and measure. If more milk is needed than results, add more hot water, reblend and strain again.

In the East Indies, they heat the grated coconut meat in its own natural liquid ♦ just to the boiling point, then remove it from the heat and cool. In the West Indies, they pour boiling water or milk over grated coconut and add the natural liquid—allowing in all about 1 pint liquid for a medium coconut. In either case, when the mixture has cooled, the coconut is drained through two thicknesses of cheesecloth, and the meat, retained in the cloth, is squeezed and kneaded until dry. The drained liquid is allowed to set, refrigerated; it solidifies into a cold butter and can be taken off in one piece. When the "cream" rises, it is skimmed off and refrigerated.

Coconut "butter," though vegetable in origin, contains completely saturated fatty acids. It is made from chilled coconut "cream"—also very rich in fat—by churning with a rotary beater or in a ⚒ blender. When the solid mass rises, force any excess water out of it with the back of a spoon. To utilize the coconut that remains, make **polvo de amor,** following. Use it as a garnish for breakfast foods and desserts.

Brown slowly in a heavy pan over low heat:

1 cup strained coconut pulp
2 tablespoons sugar

Grated fresh coconut may be soaked 6 hours refrigerated in milk to cover, and drained before use. This gives it about the same moisture content as the canned, shredded or flaked types—for which it may be substituted.

To toast grated coconut, spread it thinly on a baking sheet and heat about 10 minutes in a preheated 325° oven. Stir frequently. For a dessert or a spread made from grated coconut, see Coconut Dulcie, 571.

♦ To substitute flaked coconut, use 1⅓ cups firmly packed for 1 cup grated.

Coconut shells can make interesting food and drink containers. For a bowl, saw off the upper third of the shell. For a rack to hold this round-bottomed shell upright, cut off about one-half of the smaller piece as sketched on the left, above. For serving salads, cut the shell lengthwise. The shells can also be used to heat and serve sauced foods. Cut off the top third to serve as a lid. The food may be heated in a 350° oven by placing the lidded nutshell in a small custard cup or on an inverted canning jar lid in a pan of hot water. Baste the shell about every 10 minutes until the contents are hot. Or simply fill the shell with very hot food. The custard cup forms a base when you serve; or fold a napkin or ti leaf for support, as sketched on 245.

ABOUT FLAVORS AND SEASONINGS

"Season to taste." . . . How that time-tested direction stimulates the born cook! We know that seasonings, spices, herbs and condiments can complement and compliment food, but it is our own sense of taste that composes the symphony. Just how does it do so? The anatomy of taste is the tongue, and it differentiates between four basic sensations. The top of the tongue detects sweet and sour, the sides salt and sour, the back bitter. When we taste things, they pass so quickly over these areas that a fast sequence of tastes results, like an arpeggio or a chord. When we were young, lollipops were their sweet-

est—not without reason, because senses dull with age, and our taste buds were more impressionable then. Not only were we told to gulp our medicines fast, but we took them iced to reduce their impact. Conversely, as adults we hold chilled wine in our mouths until it has had a chance to warm up and release its flavor. And, to taste normally sweet, the ice cream we freeze must be sugared more than warm foods. It is relished more, too, when taken in small amounts and held in the mouth momentarily before swallowing. Heat seems to affect sourness and saltiness; lemon seems less acid when the tea is hottest, and soup saltier when hot than when cold. The best time to judge for salt adjustment is when food is just below 98°.

But sweet, sour, bitter and salt are only foundation tastes on which is built the complex and subtle structure whose charms are due much more to the sense of smell than to the sense of taste. Try tasting food while holding your breath; you will notice that a full and characteristic flavor is realized only when the breath is expelled through the nostrils. Since foods must be in solution for their flavors to be fully appreciated, texture plays a large part both directly and as contrast. Flavors that stand out in liquid may grow duller rather than sharper if some gumlike substance such as tragacanth or agar-agar is used as a thickener, with the intent of increasing tactile sensations related to taste. The peppers and ginger, because of their nonvolatile components, leave a somewhat painful burning sensation, along with a pleasant glow and tingle. In contrast, mint has the power to cool because of its high menthol content. Types of seasoning modify one another. Salt, for example, can make sugar less cloying and tone down acidity; as a corollary, sugar or vinegar may reduce saltiness. Ginger, brandy or sherry can lessen "gaminess" in fish and wildfowl while bringing a comforting warmth. Salt, pepper and parsley act as catalysts for other flavors. A reminder: prolonged drinking before and smoking during a meal tends to desensitize all the pathways along which food is appreciated.

The history of seasoning is an ironical one. Back in medieval days the spice routes to the Orient were fiercely contested, for spices were essential to render palatable the poorly preserved foods of Europe. Nowadays, many foods in our western world are so successfully and uniformly preserved that seasonings are needed to make them interesting enough to eat! The Greeks had recognized nine flavors: sweet, salty, sour, bitter, astringent, dry, pungent, vinous and oily. Even today no more generally acceptable categories exist. The infinite interplay of taste, aroma and texture combined with hereditary and national preferences defies exact classification, and only the familiar remains acceptable to the majority of people. Try setting your sails for new courses on this endlessly fascinating sea of taste.

◗ When adding seasoning, the greatest care must be used to enhance the natural or previously acquired flavor of the food at hand. The role of the seasoner is that of impresario, not actor: to bring out the best in his material, not to stifle it with florid, strident off-key delivery or to smother it with heavy trappings. First and best, of course, even before seasoning, are the built-in flavors of food grown in rich soils or from animals which have been nourished on flavor-inducing vegetation. Examples are the famous sea-marsh-grazed lamb of France, the heather-dieted grouse of Scotland, our own southern peach-fed pigs or northern game birds after they have taken their fill of juniper or other aromatic berries. Next come the flavors accentuated by heat: in the glazes on browned meats; in the essential roasting of coffee and cocoa beans; in the toasting of nuts, seeds and breads; in the highly treasured "ozmazome," as the gourmet calls it, which results from rich broths; as well as in the blending of tastes achieved generally through slow cooking.

Then there are the flavors induced by fermentation and bacterial activity, as in wines and cheeses; those created by distillation in extracts and liqueurs, and those brought about by smoking, 634, or marination, 180. Intensification of flavor in foods can be by purely mechanical means, too: the cracking and softening of seeds like those of poppy, anise, coriander and caraway to release their essential oils, the sources of aroma. This is also true during the mincing of herbs, the crushing of spices in a mortar, and the puréeing of pods to remove their more fibrous portions. Keep scissors handy to quickly add bits of flavorful foods such as herbs, celery, peppers and bacon. In seasoning sauces to which unseasoned or mildly seasoned solids are added, be sure to retaste after adding the food. Perhaps most important ◗ heat seasoned food with great care, since certain spices like cayenne, paprika and curry blends scorch easily, and others become bitter if overheated.

ABOUT SALTS

Salt has many powers. The interplay of salt and water is essential to life itself. The maintenance of a proper salt balance is vital to the system and different in every individual. Those for whom a low-salt or no-sodium diet has been recommended by their physician may replace the missing flavor by the skillful use of herbs, spices, lemon juice and wine. Also, they should be aware of the salt or sodium content of softened water. ◗ Salt's powers of preservation made possible our ancestors' survival in the waters, wastes and wilderness through which they forged the world's great trade routes. While its use in preserving food has become much less important with the advance

of refrigeration, it is surprising how much we still depend on it: in food processing of various kinds; in the curing of meats; in the brining and pickling of vegetables; in freezing ice cream; even, now and then, for heating oysters and baking potatoes.

In food preservation, the action of salt is twofold. It draws out moisture by osmosis, thus discouraging the microorganisms which are always more active in moist than in dry food. Afterward, the brine formed by the salt and moisture in combination further prevents or retards the growth of surface microorganisms. To cook salted meats, see (I, 609). To remove excess salt from bacon and salt pork, see 204; from anchovies, 251.

The power of salt to heighten the flavor of other foods is its greatest culinary asset. This is true even in candy making, when a pinch of salt often brings out a confection's characteristic best, and with uncooked food, as when salt is sprinkled on citrus fruits. Its reaction on cooked food is otherwise several-sided. It tends to dehydrate when added to water in

which vegetables are cooked, and firms them. It draws the moisture from meats and fish in cooking processes. And it tends to deter the absorption of water by cereals, although it helps retain the shape of the grain. It toughens eggs. And it must be used cautiously in bread making, as too much inhibits the growth of yeast and adversely affects gluten formation. For the effects of salt water on cooking, see 166.

These diverse properties of salt have provoked arguments, from time to time, as to just when this very important ingredient should be added when cooking food. It must, of course, be used very sparingly, if at all, at the start of any cooking in which liquids will be greatly evaporated—such as the making of soups, stocks and sauces. But small quantities of salt, added early to soups and stews, will help in clarification. It is obviously good practice to sear grilled, broiled or roasted meat before adding salt, to retain juices and flavor—unless the meat is floured or breaded. And since it is almost impossible to get rid of excess salt in cooked foods—although occasionally a touch of sugar will make them more palatable—the amount must be calculated with care.

We know from long experience that the flavor-enhancing power of salt is most effective if it is added judiciously toward the end of the cooking process. Don't taste with the tip of the tongue only, but with the middle and sides as well, where the greatest response to salt-stimulus lies.

Salt occurs within foods in varying amounts, animal sources having a higher salt content than vegetable. Sea fish, especially shellfish, are heavier in salt than freshwater fish. Of course, pickled, cured or corned meats and sausages; broths, catsups and extracts; brine-processed frozen fish, sardines, herrings and anchovies, as well as canned soups unless labeled "salt-free," and canned fish and meats—all are high in salt. Do watch your salting arm when dealing with any of the foods mentioned above, and in cooking artichokes, beets, carrots, celery, chard, kale, spinach, dandelion greens, endive and corn—all of which are naturally more salty than most other vegetables. And also be cautious with dates, coconut and molasses.

Various kinds of salt are mentioned in this book. When the word salt is used without qualification, it means ♦ cooking or table salt. ♦ To keep it free-flowing, put a few grains of rice in the saltcellars.

COOKING OR TABLE SALT

This is a finely ground free-flowing type, about 90% sodium chloride—to which dehydrators are frequently added.

IODIZED SALT

This is recommended for certain areas where the water and soils are lacking in iodine, an essential trace element, (I, 10).

COARSE, KOSHER OR SEA SALT

A squarish-grained salt, with natural iodine and other minerals. It is very flavorful when used in cooking and should be applied with a light touch. It is often served sprinkled over meats, after carving and just before serving, so that it does not have time to melt completely. It is also sprinkled over rolls, pretzels and bread before baking, as a sparkling garnish. ♦

Do not confuse this coarse salt with rock salt, below.

BRINE

Brine is a solution of salt and water—preferably soft water. Its purpose is to draw the natural sugars and moisture from foods and form lactic acids which protect them against spoilage bacteria. A **10% brine,** about the strongest used in food processing, is made by dissolving $1^1/2$ cups salt in 1 gallon of liquid or allowing 6 tablespoons salt to a quart of liquid. But after brining, as more liquid continues to be drawn from fruits and vegetables, the brine may be weakened. Always allow about 2 gallons of 10% brine plus enough food to fill a 4-gallon jar. ♦ A rule of thumb to test for 10% brine is that it will float a 2-ounce egg so the shell just breaks the surface of the liquid.

PICKLING OR DAIRY SALT

This is pure salt that is free from additives which might cloud the pickle liquid. It is available in both granulated and flake forms, which may be substituted pound for pound. But, if measuring by volume, use for every cup granulated salt about $1^1/2$ cups flake salt.

ROCK SALT

A nonedible, unrefined variety which is used in the freezing of ice cream—also as a base for baking potatoes or heating oysters on the half shell.

VEGETABLE SALTS

These are sodium chloride with added vegetable extracts—such as celery and onion. If you use them, cut down on the amount of salt called for in the recipes.

SEASONED SALTS

Usually a compound of vegetable salts, spices and monosodium glutamate. In using flavoring salts, be sure not to add regular cooking salt before tasting.

I.
      10 tablespoons salt
      3 tablespoons pepper
      5 tablespoons white pepper
      1 teaspoon red pepper
      1 teaspoon each nutmeg,
        cloves, cinnamon, bay, sage,
        marjoram, rosemary

II.
      4 tablespoons salt
      1 tablespoon sugar
      1 tablespoon paprika
      1 teaspoon each mace, celery
        salt, nutmeg, curry, garlic
        powder, onion powder,
        mustard

HERB SALTS

I. Blend in a mortar for 3 or 4 minutes:
      1 cup noniodized salt
      1 1/2 cups pounded fresh herbs
Spread the mixture on a heatproof tray. Preheat oven to 200°, then turn it off. Place the tray in the oven and allow salt mixture to dry.

II. You may also preserve some herbs by salting them down green in a covered crock, alternating 1/2-inch layers of salt with 1/2-inch layers of herbs. Begin and end with slightly heavier salt layers. After a few weeks, the salt will take on the flavor of the herbs you have chosen to combine and will be ready for use. The herbs which remain green may also be used.

MONOSODIUM GLUTAMATE

A concentrated form of sodium that is usually extracted from grains or beets. It is also present in bean curd and soy sauce. Long known as the magic powder of the East, where tons and tons of it are consumed annually, it is sometimes used in this country, especially in commercially processed foods, because of its power to intensify some flavors. It seems to have no effect on eggs or sweets. It may modify the acidity of tomatoes, the earthiness of potatoes and the rawness of onions and eggplant. It acts as a blending agent for mixed spices used in meat and fish cookery. It is soluble in water but not in fat. So, if you do use it, add it to the liquid ingredients. While it accentuates the saltiness of some foods, just as wine does, it lessens the saltiness of others. ◗ We detect a certain deadening similarity in foods flavored with monosodium glutamate and prefer, if a meat or vegetable is prime, to let its own choice character shine through unassisted.

Also known as MSG, this substance has been revealed as the cause of the allergic reaction known as Chinese Restaurant Syndrome which causes untoward physical side-effects in some people.

SOUR SALT

A citric acid which is sometimes used to replace a lemon flavoring or to prevent discoloration in fruits or canned foods.

SMOKED SALTS

Hickory and other scented smokes have been purified of tars and are chemically bound to these salts by an electrical charge.

SMOKY SALT MIXTURE

> 1 teaspoon smoked salt
> 1/2 cup catsup
> 1/4 cup olive oil
> 2 tablespoons mustard

SALT SUBSTITUTES

These are chlorides in which sodium is replaced by calcium, potassium or ammonium. They should be used only on the advice of a physician.

ANCHOVIES AS SEASONING

Anchovies, sometimes referred to as sardelles, discreetly added to food, can bring a piquancy the source of which is most difficult to trace. About 1/8 of an anchovy to a cup of sauce will turn the trick, or 1/8 of a teaspoon of anchovy paste. The paste is both less strong in flavor and apt to be saltier than the whole anchovies, which may be treated in several ways:

I. For use in a salad, soak anchovies in cold water or milk 1/2 to 1 hour. Drain and dry on paper toweling before using.

II. For use in a sauce, soak them in warm water 5 to 10 minutes. Drain before using. Anchovies are sometimes used as lardoons to season meats, see (I, 551).

ANCHOVY PESTO

Crush together:
> 1 anchovy fillet
> 2 tablespoons grated
>   Parmesan cheese
Combine with an equal amount of:
> Butter

BASIL PESTO

This uncooked seasoning can be made in advance. Use on pasta or on a baked potato, about 2 tablespoons to a portion, mixed with equal parts of butter. If you add a tablespoon or more per portion to Minestrone, (I, 142), as is often done, you arrive at a result close to the Provençal version called *Soupe au Pistou.*
Pound in a mortar about:
> 1 1/2 cups fresh basil leaves
Parsley may be substituted, but of course the flavor is very different. Add and pound:
> 2 cloves garlic
> 1/4 cup pine nuts
Add, until the mixture forms a thick purée:
> About 3/4 cup thinly grated
>   Sardinia or Parmesan
>   cheese
When the mixture is really thick, add very slowly, stirring constantly:
> About 3/4 cup olive oil
until of the consistency of creamed butter.
Put a film of olive oil over the top. Cover and refrigerate or freeze.

CHIFFONADE OF
FRESH HERBS

One of our very favorite ways to disguise canned soup combinations is to use a freshly gathered bouquet of tender herbs. These we mince or, if we are in a hurry, ↲ blend right in with the soup, except for chives, which we mince separately to keep them from being too pervasive. Also see Chiffonade of Herbs for Soup, (I, 172).

CHILI POWDER

A chili blend may be based on a combination of spices as varied as cumin, coriander, oregano, black pepper, cloves and sweet and hot peppers; or it may be made up quickly from a combination of:

3 tablespoons paprika
1 tablespoon turmeric
1/8 teaspoon cayenne

But, no matter how simple or how complex the mix, use with it plenty of:

Pressed garlic

To heighten the flavor of chili powder, simmer the food at least 15 minutes after combining with the seasonings.

CITRUS ZESTS, JUICES AND GARNISHES

What better name than "zest" could be found for the gratings of the colorful outer coatings of lemons, oranges, tangerines and limes—those always available, valuable, yet somehow not fully appreciated ingredients! Zest is the very quality they add to baked items, stuffings, sauces, soups, meats and desserts. ♦ Zest must, however, be used with a light touch. If you keep an easily cleaned hand grater, fifth on the right, (I, 376), hanging near the stove, you will be amazed at the subtlety you can add quickly to your seasoning. Use only the colored portions of the citrus skins; the white beneath is bitter. Citrus rinds are more intense in flavor than juice because of their heavy oil concentration. Fold them into icings, for instance, when the major beating is over, so as not to disturb the texture. Another way to get this oily residue for flavor is to grate the rinds coarsely, place them in a piece of cheesecloth and wring the oils onto sugar. Let stand about 15 minutes before using.

And enough can never be said in favor of the frequent use of small quantities of citrus juices—especially in salt-free diets where these flavors serve to obscure the lack of salt. Use them as a substitute for vinegar wherever delicacy is wanted. ♦ To get the greatest amount of juice out of citrus fruit, roll the whole fruit on a hard surface, gently but firmly pressing it with the palm while rolling, before cutting for juicing. Lemons and limes can be juiced quickly by holding the cut side against the palm and squeezing firmly. If the fruit is properly held, the seeds will be trapped.

♦ It is only the fresh rind and juice of these citrus fruits that hold the really magic seasoning power, but, if you must substitute, the following are approximations: 1 teaspoon freshly grated zest = 2 tablespoons fresh juice = 1 teaspoon dried zest = 1/2 teaspoon extract = 2 teaspoons grated candied peel.

Keep on hand for flavoring drinks and sauces Citrus-Flavored Sugars, 229. To make citrus peels for fruit sauces, take off just the colored portion of the peel with a sharp knife, a potato peeler or a special "zester" tool, shown lower right below. Blanch for 3 minutes to a limp stage. Wash in cold wa-

ter. Shred and resimmer with the sauce. ◗ To use lemons as garnishes, cut them in one of the attractive ways shown opposite and on (I, 34), or use juice from the practical pitcher also shown.

FINES HERBES

This classic phrase connotes a delicate blend of fresh herbs suitable for savory sauces and soups, and for all cheese and nonsweet egg dishes. Use equal parts of parsley, tarragon, chives and chervil—although some other mild herbs may be allowed to creep in. These mixed herbs, minced with a sharp knife and added ◗ at the last minute to the food being cooked, give up their essential oils but retain a lovely freshness.

BOUQUETS GARNIS OR FAGGOTS

Nothing helps a soup or stock so much as a combination of herbs and vegetables. They are best made of fresh materials and ◗ should be added for only the last half hour of cooking.

I. Bunch together:

> **3 or 4 sprigs parsley or chervil**
> **$1/3$ to $1/2$ bay leaf**
> **2 sprigs fresh thyme**
> **(1 leek, white portion only)**
> **(2 cloves)**

◗ To make removal easier, you may place them inside:

> **(Several overlapping celery ribs)**

and bind tightly with a white string.

II. If you cannot get fresh materials, wrap dried herbs, still on the stem, or coarsely crumbled but not powdered, in 4-inch squares of cheesecloth tied into bags as shown, 265. Store them in a tightly covered container. Allow for 12 bags:

> **2 tablespoons dried parsley**
> **1 tablespoon each thyme and marjoram**
> **2 bay leaves**
> **2 tablespoons dried celery leaves**

FOUR SPICES OR SPICE PARISIENNE

Also called **Quatre Épices.** This is the mixture that is such a favorite for sweets and meats. It varies in composition according to the will of the épicier or the whim of his customer, and frequently exceeds four. Carême's formula for **épices composés** included dried thyme, bay leaves, basil, sage, a little coriander and mace, and—at the end—the addition of one-third ground pepper. Mix:

> **1 teaspoon each cloves, nutmeg and ginger**
> **1 tablespoon cinnamon**

FIVE-SPICES POWDER

This pungent, slightly sweet mixture of ground spices is available ready-mixed in Chinese stores. Use sparingly when preparing red-stews (I, 555), and roasted meats or poultry. Mix by grinding into a powder equal amounts of:

> **Chinese star anise, fennel, pepper, cloves and cinnamon**

GREMOLATA

A mixture of seasonings for sauces and pan gravies. Mix:

> **2 tablespoons finely chopped parsley**

1 minced clove garlic
**1/2 teaspoon grated
    lemon rind**
Sprinkle this mixture on sauce or
gravy during the last 5 minutes
of cooking. Simmer, covered, over
very low heat so the flavors can be
absorbed.

SEASONED LARD

This yellow lard is called **Sofrito** in
the Caribbean, but in Italy the name
is applied to Mirepoix, below. It gets
its color from the annatto seed, a coloring often used to accentuate the
yellow in pale butter. Seasoned lard
is made in advance of use and stored
refrigerated.
Wash, drain and melt ♦ uncovered
over slow heat in a heavy pan, stirring occasionally:
    1 lb. diced salt pork
Remove from heat and strain into another heavy pan. Wash and drain:
    1/4 lb. annatto seeds
Add them to the strained melted lard
and heat slowly for about 5 minutes.
Strain the colored lard into a large,
heavy kettle. Grind and add:
    1 lb. cured ham
    **1 lb. green peppers, seeds
        and membrane removed**
    **1/4 lb. sweet chili peppers,
        seeds and membrane
        removed**
    1 lb. peeled onions
Mash in a mortar and add:
    15 fresh coriander leaves
    1 tablespoon fresh oregano
Just before cooking, place in a small
tea ball:
    6 peeled cloves garlic
and add to the lard mixture. Simmer
these ingredients over low heat, stirring frequently, for about 30 minutes
more. After the mixture has cooled,

remove garlic. Store ♦ covered and
refrigerated.

SALT PORK, BACON AND HAM
AS SEASONING

These give an interesting fillip to many
bland foods. Bacon and salt pork are
often blanched, (I, 106), to remove excess salt. Although they may be used
interchangeably, the flavors are quite
distinct. Used as a garnish, the bits are
called **grattons** or **cracklings.**
Dice:
    Salt pork
Try it out, 633, in a skillet until
brown and crisp, or place the dice in
a very slow oven until golden brown.

MIREPOIX AND MATIGNON

About 2/3 Cup
Both of these terms refer to a blend
of vegetables: diced in Mirepoix,
minced in Matignon. The blend, always made just before use, is an essential of Sauce Espagnole, (I, 391);
and it can be used either as a base or
as a seasoning for roasting meats and
fowl or for flavoring shellfish.
Dice:
    1 carrot
    1 onion
    1 celery heart: the inner ribs
Add:
    1/2 crushed bay leaf
    1 sprig thyme
    **(1 tablespoon minced raw
        ham or bacon)**
Simmer the above in:
    1 tablespoon butter
until the vegetables are soft. Deglaze
the pan with:
    Madeira

MUSHROOMS AS SEASONING

This family contributes one of the most coveted of all tastes. ◗ Never discard stems, and particularly not skins, for it is here that the greatest amount of flavor lies. Even the scrapings of their rarefied cousins, truffles, are sold at a good price and can be cooked with gelatin to form pungent garnishes for cold foods. To bring more flavor into canned mushrooms, sauté them in butter. Consider also, for seasoning, powdered or whole dehydrated mushrooms. And for a classic mushroom seasoning, see Duxelles, at right. *Agaricus campestris,* the variety most commonly found in our markets, is strengthened in flavor as it withers but must be kept free of moisture in drying, so as not to mold.

◗ To dry mushrooms for storage, select fresh, firm specimens. You may wash them, then dry on paper toweling; or simply place them on a screen or thread them on a string to sun-dry. When thoroughly dry, put in sterile, tightly sealed glass jars. Keep from all moisture until ready to use. To reconstitute, see Dried Mushrooms, below.

For mushroom types and a discussion of the dangers of collecting, see (I, 326). Mushroom spores are often sold in brick form for home culture, but unless conditions are ideal and temperatures constantly between 50° and 60°, experience has shown it is cheaper to buy your mushrooms full-grown.

DRIED MUSHROOMS

Reconstitute as follows. ◗ Wash in 3 waters to clean:

    2 oz. dried mushrooms

Drain. Pour over them:

    Boiling water to cover

and soak 15 to 30 minutes. Some types may need longer soaking, and some will still look like old leather. If they have swelled and softened somewhat, drain and use. If recalcitrant, bring them to a boil in:

    Cold water to cover
    3 teaspoons soy sauce
    1 teaspoon salt
    (2 teaspoons sugar)

Reduce heat and simmer 15 to 50 minutes, or until tender. Drain. Use as for fresh mushrooms. Utilize liquid in soups and sauces.

DUXELLES OR MUSHROOM SEASONING

This is a delicious and convenient way of using up mushroom stems and storing or preserving them for use whenever a mushroom flavor is wanted. Add to stuffings, sauces or gravies, or use in meat and fish cookery. You may strain before using. Allow 2 tablespoons for 1 cup chicken-flavored sauce.

Chop very fine:

    1/2 lb. mushrooms

Squeeze in a cloth, twisting to extract as much moisture as possible. Reserve. Cook until golden:

    1/4 cup chopped onion or
        2 tablespoons chopped shallots

in:

    2 tablespoons butter
    3 tablespoons olive oil

Add the mushrooms plus juice and:

    1/4 teaspoon grated nutmeg
    Season to taste

Sauté on high heat until the mushroom moisture is absorbed. Refrigerate duxelles in a covered jar until ready to use, but do not hold longer than 5 days.

TOMATOES AS SEASONING

Whether fresh, canned, cooked, puréed, or as paste or catsup—and even as soup—the tomato weaves its way into innumerable dishes. To get the flavor without too much moisture, cut fresh tomatoes and squeeze to release extra moisture and seeds; then skin before using, as shown on (I, 366). Canned and cooked ones are best drained, then strained so thoroughly that the tasty, pulpy part is forced through the sieve, leaving only the skin and seeds to discard. When making substitutions for purées, pastes and catsups, be sure to compensate for moisture differences and allow for the variations in strength of flavor.

TOMATO PASTE OR VELVET

About ¾ Cup

This makes a relish or a fine addition to sauces.
Wash, then mash:

   6 large ripe tomatoes
Melt:

   2 tablespoons butter
Add the tomatoes and:

   1 teaspoon brown sugar
   ¼ teaspoon paprika
   ¾ teaspoon salt
Cook the tomatoes in a double boiler ▶ over—not in—boiling water, stirring occasionally, until they are the consistency of thick paste. Put the paste through a strainer. Store refrigerated.

ITALIAN TOMATO PASTE

This flavorful paste is diluted in a little boiling water or stock and added to sauces and soups. Fine in spaghetti and noodle dishes, as a dressing for cooked vegetables or salads, and as an addition to salad dressings.

Wash and cut into slices:

   1½ pecks ripe Italian tomatoes: 6 quarts
Add:

   1 large celery rib, cut up with some leaves
   ¾ cup chopped onion
   3 tablespoons fresh herbs or 1 tablespoon dried herbs: basil, thyme, sweet marjoram or oregano
   ¾ teaspoon peppercorns
   12 cloves
   3 teaspoons salt
   1 two-inch stick cinnamon
   (1 minced clove garlic)
Simmer these ingredients until the tomatoes are soft. Stir frequently. Put the vegetables through a fine sieve. Simmer the pulp ▶ over—not in— boiling water, or over direct low heat with the use of an asbestos pad to prevent burning. Stir frequently. After several hours, when the pulp is thick and reduced by about half, spread the paste to a depth of ½ inch on moist plates. Cut into the paste to let air penetrate. Place the paste in the sun or in a 200° oven to dry. When the paste is dry enough, roll it into balls which you may dip in salad oil. Store refrigerated in airtight sterile jars.

SOYER'S UNIVERSAL DEVIL SEASONING

We have chosen this sauce from Alexis Soyer's *Culinary Campaign,* a fabulous account of the Crimean War, through which he cooked his way with abandon. No one brought more conviction to his work, whether changing the diet of the British armed forces, cooking at the Reform Club, or remolding the cooking habits of the English lower classes—which he attempted through his *Shilling Cook*

Book. The original recipe called for a tablespoon of cayenne pepper. We have changed it to a small pinch, for in Soyer's day cayenne was baked into a sort of bread and then ground, making it about the same strength as a mild paprika. Rub any deviled food with the following mixture:

- 1 **good tablespoon Durham mustard**
- 1/4 **cup chili vinegar**
- 1 **tablespoon grated horseradish**
- 2 **bruised shallots**
- 1 **teaspoon salt**
  A few grains cayenne
- 1/2 **teaspoon black pepper**
- 1 **teaspoon sugar**
- (2 **teaspoons chopped chili peppers)**
- (2 **raw egg yolks)**

Soyer's instructions are to "broil slowly at first and end as near as possible the Pandemonium Fire."

ABOUT COMMERCIAL SAUCES

Ali Baab—in his great *Gastronomie Pratique*—refers to soy, Worcestershire, catsups, tabascos and other such frequently bought condiments as "sauces violentes" which mask out all other flavors. We find them useful as occasional accents, much too powerful to use unmodified; and we indicate suitable quantities as components in various sauces.

SOY SAUCE

Known as *shoyu* in Japan, the finest of all soy sauces are oriental types made from fermenting soybeans, roasted wheat, salt, yeast or malt, and sugar. They are sometimes fermented from 12 to 18 months and range from a light, thin variety which neither colors nor overwhelms chicken, seafood or light soups, through a darker type used in so-called red stewing, (I, 555). A heavier bitter soy sauce made with molasses is almost black: it is better used as a coloring agent than for seasoning. Oriental soy sauces which are naturally fermented are preferable to domestic types produced by chemical means, which tend to be bitterer and saltier, due to additives, and may also include corn syrup or caramel and monosodium glutamate, 250.

WORCESTERSHIRE SAUCE

This sauce is claimed as original by the English. Its roots are said to be Roman and, not unlike their **Garum,** it has a base of anchovy. To make, see 688.

TABASCO SAUCE

This is made from hot tabasco peppers. ♦ Go easy—a few drops may be too much. Use in soups, cocktail sauce, piquant sauces.

ABOUT SPICES

Perhaps our interest in spices is the greater because of our descent from a sailing family, not in New England but in the old Hansa town of Lübeck, where ships with their cargoes of Kolonialwaren anchored at the wharves on the Trave. And the spices were stored in the mowlike corbie-stepped warehouses on the floors above the merchants' living quarters.

Spices, indeed, bring all the world together. Like wines and cheeses, their individuality is intense and their identification with places a vivid one. We associate the best bay leaves with Turkey; the best real cinnamon with

Ceylon; the best red hot peppers with Louisiana. And there have been lively controversies over the relative merits of Spanish and Hungarian paprika; of Mexican and Malagasy vanilla beans.

Long before the first New England farm wife bought a wooden nutmeg, spice traders have known ways to camouflage their wares. We are lucky today that both government agencies and trade associations work hard to develop and maintain high standards for these relatively costly and still most important condiments.

Pepper, like salt, because of its preservative qualities, has been at times worth its weight in gold. And we are acquainted with a treasured bay leaf that on festive occasions— all during the last war—made the rounds of ten or fifteen beleaguered English households.

Since spices are used in such small quantities, we recommend that you purchase from impeccable sources. We also suggest that ♦ if you are using ground spices, they be replenished at least within the year, as they tend in powdered form to lose strength rapidly. Be sure to date your jars when you clean and fill them. Store spices in tightly covered nonabsorbent containers and in as dark and cool an area as your kitchen provides. But have them handy! Their discriminating use will pique many a dish from obscurity to memorableness.

In cooking, put whole spices in a cloth or in a stainless metal tea ball so you can remove them more readily when the dish is done. ♦ Do not overboil spices, in particular pepper and caraway, as they become bitter. And do not use high heat for paprika or curry, for they scorch easily. Some spices are available as distilled essences, and these clear additives

are valuable in light Fruit Butters, 668, or Pickles, 676. Their flavor does not last as long as that of whole spices cooked with the food. ❀ In frozen foods, the flavors of the spices do not hold up well. And in ♦ quantity cooking, if you are enlarging household recipes, spice to taste rather than to measure. We suggest amounts considered pleasurable by the average person. You may wish to use more or less than we indicate. Spices, even when dry, can reactivate molds they may have had before, or developed during drying, so the government suggests you resist the temptation to sniff them. Below we describe spices and their uses.

ALLSPICE

In this book pimiento, the name for true peppers of the *Capsicum* family, see 276, is reserved for them. And pimento, *Pimenta dioica,* is kept for allspice only. Use allspice anywhere from soup to nuts, alone or in a combination with other spices. For within its single small reddish-brown berry lies a mixture of cinnamon, clove, nutmeg and juniper berry flavors. But do not confuse allspice with the mixture called in France Quatre Épices, or Four Spices, 253.

ANNATTO

Because of its color from the pulp surrounding the seed, annatto, *Bixa orellana,* is often used as a substitute for saffron.

THE CARDAMOMS

Powder the plump seeds of *Elettaria cardamomum* only as needed, for otherwise the aromatic loss is great. Use as for cinnamon and cloves, alone or in combination. Delicious in coffee. The smaller type, *Amamum cardamomum,* is used whole in barbecue-basting sauces and pickles.

THE CINNAMONS

True cinnamon, *Cinnamomum zeylanicum,* is the bark of a tree that flourishes in Ceylon and along the Malabar Coast. It is extremely mild whether rolled in a tight quill or stick or in powdered form. Most of the so-called cinnamon on the market is really cassia, *Cinnamomum cassia.* This is a similar bark that is not quilled, but formed as though a short scroll were rolled from both ends and left with its center portion flat. It has slightly bitter overtones compared to the warm, sweet, aromatic true cinnamon. The best forms of cassia come from Saigon. Use the stick form of either of these spices in hot chocolate, mulled wine, fruit compotes and pickles. We need hardly suggest trying cinnamon on toast, dusting it on cookie tops or incorporating it into desserts and baked items. But maybe its use in small quantities in meats and seafoods is new to you.

THE CLOVES

This spicy, dried, rich red, unopened bud of the clove tree, *Caryophyllus aromaticus,* contains so much oil that you can squeeze it out with a fingernail. Because its flavor is so strong, the heads of the cloves are sometimes removed so the seasoning will be milder. These milder portions are often used in the powdered form. Before serving a dish cooked with whole cloves, always remove them. The best cloves come from Madagascar and Zanzibar. Use in curries, stewed fruits, marmalades; in chutneys, pickles, marinades; and, in small quantities, with onions and meats; especially good with ham, as well as in spiced baked stews. An onion stuck with 3 or 4 cloves is a classic addition to stocks and stews. Oil of clove is available for use in light-colored foods, but watch out for its terrific pungency.

CURRY

We think of curry, which is really a highly seasoned sauce, mainly as a powder sitting on the shelf ready to be added when foods need a lift. But curry powders are best when the spices are freshly ground or incorporated into a paste with onion, garlic, fruits and vegetables as commonplace as apples and carrots and as exotic as tamarind and pomegranate.

The curry, in either powder or paste form, has its flavor developed in olive oil, or ghee, a clarified butter. The paste is then cooked in a low oven over a period of several hours before the final stage of preparation with the main food. Curries should be specially blended for each kind of dish: a dry one for coating meat; a sour one for marinated meats; and other mixtures for chicken or mutton, rice, beans, vegetables and fish. They range in strength from the fiercely hot curries of Madras to the mild ones of Indonesia. The mixtures below give you an idea of the variety and extent of curry bases. Amounts to use per portion are a matter of tolerance. Choose beer or a tart limeade as a beverage with curried foods. When making up the dish, use plenty of fresh garlic and onion and, if possible, fresh coconut milk, 244.

I.

    1 oz. each ginger, coriander and cardamom

¼ oz. cayenne
3 oz. turmeric

II.

2 oz. each of the seeds of
coriander, turmeric,
fenugreek, black pepper
2½ oz. cumin seed
1½ oz. each poppy and
cardamom seeds
½ oz. mustard seed
½ oz. dry ginger
2 oz. dry chilis
1 oz. cinnamon

III.

1 oz. each turmeric,
coriander and cumin
½ oz. each dry ginger and
peppercorns
¼ oz. each dried hot peppers
and fennel seed
⅛ oz. each mustard, poppy
seeds, cloves and mace

GINGER

The root of a bold perennial, *Zingiber officinale*—with the most heavenly scented lily—must be harvested at just the right moment or it will be fibrous and have a bitter aftertaste. Whole fresh or green ginger should have a smooth skin and be a uniformly buff color. It must be kept dry or it will sprout and be useless for flavoring. Refrigerated, in a plastic bag, it will keep about 3 weeks. Or you may wash the fresh ginger, cover with sherry and keep refrigerated. But it really tastes best unpeeled, sliced thin, and sautéed in oil to extract the flavor. To use in recipes, peel, grate, slice or mash.

When dry, it may be cut into ½-inch cubes and steeped for several hours in a marinade or in cold water, after which the liquid can be used as seasoning. Peeled or thinly sliced ginger can be added to stews or rubbed like garlic over duck or fish. It will do much to remove "fishy" flavors. Boiled and then preserved in syrup, it is known in this milder form as **Canton ginger** and is delicious in desserts, chopped fine and used with or without its syrup. And it is worth trying with bananas and even with tomatoes, squash, onions and sweet potatoes. Ginger is also candied or crystallized, 605, and may be used in baked goods and desserts. This form can, in a pinch, be washed of its sugar and substituted for fresh ginger. We all know the value of ground ginger for flavoring baked items. ◗ Equivalent flavoring strengths of the various forms are: ½ teaspoon ground equals 1 to 2 teaspoons thinly sliced preserved, equals 2 tablespoons syrup.

JUNIPER BERRIES

Berries from *Juniperus communis* are prized for seasoning game and bean dishes. Three to six berries suffice per serving. In fact, ½ teaspoon of these berries soaked for a long time in a marinade—or cooked long in a stew—gives a flavoring equivalent to ¼ cup gin, to which these berries lend their typical aroma.

MOCHA

This name is given to dishes flavored with a lightly roasted coffee bean. It is often paired with chocolate. We include it here, for coffee can be used profitably as a spice.

NUTMEG AND MACE

These flavors are so closely allied because they come from the same tough-husked fruit of *Myristica fragrans*. It is sun- or charcoal-dried and, when opened, has a lacy integument which is used whole in cooking fruits or desserts or ground into mace for seasoning. The hard inner kernel is the nutmeg. Use it sparingly but often, and, for its full flavor, grind it fresh from a handy nutmeg grinder that merely needs a twist—like a pepper mill. Try it not only in baked items but in spinach, with veal, on French toast—and always with eggnog. ◗ One grated whole nutmeg equals 2 to 3 teaspoons ground nutmeg.

THE WHITE AND BLACK PEPPERS

Both these peppers come from berry clusters of the vining *Piper nigrum,* the master spice. There is some difference in flavor, the white being slightly more aromatic, but their use is almost interchangeable.

The white is made from the fully ripe berry, from which the dark outer shell is buffed before the berry is ground. White pepper flavor holds up better in sausages and canned meats. This form is also used in all light-colored foods or sauces.

Black pepper is obtained from the underripe, fermented, sun-dried whole berries. The peppercorns themselves, when used in poivrade dishes, are crushed rather than ground, so the oils are not dispersed. And they are added the last few minutes before the sauce is strained. Also available for poivrade dishes are the more flavorful canned green peppercorns. Crush them before adding. But pepper, which can be used in any food except sweets—and here there is the further exception of Pfeffernüsse—is best freshly ground. It not only is a remarkable preservative but manages to strengthen food flavors without masking them as much as other spices do.

Unless otherwise specified, the word pepper in this book means black pepper. For cayenne pepper, see 277.

TURMERIC

This Indian rhizome—*Curcuma longa*—is bitterish, and its rather acrid fugitive fragrance warms the mouth, so it must be used with discretion. Its golden color gives the underlying tone to curry powders and to certain pickles. In small quantities it is used as a food coloring, often replacing saffron for this purpose.

VANILLA BEAN AND EXTRACT

Vanilla bean, before being marketed, is fermented and cured for 6 months. Vanilla extract is prepared by macerating the beans or pods in a 35% alcohol solution. To retain its greatest flavor, add it only when food is cooling. Try 2 parts vanilla to 1 part almond flavoring—a great Viennese favorite. Or try keeping vanilla beans in brandy and using the flavored brandy as a seasoning. ◗ Beware of synthetic vanillas whose cheap flavor is instantly detected and which ruin any dish that is frozen.

If you are curious about the little dark specks in a good vanilla ice cream, these are the seeds scraped from the vanilla bean, which is another way to use this flavoring. Allow about 1 inch of scraped bean for 1 teaspoon vanilla extract. For another way to flavor, see Vanilla Sugar, 229.

EXTRACTS AND FLAVORINGS USED WITH SWEETS

There are a number of other extracts, all of which should be used sparingly, such as lemon and almond. Derivatives of almond are: falernum, a syrup of lime, almond and spices dominated by ginger; grenadine, made from the juice of pomegranates; and rose and orange waters, both sweetened distillations. ♦ We do not recommend nonalcoholic liqueur flavorings.

GROWING CULINARY HERBS

Confucius, a wise man, refused to eat anything not in season. Everyone who has tasted the difference between foods served with fresh rather than dried herbs knows how wise he was. Few herbs can be bought in a fresh state at market, but the most important ones can be easily grown. We know, for we have raised and used all the culinaries in this section. Therefore, we beg you to exercise your green thumb at least on those whose evanescent oils deteriorate or almost disappear in drying. Chervil, borage, burnet and summer savory suffer the greatest losses. And the mainstays—chives, tarragon, parsley and basil—can never in their dry form begin to approach the quality of their fresh counterparts. Even the flavor of sage when fresh and discreetly used can be so delicate as to be a new sensation.

A hallmark of the Compleat Herb Grower is a love of sundials and armillary spheres—reflecting the herbs' own predilection for bright sunlight—frequently paralleled by a passion for symmetry. You might like to duplicate the sequences of plantings shown beginning at the right in the top layout opposite: in the end section is sage, followed by tarragon, parsley, dwarf basil and thyme, all partitioned by chives. You may prefer

partitions of clipped lavender, santolina or fernlike burnet which, with the sage and thyme end sections, will give your garden in winter an indication of form.

We have tried growing herbs in many patterns. Since most herbs are sun-lovers that need air and dislike competition, bed layouts, such as those shown at center and below it, suit them well.

As long ago as the seventeenth century, the herbalist Parkinson in his *Paradisi in Sole* stressed the importance of proper drainage in herb growing. We too have discovered that good drainage, whether secured by boxing or simply by the selection of terraced ground, is a primary consideration. The upper and lower sketches show raised beds, the upper crescent-shaped held high by old granite street cobbles, the lower by flue-liners which also provide containment for rampant aggressors like the mints. Shown in the partially sunken flue-liners are squares of mints, calendulas and nasturtiums, and a combination of chives and parsley—all edible yet colorful. You might also try other annual or deciduous squares, or use alternate evergreen and deciduous herbs again to allow for some winter form. Try placing the liners in Greek fret designs or any pattern that adapts to your space.

You may prefer to use squared beds. A 15-inch to 2-foot unit area for each of most culinaries is more than enough to supply household demands. Sometimes, if we want only a single specimen—for instance, a sage or a lavender—we keep it pruned to a central shrub and use the edges around it for smaller plants. Sometimes we repeat a color accent—like the gray of sage or lavender—to unify the whole complex of squares.

A more elegant solution is to use millstones which reflect the heat most herbs thrive on and which make ideal access points for the gardener to weed from. A millstone also gives the surrounding herbs freedom to spread over its edges, as well as over the flat stones that define the bed. Here in the centers are a pot of rosemary and a dwarf pepper plant, although a cherry tomato plant on a trellis would give more height to the layout. Camomiles and thymes are shown as bordering plants, but any of the dwarf creepers like dwarf savories could be used. Also to be considered, though not for patterned beds, are the unruly tousle-headed giants, the dills; the fennels, lovage, sorrel; the floppy borage and scraggly corianders; anises, sesames and mustards. If these mavericks are grown in unregimented fashion, borage, dill, fennel, chervil, coriander and parsley will self-sow. These all have less stability of condition as well as of structure, and profit by a background of fencing or a south-facing housewall which not only protects but lends unity to the plantings. These plants are always problems for the neat-minded, as are the treasured onion family shown 275, for with the exception of chives, they die back and yellow after ripening.

If you haven't room for the more extended layouts shown on 263, try setting out a few pots of annuals on your patio. Some evergreen perennials will weather the winter in a strawberry jar, 246. To prepare a jar for herbs, fill with a mixture of one-third rich friable soil and two-thirds sand. Try the thymes, sweet marjoram, burnet and chervil on the shady side. You can dwarf fennel, borage and sage by root confinement. Replace the coarse marjorams with dittany of Crete, and coarse mints with *Mentha requienii*—both tender perennials.

Pots can be used, too, for growing herbs indoors in sunny windows. We have had moderate success with rosemary, sweet marjoram, the basils, dittany of Crete, lemon verbena and scented geranium—all from late summer cuttings—and with dill and bronze fennel from seed. If you plan bringing plants indoors, pot them up in late August and put them in a partially shaded area. Bring them in before frost. Tarragon dug after cold weather dormancy and potted up indoors may show six inches of green within ten days. A small potted sweet bay is both decorative and useful. ◗ But most houseplant herbs deteriorate in flavor, just as do hothouse tomatoes.

We find that the various thymes, pot marjoram and winter savories flourish in a rock garden. Treat them with neglect and reap them for twenty years. But we also find, with our hot midwestern summers and variable winters, that sage, burnet and tarragon are more apt to hold over in well-enriched garden soil. Most perennial herbs also hold over better if they have been clipped to about two-thirds their height several times during the season prior to early August.

If they are creepers like thymes, bob them back at the base as well. Follow each clipping with a dose of liquid manure. If the herbs are evergreen varieties, treat them to a thorough watering prior to the first killing frosts.

HARVESTING, DRYING AND FREEZING HERBS

Our instinctive inclination toward the cultivation and use of herbs and our longing for a year-round supply put us in good company across the centuries: Alcuin, Charlemagne's tutor, called herbs "the friend of physicians and the praise of cooks." Which brings us to the matters of harvesting, drying and freezing of herbs—processes we must adopt to keep our kitchens in steady supply.

The first rule of harvesting herbs is to clip constantly through July; never allow the plants to reach the blossoming stage. Later heavy clipping may weaken perennials—not allowing recovery of the plant before winter. Unless otherwise indicated in the individual notes on cultivation, herbs are harvested ◗ just before their flowers emerge. At this time, when they are budding up, the leaves are at their most aromatic. Hose down the herbs the day before harvesting. Pick early next morning, as soon as the dew has dried off the leaves. If necessary, dry the leaves, without bruising.

Herbs are remarkably free from insect pests and should be grown where they are not subject to sprays. After gathering, you may tie them together and hang in small bunches until dry. You can expect about 1 pound dried herbs for every 8 pounds freshly gathered. The location traditionally recommended is a cool, airy attic.

Since such spaces are becoming scarce, a shady breezeway will do. And lacking a breezeway, room-drying at temperatures preferably below 90° is preferable to oven-drying, for even when the oven is preheated as low as possible and the herbs inserted the moment the temperature drops below 90°, their flavor is weakened. For thick-leaved varieties, the oven process may have to be repeated several times until the herbs are bone-dry.

❧ To test for dryness before packaging, put a few of the brittle sprigs or leaves in a tightly stoppered glass jar and watch for condensation, mold development or discoloration. This is important, especially with basil. ❧ Stored dried herbs in tightly stoppered lightproof glass or ceramic jars in a cool place. Should they show insect activity, discard them. You may want to strip leaves from the stems before drying or freezing herbs. If drying seeds, collect them in paper rather than plastic bags, and let them dry thoroughly before bottling in glass jars. ❧ Dried herbs retain their flavor best if pulverized in a mortar, shown opposite, just before using.

You may freeze herbs. If you do, use them before defrosting—in the same proportion as for fresh herbs. They are too limp for garnishes. Some herbs, like chives, get slimy when frozen ❧ so freeze or shot-freeze, parblanch, (I, 106), for ten seconds, plunge into ice water for one minute and dry between towels. Put them up individually in recipe-sized packets for seasoning a salad dressing or a batch of stew, or freeze mixed bouquets garnis for soups and sauces. To preserve herbs by salting, see 250. The herbs and the salt, which has become savory, will be ready to use within two weeks.

USING HERBS

Handy as an herb chart might seem, we have refrained from compiling one, because some herbs are over-powering, and it is so difficult to indicate in a general way the amounts to use. Suitable quantities of herbs are listed in the individual recipes. Below we set down detailed characteristics and helpful horticultural tips for each culinary herb. Let us add that the delicately flavored types should be placed in sauces and soups only toward the end of preparation and left just long enough to release their volatile oils. And once again, while ❧ we advocate a constant use of herbs, we don't advise too many kinds at once or too much of any one kind.

To familiarize yourself with herb flavors, some "lazy day," when you feel experimental, blend ½ pound mild cheddar cheese with 2 tablespoons sour cream and 2 tablespoons vodka. Divide the mixture into small portions and add to each an herb or herb combination. Label the cheese samples as you mix them. Let them rest for about an hour to develop flavor. Then have a testing party with your spouse or friends.

❯ To substitute dried herbs for fresh, use $1/3$ teaspoon powdered or $1/2$ teaspoon crushed for every tablespoon fresh chopped herbs. ❯ To reconstitute dried herbs and develop their flavors, soak them in some liquid you can incorporate in the recipe—water, stock, milk, lemon juice, wine, olive oil or vinegar—for ten minutes to one hour before using. Or, simmer them in hot butter. For cooking, place nonpowdered dry herbs in a cloth bag or a stainless metal tea ball for subsequent easy removal. For blends, see 250, 251 and 253.

ANGELICA

The leaves of this slightly licorice-flavored plant are candied as a garnish for desserts, 606; seeds may be added to pastry, young tips to rhubarb or gooseberries. *Angelica archangelica* grows to 4 to 8 feet. It dies after blooming but is perennial if blooming is inhibited. Seeds must be fresh, soil moist, and the locale shady.

THE ANISES

These have strangely subtle licorice overtones. Use seeds in Anise Cookies, 466; the oil is flavoring in sponge cake; or star anise in watermelon-rind pickle. To release the full flavor, crush seeds between towels with a rolling pin. *Pimpinella anisum* grows to 3 feet. Because of the long taproot, transplant into light rich soil when seedlings are young. The star anise, *Illicium anisatum,* imported from China, belongs to the magnolia family.

THE BASILS

Not without reason called *l'herbe royale,* these versatile herbs have a great affinity for tomatoes, fish and egg dishes, but are good in almost all savory dishes. They darken quickly after cutting. Serve them as they do in Italy—where basil is very popular—in a bouquet of sprigs set in water in a small vase. Be sure to try Pesto, 251, with spaghetti. *Ocinum basilicum,* which grows to 2 feet, dries poorly and should never be dried in heat above 110°. It roots in a few days in water. Make cuttings and pot up before frost in rich soil. It is worth keeping at least one plant over the winter to supply that fresh basil flavor until the new crop is ready. *Ocinum minimum,* dwarf bush basil, less than 1 foot tall, is the sweetest and mildest in flavor and the best for house culture.

THE BAYS

Always use these leaves, fresh or dry, with discretion—only $1/3$ of a fresh leaf or $1/6$ of a dry leaf in a quart of stew—and only a pinch if in powdered form. But do use them, not only in stuffings but in stocks, sauces and marinades, in the cooking of vegetables and meats, and in a Bouquet Garni, 253. Dry the leaves in August. ❯ Do not confuse the leaves of the edible bay tree, *Laurus nobilis,* highly aromatic when bruised, with those of the poisonous *Prunus laurocerasus,* the cherry laurel leaf of our gardens which is high in prussic acid.

BORAGE

Only good fresh; its flavor vanishes as it dries. Use the leaves wherever you want a cucumber flavor in fish sauces or white aspics. It is traditional in some fruit punches, and the choice blue starlike blooms, (I, 34), are beautiful floated in punches and lemonades or used in food garnishes. Young borage can be cooked like spinach, (I, 358). *Borago officinalis,* which self-seeds, grows to 2½ feet even in poor soil.

BURNET

Sometimes called salad burnet; in fact, Italians say that salad without burnet is like love without a woman. This herb has a haunting cucumberish flavor. It does not dry well, but it keeps green all winter long and can be plucked at any time. Pick the center leaves; the older ones are bitter. Use the leaves, or soak the seeds in vinegar for use in salads.

Poterium sanguisorba, a hardy evergreen perennial growing to 2 feet, is almost fernlike in habit and is easy to germinate in any well-drained soil, in sun.

CAMOMILE

Famous as a tisane, (I, 31). A small quantity is occasionally put into beef stock. Sometimes the fresh leaves are used, but it is the very center of the flower that is most prized. The petals of this tiny daisy are removed after the flower is dried. *Anthemis nobilis,* a creeping perennial, grows to 6 inches in dry light soil.

THE CAPERS AND CAPERLIKE BUDS AND SEEDS

When pickled, these bulletlike buds of the caper bush taste like tiny sharp gherkins. Use them in Tartare Sauce, (I, 421), with fish and wherever you wish a piquant note. *Capparis spinosa* is a 3-foot perennial shrub of southern Europe. ◗ Do not confuse it with the caper spurge, *Euphorbia lathyrum,* which is poisonous. Also pickled are immature or mature seeds and buds of *Tropaeolum minus* or *majus,* the nasturtium; or the buds of *Caltha palustris,* the marsh marigold. Similar in use are Chinese fermented black beans, or *toushi,* which are available in cans; and the pickled green seeds of *Martynia Proboscidea juisieui,* an annual growing to 2½ feet, with dramatic flowers and an evilly horned pod.

CARAWAY

Use the leaves of this herb sparingly in soups and stews. The seeds, similar to cumin in flavor, are classic additions to rye breads, cheeses, stews, marinades, cabbage, sauerkraut, turnips and onions. And they are the basic flavoring of kümmel. If added to borsch or other soups, put them in a bag for the last 30 minutes of cooking only, as protracted heating makes them bitter. Crush them before adding to vegetables or salads, to release their flavor. *Carum carvi* is an easily grown biennial that reaches 2 feet in the second year when the seeds develop.

THE CELERIES

The tender leaves of the celery you grow or buy can be used fresh or dried in almost all foods. Celery salt is a powdered form combined with salt. But the seeds sold for flavoring are not those of the plant we grow, but those of smallage or wild celery. These seeds, either whole or ground, have a powerful flavor and must be used sparingly: whole in stocks, court bouillon, pickles and salads; or in ground form in salad dressings, seafoods or vegetables. *Apium grave-*

olens needs rich moist soil and hilling to blanch. For celeriac, see (I, 313).

CHERVIL

One of the famous "fines herbes," this is more delicate and ferny than parsley. The leaf is used with chicken, veal, omelets, green salad and spinach—as a garnish, of course—and always in the making of a Béarnaise Sauce, (I, 412), or Vinaigrette Sauce, (I, 413). It is one of the herbs it pays to grow—for when dried at even as low a temperature as 90°, it is practically without flavor. *Pluches de cerfeuille* are sprigs of fresh or fresh blanched chervil often specified in stocks and stews. *Anthriscus cerefolium* is a self-sowing annual that grows to 2 feet. It needs some shade to keep it from turning purplish and toughening. Sow in place from April to September. Do not transplant, as this forces bolting.

COMFREY

A healing herb—its very name implies a knitting together—comfrey makes a popular tisane, (I, 31). Use its young leaves sparingly, raw in salads, or cook them as for spinach, cutting the leaves before the plant blooms. *Symphytum officinale* is a hardy perennial growing to 3 feet, preferring rich friable lime soil and moisture and shade. Propagate in spring by dividing its long white roots.

CORIANDER

Many of us identify this flavor from childhood with the seed in the heart of a "jaw breaker," in gingerbread, apple pie, sausages and pickles, or as an ingredient of curry. But few of us know the fresh leaves of this plant as Chinese parsley, as the Cilantro of the Caribbean, the Kothamille of Mexico, or the Dhuma of India, where its somewhat fetid odor and taste are much treasured. Use leaves only—no stems—and do not chop. Float the leaves in pea or chicken soups and in stews, place them on top of roasts, or use them in a court bouillon for clams. *Coriandrum sativum,* a 12- to 18-inch plant, grows in moderately heavy soil and, while needing drainage, can take some moisture.

COSTMARY

Used sparingly in sauces, soups and stuffings, this herb is sometimes substituted for mint but has bitter overtones. *Balsamita major,* a perennial, also known as alecost, grows to 4 feet and is not particular as to soil.

CUMIN

This flavor is classic in cheese, sauerkraut and unleavened bread. The seed is also used whole in marinades, chilis and tomato sauces. One of the principal ingredients of a curry, cumin is even incorporated into baked items and eggs as well as bean and rice dishes and Enchiladas, (I, 240). *Cuminum odorum,* an annual growing to 1 foot, needs near-tropical conditions for good growth.

DILL

Both seed and leaf of this feathery, pungent and slightly bitter plant are used in sour cream, fish, bean, cucumber and cabbage dishes as well as in potato salad or on new potatoes. If using dill butter sauce, do not brown the butter. The seed is also good in vinegar. The leaves make a lovely garnish. *Anethum graveolens,* an annual sometimes referred to as dillweed, grows to 3 feet and selfsows. Pull up plants when flower heads brown, and dry over paper so that the easily shattered seeds are not lost.

THE FENNELS

The leaves of common and Florence fennel can be used interchangeably where a slightly vigorous flavor is wanted. In flavoring, both the leaves and seeds are used—as for dill— especially for fat fish and in lentils, rice and potatoes and in apple pies. Fish is sometimes cooked over fennel twigs. But in sauces—as with dill— do not let the leaves cook long enough to wilt, unless they have been previously blanched. The leaves do not retain flavor in drying. *Foeniculum vulgare* and its variant, the bronze fennel, are self-sowing and grow to 5 feet. Plant in well-drained moisture-retaining soil. *F. var. dulce,* the Florence fennel or finocchio, illustrated (I, 277), is used as a vegetable, (I, 323).

FENUGREEK

This has the same odor as celery but a bitterer flavor. Popular as a tisane, (I, 31), it is also used in many African dishes. It constitutes one of the main ingredients of curries and is the base of artificial maple flavor. *Trigonella-Foenum graeca,* which grows to 1 or 2 feet, needs well-drained loam.

GERANIUMS

The sweet-scented many-flavored leaves are used in pound cake, jellies and compotes, or merely as floaters in finger bowls. Use a lime-scented leaf in custard or an apple-flavored one in baked apples. For lime flavor try *Pelargonium nervosum;* for apple, *P. odoratissimum;* for mint, *P. tomen-* *tosum;* for rose, *P. graveolens.* These geraniums are tender but grow well in pots under ordinary household conditions.

HOREHOUND

The woolly leaves of this plant are made into an extract which is combined with sugar into confections, 591. *Marrubium vulgare,* a perennial that grows to 3 feet, flourishes in poor soil.

HORSERADISH

Along with coriander, nettle, horehound and lettuce, horseradish is one of the five bitter herbs of the Passover. As the flavor is overpowering, use sparingly, and use it fresh rather than reconstituted if possible. You may grate peeled fresh root into lemon or vinegar. If the ground dried form must be used, ▶ it should be reconstituted not more than 30 minutes before serving; for, once the powder is mixed, its volatile oils are dissipated. To prepare dried ground root: soak 1 tablespoon of dried horseradish in 2 tablespoons of water and add $\frac{1}{2}$ cup heavy cream. Whether fresh, reconstituted or bought jarred—and in this book the term for the latter is "prepared horseradish"—use all horseradish promptly to avoid loss of volatile oils and development of intense bitterness. Horseradish is prized for use with Boiled Beef, (I, 576), and other fatty meats; in cocktail sauces and potato salad; or with cold meats, fish and shellfish. *Armoracia rusticana,* a perennial growing to 2 feet, is propagated from pieces of root and demands rich, moist soil. You may store roots in moist sand for winter use.

HYSSOP

The leaves of this minty, spicy, somewhat bitter herb are used sparingly with salads and fruits. The dried flowers are used in soups and tisanes. *Hyssopus officinalis,* a perennial which grows to 2 feet, prefers dry calcareous soil.

LAVENDER

The leaves and flowers of this highly aromatic plant give a bitter pungency to salads. We prefer to use it as a sachet rather than as a seasoner. But its grayness lends a lovely accent to the herb garden. Grown from cuttings or seed, *Lavandula vera,* a perennial growing to 4 feet, prefers dry lime soil and a warm climate.

LEMON BALM

Use the lemony leaves for tisane or as a garnish in fruit punch or fruit soap. *Melissa officinalis,* a perennial which reaches 2¹/₂ feet, grows in sun in any soil.

LEMON VERBENA

This, like lavender, in our opinion is better reserved for sachets or closets than for food; however, it is often used as a lemon substitute in drinks and tisanes. *Lippia citriodora* is a tender perennial growing to 5 feet; it does well in pots.

LOVAGE

The leaves of this bold herb, whose stems can be candied like Angelica, 266, or blanched and eaten like celery, are often used as a celery substitute with stews or tongue. The seeds are sometimes pickled like capers. *Levisticum officinale,* a perennial that grows to 8 feet, is not particular as to soil; it is best divided in spring.

THE MARJORAMS AND OREGANOS

These, whether called sweet or pot marjoram, oregano or oregano dulce or wild, are all very pungent. While similar in their uses, they are not quite the same in their growth habits. Use them in sausages, stews, tomato dishes; with lamb, pork, chicken and goose; with omelets, eggs, pizzas, and cream cheeses; with all of the cabbage family and with green beans; in minestrone and mock turtle soups; and, of course, don't fail to try them fresh and finely chopped for salads.

There is great horticultural confusion in regard to the oreganos of commerce, and seeds ordered under the name origanum vary enormously. *Origanum vulgare* and *O. onite,* or pot marjoram, are hardy perennials to 2 feet. *Origanum marjoram,* sweet marjoram, is a tender perennial growing about a foot high; it prefers alkaline soil.

THE MINTS

We all know peppermint and spearmint. But there are many other mints worth trying, like the curly varieties, and apple, orange and pineapple. These are less penetrating but equally refreshing. Use any of them in fruit cups, with coleslaw, peas, zucchini, lamb, veal, cream cheeses; in chocolate combinations, teas, and of course jellies and juleps. These leaves, fresh or candied, see 602, make attractive garnishes. If using fresh leaves, ¹/₄ to ¹/₂ teaspoon—crushed just before using—is enough per serving. But in the form of oil, a drop of mint flavoring is often too much—so go easy.

All of the following grow rampant in sun or partial shade, and even in dry but preferably moist soil: *Mentha viridis,* perhaps the most peppery of all; *M. piperita,* the peppermint we know best; *M. spicata* or spearmint and its preferred form *crispa;* and the woolly apple mint, *M. rotundifolia,* frosted in appearance and fine for a drink garnish.

All the mints are perennial and easily raised from root divisions. They reach 1 1/2 to 3 feet. Plant them in areas confined by metal or rock edgings sunk at least 6 inches deep to keep them from invading less sturdy neighbors in the herb garden. Keep them pruned to have bushy tops for beverage garnishes. If your growing area is confined, try *Mentha requienii* or Corsican mint—a tinyleaved plant only 1 inch high, as discreet as a moss.

And, incidentally, field mice hate mint odor and will stay away from any plant near which it is scattered.

MARIGOLD

The dried centers of pot marigolds are sometimes used as a color substitute for saffron, and the young leaves can be used in salads. The petals are used only when the recipe calls for cooking, as in stews. *Calendula officinalis* is not particular as to soil and grows to 15 inches.

THE MUSTARDS

Mustard fanciers will argue the merits of a mild champagne-based or poupon Dijon type or a Louisiana mix—against the sharp English or the fiery Jamaican or Chinese. There are many ways to prepare mustards from mustard powder, which is the dry residue left after the oil is expressed from the seed. But the freshness of the mix is an important factor. The flavor changes rapidly once moisture is added or once a bottle of prepared mustard is opened. Try keeping it fresh by putting a slice of lemon on top before closing the lid. The lemon needs renewal about once a week. Commercial mustards with their blends of flour and spices— often heavy in tumeric to color them—may be based on water, wine or vinegar. If you want to mix your own, allow 2 to 3 tablespoons liquid to 1/4 cup dry mustard. More details about preparing mustard follow.

Mustard can be added advantageously in small quantities to cheese, seasoned flour, chicken or pot roasts and to sauces, hot or cold. It is classic served with cold meats and for use in pickles—both ground and as seed.

◗ In this book prepared mustard indicates the saucelike mustard. It has about one-third to one-half the strength of dry mustard.

◗ **Hot Mustards** are based on cold liquids—water, vinegar or flat beer. Add 2 to 3 tablespoons liquid to about 1/4 cup dry mustard. If it is too hot, tone it with a little olive or vegetable oil, garlic, tarragon leaves and a pinch of sugar. To make a **Suave Mustard,** put into a heatproof glass double boiler top about 2 ounces of dry mustard. Pour water which has been brought to a rolling boil over it to cover. Place ◗ over, not in, rapidly boiling water for 15 minutes. Before covering see that the mustard has been stirred into a paste but is still covered with the hot liquid. Drain any excess water. You may add 1 teaspoon sugar and 1/4 to 1/2 teaspoon salt. If you want a bright mustard, add 1/4 teaspoon turmeric, vinegar and other spices to your taste. Put mustard in a jar. Let cool uncovered

1 to 2 hours. Then cap tightly. Keep at room temperature. Do not refrigerate.

The dark seeds come from *Brassica nigra*, the white from *Sinapsis alba*, both self-seeding and growing to 3 feet. If seed is desired, plants can tolerate poor soil. If leaves are to be used as a vegetable, *Brassica nigra*, *Sinapsis alba* and *Brassica juncea* should be grown in rich soil.

NASTURTIUM

Flowers, seeds and leaves are all used as flavorings. The leaves and lovely orange and yellow flowers are fine in salads, and the pickled pods often replace capers. The pods of *Tropaeolum* are best picked just as soon as the blossom drops, and prepared at once. To preserve nasturtium pods, see 683. *Tropaeolum majus* vines to 6 feet; *T. minus* grows to 9 inches.

THE ONIONS

Never since our first encounter with the host of alliums in a bulb catalogue have these lilies lost their allure for us as food or flower—from the thinnest chive to the enormous Schuberti with its choicest florets held captive within a flowered cage. This is a plea not only to use a variety of onions in your cooking, but to grow the perennial ones so you will always have them on hand. We have tried to indicate their use in individual recipes. To cook onions as vegetables, see (I, 333). Nothing can add such subtlety to a dish, yet none is more abused in the cooking than onions. And when we say onions, we mean any of the alliums we list below.

Use onion bulbs fresh or dry, the green tops of onions or leeks in making soups and court bouillon; and don't forget that ◗ a touch of onion freshly added to canned vegetables and soups often disguises the "canned" taste and varies the expected one.

◗ High heat and a too-long cooking period bring out the worst features. ◗ If you scorch onions, they will be bitter. ◗ Yet onions must be cooked long enough to get rid of any rawness. If you want them to taste mild in soups, like Potage St. Germain, (I, 144), or in delicate stews, the flavor of the dish can be improved and the onion odor lessened during cooking if you will follow this procedure. ◗ If they are 1 inch in diameter, parblanch the onions 5 minutes, before adding them to the soup or stew. If you want them ◗ mild in sautéing, cook them only until translucent—tender, but not flabby. If you want them ◗ penetrating, sauté until golden; if ◗ all-pervasive, brown them very slowly, as for an onion soup, (I, 133), or a Lyonnaise, (I, 392). To give color and flavor to a Petite Marmite, see (I, 131).

To shorten cooking time, onions are frequently chopped and minced fine. There are a number of ways to make this process less tearful, see (I, 333). Or when you haven't time to sauté an onion properly, but do not want a raw taste in cold dishes, hot sauces or dressings, use ◗ onion juice. Ream a cut onion on a lemon juicer, or scrape the cut center of the onion with the edge of a spoon.

To make onions milder when serving them in salads, first soak them in milk. Or put slices in a bowl and pour boiling water over them. Let stand 30 to 40 minutes. Drain, then soak them briefly in cold water with a lump of ice to crisp. Drain and serve.

The use of onions for the bacteria-destroying power of their vapor was demonstrated on a large scale in World War II. However, this antibacterial action was present only when the onion was freshly cut. This power disappeared within 10 minutes. Onions deteriorate rapidly once the outer skin is removed and ❯ should not be stored for reuse after cutting.

To rid your breath of onion traces, eat raw parsley. See 75 for a perfect raw onion-parsley canapé. Onion odor on the hands can be rubbed off with salt, vinegar or lemon juice. For onion scent on pots, moisten them, sprinkle generously with salt, let stand, then rinse with very hot water.

❯ All onions are of easy culture. They prefer sandy, moist, rich earth, with shallow planting in sun. The dry ones should all be sun-dried a few days after being dug up. You may braid the tops so the bulbs can be hung in clusters for even airing during storage. If the tops are cut, do not crop too close to the neck of the bulb. Store all onions in a cool, dark, dry, well-ventilated place. Below are descriptions of onion types used in cooking.

CHIVES

Chives are shown in bloom, first on the left on 275. Only the leaves are used. Combine them with soft white cheese and with eggs; use in green sauces. Cut and add them to hot and cold food just before serving. ❯ Do not put chives in a cottage cheese or any uncooked dish you plan storing even as long as overnight, as they get unpleasantly strong. To keep plants of *Allium schoenoprasum* looking well, cut a few of the thin tubular leaves low rather than bobbing the top, which will brown where cut. Remember that, like all bulbs, chives rely for plant renewal strength on the leaves—so don't cut any one plant more than 3 or 4 times a season. The leaves are tenderer after each cutting.

Also keep the blooms picked low so the tougher stem does not get mixed with the leaves when you use them and so you are not bothered with seeding. About 3 to 6 small bulbs set in humus-filled soil in the fall will make a good cluster 8 to 10 inches high by the following summer. A slightly larger variety, *Sibericum,* with thicker leaves is also hardy.

GARLIC CHIVES

This is a coarser plant, about 15 inches high, seen second on the left, 277, whose flatter, somewhat stronger leaves are used like chives, above. The charming, starry, honeyed white bloom cluster of this perennial can be used as a decorative garnish, or the florets sprinkled over salads. Cultivate *Allium tuberosum* as for chives.

ORIENTAL GARLIC OR AIL

This is perhaps the most controversial addition to food. Balzac, a formidable gastronome, recommended that even the cook should be rubbed with it! We couldn't live without it, and we think we have learned to use it discreetly, for our guests have sometimes been obviously relishing and unawarely eating food with garlic in it—while inveighing loudly against it. If you are fond of it ❯ keep a check on the amount used, for tolerance to it may grow apace, to the discomfort of your friends. The bulb at the base of the plant, shown last on the right, 275, is the treasure. Note the scalloped form of the bulb indicating the "cloves" within an outer skin. ❯ In this book, when we say 1 clove garlic, it is assumed that the clove is also peeled of its husk. Learn to place slivers of garlic clove on meat before cooking it; to put a clove of garlic on a skewer, cook it in a sauce or stew, and remove it before serving; to rub a salad bowl lightly with a cut clove; or to make chapons, (I, 47). Drop a peeled clove into French dressing 24 hours before serving, but do not leave it in longer, as it deteriorates. Add a small squeeze of garlic juice to sauces. This is easy to do with a garlic press, a handy kitchen utensil shown (I, 376). Should you not own a press, you may use the back of a spoon against a small bowl, or a mortar and pestle, to crush garlic with salt. The salt softens the bulb almost at once, but if you drop a whole clove into a liquid for seasoning ▶ be sure to strain it out before serving. ▶ Never allow garlic to brown. Always use fresh garlic. Powdered and salt forms tend to have rancid overtones. ▶ To blanch garlic, drop the unpeeled cloves into boiling water. Cook for 2 minutes. Drain, peel and simmer slowly in butter about 15 minutes. Mince the blanched buttered garlic and add to sauces.

True garlic bulbs, which grow 1 to 3 feet high, are not hardy. Plant bulbs of *Allium sativum* in light soil in March. They should be ready for lifting in late July. Be sure to sun-dry the cloves until the outer skin is white and parched.

GIANT OR TOPPING GARLIC, OR ROCHAMBOLE

This hardy plant, sketched second from the right, 277, has a beautiful glaucous leaf and an entrancing pointed bud carried on a furled stem. Its unwinding is a source of great pleasure to watch. The edible bulbs that bunch at the top are indistinguishable in taste and form from the tender oriental garlic described above.

Cultivate *Allium sorodoprasum* as for Chives, opposite.

SHALLOTS

The shallot, queen of the sauce onions, is not hardy but well worth growing. It is shown first on the left, 277. Shallot flavor is perhaps closer to garlic than to onions, and although it has a much greater delicacy, it must still be used with discretion. Shallots are indispensable in Bercy Butter, (I, 398), where they should be minced simultaneously with the herbs. They taste especially good in wine cookery. In sautéing them, mince fine so as not to subject them to too much heat. ▶ Never let them brown, as they become bitter. ▶ Substitute 3 to 4 shallots for 1 medium-sized onion.

Allium ascalonicum, always grown from sets, should be put in, barely covered, in the early spring. They should be harvested by late June when the leaves are no longer upright—caving in at the neck—but not yet turning in color. Allow them to dry off on the ground for several days and then braid the leaves so the shallots can be hung in strands in a dry place for use as wanted.

TOPPING ONIONS

Use these as you would any medium-sharp onion. *Allium catawissa,* unlike dry onions purchased in markets, is a perennial. It has a fibrous root system, and the onions develop early in the season at the top of the blooming stock. In fact, some even begin to sprout there too, as shown third from the right, 277, and, in turn, produce more onions at the top of the second sprout the same season. The nonsprouting bulblets can be kept for planting the following August or the next spring. The original plants may

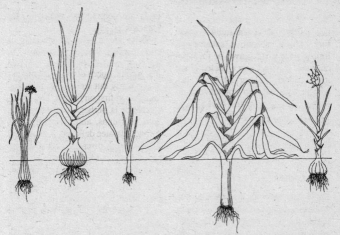

also be separated. There is really no excuse for not trying anything that easy. These are similar to the so-called Egyptian topping onion—*Cepa viviparum*—which, surprisingly, does not grow in Egypt and is hardy and has a usable bulb at the base as well.

LEEKS

The leek, the beloved French *poireau,* is king of the soup onions. It also lends itself well to braising. This biennial, *Allium porrum,* sketched second from the right, above, grows its first year with an elongated root and closely interlaced foliage. Leeks are often hilled to keep them white. This practice traps grit unless the leeks are grown with a paper collar. Be sure to rid them of this grit by washing well. They are choice the first year. A leek with a tough, hollow stem—from which the glorious silver-green bloom has been cut from the center of the foliage—and a more bulbous form at the base—is in its second year and will prove too tough to eat. However, the green portion can be utilized in soups and seasonings.

DRY ONIONS

These types of which an example is pictured second on the left, above, are the onions most available in the market; they vary greatly in flavor, color and shape. On the whole, American *cepa* varieties are smaller, have stronger flavors and keep better than foreign *cepa* types. Good raw and mild in cooking are the big yellow or white Bermudas. Even more so are the flat Spanish reds, a favorite garnish on hamburgers and salads. They mush somewhat in cooking, so if you want a mild red cooker, try the rounder, more elongated Italian redskins. Pearl onions, including the kind you find in the bottom of your Gibson cocktail, are cluster sowings of *cepa* varieties. *Allium cepa* types are biennials; they are planted in sets in February and harvested in July when the browning leaves have died down.

SCALLIONS

Use the leaves as a soup flavoring. The white flesh with about 4 inches of leaf is often braised as for Leeks, (I, 325), and they are eaten raw by self-assertive people. They are the thinnings of *Allium cepa* plantings or are grown from seeds close together and harvested before the bulb develops its characteristic shape. See them shown third on the left, 275.

WELSH ONION

These are used as a substitute for scallions, described above. See them last on the right, opposite. *Allium fistulosum,* known also as the **Japanese bunching onion** or as **Ciboules**, is usually homegrown.

WILD LEEKS, RAMPS OR
BROAD-LEAF WOOD ALLIUM

Around the bulbs of *Allium tricoccum,* seen third on the left, opposite, revolve many American folk festivals. These and the strong field garlic in your lawn—*Allium vineale*—are not recommended by us, though we frequently hear them praised.

THE PARSLEYS

These plants—root, stem and leaves— have a high vitamin A-carrying factor. They are flavorful in themselves but also valuable as an agent for blending the flavors of other herbs, and have the power to destroy the scent of garlic and onion, see 273. There is practically no salad, meat, or soup in which they cannot be used. But they should be handled with discretion, particularly the root of the Hamburg-type or soup parsley. These roots are sometimes cooked as for Parsnips, (I, 338).

There are at least 37 varieties of curly parsley, varying in strength. In mincing or deep-fat frying, remove the florets from the more strongly scented stems. The stems are used in white stocks and sauces for their strength of flavor and because they do not color the sauce, as does the leaf. *Petroselinum hortense* and its curled *crispum* varieties are the parsleys seen most frequently in the markets. Biennials, they grow to about 1 foot in rich loamy soil and sun. As they often bolt early during the second season, they are best treated as annuals.

To grow from seed, soak in water to cover about 24 hours. The uncurled or Italian type is better for fall use, as its leaves shed the snow and stay green longer. *Carum petroselinum,* a coarser-growing, heavier-rooted biennial, grows to 3 feet. Soak seeds as described above.

THE RED AND GREEN PEPPERS

These plants of the *Capsicum* family are heavy in vitamins A and C. They are also said to have bacteria-deterrent and anti-oxidant qualities that extend the keeping periods of fats, meats, and casseroles which include peppers. Native to the Americas, they are widely grown in Europe and are very different from the white and black peppers from the Orient, 261. The *Capsicums* all have this in common: the ◗ seeds and membranes are irritating and should always be removed if you are using fresh peppers. The condiments from these dried peppers are made with and without the seeds. ◗ To skin fresh peppers, place them in a 350° oven until the skin is slightly scorched and easily removed; or blanch them for a moment in deep fat at 375°. See various types on (I, 340).

The sweet or broad bell peppers, variety *C. grossum,* are frequently misnamed "mangoes" in the market. These 4- to 5-inch peppers, both green and, in their more ripened state, red, are used for stuffing and are diced for flavoring. Also to this general type belong the bonnet peppers, or *C. tetragonna,* from which paprikas are ground. The mild Hungarian types are seeded and deprived of their stalks before grinding. Paprika is sensitive to heat and should be added toward the end of the cooking period. When added to broiled food for color, paprika browns when scorched.

The longer peppers, variety *C. longum,* which include most of the chili peppers and cayenne, come in many colors, from chartreuse green to yellow to red. There are hundreds of crosses, and in the endless regional recipes for chili or mole powder, as many as 6 or 8 varieties of *Capsicum* will be indicated, with names like anchos, pasillo, chilpotle.

Cayenne, which comes from *C. annuum L.,* is often adulterated or replaced commercially by *C. fructescens,* a small red, dried tree berry, or *C. croton annuum,* known also as bird peppers. ◗ Cayenne is so very hot, it should be used only in the smallest pinches. Very hot too are the red clustered *C. fasciculatum* varieties, with fruit over 6 inches long, for which the seeds are supposed to have come from Tabasco in Mexico. Grown in southern Louisiana, they constitute the base for hot pepper sauces which are often matured 2 to 3 years. Use gloves when seeding to avoid skin irritation. Red pepper, not so hot as cayenne, is ground from this type.

◗ To prepare dried chili peppers for use in sauces, soak 6 dry chilis in 1 cup water and simmer until tender, about 20 minutes. Drain and reserve the water. When chilis are cool, split them and remove and discard seeds.

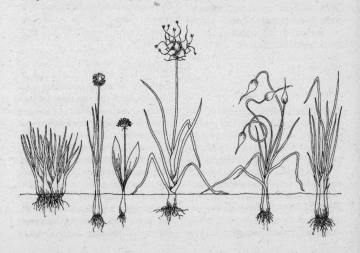

Scrape the pulp from the skin and add it to the reserved water. For other *Capsicum* recipes see Chili Powder, 251, Chili Vinegar, 180, and Sherry Peppers, 683. ♦ For decorating with pimientos, see Truffle Garnishes, (I, 332); or use them in canned form.

ROSEMARY

The stiff resinous leaves of this sub-shrub are extremely pungent and must be handled with caution. In marinades for which this flavoring is popular, allow about $1/8$ to $1/4$ teaspoon fresh for 4 servings. Use the lightly crushed leaves sparsely with lamb, duck, partridge, rabbit, capon and veal; and on peas, spinach and pizza. *Rosmarinus officinalis,* depending on the variety, grows from 2 to 6 feet and tolerates drought and lean soil but is not hardy in the North.

RUE

This herb is sometimes suggested as a flavoring for fruit or claret cups. *Ruta graveoleus,* a handsome gray-green perennial, grows to 3 feet and prefers alkaline soil. As many people are allergic to its irritant qualities, which produce symptoms comparable to poison ivy, we do not recommend its use.

SAFFRON

The golden orange stigmas of the autumn crocus, seen 246, are used to both color and flavor cakes, breads, and dressings and are classic in Risottos, (I, 193), and Bouillabaisse, (I, 161). Even a ♦ small amount of saffron has an overpoweringly medicinal flavor, so use only as directed in the recipes. If using mainly for color, just $1/4$ teaspoon in 2 tablespoons hot water will suffice for 5 to 6 cups of flour. Use only about $1/8$ to $1/4$ teaspoon in 2 tablespoons hot water or white wine to season 6 to 8 servings of a sauce. *Crocus sativus* grows in mellow soil, and, as with all bulbous plants, the foliage of this fall-blooming bulb must be allowed to ripen fully if the plant is to prosper.

THE SAGES

"The young sow wild oats; the old grow sage." Sage is perhaps the best known and loved of all American seasonings. Use for fatty meat like pork and sausages; and for duck, goose and rabbit. It is also used in cheese and chowders. There is no comparison between the flavor of the freshly chopped tender leaves and the dried ones, which lose much of their volatile oil. Dry carefully, as the leaves are thick and mold easily. Always use sages sparingly. Fresh clary sage is used in omelets and fritters and is served with lamb. *Salvia officinalis,* a perennial, grows to 2 feet and should be cut back after blooming. But prune lightly, and only on new growth. Many hybrids exist and dwarf forms are available. Clary sage is biennial.

THE SAVORIES

The leaves of winter savory are used in stews, stuffings and meat loaves. *Sauteria montana,* a rather resinous perennial evergreen sub-shrub, grows to 18 inches and tolerates lean soil. Summer savory is a much more delicately flavored herb and has many more uses. It is classic in green beans and green bean salad; in horseradish sauce and lentil soup; and even in deviled eggs. It is also used with fat fish, roast pork, potatoes, tomatoes and French dressing. *Sauteria hort-*

ensis, which grows to 18 inches, needs light, well-composted soil.

THE SORRELS

The elongated leaves of these plants are quite high in oxalic acid. They are used in small amounts to flavor soups, (I, 155), or sauces, or to combine in small quantities with other vegetables—or to use as garnishes for goose or pork. The leaves may be pounded in a mortar with sugar and vinegar to make a tart sauce. The *Rumex* species grow to 3 feet. The so-called French sorrel, *R. scutatus,* is preferred.

SWEET WOODRUFF OR WALDMEISTER

The beautiful dark green starlike whorled fresh leaves of this plant are floated in May Wine, 60, or in other cold punches, but should not be left in longer than about ½ hour. *Asperula odorata,* which grows to 1 foot, makes a charming ground cover in shady locations.

SWEET CICELY

The green seeds and fresh leaves of this soft, ferny plant may be used as a garnish in salads and cold vegetables. Use dry seeds in cakes, candies and liqueurs. *Myrrhis odorata,* a perennial growing to 3 feet, prefers partial shade and rich moist soil.

TARRAGON

Called *estragon* by the French, this herb when fresh is one of the luxuries of cooking. The flavor, chemically identical to that of anise, is pretty well lost in drying, when the leaf vein stiffens and does not resoften in cooking. So, if the dry leaf is used, it must be carefully strained out before the food is served. To avoid the need for straining and to retain flavor better than by drying, we hold tarragon in vinegar and remove the leaves as needed. Do not crowd the vinegar bottle, allowing about 3 tablespoons of leaves to 1 quart mild vinegar. This gives enough acid to keep the leaves from spoiling. Always keep them well immersed. The fresh leaves are often blanched for decorations, (I, 106). Although tarragon is too pungent to be cooked in soups, it is good added to practically everything else: eggs, mushrooms, tomatoes, sweetbreads, tartare and mustard sauces, fish or chicken. And in a Béarnaise sauce it is essential.

True tarragon, *Artemisia dracunculus,* is perennial. As it seldom sets seed, it is propagated by cuttings, or by divisions pulled—not cut—from the emerging shoots in early March. A less desirable form called Russian tarragon, *A. gmelinii* or *sacrorum,* or *A. dracunculoides,* can be grown from seed.

THE THYMES

Thymes may be used sparingly with poultry, mutton, veal, pork and rabbit; with creole and gumbo dishes; in brown sauces; with pickled beets and tomatoes; with fat fish, stews, stuffings and most vegetables; and are always found in stocks. They make lovely garnishes for hors d'oeuvre and canapés. Caraway-scented thyme or *Thymus herba-barona* is traditional with a baron of beef. There are so many of these charming *Thymus* species, and their flavors are so varied, that a collection of them makes a garden in itself. The narrow-leaf French with its upright habit and gray-green balsamic foliage; and the glistening, small-bushed, strongly scented lemon variety—*T. serpyllum citriodorus*—are the thymes most frequently found in the market. Thyme varieties, which grow best in sun, are perennial, persisting for years among rocks. Prune after blooming.

ABOUT COLOR IN FOOD

Resist the impulse to add color to food from little bottles or to retain it by the use of chemicals like soda. Instead, determine, in general, to maintain whatever color is inherent in the food itself and to heighten it by skillful cooking and effective contrast. ▶ Recent research indicates that some people are highly allergic to artificial colorings.

First steps begin with the selection of fresh, well-grown foods, properly washed, dried and trimmed, then prepared according to the "pointers" in our individual recipes. ▶ Choose utensils made of materials suitable to the foods cooked in them, (I, 119). If you have done so and are still unhappy with the results, check the kind of water you are using, 166. ▶ Never overcook foods: nothing so irrevocably dulls the kitchen palette.

Here are some further ways to keep foods colorful. While the color of soups and sauces is built into them by the way their stocks are made, see 167, it will be least affected if they are scummed while heating and cooked uncovered. Meats, if light, maintain better color if scummed. If dark, their color will be improved by browning; by greasing during roasting or broiling; by glazing or flambéing. Fish and light meat grills profit in color by a prior dusting of paprika.

Cook variety meals—or vegetables and fruits that discolor on exposure to air—in slightly acidulated water, or à blanc, (I, 555). But first sprinkle the cut surfaces of such foods with a little lemon juice. Or use an Anti-Browning Solution, 106, to prevent the discoloration of fresh fruits peeled slightly in advance of serving. Vent stews by the use of poaching paper, (I, 101). And keep in mind that color in all foods is enhanced if they are not held hot and covered after cooking.

Breads and pastries develop beautiful crust color not only through the use of fat in their doughs, but by the discreet addition of saffron or safflower. And color may also be improved just before baking by butter-brushing, 503, egg-glazing, 503, or sugar-coating. Foods served in light sauces may be gratinéed, 221, or glazed, (I, 426). And sauces may be glamorized with herb chiffonades; tomato or red pepper; lobster coral, (I, 455); Lobster Butter, (I, 399); egg yolks, saffron, meat glaze, mushrooms and browned flour.

If you are faced with really listless-looking vegetables, a green coloring additive may be very quickly made up in a blender: use spinach, parsley, or watercress mixed with a small quantity of stock.

As to color combinations and color contrasts, no one can lay down hard and fast rules, except to say that they need not be spectacular. Even so simple a combination as light and dark lettuces in a salad—or an accent of cress—will make for substantially greater interest. The occasional use of edible garnishes—suggestions for which are scattered throughout this book—will be helpful. Do consider, too, the total background: dishes and colorful tableware, table surface, linens and decor are all part and parcel of satisfactory and colorful food presentation.

ABOUT WEATHER

Weather—moist or dry, hot or cold—plays an important part in cooking. When its role is decisive, it is so noted in individual recipes. Let's review just a few instances. Since flours and cereals tend to dry out in winter, our indications for rice and flour amounts, pages (I, 188) and 209, are more variable than we would like to have them. Damp weather will greatly affect sugars after food is cooked—as in meringues and during candy making, 574. Cold and heat have a tremendous effect on the creaming of butter and sugars and on success with Puff Paste, 365, Anise Cookies, 466, or the rising of bread, 298. Threatening weather will even delay the "making" of butter, 200, and Mayonnaise, (I, 418). In storing foods, note if they are to be kept tightly lidded. It is evident that Mark Twain was wrong when he complained that nobody did anything about the weather. The circumspect cook takes account of its vagaries and acts accordingly.

ABOUT MEASURING

◗ All recipes in this book are based on standard U.S. containers: the 8-ounce cup and a tablespoon that takes exactly 16 level fillings to fill that cup level. We suggest that you test for size the tablespoon you select for this purpose, because those on sale frequently do not meet standard specifications.

All our recipes, in turn, are based on level measurements, most hedgers like "heaping" or "scant" having been weeded out of our instructions years ago. Until you are experienced, we strongly urge you to make a fetish of the level standard measure.

To prove how very much careful measurement affects quantity, conduct this simple experiment. Dip the standard spoon into flour or baking powder and then level its contents with a knife. Don't shake. Then scoop up a heaping spoonful of the same ingredients without leveling. You will find that lighter materials, if casually taken, often triple or quadruple the amounts indicated in the recipes. Ten to one the cook who prides herself on using nothing but her intuition as a guide to quantity is the same "old hand" who, for years, has used the same bowls, cups and spoons, the same stove, even the same brands of staples, and who, in addition, gets more than her share of lucky breaks. Like as not, too, she doesn't mind variations in her product.

◗ Accuracy in measuring basic ingredients is especially necessary when making bread, pies and cakes, and in using recipes which include gelatin. ◗ For dry ingredients, use a cup that measures 1 cup even—with a flush rim for leveling. ◗ No shortcuts should be adopted if the recipe requires the sifting of flour. If they are, the outcome is chancy, to say the least. In fact, frequent sifting after measurement will improve the texture of all cakes. ◗ Sifting salt, leavens and spices with the flour ensures even distribution.

Most cake recipes call for sugar to be sifted before measuring. We confess that, instead, we sometimes short-cut by spooning our granulated sugar lightly into a measuring cup and then leveling it off, see 227. To measure brown sugar, see 228.

The measurement of what we might call side-ingredients, such as flavorings and spices, is important too, but here much depends on individual taste, to say nothing of the age of the spices, and amounts may vary considerably without risking failure. To measure fats, see 199.

ABOUT SUBSTITUTIONS AND EQUIVALENTS

You're a new cook and you run out of granulated sugar. Don't think this doesn't happen to old cooks too! So you just substitute confectioners' sugar. And then when the cake is not so sweet as it should be and the texture is horrid, you wonder what happened.

Good recipes and the reasonable use of standard measures allow you to cook well without knowing that it takes about 2 cups of sugar or butter to make a pound, but that you will need about 4 cups of flour for that same pound. This you discover fast enough if you leave the United States, for almost everyone else cooks by weight, not volume.

Let's look at a few lucky volume-weight relationships that for the moment protect you, as a new cook, from the menace of that old dragon Mathematics—and his allies, Physics, Chemistry and Semantics. Here are some of our victorious, if homely, weapons, tested in many a battle with these old tricksters.

By weight, if not quite by volume, 2 tablespoons butter equal 2 tablespoons butter, melted. But try to incorporate this positive knowledge into a cake and utter failure results. See About Butter or Shortening Cakes, 409, and About Oil Cakes, 429.

By weight, 1 cup 32% whipping cream equals 1 cup 32% cream, whipped. By volume, 1 cup 32% whipping cream equals about 2 cups 32% cream, whipped.

⬥ If the recipe calls for whipped cream rather than for whipping cream, you need the airier, drier texture that results from whipping.

Let's take a closer look at sugars.

1 cup granulated weighs about 8 ounces

1 cup confectioners' weighs 4¹/₂ ounces

1 cup brown sugar weighs 6 ounces

1 cup molasses, honey or corn syrup weighs 12 ounces

These are only differences in weight. But you also have to reckon with changes in sweetening power and in texture, and—in the case of molasses and honey—with liquids that also have an acid factor. And don't forget about taste, that most important element of all.

If any of the foregoing ingredients are called for in a recipe, the recipe is written to take care of inequalities. But if you are substituting in emergencies, say, sugar for molasses, please read About Molasses first. Some substitutions work fairly well, others only under special circumstances. ⬥ But never expect to get the same results from a friend's recipe if she uses one kind of shortening and you use another. Your product may be better or worse than hers, but it won't be the same.

Before leaving you to delve into the tables that follow, like English standard measures versus those of the United States in relation to the complexities of the metric system, we introduce our ⬥ multiply-and-conquer principle for fractions.

You are preparing only ¹/₃ of a given recipe. The recipe calls for ¹/₃ cup of flour. Well, ¹/₃ cup of flour equals 5¹/₃ tablespoons. 1 tablespoon equals 3 teaspoons. So 5¹/₃ tablespoons equals 16 teaspoons, and, finally, 16 teaspoons divided by

3—you are working for $1/3$ of the recipe, remember?—gives you $5^{1}/3$ teaspoons. Now maybe you can get this result by leaving out some of these steps, but we can't.

Here is another tried and true kitchen formula—one for proportions. You want to make your grandmother's fruit cake that has a yield of 11 pounds. You'd like only 3 pounds. The recipe calls for 10 cups of flour. How much flour should you use for 3 pounds of cake? Make yourself a formula in simple proportion: 11 pounds of cake is to 3 pounds of cake as 10 cups of flour is to ? or X cups of flour: i.e., $11:3 = 10:X$. Multiply the end factors—11 x X—and the inside factors—3 x 10—to get $11X = 30$. Divide 30 by 11 to find that $X = 2^{8}/11$ or approximately $2^{3}/4$ cups. If you are in any doubt that $8/11$ is close to $3/4$, divide 8 by 11, finding the decimal closest to the standard measure. It is worth going through the same reducing process for the other basic ingredients such as egg, liquid and fruit—so the cake will hold together. Approximate the spices. But one more caution in changing recipes. ◗ Don't decrease or enlarge recipes by dividing or multiplying by any number larger than 4—purists recommend 2. This sounds and is mysterious. But the fact remains that recipes are just not indefinitely expandable or shrinkable

TABLES OF EQUIVALENTS AND CONVERSIONS

It is most unfortunate that in United States measuring systems the same word may have two meanings. For instance, an ounce may mean $1/16$ of a pound or $1/16$ of a pint; but the former is strictly a weight measure and the latter a volume measure. See the difference in weights of cups of different kinds of sugar, opposite. Except in the case of water, milk or other ingredients of the same "density," a fluid ounce and an ounce of weight are two completely different quantities. Perhaps for this reason most foreign cooks measure solid ingredients by weight. If you intend to use continental recipes frequently, a gram/ounce scale is a necessity.

UNITED STATES MEASUREMENTS

All these equivalents are based on United States "fluid" measure. In this book, this measure is used not only for liquids such as water and milk, but also for materials such as flour, sugar and shortening, since the volume measure for these is customary in the United States.

LIQUID MEASURE VOLUME
EQUIVALENTS

For U.S.-metric fluid volume, see chart on 285.

A few grains	= Less than $1/8$ teaspoon
60 drops	= 1 teaspoon
1 teaspoon	= $1/3$ tablespoon
1 tablespoon	= 3 teaspoons
2 tablespoons	= 1 fluid ounce
4 tablespoons	= $1/4$ cup or 2 ounces
$5^{1}/3$ tablespoons	= $1/3$ cup or $2^{2}/3$ ounces
8 tablespoons	= $1/2$ cup or 4 ounces
16 tablespoons	= 1 cup or 8 ounces or 2 gills
8 tablespoons	= 1 teacup or 4 ounces
$1/4$ cup	= 4 tablespoons
$3/8$ cup	= $1/4$ cup plus 2 tablespoons

⁵/₈ cup	= ½ cup plus 2 tablespoons
⁷/₈ cup	= ¾ cup plus 2 tablespoons
1 cup	= ½ pint or 8 fluid ounces
2 cups	= 1 pint or 16 fluid ounces
1 gill, liquid	= ½ cup or 4 fluid ounces
1 pint, liquid	= 4 gills or 16 fluid ounces
1 quart, liquid	= 2 pints or 4 cups
1 gallon, liquid	= 4 quarts

LINEAR MEASURES

For equipment comparison.

1 centimeter	=0.394 inch
1 inch	=2.54 centimeters
1 meter	=39.37 inches

DRY MEASURE VOLUME EQUIVALENTS

Be careful not to confuse dry measure pints and quarts with liquid measure pints and quarts. The former are about ¹/₆ larger than the latter. Dry measure is used for raw fruits and vegetables, when dealing with fairly large quantities.

	Dry Pints	Dry Quarts	Pecks	Bushels	Liters
1 Dry Pint	1	½	¹/₁₆	¹/₆₄	.55
1 Dry Quart	2	1	⅛	¹/₃₂	1.1
1 Peck	16	8	1	¼	8.8
1 Bushel	64	32	4	1	35.23
1 Liter	1.82	.91	.114	.028	1

COMPARATIVE U.S. AND BRITISH MEASUREMENTS

Many British or "Imperial" units of measurement have the same names as United States units, but not all are identical. In general, weights are equivalent, but volumes are not. The most important difference for the cook, and one we were slow to realize until we had had consistent failures using English recipes with American measures, is noted below.

Also, the variable sizes of the British teaspoon and tablespoon created a further problem. Confronted with our dilemma, a British friend laughed and told us that there were no standard household British teaspoons and tablespoons. Her own teaspoons and tablespoons had been in the family since the fifteenth century and fit the family recipes perfectly. As a result the best we can recommend is experimentation. Below are differences between U.S. and British measuring cups:

An 8-U.S.-oz. U.S. measuring cup = 2 U.S. gills of 4 U.S. oz. each, or 16 U.S. tablespoons, or 48 U.S. teaspoons.

A 10-Imperial-oz. English measuring cup = 1 English breakfast cup or 2 Imperial English gills of 5 Imperial oz. each, or 20⁴/₅ U.S. tablespoons, or 62½ U.S. teaspoons.

ABOUT METRIC CONVERSION

We all dread change and often fight it. When you look at the seemingly complicated tables below, you probably feel you want to hug to your breast more tightly than ever your good old U.S. measuring spoons and cups. These tables, which convert by both weight and volume, are handy if you want to translate American or Commonwealth recipes into metric measures.

Take heart as we face our own turnover to metric. We can use either the system already described or a much simpler volume conversion. Our food and equipment manufacturers are already planning three sizes of measures and five sizes of spoons that will give us tolerances close to our present recipes. So rest easy; when the great changeover comes, it will not prove as difficult as you may now fear.

The charts below compare common kitchen measures from metric to American Standard and vice versa. To use, we give the following example: To determine the equivalent number of U.S. cups in a recipe which calls for 500 milliliters of liquid, look at the U.S. Metric Fluid Volume chart. Find 1 ml. in the left column; follow across to cups to find .004. Multiply 500 by .004 and you will get the answer—2 cups.

U.S. METRIC FLUID VOLUME

	Fluid Drams	Tea-spoons	Table-spoons	Fluid Ounces	$1/4$ Cups	Gills $1/2$ Cups	Cups	Fluid Pints	Fluid Quarts	Gallons	Milli-liters	Liters
1 Fluid Dram	1	$3/4$	$1/4$	$1/8$ .125	$1/16$ .0625	.03125	.0156	.0078	.0039	$1/1024$	3.70	.0037
1 Tea-spoon	$1^1/3$	1	$1/3$	$1/6$	$1/12$	$1/24$	$1/48$	$1/96$	$1/192$	$1/768$	5	.005
1 Table-spoon	4	3	1	$1/2$	$1/4$	$1/8$	$1/16$	$1/32$	$1/64$	$1/256$	15	.015
1 Fluid Ounce	8	6	2	1	$1/2$	$1/4$	$1/8$	$1/16$	$1/32$	$1/128$	29.56	.030
$1/4$ Cup	16	12	4	2	1	$1/2$	$1/4$	$1/8$	$1/16$	$1/64$	59.125	.059
1 Gill $1/2$ Cup	32	24	8	4	2	1	$1/2$	$1/4$	$1/8$	$1/32$	118.25	.118
1 Cup	64	48	16	8	4	2	1	$1/2$	$1/4$	$1/16$	236	.236
1 Fluid Pint	128	96	32	16	8	4	2	1	$1/2$	$1/8$	473	.473
1 Fluid Quart	256	192	64	32	16	8	4	2	1	$1/4$	946	.946
1 Gallon	1024	768	256	128	64	32	16	8	4	1	3785.4	3.785
1 Milli-liter	.270	.203 or $1/5$	.068	.034	.017	.008	.004	.002	.001	.0003	1	.001 or $1/1000$
1 Liter	27.05	203.04	67.68	33.814	16.906	8.453	4.227	2.113	1.057	.264	1000	1

U.S. METRIC MASS (WEIGHT)

	Grams	Drams	Ounces	Pounds	Milligrams	Grams	Kilograms
1 Grain	1	.004	.002	1/7000	64.7	.064	.0006
1 Dram	27.34	1	1/16	1/256	1770	1.77	.002
1 Ounce	437.5	16	1	1/16	2835	28.35	.028
1 Pound	7000	256	16	1	"Lots"	454	.454
1 Milligram	.015	.0006	1/29,000	1/"Lots"	.1	.001	.000001
1 Gram	15.43	.565	.032	.002	1000	1	.001
1 Kilogram	15,430	564.97	.000032	2.2	1,000,000	1000	1

BRITISH—METRIC FLUID VOLUME

The British are presently using the metric system, but if you wish to use English recipes written before the early 1970s, you may find these tables a great help.

	Fluid Drams	Fluid Ounces	1/4 Cups	Gills 1/2 Cups	Cups	Fluid Pints	Fluid Quarts	Milliliters	Liters
1 Fluid Dram	1	1/8	1/20 .05	1/40 .025	1/80 .0125	1/160 .006	1/320 .003	3.55	.0035
1 Fluid Ounce	8	1	1/4	1/5 .2	1/10	1/20 .05	1/40 .025	28.4	.028
1/4 Cup	20	2.5	1	1/2	1/4	1/8	1/16	71	.07
1 Gill—1/2 Cup	40	5	2	1	1/2	1/4	1/8	142	.14
1 Cup	80	10	4	2	1	1/2	1/4	284	.28
1 Fluid Pint	160	20	8	4	2	1	1/2	568	.57
1 Fluid Quart	320	40	16	8	4	2	1	1136	1.13
1 Milliliter	.28	.035	.014	.007	.0035	.0018	.0009	1	.001 or 1/1000
1 Liter	281.5	35.19	14.08	7.04	3.52	1.76	.88	1000	1

APPROXIMATE
TEMPERATURE
CONVERSIONS

$$100°C \times 9 = 900°$$
$$900° \div 5 = 180°$$
$$180° + 32 = 212°$$

	FAHRENHEIT	CELSIUS OR CENTIGRADE
Coldest area of freezer..	−10°	−23°
Freezer....	0°	−17°
Water freezes	32°	0°
Water simmers	115°	46°
Water scalds	130°	54°
Water boils— at sea level.	212°	100°
Soft ball...	234°	112°
Firm ball ..	244°	117°
Hard ball ..	250°	121°
Very low oven......	250°-275°	121°-133°
Low oven .	300°-325°	149°-163°
Moderate oven......	350°-375°	177°-190°
Hot oven ..	400°-425°	204°-218°
Very hot oven......	450°-475°	232°-246°
Extremely hot oven......	500°-525°	260°-274°
Broil ..... *See Broiling,* 146		

To convert Fahrenheit into Centigrade, subtract 32, multiply by 5, divide by 9. To convert Centigrade into Fahrenheit, go into reverse: Multiply by 9, divide by 5, add 32.

CAN SIZES	CONTENTS	APPROXIMATE CUPS
5-oz.......	5 oz.	5/8
8-oz.......	8 oz.	1
Picnic	10½ to 12 oz.	1¼
12-oz. vacuum....	12 oz.	1½
No. 300. ...	14 to 16 oz.	1¾
No. 303. ...	16 to 17 oz.	2
No. 2......	1 lb. 4 oz. or 1 pint 2 fl. oz.	2½
No. 2½....	1 lb. 13 oz.	3½
No. 3......	46 ox.	5¾
Baby foods.	3½ to 8 oz.	
Condensed milk	14 fl. oz.	1⅓
Evaporated milk......	5⅓ and 13 fl. oz.	⅔-1⅔

AVERAGE FROZEN FOOD PACKAGES

Vegetables ....\......8 to 16 oz.
Fruits ....10 to 16 oz.
Canned frozen fruits.. 13½ to 16 oz.
Frozen juice concentrates ..... 6 oz.

EQUIVALENTS AND SUBSTITUTIONS FOR COMMON INGREDIENTS

Also check "Abouts" for individual items; see Index for further information. Some foods are sold by weight, but most **Joy** recipes give amounts in number of measuring cups or spoons and are therefore volume measurements, whether liquid or mass.

Almonds
   In shell.............∴.3½ lb.............1 lb. shelled
   Unblanched, whole ......6 oz.............1 cup

Unblanched, ground	1 lb.	2²/₃ cups
Unblanched, slivered.	1 lb.	5²/₃ cups
Blanched, whole	5¹/₃ oz.	1 cup
Blanched, slivered.	4 oz.	1 cup
Ammonium carbonate	³/₄ teaspoon ground . .	1 teaspoon baking soda
Apples	1 lb. unpared	3 cups pared, sliced
	3¹/₂ to 4 lb. raw	1 lb. dried
	About 10 apples . .	1 lb. dried
Apricots, fresh	5¹/₂ lb.	1 lb. dried
Apricots, dried.	1 lb.	3¹/₄ cups
Apricots, cooked, drained . . .	1 lb.	3 cups
Arrowroot as a thickener . .	1¹/₂ teaspoons	1 tablespoon flour
	2 teaspoons	1 tablespoon cornstarch
Baking powder		
rising equivalent	1 teaspoon	¹/₄ teaspoon baking soda plus ⁵/₈ teaspoon cream of tartar
	1 teaspoon	¹/₄ teaspoon baking soda plus ¹/₂ cup buttermilk or yogurt
	1 teaspoon	¹/₄ teaspoon baking soda plus ¹/₄ to ¹/₂ cup molasses
double-acting, SAS	1 teaspoon	1¹/₂ teaspoons phosphate or tartrate baking powder
Bananas.	3 to 4 medium-sized.	1 lb. or 1³/₄ cups mashed
Bay leaf	¹/₄ teaspoon, crushed .	1 whole bay leaf
Beans, green, fresh	1 lb. = 3 cups . . .	2¹/₂ cups cooked
Beans, kidney, dry.	1 lb. = 2¹/₂ cups . . .	6 cups cooked
Beans, lima, dry.	1 lb. = 2¹/₂ cups . . .	6 cups cooked
Beans, navy, dry	¹/₂ lb. = 1 cup	2¹/₂ cups cooked
Brazil nuts.	2 lb. in shell.	1 lb. shelled— approximately 3 cups
Bread crumbs, dry.	¹/₄ cup	1 slice bread
soft.	¹/₂ cup	1 slice bread
Butter		
1 stick	4 oz.	8 tablespoons or ¹/₂ cup
4 sticks	1 lb.	2 cups
	1 cup	1 cup margarine
		⁴/₅ to ⁷/₈ cup clarified bacon fat or drippings
		³/₄ cup clarified chicken fat
		⁷/₈ cup lard or cottonseed, corn or or nut oil, solid or liquid
Butter.	8 oz.	7.3 oz. hydrogenated fats, see 202
Butter, whipped.	1 lb. or 6 sticks	3 cups

Buttermilk . . . . 1 cup . . . . 1 cup yogurt

Cabbage . . . . 1/2 lb. minced . . . . . . 3 cups packed
                              1 lb. (1 head) . . . . 4 1/2 cups shredded

Cane syrup, *see* About Liquid Sugars, 229

Carob powder . . . . 3 tablespoons plus
                              2 tablespoons water. 1 oz. chocolate

Carrots, fresh, without tops . . 1 lb. . . . . 3 cups shredded or
                                            2 1/2 cups diced

Cheese, dry . . . . 1 lb. . . . . 4 cups

Cheese, freshly shredded . . . 1/4 lb. . . . . 1 cup

Cheese, blue . . . . 4 oz. . . . . 1 cup crumbled

Cheese, cottage . . . . 1/2 lb. . . . . 1 cup

Cheese, cream . . . . 3 oz. . . . . 6 tablespoons

Chestnuts . . . . 35 to 40 large . . . . . 2 1/2 cups peeled
                           1 lb. shelled . . . . . 1 1/2 lb. in shell

Chocolate . . . . 1 oz. . . . . 1 square
                           1 oz. . . . . 4 tablespoons grated

Chocolate, unsweetened . . . . 1 oz. . . . . 3 tablespoons cocoa plus
                                            1 tablespoon butter or fat

Chocolate, unsweetened . . . . 1 oz. . . . . 3 tablespoons carob
                                            powder plus
                                            2 tablespoons water

Chocolate, unsweetened . . . . 1 oz. plus 4 teaspoons
                              sugar . . . . 1 2/3 oz. semisweet
                                            chocolate

Cocoa . . . . 1 lb. . . . . 4 cups

Cocoa . . . . 3 tablespoons plus
                              1 tablespoon fat . . . 1 oz. unsweetened
                                            chocolate

Coconut, fine-grated . . . . . 3 1/2 oz. . . . . 1 cup

Coconut, grated . . . . 1 cup . . . . : . . 1 1/3 cups flaked

Coconut, flaked . . . . 3 1/2 oz. . . . . 1 1/3 cups

Coconut . . . . 1 tablespoon dried,
                              chopped . . . . . . 1 1/2 tablespoons fresh

Coconut . . . . 1 lb. . . . . 5 cups shredded,
                                            unsweetened

Coconut . . . . 1 lb. . . . . 4 cups shredded,
                                            sweetened

Coconut milk, see 244 . . . . . 1 cup . . . . 1 cup milk

Coconut cream, see 244 . . . . 1 cup . . . . 1 cup cream

Coffee . . . . 1 lb. . . . . 40 to 50 6-oz. cups

Coffee, instant or powdered . 2 oz. . . . . 25 6-oz. cups

Coffee, freeze-dried . . . . . . 4 oz. . . . . About 60 6-oz. cups

Corn syrup, *see* About Liquid Sugars, 229

Cornmeal . . . . 1 lb. . . . . 3 cups

Cornmeal . . . . 1 cup uncooked . . . . 4 to 4 1/2 cups cooked

Cornstarch, see Flour

Cracker crumbs . . . . 3/4 cup . . . . 1 cup bread crumbs

Cream, half-and-half, 10 to 12% butterfat........	1 cup	1½ tablespoons butter plus about ⅞ cup milk, or ½ cup coffee cream and ½ cup milk
Cream, coffee, at least 20% butterfat..........	1 cup	3 tablespoons butter, plus about ⅞ cup milk
Cream, whipping, heavy 36 to 40% butterfat......	1 cup	⅓ cup butter plus about ¾ cup milk
Cream, whipping..........	1 cup unwhipped...	2 to 2½ cups whipped
Cream, sour, *see* About Sour Cream, 190........	1 cup	3 tablespoons butter plus ⅞ cup buttermilk or yogurt
Cream, sour, cultured, *see* About Sour Cream, 190	1 cup	⅓ cup butter plus ¾ cup cultured buttermilk or yogurt
Dates	1 lb............	2½ cups pitted
Eggs, hen, extra large	4	About 1 cup
large, 2 oz...............	5	About 1 cup
medium...............	6	About 1 cup
small	7	About 1 cup
Eggs, dried, sifted	1 lb............	5¼ cups
Eggs, dried, sifted	2½ tablespoons beaten with 2½ tablespoons water..........	1 whole egg
Eggs, frozen	1 lb............	1⅞ cups
Egg whites, extra large	6	About 1 cup
large, 2 oz...............	8	About 1 cup
medium...............	10 to 11	About 1 cup
small	11 to 12	About 1 cup
Egg whites, dried, sifted	1 tablespoon plus 2 tablespoons water..........	1 egg white
Egg whites, frozen	2 tablespoons thawed	1 egg white
Egg yolks, for thickening ...	2 yolks...........	1 whole egg
Egg yolks, extra large	10 to 11	About 1 cup
large, 2 oz...............	12	About 1 cup
medium...............	13 to 14	About 1 cup
small	15 to 16	About 1 cup
Egg yolks, dried, sifted ...	1½ tablespoons plus 1 tablespoon water...........	1 egg yolk

Egg yolks, frozen . . . . 3¹/₂ teaspoons thawed . 1 large egg yolk
Eggs, bantam. . . . . 1 . . . . ²/₃ oz.
Eggs, duck. . . . . 1 . . . . 3 oz.
Eggs, goose. . . . . 1 . . . . 8 to 10 oz.
Figs, dried . . . . 1 lb. . . . . 2²/₃ cups chopped
Filberts or hazelnuts . . . . . 2¹/₄ lb. in shell. . . . . . . 1 lb. shelled or 3¹/₃ cups
Flour, *also see* About Flours, 209
   Cake . . . . 1 lb. . . . . 4³/₄ cups
   Cake . . . . 1 cup sifted . . . . . . ⁷/₈ cup sifted all-purpose
                                  flour, or 1 cup less
                                  2 tablespoons
   White or all-purpose . . . . . 1 lb. . . . . 4 cups
   White. . . . . 4 cups . . . . 3¹/₂ cups cracked wheat
   White. . . . . 1 cup. . . . . 1 cup cornmeal
                                  ⁵/₈ cup potato flour
                                  1 cup minus 2 tablespoons
                                  rice flour
                                  1¹/₄ cups rye flour
                                  ¹³/₁₆ cup gluten flour
   Graham, whole-grain or
     whole wheat . . . . 1 lb. . . . . 3³/₄ to 4 cups finely milled
Flours, for thickening . . . . . 1 tablespoon flour . 1¹/₂ teaspoons cornstarch,
                                  potato starch, rice starch
                                  or arrowroot starch
                                  1 tablespoon quick-
                                  cooking tapioca
                                  1 tablespoon waxy rice
                                  flour
                                  1 tablespoon waxy corn
                                  flour
                   ¹/₂ tablespoon flour . . 1 tablespoon browned
                                  flour, (I, 379)
Garlic. . . . . 1 small clove . . . . . ¹/₈ teaspoon powder
Gelatin. . . . . ¹/₄ -oz. envelope . . . . . About 1 tablespoon
Gelatin. . . . . ¹/₄ -oz. envelope . . . . 4 sheets gelatin, 4″ × 9″
Gelatin for 1 pint liquid. . . . ¹/₄ oz. or 1 envelope . . About 1 tablespoon
Ginger . . . . 1 tablespoon candied,
                                washed of sugar, or
                                1 tablespoon raw . ¹/₈ teaspoon powdered
Gum tragacanth. . . . . ¹/₄ oz. . . . . 1 tablespoon
Hazelnuts. . . . . 2¹/₄ lb. in shell. . . . . . . 1 lb. shelled or 3¹/₃ cups
Herbs, *see* Using
   Herbs, 265 . . . . ¹/₃ to ¹/₂ teaspoon
                         dried . . . . 1 tablespoon fresh
Honey, *see* About
   Liquid Sugars, 229 . . . . . . 1 lb. . . . . 1¹/₃ cups
Honey . . . . 1 cup . . . . 1¹/₄ cups sugar plus
                                  ¹/₄ cup liquid

Horseradish . . . . 1 tablespoon fresh,
grated . . . . 2 tablespoons bottled

Horseradish . . . . 6 tablespoons dried,
grated . . . . 10 tablespoons bottled

Lard . . . . 1 lb. . . . . 2 cups

Lemon . . . . 1 . . . . 1 to 3 tablespoons juice,
1 to 1 1/2 teaspoons
grated rind

1 teaspoon juice . . . 1/2 teaspoon vinegar

1 teaspoon grated
rind . . . . 1/2 teaspoon lemon extract

Lentils . . . . 1 lb. or 2 1/4 cups . . . 5 cups cooked

Lime . . . . 1 . . . . 1 1/2 to 2 tablespoons juice

Macaroni, uncooked . . . . . . 1 lb. . . . . 4 to 5 cups

Macaroni, 1-inch pieces . . . . 1 cup uncooked . . . . 2 to 2 1/4 cups cooked

Maple sugar, grated
and packed . . . . 1 tablespoon . . . . . . 1 tablespoon white
granulated

Maple sugar . . . . 1/2 cup . . . . 1 cup maple syrup

Maple syrup, *see* About Liquid Sugars, 229

Marshmallows . . . . 1 cup cut up . . . . . . 16 large or 160 miniature

Meat

   Beef, cooked . . . . 1 lb. . . . . 3 cups minced

   Beef, uncooked . . . . 1 lb. . . . . 2 cups ground

Milk, whole . . . . 1 cup . . . . 1/2 cup evaporated plus
1/2 cup water

1/4 cup dry whole milk plus
7/8 cup water

1 cup reconstituted nonfat
dry milk plus
2 1/2 teaspoons butter or
margarine

1 cup soy or almond milk

1 cup fruit juice or
1 cup potato water in
baking

Milk, whole . . . . 1 cup . . . . 1 cup water plus
1 1/2 teaspoons butter

1 quart . . . . 1 quart skim milk plus
3 tablespoons cream

Milk, skim . . . . 1 cup . . . . 1/3 cup instant nonfat dry
milk plus about 3/4 cup
water

Milk, whole dry . . . . 1 lb. . . . . 14 cups reconstituted

Milk, instant nonfat dry . . . . . 1 lb. . . . . About 5 quarts
reconstituted

Milk, to sour . . . . 1 cup . . . . Add 1 tablespoon
vinegar or lemon juice

to 1 cup milk minus
1 tablespoon. Let stand
5 minutes.

Molasses, *see* About Liquid Sugars, 229
Mushrooms, fresh . . . . 8 oz. or about 3 cups . About 1 cup sliced,
cooked
Mushroom, canned . . . . 6 oz. drained . . . . . 1/2 lb. fresh
Mushroom, dried. . . . . 3 oz. . . . . 1 lb. fresh
Mustard . . . . 1 teaspoon dry or
powdered . . . . 1 tablespoon prepared
mustard
Noodles, uncooked . . . . 1 lb. . . . . 6 to 8 cups
Noodles, 1-inch pieces . . . . . 1 cup uncooked . . . . . About 1 1/4 cups cooked
Nuts, *see individual names* . . 1 lb. in shell . . . . . . 1/2 lb. kernels, a little less
for heavier nuts, a little
more for lighter ones
Oatmeal . . . . 1 lb. . . . . 5 1/3 cups uncooked
1 cup uncooked . . 1 3/4 cups cooked
Oil . . . . 1 lb. fat . . . . 2 cups
Onions, *see* about Onions, 272
Orange . . . . 1 medium-sized. . . . 6 to 8 tablespoons juice
Orange . . . . 1 medium-sized . . . 3/4 cups diced
Orange rind, grated . . . . 1 medium-sized . . . 2 to 3 tablespoons
Peaches . . . . 1 lb. to 4 medium-
sized . . . . 2 cups sliced
Peanuts . . . . 1 1/2 lb. unshelled . . . . . 1 lb. shelled, about 3 cups
Pears . . . . 1 lb. or 4 medium-
sized . . . . 2 cups sliced
Peas, dried, split . . . . 1 lb. or 2 1/4 cups . . . 5 cups cooked
Pecans . . . . 2 1/2 lb. in shell . . . . . . 1 lb. shelled, about
4 1/4 cups
Peppers, green . . . . 6 oz. or 1 large . . . . 1 cup diced
Pistachios, shelled . . . . 1 lb. . . . . 3 2/3 cups
Pomegranate . . . . 1 average . . . . 1/2 cup pulpy seeds
Potatoes . . . . 1 lb. sliced or
diced . . . . 3 1/2 to 4 cups raw
Potatoes . . . . 1 lb. or 3 medium-
sized . . . . 2 1/4 cups cooked or
1 3/4 cups mashed
Prunes, dried . . . . 1 lb. . . . . 2 1/4 cups pitted
Prunes, cooked, drained . . . . 1 lb. . . . . 2 cups
Raisins
Seeded, whole . . . . 1 lb. . . . . 3 1/4 cups
Seedless, whole . . . . 1 lb. . . . . 2 3/4 cups
Rennet . . . . 1 tablet. . . . . 1 tablespoon liquid rennet
Rhubarb . . . . 1 lb. fresh . . . . 2 cups cooked
Rice . . . . 1 lb. or 2 cups
uncooked . . . . About 6 cups cooked

Rice, dehydrated or
  precooked . . . . 2 cups . . . . $2^2/3$ cups cooked
Rolled oats . . . . 1 lb. or $6^1/4$ cups
                                    uncooked . . . . 8 cups cooked
Saccharin. . . . . $^1/4$ grain . . . . 1 teaspoon sugar
Sorghum molasses, *see* About
  Liquid Sugars, 229 . . . . . . 1 lb. . . . . $1^1/3$ cups
Spaghetti . . . . 1 lb. dry . . . . 5 to 6 cups
Spaghetti, 2-inch pieces . . . . 1 cup dry . . . . About $1^3/4$ cups cooked
Spaghetti, 12-inch pieces . . . 1 lb. dry . . . . About $6^1/2$ cups cooked
Strawberries, fresh . . . . 1 quart . . . . 4 cups sliced
Sugar, in baking, *see* About Solid Sugars, 226
  and About Liquid Sugars, 229
Sugar, granulated . . . . 1 lb. . . . . 2 cups
Sugar, brown, packed . . . . . . 1 lb. . . . . $2^1/4$ cups
Sugar, brown, packed . . . . . . 1 cup . . . . 1 cup granulated sugar
Sugar, superfine. . . . . 1 cup . . . . 1 cup granulated sugar
Sugar, confectioners' or
  powdered. . . . . 1 lb. . . . . $3^1/2$ to 4 cups
Sugar, confectioners'. . . . . . $1^3/4$ cups . . . . 1 cup granulated sugar
Sweetener—noncaloric
  solution . . . . $^1/8$ teaspoon . . . . 1 teaspoon sugar
Tapioca . . . . $1^1/2$ to 2 tablespoons
                                    quick-cooking . . . 4 tablespoons pearl,
                                                        soaked
Tapioca, for thickening . . . . . 1 tablespoon quick-
                                    cooking. . . . . 1 tablespoon flour
Tea. 1 lb. . . . . 125 cups
Tomatoes. . . . . 1 cup packed . . . . . $^1/2$ cup tomato sauce plus
                                                        $^1/2$ cup water
Tomato juice . . . . 1 cup . . . . $^1/2$ cup tomato sauce plus
                                                        $^1/2$ cup water
Tomato sauce . . . . 2 cups . . . . $^3/4$ cup tomato paste plus
                                                        1 cup water
Tomato soup . . . . 1 can: $10^3/4$ oz. . . . . . 1 cup tomato sauce plus
                                                        $^1/4$ cup water
Water. . . . . 1 lb. . . . . 2 cups
Walnuts, English . . . . 2 to $2^1/2$ lb. in shell . . 1 lb. shelled, about
                                                        $4^1/2$ cups of halves
Walnuts, black . . . . $5^1/2$ lb. in shell. . . . . . 1 lb. shelled, about
                                                        3 cups broken
Wheat germ. . . . . 12 oz. . . . . 3 cups
Yeast, compressed. . . . . 1 cake, $^3/5$ oz. . . . . . 1 package active dry yeast
Yeast, active dry . . . . 1 package . . . . 1 tablespoon
Yogurt . . . . 1 cup . . . . 1 cup buttermilk

ABOUT LEFTOVERS

The minister's bride set her luncheon casserole down with a flourish and waited for grace. "It seems to me," murmured her husband, "that I have blessed a good deal of this material before."

Leftovers can, of course, stand for simple repetition; but they can also stimulate a cook's ingenuity. For our part, we feel positively blessed when we have a tidy store of them garnered away in the refrigerator. So often they give a needed fillip to a dish we are making from scratch. Sometimes they combine to make a vegetable soufflé or to dress up an omelet. And how often they turn a can of soup into a real delicacy!

One secret we have learned is to limit the number of leftover ingredients we are working with so that they retain some semblance of identity. If there is too much of a mishmash, the flavors simply cancel out—as well as the appetite.

Another secret is to watch leftovers for color. Freshen them up by presenting them with the more positive accents of tomatoes or bright greens; or with a color-contrasting sauce.

Still another secret is to be careful that you create some contrast in texture. When leftover mixtures are soft, contrast can be achieved by adding minced celery or peppers, nuts, water chestnuts, crisp bacon or freshly minced herbs.

Consult the index under the category you wish to utilize, or try one of the following suggestions:

See About Uses for Ready-Baked and Leftover Breads, Cakes and Crackers, 353; also About Crumbs, 218, and Bread Dressing, (I, 431).

For ways to use cooked cereals and pastas, see Cooked-Cereal Muffins, 346, or Garnishes for Soups, (I, 170). Also see Croquettes, 161, and Griddle Cakes, 141, or Calas, 160.

See About Stocks, 167, and About Soup Meat, (I, 129), for uses of bones, and for meat, fowl, fish and vegetable trimmings.

For cooked meat, fish and vegetables leftovers, see Brunch, Lunch and Supper Dishes, (I, 236), mousses, soufflés, timbales, meat pies, Cases for Food, (I, 236), and Stuffed Vegetables, (I, 284). See also About Economical Use of Large Cuts of Meat, (I, 562).

For cooked potatoes, see the Index; use in Shepherd's Pie, (I, 256).

Use leftover gravies and savory sauces with vegetables, pastas, meats, and hot sandwiches.

For cheese, see Soufflés, Timbales, Sauces and Au Gratin, 221.

For uses for egg yolks, see Sponge Cakes, 406, Yolk Letter Cookies, 475. Eight-Yolk Cake, 414, salad dressings, custards: and use hard-cooked yolks in sauces or riced as a garnish.

For uses for egg whites, see Angel and White Cakes, 405 and 409, meringues of all kinds, fruit whips, 526, hot and cold dessert soufflés, 516, icings, 488, insulation for pie crusts; and for breading 219, and Eggs in a Nest, (I, 217).

For citrus peels see Candies, 604, and Zests, 252.

For uses for sour or buttermilk see About Sour and Fermented Milks, 188.

For fruit juices, see fruit drinks or gelatins. Use as the liquid in cakes and custards, for meat basting, for sauces or fruit salad dressings.

For uses for leftover coffee, see coffee and mocha desserts and dessert sauces.

BREADS AND COFFEE CAKES

Once upon a time, when the English language was young, the word from which the modern English "lady" sprang meant "loaf-kneader," and the verb "to knead" has even prehistoric origins! To our own and our families' distinct profit—and with little effort—we housewives can become "ladies" again.

Begin, if you like, with a whole wheat—a flour which requires neither sifting nor kneading—and go on from there to more cunning triumphs. Try a round Swedish rye, 311, or a long crusty French loaf, 306, thin brittle Italian bread sticks, 307, or feather-light brioches, 320, all shown above. Bake quick breads such as biscuits, corn pone and scones. Or fashion a Christmas bambino of yeast bread, see illustration above and 321, kneading it by hand or with the help of an electric or a mechanical dough hook seen above in place at the rear and fully exposed in the foreground. Do become aware of the hearty flavors and varied textures of home-made breads.

ABOUT YEAST BREAD

If you have never made yeast bread, behold one of the great dramas of the kitchen. Every ingredient is a character. As a producer director, assemble your cast. Yeast is the prima donna. Her volatile temperament is capable of exploitation only within given limits of heat—and does she resent a drafty dressing room! For more intimate details, see About Yeast, 222. Wheat flour is the hero. He has a certain secret something that makes his personality elastic and gives convincing body to his performance. Rice, rye, corn, soy—no other flour can touch him for texture; but he is willing to share the stage with others—if they give him the limelight. For differences in flours, see 209. Water, milk or other liquid ingredients are the intriguers. Any one of them lends steam to the show. For effect of soft and hard water in baking, see 166. As for salt and sugar, they make essential but brief entrances. Too much of either inhibits the range of the other

actors. Fat you can enlist or leave. Use him to endow your performance with more tender and more lasting appeal. There are quite a few extras, too, which you can ring in to give depth and variety. Allow some ad-libbing with nuts and raisins, herbs and sprouts, see Additions to Yeast Doughs, 301.

Now, knowing our actors and their quality, "the play's the thing." Let's look into the types, the mixing and the baking of bread.

MIXING BREAD DOUGH

◗ To prepare the leaven, dissolve fresh compressed yeast in liquid at 85°, without stirring, 8 to 10 minutes. If instead the yeast is in active dry form, it will need liquid between 105° and 115° and should dissolve in 3 to 5 minutes. A small quantity of sugar helps activate the yeast, ◗ but do not use more than called for. Formerly milk was always scalded to kill bacteria. Now, with pasteurization, air-dried milk solids and canned milk, this operation is no longer necessary. However, scalding still does save time in dissolving the sugar and melting the fat.

Batters are the simplest of all doughs, requiring little handling. Strong beating to develop the gluten content, best done in an electric mixer, takes the place of kneading. When they come away from the sides of the bowl, these doughs have had enough beating. The breads they make are usually more porous and dry out faster than the kneaded variety. For mixing directions, see Dill Batter Loaf, 305.

Sponge breads were favorites in days when yeast strains were poorly controlled. Sponge doughs result in a lighter-textured, coarser-grained loaf or roll than those made with conventional or straight dough. To mix sponge doughs, dissolve the yeast in a larger-than-usual amount of water, to which a portion of the flour is added. When this batter has fermented—and it sometimes takes as long as one hour—it becomes foamy and spongy. Butter and eggs, if called for, additional salt and sugar and the remaining flour are then mixed into the dough with the yeast mixture.

See Gluten Bread, 312, for mixing directions.

The **Conventional** or **Straight** dough method, as given for White Bread, 302, is still our favorite for texture, keeping qualities and appearance. Also, and incidentally, we find the required kneading a healthy outlet for frustrations. Use a good-sized bowl, and start stirring the flour into the combined lukewarm liquids, shortening and dissolved yeast mixture. Mix in half the required flour gradually and beat about one minute. Then, as the rest of the flour is added, lay aside the spoon and mix by hand. When the dough begins to leave the sides of the bowl, turn it out onto a lightly floured board or pastry cloth.

◗ To flour a board lightly and evenly, allow about 1 tablespoon flour for each cup of flour in the recipe—even less for a very light dough. A damp towel placed under the board will keep it from slipping. Turn the dough several times to make it easier to handle. ◗ Cover the dough with a cloth and let it rest 10 to 15 minutes before kneading.

With the **Mixer** method: using a strong electric mixer, you may shorten preliminary preparation time by blending the active dry yeast at the very outset with part of the flour and other dry ingredients. The liquids and shortening required are heated to 120° to 130°, added to the flour-yeast mixture, and the whole beaten 2 minutes at medium speed. If eggs are called for, add them at this time with an additional cup of flour. Beat 1/2 minute at low speed, then 3 minutes at high speed Stir in the remaining ingredients and enough flour to make a soft dough; then proceed as for White Bread Plus, 302.

KNEADING AND PROOFING YEAST DOUGH

Generally speaking, flours vary in moisture content, see 209, and only experience can tell you exactly how much flour to add during the kneading process. Hence, some variations in amounts are indicated in the individual recipes. Grease your fingertips to prevent sticking. When the dough is first turned out on the board it is slightly sticky, as can be seen in the top center, 297. Then, as the gluten develops in the wheat flour through continued strong, rhythmic kneading, the dough becomes smooth and elastic.

Overkneading and long, slow risings will result in a coarse-textured bread. Using a pastry scraper, see illustration top center, 297, will help with soft doughs. The first kneading of about 10 minutes must be thorough, but ◗ the pressure exerted on the dough should be neither heavy nor rough.

Fold the dough over toward you. Then press it away from you with the floured heel of the hand, as shown below, 297; give it a quarter turn, fold it and press away again. More flour may be necessary on your hands and board to overcome stickiness. Repeat this process until the dough becomes smooth, elastic and satiny. Air blisters will appear just under the surface coating or "cloak." Try not to break the coating. The dough at this point should no longer stick to the board or cloth.

If an electric mixer is used, and particularly if you make it a regular practice to bake bread, a bread hook—as illustrated in the chapter heading—is an enormous help. Follow the manufacturer's directions. The right amount of flour has been added when the dough cleans itself

from the sides of the bowl. Turn the dough onto a floured board and knead by hand until it is smooth, elastic and satiny.

In both methods, the next step is to grease a large clean bowl evenly, put the dough into it and then turn the dough over ◗ so that the entire surface of the dough will be lightly greased. Cover the bowl with a cloth. Set the dough to rise. This process and the covering step after separating the bread into loaf sizes are shown graphically on 297 and on this page to emphasize the importance of these so-called proofing periods. During this resting time, a smooth film again develops over the surface of the dough and makes it much easier to handle.

Yeast dough should rise in a draft-free place at a temperature of about 75° to 85°. If the room is cold, you may place the dough in the bowl on a rack ◗ over a pan of warm water; near, but not on, a convector or radiator; or in an oven heated less than 1 minute, until you can just feel warmth—a quite ideal rising cabinet. Turn the heat off and keep the door closed. ◗ Be sure to remove the bread before preheating the oven to bake it.

The first time the dough rises it should double in bulk, if the loaf is to have a moist crumb. Should the dough rise to more than double its bulk, it will fall back into the bowl. Do not permit this to happen unless the recipe calls for it, as it may result in a coarse, dry bread. To make sure the dough has risen sufficiently, press it well with the fingertips. When it has doubled in bulk, usually in 1 to 2 hours ◗ the imprint of the fingertips will remain in the dough, as shown on 297 below. Now punch down the dough with a balled hand, as illustrated on the left above. Work the edges to the center and turn the bottom to the top.

▲ Yeast bread dough rises more rapidly at high altitudes and may become overproofed if it is not watched carefully and allowed to rise only until doubled in bulk. For other high-altitude baking hints, see 301.

Now you will be ready for the second kneading, if indicated in the recipe. Its purpose is to give a finer grain. It lasts only a few minutes and may be done in the bowl. Then permit the covered dough to rise again, until it has a second time ◗ almost, but not quite, doubled in bulk.

SHAPING YEAST DOUGHS

Once more for a final time, punch down the dough and divide it into the number of pieces called for in the recipe. Shape them lightly into mounds; place them on a board, cover with a cloth as shown top center, 299; and allow them to rest 10 minutes.

Meanwhile get your pans ready. Most breads call for a greased pan. To choose an appropriate one, see About Bread Crusts, opposite. Begin to form the loaf by throwing down onto the board one of the pieces of dough which has been resting. You may use a rolling pin or your palm to press it evenly first. Professional bakers start with a circle and fold the curved outer segments toward the center to make their rectangle before shaping the loaf. You may prefer to treat yours instead like a thick scroll, as shown, using the heel of your hand to press it together as you complete the roll. Then with your stiffened hands at either end of the roll, compress the short ends and seal the loaf as shown below left, 299, folding under any excess as you slide the dough, seam side down, into the greased pan. ♦ It is important that the finished dough contact the short ends of the pan to help support the dough as it rises. When the loaf is in the pan, you may grease its top lightly.

Cover the pan with a cloth. The dough will eventually fill out to the corners of the pan. While it is rising—to almost, but not quite, double in bulk—preheat your oven. When ready to bake, the loaf will be symmetrical, and ♦ a slight impression will remain when you press lightly with your fingers. To bake, see directions in the recipes. For pan placement in the oven, see (I, 115).

To encourage round loaves to rise rather than spread, use round cake pans, or encircle each loaf loosely with 1-inch-high foil. Remove foil after bread has risen about halfway.

ABOUT BREAD CRUSTS

People have passions for different kinds of crust. ♦ The choice of pan will affect the crust. Glass, darkened tin and dull aluminum will all produce a thick one; but remember ♦ glass and enamel pans require a lower temperature, see 401. Hard rolls, Vienna and rye breads sometimes are baked on a parchment-covered or greased baking sheet sprinkled with cornmeal, which prevents these low-fat breads from sticking. Milk, either used in the recipe or brushed on at the end of the baking period, gives a good all-over brown color. Cream or butter may also be brushed on after baking for color; then the bread is returned to the oven for about 5 to 10 minutes. Setting a pan of warm water in the bottom of the oven during baking will harden crusts—as will brushing them, when partially baked, with salted water. Allow 1 teaspoon salt to 1/2 cup water.

For a glazed crust, toward the end of baking you may brush the top with an Egg Wash, 503. To keep the crust soft, brush the crust with butter after the bread is baked and out of the pan; then cover it with a damp cloth.

TESTING FOR DONENESS

♦ To test for doneness, notice if the loaf has shrunk from the sides of the pan. Or test by tapping the bottom of the pan to release the loaf and then tapping the bottom of the loaf; if a hollow sound emerges, the bread is done. Otherwise, return the loaf to the pan and bake a few minutes longer.

▲ Baking time at high altitudes usually remains the same, but oven temperatures should be increased slightly, from 10 to 15 degrees.

COOLING AND STORING BREAD

When the bread has finished baking, remove it at once from the pan and place it on its side on a wire rack to cool, as shown on the right, opposite. ◗ Keep it away from drafts, which cause shrinkage. Let the bread cool completely before wrapping, storing or freezing. It is best stored in covered tins in which there are a few pinhole-sized openings for ventilation. It is sterile as it comes from the oven, but if it is not cooled sufficiently before wrapping, condensation may cause rapid molding. Keep the bread box away from any heat source. And keep it clean by washing it once a week with a baking soda solution and drying it thoroughly. Most breads can be frozen, 658 and 659, but dry out rapidly after thawing. In hot, humid weather, keep bread refrigerated in a plastic bag to help prevent the growth of mold.

ADDITIONS TO YEAST DOUGHS

Raisins, dates, dried fruits, citron, nuts, hulled sesame and roasted hulled sunflower seeds, slightly sautéed onions, dried or fresh herbs, 265, bean or grain sprouts, toasted wheat germ, milk solids and brewer's yeast—ingredients often called "improvers"—are added to yeast doughs for flavor and increased nutritional values. Improvers are seldom used in greater quantity than up to about one-value. Use this formula in your favorite bread, cookie, muffin or cake recipe. When you measure, put in the bottom of each cup of flour called for:

1 tablespoon soya flour
1 tablespoon dry milk solids
1 teaspoon wheat germ

then fill the cup with sifted un-bleached enriched flour.

WHITE BREAD

Wrote Louis Untermeyer:
"Why has our poetry eschewed
The rapture and response of food?
What hymns are sung, what praises said
To home-made miracles of bread?"
Even more constructive than versification, perhaps, are the recipes which follow: home-baked bread, in our view, can best be celebrated by repetition.

Two 5 × 9-Inch Loaves
We are partial to the straight dough or conventional method of making this even-grained all-purpose bread, which stales slowly and cuts well for sandwiches.
Scald:

1 cup milk

Add:

1 cup water
1 tablespoon shortening or lard
1 tablespoon butter
2 tablespoons sugar
1 tablespoon salt

In a separate large bowl, combine:

1/4 cup 105°–115° water
1 package active dry yeast

and let dissolve 3 to 5 minutes. If using compressed yeast, crumble 1 cake yeast into 1/4 cup 85° warm water and let stand 8 to 10 minutes. Add the lukewarm milk mixture to the dissolved yeast. Have ready:

6 1/2 cups sifted all-purpose flour

Stir in 3 cups flour, beat 1 minute, then stir or work in remaining flour by tossing the dough on a floured board and kneading well until it is smooth, elastic and full of bubbles. Place the dough in a greased bowl, turn the dough over once and cover with a cloth. Let rise in a warm place until doubled in bulk, at least 1 hour. Punch it down to its original size and, if time permits, allow the dough to rise until double once more. Otherwise, skip the second bowl rising, shape the dough lightly into 2 loaves, and place them in greased pans. Cover and let the dough rise again until almost doubled in bulk. Preheat oven to 450°.
To achieve the kind of crust you like, see 300. Bake the bread 10 minutes. Reduce heat to 350° and bake about 30 minutes longer. Test for doneness, 300. Remove loaves at once from pans and cool on a rack before storing.

WHITE BREAD PLUS

Three 5 × 9-Inch Loaves
This method of mixing bread dough calls for active dry yeast and an electric mixer. If using compressed yeast, use these same ingredients, but follow the conventional method given for White Bread, at left. As this recipe requires less yeast and more sugar than does White Bread, and because this bread, started in a cold oven, has a longer proofing period, less yeast flavor is retained.
In a large mixer bowl, mix together:

3 cups sifted all-purpose flour
1/2 cup sugar
1 tablespoon salt
1 package active dry yeast

Combine:

2¹/₂ **cups 120°–130° water**
¹/₂ **cup lard or shortening**

The shortening does not need to melt. Gradually add to dry ingredients and beat 2 minutes at medium speed, scraping bowl occasionally. Add to make a thick batter:

1 beaten egg
1 cup sifted all-purpose flour

Beat ¹/₂ minute at low speed, then at high speed 3 minutes. Stir in to make a soft dough:

3 to 4 cups sifted all-purpose flour

Turn out onto a lightly floured board and knead until smooth and elastic, about 10 minutes. Allow the bread to rise once in the mixing bowl and once in the baking pan. To bake, place loaves in a cold oven. Turn the heat to 400°. After 15 minutes, reduce heat to 357° and bake 25 minutes longer. Test for doneness, 300. Remove the loaves at once from the pans and cool on a rack before storing.

SOURDOUGH BREAD

Two 5 × 9-Inch Loaves

▶ Please read About Sourdough, 224. A variety of breads can be made by substituting 1 cup wheat germ or cornmeal, etc., for 1 cup of the white flour, or using 3 cups whole-grain flour for 3 cups white flour. About ¹/₂ teaspoon baking soda added to the whole-grain flours improves the flavor.

Combine thoroughly and let stand uncovered to ferment overnight in a warm place:

1¹/₂ **cups 85° water**
1 cup Sourdough Starter, 224
4 cups all-purpose flour
2 teaspoons sugar, honey or molasses
2 teaspoons salt

Next morning, after the sponge has risen and fallen, stir down any crust which may have formed. Add:

1 cup all-purpose flour
(2 tablespoons soft butter or shortening)
(1 to 2 beaten eggs)

When thoroughly mixed, turn out onto a board covered with:

1 cup all-purpose flour

Knead in enough of this flour to make the dough smooth and elastic. Shape the dough into 2 loaves, put into bread pans, brush lightly with butter and let rise covered until almost doubled in bulk. Bake in a preheated 400° oven 45 to 50 minutes.

RAISIN, PRUNE OR NUT BREAD

I. Add to any unflavored bread dough:

1 cup drained, cooked, chopped prunes, or 1 cup washed, well-drained seeded raisins, or 1 cup chopped nuts

Sprinkle the above with:

1 tablespoons sifted all-purpose flour
(1 tablespoon cinnamon)

II. Cook over low heat until liquid is almost absorbed:

1¹/₂ **cups raisins**
¹/₂ **cup water**
1 tablespoon cinnamon

Cool and add to the dissolved yeast with:

(1 well-beaten egg)

CINNAMON LOAF

Two 5 × 9-Inch Regular or Three Cylindrical Loaves

Follow recipe for:

White Bread, 302

While dough is rising in bowl, combine:

¹/₂ cup sugar
1 tablespoon cinnamon

After dough has been punched down, divided and rolled into two 9 × 14-inch rectangles, brush lightly with:

Melted butter

Sprinkle surfaces with the sugar mixture and roll as for Jelly Roll, 440. Place in greased 5 × 9-inch pans and proceed as for White Bread, 302. If you prefer to use a specially designed hinged or lidded cylindrical pan, it is essential that the cover be firmly bound so the loaf will not distort in the baking. The dough should be put into the cylinder before it rises a second time. This is the pan used for our children's birthday bread horse, shown on 353.

CHEESE BREAD

Two 5 × 9-Inch Loaves

For a pleasant variation, try using whole wheat flour and 2 tablespoons honey instead of the sugar indicated.
Scald:

1¹/₂ cups milk

Add to it and cool to about 105°:

¹/₃ cup sugar
¹/₄ cup butter
1 tablespoon salt

In a large bowl, dissolve for 3 to 5 minutes:

2 packages active dry yeast

in:

¹/₂ cup 105°–115° water

Stir in the cooled milk mixture. Add and beat until smooth:

1 well-beaten egg
1¹/₂ cups shredded sharp cheddar cheese
(1 teaspoon powdered thyme)
(¹/₂ teaspoon powdered marjoram)
(¹/₂ cup finely chopped pimiento)

Beat in well:

3 cups sifted all-purpose flour

Add, and then continue beating and stirring until the dough begins to leave the sides of the bowl, about:

3 cups sifted all-purpose flour

Knead the dough about 10 minutes. Allow to rise once in the bowl and once in the pans, covered, until doubled in bulk. Brush the leaves with:

(Melted butter)

Bake in a preheated 375° oven about 30 minutes. To test for doneness, to cool and to store, see 300–301.

HERB BREADS

If fresh herbs are available, triple the amounts suggested for the dry herbs given below.
Follow the recipe for:

**White Bread Plus, 302, or
Whole-Grain Bread, 309**

For each 5 × 9-inch loaf, add to dough before kneading:

1 teaspoon ground celery seeds
1 teaspoon ground caraway seeds
1 teaspoon ground dill or dillseeds

or add:

¹/₂ teaspoon marjoram or basil
¹/₄ teaspoon thyme
1 tablespoon chopped fresh parsley
(¹/₂ teaspoon oregano)

or:

¹/₄ teaspoon ginger
1 teaspoon thyme
1 teaspoon summer savory
1 teaspoon rosemary

or:

1 teaspoon nutmeg or cloves
1 teaspoon rosemary
1 teaspoon dill

1 tablespoon chopped fresh
  sage

DILL BATTER LOAF

Mix together in a large mixer bowl:
  1 package active dry yeast
  1/4 cup sifted all-purpose flour
  1/4 teaspoon baking soda
  2 tablespoons sugar
  1 teaspoon salt
  2 tablespoons dried minced
    onions or 2 teaspoons
    grated onion
  1 tablespoon dill seed or
    dillweed
Combine and gradually add to the
yeast mixture:
  1 to 2 tablespoons butter
  1/4 cup 120°–130° water
Beat 2 minutes at medium speed,
scraping bowl occasionally. Add:
  1 cup lukewarm large-curd
    cottage cheese
  1 lightly beaten egg
  1/2 cup sifted all-purpose flour
Beat at high speed 2 minutes. Beat in
to make a stiff batter:
  1 1/2 cups sifted all-purpose
    flour
Cover and let rise until doubled in
bulk. Stir down and transfer to a well-
greased 1 1/2-quart heatproof casserole.
Cover and let rise until doubled in
bulk. Bake in a preheated 350° oven
35 to 40 minutes. Top with:
  Melted butter
  A sprinkling of salt

EGG BREAD OR CHALLAH

        2 Braided Loaves
A heavier bread than the following
brioche, with good keeping qualities.
Combine:
  2 packages active dry yeast
  1 teaspoon sugar

1/4 cup 105°–115° water
Measure into a large bowl:
  6 cups sifted all-purpose
    flour
  1 tablespoon salt
Make a deep well, 366, and pour in
the yeast. Combine and add to the
flour:
  2 cups 105° water
  3 slightly beaten eggs
  1/4 cup vegetable shortening
    or oil
  3 tablespoons sugar
  (1/16 teaspoon saffron)
Beat well until a ball of dough is
formed, then turn out onto a floured
board and knead about 10 minutes
until smooth and elastic. Place in a
greased bowl, turn, cover and allow
to rise until doubled in bulk, about 1
hour. Punch down and divide dough
into two sections, kneading each for
several minutes.

Now, to make the braids. Cut each
section of dough into 3 parts and roll
between the hands or on a board into
long tapered cylinders. With the three
ropes of dough lying side by side on
a greased floured sheet, start to braid
loosely from center to end, then braid
the other portion from center to end.

Finish the ends by tucking them under. Repeat for the second loaf. Cover and let rise until almost doubled in bulk. Brush tops with:

French Egg Wash, 503

and sprinkle over all:

Poppy seeds

Bake 15 minutes in a preheated 400° oven, then reduce heat to 375° and bake about 45 minutes longer.

BRIOCHE LOAF COCKAIGNE

This light egg loaf has a feathery, tender crumb. While very similar to a true brioche, 320, it is much easier to make. Serve it right out of the oven, if possible. To cut, use an angel cake server, 405, or two forks held back to back, leaving a pulled surface rather than a cut surface. Combine and let stand 3 to 5 minutes:

2 packages active dry yeast
3 tablespoons 105°–115° milk

Beat well:

3 tablespoons sugar
3 eggs

Add:

½ cup soft butter
2 cups sifted all-purpose flour
½ teaspoon salt

Add the yeast mixture to the batter. Beat well 3 minutes. Place in a greased 9-inch tube pan. Let rise in a warm place until doubled in bulk, about 1 hour. Bake in a preheated 450° oven about 15 to 20 minutes. Test for doneness as for cake, 400.

FRENCH BREAD

To an American who travels in France, the commonest of tourist sights at the noon hour is what looks like *tout le monde* coming from the baker, afoot or a-cycle, with a couple or three long loaves of French bread, naked and gloriously unashamed, strapped on behind. French cookbooks ignore French bread, and French housewives leave the making of this characteristic loaf to the commercial baker. Why? Because he alone has the traditional wood-fired stone hearth with its evenly reflected heat, and the skilled hand with sourdough—both of which are necessary to produce the genuine article. We regard French bread as uniquely delicious and consider the closely approximate substitute recipe given below as rather more than well worth following. It was contributed some years ago by Mr. Julian Street.

2 Long Loaves

Scald:

½ cup milk

Add to it:

1 cup boiling water

While this liquid cools to 85°, dissolve:

1 cake compressed yeast

in:

¼ cup 85° water

After the yeast rests 10 minutes, add it to the milk mixture with:

1½ tablespoons melted shortening
1 tablespoon sugar

Measure into a large mixing bowl:

4 cups sifted all-purpose flour
2 teaspoons salt
2 teaspoons sugar

Make a hole in the center of these ingredients. Pour in the liquid mixture. Stir thoroughly, but do not knead. The dough will be soft. Cover with a damp cloth and set in a warm place to rise, allowing about 2 hours. Punch down the dough. Place on a floured board and pat into 2 equal oblongs. Form each into a French loaf by rolling the dough away from you, as

shown above. Continue rolling, pressing outward with the hands and tapering the dough toward the ends until a long, thin form results. Place the 2 loaves on a greased baking sheet. Cut diagonal, ¼-inch-deep slits across the tops with sharp-pointed scissors. Set in warm place to rise to ▶ somewhat less than doubled in bulk.

Preheat oven to 400°.

On bottom of oven, place a pan filled with ½ inch boiling water. Bake the bread 15 minutes, then reduce the heat to 350° and bake about 30 minutes longer. Five minutes or so before the bread is finished, brush the loaves with a glazing mixture of:

1 beaten egg white
1 tablespoon cold water

We once received a letter from a gentleman in Junction City, Kansas, which began: "My wife is too old to cook and I am too old to do anything else." It seems that he was an enthusiastic baker of French bread, but he complained that his loaves turned out too flat. We suggested that he try shaping them in the following manner: Make a long oblong of the

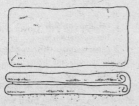

dough, fold over one edge to the center, repeat the operation for the second edge and taper the ends slightly. The bottom of the loaf may be pressed on a board which has been dusted with cornmeal and the loaf then placed on a large greased sheet for baking. This correspondent made several batches of bread and then wrote again: "Your plan works fine in shaping the loaves and I am also using ¼ cup less water. This makes the loaves come up a better shape, although it makes the dough harder to mix thoroughly. I think, however, the bread is just as good, and my French son-in-law says it is the best French bread he has eaten outside of France."

BREAD STICKS OR GRISSINI

Prepare:

French Bread, opposite

Roll into an oblong about ¼ inch thick, one dimension of which is about 8 inches. Cut into strips 2 inches wide and 8 inches long. Roll them to form sticks. Place on a greased baking sheet and brush with:

French Egg Wash, 503

Sprinkle with:

(Coarse salt)
(Caraway, sesame or
dill seeds)

Allow to rise until not quite doubled in bulk. Bake in a preheated 400° oven about 15 minutes. Try serving the sticks warm.

SALT-RISING BREAD

This unusually good formula, which has provoked the most dramatic correspondence, relies for its riser on the fermentation of a salt-tolerant bacterium in cornmeal or potato pulp. The cornmeal must be freshly stone ground. Since stone-ground cornmeal is not always available, we give also a potato-based recipe. Do not attempt this bread in damp, cold weather unless the house is adequately heated, and protect the batter well from drafts. Under the best of circumstances, it may prove to be erratic. We have had success setting a covered heavy bowl in water heated by an electric frypan or on a heating tray.

I. Cornmeal Salt-Rising Bread
Three 5 × 9-Inch Loaves
Measure into a large jar or bowl:

**½ cup fresh coarse white ▶
stone-ground cornmeal
1 tablespoon sugar**

Scald and pour over the cornmeal:

1 cup milk

Let stand overnight or longer, covered, in a warm place, 90° to 95°, until it ferments. By then it should be light and have a number of small cracks over the surface. If it isn't light in texture, it is useless to proceed, as the bread will not rise properly.
Scald:

3 cups milk

Pour it over:

**2 tablespoons sugar
5 tablespoons lard
1 tablespoon salt**

Stir in:

**3½ cups sifted all-purpose
flour**

Stir in the corn mixture. Place the bowl containing these ingredients in a pan of warm water for 1 to 2 hours,

until bubbles work up from the bottom. Keep water warm this full length of time. Stir in:

**5 cups sifted all-purpose
flour**

Knead in until smooth, but not stiff, about:

**2½ cups sifted all-purpose
flour**

Place dough in greased pans, cover and let rise until it has doubled in bulk. ▶ Watch it, for if it gets too high, it may sour. Preheat the oven to 400° and bake the bread for 10 minutes. Reduce the heat to 350° and bake 25 to 30 minutes more. To test for doneness, to cool and to store, see 300–301.

II. Potato Salt-Rising Bread
Three 5 × 9-Inch Loaves
A fan, trapped by her grandchild's measles, sent us a treatise on lessening the fantastic odors of "salt-rising." She says, "Use non-mealy 2½-inch-diameter new red-skinned potatoes for the starter. Place them in a stainless steel bowl. Set bowl in water in an electric dutch oven with heat maintained at about 90° to 95°. Perfect results are produced in 15 hours with only a mild odor—like that of good Italian cheese." As we lived for some years in an apartment with a salt-rising bread addict and shared the endless variety of smells she produced, we would settle any day for a mild cheese aroma.
Pare, then cut into thin slices:

**2½ cups new non-mealy
potatoes**

Sprinkle over them:

**1 tablespoon salt
2 teaspoons sugar
2 tablespoons white cornmeal**

Add and stir until salt is dissolved:

4 cups boiling water

Let the potato mixture stand, covered with a cloth, 15 hours. Now squeeze out the potatoes. Discard them. Drain the liquid into a bowl and add, stirring until very well blended:

1 teaspoon baking soda
1½ teaspoons salt
5 cups sifted all-purpose flour

Beat and beat "until the arm rebels." Set the sponge in a warm place to rise until light. Bubbles should come to the surface and the sponge should increase its volume by approximately a third. This will take about 1½ hours. Scald:

1 cup milk

When lukewarm, add:

2 tablespoons butter

Add this mixture to the potato sponge with:

5 to 6 cups sifted all-purpose flour

Knead dough about 10 minutes before shaping into 3 loaves. Place in greased pans. Let rise, covered, until ▶ light and not quite doubled in bulk. Bake in a preheated 350° oven about 1 hour.

WHOLE-GRAIN BREAD

Feather-lightness is, of course, by no means a prime objective in making whole-grain breads. Yet such loaves should have substance without high density. If our instructions are closely followed, you will never have occasion to level at us the reproach of Mrs. Burns, who, on viewing an impressive monument to her illustrious son, exclaimed: "Aye Robbie! Ye asked for bread, and they've gien ye a stane."

Three 5 × 9-Inch Loaves
Please read about Whole-Grain Flour, 212. Prepare the yeast as for White Bread, 302. Beat together and add to the yeast mixture:

1 beaten egg
¼ cup melted butter
2½ cups lukewarm water
1½ teaspoons salt
¼ to ½ cup sugar, honey or maple syrup

Add, without sifting, a mixture of:

4 cups whole-grain flour
4 cups all-purpose flour

To mix, knead, proof and shape, follow the arrow symbols and illustrations, 297–300, allowing the dough to rise once in the mixing bowl and once in the baking pans. Bake in a 350° oven about 45 minutes. To test for doneness, see 300.

ALL WHOLE-GRAIN BREAD COCKAIGNE

Two 4½ × 8½-Inch Loaves
A heavier, coarser bread which makes a *bonne bouche* with cheese. Sprinkle:

1 package active dry yeast
1 tablespoon brown sugar

over:

¼ cup 105°–115° water

Measure and combine:

6 cups whole-grain flour
½ cup dry milk solids

Combine:

2 cups warm water or milk
1 tablespoon salt
1 to 3 tablespoons melted bacon fat
4 to 6 tablespoons dark molasses or honey

Combine the yeast and water mixtures. Beat in the flour. Knead briefly, adding flour if necessary. Allow the dough to rise once in the bowl and once in the baking pans. Bake in a 350° oven about 45 minutes. To test for doneness, to cool and to store, see 300–301.

SPROUTED WHOLE-GRAIN BREAD

Prepare:

Whole-Grain Bread, 309

using 2 packages of yeast. Mix with the lukewarm water before adding the other ingredients:

2 cups ground sprouted wheat, soybeans, lentils or chick-peas, 241

SOY WHOLE WHEAT BREAD

Follow directions for:

White Bread, 302

but substitute for 3 cups of the sifted all-purpose flour:

1 cup soy flour
2 cups whole wheat flour

CRACKED-WHEAT BREAD

Two 5 X 9-Inch Loaves

If your cracked wheat is a coarse grind, put it in the blender to get a finer grind. Try making this good bread with cooked cereals other than cracked wheat.

Cook for 10 minutes or until the moisture is absorbed:

1 cup finely ground cracked wheat

in:

3 cups boiling water

Remove from heat and stir in:

2 tablespoons butter or shortening
1 tablespoon salt
3 tablespoons sugar or honey
1 tablespoon molasses
3/4 cup milk

While this mixture is cooling, dissolve for 3 minutes:

2 packages active dry yeast

in:

1/4 cup 105°–115° water

Combine the cooked cereal and yeast mixture, then beat in gradually:

4 cups all-purpose flour
2 cups whole wheat flour

Turn the dough out onto a floured board and knead about 10 minutes. Place in a greased bowl, cover, and let rise in a warm place until doubled in bulk. Punch down, knead a few times and shape dough to fit into 2 greased bread pans to let rise, covered, until again doubled in bulk. Preheat oven to 350°. Bake about 35 to 40 minutes or until done.

OAT BREAD COCKAIGNE

Two 5 X 9-Inch Loaves

Scald:

2 cups milk

and pour it over:

1 cup rolled oats

Add:

2 teaspoons salt
1/4 cup vegetable oil
1/2 cup brown sugar
(1/2 teaspoon ground ginger)

Cool this mixture to lukewarm. Combine:

1/4 cup 105°–115° water
2 packages active dry yeast

Add the yeast solution to the oats, plus:

1 or 2 slightly beaten eggs
1/4 to 1/2 cup wheat germ
1 cup soy flour
2 cups whole wheat or rye flour
3 to 4 cups sifted unbleached all-purpose flour

♦ To knead, proof and shape, follow the arrow symbols and illustrations on 297–300, allowing the dough to rise once in the mixing bowl and once in the baking pans. Bake in a preheated 350° oven about 1 hour. To test for doneness, to cool and to store, see 300–301.

SWEDISH RYE BREAD

2 Loaves

A moist aromatic loaf that keeps well. Combine in a large bowl:

1½ cups 105°–115° water
2 packages active dry yeast

Let rest 3 to 5 minutes until dissolved. Add:

¼ cup molasses
⅓ cup sugar
1 tablespoon salt
2 tablespoons grated orange rind
1 tablespoon fennel seed
1 tablespoon anise seed
(⅔ cup chopped raisins)

Stir in:

2½ cups sifted, finely milled rye flour
2 tablespoons softened butter

Beat all these ingredients together until smooth. Add:

2½ to 3 cups sifted all-purpose flour

If the dough is soft to handle, use the larger amount of flour. ♦ To knead, follow the arrows and illustrations, pages 297 and 298. Allow the dough to rise once in the bowl and once on the baking sheet. To shape, form into two ovals on a greased baking sheet dusted with cornmeal. To prevent spreading, see 300. Cover with a cloth and let rise until almost doubled in bulk, about 1 hour. Make four ¼-inch-deep diagonal slashes in the tops of the loaves. Bake in a preheated 375° oven 30 to 35 minutes. To test for doneness, to cool and to store, see 300–301.

ALL-RYE FLOUR BREAD

2 Rather Flat Loaves

Rye flour lacks the gluten of wheat, so a loaf made of all rye has a dense, heavy texture, similar to that of pumpernickel.

Combine:

½ cup 105°–115° water
2 packages active dry yeast

Scald:

2 cups milk

As it cools, add:

2 tablespoons butter
1 tablespoon sugar or honey
2 teaspoons salt

Add the yeast mixture and stir in:

2 cups rye flour

Let this sponge rise about 1 hour. Then add slowly, while stirring:

3 cups rye flour
(1 beaten egg)
(2 tablespoons caraway seeds)
(2 tablespoons sesame seeds)

Let rise about 2 hours. Sprinkle a board with:

1 cup rye flour

Knead the dough into it 10 minutes. Divide into 2 parts. To form, see 300. Put on a well-greased baking sheet, grease the tops of the loaves, cover and allow to rise about 2 hours more. Bake in a preheated 350° oven about 1 hour. To test for doneness, to cool and to store, see 300–301.

SOURDOUGH RYE BREAD

2 Round or 2 Long Loaves

The best-flavored rye breads call for sourdoughs, 224. We love this recipe which comes from Merna Lazier, who has run, among many other successful projects, a bakery of her own. She says: "You may object to the number of stages in this process, but I must say that old-time bakers who were proud of their rye bread really nursed it along—so there must be a reason." For this recipe, on one day you make a sourdough, using ½ cake of yeast. The following day, you make two sponges, using the other $1/2$ cake of yeast. The first day, prepare the sourdough.

Mix in a bowl and work together lightly:

$1/2$ cup rye flour
$1/4$ cup water
$1/2$ cake compressed yeast

Cover this sourdough tightly so it will not dry out, and keep it in a warm place at about 85° for 24 hours. Then work into it:

$3/4$ cup water
1 cup rye flour

The sourdough should be ready to use after it has fermented, covered, 4 hours longer.

Sponge I. Mix into the above sourdough:

$13/4$ cups rye flour
$2/3$ of $1/2$ cake compressed yeast
$1/4$ cup water

Allow this sponge to rise, covered with a damp cloth, at 85° until it doubles in bulk.

Sponge II. Add to Sponge I:

$13/4$ cups rye flour
$13/4$ cups all-purpose flour
Remaining $1/3$ of $1/2$ cake
   compressed yeast
1 cup water

Mix until smooth. Cover with a damp cloth and let rise until doubled in bulk. Then add:

1 cup water
1 tablespoon salt
$13/4$ cups all-purpose flour
1 tablespoon caraway seed

Mix until smooth, then let the mixture rest, covered, 20 minutes. Turn the dough out onto a floured board and mix and knead into it:

$11/2$ to 2 cups all-purpose flour

depending on the flour, until you have a rather firm dough—one that will not flatten or spread. Divide and shape it into 2 long or 2 round loaves. Place them on a greased pan and al-

low to rise, but not double in bulk. Too much rising will result in a flat loaf.

Preheat oven to 425°.

Place a flat pan containing about one-fourth inch water in the oven. Bake the loaves 50 to 60 minutes. You may have to replenish the water, but ▶ remove the pan after 20 minutes. As soon as the bread is done, spread it with:

Melted butter

or, if you wish a glazed crust, spread with:

Salted water—1 teaspoon
   salt to $1/2$ cup water

Cool loaves on a rack, away from drafts.

GLUTEN BREAD

Two 5 X 9-Inch Loaves

A boon for those on low-starch diets but overrated for its protein quality, as both wheat flour and the gluten made from it are deficient in lysine. See about incomplete proteins on (I, 4).

Combine:

3 cups 105°–115° water
1 package active dry yeast

After 3 to 5 minutes, when the yeast is dissolved, beat in:

2 cups gluten flour, 213

Let this sponge rise in a warm place until light and foamy. Combine, beat and then stir into the sponge:

1 beaten egg
2 tablespoons melted
   shortening
$1/2$ teaspoon salt
(2 tablespoons sugar)

Stir in:

About 4 cups gluten flour

Use only enough flour to make a dough that will knead well. After kneading, shape into 2 loaves. Let rise until doubled in bulk. Bake in a preheated 350° oven about 1 hour. To test for doneness, to cool and to store, see 300–301.

FLATBREADS

Two 8-Inch Loaves

Called **Armenian, Peda, Greek, Arab, Syrian, Euphrates Bread**, this dough can be formed into hard rolls, long thin loaves and flat envelopes for stuffing with exotic sandwich fillings. If making small sandwich-sized puffs, divide the dough into 4-inch circles and bake on a greased sheet 7 to 9 minutes until puffed and lightly browned. **Sopaipillas** can be made from this dough. Cut into 3-inch squares after the first rising and deep-fat-fried at 365°, they are seasoned with cinnamon and sugar. For a typical flatbread dough, combine in a mixing bowl and let stand 3 to 5 minutes:

> 1 **package active dry yeast**
> 1 **cup 105°–115° water**

Add and beat until smooth:

> 1½ **cups sifted all-purpose flour**
> 1 **teaspoon salt**
> (1 **tablespoon sugar**)
> 1 **tablespoon soft shortening**

Add:

> 1½ **cups sifted all-purpose flour**

If the dough is too stiff to beat, knead in the dough by hand until it is smooth and elastic, about 5 minutes. Place in a greased bowl, cover and let rise until doubled in bulk, about 45 minutes. Punch down and divide into 2 balls. Flatten the dough evenly in 2 greased 8-inch layer cake pans. Slash a decorative pattern in the dough and brush with:

> (**Milk**)

Sprinkle with:

> (**Sesame seeds**)

Let rise again until almost doubled in bulk, and bake in a preheated 425° oven about 20 minutes. Flatbread is best eaten warm, so reheat before serving.

PIZZAS

Two 14-Inch Pizza Crusts

Who would guess that this popular Italian pie began its career as a leftover improvised from surplus bread dough? In a pinch you might try pie dough or sliced English muffins as a base.

To make pizza dough, mix as for bread, 297, using the following ingredients, but do not let it rise a second time:

> 4 **cups sifted all-purpose flour**
> 1 **cake yeast in 1⅓ cups 85° water**
> 2 **tablespoons vegetable or olive oil**
> 1 **teaspoon salt**

Knead 10 minutes. Cover with damp cloth and let rise about 2 hours. Have ready two oiled 14-inch pizza pans. Sprinkle a little cornmeal over all. Pat and stretch the dough in the pans, pinching up a collar around the edge to hold the filling. Prick dough in about 6 places.

Preheat oven to 400°.

Brush each pizza lightly with olive oil to prevent crust from becoming soggy. Spread with your preferred filling and rest it about 10 minutes. At this stage the pizzas may be frozen for at least a week before baking. Bake about 25 minutes until light brown and serve at once.

I. Spread the pizza with:

> (**Thin slices of cheese**)
> **Thickened Tomato Sauce, (I, 400)**

Arrange on top:

> 12 **to 14 anchovies or sliced Italian sausage, pepperoni, prosciutto ham or salami**

Sprinkle with:

> **Oregano**
> **Olive oil**

Chopped parsley
(Parmesan or Romano
cheese)

II. Use a highly seasoned:
Italian Meat Sauce for
Pasta, (I, 402), or other
meat sauce for pasta
Cover with a layer of:
Fontina or Mozzarella
cheese

III. Use as a base:
Thickened Tomato Sauce,
(I, 400)
Add:
1 cup chopped or sliced
mushrooms

IV. Cover the base with:
Lightly sautéed onions
Black olives
Anchovies
Brush with:
Olive oil

ABOUT YEAST ROLLS

There is little difference in bread- and
roll-making, so if you are a novice
◗ please read About Yeast Bread,
296. The visual appeal of delicately
formed, crusty or glazed rolls is a
stimulant to the appetite. For varied
shaping suggestions, see the illustrations in this chapter.

Professional cooks weigh the dough
to keep the rolls uniform in size for
good appearance and even baking. If
you do not use muffin pans, place approximately equal-sized shapes of
dough at regular intervals over the entire baking sheet. Baking parchment
paper saves having a greasy pan to
wash and also cuts the grease build-up
which results in a discolored pan and
uneven browning.

You may use additions to yeast

dough, 301, and coffee cake, 331, to
vary the flavor. Sprinkle the tops with
poppy, celery, fennel, caraway, or
lightly toasted sesame seeds, depending on the rest of your menu.

To bake, follow the individual
recipes. ◗ Remove the rolls at once
from the pan to a cooling rack. ◗ To
reheat, sprinkle them lightly with water and heat, covered, in a 400° oven
or in the top of a double boiler over
hot water. Sometimes the suggestion
is made that the rolls be put in a
dampened paper bag and heated until
the bag dries. We find, however, that
some types of bags can transmit a
disagreeable flavor.

NO-KNEAD LIGHT ROLLS

Eighteen 2-Inch Rolls

These are the rolls we remember from
childhood: light as a feather and served
in a special soft linen napkin. Although
they require no kneading, they are best
chilled at least 2 hours and up to 12.
They are not true refrigerator rolls,
since this recipe is not heavy enough in
sugar to retard the rising action, and all
the dough should be baked after the 2-
to 12-hour period.
Combine and let stand 3 to 5 minutes:
¼ cup 105°–115° water
1 package active dry yeast
Place in a separate bowl:
¼ cup butter or shortening
1¼ teaspoons salt
2 tablespoons sugar
Pour over these ingredients and stir
until they are dissolved:
1 cup hot water
When they are lukewarm, add the
yeast. Beat in:
1 egg
Stir in and beat until blended:
About 2¾ cups sifted all-
purpose flour, to make a
soft dough

Put dough in a large greased bowl. Either cover with foil and chill from 2 to 12 hours, or place in a greased bowl covered with a cloth until doubled in bulk. Punch it down. Shape the rolls to fill the greased cups in a muffin pan to about one-third. Again let rise until about doubled in bulk. Bake in a preheated 425° oven 15 to 18 minutes. Cool at once.

PARKER HOUSE ROLLS

About Thirty 2-Inch Rolls
This is a basic not-too-sweet dough that can be used for variously shaped dinner rolls.
Scald:
1 cup milk
Add and stir until dissolved:
1 tablespoon sugar
2 tablespoons butter
3/4 teaspoon salt
Sprinkle:
1 package active dry yeast
over:
2 tablespoons 105°–115° water
Add the milk mixture when it has cooled to lukewarm. Beat in:
(1 egg)
Sift before measuring:
2 2/3 cups all-purpose flour
Stir in part of the flour; knead in the rest. Use only enough flour to form a dough that can be handled easily. Place in a greased bowl. Brush the top with:
Melted butter
Cover and let the dough rise in a warm place until doubled in bulk. Roll it and cut into rounds with a floured biscuit cutter. Dip the handle of a knife in flour and use it to make a deep crease across the middle of each roll. Fold the rolls over on the crease and press the edges together lightly. Place rolls in rows on a greased baking sheet. Let rise in a warm place until light, a matter of 35 minutes or so. Bake in a preheated 425° oven about 20 minutes. Remove at once from pans.

CLOVERLEAF ROLLS

Twenty-Four 2-Inch Rolls
Prepare dough for:
Parker House Rolls, above
After the first rising in the bowl, punch down the dough. Now, fill greased muffin tins about one-third with 3 small balls, as sketched below. Brush the tops with:
Melted butter
Let rise covered in a warm place until about doubled in bulk. Bake in a preheated 425° oven 15 to 18 minutes. Remove at once from pans.

HOT CROSS BUNS

About 18 Buns
Prepare dough for:
Parker House Rolls, above
increasing the sugar to 1/4 cup and including the egg. Add to the sugar:
1/4 teaspoon cinnamon
1/8 teaspoon nutmeg
1/4 cup currants or raisins
2 tablespoons finely chopped citron
After the first rising, shape dough into 18 balls and place in rows on a greased baking sheet. Cover and let rise until almost doubled in bulk.

Bake in a preheated 425° oven about
20 minutes, until golden brown. Decorate with the traditional cross, using:

Milk Glaze, 504

PALM LEAF OR SOUR CREAM ROLLS

About 4 Dozen Leaves

Sweet enough for a dessert. Serve
with coffee and fruit.

Sprinkle:

1 package active dry yeast

over:

¼ cup 105°–115° water

Sift:

3 cups all-purpose flour
1½ teaspoons salt

Cut in, until reduced to pea-sized
bits:

½ cup butter

Blend and add:

2 beaten eggs
1 cup cultured sour
cream
1 teaspoon vanilla

and the dissolved yeast. Cover and
chill for about 2 hours or more. When
ready to bake, sprinkle a board with:

½ cup Vanilla Sugar, 229

or a mixture of:

½ cup sugar
1 teaspoon cinnamon

Roll half the dough into a 6 × 18
× ¼-inch strip. Fold as sketched on
the left opposite, bringing the ends to
within about ¾ of an inch of each other.
Repeat this folding as shown in the
right foreground and again as shown
in the rear. Slice into ¼-inch-thick
"palm leaves." Repeat this process
with the other half of the dough, first
sprinkling the board with the sugar
mixture. Put leaves on an ungreased
baking sheet. Let rise, covered, about
20 minutes. Bake in a preheated 375°
oven until golden brown, about 15
minutes.

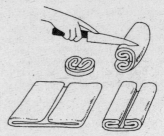

BUTTERMILK ROLLS OR FAN-TANS

About 24 Rolls

Rolls prepared in this way need not
be buttered.

Fine for a serve-yourself party.

Heat to about 110°:

1½ to 2 cups buttermilk

If the buttermilk is thick, use the
lesser amount. In ⅓ cup of the buttermilk, dissolve for 3 to 5 minutes:

1 package active dry yeast

Add the yeast mixture to the remaining buttermilk with:

¼ teaspoon baking soda
2 teaspoons salt
¼ cup sugar

Beat well; then stir in:

2 cups sifted all-purpose
flour
2 tablespoons melted
butter

Add another:

2 cups sifted all-purpose
flour

Place dough in a greased bowl and
turn it, so it is lightly greased all over.
Cover with a cloth and let rise until
more than doubled in bulk. Knead
lightly 1 minute. Separate into 2 parts.
Roll each part into a square about ⅛
inch thick. Brush the dough with
melted butter. Cut into strips 1½
inches wide. Stack them. There
should be from 6 to 8 layers of

stacked strips. Cut off pieces about 1½ inches wide, with a string, as shown below. Place them in buttered muffin tins, with the cut edges up. Let rise in a warm place until doubled in size. Bake in a preheated 435° oven 15 to 20 minutes until well browned.

KOLATCHEN

About Thirty-Six 2-Inch Rolls
Prepare the dough for:

Palm Leaf Rolls, opposite
When ready to bake, roll the dough into 2-inch balls and place on a greased baking sheet about 2 inches apart. Have ready one or more of the following:

Prune, Apricot, Date or Fig Filling, 333, jam or chopped fruit
Press an indentation into the center of each roll, leaving a ¼-inch rim. Fill with your chosen fillings, cover and let rise about 40 minutes. Preheat oven to 375°. Bake approximately 20 minutes. Sprinkle with:

(Confectioners' sugar)

OVERNIGHT ROLLS

About 48 Rolls
This is a sweet dough good for rolls and coffee cakes.
Combine and let stand 3 to 5 minutes:

1 package active dry yeast
2 teaspoons sugar
2 tablespoons 105°–115° water

Scald:

1 cup milk
Add and stir in:

7 tablespoons lard
Cool. Combine and beat well:

7 tablespoons sugar
3 beaten eggs
1 teaspoon salt

Stir in the milk and yeast mixtures. Add:

4½ cups sifted all-purpose flour
Beat the dough about 5 minutes. Place in a foil-covered bowl in the refrigerator overnight. Take out just before baking. Divide dough into 3 parts. Roll each part into a circle about 9 inches in diameter. Cut each circle into 16 wedge-shaped pieces. Before rolling further, brush with:

Melted butter
and dust with:

Sugar and cinnamon
or top with a:

Coffee Cake Filling, 331
Roll up each piece by beginning at the wide end, stretching the dough a bit as you roll it; see below. Brush with:

French Egg Wash, 503
Let rolls rise until doubled in bulk. Bake 15 to 18 minutes on a greased baking sheet in a preheated 425° oven. Take care: they burn easily.

FILLED PINWHEEL ROLLS

About 48 Rolls
Follow the recipe for:

Overnight Rolls, opposite
Prepare the dough and let rise until doubled in bulk. Roll to ¼-inch

thickness. Cut into 4-inch squares. Spread the squares generously with:

Butter

Sugar and cinnamon

Place in the center of each square:

Raisins and nuts or

2 teaspoons apricot or raspberry jam

Cut diagonally into the dough from each corner to within ³/₄ inch of the center. Fold every other point toward the center, as sketched below, overlapping and sealing the ends with a little water. Place pinwheels on a greased baking sheet. Let them rise slightly. Bake in a preheated 425° oven about 18 minutes.

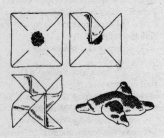

BUTTERMILK-POTATO ROLLS

About 46 Cloverleaf Rolls

Prepare:

³/₄ cup riced freshly cooked potatoes

While still hot, mix with:

¹/₂ cup butter

Heat to 105°–115°:

2 cups buttermilk

Sprinkle into about ¹/₂ cup of the buttermilk:

1 package active dry yeast

2 tablespoons sugar

Let stand 3 to 5 minutes. Add the remaining buttermilk and mix with the potatoes. Beat until light and stir in:

2 eggs

1 teaspoon salt

Sift before measuring:

7¹/₂ cups all-purpose flour

Stir in 6 cups of the flour. Knead in the rest. Place the dough in a greased bowl and turn it, so that it is greased lightly on all sides. Cover and let rise until doubled in bulk. Punch down. Shape and let rise as for Cloverleaf Rolls, 315. Glaze tops with:

(French Egg Wash, 503)

Sprinkle with:

(Poppy seeds)

Bake in a preheated 425° oven 15 to 18 minutes. Remove at once from pans.

CHEESE ROLLS

Prepare:

Cheese Bread, 304

Shape and bake as for:

Overnight Rolls, 317

LOW-FAT, EGGLESS ROLLS

About 5 Dozen Rolls

You may bake these excellent rolls in advance and reheat before serving; and, after wrapping, keep them in a refrigerator 2 weeks or in a freezer 3 months.

Scald:

2 cups milk

Add:

5 teaspoons salt

¹/₄ cup sugar

Cool this mixture to lukewarm. Combine and let stand 3 to 5 minutes:

1 cup 105°–115° water

2 packages active dry yeast

Combine above ingredients and mix well. Add gradually:

8 to 10 cups all-purpose flour

Knead the dough until smooth and elastic and let it rise, covered, until almost doubled in bulk. Shape the dough as you prefer. Let rolls rise on greased covered baking sheets until again almost doubled in bulk. Bake about 40 minutes in a preheated 275° oven. If storing, leave them in the pans to cool for 20 minutes. When they reach room temperature, wrap well. To serve: if refrigerated, reheat on a greased baking sheet about 10 minutes in a 400° oven; if frozen, bring to room temperature before reheating.

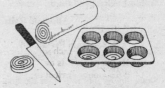

CINNAMON SNAILS AND CRISPS

Prepare:
> **Scandinavian Pastry, 330, omitting the cardamom; or Overnight Rolls, 317**

When the dough has doubled in bulk, roll into an oblong on a floured board to the thickness of ¼ inch. Spread generously with:
> **Melted butter**

Sprinkle with:
> **Cinnamon**
> **Brown sugar**

Add:
> **(Chopped nutmeats)**
> **(Seedless raisins)**
> **(Chopped citron)**
> **(Grated lemon or orange rind)**

Roll the dough like a Jelly Roll, 440. To make the snails, cut into 1-inch slices, see opposite. Rub muffin tins generously with:
> **Butter**

Sprinkle well with:
> **Brown sugar**
> **(Finely chopped nutmeats)**

Place each slice of roll firmly on the bottom of a muffin tin. Let rise in a warm place ½ hour. Bake in a preheated 350° oven about 30 minutes.

For crisps, cut the rolled dough into ½-inch slices and place on a greased baking sheet 3 inches or so apart. Flatten to about 3 inches in diameter. Allow to rise approximately 30 minutes. Now cover with waxed paper and roll to about ⅛-inch thickness. Remove paper and brush with:
> **¼ cup melted butter**

Sprinkle with a mixture of:
> **Sugar and cinnamon**
> **(Crushed nuts)**

Roll flat again, using waxed paper, and bake in a preheated 400° oven 10 to 12 minutes.

SCHNECKEN OR CARAMEL BUNS

Prepare rolls as for:
> **Cinnamon Snails, opposite**

▶ Be sure to use in the filling:
> **Grated lemon rind**
> **Raisins**
> **Pecans**

Roll as for Jelly Roll, 440. Cut into 1½-inch slices. Fill bottom of each muffin tin with a mixture of:
> **1 teaspoon melted butter**
> **1 teaspoon warmed honey**

Cover with:
> **2 teaspoons brown sugar**
> **A few chopped or whole pecans**

Lay slices of dough over sugar mixture. Let rolls rise about ½ hour. Bake in a preheated 350° oven about 20 minutes. Watch closely for signs of scorching. Remove from oven, turn pans upside down to loosen rolls and allow honey mixture to drip down over the rolls.

WHOLE-GRAIN ROLLS

About 40 Rolls

Prepare dough for:

**Whole-Grain Bread, 309,
or Oat Bread Cockaigne,
310**

Shape dough into rolls after the first rising, and let rise again until almost doubled in size. Butter the tops. Sprinkle with:

**(Coarse salt, chopped nuts
or sesame seeds)**

Bake in a preheated 400° oven 15 to 20 minutes.

RYE ROLLS

About 36 Rolls

Prepare:

Swedish Rye Bread, 311

Shape rolls after the first rising. Sprinkle tops with:

Coarse salt

For the crust of your choice, see 300. Bake in a preheated 375° oven about 20 minutes. Remove from pans at once and cool on a rack.

OAT-AND-MOLASSES ROLLS

Thirty-Eight 2-Inch Rolls

An agreeable variation on an old-time favorite formula.

Combine and cook with occasional stirring for 1 hour in a double boiler:

**1　cup steel-cut or
rolled oats
¹/₂　tablespoon shortening
³/₄　teaspoon salt
1¹/₂　cups boiling water**

Cool these ingredients until lukewarm. Combine and let stand 5 minutes in:

**1　tablespoon 105°–115° water
1　package active dry yeast**

Combine oat and yeast mixtures and add:

¹/₂　cup molasses

**4　cups sifted all-purpose
flour**

Knead the dough in the bowl until the ingredients are well blended. Cover the dough and let it rise in a warm place until doubled in bulk, about 2 hours. Pinch pieces off with buttered hands and place them in greased muffin tins. Let rise about 2 hours. Bake in a preheated 425° oven about 20 minutes.

BRIOCHE

About 15 Brioches

Due to a number of special circumstances, our recipes for French bread, while not classic, are close approximations. So, for similar reasons, is our recipe for another superb French specialty—the brioche. But we are proud of them both. The method for making brioche is more complicated to describe than to carry out. It involves good coordination between the rising of a small amount of floating yeast paste, or starter, and the working of the rest of the dough. Please read about this process before plunging in.

Cream and set aside:

6　tablespoons butter

Sift and then measure:

2　cups all-purpose flour

Make a well, see 366, with about a fourth of this flour and crumble into it:

**1　cake compressed yeast
at 70°**

◗ Be sure to use no less. A high yeast and butter content distinguishes this dough. Mix the flour and yeast with:

2　tablespoons 85° water

Gradually work the flour into a paste. When it becomes a small soft ball, snip a cross in the top with scissors and then drop it into a 2-quart pan filled with water at 85°. ◗ The ball will sink to the bottom of the pan, so be sure it is not over a burner, where additional heat might kill the yeast. As the yeast develops, the ball of paste, or starter, rises to the surface and doubles in size in about 7 to 8 minutes—if the water temperature is right. If the water chills too much, add hotter water to bring the temperature back to 85°. ♦ When the starter has doubled in bulk, it must be removed from the water. Should this state be reached before you are ready to use it, drain and cover it. Meanwhile, once you have dropped the starter into the water, shape into another well the remaining flour, mixed with:

1 tablespoon sugar
1 teaspoon salt

Break into the center of it:

2 eggs at 70°

Mix them in by gradually drawing the flour from the sides of the well. Also work in:

2 to 3 tablespoons milk

until the ingredients form a sticky but cohesive mass which you continue to work as follows. Use only one hand. Do not try to release it from the dough. Just keep picking up as much as will adhere, and throw it back hard onto the board with a turn of the wrist, gathering more from the board each time. ♦ This rough throwing process develops the gluten and should be repeated about fifty times. By then the dough should be glistening and smooth and your fingers will have become free. At this point, work the butter into the dough. When it is all absorbed, scoop the floating starter out of the water by spreading wide the fingers of one hand and ♦ drain the starter for a moment on a dry towel. Work the starter into the smooth dough, which will remain shining and of about the consistency of whipped cream.

♦ Now, get the dough ready to chill for at least 1 hour. Gather up as much as you can, including what remains on the board, releasing it with a spatula. Put it into a greased or floured bowl and chill, covered. Have ready the classic fluted and flaring brioche forms—or muffin tins. When the dough has chilled, knead it with floured hands. It should be firm enough not to require a floured board. For each brioche, make 2 balls—about 2 tablespoons of dough for one, 1 tablespoon for the other. The first ball is placed in the base of a tin. The smaller ball will form the characteristic topknot.

Mold it into a pear-shaped form. Cut a small gash in the center of the large ball, then 3 more shallow gashes radiating out from the center. Insert the point of the "pear," so it is seated firmly. The brioches should rise until almost doubled in bulk, 15 to 20 minutes. Glaze them with French Egg Wash, 503, ♦ but be sure it does not slip into the crack and bind the topknot to the base—which would keep the topknot from rising properly. Preheat oven to 450°.

Bake the brioches about 10 minutes, or until the egg-washed portions are a lovely brown. Should the topknots brown too rapidly, cover them loosely with a piece of foil. When baked they should puff to the proportionate size shown in the illustration.

Serve at once or release from the tins and cool on a rack. Reheat before serving.

BRIOCHE AU CHOCOLAT

A favorite French after-school treat. Prepare:

**Brioche, 320, or
Scandinavian
Pastry, 330**

Cut into 2-inch squares. Roll in each square a generous sliver of:

Semisweet chocolate

Bake as directed for Scandinavian Pastries, 330.

FRENCH CRESCENTS OR CROISSANTS

About 18 Crescents

Rich, somewhat troublesome, but unequaled by any other form of roll. Scald:

⅞ cup milk

Stir into it, until melted and dissolved:

**1 tablespoon lard or
vegetable oil
1½ tablespoons sugar
1 teaspoon salt**

Cool until lukewarm. Add:

1 package active dry yeast

dissolved in:

⅓ cup 105°–115° water

Stir in or knead in to make a soft sticky dough about:

**2½ cups sifted all-purpose
flour**

Knead on a lightly floured surface, using a pastry scraper to flip the soft dough end over end 10 times. The dough should now hold together. Place it in an ungreased bowl. Cover with a cloth and let rise until doubled in bulk, about 1½ hours. Then cover the dough with a lid and place in the refrigerator until thoroughly chilled,

at least 20 minutes. Roll or pat it out on a floured surface into an oblong ¼ inch thick. Now, following the directions for kneading butter and folding the dough as in Puff Paste, 365, knead:

1 cup cold butter

Spread the butter over two-thirds the surface of the dough, leaving an unbuttered border ¼ inch wide. Fold the unbuttered third over the center third. Then, fold the remaining third over the doubled portion. The dough is now in 3 layers. Swing the layered dough a quarter turn—or, directionally speaking, bring east to south. Roll it again into an oblong ¼ inch thick. Fold again in thirds as before. Sprinkle dough lightly with flour, cover with a plastic or waxed wrap and chill 1½ hours. Allow the unwrapped dough to rest on a lightly floured surface about 10 minutes. Twice again, roll into a rectangle and fold in 3 layers. Then, roll it again on a slightly floured surface to the thickness of ¼ inch.

Now, cut off any folded edges which might keep the dough from expanding. Cut the dough into 3-inch squares, and cut the squares on the bias. Roll the triangular pieces, beginning with the wide side and stretching them slightly as you roll. Shape the rolls into crescents, as sketched opposite. Place them on a baking sheet. Chill at once for ½ hour. Never allow them a final rising, as they will not have the proper flakiness.

Preheat oven to 400°.

Bake the crescents 10 minutes, then reduce the heat to 350° and bake until done—10 to 15 minutes longer.

FILLED SWEET CRESCENTS

About 28 Crescents

Prepare the dough for:

Refrigerator Potato Rolls, 326, or Scandinavian Pastry, 330

Use for each crescent:

2 teaspoons nut or fruit filling, 332 or 333

If using the refrigerator dough, roll out to ¼-inch thickness before chilling and cut into 3-inch squares. If using the Scandinavian dough, shape it after chilling. Cut the squares diagonally. Shape as shown. Place on a greased baking sheet. Let them rise until doubled in bulk. Brush lightly with:

French Egg Wash, 503

Bake in a preheated 375° oven 18 to 20 minutes. Cool on a rack or serve hot.

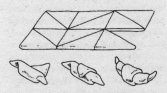

ORANGE TEA ROLLS

These must be served hot the same day they are baked.

Prepare:

Refrigerator Potato Rolls, 326

Shape them into bite-sized rolls. In the center of each roll, embed:

A section of fresh orange

which has been rolled in:

Brown sugar

Bake in a preheated 400° oven 8 to 10 minutes. If reheating, you may glaze with a mixture of equal parts of:

Sugar, water and Cointreau

HARD OR VIENNA ROLLS

Twelve 3-Inch Rolls

Sift:

4 cups all-purpose flour

Dissolve for 3 to 5 minutes in:

¼ cup 105°–115° water
1 package active dry yeast

Combine:

1 cup warm water
1 tablespoon sugar
1 teaspoon salt
2 tablespoons shortening

and the dissolved yeast mixture. Fold in thoroughly but lightly:

2 stiffly beaten egg whites

Add enough of the sifted flour to make a soft dough. To knead and proof, see 298. Allow the dough to rise twice. After the second rising, punch down and knead about 1 minute, then let rest, covered, about 10 minutes before shaping into 12 oblong pieces. Place them about 3 inches apart on a greased baking sheet. ◗ To ensure a hard crust, heat in the oven a 9 × 13-inch pan filled with ½ inch boiling water. Bake at once in a preheated 450° oven about 20 minutes or until golden brown.

ENGLISH OR RAISED MUFFINS

About Twenty 3-Inch Muffins

These are heavenly when eaten fresh and do not taste at all like "store-bought" ones. They do begin to resemble them the second day, however, so freeze leftovers immediately. You may bake these breads with or without muffin rings. The classic size is about 4 inches. We make our own rings from small unlacquered fish cans and deviled-meat cans. The tops and bottoms are removed and the rims thoroughly scrubbed. English muffins are always baked on a greased griddle.

Combine in a mixing bowl:

1 cup water
1/2 cup scalded milk
2 teaspoons sugar
1 teaspoon salt

Dissolve 3 to 5 minutes in:

2 tablespoons 105°–115°
water
1 package active dry yeast

Combine the two mixtures. Sift before measuring:

4 cups all-purpose flour

Beat 2 cups flour gradually into the milk mixture. Cover the bowl with a cloth. Let the sponge rise in a warm place, 85°, about 1 1/2 hours or ▶ until it collapses back into the bowl. Beat in:

3 tablespoons softened
butter

Beat or knead in the remaining flour. For the final rising you may put the batter into greased rings, filling the forms to a depth of no more than 1/2 inch. If not using rings, place the dough on a board lightly floured or sprinkled with cornmeal. Pat or press the dough to a thickness of about 1/2 inch, and cut it into rounds about 3 inches in diameter. Let them stand on a lightly greased cookie sheet until the dough has doubled in bulk. Carefully slip a pancake turner under the muffin rings or rounds of dough and transfer them to a fairly hot, well-buttered griddle. Remove the rings. Cook until light brown. Turn once while cooking. Cool slightly on a rack. To separate the muffins before the traditional toasting, take 2 forks back to back and pry them open horizontally. Butter generously and toast. The uneven browning gives them great charm. Serve with:

(Marmalade)

CRUMPETS

Crumpets are essentially similar to English muffins, except that greased

muffin rings must be used when preparing them, see illustration above, as the batter is more liquid. Follow the recipe for English Muffins, above, but increase the milk to 1 2/3 cups.

WHITE, WHOLE-GRAIN, GRAHAM OR RYE BREAD STICKS

Pinch off small pieces of:

Bread dough

that has risen once. This may be done with buttered hands. Roll into sticks of pencil thickness. Brush with:

• Melted butter or 1 beaten
egg

Place the sticks on a buttered baking sheet. Sprinkle with a choice of:

(Coarse salt)
(Poppy seed)
(Fresh celery seed)
(Chopped nutmeats)
(Caraway seed)

Let rise until doubled in bulk. Bake in a 425° oven until brown and crisp.

BAGELS

About 18 Rings

The classic accompaniment is cream cheese and lox or smoked salmon. But try adding to the basic dough, below, spices, raisins, finely chopped nuts or freeze-dried onions.

Combine:

1 cup scalded milk
1/4 cup butter
1 tablespoon sugar

1 teaspoon salt

When this mixture is 105°–115°, add and dissolve for 3 minutes:

1 package active dry
yeast

Blend in:

1 to 2 eggs
3³/₄ cups sifted all-purpose
flour

Knead this soft dough about 10 minutes, adding more flour if necessary to make it firm enough to handle. Let rise, covered, in a greased bowl until doubled in bulk. Punch down and divide into 18 equal pieces. Roll each piece to a rope about 7 inches long and tapered at the ends. Wet the ends to help seal. Form into doughnut-shaped rings, shown opposite. Let rise, covered, on a floured board about 15 minutes. To help firm the dough, you may chill it 2 hours. Drop rings, one at a time, into a solution of:

2 quarts almost boiling
water
1 tablespoon sugar

As the bagels surface, turn them over and cook about 3 minutes longer. Skim out and place on an ungreased baking sheet. Coat with:

Beaten egg white

Bake in a preheated 400° oven 20 to 25 minutes until golden brown and crisp. Very tasty toasted and served with butter.

BREAD PRETZELS OR STICKS

3 Dozen 6-Inch Sticks
or Twelve 6-Inch Pretzels

A chewy soft pretzel: the kind that still—praise be!—can occasionally be bought from a street-vendor. Combine in a mixer bowl:

1 cup 105°-115° water
1 package active dry yeast

When dissolved, add and beat at least 3 minutes:

1¹/₂ cups sifted all-purpose
flour
2 tablespoons soft butter
¹/₂ teaspoon salt
1 tablespoon sugar

Stir in:

1¹/₄ cups sifted all-purpose
flour

and knead until the dough loses its stickiness. Let rise in a covered greased bowl until doubled in bulk. Punch down and divide into 12 pieces for pretzels or 36 smaller pieces for sticks. With your palms, roll the 12 pretzel pieces into 18-inch lengths about pencil thickness, tapering the ends slightly. Loop into a twisted oval as shown below. Place on a greased baking sheet and let rise until almost doubled in bulk. Preheat oven to 475 °. Have ready a boiling solution of:

4 cups water
5 teaspoons baking soda

◗ Do not use an aluminum pan for this mixture. With a slotted spoon, carefully lower the pretzels into the water about 1 minute, or until they float to the top. Return them to the greased sheet. Sprinkle with:

Coarse salt

Bake until crispy and browned, about 12 minutes for the pretzels, less for the sticks. They are best served at once, but will keep about one week in an airtight container. Cool before storing.

ABOUT REFRIGERATOR DOUGHS

By "refrigerator," we mean just that—these are not freezer doughs. If it's a freezer product you're after, by all means ♦ bake before freezing for best results. We find the following recipes somewhat limited in use, because ♦ the milk-based ones can be kept chilled only three days and the water-based ones five days. Yeast action is slowed by the cold, but it does continue, so both more fat and more sugar are needed in refrigerator doughs than in other kinds to keep the yeast potent during the refrigerator period. We find that kneading before storage helps to retain rising power.

The advantage of this type of dough, of course, is that you can bake some at once and keep the rest for later. To store for chilling ♦ keep the dough in a greased plastic bag large enough to allow for some small expansion. If it rises in the refrigerator, punch the dough down. Or, place the balled dough in a greased bowl, turn it so the entire surface is evenly coated, cover it closely with waxed paper or foil, and weight it down with a plate.

After removal from refrigeration, always ♦ rest the dough, covered, 30 minutes. Then ♦ punch it down to let the gases escape before further handling. To shape or fill, see previous roll recipes and illustrations. Be sure the dough at least doubles in bulk. Allow ample time for rising because of the chilled condition of the dough. To bake, see the following individual recipes.

NO-KNEAD REFRIGERATOR ROLLS

Eighteen 2½-Inch Rolls
Sift before measuring:

3½ cups all-purpose flour
Scald:
1 cup milk
Stir in until dissolved:
6 tablespoons shortening or butter
6 tablespoons sugar
1 teaspoon salt
Cool to lukewarm. Combine and let stand for 3 to 5 minutes:
½ cup 105°-115° water
1 package active dry yeast
Beat in:
1 egg
Add these ingredients to the milk mixture. Add half the flour, beating the dough for 2 minutes. Add the remaining flour and beat the dough until it blisters. To store for chilling, to shape and to prepare for baking, see About Refrigerator Doughs, above. Bake in a preheated 425° oven about 15 minutes.

REFRIGERATOR POTATO ROLLS

About Forty 2-Inch Rolls
A sweet dough also entirely suitable for coffee cakes.
Prepare:
1 cup freshly cooked riced Boiled Potatoes, (I, 343)
Combine and let stand 3 to 5 minutes:
½ cup 105°-115° water
1 package active dry yeast
Place in a separate large bowl:
½ cup lard or shortening
Scald and pour over it:
1 cup milk
Stir until the lard is melted. When the mixture is lukewarm, add the dissolved yeast and the riced potatoes. Add:
3 beaten eggs
¾ cup sugar
2 teaspoons salt

Beat well. Sift before measuring:

5 cups all-purpose flour

Add 4 cups of the flour and beat the batter thoroughly. Stir in the remaining flour, or toss the dough on a board and knead in the flour. To store for chilling, to shape and to prepare for baking, see About Refrigerator Doughs, opposite. Bake the rolls in a preheated 425° oven about 15 minutes.

REFRIGERATOR WHOLE-GRAIN ROLLS

About Twenty 2-Inch Rolls

Please read About Flours, 209.
Combine and let stand 3 to 5 minutes:

1 cup 105°-115° water
1 package active dry yeast

Beat until creamy:

¼ cup shortening
6 tablespoons sugar

Stir in the yeast mixture. Sift before measuring:

1¾ cups all-purpose flour

Mix in:

1¼ teaspoons salt
1½ cups whole-grain flour

Stir the flour mixture gradually into the yeast mixture. Beat until well blended. To store for chilling, to shape and to prepare for baking, see About Refrigerator Doughs, opposite. Bake in a preheated 425° oven about 15 minutes.

REFRIGERATOR BRAN ROLLS

About Forty-Eight 2-Inch Rolls

These are crisp, crunchy and light.
Combine:

1 cup shortening
¾ cup sugar
1½ to 2 teaspoons salt

Pour over these ingredients and stir until the shortening is melted:

1 cup boiling water

Add:

1 cup bran or bran cereal

In a separate bowl, combine and let stand for 3 to 5 minutes:

1 cup 105°-115° water
2 packages active dry yeast

When the first mixture is lukewarm, add to it:

2 well-beaten eggs

and the dissolved yeast. Add:

6 cups sifted all-purpose flour

Beat the dough well. To store for chilling, to shape and to prepare for baking, see About Refrigerator Doughs, opposite. Bake in a preheated 425° oven about 15 minutes.

ABOUT YEAST COFFEE CAKES

Holidays are an inspiration to bakers. The Portuguese make an Easter bread, hiding within it hard-cooked eggs. Czechoslovakia has **Babka,** which is much like our Panettone, below, baked in a Turk's-head mold pan. And the Russians call our Panettone **Kulich** but bake it in a greased form similar to one of our own 1-pound metal coffee cans.

The following recipes all call for the finest of white flours, but there is no reason why flours of greater nutritional value cannot be substituted. Remember when you are baking bread and rolls that many of these doughs can be made into very acceptable coffee cake and sweet rolls. Try some with the special fillings suggested at the end of this section, 331.

NO-KNEAD YEAST COFFEE CAKE OR PANETTONE

Two 9-Inch Tube Pans

Baked in 1-pound greased coffee

cans and attractively packaged, this cake makes wonderful gifts. Combine and let stand for 3 to 5 minutes:

1 cup 105°-115° water
2 packages active dry yeast

Sift and stir in:

1 cup all-purpose flour

Cover this sponge and let rise about 30 minutes in a warm place. Beat until soft:

1/2 cup butter

Add gradually and blend until light and creamy:

1/2 cup sifted sugar

Beat in, one at a time:

2 to 3 eggs

Add:

1 teaspoon salt
2 teaspoons grated lemon rind

Beat in the sponge. Sift and beat in gradually:

3 1/2 cups all-purpose flour

Beat the dough for 5 minutes more. Add:

(1/8 cup chopped citron)
(1/4 cup golden raisins or chopped candied pineapple)
(1 cup broken nutmeats)

Cover the bowl with a cloth and let the dough rise about 2 hours or until almost doubled in bulk. Punch down, divide and place in 2 greased tube pans or in greased 1-pound coffee cans and let rise about 1/2 hour. Lightly brush the tops with:

Melted butter

If no fruit or nutmeats were added to the batter, combine and sprinkle on the dough:

(1/2 cup shredded blanched almonds)
(1/4 cup sugar)

Preheat oven to 350°.
Bake about 1/2 hour, depending on pan size. If you have omitted the top dressing of almonds and sugar, you may spread on it, after the cake has baked and cooled:

(Milk or Lemon Glaze, 504)

GLAZED FILLED COFFEE CAKE OR BIENENSTICH

· A 9 × 12-Inch Cake

Prepare half the recipe for:

Panettone, 327

After the first rising, arrange dough in a 9 × 12-inch baking pan and cover with a cooled:

Honey-Bee Glaze, 503

using 1 cup sliced almonds. Let the dough rise until almost doubled, then bake in a preheated 375° oven 15 to 20 minutes. When cool, cut pastry into 3-inch squares. Split each piece and fill with half the recipe for:

Crème Patissière I, 450

★ KNEADED FILLED COFFEE CAKE

2 Loaves

Prepare dough for:

Buttermilk-Potato Rolls, 318, or White Bread Plus, 302

adding an additional:

1/4 cup sugar

To give these breads an interesting color, use the tiniest smidgen of:

Saffron, 278

To let rise and bake, see Stollen, opposite. Consider beforehand whether to fashion your cake like a Jelly Roll, 440, to make a filled wreath, 331, or to weave a so-called **alligator,** as shown opposite. One of the most famous Christmas breads is **Vanocka,** a braided loaf supposed to resemble the Christ Child in swaddling clothes. Ironically enough, the simplified version shown in the chapter heading, 296, can be confected by adapting the "alligator" procedure. To fill, see

About Fillings for Coffee Cakes, 331.
To glaze, see 503.

★ STOLLEN OR
CHRISTMAS LOAF

2 Loaves

Have ready:

    6 to 8 cups all-purpose flour

Combine and let stand for 3 to 5 minutes:

    1½ cups 105°-115° water or milk

    2 packages active dry yeast

Add 1 cup of the flour. Cover this sponge and let it rest in a warm place until light and foamy, about 1 hour. Sprinkle a little of the sifted flour over:

    ½ lb. raisins

    ½ lb. chopped blanched almonds

    (½ cup chopped candied fruits)

Beat until soft:

    1½ cups butter

Add gradually and blend until light and creamy:

    ¾ cup sifted sugar

Beat in, one at a time:

    3 eggs

Add:

    ¾ teaspoon salt

    ¾ teaspoon grated lemon rind

Add the sponge and enough flour to knead the dough until smooth and elastic. Cover and let rise until doubled in bulk. Toss it onto a floured board. Knead in the fruit and nuts. Divide

the dough into 2 equal pieces. Roll each into an 8 × 15-inch oval. Fold in half lengthwise and place loaves on greased baking sheets. Brush the tops with:

    Melted butter

Let the loaves rise, covered, until they again almost double in bulk, about 45 minutes.

Preheat oven to 350°. Bake 30 to 40 minutes or until done. When cool, brush with:

    Milk or Lemon Glaze, 503

GUGELHUPF OR BUNDKUCHEN

A true Gugelhupf is baked in a fluted tube pan. It is the traditional Name Day cake—not your birthday, but the birthday of the saint for whom you were named. This recipe also makes an excellent Baba or Savarin, 437. For Quick Gugelhupf, see 339.

Have ready:

    4 cups all-purpose flour

Scald:

    1 cup milk

When cooled to 105°-115°, pour it over:

    2 packages active dry yeast

After the yeast has dissolved, beat in 1 cup of the sifted flour. Cover and set the sponge in a warm place until light and frothy, about 1 hour.

Beat until soft:

    1 cup butter

Add gradually and blend until light and creamy:

    ¾ cup sifted sugar

Beat in, one at a time:

    5 eggs

Add the sponge, the remaining flour and:

    1 teaspoon salt

    1 teaspoon grated lemon rind

    1 cup seedless raisins

Beat the batter well until smooth and

elastic. Spread in the bottom of a greased 10-inch tube pan:

¹/₂ cup blanched almonds

Place the dough on top of them and let rise until almost doubled in bulk. Preheat oven to 350°.

Bake the cake 50 to 60 minutes. The top and sides should be a golden brown. When cool, sprinkle the top with:

Confectioners' sugar

FRUIT-TOPPED YEAST COFFEE CAKE

Four 8-Inch Cakes

For other versions of **Galette,** see 363.

Prepare:

White Bread Plus dough, 302

adding an additional:

¹/₄ cup sugar

After the first rising, pat the dough out thin in the greased pans, prick it well and let it rest. Then make a rim by pinching up the edges all around. Brush the surface with:

Melted butter

or apply a:

French Egg Wash, 503

Although the egg wash always tends to toughen, it does prevent sogginess. Cover the entire surface of the cake with closely placed rows of:

Fruit: sliced pared apples, peeled peaches or plums or seeded cherries

Cover the fruit with:

Streusel, 502, or cinnamon and sugar mixed with butter

Or, after the last rising indicated below, in place of the butter mixture, pour around the fruit the following custard.

Beat:

1 egg yolk

¹/₄ cup cream

Let the fruit-covered dough rise only half as high as usual for bread.

Preheat oven to 375°.

Bake about 25 minutes, when the fruit should be soft and the cake done.

SCANDINAVIAN COFFEE CAKE OR PASTRY

Two 9-Inch Rings

Call them Danish, Swedish or Norwegian, these light confections fall between rich coffee cakes and rich pastries. The method of folding and rolling the dough, similar to that used in Croissants, 322, accounts for the characteristic flakiness of the superbly light crumb. The basic dough can be used for the ring shown opposite. Fillings and toppings are usually rich in nuts, with a little saffron occasionally added to the flavoring.

Beat well:

2 eggs

Add:

³/₄ cup 105°-115° water

Dissolve in this mixture:

1 package active dry yeast

Let all these ingredients rest refrigerated for about 15 minutes. Meanwhile, blend with a pastry blender or by hand:

4 cups sifted all-purpose flour
1 teaspoon salt
2 tablespoons sugar
¹/₂ cup butter
10 crushed cardamom seeds or 1¹/₂ teaspoons powdered cardamom

In a large mixing bowl, make a ring of the blended flour. Pour the chilled yeast mixture into the center and work it gradually into the dry ingredients. Knead until smooth, about 2 minutes. Form the dough into a ball and rest it, covered, about 20 minutes in the refrigerator. Roll out the dough ▶ lightly into an oblong about ³/₈ inch thick. Beat until creamy:

1¹/₃ to 1¹/₂ cups butter

To spread the butter, follow the directions for Croissants, 322, folding and rolling 4 times. Cover and chill the dough at least 2 hours. Then roll it again on a slightly floured surface, to the thickness of ³/₈ inch. Cut off any folded edges that might keep the dough from expanding. To shape the ring as shown below, roll it first into an oblong, about 29 × 11 inches. Fill it with any rich filling for coffee cake, below. It is not necessary to shape the roll on a cloth, but you may need to use a spatula or pancake turner to help lift it if the dough should stick to the lightly floured board. Bring the two ends of the roll together, using a little water for glue. Place the ring on a greased baking sheet. With floured scissors held perpendicular to the roll, cut bias gashes about 1 to 2 inches apart into the upper edges of the ring, to within one inch of the inner circle. As you cut, you may turn each partially cut slice flat onto the tin. Sometimes the slices are cut very narrow, and one slice is turned toward the outer rim, the other twisted and turned toward the inner rim; but with these variations, should the filling be generous, it tends to leak and burn on the pan. Wash the top areas with:

French Egg Wash, 503

being care not to cover the cut portions, as the glaze may harden later too rapidly in baking and inhibit further rising of the dough. Cover the cut ring with a cloth and let rise about 25 minutes, until doubled in bulk. Preheat the oven to 400° for a ring, to 375° for filled rolls or croissants. Bake a ring about 25 minutes. Bake

rolls about 15 minutes. If a Fruit Glaze, 505, is to be applied, allow the pastry to cool and apply the glaze warm. For other glazes, see 502–505.

ABOUT SEASONINGS AND FILLINGS FOR COFFEE CAKE

Home cooks often wonder why their coffee cakes and fillings seem insipid in flavor and color when compared with some of the more sophisticated commercial products. First of all, a slight touch of yellow coloring often used in commercial coffee cakes lends them a more convincing "eggy" look. Often, too, for gusto, bakers add to their crumb mixtures crushed macaroons, almond paste, rolled cake crumbs, and finely ground nuts—especially hazelnuts. Sometimes they use pecans, walnuts, almonds and, occasionally, Brazil nuts. Considerably less effective are finely chopped peanuts, coconut and cashews.

The amateur baker may also add distinction to pastry fillings with a small quantity of lemon juice, grated lemon or orange rind, dried currants, a bit of finely chopped citron or finely chopped sweet chocolate. Sometimes they may choose to avoid more solid fillings altogether and substitute a thin layer of jam or marmalade. Fillings are applied during final shaping and before the last rising. A 9-inch ring needs about one-cup-plus of filling, individual rolls about 2 teaspoons. For various Toppings, Glazes, and Streusels, see 502–505.

NUT FILLINGS FOR COFFEE CAKES

I.   For One 9-Inch Ring
If made with almonds, this is known as **Edelweiss.**
Cream:

    1/2 **cup confectioners' sugar**

    1/4 **to** 1/2 **cup butter**

Stir in:

    1/2 **teaspoon vanilla or**

       1 teaspoon grated lemon rind

    1/2 **cup shredded or ground blanched almonds or other nuts**

    (1 egg)

II.   For One 9-Inch Ring
Combine:

  1/2 **cup ground hazelnuts or other nuts**

  1/2 **cup sugar**

   2 teaspoons cinnamon

  1/2 **teaspoon vanilla**

   2 tablespoons finely chopped citron or orange peel

Beat well and add:

   1 egg

Thin these ingredients with:

   Milk

until they are of the right consistency to spread over the dough.

III.   Fór One 9-Inch Ring
Chop:

  1/4 **cup each blanched almonds, citron and raisins**

Melt:

  1/4 **cup butter, or** 1/8 **cup butter and** 1/8 **cup cultured sour cream**

After rolling the dough, spread it with the melted butter and the chopped ingredients. Sprinkle with:

   (Sugar)

   (Cinnamon)

IV.   For Three 9-Inch Rings
You may buy canned almond paste or make it, 580, for coffee cake fillings. For:

  10 oz. almond paste

allow:

   1 cup sugar

   2 unbeaten egg whites

Work these ingredients in a bowl placed over ice, (I, 186), to keep them cool and to prevent the oil in the almonds from being released.

CRUMB FRUIT FILLING

For One 9-Inch Ring
Mix well:

  3/4 **cup crushed macaroons**

   3 tablespoons melted butter

   2 tablespoons sugar

  1/2 **cup raisins or chopped dates, cooked prunes or grated coconut**

  (1/4 **cup chopped nuts)**

APPLE COFFEE CAKE FILLING

For Two 9-Inch Rings
Combine and boil for 4 minutes:

  2 1/2 **cups pared and chopped apples**

   1 cup brown sugar

  1/3 **cup butter**

   1 cup raisins

  1/2 **teaspoon cinnamon**

  1/2 **teaspoon salt**

Cool slightly and spread over dough.

PRUNE OR APRICOT FILLING
FOR COFFEE CAKE AND ROLLS

For One 9-Inch Ring

Combine:
  **1/2 cup sweetened puréed
    prunes or apricots
  2 to 4 tablespoons butter
  2 teaspoons grated orange or
    lemon rind
  (1/4 cup nuts or coconut)**

DATE OR FIG FILLING FOR
COFFEE CAKE

For One 9-Inch Ring

Melt and simmer about 2 minutes:
  **1/4 cup butter
  1/3 cup brown sugar**
Remove from heat and stir in:
  **3/4 cup chopped dates or
    dried figs
  1/4 cup Almond Paste, 580
  1/2 teaspoon cinnamon
    A grating of fresh nutmeg**
Cool slightly before using.

POPPY SEED OR MOHN
FILLINGS

I. Cockaigne

For One 9-Inch Ring

This filling is for that special occasion.
Grind or crush in a mortar:
  1/2 cup poppy seeds
Put the poppy seeds in the top of a
double boiler and, over direct heat,
bring to a boil with:
  1/4 cup milk
Remove pan from the heat and add:
  **1/3 cup brown sugar
  2 tablespoons butter**
Put the pan ▶ over—not in—boiling
water and add:
  2 egg yolks
Heat until the mixture thickens, stirring constantly. When it has cooled
slightly, add:

  **1/3 cup Almond Paste, 580, or
    1/2 cup ground almonds
  (3 tablespoons citron)
  (2 teaspoons lemon juice or
    1 teaspoon vanilla)**
Cool and have ready to add to strudel
or use for coffee cake.

II.   For Two 9-Inch Rings
Mix together well:
  **3/4 cup ground poppy seeds
  1/4 cup sugar
  1/4 cup raisins
  1/2 cup sour cream
  1/8 teaspoon cinnamon
  1 teaspoon grated lemon rind**

III.   For Four 9-Inch Rings
Grind or mash between towels with a
wooden mallet:
  2 cups poppy seeds
Mix in:
  **1 egg
  1/3 cup honey
  1 tablespoon lemon juice
  1/4 cup chopped nuts**

IV.   For One 9-Inch Ring
Grind or mash between towels with a
wooden mallet:
  1/4 cup poppy seeds
Place the ground seeds in a bowl and
add:
  About 2 tablespoons milk
just enough to make this mixture feel
buttery between your fingers. Then
add:
  **2 tablespoons melted butter
  2 tablespoons dry cake
    crumbs
  1 teaspoon cinnamon
  1 teaspoon grated lemon rind**

POT-CHEESE OR RICOTTA
FILLING

For One 9-Inch Coffee Cake Ring
Put through a ricer or a strainer:

1½ cups pot or Ricotta cheese
Mix well with:
  ¼ cup sugar
  1 slightly beaten egg yolk
  ¼ to ½ cup raisins
  2 teaspoons grated lemon
    rind
Beat until ◗ stiff but not dry, and fold in:
  1 egg white

ABOUT QUICK TEA BREADS AND COFFEE CAKES

These sweet breads are delightful but, with the exception of nut and fruit breads, should be served immediately after baking; they wither young. If you want breads that keep and reheat well, see recipes for yeast breads and yeast coffee cakes. Also see Additions to Yeast Doughs and the Cornell Formula, 301, to enrich these breads.

Nut and fruit breads are attractive baked in 6-oz. metal juice cans so that they slice prettily for tea. If you use cans, do not fill them more than three-fourths full to allow for expansion of the dough, and bake for less time than a loaf. Quick nut and fruit breads slice better if, after baking and cooling, they are wrapped in foil and refrigerated about 12 hours.

▲ When baking quick breads at high altitudes, reduce the baking powder or soda in the recipe by one-fourth. ◗ But do not decrease the soda to less than ½ teaspoon for each cup of sour milk or cream used.

QUICK NUT OR DATE BREAD

                A 9 × 5-Inch Loaf
Preheat oven to 350°.
◗ Have all ingredients at about 70°.
Sift into a bowl:
  2 cups all-purpose flour
  ⅓ cup white or ½ cup brown
    sugar

  2 teaspoons double-acting
    baking powder
  1 teaspoon salt
Melt and cool slightly:
  2 tablespoons butter
Beat until light:
  1 egg
Beat with the egg:
  1 cup milk
  (½ teaspoon vanilla)
Add the melted butter. Beat the liquid ingredients into the sifted ones until well mixed. Fold in:
  ¾ cup chopped nutmeats, or
    part dates and part
    nutmeats
Place the dough in a greased bread pan and bake about 40 minutes.

QUICK HONEY LOAF

Prepare:
  Quick Nut Bread, above
increasing the flour by ½ cup and omitting the sugar. Add:
  ¾ cup honey
  ½ teaspoon baking soda

QUICK SALLY LUNN

              A 9 × 13-Inch Pan
A light sweet bread. For an even lighter one, try Brioche Loaf Cockaigne, 306, or Brioche, 320.
◗ Have all ingredients at about 70°.
Preheat oven to 425°.
Sift together:
  2 cups sifted all-purpose
    flour
  2¼ teaspoons double-acting
    baking powder
  ¾ teaspoon salt
Combine and cream well:
  ½ cup shortening
  ½ cup sugar
Beat in, one at a time:
  3 eggs

Add the sifted ingredients to the batter in about 3 parts, alternately with:

1 cup milk

Stir the batter lightly ◗ until the ingredients are just blended. Bake in a greased pan about 30 minutes. Break the bread into squares. Serve hot.

QUICK PRUNE, APRICOT, APPLE OR CRANBERRY BREAD

A 9 X 5-Inch Loaf

◗ Have all ingredients at about 70°.
Preheat oven to 350°.
Sift together:

1¹/₂ cups sifted all-purpose flour
¹/₂ teaspoon salt
1 teaspoon baking soda

Add:

1¹/₂ cups whole-grain flour

Cream in a large bowl:

¹/₄ cup shortening

with:

¹/₂ cup sugar

Beat in:

1 egg

Add:

³/₄ cup unsweetened, cooked, mashed prune, apricot or cranberry pulp or freshly grated apple
¹/₄ cup prune, apricot or cranberry juice

Add the sifted ingredients alternately to the fruit mixture with:

1 cup buttermilk

Stir the batter ◗ with a few swift strokes, until just blended. Fold in:

1 cup broken nutmeats
(Grated rind of 1 orange)

Place the dough in a greased loaf pan. Bake the bread about 1¹/₄ hours, letting it cool in the pan.

QUICK ORANGE BREAD

Two 8¹/₂ X 4¹/₂-Inch Loaves

This is an economical, easily made tea bread. If you want a quick treat, break it apart and eat it while hot, with or without lots of good butter. If you intend it for sandwiches, bake it in cans, see About Quick Tea Breads, 334. You'll find it easier to slice on the second day.

◗ Have all ingredients at about 70°.
Preheat oven to 350°.
Sift together into a large bowl:

3 cups sifted all-purpose flour
3 teaspoons double-acting baking powder
¹/₂ teaspoon salt

Combine and add:

1 tablespoon grated orange rind
¹/₂ to ³/₄ cup sugar

For a more cakelike result, use the larger amount of sugar. Combine and beat:

1 egg
¹/₄ cup orange juice
1¹/₄ cups milk
2 tablespoons melted shortening

Add:

(1 cup chopped or broken nutmeats)

Pour the liquid mixture into the bowl. Combine all ingredients with a few swift strokes. Stir lightly until barely blended. Bake the bread in two greased loaf pans about 50 minutes or until done.

QUICK BANANA BREAD

An 8¹/₂ X 4¹/₂-Inch Loaf

◗ Have all ingredients at about 70°.
Preheat oven to 350°.
Sift together:

1³/₄ cups sifted all-purpose flour

2¼ teaspoons double-acting
    baking powder
½ teaspoon salt

Blend until creamy:

⅓ cup shortening
⅔ cup sugar
¾ teaspoon grated lemon rind

Beat in:

1 to 2 beaten eggs
1 to 1¼ cups ripe banana
    pulp

Add the sifted ingredients in about
3 parts to the sugar mixture. Beat
the batter after each addition until
smooth. Fold in:

(½ cup broken nutmeats)
(¼ cup finely chopped dried
    apricots)

Place the batter in a greased bread
pan. Bake the bread about 1 hour or
until done. Cool before slicing.

QUICK BANANA WHEAT-GERM BREAD

Prepare:

Banana Bread, above

Use in all:

1½ cups all-purpose flour

Add:

¼ cup wheat germ

QUICK PUMPKIN BREAD

One 9 X 5-Inch Loaf

Preheat oven to 350°.
Sift together:

1¾ cups sifted all-purpose
    flour
¼ teaspoon double-acting
    baking powder
1 teaspoon baking soda
1 teaspoon salt
½ teaspoon cinnamon
¼ teaspoon ground cloves

In a large bowl, beat until light and
fluffy:

1⅓ cups sugar
⅓ cup soft shortening
2 eggs

Add and beat in:

1 cup cooked or canned
    pumpkin

Now add the sifted dry ingredients in
3 additions alternately with:

⅓ cup water or milk
(½ teaspoon vanilla)

Do not overbeat between each addition. Fold in:

½ cup coarsely chopped nuts
⅓ cup raisins or chopped dates

Pour batter into a greased pan and
bake about 1 hour or until bread tests
done, see 400.

QUICK CARROT-NUT BREAD

One 5 X 9-Inch Loaf

Preheat oven to 350°.
Sift together:

1½ cups sifted all-purpose
    flour
1½ teaspoons baking soda
¼ teaspoon cinnamon

Add:

¾ cup sugar
2 beaten eggs
½ cup vegetable oil
1 teaspoon vanilla
½ teaspoon salt

Blend in with a few swift strokes:

1½ cups grated carrots
1½ cups ground pecans or
    walnuts

Bake in a greased pan about 1 hour.
Cool in the pan 10 minutes, then turn
out onto a rack for further cooling.

QUICK OLIVE-NUT BREAD

One 4½ X 8½-Inch Loaf

Sliced thin, this makes a very good
canapé or sandwich base.
Preheat oven to 350°.
Sift together:

   1¹/₂ **cups sifted all-purpose flour**
    4 **teaspoons double-acting baking powder**
   ¹/₂ **teaspoon salt**

Add:

    1 **cup whole wheat flour**

Mix together:

    1 **beaten egg**
    1 **cup milk**
    2 **tablespoons melted butter**

Combine the milk and flour mixtures with a few swift strokes, then add:

    1 **cup sliced stuffed green olives**
    1 **cup chopped nuts**

Bake in a greased pan about 45 minutes.

QUICK IRISH SODA BREAD

An 8-Inch Round Loaf

Preheat oven to 375°.
Sift together in a large bowl:

    2 **cups sifted all-purpose flour**
  1¹/₂ **teaspoons double-acting baking powder**
   ¹/₂ **teaspoon baking soda**
   ¹/₂ **teaspoon salt**
    1 **tablespoon sugar**

Cut into the flour with a pastry blender, until the mixture has the consistency of coarse cornmeal:

   ¹/₄ **cup chilled shortening**

Stir in:

   ¹/₂ **to 1 cup raisins or currants**
    2 **teaspoons caraway seeds**

Mix together:

    1 **beaten egg**
   ²/₃ **cup buttermilk**

Add to dry ingredients and stir well. Knead briefly and place in a greased 8-inch round pan. Press down so dough will fill the pan. Cut a bold cross over the top and sides so the bread will not crack in baking. Brush the top with:

     Milk

Bake 35 to 40 minutes.
To bake 🍳 outdoors, see Skillet Breads, 340.

QUICK SWEET WHOLE WHEAT BREAD

A 9 × 5-Inch Loaf

A homely coarse sweet bread, delightful served with fruit salads and cottage cheese.
Preheat oven to 375°.
Mix:

  2¹/₂ **cups whole wheat flour**
   ¹/₂ **teaspoon cinnamon**
   ¹/₄ **teaspoon salt**
    2 **teaspoons double-acting baking powder**
    1 **teaspoon baking soda**

Combine:

    1 **beaten egg**
   ¹/₂ **cup molasses**
   ¹/₄ **cup brown sugar**
   ¹/₄ **cup vegetable oil**
    1 **teaspoon grated lemon or orange peel**

Add the flour mixture, alternately with:

   ²/₃ **cup yogurt or buttermilk**

to the above ingredients. Pour into a greased pan and bake about 50 minutes.

QUICK BRAN DATE BREAD

Two 8¹/₂ × 4¹/₂-Inch Loaves

Preheat oven to 350°.
Prepare:

    2 **cups chopped dates**

Pour over them:

    2 **cups boiling water**

In a separate bowl, beat until light:

    2 **eggs**

Add slowly, beating constantly:

   ³/₄ **cup brown sugar or ¹/₂ cup molasses**

When these ingredients are creamy, add:

1 cup whole-grain flour
2 teaspoons double-acting baking powder
1 teaspoon baking soda

Add half the date mixture and:

1 cup whole-grain flour
2 cups bran
1 teaspoon vanilla

Add the remaining date mixture and:

1 cup or less chopped nutmeats

Place the dough in lightly greased loaf pans. Bake about 1 hour.

EGGLESS ALL-RYE HONEY CAKE COCKAIGNE

One 7¹/₄ × 3⁵/₈-Inch Loaf

Like a soft, deliciously spiced **Lebkuchen,** this confection keeps for weeks. The dough is stiff to beat and does not make a very high loaf, but it toasts well for tea. Age it three days or more in a plastic bag or tin tea box before eating.
Preheat oven to 350°.
Heat in the top of a double boiler until small bubbles appear through the mixture:

¹/₃ cup honey
³/₄ cup water
¹/₂ cup sugar

Remove from heat and beat it into the following mixture:

2 cups very finely milled rye flour
¹/₂ teaspoon baking soda
2 teaspoons double-acting baking powder
1 tablespoon cinnamon
¹/₂ teaspoon each cloves and allspice
¹/₈ teaspoon cardamom

Beat 10 minutes with an electric beater. Add:

¹/₄ cup pecans or blanched shredded almonds

1 tablespoon grated orange rind
¹/₄ to ¹/₂ cup finely chopped citron

Place a pan of water on the bottom shelf of the oven. Bake the cake in a greased loaf pan about 1 hour.

BAKED BROWN BREAD

One 9 × 5-Inch Loaf

Preheat oven to 350°.
Sift together:

1 cup sifted all-purpose flour
2 tablespoons sugar
³/₄ teaspoon salt
1 teaspoon baking soda

Stir in:

2 cups graham flour
1 cup buttermilk
1 cup dark molasses

You may add:

1 cup broken nutmeats and/or raisins

Combine all ingredients and bake in a greased 9 × 5-inch loaf pan about 1 hour; or in four 10-ounce buttered molds 30 to 40 minutes.

BOSTON STEAMED BROWN BREAD

Two 1-Pound Loaves or Two 1-Quart Pudding Molds

◗ Please read About Steamed Puddings, 539.
Combine:

1 cup yellow stone-ground cornmeal
1 cup rye flour
1 cup graham flour
2 teaspoons baking soda
1 teaspoon salt

Combine in a separate bowl:

2 cups buttermilk
³/₄ cup molasses
1 cup chopped raisins

One of our friends soaks the raisins

overnight in brandy! Add the liquid to the dry ingredients. Pour the batter into 2 buttered 1-quart pudding molds or fill 1-pound buttered coffee cans about three-fourths full. Butter the lids before closing molds and tie the lids on, so rising bread does not break the seal. Aluminum foil may be used as a lid; make sure the seal is tight. ◗ Steam 3 hours in 1 inch of water. To cut without crumbling, use a tough string and slice with a sawing motion.

QUICK COFFEE CAKE OR KUCHEN

A 9 × 9-Inch Pan

We prize this coffee cake for a Sunday brunch, topping it with drained sugared blueberries or pitted cherries distributed over the batter before baking.
Preheat oven to 375°.
Sift together:

    1½ cups sifted all-purpose
        flour
    ¼ teaspoon salt
    2 teaspoons double-acting
        baking powder

Cream until soft in a large bowl:

    ¼ cup butter

Add gradually and cream until light:

    ¼ to ½ cup sugar

Beat in:

    1 egg
    ⅔ cup milk

Add the sifted ingredients to the butter mixture.
Add:

    (¾ teaspoon grated lemon rind
        or ½ teaspoon vanilla)

Stir the batter until smooth. Spread in a greased pan. Cover with:

    Streusel, 502, or
        Honey-Bee Glaze, 503

or with fruits mentioned above. Bake about 25 minutes.

QUICK GUGELHUPF

A 7-Inch Tube Pan

◗ Have all ingredients at about 70°.
Preheat oven to 350°.
Sift together:

    3½ cups sifted all-purpose
        flour
    3 teaspoons double-acting
        baking powder
    ½ teaspoon salt

Cream in a large bowl until soft:

    1 cup butter

Add gradually and cream until very light:

    1 cup sifted sugar

Beat in, one at a time:

    5 eggs

Add the flour mixture in 3 parts, alternately with:

    1 cup milk

Stir the batter until smooth after each addition.
Add:

    1 cup seedless white raisins
    1 teaspoon grated
        lemon rind
    1 teaspoon vanilla

Bake the cake in a greased tube pan 45 to 50 minutes. When cool, sprinkle with:

    Confectioners' sugar

QUICK SOUR CREAM COFFEE CAKE

A 9 × 9-Inch Pan

Made on a muffin principle, this cake is wonderfully good and easy. When it is served fresh, its smooth texture approximates that of a sourdough coffee cake.
◗ Have all ingredients at about 70°.
Preheat oven to 350°.
Sift together:

    1½ cups sifted all-purpose
        flour
    1 cup sugar

2 teaspoons double-acting
baking powder
1/2 teaspoon baking soda
1/4 teaspoon salt

Combine and beat well:

1 cup cultured sour cream
2 eggs

Add the sifted ingredients to the cream mixture. Beat until just smooth ◗ as overbeating tends to toughen dough. Spread in a lightly greased pan. Sprinkle with:

Streusel, 502

Bake about 20 minutes.

BISHOP'S BREAD

Prepare the batter for:

Quick Sour Cream Coffee
Cake, 339

Add:

2 oz. grated unsweetened
chocolate
1 cup chopped dates
1 cup chopped nuts

Bake as directed.

QUICK SPICE COFFEE CAKE
WITH OIL

An 8 × 8 × 2½-Inch Pan

◗ Have all ingredients at about 70°.
Preheat oven to 350°.
Combine in a mixing bowl:

2 cups sifted all-purpose
flour
2/3 cup sugar
3/4 teaspoon double-acting
baking powder
3/4 teaspoon baking soda
1/2 teaspoon salt
1/2 teaspoon freshly grated
nutmeg
1 teaspoon cinnamon

Combine in another bowl and mix well:

1/2 cup vegetable oil

1 beaten egg
1/2 cup buttermilk or yogurt
1/3 cup light or dark corn
syrup
3/4 cup raisins

Pour this into the flour mixture, stirring rapidly until blended. All the lumps need not have vanished. Pour into a greased pan and cover with:

Streusel I, 502

Bake the cake about 35 minutes.

SKILLET OR GRIDDLE BREADS

Either:

Irish Soda Bread, 337, or
Skillet Corn Bread, 341

will make acceptable, even good, skillet bread on an open fire ▤ especially over charcoal. But our results on these heats did not compare in quality with those obtained when the same recipes were oven-baked. Bake them covered. If you prefer Irish Farls, use the Irish Soda Bread recipe and cut the bread in triangular wedges about 1 inch thick and bake on a griddle heated to about 370° and lightly rubbed with oil. Allow about 10 minutes for one side; turn and allow 10 minutes more.

ABOUT CORN BREADS

Anyone who grew up on southern corn breads hankers for a rich brown crust and a light but slightly gritty bite. We can assure you that without stone-ground cornmeal and a heavy, hot pan, the end product will be pale and lifeless. For a very crisp crust, grease the pan well and heat it in a 425° oven before filling. Whether you bake as muffins, sticks or bread, you may vary the corn and wheat proportion within a 2-cup limit, to your own taste. We like 1¼ cups cornmeal to ¾ cup all-purpose flour. Try, if you like, adding a little minced onion, shredded cheddar cheese, cream-style corn or bits of cooked ham or bacon. Many southern cooks use no sugar, but for a distinctive flavor, try dark brown sugar instead of granulated.

▲ When baking corn breads at high altitudes, reduce the baking powder or soda by one-fourth. ♦ But do not reduce soda to less than $1/2$ teaspoon for each cup of buttermilk or sour cream used.

CORN BREAD, MUFFINS OR STICKS

A 9 × 9-Inch Pan or About fifteen 2-Inch Muffins
♦ Have all ingredients at about 70°. Preheat oven to 425°.
Grease the pan with butter, oil or bacon drippings. Place it in the oven until sizzling hot.
Sift together:
  **$3/4$ cup sifted all-purpose flour
  $2^1/2$ teaspoons double-acting baking powder
  1 to 2 tablespoons sugar
  $3/4$ teaspoon salt**
Add:
  $1^1/4$ cups yellow or white stone-ground cornmeal
Beat in a separate bowl:
  1 egg
Beat into it:
  **2 to 3 tablespoons melted butter or drippings
  1 cup milk**
Combine all ingredients with a few rapid strokes. Place the batter in the hot pan. Bake sticks about 15 minutes, corn bread and muffins 20 to 25 minutes. Serve immediately.

SKILLET CORN BREAD

Prepare:
  Corn Bread, above

⊞ Cook it in a 10-inch covered skillet for about $1/2$ hour or until done. You may add to the dough:
  ($1/4$ to $1/2$ cup cooked ham or bacon bits)

BUCKWHEAT CORN BREAD

Prepare:
  Corn Bread, above
and substitute for $1/2$ cup of the cornmeal:
  $1/2$ cup buckwheat flour
and add:
  ($1/4$ cup hulled sunflower seeds)

BUTTERMILK CRACKLING CORN BREAD

A 9 × 9-Inch Pan or Twenty 2-Inch Muffins
♦ Have all ingredients at about 70°. Preheat oven to 425°.
Sift together:
  **1 cup sifted all-purpose flour
  $1/2$ teaspoon baking soda
  $1^1/2$ teaspoons double-acting baking powder
  1 tablespoon sugar
  1 teaspoon salt**
Add:
  $3/4$ cup yellow stone-ground cornmeal
Combine and beat:
  **$1^1/2$ cups buttermilk or yogurt
  2 eggs
  3 to 4 tablespoons melted butter or fresh bacon drippings**
Stir the liquid into the dry ingredients with a few swift strokes. Add:
  ($1/4$ cup salt pork cracklings)
Pour the batter into a preheated greased pan. Bake the bread 25 to 30 minutes, muffins 15.

SOURDOUGH CORN BREAD

**A 10-Inch Skillet
or Two 8-Inch Round Pans**

A moist heavy bread, best served hot from the oven.
Preheat oven to 425°.
Thoroughly mix together in a large bowl:

1 cup Sourdough Starter, 224
1½ cups yellow cornmeal
½ teaspoon salt
¾ teaspoon baking soda
2 tablespoons sugar
¼ cup melted butter
1½ cups evaporated milk
2 beaten eggs

Pour into a 10-inch greased skillet or two 8-inch round cake pans and bake 25 to 30 minutes.

CORN ZEPHYRS COCKAIGNE

About Twenty 2-Inch Puffs

In our endless search for the best recipe of its type, we welcomed the offer of a southern acquaintance to send us the Zephyr recipe she was raving about. When it arrived, it turned out to be word for word our own favorite Zephyr recipe in **Joy.** We consider this the highest of compliments. These puffs are delicate and delicious with a salad course or luncheon dish.
Combine:

1 cup white stone-ground
  cornmeal
1 tablespoon lard

Scald these ingredients by pouring over them:

4 cups boiling water

Add:

1 teaspoon salt

Cook the cornmeal over low heat 30 minutes, stirring frequently. Before cooling it, butter the top slightly to keep it from crusting. Cool.
Preheat oven to 350°.

Whip until stiff:

4 egg whites

Fold them lightly into the cornmeal mixture. Drop the batter from a teaspoon onto a greased baking sheet. Bake about ½ hour.

GOLDEN CORN PUffS

About Twenty 2-Inch Puffs

Pour:

2¼ cups boiling water

over:

1 cup yellow stone-ground
  cornmeal

Add:

1 tablespoon sugar
1 teaspoon salt
2 tablespoons butter

Cook and stir over low heat until you obtain a thick mush. Cool and beat well.
Preheat oven to 425°.
Beat in:

2 beaten egg yolks

Beat until stiff, then fold in:

2 egg whites

Drop the batter from a teaspoon onto a hot greased baking sheet. Bake the puffs about 20 minutes.

CORN DODGERS COCKAIGNE

About 24

Preheat oven to 400°.
Combine:

1 cup stone-ground cornmeal
1 teaspoon salt
1½ teaspoons sugar

Pour over the dry ingredients and stir:

1 cup boiling water

Beat in until blended:

2 tablespoons butter or
  bacon drippings
(1 beaten egg)

Drop the batter from a spoon onto a greased baking sheet; or dip your hand in cold water, fill it with batter and release the batter "splat" onto the sheet. The hand method was learned from our Sarah, who, as a child, helped her father make dodgers at the Kentucky Derby. Bake about 20 minutes.

TORTILLAS

12 Tortillas

Large tortillas are served as a substitute for bread; small ones may be filled, see Tacos, 69. A tortilla press is helpful if you are planning to make them often.

Combine by mixing well with hands:

> 2 cups corn flour: masa harina
> 1 to 1¹/₃ cups warm water
> 1 teaspoon salt

Dough should be moist but stiff enough to hold its shape. Divide into 12 balls and press each between waxed paper on a tortilla press, or between the palms of your hands, or with a flat plate, until a thin round cake is formed. Peel waxed paper from one side of the tortilla and place dough on a hot ungreased griddle. Remove other piece of waxed paper. Cook one at a time until edges begin to curl and they are very slightly browned. Turn and cook till puffs appear. Wrap in a dampened cloth and foil and keep warm in oven.

CRUSTY SOFT-CENTER SPOON BREAD

4 Servings

Preheat oven to 375°.
Sift together:

> ¹/₄ cup all-purpose flour
> 1 tablespoon sugar
> 1 teaspoon salt
> 1 teaspoon double-acting baking powder

Add:

> ³/₄ cup yellow cornmeal

Stir in until well blended:

> 1 beaten egg
> 1 cup milk

Melt in a high-rimmed 8 × 8-inch baking dish:

> 2 tablespoons butter

Pour in the batter. Pour over the top:

> ¹/₂ cup milk

Bake 45 minutes or more, until good and crusty.

BUTTERMILK SPOON BREAD

4 Servings

Pour:

> 1¹/₂ cups boiling water

over:

> 1 cup white cornmeal

Mix well and cool slightly.
Preheat oven to 350°.
Beat well before adding:

> 1 egg
> 1 tablespoon butter
> 1 cup buttermilk
> 1 teaspoon baking soda
> ³/₄ teaspoon salt

Pour the batter into a hot, greased 7-inch baking dish. Bake 30 to 40 minutes. If you wish to keep the top soft, add from time to time, while the bread is baking, a few tablespoons of milk. For this purpose, use in all:

> ¹/₂ cup milk or thin cream

This process calls for longer baking than the above, about 1 hour in all.

RICE OR MILLET SPOON BREAD

6 Servings

In Mexico, chopped green chilis or scallions and shredded cheddar cheese are added. In Italy, bits of cooked ham and cooked seafood are incorporated into the batter, which is baked until very crisp.
Preheat oven to 325°.

♦ If you use buttermilk, include the baking soda; otherwise, omit it. Combine in the order given, then stir until blended:

1 cup cooked rice or millet
¼ cup cornmeal
2 cups milk or buttermilk
(½ teaspoon baking soda)
1 teaspoon salt
2 beaten eggs
2 tablespoons melted shortening or butter

Place the batter in a greased oven-proof dish. Bake about 1 hour. The spoon bread may be served with:

Mushroom Sauce, (I, 395), or Tomato Provençale, (I, 367)

HUSH PUPPIES

About Twelve 2½-Inch Puppies

Fishermen used to cook these finger-shaped concoctions on the river bank, along with their catch. Rumor has it that they threw a large number to their clamorous dogs with the admonition, "Hush, puppy!" Sometimes we think that is still the best use for them.

Mix together:

1 cup stone-ground cornmeal
1 teaspoon double-acting baking powder
½ teaspoon salt
2 to 3 tablespoons minced onion

Beat together:

1 egg
½ cup milk

Combine with dry ingredients and form into oblong cakes or pones, about 2 × 4 × ¾ inches. Fry in deep fat heated to 370° until golden brown. Drain on paper toweling and serve at once.

ABOUT MUFFINS

Muffin batters are easily made. ♦ To mix, add in a few swift strokes the beaten liquid ingredients to the combined sifted dry ones. ♦ The mixing is held to an absolute minimum, a light stirring of from 10 to 20 seconds, which will leave some lumps. Ignore them. The dough should not be mixed to the point of pouring, ribbonlike, from the spoon, but should break in coarse globs. If the batter has been beaten too long, the gluten in the flour will develop and toughen the dough; and the grain of the muffin will be coarse and full of tunnels, as shown in the cross section on the right above.

Good muffins should be straight-sided and rounded on top, as shown on the left. The grain of the muffin is not fine but uniform and the crumb moist. The center drawings show, first, the weary muffin peak caused by oven heat that is too slow. The next drawing shows the cracked, wobbly-peaked, unsymmetrical shape caused by oven heat that is too high.

To bake, fill well-greased tins about two-thirds full. Should the dough not fill every muffin cup, put a few tablespoons of water in the empty forms, both to protect the pans and to keep the rest of the muffins moist. Unless a different indication is given in the individual recipe ♦ bake at once in a preheated 400° oven 20 to 25 minutes. ♦ If muffins remain in the tins a few moments after leaving the oven, they will be easier to remove. They are really best eaten very promptly. If you must reheat them, enclose them loosely in foil and heat about 5 minutes in a preheated 450° oven.

ADDITIONS TO MUFFINS

Muffins may be enriched by these additions, but have them all ready and beat them in so that the total beating time agrees exactly with the one described above.

I. Use any of the following as a single ingredient or in combination:

    1/4 to 1/2 cup nuts, riced
        apricots, prunes,
        dates, figs
    1/2 cup chopped cranberries
        plus 2 teaspoons grated
        orange rind
    1/2 cup mashed ripe bananas
        or chopped apples
    1/2 cup very well drained
        crushed pineapple
    6 to 8 slices cooked bacon,
        crumbled

II. Cornell Triple-Rich Formula, 301

III. For other suggestions, see Additions to Yeast Doughs, 301

MUFFINS

    About 2 Dozen 2-Inch Muffins
Please read About Muffins, opposite.
Preheat oven to 400°.
Sift together:

    1 3/4 cups sifted all-purpose
        flour
    3/4 teaspoon salt
    1/4 cup sugar
    2 teaspoons double-acting
        baking powder
Beat in a separate bowl:
    2 eggs
Add to the eggs:

    2 to 4 tablespoons melted
        butter
    3/4 cup milk
Combine the liquid and the dry ingredients with a few swift strokes. Fill well-greased muffin pans two-thirds full and bake 20 to 25 minutes.

SOUR CREAM MUFFINS

    About 2 Dozen 2-Inch Muffins
Please read About Muffins, opposite.
Preheat oven to 400°.
Sift together:

    1 3/4 cups sifted all-purpose
        flour
    1 teaspoon double-acting
        baking powder
    1/2 teaspoon salt
    2 tablespoons sugar
    1/2 teaspoon baking soda
Beat together:
    1 cup cultured sour cream
    1 beaten egg
    2 tablespoons milk or water
▶ To mix and bake, see Muffins, above.

BUTTERMILK MUFFINS

Prepare:
    Sour Cream Muffins, above
Substitute for the sour cream:
    1 cup buttermilk
Add to the milk:
    3 tablespoons melted butter

WHOLE-GRAIN MUFFINS

    Twenty 2-Inch Muffins
Please read About Muffins, opposite.
Preheat oven to 400°.
Combine:

    2/3 cup sifted all-purpose flour
    1 1/3 cups whole-grain flour.
    1 teaspoon salt
    2 teaspoons double-acting
        baking powder

(1/4 cup chopped dates, raisins
or roasted pumpkin seeds)
Beat in a separate bowl:
> 1 **beaten egg**
> 2 **tablespoons molasses or
> honey**
> 1 **cup milk**
> 2 to 3 **teaspoons melted
> butter**
◗ To mix and bake, see Muffins,
345.

BRAN MUFFINS

About Twenty-Two 2-Inch Muffins
These muffins are rather hefty.
Served with cheese, they make excel-
lent picnic companions. Please read
About Muffins, 344.
Preheat oven to 350°.
Combine and stir well:
> 2 **cups all-purpose or whole-
> grain flour**
> 1 1/2 **cups bran**
> 2 **tablespoons sugar**
> 1/4 **teaspoon salt**
> 1 1/4 **teaspoons baking soda**
> (1 to 2 **tablespoons grated
> orange rind**)
Beat:
> 2 **cups buttermilk**
> 1 **beaten egg**
> 1/2 **cup molasses**
> 2 to 4 **tablespoons melted
> butter**
Combine the dry and the liquid ingre-
dients with a few swift strokes. Fold
in, before the dry ingredients are en-
tirely moist:
> 1 **cup nutmeats, or nutmeats
> and raisins combined, or 1
> cup chopped dates**
Bake about 25 minutes.

RICE FLOUR MUFFINS

About Two Dozen 2-Inch Muffins
Please read ◗ About Rice Flour, 215,

and About Muffins, 344. Read the
recipe through before mixing.
Preheat oven to 450°.
Measure into a bowl:
> 1 **cup rice flour**
> 1/2 **teaspoon salt**
> 2 **teaspoons double-acting
> baking powder**
> 1 to 2 **tablespoons sugar**
Melt:
> 2 **tablespoons shortening**
and, when slightly cooled, add it to:
> 1 **well-beaten egg**
> 1 **cup milk**
Mix the dry ingredients well and then
with a few light strokes combine with
the liquid mixture. About 10 strokes
should suffice. The muffins are less
crumbly if you add to them, before
the dry ingredients are completely
moistened:
> 1/8 **cup raisins or 2 tablespoons
> orange or pineapple
> marmalade**
If you include the marmalade, omit
the sugar. Bake 12 to 15 minutes and
serve at once.

COOKED-CEREAL MUFFINS

About Thirty 2-Inch Muffins
A good way of utilizing leftover cere-
als or rice.
Please read About Muffins, 344.
Preheat oven to 400°.
Beat:
> 2 **egg yolks**
Add:
> 1 **cup cooked rice, oatmeal or
> cornmeal**
> 1 1/4 **cups milk**
> 2 **tablespoons melted
> butter**
Sift together:
> 1 1/2 **cups sifted all-purpose
> flour**
> 1 **tablespoon sugar**
> 1/2 **teaspoon salt**

2 teaspoons double-acting
   baking powder
Beat until stiff ◗ but not dry:
   2 egg whites
Combine the liquid and the dry ingredients with a few swift strokes, then
fold in the egg whites. To bake, see
Muffins, 345.

CHEESE MUFFINS

About Thirty-Two 2-Inch Muffins
Please read About Muffins, 344.
Preheat oven to 350°.
Sift together:
   1³⁄₄ cups sifted all-purpose
      flour
   3 teaspoons double-acting
      baking powder
   1 tablespoon sugar
   ¹⁄₂ teaspoon salt
Stir into the sifted ingredients, until
all the particles of cheese have been
separated:
   ¹⁄₂ cup grated American
      cheese
Combine and beat well:
   1 egg
   1 cup milk
   3 tablespoons melted butter
◗ To mix and bake, see Muffins, 345.

PUMPKIN OR YAM MUFFINS

About Twenty-Four 2-Inch Muffins
Prepare:
   Muffins, 345
but add to the dry ingredients:
   ¹⁄₄ cup additional sugar
   1 teaspoon cinnamon
   1 teaspoon nutmeg
Add to the milk mixture:
   1 cup canned pumpkin or 1
      cup cold cooked mashed
      yams
You may add:
   (1 cup chopped pecans)

   (2 teaspoons grated orange
      rind)
Proceed as for Muffins, 345.

BLUEBERRY OR CRANBERRY
MUFFINS

About Thirty 2-Inch Muffins
Please read About Muffins, 344.
Prepare:
   Muffins, 345
use in all:
   ¹⁄₃ cup sugar
   ¹⁄₄ cup melted butter
Fold into the batter, before the dry ingredients are completely moist:
   1 cup fresh blueberries; 1
      cup well-drained canned
      blueberries, lightly floured;
      or 1 cup chopped
      cranberries
   (1 teaspoon grated orange or
      lemon rind)
Proceed as for Muffins, 345.

POPOVERS

About 9 Popovers
Everyone enthusiastically gives us a
favorite popover recipe, and all are
equally enthusiastic, but contradic-
tory, about baking advice. We prefer
a preheated oven, but we know that
starting with a cold oven also works.
Have ready buttered deep muffin or
popover tins. If you use highly glazed
deep custard cups, grease them
lightly and—depending on what you
are serving with the popovers—dust
the cups with sugar, flour or grated
Parmesan cheese. This will give the
batter something to cling to. Have all
ingredients at 70°.
Preheat oven to 450°.
Beat just until smooth:
   1 cup milk
   1 tablespoon melted butter
   1 cup sifted all-purpose flour

¹/₄ teaspoon salt

Add, one at a time, but ◗ do not overbeat:

2 beaten eggs

The batter should be no heavier than whipping cream. Fill the buttered baking cups three-fourths full. Don't overload—too much batter in the pans will give a muffinlike texture. ◗ Bake at once. After 15 minutes, lower the heat ◗ without peeping, to 350° and bake about 20 minutes longer. To test for doneness, remove a popover to be sure the side walls are firm. If not cooked long enough, the popovers will collapse. You may want to insert a sharp paring knife gently into the other popovers to allow the steam to escape, after baking.

CHEESE POPOVERS

Preheat oven to 450°.
Prepare:

Popovers, 347

Grate into a separate bowl:

**¹/₂ cup sharp cheddar or
Parmesan cheese**

Add:

**¹/₈ teaspoon paprika
A few grains cayenne**

Pour 1 scant tablespoon of batter into each cup and cover it with a few teaspoons of cheese and another tablespoon of batter. Bake as directed for Popovers, above.

ABOUT HOT BISCUITS

Now, as in pioneer times, biscuits are popular for the speed with which they can be made. A light hand in kneading gives the treasured flaky result. The amount of liquid called for in the recipe determines whether the biscuit is a rolled or dropped type. The shortening is ◗ cut into the dry ingredients with a pastry blender or

2 knives, until the mixture is the consistency of coarse cornmeal. Make a well in the center of these ingredients. ◗ Pour all the milk or milk and water in at once. Stir cautiously until there is no danger of spilling, then stir vigorously until the dough is fairly free from the sides of the bowl. The time for stirring should be a scant ¹/₂ minute.

Turn the dough onto a lightly floured board. ◗ Knead it gently and quickly for another scant ¹/₂ minute—just long enough so it is neither knobby nor sticky, and the riser is well distributed. If it isn't, or if soda is used in excess, tiny brown spots will show on the surface of the baked biscuits. Roll the dough with a lightly floured rolling pin or pat it gently with the palm of the hand until it has the desired thickness—about ¹/₄ inch is right for the plain biscuit, ¹/₂ inch or less for a tea biscuit and 1 inch or more for shortcake. Cut the dough in typical rounds, with a biscuit cutter that has been lightly dipped in flour. ◗ Do not twist the cutter.

There are many other ways to shape biscuit dough. For easy filled biscuits, pat out 2 thin squares of dough. Put a filling on the first. Cover with the second. Glaze the top with milk. Cut into smaller squares. For a breakfast ring, see Quick Drop Biscuits, opposite. Make Biscuit Easter Bunnies for the children, 351. You may also place small rounds of dough on top of a casserole. Or cut dough in sticks for hors d'oeuvre or fill as for Pinwheels, 317. Use a spatula to place these on an ungreased baking sheet.

For a brown finish, brush the tops of the biscuits with milk or butter. Place biscuits 1 inch apart if you like them crusty all over, close together if not. Bake in a ◗ 450° preheated oven

12 to 15 minutes, depending on their thickness.

▲ At high altitude, baking powder biscuits should require no adjustment of leavening.

ADDITIONS TO BISCUITS

Biscuit flavors are easily varied to suit the menu. Dust them, before baking, with:

Cinnamon and sugar

or, just before they are finished, with:

Grated Parmesan and paprika

Or, press into the top center:

1 **lump sugar**

soaked in:

Orange juice

Or incorporate into the dough of any of the following biscuit recipes:

2 **tablespoons finely chopped parsley or chives, or**
2 **teaspoons finely chopped fresh sage, or** 1/3 **cup crumbled Roquefort or grated cheddar cheese**
3 **to 6 slices cooked, crumbled bacon, or**
3 **tablespoons chopped cooked ham, or**
4 **tablespoons sautéed chopped onions**

Prepare them like rissoles, placing between the layers one of the following:

1 **cup sugared fresh strawberries, raspberries or blueberries**
1/4 **cup nuts, dates or dried figs**
1/2 **cup raisins or currants**
1 **cup cooked, ground and seasoned poultry, sausage, ham or other meat**

ROLLED BISCUITS

About Twenty-Four 1½-Inch Biscuits

◆ Please read About Hot Biscuits, opposite.

Preheat oven to 450°.

Sift together into a large bowl:

1¾ **cups sifted all-purpose flour**
1/2 **teaspoon salt**
3 **teaspoons double-acting baking powder**

Add:

4 **to 6 tablespoons chilled butter or shortening or a combination of both**

Cut solid shortening into dry ingredients as directed above, then make a well in the center. Add, all at once:

3/4 **cup milk**

Stir until the dough is fairly free from the sides of the bowl. Turn the dough onto a lightly floured board. Knead gently and quickly, making about eight to ten folds. Roll with a lightly floured rolling pin, until the dough has the desired thickness. Cut with a biscuit cutter dipped in a very little flour. Brush the tops with:

(Milk or melted butter)

Place on an ungreased baking sheet. Bake until lightly browned—12 to 15 minutes.

QUICK DROP BISCUITS

No kneading or rolling is necessary in these two recipes. The biscuits are very palatable but less shapely, unless you drop them into muffin tins. For a good breakfast ring, prepare I, 350. Form the dough into 2 balls; roll them in melted butter. Place them in a 7-inch ring mold, into the bottom of which you have poured Caramel Roll Topping, 503. Bake at 400° about 25 minutes.

I. Preheat oven to 450°.
Prepare:

Rolled Biscuits, 349

using in all:

1 cup milk

❧ Stir the dough 1 scant minute. Drop from a spoon onto an ungreased sheet and bake 12 to 15 minutes or until lightly browned.

II.   About Twenty-Four
                  1½-Inch Biscuits

When you are obliged to use oil, it is preferable to flavor the biscuit highly. See Additions to Biscuits, 349.
Preheat oven to 475°.
Sift into a bowl:

**2 cups sifted all-purpose
     flour**
**3 teaspoons double-acting
     baking powder**
1 teaspoon salt

Pour over the top, all at once, without mixing:

⅓ cup vegetable oil
⅔ cup milk

Stir with a fork until the mixture readily leaves the sides of the bowl. Drop from a spoon onto an ungreased sheet. Bake 10 to 12 minutes.

FLUFFY BISCUITS OR SHORTCAKE DOUGH

                    About Twenty-Four
                       ½-Inch Biscuits

For other shortcakes, see Index. ❧ To mix, see About Hot Biscuits, 348.
Prepare:

Rolled Biscuits, 349

but add:

1 tablespoon sugar
½ teaspoon salt

and you may use cream instead of milk for added richness.

WHOLE WHEAT BISCUITS

                    About Twenty-Four
                       ½-Inch Biscuits

Preheat oven to 400°.
Sift together:

⅞ cup sifted all-purpose flour
**2 teaspoons double-acting
     baking powder**
½ teaspoon baking soda
2 teaspoons sugar
¾ teaspoon salt

Add and mix well:

1 cup whole wheat flour

Cut into the flour with a pastry blender:

⅓ cup butter or shortening

When the mixture has a fine-crumb consistency, stir in with a fork:

**1 cup cultured sour cream or
     buttermilk**

Turn out onto a floured board and proceed as for Rolled Biscuits, 349.

BISCUIT EASTER BUNNIES

Preheat oven to 425°.
Prepare:

Fluffy Biscuits, opposite

Pat or roll out the dough to the thickness of ½ inch. Cut it out with 3 sizes of cutters: 1—large, about 3 inches; 2—half as large; and 3—one-fourth as large. Assemble your bunnies as sketched below. Use the large biscuit for the body, the second one for the head, and roll the third one into a ball for the tail. Flatten two of the second-size biscuits slightly and shape them into ovals for the ears. Place the bunnies on a greased sheet. Bake about 15 minutes or until done.

PINWHEEL BISCUITS

Use this same form also for other fillings such as cooked meat or cheese.
Preheat oven to 450°.

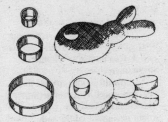

Prepare any:

Rolled biscuit dough

Roll it to the thickness of ¹/₂ inch. Spread the surface with:

¹/₄ **cup soft butter**
³/₄ **cup brown sugar**
(Chopped nuts)
(Chopped raisins)

Roll the dough like a Jelly Roll, 440, but rather loosely. Cut into 1-inch slices. Lift them carefully with a pancake turner onto a lightly greased cookie sheet. Bake about 12 minutes.

BISCUIT STICKS

Prepare dough for:

Rolled Biscuits, 349

Cut it into sticks ¹/₂ × ¹/₂ × 3 inches. Brush the sticks with:

Melted butter

Bake as directed but for a shorter period. Then to serve stack them log-cabin fashion.

BUTTERMILK BISCUITS

**About Twenty-Four
¹/₂-Inch Biscuits**

Because of the sour milk and soda, this recipe has a very tender dough.
▶ To mix, please read About Hot Biscuits, 348.

Preheat oven to 450°.

Sift together into a mixing bowl:

1³/₄ **cups sifted all-purpose
flour**

¹/₂ **teaspoon salt**
2 **teaspoons double-acting
baking powder**
1 **teaspoon sugar**
¹/₂ **teaspoon baking soda**

Cut in:

¹/₄ **cup lard or 5 tablespoons
butter**

Add and lightly mix:

³/₄ **cup buttermilk**

Turn the dough onto a floured board. Knead it gently for ¹/₂ minute. Pat the dough to the thickness of ¹/₄ inch. Cut with a biscuit cutter. Bake 10 to 12 minutes.

▤ GRIDDLE BISCUITS

Prepare any:

Rolled biscuit dough

Cook the biscuits on a lightly greased hot griddle, 1 inch apart. Brown them on one side 5 to 7 minutes; turn and brown them on the other side for the same length of time.

BEATEN BISCUITS

About Forty-Four ¹/₂-Inch Biscuits

To win unending gratitude, serve to any homesick southerner this classic accompaniment to Virginia ham. The following lines by Miss Howard Weeden in *Bandanna Ballads* sum up in a nutshell the art of making biscuits:

"O course I'll gladly give de rule
    I meks beat biscuit by,
Dough I ain't sure dat you will mek
    Dat bread de same as I.

" 'Case cookin's like religion is—
    Some's 'lected an' some ain't,
An' rules don't no more mek a cook
    Den sermons mek a saint."

Sift 3 times:

1 **tablespoon sugar**

4 cups all-purpose flour
1 teaspoon salt
(1 teaspoon double-acting
   baking powder)

Cut into the flour, with a pastry blender or 2 knives:

1/4 cup chilled leaf lard

When ingredients are the consistency of cornmeal, add to make a stiff dough:

**Equal parts of chilled milk
and ice water, approximately
1 cup in all**

Beat the dough with a mallet until it is well blistered, or put it 10 times through the coarse chopper of a meat grinder. Fold it over frequently. This is a long process, requiring 1/2 hour or more.

Miss Weeden's verse goes on to say:

"Two hundred licks is what I gives
   for home-folks, never fewer,
An' if I'm 'specting company in,
I gives five hundred sure!"

If you make these often, it might be worth investing in a biscuit machine, available from a bakers' supply company. When the dough is smooth and glossy, roll it to the thickness of 1/2 inch and cut it with a floured biscuit cutter. Spread the tops with:

Melted butter

Pierce through the biscuits with a fork. Bake about 30 minutes in a preheated 325° oven.

SHIP'S BISCUITS

**About Twenty-Four
1/2-Inch Biscuits**

These are really a simpler version of Beaten Biscuits, above. The longer they are folded and beaten, the better the results, so let the children work out with them.
Preheat oven to 325°.

Mix:

2 cups all-purpose flour
1/2 teaspoon salt

Work in with the fingertips:

1 teaspoon shortening

Stir in to make a very stiff dough:

About 1/2 cup water

Beat this dough to a 1/2-inch thinness with a mallet. Fold it into 6 layers. Beat it thin again and refold 5 or 6 times until the dough is very elastic. Before cutting with a floured biscuit cutter, roll to 1/2 inch again. Bake about 30 minutes and store tightly covered.

SCONES

About 12 Scones

These are richer than ordinary biscuits because of the addition of cream and eggs. Fine with a light luncheon.
Preheat oven to 450°.
Sift together into a large bowl:

1 3/4 cups sifted all-purpose
   flour
2 1/4 teaspoons double-acting
   baking powder
1 tablespoon sugar
1/2 teaspoon salt

Cut into these ingredients, until the size of small peas, using a pastry blender or 2 knives:

1/4 cup cold butter

Beat in a separate bowl:

2 eggs

Reserve 2 tablespoons of this mixture. Add to the remainder and beat in:

1/3 cup cream

Make a well in the dry ingredients. Pour the liquid into it. Combine with a few swift strokes. Handle the dough as little as possible. Place it on a lightly floured board. Pat until 3/4 inch thick. Cut with a knife into diamond shapes or Biscuit Sticks, 351. Brush with the reserved egg and sprinkle with:

Salt or sugar

Bake about 15 minutes.

BIRTHDAY BREAD HORSE

As our children have always demanded a piece of their birthday cake for breakfast, we concocted a bread horse to be supplemented later in the day by the candlelighted cake of richer content. This also makes a good Christmas or Fourth of July breakfast decoration.

You will need a well-rounded loaf of bread—a log-shaped Cinnamon Loaf, 303, is fine—plus an oval bun or roll about 2½ × 3½ inches; 2 braided rolls about 1 × 3½ inches; 5 peppermint candy sticks 1 × 8 inches; 2 raisins, 2 almonds and a piece of cherry or a redhot. Use the loaf for the body. Mount it on four of the candy sticks. Break off about a third or less of the fifth candy stick. Use it for the neck. Stick it into one end of the loaf at an angle. Put the oval roll on the other end or the head. Use the braided rolls for the mane and tail, the raisins for eyes, the almonds for ears, and the piece of cherry for the lips. Bed the horse on leaves or grass. Add a ribbon bridle to keep this mad steed under some sort of control.

ABOUT USES FOR READY-BAKED AND LEFTOVER BREADS, CAKES AND CRACKERS

A bread surplus can be put to many good uses—so don't throw a piece away! It can be used for Melba Toast, 355; for Stuffings, (I, 430); as a thickener in soups, see Panades, (I, 146); and for a sauce, see Bread Sauce, (I, 387). For other uses, see About Crumbs, 218; and don't forget good old Bread Pudding, 534.

Many recipes in **Joy** call for dry bread, cracker or cake crumbs. In fact, dry cake crumbs are so prized that commercial bakeries make sheets of cake solely for this purpose.

PUFFED BREAD BLOCKS

About Thirty ½-Inch Blocks

These may be prepared in advance. Keep at room temperature until soft, then blend well:

   ½ lb. cheddar cheese
   ¼ lb. butter: 1 stick

Season palatably with:

   Mustard
   Curry powder
   Caraway or celery seed
   Salt and pepper or paprika

Cut into 1½ × ¾ × ¾-inch blocks:

   Fresh bread

Cover blocks with the cheese spread. Keep them chilled until ready for use. Pop them into a 375° oven. They should brown lightly and puff.

CHEESE OR BUTTER BREAD CUBES

Serve hot as an appetizer. Also good with soup or salads.

I. Preheat oven to 375°.
Beat together:

1 egg
1½ tablespoons melted butter
Cut into cubes or blocks of any size:
>   Fresh bread
Roll the cubes in the egg mixture, then in:
>   Finely shredded American
>   cheese
>   Salt and cayenne or
>   paprika
Toast the cubes on a buttered sheet until the cheese is melted.

II. Preheat oven to 375°.
Spread bread cubes with a paste made of:
>   Butter
>   Grated Parmesan cheese
>   Caraway or celery seed
>   Salt and a few grains
>   cayenne
>   (Mustard)
Toast and serve, as above.

MELBA CHEESE ROUNDS

Especially good with Onion Soup, (I, 133).
Spread:
>   Melba Toast rounds, 355
lightly with:
>   Butter
Sprinkle generously with:
>   Grated Parmesan cheese
Just before using, run them under a broiler until toasted. Serve at once, floating one or two on top of the soup.

SEEDED CRACKERS

Brush:
>   Small crisp salt crackers
with:
>   Melted butter or partially
>   beaten egg white
Sprinkle lightly with:
>   Caraway, celery or sesame
>   seeds
Toast and serve.

TOASTED BUTTERED BREAD LOAF OR GARLIC BREAD

Preheat oven to 350°.
Slice thick or thin to taste:
>   A medium-sized loaf of
>   bread or
>   French bread
Do not slice it all the way through; leave the bottom crust intact. With a pastry brush spread the top and sides of each piece, using in all:
>   ½ cup melted butter
The butter may be flavored with:
>   (A minced clove of garlic)
>   (Herbs: basil, marjoram,
>   oregano, etc.)
You may also crush 2 cloves of garlic with a little salt, until smooth. Spread a little on each slice. Follow with melted butter as shown above. Separate the slices slightly, so that the butter will be evenly distributed. Cover the loaf with a piece of foil. Place it in the oven until the bread is light brown, about 20 minutes. Serve immediately on a napkined platter.

QUICK CINNAMON LOAF

Slice a loaf of:
>   French or Vienna bread
and spread it, as illustrated above, with the following mixture, baking 8 minutes in a 400° oven:
>   ⅓ cup melted butter
>   ⅓ cup white or light brown
>   sugar
>   2 teaspoons cinnamon

A grating of nutmeg
1/4 teaspoon grated lemon peel

applesauce flavored with cinnamon and cloves, or with maple syrup.

CINNAMON TOAST OR STICKS

Remove the crusts from bread. Spread the tops of:

Thin bread slices

or spread all 4 sides of:

3/4-inch bread sticks

with the mixture for:

Quick Cinnamon Loaf, opposite

You may sprinkle the bread sticks with:

(Rum)

Place the slices or strips in a 400° oven about 8 minutes. Be sure to toast the sticks on all sides. You may also place them under a broiler to crisp them. Applesauce is a good complement to this dish.

FRENCH TOAST

4 Servings

Beat slightly:

4 eggs

Add:

1/2 teaspoon salt
1 cup milk

Flavor with:

**(1/2 teaspoon vanilla or
1 tablespoon rum)**

Dip into this mixture:

8 slices bread

The bread may be cut in rounds with a doughnut cutter. Brown the bread, each side, on a hot, well-buttered griddle. Serve hot sprinkled with:

Sugar
Cinnamon

Garnish the cooked rounds with:

Bright red jelly

or serve with pie cherries, sweetened, slightly thickened with cornstarch, 214, and flavored with lemon; with

MELBA TOAST

Preferable to use dry bread.
Cut into the thinnest possible slices:

White or other bread

Remove crusts. Place bread in a 250° oven. Leave it in until it becomes crisp and a light golden brown and until all the moisture is withdrawn.

HONEY BUTTER TOAST

Prepare:

Honey butter, 571

Spread it on a slice of bread. Cover with another slice. Cut the bread into 1-inch strips. Toast the strips on both sides under a broiler. Serve sprinkled with:

Cinnamon

ORANGE TOAST

Very nice with tea.
Combine:

Grated rind of 1 orange
1/4 cup orange juice
1/2 cup sugar

Cut:

6 slices of bread

Remove the crusts and toast the bread. Spread it, while hot, with:

Butter

Cover it with the orange mixture. Put the toast in the oven or under a broiler, just long enough to brown the tops lightly.

ZWIEBACK, RUSKS OR TWICE-BAKED BREAD

Bake:

White Bread Plus, 302

using in all 2 eggs. Replace the 2 cups of water with 2 cups of milk.

The finished loaf should be just half as high as a normal loaf of bread, so bake in six rather than three pans. Maybe this shape was evolved to suit baby mouths, for no one enjoys this confection more than the very, very young. When the bread is cool, cut it into ½-inch slices and toast as for Melba Toast, above. You may want to glaze it before toasting with:

Lemon Glaze, 504

In the slow heat of the oven, this turns a golden brown.

PIES AND PASTRIES

At home and abroad, Americans boast about pie. It has apparently always been so; way back in the clipper era, sailors brought home not only heart-shaped boxes crusted over with tiny rare shells but the pie-jaggers they had carved to while away the doldrum days in *outre-mer.* These implements of bone, often furnished with as many as three wheels but marvelously precise all the same, sped the fancy cutting of lattice over succulent apple pies such as that shown above, lower left. Ingenious French cooks form delicate swans, shown both unbaked and assembled, lower right; or the monumental croquembouche shimmering with glaze at the right rear. Whatever the nation, skill in pastry making has been regarded worldwide as a passport to matrimony. In Hungarian villages, for example, no girl was considered eligible until her strudel dough had become so translucent that her beloved could read the newspaper through it.

First let's consider what makes for success with pastry doughs:

◗ Handle pie dough lightly, for two reasons: to incorporate as much air as possible and to inhibit the development of gluten. The aim here is a flaky and tender crust.

◗ Measure carefully—too much flour toughens pastry; too much liquid makes it soggy; too much shortening makes doughs greasy and crumbly.

◗ Chilling pastry dough, covered, up to 12 hours after mixing tenderizes it, keeps it from shrinking during baking, and makes it easier to handle. Be sure to remove the dough from the refrigerator at least one hour before shaping; otherwise you will be obliged to overhandle it. Pinch off just enough dough for one pie shell. Press it into the approximate shape needed. Roll as lightly and as little as possible, following the directions on 358. Closely covered pie dough will hold for a week or more in the refrigerator.

▶ Choose nonshiny pie pans for good browning. ▶ Always start the baking in a preheated oven. The contrast between the coolness of the dough and the heat of the oven causes rapid air expansion and contributes to the desired lightness of the texture. For various pie doughs, see 360.

▲ In making pies at high altitudes, where evaporation is greater, you may find that you achieve better results if you add a trifle more liquid.

Many pie doughs ✻ freeze well. ▶ It is better to shape them before freezing. See Freezing Baked Pies, 660, and Freezing Unbaked Pies, 659.

ROLLING PIE DOUGH

If the dough has been refrigerated, bring to room temperature before rolling. To make 2 pie shells or a double-crust pie, divide the dough evenly before rolling it. A pastry cloth and roller stocking are highly recommended. They practically do away with sticking and require the use of very little additional flour. Next to the pastry cloth, your best bet is a large wooden board. If you use either of the above methods, flour the rolling surface and the rolling pin lightly.

As to the roller, whether it's a French broomstick-type, a bottle, or the revolving type, as shown in the drawings, the important thing is how you use it. ▶ Roll the dough from the center out. Lift the roller. Do not push it to and fro, which stretches the dough. Roll the dough to a 1/8-inch thickness or less. Should it have a few tears, patch them carefully rather than trying to reroll.

CUTTING AND FORMING PIE DOUGH

To cut pie dough, allow a piece about 2 inches larger than pan dimensions, seen next page, to take care of inevitable shrinkage. It is fun to cut fancy edges on the top crust with a pastry wheel.

To form the crust, have ready a 9-inch pie pan. It's a poor pie crust that requires a greased pan, but buttering will help brown the bottom of the crust. Loosen the pastry from the board, fold it in half, lift it, lay the fold across the center of the pan and unfold it; or, after rolling it around the rolling pin, unroll it onto the pan, seen opposite, where this method is being used to form a top crust.

Ease the dough into the pan loosely, but press it in place so that no air will be left between dough and pan to form blisters in baking. You may cut a small square of dough, form it into a ball, dip it in flour and use it to press the dough down and shape it against the pan. Trim off the excess with a knife, using an easy slashing motion against the edge of the pan; or use scissors. Trimmings can be given to the children for play dough or baked up into bits for hors d'oeuvre or small pastries.

ABOUT CRUSTS FOR FILLED PIES

For crusts which are to be baked with fillings, use a deep pie pan with a wide channeled rim to catch any juices. For a one-crust pie, make a fluted edge with the dough that laps over, or build up a rim with a strip of pastry. Full it on by using a fork to press it down; or pinch it with the thumb and forefinger, as shown opposite on the right. This edge is im-

To weave, place half of the strips from left to right over the pie about ¾ inch apart. Fold back every other strip halfway, as shown below. Place a strip across the unfolded strips from front to back. Unfold the strips. Fold back the alternates. Place the next strip ¾ inch from the last. Continue until half of the pie is latticed. Then repeat the process, beginning on the other side of the center line.

When the whole pie is latticed, attach the strips to the pie edge loosely to allow for shrinkage. Moisten the ends slightly to make them stick. Cut them off before crimping the pie. We like to sprinkle a tablespoon of granulated sugar over the latticed dough before baking.

For a solid top crust, cut the rolled ⅛-inch-thick dough 1 inch larger than the pan. To allow the steam to escape, prick it with a fork in several places, double it over and gash it along the fold, or make fancy patterns with whatever cutting tool you like. Place the top crust on the pie. Full in the surplus dough and press it down around the edges with a fork. Or you may tuck it under the lower crust and press it around the edge with a fork.

portant, as it will help to hold the juices in the pie. Do not prick the lower crust. If the filling for the pie is the juicy kind, first brush the bottom crust lightly with the white of an egg, melted butter or a light sprinkling of flour. Any of these will keep the crust from becoming soggy. Putting the filling in very hot helps, too.

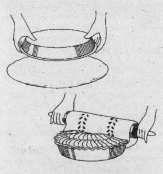

There are many attractive ways to make the lattice. You may cut plain ½-inch strips with a knife or pink them with a jagger. Or you may roll, then twist ½-inch ropelike pieces and weave any of these together or place them crisscross.

If you prefer, after sealing the edges by pressing with a fork, you may make a vent with a one-inch hollow tube of dough—3 inches high—

only partially sunk into a hole in the center of the upper crust. Support it with a round border of fulled-on dough which will hide any discoloration from juices bubbling over when you cut the vent down to the decorative support after the baking. Should any juice spill over onto the oven, sprinkle it with salt to prevent smoke and smell.

For baking filled pies, note directions in each recipe and preheat the oven to the correct temperature. Should the edge of a pie tend to brown too quickly, place a protective rim of foil lightly over it.

ABOUT CRUSTS FOR UNFILLED PIES

If the pie shell is to be baked without filling, or as the English say "blind," ◗ prick the dough generously with a fork after you have placed it in the pie pan, line it with foil or parchment paper, and weight it with dry beans or, as they do in France, with small clean round pebbles. This keeps it from heaving and baking unevenly. Remove the beans or pebbles a few minutes before the baking period is over. To cut a round for a prebaked top crust, prick it and bake it on a baking sheet.

When making individual pies, use an inverted muffin tin or, for deeper shells, inverted custard cups. Cut the rounds of dough 4 1/2 or 5 1/2 inches in diameter and fit them over the cups; or, with the help of foil as a support, create your own fancy shapes—fluted cups, simple tricornes, long barquettes. You may even make your tarts into baskets by forming handles with strips of dough molded over inverted custard cups. When baked, sink the handles into the filling just before serving. ◗ Prick the shells be-

fore baking. When you fill baked shells, spoon the filling in carefully.

Unfilled crusts may be protected from overbrowning by setting the pie pan into a larger pan or, as with filled pies, by covering the edge of the dough with a strip of aluminum foil. To glaze pie crust, giving it added flavor or color, see pages 503–504. Keep in mind, however, that glazes also tend to toughen crusts.

Baking time will vary according to the material of which the pan is made. ◗ If it is ovenproof glass or enamelware, cut the baking time indicated by one-fifth to one-fourth. When tins are used, those that are perforated, have lost their shininess, or have a base of screen material are helpful for producing a well-browned crust.

Unfilled shells, whether for individual or big pies, are baked in a preheated 450° oven, unless otherwise noted, 10 to 12 minutes or until lightly browned. Cool them before filling.

BASIC PIE DOUGH

For a double-crust 9-inch, or a single-crust pie with a generous lattice, use the following amounts. For a one-crust 9-inch pie, use half the recipe.
Sift together:

    2 cups all-purpose flour
    1 teaspoon salt
Measure and combine:
    2/3 cup chilled leaf lard or
        shortening
    2 tablespoons chilled butter
Cut half of the shortening into the flour mixture with a pastry blender, or work it in lightly with the tips of your fingers until it has the grain of cornmeal. Cut the remaining half

coarsely into the dough until it is pea size. Sprinkle the dough with:

4 tablespoons water

♦ Blend the water lightly into the dough. You may lift the ingredients with a fork, allowing the moisture to spread. If needed to hold the ingredients together, add:

1 teaspoon to 1 tablespoon water

When you can gather the dough up into a tidy ball, as shown 359, stop handling it. To fill and bake, see individual recipes. For a baked shell, see About Crusts for Unfilled Pies, opposite.

PIE DOUGH COCKAIGNE

A 9-Inch Double-Crust

A dough that refrigerates well after baking and reheats to perfection. Sift together:

2 cups all-purpose flour
1 teaspoon salt
2 teaspoons sugar

Measure and combine:

¼ cup butter
3 tablespoons shortening

Cut half the shortening into the flour mixture until it has the grain of cornmeal. Cut in the remaining half until it is pea-sized. Sprinkle the dough with:

5 tablespoons water

Proceed as for Basic Pie Dough, above.

MIXER PIE DOUGH

Using the ingredients and proportions for:

Basic Pie Dough, above

place in a large mixer bowl the flour, salt and shortening. Scraping the bowl constantly, blend at low speed 1 minute. Add the water. Mix about 10 seconds longer, or until the dough begins to cling to the beaters. Should the dough be too crumbly, incorporate 1 teaspoon to 1 tablespoon water with your hands so that the dough forms into a ball. To bake, see individual recipes. For a baked shell, see About Crusts for Unfilled Pies, opposite.

FLOUR PASTE PIE DOUGH

A 9-Inch Double-Crust

Sift into a bowl:

2 cups all-purpose flour
1 teaspoon salt

Remove ⅓ cup of this mixture and place it in a small bowl or cup. Stir into it, to form a smooth paste:

¼ cup water

Cut into the flour mixture in the first bowl with a pastry blender until the grain is the size of small peas:

⅔ cup chilled shortening

Stir the flour paste into the dough. Work it with your hand until well incorporated and the dough forms a ball. To bake, see individual recipes.

PAT-IN-THE-PAN OIL PIE DOUGH

Two 9-Inch Pie Shells or 8 Tarts

The oil gives this variant a somewhat mealy rather than a flaky texture. The shell must be baked before filling. Sift into a mixing bowl:

2 cups all-purpose flour
1¼ teaspoons salt

Mix in a cup until creamy:

⅔ cup cooking oil
3 tablespoons cold milk

Pour the mixture over the flour all at once. Stir these ingredients lightly with a fork until blended. Form them into a crust, right in the pan, by patting out the dough with a spoon, or you may roll the dough between 2 sheets of waxed paper. When ready, remove the top paper, reverse the crust into the pie pan and then remove the other paper. After pricking sides and bottom, bake 12 to 15 minutes, in a preheated 475° oven. Cool before filling.

WHEATLESS PIE DOUGH

A 9-Inch Single-Crust

This crust must be baked before filling.
◗ Sift 3 times:

    1/2 cup cornstarch
    1/2 cup finely milled rye flour

The repeated sifting is very important. Work the flour mixture as for pastry with:

    1/2 cup fine dry cottage cheese
    1/2 cup chilled butter
    1/2 teaspoon salt

Chill the dough at least 2 hours. Pat into the pan. Prick bottom and sides well and bake in a preheated 425° oven 12 to 15 minutes.

ABOUT PASTRY FOR MEATS

For meat pies, rissoles or turnovers, see About Meat Pies, (I, 557); for Meat en Croûte, see (I, 556); for Crust or Pâte for Pâtés, see (I, 630).

PÂTE BRISÉE

A 9-Inch Pie Shell

This short French pie dough has a remarkable way of withstanding a moist filling, and is best used for meat pies and pâtés. If you want a dessert crust, see Pâte Sucrée, opposite. The recipe can be doubled or tripled and stored refrigerated for a week or more before baking.
Work:

    1/2 cup chilled butter plus

    3 tablespoons lard or
        vegetable shortening

very lightly into:

    2 cups all-purpose flour
    1/2 teaspoon salt

This can be done best by working the flour and butter first with the fingers and then lightly and quickly rotating it between the palms of the hands. Make a well, 366, of the crumbly flour mixture. Pour in gradually:

    5 to 6 tablespoons cold
        water

The index finger is used to stir the liquid ◗ quickly into the flour, in a spiral fashion, beginning at the inside of the well and gradually moving to the outer edge. The dough should be soft enough to gather up into a ball but should not stick to the fingers or the board. ◗ Allow the dough to rest refrigerated from 2 to 36 hours. Cover it with a damp, wrung-out cloth for the shorter period or a piece of foil for the longer one. The resting of the dough breaks any rubbery reactions it might develop when rolled and handled. To roll, shape and bake, see 358.

VIENNA PASTRY

Eight 3-Inch Tarts

Delicious as tart shells, turnovers or thin wafers served with soup or salad.
Sift together:

    1 cup all-purpose flour
    1/4 teaspoon salt

Cut into these ingredients with a pastry blender:

    1/2 cup chilled butter
    4 1/2 oz. soft cream cheese

When these ingredients are well blended, wrap the dough in foil and refrigerate for at least 12 hours. In readying for use, roll to 1/8-inch thickness, adding as little flour as possible.

I. To use as tarts, form pastry over inverted muffin tins and bake at 450° for about 12 minutes.

II. To use as turnovers, see (I, 238).

III. To use as wafers, roll and cut the dough into rounds or put it directly into a cookie press without rolling. Before baking, dot with sesame or poppy seed. Bake 8 to 10 minutes at 450°.

PASTRY FOR CHEESE STRAWS OR WAFERS

4 Dozen

These keep for weeks in a refrigerator or freezer and are quickly sliced and baked for the unexpected guest. Or just after mixing put the dough in a pastry tube to make straws. Or use the 1½-inch ribbon disk on a cookie press to make ribbons. Cut into 2-inch lengths.
Preheat oven to 425°.
Grate or grind:

    ¼ to ½ lb. aged cheddar cheese

Combine with:

    3 to 4 tablespoons soft butter
    ¾ cup all-purpose flour
    (1 teaspoon Worcestershire sauce)
    ½ teaspoon salt
    Dash of hot pepper sauce

Form the dough into 1-inch rolls. Wrap in foil and refrigerate or freeze till cold enough to slice as thin as possible, under a quarter of an inch. Bake in a preheated 475° oven about 12 minutes.

RICH EGG TART DOUGH, PÂTE SUCRÉE OR MÜRBETEIG

Six 3-Inch Tart Shells

There are many versions of this paste, varying in richness and sweetness. This one makes a very tender paste for fresh fruit fillings. For a sweeter dough, use Roll Cookie dough, 472.
Combine:

    1 cup all-purpose flour
    2 tablespoons sugar
    ½ teaspoon salt

Work into it as you would for pastry, using a pastry blender or the tips of your fingers:

    6 tablespoons softened butter

Make a well, 366, and add:

    1 egg yolk
    ½ teaspoon vanilla
    1 tablespoon lemon juice or water

Stir with your fingers until the mixture forms one blended ball and no longer adheres to your hands. Cover it and refrigerate for at least 30 minutes. Roll to ⅛-inch thickness as for pie dough, see 358. Line the tart pans with this dough. Prick and weight down with beans or pebbles, see 360. Bake in a 400° oven 7 to 10 minutes or until lightly browned. Unmold the pastry shells and cool on a rack. Fill with fresh fruit. Glaze with:

    Melted, cooled Currant or Apricot Glaze, 505

Garnish with:

    (Whipped cream)

ABOUT GALETTE DOUGH

Fifty million Frenchmen can't be wrong; but it is hard to get any two of them to agree on the exact formula for this classic pastry. In some regions, galette is almost like a Kuchen dough. Perhaps the most famous is Galette des Rois, served on Twelfth Night. Regardless of the material used, the "Kings' Galette" has a dried bean baked in it, which is expected to bring good fortune to the guest who gets the lucky slice.

Our version of galette which, we hope, will merit majority approval is a well-pricked Rough Puff Paste, 369, rolled to 1-inch thickness and coated with a heavy French Egg Wash glaze, 503. ◗ Keep the glaze on the top surface only, for if it runs over the edge it will solidify early in the baking and prevent the dough from puffing as it should.

An alternative is to use a yeast coffee cake dough. After the last rising, pat it out thin and make a rim by pinching the dough edges all around. Put the fruit in the depression and cover it with a Streusel, 502. Bake as directed for bread. You may, as the cake cools, cover it with Apricot Glaze, 505. A less time-consuming and, we think, quite delicious solution is simply to bake Apple, Peach or Plum Cake Cockaigne, 393.

ABOUT COOKIE AND KUCHEN CRUSTS

If another type of sweet crust is desired, try Roll Cookie dough, 472. There are many, many forms of fruit Kuchen; see Apple, Plum or Peach Cake Cockaigne, 393, French Apple Cake, 394, Quick Sour Cream Coffee Cake, 339. For less sweet versions, try fruit toppings on raised coffee cake doughs, 327–331.

CHEESECAKE CRUSTS

To Line a 10-Inch Pan
This crust works well if filled before baking with dry cheesecake fillings such as Ricotta, 392.
Sift together:

    2 cups all-purpose flour
    ¹/₄ teaspoon salt
Work in with a pastry blender:
    ¹/₂ cup chilled butter
Gradually add:

    1¹/₂ to 2 tablespoons brandy
    4 tablespoons water
Mix as for pie dough. 357. Chill about 30 minutes before rolling to line the pan. Roll about ¹/₈ inch thick and, after filling, bake as directed under individual cheesecakes, 391–392.

SUGGESTED ADDITIONS TO CRUSTS

Vary your favorite basic pie crust by adding before rolling, for a double crust, one of the following sweet or savory additions that will enhance the filling:

    1 to 3 teaspoons poppy or caraway seed
    1 to 3 tablespoons toasted sesame seed
    ¹/₄ to ¹/₂ cup finely chopped nuts
    ¹/₄ to ¹/₃ cup grated aged cheese
    2 tablespoons confectioners' sugar or 1 tablespoon sugar
    ¹/₄ to ¹/₂ teaspoon cinnamon and/or nutmeg
    1 teaspoon grated citrus rind
    2 tablespoons cocoa

ABOUT CRUMB CRUSTS

These, mixed and patted into the pan, are a shortcut to pie making. An easy way to form them is first to place the crumb mixture in a pie pan, distributing the crumbs fairly evenly. Now press another pie pan of the same diameter firmly into the dough. When the top pan is removed, presto!—a crust of even thickness underneath. Trim any excess that is forced to the top edge.

Crumb crusts need not be baked before filling ◗ but, if used unbaked, must be first chilled thoroughly or the filling will immediately disintegrate the crust. If baked before filling, they require a 350° oven for about 10 minutes. ◗ It is best to cool the empty baked shell before filling.

Fill a prebaked shell with chiffon fillings, Bavarian creams or gelatin whips topped with sweetened whipped cream, or with custard or fruit filling, which may be covered with a high Meringue, 502.

GRAHAM CRACKER, ZWIEBACK OR COOKIE CRUMB CRUST

A 9-Inch Single-Crust and Topping
Crush or grind fine, or crumb in a 🗲 blender as directed until very fine:

    1½ cups crumbs of graham
        crackers, zwieback, vanilla
        or chocolate wafers, or
        gingersnaps, 218.

The flavor of the filling should determine which of the above to use. Stir into the crumbs until well blended:

    ¼ to ½ cup sifted
        confectioners' sugar
    6 tablespoons melted butter
    (1 teaspoon cinnamon)

Reserve 2 to 3 tablespoons of the crumb mixture. Pat the rest into the pan or press out to the desired thickness. To form the shell and bake, see About Crumb Crusts, opposite. When the pie is filled, scatter the reserved crumbs as a topping.

BREAD OR CAKE CRUMB CRUST

           A 9-Inch Single-Crust
A good way, this, of utilizing dry bread or cake. To be successful, the crust must be fully baked before filling.
To form the shell and bake, see About Crumb Crusts, opposite. Follow the rule for Graham Cracker Crust, above.

Substitute for the graham cracker or zwieback crumbs:

    1½ cups toasted fine bread or
        cake crumbs
    (6 tablespoons ground
        unbleached almonds)

If you use cake crumbs, omit sugar.

CEREAL PIE CRUST

           A 9-Inch Single-Crust
To form the shell and bake, see About Crumb Crusts, opposite. For a quick cereal ring mold, see 439. Roll or grind:

    6 cups flaked- or puffed-type
        breakfast cereal

There should be 1½ cups after crushing. Combine with:

    ½ cup melted butter
    ¼ cup sugar—if the cereal is
        not presweetened
    (½ teaspoon cinnamon)

PUFF PASTE OR PÂTE FEUILLETÉE

Puff paste recipes usually start: "Choose a bright, windy, chilly day . . ." We stand off unfavorable weather with an electric fan, but are careful not to train it on the work surface. If you ask, "What do commercial bakeries do about puff paste and the weather?"—the answer is: they use a highly emulsified, very impervious margarine. To become an amateur champion, keep in mind first and foremost that this most delicate and challenging of pastries must be made the way porcupines make love—that is, very, very carefully. Then shut off the telephone for an hour or two, cut yourself some paper pattern guides to the measurements below and set to work.

◗ It is best to use flour that has a high gluten content, to develop real elasticity—and this is hard to come by. We do succeed, however, with all-purpose flour by using the procedure we describe. To be "puffy" ▶ the paste must be chilled, well-kneaded, and handled in such a way as to trap air, and finally ▶ baked in a hot, thoroughly preheated oven. Then the air inside the dough expands with almost explosive effect. ▶ The surface on which you work—preferably marble—the tools, the ingredients and your fingers should be chilled throughout the operation, as it is necessary to hold the fat, which is in very high proportion to the flour, in constant suspension.

▶ The paste must not absorb undue moisture, but it must never dry out. ▶ It must entirely envelop the butter. Try not to let any cracks or tears develop, as they release the air, which is your only riser. If they do appear, mend them at once to keep the butter encased.

With these ideas firmly in mind, try making this small quantity first. As you become experienced, double or triple the recipe. Knead:

¹/₄ lb. sweet butter

in ice water or under very cold running water. The butter should become soft through kneading, but in no sense soft through melting. Quite the contrary—it must stay soft and chilled at the same time throughout the operation. The final kneading of the butter is best done on a marble

slab; or the butter may be patted briskly in the hands until no water flies. Shape it into an oblong about 4 × 6 × ¹/₄ inch. Wrap in foil and chill about 15 minutes.

Weigh, do not measure:

¹/₄ lb. all-purpose flour

On a chilled smooth surface, make a ring with the flour, allowing about a 6-inch hollow center, at left below.

Pour into the ring gradually—meanwhile forming the flour into a ball with it—a mixture of:

2 to 2¹/₂ oz. ice water
(1 teaspoon lemon juice)
¹/₄ teaspoon salt

Knead the dough lightly until smooth. The whole process should take not more than about 2 minutes if you are experienced. Cover the dough carefully and refrigerate it for 15 minutes or so. When you remove the butter and dough from the refrigerator, they should be about the same

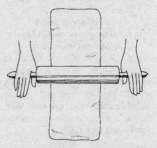

consistency—chilled but not hard. Roll the dough into a very neat oblong measuring about 6 × 16 inches and less than ¹/₃ inch thick, as in the sketch above. At this point, the dough is somewhat elastic and may have to be cajoled into the rectangle. Make the edges as even and the thickness as constant as possible. Quickly place the chilled butter pad about 1 inch from a short end and sides of the dough oblong, as shown below.

Fold the rest of the dough over the butter to make a pouch. Seal the two

layers firmly together on all three open sides, pressing with the fingers, as shown opposite, or with the sides of your hands.

With the narrow dimension always toward you as you work, roll the dough evenly, being careful not to break the layers or force the roller in such a way that the edges of the dough envelope become cracked. Should any opening develop, be sure to patch it at once with a small piece of dough taken from the long sides. Keep the pastry 6 inches in width while rolling, and extend it to about 16 inches in length.

The use of two paper patterns makes this measuring very quick to judge. Fold the pastry into three exact parts, see below.

Make sure that the corners match neatly. Compress the pack slightly with the roller. At this point, the dough should have a transparent quality. The yellow of the butter should show through but not break through anywhere. Wrap the dough, now approximately 4 × 6 × 1 inch, in foil and chill for 30 minutes. You have now made your first "turn" and, if you need a reminder, you can professionally make an initial shallow fingertip imprint in one corner before

refrigerating. Keep track of your turns by increasing the number of fingerprints after each rolling, as shown above.

When the dough has chilled, remove it from the refrigerator and repeat the rolling. ▶ Always roll with the narrow dimension of the dough toward you as you work. Roll as before, until the dough again measures about 6 × 16 inches. Fold once more into three equal parts. This time, make two fingertip impressions before refrigerating, covered, for 30 minutes. Repeat the turns until you have made five fingerprints. You may store the dough for 24 hours before baking. Wrap it first in foil and then in a dry towel. Refrigerate it.

If you prefer to bake the same day, make a sixth turn and chill the dough 30 minutes to 1½ hours. Then roll it to about 3/16 inch. This paste can be cut into many shapes. ◗ Whichever you choose, be sure to cut off a narrow slice along the folded edges. The folds have the inhibiting character of a selvage on cloth and do not allow the dough to expand evenly and freely.

◗ Always cut puff paste with a very sharp, very thin hot knife, a hot cutter or a sharp hot pastry wheel. Do not let the knife drag, as this will distort the layering.

Since making puff paste is time-consuming, you will want to use every scrap. But never, after cutting, reroll the dough for the same purpose. Get your patty shells and vol-au-vent and other classic shapes from the first cutting. Make out of rerolled scraps only those related types of pastry—such as flan, barquettes, croissants—for which the puff requirement is less exacting.

To prepare the pan for baking any of the classic shapes, sprinkle it lightly with cold water, but ◗ be sure that the side that was up when cut is now down against the wet baking surface. If properly made and cut, puff paste should rise six to eight times the height of the rolled dough.

Before baking an unsweetened paste, you may give it a lovely color by brushing the top with a combination of egg, salt and milk, see 503. ◗ Do not let this glaze spill over the edge, as the quick setting of the egg will have a deterrent effect on the rising. If the paste is to be used with sweetened food, brush with a combination of sugar and milk. For a really crispy finish, glaze also with a light sugar and water syrup just as the finished product comes from the oven.

To bake ◗ have ready an oven that has been thoroughly preheated to 500° at least 20 minutes. Bake at this temperature 5 minutes, reduce the heat to 375° and bake 25 to 30 minutes more, depending on the size of the pastry. If it colors too rapidly, place a piece of baker's paper or bond over it during the last stages of baking. The pastry is done if very light when lifted. Should it rise unevenly, the fault may lie with uneven rolling or with the uneven heat of the oven. In hot weather it may tend to slide to one side. Nothing can be done about this.

All puff paste recipes are best used fresh, but will keep closely covered and stored in a refrigerator for several days or frozen for a few weeks. For shapes to make with puff paste, see the illustration below and some of the following recipes.

Top left shows the cutting of a Vol-au-Vent, 369. It is really a larger version of the bouchée or patty shell illustrated in its dough and baked forms in the first three drawings below it.

At the top right is a Napoleon, 369. The remaining two forms are the baked and unbaked Cream Rolls, 369. ◗ Do not try to make these shapes with the Rough Puff Paste below, which is placed here because it is treated just like puff paste.

ROUGH OR HALF-PUFF PASTE, OR PÂTE DEMI-FEUILLETÉE

Do not expect this crust to rise even half so high as Puff Paste. It is made from the ingredients described below but is given fewer turns; or it is formed from the rerolled parings of true Puff Paste, when additional handling has driven off some of the trapped air. Use this paste for barquettes or croissants. Prepare:

Puff Paste, 365

using in all:

6 oz. butter
2 oz. water

Give it only 3 or 4 turns. To cut, shape and bake, see Puff Paste, 365.

PALM LEAVES

About 20 Palm Leaves

Roll into a 6 × 18-inch strip, ¼ inch thick:

Puff Paste, 365

To sugar, fold and cut, see Palm Leaf Rolls, 316. Chill and bake as noted opposite.

❀ PATTY SHELLS OR BOUCHÉES

Ten 4-Inch Shells

Prepare:

Puff Paste, 365, noting
♦ pointers

Roll the chilled paste into an oblong, 7 × 16 inches. Use a hot 3¼-inch cutter on the dough ten times. ♦ Be sure that the cutter is well within the rounded edge of the dough. Using a 2½-inch cutter and centering it in turn on each of the 3¼-inch rounds, make incisions, as shown above, about two-thirds through the dough. To chill, place and bake the dough, see Puff Paste, 365. As soon as the patty shells come from the oven, release the inner circles that were

cut two-thirds into the shell. The first third will act as the lid when the shell is filled. The second is usually damp and so is discarded. The third, uncut portion forms the base of the shell. These shells are suitable for luncheon entrées. They can be made into much smaller sizes for hors d'oeuvre, when they are called **Petites Bouchées,** or "little mouthfuls."

❀ VOL-AU-VENT

One 9-Inch Shell

Prepare:

Puff Paste, 365, noting
♦ pointers

Roll the chilled paste into an oblong, 9 × 17 inches. Use the removable bottom of an 8-inch round cake pan, or make an 8-inch cardboard circle as a cutting guide. Cut two circles with a sharp hot knife. Leave one whole. Place it upside down on a baking sheet sprinkled with water. Cut a 5-inch round out of the center of the other circle. Place the 1½-inch rim which this cut forms over the whole circle—again, upside down— and gash it diagonally along the edge, as shown upper left, opposite. You may bake the 5-inch circle separately as a lid or cut it into Petites Bouchées, see above. To chill and bake, see Puff Paste, 365. Fill at once with creamed food and serve, or cool to serve filled with:

Strawberries
Romanoff, 122

CREAM ROLLS

8 Rolls

If you visit a Konditorei in Weimar, you will find the cream rolls called Schillerlocken, named for their resemblance to the long curls worn by the renowned romantic German poet.

To make them, you need a special cone-shaped form known as a cornet. Prepare:

Puff Paste, 365, noting ♦ pointers

Roll the chilled paste into an oblong, $12^1/2 \times 9$ inches. Remove the rolled edges of the paste with a very sharp hot knife or pastry wheel. Cut the dough into eight strips 12 inches long. Roll the strips around the cones, as shown lower right in the illustration, 368. Chill the cornets, covered, at least $1/2$ hour. Glaze the tops of the strips with:

Milk Glaze, 504

Stand the cornets on a baking tin. To bake, see Puff Paste, 365.

NAPOLEONS

About Forty 2 × 3-Inch Bars

Could the Emperor conceivably have had these in mind when he contended that "an army marches on its stomach"?
Prepare:

Puff Paste, 365

Preheat oven to 450°.
Roll the chilled paste into an oblong, 24×33 inches, to a thickness of $1/8$ inch or less. ♦ Trim all folded edges carefully to a depth of $1/2$ inch. Divide the paste into three 11×24-inch oblongs. Place the 3 equal oblongs upside down on baking sheets that have been sprinkled with cold water. Prick them uniformly with a fork. Bake about 25 to 30 minutes, see Puff Paste, 365. When cool, you may glaze the layer reserved for the top with two successive coats of:

(Quick White Icing I, 496)

Let the first coat dry before applying the second, or dust the top layer with:

Confectioners' sugar

Stack the 3 layers and cut them into

2×3-inch oblongs. Put between the layers:

**Sweetened Whipped Cream, 449
or Crème Patissière, 450**

The finished pastry is shown at the top right of the illustration on 368.

ABOUT CREAM PUFF SHELLS, PÂTE À CHOUX OR POUF PASTE

Please cease thinking of this basic, quite easy paste as something for adventurous moments only. Use it unsweetened as a base for Gnocchi, (I, 185); for Dauphine Potatoes, (I, 353); as a bland foil for fillings; as soup garnishes or as hors d'oeuvre cases. Pâte à choux, when sweetened, imparts great individuality to the presentation of food. With a pastry tube you can make elegant Éclairs, 371, Beignets, 159, characteristic cabbagy or choux shapes for cream puffs, Swans, 371, dainty choux paste cases, or the towering pyramid, Croquembouche, 372, all illustrated in the chapter heading. If you serve éclair cases filled with ice cream or cream and covered with a sauce, they are called **Profiteroles,** 372.

CREAM PUFF SHELLS

Two Dozen 3-Inch Shells

Preheat oven to 400°.
Have the eggs at room temperature.
Sift before measuring:

    1 cup all-purpose flour
    $1/8$ teaspoon salt
    1 tablespoon sugar, if the puffs are to be used with a sweet filling

Place in a heavy pan:

    1 cup water or milk
    $1/3$ cup butter

Bring to a boil, add the flour mixture in one fell swoop and stir quickly with a wooden spoon. It looks rough at first, but suddenly becomes smooth, at which point you stir faster. In a few minutes the paste becomes dry and does not cling to the spoon or the sides of the pan, and when the spoon is pressed on it lightly, it leaves a smooth imprint. ♦ Do not overcook or overstir at this point, for then the dough will fail to puff. ♦ Remove pan from heat for about 2 minutes. It must never be returned to the heat; this is why, to cook properly, ♦ the eggs must be at room temperature. Add one at a time, beating vigorously after each addition:

4 or 5 eggs

Continue to beat each time until the dough no longer looks slippery. The paste is ready to bake when the last egg has been incorporated. The proper consistency has been reached when a small quantity of the dough will stand erect if scooped up on the end of the spoon. It is best to use the dough at once.

A spoon or a pastry bag will serve to form the different shapes. Be sure to press the filled bag until you are rid of all the air in the tube. Allow space for expansion around shapes, as you squeeze them onto the greased pan. To form the puff or characteristic cabbagy, choux shape, hold the tube close to the baking sheet. ♦ Do not move the tube. Simply let the paste bubble up around it until the desired size is reached. To form éclairs, draw the tube along for about 3 to 4 inches while pressing, and always finish with a lifting reverse motion. To form small pastry cups, make one-inch globules. The little point left when you lift the bag can be pressed down with a moistened finger.

Before baking sprinkle a few drops of water over the shapes on the pan—lightly—as you would sprinkle laundry. Bake cream puff shells and éclairs in a preheated 400° oven for 10 minutes. Reduce the heat to 350° and bake about 25 minutes longer. Do not remove them from the oven until they are quite firm to the touch. Cool the shells away from any draft before filling. For filling, cut them horizontally with a sharp knife. If there are any damp dough filaments inside, be sure to remove them. For suggested cream puff fillings, see 372.

CHOUX PASTE SWAN

Prepare paste for:

Cream Puff Shells, opposite

Use a simple cut-off round tube, see Decorative Icings, 490, to form the head and neck all in one piece. To force a greater quantity of paste for the head, squeeze hard at the inception of the movement, and swing the tube in an arc for the neck, as shown in the chapter heading. Head and neck sections are baked on a greased sheet for only 10 minutes in a 400° oven. For the rest of the swan's anatomy, use a serrated tube to form 3-inch éclairs. Cut them lengthwise. Just before serving, fill the bottom piece with cream. Divide the top piece lengthwise for the wings. Embed them and the neck in the fluffy cream filling. The wings are braced somewhat diagonally to steady the neck. Dust the whole swan lightly with confectioners' sugar. Perfect for a little girl's party!

CHOCOLATE ECLAIRS

To form and bake the shells, see Cream Puff Shells, opposite. For the characteristic shape, see the elongated éclair in the chapter heading. Gash the shell sufficiently to line it with filling, or squirt the filling in with a pastry tube. Fill the shells as close to serving time as possible with:

> Whipped cream, or
> Custard Chocolate or
> Coffee Fillings, 450.

Cover them with:

> A chocolate or caramel
> icing, 494.

Garnish with:

> Toasted slivered almonds

PROFITEROLES

To form and bake the shells, see Cream Puff Shells, 370. Divide the shells horizontally and fill as close to serving time as possible with:

> Crème Chantilly, 449, or
> ice cream

Cover with:

> Chocolate Sauce, 567

or fill with:

> Whipped cream, 186

and serve with a strawberry sauce.

CROQUEMBOUCHE

Serves 10 to 12

This spectacular dessert, shown in the chapter heading, is a structural marvel. It needs considerable organization, for it is best when assembled as close to serving time as possible. Caramelize:

> 2 cups sugar, 232

Form on the base of a 9-inch greased pie pan or directly on a footed cake tray a thin layer of caramelized sugar, keeping the rest soft in a 250° oven. When the thin layer has hardened, put it on the platter on which you intend to serve the dessert. Have ready:

> Cream puffs under 2 inches
> in size, made from Cream
> Puff Paste, 370

filled with:

> Whipped or flavored
> cream, 449

Remove the caramel from the oven and work quickly. If the syrup tends to harden, reheat it slowly. ♦ Dip a portion of each filled puff in turn, as you place it in circular layers of decreasing width on the caramel disk. Arrange the puffs on the outer layers so that their tops form the exposed surface. Let additional syrup drip partially over the whole as a final glaze. Serve by pulling apart with 2 forks.

ABOUT FILLINGS FOR CREAM PUFF SHELLS AND ÉCLAIRS

Use Sweetened Whipped Creams, 449, Custards, 507, Crème Patissière, 450, or almost any of the fillings in complete dessert cakes, 448. ♦ Fill as close to serving time as possible to avoid sogginess. In any case, remember ♦ that cream-based and particularly egg-based fillings must be kept refrigerated. Egg fillings, if carelessly stored, are subject to bacterial activity which may be highly toxic, even though they give no evidence of spoilage. For fillings for unsweetened puff shells, see Canapés, 68.

With a sweetened dough try one of the following:

I. For a marvelous tea-teaser, put in the base of a puff shell a layer of:

> Sweetened whipped
> cream, 449

Lightly insert with the pointed end up:

> A flawless ripe
> strawberry

II. Or fill the puffs with:

> Soft cream cheese
> A dab of bright jelly

ABOUT STRUDEL

When the last princesse slip was freshly beriboned, our beloved Hungarian laundress sometimes found time to give us a treat. She made strudel. Draping the round dining room table with a fresh cloth, she patiently worked flour into it. Neighborhood small fry gathered on the fringes of the light cast by the Tiffany dome, and their eyes would pop as she rolled the dough, no larger than a softball, into a big thin circle. Then, hands lightly clenched, palms down, working under the sheet of dough and from the center out, she stretched it with the flat planes of the knuckles, as shown below. She would play it out, so to speak, not so much pulling it as coaxing it with long, even friction, moving round and round the table as she worked.

In our household, the filling was invariably apple. But whether you make strudel dough yourself or buy it, or the similar **phyllo**—for it now comes ready to use—there are endless possibilities for "interior decoration": poppy seed, ground meat mixtures, cheese, cherries, or just pepper worked originally into the dough. This last makes an excellent hors d'oeuvre pastry.

Our Janka had organized her filling well in advance. Browned bread crumbs, lemon rind grated into sugar, raisins, currants, very finely sliced apples, almonds and a small pitcher of melted butter were all set out on a tray. These were strewn alternately over the surface of the dough. Then came the forming of the roll. Using both hands, Janka picked up one side of the cloth and, while never actually touching the dough itself, tilted and nudged the cloth and the sheet this way and that until the dough rolled over on itself—jelly-roll fashion—and completely enclosed the filling. Finally, she slid the long cylinder onto a greased baking sheet and curved it into a horseshoe. From beginning to end the process had masterly craftsmanship. Would that we could give you her skill as easily as we give you her recipe. Now are you ready? Prepare the filling ingredients. Do not feel limited by these proportions or materials. See other fillings, 331.

Mix:

    1 tablespoon cinnamon

with:

    4 to 6 tablespoons browned bread crumbs
    1 tablespoon lemon rind

grated into:

    1 cup sugar
    ³/₄ cup raisins or currants
    (¹/₂ cup shredded blanched almonds)
    6 to 8 cups finely chopped tart apples

For the dough, have ready:

6 tablespoons melted butter

part of which will be incorporated into the flour. Have a cloth ready on a large table-height surface around which you will be able to walk. Work lightly into the cloth:

Flour

Sift onto a board, making a well, as shown on 366:

1¹/₂ cups all-purpose flour
¹/₄ teaspoon salt

Pour into the center of the well:

1 well-beaten egg

mixed with:

¹/₃ to ¹/₂ cup tepid water or milk
2 teaspoons melted butter (¹/₈ teaspoon vinegar)

Depending on your flour, you may have to add a few tablespoons more of tepid water. Combine the ingredients quickly with your fingers, working from the outside of the well, and when it is consolidated, knead on a board until the dough is pliable and silky and no longer sticks to the board. Brush the surface of the ball with melted butter. Cover the dough with a warm bowl and let it rest 30 minutes to one hour. Roll it out on the board as thin as possible. Move it to the table. Begin to stretch the dough gently from the center out, trying not to tear it, as patching is difficult. If you are skillful, this should stretch to about a square yard. A heavier edge of dough or a border will develop as you work, and whatever remains of this must be cut off with a knife before the filling is spread or the pastry rolled up. Use this excess dough for making patches.

Preheat oven to 400°.

Before filling, brush the dough with some of the melted butter. Sprinkle over the surface the filling mixture above. Dust with:

Cinnamon

Form the roll as described above ◗ not too tightly, as the dough will expand. Slide it onto the greased baking sheet. Brush the surface of the roll with some of the melted butter and sprinkle lightly with water. Bake 20 minutes at 400°, then lower the heat to 350°, brush the strudel again with the remaining butter, and bake about 10 minutes longer, until golden brown. Remove from oven and dust with:

Confectioners' sugar

Cut in wide diagonal slices and serve.

PHYLLO LEAVES

Fila, phyllo, yukka, brik, malsouka—call it what you like—is the tissue-thin pastry sheet used all over the Near East. The simplest of ingredients—flour and water—are so skilfully kneaded, rested and stretched as almost to defy amateur reproduction. In recipes calling for these leaves, we have successfully used our Strudel dough, 373. Phyllo leaves may be purchased in 12 sheets to the half pound. Use at once or freeze. ◗ If frozen, thaw very slowly, still wrapped, and plan to use all exposed sheets immediately.

ABOUT MERINGUE PASTE

There are many variations of meringue—all based on egg white and sugar. Also see Meringue Toppings, 501. They include glamorous glacées and vacherins, served with ices or creams, including ice cream; Christmas meringue cookies, of which Cinnamon Stars are, perhaps deservedly, the best beloved; mountainous fluffy pie toppings; more discreet Italian types of meringue used over puddings and tarts; insulating meringues like those prepared for Omelette Soufflée Surprise and Baked Alaska; Swiss Meringue or Royal Glaze. Each calls for special treatment.

In this day of the electric mixer, showy meringue desserts have become effortless to make. They can, however, be made using a large egg whisk, but it takes endurance. ♦ Use glass, stainless steel or copper bowls for whipping the egg whites. See about Beating Eggs, 206. ♦ A word of warning: Do not attempt meringues when the humidity is high.

Ingredients and proportions do not vary. For every 4 egg whites—from 2-ounce eggs—use ½ pound sugar. As you know, sugars of the same weight differ tremendously in volume, see About Solid Sugars, 226. Eggs at about 70° should be opened, separated and whipped just before you are ready to mix the meringue. The baking is more a drying than a heating process. ♦ Use bottom heat only. A preheated 225° oven will give you a soft, crunchy meringue; a preheated 275° oven, a chewy one.

If you wonder about the indestructible meringues served in public places, they are based on confectioners' sugar: the egg whites are heated over hot water as for Génoise, 416; and the meringues are dried overnight in a warming oven, not above 175°. Whichever baking procedure is chosen, the classic confectioner does not allow his meringues to color. ♦ Store meringues immediately, tightly covered, as they absorb moisture and disintegrate easily. Do not try to freeze them.

To form meringue paste, use a spoon and spatula or a pastry bag. ♦ Do not fill meringues until just before serving. Individual kisses or rings filled with ices, ice creams or frozen desserts are called **Meringues Glacées.** Shape the paste into a large nest on a heat-resistant platter and fill it with fruits and cream for **Pinch Pie.** Baked in springform pans in shallow layers, they are called **Schaumtorten.** A **Vacherin Ring** is a flat coil of meringue with a piped edging to hold a filling of sweetened whipped cream—plain or with fruit. The top of the confection is an open meringue crown decorated at the edges with large contiguous baroque dots of meringue that are baked on. For filling suggestions, see 448, and for a cake with batter and meringue baked simultaneously, see Cream Meringue Tart, 438.

MERINGUES

Twelve 3-Inch Meringues or a 9-Inch Pie Shell

Preheat oven to 225°.
♦ Have egg whites at about 70°. Beat until foamy in an electric mixer or by hand:

4 egg whites

Add:

1 teaspoon vanilla
(⅛ teaspoon cream of tartar)

Add, while continuing to beat, 1 tablespoon at a time:

1 cup sifted, finely powdered sugar or 1 cup minus 1 tablespoon sifted sugar
(½ teaspoon cinnamon)

When the mixture stands in stiff peaks on the beater, it is ready for baking. ♦ Do not overbeat. To shape, see above. For a glaze, you may dust the meringues lightly with:

Granulated sugar

Bake on baking sheets covered with parchment paper about 1 hour or longer, depending on the size. The reason for the use of paper is not only to prevent sticking but to diffuse the heat. In some famous kitchens the meringues are baked on a thick board or a pan, both greased and floured. ♦ Do not remove from the oven at once, but turn off the oven, open the door and leave them for at least 5 minutes. Cool gradually, away from a draft. Remove them from the sheet when cool. If kisses are to be filled, crush the bottom lightly with the thumb while still warm. Shortly before serving, fill the hollows with:

> Sweetened and flavored whipped cream or a frozen mixture

covered with:

> Sweetened crushed fruit, or a chocolate sauce, 567

ABOUT BERRY AND OTHER FRUIT PIES

If you don't find the fruit combination you are looking for in our fruit pie recipes, perhaps you would like to experiment with fillings for yourself. A 9-inch fruit or berry pie needs about 4 cups of fresh fruit or 3 cups of cooked fruit. Each fruit will require its own quota of sweetening, depending on acidity and your personal taste. Four cups of gooseberries, for example, need about 1¾ cups of sugar, while the same amount of blueberries may need no more than ½ cup—plus lemon juice to heighten the flavor.

As to thickening for pie fruit: technically, each batch would require a different amount of thickener, depending on the variety of fruit, degree of ripeness, etc. For practical purposes, an often suggested formula for 4 cups of fruit is:

> ¼ cup all-purpose flour

However, acid fruits should be thickened with tapioca, cornstarch or arrowroot starch because the acidity of the fruit may neutralize the thickening

power of the flour. So for 4 cups of fruit, mix:

> 2⅔ tablespoons quick-cooking tapioca
> ⅔ to 1 cup sugar

or mix:

> 2 tablespoons cornstarch or arrowroot starch

with:

> ¼ cup water or fruit juice

until very smooth and then blend with:

> ⅔ to 1 cup sugar

Whether you use tapioca or cornstarch, let the mixture stand for 15 minutes after blending it gently into the fresh fruit. Correct the sweetening, then proceed as directed in Berry Pies, below.

Some suggested proportions are:

> ½ apple and ½ pear
> ½ apple and ½ green tomato
> ½ rhubarb and ½ strawberry
> ⅓ gooseberry and ⅔ strawberry
> ½ cherry and ½ rhubarb
> ⅓ cranberry and ⅔ apple
> ½ mincemeat, ¼ applesauce and ¼ crushed pineapple
> ½ fresh strawberries and ½ bananas
> ⅔ raspberries and ⅓ currants

Fruit pies ❀ freeze well, but ♦ do not freeze those with a custard base.

BERRY PIE WITH FRESH FRUIT

A 9-Inch Double-Crust Pie
Please read About Berry Pies, above.
Use:

> Gooseberry, currant, blackberry, raspberry, strawberry, blueberry, huckleberry or loganberry

Line a pie pan with:

A pie dough, 360–362
Prepare by picking over and hulling:
    4 cups fresh berries
Combine:
    ²/₃ to 1 cup or more sugar
    ¼ cup all-purpose flour
    (1½ tablespoons lemon juice
    or ½ teaspoon cinnamon)
If the fruit is juicy, add:
    (2 teaspoons quick-cooking
    tapioca)
Sprinkle these ingredients over the berries and stir gently until well blended. Let stand for 15 minutes. Preheat oven to 450°.
Turn the fruit into the pie shell. Dot with:
    1 to 2 tablespoons butter
Cover the pie with a well-pricked top or with a lattice. Bake the pie in a 450° oven 10 minutes. Reduce the heat to 350° and bake 35 to 40 minutes or until golden brown.

BERRY OR CHERRY PIE WITH COOKED OR CANNED FRUIT

A 9-Inch Double-Crust Pie
Allow approximately:
    2½ cups sweetened canned
    or cooked berries or
    cherries
    1 cup fruit juice
Proceed as directed in the above recipe for Berry Pie with Fresh Fruit, but for thickening use:
    1½ tablespoons quick-cooking
    tapioca
and the smaller amount of sugar. For cherry pie, see flavoring in Fresh Cherry Pie, opposite. You may bake the filling in the unbaked pie shell as in Berry Pie with Fresh Fruit, or you may thicken the fruit juice by heating it separately with the thickener. Then mix it with the fruit and put it in a baked shell to serve.

BERRY OR CHERRY PIE WITH FROZEN FRUIT

A 9-Inch Double-Crust Pie
Line a pie pan with:
    A pie dough, 360–362
Defrost until the fruit separates easily:
    Frozen berries or cherries:
    20 oz.
Mix fruit with:
    3 tablespoons quick-cooking
    tapioca
    1¼ cups sugar
    ⅛ teaspoon salt
    2 tablespoons melted
    butter
Let stand for 15 minutes before adding to shell.
Preheat oven to 450°.
Cover filling with a pricked top or a lattice and bake in a 450° oven 10 minutes. Reduce the heat to 350° and bake about 45 minutes or until golden brown.

FRESH CHERRY PIE

A 9-Inch Double-Crust Pie
Line a pie pan with:
    A pie dough, 360–362
Wash, drain and pit:
    4 cups fresh sour cherries
Combine, then mix gently with cherries:
    2²/₃ tablespoons quick-cooking
    tapioca
    1⅓ cups sugar
    (2 drops almond flavoring or
    2 tablespoons kirsch)
Let fruit mixture stand 15 minutes. Preheat oven to 450°.
Pour fruit into pie shell and dot with:
    2 tablespoons butter
Cover with a well-pricked top or a lattice. Bake 10 minutes at 450°, then reduce heat to 350° and bake about 40 minutes longer or until golden brown.

SOUR CREAM CHERRY OR BERRY PIE

A 9-Inch Single-Crust Pie or 4 Tarts

Prepare a pie shell or tart shells, using:

Graham Cracker or Zwieback Crust, 365

Chill the shell, then fill it with the following cherry custard.
Preheat oven to 325°.
Beat:

3 eggs

Add:

3/4 cup sugar
3/4 cup cultured sour cream
2 cups fresh or canned drained cherries or berries

Bake the pie until the custard is firm, about 1 hour. Serve very hot or very cold.

GLAZED BERRY PIE

A 9-Inch Single-Crust Pie

Prepare with a generous high rim:

A baked pie shell, 360

Clean and hull:

1 quart strawberries or red or black raspberries

Reserve and ✦ blend or sieve 1 cup of the fruit. Combine and cook, stirring until thickened over low heat 10 to 15 minutes:

3/4 cup sugar
2 1/2 tablespoons cornstarch
1/4 teaspoon salt
1 cup water

Add the blended fruit to give color. Put the whole berries into the baked pie shell, evenly distributed. Pour the syrup over the berries, coating them thoroughly by turning but not displacing them. Chill the pie in the refrigerator at least 4 hours. Serve garnished with:

(Whipped cream)

BLUEBERRY OR HUCKLEBERRY CUSTARD TARTS

Six to Eight 3-Inch Tarts

If seeds are small, it's blueberries you have; if many and large—huckleberries. The flavor is almost identical.
Prepare:

Pâte Sucrée, 363, or Vienna Pastry, 362

Preheat oven to 450°.
Place dough in the tart pans. Bake 8 to 12 minutes. Remove from oven and reduce heat to 375°. Fill tarts with a mixture of:

1 quart blueberries
1/2 cup sugar
(2 tablespoons lemon juice)

Bake about 10 minutes. Remove from oven. Cook and stir ✦ over—not in—boiling water until thickened:

1/2 cup cream
3 beaten egg yolks
1/2 cup sugar
1/8 teaspoon salt

Cool the custard and pour it over the slightly cooled tarts. Continue to cool and top with:

(Whipped Cream, 186)

APPLE PIE

I.   A 9-Inch Double-Crust Pie

Call it à la mode if you garnish your pie with ice cream—a real inspiration when your apples are tart.
Line a 9-inch pie pan with:

A pie dough, 360–362

Pare, core and thinly slice:

5 to 6 cups apples

If you are using dried apples, allow 1 pound apples to 1 quart water and cook 35 to 45 minutes before proceeding.
Combine and sift over the apples:

1/2 to 2/3 cup white or brown sugar

1/8 teaspoon salt
1 to 1¹/2 tablespoons
cornstarch
(¹/4 teaspoon cinnamon)
(¹/8 teaspoon nutmeg)

Only very tart apples require the larger amount of sugar. Only very juicy apples require the larger amount of cornstarch. Stir the apples gently until they are well coated. Place them in layers in the pie shell. Dot with:

1¹/2 tablespoons butter

If the apples are bland or lacking in flavor, sprinkle with:

1 tablespoon lemon juice
¹/2 teaspoon grated lemon rind
(1 teaspoon vanilla)

If you are serving the pie with cheese, omit the above flavors and use:

(1 teaspoon fennel or anise
seed)

Should the apples be very dry, add:

(2 tablespoons water or
cream)

Preheat oven to 450°.
Cover the pie with a pricked upper crust. Bake in a 450° oven 10 minutes. Reduce the heat to 350°. Bake until done, 35 to 45 minutes or until golden brown. For a delicious touch, sprinkle the top crust lightly with sugar and cinnamon as you put the pie into the oven. Some cooks brush it first with milk. Others prefer to finish the pie off, after baking, with:

(1 cup shredded cheese)

Place briefly under a broiler to melt the cheese.

II   A 9-Inch Single-Crust Pie

Follow directions for I above, using a single pie crust recipe. In place of an upper crust, top with a sprinkling of:

Streusel II, 503

Bake as directed. However, if the crumb crust is becoming too brown,

protect with a foil covering until apples are tender.

APPLE TARTS

8 Tarts

Preheat oven to 375°.
Line eight shallow 3-inch muffin cups or individual pie pans with:

A pie dough, 360–362

Fill them with:

4 cups pared, thinly sliced
apples

Combine and pour over the fruit:

¹/2 cup sugar
2 slightly beaten eggs
2 tablespoons melted butter
1 tablespoon lemon juice
1 cup cream, or ¹/2 cup
evaporated milk and ¹/2 cup
water
(¹/2 teaspoon cinnamon)
(¹/8 teaspoon nutmeg)

Bake about 40 minutes.

PEACH PIE

I   A 9-Inch Single-Crust Pie

Preheat oven to 400°.
Line a pie pan with:

A pie dough, 360–362

Combine and blend well:

1 egg or 2 egg yolks
2 tablespoons flour
²/3 to 1 cup granulated sugar
(¹/3 cup melted butter)

Pour this mixture over:

Halves of canned or peeled
fresh peaches

that have been placed cut side up in the pie shell. Bake 15 minutes at 400°, then reduce the heat to 300° and bake about 50 minutes longer. Serve hot or, if cold, garnished with:

(Whipped cream)

II   A 9-Inch Double-Crust Pie

Follow the recipe for:

Apple Pie, 378

Substitute for the apples:

 5 cups peeled, sliced peaches

Use the smaller amount of sugar.

RHUBARB PIE

I. **A 9-Inch Double-Crust Pie**

Follow the rule for baking Berry Pie with Fresh Fruit, 376, making a lattice crust for the top. This pie can also be made with half rhubarb and half strawberries.

Use:

 4 cups unpeeled, diced young rhubarb stalks
 ¹/₄ cup all-purpose flour
 1¹/₄ to 2 cups sugar
 1 tablespoon butter
 (1 teaspoon grated orange rind)

II. **A 9-Inch Single-Crust Pie**

A custardy rhubarb pie. Line a pie pan with:

 A pie dough, 360–362

Preheat oven to 400°.

Place in the pie shell:

 4 cups diced pink rhubarb

Combine and beat:

 1¹/₂ cups sugar
 3 egg yolks
 ¹/₂ cup all-purpose flour
 3 tablespoons milk
 (³/₄ teaspoon nutmeg)

Spread these ingredients over the rhubarb. Bake 20 minutes at 400°, then reduce the heat to 350° and bake another 20 minutes. When pie has cooled, use the 3 egg whites for a:

 Meringue, 502

GRAPE PIE

 A 9-Inch Double-Crust Pie

Stem:

 4 cups blue grapes

Slip the pulp out of the skins. Reserve the skins. Cook the pulp until the seeds loosen. Press through a colander to remove seeds. Combine the pulp, the skins and:

 ³/₄ cup sugar
 (1¹/₂ tablespoons lemon juice)
 1 tablespoon grated orange rind
 1 tablespoon quick-cooking tapioca

Let these ingredients stand 15 minutes. Line a pie pan with:

 A pie dough, 360–362

Preheat oven to 450°.

Fill the shell with the grape mixture and form a lattice over the top, see 359. Bake the pie 10 minutes at 450°, then reduce heat to 350° and bake about 20 minutes.

★ MINCE PIE

 A 9-Inch Double-Crust Pie

Preheat oven to 450°.

Line a pie pan with:

 A pie dough, 360–362

Fill it with:

 Mincemeat, 630, or a 28-oz. jar of mincemeat

Add to the mincemeat:

 (2 to 4 tablespoons brandy)

Cover the pie with a pricked top. Bake at 450° 10 minutes, then reduce heat to 350° and bake about 30 minutes.

★ MOCK MINCE PIE

 A 9-Inch Double-Crust Pie

Cut into pieces:

 1¹/₂ cups seeded raisins

Pare, core and slice:

 4 medium-sized tart apples or a combination of apples and green tomatoes

Combine the raisins and apples. Add:

Grated rind of 1 orange
Juice of 1 orange
1/2 **cup cider or other fruit**
juice

Cover these ingredients and simmer until the apples are very soft. Stir in until well blended:

3/4 **cup sugar**
1/2 **teaspoon each cinnamon**
and cloves
2 **or 3 tablespoons finely**
crushed soda crackers

If the apples are dry, use the smaller amount. This mixture will keep for several days. Shortly before using it, add:

(1 or 2 tablespoons brandy)

Preheat oven to 450°.
Line a pie pan with:

A pie dough, 360–362

Fill it with mock mincemeat. Cover with a pricked upper crust or with a lattice. Bake at 450° ten minutes, then reduce heat to 350° and bake about 20 minutes longer.

PRUNE OR APRICOT PIE

A 9-Inch Single-Crust Pie

Have ready:

A baked pie shell, 360

Preheat oven to 325°.
Put stewed, unsweetened prunes or apricots through a ricer. Combine:

3/4 **cup prune or apricot**
pulp
1/2 **teaspoon grated lemon**
rind
1 **tablespoon lemon juice**
1/2 **cup sugar**

Beat until stiff, but not dry:

3 **egg whites**

Beat in very slowly:

1/2 **cup sugar**

Fold the egg whites into the fruit mixture. Fill the pie shell. Bake about 20 minutes or until set.

RAISIN PIE

A 9-Inch Single-Crust Pie

Have ready:

A baked pie shell, 360

Heat to the boiling point:

1 **cup seedless or seeded**
white raisins
1 **cup water**

Add:

1/2 **cup white or brown sugar**

Cool 1/2 cup of this mixture. Stir into it gently:

2 **tablespoons butter**
2 **tablespoons all-purpose**
flour

Return it to the saucepan. Cook and stir over low heat until the mixture has thickened. Remove pan from heat. Beat in:

2 **egg yolks**
1 **teaspoon grated lemon rind**
3 **tablespoons lemon juice**

Cool the filling. Fill the pie shell. Cover with Meringue I, 502, and bake as directed.

ABOUT TRANSPARENT PIES

There is a whole galaxy of pie fillings based on brown sugar, molasses, and corn or maple syrup. These are thickened usually with egg, but sometimes with a crumb mixture or, as in Shoo-Fly Pie, with a flour base, which gives the dessert a cakelike quality. Some cooks cut the sweetness with tart jellies, lemon or vinegar. Some add butter or cream, spices, nuts and dried fruits. You may top these pies with crumb mixtures, meringues, whipped cream or icing. Some transparents claim southern, some Pennsylvania ancestry; and a few acknowledge their direct descent from English forebears—the traditional Banbury or chess tarts. To test for doneness, read About Custards, 507.

BASIC TRANSPARENT PIE

We have encountered this great southern favorite at all sorts of gatherings, from fiestas to funerals. There are many variations, but we like to use our recipe for Pecan Pie, below, omitting the pecans and replacing the vanilla with:

A grating of nutmeg or 1 tablespoon lemon juice

If you add to the filling or line the crust with ¼ cup of tart jelly, you have **Amber Pie**.

PECAN PIE

A 9-Inch Single-Crust Pie

Black walnuts for pecans makes a piquant substitution.
Preheat oven to 450°.
Line a pan with:

A pie dough, 360–362

and bake it only partially, from 5 to 7 minutes. Allow it to cool. ◗ Reduce oven heat to 375°. Combine and beat thoroughly:

    3 eggs
    1 cup sugar
    ½ teaspoon salt
    ⅓ cup melted butter
    1 cup light corn syrup

Stir in:

    1 cup pecan halves
    1 teaspoon vanilla or 1
      tablespoon rum

Fill the shell. Bake the pie 40 to 50 minutes at 375° or until a knife inserted in the filling comes out clean. Serve warm or cold. If you omit the nuts and substitute for the vanilla 3 tablespoons of bourbon whisky, you will have a **Bourbon Pie**.

BANBURY TARTS

About Six 4-Inch Tarts

Have ready:

Individual baked tart crusts, 360

Combine:

    1 cup seeded raisins
    1 cup sugar
    2 tablespoons cracker
      crumbs
    1 well-beaten egg
      Grated rind of 1 lemon
    1½ tablespoons lemon juice
    2 tablespoons butter
    ¼ cup chopped candied
      fruits
    (2 tablespoons chopped
      walnuts)

Cook and stir these ingredients over low heat until the mixture begins to thicken. Remove from the heat. Cool. Half fill the tart shells. Top with:

(Whipped cream)

You may use this filling in Turnovers, (I, 238).

JEFFERSON DAVIS PIE

A 9-Inch Single-Crust Pie

Prepare:

A baked pie shell, 360

Preheat oven to 325°.
Cream:

    ½ cup butter
    2 cups packed light brown
      sugar

Beat in:

    4 egg yolks

Mix, then add:

    2 tablespoons all-purpose
      flour
    1 teaspoon cinnamon
    ½ teaspoon allspice
    1 teaspoon freshly grated
      nutmeg

Stir in:

    1 cup cream
    ½ cup chopped dates
    ½ cup raisins
    ½ cup broken pecan meats

Fill the shell. Bake the pie until set,

about 30 minutes. When cool, top with:

Meringue I, 502

Bake as directed. Without the nuts and spices this becomes **Kentucky Pie**.

CHESS TARTS

Fill:

Baked tart crusts, 360

with filling for:

Jefferson Davis Pie, above

omitting the dates and spices. When cool, cover with:

Whipped cream

CRUMB OR GRAVEL PIE

A 9-Inch Single-Crust Pie

Use a:

Baked pie shell, 360

for this Pennsylvania Dutch specialty. Sprinkle the bottom of shell with:

(1/2 cup seedless raisins)

Combine and cook in the top of a double boiler or over low heat until thick:

    1 cup brown sugar, mild
        molasses or honey
    1/2 cup hot water
    3 beaten eggs

Cool and pour these ingredients into the pie shell.

Preheat oven to 325°.

Combine and work like pastry:

    1 cup cake or cookie crumbs
    1/3 cup all-purpose flour
    1/2 to 1 teaspoon cinnamon
    1/4 teaspoon nutmeg
    1/8 teaspoon ginger
    1/3 cup soft butter

Sprinkle this mixture over the filling. To make **Gravel Pie**, don't combine the above ingredients. Instead, sprinkle them alternately over the pie—with the crumbs on top. Bake 20 to 30 minutes. If you bake from three to

five of these shells with thin fillings, stack them and top them with Boiled White Icing, 488, flavored with lemon, or Caramel Icing, 494, you have a **Stack Pie.**

PUMPKIN OR SQUASH PIE

When Halloween comes 'round, we welcome pumpkins as symbols of harvest and sources of shivery fun. For holiday decorations, why not have each of the children carve his own small pumpkin? Then stack them into a totem pole. Use the topmost cutout as a lid, the rest for ears and noses. Stems make good features, too. Choose pumpkins of varied shapes, as shown on 357, and encourage the sculptors to vary their expressions.

Abroad, we find almost everywhere that a great diversity of puddings like the filling below, soups, (I, 154), breads, 336, and vegetable dishes, (I, 365), are prepared from these members of the squash family. Here in America we restrict their use mostly to pie.

▶ To cook pumpkin, wash and cut it in half crosswise. Remove seeds and strings. Place it in a pan, shell side up, and bake it in a 325° oven for 1 hour or more, depending on size, until it is tender and begins to fall apart. Scrape the pulp from the shell and put it through a ricer or strainer or blender.

I. **A 9-Inch Single-Crust Pie**

Line a pie pan with:

A pie dough, 360–362

Preheat oven to 425°.

Mix until well blended:

    2 cups cooked or canned
        pumpkin or squash
    1 1/2 cups undiluted evaporated
        milk or rich cream

¼ cup brown sugar
½ cup white sugar
½ teaspoon salt
1 teaspoon cinnamon
½ teaspoon ginger
¼ teaspoon nutmeg or allspice
⅛ teaspoon cloves
2 slightly beaten eggs

Pour the mixture into the pie shell. Bake 15 minutes at 425°, then reduce heat to 350° and bake about 45 minutes longer or until an inserted knife comes out clean. Serve with:

Sweetened Whipped
Cream, 449

flavored with:

(2 tablespoons bourbon)

II. Follow the directions in I, above, omitting the milk and adding:

2 tablespoons molasses
1½ cups sour cream

ABOUT CUSTARD PIES

How many puzzled inquiries we have answered about "Custard, my family's favorite pie"! In a recent one, our correspondent gloomily points out: "My mother thinks it's lumpy because I cook it too long. My husband thinks it gets watery because I put it in the icebox." How right, unfortunately, are both of this bride's critics! ◗ Custard and cream pies, unless eaten almost at once, must be kept well chilled. The lightly cooked eggs are especially subject to adverse bacterial activity, even though they may give no evidence of spoilage. It is Hobson's choice here: eat within 3 hours if the pie is left unrefrigerated or risk wateriness under refrigeration.

Again, pie dough needs a high heat, while the custard itself demands a low one. How to reconcile these contradictions? We find that the easiest way to satisfaction is to prebake

crust and filling separately; then, just before serving, to slip the cooled filling into the cooled shell. To prebake the filling, select a pie pan of the same size as the crust. Grease well. Bake the custard in the pie pan at 350°. To test for doneness, read About Custards, 507. Cool quickly. Before serving, cut the edges free with a knife and shake the pan gently to loosen the pie. Slide the filling into the crust, see below. This method takes a bit of dexterity, but after you get used to it, you will prefer it.

The filling need not even be preformed but, if precooked, can be spooned carefully into the prebaked shell. If you use a topping, see 502, no one but you will be the wiser. Two more important comments about fillings which are precooked, but not preformed, like Rich Custard, 509: ◗ always cook them over—not in—boiling water; and ◗ when they are thickened, beat them until they are cool to allow all the steam to escape. The steam will otherwise condense and thin the filling too much. Mark Twain inelegantly wrote of a frustrated crow that it was "sweating like an ice pitcher," and this is exactly what custard filling will do, unless beaten until cool. Or you may use Baked Custard, 508. When either custard is 70° or cooler, place the filling in the prebaked shell, and the pie is ready to serve.

CUSTARD PIE

A 9-Inch Single-Crust Pie

Preheat oven to 450°.
The partial baking of this pie shell before filling ensures a crisper under-crust. Line a pie pan with:

A pie dough, 360–362

Build up a fluted rim. Prick the bottom and bake it in a 450° oven just 10 minutes. Reduce heat to 325°. Pull the oven rack partway out and pour the following custard into the crust, or remove the crust from the oven only long enough to fill it.
Beat slightly:

3 eggs or 6 egg yolks

Add and stir well:

½ cup sugar
¼ teaspoon salt
2 cups milk, or milk and light cream
1 teaspoon vanilla or 1 tablespoon rum

Sprinkle the top with:

(¼ teaspoon nutmeg)

Bake the pie in the 325° oven about 30 minutes or until firm. Serve plain, with sugared fresh fruit, or garnished with curls of:

(Sweet chocolate)

QUICK CUSTARD TARTS, OR FLAN WITH FRUIT

To be assembled just before serving. Prepare:

Prebaked tart crusts, 360

Spoon into them:

½-inch layer of Baked Custard, 508

Top the custard with:

Strawberries or other berries, cooked drained apples, drained cherries,
peaches, bananas, pineapple or coconut

Coat the fruit with Glaze for Tarts, 505, to which you may add:

(1 tablespoon or more of brandy or rum)

Garnish with:

(Whipped cream)

CARAMEL CUSTARD PIE

A 9-Inch Single-Crust Pie

Prepare:

A baked pie shell, 360

and:

Caramel Custard Pudding, 514

Cool the pudding and fill the slightly cooled pie crust. Garnish with:

Sweetened Whipped Cream II, 449

CREAM PIE

A 9-Inch Single-Crust Pie

Prepare:

A baked pie shell, 360

In top of double boiler combine:

⅔ cup sugar
½ cup all-purpose flour
½ teaspoon salt

Add, stir and cook ♦ over—not in—boiling water 10 minutes or until mixture thickens:

2 cups milk

Remove from heat. Beat slightly:

3 egg yolks

Stirring well, pour half of hot mixture into eggs. When smooth, return eggs to rest of hot mixture and cook until thickened. Remove from heat and add:

2 tablespoons butter
2 teaspoons vanilla

Cool slightly before turning into the crust. Cover with:

Meringue, 502

Brown delicately as directed.

CHOCOLATE CREAM PIE

I.   A 9-Inch Single-Crust Pie

Follow the directions for:

Cream Pie, 385

with the following changes. You may increase the sugar to 1 cup. Melt in the hot milk mixture:

**2 oz. cut-up unsweetened
chocolate**

II.

Or fill the pie crust with half the recipe for:

**Pots-de-Crème, 512, or
French Chocolate Mousse,
513, or Rum Chocolate
Mousse, 513, or Chocolate
Mocha Filling, 450**

Garnish with:

Whipped cream, 186

and keep chilled until ready to serve.

FUDGE PIE

An 8-Inch Pie

A crustless pie or cake unexcelled in its delicious and devastatingly rich quality. But do not let a little devastation deter you.

Preheat oven to 325°.

Cream together:

**1 cup sugar
½ cup butter**

Beat in:

**2 egg yolks
2 oz. melted, slightly cooled
unsweetened chocolate**

Add and beat:

**⅓ cup all-purpose flour
1 teaspoon vanilla
1 cup broken nutmeats**

Whip until ♦ stiff, but not dry:

**2 egg whites
⅛ teaspoon salt**

Fold them into the batter. Pour into a greased 8-inch pie pan and bake about 30 minutes. Serve topped with:

Ice cream

BUTTERSCOTCH CREAM PIE

A 9-Inch Single-Crust Pie

Follow the directions for:

Cream Pie, 385

but substitute for the granulated sugar:

1 cup brown sugar

and decrease the vanilla to ½ teaspoon. A good addition is:

**(½ cup nutmeats or crushed
Nut Brittle or
Praliné, 593)**

Cover with:

Meringue, 502

and bake as directed; or cover with:

Whipped cream, 186

BANANA CREAM PIE

An 9-Inch Single-Crust Pie

Follow the directions for:

Cream Pie, 385

Peel and slice thinly:

2 ripe bananas

Place them in the baked pie shell. Pour the cooled filling over them.

COCONUT CREAM PIE

A 9-Inch Single-Crust Pie

You could use a crumb crust, 364, here.

Follow the directions for:

Cream Pie, 385

Add to the hot ingredients:

**½ to 1 cup grated or flaked
coconut**

Cover with:

Meringue, 502

and sprinkle over it:

¼ cup flaked coconut

Bake as directed; or you may cover the pie with:

Whipped cream, 186

COFFEE CREAM TARTS OR PIE

A 9-Inch Pie or 6 Tarts

Prepare:

6 baked tart crusts, 360, or a baked pie crust, 360

Follow the directions for:

Cream Pie, 385

adding to the hot milk:

3 tablespoons instant coffee

You may substitute for the vanilla:

(2 teaspoons rum)

Top with:

Whipped cream, 186, or Mocha Marshmallow Cream, 531

STRAWBERRY OR RASPBERRY BAVARIAN PIE

A 9-Inch Single-Crust Pie

Prepare:

A baked pie shell, 360

When cool, fill with:

Bavarian Berry Cream, 528

LEMON MERINGUE PIE

A 9-Inch Single-Crust Pie

Prepare:

A baked pie shell, 360

Sift into a 2- or 3-quart saucepan:

1½ cups sugar
6 tablespoons cornstarch
¼ teaspoon salt

Gradually blend in:

½ cup cold water
½ cup fresh lemon juice

When smooth add, blending thoroughly:

3 well-beaten egg yolks
2 tablespoons butter

Stirring constantly, gradually add:

1½ cups boiling water

Bring the mixture to a full boil, stirring gently. As it begins to thicken, reduce the heat and allow to simmer slowly 1 minute. Remove from heat and stir in:

1 teaspoon grated lemon peel

Pour into the baked pie shell. Cover with:

Meringue, 502

and bake as directed. Serve when cool.

OHIO LEMON PIE

A 9-Inch Double-Crust Pie

A very tart Shaker favorite.

Grate and reserve the yellow peel from:

2 large lemons

With a very sharp knife remove the white inner peel from the lemons and cut them into paper-thin slices. Remove seeds. Combine in a bowl the lemon slices, the grated peel and:

2 cups sugar
1 teaspoon salt

Let stand 2 to 24 hours—the longer the better.

Preheat oven to 425°.

Line a pie pan with:

A pie dough, 360–362

Add to the lemon-and-sugar mixture:

4 well-beaten eggs

After the mixture has been well stirred, pour it into the pastry-lined pan and cover with a top crust, 359. Bake ten minutes. Reduce heat to 325° and bake about 45 minutes longer. If the pie crust edges brown too fast, see 360. Cool pie before serving.

KEY LIME PIE

A 9-Inch Single-Crust Pie

This pie owes its distinctive character to the pungent citrus variety—native to Florida—called the Key lime. It may be used in any other recipe calling for either lemon or lime.

Prepare:

A baked pie shell, 360

Preheat oven to 350°.

Mix together well:

1 can sweetened condensed milk: 15 oz.
1 tablespoon grated Key lime rind
1/2 cup Key lime juice
1/4 teaspoon salt
(2 slightly beaten egg yolks)

Stir until thickened, a result of the reaction of the milk with the citrus juice.

Pour the mixture into the baked crust and cover with a meringue made by beating until ♦ stiff, but not dry:

2 egg whites
to which are gradually added:
2 tablespoons sugar

Bake pie 10 to 15 minutes or until lightly browned.

EGGLESS LEMON OR LIME PIE

A 9-Inch Single-Crust Pie

Prepare:

A baked pie shell, 360

Combine:

1 can sweetened condensed milk: 15 oz.
1/3 cup lime or lemon juice
1 tablespoon grated lime or lemon rind
1/4 teaspoon salt

♦ Stir until thickened. The thickening results from the reaction of the milk and citrus juice.

Turn the filling into the crust. Chill about 3 hours. Serve garnished with:

(Whipped cream)
(Shaved sweet chocolate)

LEMON ANGEL PIE

A 9-Inch Single-Crust Pie

Prepare a shell of:

Meringue Paste, 375

Butter the bottom of a deep 9-inch ovenproof dish and cover with the meringue, making a fluted rim. Bake

as directed. Let cool in the oven with the door open. Prepare the following filling in a double boiler ♦ over—not in—boiling water. Beat well:

4 egg yolks

Add:

1 tablespoon all-purpose flour
1/2 cup sugar
1/2 cup water
Juice and grated rind of 1 lemon

Cook until thickened, beating constantly. Cool.

Whip:

1 cup whipping cream

Fold in:

1/2 teaspoon vanilla

Put half the cream in the meringue shell, then the cooked lemon filling. Cover with the remaining cream. Chill before serving.

ABOUT CHIFFON PIES

Many chiffon pies call for raw egg whites, so please see note on uncooked eggs, 523.

Don't neglect the wonderful Bavarian Creams, 527–530, the Gelatin Puddings, 522, and the Fruit Whips, 526. All can be used in a baked pie shell.

LEMON OR LIME CHIFFON PIE

A 9-Inch Single-Crust Pie

Please see note on uncooked eggs, 523. Prepare:

A baked pie shell, 360

Combine in the top of a double boiler:

1/2 cup sugar
2/3 cup water
4 egg yolks
1 tablespoon gelatin
1/3 cup lemon or lime juice

Cook and stir these ingredients

▶ over—not in—boiling water until thick. Add:

    1 tablespoon grated lemon or lime peel

Chill mixture in refrigerator until it forms little mounds when dropped from a spoon. Whip:

    4 egg whites

until ▶ stiff, but not dry. Fold in:

    1/3 cup sugar

Fold this mixture lightly in turn into the lemon mixture. Fill the pie crust. Chill until set, which may take several hours.

ORANGE CHIFFON PIE

    A 9-Inch Single-Crust Pie

Follow directions for:

    Lemon Chiffon Pie, 388

but substitute a well-flavored orange juice for the water and lemon juice, and orange peel for the lemon peel. Indifferently flavored orange juice may be improved by the addition of 2 teaspoons of vanilla.

CHOCOLATE MOCHA GELATIN CHIFFON PIE

    A 9-Inch Single-Crust Pie

Please see note on uncooked eggs, 523.

Prepare:

    A baked pie shell, 360

Soak:

    1 tablespoon gelatin

in:

    1/4 cup cold strong coffee

Combine and stir until smooth:

    6 tablespoons cocoa or 2 oz. melted unsweetened chocolate

    1/2 cup sugar

    1/2 cup boiling strong coffee

Stir in the soaked gelatin until it is dissolved. Cool slightly and pour these ingredients gently onto:

    4 lightly beaten egg yolks

Cook and stir this mixture in a double boiler ▶ over—not in—boiling water until it thickens. Chill until about to set. Beat with wire whisk until light. Add:

    1 teaspoon vanilla

    (1 tablespoon brandy)

Whip until ▶ stiff, but not dry:

    4 egg whites

Slowly beat in:

    1/2 cup sugar

Fold the egg whites into the chocolate mixture. Fill the pie shell. Chill the pie to set the filling. Spread with:

    Whipped cream, 186

RASPBERRY OR STRAWBERRY CHIFFON PIE

    A 9-Inch Single-Crust Pie

Prepare:

    A baked pie shell, 360

Just before serving, fill with:

    Bavarian Berry Cream, 528

and serve covered with:

    Glaze for Fruit Pies II, 505

BLACK BOTTOM GELATIN PIE

    A Deep 9-Inch Single-Crust Pie

Please see note on uncooked eggs, 523. Prepare:

    A baked crumb crust, 364, or baked pie shell, 360

Soak:

    1 tablespoon gelatin

in:

    1/4 cup cold water

Scald:

    2 cups rich milk

Combine:

    1/2 cup sugar

    4 teaspoons cornstarch

Beat until light:

    4 egg yolks

Slowly stir the milk into the eggs. Stir in the sugar mixture. Cook these

ingredients ♦ over—not in—boiling
water, stirring occasionally, about 20
minutes—or until the custard coats a
spoon heavily. Take out 1 cup of the
custard. Add to it:

**1½ oz. melted unsweetened
chocolate**

Beat until well blended and cool.
Add:

½ teaspoon vanilla

Pour this into the crust. Dissolve the
soaked gelatin in the remaining hot
custard. Let it cool, but not stiffen.
Stir in:

1 tablespoon or more rum

Beat until well blended:

3 egg whites

Add:

¼ teaspoon cream of tartar

Beat the egg whites until ♦ stiff, but
not dry. Beat in gradually, a teaspoon
at a time:

¼ cup sugar

Fold the egg whites into the custard.
Cover the chocolate custard with the
rum-flavored custard. Chill to set.
Whip until stiff:

1 cup whipping cream

Add gradually:

**2 tablespoons confectioner's
sugar**

Cover custard with the cream. Top
with:

**½ oz. shaved semisweet
chocolate**

MAPLE OR CARAMEL GELATIN
CHIFFON PIE

A 9-Inch Single-Crust Pie

Prepare:

A baked pie shell, 360

Follow directions for:

**Caramel or Maple
Bavarian Cream, 529**

reducing the milk to ⅔ cup and folding in before chilling:

2 stiffly beaten egg whites

PUMPKIN GELATIN
CHIFFON PIE

A 9-Inch Single-Crust Pie

Please see note on uncooked
eggs, 523.
Prepare:

**A baked pie shell, 360, or
Graham Cracker
Crust, 365**

Soak:

1 tablespoon gelatin

in:

¼ cup cold water

Beat slightly:

3 egg yolks

Add:

**½ cup white or brown sugar
1¼ cups canned or cooked
pumpkin
½ cup milk
½ teaspoon salt
¼ teaspoon each cinnamon,
nutmeg and ginger**

Cook and stir these ingredients
♦ over—not in—boiling water until
thick. Stir in the soaked gelatin until
dissolved. Chill until mixture begins
to set. Whip until ♦ stiff, but not dry:

3 egg whites

Stir in gradually:

½ cup sugar

and fold into the pumpkin mixture.
Fill the pie shell. Chill several hours
to set. Serve garnished with:

Whipped cream, 186

ABOUT CHEESECAKE

No wonder pictures of leggy starlets
are called cheesecake! We think the
following recipes are starlets. Take
your pick, but remember to ♦ watch
temperatures. Cheesecakes are egg-
based. They need low heat and are
usually left in the turned-off oven with
the door open after baking. Expect a
slight shrinkage as they cool. If there

is great shrinkage, you have baked them at too high heat. They all profit by ❶ thorough chilling before serving, preferably 12 hours. For safe storage, keep refrigerated, lightly covered.

🔪 We have found it a time-saver to put all ingredients together in a blender except the egg whites or whipped cream, which should be folded in just before the mixture is poured into the crust. If smooth cottage cheese is not available, regular curd cottage cheese may be put through a sieve or a 🔪 blender.

A few wine-soaked currants, finely shaved almonds, or tiny pieces of angelica or citron are sometimes mixed with the filling or used as topping. Shaved curled chocolate may be added as a surface garnish. To glaze cheesecakes, see Strawberry Glaze and Apricot Glaze, 505, Sauce Cockaigne, 564, and other fruit sauces.

WHIPPED CREAM CHEESECAKE

I. 16 Servings
Prepare a double recipe of:
A crumb crust, 364
Reserve 1/2 cup of this mixture. Press the remainder with a spoon or the palm of the hand on the bottom and sides of a 12-inch spring-form pan. Chill this shell thoroughly.
Preheat oven to 350°.
To make the filling, sift:
1 1/2 cups sugar
Beat until light:
6 eggs
Add the sugar gradually. Beat these ingredients until very light. Add:
1/8 teaspoon salt
2 teaspoons grated lemon rind
1 to 2 tablespoons lemon juice
1 teaspoon vanilla
Blend well and add to the above:

1/2 cup all-purpose flour
3 1/2 pints smooth cottage cheese: 2 1/4 lb.
Whip and fold in:
2 cups whipped cream
Fill the pie crust. Sprinkle the reserved crumb mixture over the filling. Bake about 1 hour. Turn off the heat and permit the pie to stand in the oven with the door open for 1 hour longer or until cooled.

II. 10 Servings
This very delicate pie should be baked in a 2-inch-deep 9-inch pan.
Prepare:
A baked pie shell, 360, or crumb crust, 364
Make enough to also line the sides of the pan.
Preheat oven to 350°.
Combine and beat:
3 cups smooth cottage cheese
3 whole eggs
Add:
3/4 cup whipping cream
3 tablespoons melted butter
5 tablespoons sugar
1/2 teaspoon vanilla, or 1 tablespoon lemon juice plus 1/2 teaspoon grated lemon rind
(1/4 cup chopped blanched almonds)
Bake the pie until the filling is firm, about 45 minutes. Sprinkle it while hot with:
4 tablespoons confectioners' sugar
1 teaspoon cinnamon

SOUR CREAM CHEESECAKE
12 Servings
Using 2 cups crumbs, line a 2 1/2-inch-deep, 9-inch spring mold with:
Zwieback Crust, 365
Chill the crust.

Preheat oven to 375°.
Mix well, then pour into the crust:

    2 well-beaten eggs
    ³/4 lb. soft cream cheese
    ¹/2 cup sugar
    1 teaspoon vanilla
    ¹/2 teaspoon salt

Bake about 20 minutes. Remove
from oven. Dust the top with:

    Cinnamon

Let cool to room temperature. Heat
oven to 425°. Mix well and pour over
the cake:

    1¹/2 cups thick, cultured sour
         cream
    2 tablespoons sugar
    ¹/2 teaspoon vanilla
    ¹/8 teaspoon salt

Bake about 5 minutes to glaze the
cheesecake. Let it cool, then refrigerate from 6 to 12 hours before serving.

RICOTTA CHEESECAKE OR PIE

A 10-Inch Single-Crust Pie

This North Italian delight is a favorite
of our friend Jim Beard, who has generously allowed us to include it.
Prepare and line a deep pie pan with:

    Cheesecake Crust, 364

Make a fluted edge and bake about
7 minutes at 450°. Cool. Heat oven
to 375°.
Have ready:

    3 tablespoons toasted pine
         nuts
    2 tablespoons chopped
         blanched almonds
    2 tablespoons chopped citron

and dust with:

    1 tablespoon flour

Beat until light and lemony in color:

    4 eggs

Gradually add:

    1 cup sugar
    1¹/2 teaspoons vanilla

Add to the eggs and blend well:

    1¹/2 lb. Ricotta cheese

Stir in the nut mixture and pour the
filling into the crust. Bake about 40
minutes.

GELATIN CHEESECAKE

A 10-Inch Cake

This handsome and toothsome affair
will serve up to 18 persons and may
be made a day in advance. Fruit may
be incorporated, but if it is, substitute
fruit juice for the water and milk. See
note on uncooked eggs, 523. Prepare
a double recipe of:

    Graham Cracker or
    Zwieback Crumb
    Crust, 365

Reserve ¹/2 cup crumbs. Spread or
pat the rest in a thin layer over the
bottom and sides of a 3-inch-deep
10-inch spring mold. Bake the crust
about 10 minutes. Cool it. Beat in the
top of a double boiler:

    4 beaten egg yolks
    ³/4 cup sugar
    ¹/4 teaspoon salt
    ¹/3 cup milk

Heat and stir this custard ♦ over—
not in—boiling water until it thickens. Soak:

    2 tablespoons gelatin

in:

    ¹/2 cup water

Add the gelatin to the hot custard
and stir until dissolved. Cool the custard. Add:

    1¹/2 teaspoons vanilla or
         ¹/3 cup lemon juice

Beat until smooth:

    1¹/2 lb. soft cream cheese

Gradually beat the custard into the
cheese until well blended. Whip until
♦ stiff, but not dry:

    4 egg whites

Whip in gradually:

    ¹/2 cup sugar

Fold this into the custard. Beat until
stiff, then fold in:

1 cup whipping cream

Fill the crust with the custard. Sprinkle the reserved crumbs over the top. Chill well in the refrigerator until ready to serve.

ABOUT FRUIT PASTRIES

Here we include cobblers, deep-dish pies, fresh fruit cakes, shortcakes, upside-down cakes, crisps and crunches. Remember that large shortcakes, fresh fruit cakes and crunches lend themselves well to baking for individual servings.

COBBLERS AND DEEP-DISH PIES

A cobbler, first cousin to a deep-dish pie, involves a rich biscuit dough, 349–350, and fruit. Baked with the fruit either under or over it, it is usually served with rich cream, Hard Sauce, 572, or Sweetened Butters, 571; but try a fresh hot blackberry cobbler with vanilla ice cream.

Preheat oven to 425°.

Combine in a saucepan and heat:

3 cups prepared fruit: apples, peaches, plums, etc.

2/3 cup sugar—depending on sweetness of fruit

1 tablespoon all-purpose flour or 1 beaten egg

If using flour, allow the mixture to boil. If using egg, stir until it thickens somewhat, but do not allow it to boil. Have ready half the recipe for:

Fluffy Biscuit Dough, 350

Place the dough in a greased 8 × 8-inch pan or casserole and cover it closely with the hot fruit; or place the hot fruit in the bottom of an 8-inch baking dish and spoon over it the dough. Dot the fruit with:

2 tablespoons butter

Sprinkle with:

(3/4 teaspoon cinnamon)

Bake the cobbler about 1/2 hour.

APPLE, PEACH OR PLUM CAKE COCKAIGNE

A 9- or 10-Inch Round Pan

Our friend Jane Nickerson, formerly Food Editor of the New York Times, suggests using fresh guavas in this dish.

Preheat oven to 425°.

If the fruit used is very juicy, reduce the liquid in the dough by at least 1 tablespoon. Sift together:

1 cup all-purpose flour

1 teaspoon double-acting baking powder

1/4 teaspoon salt

2 tablespoons sugar

Add:

1 1/2 to 3 tablespoons butter

Work these ingredients like pastry, 360. Beat well in a measuring cup:

1 egg

1/2 teaspoon vanilla

Add:

Enough milk to make a 1/2-cup mixture

Combine with the flour and butter to make a stiff dough. You may pat the dough into the greased pan with your floured palm, or spread it in part with a spoon and then distribute it evenly by pushing it with the fruit sections when you place them closely in overlapping rows. Use about:

4 cups sliced pared apples or peaches or sliced unpared plums, preferably freestone blue

Sprinkle with a mixture of:

1 cup white or brown sugar

2 teaspoons cinnamon

3 tablespoons melted butter

Bake about 25 minutes.

FRENCH APPLE OR PEACH CAKE

A Deep 8-Inch Pie Pan

Sweet and rich.

Preheat oven to 425°.

Grease the pan or ovenproof dish and cover the bottom well with:

    2 cups or more peeled sliced apples, peaches or other fruit

Sprinkle the fruit with:

    2/3 cup sugar
    Cinnamon or nutmeg
    Grated rind and juice of 1 lemon

Dredge with:

    1 tablespoon all-purpose flour

Pour over surface:

    2 to 4 tablespoons melted butter

Prepare the following batter. Sift together:

    1 cup all-purpose flour
    1/2 cup sugar
    1 teaspoon double-acting baking powder
    1/4 teaspoon salt

Beat and add:

    2 egg yolks
    1 tablespoon melted butter
    1/4 cup milk

Beat these ingredients with swift strokes until blended. Cover the fruit with the batter. Bake the cake for about 30 minutes. Reverse it on a platter. Cool slightly. Use the egg whites for:

    (Meringue ll, 502)

and brown as directed.

SKILLET OR UPSIDE-DOWN CAKE

A 9- or 10-Inch Heavy Skillet

Vary this recipe, which conventionally calls for canned pineapple, by using canned or frozen raspberries, peaches or apricots. The last two require only 1/2 cup sugar. Fresh fruit—peaches, cherries, apples, etc.—may require more than 1 cup, depending on the acidity of the fruit.

Preheat oven to 350°.

Melt in a skillet:

    1/4 to 1/2 cup butter

Add, cook gently and stir until dissolved:

    1/2 to 1 cup packed brown sugar

Remove the pan from the heat and add:

    (1 cup pecan meats)

Place over the butter and sugar mixture:

    Slices or halves of drained canned fruit:
    No. 2 1/2 can

Cover the fruit with the following batter. Sift together:

    1 cup cake flour
    1 teaspoon double-acting baking powder

Beat in a separate bowl:

    4 egg yolks

Add:

    1 tablespoon melted butter
    1 teaspoon vanilla

Sift in a separate bowl:

    1 cup sugar

Whip until stiff ♦ but not dry:

    4 egg whites

Fold in the sugar, 1 tablespoon at a time; then fold in the yolk mixture, and finally the sifted flour, 1/4 cup at a time. Bake the cake about 30 minutes. Immediately upon removal from the oven, reverse the cake onto a serving plate. Allow pan to remain over the cake briefly to let brown sugar mixture coat the cake. Remove pan and serve upside down, after sprinkling the fruit with:

    (Brandy or rum)

The cake may be garnished with:

**(Whipped cream or a
dessert sauce)**

For individual servings, try this
method: Put butter, sugar and fruit in
base of custard cups, run batter given
above on top of the fruit and bake in
a 350° oven until done.

APPLE CRISP OR FRUIT PARADISE

6 Servings

This dessert can be baked in an ovenproof dish from which you may serve
at table. Its success, when made with
apples, depends on their flavor. See
About Apples, 115.

Preheat oven to 375°.

Pare, core and slice into a 9-inch pie
pan or dish:

4 cups tart apples

or use the same amount of:

**Peaches, slightly sugared
rhubarb or pitted
cherries**

Season with:

**(2 tablespoons lemon juice or
kirsch)**

Work like pastry with a pastry
blender or with the fingertips:

**1/2 cup all-purpose flour
1/2 cup packed brown sugar
1/4 cup butter
1/2 teaspoon salt, if butter is
unsalted
(1 teaspoon cinnamon)**

The mixtures must be lightly worked
so that it does not become oily.
Spread these crumbly ingredients
over the apples. Bake about 30 minutes. Serve hot or cold with:

**(Sweet or cultured sour
cream)**

GINGER CRISP

Substitute for the flour in the recipe
above:

**1 1/2 cups crushed gingersnap
cookies**

and proceed as directed.

APPLE-MINCE-OAT CRISP

Add to the recipe for Apple Crisp,
opposite:

1 cup moist mincemeat

and reduce the flour to 1/3 cup. Add to
the flour mixture:

**1 cup rolled oats
1/4 teaspoon nutmeg**

and proceed as directed above.

QUICK CHERRY CRUNCH

A 9 X 9 X 2-Inch Pan

A well-flavored, easy cherry pastry.
Preheat oven to 350°.

Mix and let stand 15 minutes:

**1/2 cup cherry juice
1 1/2 tablespoons quick-cooking
tapioca**

Melt in a large pan:

1/2 cup butter

Mix with it:

**1 to 1 1/2 cups packed brown
sugar
1 cup all-purpose flour
1 cup quick-cooking oatmeal
1/4 teaspoon each double-
acting baking powder, salt,
and baking soda**

Put half of this mixture into the baking pan. Scatter over it:

**2 cups drained canned red
cherries**

and the juice and tapioca mixture.
Cover the fruit with the other half of
the pastry mixture. Bake 30 to 35
minutes or until brown.

SWEET FRUIT TURNOVERS

To shape these tea pastries, see Filled
Cookies, 481. The pastry may be:

Rough Puff Paste, 369

or use any pie dough. A cutting into shapes, place in the center of each pastry 1 teaspoonful or more of one of the following fillings:

> **Well-flavored applesauce**
> **Preserves or ja**
> **Mincemeat, 630**
> **Banbury Tart Filling, 382**
> **Filled Cookie Filling, 481**

Preheat oven to 450°.
Brush the edges lightly with water. Fold the dough over into triangles or crescents and press edges to seal. Brush the tops with:

> **1 egg yolk diluted with**
> **2 tablespoons cream**

Bake about 15 minutes. While still warm dust pastries with:

> **Powdered sugar**

FRUIT DUMPLINGS

4 Dumplings

Prepare:

> **A pie dough, 360–362, or**
> **Biscuit Dough, 349**

Chill it. Pare and core:

> **4 medium-sized apples or 4**
> **peeled, pitted and halved**
> **peaches or apricots**

If using canned fruit, drain well and sprinkle with:

> **Lemon juice or rum**

and use less sugar. Combine until blended:

> **3/4 cup packed brown sugar**
> **1/4 cup soft butter**
> **1/2 teaspoon salt**
> **1/2 teaspoon cinnamon**
> **(Grated lemon rind or**
> **citron)**

Fill the core hollows with this mixture or with:

> **Raspberry jam**

and spread the remainder over the fruit.
Preheat oven to 450°.
Roll out the dough in a thin sheet, 1/8

inch for pastry, 1/4 inch for biscuit dough. Cut it into 4 squares, large enough to enclose the apple entirely. Brush squares with the white of an egg to keep the dough from becoming soggy. Place an apple on each square. Bring up the four corners of the dough to cover the apple and press the edges together, using a little water, if necessary, to make them stick. Prick the tops of the dumplings in several places. They may be chilled for several hours or baked at once. Brush the tops with milk. Bake about 10 minutes at 450°, reduce the heat to 350° and bake about 45 minutes longer, until the apples are tender. Test them with a wooden pick. Serve with:

> **Brown Sugar Butter**
> **Sauce, 570**

If you wish to bake the dumplings in sauce, combine and simmer 5 minutes:

> **1 cup water**
> **1/2 cup sugar**
> **2 tablespoons butter**
> **1/2 teaspoon cinnamon**

For enhanced flavor, if you are using apples, you may simmer the cores and peelings in 1 1/2 cups water 15 minutes. Drain and use the fruit liquid in place of the water. Pour it boiling hot over the dumplings when they begin to color. Dumplings that are not baked in sauce may be served hot or cold with:

> **Fluffy Hard Sauce with**
> **Rum, 572, Foamy**
> **Sauce, 573, Lemon Sauce,**
> **563, or cream**

RAISED DUMPLINGS OR DAMPFNUDELN

About 16 Dumplings

It was fun digging into old cookbooks for this recipe, if only because it made us realize that the modern method of writing for cooks is an immense improvement over the old. Our grandmothers had to hack through a labyrinth, undoubtedly armed with a ball of string, plus a rabbit's foot, in order to arrive at their culinary goals. This homely old-time favorite is worth resurrecting. Try it in its modern form. A well-known Cincinnati hostess serves it as a dessert at formal dinners with much success.

Combine:

　½ tablespoon active dry yeast
　1 tablespoon sugar
　1¼ cups all-purpose flour

Add:

　½ cup 110°–115° milk

Let this heavy sponge rise, covered with a cloth in a warm place, until light, for about 1 hour. Cream:

　1 tablespoon butter
　2 tablespoons sugar
　½ teaspoon salt

Beat in and stir until light:

　1 whole egg

Add this to the sponge and work in about:

　½ cup all-purpose flour

or enough to stiffen, as for yeast cake. Cover the bowl with a cloth. Allow the dough to rise until doubled in bulk. Shape it into about 16 biscuits. They may be rolled out and cut. If you have time, permit them to rise again. From here on, there is a great

divergence in treatment. The old method required the use of a Dutch oven, but a covered deep 10-inch ovenproof glass baking dish is preferable, as it enables you to watch the cooking process. Place in it one of the hot liquids indicated below and then the dumplings. If they are to be served with a meat course with lots of gravy, use ½ cup butter and ½ cup milk. If they are to constitute a dessert, use 1½ cups syrup, fruit juice, preserves or stewed fruit.

◗ Cover the pot closely, place it in a 275° oven and cook the dumplings about 1½ hours. If you have not used a glass baker, do not lift the lid, even to peek. Old recipes add that your sense of smell must be your guide as to when to uncover. Do it when the dumplings begin to give off a tempting fragrance of finality and all sizzling noises have ceased, telling you that the liquid has been absorbed. Test the dumplings with a wooden pick to be sure they are dry. Remove them from the pot and serve at once.

An outstanding accompaniment for this dessert is stewed blue plums or prunes. Use part of the syrup in the pot. Serve the dumplings with:

　Plums or prunes stewed with part white wine and part water

In addition, it is customary to serve:

　Custard Sauce, 565, or Rich Custard, 509

CAKES, CUPCAKES, TORTEN AND FILLED CAKES

A gaggle of cakes can be oven-ready in short order with the sensitive use of an electric mixer, above. Whip up a Lightning Cake, 424, which should be eaten warm from the oven, with its baked-on garnish of cinnamon, sugar and almonds, or Honey-Bee Glaze, 503. Above center is a perfectly textured Bundkuchen, 329, needing only a dusting of powdered sugar, and in the right foreground a pan for Madeleines, 447, which are perfect unadorned. Bake a fresh Coconut Cake, 412; cut it into a swirl, and highlight it with one tactful candle, as a birthday treat. For other special occasions, you may want to try your hand at a classic Yule Log, 441, or a towering Kransekake, 435.

For all these cakes, start, of course, with high-quality materials. Pay attention to the ♦ measurements and proportions you use, ♦ the temperature of the ingredients, and ♦ the heat of your oven, 401. Most recipes call for ingredients at room temperature. As kitchen temperatures vary, we suggest that ♦ ingredients be about 70°, the ideal recommended by professional bakers. ♦ Pay attention also to the physical states you induce by stirring, creaming and folding. Our drawings and descriptions can do no more than get you off to a flying start. The proper "look" of well-creamed butter and eggs, of batter ready for the oven—these and other critical stages in cake making you will learn to recognize most effectively through practice.

If you are concerned with the amount of sugar in most cakes, we suggest you consider Quick Breads, 334, and muffin recipes, 344. Whole grains, the Cornell Formula, 301, and other substitutions may be used to enrich cakes as well as breads. When using whole wheat flour for cakes, sift to remove the coarse bran. Use the bran in cereals or soups.

CAKE TYPES

We divide cakes according to their leavens. If you know what makes them rise, it will help you to safeguard this lifting action during the mixing period. Angel and sponge cakes are sometimes called ♦ foam cakes, because they depend for their leavening exclusively on the expansion of the vapor trapped in their light egg-rich doughs. Egg yolk contains fat; egg white does not. As a consequence, angel cakes are fat-free; ♦ but sponge cakes, though light in texture, contain an appreciable amount of fat by reason of their yolk content, (I, 8).

♦ Butter and shortening cakes need baking powder for proper leavening. We feel that most cakes in this category are more delicious if butter alone is used as the shortening. One exception may be spice cakes, where the strong flavors overwhelm the taste of butter. If you care to use, instead, one of the bland vegetable shortenings now on the market, you will trade distinctive flavor for a measure of economy, a spongier texture and a somewhat greater volume.

In cakes made with ♦ melted butter, such as the classic Génoise, 416, the butter is put in last. In cakes made with oils, special mixing procedures are employed to allow the incorporation of air into the batter.

Torten often depend on egg yolks instead of butter for their fat content and on egg whites for their leavening; ground nuts and bread crumbs replace flour as their base. Our cake recipes are all adjusted in method to the specific demands of the ingredients. So, for success, please follow directions as given.

All these cake types may be ❅ frozen, see 658, but dry out rapidly after thawing.

▲ To bake cakes at high altitude, see 442.

CAKE MIXING

After reading About Leavens, 222, look at the drawing on 400. ♦ To cream, work 70° shortening lightly with the fingertips—or use the back of a wooden spoon. Press the mixture between the back of the spoon and the side of the bowl in a gently gliding motion. Use short rocking strokes over a rather limited area, as shown between the arrows in the sketch. When thoroughly creamed, the sugar mixture should become light in color; smooth, even, and creamy in texture. If it looks curdled and frothy, you have worked it too long; the oil in the butter has separated, and the result will be a coarsely grained cake. In the center, you see how to ♦ stir a batter. Begin at the center of the bowl, using a circular motion; widen the circle as the ingredients become blended. The entire operation of adding and blending the dry and liquid ingredients should take no more than 2 minutes, or the result may be a too finely grained cake. To beat or whip, ♦ use a long, free-swinging, lifting motion, which brings the bottom mass constantly to the top, trapping as much air as possible in the mixture, as shown on the right. A slotted spoon makes the work quicker; a wooden, rather than a metal, spoon keeps the ingredients in the best condition. Whipping is done rapidly with an increasing tempo. For best results in handling egg whites, use a long, thin whip, such as the one shown, on 400, on the right above or as shown on the right below. For beating cream, use a wider whisk like the one on the left above. In choosing a mechanical mixer, see that the beaters have many wires that are as thin as is consistent with durability.

Folding in is one of the most delicate

of cakemaking operations: the objective is to blend thoroughly, yet not lose any of the air you have previously worked into your materials.

◗ To fold, first of all have a large enough bowl. A flat whip as shown below is usually recommended, but this tool can be maddening because it cuts through the whites, and its too widely spaced wires allow the heavier substances to fall through. We commonly dispense with tools for this step and use the flat of the hand both to scoop and to slice. Begin by folding into the dough a small quantity of the whites. When thoroughly mixed, fold in the rest of the whites by scooping up some of the more solid material and covering the whites. Then, cut it in with a gentle but determined slicing motion to the base of the mixing bowl. Turn the bowl slightly with the other hand each time you repeat the folding motions. It is surprising how quickly blending is achieved by this simple procedure.

TESTING CAKES FOR DONENESS

Insert a wire cake tester or a wooden pick in the center of the cake; if it emerges perfectly clean, the cake is done. The cake should be lightly browned and beginning to shrink from the sides of the pan. If pressed lightly with a finger, it should at once come back into shape, except in very rich cakes and chocolate cakes, which may dent slightly and still be done.

When removed from the oven, the cake is cooled in the pan on a rack—plain cakes about 5 minutes and rich cakes 10 to 15 minutes—and then cooled out of the pan, on a rack, until all heat has left. For exceptions, see About Angel, 404, Sponge, 406, Génoise, 416, and Fruit Cakes, 426. If cakes are left in pans too long, they become soggy and obstinate. You may set the pan on a cloth wrung out in hot water. This often helps in removing the cake from the pan.

A towel placed on the cooling rack will prevent the wire from indenting

the fragile top of the cake when it is turned out of the pan. Do not leave the cake resting on its top, but immediately turn it right side up onto another rack.

ABOUT CAKE PANS

If you want a thin, evenly browned crust, try using ◗ medium-weight shiny metal pans. If you prefer heavier, browner crusts, use glass or enamel pans or those that are dark in color—all of which absorb and hold more heat. Should you choose from the second group ◗ reduce the oven heat by 25°, but use the same baking time. In baking layer cakes, use pans with straight sides. Note also that too-high sides will prevent good browning. But even more important to the crumb and volume of your cake is the relation of dough to the size of the pan. All our cake recipes indicate the proper pan sizes.

If the recipe calls for a greased pan, use solid shortening, but not butter, margarine or oil. Use a pastry brush or waxed paper to apply evenly about 1/2 tablespoon of shortening to the bottom only of each layer or tube pan. You may dust each greased pan with flour—about 1/2 tablespoon—and remove any excess by tapping the overturned pan gently. If using nonstick pans, follow the manufacturer's directions. For pan placement in the oven, see (I, 115).

The batter, for a velvety texture, should be at least 1 inch deep in the pan. If the pan is too big, the cake will not rise properly and may brown unevenly. If the pan is too small, the texture will be coarse and the batter may overflow before it sets. If it doesn't overflow, it will probably sink in cooling. More pans are filled at least half full, but not more than two-thirds. Loaf and tube pans can be filled higher. If you have no pan corresponding to the size called for in the recipe, see the chart below to find the corresponding square-inch area of pan size. Then substitute a pan of that approximate size. For instance, a recipe calls for a 9-inch round pan which has an area of approximately 64 square inches. From the tables you see that you could equally well use an 8 × 8-inch square pan, which offers also an area of 64 square inches. ◗ Note, below, that a round 9-inch-diameter pan equals only about three-fourths the area of a square 9-inch pan. Should your pan be too large, you can reduce the baking area of a rectangular pan by folding a piece of foil as shown in the drawing on the right, 402. The batter will help to hold the divider in place on one side. Place dry beans or rice on the other, see center sketch.

◗ To determine how much batter to mix for oddly shaped pans or molds, first measure their contents with water. Then make up two-thirds as much dough as the amount of the water measured.

COMPARATIVE PAN SIZES

Cake pans are measured across the top between the inside edges.

ROUND CAKE PANS

8 × 1½	50 sq. inches
9 × 1½	64 sq. inches
10 × 1½	79 sq. inches

SQUARE AND RECTANGULAR CAKE PANS

7¾ × 3⅝ × 2¼	28 sq. inches
8 × 8 × 1½	64 sq. inches
9 × 5 × 2¾	45 sq. inches
9 × 9 × 1½	81 sq. inches

11 × 4½ × 2¾ ...... 50 sq. inches
11 × 7 × 1½ .... 77 sq. inches
13 × 9 × 2 .... 117 sq. inches
15 × 10 × 2 .... 150 sq. inches
15½ × 10½ × 1 .... 163 sq. inches
16 × 5 × 4 .... 80 sq. inches

ABOUT CAKES IN A MIXER

Electric mixers are the greatest boon to cake bakers, but, because models vary in speed and efficiency, ◗ be sure to read the manual which comes with your particular appliance. Having an extra mixer bowl is a great convenience if you bake often. The following comments can give only approximate speeds and times. So-called one-bowl cakes can be mixed in as little as three minutes. Butter cakes may take as long as 8 to 10 minutes. Basically, you apply the same principles that you use in hand mixing. ◗ Have all ingredients assembled. If chocolate, honey or molasses mixtures are called for, melt or heat them ◗ and cool, before using, to about 70°, which should be the approximate temperature of all your ingredients. Sift and measure the flour; sift it once again with the baking powder, the soda, the spices and the cocoa, if called for. You may then mix just as though you were working by hand, or use the one-bowl method described below. ◗ The main things to observe are the beating speed and the timing of each process. We find it

wise to stop the beating during the addition of most ingredients. During these breaks is the time, too, when the sides of the bowl should be scraped down with a rubber or plastic scraper, unless you have a heavy-duty mixer which revolves with an off-center motion, covering every bit of the mixing area.

To mix a typical butter cake, cream the 70° butter until light, at low speed. Then cream it with the sugar at medium speed until the mix is the consistency of whipped cream. If the recipe calls for whole eggs, they may be creamed from the beginning with the sugar and butter. If the eggs are separated, add the yolks at the end of about a 3- to 5-minute creaming period of the butter and sugar. The whites are added later. For descriptions of the textures that these ingredients should have, read about Cake Mixing, 399. Then ◗ using low speed and stopping the mixing between additions, add the flour mixture in 3 parts and the milk in 2 parts. Begin and end with the flour. Mix until just smooth after each addition. The whole operation should not take more than about 2 minutes or you will have a too finely grained cake. If nuts and other lumpy substances are to be added, fold them in lightly with a fork at the end of the mixing period, or briefly use the low speed on the beater.

Be sure ◗ before you begin beating

the egg whites that your oven has reached the right temperature and that your pans are greased. Beat the whites, in a grease-free bowl, at medium speed for about 1/2 minute—until foamy. Now the cream of tartar, if called for, is added. Then beat at high speed for another 1/2 minute until the whites are ♦ stiff, but not dry, see 207. For the best results from this point on, the beater is no longer used and the beaten whites are folded in by hand, see 400.

To mix so-called one-bowl cakes with unseparated eggs and solid shortenings, put sifted flour, baking powder, spices and cocoa, if called for, the fat and 2/3 of the liquid into the mixer bowl at once. Beat on medium speed about 2 minutes. Add the rest of the liquid. Add, unbeaten, the whole eggs, the yolks, or the whites, as called for in the recipe, and beat for 2 minutes more. ♦ Scrape the bowl several times during this beating period. ♦ Overbeating will reduce the volume and give a too densely grained cake.

ABOUT PACKAGED BAKING MIXES

We know that people think they save time by using mixes—just how much time is a sobering consideration—but we also know they do not save money, nor are they assured of good ingredients and best results. Use mixes, if you must, in emergencies. But consider that, under present distribution methods, the mix you buy may be as old as 2 years—if the store has a slow turnover. Remember that, in contriving the mix originally, everything was done to use ingredients that would keep. Egg whites were used in preference to whole eggs, as the fat from the yolks might

turn rancid. For the same reason, non-fat dry milk solids were preferred. Even when the natural moisture content of flour has been greatly lowered, what remains in the packaged mix can still deteriorate baking powders, flavorings and spices. Furthermore, even the most elaborate packaging is not proof, over a protracted storage period, against spoilage by moisture from without. So why not become expert at a few quick cakes and hot breads? Build up your own baking speed, control your ingredients, create really topnotch flavor and save money.

ABOUT WEDDING AND OTHER LARGE CAKES

Be sure for any big cake to ♦ choose a recipe that enlarges successfully, see comment under White Cake I, 409, or use a large fruit-cake recipe. We find that when rather shallow pans are used—not more than 2 inches deep for each layer—the cake bakes more evenly and cuts more attractively. For any large cake, lower the indicated oven temperature by 25°. For more even baking, turn the pans in the oven frequently during the necessarily longer baking period. To help support the tiers of cakes, bake three

1-inch-wide dowels in the lower layers, as long in length as the pan is high. Place the dowels upright within the diameter of the succeeding layer. Test for doneness as you would with any cake, see 400. To ice, see Decorative Twice-Cooked or Cream Icings, 492, or Royal Glaze, 496. Top the cake with the traditional bride-and-groom figurines, with an icing flower or with a miniature vase of fresh flowers.

After the bride's first slice, whether the wedding cake is round or rectangular, the cutting begins at the lowest tier. To make the cuts even in depth, run a knife perpendicularly through the bottom layer, where it abuts the second layer. Continue this process at each tier. Cut successive slices until a single cylindrical central core remains, crested by the ornate top, as shown on the preceding page. Remove and save this, or freeze it for the first anniversary party. Then finish slicing the central core, beginning at the top.

ABOUT ANGEL CAKES

Laboratory research in some types of recipes—and no cake has a larger bibliography than angel cake—has become so elaborate as to intimidate the housewife, who can rarely know the exact age of the eggs she uses or the precise blend of flour. Yet, working innocently as she must, she can still contrive a glamorous result with a little care. The main risers in angel cake are air and steam, so the egg-white volume is important. See Beating Eggs, 206, for the type of bowl and preparation of equipment.

◗ Have egg whites ready. They should be at least 3 days old, at about 60° to 70°, and separated just before use. These are preferable to leftover egg whites. Divide the beating time into 4 quarters. During the first quarter, beat whites gently ◗ until foamy. Add salt, cream of tartar and liquid flavoring. Be sure the cream of tartar has been stored in a closely covered container. It is added midway during the first quarter of the beating and controls both the stabilizing of the foam and the whiteness of the cake. End the first quarter of the beating with an increasing speed and gradually add, while continuing to beat at high speed, three-fourths of the sugar called for in the recipe. Finely granulated fruit or berry sugar, 227, is best.

If you are using an electric mixer, this sugar addition begins in the second quarter because it guards against overbeating the whites. If you are beating by hand with a flat whip—and this gives the best results—or a rotary one, the gradual addition of sugar is made in the last half of the beating time. In either case, the remaining one-fourth of the sugar is sifted with the cake flour to keep the flour well dispersed when it is folded into the egg and sugar mixture. ◗ The folding should never be done mechanically, unless you are using a mix, in which case follow the package directions. As in all hand-folding, the movement is both gentle and firm but rapid. Avoid breaking down the cellular structure of the egg whites which have trapped air.

The choice of pan and its careful preparation are essential to good results. Choose a tube pan with a removable rim. Since the dough is light, a central tube helps to give it additional support while it rises. ◗ Don't grease the pan. If it has been used for other purposes and any grease remains, the batter will not rise. Wash a suspect pan with detergent, scrubbing well to remove every trace of grease. After putting the batter in the pan, draw a thin spatula gently through the dough to destroy any large air pockets.

Endless experiments have been performed for baking angel cakes—starting with a cold oven and ending with a very hot one. But ♦ the best oven is one that is not so slow that it will dry and toughen the cake and not so hot that it will set the protein of the whites before they can expand to their fullest volume. In other words, the ideal is a preheated moderate oven. We use 350° for about 45 minutes for the recipes given here. Set the pan on a rack placed in the lower third of the oven. When the cake is done ♦ reverse the pan when you remove it from the oven, as shown in the illustration. Use an inverted funnel or a soft-drink bottle to rest the pan on, if the tube is not high enough to keep the cake above the surface of the table. Let the cake hang for about 1½ hours until it is thoroughly set. Be sure to remove it from the pan before storing. Do not cut a fresh angel or sponge cake with a knife, but use a divider such as the one shown on the left, or 2 forks inserted back to back to pry the cake gently apart.

To make an angel cake for a jelly roll, use half the recipe for a 10½ × 15½-inch pan. Here we make an exception and grease the bottom of the

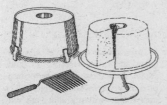

roll pan. To fill an angel cake with a secret filling, see About Filled Cakes, 434. Or decorate the cake with one of the Glazes Applied After Baking, 504, or one of the luscious Icings, 487–501.

ANGEL CAKE

I.   A 9-Inch Tube Pan
Preheat oven to 350°.
Sift twice:

    1¼ cups sugar
Sift separately before measuring:

    1 cup cake flour
Resift the flour 3 times with ¼ cup of the sifted sugar and:

    ½ teaspoon salt
Whip until foamy:

    1¼ cups egg whites: about
       10 egg whites (2
       tablespoons water or
       1 tablespoon water and
       1 tablespoon lemon
       juice)
Add:

    1 teaspoon cream of tartar
Whip the egg whites ♦ until stiff, but not dry.
Fold in:

    ½ teaspoon vanilla
    ½ teaspoon almond
       extract
Gradually whip in, about 1 tablespoon at a time, the remaining sifted sugar. Sift about ¼ cup of the flour and sugar mixture over the batter. Fold it in gently and briefly. Continue until all the mixture is used. Pour the batter into an ungreased tube pan. Bake about 45 minutes. To cool, see About Angel Cakes, opposite. Over this cake we like to dribble:

    European Chocolate
    Icing, 499
thinned a bit by an additional tablespoon of whipping cream.

A 10-Inch Tube Pan

II. An electric mixer method.
Preheat oven to 350°.
Sift, then measure:

    1 cup cake flour

Add and resift 6 times:

    **¹/₂ cup sugar or confectioners'
    sugar**

Combine:

    **1¹/₂ cups egg whites: 10 to 12
    egg whites**
    2¹/₂ tablespoons cold water
    1¹/₂ teaspoons cream of tartar
    ¹/₄ teaspoon vanilla
    **1 teaspoon almond extract or
    1 or 2 drops anise flavoring**
    ¹/₂ teaspoon salt

Beat ♦ until stiff, but not dry. Stop
while the mixture is still glossy. Fold
in, about 2 tablespoons at a time:

    1 cup sifted sugar

Fold in the flour and sugar mixture
lightly, a little at a time. Bake the batter in an ungreased tube pan about 45
minutes. To cool, see About Angel
Cakes, 404.

COCOA ANGEL CAKE

A 9-Inch Tube Pan

This cake is incredibly delicate.
Preheat oven to 350°.
Sift before measuring:

    ³/₄ cup cake flour

Resift 5 times with:

    ¹/₄ cup cocoa
    ¹/₄ cup sugar

Sift separately:

    1 cup sugar

Whip until foamy:

    **1¹/₄ cups egg whites: about 10
    egg whites**

Add:

    1 teaspoon cream of tartar

Whip ♦ until stiff, but not dry. Fold in
the sifted sugar, 1 tablespoon at a
time. Add:

    1 teaspoon vanilla

    ¹/₂ teaspoon lemon extract

Sift a small amount of the flour mixture over the batter and fold it in. Repeat this process until the flour is
used up. Bake the cake in an ungreased tube pan about 45 minutes.
To cool, see About Angel Cake, 404.
Cover the cooled cake with:

    **Chocolate Coating over
    Boiled White Icing, 493, or
    with Coffee Icing, 499**

FLAVORED ANGEL CAKE

Try using flavored angel cake batter
for cupcakes, 445.
Add to the flour for Angel Cake I or
II, 405:

    1 teaspoon cinnamon
    ¹/₂ teaspoon nutmeg
    ¹/₄ teaspoon cloves

Or, crush with a rolling pin:

    ¹/₃ cup soft peppermint sticks

Fold the candy into the egg and flour
mixture. This is good iced with
Boiled White Icing, 489, to which
you may add more crushed candy for
color, or, if using the spiced cake:

    **(1 to 2 teaspoons instant
    coffee)**

MARBLE ANGEL CAKE

Prepare:

    Angel Cake I, 405

and:

    Cocoa Angel Cake, at left

Alternate the batters in 2 ungreased
9-inch tube pans. Bake as directed in
Angel Cake I.

ABOUT SPONGE CAKES

In true sponge cakes, as in angel
cakes, the main riser is air, plus
steam, so all the suggestions for trapping air given in About Angel Cakes
apply here—with this added admoni-

tion: egg yolks beat to a greater volume if they are at about 70°. Beat the yolks until light and foamy; add the sugar gradually, while continuing to beat, until the mixture is pale in color and thick in texture. It has reached proper consistency when a sample dropped from a spoon remains raised for a moment above the rest of the batter and then rather reluctantly settles down to the level in the bowl.

♦ In sponge cakes, an electric or rotary beater gives a better result than a hand whip. You can beat the egg and sugar mixture mechanically as long as 7 minutes with good results for the amounts given in the recipes here. Then stir in the dry ingredients carefully by hand. When they are blended, use the folding technique illustrated on 400. For pan preparation and baking, see About Angel Cakes, 404.

True-blue sponge cake enthusiasts scorn baking powder, but it does give added volume in the basic recipe just below. See Flavored Angel Cake, opposite, for additions to vary the usual sponge cake.

SPONGE CAKE

A 9-Inch Tube Pan

Economical, if you use the minimum number of eggs. Especially delightful if you vary the flavors. To prepare the pan, bake and cool, see About Angel Cakes, 404.
Preheat oven to 350°.
Grate, then stir:

   1 teaspoon lemon or orange
      rind
into:
   1 cup sifted sugar
Beat until very light:
   3 to 6 egg yolks
Beat in the sugar gradually. Beat in:
   1/4 cup boiling water or coffee

When cool, beat in:
   1 tablespoon lemon juice or
   1 teaspoon vanilla or
   3 drops anise oil
Sift before measuring:
   1 cup cake flour
Resift with:
   1 1/2 teaspoons double-acting
      baking powder
   1/4 teaspoon salt
Add the sifted ingredients gradually to the yolk mixture. Stir the batter until blended. Whip ♦ until stiff, but not dry.
   3 to 6 egg whites
Fold them lightly into the batter. Bake the cake about 45 minutes.

RICE- OR POTATO-FLOUR SPONGE CAKE

A 9-Inch Round Pan

Because rice and potato flours lack the gluten of wheat, do not expect the same cake texture.
Preheat oven to 325°.
Sift 3 times or more:
   1 cup potato or rice flour
Beat until light and creamy:
   4 egg yolks
Blend in:
   1 cup sugar
Add the sifted flour and:
   1/8 teaspoon salt
   2 tablespoons lemon juice
   1 1/2 teaspoons vanilla
Whip ♦ until stiff, but not dry:
   4 egg whites
Fold the egg whites into the batter. Bake in a greased and floured pan 20 minutes at 325°, then 15 minutes longer at 350°.

SUNSHINE CAKE

A 9-Inch Tube Pan

To prepare pan, bake and cool, see About Angel Cakes, 404.

Preheat oven to 350°.
Sift before measuring:

1 cup cake flour

Resift with:

¹/₂ teaspoon cream of tartar

Boil to the soft-ball stage, 240°,
see 576:

¹/₃ cup water
1¹/₄ cups sugar

Whip ♦ until stiff, but not dry:

5 to 7 egg whites

Pour the syrup over them in a fine
stream. Beat constantly until the mixture is cool. Add:

1 teaspoon vanilla

Beat well and fold in:

5 to 7 egg whites

Fold in the sifted flour, 1 tablespoon
at a time. Bake the cake about 45
minutes.

CHOCOLATE SPONGE CAKE

A 7-Inch Tube Pan

Butterless but rich in taste. To pre-
pare pan, bake and cool, see About
Angel Cakes, 404.
Preheat oven to 350°.
Melt:

4 oz. unsweetened chocolate

in a pan with:

1 cup milk

Sift before measuring:

1¹/₄ cups cake flour

Resift with:

**2¹/₂ teaspoons double-acting
baking powder**
¹/₂ teaspoon salt

When the chocolate mixture is cool,
add it to:

4 beaten egg yolks

creamed with:

**2 cups sifted confectioners'
sugar**
1 teaspoon vanilla

Stir in the sifted flour. Beat ♦ until
stiff, but not dry:

4 egg whites

Fold the beaten whites into the
chocolate mixture. Bake about 50
minutes.

CHOCOLATE DATE CAKE

A 9-Inch Tube Pan

An unusual flavor combination.
Prepare batter for:

**Chocolate Sponge Cake,
above**

but wait to add the beaten egg whites
until after incorporating the date mixture below. Sprinkle:

**2 tablespoons sifted all-
purpose flour**

over:

³/₄ cup chopped dates
**1 tablespoon grated orange
rind**
(¹/₂ cup chopped nutmeats)

Stir these ingredients into the cake
batter before folding in the egg whites.
Bake as directed. Sprinkle with:

Powdered sugar

We serve this to everybody's intense
satisfaction with:

**Liqueur Cream Sauce, 573,
or Foamy Sauce, 573**

DAFFODIL CAKE

A 9-Inch Tube Pan

A yellow and white marble cake. To
prepare pan, bake and cool, see
About Angel Cakes, 404.
Preheat oven to 350°.
Sift before measuring:

1¹/₈ cups cake flour

Resift it twice more. Sift separately:

1¹/₄ cups sugar

Whip until frothy:

10 egg whites

Add:

¹/₂ teaspoon salt
1 teaspoon cream of tartar

Whip until egg whites hold a peak.
Fold the sifted sugar in gradually.

Separate the mixture into halves. Fold into one half, a little at a time, 3/4 cup of the sifted flour and:

6 beaten egg yolks
Grated rind of 1 orange

Fold into the other half, a little at a time, the remaining sifted flour and:

1 teaspoon vanilla

Place the batters, a cupful or more at a time, in the ungreased tube pan, alternating the colors. Bake about 45 minutes or until done.

ABOUT BUTTER OR SHORTENING CAKES

For flavor and texture, butter is our strong preference. It is not a very novel one, for way back when the cathedrals were white, one of the spires at Rouen was nicknamed the Butter Tower, having been built, reputedly, with money paid for indulgences permitting the use of butter during Lent.

The butter, margarine or shortening—but not lard, as it is best reserved for pastries—should be at ◗ about 70° when ready to cream. If much cooler, it fails to disperse properly into the other ingredients. If melted, it prevents the proper incorporation of air into the batter. ◗ So don't try to hasten the conditioning of shortenings with heat.

Creaming softens and lightens cake ingredients. If the weather is very hot, cream butter and sugar in a bowl immersed in a pan of 60° water. Add the sugar ◗ gradually, continuing to cream with a light touch.

Add beaten egg yolks gradually, or, as in Quick Cakes, 424, add egg yolks unbeaten, one at a time, beating well after each addition. The sifted dry ingredients and the 70° liquids are added in 3 or more alternating periods, usually beginning with the dry ingredients. After the addition of flour the blending should be gentle so as not to develop the gluten, and continued until the flour is no longer dry. ◗ Overblending will cause too fine a crumb. We suggest, for a cake made with double-acting baking powder, about 200 strokes by hand or 2 minutes at medium speed with an electric mixer; be sure to consult the directions that come with the mixer. If you use other baking powders, they may require about one-third less beating. Just before being incorporated into the batter, the whites are beaten to a state described as "stiff, but not dry." ◗ The whites are then simultaneously folded and cut in gently but quickly, as shown in the illustrations on 400. For a more stable foam, reserve one-fourth of the sugar called for in the recipe and beat it in as described in Fudge Meringue Cake, 416. Bake in a preheated oven. Grease and flour bottoms of pans but ◗ not sides. Use the pan sizes indicated for each recipe or adjust by consulting the Pan Size Chart, 401.

WHITE CAKE

This recipe is amazing: it can be multiplied by 8 and still give as good a result as when made in the smaller quantity below. See hints under About Large Cakes, 403. We once saw a wedding cake made from this recipe which contained 130 eggs and was big enough to serve 400 guests. This formula is also the classic base for Lady Baltimore Cake, 410, for which, in the Good Old Days, 5 layers were considered none too many.

I.   Three 8-Inch Round Pans
Preheat oven to 375°.

◗ Have all ingredients at about 70°.
Sift before measuring:

3¹/₂ cups cake flour

Resift it twice with:

**4 teaspoons double-acting
baking powder**

¹/₂ teaspoon salt

Cream well:

1 cup butter

Add gradually and cream until very light:

2 cups sifted sugar

Add the flour mixture to the butter mixture in 3 parts, alternately with:

1 cup milk

Stir the batter until smooth after each addition.
Beat in:

1 teaspoon vanilla

(¹/₄ teaspoon almond extract)

Whip ◗ until stiff, but not dry:

7 or 8 egg whites

Fold them gently into the cake batter.
Bake in greased pans about 25 minutes. Spread the cake when cool with:

**A choice of Icings,
487–500**

II.   Two 9-Inch Round Pans

This batter, which we use for our Easter Bunny, see 411, is enough to fill a 7-cup-capacity mold.
Preheat oven to 375°.
◗ Have all ingredients at about 70°.
Sift before measuring:

2¹/₄ cups cake flour

Resift with:

**2¹/₂ teaspoons double-acting
baking powder**

¹/₂ teaspoon salt

Cream until fluffy:

1¹/₄ cups sugar

¹/₂ cup butter

Combine:

1 cup milk

1 teaspoon vanilla

Add the sifted ingredients to the butter mixture in 3 parts, alternating

with the liquid combination. Stir the batter until smooth after each addition. Whip ◗ until stiff, but not dry:

4 egg whites

Fold them lightly into the batter and bake in layers, about 25 minutes. When cool, ice with:

**Luscious Orange, 494, or
Quick Chocolate Icing, 499**

LADY BALTIMORE CAKE

Prepare the batter for:

White Cake I, 409

Bake it in 3 layers. When cool, place the following filling between the layers. Chop:

6 dried figs

¹/₂ cup seeded raisins

1 cup nutmeats

Prepare:

**Boiled White Icing, 489, or
Seven-Minute White Icing,
493**

Reserve a generous portion of this. To the rest, add the nuts, figs and raisins for the filling between the layers. Spread the reserved icing over the top and sides.

MARBLE CAKE

A 9-Inch Tube Pan

This old-fashioned cake is still a great favorite.
Preheat oven to 350°.
Prepare:

White Cake II, at left

Before whipping the egg whites, separate the batter into 2 parts. Add to half the batter:

**1¹/₂ oz. melted, cooled
unsweetened chocolate**

1 teaspoon cinnamon

¹/₄ teaspoon cloves

¹/₈ teaspoon baking soda

Whip the egg whites as directed and fold half into the light and half into the dark batter. Grease the bottom of a tube pan. Place large spoonfuls of batter in it, alternating light and dark batter. Bake about 45 minutes. Spread when cool with:

> **Boiled White Icing, 489, or**
> **Raisin or Nut Icing, 489**

ABOUT TWO-PIECE CAKE MOLDS

To prepare a new cast iron mold, see directions on (I, 120). Lambs, bunnies, and Santas need firm, compact batters. Prepare:

> **White Cake II, opposite**

Keep nuts, raisins, etc., for decorations, rather than using them in the batter itself, because these solid ingredients, while they make the cake more interesting, tend to break down the tensile strength of the batter. Ground spices, however, are a good addition. Grease the mold with unsalted fat or oil. Use a pastry brush and be rather lavish. Then dust the greased surface with flour, reversing the mold to get rid of any excess. Fill the face side of the mold with batter. Leftover batter may be used for cupcakes or cake eggs. If the mold has steam vents, fill the solid section with the batter to just below the joint. Using the following directions, we have baked successfully in cake molds even when they had no steam vents. Move a wooden spoon gently through the batter to release any air bubbles. ◖ Be careful not to disturb the greased and floured surface of the mold. You may insert wooden picks into the snout and into the ears where they join the head, ◖ but be sure to remove the picks when you cut the cake. Put the lid on the mold, making sure it locks, and tie or wire together so the steam of the rising batter will not force the two sections apart.

To bake, put the filled mold on a cookie sheet in a 375° preheated oven for about 1 hour. Test as you would for any cake, inserting a thin metal skewer or wooden pick through a steam vent. Put the cake, still in the mold, on a rack for about 15 minutes. Carefully remove the top of the mold. Before you separate the cake from the bottom, let it continue to cool about 5 minutes more to let all steam escape and to allow the cake to firm up a little. After removing, continue to cool on a rack. ◖ Do not try to let it sit upright until it is cold. If the cake has constitutional weaknesses, reinforce it with a wooden or metal skewer before icing. Ice with:

> **Boiled White Icing, 489,**
> **or Seven-Minute White**
> **Icing, 493**

As a variation to coat a bunny mold, you may use:

> **Caramel Icing, 494**

Or, if you are in a hurry, try:

> **French Icing, 497**

Increase the recipes by half for a heavy coat. For woolly or angora effects, press into the icing:

> **1/2 to 1 cup shredded coconut**

To accentuate the features, use:

> **Raisins, nuts, cherries,**
> **citron and gumdrops**

Surround your animals with seasonal

flowers and ferns. If bunnies or lambs are made for Easter, you may want to confect cake eggs and decorate them with icings of different colors. See Angel Cake Balls, 446.

LADY CAKE

A 9-Inch Tube Pan

Another white cake using egg whites only, this makes a tube or loaf cake or an excellent batter for Petits Fours, see 447. It tastes and looks a lot like a conventional white wedding cake.
Preheat oven to 350°.
Have all ingredients about 70°. Sift before measuring:

    1³/₄ cups cake flour

Resift twice with:

    2 teaspoons double-acting
        baking powder
    ¹/₄ teaspoon salt

Cream until soft:

    ³/₄ cup butter

Add gradually and cream until very light:

    1 cup sifted sugar

Add the flour mixture to the butter mixture in 3 parts, alternating with:

    ¹/₂ cup milk

Stir the batter a few minutes after each addition.
Add:

    1 teaspoon almond extract
    Grated rind of 1 lemon

Whip ◗ until stiff, but not dry:

    3 egg whites

Fold them lightly into the cake batter. Bake in a greased tube pan about 45 minutes. Sprinkle with:

    Powdered sugar

or spread, when cool, with:

    Quick Lemon Icing, 497

WHIPPED CREAM CAKE

Two 9-Inch Layers

Preheat oven to 350°.

◗ Have all ingredients except the whipping cream about 70°. Sift before measuring:

    2 cups cake flour

Resift twice with:

    2³/₄ teaspoons double-acting
        baking powder
    1¹/₃ cups sugar
    ³/₄ teaspoon salt

Whip until stiff:

    1 cup cold whipping cream

and add gradually, stirring gently until smooth:

    ¹/₂ cup water
    1¹/₂ teaspoons vanilla or
        almond flavoring

Whip ◗ until stiff, but not dry:

    3 egg whites

Combine the cream and the egg whites. Fold the sifted ingredients into the cream mixture, about one-third at a time. Bake in greased layer pans about 25 to 30 minutes. Fill with:

    Ginger Fruit Filling, 452

Dust cake with:

    Powdered sugar

COCONUT MILK CAKE COCKAIGNE

Three 8-Inch Round Pans

Some years ago we gave a pet recipe to a friend who later presented us with the one which follows—best made with fresh coconut milk. She said that, in her family, whenever a treasured recipe was received, an equally treasured one was given in return. We love this festive adopted child.
Preheat oven to 350°.

◗ Have all ingredients about 70°. Have ready, reserving the coconut milk:

    1¹/₂ cups freshly grated coconut

Sift before measuring:

    3 cups cake flour

Resift it with:

3 teaspoons double-acting
baking powder
1/2 teaspoon salt

Cream well:

3/4 cup butter

Add gradually and cream until very light:

1 1/2 cups sifted sugar

Beat in:

3 egg yolks

Add the sifted flour mixture in 3 parts to the butter mixture, alternately with:

3/4 cup coconut milk or milk
1/2 teaspoon vanilla

Stir the batter until smooth after each addition. Then add 3/4 cup of the grated coconut. Whip ◗ until stiff, but not dry:

3 egg whites

Fold the egg whites gently into the batter. Bake in greased layer pans about 25 minutes. To serve, spread between the layers:

Currant, strawberry or
raspberry jelly

Cover the cake with:

Seven-Minute Sea Foam
Icing, 494

Coat it with the remaining 3/4 cup grated coconut.

SOUR CREAM CAKE

Two 8-Inch Round Pans

Preheat oven to 375°.
◗ Have all ingredients about 70°. Sift before measuring:

1 3/4 cups cake flour

Resift with:

1/4 teaspoon baking soda
1 3/4 teaspoons double-acting
baking powder
1/4 teaspoon salt

Cream until soft:

1/3 cup butter

Add gradually and cream until light:

1 cup sifted sugar

Beat in:

2 egg yolks
1 teaspoon vanilla

Add the sifted flour mixture to the butter mixture in 3 parts, alternating with:

2/3 cup yogurt or 1 cup
cultured sour cream

Stir the batter after each addition until smooth.
Whip until ◗ stiff, but not dry:

2 egg whites
1/4 teaspoon salt

Fold them lightly into the batter. Bake in greased pans about 25 minutes. When cool, spread with:

Almond and Fig or Raisin
Filling, 453

Cover with:

Boiled White Icing, 489

CAROB CAKE

Two 8-Inch Round Pans

A delicate distinctive flavor resembling chocolate. Please read about Carob Flour, 218.
Prepare the batter for:

Sour Cream Cake, at left

Omit 1/4 cup of the cake flour and substitute:

1/4 cup sifted carob flour

You may use either white or brown sugar. The latter gives the cake a butterscotch flavor.

GOLD LAYER CAKE

Two 8-Inch Round Layers

A delicious way to utilize leftover egg yolks.
Preheat oven to 375°.
◗ Have all ingredients about 70°. Sift before measuring:

2 cups cake flour

Resift with:

2 teaspoons double-acting
baking powder
¼ teaspoon salt

Cream until soft:

½ cup butter

Add gradually and cream until light:

1 cup sifted sugar

Beat in:

3 egg yolks

Add:

1 teaspoon vanilla or 1
teaspoon grated lemon rind

Add the flour mixture to the butter
mixture in 3 parts, alternating with:

¾ cup milk

Stir the batter until smooth after each
addition. Bake in greased layer pans
about 25 minutes. Spread between
the layers, when cool:

**Lemon-Orange Custard
Filling, 452, or Lemon
Filling, 451**

Dust the top with:

Powdered sugar

This cake is also delicious filled with
a layer of good raspberry jam.

FOUR-EGG CAKE

Three 9-Inch Round Pans

This is the old-time One-Two-Three-
Four Cake, slightly modernized.
Preheat oven to 350°.
◗ Have all ingredients about 70°. Sift
before measuring:

2⅔ cups cake flour

Resift with:

2¼ teaspoons double-acting
baking powder
½ teaspoon salt

Cream until soft:

1 cup butter

Add gradually and cream until light:

2 cups sifted sugar

Beat in, one at a time:

4 egg yolks

Add:

1½ teaspoons vanilla, or 1

teaspoon vanilla and ½
teaspoon almond extract

Add the flour mixture to the butter
mixture in about 3 parts, alternating with:

1 cup milk

Stir the batter until smooth after
each addition. Whip ◗ until stiff, but
not dry:

4 egg whites

Fold them lightly into the batter.
Bake in greased layer pans from 30
to 35 minutes. Spread the layers,
when cool, with:

**Ginger Fruit Filling, 452,
or Almond Custard Filling,
453**

Cover with:

Whipped cream

COCONUT LOAF OR LAYER CAKE

Follow the recipe for:

Four-Egg Cake, above

Add to the batter, before folding in
the egg whites:

¾ cup shredded coconut
1½ teaspoons grated lemon
rind
¼ teaspoon salt

Bake in a greased 10-inch tube pan or
two 9 × 5-inch loaf pans about 50
minutes.

EIGHT-YOLK CAKE

Three 9-Inch Layers

Bake it as a second cake after making
Angel Food Cake with the whites.
Preheat oven to 375°.
◗ Have all ingredients about 70°. Sift
before measuring:

2½ cups cake flour

Resift 3 times with:

2½ teaspoons double-acting
baking powder
¼ teaspoon salt

Cream until soft:

¾ cup butter

Add gradually and cream until light:

1¼ cups sifted sugar

In a separate bowl, beat until light and lemon colored:

8 egg yolks

Beat them into the butter mixture. Add the flour mixture in 3 parts, alternating with:

¾ cup milk

Stir the batter after each addition. Add and beat 2 minutes:

1 teaspoon vanilla
1 teaspoon lemon juice or grated lemon rind

Bake in greased layer pans about 20 minutes. Sprinkle with:

Powdered sugar

Or, when cool, spread with:

Quick Orange Icing, 498, or with one of the Seven-Minute Icings, 493–494

POUND CAKE

Two 9 × 5-Inch Pans or One 10-Inch Tube Pan

An electric mixer is a true aid for creaming this batter. You may add the eggs whole to give the traditional dense pound cake, or separate the yolks and whites for a fluffy texture. Preheat oven to 325°.

◗ Have all ingredients about 70°.

Cream:

2 cups butter, no substitutes

Add slowly and cream well:

2 cups sugar

Beat in one at a time:

9 egg yolks, see note above

Beat the batter well after each addition. Add:

1 teaspoon vanilla
½ teaspoon mace

You may add:

(2 tablespoons brandy or 8 drops rose water)

Sift before measuring:

4 cups cake flour

Resift with:

½ teaspoon cream of tartar
½ teaspoon salt

Add the sifted ingredients slowly, at lowest speed, mixing only until thoroughly blended. Whip in a separate bowl ◗ until stiff, but not dry, then fold in:

9 egg whites

Pour the batter into a greased tube pan or into 2 greased loaf pans lined with parchment paper as shown or into a greased and floured hinged loaf pan. Bake the cake about 1 hour for pans; 15 minutes longer for tube pan.

Sometimes we add to half the mixture ½ cupful each of candied cherries, pineapple, citron and white raisins—and have a delicious fruit cake.

SEED CAKE

A cake that reminds us of antimacassars and aspidistras.

Prepare:

Pound Cake, above

Add:

2 teaspoons caraway seed
⅓ cup shaved citron or candied orange peel
1 teaspoon grated lemon rind

❋ GÉNOISE

Two 9-Inch Round Pans

This rich, moist Italian cake, which the French and we have borrowed, has no equal for versatility. It also keeps well and freezes well. If not overbaked it may be used for dessert rolls with cream or jelly fillings, see About Roll Cakes, 439, or Baked Alaska, 520; also with butter icings or as a foil for fruit. You may bake it as Ladyfingers, 448, or in layers. For a very elaborate Génoise, sprinkle it after cooling with Cointreau or kirsch, fill it with Sauce Cockaigne, 564, or cover it with whipped cream or with European Chocolate Icing, 499. For a children's party, bake favors in the cake, see Galette des Rois, 363.

Preheat oven to 350°.
Melt and put aside:
    ¼ cup butter
Do not let it get cooler than about 80°. Break into the top of a double boiler ❱ over—not in—boiling water until they are lukewarm:
    6 eggs
Add:
    ⅔ cup sugar
Beat with a rotary or electric mixer at medium speed 7 minutes. Add:
    ⅓ cup sugar
Increase speed and beat 2 minutes longer or until the mixture is lemony in color and has reached the stage known as **au ruban**—like a continuous flat ribbon when dropped from a spoon. Add:
    1 teaspoon vanilla
Fold in:
    1 cup sifted cake flour
Add the melted butter with a folding motion. Pour the batter into greased and floured pans and bake about 30 to 40 minutes or until done. ❱ Turn out at once onto a rack to cool.

CHOCOLATE CAKE

A 9 × 13-Inch Pan

A mild light chocolate cake known as "Rombauer Special."
Preheat oven to 350°.
❱ Have ingredients about 70°. Sift before measuring:
    1¾ cups cake flour
Resift with:
    3 teaspoons double-acting baking powder
    ¼ teaspoon salt
    (1 teaspoon cinnamon)
    (¼ teaspoon cloves)
    (1 cup coarsely chopped nuts)
Melt over hot water:
    2 oz. unsweetened chocolate
Add:
    5 tablespoons boiling water
Cream until soft:
    ½ cup butter
Add and cream until light:
    1½ cups sifted sugar
Beat in, one at a time:
    4 egg yolks
Add the cooled chocolate mixture. Add the flour mixture to the butter mixture in 3 parts, alternating with:
    ½ cup milk
Stir the batter until smooth after each addition.
Add:
    1 teaspoon vanilla
Whip ❱ until stiff, but not dry:
    4 egg whites
Fold them lightly into the cake batter. Bake in a greased pan about ½ hour. Spread with thick:
    Chocolate Coating over Boiled White Icing, 489; or Quick Chocolate Icing with chocolate peppermints, 499

FUDGE MERINGUE CAKE

A 9 × 13-Inch Pan

Preheat oven to 350°.

◗ Have all ingredients about 70°. Sift:

2 cups cake flour

Resift with:

1 tablespoon double-acting baking powder

¹/₄ teaspoon salt

Melt ◗ over—not in—boiling water:

4 oz. unsweetened chocolate

Cream:

¹/₄ cup butter

Add gradually; continue to cream and mix:

1¹/₂ cups sugar

Beat in:

3 egg yolks

1 teaspoon vanilla

and the cooled chocolate. Then add the sifted flour in 3 parts, alternating with:

1 cup milk

Stir well after each addition. Whip ◗ until stiff, but not dry:

3 egg whites

Fold in:

¹/₂ cup sugar

Beat to a meringue consistency. Fold into batter. Bake about 35 minutes in a greased pan. When cool, ice with:

French Icing, 497

DEVIL'S FOOD CAKE COCKAIGNE

Two 9-Inch Round Pans

The best chocolate cake we know. Whether made with 2 or 4 oz. chocolate, it is wonderfully light, but rich and moist.

Preheat oven to 350°.

Prepare the following custard:

Cook and stir in a double boiler ◗ over—not in—boiling water:

2 to 4 oz. unsweetened chocolate

¹/₂ cup milk

1 cup light brown sugar, firmly packed

1 egg yolk

Remove from the heat when thickened. Have other ingredients at about 70°. Sift before measuring:

2 cups cake flour

Resift with:

1 teaspoon baking soda

¹/₂ teaspoon salt

Beat until soft:

¹/₂ cup butter

Add and cream until light:

1 cup sifted sugar

Beat in, one at a time:

2 egg yolks

Add the flour to the butter mixture in 3 parts, alternating with the following mixture:

¹/₄ cup water

¹/₂ cup milk

1 teaspoon vanilla

Stir the batter until smooth after each addition. Stir in the chocolate custard. Whip ◗ until stiff, but not dry:

2 egg whites

Fold them lightly into the cake batter. Bake in greased pans about 25 minutes. Spread when cool with:

Coconut Pecan Icing, 495,
Caramel Icing, 494, or
Chocolate-Fudge Icing, 495

COCOA DEVIL'S FOOD CAKE

One 9-Inch Tube or
Two 9-Inch Round Pans

During wartime shortages, a foreign fan had success with this long-keeping cake using cassava flour when no other flour was available.

◗ Have all ingredients about 70°. Combine, beat until well blended, and set aside:

1 cup sugar

¹/₂ cup cocoa

¹/₂ cup buttermilk or yogurt

Beat until soft:

¹/₂ cup butter

Add gradually and cream until light:

1 cup sifted sugar

Beat in, one at a time:

2 eggs

Beat in cocoa mixture. Sift before measuring:

2 cups cake flour

Resift with:

1 teaspoon baking soda
¹/₂ teaspoon salt

Add the flour in 3 parts to the butter mixture, alternately with:

¹/₂ cup buttermilk or yogurt
1 teaspoon vanilla

Beat batter after each addition just until smooth. Grease the tube pan and sprinkle sugar over the bottom. Bake the cake about 1 hour in a preheated 350° oven. It may be baked in 2 layer pans about 35 minutes in a 375° oven. Spread the cake with:

A white, 489, or chocolate icing, 498

Add to the icing:

(Nutmeats)

SOURDOUGH CHOCOLATE CAKE

One 9-Inch Square Pan or Two 8-Inch Round Pans

Please read About Sourdough, 224.
◗ Have all ingredients about 70°.
Preheat oven to 350°.
Cream thoroughly:

6 tablespoons butter
1 cup sugar

Add and beat:

2 eggs

Stir in, then beat well:

1 cup Sourdough Starter, 224
³/₄ cup milk
3 oz. melted semisweet chocolate
1 teaspoon vanilla

Sift together:

1³/₄ cups sifted all-purpose flour

1 teaspoon baking soda
¹/₂ teaspoon salt

Fold the flour mixture into the batter and stir until smooth. Pour into greased pans and bake about 40 minutes for one square pan or 25 minutes for two round pans. Sprinkle over this moist cake:

Sifted powdered sugar

★ OLD-WORLD CHOCOLATE SPICE CAKE WITH CITRON

A 9-Inch Tube Pan

A tempting tube cake with a rather heavy crumb.
Preheat oven to 350°.
◗ Have all ingredients about 70°. Sift before measuring:

2¹/₃ cups cake flour

Resift with:

1¹/₂ teaspoons double-acting baking powder
¹/₂ teaspoon cloves
1 teaspoon cinnamon
¹/₂ teaspoon freshly grated nutmeg

Cream until soft:

¹/₂ cup butter

Add gradually and cream until light:

1¹/₂ cups sugar

Beat in, one at a time:

4 eggs

Stir in:

4 oz. grated sweet chocolate
¹/₂ cup very finely shaved citron, candied orange or lemon peel

Stir the flour mixture into the butter mixture in about 3 parts, alternating with:

⁷/₈ cup milk

Stir the batter after each addition until smooth. Most European cakes are stirred a long time. This gives them a close, sandy texture. Bake the cake in a greased tube pan or in a loaf pan about 1 hour. When cool, simply dust with:

Powdered sugar
or ice with:
   Chocolate Butter Icing, 498

SPICED CHOCOLATE PRUNE CAKE

       A 9 × 13-Inch Pan
A moist, fruity loaf cake which makes a delightful dessert when served with whipped cream or pudding sauce.
Preheat oven to 350°.
◗ Have all ingredients about 70°.
Cook and cool:
   **1 cup lightly sweetened
      drained puréed prunes**
◗ Canned puréed prunes will not do, because they are too liquid. Sift before measuring:
   1½ cups cake flour
Resift with:
   **1½ teaspoons double-acting
      baking powder**
   ¼ teaspoon baking soda
   ¼ teaspoon salt
   (1 teaspoon cinnamon)
   (½ teaspoon cloves)
Cream until soft:
   ⅓ cup butter
Add gradually and cream until light:
   ¾ cup sifted sugar
Melt and add when cool:
   **1 oz. unsweetened
      chocolate**
Beat well and add to the butter mixture:
   2 eggs
Add the flour mixture to the butter mixture in 3 parts, alternating with:
   ½ cup milk
Stir the batter until smooth after each addition.
Add the prunes and:
   ½ teaspoon vanilla
Bake in a greased pan about 25 minutes. Spread, when cool, with:
   French Icing, 497

CHOCOLATE APRICOT CAKE

Follow the recipe for:
   **Spiced Chocolate Prune
      Cake, opposite**
Substitute for the prunes:
   **1 cup cooked, lightly
      sweetened, well-drained
      puréed apricots**
Omit the spices. Ice, when cool, with:
   Whipped cream
or serve with:
   Foamy Sauce, 573

HONEY CAKE

      A 9 × 9-Inch Square Pan
Well wrapped and kept in a cool place, this cake improves with age.
◗ Have all ingredients about 70°.
Preheat oven to 350°.
Cream thoroughly:
   ½ cup butter or shortening
   ½ cup sugar
Add and continue creaming until light and fluffy:
   2 eggs
Sift together:
   **2 cups sifted all-purpose
      flour**
   ½ teaspoon baking soda
   **1 teaspoon double-acting
      baking powder**
   ½ teaspoon cinnamon
   ¼ teaspoon ginger
   ¼ teaspoon salt
Add the sifted ingredients to the egg mixture alternately in 3 parts with:
   ½ cup honey
   ½ cup cool strong coffee
Stir in:
   ½ teaspoon vanilla
   ¾ cup chopped walnuts
   (Grated rind of ½ orange)
Pour batter into a greased pan and bake about 30 minutes. Dust with:
   Confectioners' sugar
or spread with:

Three-Minute Icing, 497, or
French Icing, 497

VELVET SPICE CAKE

A 9-Inch Tube Pan

This cake has a very delicate consistency. Among spice cakes its flavor is unequaled. ◗ Be sure to bake it in a 9-inch tube pan.

Preheat oven to 350°.

◗ Have all ingredients about 70°. Sift before measuring:

2¹/₃ cups cake flour

Resift twice with:

**1¹/₂ teaspoons double-acting
    baking powder**
¹/₂ teaspoon baking soda
**1 teaspoon freshly grated
    nutmeg**
1 teaspoon cinnamon
¹/₂ teaspoon cloves
¹/₂ teaspoon salt

Cream:

³/₄ cup butter or shortening

Add gradually and cream together

1¹/₂ cups sifted sugar

Beat in:

3 egg yolks

Add the sifted ingredients to the butter mixture in 3 parts, alternating with:

⁷/₈ cup yogurt or buttermilk

Stir the batter after each addition until smooth. Whip ◗ until stiff, but not dry:

3 egg whites

Fold them lightly into the cake batter. Bake in a greased tube pan 1 hour or more. Spread, when cool, with:

**Chocolate Butter Icing,
    498, or Boiled White
    Icing, 489**

BROWN-SUGAR SPICE CAKE

Prepare:

Velvet Spice Cake, above

substituting for the granulated sugar:

**1¹/₂ cups packed brown
    sugar**

and adding to the batter:

**2 to 3 teaspoons grated
    orange rind**

BURNT-SUGAR CAKE

Two 9-Inch Round Pans

A caramelized flavor and a taste sensation.

◗ Have all ingredients about 70°. Caramelize, 232:

¹/₂ cup sugar

and add ◗ very slowly:

¹/₂ cup boiling water

Boil the syrup until it has the consistency of molasses. Cool it.

Preheat oven to 375°.

Sift together:

2¹/₂ cups sifted cake flour
**2¹/₂ teaspoons double-acting
    baking powder**
¹/₄ teaspoon salt

Cream:

¹/₂ cup butter

Add gradually and cream until light:

1¹/₂ cups sifted sugar

Beat in, one at a time:

2 egg yolks

Add the flour mixture in 3 parts to the butter mixture, alternating with:

1 cup water

Stir the batter after each addition until smooth. Stir in:

**3 tablespoons of the
    caramelized syrup**
1 teaspoon vanilla

Whip ◗ until stiff, but not dry:

2 egg whites

Fold them lightly into the cake batter. Bake in greased pans about 25 minutes. Spread when cool with:

A white icing, 489

In making the icing, flavor it with:

**4 teaspoons of the
    caramelized syrup**

in addition to the vanilla.

Place any remaining syrup in a closed jar. It will keep indefinitely.

APPLESAUCE CAKE

A 9-Inch Tube Pan

If someone in your family is allergic to eggs, omit the egg and add an additional teaspoon of soda.
Preheat oven to 350°.
◗ Have all the ingredients about 70°.
Sift before measuring:

    1³/₄ cups cake flour

Sift a little of the flour over:

    1 cup raisins
    1 cup currants, nutmeats or dates

Resift the remainder with:

    ¹/₂ teaspoon salt
    1 teaspoon baking soda
    1 teaspoon cinnamon
    ¹/₂ teaspoon cloves

Cream until soft:

    ¹/₂ cup butter or shortening

Add gradually and cream until light:

    1 cup white or packed brown sugar

Beat in:

    1 egg

Stir the flour mixture gradually into the butter mixture until the batter is smooth. Add the raisins, nutmeats, and:

    1 cup thick, lightly sweetened applesauce

Stir it into the batter. Bake in a greased tube pan 50 to 60 minutes. Spread when cool with:

    Caramel Icing, 494

FIG SPICE CAKE

A 9-Inch Tube Pan

◗ Have all the ingredients about 70°. Cool, drain, then cut into ¹/₄-inch cubes and reserve the syrup:

    1 lb. cooked dried figs

There should be 2 cups of figs. Combine.

    ¹/₂ cup fig juice
    ¹/₂ cup buttermilk or yogurt

Preheat oven to 350°.
Sift before measuring:

    1¹/₂ cups cake flour

Resift with:

    1 teaspoon double-acting baking powder
    1 teaspoon salt
    ¹/₂ teaspoon cinnamon
    ¹/₄ teaspoon cloves
    ¹/₂ teaspoon baking soda

Cream until soft:

    ¹/₂ cup butter or shortening

Add gradually and cream until light:

    1 cup sifted sugar

Beat in, one at a time:

    2 eggs

Add the flour mixture to the butter mixture in 3 parts, alternating with the milk and fig juice. Stir the batter after each addition until smooth. Add the figs and:

    1 teaspoon vanilla
    (1 cup broken nutmeats or raisins)

Bake in a greased tube pan about 50 minutes. Spread when cool with:

    Coffee or Mocha Icing, 499

DATE SPICE CAKE

An 8¹/₂ × 4¹/₂-Inch Loaf

Preheat oven to 325°.
◗ Have all ingredients about 70°. Cut into small pieces:

    1 cup dates

Pour over them:

    1 cup boiling water or coffee

Cool these ingredients. Sift before measuring:

    1¹/₂ cups cake flour

Resift with:

    1¹/₂ teaspoons double-acting baking powder

³/₄ teaspoon freshly grated
    nutmeg
¹/₄ teaspoon salt
¹/₄ teaspoon baking soda
Cream together:
    3 tablespoons butter or
        shortening
    1 cup sifted sugar
    1 egg
Add the flour mixture to the butter
mixture in 3 parts, alternating with
the date mixture. Stir the batter well
after each addition. Fold in:
    1 cup raisins
    1 cup broken pecan meats
Bake in a greased loaf pan about
50 minutes. Test for doneness, 400.
Dust with:
    Powdered sugar

EGGLESS, MILKLESS SPICE
CAKE

            A 7-Inch Tube Pan
Preheat oven to 325°.
Boil for 3 minutes:
    1 cup water or beer
    2 cups seeded raisins
    1 cup packed brown sugar
    ¹/₃ cup butter or shortening
    ¹/₂ teaspoon each cinnamon
        and allspice
    ¹/₂ teaspoon salt
    ¹/₈ teaspoon nutmeg
Cool these ingredients. Sift before
measuring:
    2 cups cake flour
Resift with:
    1 teaspoon double-acting
        baking powder
    1 teaspoon baking soda
Stir the flour gradually into the other
ingredients.
Stir the batter until smooth. Add:
    (1 cup chopped almonds)
By the addition of 1 cup chopped
dates, figs and citron, this becomes

an acceptable fruit cake. Bake in a
greased tube pan for 1 hour or more.
Spread with:
    Caramel Icing, 494

ROMBAUER JAM CAKE

            A 7-Inch Tube Pan
Preheat oven to 350°.
◗ Have all ingredients about 70°. Sift,
then measure:
    1¹/₂ cups all-purpose flour
Resift with:
    1 teaspoon double-acting
        baking powder
    ¹/₂ teaspoon baking soda
    ¹/₂ teaspoon cloves
    1 teaspoon each cinnamon
        and nutmeg
Cream until light:
    6 tablespoons butter or
        shortening
    1 cup packed brown sugar
Beat in, one at a time:
    2 eggs
Beat in:
    3 tablespoons cultured sour
        cream
Stir the flour mixture into the butter
mixture until barely blended. Stir in:
    1 cup rather firm raspberry
        or blackberry jam
    (¹/₂ cup broken nutmeats)
Pour the batter into a greased tube
pan. Bake it about ¹/₂ hour or until
done. When cool, ice the cake with:
    **Quick Brown Sugar
    Icing, 498**

OATMEAL CAKE

            A 9 X 13-Inch Pan
Make this cake a day or two before
eating. For another oat cake, see Guy
Fawkes Day Cake, 426.
Preheat oven to 350°.
◗ Have all ingredients about 70°.

Combine and let stand at least 20 minutes:

1 cup rolled oats
1½ cups boiling water

Cream together:

½ cup butter
1 cup sugar
1 cup packed brown sugar

Add, mixing thoroughly:

2 eggs
1 teaspoon vanilla

and the oat mixture. Sift together:

1⅓ cups all-purpose flour
1 teaspoon baking soda
½ teaspoon salt
1 teaspoon cinnamon
½ teaspoon nutmeg

Stir flour mixture into the egg mixture. Beat about 2 minutes, then turn into a greased cake pan and bake 30 minutes or until done. To ice the warm cake, make up a double portion of:

Broiled Icing, 501

and put under the broiler until light brown.

TOMATO SOUP OR MYSTERY CAKE

A 9-Inch Tube Pan

This curious combination of ingredients makes a surprisingly good cake. But why shouldn't it? The deep secret is tomato, which after all is a fruit.

Preheat oven to 350°.

Have all ingredients about 70°. Sift before measuring:

2 cups all-purpose flour

Resift with:

½ teaspoon salt
1 teaspoon cinnamon
½ teaspoon each nutmeg and cloves
1 teaspoon baking soda

Sift:

1 cup sugar

Cream until soft:

2 tablespoons butter

Add the sifted sugar gradually and cream these ingredients well. Stir the flour mixture in 3 parts into the sugar mixture, alternating with:

1 can condensed tomato soup: 10½ oz.

Stir the batter until smooth after each addition.

Fold in:

1 cup nutmeats
1 cup raisins

Bake in a greased tube pan about 45 minutes. Spread, when cool, with:

Boiled White Icing, 489, or Cream Cheese Icing, 497

TUTTI-FRUTTI CAKE

A 9-Inch Tube Pan

A well-flavored summer fruit cake.

Preheat oven to 350°.

◗ Have all ingredients about 70°.

Sift before measuring:

2 cups and 2 tablespoons cake flour

Resift with:

1 teaspoon each cloves, cinnamon, nutmeg
1 teaspoon baking soda
½ teaspoon salt

Cream:

½ cup butter or shortening

Add gradually and cream until light:

1½ cups packed brown sugar

Beat in, one at a time:

2 eggs

Stir the flour mixture into the butter mixture in 3 parts, alternating with:

1 cup lightly drained crushed pineapple

Stir in:

½ cup each raisins and currants
1 cup broken nutmeats

Bake in a greased tube pan about 1 hour.

BANANA CAKE COCKAIGNE

Two 9-Inch Round Pans

Do try this if you like a banana flavor.
Preheat oven to 350°.

◗ Have all ingredients about 70°. Sift before measuring:

> **2¼ cups cake flour**

Resift with:

> **½ teaspoon double-acting baking powder**
> **¾ teaspoon baking soda**
> **½ teaspoon salt**

Cream:

> **½ cup butter**

Add gradually and cream until light:

> **1½ cups sifted sugar**

Beat in, one at a time:

> **2 eggs**

Prepare:

> **1 cup lightly mashed ripe bananas**

Add:

> **1 teaspoon vanilla**
> **¼ cup yogurt or buttermilk**

Add the flour mixture to the butter mixture in 3 parts, alternating with the banana mixture. Stir the batter after each addition until smooth. Bake in greased pans about ½ hour. When cool, place between the layers:

> **2 sliced ripe bananas**

Spread the cake with:

> **A white icing, 489**

If served at once, this cake is good without icing—just sprinkled with:

> **Powdered sugar**

or served with:

> **Whipped cream, Caramel Cream Sauce, 570, or Custard Sauce, 565**

ABOUT QUICK CAKES

We all want a good cake in a big hurry. But let's not delude ourselves that shortcuts make for the best textures or flavors. Any cake in the following group can be mixed in one bowl and successfully beaten with an electric mixer. However, ◗ never try to use the one-bowl method for just any recipe.

QUICK OR LIGHTNING CAKE

Two 8-Inch Square or Two 8-Inch Round Pans

Vary the flavor of this cake—the German **Blitzkuchen**—by using the suggestions below.
Preheat oven to 375°.

◗ Have all ingredients about 70°.
If you want a wonderful, thin tea cake, have ready a topping of:

> **½ cup confectioners' sugar**
> **1 tablespoon cinnamon**
> **¼ cup chopped pecans**

and prepare the 8-inch square pans. If you want a thicker layer cake to ice, use the 8-inch round pans and omit the topping. Let soften to the consistency of mayonnaise:

> **½ cup butter**

Sift into a beater bowl:

> **1¾ cups cake flour**
> **½ teaspoons salt**
> **1 cup sugar**

Add:

> **2 eggs**
> **¼ cup plus 2½ teaspoons milk**

and the softened butter. Using the ◗ whip attachment of your beater, whip for 1 minute at low speed. Scrape the bowl. Whip for 1½ minutes at slightly higher speed. Scrape the bowl again and fold in:

> **1½ teaspoons double-acting baking powder**
> **(1 teaspoon vanilla)**

Whip for 30 seconds on first speed. Pour the batter into 2 greased pans, sprinkle with the topping and bake 20 minutes.

QUICK CARAMEL CAKE

Prepare:
>**Quick Cake, opposite,
>omitting the topping**

Substitute for the white sugar:
>**1 cup packed brown sugar**

You may add to the batter:
>(**3/4 cup nutmeats**)
>(**3/4 cup chopped dates**)

Spread the cake when cool with:
>**Caramel Icing, 494**

QUICK COCOA CAKE

Prepare:
>**Quick Cake, opposite,
>omitting the topping**

Substitute for 1/4 cup of the cake
flour:
>**1/4 cup Dutch process cocoa**

Ice the cake, when cool, with:
>**European Chocolate Icing,
>499**

QUICK SPICE CAKE

Prepare:
>**Quick Cake, opposite,
>omitting the topping**

Add:
>**1 teaspoon cinnamon**
>**1/2 teaspoon cloves**

When cool, dust the cake with:
>**Confectioners' sugar**

ONE-EGG CAKE

>**Two 8-Inch Round Pans**

Preheat oven to 375°.
▶ Have all ingredients about 70°. Sift
into an electric-mixer bowl:
>**1 3/4 cups sifted all-purpose
>flour**
>**1 1/4 cups sugar**
>**2 1/2 teaspoons double-acting
>baking powder**
>**1 teaspoon salt**

Add and mix for 2 minutes at
medium speed:
>**1/3 cup soft butter**
>**2/3 cup milk**

Add and mix for ▶ 2 minutes more,
scraping bowl constantly:
>**1 egg**
>**1/3 cup milk**
>**1 teaspoon vanilla**

Pour the batter into greased pans and
bake about 25 minutes. See Quick Icings, 496, for a choice; apply when
cake is cool.

GINGERBREAD

>**A 9 X 9 X 2-Inch Pan**

Preheat oven to 350°.
Melt in a heavy pan and let cool:
>**1/2 cup butter**

Add and beat well:
>**1/2 cup sugar**
>**1 egg**

Sift together:
>**2 1/2 cups sifted all-purpose
>flour**
>**1 1/2 teaspoons baking soda**
>**1 teaspoon each cinnamon
>and ginger**
>**1/2 teaspoon salt**

Combine:
>**1/2 cup light molasses**
>**1/2 cup honey**
>**1 cup hot water**
>(**1 tablespoon grated orange
>rind**)

Add the sifted and liquid ingredients
alternately to the butter mixture until
blended. Bake in a greased pan about
1 hour.

WHEATLESS GINGERBREAD

>**A 9 X 9 X 2-Inch Pan**

Unusual, yet perhaps the best of all.
Preheat oven to 325°.
Sift together 6 times:

1¼ cups rye or rice flour
1¼ cups cornstarch
2 teaspoons baking soda
1 teaspoon cinnamon
¼ teaspoon each cloves and
    ginger
Mix together:
½ cup sugar
1 cup molasses
½ cup soft butter
1 cup boiling water
Add and stir well:
2 well-beaten eggs
Combine all ingredients and beat until thoroughly mixed. Bake in a greased pan 60 to 70 minutes or until it tests done.

GUY FAWKES DAY CAKE

An 8 × 8-Inch Pan

Also called **Parkin**—a not-too-sweet cake.
Preheat oven to 350°.
Heat ◗ over—not in—boiling water, until the butter is melted:
½ cup butter
⅔ cup treacle
Mix in a bowl:
⅔ cup rolled oats
1 cup all-purpose flour
1 tablespoon sugar
½ teaspoon ginger
¼ teaspoon cloves
½ teaspoon salt
½ teaspoon baking soda
(1 teaspoon grated lemon
    rind)
Add alternately with the melted butter mixture:
⅔ cup milk
Combine until the dry ingredients are just moist. The batter will be thin. Bake in a greased pan about 35 minutes or until the cake begins to pull from the sides of the pan.

ABOUT FRUIT CAKES

Many people feel that these cakes improve greatly with age. When they are well saturated with alcoholic liquors, which raise the spirits and keep down mold, and are buried in powdered sugar in tightly closed tins, they have been enjoyed as long as 25 years after baking.

Fruit cakes are fundamentally butter cakes with just enough batter to bind the fruit. Raisins, figs and dates can be more easily cut if the scissors or knife used is dipped periodically in water. If you do not care for the usual candied fruits, do as one fan wrote us. She cooked chopped dried apricots, dates, raisins and currants in orange juice, used whole wheat flour and added pumpkin and sunflower seeds.

For a 2½-pound cake, use an 8-inch ring mold or a 4½ × 8½-inch loaf pan, either filled to about 2½ inches. To prepare loaf pans, see Pound Cake, 415. To prepare a tube pan, line the bottom with a round of greased parchment paper or foil and cut a straight strip for the sides. Bake as long as indicated in individual recipes or until the cake tests done by pressing lightly with a finger, see 400.

Fruit cakes, still in the pan, are cooled from 20 to 30 minutes on a rack. After removing the cakes from pans, the parchment or foil in which they are baked is carefully peeled away and the cake rack-cooled further until entirely free from heat. To decorate the cakes with candied fruit or nutmeats, dip the undersides of the decorations into a light sugar syrup before applying them, or simply cover the cake with a sugar syrup glaze and arrange the trimming on it.

To store, wrap the loaves or tubes

in brandy or wine-soaked linens. If you prefer, you may make a few fine skewer punctures in the cake and pour over it very slowly, drop by drop, $1/4$ to 1 cup heated, but not boiling, brandy or wine. However you glaze or soak the cake, wrap it in liquor-soaked linen, then in foil. For very long storage, bury the liquor-soaked cake in powdered sugar. In any case, place it in a tightly covered tin in a cool place.

▲ In baking fruit cakes at high altitude, omit any leavening.

★ FRUIT CAKE COCKAIGNE

Two 4 × 8¹/₂-Inch Loaves

Not unlike a pound cake. The fruits stay light in color.
◗ Please review About Butter Cakes, 409, and About Fruit Cakes, opposite.
Preheat oven to 350°.
◗ Have all ingredients about 70°. Sift before measuring:

4 cups all-purpose flour

Mix $1/2$ cup of the sifted flour with 4 cups nuts and fruits. We particularly like:

1¹/₃ cups pecans or hickory nuts
1¹/₃ cups white raisins
1¹/₃ cups seeded and chopped preserved kumquats or dried apricots

Resift the remainder of the flour with:

1 teaspoon double-acting baking powder
¹/₂ teaspoon salt

Cream until light:

³/₄ cup butter

Then cream it with:

2 cups sugar

Beat in one at a time:

5 eggs

Add:

1 teaspoon vanilla

and continue to beat until light. Stir the flour mixture into the egg mixture

and continue beating until thoroughly mixed. Fold in the reserved floured nuts and fruits. Bake about 1 hour.

★ CURRANT CAKE

Prepare the batter for:

Fruit Cake Cockaigne, above

Add instead of the suggested fruit mixture:

1 to 1¹/₂ cups currants

Bake, cool and store as for the above cake.

✿ WHITE FRUIT CAKE

Two 4 × 8¹/₂-Inch Loaves

Preheat oven to 350°.
Prepare the batter for:

Fruit Cake Cockaigne, above

Substitute for the fruits and nuts:

1 cup chopped nutmeats, preferably blanched, slivered almonds
¹/₂ cup finely sliced citron, candied orange or lemon peel
1 cup white raisins
¹/₄ cup chopped candied pineapple
¹/₄ cup chopped candied cherries
(¹/₂ cup finely shredded coconut)

Bake about 1 hour. To prepare pans, cool and store, see About Fruit Cakes, opposite.

✿ DARK FRUIT CAKE

I. **Two 4¹/₂ × 8-Inch Loaves, plus Two 9-Inch Tube Pans— About 12 Pounds**
◗ Please review About Butter Cakes, 409, and About Fruit Cakes, opposite.
Preheat oven to 275°.

◗ Have all ingredients about 70°. Sift before measuring:

4 cups all-purpose flour

Reserve 1 cup. Resift the remainder with:

1 tablespoon each of cinnamon, cloves, allspice and nutmeg

1/2 tablespoon mace

1 1/2 teaspoons salt

Wash:

2 1/2 lb. currants

Cut up:

2 1/2 lb. raisins

1 lb. citron

Break coarsely:

1 lb. pecan meats

Sprinkle these ingredients well with the reserved flour. Sift:

1 lb. brown sugar: 2 2/3 cups, packed

Cream until soft:

1 lb. butter

Add the sugar gradually. Cream until very light.

Beat in:

15 beaten egg yolks

Add the flour mixture to the butter mixture, alternately with:

1/4 cup bourbon whisky and 1/4 cup wine, or 1/2 cup thick fruit juice: prune, apricot or grape

Fold in the floured fruits and nuts. Beat ◗ until stiff, but not dry:

15 egg whites

Fold them into the butter mixture. Bake a 2 1/2-pound cake in prepared pans, for 1 1/2 to 3 hours, depending on pan size. For over 5 pounds, allow at least 5 hours. Place a shallow pan filled with water in the oven. Remove it the last hour of baking. Cool cakes and store.

II.   Two 4 1/2 × 8 × 2 1/2-Inch Loaves, Plus Two 8-Inch Tube Pans— About 11 Pounds

In this recipe the fruit is preconditioned, so it does not draw moisture from the cake during or after baking. Place and cook in a heavy pot for 5 minutes, stirring constantly:

1 1/2 cups apricot nectar

2 1/2 cups seedless white raisins

2 1/2 cups seedless raisins

1 cup pitted, chopped dates

1 cup diced candied pineapple

2 cups diced candied cherries

1 cup diced candied apricots

Remove from heat, cover and let stand 12 to 15 hours.

◗ Please review About Butter Cakes, 409, and About Fruit Cakes, 426.

◗ Have all ingredients about 70°. Preheat oven to 300°.

Sift before measuring:

6 cups all-purpose flour

Resift with:

2 teaspoons salt

1/2 teaspoon baking soda

2 teaspoons cinnamon

1 teaspoon each allspice and nutmeg

1/2 teaspoon cloves

1/4 teaspoon cardamom

Cream until light:

2 cups butter

2 cups sugar

Add and beat in well:

10 beaten eggs

2 tablespoons vanilla

Stir in the sifted flour mixture. Combine the batter with the fruit syrup and fruit and:

3 cups coarsely chopped pecans

until well mixed. Pour into the loaf and tube pans and bake 3 to 3 1/2 hours or until the tests indicate that the cake is done. Cool and store.

ABOUT OIL CAKES

In this book, all cakes made with cooking oil carry the word "oil" in the title. Have all ingredients about 70°. If liquid fats are used in cake mixing, they demand special mixing processes. The egg whites must be beaten so stiff that they begin to lose their gloss.

▶ Olive oil should never be used, because its flavor is too strong. To achieve a light texture, oil cakes often need a disproportionate amount of sugar and egg, and consequently the calorie and saturated-fat content approximates that of butter cakes. Because of the difference in mixing ▶ do not try to substitute oil for solid fats in other cake recipes. You may vary the recipes given for oil cakes, however, by the addition of spices, flavorings, nuts and raisins.

CHIFFON OIL CAKE

A 10-Inch Tube or a 9 × 13-Inch Oblong Pan

Please read About Oil Cakes, above, and ▶ mix exactly as indicated.
▶ Have all ingredients about 70°.
Preheat oven to 325°.
Sift twice and put into a beater bowl:

    2¼ cups sifted cake flour
    1½ cups sugar
    3 teaspoons double-acting baking powder
    1 teaspoon salt

Beat until smooth and fold in all at once:

    ½ cup vegetable oil
    5 egg yolks
    ¾ cup water
    1 teaspoon grated lemon rind
    1 teaspoon vanilla

Beat until foamy:

    6 to 10 egg whites

Add:

    ½ teaspoon cream of tartar

Now beat until the whites are so stiff that they begin to lose their gloss. Fold the flour, egg and oil mixture gently into the egg whites. Do this by hand, not in the mixer, see 400. Bake the cake in an ungreased tube pan about 1 hour and 10 minutes or in an ungreased 9 × 13-inch pan 30 to 35 minutes. Reverse the tube pan to cool the cake, as shown on 405, or set the oblong pan reversed and supported at the edges by two other pans while the cake cools. Ice with:

    Quick Lemon Icing, 497

CHIFFON CHOCOLATE-MOCHA OIL CAKE

A 10-Inch Tube or a 9 × 13-Inch Oblong Pan

Mix and bake as for preceding cake.
▶ Have all ingredients about 70°.
Preheat oven to 325°.
Melt over hot water:

    3 oz. unsweetened chocolate

Sift twice and put into a beater bowl:

    2¼ cups sifted cake flour
    1⅔ cups sugar
    3 teaspoons double-acting baking powder
    2 teaspoons instant coffee
    1 teaspoon salt
    ¼ teaspoon cinnamon

Beat until smooth and fold in all at once:

    ½ cup vegetable oil
    6 egg yolks
    ¾ cup milk
    1 teaspoon vanilla

and the cooled melted chocolate. Blend well. Beat until frothy:

    8 egg whites

Add:

    ½ teaspoon cream of tartar

Continue to beat until the whites are very stiff. Gently fold the egg whites into the flour, egg and oil mixture.

Pour the batter into an ungreased pan and bake as for the cake above. Ice with:

Luscious Orange Icing, 494

CARROT OIL CAKE

One 8-Inch Square Pan

♦ Have all ingredients about 70°.
Preheat oven to 325°.
Sift before measuring:

1 cup all-purpose flour

Resift with:

1 teaspoon baking soda
1 teaspoon double-acting baking powder
1 teaspoon cinnamon
1/2 teaspoon salt

Mix together and add to flour, stirring well:

2/3 cup vegetable oil
1 cup sugar
2 beaten eggs

Add and blend in well:

1/2 cup chopped nuts
1 1/2 cups grated carrots

Bake in a greased and floured pan about 1 hour and 25 minutes.

ABOUT TORTEN

So many people speak of baking torten as unattainably difficult, not realizing that mixing a torte is just a matter of replacing the flour in certain recipes with dry bread or cake crumbs and nuts ground to a fine meal. Here are some tricks in making torten: ♦ Do not use ground commercial bread crumbs; they are too fine. Prepare your own, using a medium blade in the meat grinder. ♦ The nuts should never be ground in a meat grinder, which simply crushes them and brings up the oil. A small hand grinder with a sharp cutting edge like the one shown in About Nuts, 236, will produce the light, dry, fluffy particles needed. Or, you may grind nuts at very high speed in the ⚙ blender. Do no more than 1/4 cup at a time.

♦ Use a pan with a removable rim—either a spring-form or a tube from which you can remove the bottom, because this kind of pastry is often too delicate in texture to withstand much handling. The sketch at left shows you a cross section of the bottom separate and unlocked, the open rim unlocked, and the entire assembly locked into place. If baking in a tube or in layers, use pans with removable rims. ♦ Never grease the pan sides. Torten are good just as baked, with black coffee. But who can possibly object to a whipped cream or fruit-sauce garnish?

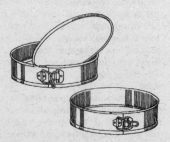

❊ ALMOND TORTE COCKAIGNE

An 8-Inch Removable-Rim Pan or Two 8-Inch Layer Pans

The following recipe is the well-known German **Mandeltorte**.
♦ Please read About Torten, above.
Preheat oven to 350°.
♦ Have all ingredients about 70°. Sift:

1 cup sugar

Beat:

6 egg yolks

Add the sugar gradually and beat until very creamy. Add:

Grated rind and juice of 1 lemon or of 1 small orange

1 teaspoon cinnamon
1 cup ground unblanched
   almonds
1/2 cup toasted or dry white
   bread crumbs
(1/2 teaspoon almond extract)
Whip ♦ until stiff, but not dry:
6 or 7 egg whites
The extra egg white makes a much lighter cake. Fold them lightly into the batter. Bake about 40 minutes in an ungreased removable-rim pan or loaf pan. Let cool in the pan. Spread with:
Chocolate Butter Icing, 498
Or, bake it about 20 minutes in two 8-inch ungreased layer pans. Spread between the layers:
Lemon-Orange Custard
Filling, 452
Spread the top with:
Sifted confectioners' sugar
or with one of the fillings suggested on 448. This cake is very light and consequently difficult to remove from the pan, so be careful.

❀ PECAN TORTE

For a richer, moister cake, prepare:
Almond Torte, above
substituting pecans for the almonds.
♦ Be sure to grind the nuts in a nut grinder.

❀ BREAD TORTE OR
BROTTORTE

A 9-Inch Removable-Rim Pan
In the following recipe for a celebrated German confection, the ingredients differ only slightly from those in the preceding Mandeltorte, but the results, thanks to the wine bath, are gratifyingly different. You might try substituting walnuts for the almonds. Preheat oven to 350°.
♦ Have all ingredients about 70°. Sift:
1 cup sugar
Beat:

6 egg yolks
Add the sugar gradually. Beat until creamy. Combine and add:
1 1/4 cups dry bread crumbs
1/2 teaspoon double-acting
   baking powder
1/2 teaspoon cinnamon
2 oz. citron, cut fine
1 cup unblanched almonds,
   ground in a nut grinder
   Grated rind and juice of 1
   lemon
Whip ♦ until stiff, but not dry:
6 egg whites
Fold them lightly into the cake batter. Bake 1 hour or more in an ungreased pan. Heat but do not boil for about 10 minutes:
3/4 cup dry sherry
2 tablespoons water
2 whole cloves
1 stick cinnamon
1/4 cup sugar
Strain these ingredients and place the syrup in a small pitcher. Pour it very slowly onto the hot cake. When all the liquid has been absorbed, cool the cake and remove it from the pan. Spread with:
A flavored Crème
Patissière, 450

DOBOS OR DRUM TORTE

The many-tiered Hungarian chocolate-filled torte that looks rich, is rich and enriches everyone who eats it. We like to think of it as "drummer's" torte because of its hard glazed top, but it seems its name refers to its creator, a patissier named Dobos.
♦ Have all ingredients about 70°. Prepare:
Génoise, 416
Using well-greased 8-inch cake pans, bake the cake in 9 thin layers, 5 to 9 minutes each. If your oven will not hold so many layers, bake thicker

ones and slice them in two, in the professional manner, holding them as shown on 435. Stack them so that the icing is applied to the uncut surfaces. When cool, spread between the layers the following filling. Place in a double boiler ♦ over—not in—boiling water:

> ½ cup sugar
> 4 eggs
> 1-inch vanilla bean

or omit the vanilla bean and add 1 teaspoon vanilla after the filling has cooled. Beat until the eggs begin to thicken. Cool the filling slightly. Cut into pieces and dissolve:

> 4 oz. unsweetened chocolate

in:

> 2 tablespoons boiling water

Keep this warm. Cream until light:

> ⅞ cup butter: 1¾ sticks

Add the chocolate mixture. Beat this into the egg mixture. This filling may also be spread over the top and sides of the cake, but the true Hungarian will spread it between layers only, reserving the best-looking layer for the top. Glaze this chef d'oeuvre with:

> ½ cup Clear Caramel
> Glaze, 505

Before the caramel sets, use a hot buttered knife to cut 12 to 18 radial lines into the top glaze, so the cake may be easily sliced. "Rest" the cake in a chilled place 12 hours or more before serving.

❊ HAZELNUT TORTE

A 10-Inch Removable-Rim Pan
♦ Please read About Torten, 430.
Preheat oven to 350°.
♦ Have all ingredients about 70°. Sift:

> 1 cup sugar

Beat:

> 12 egg yolks

Add the sugar gradually. Beat well until ingredients are very creamy.

Grind in a nut grinder and add to the yolk mixture:

> ¼ lb. hazelnuts
> ¼ lb. pecans or walnuts

Add:

> (2 tablespoons bread crumbs)

Whip ♦ until stiff, but not dry:

> 8 egg whites

Fold them lightly into the other ingredients. Bake the cake in an ungreased pan about 40 minutes. When cool, serve with:

> Whipped cream, flavored
> with vanilla or sweet sherry

or spread the cake with:

> (Coffee or Caramel Icing,
> 499, 494)

CHOCOLATE WALNUT TORTE

A 9-Inch Removable-Rim Pan
♦ Please read About Torten, 430.
Preheat oven to 325°.
♦ Have all ingredients about 70°. Sift:

> ⅞ cup sugar

Beat until light:

> 6 egg yolks

Add the sugar gradually. Beat until well blended. Add:

> ½ cup finely crushed cracker
> crumbs
> ¼ cup grated unsweetened
> chocolate
> ¾ cup chopped walnut meats
> 2 tablespoons brandy or rum
> ½ teaspoon double-acting
> baking powder
> ½ teaspoon cinnamon
> ¼ teaspoon each cloves and
> nutmeg

Whip ♦ until stiff, but not dry:

> 6 egg whites

Fold them lightly into the cake batter. Bake in an ungreased pan about 1 hour. Spread with:

> Chocolate Butter Icing, 498

or serve with:

> Wine Custard, 511

FLOURLESS ANGEL ALMOND CAKE

A 7-Inch Tube Pan

◗ Have all ingredients about 70°.
Preheat oven to 350°.
Blanch, then grind in a nut grinder:

1¹/₂ cups almonds

Sift:

1¹/₂ cups confectioners' sugar

Beat until stiff:

7 egg whites

Fold in the sugar and almonds. Bake in a greased pan about 45 minutes or until done. To cool, see About Angel Cakes, 404.

❋ LINZERTORTE

A 9-Inch Pie or Cake

The following is a delicious German "company" cake or pie. It looks like an open jam pie and, being rich, is usually served in thin wedges. It should serve 12.
Have all ingredients about 70°. Sift:

1 cup sugar

Beat until soft:

³/₄ cup butter

Add the sugar gradually. Blend these ingredients until very light and creamy. Add:

1 teaspoon grated lemon rind

Beat in, one at a time:

2 eggs

Stir in gradually:

1¹/₄ cups sifted all-purpose flour
1 cup unblanched almonds, ground in a nut grinder or a ⅄ blender
¹/₂ teaspoon cinnamon
¹/₄ teaspoon cloves
1 tablespoon cocoa
¹/₄ teaspoon salt

The old recipe reads, "Stir for one hour," but of course no high-geared American has time for that. If the dough is very soft, chill it. Pat half the dough into an ovenproof dish to the thickness of ¹/₈ inch. Rechill it until firm. Cover this part of the cake generously with good-quality:

Raspberry jam or preserves, or apple butter

Preheat oven to 325°.
Place the remaining dough in a pastry tube. Forcing the dough through the bag, form a good edge and lattice. Bake the cake about 50 minutes. Before serving, fill the hollows with additional preserves. You may also dust the top with:

Confectioners' sugar

SACHERTORTE

A 9-Inch Removable-Rim Pan

Frau Sacher, one of the great personalities of Vienna, fed the impoverished Austrian nobility in her famous restaurant long after they had ceased to pay. Today she is remembered throughout the world for her chocolate torte, for which endless recipes, all claiming authenticity, abound. We make no claims but think the following delicious. ◗ Please read About Torten, 430.
◗ Have all ingredients about 70°.
Preheat oven to 325°.
Grate:

5 to 6 oz. semisweet chocolate

Cream well:

¹/₂ cup sugar
¹/₂ cup butter

Beat in one at a time until mixture is light and fluffy:

6 egg yolks

Add the grated chocolate and:

³/₄ cup dry bread crumbs
¹/₄ cup finely ground blanched almonds
¹/₄ teaspoon salt

Beat until stiff, but not dry, and fold in:

6 to 7 egg whites

The extra egg white makes a lighter cake.

Bake in an ungreased removable-rim or spring-form pan 50 minutes to 1 hour. When well cooled, slice the torte horizontally through the middle. Should the top be mounded, reverse the layers so the finished cake has a flat top. Place between the layers:

1 cup apricot jam or preserves

Cover the cake with:

Chocolate Glaze, 504

which should retain its glossy sheen. For a really Viennese effect, garnish each slice with a great gob of "Schlag" or whipped cream.

ABOUT FILLED CAKES

Filled cakes are especially appropriate for buffets; they serve as complete desserts, combining ice cream and cake, pudding and cake or fruit and cake. They may also be as rich and substantial or as light in texture and calorie content as you choose.

We have assembled in the next pages some individual recipes that we enjoy serving as complete desserts. We also suggest a number of ways that basic cakes can be combined with fillings. Read about Roll Cakes, 439, Torten, 430, Filled Rolled Cookies, 471, and Charlottes, 530. See illustrations for making a secret filling, opposite, lining pudding molds, 522, or turning a simple Baked Alaska into an Omelette Surprise, 521.

If you must, buy your basic angel and sponge cakes, ice cream and ice fillings. But when you combine them, make a delicious sauce of your very own with fresh eggs or fruit and—most important of all—real vanilla, fresh spices and quality spirits. All the recipes for sponge, angel cakes, Génoise, Daffodil Cake, roll cakes, nut torten, ladyfingers and rolled cookies are suitable for mold linings. For additional fillings and combinations, see About Cake Fillings, 448–453.

To prepare a tube cake for a secret filling, see the illustrations opposite. Have ready a serrated knife or a long piece of thread. Marking the section to be separated with wooden picks, as shown, cut a 1-inch incision at the pick level all around the cake. Then cut through or if using a thread hold it taut and with a sawing motion cut the 1-inch-high section free. Reserve this top slice for the lid.

Then start to cut a smooth-rimmed channel in the remaining section, to receive the filling. Allow for 1-inch walls by making 2 circular, vertical incisions, to within 1 inch of the base. To remove the cake loosened by these incisions, next insert your knife diagonally, first from the top of the inside of the outer rim to the base cut of the inner rim, and continue to cut diagonally all around through the channel core. Then reverse the action and repeat the cut from the top of the inside of the inner rim to the base cut of the outer rim. Performed with a saw-bladed knife, these two cuts bisect each other in an X operation and give you 3 loose triangular sections which are easily removed. The fourth triangle still attached at the base is then cut free one inch from the base of the cake. A curved knife is a help here. The cake which formed the channel area can be used for Angel Balls, 446, or some of it may be shredded and mixed with the filling. Ladle the filling of your choice into the channel as shown in the center.

Replace the lid. Top this whole cake with whipped cream or icing. When you cut the cake, each slice will look like the cross sections sketched on the cake-stand.

REFRIGERATED FILLED CAKE

Line molds with cakes suggested above, or make a cake with a secret filling, shown below. Fill with:

> Bavarians, 527, or
> mousses, 513
> Whipped gelatin pud-
> dings, 522

> Pastry creams, 450, or
> Charlotte mixtures, 530
> Fillings for cream pie, 385,
> or chiffon pie, 388
> Sweetened whipped
> creams, 449

Refrigerate at least 6 hours, covered, before serving. Garnish with:

> Fruits and nuts

or serve with:

> Sauce or whipped cream

Dust with:

> Toasted nuts
> Shredded coconut or
> Praliné, 593

❄ QUICK MOCHA-CHOCOLATE FREEZER CAKE

About 10 to 12 Servings

Cut:

> Angel Cake, 405

into 4 layers. Soften:

> ½ gallon Mocha Ice
> Cream, 552

Stir in:

> 3 shaved sweet chocolate and
> almond bars

Put the ice cream between the layers and cover the cake all over with it. Put into the ❄ freezer and allow to set for about an hour. If you make this the day before and keep it in the freezer, be sure to unfreeze ½ hour before serving.

KRANSEKAKE OR PYRAMID CAKE

A tiered cake usually served at weddings and confirmations in Norway; in America, a spectacular finale to a dinner party; see illustration in chapter heading on 398.

Preheat oven to 375°.

Mix together:

> 1 cup sugar
> 4 hard-cooked egg yolks,
> mashed

Set aside this mixture and beat together:

> 4 whole eggs
> 2 cups butter

Combine the two egg mixtures. Gradually add, kneading well:

> 5 cups sifted all-purpose
> flour
> 3 cups ground almonds

The dough is delicate and rather difficult to handle. With lightly floured hands, roll a small lump on a pastry cloth into a ½-inch-thick strip, long enough to form a circle eight or nine inches in diameter. This is for the bottom ring of the pyramid. It is best to roll out all the strips first, making each one a little shorter than the one before. To join the ends of the strips of dough, dip them in:

A little egg white, slightly beaten

Place the rings on several slightly floured cookie sheets. You can manage three or more rings to a sheet. Sprinkle with:

Granulated sugar

Bake about 7 minutes or until light brown. When removed from the oven, immediately place one ring on top of the other so they will stick together. Decorate with:

Lemon Glaze, 504

by piping a thin line of glaze at the point where two rings meet. Then continue in an irregular zigzag fashion all over the cake. This pastry is delightful served with:

Fresh strawberries or other fruit

CASSATA ALLA SICILIANA

Prepare:

Pound Cake, 415

Cut off and reserve crusts for cookie crumbs, 353. Cut the cake horizontally into 4 long even slices. Prepare a filling by mixing in a 🥄 blender until very smooth:

1 lb. Ricotta cheese
2 tablespoons cream
¼ cup sugar
3 tablespoons crème de cacao or Grand Marnier

Fold in:

2 tablespoons coarsely chopped candied orange or lemon peel
2 squares coarsely chopped semisweet chocolate

Divide the filling in about three parts so as to cover all but the top layer.

Firm up the filled cake by refrigerating, wrapped, about 2 hours. Depending on how rich a dessert you want, dust with:

(Powdered sugar)

or cover the cake with:

(Chocolate Butter Icing, 498)

using coffee as the liquid.

MOHRENKÖPFE OR MOORS' HEADS

These Moors' heads, along with Individual Nut Tarts, 482, and Macaroon Jam Tarts, 482, were specialities of a famous St. Louis bakery, now extinct, and these cakes graced a thousand Kaffee klatsches. While the true Mohrenkopf is baked in a special half-round mold, then filled and the halves joined, the full taste effect can be gained by the following method. Cut in rounds or squares:

Thin Génoise, 416

Make a "sandwich" filling of:

Hazelnut-flavored whipped cream

placed between 2 slices of cake. Ice with:

European Chocolate Icing, 499, or Chocolate Sauce Cockaigne, 567

TRIFLE OR RASPBERRY RUM CAKE

A good use for dry cake. Combine it with raspberries, which are traditional. But apricot jam or other preserves, thickened pie cherries, or fresh or cooked drained fruit may be substituted.
Place in a deep dish:

Rounds of yellow, sponge or layer cake

You may sprinkle the cake with:

(2 tablespoons rum or sherry)

Spread the pieces with:

¹/₂ cup jam or jelly or
1 to 2 cups sweetened fruit
(¹/₄ cup blanched, slivered
almonds)

Prepare:

Rich Custard, 509

Pour the custard over the cake. If desired, garnish with:

(Whipped cream)

BABA AU RHUM OR SAVARIN

Beloved by the French, who frequently serve babas with tea. This is an American version. Savarin is really a larger version of Baba au Rhum. The same dough and the same syrup are used, but the Savarin is baked in a ring mold with a rounded base, and it is often flavored with kirsch instead of rum. When it is turned out, the center is filled with fruit. If you fill it with tart red cherry compote, you need hardly be told it will have become **Savarin Montmorency**!

Prepare the dough for:

Bundkuchen, 329, or
Brioche, 320

Place it in a greased 8-inch tube pan. Let rise, and bake as directed. Remove from the pan, cool and return to the pan. Prepare a syrup by boiling for 10 minutes:

¹/₂ cup water
1 cup sugar

Cool it to lukewarm. Flavor it generously with:

Dark rum, whisky or
kirsch: at least ¹/₄ cup

Place the syrup in a small pitcher. One hour before serving, pour the syrup slowly, drop by drop, onto the baba. Use as much as will be absorbed. Remove the cake from the pan and let it drain on a rack until ready to serve. If it is to be a dessert, top it with:

(Whipped cream or Crème
Chantilly, 449)

You may serve individual baba cakes. Bake them in greased muffin or popover tins. Soak them with syrup as directed or cut a slice from the top, hollow the cakes slightly and fill the hollows with raspberry or apricot jam. Serve with:

Lemon Sauce, 563

Or slice the babas in half. Cover each half with a slice of fresh pineapple and currant jelly, sprinkled with confectioners' sugar and kirsch.

POPPY SEED CUSTARD CAKE COCKAIGNE

Two 9-Inch Round Pans

A delightful filled tea cake.
♦ Have all ingredients about 70°.
Combine and soak ♦ 2 hours:

²/₃ cup poppy seed
³/₄ cup milk

Preheat oven to 375°.
Beat until soft:

²/₃ cup butter

Add gradually and cream until fluffy:

1¹/₂ cups sugar

Sift before measuring:

2 cups cake flour

Resift with:

2¹/₂ teaspoons double-acting
baking powder
¹/₂ teaspoon salt

Combine the poppy seed-milk mixture with:

¹/₄ cup milk
1 teaspoon vanilla

Add the sifted ingredients to the butter mixture in 3 parts, alternating with the liquid ingredients. Beat the batter after each addition until blended. Whip ♦ until stiff, but not dry, then fold in:

4 egg whites

Bake about 20 minutes in pans with

greased bottoms. Place between the layers:

Crème Patissière, 450

Dust with:

Powdered sugar

Or serve with:

(Chocolate Sauce Cockaigne, 567)

ORANGE-FILLED CAKE

Three 9-Inch Round Pans

Most recipes for orange cake prove to be disappointing, for upon reading them you find that they are merely sponge or butter cake with an orange filling. This one calls for orange juice in the batter plus orange filling and icing. Earrings for an elephant with no apologies!

Preheat oven to 375°.

◗ Have all ingredients about 70°. Sift before measuring:

3 cups cake flour

Resift with:

3/4 teaspoon salt

3 1/2 teaspoons double-acting baking powder

Grate:

Rind of 1 orange

into:

1 1/2 cups sugar

Cream this until light with:

3/4 cup butter

Beat in, one at a time:

3 eggs

Measure:

1/2 cup orange juice

1/2 cup water

2 tablespoons lemon juice

Add the flour mixture in 3 parts to the butter mixture, alternately with the liquid. Stir the batter after each addition until smooth. Bake the cake about 1/2 hour in 3 layer pans with greased bottoms. When the cake is cool, spread between the layers:

Orange Cream Filling, 451

BOSTON CREAM PIE OR CAKE

Traditionally called a pie, this is really a 2-layer cake. There are many versions, but the most prevalent one today reads as follows.

Place between 2 layers of:

Gold Layer Cake, 413

a thick coating of:

Crème Patissière, 450

Leave the sides exposed, but cover the top with:

A chocolate icing, 498

CREAM MERINGUE TART COCKAIGNE

Two 8-Inch Layer Pans

The following recipe is not at all difficult to make, yet it is an optical as well as a gastronomic treat. A cake batter and a meringue are baked at the same time.

Preheat oven to 325°.

◗ Have all ingredients about 70°.

Blanch and shred:

(1/3 cup almonds)

Sift:

1 1/2 cups sugar

Beat until soft:

1/4 cup butter

Add 1/2 cup of the sifted sugar gradually. Blend until light and creamy. Beat in, one at a time:

4 egg yolks

Add:

1/2 teaspoon vanilla

Sift before measuring:

1 cup cake flour

Resift with:

1 teaspoon double-acting baking powder

1/4 teaspoon salt

Add the sifted ingredients to the butter mixture, alternately with:

5 tablespoons cream

Beat the batter until smooth. Spread it in 2 greased pans with 1 1/2-inch sides.

Cover it with the following meringue. Whip ◗ until stiff, but not dry:

4 egg whites

Add the remaining cup sifted sugar slowly, about 1 tablespoon at a time. Beat constantly. When all the sugar has been added, continue to beat for several minutes. Fold in:

1 teaspoon vanilla

Spread the meringue lightly over the cake batter in both pans. If using the almonds, stud one meringue with the blanched, shredded almonds, placing the shreds upright and close together. Bake the layers about 40 minutes. Remove them from the oven and let them cool in the pans. Shortly before serving the cake, place the unstudded layer, meringue side down, on a cake plate. Spread one of the following fillings over it, reserving 1/4 cup to garnish the top. Place the almond-studded layer, meringue side up, on the filling and place the reserved filling in the center on top, using:

**A cream filling, 450;
Sauce Cockaigne, 564;
or whipped cream**

CARAMEL CORNFLAKE RING

A 7-Inch Ring Mold

Stir and melt in a large saucepan:

**1 cup packed brown
sugar
3 tablespoons butter
(1/4 teaspoon salt if butter is
unsalted)**

Fold in until well coated:

4 cups uncrushed cornflakes

Press the mixture lightly into a 7-inch ring mold. Invert the ring onto a platter before the mixture is cold. When set, fill with sweetened fruits and whipped cream, coffee ice cream dribbled with chocolate sauce, or a fruit ice laced with liqueur.

FRUIT SHORTCAKES

Prepare:

**Fluffy Biscuit dough, 350,
Scone dough, 352, or any of
the plain sponge cakes, 407**

For small shortcakes, the dough should be baked in 3-inch rounds, split while hot and spread with butter. The sponge cake should be cut to size after baking. For large shortcakes, bake in 2 layers. Place between the layers and over them:

Sugared or cooked fruit

Garnish with:

Whipped cream

ABOUT ROLL CAKES

Any number of batters lend themselves to rolling, see 440–441. For easy removal, they should be baked in sheets, $10^{1}/_{2} \times 15^{1}/_{2} \times 1$ inch. Grease the baking sheet, then line the bottom with a long strip of parchment paper or foil which extends over the ends of the pan. Grease the paper also and pour in the batter so it covers all corners. Bake in a 375° oven about 12 minutes. Loosen the edges as soon as the cake comes from the oven. Reverse the pan onto a clean towel that has been dusted with:

Sifted confectioners' sugar

Immediately peel off the paper or foil. Trim any crusty edges and roll before the cake cools. If the filling is a perishable one, roll the unfilled cake while it is still hot, with the towel, as shown in the illustration on 440. Place the cake, still wrapped in the towel, on a rack to cool. Later, when ready to fill, unroll the cake, fill it and use the towel to roll it again, as shown in the lower sketch. If the filling is jam or jelly, it can be put on the warm cake immediately before rolling. When the cake is rolled after

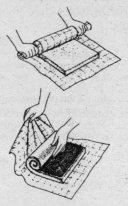

filling ◗ place it on the serving plate with the loose edge down.

JELLY ROLL

A 10¹/₂ X 15¹/₂ X 1-Inch Pan

This standard roll cake, or jelly roll, recipe also bakes well in two 8-inch round layer pans. To prepare pan, bake and roll, see About Roll Cakes, 439.

◗ Have all ingredients about 70°.
Preheat oven to 375°.
Sift:
     ³/₄ cup sugar
Beat until light:
     4 egg yolks
Add the sugar gradually. Beat until creamy. Add:
     1 teaspoon vanilla
Sift before measuring:
     ³/₄ cup cake flour
Resift with:
     **³/₄ teaspoon double-acting
          baking powder**
     ¹/₂ teaspoon salt
Add the flour gradually to the egg mixture. Beat the batter until smooth. Whip ◗ until stiff, but not dry:
     4 egg whites
Fold them lightly into the cake batter.

You may add:
     (¹/₂ cup finely chopped nuts)
Bake about 12 minutes. When cold, spread with at least:
     **¹/₂ cup jelly or tart jam or
          1 cup or more cream or
          custard filling, 450**
Or for an unusual touch, try:
     Ginger Fruit Filling, 452

LEMON ROLL

Prepare:
     Jelly Roll, above
Substitute for the jelly:
     Lemon Filling, 451
Roll and fill as directed above.

BUTTERSCOTCH SPICE ROLL

A 10¹/₂ X 15¹/₂ X 1-Inch Pan

◗ To prepare pan, bake and roll, see About Roll Cakes, 439. ◗ Have all ingredients about 70°.
Preheat oven to 400°.
Place in a bowl over hot water:
     4 eggs
     ¹/₄ teaspoon salt
Beat until the eggs are thick and lemon colored. Beat in gradually:
     ³/₄ cup sugar
Remove from the heat. Sift before measuring:
     ³/₄ cup cake flour
Resift with:
     **³/₄ teaspoon double-acting
          baking powder**
     1 teaspoon cinnamon
     ¹/₂ teaspoon cloves
Fold the sifted ingredients into the eggs with:
     1 teaspoon vanilla
Bake the batter about 12 minutes. A good filling is:
     **Butterscotch
     Filling, 450**

ALMOND SPONGE ROLL

A 10½ X 15½ X 1-Inch Pan
♦ To prepare pan, bake and roll, see
About Roll Cakes, above. ♦ Have all
ingredients about 70°.
Preheat oven to 325°.
Beat until light:
  8 egg yolks
Beat in gradually:
  ½ cup sugar
Add:
  **½ cup blanched ground
      almonds**
Beat ♦ until stiff, but not dry:
  8 egg whites
  ¼ teaspoon salt
Fold in:
  1 teaspoon vanilla
Fold the egg whites into the yolk
mixture. Bake about 15 minutes, roll
and, when cold, spread with any desired filling, see 448–453.

ANGEL CAKE ROLL

A 10½ X 15½ X 1-Inch Pan
To prepare pan, bake and roll, see
About Roll Cakes, 439. The pan is
greased here in order to free the cake
intact for rolling.
Prepare half the recipe for:
  Angel Cake I, 405
Bake in a 300° oven about 20 minutes. Use any of the fillings suggested
for the various Cake Rolls in this
chapter. Raspberry or apricot jam and
whipped cream are fine.

CHOCOLATE-FILLED ROLL

A 10½ X 15½ X 1-Inch Pan
Prepare:
  Jelly Roll, opposite
When rolled and cooled, spread with:
  **Chocolate Sauce
  Cockaigne, 567**

Serve with:
  Whipped cream

★ CHOCOLATE CREAM ROLL
OR BÛCHE DE NOËL

An 8 X 12-Inch Pan
For Christmas this can be made into a
Yule Log, shown in the chapter heading. Trim it without the mushrooms
for Washington's Birthday. To prepare pan, bake and roll, see About
Roll Cakes, 439.
♦ Have all ingredients about 70°.
Preheat oven to 325°.
Sift:
  ½ cup powdered sugar
Beat until light:
  3 to 6 egg yolks
Add the sugar gradually and beat
these ingredients until creamy. Add:
  1 teaspoon vanilla
Sift and add:
  2 to 6 tablespoons cocoa
If you use less than 4 tablespoons cocoa, add:
  **(2 tablespoons all-purpose
      flour)**
  ⅛ teaspoon salt
Whip ♦ until stiff, but not dry:
  3 to 6 egg whites
  ½ teaspoon cream of tartar
Fold lightly into the cake batter.
Spread the dough in the greased pan
to the thickness of ¼ inch. Bake the
cake about 25 minutes. Let it cool in
the pan 5 minutes before rolling.
Fill with:
  **A sweetened whipped
  cream, 449**
Cover with:
  Chocolate Sauce, 567
For the Yule Log, cover with a
roughed-up:
  Chocolate Butter Icing, 498
sprouting small:
  Macaroon mushrooms

▲ ABOUT HIGH-ALTITUDE CAKE BAKING

Cake batters at high altitudes are subject to pixie-like variations that often defy general rules. Read the comments and then launch forth on your own, keeping records at first until you know what gives you the greatest success. On the whole, ♦ cupcakes and layer cakes are better textured than loaf cakes.

Up to 3000 feet, if you reduce the air in the cakes by ♦ not overbeating eggs, you will probably need no adjustment of the cake formula. ♦ Also raise the baking temperature about 25°. In elevations higher than 3000 feet, continue to underbeat the eggs as compared to sea level consistency. Another way to reduce their volume is to keep the eggs refrigerated until almost ready to use.

At around 5000 feet, it will also help to reduce the double-acting baking powder or baking soda by ⅛ to ¼ teaspoon for each teaspoon called for in the recipe. Decrease sugar 1 to 2 tablespoons for each cup called for, and increase liquid 2 to 3 tablespoons for each cup indicated. Raise the baking temperature about 25°.

At 7000 feet, decrease double-acting baking powder or baking soda by ¼ teaspoon for every teaspoon called for. Decrease sugar by 2 to 3 tablespoons for each cup indicated and increase liquid by 3 to 4 tablespoons for each cup called for. Increase the flour 1 tablespoon for each cup called for. Raise the baking temperature about 25°.

At 10,000 feet, decrease the double-acting baking powder or baking soda by ¼ to ½ teaspoon for every teaspoon called for in the recipe, and add an extra egg, but do not overbeat the eggs. Decrease the sugar 2 to 3 tablespoons for each cup in the recipe. Increase the liquid by 3 to 4 tablespoons for each cup liquid indicated. Increase the flour by 1 to 2 tablespoons for each cup called for. Increase the baking temperature about 25°.

Following are some basic high-altitude recipes from government sources. But if you are reluctant to give up your own recipes from home, we also throw in as a talisman the homely formula of a friend who has for years had luck with it at 7000 to 8000 feet, using her old Chicago favorites. She merely uses three-fourths the amount of double-acting baking powder or baking soda called for, adds 1 additional tablespoon flour and 1 extra egg, decreases the butter by a few tablespoons if the recipe is very rich, and increases the oven heat by about 25°.

But whatever formula you use ♦ grease your baking pans well and dust them with flour or line them with parchment paper. For, at high altitudes, cakes have a tendency to stick to the pan. Exceptions are angel and sponge cakes, see recipes below. Fill cake pans only half full of batter, as high-altitude cakes may overflow.

▲ HIGH-ALTITUDE ANGEL CAKE

10-Inch Tube Pan

This recipe is for baking at 5000 feet. If baking at 7000 feet, add 1 tablespoon cake flour and decrease sugar by 2 tablespoons. If baking at 10,000 feet, add 2 tablespoons cake flour and decrease sugar by 4 tablespoons.

♦ Please read About Angel Cakes, 404. Preheat oven to 375°.

Mix and sift together 3 times:

**1 cup plus 2 tablespoons
sifted cake flour**

¹/₂ cup sugar

Keep refrigerated until ready to use:

1¹/₂ cups egg whites: 10 to 12 eggs

Beat the egg whites until foamy and add:

1¹/₂ teaspoons cream of tartar
¹/₂ teaspoon salt

Continue beating until egg whites are glossy and ♦ form peaks which just barely fall over. Fold in, with about 25 strokes:

1 cup sugar

Beat until mixture is fluffy and meringuelike. Beat briefly while adding:

1¹/₂ teaspoons vanilla

Add the dry ingredients about one-fourth at a time by sifting them over the egg mixture, using about 15 folding strokes after each addition. After last addition, use about 10 more strokes to blend completely. Pour into ungreased tube pan. Cut through batter with knife to release air bubbles. Bake about 40 minutes. Invert pan, as shown on 405, and allow cake to cool before removing it from the pan.

▲ HIGH-ALTITUDE CHOCOLATE ANGEL CAKE

Prepare:

High-Altitude Angel Cake, above

Use in all 1 cup cake flour and add:

¹/₄ cup cocoa
¹/₄ cup sugar

▲ HIGH-ALTITUDE SPICE ANGEL CAKE

Prepare:

High-Altitude Angel Cake, above

Omit the vanilla and substitute by sifting with dry ingredients:

¹/₄ teaspoon cloves
¹/₂ teaspoon nutmeg
1 teaspoon cinnamon

▲ HIGH-ALTITUDE WHITE CAKE

Two 8-Inch Round Pans

This formula is for baking at 5000 feet. If baking at 7500 feet, reduce baking powder by ¹/₂ teaspoon. If baking at 10,000 feet, reduce baking powder by 1 teaspoon.

♦ Please read About Butter or Shortening Cakes, 409.

Preheat oven to 375°.

Place in a mixer:

¹/₂ cup soft butter

Sift together twice and then sift into the beater bowl with the butter:

2 cups sifted cake flour
2 teaspoons double-acting baking powder
¹/₂ teaspoon salt
1 cup sugar

Add and mix 2 minutes:

³/₄ cup milk
1 teaspoon vanilla

Beat until foamy:

4 egg whites

Add and beat ♦ until stiff, but not dry:

¹/₄ cup sugar

Add this meringue to batter with:

3 tablespoons milk

and beat 1 minute. Grease the pans and dust well with flour or line with foil, pour in the batter and bake about 30 minutes or until done.

▲ HIGH-ALTITUDE FUDGE CAKE

A 9 X 13-Inch Pan

This recipe is for baking at 5000 feet. If baking at 7500 to 10,000 feet, decrease baking powder by 1 teaspoon, and if baking at 10,000, also decrease sugar by ¹/₄ cup.

◗ Please read About Butter or Shortening Cakes, 409.

Preheat oven to 350°.

Melt over hot water:

4 squares unsweetened chocolate

Mix and sift together 3 times:

**2 cups sifted cake flour
2 teaspoons double-acting baking powder
1 teaspoon salt**

Soften:

1/2 cup butter

Add slowly to butter, and cream longer than you would at sea level:

2 1/4 cups sugar

Remove from the refrigerator and separate:

3 eggs

Beat and add the yolks and the cooled melted chocolate. Add alternately by thirds the dry ingredients and:

**1 1/2 cups milk
2 teaspoons vanilla**

After each addition of flour, beat about 25 strokes. After each addition of liquid, beat about 75 strokes. Whip the egg whites ◗ until stiff, but not dry. Fold them into the batter. Grease pan and dust well with flour or line with foil. Pour in the batter and bake about 45 minutes or until done.

▲ HIGH-ALTITUDE TWO-EGG CAKE

Two 8-Inch Pans

The following high-altitude recipe is for a cake baked at 5000 feet. If baking at 7500 feet, decrease baking powder by 1/4 teaspoon and add 2 tablespoons milk. If baking at 10,000 feet, decrease baking powder by 1/2 teaspoon and add 2 tablespoons milk. Preheat oven to 375°.

Mix and sift together 3 times.

2 cups sifted cake flour

**1 1/2 teaspoons double-acting baking powder
1/2 teaspoon salt**

Cream:

1/2 cup butter

Add gradually to the butter:

**1 cup sugar
1 teaspoon vanilla**

Cream until light and fluffy, somewhat longer than you would at sea level. Add to creamed mixture and mix thoroughly:

2 eggs

which were refrigerated until ready to use. Add alternately by thirds the sifted dry ingredients and:

3/4 cup plus 1 tablespoon milk

using about 50 strokes each time the liquid is added. Grease the layer pans, dust them well with flour or line them with foil. Release air pockets by cutting through batter 3 or 4 times. Bake about 25 minutes or until done.

▲ HIGH-ALTITUDE SPICED COCOA CAKE

Prepare:

High-Altitude Two-Egg Cake, above

observing the adjustments for the altitude at which you are baking. Add to the dry ingredients before the final sifting:

**1/2 teaspoon nutmeg
1/4 teaspoon cloves
1 teaspoon cinnamon**

Replace 1/2 cup cake flour with:

1/2 cup cocoa

▲ HIGH-ALTITUDE SPONGE CAKE

An 8-Inch Tube Pan

This recipe is for an altitude of 5000 to 7500 feet. If baking at 10,000 feet, add 5 tablespoons sifted cake flour.

♦ Please read About Sponge Cakes, 406.

Preheat oven to 350°.

Remove from the refrigerator and separate:

6 eggs

Beat the yolks slightly. Add to them:

1¹/₂ tablespoons water
1 teaspoon vanilla
¹/₂ teaspoon salt

Continue to beat while adding gradually:

¹/₂ cup sugar

Beat until thick and lemon-yellow in color. Beat the egg whites until foamy and add:

¹/₂ teaspoon cream of tartar

Then add gradually to egg whites:

¹/₂ cup sugar

♦ Beat just until peaks form and fall over slightly when beater is removed from mixture. Fold yolk mixture into the beaten whites. Add one-fourth at a time, using about 15 strokes after each addition:

1¹/₄ cups plus 1 tablespoon sifted cake flour

After fourth addition, mix for about 10 more strokes. Fold in:

1¹/₂ tablespoons lemon juice
1 tablespoon grated lemon rind

Bake in an ungreased tube pan 40 to 50 minutes. Invert pan as shown on 405 and allow cake to cool completely before removing from pan.

▲ HIGH-ALTITUDE GINGERBREAD

A 9-Inch Square Pan

This recipe is for baking at 5000 feet. If baking at 7500 feet, decrease baking soda by ¹/₄ teaspoon. If baking at 10,000 feet, reduce soda by ¹/₂ teaspoon, sugar by 3 tablespoons and molasses by 2 teaspoons.

Preheat oven to 350°.

Mix and sift together 3 times:

2¹/₃ cups sifted all-purpose flour
³/₄ teaspoon baking soda
¹/₂ teaspoon salt
¹/₄ teaspoon each cinnamon, nutmeg and allspice
1 teaspoon ginger

Beat:

¹/₂ cup soft shortening

Add gradually to shortening, and cream somewhat longer than you would at sea level, until light and fluffy:

¹/₂ cup sugar

Add 1 at a time and beat well after each addition:

2 eggs

Add and mix in thoroughly:

³/₄ cup molasses

Add the dry ingredients alternately by fourths with:

²/₃ cup boiling water

Beat about 20 strokes after each addition of flour and 30 strokes after each addition of liquid. Grease and flour the pan well or line with foil, pour in the batter and bake about 45 minutes.

ABOUT CUPCAKES

Nearly all cake batters lend themselves to baking in individual portions; only the baking time will differ, and this depends on the size of cupcakes being made. Bake them in muffin, madeleine or ladyfinger molds. On informal occasions like children's parties, bake and serve in fluted paper baking cups. If the papers are set in muffin tins, the cakes will retain their shape and you do not have to grease the pans. If not using paper cups, grease the pans and fill the molds about halfway. Bake in a 375° preheated oven 20 to 25 minutes. Another suggestion for children: bake in cup-shaped ice cream cones.

Fill cones about half with batter. Set them on a baking sheet and bake as for cupcakes.

Cupcakes can be filled and iced, see About Cake Fillings, 448, and About Quick Icings, 496. Or garnish the cakes with nuts, diced dried fruits, or a dusting of powdered sugar.

YELLOW CUPCAKES

About Two Dozen 2-Inch Cakes
See About Cupcakes, 445.
Prepare:
> **Gold Layer Cake, 413,**
> **Lightning Cake, 424, or**
> **One-Egg Cake, 425**
Add to the batter:
> **(1 cup raisins or washed,**
> **dried currants)**
When cool, sprinkle the tops with:
> **Confectioners' sugar**

SPONGE CUPCAKES

See About Cupcakes, 445.
Prepare:
> **Any sponge cake, 406**
Permit the cakes to cool in the pans, then remove and sprinkle with:
> **Powdered sugar**

ANGEL CUPCAKES OR BALLS

About Sixteen 2½-Inch Cupcakes
See About Cupcakes, 445.
Prepare the batter for:
> **Angel Cake, 405, or**
> **Flavored Angel Cake, 406**
Place it in deep muffin tins with greased bottoms. Bake about 20 minutes. When cold, split the cupcakes horizontally and fill them. See Filled Cakes, 434, and Torten, 430, for suggestions. For a luxurious tea cake, ice with a rather soft icing and roll in

chopped nuts or shredded chopped coconut.

CHOCOLATE CUPCAKES

See About Cupcakes, 445.
Prepare any recipe for:
> **A chocolate cake,**
> **416–419**
When cool, spread cupcakes with:
> **Quick White Icing, 496, or**
> **Chocolate Butter Icing,**
> **498, or Coffee Icing, 499**

CARAMEL CUPCAKES

About Twenty-Four 2-Inch Cakes
See About Cupcakes, 445.
Prepare the batter for:
> **Quick Caramel Cake, 425**
Spread when cool with:
> **Caramel Icing, 494**

SOUR CREAM SPICE CUPCAKES

About Two Dozen 2-Inch Cakes
See About Cupcakes, 445.
Prepare the batter for:
> **Sour Cream Cake, 413**
substituting for the white sugar:
> **Brown sugar**
Add:
> **½ teaspoon cinnamon**
> **¼ teaspoon cloves**
Fold in:
> **¾ cup nutmeats**
Good served plain or iced.

JAM CUPCAKES

About Twenty 2-Inch Cakes
See About Cupcakes, 445.
Prepare the batter for:
> **Rombauer Jam Cake, 422**
Spread over the cooled cupcakes:
> **Quick Brown Sugar**
> **Icing, 498**

PEANUT BUTTER CUPCAKES

About Twenty-Two 2-Inch Cakes

Delicate and well flavored. See About Cupcakes, 445. ◗ Have all ingredients about 70°.
Preheat oven to 350°.
Beat until soft:

⅓ cup butter

Add gradually:

1 cup packed brown sugar

When these ingredients are light and fluffy, beat in and blend well:

½ cup peanut butter

Combine and beat until light:

2 eggs
½ cup packed brown sugar
1 teaspoon vanilla

Sift before measuring:

2 cups all-purpose flour

Resift with:

½ teaspoon salt
2 teaspoons double-acting baking powder

Beat the egg mixture into the butter mixture. Add the sifted ingredients in 3 parts alternately with:

¾ cup milk

Bake the cakes about 25 minutes. Ice them with:

Quick Maple Icing, 499

COCONUT CUPCAKES

Three Dozen 2-Inch Cakes

See About Cupcakes, 445.
Prepare batter for:

Coconut Loaf Cake, 414

Serve plain or iced.

✿ PETITS FOURS

Prepare the batter for:

Lady Cake, 412, or Génoise, 416

Pour the batter into greased pans, so that you can cut the cake into small cubes. You may cut the cubes in half horizontally and apply a filling, 448. To apply Fondant, the traditional icing, see 494 and the illustration below.

MADELEINES

About 15 Cakes

It was Proust's fortuitous nibble of a madeleine with tea that awakened from the subconscious the sensitive recollections of his childhood in a French provincial town—and from there, the long pageant of *Remembrance*.

These light-as-a-feather French tea cakes are usually baked in greased and lightly floured scalloped madeleine shells or muffin tins, see illustration in chapter heading, 398. Who could guess that their tender crumb results from an overdose of butter? The method of making them is just like that of Génoise, 416.
Preheat oven to 350°.

Melt and allow to cool to lukewarm:

¾ cup clarified butter, (I, 396)

Heat until lukewarm in the top of a double boiler ◗ over—not in—boiling water:

2 eggs
1 cup sugar

Stir constantly. Remove from heat and beat until thick but light and creamy, incorporating as much air as possible. When cool, sift and add gradually:

1 cup sifted cake flour

Add the melted butter and:

1 tablespoon rum or brandy

1 teaspoon vanilla or 1 teaspoon grated lemon rind

Bake shell forms about 8 minutes; muffins about 15 minutes, until a delicate brown. Cool on a rack, shell side up.

LADYFINGERS

About 15 Ladyfingers

Preheat oven to 375°.

◗ Have ingredients about 70°. Sift before measuring:

1/3 cup cake flour

Resift it 3 times. Sift:

1/3 cup confectioners' sugar

1/8 teaspoon salt

Beat until thick and lemon colored:

1 whole egg

2 egg yolks

1/2 teaspoon vanilla

Whip until stiff, but not dry:

2 egg whites

Fold the sugar gradually into the egg whites. Beat the mixture until it thickens again. Fold in the egg-yolk mixture. Fold in the flour. With a pastry tube, shape the dough into strips 3 1/2 to 4 inches long by 1 1/4 inches wide on ungreased paper placed on a sheet pan; or pour it into greased ladyfinger or small muffin tins. Or you may put it through a cookie press. Bake about 12 minutes. When cool, dust with:

Confectioners' sugar

Serve plain, or enclose a filling between the flat surfaces of two ladyfingers pressed together.

CORNSTARCH PUFF CAKES

Fifteen Small Cupcakes

Preheat oven to 350°.

Have ingredients about 70°. Cream:

1/2 cup butter

1 cup sifted powdered sugar

Add and beat until light:

4 eggs

1 teaspoon vanilla

Sift before measuring:

1 cup cornstarch

Sift 3 times again, with:

2 teaspoons double-acting baking powder

Combine the creamed and the sifted ingredients until blended. Fill muffin tins with greased bottoms half full and bake about 15 minutes.

ABOUT CAKE FILLINGS

If you happen to be pressed for time or are just plain lazy, you may prefer to buy the "baked goods"—sponge, angel cakes, macaroons, ladyfingers—which make the foundation for many and varied fancy desserts. Such pastries may be filled with seasonally flavored creams, pastry creams, Bavarians, mousses, zabagliones or layers of jam or jelly. Garnish these desserts with candied fruits and creams. Many pie fillings—fruit, custard and chiffon—as well as whipped gelatin puddings also lend themselves to use with cake bases. Thickened fillings, such as those having the word custard in the title, or the heavier nut and fruit fillings can stand somewhat longer storage before serving; but do not hold them more than 24 hours. Should you choose flavored creams and the less-stable fillings such as gelatins or ice creams, add them to your cake just before serving to forestall sogginess. For the same reason, be sure to choose fillings heavy in cream for freezing.

Fillings seem to adhere better if the layers are placed with the bottom crusts facing each other. For a charming but not rich finish, coat filled cakes with a dusting of confectioners' sugar, see 501. Filling yields are given in cups. For approximate coverage, see Icing Yields, 487.

SWEETENED WHIPPED CREAM OR CRÈME CHANTILLY FILLINGS

About 2¹/₂ to 3 Cups

I. Whip until stiff, see 186:
   1 cup whipping cream
Fold in:
   ¹/₂ teaspoon vanilla
   (1 to 3 tablespoons sifted confectioners' sugar or 2 teaspoons strained honey)
You may use as is or add any one of the following:

II. Fold into the whipped cream:
   ¹/₂ cup walnuts, pecans, pistachios, hazelnuts or blanched, slivered, toasted almonds, or ¹/₄ cup nut paste

III. ¹/₂ cup lightly toasted coconut
   1 tablespoon rum or crème de cacao

IV. ¹/₂ cup jam or orange or ginger marmalade

V. ³/₄ cup fresh, canned or frozen fruit purée
   (2 tablespoons kirsch)

VI. ³/₄ cup drained, chopped fresh fruit
Reserve ¹/₄ cup of perfect berries or fruit slices for garnish.

VII. ¹/₂ cup crushed soft peppermint stick candy

VIII. ²/₃ cup brown sugar or ¹/₂ cup maple sugar
   1 teaspoon vanilla or
   ¹/₄ teaspoon nutmeg

IX. 1 teaspoon instant coffee
   ³/₄ cup crushed nut brittle

X. ¹/₄ cup Almond or Filbert Paste, 580

XI. Prepare an angel or sponge cake shell, see 434. Shred the removed cake. Combine some of it with the whipped cream. Then add:
   2 cups drained crushed pineapple
   1 cup shredded coconut
   (20 diced marshmallows)
   2 teaspoons melted semisweet chocolate
   2 teaspoons rum or Cointreau
Chill the filled cake 6 hours before serving.

XII. Heat in the top of a double boiler ♦ over—not in—boiling water, 2 tablespoons of the whipped cream and:
   ¹/₄ cup sugar
   ¹/₈ teaspoon salt
   1 oz. unsweetened chocolate, cut in pieces
When the sugar is dissolved and the chocolate melted, beat the filling with a wire whisk until well blended. Cool. Blend in the remainder of the whipped cream.

XIII. Before whipping the cup of cream, mix in:
   ¹/₃ cup sifted confectioners' sugar
   3 tablespoons cocoa

1/8 teaspoon salt
1/2 teaspoon vanilla

Thoroughly chill 2 to 3 hours, then whip until it holds its shape. You may sprinkle the filling with:

  2 tablespoons chopped toasted
    pistachio or other nuts

CUSTARD CREAM PASTRY FILLING OR CRÈME PATISSIÈRE

About 2 Cups

The custardy pastry fillings below can all be varied. Enrich them by folding in 1/4 to 3/4 cup of whipped cream and/or chopped nuts, candied fruits and liqueur flavorings.

I. Vanilla
Scald:

  1 1/2 cups milk
    A vanilla bean

Mix in the top of a double boiler ▶ over—not in—boiling water:

  1/2 cup sugar
  1/4 cup all-purpose flour
    3 to 4 well-beaten egg yolks
      or 2 eggs and 2 yolks

Beat this mixture until light. Now remove the vanilla bean and add the scalded milk gradually. Stir until all is well blended. Cook, stirring constantly, until it begins to thicken. Remove from the heat and continue to stir to release the steam and prevent crusting. Cool mixture before filling pastry.

II. Chocolate
When scalding the milk, above, add to it:

  2 to 4 oz. semisweet chocolate

III. Coffee
When scalding the milk, above, add to it:

  1 to 2 teaspoons instant
    coffee
    (Ground hazelnuts)

IV. Banana
Before spreading the custard, above, add to it:

  2 or more thinly sliced
    bananas

FRANGIPANE CREAM

Prepare Crème Patissière I, above, but after removing from the heat, beat in:

  2 tablespoons butter
  1/4 cup crushed macaroons or
    chopped blanched almonds
    2 teaspoons chopped candied
      nuts

BUTTERSCOTCH FILLING

About 2 Cups

Prepare:

  **Butterscotch Cream Pie
    Filling, 386**

using in all:

  1 1/2 cups milk

CHOCOLATE MOCHA FILLING

About 2 1/2 Cups

Combine, cook and stir in the top of a double boiler ▶ over—not in—boiling water, until smooth:

  2 oz. unsweetened
    chocolate
  2/3 cup cream
  1 1/3 cups strong coffee

Then add and stir into this mixture a smooth paste of:

  3 tablespoons cornstarch
  2 tablespoons cold coffee

Stir and cook the filling about 8 minutes. Cover and continue to cook 10 minutes more. Meanwhile, combine and beat:

  4 egg yolks
  1 egg
  1/4 teaspoon salt

Beat in gradually:

1³/4 cups sugar

Pour some of the hot cornstarch mixture over the egg mixture and then gradually return it to the double boiler. Cook 2 to 3 minutes, stirring lightly. Remove the filling from the heat and stir gently until cool and thickened.

RICOTTA CHOCOLATE FILLING

About 3¹/2 Cups

Combine and beat until light and fluffy:

2³/4 cups ricotta cheese: 1¹/4 lb.
2 cups sugar
1 teaspoon vanilla
2 tablespoons crème de cacao

Fold in:

2 tablespoons shaved
  semisweet chocolate
2 tablespoons chopped
  candied fruit

LEMON FILLING

About 1¹/2 Cups

Mix in the top of a double boiler:

2¹/2 tablespoons cornstarch
³/4 cup sugar
¹/4 teaspoon salt

Gradually stir in:

¹/2 cup water or orange juice
3 tablespoons lemon juice
¹/2 teaspoon grated lemon rind
1 tablespoon butter

Cook ♦ over—not in—boiling water about 5 minutes, stirring constantly. Cover and cook gently 10 minutes longer without stirring. Remove from heat and stir in gently:

3 slightly beaten egg yolks

Return to heat and cook about 2 minutes longer, stirring gently and constantly. Remove the filling from the heat and stir gently until cool.

ORANGE CUSTARD FILLING

About 1¹/2 Cups

Mix in the top of a double boiler ♦ over—not in—boiling water:

¹/3 cup sugar
5 tablespoons all-purpose
  flour
¹/4 teaspoon salt

Stir in until smooth:

1 cup milk

Then stir in:

¹/2 cup orange juice

Cook about 10 minutes, stirring frequently. Beat slightly:

1 egg

Beat about a third of the sauce into the egg. Return it to the pan. Continue to cook and stir about 2 minutes or until it thickens. Cool the filling before spreading.

ORANGE CREAM FILLING

About 2¹/2 Cups

Soak about 5 minutes:

1 teaspoon gelatin

in:

1 tablespoon water

Combine in the top of a double boiler:

2 tablespoons cornstarch
2 tablespoons all-purpose
  flour
³/4 cup sugar

Add:

³/4 cup hot water

Cook these ingredients ♦ over—not in—boiling water 8 to 12 minutes. Stir constantly. ♦ Cover and cook undisturbed 10 minutes more. Add:

1 tablespoon butter

Pour part of this mixture over:

2 beaten egg yolks

Beat and pour back into the double boiler. Cook and stir the custard gently, about 2 minutes, to let the yolks thicken. Add the soaked gelatin. Stir

until dissolved. Remove custard from
heat. Add:

> **Grated rind of orange**
> **3 tablespoons each orange**
> **and lemon juice**

Cool the custard. Beat until stiff:

> **¹/₂ cup whipping cream**

Fold it into the custard. Chill 1 hour.
If spread between the layers of a
cake, ice with:

> **Luscious Orange Icing, 494**

LEMON-ORANGE CUSTARD FILLING

About 1¹/₂ Cups

Stir and cook in the top of a double
boiler ◗ over—not in—boiling water,
until thick:

> **2¹/₂ tablespoons lemon juice**
> **6 tablespoons orange juice**
> **¹/₃ cup water**
> **¹/₂ cup sugar**
> **2 tablespoons all-purpose**
> **flour**
> **¹/₈ teaspoon salt**
> **3 beaten egg yolks or 1 egg**
> **and 1 yolk**
> **(¹/₂ teaspoon grated lemon or**
> **orange rind)**

Cool the filling.

APRICOT CUSTARD FILLING

About 2 Cups

Prepare:

> **Lemon-Orange Custard**
> **Filling, above**

Add:

> **¹/₂ to ²/₃ cup sweetened thick**
> **cooked apricot pulp**

CHOPPED FRUIT FILLING

About 1³/₄ Cups

I. Cook in the top of a double boiler
◗ over—not in—boiling water:

> **³/₄ cup evaporated milk**
> **¹/₄ cup water**

> **³/₄ cup sugar**
> **¹/₈ teaspoon salt**

When the sugar is dissolved, add and
cook until thick:

> **¹/₄ cup each chopped dates**
> **and figs**

Cool these ingredients and add:

> **1 teaspoon vanilla**
> **¹/₂ cup chopped nutmeats**

II.   **About 2 Cups**

Combine and cook until it thickens:

> **²/₃ cup puréed or mashed**
> **cooked apricots**
> **²/₃ cup sugar**

Remove from the heat and add:

> **2 tablespoons orange**
> **juice**
> **2 tablespoons grated**
> **orange rind**
> **³/₄ cup chopped raisins**
> **¹/₄ cup chopped dates or figs**

GINGER FRUIT FILLING

About 1¹/₂ Cups

Mix well in the top of a double boiler
and cook, stirring constantly ◗ over—
not in—boiling water about 8 to 10
minutes or ◗ until the mixture thickens:

> **¹/₄ cup sifted confectioners'**
> **sugar**
> **3 tablespoons cornstarch**
> **¹/₂ teaspoon salt**
> **1 cup canned pineapple juice**

Cover and cook about 10 minutes
longer. Remove from the heat and
add:

> **¹/₂ cup mashed banana**
> **¹/₂ cup drained canned**
> **crushed pineapple**

Return to heat 2 minutes, stirring
gently. Add:

> **3 tablespoons finely chopped**
> **drained candied ginger**
> **1 teaspoon vanilla**
> **(¹/₄ cup slivered, blanched**
> **almonds)**

ALMOND AND FIG OR RAISIN FILLING

About 1½ Cups

Blanch, sliver, then toast:

¾ **cup almonds**

Combine:

½ **cup sugar**

1 **tablespoon grated orange rind**

½ **cup orange juice**

2 **tablespoons all-purpose flour**

½ **cup water**

1½ **cups chopped or ground dried figs or seeded raisins**

⅛ **teaspoon salt**

Simmer these ingredients 5 minutes. Stir constantly. Add the almonds and:

½ **teaspoon vanilla**

TOASTED WALNUT OR PECAN FILLING

About ¾ Cup

Combine, stir and heat in the top of a double boiler ♦ over—not in—boiling water until sugar is dissolved:

½ **cup packed brown sugar**

¼ **teaspoon salt**

2 **tablespoons butter**

1 **tablespoon water**

Stir part of this into:

1 **slightly beaten egg yolk**

Return it to the double boiler. Stir and cook until the mixture is slightly thickened. Cool. Add:

¾ **cup toasted walnuts or pecans**

½ **teaspoon vanilla**

(¼ **cup finely flaked coconut**)

ALMOND OR HAZELNUT CUSTARD FILLING

About 1½ Cups

Stir and heat in the top of a double boiler ♦ over—not in—boiling water:

1 **cup sugar**

1 **cup cultured sour cream**

1 **tablespoon all-purpose flour**

Pour one-third of this mixture over:

1 **beaten egg**

Return it to the double boiler. Stir and cook the custard until thick. Add:

1 **cup blanched or unblanched, shredded or ground almonds or ground hazelnuts, 239**

When the custard is cool, add:

½ **teaspoon vanilla or**

1 **tablespoon liqueur**

COOKIES AND BARS

★ ABOUT CHRISTMAS COOKIES

Christmas and cookies are inseparable. Stars, angels, bells, trees, Santas
and even pretzels—the pilgrim's
token—are memorialized . in rich
holiday confections. Why not make
use of these charming cookie shapes
to decorate a small table tree at
Christmas, or get a gifted friend to
make you a wooden mold. of the
three kings bearing gifts. To cut your
own molds, see Gingerbread Men,
473, and to build a cookie house, see
461. You can bake the strings for
hanging right into the cookies. It
irks us that such delightful sweets as
Christmas cookies should be relegated to a period of a few weeks. In
the hope that you will prolong the
season, we have marked with this
symbol ★ recipes that are generally
recognized as traditional, as well as
some that have become traditional
with us, if for no other reason than
that they can be baked in advance of
a busy season.

MIXING AND DECORATING COOKIES

If you are planning to bake a number
of kinds of cookies, see that they
complement each other in texture and
flavor and that they use up ingredients economically. Choose shapes
that will look attractive on serving
dishes. Many of these recipes call for
butter as the basic fat. ◗ If you feel
that, for reasons of economy, you
cannot afford all butter, do try to use
at least one-third butter. You will notice a marked superiority in flavor.

The mixing of cookies is usually
quick and easy: Some ingredients
must be well stirred together; some
are creamed like cakes and, abroad,
are called biscuits; others are blended
like pastry. Use whatever mixing
process the recipe calls for.

You may want to combine different flours. If you do so ◗ be sure to
see the note on flour substitutions,
301. Because of variations in the size
of eggs and in the moisture content
of honey, molasses and flour, the

consistency of your dough may have to be modified. ♦ Chill cookie doughs well and keep them covered until ready to bake.

▲ In altitudes up to 5000 feet, simple cookies usually need no adjustment. But for cookies rich in chocolate, nuts, or dates, a reduction of about one-half the baking powder or soda may be advisable. And at very high altitudes a slight reduction in sugar may help. ♦ But the soda should not be reduced beyond 1/2 teaspoon for each cup of sour milk or cream used.

To decorate cookies, dip the garnish before baking into either a simple syrup or unbeaten egg white. Then press the garnish firmly onto the cookie surface. Or dust sugar onto the cookies after placing them on the sheet and press it in with a wide spatula. Try icing cookies with flowers, patterns, names and holiday messages. To color cookies for special occasions, stir 1/4 teaspoon water into 1 egg yolk. Divide the mixture into several custard cups and tint each one with a drop of different vegetable food coloring. (The yolk color will affect only the blue, which can be added to the egg white if you wish.) This coloring applied with a soft brush before baking allows you to make elaborate patterns.

BAKING COOKIES

If you wonder why commercial cookies are often large, the answer lies in handling and oven costs. A true sign of home baking is a delicate small cookie. Successful baking depends on the preheating of the oven, as well as on the kind of baking sheet used, its size, the material of which it is made—even its temperature. Choose a heavy flat baking sheet, or

use the bottom of a reversed baking pan, as shown illustrated on the left, 472; or if you prefer, cut the cookies on a board and transfer them to the reversed pan bottom. The heat can then circulate directly and evenly over the cookie tops. A pan with high sides will both deflect the heat and make the cookies hard to remove when baked. The very best aluminum sheets have permanently shiny baking surfaces and specially dulled bottoms to produce an even browning. If only dark thin sheets are available, a second empty sheet may be placed under the first while baking.

Grease cookie sheets with unsalted fats, preferably sweet butter or beeswax. Warm the baking sheet and rub a lump of beeswax lightly over the surface. It will eventually acquire a permanent coat of wax and will not require further greasing. ♦ When baking cookies with a large amount of shortening, you may find it unnecessary to grease the cookie sheets. For delicate cookies, use a greased parchment paper or foil liner. They will peel off easily when slightly cooled. ♦ The baking sheet should always be cold when cookies are put on it, so they will not lose their shape. ♦ Always fill out a sheet, placing cookies of even size and thickness about 1 inch apart, unless otherwise indicated. On a partially filled sheet the heat is drawn to the area where the cookies lie, and the batch may burn on the bottom. If you haven't enough dough on your last baking to fill a whole baking sheet, reverse a pie pan or turn a small baking pan upside down.

♦ The placement of the pans during baking is very important. Bake 1 sheet of cookies at a time, at least 2 inches from the oven walls. If using two smaller pans, see that they are spaced evenly from the walls and from each other. Heat should circulate all around the pans. Few ovens are so nearly perfect that they will brown a large sheet evenly. During the baking process, do turn the sheet sometimes to compensate for uneven baking. Oven thermostats are also variable, so watch closely, especially when baking molasses and brown-sugar cookies, which burn easily. When cookies are done, remove them from the baking sheet at once or they will continue to cook. Should they harden on the pan, return the baking sheet for a moment to the oven before trying to remove them. ♦ Always cool cookies on a rack ♦ not overlapping, and store as suggested below.

STORING COOKIES

Most cookies and bars tend to dry out or go limp. To restore freshness, cookies can be heated briefly before serving, but it is wiser to use good storage practices from the start. Keep cookies in tightly covered tins or containers. If for immediate use, store bar cookies in the pan in which they are baked. Cover with aluminum foil. Or store them in an aluminum pan with its own lid, shown on 487. However, to prolong freshness, be sure to wrap these bars individually in foil after cooling and cutting. They are then all ready for serving, freezing, or packing in lunch boxes.

To soften hard dry cookies, put them with a piece of bread or apple into a tightly closed container. Replace the bread or apple every few days, for they mold easily. Another way to restore moisture is to use a dampened paper napkin, wrapped in punctured foil.

If you have frozen baked cookies and want them for immediate consumption ♦ thaw them unwrapped, then heat them for a moment on a cookie sheet in a 300° oven to restore crispness. This is also a good plan for weary "bought" cookies.

If you are sending cookies or cakes to out-of-towners, wrap them individually or put them into a polyethylene bag and bed them down in popcorn. Fill all the crannies of the box with the corn, until it just touches the lid.

We find that egg-white cookies, a natural by-product of Christmas baking, need special handling. Some of the meringues heavy in nuts, like Cinnamon Stars, 477, keep well if tightly tinned. In packing mixed boxes, though, be sure to ♦ add meringue-based cookies at the last moment, for, unwrapped, they dry out quickly; and, if freshly made and stored with cookies rich in fruit, they may disintegrate.

ABOUT SQUARES AND BARS

The quickest and most easily produced uniform small cakes are squares and bars. Bake them in greased pans at least 1¹/₂ inches deep. ♦ Do observe pan sizes indicated in recipes, because the texture is much affected by thickness. A pan smaller than indicated in the recipes will give a cakey result—not a chewy one. A too large pan will give a dry, brittle result. If your pan is too large, divide it with a piece of foil folded as illustrated on 402. The dough placed on the horizontal lap will help hold the divider in place. Most bars, unless meringue-based, bake about 25 minutes in a preheated 350° oven. To prepare filled bars, line a 9 × 13-inch pan with two-thirds of the dough;

spread the filling over it, see Cookie
Fillings, 481; and cover the filling
with the remaining one-third dough.
We suggest the use of muffin tins for
individual servings, or pie tins to
make larger festive rounds under ice
cream. See chart of comparative pan
sizes on 401.

Squares or bars of different flavors
wrapped in colored foils, or one dull
side up and one shiny side up in regular foil, make an attractive dessert to
pass at an informal outdoor buffet.

BROWNIES COCKAIGNE

About 30 Brownies

Almost everyone wants to make this
classic American confection. Brownies may vary greatly in richness and
contain anywhere from 1½ cups of
butter and 5 ounces of chocolate to 2
tablespoons of butter and 2 ounces of
chocolate for every cup of flour. If
you want them chewy and moist, use
a 9 × 13-inch pan; if cakey, a 9 × 9-
inch pan. We love the following.
Preheat oven to 350°.
Melt in a double boiler:

> ½ cup butter
> 4 oz. unsweetened chocolate

♦ Cool this mixture. If you don't,
your brownies will be heavy and dry.
Beat until light in color and foamy in
texture:

> 4 eggs at 70°
> ¼ teaspoon salt

Add gradually and continue beating
until well creamed:

> 2 cups sugar
> 1 teaspoon vanilla

With a few swift strokes, combine the
cooled chocolate mixture and the
eggs and sugar. ♦ Even if you normally use an electric mixer, do this
manually. Before the mixture becomes uniformly colored, fold in,
again by hand:

> 1 cup sifted all-purpose flour

And before the flour is uniformly colored, stir in gently:

> 1 cup pecan meats

Bake in a greased 9 × 13-inch pan
about 25 minutes. Cut when cool, as
interiors are still moist when fresh
from the oven.

Good ways to serve Brownies are
to garnish with whipped cream, ice
cream or an icing.

RICE OR POTATO FLOUR BROWNIES

Prepare:

> **Brownies Cockaigne, above**

substituting for the flour:

> 1⅓ cups rice or potato flour

Proceed as directed. The baking time
may be longer, so watch carefully.

BUTTERSCOTCH BROWNIES

About 16 Thin 2¼-Inch Squares

An all-time favorite, easily made.
Preheat oven to 350°.
Melt in a saucepan:

> ¼ cup butter

Stir into it until dissolved:

> 1 cup sugar

Cool these ingredients slightly, then
beat in well:

> 1 egg
> 1 teaspoon vanilla

Sift, then measure:

> ½ cup all-purpose flour

Resift it with:

> 1 teaspoon double-acting
> baking powder
> ½ teaspoon salt

Stir these ingredients into the butter
mixture. Add:

> ½ to 1 cup finely chopped
> nuts or ¼ cup grated
> coconut

Chopped dates and figs may be substituted for the nuts. Use a little of the

flour over them. Pour the batter into a greased 9 × 9-inch pan. Bake about 20 to 25 minutes. Cut into bars when cool.

CAROB BARS

About 16 Thin 2¼-Inch Squares
A nonchocolate chocolate bar.
Prepare:

> **Butterscotch Brownies, 457**

using either white or brown sugar.
Sift into the flour mixture:

> **3 tablespoons carob powder**

and proceed as directed.

RAISIN MOLASSES BARS

About Thirty 2½ × 2-Inch Squares
Preheat oven to 375°.
Melt:

> **6 tablespoons butter**

When cooled slightly, stir in:

> **⅓ cup sugar**
> **⅔ cup dark molasses**
> **1 slightly beaten egg**
> **1 teaspoon vanilla**

Sift together:

> **1 cup all-purpose flour**
> **⅛ teaspoon each salt and baking soda**
> **1 teaspoon cinnamon**
> **⅛ teaspoon each cloves and ginger**

Add to the flour:

> **1 cup raisins**
> **(½ to 1 cup chopped nutmeats)**

Combine all ingredients until well blended, then pour into a greased 10½ × 15½-inch cookie sheet and bake about 12 minutes. Cut the cake into bars when cool and dust with a combination of:

> **2 teaspoons cinnamon**
> **⅓ cup sugar**

or cover with:

> **Lemon Glaze, 504**

★ CHRISTMAS CHOCOLATE BARS COCKAIGNE

About 108 Bars, 1 × 2 Inches
Preheat oven to 350°.
Sift:

> **2¾ cups packed brown sugar: 1 lb.**

Beat until light:

> **6 eggs**

Add the sugar gradually, beating until well blended. Grate and add:

> **4 oz. unsweetened chocolate**

Combine and sift:

> **3 cups all-purpose flour**
> **1 tablespoon cinnamon**
> **1½ teaspoons cloves**
> **½ teaspoon allspice**
> **1 teaspoon each baking soda and salt**

Add the sifted ingredients to the egg mixture, alternately with:

> **½ cup honey or molasses**

Chop and add in all:

> **2½ cups mixed citron, candied lemon, orange, pineapple and nuts—preferably blanched almonds**

Spread the dough with a spatula into two 9 × 13-inch greased pans. Bake about 20 minutes. When cool, ice one pan with:

> **Lemon Glaze, 504**

and the other with:

> **Chocolate Butter Icing, 498**

Cut into bars.

CHOCOLATE OAT BARS

About 6 Dozen 1 × 2-Inch Bars
Preheat oven to 350°.
Cream together:

> **1 cup butter**
> **2 cups packed brown sugar**

Beat in:

> **2 eggs**
> **2 teaspoons vanilla**

Sift together:

2¹/2 **cups sifted all-purpose flour**
1 **teaspoon baking soda**
1 **teaspoon salt**

Add:

3 **cups rolled oats**

Over low heat combine:

2 **cups semisweet chocolate pieces: 12 oz.**
1 **can sweetened condensed milk: 14 oz.**
2 **tablespoons butter**
¹/4 **teaspoon salt**

Stir until smooth, then add:

1 **cup chopped walnuts or pecans**
1 **teaspoon vanilla**

Now combine the egg and flour mixtures and pat about two-thirds of it into a 10¹/2 × 15¹/2-inch cookie sheet. Pour the chocolate mixture over all, then dot with the remaining one-third batter. Bake about 25 minutes.

★ NUT BARS

About Forty-Eight
1 × 2-Inch Sticks

These, like the following Pecan Slices, are made on a rich, sweet pastry base.
Preheat oven to 350°.
Cream until well blended:

¹/2 **cup butter**
¹/4 **cup sugar**

Beat in well:

1 **egg**
¹/2 **teaspoon vanilla**

Combine:

1¹/4 **cups sifted all-purpose flour**
¹/8 **teaspoon salt**

Add these dry ingredients in about 3 parts to the butter mixture, blending them well. Use your hands to pat the dough evenly in a greased 9 × 12-inch pan. Bake about 15 minutes. In a

heavy saucepan, beat until they begin to froth:

4 **egg whites**

Stir in:

2¹/4 **cups finely chopped pecans**
1 **cup sugar**
1¹/2 **teaspoons cinnamon**

Cook and stir this mixture over low heat. After the sugar has dissolved, increase the heat slightly. Stir and cook until the mixture leaves the sides of the pan, but remove it from the heat before it is dry. Spread it over the pastry base. Bake the cake about 15 minutes longer. When cool, cut into sticks.

★ PECAN OR ANGEL SLICES

About Forty-Eight
1 × 2-Inch Bars

Many a copy of the **Joy** has been sold on the strength of this recipe. One fan says her family is sure these are the cakes St. Peter gives little children at the Gates of Heaven, to get them over the first pangs of homesickness. Her family has dubbed them Angel Cookies.
Preheat oven to 350°.
Line a pan with dough for:

Nut Bars, above

Bake as directed. Spread with the following mixture:

2 **beaten eggs**
1¹/2 **cups brown sugar**
¹/2 **cup flaked coconut**
1 **cup chopped pecan meats**
2 **tablespoons all-purpose flour**
¹/2 **teaspoon double-acting baking powder**
¹/2 **teaspoon salt**
1 **teaspoon vanilla**

If preferred, omit the coconut and use 1¹/2 cups nutmeats instead. Bake the cake about 25 minutes. When cool, ice with:

1½ cups sifted confectioners'
sugar

thinned to a good spreading consistency with:

Lemon juice

Cut the cake into oblongs.

APRICOT MERINGUE BARS

**About Forty-Eight
1 × 2-Inch Sticks**

Preheat oven to 350°.
Line a pan with dough for:

Nut Bars, 459

Cover the unbaked batter with:

1 cup apricot preserves

Beat until stiff but not dry:

2 egg whites

Add gradually, continuing to beat:

½ cup sugar

When the mixture stands in peaks,
fold in:

½ cup chopped pecans or
walnuts

Spread the meringue over the apricot
jam and bake 35 to 40 minutes or until firm. Cool slightly before cutting
into squares.

DATE BARS COCKAIGNE

About Forty 2-Inch Squares

Preheat oven to 325°.
Cream:

½ cup butter
½ cup packed brown sugar

Add and beat well:

1 egg
6 tablespoons milk
1 cup chopped dates
1 cup chopped pecans

Sift together:

¼ cup sifted all-purpose flour
¼ teaspoon salt
½ teaspoon double-acting
baking powder
1 teaspoon cinnamon
¼ teaspoon cloves

½ teaspoon allspice

Add to the sifted ingredients:

¾ cup rolled oats

Combine all ingredients. You may
add:

**(Juice and grated rind of
1 lemon)**

Let dough stand about 15 minutes,
then spread it into a 10½ × 15½-
inch greased cookie sheet. Bake 15 to
20 minutes or until the dough begins
to leave the sides of the pan. Cut into
squares.

LEMON CURD SQUARES

About 16 Squares

Preheat oven to 350°.
Sift together:

1 cup sifted all-purpose flour
¼ cup confectioners' sugar

Add and combine:

½ cup melted butter

Press the mixture into a 8 × 8-inch
greased baking pan and bake 20 minutes. Meanwhile combine:

1 cup sugar
½ teaspoon double-acting
baking powder
2 slightly beaten eggs
2 tablespoons lemon juice
2 teaspoons grated
lemon peel
(½ cup flaked coconut)

Pour these ingredients over the baked
warm crust and bake 25 minutes.
Chill. Before serving, cut into 2-inch
squares and sprinkle with:

Confectioners' sugar

★ LEBKUCHEN OR GERMAN
HONEY BARS

**About One 8 × 8-Inch Cake
Plus One 10½ × 15½-Inch Cake**

Honey, like molasses, may be troublesome. Old German cooks used to insist on its being over a year old. Very good cakes are made with fresh honey, but then the amount of flour is a little hard to gauge. If a crisper bar is desired, substitute carbonate of ammonia, 226, for the baking powder and soda given below. Use 1 teaspoon carbonate of ammonia dissolved in 2 tablespoons warm water, rum or wine. These German Honey Bars will keep 6 months in a tightly closed tin, especially if, as our grandmother used to say with a twinkle, "locked up."

Heat slightly in a large saucepan:

1¹/₃ cups honey or molasses
³/₄ cup sugar

Add and melt:

3 tablespoons butter

Sift together and add:

About 2 cups sifted all-purpose flour: enough to make a semiliquid dough
1 teaspoon double-acting baking powder
¹/₂ teaspoon baking soda

Add:

¹/₂ cup blanched almonds
¹/₄ cup each chopped citron and chopped candied orange or lemon peel
¹/₄ teaspoon ginger
¹/₂ teaspoon cardamom
2 teaspoons cinnamon
¹/₈ teaspoon cloves

Add:

1¹/₂ to 2 cups more flour

The dough should be sticky to the touch. You may age the dough overnight, refrigerated, in a covered crock, or pat it out at once into a ¹/₄-inch thickness in buttered pans. If you age it, you may find it necessary to heat it slightly before working it into the pans. Bake about 25 minutes in a preheated 350° oven. Cut into squares and ice with:

Lemon Glaze, 504

ABOUT CAKE AND COOKIE HOUSES

No matter how peculiar the medium or incongruous the scale, the instinct to build persists. We have tried and discarded many cake construction methods. Professionals use Pastillage, 597, and Royal Glaze, 496, thus achieving rather cold-looking but clean-cut and intricate models. We prefer a simple approach.

Prepare any close-grained cake such as:

Gingerbread, 425, German Honey Bars, opposite, or Eggless All-Rye Honey Cake, 338

You will need 2 sheets of cake baked in an 11 × 17-inch pan, and a third sheet if also using cake for the foundation. The baking can be done over a period of days, but cut the cakes while still warm. Either use your own ingenuity or cut a paper pattern as illustrated below.

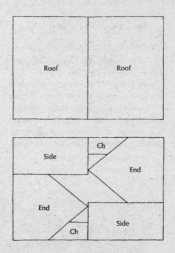

When ready to assemble, find an extra pair of hands, and with the help of plenty of "glue" made of:

Royal Glaze, 496

start to build. This icing, which dries hard and colors easily, makes a perfect bond for the various building elements and whatever decorations you want to add onto the house. Mitre the edges where the walls meet and shamelessly drive wooden pick "nails." ◗ Watch for these when the cake is eaten. When the walls are in place, use slabs for the roof, nailing them again with picks where they touch the side walls. You could decorate the whole with icing, contrasting color of windows and door, shingle tile, etc. Or build up overlapping roof tiles and make doors and shutters of thin:

Molasses Crisps Cockaigne, 480

Afix these with the glaze. Colored hard candies and gumdrops also make festive decorations for your holiday house.

ABOUT DROP COOKIES

Almost any cookie dough can be baked as a drop cookie if additional liquid is added to the batter. Drop cookie doughs vary in texture. Some fall easily from the spoon and flatten into wafers in baking. Stiffer doughs need a push with a finger or the use of a second spoon to release them, as seen second on the left. To make uniform soft drops, use a measuring teaspoon. When chilled, these doughs may be formed into balls and flattened between palms, as shown on the left. First dust your hands with flour or powdered sugar; or, if the cookies are a dark or chocolate dough, use cocoa for dusting. Or, to flatten the balls, use a glass tumbler greased lightly on the bottom or dusted with flour, powdered sugar or cocoa as shown below, or a spatula dipped in ice water.

To prepare the pans, grease them lightly and dust with flour. For chocolate cookies, dust with cocoa. Shake off excess flour or cocoa.

DROP BUTTER WAFERS

About Forty-Eight 2¹/₄-Inch Wafers

These, when baked, automatically produce a lovely paper-thin brown rim.

Preheat oven to 375°.

Cream until light:

¹/₂ **cup butter**
¹/₂ **cup sugar**

Beat in:

1 **egg**
1 **teaspoon vanilla**
¹/₄ **teaspoon grated lemon rind**

Add:

³/₄ **cup sifted cake flour**
(1¹/₂ **tablespoons poppy seed or**
1 **teaspoon grated orange rind**)

Drop the cookies from a teaspoon

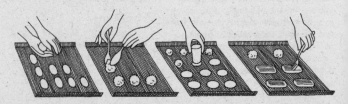

◗ well apart on a greased cookie sheet. Bake about 7 minutes or until the rims brown.

CHOCOLATE-CHIP DROP COOKIES

About Forty-Five 2-Inch Cookies
Preheat oven to 375°.
Cream:

1/2 **cup butter**

Add gradually and beat until creamy:

1/2 **cup brown sugar**
1/2 **cup white sugar**

Beat in:

1 **egg**
1/2 **teaspoon vanilla**

Sift and stir in:

1 **cup plus 2 tablespoons
   sifted all-purpose flour**
1/2 **teaspoon salt**
1/2 **teaspoon baking soda**

Stir in:

1/2 **cup chopped nutmeats**
1/2 **cup semisweet chocolate
   chips**

Drop the batter from a teaspoon, well apart, on a greased cookie sheet. Bake about 10 minutes.

SUGAR DROP COOKIES WITH OIL

About 5 Dozen Cookies
Preheat oven to 375°.
Sift together:

2 1/2 **cups sifted all-purpose
   flour**
1 1/2 **teaspoons double-acting
   baking powder**
3/4 **teaspoon salt**
1 **teaspoon cinnamon or 1/4
   teaspoon freshly grated
   nutmeg**

Combine:

1 **cup sugar**
3/4 **cup vegetable oil**

Add to this mixture and beat well after each addition:

2 **eggs**
1 **teaspoon vanilla**

Add the flour mixture all at once and beat well. Shape the dough into 1/2-inch balls. Dip the balls in:

Granulated sugar

or, flatten the balls as thin as you can between very lightly floured hands. To give a corrugated effect, score them in parallel lines, as shown opposite right, with a fork dipped in flour. Sprinkle with:

Granulated sugar

Bake about 10 to 12 minutes on a lightly greased cookie sheet.

ABOUT NUT DROP COOKIES

The following four recipes, all delicious, may read as though they are much alike, yet they differ greatly when baked. They have in common a brown sugar and egg base ◗ so don't try to bake them in hot humid weather. In such weather, choose, instead, Pecan Puffs or Florentines. To prepare nuts, please read About Nuts, 236.

Most of these cookies are fragile. But if made small, and baked on a beeswaxed sheet, 455, or a foil pan liner, they are easy to remove intact.

◗ Should they harden on the pan, return the baking sheet to the oven for a moment before trying to remove them.

PECAN OR HAZELNUT DROP COOKIES

About Fifty 1 1/2-Inch Wafers
If made with hazelnuts, these are very like **Nürnberger Lebkuchen**.
Preheat oven to 325°.
◗ Read About Nut Drop cookies, above. Grind in a nut grinder:

1 cup pecan meats

Put through a sieve:

1¹/₃ cups firmly packed brown sugar

Whip until stiff, but not dry:

3 egg whites

Add the sugar very slowly, beating constantly. Fold in the ground pecans and:

1 teaspoon vanilla

Drop the batter from a teaspoon, well apart, onto a greased and floured cookie sheet. Bake about 15 minutes.

PECAN OR BENNE WAFERS

About Fifty 2¹/₂-Inch Wafers

Preheat oven to 375°.

◗ Read About Nut Drop Cookies, 463. Whip until light:

2 eggs

Add gradually:

1¹/₃ cups firmly packed brown sugar

Beat these ingredients until they are well blended. Add:

5 tablespoons all-purpose flour
1/8 teaspoon salt
1/8 teaspoon double-acting baking powder
1 teaspoon vanilla

Beat the batter until smooth, then add:

1 cup broken nutmeats or 1/2 cup toasted benne seeds

Grease and flour cookie sheets. Drop the batter on them, well apart, from a teaspoon. Bake about 8 minutes. Remove from sheets while still warm.

MOLASSES NUT WAFERS

About Fifty 2¹/₂-Inch Wafers

Preheat oven to 375°.

◗ Read About Nut Drop Cookies, 463.

Sift:

1 cup firmly packed dark brown sugar

Whip until light:

2 eggs

Add the sugar gradually. Beat these ingredients until well blended. Add:

1 tablespoon dark molasses
1/4 teaspoon double-acting baking powder
6 tablespoons all-purpose flour
1/8 teaspoon salt

Beat the batter until smooth. Stir in:

1 cup chopped black or English walnuts, hazelnuts or mixed nutmeats

Drop the batter, well apart, from a teaspoon onto a well-greased cookie sheet. Bake about 8 minutes.

★ FLOURLESS NUT BALLS

About Thirty-Six 1¹/₄-Inch Balls

Preheat oven to 325°.

◗ Read About Nut Drop Cookies, 463.

Grind in a nut grinder:

1¹/₂ cups almonds or pecans

Combine in a pan with:

1 cup firmly packed brown sugar
1 egg white
1¹/₂ teaspoons butter

Stir these ingredients over very low heat until well blended. Cool the mixture. Shape the dough into small balls or roll it out and cut it into shapes. If the dough is hard to handle, dust the hands with a little confectioners' sugar. Place the cookies on a very well-greased cookie sheet. Bake 30 to 40 minutes. Leave on the sheet until cool. Ice with:

Lemon Glaze, 504, or a chocolate icing, 498 or 499

PECAN PUFFS

About Forty 1½-Inch Balls

Rich and devastating.
Preheat oven to 300°.
Beat until soft:

½ cup butter

Add and blend until creamy:

2 tablespoons sugar

Add:

1 teaspoon vanilla

Measure, then grind in a nut grinder:

1 cup pecan meats

Sift before measuring:

1 cup cake flour

Stir the pecans and the flour into the butter mixture. Roll the dough into small balls. Place balls on a greased cookie sheet and bake about 30 minutes. Roll while hot in:

Confectioners' sugar

To glaze, put the sheet back into the oven for a minute. Cool and serve.

FLORENTINES COCKAIGNE

About 18 Thin 2½- to 3-Inch Patties

A great European favorite—really choice!
Preheat oven to 350°.
Place in a blender:

4 tablespoons brown sugar
4 tablespoons honey
½ cup slivered almonds
⅛ teaspoon salt
½ teaspoon vanilla

Add:

1¼ cups packed mixed candied fruits

that have been thoroughly separated by working them over with the hands in:

½ cup flour

Blend this mixture until fruits and nuts are about ¼-inch size. Add:

4 tablespoons melted butter

and reblend briefly, reducing fruits and nuts to about ⅛-inch size. Form dough into 1-inch balls and place on 2 buttered cookie tins. Flatten the balls to 2½- to 3-inch patties. Bake 7 to 8 minutes or until golden brown. Allow the patties to cool very briefly, then turn them onto wire racks. Meanwhile, melt over hot water:

4 ounces semisweet chocolate

and cover the bottoms of the slightly cooled patties with the chocolate. Cool completely and store covered.

OLD-FASHIONED MOLASSES COOKIES

About Forty 2-Inch Cookies

These are highly spiced.
Preheat oven to 350°.
Beat until soft:

½ cup butter or shortening

Add gradually and blend until light and creamy:

½ cup sugar

Beat in:

1 egg
½ cup molasses

Have ready:

½ cup buttermilk

Sift together:

2½ cup sifted cake flour
1 teaspoon baking soda
1 teaspoon each cinnamon and ginger
¼ teaspoon cloves
¼ teaspoon salt

Add the sifted ingredients in 3 parts to the sugar mixture alternately with the buttermilk. Beat the batter until smooth after each addition. Add:

(½ cup chopped raisins)

Drop the batter from a teaspoon onto a greased cookie sheet. Bake 8 to 12 minutes.

GINGERSNAPS

About 10 Dozen 2-Inch Cookies
Like "boughten" ones in texture, but
with a dreamy flavor.
Preheat oven to 325°.
Cream together:

> 3/4 cup butter
> 2 cups sugar

Stir in:

> 2 well-beaten eggs
> 1/2 cup molasses
> 2 teaspoons vinegar

Sift and add:

> 3 3/4 cups all-purpose flour
> 1 1/2 teaspoons baking soda
> 2 to 3 teaspoons ginger
> 1/2 teaspoon cinnamon
> 1/4 teaspoon cloves

Mix ingredients until blended. Form
dough into 3/4-inch balls. Bake on a
greased cookie sheet about 12 minutes. As the ball melts down during baking, the cookie develops the
characteristic crinkled surface. When
cool, ice to taste. A topping to delight
the children is half a marshmallow,
cut side down, on the almost baked
cookies. Return to oven about 4
minutes.

★ GINGER THINS

**About Three Hundred
3/4-Inch Wafers**
Mme. Bu Wei, in her charming book,
How to Cook and Eat in Chinese,
tells us that little cakes served between meals in her native country are
called "dot hearts." They should have
the diameter of a quarter when baked,
for they toughen if they are larger.
Preheat oven to 325°.
Cream:

> 3/4 cup butter
> 1 cup brown sugar
> 1 beaten egg
> 1/4 cup molasses

Sift together:

> 1 1/2 cups sifted all-purpose
> flour
> 1/4 teaspoon salt
> 1/2 teaspoon baking soda
> 1/2 teaspoon each cloves,
> cinnamon and ginger

Combine the above ingredients and
stir until smooth. Puts dots of 1/8 teaspoon of dough 1 inch apart on a
greased cookie sheet and bake 5 to
6 minutes. Cool on a rack. Cookies
snap off if you twist the sheet
slightly.

★ ANISE OR BUTTERLESS
DROP COOKIES

About Ninety-Six 1-Inch Cookies
These professional-looking self-
glazing cookies with the charming
puffed tops are best made in cool
weather. They do not turn out well if
the humidity is over 50%.
Beat until light:

> 3 eggs

Add gradually:

> 1 cup sifted sugar

Beat at least 3 to 5 minutes on
medium speed with an electric beater,
longer if beating by hand, then add:

> 1/2 teaspoon vanilla

Sift before measuring:

> 2 cups all-purpose flour

Resift with:

> 1 teaspoon double-acting
> baking powder

Add:

> 1 1/2 tablespoons crushed anise
> seed

Add flour ingredients to egg mixture
and beat the batter another 5 minutes. Drop 1/2 teaspoon at a time, well
apart on a cookie sheet lined with
foil. The dough should flatten to a
1-inch round but should not spread
more. If it does, add a little more
flour. Let the drops dry at room tem-

perature 18 hours. Bake the cakes in a preheated 325° oven until they begin to color, about 12 minutes. When done, they will have a puffed meringuelike top on a soft cookie base.

HERMITS

About Fifty 2-Inch Cookies
Preheat oven to 375°.
Beat until soft:
    1/2 cup butter
Add gradually:
    1 cup packed brown sugar
Blend until light and creamy. Beat in:
    1 egg
    1/2 cup cultured sour cream or buttermilk
Sift before measuring:
    1 1/3 cups all-purpose flour
Resift with:
    3/4 teaspoon cinnamon
    1/2 teaspoon cloves
    1/4 teaspoon baking soda
Add the sifted ingredients to the butter mixture and beat until smooth. Stir in:
    1/2 cup chopped raisins, dates, figs, dried apricots or citron
    1/4 cup hickory or other nutmeats
    (1/4 cup coconut)
Drop batter from a teaspoon onto greased cookie sheets. Bake about 15 minutes.

★ PFEFFERNÜSSE

One Hundred Eighty 1-Inch Balls
Sift together:
    2 cups plus 2 tablespoons sifted all-purpose flour
    3/4 teaspoon double-acting baking powder
    1/8 teaspoon baking soda
    1/4 teaspoon salt

    1/4 teaspoon freshly ground black pepper
Add:
    1/4 teaspoon each nutmeg and ground cloves
    1 teaspoon cinnamon
    1/4 teaspoon anise seeds or 1 teaspoon crushed cardamom seeds
Cream together:
    1/2 cup butter or shortening
    1/3 cup sugar
Add and beat well until light:
    1 egg
Add:
    1/4 cup finely chopped almonds
    (1 tablespoon finely chopped citron)
    (1/4 cup finely chopped candied orange peel)
Add the flour mixture to the above ingredients in thirds, alternately with:
    1/3 cup molasses
    1 tablespoon corn syrup
    1/3 cup brandy
    1 teaspoon grated lemon rind
    1 tablespoon lemon juice
Beat well, then set aside overnight.
Preheat oven to 350°.
Shape into 1-inch balls and bake on a greased cookie sheet 10 to 15 minutes. Roll while warm in:
    Confectioners' sugar

★ GERMAN HONEY COOKIES

About Two Hundred 2 1/2-Inch Cookies
Cut into small pieces and combine:
    3 oz each of citron, candied orange peel and candied lemon peel
Add:
    1 cup chopped blanched almonds
    1 teaspoon grated lemon rind
    3 tablespoons cinnamon
    1 tablespoon cloves

3¹/₃ **cups confectioners' sugar**
Beat until light and add:
    6 eggs
    ¹/₄ **cup orange juice**
Bring to the boiling point and cool until lukewarm:
    1 pint honey
    2 tablespoons hot water
Stir this into the egg mixture with:
    5 cups sifted all-purpose flour
    1 tablespoon baking soda
Cover the dough and let it stand 12 hours or more.
Preheat oven to 350°.
Drop the dough from a spoon, well apart, onto a greased cookie sheet. Bake about 8 minutes or until light brown. When cool, decorate with:
    Lemon Glaze, 504
or decorate before baking with:
    Blanched almonds

QUICK OATMEAL OR WHEAT FLAKE COOKIES

    About 3 Dozen 2-Inch Cookies
Preheat oven to 350°.
Cream:
    ¹/₂ **cup butter**
Add and cream well:
    ¹/₂ **cup firmly packed brown sugar**
    ¹/₂ **cup granulated sugar**
Combine and beat in until smooth:
    1 egg
    1 teaspoon vanilla
    1 tablespoon milk
Sift together and add to the above ingredients:
    1 cup sifted all-purpose flour
    ¹/₂ **teaspoon baking soda**
    ¹/₂ **teaspoon double-acting baking powder**
    ¹/₂ **teaspoon salt**
When beaten smooth, add:
    1 cup uncooked quick rolled oats or wheat flakes

For a different flavor or texture, try adding one of the following:
    (³/₄ **cup chocolate chips**)
    (**1 teaspoon grated orange rind**)
    (¹/₂ **cup raisins**)
    (**1 can flaked coconut**)
Beat the mixture well. Drop cookies 2 inches apart on a well-greased cookie sheet and bake 10 to 12 minutes or until light brown.

GLAZED OR FLOURLESS OATMEAL LACE WAFERS

    About 8 Dozen 2-Inch Wafers
A pale yellow, crisp yet chewy cookie with a shiny bottom.
Preheat oven to 350°.
Beat:
    3 whole eggs
Add gradually, beating constantly:
    2 cups sugar
Stir in:
    2 tablespoons melted butter
    ³/₄ **teaspoon vanilla**
    1 teaspoon salt
    1 cup shredded coconut
    2 cups uncooked rolled oats
Line cookie sheet with foil. Drop the dough by half-teaspoons 1 inch apart. Bake about 10 minutes or until the edges are lightly browned. Lift foil from pan; cool until wafers can be easily removed.

ORANGE MARMALADE DROPS

    About Forty-Eight 2-Inch Cookies
This chewy cookie needs a tart marmalade. It is difficult to prescribe the right amount of flour, as marmalades differ a great deal in consistency. Follow the recipe, then try out 1 or 2 cookies. If they are too dry, add a little more marmalade; if too moist, a little more flour.

Preheat oven to 375°.
Beat until soft:

   1/3 **cup butter**

Add gradually:

   2/3 **cup sugar**

Blend until light and creamy. Beat in:

   1 **whole egg**
   6 **tablespoons tart orange marmalade**

Sift:

   1 1/2 **cups all-purpose flour**

Resift with:

   1 1/4 **teaspoons double-acting baking powder**

Stir the sifted ingredients into the butter mixture. Drop the batter from a teaspoon, well apart, onto a greased cookie sheet. Bake about 8 minutes.

PUMPKIN COOKIES

About 5 Dozen Cookies

A spicy cookie with a mealy, rather unusual texture.
Preheat oven to 375°.
Cream together:

   1 **cup butter or shortening**
   1 **cup sugar**

Add and mix well:

   1 **cup cooked pumpkin**
   1 **egg**
   1 **teaspoon vanilla**

Sift together and add to above mixture:

   2 **cups sifted all-purpose flour**
   1 **teaspoon double-acting baking powder**
   1/2 **teaspoon baking soda**
   1/2 **teaspoon salt**
   1 **teaspoon cinnamon**
   1/2 **teaspoon allspice**

Stir in:

   1 **cup chopped nuts**
   1 **cup raisins**

Drop cookies onto a well-greased cookie sheet and bake about 15 minutes.

PEANUT BUTTER COOKIES

About Sixty 1 1/2-Inch Cookies

For those who dote on peanut butter cookies, try these rich and crumbly ones. Use the greater amount of flour if your peanut butter is heavy in oil.
Preheat oven to 375°.
Beat until soft:

   1/2 **cup butter or shortening**

Add gradually and blend until creamy:

   1/2 **cup firmly packed brown sugar**
   1/2 **cup granulated sugar**

Beat in:

   1 **egg**
   1 **cup peanut butter**
   1/2 **teaspoon salt**
   1/2 **teaspoon baking soda**
   1/2 **teaspoon vanilla**

Sift before measuring and add:

   1 **to** 1 1/2 **cups all-purpose flour**

Roll the dough into small balls. Place them on a greased cookie sheet. Press flat with a fork, as illustrated on 462. Bake about 10 to 12 minutes.

BUTTERSCOTCH NUT COOKIES

Preheat oven to 375°.
For flavor, chewiness and ease of making, we suggest using the recipe for:

   Butterscotch Brownies, 457

and adding:

   2 **tablespoons flour**

Drop well apart on a greased cookie sheet and bake about 6 minutes.

MACAROONS

About 2 Dozen Cookies

Preheat oven to 325°.
Cut into a bowl thin slices of:

   1 **cup almond paste:** 1/2 **lb.**

Gradually knead into the paste:

1 cup sugar

and when the mixture gets too stiff, add in small amounts:

3 unbeaten egg whites

until all the above ingredients are thoroughly mixed, with no lumps remaining. Line a cookie sheet with parchment paper. Put the batter into a pastry bag and squeeze out small thick drops about the size of a half-dollar, 2 inches apart. Bake 25 to 30 minutes. After cooling, dampen the underside of the paper, using a moist cloth. After a few minutes remove the cookies from the paper.

COCONUT MACAROONS

About Twenty 1-Inch Cookies

Preheat oven to 350°.

Have ready in a bowl:

3 cups moist shredded coconut: 8 oz.

Add:

1 teaspoon vanilla or almond extract

1/8 teaspoon salt

Combine these ingredients with:

2/3 cup sweetened condensed milk

to make a thick paste. These cookies are much improved by folding into the batter:

(1 to 2 stiffly beaten egg whites)

Roll the paste into balls or drop it from a teaspoon onto well-greased cookie sheets, about 2 inches apart. Bake 8 to 10 minutes, until edges are lightly browned. They may be rolled in:

Sifted confectioners' sugar

CHOCOLATE COCONUT MACAROONS

Prepare the recipe for:

Coconut Macaroons, above

heating the milk and adding:

2 tablespoons cocoa or 3/4 oz. grated chocolate

Cool the mixture before adding it to the coconut.

★ ALMOND MERINGUE RINGS

About 36 Rings

Decorative in Christmas boxes, but add them at the last minute, because they do not keep well.

Preheat oven to 300°.

Blanch:

1/4 lb. almonds

Cut them lengthwise into thin shreds. Toast lightly. Whip:

2 egg whites

Add gradually, beating constantly:

1 cup sifted confectioners' sugar

Our old recipe says "stir" for 1/2 hour, but of course you won't do that, so whip until you are tired, or use an electric beater. Fold in the almonds and:

1 teaspoon vanilla

Shape the batter into rings on a greased cookie sheet. Bake until the rings just begin to color.

KISSES

About Thirty-Six 1-Inch Kisses

Preheat oven to 375°.

Whip until frothy:

2 egg whites

Continue to beat while adding gradually:

1/2 cup sugar

When the mixture is quite stiff, fold in:

1/2 cup chopped nuts and cinnamon

Drop from a teaspoon onto a greased cookie sheet and put into the oven. ▶ Immediately turn heat off, and do not open oven door for at least 1 1/2 hours, preferably overnight.

COCOA KISSES

About Forty 1-Inch Meringues
Preheat oven to 250°.
Sift:
   1 cup sugar
Whip until stiff, but not dry:
   3 egg whites
   1/8 teaspoon salt
Add gradually half of the sugar.
Combine.
   2 teaspoons water
   1 teaspoon vanilla
Add the liquid, a few drops at a time,
alternately with the remaining sugar.
Whip constantly. Fold in:
   3 tablespoons cocoa
   3/4 cup chopped pecans
Drop the batter from a spoon onto a
lightly greased cookie sheet and
shape into cones. Bake until the
kisses are firm to the touch but soft inside. Remove from the pan while hot.

CHOCOLATE CRACKER KISSES

About Sixty 1-Inch Kisses
The only people who will be wise to
these ingredients are those who, in
adolescence, were addicted to the
consumption of thin chocolate candy
bars between salted soda crackers.
Preheat oven to 300°.
Beat until frothy:
   2 egg whites
Add:
   1/4 teaspoon vanilla
   1/4 teaspoon cream of tartar
Continue beating while adding:
   2/3 cup sugar
When the mixture is quite stiff, fold
in gently:
   **3 tablespoons crushed salted
      soda crackers**
   **2/3 cup semisweet chocolate
      chips or peppermint-
      flavored chocolate morsels**
Drop the meringuelike dough, 1 tea-

spoon at a time, onto a well-greased
cookie sheet. Bake about 20 minutes.
When cool, store in a tightly closed
container.

ABOUT ROLLED AND MOLDED COOKIES

Aunties and grandmothers who roll
cookies for and with children are
scarce these days. But shaping cookies is such fun that children should be
encouraged to learn to make them
for themselves. Inexperienced bakers
often ruin rolled cookies by using too
much flour in the rolling process. To
use as little extra flour as possible
♦ chill the dough at least 1 hour
before rolling it, and ♦ use a pastry
cloth and rolling pin cover, 358.
These practically do away with sticking and require the use of very little
additional flour. Grease the pan, but
♦ remember never to use a pan with
deep rims for cookie baking. Removing the cookies from such a pan is
very difficult.

♦ Use cutters that interlock, as
shown on 472, so that dough need be
handled as little as possible. An even
easier way to form fancy shapes that
will not be distorted by handling:
grease the back of a baking pan.
Spread dough on pan as shown on
left, 472. Place cutters for maximum
yield. Lift out the dough scraps between the shapes and reroll or reform them on another pan to make
more cookies.

A roller cutter speeds cookie-
cutting. Two time-saving molds are
an old French one of dovetailed
hearts and diamonds, and a wheel
cutter, which spins out the shapes
shown on the right, with great rapidity. Amusing cutters lurk in antique
shops. We wish a designer today
would charm us with something con-

temporary. If you have a yen to do your own, take your designs to a tin-smith or make them from cardboard or plastic. See Gingerbread Men, 473.

ROLL COOKIES

About Forty 2-Inch Cookies
Remarkable for its handling quality, this dough can be shaped into crusts for filled cookies or tarts, as well as cut into intricate patterns.
Cream:

>   1/2 cup white or brown
>   sugar

with:

>   1/2 cup butter

Beat in:

>   1 teaspoon vanilla
>   2 eggs
>   2 1/2 cups sifted all-purpose
>   flour
>   2 teaspoons double-acting
>   baking powder
>   1/2 teaspoon salt

Chill the dough 3 to 4 hours before rolling.
Preheat oven to 375°.
To roll and cut, see About Rolled Cookies, 471. Place cookies on a greased cookie sheet. You may deco-rate them with:

>   (Sugar, sugar and
>   cinnamon, or colored
>   sugar)
>   (1/2 nutmeat or candied
>   cherry)

Bake 7 to 12 minutes.

RICH ROLL COOKIES

About Sixty 2-Inch Cookies
Just what they are named, and delicious!
Cream:

>   1 cup butter
>   2/3 cup sugar

Beat in:

>   1 egg
>   1 teaspoon vanilla or almond
>   extract

Combine and add:

>   2 1/2 cups sifted all-purpose
>   flour
>   1/2 teaspoon salt
>   (1/2 teaspoon grated lemon
>   rind, or 1 tablespoon
>   cinnamon, or 2 tablespoons
>   poppy seeds)

Chill dough 3 to 4 hours before rolling.
Preheat oven to 350°.
To roll and cut, see About Rolled Cookies, 471. Bake on a greased cookie sheet 8 to 10 minutes or until slightly colored.

SAND TARTS

About Eighty 1 1/2-Inch Cookies
When touring in Normandy we met up with a famous local specialty which, curiously enough, proved to be our very own sand tarts.
Beat until soft:

>   3/4 cup butter

Add gradually and blend until creamy:

  1¼ cups sifted white sugar

Beat in:

  1 egg
  1 egg yolk
  1 teaspoon vanilla
  1 teaspoon grated lemon rind

Sift before measuring:

  3 cups all-purpose flour

Resift with:

  ¼ teaspoon salt

Stir the flour gradually into the butter mixture until well blended. The last of the flour may have to be kneaded in by hand. Chill the dough several hours.
Preheat oven to 400°.
Roll the dough until very thin, see About Rolled Cookies, 471. Cut into rounds and place on greased cookie sheets. Brush the tops of the cookies with:

  The white of an egg

Sprinkle generously with:

  Sugar

Garnish with:

  (Blanched, split almonds)

Bake about 8 minutes. A good sand tart with a slightly different flavor may be made by following this recipe, but substituting for the white sugar 1⅓ cups firmly packed brown sugar.

WHOLE WHEAT SEED WAFERS

            About 5 Dozen Cookies
For best flavor, try storing these cookies a few days—usually a futile effort in our cookie-loving family.
Preheat oven to 350°.
Cream together:

  1 cup soft butter or
    shortening
  ⅔ cup sifted sugar

Sift together:

  2 cups sifted all-purpose
    flour
  1 teaspoon double-acting
    baking powder
  1 teaspoon salt

Add to flour mixture:

  1 cup whole wheat flour
  (2 teaspoons grated orange or
    lemon peel)

With a fork or pastry blender, lightly combine the butter and flour mixtures, adding:

  6 or 7 tablespoons water

until the dough holds together. Roll it out to ⅛-inch thickness. Have ready a topping made from a mixture of:

  2 tablespoons finely ground
    seeds: anise, coriander,
    sesame, caraway, hulled
    sunflower or cardamom
  ¼ cup sugar

Sprinkle the dough with the topping, pat it in gently with fingers, then cut into individual shapes. Bake on a greased cookie sheet 10 to 12 minutes, until edges are slightly browned.

★ GINGERBREAD MEN

      **About Eight 5-Inch-Long Fat Men
          or 16 Thinner Ones**
Even quite young children are good at making these if the modeling method suggested below is followed.
Preheat oven to 350°.
Blend until creamy:

  ¼ cup butter
  ½ cup white or brown
    sugar

Beat in:

  ½ cup dark molasses

Sift:

  3½ cups all-purpose flour

Resift with:

  1 teaspoon baking soda
  ¼ teaspoon cloves
  ½ teaspoon cinnamon
  2 teaspoons ginger

¹/₂ **teaspoon salt**

Add the sifted ingredients to the butter mixture in about three parts, alternately with:

¹/₄ **cup water if you roll the dough, or ¹/₃ cup if you model it**

You may have to work in the last of the flour mixture with your hands if you are not using an electric mixer. If you are satisfied with a crude approximation, roll a ball for a head, a larger one for the body, and cylinders for the arms and legs. Be sure to overlap and press these dough elements together carefully on the greased pan, so they will stay in one piece after baking. If you want something looking less like Primitive Man, roll the dough first to any thickness you like. A good way to do this is to grease the bottom of a baking sheet and to roll the dough directly onto it. Now, cut out your figures, either by using a floured cookie cutter or by making a pattern of your own, as follows:

Fold a square of stiff cardboard or light plastic lengthwise and cut it. Unfold it and you have a symmetrical pattern. Grease or flour one side of the pattern and place it on the rolled dough. Cut around the outlines with a sharp knife. Remove the scraps of dough between the figures, using them to make more men. Decorate before baking with small raisins, bits of candied fruits, red-hots, marshmallows and citron, indicating features or buttons. The men may receive further decorations after baking, as described later. Bake the cookies about 8 minutes or longer, according to their thickness. Test for doneness by pressing the dough with your finger. If it springs back after pressing, they are ready to be cooled on a rack. Stir in a small bowl, to make a paste:

¹/₄ **cup confectioners' sugar**
A few drops water

You may add:

(A drop or two of vegetable coloring)

Apply the icing with a wooden pick or a small knife for additional garnishes—caps, hair, mustaches, belts or shoes.

ALMOND CRESCENTS

About 5 Dozen Cookies

Sift:

³/₄ **cup confectioners' sugar**

Add the sugar gradually and cream with:

1 cup butter

Add:

2 teaspoons vanilla
(1 teaspoon cinnamon)
1 cup ground blanched almonds

Knead in by hand until completely mixed:

2¹/₂ **cups sifted all-purpose flour**

Chill the dough and roll it to the thickness of ¹/₄ inch. Cut or form into crescent shapes. Bake the cakes on a greased cookie sheet in a preheated 350° oven, about 15 minutes. When baked, dip them in:

Confectioners' sugar or Vanilla Sugar, 229

★ ALMOND PRETZELS OR MANDELPLÄTTCHEN

About 2 Dozen 2-Inch Pretzels

Beat until soft:

    1 cup butter

Add gradually and blend until creamy:

    1 cup sifted sugar

Beat in:

    1 to 2 egg yolks

    2 eggs

    ¼ cup cultured sour cream

Sift together and stir in:

    2½ cups sifted all-purpose flour

    1 teaspoon double-acting baking powder

    1 teaspoon cinnamon

    1 teaspoon grated lemon rind

Chill the dough several hours until easy to handle.

Preheat oven to 375°.

Shape the dough into long thin rolls and twist these into pretzel shape, see 325. Place on a greased cookie sheet. Brush with:

    French Egg Wash, 503

Sprinkle the tops with:

    Chopped blanched almonds

    Sugar

Bake at once 10 to 15 minutes. Do not let the pretzels color.

SCOTCH SHORTBREAD

About 20 Squares

Preheat oven to 325°.

Cream:

    1 cup butter

Sift together:

    2 cups sifted all-purpose flour

    ½ cup sifted confectioners' sugar

    ¼ teaspoon salt

Blend the dry ingredients into the butter. Pat the stiff dough into an ungreased 9 × 9-inch pan and press edges down. Pierce with a fork through the dough every half-inch. Bake 25 to 30 minutes. Cut into squares while warm.

YOLK LETTER COOKIES

About 100 Initials or Thin 1½-Inch Cookies

A great lexicographer said that an expression such as "It's me" was a sturdy indefensible. These cookies are our version of a sturdy indefensible. While not unusual, they use up leftover yolks. They have good tensile strength and make an excellent base for filled nut or jam tarts. We have used them as "initial" cookies for engagement parties.

Beat until soft:

    1 cup butter

    ½ teaspoon salt

Add gradually and blend until creamy:

    1 cup sifted sugar

Add:

    ½ teaspoon grated lemon rind

    1½ tablespoons lemon juice

Beat in:

    8 egg yolks

Stir in:

    4 cups sifted all-purpose flour

Chill the dough 1 hour.

Preheat oven to 375°.

Roll the dough into sticks ¼ inch in diameter. Shape these into letters. Brush them with:

    Yolk of an egg

Sprinkle with:

    Colored or white sugar

Bake on a greased cookie sheet 6 to 8 minutes.

★ SPRINGERLE

About 5 Dozen Cookies

This recipe produces the well-known German anise cakes which are stamped with a wooden mold, shown in the chapter heading, 454, middle right, or roller, into quaint little designs and figures. If you have no mold, cut the dough into 3/4 × 2 1/2-inch bars.

Beat until light:

4 eggs

Add gradually and beat until creamy:

2 cups sifted sugar

Sift together and add:

3 cups sifted all-purpose flour

1/2 teaspoon double-acting baking powder

Sprinkle 1/2 cup flour on a pastry cloth. Turn the dough onto the cloth and knead in enough flour—about 1/2 cup more—to stiffen dough. Roll to the dimensions of your mold, 1/3 thick. Use the floured springerle board and press it hard upon the dough to get a good imprint. If the dough is too soft, pick it up and add more flour. Separate the squares, place them on a board and let dry 12 hours, uncovered, in a cool dry place.

Preheat oven to 300°.

Grease cookie sheet and sprinkle with:

2 tablespoons crushed anise seed

Place the squares of dough on the pan and bake about 15 minutes or until the lower part is light yellow. To store, see 456.

★ SPECULATIUS

About Twenty-Eight 2 × 4-Inch Thin Cookies

A rich cookie of Danish origin, pressed with carved wooden molds into Santas and Christmas symbols.

Work as for pie dough, until the particles are like coarse cornmeal:

2/3 cup butter

1 cup flour

Cream:

1 egg

with:

1/2 cup firmly packed brown sugar

Add:

1/8 teaspoon cloves or

1/16 teaspoon cardamom

1 teaspoon cinnamon

Combine the egg and butter mixtures well. Spread the dough on a 14 × 17-inch baking sheet. Let it rest chilled 12 hours.

Preheat oven to 350°.

Stamp the figures with the floured molds. Bake about 10 minutes or until done.

COOKIE-PRESS OR SPRITZ COOKIES

About 5 Dozen Cookies

These may also be made in a pastry bag, illustrated 482.

Sift together:

2 1/4 cups all-purpose flour

1/2 teaspoon salt

Cream together:

3/4 cup sugar

1 cup butter

Add:

2 egg yolks

1 teaspoon vanilla or almond extract

Stir the flour.

Beat well, then chill. Put dough through cookie press onto ◗ an ungreased cookie sheet. ◗ The dough should be pliable, but if it becomes too soft, rechill it slightly. Bake about 10 minutes in a 350° oven until lightly browned.

LANGUE DE CHAT OR CAT'S TONGUE

About 2 Dozen

There are special pans for these lady-finger-shaped wafers. To turn them into **Maquis,** put between two of these cookies a filling made of 3 parts chocolate icing, 498, and 1 part crushed nut brittle, 593.
Preheat oven to 350°.
Cream:

1/4 cup butter
1/4 cup sifted sugar

Beat in:

2 eggs
1 teaspoon vanilla

Fold in:

1/2 cup sifted all-purpose flour

Bake in greased molds about 15 minutes. You may dip one end of each wafer in:

(European Chocolate
Icing, 499)

★ CHOCOLATE ALMOND SHELLS

About Sixty 1 1/2-Inch Cookies

This dough is usually pressed into little wooden molds in the shape of a shell, but any attractive ones like individual butter molds will do. ◗ The batter must stand for 12 hours.
Grind in a nut grinder:

1/2 lb. unblanched almonds

Whip until stiff:

4 egg whites
1/4 teaspoon salt

Add gradually, whipping constantly:

1 cup sifted sugar

Fold in the ground almonds and:

1 1/2 teaspoons cinnamon
1/8 teaspoon cloves
1 teaspoon grated lemon rind
1 tablespoon lemon juice
2 1/2 oz. grated unsweetened chocolate

Let this batter stand uncovered in a cool dry place 12 hours.
Preheat oven to 300°.
Shape the batter into balls. Dredge molds with equal parts of:

Sugar and flour

Press the balls into the molds. Unmold them. Bake on a greased cookie sheet about 30 minutes.

★ CINNAMON STARS

About Forty-Five 1 1/2-Inch Stars

Deservedly one of the most popular Christmas cakes; also one of the most decorative. See About Nut Drop Cookies, 463.
Preheat oven to 300°.
Sift:

2 cups confectioners' sugar

Whip until ◗ stiff but not dry:

5 egg whites
1/8 teaspoon salt

Add the sugar gradually, continuing to whip. Add:

2 teaspoons cinnamon
1 teaspoon grated lemon rind

Whip constantly. Reserve one-third of the mixture. Fold into the remainder:

1 lb. ground unblanched almonds

Dust a board or pastry canvas lightly with confectioners' sugar. Pat the dough to the thickness of 1/3 inch; it is too delicate to roll. If it tends to stick, dust your palms with confectioners' sugar. Cut the cakes with a star or other cutter, or simply mold them into small mounds. Glaze the tops with the reserved mixture. Bake on a greased cookie sheet about 20 minutes.

TEA WAFERS

About 100 Paper-Thin Wafers

Sometimes when a recipe looks as innocuous as this one, it's hard to believe the result can be so outstanding. These tender, crisp squares are literally paper-thin. ‣ As soon as cool, they must be placed in a tightly covered tin. They keep several weeks this way, but we have a hard time hiding them successfully enough to prove it.

Preheat oven to 325°.

Cream:

¹/₂ cup butter

Sift, then measure and beat in:

1 cup confectioners' sugar

Beat until smooth. Add:

1 teaspoon vanilla

Sift, then measure:

1³/₄ cups all-purpose flour

Resift and add to the creamed mixture, alternately with:

¹/₂ cup milk

Beat until creamy. Lightly butter a 16¹/₂ × 14-inch cookie sheet. Chill the sheet. With a spatula, spread only about 2 tablespoons of the mixture over it as thinly and evenly as possible. You may sprinkle the dough with:

(Chopped nutmeats or cinnamon and sugar or grated lemon rind)

It is well to press the nuts in a bit so that they will stick. Take a sharp knife and mark off the dough in 1¹/₂-inch squares. Bake about 5 minutes or until brown. When done, take from oven and, while still hot, quickly cut through the marked squares. Slip a knife under to remove from sheet. The cakes grow crisp as soon as they cool, and they break easily, so you have to work fast.

LEAF WAFERS

Although a metal stencil available at confectionery suppliers is used for these thin crisp cookies, they add great distinction to a tray when dipped like Florentines Cockaigne, 465, in chocolate or in icing or glaze. Place the stencil on a well-greased cookie sheet. Spread the dough over the stencil with a wet spatula. Remove excess dough and lift the stencil. If you have no stencil, spread the dough thinly, using the palm of your hand, onto greased cookie sheets. Score the dough in diamond shapes before baking and cut wafers after baking. Bake at 375° 5 to 7 minutes. Remove from pan while still warm.

I.   Black Walnut Leaves
About 60 Thin Leaves

Preheat oven to 375°.

Cream together:

¹/₄ cup butter
1 cup brown sugar

Add and mix well:

1 beaten egg
¹/₄ teaspoon each baking soda, cream of tartar and salt
¹/₂ teaspoon vanilla
1³/₄ cups sifted cake flour

Stir in:

¹/₂ cup ground black walnuts

To form and bake, see above.

II.   Almond Leaves
About 50 Thin Leaves

Preheat oven to 375°.

Cut into thin slices:

¹/₂ lb. almond paste: 1 cup

Knead in gradually and work until the mixture is very smooth:

2 egg whites
1 tablespoon water

Stir in and beat well:

³/₄ cup sifted confectioners' sugar
¹/₄ cup cake flour

To form and bake, see above.

ABOUT REFRIGERATOR COOKIES

An advantage of these doughs is that they can all be baked as drop cookies, 462, without chilling, if you want to make up a batch immediately. After mixing the dough, form it into a 2-inch-diameter roll on a piece of foil or waxed paper, in which you wrap it securely. Chill the roll 4 to 12 hours, after which time it can be very thinly sliced with a sharp knife. You may hasten the chilling by placing the roll in the freezer. Whole nutmeats may be combined with the dough or used to garnish the slices; or, the entire roll of dough may be rolled in chopped nuts, so as to make a border when the cookie is cut, as shown on the left, below. Two sheets of differently colored dough may be rolled together, see below. These, when sliced, become pinwheel cookies.

Bake the refrigerated cookies on a greased cookie sheet in a 400° oven 8 to 10 minutes, unless otherwise directed. Refrigerator cookies ❄ freeze well baked or unbaked. See Freezing Unbaked Cookies, 658.

VANILLA REFRIGERATOR COOKIES

About Forty 2-Inch Cookies
This dough makes a good filled cookie, 481, or rich drop cookie if the lesser amount of flour is used.
Beat until soft:
    ¹/₂ **cup butter**

Add gradually and blend until creamy:
    1 cup sifted sugar
Mix in:
    1 beaten egg
    1 teaspoon vanilla
    (¹/₂ teaspoon grated lemon rind or cinnamon)
Sift before measuring:
    1¹/₄ to 1¹/₂ cups all-purpose flour
Resift with:
    ¹/₄ teaspoon salt
    1¹/₂ teaspoons double-acting baking powder
Stir the sifted ingredients into the butter mixture. You may add:
    (¹/₂ cup nutmeats)
To chill, form and bake, see About Refrigerator Cookies, at left. Before baking, sprinkle the cookies with:
    (Sugar)
to make them sandy, or with:
    (Chopped or half nutmeats)

BUTTERSCOTCH REFRIGERATOR COOKIES

Prepare:
    Vanilla Refrigerator Cookies, above
Substitute for the white sugar:
    1¹/₄ cups firmly packed brown sugar
You may substitute for the nutmeats:
    (1 cup grated coconut)

CHOCOLATE REFRIGERATOR COOKIES

Prepare:
    Vanilla Refrigerator Cookies, at left
Melt, then cool and mix into the dough:
    2 oz. unsweetened chocolate
    (1 tablespoon brandy or rum)

PINWHEEL REFRIGERATOR COOKIES

Prepare:

**Vanilla Refrigerator
Cookies, 479**

Divide the dough in half. Add to half the dough:

**1 oz. melted unsweetened
chocolate**

If the dough is soft, chill until easily rolled. Then roll the white and brown dough separately into oblongs to the thickness of $1/8$ inch. Place the dark dough on the light dough and roll the layers like a jelly roll, see illustration, 440. To chill, form, slice and bake the rolled layers, see About Refrigerator Cookies, 479.

CREAM CHEESE REFRIGERATOR COOKIES

About Sixty 2-Inch Cookies

Blend until creamy:

**$1/2$ cup butter
1 cup sugar
1 well-beaten egg**

Soften slightly:

**1 package cream cheese:
3 oz.**

Beat it into the butter mixture with:

**2 tablespoons buttermilk or
yogurt
1 teaspoon vanilla**

Beat in:

**2 cups sifted all-purpose
flour
$1/8$ teaspoon baking soda
$1/2$ teaspoon double-acting
baking powder
$1/2$ teaspoon salt**

After being chilled, see About Refrigerator Cookies, 479, this dough may be rolled to paper-thinness, cut into shapes and baked. Sprinkle before baking with:

Sugar and cinnamon

Preheat oven to 350° and bake from 12 to 15 minutes.

MOLASSES CRISPS COCKAIGNE

About 6 Dozen 2 × 3-Inch Cookies

Heat to the boiling point in a double boiler ◗ over, not in, boiling water:

$1/2$ cup dark molasses

Remove from heat, add and beat until blended:

**$1/4$ cup sugar
6 tablespoons butter
1 tablespoon milk
2 cups all-purpose flour
$1/2$ teaspoon salt
$1/2$ teaspoon double-acting
baking powder
$1/2$ teaspoon each fresh ground
nutmeg and cloves
2 teaspoons cinnamon**

Wrap in foil and cool until firm, see About Refrigerator Cookies, 479. To form, slice very thin and, if necessary, pat thin on a greased cookie sheet with fingers until dough is translucent. Press into the center of each cookie:

**$1/2$ a pecan or blanched
almond**

Preheat oven to 325° and bake 10 to 12 minutes.

★ JUBILEE WAFERS

About Seventy 2-Inch Wafers

Good for all those festive anniversaries. Soften and mix in the top of a double boiler ◗ over, not in, boiling water:

**$2/3$ cup honey
1 cup sugar
$1/4$ cup butter**

Sift together and add:

**$2^1/2$ cups all-purpose flour
1 teaspoon double-acting
baking powder**

¹/₄ teaspoon each mace and
    cardamom
¹/₄ teaspoon baking soda
  2 teaspoons cinnamon
¹/₂ teaspoon cloves

Combine with all the above
ingredients:

¹/₃ cup whisky or brandy

Add:

  1 cup grated blanched
    almonds
  2 tablespoons each chopped
    citron, candied orange and
    lemon peel

To make into a roll, chill, slice and
bake, see About Refrigerator Cookies, 479.

ABOUT FILLED COOKIES

The recipes that follow describe individual ways to shape and fill cookies.
But first, look at simple and basic ways
to shape and fill them as sketched
on 482.

Prepare:

Roll Cookies, 472; Vanilla
Refrigerator Cookies, 479;
Sand Tarts, 472, or Yolk
Letter Cookies, 475

Form a ball and make an imprint with
your thumb to hold a filling as shown
on the left, below. Or roll the dough
thin and cut into rounds. For a
turnover, use a single round of dough
and less than a tablespoon of filling.
Fold over and seal edges firmly by
pressing with a floured fork. A closed
tart takes 2 rounds of dough. Place a
tablespoon of filling on one and
cover with the other, then seal. For a
see-through tart, employ the same
bottom round and filling, but cut the
top with a doughnut cutter and seal
outer edge in the same way.

Here are 4 basic fillings. For others, see Nut Bars, 459, or Pecan

Slices, 459; or try Ricotta Chocolate
Filling, 451.

I. Raisin, Fig, or Date Cookie Filling

Boil and stir until thick:

  1 cup chopped raisins, figs,
    or dates
  6 tablespoons sugar
  5 tablespoons boiling water
¹/₂ teaspoon grated lemon
    rind
  2 teaspoons lemon juice
  2 teaspoons butter
¹/₈ teaspoon salt

II. Apricot-Orange Cookie Filling

Combine and cook until thick:

²/₃ cup drained mashed
    cooked apricots
²/₃ cup sugar

Remove from heat and add:

  2 tablespoons orange juice
  2 tablespoons grated orange
    rind
¹/₂ cup chopped raisins
(¹/₄ cup chopped dates or figs)

III. Coconut Cookie Filling

Combine:

  1 slightly beaten egg
¹/₂ cup brown sugar
  1 tablespoon flour
1¹/₂ cups flaked or chopped
    shredded coconut

IV. ★ Drained Mincemeat, 630

JELLY TOTS

About Forty-Two
1¹/₄-Inch Cookies

You may call these **thimble cookies,
Hussar balls, jam cookies, thumb-
print cookies, deep-well cookies or
pits of love**—the latter borrowed, of
course, from the French—but a rose
by any other name . . .
Preheat oven to 375°.

Prepare the dough for:

Roll Cookies, 472

Roll the dough into a ball. You may chill it briefly for easier handling. Pinch off pieces, to roll into 1-inch balls. Roll the balls in:

Sugar

Or, for a fancier cookie, roll the balls in:

1 slightly beaten egg white

then in:

1 cup finely chopped nutmeats

Place them on a lightly greased and floured sheet. Bake 5 minutes. Depress the center of each cookie with a thimble or your thumb, as shown in sketch below. Continue baking until done, about 8 minutes. When cool, fill the pits with:

> **A preserved strawberry, a bit of jelly or jam, a candied cherry or pecan half, or a dab of icing**

MACAROON JAM TARTS

About Fourteen 3-Inch Cakes

The star of stars.

Blend until creamy:

2 tablespoons sugar
1/2 cup butter

Beat in:

1 egg yolk
1/2 teaspoon grated lemon rind
1 1/2 tablespoons lemon juice

Stir in gradually, until well blended:

1 1/2 cups sifted all-purpose flour

alternately with:

2 tablespoons cold water

Chill the dough 12 hours.
Preheat oven to 325°.
Roll out dough 1/8 inch thick. Cut into 3-inch rounds and place on a greased cookie sheet. Whip until foamy:

3 egg whites

Beat in gradually, until stiff but not dry:

1 1/3 cups sifted confectioners' sugar
1 teaspoon vanilla

Fold in:

1/2 lb. almonds, blanched and ground in a nut grinder

Place mixture around the edge of each cookie, making a 3/4-inch border, and, if you like, add two crossed lines on top as illustrated below. Use a pastry bag, a spatula or spoon, as sketched. Bake 20 minutes or until done. When cool, fill centers with:

A thick jam

INDIVIDUAL NUT TARTS

About 10 to 12 Tarts

Prepare and chill 12 hours:

Vanilla Refrigerator Cookie Dough, 479

Preheat oven to 350°.
Pat or roll the dough until very thin. Line shallow muffin pans with it. Beat until light:

3 egg yolks

Beat in gradually:

1 cup sifted sugar
1/4 teaspoon salt

Grind in a nut grinder and add:

1 cup blanched almonds or
other nuts

Stir in:

1½ tablespoons lemon juice

Fold in:

3 stiffly beaten egg whites

You may place in the bottom of
each tart:

(1 teaspoon Apricot
Glaze, 505)

Fill the lined muffin pans with the
nut and egg mixture. Bake about 20
minutes.

FILLED PRUNE COOKIE

About Forty 2-Inch Cookies

Have ready a double recipe of:

**Prune Filling for Coffee
Cakes, 333**

Prepare dough for:

Roll Cookies, 472

After chilling, roll to ⅛-inch thickness on a floured board, then cut into
2-inch rounds. Place 1 teaspoon filling on each round. Bring edges together and pinch to form a triangle.
Bake 10 to 12 minutes in a 375° oven.

ABOUT CURLED COOKIES

Some curled cookies are simply
dropped on a baking sheet; others
require a special iron. In either
case they are very dressy-looking—
whether they make a tube or cornucopia or are just partially curled, after

being shaped over a rolling pin or
wooden spoon handle while still
warm. Filled ♦ just before serving,
they make a complete dessert. Use
flavored whipped cream fillings, 449,
a cake filling, 450, or cream cheese.
Serve them as tea cakes with a contrasting butter-cream filling, 571. Dip
the ends in:

Ground pistachio or
chocolate shot "gimmies"

to lend a most festive look.

SCANDINAVIAN KRUMKAKES

To make these fabulously thin wafers,
you will need the inexpensive iron
shown below. It fits over a 7-inch surface burner, either gas or electric, and
is ♦ always used over moderate heat.
For each baking period the iron
should be lightly rubbed at the beginning with unsalted butter; but after
this initial greasing, nothing more is
required. The batter needs a preliminary testing, as it is quite variable, depending on the condition of the flour;
so do not add at once all the flour
called for in the recipe. Test the batter
for consistency by baking 1 teaspoonful first. The iron is geared to use 1
tablespoon of batter for each wafer,
and it should spread easily over the
whole surface but should not run over
when pressed down. If the batter is
too thin, add more flour. Should any

batter drip over, lift the iron off its frame and cut off the excess batter with a knife run along the edge of the iron. Cook each wafer about 2 minutes on each side or until barely colored. As soon as you remove it from the iron, roll it on a wooden spoon handle or cone form as illustrated and, when cool, fill it. You may prefer to use these cookies as round filled sandwich cookies, see Frankfurter Oblaten, below. For a toasted sesame seed effect, a fan suggests sprinkling ¼ teaspoon sesame seeds over the batter before closing the iron. For suggestions for fillings, see Curled Cookies, 483.

I. Butter Krumkakes
About Thirty 5-Inch Wafers
A teen-age neighbor recommends an ice cream filling. We like cultured sour cream with a spot of tart jelly, or a flavored whipped cream, 449.
Beat until light:
> 2 eggs

Add slowly and beat until pale yellow:
> ⅔ cup sugar

Melt and add slowly:
> ½ cup butter

Stir in until well blended:
> 1¾ cups sifted all-purpose
> flour
> 1 teaspoon vanilla

To bake, form and fill, see Krumkakes, 483.

II. Lemon Krumkakes
About Thirty 5-Inch Wafers
Cream:
> 1 cup sugar
> ½ cup butter

Combine and add:
> 3 beaten eggs
> 1 cup whipped cream
> ½ teaspoon grated lemon rind

Add enough flour to make a dough that spreads easily on the iron—not more than:
> ½ cups sifted all-purpose
> flour

To bake, form and fill, see Krumkakes, 483.

III. Almond Krumkakes
About Twelve 5-Inch Wafers
Fortune cookies can be made from this batter, see Almond Curls, opposite.
Cream and beat well:
> ¼ cup butter
> ½ cup sifted confectioners'
> sugar

Add by degrees:
> 3 unbeaten egg whites
> 2 tablespoons ground
> almonds
> ½ cup sifted all-purpose flour
> 1 teaspoon vanilla

To bake, form and fill, see Krumkakes, 483.

FRANKFURTER OBLATEN

Prepare:
> **Butter Krumkakes, at left**

Fill in between two wafers a thin layer of flavored soft fondant or French Icing, 497.

ICE CREAM CONES OR GAUFRETTES
7 Large or 12 Small Cones
If made on a krumkake iron, as illustrated, this dough can be rolled into delicious thin-walled cones. If made on an oblong waffled gaufrette iron, they become the typical French honey-combed wafer or gaufrette so often served with wine or ices.

Preheat the krumkake or gaufrette iron over a moderate surface burner.
Melt and let cool:
> ¼ cup butter

Beat until very stiff:

    2 egg whites

Fold in gradually:

    3/4 cup sifted confectioner's sugar

    1/8 teaspoon salt

    1/4 teaspoon vanilla

Fold in:

    1/2 cup sifted all-purpose flour

Add the cooled butter, folding it in gently. Put 1 tablespoon of this batter into the preheated iron. After about 1 1/2 minutes, turn the iron and bake on the other side until a pale golden beige in color. Remove and use flat or curl the wafer into a cone. When cool, fill and serve. Or serve plain in the French fashion, as described above.

ALMOND CURLS OR FORTUNE COOKIES

About 5 Dozen Cookies

These cookies and Almond Krumkakes, opposite, may be made into a western version of fortune cookies for a party. Have your remarks printed on thin papers, 3 × 3/4 to 1 inch in size. After the cookies are curled, insert a slip in each, letting part of the paper project. Pinch the ends of the roll closed while the cookie is still warm.

Preheat oven to 350°.

Combine and mix until sugar is dissolved:

    3/4 cup unbeaten egg whites: 5 to 6

    1 2/3 cups sugar

    1/4 teaspoon salt

Stir in separately and beat until well blended:

    1 cup melted butter

    1 cup all-purpose flour

    3/4 cup finely ground blanched almonds

    1/2 teaspoon vanilla or 1 tablespoon lemon juice

Drop the dough in tablespoonfuls, well apart, onto a greased baking sheet. Bake about 10 minutes or until the edges are a golden brown. Mold cookie over a wooden spoon handle, see 483; see also Curled Caramel Cookies, 486.

BRANDY SNAPS

About Twenty 3 1/2-Inch Cookies

Preheat oven to 300°.

Stir over low heat:

    1/2 cup butter

    1/2 cup sugar, or 1/4 cup sugar plus 1/4 cup packed, grated maple sugar

    1/3 cup dark molasses

    1/4 teaspoon ginger

    1/2 teaspoon cinnamon

    1/2 teaspoon grated lemon or orange rind

Remove from heat and add:

    1 cup sifted all-purpose flour

    2 teaspoons brandy

Roll into 3/4-inch balls.

Bake on an ungreased cookie sheet about 12 minutes. Remove cookies from pan, after a minute or so, with a spatula. Roll over a spoon handle, see sketch, 483. Store in a tightly covered tin.

MAPLE CURLS

About Fifteen 3-Inch Curls

Preheat oven to 350°.

Bring to a hard boil for about 1/2 minute:

    1/2 cup maple syrup or maple-blended syrup

    1/4 cup butter

Remove from heat and add:

    1/2 cup sifted all-purpose flour

    1/4 teaspoon salt

When well blended, drop the dough onto a greased cookie sheet, 1 tablespoonful at a time, 3 inches apart.

Bake from 9 to 12 minutes or until the cookie colors to the shade of maple sugar. Remove pan from oven. When slightly cool, remove cookies with a spatula, roll as shown on 483, and cool on a rack.

CURLED CARAMEL COOKIES

About 24 Cornucopias
Preheat oven to 400°.
Cream well:

- ¼ cup butter
- ½ cup firmly packed brown sugar

Beat in:

- 1 egg

When well blended, beat in:

- ½ teaspoon vanilla
- ⅛ teaspoon salt
- 3 tablespoons all-purpose flour

Stir in:

- ¼ cup ground or minced nutmeats

Black walnuts or hazelnuts are excellent. Drop the batter from a teaspoon, well apart, on a greased cookie sheet—about 6 to a sheet. Flatten the cookies with the back of a spoon. Bake 8 or 9 minutes. Cool slightly and remove from pan with a small pancake turner. Then roll the cookies over a wooden spoon handle or a rolling pin, or roll them with your hands. If they cool too quickly to manipulate, return them ♦ for a minute to the oven.

CURLED NUT WAFERS

About 20 Wafers
Preheat oven to 375°.
Beat until soft:

- 2 tablespoons butter
- 2 tablespoons shortening

Add gradually:

- ⅔ cup sifted sugar

Blend these ingredients until very light and creamy. Beat in:

- 1 egg
- 2 tablespoons milk
- ½ teaspoon vanilla
- ¼ teaspoon almond extract

Sift before measuring:

- 1⅓ cups all-purpose flour

Resift with:

- 1 teaspoon double-acting baking powder
- ½ teaspoon salt

Add the sifted ingredients to the butter mixture. Beat batter until smooth. Grease a cookie sheet. Spread the batter evenly, to the thickness of ⅛ inch, over the pan with a spatula. Sprinkle dough with:

- ½ cup chopped nutmeats

Bake about 12 minutes. Cut the cake into ¾ × 4-inch strips. Shape the strips, while hot, over a rolling pin. If the strips become too brittle before they are shaped, return them to the oven until they become pliable again.

ICINGS, TOPPINGS AND GLAZES

To decorate certain kinds of cake is to gild the lily. If the cake dough is rich and sweet, as in Old-World Chocolate Spice Cake with Citron, 418, or baked in a Bundkuchen mold as shown on 398, a plain dusting of powdered sugar, or a fancy one repeating the pattern of its lace plate doily, shown in the foreground above, is enough. To make such a sugar design, see 501. One form of gilding—for the less self-sufficient kinds of cake—is an ornamental icing whose design indicates portion servings, like the jacquard decoration on the flat loaf-cake shown above, baked in a pan with its own handy storage lid. Or show descending radials such as those on the high loaf-cake on the upper right. Or make the icing delightfully frilly to harmonize by designs sympathetic to the stand; or, as on the Valentine cake, let it capture the gaiety of the occasion.

In the icing operation—if you are working directly on the serving platter—you can cope with the spillage problem by tucking narrow overlapping pieces of waxed paper or foil just under the cake to the edge of the platter, removing them as the icing sets. If you are using a turntable or another work surface, you may place on it several strips of sturdy paper or foil projecting beyond the cake on either side. After the cake has been iced, lift it by the paper strips onto the serving platter; pull out the strips and discard. In both filling and icing, layers should be turned topside down for both a flatter and a rougher surface. If the cake is uneven, you may want to trim it slightly. Use about a fourth to a third of the total icing as filling between the layers. Then, depending on the consistency of your icing, either pour it over the top and smooth with a spatula, correcting the overflow on the sides; or slather the icing around the sides first and then apply to the top.

ABOUT ICING YIELDS

Yields on icing and filling recipes are given in numbers of cups, so you can mix or match your choice according to the size of your cake. For comparative pan sizes and areas, see 401. We consider the following amounts a sufficient coverage but suggest that for fluffy frostings you choose the greater amounts, for butter icings the lesser.

For the top and sides of one 9-inch round layer cake, use ³/₄ to 1¹/₄ cups.

For the tops and sides of two 9-inch round layers, use 1¹/₂ to 2²/₃ cups.

For the tops and sides of three 9-inch round layers, use 2¹/₄ to 3 cups.

For the top and sides of a 9¹/₂ X 5¹/₂ X 3-inch loaf pan, use 1 to 1¹/₂ cups.

For a 16 X 5 X 4-inch loaf pan, use 2 to 2¹/₂ cups.

For the top and sides of a 9- or 10-inch tube, use 3 cups.

For 16 large or 24 small cupcake tops, use 1¹/₂ to 2¹/₄ cups.

For glazing a 9- or 10-inch cake, use 1 cup.

For glazing a 10 X,15-inch sheet, use 1¹/₃ cups.

For filling a 10 X 15-inch roll, use 2 cups.

ABOUT BOILED ICINGS

Just as in candy making, success with boiled icing depends on favorable weather and the recognition of certain stages in preparing sugar syrup, see 575. If the icing is too soft or too hard, take the corrective steps suggested below. ◗ Never ruin a good cake with a doubtful icing.

Boiled white icings are based on a principle known as Italian meringue—the cooking of egg whites by beating into them ◗ gradually, a hot but not boiling syrup.

For boiled icings ◗ the cake must be cooled before the icing is applied.

◗ Have all utensils absolutely free of grease, and eggs at room temperature. Separate the whites ◗ keeping them absolutely free of yolk, and put them in a large bowl. You may start with unbeaten, frothy, or stiffly whipped whites. ◗ Have available a stabilizer: lemon juice, vinegar, cream of tartar or light corn syrup; and also a small quantity of boiling water—in case the icing tends to harden prematurely.

Cook the syrup to 238° to 240°. It will have gone through a coarse thread stage and, when dropped from the edge of a spoon, will pull out into thickish threads. When the thick thread develops a hairline appendage that curls back on itself, remove the syrup from the heat. Hold the very hot, but not bubbling, syrup above the bowl and let it drop in a slow and gradual thin stream onto the whites as you beat them. In an electric mixer, this is no trick. If you are beating by hand, you may have to steady your bowl by placing it on a folded wet towel.

As the egg whites become cooked by the hot syrup, the beating increases the volume of the icing. By the time the syrup is used up, you should have a creamy mass, almost ready for spreading. At this point, add any of the stabilizers—a few drops of lemon juice or vinegar, a pinch of cream of tartar or a teaspoon or two of light corn syrup. These substances help to keep the icing from sugaring and becoming gritty. Then beat in the flavoring of your choice. When the icing begins to harden at the edges of the bowl, it should be ready to put on the cake. ◗ Do not scrape the bowl.

If the syrup has not been boiled long enough and the icing is somewhat runny, beat it in strong sunlight.

If this doesn't do the trick, place the icing in the top of a double boiler or in a heatproof bowl ▶ over—not in—boiling water, until it reaches the right consistency for spreading. If the syrup has been overcooked and the icing tends to harden too soon, a teaspoon or two of boiling water or a few drops of lemon juice will restore it. If raisins, nutmeats, zest or other ingredients are to be added to the icing, wait until the last moment to incorporate them. They contain oil or acid which will thin the icing.

▲ In high altitudes it helps to add to the sugar ⅛ teaspoon glycerin and to allow a longer cooking period.

BOILED WHITE ICING

About 2 Cups

Stir until the sugar is dissolved and bring to a boil:

> 2 cups sugar
> 1 cup water

▶ Cover and cook about 3 minutes, until the steam has washed down any crystals which may have formed on the sides of the pan. ▶ Uncover and cook to 238° to 240°. At that temperature the syrup will spin a very thin thread on the end of a coarser thread. This final thread will almost disappear, like a self-consuming spider web. Whip until frothy:

> 2 egg whites
> ⅛ teaspoon salt

Add the syrup in a thin stream, whipping eggs constantly. When these ingredients are all combined, add:

> (⅛ teaspoon cream of tartar or a few drops lemon juice)
> 1 teaspoon vanilla

WHITE-MOUNTAIN ICING

About 1¾ Cups

You need an electric mixer for this recipe. Stir until the sugar is dissolved, then cook covered until the syrup boils rapidly:

> 1 tablespoon white corn syrup
> 1 cup sugar
> ⅓ cup water

Beat about 2 minutes in a small bowl at high speed:

> 1 egg white

Add 3 tablespoons of the boiling syrup. Let the mixer continue to beat. Meanwhile ▶ cover the remaining syrup and cook covered about 3 minutes, until the steam has washed down from the sides of the pan any crystals which may have formed. ▶ Uncover and cook until the syrup reaches 238° to 240°. Pour the remaining syrup gradually into the egg mixture, while continuing to beat at high speed. While still beating, add:

> 1 teaspoon vanilla

Now beat the icing until it is ready to spread—4 to 6 minutes.

RAISIN OR NUT ICING

Chop:

> 1 cup seeded raisins, or ½ cup raisins and ½ cup nuts

Add them at the last minute to:

> Boiled White Icing, above

or sprinkle raisins and nuts on the cake and spread the icing over them.

NUT OR COCONUT ICING

To make a nut or coconut coating, have chopped nuts or fresh or dried shredded or grated coconut ready to press gently into the icing. Or, while the icing is still soft, proceed as follows: hold the cake on the palm of the left hand and, cupping the right hand to the curve of the cake, apply grated coconut or nuts to the icing as shown. Have a bowl underneath to catch the reusable excess. To prepare fresh coconut, see 244. To chop nuts, see 237.

ABOUT DECORATIVE ICINGS

Several types of pastry bags made of canvas or plastic are available in stores. And there is also a rigid metal "bag" on the market. If you choose canvas, be sure to use it with the ragged fabric seam outside. Several metal tips with different patterns are included in pastry bag kits. The most useful have a rose, star and round cutout.

Here's how to make your own decorating bag: Using heavy bond or bakery paper, cut an oblong about 11 × 15 inches. Fold the oblong diagonally as shown on the left, opposite. Keep the folded edge away from you. Roll the paper from the right side into a cornucopia with a tight point at the center of the long fold, as seen in upper right of sketch. With the left hand, continue to roll the paper until the cornucopia is complete. Turn it with the seam toward you and the point away from you. The seam should lie in a direct line with the point of one of the highest peaks of the bag, so that, by folding the peaks outward and away from you, you stabilize the shape of the cornucopia and the seam. This is shown by the two horizontal bags illustrated. If you

could see through the lower one, you would find the hollow cone ready to receive the icing. The upright bag at the end shows the final double fold that tightly closes the top of the filled bag. The peaks have already been turned inside to help make the cornucopia leakproof at the top when pressure is applied. Before filling, press the tip of the paper bag flat and cut off the end. If you plan to use the metal tips from your pastry bag kit, be sure the opening is large enough to hold the tip, but not so large that it will slip through under pressure. If you plan to use the paper point rather than a metal tip to make the designs, make three paper cornucopias. Cut one point straight across to make a small round opening; clip the others with a single and a double notch, to achieve the star and rose cutouts. These three cuts will make all of the patterns shown in the drawings on 492, depending on the angle at which the bags are held and the amount of pressure applied. You can control the scale of the decoration by the size of the cut.

Now for the actual decorating. You have a choice of three fine icings: Royal Glaze, 496, Decorative Icing, 492, and Creamy Icing, 493. Decorative Icing is tastier but not so easy to handle and does not keep so well as the others. In any case, apply a smooth base coat to the cake. ◗ For Decorative Icing and Royal Glaze you may use a spatula dipped in tepid water for a glossy finish. ◗ Allow the base coat to dry. If using several colors for decoration, divide the icing into small bowls and tint with vegetable paste or liquid vegetable coloring. ◗ Keep the bowls covered with a damp cloth. Never fill the bag to more than two-thirds of its capacity. For colors needed in small quantities,

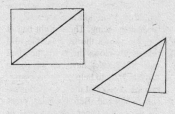

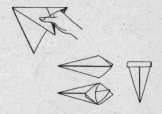

make the bags half size. Use a small spatula to push the icing well down into the point of the bag.

Before beginning any trimming, press the bag to equalize the icing in it and to force any unwanted air toward the tip, so that no bubbles will later destroy the evenness of your decorations. If the bag becomes soft through use or has been unsatisfactorily made, cut a generous piece off the point and press the icing directly into a new bag.

Practice making and filling bags. Then apply the icing on an inverted cake pan. For practice, the icing can be scraped off repeatedly and reused. Make patterns like old-fashioned Spencerian-writing doodles until you have achieved some ease. ◗ Experiment with the feel of the bag, until you can sustain the pressure evenly for linear effects and with varying force for borders, petals and leaves. With the bag in your right hand, you may work with as much freedom as in drawing.

Now you are ready to make the designs. It is a great help if the cake is on a turntable or lazy susan. In any case, when working on the sides, try to have the cake just above elbow level as you work. Pressure and movement, as we said before ◗ are controlled by the right hand. ◗ The left is used only for steadying. As shown in the sketch on 492, grasp the bag lightly but firmly in the palm of

the hand ◗ with the thumb resting on top, leaving the fingers free to press the bag as the hand and wrist turn to form the designs.

Sometimes the bag rests in the scissorlike crotch of the first two fingers. At other times the bag is merely guided, as shown in the second to last figure, 492. As the icing diminishes, refold the bag at the top, pushing the icing down.

First shown below left, 492, are forms executed from a bag with simple crosscut at the tip—making a small round opening. The second group was achieved with a notch like a V, and the elaborate composite-type flower needed a double notch, like a W. The decoration on the cake involves the use of all three types of cuts.

As in any work of art, the concept must dominate the technique. Make a sketch first of what you intend to do, or have it clearly in mind. The patterns shown below are conventional ones; try them, and then develop your own style. We remember a cake that Alexander Calder did for a mutual friend—complete with mobile and showing a clarity of line so characteristic of his talent.

It is a great temptation when decorating cakes to overload them. Try out some asymmetrical compositions. Partially bind the top and sides of the cake with garlands, heavy in relief but light in values, and remem-

ber to leave plenty of undecorated space to set them off. At first, you may make some of the more complicated designs separately on a piece of wax paper and let them dry before applying them to the cake. For those items made separately, use as an adhesive a little of the reserved fresh icing.

DECORATIVE ICING OR TWICE-COOKED ICING

About 1¾ Cups

This is a fine recipe for decorative icing. It will keep for a long time without hardening if closely covered with waxed paper. ▶ Please read About Boiled Icings, 488.

Stir until the sugar is dissolved, then boil without stirring:

   1 cup sugar
   ½ cup water

Meanwhile, whip until ▶ stiff, but not dry:

   2 egg whites
   ⅛ teaspoon salt

Sift and add very slowly, whipping constantly:

   3 tablespoons sugar

When the syrup begins to fall in heavy drops from a spoon, add a small quantity of it to the eggs and sugar; continue beating. Repeat this process, adding the syrup to the eggs in 4 or 5 parts. If these additions are properly timed, the last of the syrup will have reached the thread stage. Beat the icing constantly. Have a pan ready, partly filled with water. Place it over heat. The bowl in which the icing is being made should fit closely into this pan, so that the bowl will be over—but not in—the water. When the water in the pan begins to boil, add to the icing:

   ¼ teaspoon icing powder:
     equal parts of baking
     powder and tartaric acid

Continue to beat the icing until it sticks to the sides and the bottom of the bowl and holds a point. Remove from heat. Place as much as is required for the decoration, usually about a third, in a small bowl. Cover it closely with waxed paper. To the remainder, add:

   1 teaspoon or more hot water

thinning it to the right consistency for spreading. Beat it well and spread it on the cake. To decorate, see About Decorative Icings, 490.

CREAMY ICING

A highly manageable icing for intricate, precise decorations that keeps well if stored covered. Enough to frost and lightly decorate a 9-inch cake. Sift:

> **1 lb. confectioners' sugar**

Add and mix well with electric mixer:

> **¹/₂ cup white vegetable shortening**
> **5 to 6 tablespoons milk or cream**
> **1 teaspoon vanilla, or ¹/₂ vanilla and ¹/₂ almond extract**

Continue beating until icing is evenly smooth. It will be slightly stiff, which is the proper consistency for making decorations.

CHOCOLATE COATING OVER BOILED WHITE ICING

About 2¹/₄ Cups

The supreme touch to something that is already good in itself. Melt:

> **2 oz. chocolate**

Cool and spread with a broad knife or spatula over:

> **Boiled White Icing, 489, or Seven-Minute White Icing, at right**

This may be done as soon as the white icing is set. Allow several hours for the coating to harden. In summer or in moist weather, add to the chocolate before spreading it:

> **(¹/₄ teaspoon melted paraffin)**

This coating is always thin when applied, and hardens more rapidly if refrigerated. ♦ It is not recommended for use in damp hot weather. Transfer the cake to a fresh plate before serving.

SEVEN-MINUTE WHITE ICING

I.   **About 2 Cups**

A very fluffy, delightful icing that never fails. ♦ Please read About Boiled Icings, 488. Place in the top of a double boiler and beat until thoroughly blended:

> **2 unbeaten egg whites**
> **1¹/₂ cups sugar**
> **5 tablespoons cold water**
> **¹/₄ teaspoon cream of tartar**
> **(1¹/₂ teaspoons light corn syrup)**

Place these ingredients ♦ over rapidly boiling water. Beat them constantly with a rotary beater or with a wire whisk 7 minutes. Remove icing from heat. Add:

> **1 teaspoon vanilla**

Continue beating until the icing is the right consistency for spreading. You may add to it at this point:

> **(¹/₂ cup chopped nutmeats or grated coconut or 1 stick crushed peppermint candy)**

II. Made with an electric mixer. Stir, then boil in a covered pan until the sugar is dissolved:

> **3 tablespoons hot water**
> **1 cup confectioners' sugar**

Place in a small mixing bowl:

> **1 unbeaten egg white**
> **¹/₄ teaspoon cream of tartar**
> **¹/₈ teaspoon salt**

Add the hot syrup. Beat these ingredients at high speed until the icing is the right consistency to spread, 3 to 4 minutes. Add while beating:

> **1 teaspoon vanilla**

SEVEN-MINUTE LEMON ICING

Prepare:
> **Seven-Minute White Icing I, 493**

Use only:
> 3 tablespoons water

Add:
> 2 tablespoons lemon juice
> ¼ teaspoon grated lemon rind

SEVEN-MINUTE ORANGE ICING

> **About 1½ Cups**

Place in the top of a double boiler and beat until thoroughly blended:
> 1½ cups sugar
> 2 egg whites
> 1 tablespoon lemon juice
> ½ teaspoon orange rind
> ¼ cup orange juice

Follow the recipe for Seven-Minute White Icing I, 493.

SEVEN-MINUTE SEA-FOAM ICING

Cook:
> **Seven-Minute White Icing I, 493**

for 8 minutes. Fold in:
> 4 teaspoons Caramelized Sugar I, 232

Don't forget the vanilla.

FONDANT ICING

> **About 2 Cups**

This is the classic icing for petits fours. It is tricky to apply evenly. Prepare:
> **Basic Fondant, 577**

Just before you are ready to use it, heat the fondant ◗ over—not in— boiling water, beating it constantly until it melts. Then add any desired flavoring or coloring. Spread at once, as this icing tends to glaze over

rapidly and then needs reheating. Let the icing drip across, from one narrow edge of the cake to the other, as shown on 447, repeating until covered. Reheat and reuse any icing that falls onto the sheet below. If you have only a very few cakes to frost, place them one at a time on a slotted pancake turner or spoon held over the pot and ice them individually.

LUSCIOUS ORANGE ICING

> **About 1½ Cups**

This icing becomes firm on the outside and remains soft inside. ◗ Please read About Boiled Icings, 488.
Stir over heat until dissolved:
> 1 cup granulated sugar
> 1 tablespoon white corn syrup
> ⅛ teaspoon cream of tartar
> ½ cup water

◗ Cover and cook about 3 minutes or until the steam has washed down any crystals that may have formed on the sides of the pan. ◗ Uncover and cook to 238° or 240° without stirring. Pour the syrup in a slow stream over:
> 2 beaten egg whites

Beat for 10 minutes. Add:
> ¼ cup powdered sugar
> 1 teaspoon grated orange rind
> 1 tablespoon orange juice or ¾ teaspoon vanilla

Beat the icing to a spreading consistency.

CARAMEL ICING

> **About 1½ Cups**

◗ Please read About Boiled Icings, 488.
Stir until the sugar is dissolved:
> 2 cups brown sugar
> 1 cup cream, or ½ cup butter plus ½ cup milk

◗ Cover and cook about 3 minutes or until the steam has washed down any crystals that may have formed on the sides of the pan. ◗ Uncover and cook without stirring to 238° to 240°. Add:

3 tablespoons butter

Remove the icing from the heat and cool to 110°. Add:

1 teaspoon vanilla

Beat the icing until thick and creamy. If it becomes too heavy, thin it with a little:

Cream

until it is of spreading consistency. Top with:

(Chopped nuts)

MAPLE SUGAR ICING

About 1½ Cups

◗ Please read About Boiled Icings, 488.

Combine and cook, stirring frequently, until the mixture reaches a boil:

2 cups maple sugar
1 cup cream

Then ◗ cover and cook about 3 minutes or until the steam has washed down any crystals that may have formed on the sides of the pan. ◗ Uncover and cook to 234°. Remove the icing from the heat. Cool to 110°. Beat well until creamy. Fold in:

½ cup chopped nutmeats, preferably butternuts or slivered toasted almonds

COCONUT PECAN ICING

About 2½ Cups

Combine in a pan:

⅔ cup sugar
⅔ cup evaporated milk
2 egg yolks
⅓ cup butter
½ teaspoon vanilla

Cook and stir constantly over low heat about 10 minutes or until the egg

thickens. ◗ Do not boil. Remove from heat and add:

1⅓ cups flaked coconut
⅔ to 1 cup chopped pecans

CHOCOLATE MARSHMALLOW ICING

About 2 Cups

◗ Please read About Boiled Icings, 488.

Stir until the sugar is dissolved:

1½ cups sugar
1½ cups water

Then ◗ cover and cook about 3 minutes or until the steam washes down any crystals that may have formed on the sides of the pan. ◗ Uncover and cook without stirring to 238° to 240°. Remove from heat and add:

2 oz. grated unsweetened chocolate
1 dozen large marshmallows, cut into eighths and steamed until soft

Let these ingredients stand until the mixture no longer bubbles. Add:

⅛ teaspoon cream of tartar

Whip until ◗ stiff, but not dry.

2 egg whites
⅛ teaspoon salt

Pour the syrup over the egg whites in a thin stream. Whip constantly, until the icing is of the right consistency for spreading.

CHOCOLATE FUDGE ICING

About 2 Cups

Prepare:

Fudge Cockaigne, 582

Use in all:

1 cup milk

Beat until the icing is of the right consistency to be spread.

BROWN SUGAR MARSHMALLOW ICING

About 1¹/₂ Cups

◗ Please read About Boiled Icings, 488.

Cut into small cubes:

12 large marshmallows

Stir over low heat until dissolved:

2 cups brown sugar
¹/₂ cup milk

◗ Cover the syrup for about 3 minutes or until the steam has washed down any crystals which may have formed on the sides of the pan. ◗ Uncover and cook without stirring to 238°. Remove from the heat and add the marshmallows and:

¹/₄ cup butter

When these ingredients are melted and the icing has cooled to 110°, beat until it is of a good consistency for spreading. If too heavy, thin with a little:

Cream

Pour the cream a few drops at a time. Add:

(¹/₂ cup chopped nutmeats)

ABOUT QUICK ICINGS

Most quick icings, unless heavy in butter, are best spread on warm cakes. ◗ Those which have eggs in them, if not consumed the day they are made, should be refrigerated. Recipes calling for confectioners' sugar are tastier when ◗ allowed to stand over—not in—boiling water for 10 to 15 minutes, to cancel out the raw taste of the cornstarch filler. If you don't mind that taste, you can mix these icings more quickly in a ⚶ blender. ◗ Any delicate flavoring should be added after the icing leaves the heat. A glossy finish can be achieved by dipping your spatula frequently in hot water while icing the cake.

QUICK WHITE ICING

I.   About 1 Cup

See About Quick Icings, at left.

Cream together:

2 cups sifted confectioners' sugar
¹/₄ cup soft butter or 3 tablespoons hot whipping cream

Add and beat until smooth:

¹/₄ teaspoon salt
1 teaspoon vanilla
3 to 4 tablespoons milk, dry sherry, rum, or coffee

If the icing is too thin, add more:

Confectioners' sugar

If too thick, add:

A little cream

II.   About ³/₄ Cup

Melt and stir in a skillet until golden brown:

6 tablespoons butter

Blend in gradually:

1¹/₂ cups confectioners' sugar

Add 1 tablespoon at a time, until the icing is of a good spreading consistency:

Hot water

Flavor with:

1 teaspoon vanilla

ROYAL GLAZE, SWISS MERINGUE OR QUICK DECORATIVE ICING

About 2 Cups

This icing will become very hard. To avoid the naturally grayish tone that develops during preparation, add to portions that you want to keep white a slight amount of blue vegetable coloring. Do not use blue in any icing that you plan to color yellow, orange or any other pale, warm tint. Sift:

3¹/₂ cups confectioners' sugar

Beat until ◗ stiff, but not dry:

2 egg whites

Gradually add the sifted sugar and:

Juice of a lemon
1 to 2 drops glycerin

until it is of a good consistency to spread. Cover with a damp cloth until ready to use.

To apply as piping or for decorative effects, see About Decorative Icing, 490. Should you want the icing stiffer, add a little more sifted sugar. To make it softer, thin it ▶ very, very gradually with lemon juice, more egg white or water.

LEMON TOPPING FOR COOKIES OR BARS

About 1½ Cups

Whip until ▶ stiff, but not dry:

2 egg whites
⅛ teaspoon salt

Sift and add gradually:

2 to 2½ cups confectioners' sugar
Grated rind and juice of 1 lemon

QUICK LEMON ICING

About 1 Cup

Please read About Quick Icings, opposite.

A very subtle flavor may be obtained by coarsely grating the rind of an orange or lemon, wrapping the rind in a piece of cheesecloth, and wringing the citrus oils into the sugar before it is blended. Stir the oils into the sugar and allow it to stand 15 minutes or more.

Blend well:

2 cups confectioners' sugar
¼ cup soft butter

Beat in:

1 or more tablespoons cream

If you have not treated the sugar as suggested above, add:

Grated rind and juice of 1 lemon or 3 tablespoons liqueur such as apricot or crème de cacao

THREE-MINUTE ICING

Use this soft icing as a substitute for whipped cream or meringue.

Beat until blended, then place in a double boiler over boiling water:

2 egg whites
½ cup sugar
⅛ teaspoon salt
2 tablespoons cold water

Beat these ingredients with a wire whisk 3 minutes, or until stiff. Remove the icing from the heat. Add:

1 teaspoon vanilla or almond extract

Beat the icing well. Spread it over jellied fruit, pies or tarts, cakes, etc., that have been cooled Top it with:

Chopped nutmeats or coconut

FRENCH ICING

About 1½ Cups

See About Quick Icings, opposite. Sift:

2 cups confectioners' sugar

Beat until soft:

¼ cup butter

Add the sugar gradually. Blend these ingredients until creamy. Beat in:

1 egg
1 teaspoon vanilla

Place the mixture ▶ over—not in—boiling water 10 to 15 minutes.

CREAM CHEESE ICING

About ¾ Cup

▶ Please read About Quick Icings, opposite.
Sift:

¾ cup confectioners' sugar

Work until soft and fluffy:

3 oz. cream cheese
1½ tablespoons cream or milk
Beat in the sugar gradually. Add:
    1½ teaspoons grated lemon or
        orange rind
or:
    1 teaspoon vanilla and
    ½ teaspoon cinnamon
or:
    A good dash liqueur, lemon
    or orange juice and grated
    rind

QUICK ORANGE ICING

About 1 Cup

See About Quick Icings, 496.
Place in the top of a double boiler:
    2 cups sifted confectioners'
        sugar
    1 tablespoon melted butter
    1 tablespoon grated orange
        rind
    ¼ cup orange juice, or 3
        tablespoons orange juice
        and 1 tablespoon lemon
        juice
Place these ingredients ▶ over—not
in—boiling water 10 minutes. Then
beat the icing until cool and of a good
spreading consistency.

BUTTERSCOTCH OR PENUCHE ICING

About 1¼ Cups

Combine, stir and heat in a double
boiler until smooth:
    ¼ cup butter
    ½ cup brown sugar
    ⅛ teaspoon salt
    ⅓ cup light cream or
        evaporated milk
Cool this slightly. Beat in, to a good
spreading consistency:

2 cups, more or less, of
    confectioners' sugar
You may add:
    (½ teaspoon vanilla or
      1 teaspoon rum)
    (½ cup chopped nutmeats)

CHOCOLATE BUTTER ICING

About 1½ Cups

This icing can be used for decorating.
▶ Please read About Quick Icings, 496.
Melt over very low heat:
    2 to 3 oz. unsweetened
        chocolate
Melt in:
    2 teaspoons to 3 tablespoons
        butter
Remove these ingredients from the
heat and add:
    ¼ cup hot water, cream or
        coffee
    ⅛ teaspoon salt
Add gradually:
    2 cups, more or less, sifted
        confectioners' sugar
    1 teaspoon vanilla
You may not need quite all the sugar.

QUICK BROWN SUGAR ICING

About ¾ Cup

A quickly made but rather coarse
icing.
Combine, stir and cook slowly to the
boiling point:
    1½ cups brown sugar
    5 tablespoons cream
    2 teaspoons butter
    ⅛ teaspoon salt
Remove from the heat. Cool slightly
and add:
    ½ teaspoon vanilla
Beat the icing until it can be spread.
You may add:
    (½ cup chopped nutmeats)

CHOCOLATE CREAM CHEESE ICING

About 2 Cups

Melt:

3 oz. unsweetened chocolate

Soften:

3 oz. cream cheese

in:

¼ cup milk

Add gradually:

**4 cups confectioners' sugar
½ teaspoon salt**

Combine this mixture with the melted chocolate and heat until smooth and ready to be spread.

☘ EUROPEAN CHOCOLATE ICING

About ⅔ Cup

A letter from a homesick American bride made us realize that familiar tastes abroad have an accent as foreign as English words spoken by other nationals. Where to get bitter chocolate for icing, to make it taste the way she thought it should? Chef James Gregory made her feel almost at home with this semisweet answer. Melt in a double boiler ♦ over—not in—boiling water:

**1 tablespoon butter
4 oz. semisweet chocolate**

When melted, add and beat well or ☘ blend:

6 tablespoons whipping cream

Sift and add, until the desired sweetness is reached and the icing is smooth, about:

**1½ cups confectioners' sugar
1 teaspoon vanilla**

Spread while warm.

QUICK CHOCOLATE ICING

Melt over hot water:

Sweet chocolate bars or chocolate peppermints

Cool slightly, then spread the icing. If the chocolate seems stiff, beat in a little:

Cream

and, to perfect the flavor, add:

Vanilla

CAROB ICING

Prepare:

French Icing, 497

and sift with the confectioners' sugar:

¼ carob powder

You may add:

(½ teaspoon instant coffee)

Proceed as for French Icing.

COFFEE OR MOCHA ICING

About 1¼ Cups

Sift:

**1⅔ cups confectioners' sugar
1 to 2 tablespoons cocoa**

Beat until soft:

¼ to ½ cup butter

Add the sugar gradually. Blend these ingredients until creamy. Add:

**⅛ teaspoon salt
3 tablespoons strong hot coffee**

Beat for 2 minutes. When the icing is cool, add:

1 teaspoon vanilla, almond flavoring or rum

Let stand 5 minutes. Beat well and spread.

QUICK MAPLE ICING

About 1 Cup

Sift:

2 cups confectioners' sugar

Add and blend:

1 tablespoon butter
¼ teaspoon salt
½ teaspoon vanilla

Add and beat to a good consistency for spreading:

Maple syrup
(½ cup toasted coconut)

QUICK HONEY-PEANUT BUTTER ICING

About 1 Cup

This appeals mainly to the small fry. Combine and bring to a boil:

2 tablespoons shortening
2 tablespoons butter
¼ cup honey

Remove from heat and add:

½ cup coarsely ground peanuts

Stir until well blended. Spread on a warm cake. Toast very lightly under a broiler at medium heat; watch carefully.

APRICOT OR PINEAPPLE ICING

About 1 Cup

A soft icing.
Stir until smooth:

½ cup sweetened, cooked dried apricot pulp or drained crushed pineapple

with:

1½ to 2 cups sifted confectioners' sugar

Beat in:

1 to 3 tablespoons soft butter
½ tablespoon lemon juice

Add more confectioners' sugar if needed.

PINEAPPLE ICING

About 1½ Cups

Sift:

2 cups confectioners' sugar

Beat until soft:

¼ cup butter

Add the sugar gradually. Blend until creamy.
Beat in:

1 teaspoon lemon juice
⅛ teaspoon salt
½ teaspoon vanilla
½ cup drained crushed pineapple

Let stand 5 minutes. Beat the icing until creamy. Add more sugar, if necessary.

ABOUT ICING SMALL CAKES AND COOKIES

There are a number of ways to ice and garnish small cakes quickly. Some are shown below. **I.** Place on a hot cupcake small bits of semisweet or sweet chocolate. Spread as it melts. **II.** Just before removing cookies from the oven, put on each one a mint-flavored chocolate candy wafer and return the cookie sheet to the oven until the wafer melts. **III.** To ice cupcakes or leaf cookies, dip them quickly into any soft icing. Swirl the cakes as shown. Cookies are most easily iced if impaled on a skewer.

IV. For cupcakes, sift confectioners' sugar over them through a strainer, as shown opposite. **V.** Or ice as for Petit Fours, 447.

QUICK LACE TOPPING

A good, quick decorative effect on any cake can be gained with a slightly rough top, see sketch, below. Place a paper doily or monogrammed cut paper pattern on top of the cake and fill the interstices with sugar. Be sure that the sugar, confectioners' or colored, is dusted lavishly over the doily and filters down into all the voids. Lift the doily or pattern off gingerly, with a straight upward motion, and you will find a clearly marked lacy design on your cake top. Shake into a bowl any surplus sugar left on the pattern. Reserve it for future use. You may also follow this principle in applying finely grated semisweet chocolate on an iced cake.

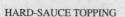

HARD-SAUCE TOPPING

Soften slightly, then apply a thin layer of brandied:

   Hard Sauce, 572

to any cooled cake or coffee cake.

BAKED ICING

   Glaze for an 8 × 8-Inch Cake

This icing is baked at the same time as the cake. Use it on a thin cake only, one that will require 25 minutes of baking or less—such as spice, ginger or coffee cake.

Preheat oven to 375°.

Sift:

   ¹/₂ cup brown sugar

Whip until ♦ stiff, but not dry:

   1 egg white
   ¹/₈ teaspoon salt

Fold in the sugar or beat it in slowly. For an exciting new taste, fold in:

   (2 tablespoons cocoa)

Spread the icing on the cake. Sprinkle it with:

   ¹/₄ cup broken nutmeats

Bake the cake as indicated in the recipe.

BROILED ICING

   For an 8 × 8-Inch Cake

Combine and spread on a cake, coffee cake or cookies, while they are warm, a mixture of:

   3 tablespoons melted butter
   ²/₃ cup brown sugar
   1 to 2 tablespoons cream
   ¹/₈ teaspoon salt
   ¹/₂ cup shredded coconut or nutmeats

Place the cake 3 inches below a broiler, with the heat turned low. Broil the icing until it bubbles all over the surface, but see that it does not burn.

ABOUT MERINGUE TOPPINGS

Pie and pudding meringues are delicate affairs that ♦ are best made and added to pastry shortly before serving. Since meringue is beaten constantly until the moment to spread it, have the ♦ oven preheated to between 325° and 350°. Lower heat will dry the meringue. Higher heat will cause

egg protein to shrink or shrivel. The two toppings below differ greatly in volume, texture and method. The first is cooked on the pie or dessert itself. The second is cooked separately and beaten until cool before applying; it may or may not be browned later. As volume in the egg white is essential, please follow these suggestions:
◗ Have the utensils absolutely free of grease, with ◗ egg whites at about 70° and ◗ without a trace of yolk. Add sugar as specified in each recipe. Excess sugar beaten into the meringue will cause gumminess and "beading." If you prefer a topping sweeter than these, you may glaze the surface, after the meringue is in place, by sprinkling it with additional sugar. This also makes the meringue easier to cut cleanly when serving. You may also top it with a sprinkling of coconut or slivered almonds before baking.

Meringue toppings for small tarts may be baked on foil and slipped onto a cooked or fresh pie filling just before serving. For a large pie, spread the meringue lightly from the edges toward the center of the pie. ◗ Should it not adhere well to the edges at all points, it will pull away during the baking. ◗ To avoid shrinkage, cool meringues in a warm place, away from drafts.

lean over slightly when the beater is removed. Beat in, 1 tablespoon at a time:

> **3 tablespoons sugar or
> 4 tablespoons confectioners'
> sugar**

◗ Do not overbeat. Beat in:

> **1/2 teaspoon vanilla**

Spread on pie and bake 10 to 15 minutes, depending on the thickness of the meringue.

II.   About 1 1/4 Cups

This classic Italian meringue does not require baking, because the egg whites are already cooked by the hot syrup. You may want to brown it lightly in a 350° oven. This meringue is not so stiff as the preceding one.
Heat in a heavy pan and stir until dissolved:

> **1/2 cup water
> 1/4 teaspoon cream of tartar
> 1 cup sugar**

When the syrup is boiling ◗ cover and cook about 3 minutes or until steam has washed down any crystals that may have formed on the sides of the pan. ◗ Uncover and cook without stirring to 238° to 240°. Pour the syrup ◗ very gradually onto:

> **3 well-beaten egg whites**

beating constantly, until this frosting meringue is cool and ready to be spread on the pie filling or pudding.

MERINGUE TOPPING

I.   For a 9-Inch Pie

Preheat oven to 325° to 350°.
Whip until frothy:

> **2 egg whites**

Add:

> **1/4 teaspoon cream of tartar**

Whip them until they are ◗ stiff, but not dry; until they stand in peaks that

STREUSEL AND TOPPINGS APPLIED BEFORE BAKING TO COFFEE CAKES, PIES AND SWEET ROLLS

I. Streusel

For an 8 × 8-Inch Cake

Prepare:

> **Any coffee cake dough,
> 327–331**

After spreading it with butter, combine:

> **2 tablespoons all-purpose or rice flour**
> **2 tablespoons butter**
> **5 tablespoons sugar**

Blend these ingredients until they crumble. Add:

> **1/2 teaspoon cinnamon**

Sprinkle the crumbs over the cake and bake as directed. Add:

> **(1/4 to 1/2 cup chopped nuts)**

II. Streusel   For a 9-Inch Pie

Frequently called Danish or Swedish and much like the topping for Apple Paradise. This is a crumb topping usually served in place of a top crust on apple or tart fruit pie, but which does well for coffee cakes. Melt:

> **6 tablespoons butter**

Stir in and brown lightly:

> **1 cup fine dry cake crumbs**
> **3/4 teaspoon cinnamon**

III. Honey Glaze
For a 9 × 13-Inch Cake

Cream:

> **1/2 cup sugar**
> **1/4 cup butter**

Blend in:

> **1 unbeaten egg white**

Add:

> **1/4 cup honey**
> **1/2 cup crushed nutmeats**
> **1/2 teaspoon cardamom**

Spread these ingredients on coffee cakes that are ready to be baked.

IV. Honey-Bee Glaze
For Two 9-Inch Square Cakes

Stir and bring to the boiling point over low heat:

> **1/2 cup sugar**
> **1/4 cup milk**
> **1/4 cup butter**
> **1/4 cup honey**
> **1/2 cup crushed nutmeats**

Spread these ingredients on coffee cakes that are ready for baking.

V. Caramel Roll Topping
For 12 Rolls

This heavy topping is put in the bottom of the pan, and when the cake or rolls are reversed, it becomes the topping.
Melt:

> **1/4 cup butter**

Stir in until dissolved:

> **1 cup packed brown sugar**
> **2 tablespoons honey or corn syrup**
> **1 to 2 teaspoons cinnamon**
> **1/2 teaspoon chopped lemon rind**
> **1/2 cup chopped nuts**

Add:

> **(2 tablespoons finely chopped citron)**

GLAZES APPLIED BEFORE OR DURING BAKING

I. To give color to yeast dough or pastry, brush with:

> **Milk or butter or a combination of milk and sugar**

II. French Egg Wash or Dorure

To give color and gloss to yeast dough or pastry, brush with:

> **1 egg yolk diluted with**
> **1 to 2 tablespoons water or milk**

III. To sparkle a glaze, sprinkle before baking with:

> **Granulated sugar**

IV. For a clear glaze, just before the pastry has finished baking, apply with brush dipped in:

> **1/4 cup sugar**

dissolved in:

¼ **cup hot water or strong hot coffee**

(½ **teaspoon cinnamon**)

and return to oven.

V. To give yeast dough or pastry a glow and flavor, brush with sweetened fruit juice and lemon rind.

VI. To gloss and harden crust of yeast dough, brush with a cornstarch and water glaze several times during the baking.

VII. Broiled Icing, 501.

VIII. Baked Icing, 501.

GLAZES APPLIED AFTER BAKING

Just after these glazes are applied, decorate with:

Whole or half nuts, cherries, pineapple bits and citron

When it dries, the glaze will hold the decorations in place on cakes and sweet breads.

I. Milk Glaze   About ⅓ Cup

This can be used as a substitute on small cakes similar to petits fours, which are classically iced with fondant. Sift:

½ **cup confectioners' sugar**

Add:

2 **teaspoons hot milk**
¼ **teaspoon vanilla**

II. ★ **Lemon Glaze**

About ½ Cup

Enough glaze to cover four 8 × 8-inch cakes. This glaze needs no heating but is spread directly on warm cakes or Christmas cookies. It is of a fine consistency for imbedding decorative nuts and fruits.

Mix or ⌁ blend:

1¼ **cups confectioners' sugar**

with:

¼ **cup lemon, orange or lime juice**
1 **teaspoon vanilla**

Mix until smooth.

III. Honey Glaze

About ⅓ Cup

Combine and bring to a boil:

2 **tablespoons sugar**
¼ **cup honey**
1 **tablespoon butter**

IV. Chocolate Glaze

About 1¼ Cups

This retains a glossy sheen.

Melt in a double boiler ⌁ over—not in—boiling water:

6 **to 7 oz. semisweet chocolate**
(1 **tablespoon butter**)

Cook to the thread stage (230°):

1 **cup sugar**
⅓ **cup water (of which 3 tablespoons may be strong coffee)**

Pour the syrup slowly into the chocolate, stirring constantly until the mixture coats the back of the spoon. Pour the glaze over the cake.

V. ⌁ **Blender-Whipped Cheese Topping**

About ⅓ Cup

Soften:

3 **oz. cream cheese**

with:

1 **tablespoon cream**
½ **teaspoon vanilla**

Blend in and cream well:

3 **tablespoons confectioners' sugar**

VI. Liqueur Glaze

About ⅔ Cup

Combine and mix well:

2 cups sifted confectioners'
   sugar
3 tablespoons liqueur
2 tablespoons melted butter

Spread over cake or cookies.

VII. Glaze for Breads

To make a crisp crust, brush with
water immediately when taken from
oven.

VIII. Glaze for Puff Paste

For a crisp crust, brush with a light
sugar syrup immediately upon removal from oven.

GLAZES FOR FRUIT PIES, TARTS AND COFFEE CAKES

I. Apricot, Peach or Raspberry Glaze
About 4½ Cups

For already baked pastries, the simplest glazes are melted preserves or
jellies such as currant, quince or apple. Below is a useful glaze to keep
on hand in the refrigerator.
Prepare:

3 cups strained apricots,
   peaches or raspberries

Cook until the sugar is dissolved,
with:

1 cup sugar
1 cup light corn syrup

While the mixture is still warm, glaze
the cooled pastry.

II. Fruit Glaze
Sufficient for Glazing 3 Cups of Berries or Fruit

Boil to the jelly stage, 663, then
strain these ingredients:

¼ cup water
1 cup sugar
1 cup cleaned fruit
2 medium-sized chopped
   apples
   A little red vegetable
   coloring

(1 tablespoon butter)

The butter will keep the glaze supple.
Cool. When the jelly is about to set,
pour it or spread it over the fruit to be
glazed.

III. Strawberry Glaze
Sufficient for a 9-Inch Pie Shell or Six 2½-Inch Tarts

Hull and crush:

3 cups strawberries

Strain them first through a ricer, then
through a fine sieve. Add to the juice:

⅓ cup sugar
1 tablespoon lemon juice
1 tablespoon cornstarch
   A little red vegetable
   coloring

Cook and stir these ingredients over
low heat until thick and transparent.
Cool. Spread over the fruit to be
glazed.

IV. Thickened Fruit Glaze

Glaze may also be made of canned
fruit syrups or of jellies. Boil the
syrup or jelly until thick. To each ½
cup, add:

1 teaspoon cornstarch or
   arrowroot

blended with:

1 tablespoon sugar

The cornstarch will give a smooth
glaze, the arrowroot a more transparent and stickier one.

CLEAR CARAMEL GLAZE
About 1 Cup

This brittle topping is used on many
European cakes, especially the famous Dobos or Drum Torte, 431.
Place in a large, heavy skillet over
low heat:

1 cup sugar

Cook and stir with a wooden spoon,
using the same kind of gentle motion
you use for scrambling eggs. ▶ Keep

agitating the pan to prevent scorching. When the sugar bubbles, remove the pan from the heat. The glaze should be clear, light brown and smooth, and should have reached a temperature of about 310°. Spread it at once with a hot spatula. ♦ If you work quickly, you may score it in patterns for easier cutting later. Use a knife dipped in cold water.

FRESH FLOWERS FOR CAKES

Cake decorations can be made from flowers, if you are sure they were not sprayed. Place on the cake just before it is served. Choose delicately colored open-petaled flowers like hollyhocks. Remove the stamens. Cut off all but ³/₄ inch of the stem. Arrange the flowers on an iced cake. Place a small candle in the center of each one. A hemerocallis wreath is good for daytime decorations but closes at night. Field daisies and African daisies hold up well. ♦ Beware of flowers like lilies of the valley or Star of Bethlehem, which have poisonous properties.

DESSERTS

A family we know had a cook who always urged the children to eat sparingly of the main course, so as to leave a little room for the "hereafter." Desserts can indeed be heavenly. They also give the hostess a chance to build a focal point for a buffet, such as the flambéed plum pudding shown above, or to produce a startling soufflé. Serve a rich chocolate custard in Empire pots-de-crème, 512, as shown in foreground. Remember, too, fruits and fruit fondues, 113, and dessert cheeses, 542. See also Filled Cakes, 434, and Torten, 430, that serve as complete desserts, and Crêpes, 143, and Beignets, 157, and by all means Compotes, 111.

ABOUT CUSTARDS

Custard puddings, sauces and fillings accompany the seven ages of man in sickness and in health. To prepare them in ways that enhance their charm, remember these simple precautions. ◗ When pasteurized milk is used in making custards, it is not nec-essary to scald it; but scalding does shorten the cooking time. If scalded, cool the milk enough afterward to keep the eggs, when added, from curdling; or temper the beaten eggs by adding a small quantity of the hot liquid to them before gradually adding the eggs to the hot mixture.

For baked custard, simply whip the ingredients together well and pour them into custard cups. We prefer cups of heavy ceramic glaze like those shown on 509, with their pottery tray. Or cups may be set on a rack or on a folded towel in a pan. In either case, pour an inch of hot, but not boiling, water into the cooking container. Bake them 50 to 60 minutes at low heat, around 300°. If you have used homogenized milk, allow about 10 minutes longer. To test for doneness, insert a knife ◗ near the edge of the cup. If the blade comes out clean, the custard will be solid all the way through when cooled. There is sufficient stored heat in the cups to finish the cooking process. Remove the custards from the pan and cool on a rack. ◗ However, should you suspect that they are overcooked, test them at the centers. If they are as well done as at the edges, set the cups in ice water at once to arrest further cooking.

For softer top-of-the-stove custards and sauces, use a double boiler, cooking ◗ over—not in—boiling water. Too high heat will toughen and shrink the albumen in the eggs and keep it from holding the liquid in suspension as it should. Beat the eggs well. Add about ¼ cup of the hot liquid to them and then slowly add the rest of it, stirring constantly. Cook until the custard is thick enough to coat a spoon. Remove pan from heat. Strain. Then continue stirring to release steam. If the steam is allowed to condense, it may make the custard watery. Should you have reason to believe that the custard has become too hot, turn it into a chilled dish and whisk it quickly, or put it in the blender at high speed to cool rapidly. ◗ Always store custards or custard-based dishes like pies and éclairs covered in the refrigerator, as they are highly susceptible to bacterial activity even though they may give no evidence of spoilage.

CUSTARD

5 Servings

This artless confection, often referred to as "boiled" custard, is badly nicknamed, because ◗ it must not be permitted to boil at any time. It is never so firm as baked custard but is more like a thick custard sauce.

Scald in the top of a double boiler.

2 cups milk

Stir in slowly:

3 or 4 slightly beaten egg yolks

¼ cup sugar

⅛ teaspoon salt

Place the custard ◗ over—not in—boiling water. Stir it constantly until it begins to thicken. As it cools, beat to release the steam. Add before chilling thoroughly:

1 teaspoon vanilla, rum or dry sherry, or a little grated lemon rind

⅄ BAKED OR CUP CUSTARD

5 Servings

Delicious served in solitary glory. Use it also to top a summer brunch of unsweetened dry cereal and fresh berries; or as a filling in cored pear halves, fresh or stewed, sprinkled with rum and garnished with a stewed pitted prune dusted in cinnamon. Preheat oven to 300°.

Blend together:

2 cups milk

¼ to ½ cup sugar or ¼ cup honey

⅛ teaspoon salt

Should the milk be unpasteurized, be sure to see About Custards, above. Add and beat well:

2 whole eggs or 4 egg yolks

If you want to unmold the custard, add an extra egg. The greater the proportion of yolk, the tenderer the custard will be. If you use 2 egg whites to 1 yolk, quite a stiff custard results. Add:

½ teaspoon vanilla or almond extract, or the scraped seeds from a 1-inch length of vanilla bean

When this is all well beaten, pour it into a baking dish or into individual custard cups. Dust with:

(Nutmeg)

A nutmeg grater is shown at the right, 509.

Place the molds in a pan of hot water on a rack or in a heavy ceramic baking dish, shown below. Bake an hour or more for the casserole and 50 to 60 minutes for the cups. To test, see About Custards, 507. Chill and serve with:

> **Caramel Syrup, 597, berries, a fruit sauce, or Maple Syrup Sauce, 569**

⚘ COFFEE CHOCOLATE CUSTARD

4 Servings

A sophisticated dessert easily made in a blender.

Put into blender:

> 1/2 **to 1 oz. finely cut-up unsweetened chocolate**

Pour over it:

> 1 **cup strong, hot coffee**

Add:

> 1 **cup milk**
> 4 **to 6 tablespoons sugar**
> 1/8 **teaspoon salt**
> 2 **whole eggs or 3 egg yolks**

Blend this mixture. Bake as for Baked Custard, opposite.

CARAMELIZED CUSTARD OR CRÈME CARAMEL

4 to 5 Servings

Caramelize:

> 1/2 **cup sugar, see Caramelized Sugar I, 232**

Place it in a 7-inch ring mold or custard cups. Turn the mold so the caramel spreads evenly, then push the coating with a wooden spoon until

the entire base of the dish is covered. At this point the syrup should be, and should remain, thick if you have caramelized the sugar properly.

Prepare:

> **Baked Custard, opposite**

Bake as directed in the caramelized mold or cups. Invert it when cold onto a platter. To ensure that the caramel comes out intact, dip the mold to the depth of the caramel ▶ quickly into hot water, as you would in releasing a gelatin. Now the center may be filled with:

> **(Whipped cream)**

Sprinkle the top with:

> **Shredded toasted almonds or crushed nut brittle**

CARAMEL CUSTARD

Prepare:

> **Baked Custard, opposite**

omitting the sugar. Mix with it:

> 1/2 **cup Caramelized Sugar I, 232**

Bake as directed.

RICH CUSTARD

6 Servings

Mix in the top of a double boiler:

> 3/4 **cup sugar**
> 2 **tablespoons cornstarch**
> 1/8 **teaspoon salt**

Gradually stir in:

> 2 **cups milk and cream, mixed**

Cook covered ▶ over—not in— boiling water 8 minutes without stirring. Uncover and cook for about 10 minutes more. Add:

> 4 **well-beaten egg yolks**
> 2 **tablespoons butter**

Continue to cook and stir these ingredients 2 minutes longer. Cool, stirring occasionally to release steam, then add:

1¹/₂ teaspoons vanilla

Fold in:

1 cup whipped cream

Chill the custard. It will have the consistency of a heavy whipped cream. It is divine with:

**Dampfnudeln, 396, or
drained Tutti-Frutti, 674**

FLOATING ISLAND

4 Servings

The French call this dish **Oeufs à la Neige** or **Snowy Eggs**.

Whip until stiff:

3 egg whites

Beat in gradually:

¹/₄ cup sugar

Scald:

2 cups milk

Drop the meringue mixture from a tablespoon in rounds onto the milk. Poach them gently, without letting the milk boil, for about 4 minutes, turning them once. Lift them out carefully with a skimmer onto a towel. Use the milk and egg yolks to make:

Custard, 508

Cool the custard. Place the meringues on top. Chill before serving.

Or you may heap the meringue on the cooled custard. Place the custard dish in a pan of ice water and put the whole into the hot oven just long enough to brown the tips of the meringue. Dribble over the tops of the "eggs":

(Caramelized Sugar I, 232)

CRÈME BRÛLÉE

6 Servings

A rich French custard—famous for its hard, caramelized sugar glaze.

Heat in a double boiler until hot:

2 cups whipping cream

Pour it slowly over:

4 well-beaten eggs

Beat constantly while pouring. Return the mixture to the double boiler. Stir in:

(2 tablespoons sugar)

Heat, stirring constantly, until the eggs thicken and the custard coats a spoon heavily. Place the mixture in a greased baking dish or custard cups. Some people insist this custard should be made and chilled the day before it is caramelized. In any case, chill it well. Cover the custard with:

¹/₄ to ¹/₃-inch layer of sieved light-brown sugar or maple sugar

Be sure to cover the custard with the sugar to the very edges of the dish. To avoid a mess, place a piece of paper under the dish. Place the custard cups or dish in a shallow pan. If the custard has been chilled for 12 hours, put it in a cold oven. Turn the heat to 250° and heat until the sugar is caramelized. If the custard has been chilled a shorter time, put the dish in a shallow pan. Surround it with ice. Place it under a hot broiler just long enough to let the sugar form a crust. Keep the oven door open, and regularly rotate the dish to even the heating. While the sugar caramelizes, watch carefully, because it may scorch. Serve at once. A delicate garnish is:

A compote of greengage plums and apricots

BRÛLÉE CRUST

Making the brûlée crust in advance, separately, relieves tension and assures a professional look. Cut a piece of aluminum foil the exact size of the dish in which you want to serve the brûlée. Grease the foil on one side with:

Butter

Pat onto the buttered side in a firm, lacy disk pattern about ¼ inch thick:

Brown sugar

Put the sugar-covered foil on a cookie sheet. ◗ At this point the operation needs your entire attention. Put the cookie sheet under broiler heat until the sugar is caramelized or glazed. Remove it from the oven and reverse the foil, with the sugar disk, onto a cake rack to cool. When it is slightly cooled, the foil should peel off, leaving a large praline. Place the praline on the custard just before serving. The crust will disintegrate if put on the custard too soon.

ZABAGLIONE OR SABAYON

6 Servings

Served as sauce, dessert or beverage. Marsala is the classic wine, but Madeira or sherry is also used. If for a sauce, you might even try a good dry white wine and a little Cointreau. For Cold Sabayon Sauce, which can be made in advance and held, see 566. Beat until very light:

8 egg yolks
1 cup confectioners' sugar

Place these ingredients in the top of a double boiler ◗ over—not in— boiling water. Beat the custard constantly with a wire beater. When foamy, add gradually:

½ cup dry Marsala, Madeira or sherry

Continue to beat the custard until it doubles in bulk and begins to thicken. Remove it from the heat. If you want a fluffier result, whip until ◗ stiff, but not dry:

(8 egg whites)

Fold into the custard. Serve the Zabaglione at once in sherbet glasses.

WINE CUSTARD OR WEINSCHAUM

6 Servings

Similar to Sabayon, at left, but less sweet. Place in the top of a double boiler ◗ over—not in—boiling water:

2 cups dry white wine
½ cup water

Add:

4 unbeaten eggs
½ cup sugar

Beat these ingredients vigorously with a wire whisk. Cook the custard until it thickens, beating it constantly. Serve hot or cold.

ORANGE CUSTARD WITH MERINGUE

6 Servings

Mix together:

2 tablespoons grated orange rind
⅓ cup sugar

Peel:

6 oranges

Separate the sections and remove the membrane as illustrated on 125. Place sections in a baking dish. Scald:

3 cups milk

Pour over:

3 beaten egg yolks

Beat these ingredients until well blended. Combine the sugar with:

2 tablespoons cornstarch
¼ teaspoon salt

Stir this mixture into the custard. Cook and stir in the top of a double boiler until thick, about 7 minutes. Cool. Pour over the oranges. Preheat oven to 325°. Top the custard with:

Meringue Topping I, 502

Bake about 15 minutes. Serve chilled.

ABOUT SPONGE CUSTARDS

From a fan came a drawing of an elaborate mold and the question, "Can you tell me how my great-aunt used to make a dessert that had a spongy bottom and a clear quivery top?" Her aunt's creation must have been a sponge custard baked and unmolded. This batter holds together when put into the baking dish, but magically separates while cooking. If you serve it in the dish, the sponge will form a decorative top. If you prefer a meringue-like quality rather than a spongy one, reserve 1/4 cup sugar to beat slowly into the stiff egg whites before folding them into the egg-yolk mixture.

PINEAPPLE SPONGE CUSTARD

4 Servings

Please read About Sponge Custards, above.

Preheat oven to 350°.

Combine and stir in the order given:

    5 tablespoons sugar
    3 tablespoons all-purpose flour
    1/2 cup pineapple syrup
    1 teaspoon grated lemon rind
    2 tablespoons lemon juice
    2 or 3 beaten egg yolks
    1/2 cup milk
    1 1/2 tablespoons melted butter

Whip until ◗ stiff, but not dry, then fold in:

    2 or 3 egg whites

Place in the bottom of a buttered 7-inch ovenproof dish or in four buttered 3 1/2-inch individual ones:

    1 1/4 to 1 1/2 cups drained crushed pineapple

Pour the custard mixture over the fruit. Place the dishes on a rack in a pan in 1 inch of hot water. Bake the custard for about 1 hour for the dish and 45 minutes for the cups. Serve hot or cold.

ORANGE OR LEMON SPONGE CUSTARD

4 to 6 Servings

Please read About Sponge Custards, at left.

Preheat oven to 350°.

Cream:

    3/4 cup sugar
    1 1/2 tablespoons butter
    1 tablespoon grated orange rind or 2 teaspoons lemon rind

Add and beat well:

    2 or 3 egg yolks

Stir in:

    3 tablespoons all-purpose flour

alternatively with:

    1/3 cup orange juice or 1/4 cup lemon juice
    1 cup milk

Beat until ◗ stiff, but not dry:

    2 or 3 egg whites

Fold them into the yolk mixture. Place the batter in buttered custard cups or in a buttered 7-inch ovenproof dish. Set on a rack in a pan filled with 1 inch of hot water. Bake about 45 minutes for the cups and about 1 hour for the baking dish, or until set. Serve hot or ice cold with:

    (Thick cream or raspberry sauce)

CHOCOLATE CUSTARD OR POTS-DE-CRÈME

Some custard recipes are perfect for use in lidded pots-de-crème like those illustrated in the chapter heading. Although the classic procedure is baking, the consistency is simpler to control by this top-of-the-stove method. ◗ Be sure the eggs are at room temperature.

I.   **6 Servings**

Combine and cook in the top of a

double boiler, over—not in—boiling water:

>2 **cups milk or cream, or half milk and half cream**
>
>5 **to 8 oz. best quality sweet chocolate, grated**
>
>(2 **tablespoons sugar**)

Cook and stir these ingredients until they are blended and the milk scalded. Beat lightly:

>6 **egg yolks**

Before adding the eggs to the above mixture, temper them by stirring in about 1/2 cup of the hot milk mixture. Then stir the eggs into the mixture in the double boiler. Add:

>1 **teaspoon vanilla or grated rind of 1 orange**

Continue to stir until the custard begins to thicken. You may strain the custard. Pour into custard cups. Cool uncovered until steam is out, then cover and refrigerate.

II. Pots-de-Crème Café
4 Servings

Cook and serve as above, using:

>1/2 **cup whipping cream**
>
>1/2 **cup sugar**
>
>1 **tablespoon instant coffee**
>
>6 **egg yolks**
>
>1 **tablespoon brandy or lemon zest, 252**

III. ⅄ Blender Pots-de-Crème
4 Servings

⅄ Blend together:

>3/4 **cup semisweet chocolate bits**
>
>3/4 **cup hot milk**

Add when the chocolate is melted:

>1 **egg**

Pour into 4 pot-de-crème cups. Chill 2 to 3 hours and serve garnished with:

>(**Whipped cream**)

FRENCH CHOCOLATE MOUSSE
6 Servings

The director of a boys' camp in Maine recently reported to us the crestfallen faces in the dining room when it turned out that the "moose" promised for evening dessert had emerged from the pages of **Joy** instead of from the woods.

Scald and stir in a saucepan over low heat:

>2 **cups milk**
>
>1/4 **cup sugar**
>
>3 **oz. grated sweet chocolate**

Pour part of these ingredients over:

>4 **beaten egg yolks**

Return the sauce to the pan. Stir the custard constantly over low heat until it thickens slightly. Do not overcook. You may strain it. Cool by placing the pan in cold water and then in the refrigerator. In a separate bowl, whip until stiff:

>3/4 **cup whipping cream**

Add:

>1 **teaspoon vanilla**

Fold the cold custard into the whipped cream mixture until well blended. Fill custard cups with the mousse. Chill thoroughly before serving, but do not expect it to become firm.

RUM CHOCOLATE MOUSSE
8 to 10 Servings

A phenomenally smooth, rich dessert that is quickly confected. A specialty of our friend Chef Pierre Adrian.
Cook over very low heat until dissolved but not brown in color:

>1/4 **cup sugar**
>
>2 **to 4 tablespoons rum**

Melt in a double boiler:

>1/4 **lb. semisweet or sweet chocolate**

When the chocolate is melted, stir in:

>2 **to 3 tablespoons whipping cream**

Add the syrup to the melted chocolate and stir until smooth. When the mixture is cool but not chilled, fold into it:

2 stiffly beaten egg whites

and then fold this combination very gently into:

2 cups whipped cream

Chill in sherbet glasses at least 2 hours before serving.

CHESTNUT MOUND OR MONT BLANC

6 Servings

A typical European recipe needing lots of time.

Boil in water 8 minutes:

2 lb. chestnuts, see 238

Remove shells. Cook the shelled nuts until mealy in a double boiler over—not in—boiling water in:

1 quart milk

Drain, discard milk, then cook the drained chestnuts in a sugar syrup made of:

1 cup water
1 cup sugar

until the syrup is reduced by a third. Add:

(1/4 cup Almond Paste, 580)

When partially cool, add:

1 teaspoon vanilla or 2 more tablespoons brandy, curaçao, etc.

Put the mixture through a ricer. Let it fall lightly onto a large service platter into a mound. If necessary to touch it, try to do so very lightly, so that the chestnuts will not pack. Chill well, and when ready to serve, whip until stiff:

1 cup whipping cream

Fold in:

1 teaspoon vanilla
2 tablespoons sifted confectioners' sugar

Place the cream on the mound and let it overflow onto the sides. You may cover the top of the cream with a grating of:

(Sweet chocolate)

CORNSTARCH CUSTARD PUDDING OR BLANCMANGE

8 Servings

To be really good, this pudding needs loving care. For success, see about cornstarch, 214.

Mix in the top of a double boiler:

1/2 cup sugar
6 tablespoons cornstarch
1/4 teaspoon salt

Gradually add while stirring well:

4 cups milk

Place the mixture ♦ over—not in—boiling water and stir constantly 8 to 12 minutes, at which time it should have begun to thicken. Cover and continue to cook for about 10 minutes more. Stir 1 cup of this thickened mixture slowly into:

2 well-beaten eggs

Return it to the milk mixture and continue to cook 2 minutes, stirring constantly. Do not overcook. The pudding will thicken more as it cools. Remove from heat, and when slightly cooled by gentle stirring to release the steam, add:

1 teaspoon vanilla

Place in prepared molds, 521.

CARAMEL CUSTARD CORNSTARCH PUDDING

8 Servings

♦ Please read about cornstarch, 214. Heat slightly in the top of a double boiler over direct heat:

3 cups milk

Caramelize as in Caramelized Sugar I, 232:

1 cup sugar

Add it gradually to the warm milk

and heat to the boiling point. Gradually pour:

1 cup cold milk

over:

4 tablespoons cornstarch

stirring to make a thin paste. When this is smooth, combine the two mixtures by pouring the hot one ▶ gradually into the cold one and stirring until smooth again. Place in the top of the double boiler ▶ over—not in—boiling water and stir constantly 10 minutes until the mixture begins to thicken. Cover and continue to cook for 10 minutes more. Mix 1 cup of this thickened mixture slowly into:

2 well-beaten eggs

Return to the pan and continue to cook 2 minutes, stirring constantly. Then remove pudding from heat. Stir gently until slightly cooled, then add:

1 teaspoon vanilla

Place in prepared molds, 521.

CHOCOLATE CORNSTARCH PUDDING

4 Servings

▶ Please read about cornstarch, 214.
Melt in the top of a double boiler:

1 oz. unsweetened chocolate

Stir in slowly:

1/2 cup sugar
1 3/4 cups milk
1/8 teaspoon salt

Heat these ingredients to the boiling point.
Dissolve:

3 tablespoons cornstarch

in:

1/4 cup milk

Stir the cornstarch slowly into the hot milk mixture. Cook over boiling water for 10 minutes, stirring constantly. Cover and cook 10 to 12 minutes more. Cool by stirring very gently. Add:

1 teaspoon vanilla

Place in prepared molds, 521. Serve with:

Cream

FRIED CREAM OR CRÈME FRITE

Thirty-six 1 1/2-Inch Squares

▶ Please read about cornstarch, 214.
Place in the top of a double boiler:

A 2-inch piece of
vanilla bean
1 cinnamon stick
1 1/2 cups milk

Bring to a boil over direct heat and then cool slightly. Mix in a bowl until smooth:

1/4 cup sugar
1 tablespoon all-purpose
flour
1/4 cup cornstarch
1/2 cup milk

Remove vanilla bean and cinnamon stick from the slightly cooled milk and stir the smooth cornstarch mixture into the milk. ▶ Cook over—not in—boiling water until it begins to thicken—about 10 minutes. Pour some of this mixture over:

3 beaten egg yolks

Return the egg mixture to the pan and ▶ cook, stirring gently, about 3 minutes. Beat in:

1 tablespoon butter
1/4 teaspoon salt

Pour the thickened cream into a 9 × 9-inch buttered pan. Cool. Cut into diamonds or squares about 1 1/2 inches long. Beat:

1 egg

Dust cream with:

Finely crushed bread or
cake crumbs

Dip the pieces of cream in the egg, then again in the crumbs. Fry in deep fat heated to 370°. Drain and roll in:

Powdered Vanilla
Sugar, 229

Serve at once sprinkled with:
Rum
or with:
A fruit sauce, 563

ABOUT DESSERT SOUFFLÉS

If you have never made soufflés before ▶ please read the directions for making and baking them on (I, 225). ▶ To prepare a dish for a sweet soufflé, use a straight-sided ovenproof baker. Butter it and dust the inside with powdered sugar. Or, as an added touch, caramelize sugar in the base of the soufflé dish as for Crème Caramel, 509.

Some fruit and nut soufflés are very close in texture to omelets and whips, having no binding sauce. For such soufflés, the proper beating of the egg whites and the right baking temperatures are more important than ever. If the egg whites are under- or overbeaten or the baking heat is too high, they have the look and texture of an old leather belt. If mixed and baked with care, these same ingredients produce a delicacy and strength that remind us of dandelion seed puffs just before they blow. Some soufflés, like Apricot Omelette Soufflé, 521, are made on choux-paste base.

If you decide to add liqueurs as a flavoring, allow an extra egg yolk for every 2 tablespoons of liqueur. Otherwise, the mixture will be thinned too much.

To glaze a soufflé, dust it with confectioners' sugar 2 or 3 minutes before it is to come from the oven. The soufflé should have doubled in height and be firm before the glaze is applied. Watch it closely with the oven door partially open. The glaçage will remain fairly shiny when the soufflé is served.

Cold soufflés are based on gelatins and resemble mousses or Bavarians, 527.

Note carefully the size of the baking dish indicated, as this affects the lightness and volume of the result. A 7-inch dish should serve 3 to 4; a 10-inch dish, 8 to 10.

VANILLA SOUFFLÉ

A 9-Inch Soufflé Dish
▶ Please read About Dessert Soufflés, at left, to prepare a soufflé baker.

This soufflé has a versatile wardrobe and many aliases. You may add a very few drops of oil of anise or a few marrons glacés; or you may replace the sugar with ⅓ to ½ cup of syrup from preserved ginger; also, add about ¼ cup very finely chopped candied fruits that have been soaked in Danziger Goldwasser or kirsch. In the latter guise, it is called **Soufflé Rothschild**. Sift before measuring:
½ cup all-purpose flour
Resift with:
¼ cup sugar
¼ teaspoon salt
Stir in until smooth:
½ cup cold milk
Scald:
2 cups milk
with:
A vanilla bean
Remove the bean and stir in the flour mixture with a wire whisk. Cook and stir these ingredients over low heat until they thicken. Remove from the heat. Stir in:
¼ cup butter
4 to 5 beaten egg yolks
You may add:
(¾ cup chopped nutmeats)
Cool the mixture.
Preheat oven to 350°.
Whip until ▶ stiff, but not dry:
5 egg whites

Fold them lightly into the batter. Bake soufflé about 25 minutes. Serve with:

> **A fruit sauce, a rum-flavored sauce, or Maple Syrup Sauce, 569**

SOUFFLÉ GRAND MARNIER

An 8-Inch Soufflé Dish

▶ Please read About Dessert Soufflés, opposite, to prepare a soufflé baking dish.
Preheat oven to 400°.
Beat in a double boiler over boiling water:

> **8 lightly beaten egg yolks**
> **²/₃ cup sugar**

Continue to beat until the mixture forms a broad ribbon as it runs from a lifted spoon. Add:

> **¹/₂ cup Grand Marnier liqueur**

To arrest the cooking, transfer the mixture to a bowl and beat it over ice until cooled. Beat until foamy:

> **10 egg whites**

Add:

> **¹/₄ teaspoon cream of tartar**

Continue to beat until ▶ stiff, but not dry. Fold the egg yolk mixture into the whites, see illustration, 400. Mound the mixture in a soufflé dish. Bake 12 to 15 minutes, until firm, and serve at once.

PINEAPPLE SOUFFLÉ

A 7-Inch Soufflé Dish

▶ Please read About Dessert Soufflés, opposite, to prepare a soufflé baking dish.
Melt over low heat:

> **3 tablespoons butter**

Stir in:

> **3 tablespoons all-purpose flour**

When blended, stir in:

> **1 cup drained crushed pineapple**

Cook until thick; cool slightly and stir in:

> **²/₃ cup crushed dry macaroons**
> **3 beaten egg yolks**

Heat again until the yolks thicken slightly. Cool the mixture.
Preheat oven to 325°.
Beat until ▶ stiff, but not dry:

> **3 to 4 egg whites**

Beat in gradually:

> **2 tablespoons sugar**
> **¹/₂ teaspoon vanilla**

Fold this into the soufflé mixture. Bake in a soufflé dish about 30 minutes or until firm.

CHOCOLATE SOUFFLÉ

A 9-Inch Soufflé Dish

▶ Please read About Dessert Soufflés, opposite, to prepare a soufflé baking dish.
Melt:

> **2 tablespoons butter**

Stir in until blended:

> **1 tablespoon all-purpose flour**

In a separate saucepan, heat but do not boil:

> **1 cup milk**
> **1 oz. unsweetened chocolate, cut into pieces**
> **¹/₃ cup sugar**

Slowly add the hot milk mixture to the flour mixture, stirring constantly until well blended. Beat until light:

> **3 egg yolks**

Beat part of the sauce into the yolks, then add the yolk mixture to the rest of the sauce and stir the custard over very low heat until the yolks thicken slightly. Cool the custard well.
Preheat oven to 350°.
Add to the cooled chocolate mixture:

> **1 teaspoon vanilla**

Whip until ▶ stiff, but not dry:

> **3 egg whites**

Fold them lightly into the cooled chocolate mixture. Bake in a soufflé dish set in a pan of hot water about 20 minutes or until firm. Serve at once with:

> Cream; Vanilla Sauce, 571; Foamy Sauce, 573; or Weinschaum Sauce, 566

LEMON SOUFFLÉ

An 8-Inch Soufflé Dish

♦ Please read About Dessert Soufflés, 516, to prepare a soufflé baking dish.

Preheat oven to 350°.

Sift:

> ¾ cup sugar

Beat until very light:

> 5 egg yolks

Add the sugar gradually. Beat constantly until the eggs are creamy. Add:

> 1 teaspoon grated lemon rind
> ¼ cup lemon juice
> (½ cup chopped nutmeats)

Whip until ♦ stiff, but not dry:

> 5 egg whites

Fold them lightly into the yolk mixture. Bake in an ovenproof dish set in a pan of ♦ hot, but not boiling, water about 35 minutes, or until firm. Serve at once with:

> Cream

FRESH FRUIT SOUFFLÉ

A 7-Inch Soufflé Baker

♦ Please read About Dessert Soufflés, 516, to prepare a soufflé baker.

Preheat oven to 350°.

Prepare by peeling and mashing ripe fruits to make:

> 1 cup sweetened fruit pulp: fresh apricots, nectarines, peaches, plums, raspberries or strawberries

Add:

> 1½ tablespoons lemon juice
> 4 beaten egg yolks
> ⅛ teaspoon salt

> (1 tablespoon grated orange rind)

Beat until ♦ stiff, but not dry, and fold in:

> 4 egg whites

Beat the soufflé in a dish set in a pan of ♦ hot, but not boiling, water about 30 minutes or until it is firm. Serve hot with:

> Cream

PRUNE OR APRICOT SOUFFLÉ OR WHIP

A 9-Inch Soufflé Baker

♦ Please read About Dessert Soufflés, 516, to prepare a soufflé baker.

Preheat oven to 350°.

Have ready:

> 1 cup sweetened, thick cooked prune or apricot purée

Whip until ♦ stiff, but not dry:

> 5 egg whites

Add:

> ¼ teaspoon cream of tartar

Fold in the prune or apricot pulp and:

> (½ cup broken nutmeats)
> (1 teaspoon grated lemon rind)

Bake the soufflé in a baking dish set in a pan of ♦ hot, but not boiling, water. Bake about 1 hour or until firm. Serve hot with:

> Cream or Custard Sauce, 565

HAZELNUT SOUFFLÉ

An 8-Inch Soufflé Baker

♦ Please read About Dessert Soufflés, 516, to prepare a soufflé baker.

Preheat oven to 350°.

Put through a nut grinder:

> ¾ cup hazelnuts

Heat to just below the boiling point and pour over the nuts:

> 1 cup milk

Beat until light:

3 egg yolks

Beat in gradually:

3 tablespoons sugar

3 tablespoons all-purpose flour

¹/₈ teaspoon salt

Stir a small quantity of the hot mixture into the eggs, then return this combination to the rest of the hot mixture. Stir and cook these ingredients over low heat to let the yolks thicken slightly. Stir in:

3 tablespoons butter

Cool. Beat in:

¹/₂ teaspoon vanilla or 1 tablespoon rum

Beat until ▶ stiff, but not dry:

3 egg whites

Fold these into the cooled custard. Bake in a soufflé dish about 30 minutes or until firm. Serve hot with:

1 cup whipped cream

flavored with:

Caramel or coffee

NUT SOUFFLÉ

A 12-Inch Soufflé Baker

▶ Please read About Dessert Soufflés, 516, to prepare a soufflé baker. Preheat oven to 350°.

Sift:

1 cup confectioners' sugar

Beat until very light:

8 egg yolks

Add the sugar gradually. Beat constantly until the yolks are creamy. Fold in:

2 teaspoons grated lemon rind or 1 teaspoon vanilla

¹/₂ lb. ground blanched almonds or walnuts

Whip until ▶ stiff, but not dry:

8 egg whites

Fold them lightly into the yolk mixture. Bake the soufflé in a baking dish set in a pan of ▶ hot, but not boiling,

water. Bake until firm, about 45 minutes. Serve with:

Sabayon Sauce, 565–566, or a fruit sauce, 563

SOUR CREAM APPLE CAKE SOUFFLÉ COCKAIGNE

A 12 X 17-Inch Pan or Ten 4-Inch Round Baking Dishes

The specialty of our great-grandmother, who came from Lübeck. It was once served to us in a pie crust, as a renowned confection of Lyons. We feel the pie shell makes an attractive container. However, the crust does not greatly improve the flavor. Prepare:

5 to 6 cups pared, cored and sliced tart apples

Melt in a large heavy skillet:

¹/₄ cup butter

Add the apples and cook them uncovered over medium heat, stirring them often until they are tender. Do not let them brown. Combine and pour over the apples:

¹/₂ cup cultured sour cream Grated rind and juice of 1 lemon

1 cup sugar, scant unless apples are very tart

2 tablespoons all-purpose flour

8 beaten egg yolks

(¹/₂ cup shredded blanched almonds)

Stir these ingredients over low heat until they thicken. Cool the mixture. Preheat oven to 325°. Whip until ▶ stiff, but not dry:

8 egg whites

Fold them lightly into the apple mixture. Spread the mixture to a thickness of 1 inch in a large pan or ovenproof dish. Sprinkle the top with a combination of:

¹/₄ cup sugar

1 tablespoon cinnamon
¼ cup dry bread crumbs
¼ cup shredded blanched
    almonds

Bake about 45 minutes or until firm. The cake may be served hot, but it is best very cold, covered with:

**Whipped cream flavored
with vanilla, or with
Angelica Parfait, 552**

OMELETTE AUX CONFITURES

2 Servings

To prepare, please read about French Omelet, (I, 222).
Beat until light:

2 egg yolks

Beat in gradually:

¼ cup confectioners' sugar

Add:

½ teaspoon vanilla or a
    grating of orange or lemon
    rind

Whip until ◗ stiff, but not dry:

4 egg whites

Fold them lightly into the yolk mixture.
Melt in a skillet:

2 tablespoons butter

When the butter is very hot, pour in the omelet mixture. To cook and fold, see (I, 221). When done, sprinkle with:

Confectioners' sugar

Serve with:

Preserves or jelly

or fold the omelet and spread with:

**Applesauce, prune or
apricot pulp, drained
canned fruit or sugared
berries**

BAKED ALASKA

12 Servings

This tour de force speaks several languages and always seems gala. It needs last-minute preparation to be *à point*—the meringue glazed and delicately colored, the ice cream firm, the cake not soggy—in other words, "Just right!" There are individual or large pans, and also ovenproof dishes, shown 562, made especially for this dessert. Or you may also build a similar "cake case" on an oval heatproof dish.
Preheat broiler.
Line the dish with a half-inch layer of:

**Génoise, 416, or sponge or
angel cake, 405–407**

Three-day-old cake dry enough to absorb any liquid from the ice cream is suggested. You may sprinkle it lightly with:

(Brandy)

Have ready:

¾ -inch thick pieces of
    Génoise, sponge or angel
    cake to cover the ice cream
    later

Make a meringue as follows. Beat until frothy:

6 egg whites

Add and beat until almost stiff:

½ teaspoon cream of tartar
¼ teaspoon salt

Beat in, a tablespoon at a time:

¾ cup superfine sugar

Continue to beat and add:

1 teaspoon vanilla

When the meringue is stiff, quickly form on the cake base an oval mound made of:

1½ quarts ice cream

◗ softened just enough so that you can shape it. Cover this melon-mold shape with the cut strips of cake. Cover it at once with the meringue, so the cake surface is entirely coated to at least a three-fourths-inch thickness. Bring the meringue right down to the dish surface.. You may use some of the meringue in a pastry bag to pipe on fluted edges and patterns. Accent them with:

(Candied fruit)

Run this meringue-covered confection under a 500° broiler—not more than 3 minutes—to brown. Watch it very closely! Serve at once.

You may like to try out this baked meringue covering by using orange cups instead of cake as a base to hold the ice cream. Bring the meringue well down over the edge of the orange cups.

NORWEGIAN OMELET OR OMELETTE SOUFFLÉE SURPRISE

An unusual meringue because it includes egg yolks. This is another version of Baked Alaska.
Prepare the cake and ice cream as directed above, but make the meringue as follows. Beat:

4 egg yolks

Beat in:

¼ cup sugar
½ teaspoon grated lemon rind

Whip until ♦ stiff, but not dry, and fold in:

6 egg whites

Continue as directed for Baked Alaska, opposite.

APRICOT OMELETTE SOUFFLÉE

6 Servings
Two 9-Inch Round Pans with Removable Rims

Blend together in the top of a double boiler and heat ♦ over—not in—boiling water until the mass leaves the sides of the pan:

¼ cup butter
1 cup all-purpose flour
1 tablespoon sugar
1¼ cups cream
¾ cup milk

Cool the mixture. Preheat oven to 325°. Add one at a time, beating after each addition:

6 egg yolks
1 teaspoon vanilla

Beat until ♦ stiff, but not dry, and fold in:

6 egg whites

Pour the omelette mixture into the pans and bake 25 to 30 minutes. While baking, heat in the top of a double boiler:

1½ cups apricot jam

Have ready a heated serving dish on which to reverse one of the omelette layers. Cover it lightly with the jam. Reverse the second layer over it. Cover second layer with jam and serve at once with:

(Whipped cream)

ABOUT DESSERT MOLDS

Almost any bowl that splays out is suitable for a pudding mold. Be sure the slanted sides allow molded ingredients to slide out easily when the mold is inverted. For straight-sided desserts, use spring forms, shown on 430. One of the favorite shapes for Bavarians is the melon mold. To prepare the mold, rinse it out with cold water.

Dessert molds are often cake-lined. To make a pudding mold from a cake itself, see description below and illustration opposite. If the mold is deep and the pudding or cake surface very tender, always use a paper lining as a safety measure, see opposite, left. First cut a piece of paper for the base. Then, for the sides, notch the bottom and fold in at the base line. The simplest cake linings are made with thin sheets of Génoise, 416, or large areas cut from Jelly Rolls, 440, while they are still flat, before filling. Shown on the right is a

mold lined with filled jelly roll slices. Macaroons and cookies can also be used in this pattern. In the center, you see ladyfingers, either whole or split, forming the mold. If they are split, be sure to put the curved sides against the form. To make an even top, slice each section to a point by cutting it diagonally, as shown, and placing it with the pointed end toward the middle, until the base of the mold is filled. You may want to cut a small round for the very center.

If the ladyfingers are sparsely sprinkled with a liqueur or a fruit juice after placing, they will soften enough to fill any crevices. If moistened too much, they will disintegrate.

For fillings in such molds, see suggestions on 448. Whatever fillings you choose, be sure to ◗ refrigerate them, preferably 12 hours, before unmolding. Garnish the molded food with flavored creams, sauces or fruit and serve at once.

ABOUT CARAMEL-COATED MOLDS

I. Sprinkle the bottom of a mold with:

> Sugar

Heat in a slow—250° to 300°—oven or over low heat until the sugar is brown and bubbling. This is a simple method to be used if only the top of the custard or pudding is to

be caramelized when the mold is reversed.

II. Spread the mold with:

> Caramelized Sugar I, 232

before the syrup hardens. If necessary, spread the caramel around with a wooden spoon to coat the sides. Let the caramel harden before adding the filling.

SEMISWEET CHOCOLATE CASES

6 Servings

Melt in the top of a double boiler over hot, not boiling, water:

> 6 squares semisweet
> chocolate
> 1 tablespoon butter

When melted, beat thoroughly. Swirl the mixture into the insides of crinkled paper baking cups. Place cups in muffin tins and chill to allow the chocolate to harden. To serve, carefully remove the paper and fill the chocolate cases with:

> Ice cream or Custard, 508

ABOUT GELATIN PUDDINGS

◗ For details about handling gelatin, see About Gelatin, 233. These desserts vary greatly in texture. Easiest to prepare are the clear jellies, to which you may add fruit and nuts. If you add puréed fruits, you lose clarity at once, and the dessert bears some similarity to a mousse. When gelatins are allowed to set partially until slightly thicker than unbeaten egg whites, and are then beaten or combined with egg whites, they are known as **whips, sponges** or **snows.** Whipped gelatins double in volume; snows and sponges, which include egg white, may triple. We also indicate in Molded Custard, 526, a method whereby you can get a jellied effect in the bottom of the mold and a custard on top.

For very rich gelatin puddings, see Bavarians, 527. For both Bavarians and clear fruit gelatins, you may line the mold with macaroons. Sprinkle them lightly with fruit juice, rum or cordial before adding the pudding or gelatin.

A word of caution: gelatin puddings with uncooked egg whites are often served to children or invalids over protracted periods of time. Since it has been discovered that biotin deficiency is occasionally induced by overproportionate quantities of raw egg white, we suggest varying such diets. Substitute instead some of the puddings we describe in which the egg whites are cooked like meringues.

To get a snow or whip texture, begin as for clear gelatin. Chill to a syrupy consistency. Using an electric mixer, a rotary beater or a ♎ blender, mix in a ♦ cold bowl or over ice. ♦ If the gelatin is not sufficiently chilled before whipping or before adding the egg white, it may revert to a clear jelly. Gelatins without cream or eggs ♦ must be refrigerated, but cannot be frozen. But Bavarians, mousses and ice creams, rich in cream and eggs, with gelatin as a stabilizer, may be solidified and stored in the freezer ♦ for not longer than 3 or 4 days. The use of gelatin in these puddings prevents the formation of

coarse crystals and produces a lovely smooth texture.

LEMON GELATIN

4 Servings

Soak:
  1 tablespoon gelatin
in:
  ¼ cup cold water
Dissolve it in:
  1½ cups boiling water
Add and stir until dissolved:
  ¾ cup sugar
  ¼ teaspoon salt
Add:
  ½ cup lemon juice
  (1 teaspoon grated lemon rind)
Pour the jelly into a wet mold. ♦ Chill 4 hours or more. Serve with:
  Cream or Custard Sauce, 565

ORANGE GELATIN

4 Servings

Soak:
  1 tablespoon gelatin
in:
  ¼ cup cold water
Dissolve it in:
  ½ cup boiling water
Add and stir until dissolved:
  ½ cup sugar
  ¼ teaspoon salt
Add:
  6 tablespoons lemon juice
  1½ cups orange juice
  (1½ teaspoons grated orange rind)
Pour jelly into a wet mold. Chill 4 hours or more. Unmold and serve with:
  Cream or Custard Sauce, 565

FRUIT MOLDED INTO LEMON OR ORANGE GELATIN

Prepare:

Lemon or Orange Gelatin, 523

◗ Chill it until nearly set. It will fall in sheets from a spoon. Combine it with well-drained:

Cooked or raw fruit

◗ Fresh pineapple must be poached before it is added to any gelatin mixture. Add:

(Nutmeats)

(Marshmallows cut into quarters)

◗ Do not use more than 2 cupfuls of solids in all. Pour jelly into a wet mold and ◗ chill 4 hours or more before serving.

PINEAPPLE GELATIN

8 Servings

◗ Note that fresh pineapple must be poached before it is added to any gelatin. Soak:

2 tablespoons gelatin

in:

1 cup cold water

Dissolve it in:

1 1/2 cups boiling pineapple juice

Add:

1 cup boiling water

Add and stir until dissolved:

3/4 cup sugar

1/8 teaspoon salt

◗ Chill the gelatin until it is about to set. It will fall in sheets from a spoon. Add:

2 1/2 cups canned, drained crushed pineapple

3 tablespoons lemon juice

Pour the jelly into a wet mold. ◗ Chill 4 hours or more. Unmold and serve with:

Cream or Custard Sauce, 565

FRUIT JUICE GELATIN

4 Servings

Soak:

1 tablespoon gelatin

in:

1/4 cup cold water

Dissolve it in:

3/4 cup boiling water

Add:

1 cup sweetened fruit juice: prune, apricot, peach or cooked pineapple

(2 tablespoons lemon juice)

and if not sweet enough, add:

Sugar

Chill gelatin. When gelatin is ◗ about to set, it will fall in sheets from the spoon. Add:

Drained diced fruit

Pour jelly into a wet mold and chill for 4 hours or more before serving.

QUICK FRUIT GELATIN

4 Servings

Dissolve:

1 package fruit-flavored gelatin

in:

1 cup boiling water

Chill rapidly by adding any but pineapple:

1 can frozen fruit juice: 6 oz.

Pour jelly into sherbet glasses. Chill further until firm.

MOCHA GELATIN

4 Servings

The subtle flavor of this gelatin comes from coffee combined with a syrup from canned fruit. Dress it up if you want with nuts or cream, but we like it served simply with a light custard sauce.

Prepare:

Fruit Juice Gelatin, above

substituting for the water:

1 cup very hot double-
    strength coffee
Omit the lemon juice. Serve with:
    Custard Sauce, 565

WINE GELATIN

                                  8 Servings
The proportions of water, fruit juice
and wine may be varied. If the wine
is not strong, use less water to dissolve the gelatin and increase the
amount of wine accordingly. This
makes a soft jelly of a very good consistency, suitable for serving in sherbet glasses or from a bowl. If a stiff
jelly is desired for molds, increase
the gelatin to 3 tablespoons.
Soak:
    2 tablespoons gelatin
in:
    ¼ cup cold water
Dissolve it in:
    ¾ cup boiling water
Stir in until dissolved:
    ½ cup or more sugar
It is difficult to give an accurate sugar
measurement. One-half cup is sufficient if both the orange juice and the
wine are sweet. Taste the combined
ingredients and stir in additional
sugar if needed. Cool these ingredients. Add:
    1¾ cups orange juice
    6 tablespoons lemon juice
    1 cup well-flavored wine
Pour the jelly into sherbet glasses.
Chill until firm.
Serve with:
    Cream, whipped cream, or
    Custard Sauce, 565

BLANCMANGE

                                  8 Servings
Blancmange, in America, is often a
cornstarch pudding, see 514, but the
true French type is made with almond milk and gelatin.

To prepare **Almond Milk**, pound in a
mortar to extract as much flavor as
possible from the almonds:
    ½ lb. blanched almonds
adding gradually:
    ¼ cup water
    ½ cup milk
Strain the liquid through a cloth.
Soak:
    1 tablespoon gelatin
in:
    ¼ cup water
Heat until scalded:
    1 cup cream
    ½ cup sugar
Dissolve the gelatin in the hot cream
mixture. Stir in the almond milk.
Add:
    1 tablespoon kirsch
▶ Chill it about 4 hours. Serve the
pudding in sherbet cups with:
    Fresh or stewed fruit

PERSIAN CREAM

                                  6 Servings
Soak:
    1 tablespoon gelatin
in:
    ¼ cup cold milk
Scald:
    1½ cups milk
Dissolve the gelatin in it. Beat:
    2 egg yolks
    ⅓ cup sugar
Beat a little of the hot milk into the
yolks, then return to saucepan. Cook
and stir these ingredients over ▶ very
low heat until they begin to thicken.
Cool. Add:
    1 teaspoon vanilla or rum
Whip until ▶ stiff, but not dry:
    2 egg whites
Fold them lightly into the gelatin
mixture. Chill for 4 hours or more.
Serve very cold with:
    Crushed fruit or fruit sauce

MOLDED CUSTARD

8 Servings

Place in the top of a double boiler ▶ over—not in—boiling water:

3 cups milk

Sprinkle over it:

1 tablespoon gelatin

1/2 cup sugar

Stir until ingredients are dissolved. Beat:

3 egg yolks

1/4 teaspoon salt

Pour a small quantity of the hot milk over the eggs to temper them, then add this mixture to the rest of the milk. Cook until thickened somewhat, stirring constantly. Remove from heat and add:

1 teaspoon vanilla

At this point decide if you want a molded custard all of one texture or if you prefer a clear jellied base with an opaque layer at the top of the mold. To get a mold of uniform texture, add while the gelatin mixture is hot:

3 stiffly beaten egg whites

If you prefer the clear jellied base and opaque top, cool the gelatin mixture slightly before adding the stiffly beaten whites. In either case, turn the mixture into a large mold or individual molds that have been rinsed in cold water. When set, unmold and serve with:

A fruit sauce, 563

FRUIT WHIPS

6 to 8 Servings

▶ Please read About Gelatin Puddings, 522. Oranges, raspberries, peaches, strawberries, apricots, prunes, etc.—raw or cooked—may be used alone or in combination. ▶ If fresh pineapple is preferred, it must be poached before being added to any gelatin mixture.

Stir:

1 teaspoon grated lemon rind

into:

7/8 cup sugar

Soak, according to the juiciness of the fruit:

2 1/2 teaspoons to 1 tablespoon gelatin

in:

1/4 cup cold water

Dissolve it in:

1/4 cup boiling water

Stir in the sugar until dissolved. Add:

3 tablespoons lemon juice

1 cup crushed or ᛘ blended fruit

Place the pan holding these ingredients in ice water. When they are chilled ▶ to a syrupy consistency, whip them with an eggbeater until frothy. Whip until stiff:

4 egg whites

Whip these ingredients into the gelatin mixture until the jelly holds its shape. Pour it into a wet mold. ▶ Chill 4 hours or more. Serve with:

Cream or Custard Sauce, 565

ᛘ BLENDER FRUIT WHIP

4 Servings

Cut into 16 pieces the contents of:

1 package frozen fruit: 10 oz.

Put into an electric blender:

1 tablespoon gelatin

2 tablespoons lemon juice

1/2 cup boiling water

Cover and blend for 40 seconds. Add:

2 unbeaten egg whites

Cover and blend 10 seconds. Continuing to blend, uncover the container and drop in, a few at a time, the pieces of still frozen fruit until they are all mixed in. Pour into a wet mold and chill 4 hours or more.

MARSHMALLOW PUDDING

6 to 8 Servings

Although this pudding calls for no marshmallows, the consistency is similar.

Sift:

1 cup sugar

Soak:

1½ tablespoons gelatin

in:

½ cup cold water

Dissolve it in:

½ cup boiling water

Cool these ingredients. Whip until stiff:

4 egg whites

Add the gelatin to the egg whites in a slow stream, whipping the pudding constantly. Add the sugar, ½ cupful at a time. Whip well after each addition. Add:

1 teaspoon vanilla

Continue to whip until the pudding thickens. ♦ Chill 4 hours or more. Serve with:

Custard Sauce, 565

Flavor the custard when it is cold with:

Cointreau, rum or sherry

or serve the pudding with:

Crushed sweetened fruit

★ PINEAPPLE SNOW

8 Servings

A refreshing Christmas pudding.

Soak:

1 tablespoon gelatin

in:

¼ cup cold water

Heat:

2 cups canned crushed pineapple

♦ If fresh pineapple is used, be sure it is poached before adding it to the gelatin mixture. Stir in:

1 cup sugar

⅛ teaspoon salt

When these ingredients are boiling, add the soaked gelatin. Remove pan from heat and stir until the gelatin is dissolved. ♦ Chill until it is about to set. Whip until stiff:

1 cup whipping cream

Add:

½ teaspoon vanilla

Fold in the pineapple mixture. Place pudding in a wet mold. Chill 4 hours or longer. Unmold and serve with:

(Maraschino cherries)

ABOUT BAVARIAN CREAMS

You can count on finding eggs combined with gelatin and cream as ingredients in a classic Bavarian. The additions of egg and cream are made when the gelatin mixture mounds slightly if dropped from a spoon. They are then chilled until firm. ♦ If Bavarian puddings are to be unmolded, chill them 12 hours or more. If served in sherbet glasses, chill 4 hours. Bavarians are often called "Cold Soufflés." If very heavy in egg and cream content, they may be frozen for a few days. They are frequently heightened by a collar or band of paper tied around the outside of the dish in which the soufflé is to be served, and extending a few inches above it. Remove the collar just before serving.

CABINET PUDDING OR BAVARIAN DE LUXE

10 Servings

Whose Cabinet? Cabinet de Diplomate. Where else could you find anything so smooth and suave?

Heat in the top of a double boiler ♦ over—not in—boiling water, until lukewarm:

5 eggs

Beat at medium speed for 7 minutes; then beat in:

¼ cup sugar

until a mayonnaise consistency is reached. Beat in an additional:

¼ cup sugar

◗ but do not overbeat or overheat. The somewhat thickened eggs should stand in soft peaks. Dissolve over hot water:

1½ tablespoons gelatin
¼ cup cold water

Fold the cooled gelatin very gently into the egg mixture. Chill the mixture, while you beat over a bowl of ice until stiff:

2 cups whipping cream

◗ Do not overbeat the cream. Let it still have a glistening finish when you combine it with the egg mixture. Dribble onto it:

2 teaspoons vanilla or 1 tablespoon kirsch or Grand Marnier

You may fold into it:

(⅓ cup preserved ginger or ½ cup sliced candied kumquats)

Chill this mixture until it is like heavy cream. Line a mold with:

Ladyfingers, 448

Build layers of rum- or lemon-sprinkled fruits and berries with ladyfinger crumbs, alternating with the Bavarian mixture. Repeat these layers until the mold is complete, with ladyfingers on top. ◗ Refrigerate about 12 hours before unmolding.

NESSELRODE PUDDING

Prepare:

Cabinet Pudding, above

You may use the fruits or not, as you like. Fold into it, after putting through a ricer:

2 cups slightly sweetened Boiled Chestnuts II, (I, 313)

5 oz. crumbled Glazed Chestnuts, 605

Serve it garnished with:

Crème Chantilly, 449

BAVARIAN BERRY CREAM

8 Servings

Crush:

1 quart hulled strawberries or raspberries

Add:

1 cup sugar

Let them stand 30 minutes. Soak:

2 teaspoons gelatin

in:

3 tablespoons water

Dissolve it in:

3 tablespoons boiling water

Stir this into the berries. You may add:

(1 tablespoon lemon juice)

Cool the gelatin. When it is about to set, whip and fold in lightly:

1 cup whipping cream

Pour the Bavarian cream into a wet mold. ◗ Chill for 12 hours if you plan to unmold it. Serve with:

Strawberry or Fruit Glaze, 505

HAZELNUT BAVARIAN CREAM

8 Servings

Soak:

1 tablespoon gelatin

in:

2 tablespoons cold water

Scald:

½ cup milk

Beat together:

¼ cup sugar
4 egg yolks
⅛ teaspoon salt

Combine the milk with the egg mixture ◗ by first pouring a little of the hot milk over the mixture and adding the rest gradually. Stir ◗ over—not in—boiling water until the ingredients begin to thicken. Stir in the soaked gelatin until dissolved. Grind and add:

³/₄ cup hazelnuts

Add:

1 teaspoon vanilla

Chill these ingredients until they are about to set.

Whip until stiff:

1 cup whipping cream

Fold into the other ingredients. Place the pudding in the dish from which it is to be served, or in a wet mold. Chill thoroughly if you plan to unmold it—12 hours or more. Serve with:

Raspberry syrup

CARAMEL OR MAPLE BAVARIAN CREAM

8 Servings

Soak:

1 tablespoon gelatin

in:

¹/₄ cup water

Prepare:

³/₄ cup Caramelized Sugar I, 232, or ¹/₂ cup maple syrup

When the sugar is slightly cooled, put it or the maple syrup in the top of a double boiler with:

1 cup hot milk

¹/₄ cup sugar

¹/₄ teaspoon salt

Stir over boiling water until these ingredients are dissolved. Pour part of this over:

3 beaten egg yolks

Return the sweetened yolks to the double boiler. Stir and cook the mixture over boiling water until it coats a spoon heavily. Stir in the soaked gelatin until it is dissolved. Cool the custard. Add:

1 teaspoon vanilla or 1 tablespoon rum

Whip and fold in:

1 cup whipping cream

Place the Bavarian in a wet mold. Chill at least 12 hours if you plan to unmold it.

CHOCOLATE OR COFFEE BAVARIAN

Add to any of the Bavarians calling for scalded milk:

2 oz. melted sweet chocolate and/or 2 teaspoons instant coffee

EGGLESS BAVARIAN CREAM

8 Servings

Not classic, but pleasant, and it will lend itself to all the variations in the previous recipes.

Soak:

1 tablespoon gelatin

in:

2 tablespoons cold water

Scald:

1¹/₂ cups milk

If a richer pudding is preferred, use instead ¹/₂ cup milk and 1 cup whipping cream. Add:

¹/₃ to ¹/₂ cup sugar

¹/₄ teaspoon salt

Stir the gelatin into this mixture until dissolved. Chill. As it thickens, flavor it with:

1¹/₂ teaspoons vanilla

(¹/₄ teaspoon almond extract)

Whip it with a wire whisk until fluffy. Beat until stiff:

1 cup whipping cream

Fold into gelatin mixture. Place pudding in a wet mold. If desired, alternate the pudding mixture in layers with:

6 broken macaroons or ladyfingers soaked in rum or dry sherry and

½ cup ground nutmeats,
  preferably almonds

♦ Chill the pudding at least 12 hours
if you plan to unmold it. Serve with:

Whole or crushed berries
  or stewed fruit and
  whipped cream

RENNET PUDDING OR JUNKET

4 Servings

♦ Please read about rennet, 236, before making this favorite English
dessert.
Put into the bowl in which the pudding will be served:

2 cups milk

warmed to exactly 98°. Add:

2 teaspoons sugar

Stir in:

2 teaspoons essence of rennet
  or 1 teaspoon prepared
  rennet
(2 teaspoons brandy)

Let the pudding stand about 1½
hours until it coagulates. Sprinkle
with:

Cinnamon or nutmeg

Serve cold.

MOLDED PINEAPPLE CREAM

4 Servings

Soak:

1 tablespoon gelatin

in:

¼ cup cold water

Combine and stir constantly over very
low heat until slightly thickened:

2 egg yolks
½ cup sugar
2 cups unsweetened cooked
  pineapple juice
⅛ teaspoon salt

Add the soaked gelatin. Stir until dissolved. Pour half of this mixture into
a wet mold. Chill it. Chill the remain-

ing gelatin until it begins to set. Then
whip and fold in:

½ cup whipping cream

Fill the mold. Chill until firm.

ABOUT CHARLOTTES

How dull seem the charlottes of our
youth, with only a cream and a
cherry, when compared with those
put together in the sophisticated soci-
ety we now seem to frequent!

Today's fillings include all kinds of
creams and Bavarians, nuts, angelica,
citron, jams, chestnuts, fruits and
ices. Whether the mold is lined with
ladyfingers, sponge or Génoise, it
may still be called a charlotte. For
combinations, see below.

CHARLOTTE RUSSE

6 Servings

Soak:

¾ tablespoon gelatin

in:

¼ cup cold water

Dissolve it in:

⅓ cup scalded milk

Beat in:

⅓ cup powdered sugar

Cool. Flavor with:

2 tablespoons strong coffee

Whip until stiff:

1 cup whipping cream

Fold it lightly into the chilled ingredients. Line a mold with:

Ladyfingers, 448

Pour the pudding into it. Chill thoroughly. Unmold and serve with:

Custard Sauce, 565,
  flavored with rum

CHOCOLATE CHARLOTTE

Prepare:

French Chocolate Mousse,
513 or Rum Chocolate
Mousse, 513

adding:

(**³/4 cup ground nut meats**)

Line a mold as described in About Dessert Molds, 521. Fill the lady-finger-lined mold with the mousse.

MAPLE CHARLOTTE

10 Servings

Soak:

1 tablespoon gelatin

in:

¹/4 cup cold water

Dissolve it in:

³/4 cup hot maple syrup

Chill until it falls in heavy sheets from a spoon.

Whip until the cream holds soft peaks:

2 cups whipping cream

Fold in with a spoon:

(**¹/2 cup chopped, blanched almonds**)

Fold in the gelatin until well blended. Line a bowl with pieces of:

Sponge Cake, 407, or Ladyfingers, 448

Pour the gelatin into it. Chill until firm. Unmold and serve garnished with:

Whipped cream

MOCHA MARSHMALLOW CREAM

6 Servings

Melt in the top of a double boiler ▸ over—not in—boiling water:

1 lb. diced marshmallows
2 oz. unsweetened chocolate
1 tablespoon sugar

in:

1 cup double-strength coffee

Stir and cook these ingredients until the marshmallows are dissolved. Chill the mixture until it is about to set. Whip and fold in:

1 cup whipping cream

Place in a wet ring mold. Chill at least 4 hours.

Invert and cover the top of the cream with:

Slivered toasted Brazil nuts or crushed nut brittle

INDIAN PUDDING

8 Servings

This dish is sometimes made with apples. In that case, add 2 cups thinly sliced apples and use, in all, 2 cups milk.

Preheat oven to 300°.

Boil in the top of a double boiler over direct heat:

4 cups milk

Stir in:

¹/3 cup cornmeal

Place these ingredients over boiling water. Cook them for about 15 minutes. Stir into them and cook for about 5 minutes:

³/4 cup dark molasses

Remove from heat. Stir in:

¹/4 cup butter
1 teaspoon salt
1 teaspoon ginger
3 tablespoons sugar
(**1 well-beaten egg**)
(**¹/2 cup raisins**)
(**¹/2 teaspoon cinnamon**)

Pour into a well-greased baking dish. To achieve a soft center, after 1 hour of baking, float over the top without stirring:

(**1 cup cold milk**)

Bake the pudding from 1¹/2 to 3 hours, the latter if you added milk. Serve pudding hot with:

Hard Sauce, 572, cream or ice cream

FARINA PUDDING

6 Servings

Try this for a finicky breakfaster.

Boil:

2 cups milk
¼ cup sugar
Add:
½ cup farina
Stir and cook the farina over low heat until thick.
Add and stir until melted:
1 tablespoon butter
Remove pan from heat. Beat in, one at a time:
2 egg yolks
Cool. Add:
1 teaspoon vanilla
(½ teaspoon grated lemon rind)
Whip until ◗ stiff, but not dry:
(2 egg whites)
Fold into the farina mixture. If used as a dessert, serve the pudding cold with:

> **Cream, tart fruit juice,
> stewed fruit, crushed
> sweetened berries or Hot
> Wine Sauce, 566, using
> claret**

ROTE GRÜTZE

4 Servings
This good German fruit pudding, Rote Grütze, long popular in our family, is usually made with rasp-berry juice. It is designed to end a meal; not, like the less sweet Fruit Soups, 114, to begin it. Strawberries, cherries or black currants may be used, but our favorite base is a combination of raspberry and strawberry juice, which may be strengthened with raspberry jelly or red wine. In winter a wonderfully fresh taste may be obtained if you cook frozen raspberries and strawberries and strain off the juice.
I. Bring to a boil:
2 cups fruit juice
Sweeten it palatably with:

Sugar
Season with:
⅛ teaspoon salt
Stir into the boiling juice:
⅓ cup farina
Cook this mixture in the top of a double boiler ◗ over—not in—boiling water about 20 minutes. Stir until it thickens. Pour into individual serving dishes. Chill. Serve very cold with:
Heavy cream
II. Substitute for the farina, above:
2½ tablespoons tapioca

CREAMY RICE PUDDING

12 Servings
This dessert is frequently served in Europe, where rice puddings are highly appreciated. Steam covered in the top of a double boiler over—not in—boiling water about 1 hour:
1 cup short- or medium-grain rice
6 cups hot milk
1 teaspoon salt
Stir frequently and watch that the water in the bottom pan does not boil off. When the rice is tender, cool slightly and add:
2 tablespoons butter
**2 teaspoons vanilla, or 1
teaspoon vanilla and 1
teaspoon lemon rind,
grated**
2 teaspoons sugar
Serve as a pudding, hot or cold, with:
> **Stewed or canned fruit,
> crushed sweetened berries
> or Jelly Sauce, 565, using
> quince jelly**
or serve with a combination of:
4 tablespoons sugar
1 tablespoon cinnamon

RICE PUDDING

6 to 8 Servings

Preheat oven to 325°.
Have ready:

    **2 cups short- or medium-
    grain Boiled Rice, (I, 189)**

Combine, beat well and add:

    1¹/₃ cups milk
    ¹/₈ teaspoon salt
    **4 to 6 tablespoons sugar or
    ¹/₂ cup brown sugar**
    1 tablespoon soft butter
    1 teaspoon vanilla
    2 to 4 eggs

Add:

    **¹/₂ teaspoon grated lemon
    rind**
    1 teaspoon lemon juice
    (¹/₃ cup raisins or dates)

Combine these ingredients lightly
with a fork. Grease a baking dish.
Cover the bottom and sides with:

    (Cake or cookie crumbs)

Put rice in dish and cover top with
more crumbs.
Bake the pudding until set—about 50
minutes. Serve hot or cold with:

    **Cream, Fruit Fondue
    Sauce, 563, fruit juice or
    Hot Wine Sauce, 566**

RICE AND FRUIT CREAM

5 Servings

Combine:

    **1 cup short- or medium-
    grain Boiled Rice, (I, 189)**
    **1 cup drained apricots,
    pineapple, etc.**

Whip until stiff:

    ¹/₂ cup whipping cream

Fold in the rice mixture. Add:

    (12 diced marshmallows)

Place the cream in individual dishes.
Chill thoroughly. You may top it
with:

    (Crushed nut brittle)

RICE PUDDING WITH WHIPPED CREAM

10 Servings

Have ready:

    **1 cup short- or medium-
    grained Boiled Rice, (I,
    189)**

Soak for 5 minutes:

    2 teaspoons gelatin

in:

    ¹/₄ cup cold water

Dissolve over heat. Add to the rice.
Stir in:

    6 tablespoons sugar
    **(¹/₂ cup shredded blanched
    almonds)**

Chill. Whip until stiff:

    2 cups whipping cream

Fold into the cream:

    2 teaspoons vanilla

Fold the cream into rice. Place in a
wet mold.
Chill 4 hours or more. Unmold and
serve very cold with:

    **Cold Jelly Sauce, 565, or
    hot Butterscotch Sauce, 569**

QUICK TAPIOCA CUSTARD

4 Servings

Combine and stir in the top of a double boiler:

    **3 tablespoons quick-cooking
    tapioca**
    ¹/₂ cup sugar
    ¹/₄ teaspoon salt
    1 or 2 beaten eggs
    2 cups milk

Cook these ingredients without stirring ♦ over—not in—rapidly boiling
water for 7 minutes. Stir and cook 5
minutes longer. Remove from heat.
The tapioca thickens as it cools. Fold
in gradually:

    **¹/₂ teaspoon vanilla or
    1 teaspoon grated orange
    or lemon rind**

Chill. Serve with:
>   Cream, fresh berries,
>   crushed or canned fruit, or
>   Chocolate Sauce, 567

Additions may be made to this recipe. In that case, the eggs may be omitted. Suggestions:
>   1/4 cup or more coconut or
>   toasted almonds
>   1/2 cup or more chopped dates
>   1 crushed or diced banana
>   1 cup sliced, drained, cooked
>   apples
>   1/2 cup fruit, soaked in wine or
>   liqueur

If the eggs are omitted, serve with:
>   Custard Sauce, 565

BUTTERSCOTCH TAPIOCA CUSTARD

4 Servings

Follow the preceding recipe for:
>   Quick Tapioca Custard

but omit the sugar. Melt:
>   2 tablespoons butter

Stir in until it melts and bubbles:
>   1/3 cup packed brown sugar

Add this mixture to the cooked tapioca.

EGGLESS CRUSHED-FRUIT TAPIOCA PUDDING

8 Servings

This may be made with pineapple, prunes, berries, etc.
Boil in the top of a double boiler over direct heat:
>   2 cups water

Combine and stir in gradually:
>   1/3 cup quick-cooking tapioca
>   1/2 cup sugar
>   1/4 teaspoon salt

When these ingredients are boiling, place them ♦ over—not in—rapidly boiling water. Cook and stir them

about 5 minutes. Remove from heat. Cool slightly. Fold in:
>   2 1/2 cups canned crushed
>   pineapple or 2 cups cooked
>   prune or apricot pulp or 2
>   cups crushed sweetened
>   berries
>   2 tablespoons lemon juice

Chill. This may be served in sherbet glasses with:
>   Whipped cream, plain
>   cream or Custard Sauce,
>   565

PEARL TAPIOCA PUDDING

8 Servings

Soak overnight, refrigerated:
>   1 cup pearl tapioca
in:
>   1 cup milk

Add these ingredients to:
>   3 cups milk
and cook them 3 hours in a double boiler ♦ over—not in—boiling water. Cool.
Preheat oven to 325°.
Beat and add:
>   5 egg yolks
>   Grated rind of 1 lemon
>   Juice of 1/2 lemon
>   3/4 cup sugar

Beat until ♦ stiff, but not dry:
>   5 egg whites

Line a baking dish with a layer of the tapioca mixture, a layer of the egg whites, another layer of tapioca and end with the egg whites on top. Bake about 15 minutes. Serve hot or cold without a sauce, or with one such as:
>   a hot fruit sauce, 563, 564

BREAD PUDDING WITH MERINGUE

6 Servings

Preheat oven to 350°.
Cut bread into slices and trim away

crusts. It should be measured lightly, not packed. Soak for 15 minutes:

> 3 **to 5 cups diced fresh bread or 3¹/₂ cups stale bread or stale cake**

in:

> 3 **cups warm milk, or 2 cups milk and 1 cup fruit juice**
> ¹/₄ **teaspoon salt**

Combine and beat well:

> 3 **egg yolks**
> ¹/₃ **to ¹/₂ cup sugar**
> 1 **teaspoon vanilla**
> (¹/₂ **teaspoon nutmeg)**

Add:

> **Grated rind and juice of ¹/₂ lemon**
> (¹/₄ **cup raisins, dates or nutmeats, or ¹/₂ cup drained crushed pineapple, or ¹/₄ cup orange marmalade)**

Pour these ingredients over the soaked bread. Stir them lightly with a fork until well blended. If preferred, the meringue may be dispensed with and the stiffly beaten egg whites may be folded in at this time. Bake the pudding in a baking dish set in a pan of hot water about 45 minutes. Cool pudding. Cover with:

> **(Meringue I, 502)**

Bake in a 300° oven until the meringue is set, about 15 minutes. Serve hot with:

> **Hard Sauce, 572, Jelly Sauce, 565, or cream, fruit juice or dabs of tart jelly**

BROWN BETTY

5 Servings

Preheat oven to 350°.
Combine:

> 1 **cup dry bread or graham cracker crumbs**
> ¹/₄ **cup melted butter**

Line the bottom of a baking dish with one-third of the crumb mixture. Prepare:

> 2¹/₂ **cups peeled, diced or sliced apples or peaches; or cherries or cranberries**

Sift:

> ³/₄ **cup packed brown sugar**
> 1 **teaspoon cinnamon**
> ¹/₄ **teaspoon each nutmeg and cloves**
> ¹/₂ **teaspoon salt**

Add:

> 1 **teaspoon grated lemon rind**
> (1 **teaspoon vanilla)**

Place half of the apples in the dish. Cover the layer with half of the sugar mixture. Sprinkle with:

> 1 **tablespoon lemon juice**

Add:

> 2 **tablespoons water**

Cover the apples with a third of the crumb mixture and:

> (¹/₄ **cup raisins or currants)**

Add the remaining apples and sprinkle them as before with the sugar mixture and:

> 2 **tablespoons lemon juice**
> 2 **tablespoons water**
> (¹/₄ **cup raisins or currants)**

Place the last third of the crumb mixture on top. Cover the dish and bake about 40 minutes, until the apples are nearly tender. Remove cover, increase heat to 400° and let pudding brown for about 15 minutes. Serve hot with:

> **Cream, Hard Sauce, 572, or Lemon Sauce, 563**

PRUNE OR APRICOT BETTY

Follow the preceding recipe for:

> **Brown Betty**

Use only:

> 2 **tablespoons sugar**

Substitute for the apples:

1½ cups stewed, drained,
      sweetened prunes or
      apricots
Substitute for the lemon juice and
water:
   ¾ cup prune or apricot juice

BAKED PINEAPPLE BETTY

4 Servings

This may be made in advance. It is
equally good served hot or very cold.
Preheat oven to 325°.
Cream until light:
   ½ cup butter
   ¾ cup sugar
Beat in:
   5 egg yolks
   ¼ cup dry bread crumbs
   1 cup drained crushed
      pineapple
   1 tablespoon lemon juice
Whip until stiff, then fold in:
   3 egg whites
Place the mixture in a baking dish.
Cover with Meringue I, 502, and
bake it, set in a pan of hot water,
about 30 minutes. Serve with:
   Cream or whipped cream

★ BAKED FIG PUDDING

14 Servings

Preheat oven to 325°.
Beat until soft:
   ½ cup butter
Add and beat until fluffy:
   2 eggs
   1 cup molasses
Add:
   2 cups finely chopped dried
      figs
   ½ teaspoon grated lemon rind
   1 cup buttermilk
   (½ cup broken black walnut
      meats)
Sift before measuring:
   2½ cups all-purpose flour

Resift with:
   ½ teaspoon baking soda
   2 teaspoons double-acting
      baking powder
   1 teaspoon salt
   1 teaspoon cinnamon
   ½ teaspoon nutmeg
One teaspoon ginger may be substituted for the cinnamon and nutmeg.
Stir the sifted ingredients into the pudding mixture. Bake in a greased 9-inch
tube pan about 1 hour. Serve hot with:
   **Brown-Sugar Hard Sauce,
      572, Sabayon Sauce,
      565–566, or Hot Wine
      Sauce, 566**

★ BAKED DATE RING OR CHRISTMAS WREATH

6 Servings

You may bake this in a ring mold.
When cold, unmold it onto a platter,
cover it well with whipped cream and
stud it with maraschino cherries. Surround it with holly leaves. Although
very effective this way, it tastes almost as good baked in a shallow pan,
cut into squares and served with
Foamy Sauce, 573.
Preheat oven to 350°.
Prepare:
   1 cup pitted minced dates
   1 cup chopped nutmeats
Combine these ingredients with:
   ½ cup white or packed brown
      sugar
   1 tablespoon all-purpose
      flour
   1 teaspoon double-acting
      baking powder
   2 beaten egg yolks
   1 teaspoon vanilla
Fold in:
   2 stiffly beaten egg whites
Bake the pudding in a well-greased
9-inch ring mold about 30 minutes.
You may sprinkle over it, while hot,

¹/₄ cup Madeira or sherry or 3 table-spoons brandy or rum. Let it cool in the pan.
Whip until stiff:
> **1 cup whipping cream**

Fold in:
> **2 teaspoons powdered sugar**
> **1 teaspoon vanilla**

Garnish the ring as suggested above.

★ BAKED PLUM PUDDING

10 Servings

Not for Jack Horner's legendary thumb, but a rewarding confection just the same.
Preheat oven to 375°.
Beat until soft:
> **¹/₂ cup butter**

Add gradually and cream
> **1 cup sugar**

Beat in, one at a time:
> **6 eggs**

Combine:
> **1 cup raisins, currants and pecans**

Sprinkle lightly with:
> **Flour**

Add these ingredients to the butter mixture. Combine:
> **2 cups bread crumbs**
> **2 teaspoons cinnamon**
> **¹/₂ teaspoon cloves**
> **¹/₂ teaspoon allspice**

Stir these ingredients into the butter mixture. Bake in a greased pan or baking dish about 30 minutes. Serve with:
> **Hard Sauce, 572, Lemon Sauce, 563, or Hot Wine Sauce, 566**

COTTAGE PUDDING

6 Servings

Preheat oven to 400°.
Follow the recipe for:
> **One-Egg Cake, 425**

For a new fillip, line a greased 8 × 8-inch pan with:
> **(1 cup heated marmalade)**

Pour the batter over the marmalade. Marmalade or none, bake the pudding about 25 minutes. Serve cut into squares with:
> **Crushed fruit, stewed fruit, Fluffy Hard Sauce, 572, Raisin Sauce, 564, Coffee Sauce, 570, Hot Wine Sauce, 566, or Hot Brown-Sugar Sauce, 569**

PANCAKE AND WAFFLE DESSERTS

Serve:
> **Pancakes or waffles**

spread with:
> **Thick cultured sour cream**
> **Strawberry or other preserves**

or serve with:
> **Crushed sweetened berries or fruit, or with Sauce Cockaigne, 564**

CHOCOLATE FEATHER PUDDING

8 Servings

Perhaps this should be placed among the steamed puddings, but they are more troublesome and this one might be neglected in such company. It is an inexpensive and delightful dessert.
Preheat oven to 350°.
Sift:
> **1 cup sugar**

Beat until light:
> **1 egg**

Stir in sugar gradually. When these ingredients are well blended, stir in:
> **1 cup milk or coffee**
> **1 tablespoon melted butter**
> **1¹/₂ oz. melted unsweetened chocolate**

Sift:

1¹/₂ cups all-purpose flour

Resift with:

¹/₄ teaspoon salt

**1¹/₂ teaspoons double-acting
baking powder**

Stir these ingredients into the egg mixture. Add:

¹/₂ teaspoon vanilla

Place the batter in well-greased deep custard cups—about two-thirds full. Cover with foil. Steam in the oven by setting cups in a pan of hot water, about 30 minutes, or place pan over low heat on top of stove for same length of time. Remove foil and serve pudding at once with:

Vanilla Sauce, 571

flavored with:

(Rum)

SWEET-POTATO PUDDING

6 Servings

Preheat oven to 350°.

Combine and beat well:

**2 cups cooked, mashed sweet
potatoes**

1 cup sugar

¹/₂ cup melted butter

6 beaten egg yolks

**1¹/₂ teaspoons grated lemon
rind**

1 cup orange juice

**¹/₄ teaspoon nutmeg or 2
tablespoons rum**

Fold in:

2 stiffly beaten egg whites

Bake pudding in a greased baking dish about 1 hour. Before baking, the top may be sprinkled with:

(Sliced citron)

(Broken nutmeats)

After the pudding is baked and cooled, it may also be topped with Meringue I, 502, made with the remaining egg whites. Bake in a 325° oven about 15 minutes.

PERSIMMON PUDDING

8 Servings

Best made with the small native *Diospyros virginiana,* which give a waxy but not tough consistency to the pudding. The large Japanese *Diospyros kaki* do not have enough flavor to warrant using.

Preheat oven to 325°.

Put through a colander:

Persimmons

There should be about 2 cups of pulp.

Beat in:

3 eggs

**1¹/₄ cups sugar: white or light
brown**

1 cup all-purpose flour

**1 teaspoon double-acting
baking powder**

1 teaspoon baking soda

¹/₂ teaspoon salt

¹/₂ cup melted butter

2¹/₂ cups light cream

2 teaspoons cinnamon

1 teaspoon ginger

**¹/₂ teaspoon freshly grated
nutmeg**

One cupful raisins or nutmeats may be added to the batter. Bake the pudding in a greased 9 × 9-inch baking dish about 1 hour or until firm. Serve with:

Cream or Hard Sauce, 572

UNCOOKED DATE LOAF

12 Servings

Crush:

¹/₂ lb. graham crackers

Remove pits and cut into pieces:

1 lb. dates: 2 cups

Cut into pieces:

¹/₂ lb. marshmallows

Chop fine:

1 cup pecan meats

Whip until stiff:

1 cup whipping cream

Fold in:
1 teaspoon vanilla
Combine half the cracker crumbs with the dates, marshmallows, nuts and whipped cream. Shape into a roll. Roll it in the remaining cracker crumbs. Chill 12 hours. Cut into slices and serve with:
Cream or whipped cream

ABOUT STEAMED PUDDINGS

To steam pudding mixtures in a steamer, use pudding molds or cans with tightly fitting lids. First, grease insides of molds well, then sprinkle with sugar. Containers should be ◗ only two-thirds full. Place molds on a trivet in a heavy kettle over 1 inch of boiling water. Cover kettle closely. Use high heat at first, then, as the steam begins to escape, low heat for the rest of the cooking.

◗ To steam pudding mixtures in a ✪ pressure cooker, use tightly lidded molds or cans as described above and ◗ fill only two-thirds full. Place them on a rack in the bottom of the cooker, allowing space between both the molds and the walls of the cooker. Add boiling water ◗ until it is halfway up the sides of the molds.

If the steaming period for a regular steamer is 30 minutes, steam with vent off for 5 minutes, then pressure-cook at 15 pounds for 10 minutes. If steaming for 45 minutes to 1¹/₂ hours is called for, steam without closing the vent for 25 minutes, then pressure-cook at 15 pounds pressure for 25 minutes. If steaming for 2 to 4 hours is called for, steam without closing the vent for 30 minutes, then pressure-cook at 15 pounds pressure for 50 minutes. ◗ After steaming, re-

duce the heat at once. True steamed puddings need complete circulation of steam, so do not expect good results if you use a greased double boiler. Always ◗ before unmolding, take the lid from the mold and allow the pudding to rest long enough to let excess steam escape. The pudding will be less apt to crack in unmolding.

▲ In high altitudes, reduce the leavening by half the required amount.

STEAMED BROWN PUDDING

14 Servings
To steam or ✪ pressure-cook and unmold, see About Steamed Puddings, at left.
Combine and blend well:
1 cup packed brown sugar
¹/₂ cup shortening
Add:
1 cup milk
1 cup molasses
1 cup dry bread crumbs
2 beaten eggs
2 cups chopped seeded raisins
Sift before measuring:
2 cups all-purpose flour
Resift with:
2 teaspoons double-acting baking powder
¹/₂ teaspoon baking soda
1 teaspoon cinnamon
¹/₂ teaspoon each ginger, cloves and grated nutmeg
Add sifted ingredients to the molasses mixture. Pour batter into a well-greased pudding mold. Steam 1¹/₂ hours. Serve hot with:
Hard Sauce, 572, or Foamy Sauce, 573

★ STEAMED FRUIT SUET
   PUDDING

                    12 servings

Less cooking is needed here, as the
thickener is bread crumbs. To steam
or ✪ pressure-cook and unmold, see
About Steamed Puddings, 539.
Beat until soft:

   **1 cup very finely chopped
       beef suet: ¹/₂ lb.**

Add gradually:

   1 cup sugar

When these ingredients are well
blended, beat in:

   3 egg yolks

Stir in:

   **1 cup milk
   3 tablespoons brandy**

Put through a grinder and add:

   **1 lb. figs or dates or 2 cups
       peeled sliced apples
   (1 cup chopped pecans or
       walnuts)**

Grate and add:

   **2 teaspoons orange rind
   1 teaspoon freshly ground
       nutmeg or ginger**

Combine and add:

   **1¹/₂ cups dry bread crumbs
   2 teaspoons double-acting
       baking powder**

Whip until stiff, then fold in:

   3 egg whites

Pour the ingredients into a greased
mold. Steam slowly 4 hours. Serve
with:

       **Hot Sabayon Sauce, 565, or
       Hot Wine Sauce, 566**

Flavor the sauce with:

   (2 teaspoons or more brandy)

★ STEAMED DATE PUDDING

                    8 Servings

Not so rich as Steamed Fruit Suet
Pudding. To steam or ✪ pressure-
cook and unmold, see About Steamed
Puddings, 539.
Sift:

   1 cup packed brown sugar

Beat until soft:

   ¹/₄ cup butter

Add the sugar gradually. Blend these
ingredients until they are creamy.
Beat in:

   **1 egg
   ¹/₂ teaspoon vanilla**

Sift before measuring:

   1¹/₄ cups all-purpose flour

Resift with:

   **2²/₃ teaspoons double-acting
       baking powder
   ¹/₂ teaspoon salt**

Add sifted ingredients to butter mixture in 3 parts, alternately with:

   1 cup milk

Beat batter until smooth after each
addition. Fold in:

   **1 cup chopped dates
   1 cup broken nutmeats**

Pour into a greased pudding mold.
Cover closely. Steam 2 hours. Serve
hot with:

       **Foamy Sauce, 573, or Hard
       Sauce, 572**

STEAMED CHOCOLATE
PUDDING

                    6 Servings

This is richer than Chocolate Feather
Pudding, which may also be steamed
in a mold. To steam or ✪ pressure-
cook and unmold, see About Steamed
Puddings, 539.
Beat until light:

   6 egg yolks

Beat in gradually:

   1 cup sugar

Stir in:

   **³/₄ cup grated unsweetened
       chocolate
   2 tablespoons finely crushed**

crackers or toasted bread
crumbs
  1 teaspoon double-acting
baking powder
  1 teaspoon vanilla
  1/2 teaspoon cinnamon
  (1/2 cup grated nutmeats)
Beat until ◗ stiff, but not dry:
  6 egg whites
Fold them lightly into the batter. Pour
into a greased pudding mold. Steam
1 1/2 hours. Serve with:
  Hard Sauce, 572, or cream

STEAMED CARAMEL PUDDING
      6 Servings
Try this as a company pudding. To
steam or ◒ pressure-cook and unmold, see About Steamed Puddings,
539.
Melt in a heavy skillet:
  1/3 cup sugar
When it is light brown, stir in ◗ very
slowly:
  3/4 cup hot milk
Cool this syrup. Beat until soft:
  2 tablespoons butter
Beat in one at a time:
  5 egg yolks
Add the syrup and:
  1 teaspoon vanilla
  1 1/2 tablespoons all-purpose
flour
  1 cup ground unblanched
almonds
Beat batter until smooth. Whip ◗ until
stiff, but not dry:
  5 egg whites
Fold them lightly into the batter. Pour
into a greased pudding mold sprinkled with:
  Sugar
Cover closely. Steam 1 hour. Serve
hot with:
  Whipped cream or Sauce
Cockaigne, 564

STEAMED APPLE MOLASSES
PUDDING
      6 Servings
To steam or ◒ pressure-cook and unmold, see About Steamed Puddings,
539.
Cream until fluffy:
  1/4 cup butter
  1/2 cup packed brown sugar
Beat in:
  1 egg
  1/2 cup molasses
  1 tablespoon grated orange
rind
Measure:
  1 1/2 cups sifted all-purpose
flour
Resift with:
  1/2 teaspoon baking soda
  1 teaspoon double-acting
baking powder
  1 teaspoon each ginger and
cinnamon
Add these ingredients to the butter
mixture, alternately with:
  1/2 cup buttermilk
Stir in:
  1 cup chopped apples
Place the pudding in a greased mold.
Steam it 1 1/2 hours. Serve with:
  Lemon Sauce, 563, or Hard
Sauce, 572

★ STEAMED PLUM PUDDING
      24 Servings
A truly festive Christmas dish that
needs patience in the making. ◗ The
slow six-hour cooking is necessary,
so that all the suet melts before the
flour particles burst. If the pudding
cooks too fast and the flour grains
burst before the fat melts, the pudding will be close and hard. To steam
and unmold, see About Steamed Puddings, 539.
Sift:

1 cup all-purpose flour

Prepare and dredge lightly with part of the flour:

1 lb. chopped suet: 2 cups
1 lb. seeded raisins
1 lb. washed dried currants
1/2 lb. chopped citron

Resift the remaining flour with:

1 grated nutmeg
1 tablespoon cinnamon
1/2 tablespoon mace
1 teaspoon salt
6 tablespoons sugar or 1/2 cup packed brown sugar

Combine the dredged and the sifted ingredients.

Add:

7 egg yolks
1/4 cup cream
1/2 cup brandy or sherry
3 cups grated dry bread crumbs, white or rye

The bread crumbs help make the pudding light.

Whip until stiff:

7 egg whites

Fold them lightly into the raisin mixture. Pour the batter into a covered greased gallon mold and steam 6 hours. Serve with:

Hot Wine Sauce, 566, or Hard Sauce, 572

To store plum pudding for future use, cool, and pour over it:

1/2 cup brandy or applejack

Cover and store. Heat through in double boiler at least an hour before serving.

ABOUT SAVORIES

To most Americans, savories seem curious desserts. Of course, ours must also seem strange to the English—for, to them, the word "dessert" signifies fruit. Their term for our cold desserts is "sweets," and they call our hot ones "puddings."

Traditionally English, savories are a course presented before the fruit or after the sweet to cut the sugar taste before the port is served. They function like an hors d'oeuvre, although they are slightly larger in size. Try oysters or chicken livers in bacon; also sardine, caviar and roe crêpes; or pancakes or a tomato tart; deviled or curried seafood tarts or toasted cheese rolls. If you are serving wine, choose cheese straws or cheese-and-cracker combinations rather than the fishy savories.

ABOUT DESSERT CHEESES

Dessert cheeses may be served after the roast, with the same red wine that has accompanied that course; or after the salad, if, of course, the salad has not been served as a first course. Cheeses may also be served following the sweet or with a suitable dessert fruit such as apples, pears, grapes, cherries, plums or melons. Cheeses should always be served at a temperature of about 70°. Some types which are best when *coulant*, or runny, should be removed from refrigeration 3 to 6 hours before serving.

Usually some pats of sweet butter are added to the cheese-board. Toast, crackers, pumpernickel, crusty French Bread, 306, or Sour Rye, 311, follows the cheese on a separate tray. Salted, toasted or freshly shelled nuts, roasted chestnuts, celery or fennel make pleasant accessories. Try mixing mild cheeses with the more highly ripened aromatic or smoked ones.

Above all, remember that cheeses have their own seasons. And choose varieties that are in season. If you must store them, see 194. Below are listed some favorite dessert cheeses.

Soft types include uncrusted, unripened cheeses like Petit Gervais and Petit Suisse, Ricotta and Coulommiers; as well as those which are ripened and have soft edible crusts, such as Brie, Camembert, Liederkranz and Poona.

Among the semihards are the famous *fromages persillés*, or mold-ripened blue-greens, in which the mold patterns the cream-colored bases in traceries resembling parsley. The interior mold, which contributes to the characteristic flavor, must be distinguished from green mold on the exterior of the cheese, which may be harmless but should be removed.

The famous blues include Stilton, Gorgonzola, Bleu, Dorset Vinney and Roquefort. Other well-known semihard dessert cheeses are Muenster, Port du Salut, Bel Paese and Gammelost.

Hard types, from which come the very best cheeses for cooking, afford many choice ones for dessert: cheddar, Gruyère, Provolone, Gjetost, Emmentaler, Cheshire and Edam, to name a few.

DESSERT CHEESE MIX

Many people like to mix sweet butter with the stronger cheeses in serving them for dessert. The combinations are legion; for others, see 74. This one is a favorite of our friend Helmut Ripperger, who likes to prepare it at the table. However, sometimes these mixtures are made in advance, formed into a large ball, and rolled in toasted bread crumbs or nuts.

▶ Have ingredients at room temperature.

Mix:

   2 parts Roquefort cheese
   1 part sweet butter

Add enough:

   Armagnac or your favorite
   brandy

to make a spreadable soft paste. Serve with:

   Toasted crackers

POTTED CHEESE

                              About ³/₄ Cup

If you would like to make up a combination of cheeses to keep, try one based on a mixture of:

   4 oz. cheese
   2 oz. butter
   3 tablespoons port, sherry or
   brandy

Season to taste with:

   Pepper or cayenne
   (Mace)

COEUR A LA CRÈME OR
FRENCH CHEESE CREAM

                                   6 Servings

When the fruit is prime, this very simple dessert is as good as any elaborate concoction we know of or use.

Beat until soft:

   1 lb. rich firm cream cheese
   2 tablespoons cream
   ¹/₈ teaspoon salt

Have ready:

   1 cup cultured sour cream or
   whipped cream

Fold the cheese into the cream. Place these ingredients in a wet mold, in individual molds, or in the traditional heart-shaped wicker basket, shown here, lined with moistened cheesecloth. Chill the cheese thoroughly. Unmold it. Serve with:

> Fresh unhulled
> strawberries, or
> raspberries or other fresh
> fruit, or Cherry Sauce, 563

COTTAGE OR CREAM CHEESE OR YOGURT DRESSING

Sweeten:

> Cottage or cream cheese or
> yogurt

with:

> White or brown sugar
> Vanilla

Sprinkle the top with:

> Cinnamon

Serve the mixture very cold with:

> Stewed cherries, crushed
> strawberries, skinned,
> sliced apricots or peaches,
> pared apples,
> pomegranates, green
> grapes or sliced melon

BAR-LE-DUC

About 1 Cup

A pleasant summer dish. Serve it with toasted crackers.

Stir to a smooth paste:

> ³/₄ cup firm cream cheese
> 1 or 2 tablespoons cream

Fold in:

> 2 tablespoons currant
> preserves or Bar-le-Duc
> Preserves, 672

Refrigerate to firm the dessert, but serve at about 70°.

LIPTAUER CHEESE

About 2 Cups

If you can't buy the real thing, try this savory cheese made by mixing together, until well blended:

> ¹/₂ lb. dry cottage cheese
> ¹/₂ lb. soft butter
> ¹/₂ teaspoon paprika
> ¹/₂ teaspoon caraway seeds
> 1 teaspoon chopped capers
> ¹/₂ teaspoon anchovy paste
> ¹/₂ teaspoon mild prepared
> mustard
> 1 tablespoon chopped
> chives

Mold. Serve within 6 hours of mixing, as the taste of the chives may grow strong.

FROZEN DESSERTS AND
SWEET SAUCES

Molds, whether of metal—such as the proud rooster and the classic melon on the left—or of ceramic, on the right, do much to enhance bombes, 551, mousses, 554, and Bavarians, 527. Also presented above on a raised milk glass platter is a bombe whose white mold is shown reversed and used as a sympathetic flower container with a white and green arrangement of caladium, calla leaves and spathiphyllum blooms. The antique sauceboat in the left middle-ground holds a variety of sweet sauces. Between the rooster and the melon mold are individual Frozen Orange Surprises, 558. In the foreground lies the dasher from the ice cream freezer shown 548. The texture of frozen desserts depends on how long and at what speed you turn this vital tool.

CHURNED ICE CREAMS
AND ICES

A century and a half ago the youthful Stendhal, when he first tasted ice cream, exclaimed: "What a pity this isn't a sin!" Nowadays, with electric churning and plentiful ice, few people recall the shared excitement of the era when making ice cream was a rarely scheduled event. Then the iceman brought to the back door, on special order, a handsome 2-foot-square cube of cold crystal, and everyone in the family took a turn at the crank. The critical question among us children was, of course, who might lick the dasher—that portion of the freezing equipment which defies modernization and which is shown in the foreground above. For no power-driven machine has yet been invented that can achieve a comparable texture. Even French Pot, the very best commercial method for making ice cream, calls for finishing by hand.

Ice creams are based on ♦ carefully cooked ♦ well-chilled syrups and heavy custards, added to ♦ unwhipped cream. ♦ No form of vanilla flavoring can surpass that of vanilla sugar or of the bean itself, steeped in a hot syrup. If sweetened frozen fruits are incorporated into the cream mixture instead of fresh fruits, be sure to adjust sugar content accordingly.

◗ Make up mixtures for churn-frozen ice creams the day before you freeze, to increase yield and to produce a smoother-textured cream. ◗ In churn-freezing ice creams and ices, fill the container only two-thirds full to permit expansion. ◗ To pack the freezer, allow 4 parts chipped or cracked ice to 1 part coarse rock salt. Pack about one-third of the freezer with ice and add layers of salt and ice around the container until the freezer is full. Allow the pack to stand about 3 minutes before you start turning—slowly at first, about 40 revolutions a minute, until a slight pull is felt, then triple speed for 5 or 6 minutes. If any additions, such as finely cut candied or fresh fruits or nuts, are to be made, do so at this point. Then repack and taper off the churning to about 80 revolutions a minute for a few minutes more. The cream should be ready in 10 to 20 minutes, depending on quantity.

If the ice cream or ice is to be used at once, it should be frozen harder than if you plan to serve it later. Should the interval be 2 hours or more, packing will firm it. ◗ To pack, pour off the salt water in the freezer and wipe off the lid. Remove the dasher carefully, making sure that no salt or water gets into the cream container. Scrape the cream down from the sides of the container. Place a cork in the lid and replace the lid. Repack the container in the freezer with additional ice and salt, using the same proportions as before. Cover the freezer with wet newspapers, burlap or other heavy material.

The cream should be smooth when served. If it proves granular, you used too much salt in the packing mixture,

overfilled the inner container with the ice cream mixture, or turned too rapidly. ✳ If making a large quantity with the idea of storing some in the deep-freeze, package in sizes you plan serving. Do not store longer than 1 month. Should ice cream be allowed to melt even slightly and then be refrozen, it loses in volume and even more in good texture. As we have said, texture also suffers if you use an electric freezer. If you do so, follow manufacturer's directions.

GARNISHES AND ADDITIONS TO ICE CREAM

You may add to ice cream, when it is in a partially frozen state, allowing the following amounts per quart:

> **1 cup toasted chopped nuts**
> **1 cup finely crushed Nut Brittle, 593**
> **1/8 cup preserved chopped ginger and 1 tablespoon of the syrup**
> **1 cup crushed chocolate molasses chips**
> **1 cup crushed Macaroons, 469, plus 2 tablespoons sherry or liqueur**
> **1/2 cup Polvo de Amor, 245**

For fruit additions, see Fruit Ice Creams, 548. To garnish ice cream, add just before serving:

> **Chopped nuts or shredded coconut**
> **Candied violets**
> **Chopped candied citrus peel or other candied fruits**
> **Crystallized angelica, cut in tiny fancy shapes**
> **Decorettes**
> **Shaved or chopped sweet or bitter chocolate**
> **Marzipan fruits or rosettes**
> **Sweet Sauces, 563**

VANILLA ICE CREAM I

About 9 Servings

Scald over low heat, but do not boil:

1 cup cream

Stir in, until dissolved:

¾ cup sugar

⅛ teaspoon salt

If you have a vanilla bean, add to the hot mixture:

Seeds scraped from a 2-inch section of vanilla bean

If you do not have a bean, add after chilling:

1 ½ teaspoons vanilla

Chill, Add:

3 cups cream

To churn-freeze the ice cream, see 546. Serve with:

Tutti Frutti, 674, Cherry Jubilee Sauce, 564, a heavy liqueur, or a chocolate sauce, 567

DELMONICO ICE CREAM I, OR CRÈME GLACÉE

About 9 Servings

Scald over low heat, but do not boil:

1 ½ cups milk

Stir in, until dissolved:

¾ cup sugar

⅛ teaspoon salt

Pour the milk slowly over:

2 or 3 beaten egg yolks

Beat these ingredients until well blended. Stir and cook in a double boiler ◗ over—not in—boiling water until thick enough to coat the back of a spoon. Chill. Add and fold into the custard:

1 tablespoon vanilla

1 cup whipping cream

1 cup cream

To churn-freeze the ice cream, see 546. Serve with:

Crushed Nut Brittle, 593

CARAMEL ICE CREAM

Prepare:

Vanilla or Delmonico Ice Cream, at left

Add:

2 to 4 tablespoons Caramelized Sugar I, 232

To churn-freeze and serve, see 546. Garnish with:

Chopped pecans or toasted almonds

PEPPERMINT-STICK ICE CREAM

About 12 Servings

Grind or crush:

½ lb. peppermint-stick candy

Soak for 12 hours, refrigerated, in:

2 cups milk

Add:

1 cup cream

1 cup whipping cream

To churn-freeze and serve, see 546. Serve with:

Shaved sweet chocolate, 243, or Chocolate Sauce Cockaigne, 567

CHOCOLATE ICE CREAM

About 8 Servings

Dissolve in the top of a double boiler ◗ over—not in—boiling water:

2 oz. unsweetened chocolate

in:

2 cups milk

Stir in:

1 cup sugar

⅛ teaspoon salt

Remove from heat. Beat with a wire whisk until cool and fluffy. Add:

1½ teaspoons vanilla

1 cup whipping cream

1 cup cream

To churn-freeze and serve, see 546. You may serve it in:

(Meringues, 375)

with:

(A chocolate sauce, 567)

COFFEE ICE CREAM

About 9 Servings

Scald over low heat, but do not boil:

2¹/₂ cups milk

Stir in, until dissolved:

1¹/₂ cups sugar

Pour the milk slowly over:

2 beaten eggs

Beat until well blended. Stir and cook in a double boiler ♦ over—not in—boiling water until thick enough to coat the back of a spoon. Chill. Add:

¹/₂ cup strong cold coffee
¹/₂ teaspoon salt
1 cup whipping cream

Partly churn-freeze these ingredients, 546, and when almost frozen, add:

1 teaspoon vanilla
3 tablespoons rum

Finish freezing.

Garnish with:

Shaved sweet
chocolate, 243

★PISTACHIO ICE CREAM

About 9 Servings

A pretty Christmas dessert served in a meringue tart garnished with whipped cream and cherries. Shell and blanch, 237:

4 oz. pistachio nuts

Pound them in a mortar with:

A few drops rose water

Add to them:

¹/₄ cup sugar
¹/₄ cup cream
1 teaspoon vanilla
¹/₂ teaspoon almond extract
A little green vegetable
coloring

Stir these ingredients until the sugar is dissolved. Heat, but do not boil:

1 cup cream

Add and stir until dissolved:

³/₄ cup sugar
¹/₈ teaspoon salt

Chill these ingredients. Add the pistachio mixture and:

2 cups whipping cream
1 cup cream

To churn-freeze and serve, see 546.

FRUIT ICE CREAMS

About 9 Servings

Delicious fruit creams can be made using:

2 cups sweetened puréed or
finely sliced fruit—
greengage plums, mangoes,
peaches, apricots or
bananas

Add:

¹/₄ teaspoon salt
Lemon juice to taste
2 cups whipping cream
1 cup cream

To churn-freeze the cream, see 546.

APRICOT OR PEACH ICE CREAM

About 9 Servings

Peel, slice and mash:

4 lb. ripe peaches or apricots

Stir in:

$1/2$ to $3/4$ cup sugar
$1/8$ teaspoon salt

Cover the fruit closely and keep it refrigerated until the sugar is dissolved. Combine:

1 teaspoon vanilla
$1/2$ cup sugar
2 cups cream
2 cups whipping cream

Partly churn-freeze these ingredients, see 546. When half-frozen, add the fruit mixture and finish freezing.

ORANGE ICE CREAM

About 9 Servings

Heat but do not boil:

$1^1/2$ cups cream

Stir in until dissolved:

$1^1/2$ cups sugar

Chill. Add:

$1^1/2$ cups whipping cream

Churn-freeze the cream, see 546, until it has a slushy consistency. Add:

3 tablespoons lemon juice
$1^1/4$ cups orange juice

Finish freezing. Serve with:

Polvo de Amor, 245

STRAWBERRY OR RASPBERRY ICE CREAM

About 9 Servings

Hull:

1 quart berries

Sieve them. Stir into the pulpy juice:

$7/8$ cup sugar

Chill thoroughly. Combine with:

2 cups cream
2 cups whipping cream

To churn-freeze, see 546.

ABOUT STILL-FROZEN ICE CREAMS, ICES, BOMBES, MOUSSES AND PARFAITS

In our family, a richly loaded bombe, even more than a churned ice cream, betokened festivity—the burst of glory that topped off a party dinner. Fancy molds such as those illustrated in the chapter heading, 545, were reserved for these occasions. We children always hoped they might be chilled in the backyard, under snow: such fun finding them!

Then, as now, these still-frozen desserts ♦ needed an emulsifying agent—eggs, cornstarch, gelatin or corn syrup—to keep large crystals from forming during the freezing process. Some classic French recipes specify at least 8 eggs for each cup of sugar syrup to obtain the requisite smoothness. Whatever the proportions, count on a very different texture in these still-frozen desserts from those made by churning.

Here are some good combinations:

> **Strawberry ice outside, Delmonico with strawberries in kirsch inside**
> **Raspberries and pistachios**
> **Coffee and vanilla praliné**
> **Coffee and banana mousse**
> **Chocolate and angelica**
> **Vanilla, orange and chocolate**

♦ To still-freeze creams and ices ♦ whip the cream only to the point where it stands in soft peaks. Any further beating will make the dessert disagreeably buttery. The whipped cream and any solids such as nuts and candied fruits are incorporated when the rest of the mixture is partially frozen, and liqueurs are usually added almost at the end of the freezing period.

Chill the mold before packing. Pack the ice cream firmly so no air spaces remain.

When the mixtures are in the mold, rest them at least 6 hours in the deep freeze on top of other packages, not directly on the freezer shelves. They may be made the day before you plan to use them, but ♦ they do not keep well much longer than this. ♦ Remove them from the freezer about ¹/₂ hour before use, leaving them in the mold until ready to serve. Then garnish with meringues, fruits, sauces or cakes. ♦ To make ornamental bombes, put the cream into tall fancy or melon molds or in the special ones from which they took their playfully sinister name.

Churn-frozen ices or ice creams may form a single or double outside coating. They are applied as a rather thin layer to the inside surface of the mold, each layer being, in turn, individually frozen, see Gelatin Molds, 234. The softer, still-frozen bombe, mousse or Bavarian mixtures are then filled into the center and the mold covered before placement in the freezer for at least 6 hours. To unmold, let cool water run briefly over the mold, and have a cooled platter ready to receive the molded cream.

To make still-frozen ice cream in freezer trays, prepare as in the following recipes. After about 2 hours of freezing, remove tray from freezer and beat contents well. Return to freezer. Repeat the beating in about 2 hours and again in 2 more hours if crystals appear on the surface. Refreeze after each beating. Cover the tray closely each time with plastic or foil. ♦ Do not store more than 24 hours if you want a satisfactory texture. You may form individual parfaits before the last freezing in stemmed tall parfait glasses, layering the ice

creams between preserved fruits and sauces. When serving, top them with freshly whipped cream and a maraschino cherry.

♦ In the absence of a freezer, set the well-covered mold in a bed of cracked ice. Allow from 2 to 4 parts ice to 1 of salt and use a bucket or a pail that will ensure complete coverage—about 3 inches on top, bottom and sides. Chill the cream 4 to 6 hours.

VANILLA ICE CREAM II

About 9 Servings

Soak:

2 teaspoons gelatin

in:

¹/₄ cup cold water

Scald over low heat but do not boil:

³/₄ cup milk

with:

**Seeds scraped from a 2-inch
section of vanilla bean**

Stir into it, until dissolved:

³/₄ cup sugar

¹/₈ teaspoon salt

Stir in the soaked gelatin. Cool and place this mixture in refrigerator trays until thoroughly chilled. Then whip with a wire whisk until thickened, but not stiff:

3 cups whipping cream

Fold cream into the chilled and beaten gelatin mixture. ♦ Still-freeze the dessert in a mold or in a foil-covered refrigerator tray. Serve with:

**Chocolate Mint Sauce, 569,
or Maple Sugar Sauce, 569**

or cover with:

**Shredded coconut
A chocolate sauce, 567**

An attractive way to serve vanilla ice cream in summer is to place balls of cream in the center of a large platter and surround them with mounds of red raspberries, black raspberries and fresh pineapple sticks, using green leaves as a garnish. You may also use any of the additions suggested in Vanilla Ice Cream I, 547.

VANILLA ICE CREAM III

4 Servings

Start to make this the day before you need it, as the evaporated milk needs to chill 12 hours. Prepare for whipping by the method on 187:

1¼ cups evaporated milk

During the process of evaporating milk, a caramel overtone develops which plays hob with the delicate flavor of vanilla. We prefer to accentuate the caramel by adding:

**2 to 4 tablespoons or more
Caramel Syrup, 597**

Or you may transform the caramel flavor with:

1 to 2 teaspoons instant coffee

To prepare the ice cream, stir over heat, but do not boil:

**⅓ to ½ cup sugar
¼ cup cream**

Chill. Add:

1½ teaspoons vanilla

Whip the evaporated milk and combine lightly with the sugar mixture. To still-freeze and serve, see 550.

DELMONICO ICE CREAM II

6 Servings

Beat:

2 egg yolks

Beat in until well blended:

**½ cup confectioners' sugar
¼ cup cream**

Cook and stir in a double boiler
♦ over—not in—boiling water until the mixture coats the back of a spoon. Chill. Add:

**1 teaspoon vanilla or
1 tablespoon or more dry
sherry**

♦ Whip until thickened, but not stiff:
1 cup whipping cream
In a separate bowl, whip until stiff
♦ but not dry:
2 egg whites
Fold the cream and the egg whites into the custard. ♦ Still-freeze the ice cream in a mold or in foil-covered refrigerator trays, see 550. Serve with:
Jelly Sauce, 565

❊ FROZEN EGGNOG

Prepare:
**Delmonico Ice Cream I,
547, or II, at left**
When almost frozen, make a funnel-shaped hole in the center. Place in it:
**Several tablespoons rum,
brandy or whisky**
Stir the liquor into the ice cream. Let the mixture continue to freeze.

MANGO ICE CREAM

Prepare:
**Delmonico Ice Cream, 547,
or II, at left**
Before freezing, fold in:
2 cups mango purée
Freeze in refrigerator trays, see 550.

DELMONICO BOMBE

About 15 Servings

Soak:
1½ teaspoons gelatin
in:
¼ cup cold water
Stir and bring to the boiling point:
**2 cups milk
1½ cups sugar**
Dissolve the gelatin in the hot milk. Pour part of this mixture over:
2 beaten egg yolks
Beat until blended, then add the rest of the mixture. Stir and cook in a

double boiler ◗ over—not in—boiling water until the custard coats the back of a spoon. Cool. Add:

1 teaspoon vanilla

Chill until about to set. ◗ Whip until thickened, but not stiff:

4 cups whipping cream

In a separate bowl, whip until ◗ stiff, but not dry:

2 egg whites

Fold the cream and the egg whites lightly into the custard. Have ready:

18 Macaroons, 469

Sprinkle them with:

Cointreau or kirsch

Spread them with:

Tart jelly

Place alternate layers of cream and macaroons in a mold or in refrigerator trays. To still-freeze the ice cream, see 550.

BISCUIT TORTONI OR MACAROON BOMBE

4 Servings

Combine:

3/4 cup crushed Macaroons, 469
3/4 cup cream
1/4 cup sifted confectioners' sugar
A few grains of salt

Let these ingredients stand 1 hour. ◗ Whip until thickened, but not stiff:

1 cup whipping cream

Fold in the macaroon mixture and:

1 teaspoon vanilla

Place in paper muffin cups set in a refrigerator tray. To still-freeze, see 550. Either before freezing or when partly frozen, decorate tops with:

Candied cherries
Unsalted toasted almonds
Crystallized angelica

ANGELICA PARFAIT

About 12 Servings

Try combining layers of angelica, chocolate and lime sherbet.
Boil to the thread stage, 576:

1 1/2 cups sugar
1/2 cup water

Whip ◗ until stiff, but not dry:

2 egg whites

Pour syrup over them in a slow stream. Whip constantly. When cool, add:

1 teaspoon vanilla or 1 tablespoon or more Cointreau

◗ Whip until thickened, but not stiff:

3 cups whipping cream

Fold lightly into egg mixture. Still-freeze in a mold or in foil-covered refrigerator trays, see 550. Serve with:

Raspberry syrup, or
A chocolate sauce, 567

MOCHA ICE CREAM

8 Servings

In spite of an almost lifelong prejudice against marshmallows, we give the next two recipes more than grudging approval.
Melt in a double boiler ◗ over—not in—boiling water:

18 average-sized Marshmallows, 581: 1/4 lb.
1/2 lb. semisweet chocolate

Cool slightly and stir in:

2 cups whipping cream
3/4 cup strong coffee

Pour this mixture gradually over:

4 well-beaten egg yolks

◗ Be sure that the mixture is not so hot as to curdle the eggs. To still-freeze and serve, see 550.

CHOCOLATE ICE CREAM II

4 Servings

Chill until ice-cold so it will whip, 187:

1 cup evaporated milk

Combine:

6 tablespoons cocoa or
1½ oz. melted unsweetened
chocolate

6 tablespoons sugar

¼ teaspoon salt

Stir in gradually:

½ cup evaporated milk

½ cup water

Stir and cook these ingredients in a double boiler ♦ over—not in—boiling water until smooth. Add and stir until melted:

18 average-sized
Marshmallows, 581: ¼ lb.

Cool this mixture. Whip the chilled milk until stiff, then fold it in. To still-freeze the ice cream in a mold or in foil-covered refrigerator trays, see 550.

CHOCOLATE BOMBE

About 10 Servings

Soak:

1½ teaspoons gelatin

in:

1 cup cold water

Stir and bring to the boiling point:

1 cup milk

1½ cups sugar

2 to 4 tablespoons cocoa

Dissolve the gelatin in the mixture. Cool. Add:

1 teaspoon vanilla

Chill until about to set. ♦ Whip until thickened, but not stiff:

2 cups whipping cream

Fold lightly into the gelatin mixture. To still-freeze the bombe in a mold or in foil-covered refrigerator trays, see 550.

BUTTER PECAN ICE CREAM

About 6 Servings

Boil for 2 minutes:

1 cup light brown sugar

½ cup water

⅛ teaspoon salt

Beat:

2 eggs

Beat in the syrup slowly. Cook in a double boiler ♦ over—not in—boiling water, stirring constantly until the mixture coats the back of the spoon. Add:

2 tablespoons butter

Cool, then add:

1 cup milk

1 teaspoon vanilla extract

1 tablespoon sherry

Beat until ♦ thickened, but not stiff:

1 cup whipping cream

Fold it into the egg mixture. To still-freeze, see 550. When partially frozen, fold in:

½ cup broken toasted pecan
meats

If the nuts are salted, a very special piquancy results.

CARAMEL PARFAIT

About 9 Servings

Soak:

1½ teaspoons gelatin

in:

½ cup cold water

Prepare:

¾ cup warm Caramelized
Sugar I, 232

Beat:

2 egg yolks

Beat in slowly:

½ cup sugar

Beat these ingredients until well blended. Add the caramel mixture. Stir in a double boiler ♦ over—not in—boiling water until the custard coats the back of a spoon. Stir in the soaked gelatin. Cool. Add:

2 teaspoons vanilla

Chill until about to set. ◗ Whip until thickened, but not stiff:

2 cups whipping cream

Fold lightly into the custard. Still-freeze in a mold or in foil-covered refrigerator trays, see 550. Garnish with:

Toasted slivered almonds

BUTTERSCOTCH PARFAIT

About 6 Servings

Stir and melt in a saucepan over low heat, then boil for 1 minute:

²/₃ cup brown sugar
2 tablespoons butter
¹/₈ teaspoon salt

Add:

¹/₂ cup water

Cook the butterscotch until smooth and syrupy.

Beat:

4 egg yolks

Add the cooled syrup slowly, beating constantly. Cook and stir in a double boiler ◗ over—not in—boiling water until the mixture coats the back of a spoon. Whip until fluffy. Chill. ◗ Whip until thickened, but not stiff:

1 cup whipping cream

Add:

2 teaspoons vanilla

Fold into egg mixture. Still-freeze in a mold or in foil-covered refrigerator trays, see 550.

MAPLE PARFAIT

About 9 Servings

Cook and stir ◗ over—not in—boiling water until thick:

6 egg yolks
³/₄ cup maple syrup
¹/₈ teaspoon salt

When the custard coats the back of a spoon, remove it from the heat. Pour into a bowl and beat with a wire whisk until cool. ◗ Whip until thickened, but not stiff:

2 cups whipping cream

Fold it lightly into the custard. When partially frozen, add:

(¹/₂ cup crushed Nut Brittle, 593)

Still-freeze in a mold or in foil-covered refrigerator trays, see 550.

COFFEE PARFAIT

About 6 Servings

Combine:

2 tablespoons cornstarch
²/₃ cup sugar
¹/₈ teaspoon salt

Stir into this mixture:

2 tablespoons milk

Add:

2 beaten egg yolks
1 cup strong coffee

Stir and cook this custard in a double boiler ◗ over—not in—boiling water until it coats the back of a spoon. Chill. ◗ Whip until thickened, but not stiff, and fold in:

1¹/₂ cups whipping cream

To still-freeze in foil-covered refrigerator trays, see 550. Serve in tall glasses, topped with:

Whipped cream
(Grated chocolate)

FRUIT MOUSSE

About 9 Servings

Prepare:

2 cups crushed fruit—peaches, apricots, bananas, strawberries or puréed black or red raspberries

Stir in:

¹/₈ teaspoon salt
³/₄ to 1 cup confectioners' sugar

Soak:

    1¹/₂ teaspoons gelatin

in:

    2 tablespoons cold water

Dissolve it in:

    ¹/₄ cup boiling water

Cool and add:

    2 tablespoons lemon juice

Stir into the fruit mixture. ◗ Whip until thickened, but not stiff:

    2 cups whipping cream

Fold into the fruit and gelatin mixture. Still-freeze in a mold or in foil-covered refrigerator trays, see 550.

APRICOT MOUSSE

      About 6 Servings

Surprisingly good—the fruit flavor being decided enough to disguise the evaporated milk taste. Prepare for whipping, 187:

    1¹/₄ cups evaporated milk

Put through a ricer or blender:

    ³/₄ cup cooked sweetened drained dried apricots

We do not like to substitute the canned ones, as the flavor is not strong enough. Soak:

    1 teaspoon gelatin

in:

    2 tablespoons cold apricot juice

Dissolve it in:

    2 tablespoons hot apricot juice

Add the gelatin to the apricot purée. Chill until about to set. Whip the chilled evaporated milk and add to it:

    ¹/₂ teaspoon vanilla

    ¹/₈ teaspoon salt

Fold lightly into gelatin mixture. To still-freeze in foil-covered refrigerator trays, see 550.

STRAWBERRY OR RASPBERRY BOMBE

Prepare:

    Bavarian Berry Cream, 528

using in all:

    1¹/₂ cups sugar

To still-freeze the ice cream, see 550.

RASPBERRY PARFAIT

      About 9 Servings

Crush and strain through two thicknesses of cheesecloth:

    1 quart raspberries: about 1 cup juice

Discard the pulp. Boil to the thread stage, 576:

    ³/₄ cup water

    1 cup sugar

Whip until stiff ◗ but not dry:

    3 egg whites

Pour the syrup over them in a slow stream. Whip constantly until cool. Fold in juice. In a separate bowl ◗ whip until thickened, but not stiff:

    2 cups whipping cream

Fold lightly into other ingredients. Still-freeze in a mold or in foil-covered refrigerator trays, see 550.

GREENGAGE PLUM ICE CREAM

      12 Servings

Drain:

    3¹/₂ cups canned pitted greengage plums

Put them through a ricer. There should be about 1¹/₂ cups of pulp. Soak:

    1¹/₂ teaspoons gelatin

in

    ¹/₄ cup cold water

Heat to the boiling point:

    2 cups milk

    ³/₄ to 1 cup sugar

    ¹/₈ teaspoon salt

Dissolve the gelatin in the hot milk. Cool, then add the plum pulp and:

2 tablespoons lemon juice

Chill the mixture until slushy. Whip until thickened, but not stiff, and add to above ingredients:

2 cups whipping cream

Still-freeze the ice cream in a mold or in foil-covered trays, see 550.

PERSIMMON ICE CREAM

About 6 Servings

A California creation.

Put through a ricer:

4 ripe Japanese persimmons

Add:

2 tablespoons sugar
6 tablespoons lemon juice

◗ Whip until thickened, but not stiff, and fold in:

2 cups whipping cream

Still-freeze in a mold or in foil-covered refrigerator trays, see 550.

TUTTI-FRUTTI PARFAIT

About 6 Servings

Cover and soak for several hours:

1 cup chopped candied fruit

in a combination of:

Brandy, rum, liqueur and
syrup from canned stewed
fruit

Drain well. Reserve liquid for flavoring other puddings. Soak:

1 teaspoon gelatin

in:

2 tablespoons water

Dissolve it over hot water. Boil to the thread stage, 576:

1/2 cup water
1/2 cup sugar

Beat ◗ until stiff, but not dry:

2 egg whites

Pour the syrup over the egg whites in a fine stream, beating constantly. Add the dissolved gelatin and continue beating until mixture thickens somewhat. Beat in drained fruit. ◗ Whip until thickened, but not stiff:

1 cup whipping cream
1 teaspoon vanilla

Fold into fruit and egg mixture. Still-freeze in a mold or in foil-covered refrigerator trays, see 550. Serve topped with:

Whipped cream

FRUIT-BUTTERMILK ICE CREAM

About 5 Servings

For girth-watchers: a quite acceptable low-fat variation.

Combine:

1 cup sweetened fruit purée:
apricot, peach or
strawberry

with:

3 tablespoons lemon juice
1/8 teaspoon salt
1 1/2 cups buttermilk

To still-freeze, see 550.

ABOUT ICES AND SHERBETS

Ices, or glaces, are made simply of fruit juice, sugar and water. Sherbets have variants, like the Italian **Granite** and French **Sorbets**. These may have added egg white, milk or cream and are generally less sweet. Sherbets may be appropriately served with the meat course, as well as for dessert. Both are best when churn-frozen. Some types may be still-frozen without the addition of gelatin or egg white, but their texture is considerably lighter and less flinty when these modifying ingredients are included.

Freezing diminishes flavoring and sweetening, so sugar your base accordingly. ◗ However, if ices are too sweet they will not freeze. A safe proportion is approximately 1 part sugar to 4 parts liquid. ◗ Stir in any liqueurs after the ices have begun to freeze.

◗ To churn-freeze ices and sherbets, follow the directions for processing ice cream, 546. Like ice creams, they can be molded, after freezing, into attractive shapes like those shown in the chapter heading, 545. Pack a mold in salted ice for 3 hours. Remove the ice or sherbet from it about 5 minutes before serving.

◗ To still-freeze ices and sherbets, put them in a covered mold or a refrigerator tray covered with foil and place them in the freezer. While they are still slushy, they should be stirred or beaten from front to back in the tray to reduce the size of the crystals. Repeated beating at half-hour intervals will give them the consistency of a coarse churn-frozen water ice. ◗ Remove them from freezer to refrigerator about 20 minutes before serving. Ices and sherbets are especially delectable when served in fruit shells—fancy-cut and hollowed-out lemons, tangerines or oranges—garnished with leaves. See also Frozen Orange Surprise, 558.

Of course, meringues topped with whipped cream are containers as wonderful as crystal coupes or frappé goblets. Ices and sherbets lend themselves particularly to combinations with fruits—fresh, poached, preserved and candied: to chestnut garnishes with touches of liqueur; and if you are really professional, to veils of spun sugar.

FRUIT ICE

About 10 Servings

Have ready:
> 1 cup any sweetened fruit
> purée

Add to taste:
> (Lemon juice)

Combine with:
> 4 cups water

To churn-freeze, see 546. If adding:
> (Liqueur)

◗ have the ice almost completely churned before you do so: the high alcoholic content tends to inhibit freezing.

RASPBERRY OR STRAWBERRY ICE I

About 10 Servings

This method makes delicious linings for bombes. Cook until soft:
> 2 quarts strawberries or
> raspberries

Strain the juice through 2 thicknesses of cheesecloth. There should be about 2 cups of thick juice. Combine, stir over heat until the sugar is dissolved, then boil 5 minutes, covered, without stirring, to avoid crystallization:
> 4 cups water
> 2 cups sugar

Chill. Add the thick berry juice and:
> 1 tablespoon lemon juice

To churn-freeze, see 546.

PEACH ICE

About 12 Servings

Combine:
> 2 cups peach pulp: fresh
> peaches, peeled and
> riced
> 6 tablespoons lemon
> juice
> 3/4 cup orange juice

Stir over heat until sugar is dissolved:
> 3 cups water
> 1 cup sugar

Then boil 5 minutes, covered, without stirring, to avoid crystallization. Chill. Combine with the fruit pulp and juices. To churn-freeze, see 546. Top each serving with:
> 1 teaspoon cassis or Melba
> Sauce, 564

APRICOT ICE

About 9 Servings

Put through a ricer or a sieve:

**3¹/2 cups drained canned
    apricots**

Add:

**2¹/4 cups orange juice
6 tablespoons lemon juice**

Stir in over heat until dissolved:

1 cup sugar

Then boil 5 minutes, covered, without stirring, to avoid crystallization. Chill. To churn-freeze, see 546.

PINEAPPLE ICE

About 9 Servings

Stir over heat until sugar is dissolved:

**1 cup sugar
4 cups water**

Boil 5 minutes, covered, without stirring, to avoid crystallization. Chill the syrup and add:

**1 cup drained canned
    crushed pineapple
6 tablespoons lemon juice**

To churn-freeze, see 546. Garnish with:

Mint leaves

LEMON ICE

About 9 Servings

Grate:

2 teaspoons lemon rind

onto:

2 cups sugar

Add:

**4 cups water or tea
¹/4 teaspoon salt**

Stir over heat until sugar is dissolved, then boil 5 minutes, covered, without stirring, to avoid crystallization. Chill. Add:

³/4 cup lemon juice

To churn or still-freeze, see 546 or 550. Serve in a mound or ring with:

**Fruit or canned fruit used
in some attractive
combination, flavored
with curaçao, Cointreau
or rum**

LEMON AND ORANGE ICE

About 12 Servings

Combine and stir over heat until sugar is dissolved:

**2 teaspoons grated orange
    rind
2 cups sugar
4 cups water
¹/4 teaspoon salt**

Boil for 5 minutes, covered, without stirring, to avoid crystallization. Chill. Add:

**2 cups orange juice
¹/4 cup lemon juice**

To churn-freeze, see 546. Top each serving with:

**1 teaspoon rum or orange
    marmalade**

FROZEN ORANGE OR LEMON
SURPRISE

This dessert can be made well in advance. If it is removed from the freezer and set in place just before the guests are served, it may even be used as a centerpiece or table decoration, bedded on a shallow tray of cracked ice. Choose:

**Navel oranges or heavy-
    skinned lemons**

Cut a fancy opening near the top, which later serves as a lid. ◖ Keep lids and bottoms matched until ready to fill. Hollow out the pulp. Use it for juice or for making fruit ice or sherbet. When ready to fill the orange case, have all ingredients ready so you can work fast to avoid undue melting. Fill the cases with:

Fruit ice or sherbet

or a combination of:

Fruit ice
Ice cream
Partially frozen
raspberries, peaches,
strawberries
A touch of liqueur

Wrap fruits individually in foil and deep-freeze at once. Depending on the temperature of the room, allow about $1/2$ hour or more to defrost, uncovered, before serving. Garnish the cases with fresh green leaves stuck in the lids and around the bases, see sketch on 545.

RASPBERRY OR STRAWBERRY ICE II

About 4 Servings

This combines well with Angelica Parfait, 552. Press through a sieve or a ricer:

1 quart strawberries or
raspberries

Soak:

1 teaspoon gelatin

in:

1 tablespoon cold water

Stir over heat until sugar is dissolved:

1 cup water or $1/2$ cup water
and $1/2$ cup pineapple juice
$3/4$ to 1 cup sugar

Boil 5 minutes, covered, without stirring, to avoid crystallization. Add:

1 to 2 tablespoons lemon
juice

Dissolve the gelatin in the hot syrup. Chill. Combine juice with syrup. To still-freeze, see 550.

MINT ICE

About 9 Servings

A refreshing alternate for the mint jelly that traditionally accompanies lamb.

Prepare:

Any orange or lemon ice

After the syrup reaches the boiling point, pour it over:

$1/2$ cup chopped fresh mint
leaves

Steep 1 to 2 minutes, drain out the mint leaves, and proceed as for the recipe you have chosen.

LEMON SHERBET

About 5 Servings

Soak:

2 teaspoons gelatin

in:

$1/4$ cup cold water

Stir over heat until sugar dissolves:

$2^{1}/4$ cups water
$3/4$ cup sugar

Boil 5 minutes, covered, without stirring, to avoid crystallization. Dissolve gelatin in hot syrup. Chill. Grate:

1 teaspoon lemon rind

Add:

$3/4$ cup lemon juice

Add these ingredients to the syrup. Beat ♦ until stiff, but not dry, and fold into the chilled mixture:

2 egg whites

To still-freeze, see 550. Serve topped with:

(Finely chopped candied
orange or lemon rind)

ORANGE SHERBET

About 5 Servings

Soak:

2 teaspoons gelatin

in:

$1/4$ cup cold water

Stir over heat until sugar dissolves:

1 cup water
$2/3$ to $3/4$ cup sugar, depending
on sweetness of fruit

Boil 5 minutes, covered, without stirring, to avoid crystallization. Dissolve gelatin in hot syrup. Cool. Add:

1 teaspoon grated lemon rind
1 teaspoon grated orange
   rind
1½ cups orange juice
⅓ cup lemon juice

Beat ◗ until stiff, but not dry, and add:

2 egg whites

To still-freeze, see 550. Garnish with:

Fresh pineapple slices

LIME SHERBET

About 6 Servings

Soak:

1¼ teaspoons gelatin

in:

¼ cup cold water

Stir over heat until sugar dissolves:

⅔ cup sugar
1¾ cups water

Boil 5 minutes, covered, without stirring, to avoid crystallization. Add the gelatin mixture. Chill and add:

½ cup lime juice
2 drops green vegetable
   coloring

Beat until ◗ stiff, but not dry, and add:

2 egg whites

To still-freeze, see 550. Serve in:

Lemon shells

Garnish with:

Green leaves

GRAPEFRUIT SHERBET

About 4 Servings

Soak:

2 teaspoons gelatin

in:

½ cup cold water

Stir over heat until sugar dissolves:

1 cup sugar
1 cup water

Boil 5 minutes, covered, without stirring, to avoid crystallization. Dis-

solve the gelatin in the hot syrup. Chill. Add:

¼ cup lemon juice
2 cups fresh grapefruit juice
⅓ cup orange juice
¼ teaspoon salt

Beat until ◗ stiff, but not dry, and add:

2 egg whites

To still-freeze, see 550.

RASPBERRY OR STRAWBERRY SHERBET

About 5 Servings

Soak:

2 teaspoons gelatin

in:

¼ cup cold water

Press through a sieve or a ricer:

1 quart fresh berries

Add to them:

¼ cup lemon juice

Stir over heat until sugar dissolves:

1¾ cups water
¾ cup sugar

Boil 5 minutes, covered, without stirring, to avoid crystallization. Dissolve the gelatin in the hot syrup. Cool and add berries. Chill. Beat until ◗ stiff, but not dry, and add:

2 egg whites

To still-freeze, see 550.

BANANA-PINEAPPLE SHERBET

About 8 Servings

Combine and stir until sugar is dissolved:

1½ cups crushed pineapple
¾ cup confectioners' sugar

Add:

1½ cups banana pulp: about 3
   large bananas
½ cup orange juice
6 tablespoons lemon juice

Place in refrigerator trays. Freeze un-

til nearly firm. ◖ Beat until stiff, but
not dry:

> 2 egg whites

Add fruit mixture gradually. Beat
sherbet until light and fluffy. Return
to trays. To still-freeze, see 550.

★ CRANBERRY SHERBET

About 8 Servings

Simmer until soft and ready to pop:

> 1 quart cranberries

in:

> 1³/₄ cups water

Force the berries through a sieve or
blend in an electric blender. Add to
them and boil, covered, 5 minutes,
without stirring:

> 1³/₄ cups sugar
> 1 cup water or pineapple
>   juice

Soak:

> 2 teaspoons gelatin

in:

> ¹/₄ cup cold water

Dissolve the gelatin in the hot juice.
Chill. Beat until ◖ stiff, but not dry,
and add:

> 2 egg whites

To still-freeze, see 550. Serve in:

> Orange cups

WINE SHERBET

About 8 Servings

A dry sherbet—delightful served after roasted meat or as a garnish for a
fruit compote.

Soak:

> 1 tablespoon gelatin

in:

> ¹/₄ cup cold water

Stir over heat until sugar dissolves:

> 1 cup water
> ³/₄ cup sugar

Boil 5 minutes, covered, without stirring, to avoid crystallization. Dissolve gelatin in hot syrup. Chill. Add:

> 2 cups dry white wine
> 1 cup unstrained lime juice
> 1 tablespoon crème de
>   menthe

Beat until ◖ stiff, but not dry, and fold
into this chilled mixture:

> 1 egg white

To still-freeze, see 550.

CHAMPAGNE SHERBET

About 8 Servings

Stir over heat until sugar dissolves:

> 1¹/₄ cups sugar
> 1 cup water

Boil 5 minutes, covered, without stirring, to avoid crystallization. Cool.
Stir in:

> 1¹/₂ cups champagne
> 3 tablespoons lemon juice

Churn-freeze, 546, until almost set.
Fold in:

> Meringue I, 502

When ready to serve, pour over each
portion:

> 2 tablespoons champagne

LEMON MILK SHERBET

About 9 Servings

Dissolve:

> 1¹/₃ cups sugar

in:

> 7 tablespoons lemon juice

Stir these ingredients slowly into:

> 3¹/₂ cups milk or milk and
>   cream

If the milk curdles, it will not affect
texture after freezing. To churn-
freeze, see 550.

ORANGE MILK SHERBET

About 10 Servings

Combine and stir:

> 1¹/₂ teaspoons grated orange
>   rind
> 1¹/₂ cups sugar

Stir into:

>**¼ cup lemon juice**
>**1½ cups orange juice**
>**(1½ bananas, riced)**

until sugar is dissolved. Stir these ingredients gradually into

>**4 cups very cold milk**

If the milk curdles slightly, it will not affect the texture after the sherbet is frozen. To churn-freeze, see 546.

PINEAPPLE MILK SHERBET

About 10 Servings

Combine and stir until sugar is dissolved:

>**1 cup unsweetened pineapple juice**
>**1 teaspoon grated lemon rind**
>**¼ cup lemon juice**
>**1 cup sugar**
>**⅛ teaspoon salt**

Stir these ingredients slowly into:

>**4 cups chilled milk**

To churn-freeze, see 546.

PINEAPPLE BUTTERMILK SHERBET

About 6 Servings

A low-fat version, well worth trying. Combine:

>**2 cups buttermilk**
>**½ cup sugar**
>**1 cup crushed pineapple**

Freeze these ingredients until they have a slushy consistency. Place them in a chilled bowl. Add:

>**1 slightly beaten egg white**
>**1½ teaspoons vanilla**

Beat until light and fluffy. Return to freezer in foil-covered refrigerator trays. To still-freeze, see 550.

FROZEN SUCKERS

Fourteen 1½-inch Suckers

Quickly made from canned baby fruits, and definitely for the very young.

When these mixtures are partially frozen in a compartmented ice tray or in individual paper cups, insert a looped paraffined string or a paper spoon into each unit to form a handle. Then freeze until hard.

I. Mix and stir well:

>**2 cups sweetened puréed fruit**
>**1 cup orange juice**
>**2 tablespoons sugar**

Freeze as described above.

II. Mix and freeze, as described above:

>**¾ cup orange or grape juice**
>**1 cup yogurt**
>**½ teaspoon vanilla**
>**(1 tablespoon lemon juice)**

SNOW ICE CREAM

The ancestor of all frozen delights and a favorite of small fry.

Arrange attractively in a chilled bowl trying not to compact it:

>**Fresh, clean snow**

Pour over it:

>**Sweetened fruit juice or maple syrup**

Or, for a gallon of snow, stir in:

1 cup cream
³/₄ cup sugar
¹/₂ teaspoon vanilla

For this kind of frozen delight, as well as for packing frozen desserts in general and for serving them attractively on a dish in thin slabs, the shovel scoop shown at the bottom opposite is useful. A spring-release scoop, also shown, turns out uniform ball shapes, and is a great help in molding single portions quickly at dessert time, provided the entire utensil is dipped into very hot water between dollops.

ABOUT SWEET SAUCES

With dessert sauces, "the object all sublime" is to "let the punishment fit the crime." In fact, unless the sauce can complement the dessert, omit it. Should the latter be tart, tone it down with a bland sauce; if bland, use a sauce to which a tablespoon of liqueur imparts the final sprightly touch. Sauces based on sugar are usually very simple to confect. They have distinct family branches similar to those of their unsweetened counterparts. The main things to remember are ♦ don't overbeat cream bases or cream garnishes and ♦ do cook egg sauces over—not in—boiling water. ♦ Be sure that sauces thickened with flour and cornstarch are free from lumps, and cook them thoroughly to avoid any raw taste. See flour paste, (I, 379), and cornstarch, (I, 379). ♦ In preparing heavy syrups, guard against sugaring, see 574.

LEMON, ORANGE OR LIME SAUCE

About 1 Cup

A lovely, translucent foil for puddings and gelatins. Combine and stir in a double boiler ♦ over—not in—boiling water until thickened:

¹/₄ to ¹/₂ sugar
1 tablespoon cornstarch
1 cup water

Remove sauce from heat. Stir in:

2 to 3 tablespoons butter
¹/₂ teaspoon grated lemon or
    orange rind
1¹/₂ tablespoons lemon or lime
    juice or
3 tablespoons orange juice
¹/₈ teaspoon salt

FRUIT FONDUE SAUCE

About 1¹/₂ Cups

If you omit the crushed fruit, this sauce can serve as a hot sweet fondue sauce for fruits or bits of cake.
Combine and stir in a double boiler over—not in—boiling water until thickened:

1 cup unsweetened fruit juice
¹/₂ to ³/₄ cup sugar
1 tablespoon cornstarch or
2 tablespoons flour

Remove mixture from heat. Stir in:

2 teaspoons lemon juice
(2 tablespoons butter)

Cool. You may add:

(1 cup crushed, shredded
    fruit, fresh or stewed)

Flavor with:

Sherry or other wine or
    liqueur

Serve cold or hot.

CHERRY SAUCE

About 2¹/₂ Cups

Drain well, reserving juice:

2 cups canned sweet cherries

Add to the cherry syrup and simmer about 10 minutes in the top of a double boiler over direct heat.

¹/₄ cup sugar
¹/₄ cup corn syrup

1 stick cinnamon: 2 inches
1 tablespoon lemon juice

Remove the cinnamon. Mix:

2 teaspoons cornstarch
1 tablespoon cold water

Stir this mixture into the hot cherry juice. Cook ♦ over—not in—boiling water and stir until it thickens. Add the cherries. Serve hot or cold.

CHERRY JUBILEE SAUCE

About 1¼ Cups

This recipe always involves the use of liqueurs. If you do not wish to ignite the brandy, you may soak the cherries in it well ahead of time. If you flambé, be sure that the fruit is at room temperature, and the brandy warm, see 112. Other preserved fruits may be substituted for the cherries. Heat well:

1 cup preserved pitted Bing
   or other cherries

Add:

¼ cup slightly warmed
   brandy

Ignite the brandy. When the flame has died down, add:

2 tablespoons kirsch

You may serve the sauce hot on:

Vanilla ice cream

MELBA SAUCE

About 1¾ Cups

Combine and bring to the boiling point in the top of a double boiler over direct heat:

½ cup currant jelly
1 cup sieved raspberries

Mix and add:

1 teaspoon cornstarch
⅛ teaspoon salt
½ cup sugar

Cook ♦ over—not in—boiling water until thick and clear. Chill before using.

⅄ QUICK AMBROSIA SAUCE

About 1¾ Cups

Mix:

¾ cup sweetened puréed
   apricots
¾ cup sweetened puréed
   peaches

Add:

¼ cup orange juice
1 teaspoon grated lemon rind
2 tablespoons rum or sloe gin

SAUCE COCKAIGNE

About 8 Cups

A sauce for all seasons—its ingredients are always available. Great with custards, glazed bananas, cottage pudding and waffles, by itself or combined with a little liqueur or whipped cream.

Cook gently in a wide-bottomed covered pan until the fruit is pulpy and disintegrates easily when stirred with a wire whisk:

2 cups dried apricots
1¼ cups water

Add:

1½ cups sugar

Stir until dissolved. Add:

5 cups canned crushed
   pineapple

Bring the mixture to a boil. Pour into jars and cover. Keep under refrigeration.

RAISIN SAUCE

About 1⅔ Cups

Boil 15 minutes:

1½ cups water
½ cup seeded raisins
¼ cup sugar
⅛ teaspoon salt

Melt:

2 tablespoons butter

Stir in, until blended:

1 teaspoon flour
Add the hot sauce slowly. Stir and
cook until it boils. Mix in:

A grating of nutmeg or
lemon rind

Serve over:

Steamed puddings, 539

JELLY SAUCE

About ¾ Cup

For steamed and cornstarch puddings, or use as a fondue sauce.
Dilute over hot water in double
boiler:

¾ cup currant or other jelly

Thin with:

¼ cup boiling water or wine

Serve hot or cold. This sauce may be
thickened. Melt:

1 tablespoon butter

Blend in:

1 tablespoon floor

Add the jelly mixture. Stir over low
heat until.it reaches the consistency
desired. You may spice the sauce
with:

1 teaspoon cinnamon
⅛ teaspoon ground cloves
⅛ teaspoon grated lemon rind

JAM SAUCE

About ¾ Cup

Combine in a small saucepan:

¼ cup raspberry, damson,
gooseberry, grape or
peach jam

½ cup water

Stir and boil these ingredients 2 minutes. Remove from heat and add:

1 teaspoon kirsch or ¼
teaspoon almond extract

Serve hot or cold. Use on:

Bread, farina and other
cereal puddings, 531

CUSTARD SAUCE OR CRÈME ANGLAISE

Prepare:

Custard, 508

using 5 egg yolks and ⅔ cup sugar.
You may add:

(½ cup slivered almonds)

QUICK FRUIT CUSTARD SAUCE

About 3 Cups

Cream:

¼ cup butter

Add gradually and beat until fluffy:

1 cup sugar

Beat in, one at a time:

2 eggs

One or two extra eggs will add richness. Beat in slowly and thoroughly
and cook in a double boiler ♦ over—
not in—boiling water:

1 cup scalded milk
1 teaspoon vanilla
1 teaspoon nutmeg

Fold in:

1 cup crushed berries, sliced
peaches, etc.

CLASSIC SABAYON SAUCE

About 3 Cups

Prepare:

Zabaglione or Sabayon, 511

You may omit the egg white if you
prefer a richer and denser mixture. If
you do, use in all:

1 cup wine

HOT SABAYON SAUCE

About 2 Cups

Excellent with beignets or fruit cake.
Marsala is traditional in Italian
recipes. We find that it gives the
sauce a rather dull color and prefer
to use, instead, a sweet white wine—
after the French fashion. This mix-

ture should be creamy rather than fluffy. For a fluffy sauce, see the next recipe.

Stir constantly until thick in the top of a double boiler ◗ over—not in—boiling water:

    6 egg yolks
    1/3 cup sugar
    1 cup white wine or 1/2 cup water and 1/2 cup Cointreau or Grand Marnier

COLD SABAYON SAUCE

          About 1 1/4 Cups

The advantage of this sauce over the classic version is that it will keep for several days in the refrigerator. Use it over fresh fruits.

Combine, beat and heat in the top of a double boiler ◗ over—not in—boiling water:

    4 egg yolks
    3/4 cup sugar
    3/4 cup dry sherry or other dry wine

Beat with a whisk until very thick. Set the double boiler top in a pan of cracked ice and continue to beat the sauce until cold. Add:

    (1/4 cup lightly whipped cream)

WEINSCHAUM SAUCE

Prepare:

    Wine Custard or Weinschaum, 511

RUM SAUCE

          About 2 1/2 Cups

Beat:

    2 egg yolks

Add and beat until dissolved:

    1 cup sifted confectioners' sugar

Add slowly:

    6 tablespoons rum

Beat these ingredients until well blended. Whip until stiff:

    1 cup whipping cream

Fold in:

    1 teaspoon vanilla

Fold the egg mixture into the cream.

RED WINE SAUCE

          About 2 Cups

Boil for 5 minutes:

    1 cup sugar
    1/2 cup water

Cool and add to the syrup:

    1/4 cup claret or other red wine
    1/2 teaspoon grated lemon rind

HOT WINE OR PLUM PUDDING SAUCE

          About 1 1/2 Cups

Cream:

    1/2 cup butter
    1 cup sugar

Beat and add:

    1 or 2 eggs

Stir in:

    3/4 cup dry sherry, Tokay or Madeira
    1 teaspoon grated lemon rind
    (1/4 teaspoon nutmeg)

Shortly before serving, beat the sauce over—not in—boiling water in a double boiler. Heat thoroughly.

CRÈME DE MENTHE OR LIQUEUR SAUCE

Allow, for each serving, about:

    1 1/2 tablespoons crème de menthe or other liqueur

Pour it over:

    Ice cream, ices or lightly sugared fruits

NESSELRODE SAUCE

About 4 Cups

Combine and stir well:

 3/4 cup chopped maraschino
  cherries
 1/3 cup chopped citron or
  orange peel

Add:

 1 cup orange marmalade
 1/2 cup coarsely chopped
  candied ginger
 2 tablespoons maraschino
  cherry juice
 1 cup chopped Boiled
  Chestnuts, (I, 313)
 1/2 cup or more rum, to make
  the sauce of a good
  consistency

Place in jars and seal. Ripen for 2
weeks before serving.

CIDER SAUCE

About 2 Cups

Melt over low heat:

 1 tablespoon butter

Blend in and simmer 3 to 5 minutes:

 3/4 tablespoon flour

Add:

 1 1/2 cups cider

Add, if needed:

 (Sugar)
 (1 teaspoon cinnamon)
 (1/4 teaspoon cloves)

Stir and boil these ingredients about
2 minutes. Serve hot or cold on a
bland pudding.

CHOCOLATE SAUCE
COCKAIGNE

About 1 3/4 Cups

Dreamy on vanilla, coffee or chocolate ice cream. Melt in the top of
a double boiler ◗ over—not in—
boiling water:

 3 oz. unsweetened chocolate

Combine, then stir into the chocolate:

 1 well-beaten egg
 3/4 cup evaporated milk
 1 cup sugar

Cook about 20 minutes. Remove
from heat and beat with a rotary
beater 1 minute or until well blended.
Stir in:

 1 teaspoon vanilla
 (1/4 teaspoon cinnamon)

Cool sauce before using. If tightly
covered and placed in the refrigerator, it will keep several days.

CHOCOLATE SAUCE

About 1 Cup

Stir until dissolved, then cook, without stirring, to the syrup stage, about
5 minutes:

 3/4 cup water
 1/2 cup sugar or 1/3 cup honey

Melt in the syrup:

 1 to 2 oz. unsweetened
  chocolate

Cool. Add:

 1 teaspoon vanilla

You may add a small amount of:

 Cream, dry sherry or
  brandy

Serve hot. If made in advance, keep
the sauce hot in a double boiler.

HOT FUDGE SAUCE

About 1 Cup

The grand kind that, when cooked for
the longer period and served hot,
grows hard on ice cream and enrap-
tures children.

Melt in a double boiler ◗ over—not
in—boiling water:

 2 oz. unsweetened chocolate
 1 tablespoon butter

Stir and blend well, then add:

 1/3 cup boiling water

Stir well and add:

 1 cup sugar

2 tablespoons corn syrup

Let the sauce boil readily, but not too furiously, over direct heat. Do not stir. If you wish an ordinary sauce, boil it ♦ covered for about 3 minutes to wash down any crystals which may have formed on the sides of the pan. Uncover, reduce the heat, and cook 2 minutes more without stirring. If you wish a hot sauce that will harden over ice cream ♦ boil it, uncovered, about 3 minutes more. Add just before serving:

1 teaspoon vanilla or
2 teaspoons rum

When cold, this sauce is very thick. It may be reheated over—not in—boiling water.

CHOCOLATE CUSTARD SAUCE

About 2¹/₄ Cups

Heat in a double boiler ♦ over—not in—boiling water until melted:

2 oz. chopped unsweetened
chocolate
2 cups milk

Beat well:

4 egg yolks
³/₄ cup sugar
¹/₈ teaspoon salt

Beat the hot mixture gradually into the yolks. Return to double boiler. Cook gently, stirring constantly ♦ over—not in—boiling water, about 5 minutes or until thickened. Cool. Add:

1 teaspoon vanilla

Serve hot or cold over:

Puddings, ice cream, or
filled cream puffs

CHOCOLATE NUT-BRITTLE SAUCE

About 1¹/₂ Cups

Melt in a double boiler ♦ over—not in—boiling water:

3 oz. sweet chocolate

Stir in slowly:

¹/₂ cup boiling water

Add:

1¹/₄ cups crushed nut brittle

Cool slightly. Before serving, add:

1 tablespoon brandy

Serve over:

Ice cream

QUICK CHOCOLATE FONDUE SAUCE

I.   **About 1¹/₄ Cups**

Combine and stir in a heavy saucepan over low heat until smooth:

1 cup semisweet chocolate
pieces
¹/₂ cup evaporated milk
(¹/₄ cup marshmallows)

Keep warm in a fondue pan, (I, 243), and use for dipping fruit: pieces of pineapple, banana or orange, or small squares of cake.

II.   **About 1 Cup**

Put into an ⅄ electric blender:

2 squares chopped
unsweetened chocolate
¹/₂ cup sugar
6 tablespoons warm milk,
cream, coffee or sherry
¹/₂ teaspoon vanilla or rum
¹/₈ teaspoon salt

Blend until smooth. Heat in a fondue pan, see I, above.

MOCHA SAUCE

About 1¹/₂ Cups

Bring to a boil and cook over moderate heat about 3 minutes, stirring occasionally:

¹/₂ cup cocoa
¹/₈ teaspoon salt
1 cup dark corn syrup
¹/₄ cup sugar or 16 average-
sized Marshmallows, 581
¹/₄ cup water

1 teaspoon instant coffee
Swirl in:
  2 tablespoons butter
When slightly cool, stir in:
  1/2 teaspoon vanilla
Serve hot or cold.

CHOCOLATE MINT SAUCE

6 Servings

Melt in a double boiler ♦ over—not in—boiling water:
  **10 large chocolate peppermint
     creams**
Add:
  3 tablespoons cream
Stir well.

CHOCOLATE CARAMEL SAUCE

About 1 Cup

Melt over low heat:
  4 oz. semisweet chocolate
Stir in and cook until sauce is thick:
  1 cup brown sugar
  1/2 cup cream
  1 tablespoon butter
Cool slightly and add:
  1 teaspoon vanilla

MAPLE SYRUP SAUCE

About 3/4 Cup

Heat, but do not boil:
  1/2 cup maple syrup
Add:
  1/2 teaspoon grated lemon peel
  **1/4 teaspoon freshly grated
      nutmeg or 1/8 teaspoon
      ginger or cloves**
  **(2 to 3 tablespoons chopped
      nutmeats)**
Chill and serve cold. If you care to serve it hot, swirl in:
  1 to 2 tablespoons butter

MAPLE SUGAR SAUCE

About 2 Cups

Stir over low heat until dissolved, then cook to a thin syrup without stirring:
  1 lb. maple sugar
  1/2 cup evaporated milk
  1/4 cup light corn syrup
Add when cooked:
  1/2 teaspoon vanilla
  1/2 cup shredded nutmeats

BUTTERSCOTCH SAUCE

About 3/4 Cup

Boil to the consistency of heavy syrup:
  1/3 cup light corn syrup
  5/8 cup light brown sugar
  2 tablespoons butter
  1/8 teaspoon salt
Cool these ingredients. Add:
  **1/3 cup evaporated milk or
      cream**
Serve the sauce hot or cold. It may be reheated in a double boiler.

HOT BROWN-SUGAR SAUCE

About 1 1/2 Cups

Cook 5 minutes, stirring occasionally:
  1 cup brown sugar
  1/2 cup water
Pour a little of the syrup in a fine stream over:
  1 beaten egg
Beat constantly, adding the rest of the syrup gradually so the egg thickens. Add:
  3 tablespoons dry sherry
  1/8 teaspoon salt
Serve at once, or hold in a double boiler ♦ over—not in—hot water.

BROWN-SUGAR BUTTER SAUCE

About 1 Cup

Fine with hot puddings or waffles.
Cream in a small saucepan:

¼ cup butter
1 cup brown sugar

Add gradually:

1 cup warm half-and-half or light cream

Stir over low heat until it boils. Remove from heat. Add:

¼ cup bourbon or brandy

Beat with a wire whisk until smooth.
Add and mix in:

(⅓ cup chopped nuts)

RICH BROWN-SUGAR SAUCE

About 1½ Cups

Place in a double boiler ♦ over—not in—boiling water:

3 beaten egg yolks
¾ cup cream
¾ teaspoon salt
½ cup brown sugar

Stir and cook until thick and creamy.
Add a little at a time, stirring constantly:

3 tablespoons butter
1½ tablespoons lemon juice

BROWN-SUGAR ORANGE SAUCE

About 1 Cup

Superfine for filling coffee cakes or for pouring over pancakes and waffles.
Combine in a saucepan:

¾ cup brown sugar
¼ cup butter
½ cup orange juice

Stir constantly and heat for 3 minutes, then cool.

CARAMEL MOCHA SAUCE

About 1 Cup

Prepare and cool, so as not to curdle the cream:

½ cup Caramel Syrup, 597

Add:

1 cup cream or strong coffee
1 teaspoon vanilla
⅛ teaspoon salt

If you use coffee instead of cream, swirl in:

2 tablespoons butter

You may keep the sauce hot over hot water.

CARAMEL CREAM SAUCE

About 1½ Cups

Combine and stir in a double boiler ♦ over—not in—boiling water until melted:

½ lb. Caramels, 586
1 cup whipping cream or evaporated milk

COFFEE SAUCE

About 1½ Cups

Beat:

2 eggs

Beat into them, very slowly:

½ cup strong boiling coffee

Add:

¼ cup sugar
⅛ teaspoon salt

Cook ♦ over—not in—boiling water and stir the sauce in the top of a double boiler until it coats a spoon. Chill. Shortly before serving, fold in:

½ cup whipped cream
(¾ cup chopped candied ginger)

HONEY SAUCE

About 1 Cup

Combine and stir well:
    1/4 **cup hot water**
    1/2 **cup honey**
    1/4 **cup chopped nutmeats**
    1/4 **cup minced candied orange
        or lemon peel or candied
        ginger**
Chill.

HONEY MINT SAUCE

About 3/4 Cup

Recommended for fruit compotes.
Combine:
    1/2 **cup orange juice**
    2 **tablespoons lemon juice**
    2 **tablespoons honey**
    1/8 **cup finely chopped fresh
        mint**

VANILLA SAUCE

About 1 Cup

Combine and stir in a double boiler
over—not in—boiling water until
thickened:
    1/4 **cup sugar**
    1 **tablespoon cornstarch**
    1 **cup water**
Remove sauce from heat. Stir in:
    2 **to 3 tablespoons butter**
    1/8 **teaspoon salt**
    1 **to 2 teaspoons vanilla or
        the seeds scraped from a
        2-inch length of vanilla bean,
        261, or 1 tablespoon rum**

MARSHMALLOW SAUCE

About 2 Cups

Stir over low heat until the sugar is
dissolved:
    3/4 **cup sugar**
    1 **tablespoon light corn syrup**
    1/4 **cup milk**

Bring to a boil, then simmer gently
about 5 minutes. Dissolve in top of
double boiler by stirring ♦ over—not
in—boiling water:
    1/2 **lb. Marshmallows, 581**
    2 **tablespoons water**
Pour the syrup over the dissolved
marshmallows, beating well.
Add:
    1 **teaspoon vanilla**
Serve the sauce hot or cold. It may be
reheated in a double boiler. Beat well
before serving.

COCONUT DULCIE

About 4 1/2 Cups

Good by itself over fruit puddings, or
combined as a sauce with purées of
tart fruit such as guava and currant.
Boil to a thick syrup:
    4 **cups water**
    3 **cups sugar**
Add:
    1 **freshly grated coconut, 244**
Cook slowly about 25 minutes until
the mixture is translucent. Pour into
sterile jars and seal.

SWEETENED BUTTERS

I.   **About 1/4 Cup**

Cream, then chill:
    3 **tablespoons butter**
    1/2 **cup sifted confectioners'
        sugar**
    3/4 **teaspoon cinnamon**

II. Honey Butter

About 1/2 Cup

Delicious on waffles or toast.
Beat well:
    1/4 **cup honey**
    2 **tablespoons soft butter**
    2 **tablespoons whipping
        cream**

**III. See Butter Sauce for Crêpes
Suzette, 145.**

HARD SAUCE

About 1 Cup

Basic ingredients are always the same, although proportions and flavoring may vary. In this recipe, the larger amount of butter is preferable. An attractive way to serve hard sauce on cold cake or pudding is to chill it and mold it with a small fancy cutter—or to put it through the individual butter mold illustrated on 202.
Sift:

> 1 cup confectioners' sugar

Beat until soft:

> 2 to 5 tablespoons butter

Add the sugar gradually. Beat these ingredients until well blended and fluffy. Add:

> 1/8 teaspoon salt
> 1 teaspoon vanilla or
> 1 tablespoon coffee, rum, whisky, brandy or lemon juice

You may beat in:

> (1 egg or 1/4 cup cream)

When the sauce is very smooth, chill thoroughly.

SPICY HARD SAUCE

About 1 Cup

Prepare:

> Hard Sauce, above

Beat into it:

> 1/2 teaspoon cinnamon
> 1/4 teaspoon cloves
> (Liqueur, to taste)

Chill.

BROWN-SUGAR HARD SAUCE

About 1 2/3 Cups

Sift:

> 1 1/2 cups brown sugar

Beat until soft:

> 1/2 cup butter

Add the sugar gradually. Beat these ingredients until well blended. Beat in slowly:

> 1/3 cup cream

Beat in, drop by drop:

> 2 tablespoons dry wine or
> 1 teaspoon vanilla

Chill well. Add for garnish:

> (1/4 cup chopped nuts)

FRUIT HARD SAUCE

About 1 2/3 Cups

Sift:

> 1 cup confectioners' sugar

Beat until soft:

> 1/3 cup butter

Add the sugar gradually. Beat until well blended.
Beat in:

> 1/4 cup cream
> 2/3 cup crushed strawberries, raspberries, apricots or bananas

Chill thoroughly.

FLUFFY HARD SAUCE

About 1 1/2 Cups

Sift:

> 1 cup sugar

Beat until soft:

> 1 tablespoon butter

Add the sugar gradually and:

> 1 tablespoon cream

Beat until well blended. Whip until stiff:

> 3 egg whites

Fold them into the sugar mixture. Add:

> 2 tablespoons cream
> 1 teaspoon or more vanilla, rum or port

Beat the sauce well. Pile it in a sauceboat. Chill thoroughly.

FOAMY SAUCE

About 2 Cups

Sift:

    1 cup confectioners' sugar

Beat until soft:

    1/3 to 1/2 cup butter

Add the sugar slowly. Beat until well blended.

Beat in:

    1 egg yolk

    1 teaspoon vanilla or 2 tablespoons port or 1 tablespoon Grand Marnier

Place the sauce in a double boiler ▶ over—not in—boiling water. Beat and cook until the yolk has thickened slightly. Whip until stiff:

    1 egg white

Fold it lightly into the sauce. Serve hot at once, or cold—but do not try to reheat.

LIQUEUR CREAM SAUCE

About 1 1/2 Cups

So zestful that it will glorify the plainest cottage pudding, cake or gingerbread. Less extravagant, too, than it sounds; only a small amount is needed.

Beat until soft in the top of a double boiler ▶ over—not in—boiling water:

    1/3 cup butter

Add gradually and beat until creamy:

    1 cup sifted confectioners' sugar

Beat in slowly:

    3 tablespoons brandy or other liqueur

Beat in, one at a time:

    2 egg yolks

Add:

    1/2 cup cream

Cook until slightly thickened.

SOUR CREAM SAUCE

About 1 1/2 Cups

Use as dressing for berries, or combine berries with it and serve over cake or fruit gelatin.

Combine:

    1 cup cultured sour cream

    1/2 cup brown sugar

    (1 cup berries)

    (1/2 teaspoon vanilla)

CANDIES AND CONFECTIONS

The fudge pot is responsible for the beginnings of many a good cook. So be tolerant when, some rainy day, your children take an interest in the sweeter side of kitchen life. Weather and altitude play important roles for confectioners, young and old. On humid days, candy requires longer cooking and ingredients must be brought to a heat at least 2 degrees higher than on dry days. In fact, clear, cool weather is a near-precondition for a large group of confections, such as hard candies, glazes, divinities, fondant, nougats and those made with honey.

To avoid a mess ◗ always choose a pan with about four times as great a volume as that of the ingredients used, so that the candy will not boil over. ◗ To keep from burning the candy, see that the pan has a heavy bottom or is lined with a nonstick material. ◗ To keep from burning yourself, use a long wooden spoon that will not heat up during the prolonged cooking period.

Be adventurous about shaping can-dies. A maple sugar mold and a double chocolate rabbit mold with its clips are shown above. As sugar is highly hygroscopic, be sure to store candies tightly covered in glass, ceramic or tin; or serve candies wrapped as temptingly as possible. The illustration above shows a sumptuous and lighthearted silver bonbon-nière, filigreed and spoon-shaped. The utilitarian object in the left foreground is a candy hook for taffy-making, 588.

ABOUT SUGARING IN CANDIES

When we were inexperienced, we were constantly baffled by the tendency of smooth, promising candy syrups to turn with lightning speed into grainy masses. We did not realize that one cause of this calamity was that we had stirred down the sugar crystals that had formed on the sides of the pan into crystals of quite different structure in the liquid below it.

Here are other tips to ward off

sugaring. ◗ If the recipe calls for
butter—and remember, always use
unsalted butter—a good precaution
is to grease the sides of the pan with
some of it before putting in the
other ingredients. Again, in cooking
any candy, we achieve never-fail results by adopting the following procedure, adding other ingredients
along the way as called for in specific individual recipes. Mix liquid
and sugar ◗ stirring until the sugar is
dissolved. Place pan on heat. Bring
mixture to a boil and ◗ cover it
until the candy develops enough
steam to wash down crystals from
the walls of the pan. This is a matter
of 2 or 3 minutes only. Now ◗ uncover the pan to allow for evaporation. ◗ Reduce the heat to medium if
the liquid is milk. ◗ Do not stir after
uncovering, but continue cooking
until the mixture has reached the
desired temperature. When you do
test for temperature, be sure to use
an absolutely clean spoon or thermometer, the reason being, as before, to avoid introducing extraneous
sugar crystals. Should the candy
start to sugar, add a small quantity
of water and begin over again.

Those who make candy frequently
will do well to provide themselves
for the finishing step with a marble
slab of generous proportions. For
candies that require rapid cooling,
this material absorbs heat quickly
and evenly, but not so rapidly as to
hasten and so adversely affect crystallization. The next best base is a
heavy stoneware platter or a flat pan
elevated on a cooling rack so that air
can circulate around it. Surfaces
should be buttered in advance, except
in making fondant.

CANDIES AND CONFECTIONS 575

ABOUT CANDY THERMOMETER TEMPERATURES

Producing varied and distinctive
kinds of candy depends entirely on
arriving at certain established stages
of crystallization; and crystallization,
in turn, depends on temperature. For
this reason ◗ an accurate professional
candy thermometer, properly used, is
invaluable. To test your thermometer for accuracy, heat it in water—
gradually to avoid breakage—and
keep it in boiling water for 10 minutes. It should register 212°. If there
is any variation, add or subtract the
number of degrees necessary to correct
its reading.

When actually using the thermometer, warm it, as for testing, before inserting it into the candy. Place
it near the center of the pan, and do
not let the bulb touch the bottom.
Also keep it from rolling around
in the syrup, for this can trigger
crystallization. Have a spoon ready
when you remove the thermometer
to catch any syrup drops that might
fall back into the pan. Clean the
thermometer after each use by letting it stand in warm water. Heat
rises slowly to 220°, then takes a
spurt—so watch carefully. ◗ For true
accuracy, read at eye level, which of
course means some gymnastics on
your part.

If you have no thermometer, practice can make you expert in recogniz-
ing the subtle differences in color,
bubbling and threading that reveal
crucial temperatures. Always remove
the pot from the heat while testing so
as not to overcook, as a few extra degrees can bring the candy up into the
next stage of crystallization. Use fresh
chilled water for each test.

THREAD—Begins at 230°
The syrup makes a 2-inch coarse thread when dropped from a spoon.

SOFT BALL—Begins at 234°
A small quantity of syrup dropped into chilled water forms a ball which does not disintegrate but flattens out of its own accord when picked up with the fingers.

FIRM BALL—Begins at 244°
The ball will just hold its shape and will not flatten unless pressed with the fingers.

HARD BALL—Begins at 250°
The ball is more rigid but still pliable.

SOFT CRACK—Begins at 270°
Drop a small quantity of syrup into chilled water. It will separate into hard threads, which, when removed from the water, will bend.

HARD CRACK—Begins at 300°
The syrup separates into threads that are hard and brittle.

CARAMELIZED SUGAR—310° to 338°
Between these temperatures syrup turns dark golden, but it will turn black at 350°.

▲ For each increase of 500 feet above sea level, cook candy syrups 1° lower than indicated in the following recipes. For instance, if 234° is given and you are at 2000 feet, your syrup should be brought to 230°; at 5000 feet, to 224°.
◗ Do not jostle the pan when removing it from heat or during the cooling period. ◗ The candy should never be beaten until it has cooled to 110°. There are two ways of cooling. If you are the impatient type, place the pot gently—the minute you take

if from the heat—into a pan of ice-cold water and allow it to remain until you can touch the bottom without discomfort. The other way is to pour the candy onto a marble slab or a heavy buttered platter. If it is taffy, caramel or brittle, hold the pouring edge of the pan away from you and only a few inches above the slab to avoid spattering. With these candies, too, let the mix run out of the pan of its own accord. ◗ To avoid sugaring, do not scrape the dregs from the pan. There is a difference in crystallization rate between the free-flowing portion and the other, near the bottom of the pan, which was exposed to greater heat. If you have neglected to add the called-for butter, you may drop it onto the surface of the hot candy and beat it in after the candy reaches 110°.

These are general principles. For particulars, follow the individual recipes carefully. Should you substitute honey in part for sugar, remember that honey needs a higher degree of heat and longer beating. When used as a candy ingredient, it will attract even more atmospheric moisture than sugar. For this reason honey-based confections must be wrapped with special care.

◗ In gauging yields for the following recipes, we have not included nuts, fruits and other additions where such additions are optional.

ABOUT CANDY WRAPPINGS

For that professional look, wrap candies in attractive foils, or buy, at small cost, fancy fluted foil cups into which you can pour directly. Delight the children by inserting lollipop cords. Or let them form candy chains by cutting 2 long narrow strips of thin self-sealing transparent wrap, laying out squares of candy—rather generously spaced—on one, placing the other neatly on top, then sealing in the candy bits, sausage-fashion. By twisting the wrap between the candy segments, colorful ★ Christmas-tree chains can be made and the links cut apart later for individual distribution.

ABOUT FONDANT AND CREAM CENTERS

One of the charms of fondant is that a batch can be made and ripened and then used at will over a period of weeks, with varying flavors, colors and shapes to suit the occasion. Basic Fondant also lends itself to variations during cooking. You may replace the water in the recipe with strong coffee, or use half white and half brown sugar, or half white and half maple sugar. But in case you don't want to make up a large batch of Basic Fondant, read the alternate processes given after the basic recipe—or use recipes carrying the word "center" in the title.

After removing fondant or centers from refrigeration, cover for several hours to keep them from absorbing atmospheric moisture as they reach room temperature.

BASIC FONDANT

About 1¹/₄ Pounds

Bring to a boil in a large heavy pan:

1 cup water

Remove from heat and stir in until dissolved:

3 cups sugar

Return to heat and have ready:

¹/₁₆ teaspoon cream of tartar

More will make the fondant harder to work later. ◗ Just as the syrup comes up to a boil, add the cream of tartar to the mixture by tapping it from the spoon on the edge of the pan. Be ready to stir, as it will tend to make the syrup boil over. ◗ Cover 2 to 3 minutes until the steam can wash down the sides of the pan. Then cook this mixture ◗ uncovered, without stirring, until it reaches the soft-ball stage, 234°. Remove pan gently from heat. Pour syrup onto a marble slab or platter moistened with ice water by snapping the water off your fingers as though you were sprinkling laundry. ◗ Do not scrape pan. ◗ Let the syrup cool at least until it holds a fingerprint momentarily.

Work the syrup with a candy scraper or a wooden spoon by lifting and folding, always from edges to center. When the syrup loses its translucency and begins to become opaque and creamy, knead it well with your hands, dusting them with confectioners' sugar if necessary.

Even experts sometimes cook fondant too hard to knead it. If you have done so, add ²/₃ of a cup of water. Melt the mixture very slowly in the top of a double boiler ◗ over—not in—boiling water, stirring constantly until it has thoroughly liquefied. Return it to pan and heat to the boiling point again. Then proceed by covering, letting the steam wash down the sides of the pan and recooking to the soft-ball stage, 234°.

After kneading fondant, put it in a tightly covered container. Allow it to remain in a cool place for from 24 hours to a week or more. To prepare it for shaping, put it in a double boiler ◗ over—not in—hot water. Heat it slowly, with the water at 170° to 180°, until you can shape it, then put it on a slab for forming and cutting.

If you want to color fondant, make a depression in the mass and pour in a few drops of vegetable food coloring. Gash it in several places but not all the way through to the slab—allowing the color to spread through the candy. Continue slashing and folding to complete the spreading process. Flavoring can be worked in in the same way. At this time you may also incorporate chopped or whole nuts, candied fruits, ginger, coconut or jam. The amount of such additions should about equal that of the fondant. Correct to the proper consistency with confectioners' sugar if necessary.

Form fondant by rolling it into 1/2-inch rods, then cutting them into round or oval pieces. You are now ready to dip them in:

Chocolate Coating, 582

◗ Be sure to have centers at room temperature to keep chocolate from developing gray streaks.

SOFT-CENTER FONDANT

About 1 Pound

The type of fondant often used around a candied cherry in a chocolate coating. It is not allowed to ripen but must be molded and dipped at once. After dipping, the egg white causes it to become liquid inside its coating.

Bring to a boil in a large, heavy pan:

  2 cups sugar
  1 cup water
  1/4 teaspoon glycerin
  1 tablespoon light corn syrup

Stir these ingredients until the sugar is thoroughly dissolved. Place the pan over low heat. ◗ When the mixture begins to boil, cover it, so that the steam will wash down any crystals that may have formed on the sides of the pan. Cook the syrup about 3 minutes. ◗ Uncover and continue cooking syrup without stirring until it reaches the soft-ball stage,

234°. Remove it gently from heat. Pour onto a wet slab or platter. Cool syrup to 110°. Spread over it with a spatula:

  1 well-beaten egg white

To work, flavor, form and dip, see Basic Fondant, above. These processes must be done as quickly as possible.

UNCOOKED FONDANT

About 1 1/2 Pounds

"Candy," as Dorothy Parker reminded us, "is dandy." But the chocolate-coated balls below are nothing short of seditious.

Beat until soft:

  1/2 cup butter

Add very slowly and cream until very light:

  1 lb. sifted confectioners' sugar

Add:

  1/4 cup whipping cream
  3/4 teaspoon vanilla

Work the fondant well with the hands and shape it into 1-inch balls. To roll the balls, use about:

  1/4 lb. sifted confectioners' sugar

Raisins, nutmeats or bits of candied fruit may be used as centers. Place balls on foil in the refrigerator, covered, until they harden. To dip, see Chocolate Coating, 582.

When coating has hardened, store balls covered and refrigerated until ready to serve.

CARAMEL FONDANT

About 1 1/4 Pounds

Heat in a large, heavy pan:

  1/2 cup milk

Remove from heat and stir in until dissolved:

  1 1/2 cups sugar

¹/₄ **cup butter**
Return to heat and bring very slowly to a boil. Meanwhile, caramelize, 232, in a heavy skillet:

¹/₂ **cup sugar**
When the sugar and butter mixture boils, stir in the caramelized sugar very slowly. Boil, then ◗ cover about 3 minutes until any crystals on the sides of the pan have been washed down by the steam. Uncover and cook candy to soft-ball stage, 234°, without stirring. Cool candy to 110°. Beat it until creamy. Pour it into a pan and mark it into squares or form candy into small balls. Place between the squares:

Nutmeats
or dip squares or balls in:

Chocolate Coating, 582

NEWPORT CREAMS OR CENTERS

About 1¹/₂ Pounds
Much like an opera cream in texture. Bring to a boil in a large, heavy pan, stirring until the sugar is dissolved:

²/₃ **cup light corn syrup**
2 **cups light brown sugar**
6 **tablespoons hot water**
◗ Cover about 3 minutes until any crystals on the sides of the pan have been washed down by the steam. ◗ Uncover and cook, without stirring, to the thread stage, 230°. Whip until stiff:

1 **egg white**
A few grains of salt
Pour syrup slowly into the egg white, whipping constantly. Add:

1 **teaspoon vanilla**
1¹/₄ **cups nutmeats**
When you can no longer stir the candy, flatten it out on a buttered tin. When cold, cut it into squares.

OPERA CREAMS OR CENTERS

About 1¹/₄ Pounds
Bring to a boil in a large, heavy pan, stirring until the sugar is dissolved:

2 **cups sugar**
³/₄ **cup whipping cream**
1 **cup milk**
2 **tablespoons light corn syrup**
¹/₈ **teaspoon salt**
◗ Cover and cook about 3 minutes until the steam has washed down any crystals on the sides of the pan. ◗ Uncover and cook over low heat to the soft-ball stage, 234°. Remove from heat. Cool to 110°. Add:

1 **teaspoon vanilla**
Beat the mixture until creamy. Pour it into special rubber-sheet candy molds or a buttered pan. When cold, cut into squares. Place in an airtight container. This candy improves if aged at least 24 hours. When it has ripened, you may dip it in a:

Chocolate Coating, 582

PEPPERMINT CREAM WAFERS

About 1¹/₄ Pounds
These are delightful decorated or initialed for teas. See About Decorative Icings, 490.
Stir over low heat in a large, heavy pan until the sugar is dissolved:

2 **cups sugar**
¹/₄ **cup light corn syrup**
¹/₄ **cup milk**
¹/₄ **teaspoon cream of tartar**
Cook and stir these ingredients slowly until they boil. ◗ Cover about 3 minutes until any crystals on the sides of the pan have been washed down by the steam. ◗ Uncover and cook without stirring to the soft-ball stage, 234°. Remove from heat. Cool slightly. Beat until creamy. Flavor with:

8 **to 12 drops oil of peppermint**

Tint lightly with vegetable coloring if desired. Drop the mixture from a teaspoon onto foil to form patties the size you want.

For more uniform shapes, make use of a wooden-handled funnel. Pouring the hot mixture into the funnel requires two people—one to hold the stopper and funnel, the other to pour. As the funnel is filled, keep the stopper in place. Immerse the funnel in hot water just past the neck to avoid chilling and stoppage of the mixture. Then, periodically removing the funnel from the hot water, release the candy onto a wax-paper-covered tray. When an adequate amount has dripped through, as shown, replace the stopper.

MAPLE CREAM CANDY

About 1 Pound

Who would ever suspect this delicious confection to be just plain maple syrup in a more solid—and definitely more delectable—form?
Boil over very low heat without stirring:

2 cups maple syrup

until it reaches about 233°. Pour into a shallow pan and cool to 110°, or lukewarm, without stirring. Beat until it becomes lighter in color and creamy in texture. Pour into a greased pan. This candy dries out on exposure to air, so box tightly as soon as cool.

★ ALMOND OR FILBERT PASTE

About 2 Pounds

In some parts of Europe this almond confection is traditional at Christmas time. It is molded into fancy shapes or into flat cakes that are pie-shaped and elaborately decorated. A thin wedge is served to visitors, together with a glass of dessert wine. You may also prepare filberts this way for cake fillings.
Blanch, 237:

1 lb. almonds or filberts

Grind them. All our other recipes for grinding almonds read: "Put through a nut grinder." This is the only recipe that says: "Put them through a meat grinder." This time you want the nuts to be oily. Use the finest blade and grind the nuts at least 4 times. If you use a ♣ blender, use the orange juice or kirsch called for to start the blending action. Cook to the end of the soft-ball stage, 240°, in a large heavy pan:

2 cups sugar
1 cup water

Add the ground nuts and:

6 to 8 tablespoons orange
juice or kirsch
(A few drops rose water)

Rose water is a traditional flavoring. Stir these ingredients until thoroughly blended and creamy. Let them cool until you can knead them. Here are two things you can do to make kneading easier: put confectioners' sugar on your hands, or cover the paste and allow it to rest about 12 hours. Flatten it on a hard surface dusted with confectioners' sugar, then mold it into any desired shape. Pack in a closely covered tin or jar. Ripen from 6 to 8 days.

Should you buy rather than make almond paste, see that it is marked "genuine." If it is not so marked and has a slightly bitter taste, it may be made of crushed apricot, peach or plum seeds treated to destroy the prussic acid content. Once opened, keep refrigerated.

★ MARZIPAN OR MARCHPANE

About ¹/₂ Pound

The Arabs brought this confection to Europe. In tribute to its preciousness, the word which describes it has meant "a seated king," "a little box," "a stamped coin."

Marzipan cake and dessert decorations made in advance are useful to have on hand, and those prepared by the first method can be ❄ frozen for future use.

I. Whip until fluffy:

    1 egg white

Work in gradually:

    1 cup Almond Paste, opposite

Add:

    1¹/₂ cups sifted confectioners' sugar

Use more if necessary to make a paste that is easy to handle. Should it become too thick, work in drop by drop:

    Lemon juice

Should it become too oily, work it in a dish over ice. In either case, knead the paste. Mold it into any desired shape. Small fruit shapes are great fa-vorites. If you wish to color it, use a pastry brush with a little diluted vegetable coloring. Glaze the "fruits" with a solution of:

    Gum arabic, 603

Also, you may roll the paste in:

    Equal parts of cocoa and powdered sugar

or use it as a center for dipping. Wrap each piece separately in foil. Store in a cool place.

II. Use:

    Equal parts of almond paste and fondant

Knead, mold and color as above.

MARSHMALLOWS

About 1³/₄ Pounds

This recipe requires the use of an electric mixer. Results are also much improved if you can get, at a professional outlet, gelatin of 250 bloom—a more concentrated form than that sold to the housewife.

Put in the mixer bowl and let stand for 1 hour:

    3 tablespoons gelatin

    ¹/₂ cup cold water

In about ¹/₂ hour start to prepare a syrup. Place in a heavy pan over low heat and stir until dissolved:

    2 cups sugar

    ³/₄ cup light corn syrup

    ¹/₂ cup water

    ¹/₄ teaspoon salt

When the mixture starts to boil
◗ cover it about 3 minutes to allow

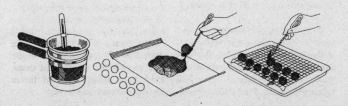

any crystals which have formed to be washed down from the sides of the pan. Continue to cook ◗ uncovered and unstirred over high heat to the firm-ball stage, 244°. Overcooking will make marshmallows tough. Remove the mixture from heat and pour slowly over the gelatin, beating constantly. Continue to beat about 15 minutes after all the syrup has been added. When the mixture is thick but still warm add:

2 tablespoons vanilla

Put the mixture into an 8 × 12-inch pan that has been lightly dusted with cornstarch. When it has dried for 12 hours, remove it from the pan, cut it into squares with scissors dusted with cornstarch, and store the fully dusted pieces in a closed tin.

CHOCOLATE COATING

For a long time our attempts to dip candies attractively were not an unqualified success. We finally sought the advice of Larry Blumenthal, whose family has been "in chocolate" for generations. He finds our procedure solid, but warns us that when you heat chocolate and cool it to dipping temperature, you have "tempered" it, and that its reactions from this point on are somewhat unpredictable. In the candy trade, dipping is turned over to a "handcoater," who uses no specially processed chocolate, although he may thicken his mix adroitly by adding at just the right moment a few drops of water at 65° to 70°.

◗Choose crisp dry weather for dipping. ◗ Work in a room where the temperature is 60° to 70°, the humidity below 55 percent, and where there are no drafts.

Grate about:

1 lb. chocolate: sweet, unsweetened, semisweet or milk

Melt it very, very slowly in the top of a 1¹/₂-quart double boiler ◗ over—not in—boiling water. ◗ Stir the chocolate until its temperature reaches 130°. If you do not stir constantly at temperatures over 100°, the cocoa butter will separate out. Remove from the heat and cool to about 88°. Heat water to 90° in the bottom of the double boiler. Place chocolate in the upper part.

Before dipping into chocolate, be sure candy centers or fillings are about 70°. Otherwise, the chocolate may streak with gray. Coat the centers one at a time in a small quantity of the chocolate, as shown at center, 581. Lift them out with a fork or a candy-dipping fork onto a ¹/₄-inch wire rack above a pan or tray—to catch chocolate drippings, which may be remelted and reused. There is always a surplus on the dipping fork. This is lifted directly above the candy and dripped to make designs which identify the various fillings.

FUDGE COCKAIGNE

About 1¹/₄ Pounds

Bring to a boil in a large heavy pan:

1 cup minus 1 tablespoon milk

Remove from heat and stir in until dissolved:

2 cups sugar
¹/₈ teaspoon salt
2 oz. grated unsweetened chocolate

◗ Bring to a boil and cook covered 2 to 3 minutes until the steam washes down from the sides of the pan any crystals which may have formed. ◗ Uncover, reduce heat and cook without stirring to soft-ball stage,

234°. When nearing 234°, there is a fine overall bubbling with, simultaneously, a coarser pattern, as though the fine bubbled areas were being pulled down for quilting into the coarser ones. Remove from heat without jostling or stirring. ♦ Cool the candy to 110°. You may hasten this process by placing the hot pan in a larger pan of cold water until the bottom of the pan has cooled. Add:

2 to 4 tablespoons butter

Beat fudge partially. Add:

1 teaspoon vanilla

Then beat until it begins to lose its sheen. At this point the drip from the spoon, when you flip it over, holds its shape against the bottom of the spoon. Quickly add:

¹/₂ to 1 cup broken nutmeats

Pour the fudge into a buttered pan. Cut into squares before it hardens. To use fudge for centers, beat until thick, knead and shape.

COCOA FUDGE OR CENTERS

About 1¹/₂ Pounds

An unusually interesting texture for centers.

Melt in a large, heavy pan over medium heat:

¹/₄ cup butter

Add:

1¹/₂ cups boiling water

Mix and stir into the hot mixture:

3 cups sugar
²/₃ cup cocoa
¹/₈ teaspoon cream of tartar

♦ Continue to stir until the mixture boils. Cover about 3 minutes to allow steam to wash down any crystals that may have formed on sides of pan. ♦ Uncover, lower heat and cook slowly ♦ without stirring to the soft-ball stage, 234°. Do not stir after removing candy from heat. When the mixture has cooled to 110°, add:

6 tablespoons whole or skim milk solids
1 teaspoon vanilla

Beat until creamy. Pour into an 8 × 8-inch buttered pan. When it becomes firm, cut into squares or knead into 1-inch balls. If it seems too stiff to knead, cover with damp cloth about an hour.

CARAMEL CREAM FUDGE

About 1¹/₄ Pounds

Who would guess that this candy has no maple sugar or maple flavoring at all? Sleight-of-hand? The deception is accomplished more easily with an electric beater.

Put in a large heavy pan:

1 cup brown sugar
1 cup sugar
¹/₈ teaspoon salt
¹/₃ cup corn syrup
1 cup milk

Cook these ingredients quickly, stirring them constantly until they boil. ♦ Cover and cook 2 to 3 minutes. Remove the lid, reduce heat and cook until the mixture reaches the soft-ball stage, 234°.

Place in bottom of a mixing bowl, or your mixer bowl if you are using an electric mixer:

2 tablespoons butter

Remove pan from heat and at once pour mixture over butter. ♦ Do not stir. When cool, add:

1 teaspoon vanilla

and beat until creamy. Just as the mixture loses its gloss, stir in:

1 cup broken black walnuts

Pour onto an oiled marble slab. Cut into squares when set. Store tightly covered.

COFFEE FUDGE

About 1 Pound

Bring to a boil in a large, heavy pan:

1 cup strong coffee

Remove from heat and stir in until dissolved:

2 cups sugar
1 tablespoon cream
1 tablespoon butter
1/8 teaspoon salt
1/4 teaspoon cream of tartar

Cook these ingredients quickly, stirring them constantly until they boil. ◗ Cover and cook for about 3 minutes, until the steam washes down any crystals which may have formed on the sides of the pan. ◗ Uncover and cook over moderate heat to the soft-ball stage, 234°. Remove from heat. Cool to 110°. Add:

1/2 teaspoon almond extract or
1/2 teaspoon cinnamon

Beat until the mixture begins to solidify. Add:

1 cup broken pecan or
hickory nuts

Pour onto a buttered surface. Let the candy cool and harden before cutting it into squares.

COCONUT FUDGE OR CENTERS

About 1 1/4 Pounds

Combine in a deep saucepan:

1 1/2 cups sugar
1/2 cup corn syrup
1/2 cup milk
1/4 cup molasses
(1 tablespoon vinegar)
1/8 teaspoon salt

Stir these ingredients over medium heat until the sugar is dissolved. Bring to a boil and ◗ cook covered for about 3 minutes, until the steam has washed down from the sides of the pan any crystals which may have formed. ◗ Uncover and cook slowly to the soft-

ball stage, 234°, without stirring. Remove from heat and stir in:

1 1/4 cups moist shredded
coconut
3 tablespoons butter

Pour candy onto a buttered platter. When cool enough to handle, shape into small balls or centers. Place them on foil to dry.

CAROB FUDGE

About 1 Pound

Combine in a saucepan over medium heat:

2 cups brown sugar
6 tablespoons carob powder

Add:

2 tablespoons butter
2/3 cup milk
1/8 teaspoon salt

When the mixture begins to boil ◗ cover and cook 2 or 3 minutes, until the steam washes down any crystals which may have formed on the sides of the pan. ◗ Uncover, reduce heat and cook without stirring to the thread stage, about 230°. Remove from heat and add:

1 1/2 teaspoons vanilla

Beat well and add:

1/2 cup broken nutmeats

Let harden in an 8 × 8-inch buttered pan.

WHITE FUDGE COCKAIGNE

About 1 1/2 Pounds

Stir in a large heavy pan over medium heat until dissolved:

2 1/2 cups sugar
1/2 cup cultured sour cream
1/4 cup milk
1 tablespoon light corn syrup
1/4 teaspoon salt

When the mixture begins to boil ◗ cover and cook for 2 to 3 minutes, until the steam washes down any crystals which may have formed on the sides of the pan. ♦ Uncover, reduce heat and cook without stirring to the soft-ball stage, 234°. Pour at once into an electric mixer bowl. Do not scrape the pan. While the mixture is cooling, float on top:

2 tablespoons butter
1 teaspoon vanilla

In about 1 hour, when cool, beat until the mixture begins to lose its gloss. Quickly beat in:

(³/₄ cup broken nutmeats)
(¹/₄ cup finely cut dried apricots)

Let harden in an 8 × 8-inch buttered pan. Cut into squares. Store tightly covered.

DIVINITY

About 1¹/₂ Pounds

Pick a dry day. This candy does not keep well. If you use the brown sugar and vinegar, you may prefer to call this Sea Foam. Bring to room temperature:

2 egg whites

Bring to a boil in a heavy pan:

¹/₂ cup water
¹/₂ cup light corn syrup

Dissolve in it:

2 cups white or brown sugar
(1 tablespoon vinegar)

When boiling ♦ cover pan and cook about 3 minutes until the steam has washed down any crystals that may have formed on the sides of the pan. ♦ Remove lid and cook over moderate heat, without stirring, to the hard-ball stage, about 250°. While syrup is cooking, beat egg whites in a large bowl until they just hold their shape. When the syrup is ready, pour it slowly over the egg whites in a steady thin stream, whipping slowly at the same time. Toward the end, add the syrup more quickly and whip

faster. ♦ Do not scrape pan. After all the syrup has been added, put in:

1 cup broken nutmeats
(1 cup white raisins)

As a variation try omitting nuts and raisins and add:

(1 cup crushed Peppermint Hard Candy, 590)

Beat until candy can be dropped onto a buttered surface into patties which hold their shape.

CARAMEL CREAM DIVINITY

About 2 Pounds

A smooth, rich candy which keeps better than divinity. Bring to a boil in a large heavy pan:

2 cups cream

♦ Remove from heat and stir in:

3 cups sugar
1 cup white corn syrup

Return to heat and cook slowly. When the candy boils ♦ cover and cook about 3 minutes until the steam washes down any crystals which may have formed on the sides of the pan. ♦ Uncover and cook slowly, without stirring, to the soft-ball stage, 234°. Remove syrup from heat. Cool to 110°. Beat until very stiff. Beat in:

1 cup broken pecan meats

Pour the candy into a buttered pan. Cut it when cool.

NOUGAT

About 1¹/₄ Pounds

Southern France and Italy are famous for luscious nougats with distinctive flavors dues to regional honey variations. So, why is there no honey in our recipe? For the answer, see About Honey, 229. Pick a dry day. This is a two-part process, and an electric mixer is almost imperative.

First, cook in a 2-quart heavy saucepan:

6 tablespoons sugar
1 tablespoon water
1/3 cup light corn syrup

Blend over low heat and stir until the mixture boils. ◗ Cover and cook about 3 minutes until the steam has washed down any crystals which may have formed on the sides of the pan. Cook ◗ uncovered over medium heat, without stirring, to the soft-ball stage, 234°. Remove pan from heat and let stand while you beat in a mixer until very stiff:

1/4 cup egg whites

Add the hot syrup gradually to the whites, continuing to beat at least five minutes until the mass thickens. Blend in a heavy 1-quart pan and stir over low heat to boiling point:

1 cup light corn syrup
1 cup sugar

Stop stirring. ◗ Cover again for 3 minutes, then uncover and boil rapidly, without stirring, to just under the hard-crack stage, about 285°. Remove from heat and let stand until syrup stops bubbling. Now pour the second mixture into the first and beat until well combined. Beat in:

2 tablespoons butter cut into
small chunks

Add:

1 cup blanched almonds, 237
1/2 cup blanched pistachio
nuts, 237
(1/2 cup chopped candied
cherries)

Pour into an 8 × 8-inch buttered pan dusted with confectioners' sugar or lined with baker's wafer paper. Let set in a cool place 12 hours. If hard to get out of pan, release sides with a knife. Then hold bottom of pan briefly over heat and reverse the block onto a board for slicing.

VANILLA CREAM CARAMELS

About 2 1/2 Pounds

Dissolve over low heat in a large heavy pan, stirring until the mixture boils:

2 cups sugar
2 cups dark corn syrup
1 cup butter
1 cup cream

Cook over moderate heat, stirring constantly, to just under the firm-ball stage, 244°. Remove from heat and add very gradually:

1 cup cream

Return to heat and cook to the firm-ball stage, 244°. Pour the mixture at once, without stirring, into a buttered pan. When firm, about 3 hours later, invert the candy onto a wooden board and cut into squares with a thin-bladed knife. Use a light sawing motion.

MAPLE CARAMELS

About 1 1/2 Pounds

Stir in a large heavy pan over quick heat until the sugar is dissolved:

2 cups brown sugar
1 1/2 cups maple syrup
1/2 cup cream

Stir and cook these ingredients slowly to the firm-ball stage, 244°. Add:

1 tablespoon butter

Pour candy into buttered tin. Cut into squares as it hardens. Nuts may be added to the candy just before removing it from the heat, or they may be sprinkled in the buttered tin before pouring the candy. When cool, about 3 hours later, invert onto a board and cut squares free along lines previously indicated.

CHOCOLATE CARAMELS

About 1 1/2 Pounds

Stir over quick heat until the sugar is dissolved:

3 **cups sugar**
1 **cup light corn syrup**
1 **cup milk**
1 1/2 **tablespoons butter**

Cut into small pieces and stir in:

3 **oz. unsweetened chocolate**

Stir and boil these ingredients slowly to the firm-ball stage, 244°. Add:

1 **teaspoon vanilla**

Pour candy into a lightly buttered 9 × 9-inch tin. When firm—about 3 hours later—invert onto a board and cut into 3/4-inch squares.

CHOCOLATE CREAM CARAMELS

About 1 Pound

Stir over high heat until the sugar is dissolved:

1 **cup sugar**
3/4 **cup light corn syrup**
3 **oz. unsweetened chocolate**
1/4 **teaspoon salt**
1/2 **cup cream**

Bring the ingredients to the soft-ball stage, 234°, over moderate heat. Stir constantly. Add:

1/2 **cup cream**

Cook candy until it again reaches the soft-ball stage, 234°. Add:

1/2 **cup cream**

Cook to the firm-ball stage, 244°. Remove candy from heat and pour into an 8 × 8-inch buttered pan. Do not scrape pan. When candy is firm, about 3 hours later, invert onto a board and cut into squares.

FILLED CARAMELS COCKAIGNE

Prepare:

**Chocolate Cream
Caramels, above**

Pour half the candy into one 8 × 8-inch buttered pan, the other half into

a second buttered pan. When it holds its shape, remove from pans. Slice a 1/4-inch layer of:

Basic Fondant, 577

Place it over the surface of one layer. Cover with the other layer. Cut the caramels in 1/2- or 3/4-inch squares, using a sharp knife and a sawing action. Wrap individually.

OLD-FASHIONED BUTTERSCOTCH

About 1 Pound

Place in a heavy pan large enough to allow for foaming:

2 **cups brown sugar**
1/4 **cup molasses**
1/2 **cup butter**
2 **tablespoons water**
2 **tablespoons vinegar**

Stir these ingredients over high heat until the sugar is dissolved. Boil quickly—stirring frequently—to the hard-crack stage, 300°. Drop candy from a teaspoon onto a buttered slab or foil to form patties.

BUTTERSCOTCH

About 1 3/4 Pounds

Stir in a large, heavy saucepan until dissolved:

2 **cups sugar**
2/3 **cup dark corn syrup**
1/4 **cup water**
1/4 **cup cream**

Cook these ingredients to just below the hard-ball stage, about 250°, then stir constantly until they almost reach the hard-crack stage, about 300°. Pour candy into a buttered pan. When cool and almost set, mark into squares or bars. When cold, cut or break apart.

COFFEE DROPS

About 1¹/₄ Pounds

Use same ingredients as in recipe for Butterscotch on 587, but cook to 295°. Have ready an essence made of:

> **6 to 8 tablespoons instant coffee**
>
> **3 tablespoons water**
>
> **1 tablespoon vinegar**

Add:

> **¹/₂ teaspoon glycerin**

Remove sugar syrup from heat. When it is ready to pour, sprinkle coffee essence over the surface. Stir it in very gently. Drop syrup into ³/₄-inch patties from the edge of a spoon onto a buttered surface. When cool, wrap individually and store in a tightly covered container.

ABOUT TAFFIES

If you hanker to re-create an old-time candy pull, be sure you have a reasonably stout pair of arms or an adolescent in the family who wants to convert from a puny weakling to a muscle-man. However, should you make taffy-pulling a frequent practice, you may find that a candy hook, shown on 574, is well worth the investment. The hook is normally placed at least 6 feet from the floor. The rope of candy is thrown over it repeatedly, while gravity does the rest.

When syrup for taffy has cooked to the indicated temperature ◗ pour it slowly onto a buttered slab. ◗ Hold the pouring edge of the pan away from you and only a few inches above the slab, so you won't be spattered with the dangerously hot syrup. Allow the syrup to cool briefly. ◗ This is the moment to flavor the taffy. Because of the great heat, use flavoring essences based on essential oils. See flavoring of hard candies, 590. Sprinkle these over the surface of the hot syrup. Go easy, as they are very strong. If chocolate is to be added, grate it on the buttered slab before pouring. Nuts, fruits and coconut can be worked in during the pulling process.

Begin to work the syrup up into a central mass, turning it and working it with a candy scraper until it is cool enough to handle with your oiled fingertips. ◗ Take care in picking up the mass. It may have cooled on the surface and still be hot enough to burn as you press down into it. Taffy cooked to 270° should be pulled near a source of heat. When you can gather it up, start pulling it with your fingertips, allowing a spread of about 18 inches between your hands. Then fold it back on itself. Repeat this motion rhythmically. As the mass changes from a somewhat sticky, side-whiskered affair to a glistening crystal ribbon, start twisting, while folding and pulling. ◗ Pull until the ridges on the twist begin to hold their shape.

The candy will have become opaque, firm and elastic but will still

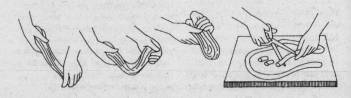

retain its satiny finish. Depending on proper cooking, the weather and your skill, this pulling process may last from five to twenty minutes.

◗ Have ready a surface dusted with confectioners' sugar or cornstarch. Then form the candy into a ball in your hands and press it into a narrow point at the fingertip end. Grasping the narrow point in one hand, pull it away from the rest of the ball into a long rope about one inch thick. Let the rope fall out onto the dusted board like a snake. With well-buttered shears, cut up into segments of a size you prefer. Let it cool. If you do not want to wrap it separately, put the candy into a tightly covered tin, dusting and all. Some taffies, especially those heavy in cream, will, of their own accord, turn from a pulled chewy consistency to a creamy one. This happens sometimes a few minutes after cutting, sometimes as long as 12 hours later. After creaming takes place, be sure to wrap the taffies in foil and store them in a closed tin, because in this state they dry out readily on exposure to air.

VANILLA TAFFY

About ¹/₂ Pound

If you allow this candy to become creamy, it rivals the very rich Cream Pull Candy, next page. Stir over low heat until the sugar is dissolved:

1¹/₄ cups sugar
¹/₄ cup water
2 tablespoons mild vinegar
1¹/₂ teaspoons butter

Cook these ingredients quickly, without stirring, to just between the hard-ball and the soft-crack stages, about 265°. Pour candy on buttered platter or marble slab and let cool until a dent can be made in it when pressed with a finger. Gather it into a lump

and pull it, as seen opposite, with fingertips until porous. Pull into the candy any desired flavoring or coloring, such as:

1 teaspoon vanilla or a few
drops peppermint or other
flavoring oil

Roll it into long thin strips and cut into 1-inch pieces. Place candy in a tightly covered tin if you want it to become creamy.

MOLASSES TAFFY

About 1 Pound

Stir over high heat until the sugar is dissolved, then stir until the mixture boils:

1 cup molasses
2 teaspoons vinegar
1 cup sugar
¹/₈ teaspoon salt

Cover pan and, without stirring, cook syrup rather quickly to just below the firm-ball stage, 242°. Add, by dropping in small pieces:

2 tablespoons butter

Boil syrup slowly—just below the soft-crack stage, about 268°. Holding the pouring edge of the pan away from you and a few inches above the slab, allow syrup to spread over slab. ◗ Do not scrape pan. Sprinkle surface of taffy with:

4 drops oil of peppermint

To work, pull and form, see About Taffies, opposite. To make chips, pull in long, very thin strips. To cover, see:

Chocolate Coating, 582

PULLED MINTS

About 1 Pound

Like the old-fashioned little cushions we used to buy in tins. Combine in a large, heavy pan and stir until it reaches a boil:

1 cup boiling water

2 **cups sugar**
1/4 **teaspoon cream of tartar**

♦ Cook covered about 3 minutes until the sides of the pan are washed free of crystals. ♦ Uncover and cook without stirring to mid-hard-ball stage, 262°. Remove from heat and pour onto buttered marble slab. Sprinkle with:

**A few drops oil of
peppermint**

To work, pull, form and cream, see About Taffies, 588.

SALTWATER TAFFY

About 1 1/2 Pounds

Combine and stir over low heat until sugar is dissolved:

2 **cups sugar**
1 1/2 **cups water**
1 **cup light corn syrup**
1 1/2 **teaspoons salt**
2 **teaspoons glycerin**

Bring to a boil. Cook covered about 3 minutes until the sides of the pan are washed free of crystals. ♦ Uncover and cook the syrup, without stirring, to the late-hard-ball stage, 265°. Remove from heat. Add:

2 **tablespoons butter**

Holding the pouring edge of the pan away from you, and a few inches above the oiled slab, allow the syrup to spread. ♦ Do not scrape pan. To work, pull, flavor and form, see About Taffies, 588.

CREAM PULL CANDY

About 1 1/2 Pounds

Do not try this in hot or humid weather.

Combine in a heavy saucepan and stir over low heat until dissolved and boiling:

3 **cups sugar**
1 **cup boiling water**

1/8 **teaspoon soda**
1/2 **teaspoon salt**

♦ Cover about 3 minutes until steam has washed crystals from sides of pan. ♦ Uncover and cook without stirring to the soft-ball stage, 234°. ♦ Reduce heat—but not below 225°— while adding almost drop by drop:

1 **cup cream**
(1/4 **cup butter cut into small
bits)**

Cook over moderate heat ♦ without stirring, to 257° and pour syrup at once onto buttered marble slab. Hold the pouring edge away from you and a few inches from the slab. Allow syrup to spread over the slab. ♦ Do not scrape pot. To work, pull, flavor, form and cream, see About Taffies, 588.

HARD CANDY OR LOLLIPOPS

About 1 1/2 Pounds

All hard candies become sticky unless individually wrapped.

Bring to a boil in a large heavy pan:

1 **cup water**

Remove from heat. Add and stir until dissolved:

2 **cups sugar**
3/4 **cup light corn syrup**
1 **tablespoon butter**

Return to heat. When boiling ♦ cover about 3 minutes so the steam can wash down any crystals on the sides of the pan. ♦ Uncover and cook at high heat, without stirring, to hard-crack stage, 300°. Prepare a slab or molds by brushing them well with butter or oil. If you are going to make lollipops, have stiffened lollipop cords on the oiled slab ready to receive patties. Remove candy mixture from heat and cool to 160°. Add:

**A few drops vegetable
coloring**

Choose a vegetable color suitable to the flavor you have decided to use.

An alcohol-based flavor like vanilla will evaporate in the intense heat, so be sure to use a flavor based, instead, on essential oils. For the above recipe, for instance, we suggest one of the following:

1/4 **teaspoon oil of peppermint, cassia or cinnamon**

1 **teaspoon oil of orange, lime or wintergreen**

1/8 **teaspoon oil of anise**

To heighten fruit flavors, add:

(1 **teaspoon powered citric acid)**

If you have no molds, form into balls by pouring a small amount of the candy onto an oiled slab. Keep the rest in the pan over very low heat. Cut candy on the slab into squares with a scissors and roll quickly into balls. Continue to pour the candy onto the slab as needed, but do not scrape the pan. If you have made lollipops, remove them from the slab just as soon as they are firm so as not to crack them.

ROCK CANDY

Broken into small pieces and piled in an open bowl, this makes a sophisticated-looking sugar substitute for coffee. Small clumps clustered on 1/8-inch dowels make attractive swizzle sticks for drinks. Whether the candy be on sticks or on strings, the process of making it is a fascinating experiment in crystallization. Punch holes at the top edge of a thin 8-inch square pan and lace about seven strings from one side to the other as shown below. Place the laced pan in a pan deep enough to catch any leaking syrup. Dissolve:

21/2 **cups sugar**

in:

1 **cup water**

and cook without stirring to about

hard-ball stage, 247°–252°. Pour syrup into laced pan. It should reach a level about 3/4 inch above the strings. Cover the surface with a piece of foil. Watch and wait. The syrup sometimes takes a week to crystallize. Lift out the laced pan. Cut the strings and dislodge the rock candy. Rinse quickly in cold water, and put on racks in a very low oven to dry.

HOREHOUND CANDY

About 21/2 Pounds

Make an infusion of:

8 **cups boiling water**

11/2 **quarts loosely packed horehound leaves and stems**

Steep covered 20 minutes. Drain and discard leaves and stems. To 2 quarts of this bitter dark brew, add:

4 **cups sugar**

11/4 **cups dark cane syrup**

1 **tablespoon butter**

(1 **teaspoon cream of tartar)**

Cook these ingredients until they reach the hard-crack stage, 300°. Skim off any scum. Pour into a buttered 15 × 10 × 1-inch pan and score into pieces before it sets. Allow to cool.

NUT CRUNCH

About 2 Pounds

Sliver large, dense nuts like almonds and Brazil nuts. Others can be left whole. You may add them at once to the mixture if you like a roasted quality in the nut. If not, spread them on a buttered slab or pan and pour the syrup over them after cooking. Heat in a large, heavy skillet:

  1 cup sugar
  1 cup butter
  3 tablespoons water

Cook rapidly and stir constantly about 10 minutes or until the mixture reaches the hard-crack stage, 300°. Add:

  1 to 1½ cups nutmeats

Turn the candy quickly onto the buttered slab. Form into a shape about 1 foot square. When almost cool, brush with:

  ¼ lb. melted semisweet
    chocolate

Before the chocolate hardens, dust with:

  ¼ cup finely chopped nuts

Break into pieces when cold.

ENGLISH TOFFEE

About 1½ Pounds

Combine in a large heavy saucepan and stir over high heat until the sugar is dissolved:

  1¾ cups sugar
  ⅛ teaspoon cream of tartar
  1 cup cream

Stir and boil these ingredients for about 3 minutes. Add:

  ½ cup butter

Cook and stir the syrup to the soft-crack stage, about 270°. It will be light-colored and thick. Remove from heat. Add:

  1 teaspoon vanilla or
  1 tablespoon rum

Pour candy into a buttered pan. When cool, cut into squares. To cover it with semisweet chocolate and nuts, see Nut Crunch, at left.

ABOUT PENUCHE AND PRALINES

The taste of these candies is very similar. Penuche is often cut into squares, like fudge, while pralines are usually made into 3- to 4-inch patties. Why so large, we wonder. We prefer small sugared nuggets made by separating the nuts as the sugar begins to harden. They are best when freshly made with nuts of finest quality. Sometimes coconut or raisins are added. Pralines do not keep well unless wrapped in foil and stored in tightly covered containers.

PENUCHE

About 1 Pound

Dissolve in a large heavy pan and stir constantly until boiling:

  3 cups brown sugar
  ¼ teaspoon salt
  1 cup milk or cream

◗ Cover and cook about 3 minutes, until the steam has washed down any crystals from the sides of the pan. ◗ Uncover and cook slowly, without stirring, to the soft-ball stage, 234°. Remove candy from heat and add:

  1 to 2 tablespoons butter

Cool to 110°. Beat until smooth and creamy. Add:

  1 teaspoon vanilla
  1 to 1½ cups nutmeats

In summer try adding instead:

  (½ cup grated fresh pineapple)
  (1 teaspoon lemon juice)

Pour into a buttered pan and cut into squares.

PLAIN OR SHERRIED PRALINES

About 2 Pounds

Dissolve in a large heavy pan over low heat until boiling:

1¹/₃ cups sugar
²/₃ cup brown sugar
1¹/₃ cups water or sherry
¹/₈ teaspoon salt

◆ Cover and cook about 3 minutes to allow the steam to wash down any crystals from the sides of the pan.
◆ Uncover and cook to the soft-ball stage, 234°. Remove pan from heat and cool candy to 110°. Beat until it thickens and begins to lose its gloss. Quickly stir in:

2 to 3 cups pecans

Drop candy in patties from a spoon onto a buttered platter. When hardened, wrap them individually in foil. Or, pour the candy onto a greased sheet, and before it is fully hardened, roll it to separate the nuts. Store tightly closed in glass jars.

PEANUT OR NUT BRITTLE

About 2 Pounds

Have ready a pair of clean white cotton gloves. It is best to use raw nuts and cook them in the syrup. Should only roasted nuts be available, add them after the syrup is cooked. In this case the candy is best if aged 24 hours. If the nuts are salted, rub them between paper towels and omit salt from the recipe. This recipe makes a tender clear brittle. For a porous one, combine ¹/₄ teaspoon cream of tartar with the sugar, and sprinkle ¹/₂ teaspoon of soda all over the hot syrup just before pouring. Bring to a boil in a large heavy pan:

1 cup water

◆ Remove from heat and stir in until dissolved:

2 cups sugar

Then add and stir in:

1 cup corn syrup

Cook to hard-ball stage, 250°, then add:

2 cups raw Spanish peanuts, pecans and chopped Brazil nuts, or some other nut combination
1 teaspoon salt

Stir occasionally to submerge any exposed nuts so that they cook thoroughly and so the candy does not burn. Cook to almost hard-crack stage, 295°. Remove from heat. Stir in lightly:

1 to 3 tablespoons butter
¹/₄ teaspoon baking soda
(1 teaspoon vanilla)

Pour onto a well-buttered slab at once, scraping out bottom of pan. Spread mixture rapidly with a spatula. At this point, don the cotton gloves. Loosen the mass from the slab with a scraper, reverse it and, discarding the scraper, stretch and pull the brittle so thin that you can see through it. When cool, crack into eating-size pieces and store at once in a tightly covered tin.

NUT BRITTLE, GLAZED NUTS AND PRALINÉ FOR GARNISH

I. **About ¹/₂ Pound**

This clear candy when ground or crushed is called **praliné.** Delicious over ice cream or added to icings and dessert sauces.

Melt in a skillet over low heat:

1 cup sugar

Stir constantly. When the sugar is caramelized, 310°, stir in until well coated:

1 cup toasted almonds or hazelnuts or toasted benne seeds

Pour the candy onto a buttered platter. When cool, crack into pieces.

II. For other syrups to use with nuts, see:

> Glazed Fresh Fruits,
> 602–603

ALMOND CREAMS

Blanch and toast lightly:

> Almonds or hazelnuts

Cover them first with:

> Basic Fondant, 577, or
> Uncooked Fondant, 578

then dip them at once in:

> Chocolate Coating, 582

Place them on a wire rack to dry.

SPICED CARAMEL NUTS COCKAIGNE

Have ready:

> Toasted blanched almonds,
> hazelnuts or pecans, 237

Prepare:

> Chocolate Cream
> Caramels, 587

Add to the dissolved ingredients:

> 1 teaspoon cinnamon

When the candy has cooked almost to the hard-ball stage, 250°, remove it from heat and spread to a ¼-inch thickness on a marble slab. Score the candy in 1-inch squares. Place a whole toasted nut on each square. Before candy hardens, enclose each nut in its candy square, shaping it to the nut.

BURNT ALMONDS AND OTHER NUTS

About 2 Pounds

Cook over low heat, stirring constantly until dissolved:

> 2 cups sugar
> ½ cup water
> 1 teaspoon cinnamon

Boil the syrup rapidly. When it is clear and falls in heavy drops from a spoon, add:

> 1 lb. unblanched almonds,
> hazelnuts or peanuts

Stir the nuts until well coated. Remove the mixture from heat and pour onto a marble slab. Stir until nuts are coated and dry. Sift them to remove any superfluous sugar. Put this excess sugar in a pan and add a very little water and:

> A few drops of red
> vegetable coloring

Boil syrup until clear, then add nuts and stir them until they are well coated. Drain and dry.

SPICED NUTS

About ¼ Pound

Preheat oven to 250°.
Sift into a shallow pan:

> ½ cup sugar
> ¼ cup cornstarch
> ⅛ teaspoon salt
> 1½ teaspoons cinnamon
> ½ teaspoon allspice
> ⅓ teaspoon each ginger and
> nutmeg

Combine and beat slightly:

> 1 egg white
> 2 tablespoons cold water

Dip into the liquid:

> ¼ lb. nutmeats

Drop them one at a time into the sifted dry ingredients. Roll them about lightly. Keep nutmeats separated. Place them on a cookie sheet. Bake at least 1 hour. Remove from oven and shake off excess sugar. Store tightly covered.

CHOCOLATE TRUFFLES

About ⅓ Pound

Definitely a brisk-weather confection.
Coarsely grate:

> 3 oz. unsweetened chocolate

Melt it with:

 1/4 cup butter

Add:

 2 tablespoons cream

Gradually stir in until lump-free:

 7 tablespoons sifted
  confectioners' sugar
 2 tablespoons finely ground
  hazelnuts

Cover and refrigerate 12 to 24 hours. Make individual balls by rolling about a teaspoonful of the mixture in the palm of the hand. This friction and warmth will cause the chocolate to melt slightly, so that the final coating will adhere. Roll balls in:

 Cinnamon-flavored cocoa, or
 Chocolate pastilles or shot

This covering will stick to them very satisfactorily. Keep refrigerated, but for best flavor remove 2 hours before serving.

★ BOURBON BALLS

                    About 1/3 Pound

Sift together:

 2 tablespoons cocoa
 1 cup powdered sugar

Combine and stir in:

 1/4 cup bourbon whisky
 2 tablespoons light corn
  syrup

Add and mix thoroughly:

 2 1/2 cups crushed vanilla wafers
 1 cup broken pecans

Roll mixture into small balls. Dredge in:

 1/2 cup powdered sugar

RUM DROPS, UNCOOKED

 About Forty-Five 1-Inch Balls

Fine served with tea or with lemon ice. Place in a mixing bowl:

 2 cups finely sifted crumbs of
  toasted sponge cake,
  zwieback or graham
  crackers

Add:

 2 tablespoons cocoa
 1 cup sifted confectioners'
  sugar
 1/8 teaspoon salt
 1 cup finely chopped
  nutmeats

Combine:

 1 1/2 tablespoons honey or syrup
 1/4 cup rum or brandy

Add the liquid ingredients slowly to the crumb mixture. Use your hands in order to tell by the "feel" when the consistency is right. When the ingredients will hold together, stop adding liquid. Roll the mixture into 1-inch balls. Roll them in:

 Confectioners' or
 granulated sugar

Set the drops aside in a tightly covered tin box at least 12 hours to ripen.

HEAVENLY HASH CANDY

                    About 1 1/4 Pounds

At least a child's idea of heavenly! Dice:

 12 large or 48 miniature
  marshmallows

Chop:

 1 cup nutmeats

Boil water in bottom of a double boiler. Turn off heat. Place in top:

 1 lb. milk chocolate

Stir occasionally. Line a tray with waxed paper. Pour in half the chocolate when melted. Cover with marshmallows and nutmeats. Pour rest of chocolate over this. Cool and break candy into pieces.

CHOCOLATE CLUSTERS

                    About 3/4 Pound

Melt over hot water:

 1/2 lb. semisweet chocolate

Stir in slowly:

¾ cup sweetened condensed
   milk
When well blended, add:
   1 cup nutmeats or
      unsweetened ready-to-eat
      cereal, sesame seed or
      wheat germ
Drop candy from a teaspoon onto foil.

PEANUT BUTTER FUDGE OR CENTERS

About 2 Pounds

Mix and stir until blended:
   1 cup peanut butter
   1 cup corn syrup
   1¼ cups nonfat milk solids
   1¼ cups sifted confectioners'
      sugar
Mix, then knead. Form into balls.

POPCORN

Kernels of popcorn have been found
in the remains of Central American
settlements almost 7000 years old,
and most archeologists believe that it
may have been the earliest variety
eaten. Keep unpopped corn tightly
covered and refrigerated. ◗ One-half
cup corn equals about 1 quart when
popped. If popcorn has the right
moisture content, you will hear it in a
minute—popping gently. It will be
completely fluffy and ready in another minute. For best results, never
overload the popper. Wire poppers
similar to the one seen opposite, used
over coals or burner heat, call for no
butter or oil before popping, and a
drier popcorn results. They will
process about ¼ cup of kernels at a
time; a heavy-lidded or electric skillet
or a 4-quart pressure pan, ½ cup.
With an electric popper, follow the
manufacturer's directions. Unless you
are using a cage-type popper, add to
the preheated pan for each cooking:
   1 tablespoon vegetable oil
◗ Cook over high heat. ◗ Keep pan
moving constantly. When corn stops
popping, discard all imperfect kernels. For each 4 cups of hot popcorn,
sprinkle with:
   ¼ to ½ teaspoon salt
   2 tablespoons or more melted
      butter or grated cheese

CANDIED POPCORN

Besides making a tasty confection,
candied popcorn lends itself well to
large, but largely inedible ★ Christmas decorations. For other seasons,
use a well-oiled or buttered fancy
two-piece cake mold such as a lamb
or rabbit form, ramming the corn
tightly into all the nooks and crannies
after you have coated it with one of
the syrups below. If you want to color
popcorn, use plenty of vegetable coloring to counteract the whiteness of
the basic material.
To prepare popcorn for shaping, have
ready in a large bowl:
   6 cups popped corn, at left
Prepare any of the syrups below.
When the liquid has been taken from
the heat, pour it over the corn. Stir

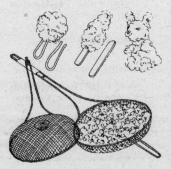

corn gently with a wooden spoon until well coated. Then, when you are sure the corn is cool enough to handle with lightly buttered fingers, press it into balls or lollipops with an embedded loop of string or wooden stick as illustrated opposite.

WHITE SUGAR SYRUP

Stir until the sugar is dissolved:

  2/3 **cup sugar**
  1/2 **cup water**
  2 1/2 **tablespoons light corn syrup**
  1/8 **teaspoon salt**
  1/3 **teaspoon vinegar**

Bring to a boil. ♦ Cook covered for about 3 minutes until steam washes down sides of pan. ♦ Uncover and cook, without stirring, nearly to the hard-crack stage, about 290°.

MOLASSES SYRUP

Melt:

  1 **tablespoon butter**

Add:

  1/2 **cup molasses**
  1/4 **cup sugar**

Stir these ingredients until sugar is dissolved. Bring to a boil. ♦ Cover and cook for about 3 minutes until the steam has washed down the sides of the pan. ♦ Uncover and cook, without stirring, nearly to the hard-crack stage, about 290°.

CARAMEL SYRUP

Melt:

  1 1/2 **tablespoons butter**

Add:

  1 1/2 **cups brown sugar**
  6 **tablespoons water**

Stir these ingredients until sugar is dissolved. Bring to a boil. ♦ Cover and cook for about 3 minutes until the

steam has washed down the sides of the pan. ♦ Uncover and cook, without stirring, to the soft-ball stage, 234°.

PASTILLAGE OR GUM PASTE

About 3 Cups

A favorite mixture for decorations, especially on wedding cakes. It makes lovely molded leaves and flowers. The shapes are separately formed and held together later with Quick Decorative Icing, 496. Gum paste can be rolled out like pie crust, but never more at a time than you plan to shape immediately, because it dries rapidly and becomes cracked and grainy.

Dissolve in the top of a double boiler over, not in, boiling water:

  1 **tablespoon gelatin**
  1/2 **cup water**
  1 **teaspoon cream of tartar**
  1 **teaspoon powdered gum tragacanth**

To keep paste white, add:

  1 **or 2 drops blue vegetable coloring**

Mix and knead the mixture with:

  4 **cups confectioners' sugar**

working various vegetable colorings, if you wish, into separate portions of the mix as you complete this operation. Store the paste in a bowl covered with a damp cloth and let it rest at least 1/2 hour. When you are ready to use it, dust a board, a roller and your hands with cornstarch. Roll to the desired thickness as much paste as you will immediately use. Cut into shapes. Large flat ones are allowed to dry on the cornstarch-covered board for at least 24 hours. Cover top surfaces of paste with cornstarch also. Petals, leaves, etc., are shaped and stored in cornstarch or cornmeal until dry and ready to assemble.

TURKISH FRUIT PASTE, TURKISH DELIGHT, OR RAHAT LOUKOUM

I.   About 1½ Pounds

In the Middle East, this sweet is served with coffee to friends who drop in for a visit. It calls for simultaneous cooking and stirring in 2 pans. ◗ Have everything ready before you turn on the heat.

Put into a very heavy 2-quart pan:

    2 tablespoons water
    ¾ cup liquid fruit pectin

Stir in:

    ½ teaspoon baking soda

The soda will cause foaming. Do not be alarmed.

Put into another pan:

    1 cup light corn syrup
    ¾ cup sugar

Put both pans on high heat. Stir alternately 3 to 5 minutes or until foaming has ceased in the pectin pot and boiling is active in the other. Then, still stirring the corn syrup mixture, gradually and steadily pour the pectin mixture into it. Continue stirring and boiling, and add during the next minute:

    ¼ cup any jelly: apple,
      currant, apricot,
      raspberry, peach or
      quince

Remove the mixture from heat and stir in:

    1 tablespoon lemon juice
    (1 teaspoon grated lemon
      rind)
    (½ cup broken pistachio or
      other nutmeats)

Pour into an 8 × 8-inch pan. Let stand at room temperature about 3 hours. When the mixture is very firm, sprinkle with:

    Confectioners' sugar

Cut into shapes or squares by pressing down with a buttered or sugared knife. Release the candies onto a sugared tray so all sides become coated. If you plan packing these candies, let them stand sugared 12 hours or more on a rack. Redust on all sides and pack, then store tightly covered. Should you want to dip them in chocolate, remove excess sugar first.

II.

Combine in a measuring cup and let stand at least 5 minutes:

    ⅓ cup lemon or lemon and
      lime juice
    3 tablespoons cold water
      Grated rind of 1 lemon
    2 tablespoons gelatin

Place in a large heavy pan over moderate heat:

    ⅔ cup water
    2 cups sugar

Stir until sugar is dissolved. When boiling starts ◗ cover and boil 2 to 3 minutes. Uncover and cook to the soft-ball stage, 234°, without stirring. Remove from heat and add the gelatin mixture. Return to heat and stir until thermometer registers 224°. If you wish, add:

    (A few drops of vegetable
      food coloring)

Pour the mixture into a lightly oiled 8 × 8-inch pan in which you have scattered:

    (1 cup chopped nuts)

Let stand 12 hours. To cut and store, see I above. You may vary the flavor of fruit paste by using juices other than lemon and lime, such as reduced unsweetened apricot or apple, raspberry or strawberry juice, if the liquid proportions are not altered. You may also replace 1 tablespoon of the cold water used for soaking the gelatin with 1 tablespoon of lemon or lime juice to give additional tartness.

MEXICAN ORANGE DROPS

About 2 Pounds

Heat in the top of a double boiler:

1 cup evaporated milk

Melt in a deep saucepan:

1 cup sugar

When the sugar is a rich brown, stir in slowly:

¹/₄ cup boiling water or orange juice

Add the hot milk. Stir in until dissolved:

2 cups sugar

¹/₄ teaspoon salt

◗ Bring to a boil and cook covered 3 minutes until the steam washes down any crystals on the sides of the pan.◗ Cook uncovered over low heat, without stirring, to the soft-ball stage, 234°. Add:

Grated rind of 2 oranges

Cool these ingredients. Beat until creamy. Stir in:

1 cup broken nutmeats

Drop the candy from a spoon onto foil.

GINGER CANDY OR CENTERS

About 1³/₄ Pounds

Bring to a boil in a large heavy pan:

³/₄ cup milk

◗ Remove from heat. Add and stir until dissolved, then cook until boiling:

2 cups white sugar

1 cup brown sugar

2 tablespoons white corn syrup

◗ Cover and cook for about 3 minutes until the steam washes down any crystals which may have formed on the sides of the pan. ◗ Uncover and cook to the soft-ball stage, 234°. Remove from heat and drop on surface of syrup:

2 tablespoons butter

Cool to 110°. Beat until it begins to thicken. Add:

1 teaspoon vanilla

¹/₄ lb. finely chopped ginger

If preserved ginger is used, drain it well first. If candied ginger is preferred, wash the sugar from it, then dry it in paper towels and chop it. Pour candy onto a buttered platter. Cut into squares before it hardens. These squares may be dipped in:

Chocolate Coating, 582

HAWAIIAN CANDY OR CENTERS

About 1 Pound

A great combination—the tart flavor of pineapple with the spicy taste of ginger.

Bring to a boil in a large heavy pan:

1 cup cream

◗ Remove from heat, add and stir until dissolved:

¹/₂ cup brown sugar

1 cup sugar

¹/₂ cup drained crushed pineapple

Bring to a boil, stirring constantly. ◗ Cover and cook for about 3 minutes, until the steam washes down any crystals which may have formed on the sides of the pan. ◗ Uncover and cook over low heat, stirring only if necessary, to the soft-ball stage, 234°. Remove from heat and add:

1 tablespoon butter

1 teaspoon finely chopped preserved ginger

¹/₂ cup broken pecan meats

1 teaspoon vanilla

Cool to 110°. Beat until creamy. Pour into a shallow buttered pan, and cut into squares before it completely cools.

★ CANDY FRUIT ROLL OR CENTERS

About 5 Pounds

Bring to a boil in a large heavy pan:

1 cup cream
¼ cup water

◗ Remove from heat and stir in until dissolved:

5 cups light brown sugar
¾ cup light corn syrup
1 tablespoon butter
¼ teaspoon salt

Bring these ingredients slowly to a boil, stirring constantly. ◗ Cover and boil about 3 minutes, until the steam has washed down any crystals which may have formed on the sides of the pan. ◗ Uncover and cook without stirring to the soft-ball stage, 234°. Remove from heat and add:

1 lb. blanched shredded almonds
¼ lb. chopped dried figs
1 lb. seeded chopped raisins

Cool to 110°. Beat mixture until it begins to cream. Shape into a roll. Cover with foil and refrigerate. When cold and firm, remove foil. You may roll it in:

(Melted semisweet chocolate)

★ PERSIAN BALLS OR CENTERS

Put through the coarsest cutter of a meat grinder:

½ lb. pitted dates
1 lb. dried figs with stems removed
1 lb. seeded raisins
1 lb. pecan meats
½ lb. crystallized ginger or candied orange peel

If the mixture is very stiff, add:

1 or 2 tablespoons lemon juice

Shape these ingredients into balls or centers for dipping, or form them into a roll to be sliced. Coat with:

Confectioners' sugar

then wrap in foil.

★ DATE ROLL OR CENTERS

Boil to the soft-ball stage, 234°:

3 cups sugar
1 cup evaporated milk

Stir in:

1 cup chopped dates
1 cup chopped nutmeats

When cool enough to handle, form these ingredients into a roll with buttered hands. Wrap the roll in foil. Chill and slice later.

★ STUFFED DRIED FRUITS

Steam over hot water in a covered colander for 10 to 20 minutes:

1 lb. apricots, prunes, dates or figs

Stuff fruits as soon as cool with one or two of the following:

Fondant, 577
Hard Sauce, 572
Nutmeats
Candied pineapple
Candied ginger
Marshmallows
Marzipan, 581, and Orange Zest, 252

I. After steaming and stuffing, the fruits may be rolled in:

Granulated or powdered sugar or grated coconut

II. Or you may coat the fruits in a meringue glaze. Preheat oven to 250°. Beat until very stiff:

2 egg whites

Add gradually, beating steadily:

½ cup sugar
½ teaspoon vanilla

Place the stuffed fruits on a fork. Dip them one by one into the egg mixture until well coated. Place on a wire rack with a baking sheet underneath. Sprinkle tops with:

Grated coconut

Bake about ½ hour.

★ APRICOT ORANGE BALLS

About 2 Pounds

Placed in Christmas boxes, these confections keep the tougher cookies from drying out. Use best quality, slightly soft dried apricots. Steam any that seem too hard and dry. Grind twice in a meat grinder using the finest blade:

1 lb. apricots

1 whole seedless orange or 5 seeded preserved kumquats

You may also grind with them a choice of:

(1/4 lb. candied lemon rind)

(1/4 lb. candied citron)

(1/2 cup shredded coconut)

(1/2 cup nutmeats)

Shape the mixture into balls or patties. Dust in:

Granulated sugar

Store closely covered.

★ APRICOT OR PEACH LEATHER

About 2 Pounds

An old-time Southern Seaboard favorite.
Cover with:

1 cup boiling water

and soak for 12 hours in a glass dish:

1 lb. dried apricots, or 3/4 lb. dried apricots and 1/4 lb. dried peaches

If tenderized fruit is used, omit soaking. Grind fruit with finest blade. Mix in:

(2 teaspoons grated lemon rind)

Sprinkle on a board:

Powdered sugar

You will need about 2 cups sugar in all. Start rolling a small quantity of the fruit pulp with a rolling pin. Sprinkle a little powdered sugar on the surface if the mass sticks. Continue to roll and to add sugar, as necessary, until you have

a very thin sheet resembling leather in texture. This amount should make about a 12 × 16-inch sheet, 1/16 inch thick. Cut it into 1 1/4 × 2-inch strips and roll the powdered strips very tightly. Store closely covered.

BAKLAVA

About 100 2 1/2-Inch-Long Diamonds

A confection prevalent throughout the Near East.
Simmer a syrup of:

1/2 cup sugar or honey

3/4 cup water

1/2 lemon

until it is thick enough to coat the back of a spoon. Remove the lemon. Add:

(1 tablespoon orange blossom water)

and simmer a few minutes longer. Cool and refrigerate.
Prepare a filling of:

1 1/2 cups coarsely chopped nuts: almonds, pistachios and walnuts in any proportion

Sprinkle the nuts with a mixture of:

2 tablespoons sugar

1 teaspoon cinnamon

1/8 teaspoon cloves

Melt:

1 cup sweet butter

Have ready:

24 sheets phyllo, 373: 1 lb.

Layer 12 of them on an 11 × 15-inch buttered baking pan, brushing the sheets of dough with about half the butter. Spread the filling on top and cover with the remaining 12 similarly buttered sheets.
Preheat oven to 350°.
Cut the top layered sheets and filling diagonally into 2-inch-long diamonds, but leave the bottom few layers of sheets uncut. Bake about 30 minutes. Raise oven temperature to

475° and bake about 15 minutes longer or until golden. Remove from oven. Pour the refrigerated syrup over the top of the puffed dough. Cut, using the same diagonals, through the uncut layer of dough and serve the diamond-shaped slices when cooled.

ABOUT CANDIED, CRYSTALLIZED OR GLAZED FRUITS, LEAVES AND BLOSSOMS

There are a number of different methods suggested in the following recipes, and the "keeping" qualities of the product vary. Some fruits and leaves are glazed for temporary decorative effects, which involves a superficially applied covering of syrup or of egg and sugar. Unless used on ♦ very thin leaves and blossoms, they will hold for only a day. If the leaves or flowers are thin and are stored ♦ after thoroughly drying, in a tightly covered container, they may be kept several months.

The other methods described call for ♦ sugar penetration as well as glazing, and the fruits will keep about 3 months. Different syrup weights and different time intervals of drying are suggested, but the principles in these recipes remain the same.

There is a third method for blossoms, using a syrup much like that for Candied Kumquats, 604—especially for the imported violet, *Viola odorata*. Our native violets are too tender to use.

♦ In every operation, keep the fruit or other material covered with the syrup to avoid any hardening or discoloration. To begin with, the fruit is dropped into a thin syrup which can penetrate the skins and cells. Then the liquid is reduced or is replaced with a heavier one. This also penetrates, after the thin syrup has opened

the way, and finally sugars out or dries into a crystal coating.

GLAZED FRESH FRUITS

**Enough to Cover About
1 Cup of Solids**

The beauty of these sparkling confections depends on sparkling weather and last-minute preparation. They must be eaten the very day they are prepared. Use only fresh fruits that are in prime and perfect condition. If you are covering a large quantity of fruit, divide it into several batches for successive syrup cooking. All fruit must be at room temperature and very dry; orange sections, if used, must be dried for at least 6 hours in advance. Work very quickly to keep the syrup effective. Stir in a heavy saucepan, over low heat, until dissolved:

    1 cup sugar
    1/2 to 3/4 cup boiling water
    1/16 teaspoon cream of tartar

Bring syrup to the boiling point. ♦ Cover and cook, without stirring, about 3 minutes to allow steam to wash down any crystals that may have formed on sides of pan. Uncover, lower heat and cook to the hard-crack stage, 300°. Remove pan from heat and place over hot water. Dip only a few fruits at a time and remove them with a fork. Place them on a wire rack until the coating hardens. Should syrup in the pan begin to solidify, reheat it over hot water and repeat the dipping.

GLAZED MINT LEAVES

Have ready the following solution. Dissolve and cook over low heat until clear:

    1 cup sugar
    1/2 cup water

Cool the syrup slightly, before blending in thoroughly:

4 teaspoons powdered acacia

This mixture is called **gum arabic**.
♦ Before using, refrigerate it until chilled. The unsprayed mint leaves should be freshly picked and kept cold, so as not to wilt. Prepare by carefully stripping from the main stem individual leaves, with their small stems attached. Wash and dry thoroughly. Put on a napkin over ice. Dip each leaf in the gum arabic and sugar solution; using your forefinger gently, make a smooth, thin coating. ♦ Be sure every bit of leaf is covered, top and bottom, for any uncoated area will turn brown later. Place leaves carefully on a rack. Turn with a spatula after 12 hours. When the coated leaves become thoroughly dry, store them in tightly covered containers.

CANDIED APPLES

**I.   Enough for
                         5 Medium-Sized Apples**

Combine in a saucepan:

2 cups sugar
2/3 cup light corn syrup
**1 cup water
(A 2-inch piece stick
cinnamon)**

Stir until dissolved. Bring to a boil. ♦ Cook covered for about 3 minutes until the steam has washed down any crystals that may have formed on the sides of the pan. ♦ Uncover and cook, without stirring, nearly to the hardcrack stage, 290°. Remove cinnamon stick if used. Add:

**A few drops of red
vegetable coloring**

After cooking glaze, keep it in a double boiler ♦ over—not in—boiling water. Now, work quickly.
Dip in:

Apples on skewers

Place them on a metal flower holder to harden. Or, to make these lollipops easier to handle after dipping, dust the tips with finely chopped nutmeats or with sugared puffed dry cereals; or arrange on the top of each a trefoil decoration of three pecan or walnut halves, and allow the apples to dry upside down on a piece of foil, as shown.

II. Wash, dry and insert a skewer in the stem end of:

5 medium-sized apples

Place in the top of a double boiler:

1 lb. Caramels, 586
2 tablespoons water

Heat and stir these ingredients until they melt into a smooth coating. Dip the skewered apples into the sauce, twirling them until completely coated. Dry as above. If refrigerated, they will harden in a few minutes.

GLAZED PINEAPPLE

Drain and reserve juice from:

**3½ cups sliced cooked or
canned pineapple**

Dry slices with a cloth or paper towel. Add to the juice:

2 cups sugar
1/3 cup light corn syrup

Stir and bring these ingredients to a boil in a large heavy pan. Add the fruit but do not crowd it. Simmer until it is transparent. Lift fruit from syrup. Drain it on racks until thoroughly dry. Place between waxed paper and store tightly covered.

★ CANDIED CITRUS PEEL

This confection may be grated for zest, 252, in cakes and desserts.

I. A moist peel.
Grate fruit slightly to release oil from cells. Cut into thin strips and place in a heavy pan:

> **2 cups grapefruit, orange,
> lime or lemon peel**

Cover with:

> **1¹/₂ cups cold water**

Bring slowly to the boiling point. Simmer 10 minutes or longer if you do not like a rather bitter taste. Drain. Repeat this process 3 to 5 times in all, draining well each time. For each cup of peel, make a syrup of:

> **¹/₄ cup water**
> **¹/₂ cup sugar**

Add peel and boil until all syrup is absorbed and the peel is transparent. Roll it in:

> **Powdered sugar**

and spread on racks to dry. When ▶ thoroughly dry, you may dip it into:

> **(Chocolate Coating, 582)**

II. This quicker process makes a softer peel which does not keep as well as the one above.
Cut into strips:

> **Grapefruit or orange peel**

Soak for 24 hours in:

> **Salt water to cover**

Use 1 tablespoon salt to 4 cups water. Drain peel. Rinse and soak for 20 minutes in fresh water. Drain, cover with fresh water and boil 20 minutes. Drain again. Measure in equal parts with the peel:

> **Sugar**

Cook the peel. Add a very little water—but only if necessary—until the peel has absorbed the sugar. Shake the pot as the syrup diminishes, so that the peel does not burn. ▶ Dry thoroughly and store tightly covered.

★ CANDIED OR PRESERVED
KUMQUATS OR CALAMONDINS

These miniature oranges should first be washed well in warm soapy water. Rinse, cover with fresh water and boil 15 minutes:

> **1 lb. kumquats or
> calamondins**

Drain well and repeat twice. Make a syrup of:

> **1¹/₂ cups sugar**
> **4 cups water**

Boil 5 minutes. Place drained kumquats in hot syrup and bring syrup to the soft-ball stage, 234° or boil gently until the kumquats are transparent. To plump up the fruit, cover pan just before heat is turned off and allow fruit to remain covered in hot syrup about half an hour. At this point, you have Preserved Kumquats or Calamondins. Pack in sterile jars. Serve as a meat garnish or with desserts. If you chop them, be sure to slit them first and take out the seeds.

To candy the kumqauts, remove from syrup and drain. You may prick a hole in the stem end and force out the seeds. Bring to a boil a heavier syrup of:

> **1 part water to**
> **1 part sugar**
> **(¹/₈ teaspoon cream of tartar
> for every quart of liquid)**

Reboil the kumquats for 30 minutes. Remove them from heat but allow them to stand in the syrup 24 hours.

Bring them to a boil again. Cook for 30 minutes more. Drain, dry on a rack and roll in:

(Granulated sugar)

CANDIED GINGER

5¹/₂ Pints Preserved

Our friend Cecily Brownstone has graciously allowed us to use this recipe from her *Associated Press Cook Book*. This is either a single long-day or an intermittent four-day procedure. If you settle for one day, allow several hours between each of the four cookings. ◗ See About Ginger, 260. Scrape and cut into ¹/₄-inch slices enough fresh nonfibrous young:

Gingerroot

to make 1 quart. Put the slices into a large stainless steel pan and cover generously with:

Water

Bring water slowly to a boil and simmer covered until tender, about 20 minutes. Add:

1 cup sugar

and stir until mixture boils. Remove from heat. Cover and let stand overnight at room temperature. Recook, simmering gently for about 15 minutes after the ginger has again come to a boil. Add:

1 seeded sliced lemon
1 cup light corn syrup

Uncover and simmer 15 minutes longer, stirring occasionally. Remove from heat and let stand covered overnight. During the third cooking, the ginger must be stirred often to avoid scorching. Bring the syruped ginger to a boil. Stir in:

1 cup sugar

Simmer 30 minutes. Stir in:

1 cup sugar

and bring mixture again to a boil. Re-

move from heat. Cover and let stand overnight.

In the fourth cooking, bring the mixture to a boil once more. When the syrup drops heavily from the side of a spoon, 664, and the ginger is translucent, pour the mixture into sterile wide-mouthed jars. Seal, 617. You should now have about 5 cups of **Canton Ginger**. Should you want **Candied Ginger**, drain the ginger after the last cooking. Reserve the syrup for flavoring sauces. Dry the ginger slices on a rack over a tray, uncovered, overnight. When well dried, roll the slices in:

Granulated sugar

Store in tightly covered glass jars.

★ GLAZED CHESTNUTS OR MARRONS GLACÉS

Shell:

Boiled Chestnuts, (I, 313)

Soak them overnight, covered with cold water to which you have added:

Juice of 1 lemon

Next morning, drain them and drop into boiling:

Water or milk

Simmer until tender but firm. Drain chestnuts and discard water or milk. For every cup of nuts, make a syrup by cooking to the soft-ball stage, 234°:

1 cup sugar
1 cup water
¹/₄ teaspoon cream of tartar

Drop nuts into boiling syrup and simmer about 10 minutes. Remove from heat and let stand, covered, 24 hours. Drain nuts, reserving syrup. While preparing the sauce, put nuts in a 250° oven to dry. Reduce the syrup until very thick. Place nuts in jars. Add to each jar:

1 to 2 tablespoons cognac

Fill jars with the heavy syrup and

seal. To candy the nuts, they must be dried not once but three times, dipping them between dryings in the reduced syrup. After the final drying roll them in:

Granulated sugar

Store in tightly covered tins.

CANDIED CRANBERRIES

Because of their innate keeping qualities cranberries can be candied by a rather simple method, after which they will store for 3 months if kept covered.

Stir until dissolved and bring to a boil:

2½ cups sugar
1½ cups water

Have ready in a heat-resistant bowl:

1 quart cranberries

Pour the boiling syrup over the berries. Put the bowl in a steamer, (I, 281), for 45 minutes. Remove and cool without stirring. Leave in a warm, dry room 3 to 4 days. Stir at intervals. When the syrup reaches a jellylike consistency, remove berries and let them dry 3 days longer—out of the syrup. Turn them for uniform drying. When the fruit can be handled easily, store in a tightly covered container. Use the berries on picks to stud a ham or for other garnishing.

FRUIT PASTE

You find this delicacy in Italy, Spain, the American tropics, and in Germany, where it bears the quaint name of **Quittenbrod** or **Quittenwurst** because quince is a favorite flavor. The trick is to reduce, very radically, equal parts of:

> **Fruit pulp—guava, quince,**
> **apricot, etc.**
> **Sugar**

The real trick, of course, is to find the patience and time to watch this mixture so it won't scorch. When it is stiff, spread it to a ½-inch thickness in pans that have been dipped in cold water. Cut into squares and dry in racks in a cool place, turning once a day for 3 to 4 days. Dust the squares with:

Granulated sugar

Or stuff the stiff pulp without drying into cellophane sausage casings. Before pouring or stuffing, you may add at the last minute:

> **Ground cinnamon, cloves,**
> **citron or almonds**

The slices or squares look attractive when served on a green leaf.

CANDIED ANGELICA AND OTHER ROOTS AND STALKS

About 1 Pound

Wash:

> **2 cups edible young roots and**
> **stalks such as angelica or**
> **Acorus calamus**

Place them in a crock. Pour over to cover:

⅓ cup salt
2 cups boiling water

Cover crock and let them soak for 24 hours. Drain, peel and wash in cold water. Cook to the soft-ball stage, 234°:

2 cups sugar
2 cups water

Add the cleaned roots and stems. Cook for 20 minutes. Drain them, but reserve syrup. Put them on a wire rack in a cool, dark place for 4 days. Bring the syrup and roots to 234° and cook 20 minutes or until the syrup candies the roots. Drain on a rack until ▶ thoroughly dry. Store tightly covered.

THE FOODS WE KEEP

As modern living moves many of us farther and farther from primary sources of food, we more easily take for granted the marvels of modern packaging. Gone is the close awareness of growth and decay, of the fragile balance between the heat that halts enzymatic growth and the chill that retards decomposition, of the interaction of humidity and ventilation that discourages molds. No matter what method of preservation we investigate—freezing, canning, salting, smoking, drying, preserving or storing—we still find intricate reactions at work, confronting us with the very same problems that have faced conservers from time immemorial. In the following chapters we give you the safest methods we have found to keep food from season to season. In carrying out these procedures you will experience almost complete success, but unexpected contingencies may lead to a rare and potentially dangerous failure. Such failures may occur in commercial packaging as well. ▶ Whenever kept foods show even the slightest sign of spoilage, such as leakage, off-odor, bulging can ends, or liquid that spurts out when a can is opened, please accept the best advice we know: **If in doubt, throw it out.** Do not even taste the smallest bit of the contents.

Rare is the climate or circumstance that allows man to live the year around on varied, fresh and abundant foodstuffs with bounteous quotas of valuable nutritive elements. So food preservation by home and by commercial methods must loom large on our horizon. As with all foods not eaten when fresh, both processing and storage time usually work against the retention of nutritive values. The following chapters discuss how best to freeze, can, dry, salt, smoke and preserve foods for which we, as housekeepers, must assume the responsibility of safe preparation.

Of all these processes, whether home or commercial, freezing—if its time limitations are observed, 643—seems to give us superior flavor and nutritive values; canning comes in second generally in both flavor and nutrition but wins in superior long-term keeping qualities; while drying, salting and smoking follow in decreasing nutritive and taste values.

In addition to freezing, canning, drying, smoking and salting foods, there are two more recent commercial processes capable of extending shelf life, neither of which can be performed by the householder. One involves commercial dehydration equipment capable of removing 98% of the moisture from a food as opposed to the 25 to 30% extracted in home drying. The **commercially dehydrated foods** resulting are nonfat dried milk, eggs and gelatins; dried soup and cake mixes; dehydrated grains, fruits and vegetables; dried fruit juices, and textured vegetable proteins. As 98% of the moisture is extracted from these commercially dehydrated foods, they shrink in size, and their contracted state helps to protect nutritive values. Extravagant claims are made that commercially dehydrated foods will last fifteen years if properly packaged and stored at proper temperatures. A safer estimate seems to be closer to five years if they are packed in coated cans in a nitrogen atmosphere with less than 2% oxygen.

Compare commercially dehydrated foods with the more expensive, bulkier **freeze-dried foods** for which exorbitant storage claims are also made. Freeze-dried foods result when food sliced or processed prior to immersion in or spraying with a preserving agent is frozen, placed in a vacuum chamber and heated. As the ice crystals in the frozen food melt they are "vacuumed" away, but the cellular structure of the food remains lightweight, porous and ready for quick reconstitution. This freeze-dried process, relatively more expensive than commercial dehydration, retains higher food values during the first six months of storage. Valid total shelf life for freeze-dried foods is estimated at twelve to eighteen months.

Most purchased staples come under state and local sanitary laws, and any that are in interstate commerce are covered by federal food and drug legislation. The integrity of certain additives, like seasonings, salts and flavorings, has been traditionally taken for granted. Since 1960, approved substances "generally recognized as safe" have appeared on the government's so-called GRAS list. Under the Delaney Amendment, however, any substance, new or old, proved to be cancer-inducing may lose its acceptance. This applies, for instance, to sassafras as well as to cyclamates.

A special subject of federal concern is those extra substances that are present in food as a result of the manufacturers' determination to boost nutritive or color content or of special conditions growing out of processing, packaging or storage. An entirely different kind of additive is the unintentional or accidental kind—the one that results from improper processing, contamination, imperfect sealing, or careless keeping. In this area, again, there is a whole series of federal rulings.

A change in the nature of legal concepts during the past decade now puts the burden of proof for the safety of additives on the manufacturer and thus provides more immediate and positive protection for the consumer. It is the business of every one of us to support all legislation controlling amounts and kinds of food additives so that we may be sure they will not increase beyond human tolerance. ◗ Read the labels and carefully note both contents and weight and nutritive claims of all the packaged or preserved food you buy.

For most of us, the responsibility of keeping food in good condition starts as we roll our baskets past the checker. And what a lot we push! In one week, a single normally well fed American uses a minimum of 3½ quarts of milk, ½ pound of fat, 4½ pounds of meat, poultry, fish, cheese, beans or nuts, 3 pounds of cereals and ½ pound of sugar. Add fruits and vegetables and multiply by 52, then by the number of persons in your family. If there are four of you, the total will stand at something like a ton and a half a year. This is an impressive investment in hard currency: an item, in fact, amply huge to warrant protecting your market purchases to the very best of your ability.

But all of us are guilty on occasion of picking up Junior at the tennis club after shopping and getting involved in some friendly gossip—while the lettuces back in the car wilt down and the frozen foods begin disastrously to thaw. Remember that heat and moisture encourage spoilage, bacteria, insect infestation and mold. And sunlight may destroy vitamin content, as in milk; or cause flavor deterioration, as in spices. Keep an insulated cooler in your car to transport purchases that should be kept cold.

Many molds need no light and thrive on acids; some occur only on the surface but give off gases that may adversely affect flavor. ◗ Store most staples in a cool, dark, dry place, preferably with a constant temperature around 70°; or, if indicated, refrigerate. ◗ Any stockpiled food should be kept on a rotating system. Place the new food at the back of the shelves and use the older purchases from the front for the day-to-day needs of the household. ◗ Although we know some stored foods may not spoil for years, flavor and nutritive qualities in all of them are progressively lessened as the months roll by. And if a large portion of your diet comes from freeze-dried or dehydrated foods, be sure to include enough fresh foods high in vitamin C and in essential fatty acids to make up for these losses in processing.

We do urge you to ◗ use a preponderance of fresh foods whenever possible. Build your menus around government "best buys" on produce that appear regularly in the newspapers. These items are apt to be both reasonable in price and fresh, because they are seasonal. After buying, store them in the ways we suggest below, and cook them carefully, following the "pointers" ◗ so as to assure retention of topmost taste and nutritive value.

STOCKING THE KITCHEN

For pots and pans and all the other cooking equipment so necessary to our western culture, see (I, 114, 119, and 122), and the equipment illustrated at the point of use in recipes. Use the following list to stock the larder of a new or second home or to surprise a bride with a basket full of staples. Campers, too, will find the list useful to check before going into the wilderness. Try to buy products that are package-dated: there is no way otherwise to tell how long food has been on a shelf or even before that in a storage warehouse. And be wary of packages bought in obscure places or shops where turnover may be slow.

STAPLES FOR THE AVERAGE FAMILY

Beverages: coffee, tea
Cereals: breakfast foods, rice, macaroni, spaghetti, noodles, farina, cornmeal, tapioca
Cheeses
Chocolate, cocoa
Coconut
Butter, lard, cooking oil or other shortening
Flour: whole-grain, all-purpose, cake
Sugar: granulated, confectioners', brown
Bread, crackers
Fruits: fresh, dried, canned, frozen
Fruit and vegetable juices: frozen, canned
Potatoes: white, sweet
Onions, garlic, shallots, chives
Syrups: corn, molasses, maple
Mayonnaise and French dressing
Salad oils, vinegars
Milk, cream, eggs
Milk solids, evaporated and condensed milk
Frozen and canned meats, fish
Beef, chicken and vegetable cubes
Nuts
Vegetables: fresh, frozen, canned
Honey, preserves, marmalade, jellies
Soups: frozen, canned, dried
Raisins, currants
Peanut butter
Active dried yeast
Worcestershire and hot pepper sauces
Gelatin: flavored, unflavored
Catsup, chili sauce, horseradish
Flavorings: vanilla, almond, etc.
Baking powder, baking soda
Cornstarch
Ground and stick cinnamon
Ground and whole cloves
Ground and crystallized ginger
Allspice
Whole nutmeg
Bay leaves
Salt
Celery seed
Celery salt
Dry and prepared mustard
Black and white peppercorns
Paprika, cayenne
Curry powder
Garlic and onion salt
Chili powder
Dried herbs: tarragon, basil, savory, sage, etc. See Herbs, 262

STORAGE OF PRESERVED FOODS

You may store in an area that ♦ stays around 70° for:

♦ About 5 years: dehydrated foods if properly packaged, see 608.

♦ About 2 years: Salt, sugar, whole pepper.

♦ About 18 months: Canned meat, poultry and vegetables—except sauerkraut and tomatoes—alone or mixed with cereal products. Canned fruit—except citrus fruits and juices and berries. Dried legumes, if stored in stainless steel or aluminum containers, and freeze-dried foods if properly packaged.

♦ About 12 months: Canned fish, hydrogenated fats and oils, flour, ready-to-eat dry cereals stored in stainless or aluminum containers, uncooked cereal in original container, canned nuts, instant puddings, instant dry cream and bouillon products, soda and baking powder.

♦ About 6 months: Evaporated milk, nonfat dry whole milk in metal containers, condensed meat and beef soups, dried fruits in metal container, canned citrus fruits and juices, canned berries. To store water, see 167.

If temperatures are lower than 70° but still above freezing, the permissible storage period for most of these items is longer.

WINTERING FRESH PRODUCE

The earliest agricultural societies realized how urgent it was to protect seed grains from deterioration between harvest and planting time, and they evolved many ingenious methods for storing them against rodents, rain, insect infestation and decay. The same enemies plagued them that plague us in our effort to winter over fresh produce: to find areas cool enough to stave off enzymatic action and ventilated sufficiently to prevent decay. Root cellars with stone walls and earthen floors are now as they were then the most practical solution if the climate is not too cold, too damp, or too dry, since they allow easy access and adequate space in which to segregate fruits from vegetables. When floors and walls are of concrete, produce must be kept freestanding from these surfaces to prevent mildew. Should a basement area be heated, through proximity to a furnace or otherwise, steps must be taken to compensate for this situation; but the precautions necessary depend on so many individual factors that they cannot be spelled out here.

The latest possible mature crops are best for any wintering over, but they should not be overripe. Harvest them on a dry day. Most crops for storage do best if allowed to cool in the field overnight. There are some exceptions: for example, onions need about a week after harvesting to attain regular storage status; with root vegetables like carrots, beets, rutabagas and kohlrabi, be sure to leave on an inch of the tops, discarding the rest.

Unbruised and unblemished produce—no other—may then be stored, for the most part in temperatures between 35° and 40°. Sweet potatoes and yams, however, respond best to somewhat higher temperatures—40° to 50°. They need moderately dry storage, while late cabbage, potatoes, pumpkins, winter squash, root crops, hard apples and pears require moderately moist conditions. Some people prefer to wash vegetables before storing; others refrain, from fear of vitamin loss. In any case, ◗ the surface of the produce should be dry before storage. It can be insulated and kept at more even temperatures if packed in dry sand or sawdust, although we have heard complaints that sand imparts off-flavors. Fruits such as apples and pears may be wrapped separately in paper to keep down contact spoilage from any unnoticed bruises. Whatever material is used, packing should be relegated to the compost heap after one season's use.

Outdoor storage in reinforced sodhouse mounds is tricky wherever temperatures average 30° or higher. Fruits and vegetables should be stored in separate structures. In climates where the ground freezes, if the mound does not have an insulated entry door, it should be kept small, because, once opened, the earth covering cannot be made cold-impervious again. Should this happen, all produce should be removed, used quickly and/or, if suitable, refrigerated. Mounds should be located in well-drained areas with a drainage trench dug around the outside. Line the mound bottom with at least 6 inches of straw or dry leaves. To protect produce against rodents, place over the base insulation a piece of hardware cloth which can be shaped up against the sides of the conelike pile of vegetables or fruits you will be placing on it. ◗ Never store fruits and vegetables in the same mound. Then cover the whole with about 6 inches of straw or dry leaves. Shape over this a 6-inch layer of earth, leaving at the top of the cone a chimneylike opening which will allow sufficient ventilation, even when filled with straw and weighted down with a piece of board or metal held in place by a rock. Finally, cover the sides of the produce-cone with one more layer of leaves or straw as further insulation and erosion control.

You may prefer pit rather than mound storage. In a well-drained shady area, dig a hole deep enough to accommodate an 18-inch-diameter by 30-inch-long section of ceramic tile set on a hardware-cloth base, insulating the base beforehand with a layer of straw or dry leaves. Put in the produce. After filling the tile,

keep it covered with a thick layer of straw and an outer one of soil and straw, and proceed to make a chimney in the center as described at left. Dig a drainage ditch around the finished mound. Whether you use a mound or a pit, if you are in snow country, mark the location of your storage area with a tall pole.

The simplest method of all for storing root-crops, of course, is to leave them in the ground where they were grown and cover them with 15 to 18 inches of straw. This mulch applied on late crops just before frost should keep the ground from freezing hard. Again mark your rows with tall poles and keep a plan of your planting. It is surprising how easy it is to lose the location of the storage rows once the tops have shrunk in colder weather or are snow covered.

CANNING, SALTING, SMOKING AND DRYING

It is a thrill to possess shelves well stocked with home-canned food. In fact, you will find their inspection—often surreptitious—and the pleasure of serving the fruits of your labor comparable only to a clear conscience or a very becoming hat.

In fact, you must carry a clear conscience right with you through the processing itself, making absolutely sure that the food you keep is safe to eat. Great care must be exercised in the canning of all foods to avoid spoilage. Even greater care is required in the canning of nonacid foods—for which pressure-canning is the only recommended process—to prevent the development of Clostridium botulinum, a germ so deadly that "1 oz. could theoretically kill 100 million people." The spores of botulinus may resist 212°, or boiling temperature, even after several hours of processing and may produce a fatal toxin in the canned product. Botulinus poisoning may be present even if no odor, gas, color change or soft- ness in food texture indicates its presence.

Whether or not your suspicions are aroused, ▶ do not test home-canned nonacid food by tasting it out of the container. Instead, before tasting or serving, follow the recommendations of all reputable authorities, and—without exception—cook home-canned vegetables for 15 minutes, meat, poultry and fish for 20 minutes, in boiling liquid, uncovered, stirring closely packed produce to allow heat penetration. By this means, botulinus toxin is positively destroyed.

▶ For maximum nutritional value, only the freshest and best food should be canned. Inspect it with an eagle eye, discarding all blemished or rotted portions and washing or scrubbing the selected remainder to remove spray, soil or insects. Produce that is imperfect before processing may spoil the rest of the food in its container afterward, producing color changes and encouraging the formation of mold or gases. If, as a result of any careless preliminary handling, your jars show evidences of any spoilage or mold, ▶ discard them at once, preferably without opening.

▶ Good organization and proper equipment simplify canning and give you, with a minimum of effort, gay-looking shelves of glistening, jewel-like jars filled with canned fruits and vegetables, all labeled, dated and ready to use.

Seasonal heat and heat from the stove inevitably accompany canning. Hot fluids in hot jars and heavy pans have to be handled carefully.

Seen in the chapter heading are a fruit press, a glazed crock for salting, a wooden sauerkraut fork, a salt container, both narrow and wide-mouthed tempered glass jars, and a wide-mouthed funnel used for filling them. ▶ Plenty of pot holders, strong tongs or jar lifter, 124, and paraffin are added aids. When using special equipment, follow the manufacturer's directions.

CANNING PROCESSES

▶ Remember that all nonacid vegetables and all meats and fish must be pressure-processed, 616.

▶ The boiling-water bath, 616, is not recommended for any nonacid foods.

▶ Oven canning is not recommended under any circumstances. The open-kettle method has been abandoned by officialdom but is still used by some housewives for acid fruits. To can specific foods, see alphabetical listings in this chapter.

In canning, follow these general steps. ▶ Line up your equipment and read below about the type you are using. ▶ Sterilize all equipment and keep it sterile all during the processing. ▶ Should you be using a pressure canner—see illustration, 616—make sure that the jars are the type that can stand 240° or more of heat. Do not use ordinary jars that are not tempered for canning or freezing.

▶ In any case, check all jars against chipping, cracking or other defects. Next, check the closures between the jars and lids. If using screw types, first place them on sound jars without a rubber. Screw them tight. They are usable if it is impossible to insert a thin penknife blade or a thumbnail between the jar and the lid. Unscrew them. Put the rubbers in place and fill the jars with water. Screw down the lids. Invert the jars. If there is no seepage, the jars and lids are safe to use. This test may also be applied to the clamp or wire-bail type of closure, seen in narrow and wide-mouthed styles at either end of the drawing opposite.

Lids are of two main types—those which need separate rubbers and adjustment both before and after processing, and those which have an attached rubberlike sealing compound and are adjusted once before processing and then close automatically by vacuum when cooling. The vacuum types are sketched second and third on the left. The first has a wider mouth and straight sides which make filling and emptying easier than with the shouldered jar shown next. This wide-mouthed jar is recommended for freezing. Lids with attached rubbers should never be sterilized. Merely wash, rinse well and cover with water brought to a simmer, but not to a boil. Remove from heat but leave in hot water until ready to use.

If the lids call for separate rubbers, have clean new rings of the right size. Rubber rings should never be reused. ♦ Unless you are pressure-canning or using a boiling-water bath, jars and lids shown with separate rubbers should be sterilized 15 minutes in boiling water. Also sterilize reused zinc caps. If pressure-canning, wash glass jars and new rubber rings in hot soapy water, rinse well and keep in hot water until ready to fill.

Lids two through five shown below fit on the regular threaded-top canning jars, whether of pint, quart or half-gallon size. The zinc- and glass-disk tops, shown fourth and fifth below, are placed on the rubber ring, screwed clockwise as tightly as possible, and then turned counterclockwise 1/4 inch before putting them in the canner.

The jars with the all-glass lids shown next have wire-bail or clamp closures. While processing, the longer wire rests in the groove of the lid. The shorter wire is not snapped down in its final position until after processing. ♦ The slight openings provided by all these adjustments are temporary. They allow excess air to be forced out of the jars during processing, and thus avoid possible explosion. See Sealing Jars, 617.

PREPARING FOOD FOR CANNING

♦ To prepare food for canning, wash, clean, pare and cut up food just as you would if planning to cook it for immediate use. ♦ Remember that vitamins escape quickly, so prepare only small batches of food, about 1 quart at a time. The size in which pieces are cut may depend on convenience in packing.

♦ To blanch or precook foods for canning, put large fruits and all vegetables in a wire basket and immerse them, about 1 quart at a time, in boiling liquid for 5 minutes, counting from the time the water begins to boil again after immersion. Then dip them up and down quickly in cold water 2 or 3 times to reduce the heat. This will keep the food shapely and make handling easier. Blanching shrinks food and drives out air so that produce may be packed more closely. Its most important role, however, is to arrest some undesirable kinds of enzymatic action. ♦ The liquid in which the foods were precooked or steamed should be used to fill the jars, thus saving valuable minerals.

Berries, soft fruits and tomatoes may be canned without blanching. Meat may be partially cooked—about two-thirds done—by simmering or roasting. For more details about meat, see 629.

◗ To steam foods for canning, use a steamer or steam basket, (I, 281). Steam only a small quantity at a time. ◗ Do not crowd the food, as the steam must penetrate all of it. Use a kettle with a tightly fitted lid. Have in the kettle several inches of boiling water. Close the lid tightly and steam food the length of time given in individual recipes for fruit or vegetables.

PACKING JARS

There are two methods of filling the jars before they go into the pressure canner or boiling-water bath. ◗ With **Cold or Raw Pack,** the hot jars are filled with raw food and covered with boiling syrup, juice or water; they begin their processing treatment in hot, not boiling, water. ◗ With **Hot Pack,** the hot jars are filled with precooked hot food, then processed. More food can be packed into a jar using this method.

◗ In canning, pack jars firmly, but not so tightly that the produce is crushed. ◗ Pack fruits and acid vegetables to within $1/2$ inch of jar tops. Lima beans, dried beans, peas, corn and other low-acid foods which swell considerably more than other vegetables, plus meats canned under pressure, should be packed loosely to within 1 inch of jar tops. Add boiling liquid to completely cover the food solids, but leave headroom for expansion above the liquid, as indicated in individual recipes. You may add salt to meats and vegetables at the rate of 1 teaspoon per quart.

Fill jars of fruit with sugar syrup to within $1/2$ inch of top. For sugar syrup formulas, see 619. ◗ Before putting on lids, make sure that any air that may be trapped in the liquid is expelled. Run a long thin spatula down between the inside of the jar and the produce, changing the position of the contents enough to release any trapped air as shown above. Then carefully wipe the top of the jar before lidding.

PRESSURE-CANNING

◗ Pressure-canning at a temperature of 240° F. at 10 pounds pressure at sea level is the only method recommended for nonacid fruits, vegetables, fish and meats. Detailed directions for the use of such appliances—of which a typical one is shown—are furnished by the manufacturer and should be followed carefully—especially the checking of pressure gauges. ◗ Be sure also to exhaust the air from the canner for at least 10 minutes before closing the petcock or steam vent so that no cold spots develop to cause the food to be

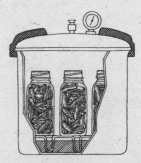

underprocessed. Bring pressure to 10 pounds and start counting processing time, keeping pressure constant. Remove canner from heat and let pressure fall to zero before opening. To remove jars, see directions under Canning in a Boiling-Water Bath, below. ♦ If using a small steam-pressure saucepan, keep the heat constantly at 10 pounds pressure, and be sure to add 20 minutes to the processing time. For vegetable pressure-canning, see 623; and for meats, see 628.

▲ If canning at high altitudes in a pressure canner ♦ add ½ pound to the pressure gauge for each additional 1000 feet. For instance, if processing requires 10 pounds pressure at sea level, use 12 pounds at 4000 feet, 14 pounds at 7500 feet; if 15 pounds at sea level, use 17 pounds at 4000 feet, 19 pounds at 7500 feet.

CANNING IN A BOILING-WATER BATH

♦ The boiling-water-bath process is used only for acid fruits and brined or pickled vegetables. A regular hot-water canner, see below, or a clean washboiler or lard can may be used if it has a tight-fitting lid and enough headroom for briskly boiling water.

An important utensil in canning is a ♦ rack for the bottom of the boiler to keep the jars from cracking when they come in contact with heat. Have ready

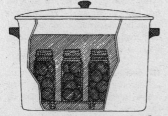

a holder for lifting jars out of boiling water, see illustration on (I, 124). Half fill the boiler with hot or boiling water. For Raw Pack in glass jars, have water in canner hot but not boiling; for all other packs, have water boiling. Lower the jars into the boiler. ♦ The jars must not touch one another, the base or the sides of the container, see above. Leave a 2-inch space between them. ♦ The jars should rest on the rack. Add more hot or boiling water to cover them at least 2 inches above the tops. Don't pour water directly onto jars. When the water comes to a rolling boil, cover the canner and process the required length of time for the particular food chosen. ♦ To remove the jars from the boiling water, use tongs or a jar lifter as soon as the time is up. ♦ Do not lift the jars by the lids. ♦ Place the jars on wood, a paper pad, or a cloth surface, allowing several inches between them. See that there is no draft on the hot jars, as sudden cooling may cause the glass to crack.

▲ Canning at high altitudes in a boiling-water bath ♦ requires a 1-minute increase in processing time for every 1000 feet above sea level if the total time is 20 minutes or less, and 2 minutes per 1000 feet if the total time is more than 20 minutes.

SEALING, LABELING AND STORING JARS

♦ Seal all jars according to manufacturer's directions. With the types of lids described on 615, the rubber-attached metal lid is self-sealing and is held in place by a metal screw band. This is screwed down completely before processing. The seal automatically tightens itself and should not be touched after processing. After the jar has cooled 12 hours or more, the band may be removed for reuse.

The zinc-screw type and the glass-disk and metal-ring lids should be turned clockwise as far as possible, then loosened 1/4 inch before being processed. Be sure to screw lids with a slow, steady turn, so as not to displace the rubbers. After removal from the canner, tighten the lids or bands again. This is referred to in the recipes as "Complete seals if necessary."

The longer wire on the bail or clamp type should be snapped into place during processing, and the shorter wire snapped down on the shoulder of the jar after removal from the canner.

◗ Whatever type you use, be sure to leave the jars upright and undisturbed for 12 hours. ◗ Do not tighten caps after jars have cooled. While the jars are still hot after sealing, you may see active bubbling going on. This is merely continued boiling caused by the lowered boiling point produced by the vacuum in the jar; it will cease as the contents cool.

◗ Test-seal the metal tops by tapping the lids lightly with a metal spoon or knife. A ringing note indicates a safe seal. If the contents touch the inner side of the lid, the sound may be dull but not hollow. ◗ If the note is both dull and hollow, reprocessing with a new lid is in order. Or, if you prefer, use the food right away.

◗ Label and store jars in a cool, dark, airy place. Storage temperatures between 45 ° and 60 ° maintain good color and are generally suitable for all properly heat processed foods.

FRUIT CANNING

All acid fruits should be processed in a hot-water canner, see 616. All nonacid fruits should be pressure-canned, see 616. ◗ Choose fresh, firm fruit that is not overripe. Imperfect fruit may be used, but it must be carefully gone over and all blemishes removed. Wash the fruit. Prepare as for table use. If it is to be pared, it may be dipped in boiling water until the skins loosen, and then dipped for a moment in cold water. It is best to process only enough produce for one canner load at a time.

To keep fruit from discoloring until you can pack it, mist it over with Anti-Browning Solution, below. Leave 1/2 inch headroom in the jars after packing with fruit and syrup. Enough liquid will develop during processing to cover the fruit and prevent darkening.

ANTI-BROWNING SOLUTION FOR CANNING

I. Drop prepared fruit into a solution of 2 tablespoons salt and 2 tablespoons vinegar to 1 gallon water. Do not leave the fruit in the solution longer than 20 minutes, and ◗ rinse before packing.

II. Commercially packaged ascorbic acid—vitamin C—is a concentrated natural constituent of fruit. It should be mixed well with the sugar in the syrup so as not to lose the delicate fruit flavor. Dissolve 1/2 teaspoon crystalline ascorbic acid, or 1500 milligrams in tablet form, in a little water and add to 1 quart syrup.

III. Just before lidding the jar, sprinkle ascorbic acid over the contents. Allow 1/4 teaspoon to each quart of fruit.

APPROXIMATE YIELD OF COMMON FRUITS

	POUNDS PER QUART JAR	QUART JARS PER BUSHEL OR CRATE
Apples	2¹/₂–3	16–20
Apricots	2–2¹/₂	7–11
Berries	1¹/₂–3	12–18
Cherries	2–2¹/₂	(unpitted) 22–32
Peaches	2–3	18–24
Pears	2–3	20–25
Plums	1¹/₂–2¹/₂	24–30
Tomatoes	2¹/₂–3¹/₂	15–20

SYRUPS FOR CANNING

Sugar helps fruit keep its shape, flavor and color, but you may can fruit without sweetening it. Syrup for canned fruit varies in consistency, depending on the fruit or the use to which it will be put. The following formulas will help you decide on the most appropriate blend of sugar and water. Cook until the sugar dissolves and keep hot until needed. Do not let the syrup boil down. Allow 1 to 1¹/₂ cups syrup for each quart of fruit. Light corn syrup or mild-flavored honey may be used to replace up to one-half the specified amount of sugar.

THIN SYRUP

About 5 Cups

2 cups sugar to 4 cups water. Stir well before heating and bring slowly to a boil, 236°. Use for naturally sweet fruits and to approximate the quality of fresh fruits.

MEDIUM SYRUP

About 5¹/₂ Cups

3 cups sugar to 4 cups water. Prepare as for thin syrup. Good for canning fruits that are not highly acid.

HEAVY SYRUP

About 6¹/₂ Cups

Use 4³/₄ cups sugar to 4 cups water. ▶ Dissolve and boil very carefully to prevent crystallization and scorching. Use for very sour fruits like rhubarb; also suitable for dessert use. If too heavy a syrup is used the fruit may rise to the top of the jar during processing.

SYNTHETIC SWEETENER

Some artificial sweeteners may be used in canning. Check manufacturer's recommendations and do not use without a doctor's consent.

PROCESSING FRUITS

I. NONACID FRUITS

Use a pressure canner. Place jars as described on 616. Vent canner for 10 minutes. Process fruits 5 minutes at 10 pounds pressure.

II. ACID FRUITS

The following directions are for quart jars processed in a boiling-water bath, 617. Start counting time when the water surrounding the lidded jars reaches a fast boil. Reduce the processing time by 10% if pint jars are used. Increase the processing time by 15 minutes for half-gallon jars. ▶ When fruit is hot-packed, use stainless or enamel pans for the precooking. After removing jars from canner, complete seals if necessary, 617.

III. FRUIT PURÉES AND PASTES

Use ripe, firm, unblemished fruit. Add 1 cup boiling water to each quart fruit. Simmer until it can be forced through a sieve or food mill, shown in chapter heading, 661. If you are using a blender, the fruit should be peeled. You may add sugar to taste, unless you are puréeing tomatoes. Reheat the purée and fill the hot jars, leaving 1/4-inch headroom. For acid fruits, seal and process 20 minutes in a boiling-water bath for each half-pint. ◗ For less acid fruits and tomato purées, allow 1/4-inch headroom. Pressure-can 15 minutes for each half-pint at 10 pounds pressure.

APPLES

Use Hot Pack, 616. Select firm, sound, tart varieties. Wash, pare and core; cut into quarters or halves. Drop into Anti-Browning Solution, 618. Drain. Boil 5 minutes in thin or medium syrup. Pack in hot jars, cover with boiling syrup and process 20 minutes in boiling-water bath. Apples may also be baked, packed, covered with boiling syrup and processed 15 minutes in boiling-water bath.

APPLE CIDER

Use Raw Pack only. Use a blend of 3 or more varieties of firm, ripe apples, making sure to balance the sweet apples against those that are acid. Because crab apples are astringent, use them in small proportions. After putting apples through a cider mill or fruit press, shown in chapter heading on 613, strain and put into hot sterile jars. Process 30 minutes in hot-water bath at 185° F.

APPLESAUCE

Use Hot Pack, 616. Prepare Applesauce, 118; pack boiling hot. To prevent darkening at top of jar, add 1 teaspoon lemon juice at the last moment before sealing. Process 10 minutes in boiling-water bath.

APRICOTS

Use Raw or Hot Pack, 616. Select ripe, firm fruit. Blanch to remove skins, then heat through and treat to prevent darkening. 618. Drain. Pack whole or in halves into hot jars and cover with boiling medium syrup; process 25 minutes in boiling-water bath for Hot Pack, 30 minutes for Raw Pack.

BERRIES

Use Raw Pack for soft berries: **blackberries, boysenberries, dewberries, loganberries** and **raspberries.** Pick over, wash if gritty, stem, pack closely in hot jars, fill with boiling medium syrup and process 15 minutes in boiling-water bath.

Blueberries should be blanched, 615, and may be packed without sugar, then processed as above.

Use Hot Pack for **currants, elderberries, gooseberries** and **huckleberries.** They should be added to boiling medium or thick syrup for 1/2 minute, then packed in hot jars. Cover with the boiling syrup and process 15 minutes for all except huckleberries, which need 20 minutes in a boiling-water bath. For **strawberries,** the following more complicated procedure will yield plump, bright-colored fruit. Wash if gritty, then hull. Add 1 cup sugar to each quart prepared berries, placing in alternate layers in shallow pans, and let stand 2 hours. Simmer 5 minutes in the juice they have drawn while standing. Fill hot jars full and add boiling thin syrup if additional liquid is needed. Process 15 minutes in boiling-water bath.

CHERRIES

For Raw Pack, wash and stem. Can whole or pitted. To seed, use a cherry pitter, shown in the heading on 607, or the rounded end of a paper clip. If not seeded, prick with a pin. Use heavy syrup for sour cherries; medium syrup for sweet. Pack, cover with boiling syrup and process 25 minutes in boiling-water bath.

CRANBERRIES

Use Hot Pack. Wash and stem. Boil 3 minutes in heavy syrup. Pack in hot jars. Cover with boiling syrup. Process 10 minutes in boiling-water bath.

CITRUS FRUITS: GRAPEFRUIT, ORANGES

Use Raw Pack only. Prepare sections as shown, 125, and pack in hot jars. Add boiling thin syrup and process 10 minutes in boiling-water bath.

CURRANTS

See berries, 620.

FIGS

Use Hot Pack only. Wash ripe, firm figs, leaving peels and stems intact. Let simmer with water to cover 5 minutes. Drain. Pack in hot jars and add boiling thin syrup and ◗ 2 teaspoons lemon juice to each quart to increase acidity. Process 30 minutes in boiling-water bath.

GRAPES

Use Raw or Hot Pack. Use only sound, firm, preferably seedless, grapes. Wash and stem. For Hot Pack bring to a boil in medium syrup. Pack in hot jars. Cover with boiling syrup. Process 20 minutes in boiling-water bath. For Raw Pack, process 30 minutes.

GRAPE JUICE

I. Use Hot Pack only.
Wash sound, ripe grapes. Cover with boiling water and heat slowly to simmering. ◗ Do not boil. Cook slowly until fruit is very soft, then strain through a jelly bag as shown in chapter heading, 661. Let stand 24 hours refrigerated. Strain again. Add $1/2$ cup sugar to each quart juice. Reheat to simmering and pour into hot jars. Process 30 minutes in hot-water bath held at 190°.

OTHER FRUIT JUICES

Use Hot Pack only. Select sound, ripe fruit, crush and heat slowly to simmering point. Strain through several layers of cheesecloth. Add 1 cup sugar to each gallon juice for moderate sweetness. Heat again to about 190° and simmer 10 minutes. ◗ Do not boil, as it ruins the flavor. Pour into hot jars, seal, and process in hot-water bath held at 190° for 30 minutes. Do not allow water to boil.

Juices from uncooked fruit may be pressed out in a cider press and heated to lukewarm before being poured into jars and processed as above. Peach, cherry and apple juice and cider canned this way are less likely to taste flat.

PEACHES

Use Raw or Hot Pack. Use firm, ripe fruit. Scald to remove skins. Halve peaches and discard pits, 132. You may scrape out reddish areas, which brown in canning. Treat to prevent darkening, 618. For Raw Pack, arrange, pit side down, in hot jars, cover with boiling thin or medium syrup and process 30 minutes in boiling-water bath. For Hot Pack, process 25 minutes.

PEARS

Use Raw or Hot Pack. Pare, core and halve, quarter or slice. Treat to prevent darkening, 618. For Hot Pack, boil gently about 5 minutes in thin or medium syrup. Pack into hot jars, cover with boiling syrup and process 25 minutes in boiling-water bath. Hard pears are best if cooked in water only until nearly tender. The sugar is then added to the cooking water in the same proportions as for a medium syrup and the whole brought to a boil. Pack into hot jars, cover with boiling syrup and process 25 minutes in boiling-water bath. For Raw or Cold Pack, process 30 minutes.

PERSIMMONS

Use Hot Pack only. Wash ripe wild persimmons and steam until soft. Put through a colander or food mill. Reheat to boiling and pour into hot jars. Process 20 minutes in boiling-water bath. You may sweeten the pulp before processing if it is to be used as a sauce.

PINEAPPLE

Use Hot Pack only. Slice, pare, core, remove eyes. Shred or cut into cubes. Simmer in light or medium syrup about 5 minutes or until tender. Pack into hot jars and cover with boiling syrup. Process 20 minutes in boiling-water bath.

PINEAPPLE JUICE

Discarded eyes, cores and skins of fresh fruit can be used in making pineapple juice. Cover with cold water. Cook slowly in covered kettle from 30 to 40 minutes. Strain through a jelly bag, shown 661. Measure juice; heat.

For each cup of juice add 1/8 cup sugar. Boil rapidly 10 minutes and process 5 minutes in boiling-water bath. Juice may also be extracted from pineapple by putting the pared fruit through the fine blade of a food chopper, with a large bowl beneath to catch the liquid. After sweetening, process as for strained juice above.

PLUMS

Use Raw or Hot Pack method. Use moderately ripe fruit. Meaty instead of juicy plums are best for canning. Wash and prick skins. For Hot Pack, cover with boiling syrup: thin for sweet plums, medium for tart varieties. Cover and let stand 20 to 30 minutes. Pack drained fruit firmly into hot jars, but do not crush. Reheat syrup to boiling and pour over plums. Process 25 minutes in boiling-water bath for Hot Pack, 30 minutes for Cold or Raw Pack.

QUINCES

"Preserved," noted an herbalist optimistically in 1562, "they do mightily prevail against drunkenness." Use well-ripened fruit. Wipe the fuzz from the quince, cut out the stem and blossom ends and cook the fruit gently in several inches of water, covered, 20 minutes. Drain the water and use to make a medium syrup. Pare, or simply cut the fruit from the core unpared. Pack into hot jars, cover with boiling syrup, and process 60 minutes in boiling-water bath.

RHUBARB

Use Hot Pack only. Wash stalks and cut into 1/2-inch pieces. Add and mix well 1/2 to 1 cup sugar for each quart fruit. Let stand 3 to 4 hours, then heat slowly to boiling for ¹/₂ minute. Pack in hot jars and process 10 minutes in hot-water bath.

TOMATOES

Use Raw or Hot Pack. Use firm, fresh tomatoes. Scald 1 minute and then dip 1 minute into cold water to remove skins. Cut out cores. Halve, quarter, or leave whole. You may add ¹/₂ teaspoon salt per quart if desired. If Cold-Packing, press tomatoes gently into hot jars to within ¹/₂ inch of top of jar. Add no water. For Hot Pack, place tomatoes in hot jars; fill with boiling water or tomato juice. As it is difficult to judge the acidity of the many new tomato hybrids, we recommend pressure-canning only at 10 pounds pressure for 10 minutes.

TOMATO JUICE

Use Hot Pack only. Use firm, ripe perfect tomatoes. Wash; remove stem ends and cores. Chop or cut into small pieces. Cook gently, covered, until the juice flows freely. Put through a fine sieve or food mill. If there is no residue in the juice, pack into hot jars to within ¹/₂ inch of top. Process in boiling-water bath 10 minutes. Flavor just before serving. If some residue remains after straining the juice, we recommend pressure-canning at 10 pounds pressure for 10 minutes.

APPROXIMATE YIELD OF COMMON VEGETABLES

RAW VEGETABLE	POUNDS PER QUART JAR	QUART JARS PER BUSHEL
Beans, lima in the pod	4–5	6–8
Beans, snap	1¹/₂–2	15–20
Beets	2¹/₂–3	17–20
Carrots	2¹/₂–3	16–20
Corn cut off cob	7 ears	8
Greens	2–3	6–9
Okra	1¹/₂–2	17
Peas in the pod	2–2¹/₂	5–10
Squash, summer	2–2¹/₂	16–20
Sweet potatoes	2¹/₂–3	18–22
Tomatoes	2¹/₂–3¹/₂	15–20

VEGETABLE PRESSURE CANNING

▶ Pressure canning, 616, is the only process recommended for vegetables. As with all fruits, vegetables must be very carefully and quickly washed, through several waters if necessary or under running water, to remove all soil. Prepare only one pressure canner load at a time and work quickly. You may add about 1 teaspoon salt to each quart before processing. Pack the vegetable in the water used for blanching or steaming because this contains dissolved vitamins and minerals.

Great care must be exercised in the canning of nonacid foods to prevent the development of Clostridium botulinum, a deadly germ that may be present even though no odor or color change indicates its presence. The U.S. Government warns that all nonacid home-canned vegetables should be boiled in an open pan for 15 minutes before tasting or serving. They should be stirred frequently during cooking.

▶ The following directions are for 1-quart glass jars, unless otherwise specified, processed in a steam pressure canner at 10 pounds pressure at 240° F. One exception is Pickled Beets, which, because of the acidity of the vinegar, may be safely processed in a boiling-water bath. Vegetables may be canned either by

Raw Pack or Hot Pack; however, our preference for the recipes below is the Hot Pack method.

The Department of Agriculture does not recommend home canning the following vegetables:

> Cabbage, except
>   sauerkraut
> Cauliflower
> Celery
> Cucumbers
> Eggplant
> Lettuce
> Onions
> Parsnips
> Turnips
> Vegetable mixtures

ARTICHOKES

Wash and trim well 2-inch or smaller artichokes. Precook 5 minutes in brine of ³/₄ cup vinegar or lemon juice and 3 tablespoons salt to 1 gallon water. Pack in hot jars. Fill boiling brine to ¹/₂ inch of top. Process 25 minutes at 10 pounds pressure.

ASPARAGUS

Wash; remove loose scales and tough ends. Grade for uniformity. Place upright in wire basket. Hold in boiling water reaching just below tips for 3 minutes. Or cut into 1-inch lengths and boil 2 to 3 minutes. Pack hot jars and cover with boiling water, leaving ¹/₂-inch headroom. Process 30 minutes at 10 pounds pressure.

BEANS, GREEN, SNAP OR WAX

Wash; remove strings and tips. Break into small pieces. Precook 5 minutes. Reserve water. Pack hot jars and cover with boiling reserved water, leaving ¹/₂-inch headroom. Process 25 minutes at 10 pounds pressure for

young tender pods. Old beans should be processed for 40 minutes.

BEANS, FRESH LIMA

Shell, sort and grade for size and age. Boil young beans 5 minutes, older beans 10 minutes. Pack loosely. Cover with boiling water, allowing 1-inch headroom. Process young beans 50 minutes, older beans 60 minutes, at 10 pounds pressure.

BEANS OR PEAS, DRIED

Cover beans or peas with cold water and let stand in a cool place 12 to 18 hours. Boil 30 minutes, then pack into hot jars. Cover with boiling water, leaving 1-inch headroom. Process 90 minutes at 10 pounds pressure.

BEETS

Select and prepare small whole beets with 1-inch stem and all the root. Boil 15 minutes. Trim off roots and stems. Slip off skins. Pack whole, sliced or diced, into hot jars. Add boiling water, leaving ¹/₂-inch headroom. Process 35 minutes at 10 pounds pressure.

BEETS, PICKLED

Prepare a boiling pickling syrup of 2 parts vinegar, 2 parts sugar. Dilute with water according to taste. Prepare cooked beets, see above. Fill hot jars and cover with boiling syrup, leaving ¹/₂-inch headroom. Process in boiling-water bath 30 minutes.

CARROTS

Sort and grade for uniformity. Wash and scrape. Boil 5 minutes. Reserve water. Slice or pack whole. Fill jars with boiling reserved water, leaving

1-inch headroom. Process 30 minutes at 10 pounds pressure.

CORN, WHOLE-KERNEL

Use tender, freshly gathered corn. Cut from cob. Do not scrape cobs. To each quart of corn add only 2 cups boiling water. Heat to boiling. Pack at once, adding no more water. Leave 1-inch headroom. Process 85 minutes at 10 pounds pressure.

CORN, CREAM-STYLE

Pack in pints only, see Peas, right. Cut off the tops of kernels and scrape cobs with back of knife or corn scraper—see (I, 315)—to remove all pulp. To each pint of corn add 1 cup boiling water. Heat to boiling. Pack at once, leaving 1-inch headroom. Process pints 85 minutes at 10 pounds pressure.

GREENS

Use fresh, tender greens. Wash thoroughly; discard any decayed leaves and tough stems. Steam about 8 minutes, or until wilted. Cut through greens several times with a knife. Pack quickly and loosely. Fill jars with boiling water, leaving 1-inch headroom. Process 90 minutes at 10 pounds pressure.

MUSHROOMS

Pack in pints only, see Peas, right. Wash well. Peel if wilted. If old, discard. Let stand 10 minutes in cold water. Wash again. Steam 4 minutes. Pack into hot jars with the hot liquid from the mushrooms and enough added boiling water to cover. Add 1/2 teaspoon salt and 1/8 teaspoon ascorbic acid to each pint to prevent darkening. Leave 1-inch headroom.

Process 30 minutes at 10 pounds pressure.

NUTMEATS

Dry nuts in a 250° oven. Stir occasionally and do not let them brown or scorch. While still hot, fill dry sterilized half-pint or pint self-sealing jars, leaving 1/2-inch headroom. Process 10 minutes at 5 pounds pressure.

OKRA

Use tender pods only. Wash and remove caps without cutting into pod. Cover with boiling water and bring to a boil for 2 minutes. Pack hot. Cover with boiling liquid, leaving 1-inch headroom. Process 40 minutes at 10 pounds pressure.

PEAS, GREEN OR "ENGLISH"

Pack only in pint jars because they overcook and become mushy if packed in quarts. Shell; sort for size. Cover with boiling water; boil small ones 3 minutes, larger ones 5 minutes. Pack loosely into jars. Cover with boiling cooking liquid to within 1 inch of tops of jars. Process 40 minutes at 10 pounds pressure.

PEAS, BLACKEYE, CROWDER, ETC.

Same as Green Peas, above, but leave 1 1/2-inch headroom.

PEPPERS, GREEN

Wash; remove stems, white cores and seeds. Boil 3 minutes in water. Drain and pack into hot jars. Add 1 tablespoon vinegar or 1 1/2 teaspoons lemon juice. Cover with boiling water, leaving 1/2-inch headroom. Process 35 minutes at 10 pounds pressure.

PIMIENTOS

Scald in boiling water or roast in a 450° oven until skins can be rubbed off. Remove stem and blossom ends. Pack hot in dry hot half-pint or pint jars. Do not add water. Process 20 minutes at 10 pounds pressure.

POTATOES, WHITE OR IRISH

Wash, pare, and cook in boiling water for 10 minutes. Drain. Pack into hot jars. Add 1 teaspoon salt to each quart. Cover with boiling water, leaving 1-inch headroom. Process 40 minutes at 10 pounds pressure.

PUMPKIN AND WINTER SQUASH

Bake as on 383, or pare and cut into 1-inch cubes. Add enough water to prevent sticking. Cook or steam until tender. Put through food mill or strainer and pack hot into hot jars, leaving 1-inch headroom. Process 80 minutes at 10 pounds pressure.

SQUASH, SUMMER

Wash, but do not pare. Trim ends and cut into small pieces. Steam or boil 3 minutes. Pack loosely into hot jars and cover with boiling water, leaving 1/2-inch headroom. Process 40 minutes at 10 pounds pressure.

SWEET POTATOES

Wash well and sort for size. Boil or steam slowly about 15 minutes or until skins will slip off easily. Do not pierce with a fork. Skin and cut into pieces. Pack hot. Cover with fresh boiling water or thin or medium syrup, 619, leaving 1-inch headroom. Process 95 minutes at 10 pounds pressure.

TOMATOES

See comments under Tomatoes and Tomato Juice on 623, and Fruit Purées on 619. For Green Tomato Mock Mincemeat, see 682.

PREPARING GAME

The hunter not only must familiarize himself with season, limit and holding laws but must almost of necessity learn how to clean, cut and store his bag, since many states forbid the use of packing plants or butcher shops for this purpose. Quick cooling, scrupulous cleaning and careful preservation greatly enhance that deliciously and legitimately gamy flavor which derives from the fruit, the seeds, the berries or the grasses on which the animal has fed. All too often, gaminess is just the unpleasantly exaggerated result of improper care and manipulation before cooking.

To guard against such diseases as trichinosis, (I, 601), in bear; tularemia, (I, 660), in rabbit; and salmonella, (I, 550), the hunter should wear gloves when handling raw meat. Some of these factors can be counteracted by proper cooking. But whether you go in for little rabbits or big deer, your procedures are basically similar—to bleed, clean, skin, cool, hang or freeze as quickly as possible. It is important, too, to remove the fat of wild animals as soon as possible, as it turns rancid quickly, and to keep any loose hair from the flesh, for the oils in the hair produce off-flavors. Also, in any areas where shot has damaged the flesh, all traces of blood must be removed by scraping or cutting, washing with salted water and drying well. Edible variety meats, (I, 638), should be used at once in camp cooking or should be frozen. For small game like birds, squirrel and rabbit, see (I, 543, 663, and 660). With larger game the logistics of butchering are similar to those for domestic cattle; a careful study of the meat chart on (I, 561) will familiarize you with the bone structure. The ease of further preparation depends somewhat on the skill or luck of your shot.

Immediately after the kill, the animal should be bled. Behead it or cut the jugular vein at the base of the neck, slightly to the left of center. Have a bowl ready underneath to save the blood. You can use it at once or refrigerate it to use later for blood sausage, (I, 635), or as a thickener for gravies, (I, 380). To store see (I, 380).

If the animal is large, place it on a slope with its head at the lowest point. Cut the vein as described above and make sure the blood is flowing freely. Should the animal have been shot in a vital organ, the blood may not be released through the neck but inwardly. It will then be necessary to gut the carcass as quickly and as cleanly as possible to avoid taint from the bullet-ruptured organs. In this case discard the blood. Whatever procedure you use ♦ clean and cool the meat as rapidly as possible.

Leaving the animal with its head lower than the body, you may cut off the feet, pierce the legs and turn it on its back. Tie a rope or wire to each leg and attach them to a shrub or tree nearby, so that when you split the breast bone and cut all the way down the center the animal will be steadied. You may prefer to brace the animal by putting rocks or logs on either side of it.

A good way to start the center cut is to slit the skin for about 3 or 4 inches at the breast bone. Insert your free hand and press the inner organs down out of the way as you continue

to cut, now turning the blade of the knife upward so as not to pierce the intestines.

Continue to press downward with your free hand as you go, and cut almost to the end of the gut cavity where the meat of the hindquarters begins. When this long slit is made, roll the skin back about 3 or 4 inches on either side of the cut, keeping the loose hairs away from the flesh. At this point the innards and intestines will be protruding. But before trying to remove them, hold the hind legs apart and continue a skin-deep cut down the center all the way to the anus. If you are working on a buck, cut off the genitals. Then make a very deep cut through the skin all around the anus. Next prepare to remove the lower alimentary canal. This long tract continues from the mouth to the anus. It is more easily taken out if the animal is lying on its side with its legs downhill. Start at the base of the gut cavity near the hindquarters and pull out enough of the intestines to make room for your hand. These are attached only randomly by not very strong tissue. Find and take hold of the large intestine as near as possible to the already loosened anus and pull the tract into and out through the gut cavity past the incision you have made in the abdomen. Care must be taken during this process not to rupture the thin-walled urine sac. Locate this by tracing the tube that leads to the outside. Grasp the tube, pinching it together to close off the bladder, and after further freeing the bladder, retain your grasp on the tube as you ease out the bladder carefully. The alimentary tract is still attached at the upper end, but the lower mass lies outside the carcass. The liver can be found at the upper edges of the stomach toward the back near the thin, tough diaphragm membrane. In animals other than deer, which have no gall, be careful in reconnoitering for the liver not to pierce the gall-bladder. Now dispose of all the lower alimentary tract by cutting it loose above the stomach at the base of the thin, tough membrane that forms the diaphragm between the lower cavity and the rib cage. Then remove the diaphragm, heart, lungs and upper alimentary canal. Work if possible in such a way that after the removal of the internal organs you will merely have to wipe the cavity with a dry cloth. But where internal bleeding has taken place and fluids from the organs or blood have touched the flesh, or where the flesh has been bullet-pierced, scrape or cut the areas as clean as possible. Do not allow any blood to remain, as it will produce "fishy" flavors. Wipe such areas with salted water. Dry carefully. If the weather is warm, dust the entire cavity with black pepper or powdered charcoal. To shorten the cooling time of large animals, prop the cavity open with sticks. Skin furry animals as quickly as possible. With deer the musk sacs will pull off with the skin. For other game, see individual recipes.

After cleaning, game and poultry should be cooled to below 40°, preferably for a minimum of 24 hours, before canning. Beef is better if allowed to age for a week or 10 days at 34° to 38°. Large game animals are prepared and processed like beef, small game like poultry. ◗ In processing, use enamel or stainless steel cooking ware.

◗ Spices should be used sparingly in this type of preservation, and vegetables omitted altogether. White pepper retains a better flavor than black pepper in meat products. If you like, you may place 1 teaspoon salt in each empty quart container. This amount flavors but does not help to preserve the meat. ◗ Any canned game should be pressure-processed, see below.

MEAT, POULTRY, GAME AND FISH PRESSURE-CANNING

Methods for canning fish are not given in this book because the various recommended processes are controversial. Government bulletins call for long processing and, in addition, before the food is served, for prolonged cooking of home-canned fish and seafood. This causes great loss of flavor and food value. ◗ The freezing of fish is recommended as an alternative for better retention of both qualities, see 654. But the canning of meats, poultry and game in homes can be both a safe and economical procedure and a much more convenient one than the old-fashioned method of preserving by salting and smoking, although again not nearly so satisfactory as freezing, see 652. **The government warns that all home-canned meats should be boiled in an open pan for 20 minutes before tasting or eating.**

For safe serving of home-canned meat products, process all these nonacid foods in a pressure canner. ◗ Make sure that the temperature reaches at least 240° during processing.

It is best to can only fresh, not brined or salted meats. For brined and salted meats, smoking is considered a more satisfactory method than canning. To butcher meat for canning, see Preparing Game, above.

As the packing of cooked meats involves both cooking them first and processing them the same length of time as for Raw Packed meats, and since both must be boiled in an open pan for 15 minutes again before use, we prefer the Raw Pack method.

◗ To **Raw Pack** fresh meats and poultry, prepare jars, 614. Cut meat from bone. Use bones and scraps to prepare Stock, 168. For chicken, separate pieces at the joints. Trim fat carefully, as it may cause meat to have a strong flavor as well as ruin the sealing rubber of the jar. If necessary, wipe meat clean with a damp cloth. ◗ Do not soak it. Cut meat against the grain into 1-inch strips or chunks. Pack into the sterile jars. Cover with boiling stock or tomato juice. ◗ Never use a thickened gravy. You may add 1 teaspoon salt to each quart for seasoning. Allow 1-inch headroom. Now exhaust the air from the open filled jars by setting them on a rack in a pan of boiling water. Keep water level 2 inches below jar tops. Put a thermometer in the center of a jar, cover the pan and heat the meat slowly to 170° F. If not using a thermometer, heat slowly for 75 minutes. Remove jars from the pan and wipe off tops and threads of jars before lidding, 805. Process in a pressure canner at 10 pounds pressure 75 minutes for pints and 90 minutes for quarts. To remove jars from canner, seal, test closure and store, see 617–618.

PRECOOKING AND PACKING MEATS AND POULTRY FOR CANNING

Roasts, steaks, meatballs or patties and sausage cakes may be processed and canned. Use beef, veal, lamb, mutton, pork, chevon, (I, 592), or venison. To bake, preheat oven to 350°. Cut the meat into pieces about 1 pound each. Remove bones, gristle,

and all surface fat. Place in uncovered pans in the oven. Roast until the red or pink color of the meat has almost disappeared at the center, about 20 to 40 minutes. Cut the meat into pieces small enough to fit the jars. Pack closely while still hot into hot, sterile jars, at least 2 pieces to a pint jar. Skim fat from drippings. Add enough boiling water or broth to the drippings to cover the meat, leaving 1-inch headroom. Remove air bubbles, see at left. Wipe jar rim carefully to remove any fat. Adjust the lids and pressure-process at 10 pounds pressure, pints 75 minutes, quarts 90 minutes.

To stew, cut meat into uniform pieces about 1 pound each, drop into boiling water and simmer 12 to 20 minutes or until the raw color has disappeared at center. Liver should be simmered about 5 minutes, tongue about 45 minutes, or until skin can be removed. Cut meat into smaller serving pieces. Remove fat and gristle, then salt, pack closely in hot jars and cover with the boiling broth. ◗ To remove air bubbles, see left. Wipe jar rim carefully.

Frying is the least desirable method of precooking. It makes the surface of the meat hard and dry and often gives an undesirable flavor to the finished product.

◗ Meat that is not covered with liquid will discolor and lose some flavor in storage. Depending on the shape of the pieces, 1 to 1¹/₂ pounds of meat will fill a pint jar and still remain submerged. ◗ Pint jars are preferable to larger containers, as the heat penetrates more readily to the center of the container. Process pints 75 minutes, quarts 90 minutes at 10 pounds pressure.

To precook chicken, simmer meaty pieces in a broth until medium done.

Cover with boiling broth, leaving 1-inch headroom. With bone, process pints 65 minutes, quarts 75 minutes at 10 pounds pressure. Without bone, process 75 and 90 minutes. Gizzards and hearts should be canned together, but separate from the meat, in boiling chicken broth. Process pints 75 minutes at 10 pounds pressure.

★ MINCEMEAT

This is enough filling for about 20 pies. Some of our fans make this recipe for Christmas gifts. It is best if prepared at least 2 weeks before using. Prepare:

9 quarts sliced, peeled apples

Combine with:

4 lb. chopped lean beef or chopped ox heart
2 lb. chopped beef suet
3 lb. sugar
2 quarts cider
4 lb. seeded raisins
3 lb. currants
1½ lb. chopped candied citron
½ lb. dried, chopped, candied orange peel
½ lb. dried, chopped, candied lemon peel
Juice and rind of 1 lemon
1 tablespoon each cinnamon, mace, cloves
1 teaspoon each salt and pepper
2 whole nutmegs, grated
1 gallon sour cherries with juice
2 lb. broken nut meats
(1 teaspoon powdered coriander seed)

Simmer these ingredients about 2 hours. Use an asbestos pad to avoid scorching the mincemeat. Stir frequently. Ladle into hot jars, allowing ½-inch headroom. Process 20 minutes at 10 pounds pressure. If using a boiling-water bath, process 90 minutes. Before serving, season with:

Brandy

SAUSAGE MAKING

There are three major types of sausage: fresh, or "country"; cooked, lightly cured; and partially dried or dry sausage, all described more fully on (I, 633). The preparation for all three types requires using the freshest of meat or game combinations and preferably hard back fat. Best flavor results from the use of a special mechanism whose blades cut and chop rather than grind and crush, as a typical home meat grinder does. Such a machine, seen on 607, is available at butchers' supply houses; and here, too, the blades may be resharpened. This is the place, also, to get special hand stuffers and various sausage casings. For home use, ◗ we do not recommend impervious plastic casings which may allow the development of anerobic organisms, such as those causing botulism. ◗ To avoid trichinosis when making sausage, see (I, 634).

The long natural casings made from the intestines of sheep, hogs and cattle are preferred because they are edible; and more important, because they shrink during smoking so as to adhere to the meat as it dehydrates. These natural casings come dry-salted or brined, if from sheep and hogs; brined only if from beef. ◗ They should be kept refrigerated or frozen until ready to use. Brined casings, however, will not freeze tight because of the strength of the solution. Dry-salted casings should be washed before use; brined casings need not be. All natural casings must be handled with skill and care during the stuffing procedure. While they are available in 1- to 4-

inch diameters, we recommend them especially for link sausages.

Sewn casings of unbleached muslin, while not edible, are practical for home preparation of large sausages. These tubular casings, rounded at one end, open at the other, may be stitched together on a sewing machine. For a 2-inch-diameter sausage, tear to size 8-inch strips of unbleached muslin. This width allows for 1/2-inch seams. Cut the muslin in 9- to 18-inch lengths, depending on the size of your smoker. Cloth casings should be used only after soaking in water and wringing out excess moisture. They usually turn a tawny brown when the sausages have been sufficiently cold-smoked.

▶ Throughout the grinding and mixing process, sausage ingredients should be kept chilled. See the chapter heading on 607, which illustrates the ingredients held over ice. Successful filling depends on the consistency of the sausage mix. If it seems dry, work a little wine or water into the seasoned chopped meat. The trick in stuffing is to keep air from being trapped in the casings, for decay is apt to develop in air pockets. On the other hand, in forcing air out, continuous gentle manipulation is necessary to avoid too great tension in the casings and kinking as the casings fill. Tie off the plumply filled casings in links with string as you fill enough casing for each link, and make the final tie so tight that some of the meat is forced out of the end. Cut this last tie with enough extra cord to make a loop for hanging the sausage during smoking. All these precautions apply to muslin-enclosed sausage, although for larger single units the mix may be somewhat drier.

After stuffing, sausages should hang in a 35° temperature about two days. If using a refrigerator for storage, S-shaped hooks from the shelf grids make a handy means of suspension. If the sausage is to be smoked, allow 12 to 15 hours of cool smoking, 634. During this time it will lose a very appreciable amount of weight. Before eating sausages after smoking, hang them at a 35° temperature at least two weeks to mature. Sausages so prepared may then be kept for many months in a cool, dry, dark place. If a casing mold develops, wipe it off with a vinegar-dampened cloth and discard the casing before serving the sausage.

DRY OR SUMMER SAUSAGE

A great favorite in hot climates. It is called summer sausage even though it is made in winter, because it holds over through the next spring and summer.

Cut into 2-inch cubes:

6 lb. lean beef
2 lb. lean pork

Soak the meat in a 10% brine, 249, in a glass, enamel or stone crock. Weight the meat with a plate held in place with a clean brick or stone, making sure the meat is continually covered with brine. Keep at 35°, stirring every two or three days. Remove the meat after 8 to 12 days; rinse briefly in cold water, and dry; then store refrigerated at 35° on a stainless mesh rack. After four hours or more, when the meat is well dried and chilled, cut it into pieces that will fit your grinder, see opposite. Add to it:

2 lb. hard back fat

Season with:

3 tablespooons salt
1/2 teaspoon each cloves, ginger, nutmeg and coriander
2 teaspoons white pepper
2 cups red wine or water

CANNING, SALTING, SMOKING AND DRYING

To stuff, hang, smoke and mature, see Sausage Making, 630.

DRY-CURING MEAT, GAME AND FOWL

There are two chief ways to salt these meats at home: brining, see Corned Beef, opposite, and dry-curing. When meat is soaked in brines, or, in the more modern technique, unfortunately not practical for home processing, when brine is forced through the arterial system under pressure, temperatures must be very carefully controlled.

Dry-cured meats are more tolerant of fluctuating temperatures under processing than those treated with brine. Ideally, the curing and storing of meats should take place in a 36° to 40° temperature. Even considering the somewhat inconveniently higher temperatures in which most of us are obliged to work, we recommend dry-curing as safer than brining in home-processing. ♦ The three recipes below call for saltpeter, a substance currently questioned by the USDA, but in use to prevent botulism until an effective substitute is available.

♦ To dry-cure, allow the meat to cool as naturally and rapidly as possible after butchering. Spread the pieces out on racks, never allowing them to overlap. Sprinkle them at once ♦ very lightly with salt. Do not blanket them at this time with the salt, as this would retard cooling. When cool, rub them repeatedly with the following salt mixture, being sure to coat the entire surface well in the process. Put the meat into a sterilized crock, being careful not to disturb the salt coating. Cover with a loose-fitting lid or cheesecloth. Six to eight days later resalt the heavier cuts with more

of the curing mixture. Allow for every 10 pounds of meat a mixture of:

> 1 **cup salt**
> 1/4 **cup sugar**
> 2 **teaspoons saltpeter, see comment at left**

with:

> (2 **bay leaves**)
> (2 **coriander seeds**)
> (3 **cloves**)
> (6 **peppercorns**)

which you have crushed in a mortar.

To secure effective salt-penetration, cure the salted meat three days for each pound of meat in the piece. Boned hams and other meat and small pieces will of course cure more rapidly. If the temperature should go below 36° at any time, be sure to add an equal length of time to the curing period, as salt-penetration is slowed to a standstill in freezing temperatures. Leave the meat in the curing container even after all surface salt is absorbed. You may turn the meat occasionally and make a second salt application.

When the prescribed time is up, the meat may be left in the dry salt until used, or it may be scrubbed well and hung in a cool ventilated place to dry out before storing or smoking, 634. Hams should be hung at least 25 days before smoking. Smoking gives that wonderful "country" taste to dry-cured and brined foods. If not to be smoked, wrap each piece of meat individually, first in muslin, then in layers of heavy paper. Hang in a dark, cool, well-ventilated room. When properly cured, hams are at their best after a year. But bacon and shoulder meat should be used before hanging that long.

CORNED BEEF

This salted beef actually has nothing to do with corn but got its name in Anglo-Saxon times when a granular salt the size of a kernel of wheat—"corn," of course, to a Briton—was used to process it. To corn, combine:

> **4 quarts hot water**
> **2 cups coarse salt**
> **1/4 cup sugar**
> **2 tablespoons pickling spice**
> **1 1/2 teaspoons saltpeter or sodium nitrate, see comment opposite**

When cool, pour over:

> **A 5-lb. piece of beef: brisket or tongue**

which has been placed in a deep enameled pot or stoneware jar. Add:

> **3 cloves garlic**

Weight meat to keep it submerged, and cover pot. Cure in refrigerator 3 weeks, turning meat every 5 days.
◗ To cook corned beef, see (I, 584). If it is to be stored, wash in lukewarm water, dry thoroughly, then wrap in layers of heavy paper and hang in a cool, dry place.

SALT OR PICKLED PORK

◗ Please read about Pickling Equipment, 676. Known as **white bacon** in some parts of the country, salt pork may be sliced and used as bacon, but it is more often used for seasoning vegetables or for larding roasts.
Cut into pieces 6 inches square:

> **Fat back or other thin pieces of fat pork**

Rub each square well all over with:

> **Pickling Salt, 249**

Pack the salted pork tightly in a clean crock and let stand 12 hours. For each 25 pounds of meat, mix and cool the following brine:

> **2 1/2 lb. salt**
> **1/2 oz. saltpeter, see comment opposite**
> **4 quarts boiling water**

Pour the ◗ cooled brine over the meat to cover. Store the pork ◗ weighted and covered at 35° to 38° until ready to use. Keep refrigerated and use within 3 weeks.

JERKY

Use jerky when backpacking or for high-protein snacking. This chewy well-flavored item is a great extravagance, for you will end up by weight with only one-third the amount of meat you started with. Slice lean meat on the bias 6 inches long, 3 inches wide and 1/8 to 1/4 inch thick. This makes drying faster, and the end product is easier to chew or reconstitute in stews. Cut away pieces of fat and any muscle membrane left on the meat. Salt and pepper lightly, or marinate the strips, 180, then hang them from the bars of an oven rack in a 175° oven or on "warm." It is advisable to place aluminum foil on the bottom of the oven to catch any juices. But if the meat is of good quality, there should be none unless marinated. Leave the oven door ajar to allow moisture to escape and to ensure the best drying process. The jerky should be ready in 4 to 5 hours, depending on the thickness and leanness of the meat and the humidity of the environment. Make sure that the jerky is ◗ very dry—not more than 2% moisture—or bacteria will grow. It should be slightly flexible, bending before it breaks. Let cool, place in a lidded dry container and store in a cool area.

ABOUT PREPARING ROE FOR CAVIAR

Remove from very fresh fish as soon as possible:

Roe

Tear the egg masses into small-sized pieces. Work them through a $^1/_4$-inch or finer screen to free the eggs from the membrane. Place them for 15 to 20 minutes in a cold-water brine made of:

$1^1/_8$ cups Pickling Salt, 249 to every quart of cold water

If you use a salinometer, the reading should be 28.3. There should be twice as much brine as roe in volume. Remove from liquid and drain thoroughly by allowing to drip through a strainer for about 1 hour. Keep refrigerated during this operation. Place in an airtight nonmetal container and store at 34° for 1 to 2 months. Remove, drain and repack, storing at 0° Fahrenheit in the freezer until ready to use.

PRESERVED EGGS

Preserve eggs at home only if you have no alternative. The commonest method is immersion in waterglass or sodium silicate. If possible, use non-fertile eggs that are at least 12 hours old. Do not pack too many layers on top of each other, as the weight might crack those below. Eggs so kept are not good for boiling, as the shells become too fragile—nor do the whites beat well for meringues, or soufflés or for baking cakes dependent on egg alone as a riser.

To preserve 10 dozen eggs, pour 9 quarts of boiling water into a 5-gallon sterile crock. Add 1 quart waterglass, stir thoroughly and add the eggs. The waterglass should cover the eggs 2 inches above the top egg. Cover crock and store in a cool place no longer than 6 months.

SMOKING FOOD

Hot smoking completely cooks food. **Cold-smoking** preserves the food, often for a considerable time. Both methods add flavor. Cold-smoking is fundamentally a drying process during which brined foods, 249, such as meat, game, fish and fowl are smoked for as short a period as 24 hours or as long as 3 weeks. Length of smoking time depends on the size of the food unit being processed and the steadiness of the temperature. Cold-smoking should never exceed 80° to 85°. If the heat climbs as high as 90°, the fats begin to liquefy and spoilage results. To prepare cured meat, 632, for any smoking process, dry it out first under refrigeration and wipe the surface dry. Hams should be hung to dry out at least 25 days before smoking. Individual taste determines whether to smoke longer than about 72 hours for a ham, 60 hours for a pork shoulder and about 45 hours for a thinner piece of meat like bacon. Food has been sufficiently smoked if it has lost at least one-fourth of its weight during the process. Another test—for unboned meat: a stiff slender wire inserted along the bone to the center of the cut smells sweet when withdrawn.

Hot-smoking is more like a flavorful cooking of brined foods, never producing enough drying to ensure safe keeping qualities. It may last from a very short period to an exposure of 4 to 5 hours, depending again on the size of the unit processed and how steadily the temperature has been maintained. Generally speaking, hot-smoking involves shorter and weaker brining, with temperatures ranging from 250° to 300°.

In another method of hot-smoking, perfected by the Chinese, foods, usually marinated, are cooked in almost sealed smoke pots. A simplified western adaptation is, first, to line a large iron pot generously with foil and sprinkle on it a mixture of brown sugar and condiments. Marinated food is then placed on a rack above the sugar, and the foil closed with a tight seam around the entire contents of the pot—sugar, rack, food and all. After a single tiny hole has been pricked in the top of the foil with a thin skewer, the pot is heated 5 to 7 minutes. As the sugar and spices char, the smoke flavors the food. After smoking, the food is eaten at once. This is the best policy, in fact, with food hot-smoked by any procedure. If not immediately served, the food should be refrigerated without delay. Hot-smoked food—but not that produced by our western version of the Chinese technique—may be kept refrigerated about three weeks. ♦ Freezing is never recommended for any smoked foods.

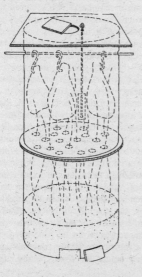

The equipment at left may be used for both cold- and hot-smoking. Some cold-smoking enthusiasts build a separate fire pit joined to the smoke chamber by an inclined buried 12-foot length of stove pipe that elbows up into the smoking cavity. This pit is fired with fruitwood, oak, hickory or any other hardwoods or hardwood chips. ♦ Never use a green or a resinous wood. We do not recommend electrical smokers which depend on smoking chemicals and liquids but suggest, as shown at left, a simple device that involves 2 metal drums placed one on top of the other and shown as though the drums were transparent. Remove the bottom of the lower drum and cut a small vent at the base of the side where the fire can be ignited. The strength of the draft can subsequently be controlled by partially closing off the vent with the piece of metal you have removed. The lid of the lower drum is perforated with about fifteen or more 1-inch holes, allowing the smoke to flow up from the lower drum, while it forms a baffle against direct heat. The lower drum itself is kept filled about one-fourth with hardwood sawdust. To replenish sawdust during the smoking period the upper drum and the perforated lid are lifted off. Prepare the second drum by cutting out the bottom and punching holes opposite each other in the sides near the top, to support staggered rods as shown. From these rods the foods to be smoked are suspended on S-shaped hooks so as to keep the food well spaced.

Preheat the lower drum to 85°. Place the upper drum over the baffle and clap a piece of sheet iron over the top of the second drum. This should have a small aperture toward the top center, and smoke emission can be controlled as needed by partial coverage with a small piece of movable metal. In the upper drum, on a line with the lowest piece of meat, hang a thermometer near the vent so you can retract it for continual reading. It is also wise during smoking to shift the various meats to give them all fairly uniform smoke exposure.

After smoking, then hanging until cool in temperatures not exceeding 60°—which for large pieces sometimes takes a week or longer, depending on the weather—the food is ready for storing. Should any salt crystals have accumulated on the surface, wipe them off, as this crystallization will reattract moisture. The food should then be wrapped first in parchment and then in muslin and stored in a dark north-facing ventilated area where the temperatures stay between 35° and 60°. Or for more even temperature control, wipe off any crystallization and store the smoked unwrapped food in a wooden box raised off the floor, using cooled wood ashes as the packing medium. To cook smoked meats and other smoked foods, see Index.

PASTRAMI

To convert basic Corned Beef, 633, to pastrami, the meat must be smoked. You may also wish to experiment with a more elaborate marinade, substituting for half the water ingredient a red wine vinegar and adding one or more of the following:

(2 tablespoons ginger)
(1 tablespoon coriander)
(1 tablespoon paprika)
(1 teaspoon pepper)

After marination, commercial pastrami is cooked entirely by Hot-Smoking, 634, at 320° for 6 or 7 hours. Because the relatively high heat required is hard to maintain in domestic appliances, one of our correspondents produces pastrami by attaching the marinated meat to a continually revolving rotisserie and smoking it outdoors over his "charbroil" barbecue grill, using plenty of charcoal and oak and hickory chips. This procedure takes about 10 hours and may or may not meet with complete neighborhood approval.

SMOKING FOWL AND COOKING SMOKED FOWL

To prepare birds for smoking, bleed, (I, 535), cool rapidly and pluck, (I, 536), clean, (I, 536), and wash quickly but thoroughly in running cold water. Dry-cure, 632, or prepare a brine, 249. Chicken and game birds are steeped in the brine 24 to 48 hours, depending on size; ducks and geese for about 3 days, and a 12- to 20-pound turkey for 5 days. Cover the brining birds with a plate weighted with a stone, and check during the brining process to make sure they are brine-covered at all times.

On removal wash quickly in running cold water, wipe well, and further dry by hanging for at least 3 hours in a 38° temperature. If not refrigerated protect from insects. If you wish to serve the meat or fowl at once, roast in a preheated 350° oven about three-fourths the usual roasting time. Remove to a smoke oven and flavor by hot-smoking at 200° to 225° until the skin takes on a pleasing rich color. Although the meat will retain a certain redness, it is done when with gentle twisting you can turn the leg of the fowl in the socket. Before cold-smoking birds which are smoked as for meats, 634, they must be brined, see above. After smoking and before the final cooking, they should be steamed for about 10 minutes to remove excess salt.

SMOKING FISH

Use fat fresh fish, (I, 469), for smoking. Under 3 pounds they may be left whole after cleaning, (I, 471). If you cut the heads off, do so just above the bony collar. It is best to split small fish down the belly side and, before hanging them in the smoker, insert small pointed wooden wedges into the chest cavity to hold it and the split edges below from touching and closing off circulation as the fish smoke. Fish over 3 pounds are best filleted, (I, 471), with the skin left on. Place the fillets ♦ on oiled racks, skin side down, during the entire smoking period.

Whether hot- or cold-smoked, 634, fish must first be brined as for fowl, opposite. Fish under 1/4 pound need 30 minutes, from 1 to 2 pounds 2 hours, and 4 to 5 pounds 5 hours. Immediately after brining, rinse the fish quickly in cold water. Dry them off carefully and then dry them further, either hung or racked, in a minimum temperature of 38° and, in any case, protected from insects. During this second drying of about 3 hours a shiny hard glaze should form over the entire surface of the fish. Since the flesh of fish is so fragile, we recommend hot-smoking only when the fish is to be eaten at once. The fish is safe to eat when the flesh flakes when pierced with a fork.

Cold-smoking where the temperature must not go over 80° uses the same equipment and fuel described on 634. Smoking time depends on the storage period desired. For 2-week storage, smoke steadily for 24 hours; for 1-year storage, smoke steadily for a week. Cold-smoked fish can be

eaten without further cooking. Store at about 35° in nonairtight, nonplastic packaging.

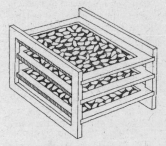

DRYING FOOD

Few climates lend themselves ideally to sun-drying of foodstuffs, ancient as this custom is. Under modern conditions, as we have stated before, freezing and canning are preferred methods of storage. But if harvests are heavy and your freezer and storage space is already preempted, dried foods demand only one-third to one-sixth as much storage space. Albeit there is some vitamin loss due to heat during drying, dried fruits that are eaten without moisture reconstitution have greater caloric value, weight for weight, than either fresh or otherwise processed fruits. In order to discourage spoilage organisms, enzymes, molds, bacteria and yeasts that are present in all foods, at least 80% of the water must be removed from fruit and about 90% from vegetables, which are apt to be less acid. To dry herbs, see 264. Meats and fish which require even greater moisture loss are discussed later. This loss is achieved often by a combination of processes, such as recommended prior steamblanching, described later; sulfuring, a moot process; and salting, most often in the case of meats and fish, before final drying both in the sun and by other heat means. But home methods never achieve the degree of dryness produced by commercial methods, in which moisture content must measure between 2.5% and 6% in order to qualify for sale as dehydrated.

Steam-blanching, 616, which stops enzymatic action, discourages oxidation, and produces some moisture loss, is ♦ necessary for vegetables but, though recommended, is optional for fruits. Whether or not you steam-blanch fruits, wash them first in cold water. Furthermore, to remove the waxy coatings on fruits like apricots, nectarines, plums and blueberries and to avoid cracking of the skins on berries, cherries, figs and grapes, you may place the fruit in a colander and dip it into rapidly boiling water for about 35 seconds. To test for length of steam-blanching, take a sample from the center of the food. It should be wilted and heated through. Remove the food and let it dry on and covered with paper toweling. It is then ready to be spread on the drying trays.

Whether sun- or heat-drying foods, every effort must be made to hasten matters sufficiently to outrun decomposition, so if your sun source is not steady it must be supplemented by oven or other heat at temperatures below actual cooking or scorching. The heat should never go over 140°. It should be maintained for at least two-thirds of the drying time. The heat buildup should begin slowly from not more than 120° so the outside of the food is not hardened, inhibiting the release of moisture from the center. So for best results make your drying racks of such size that they can be moved from sun heat to oven heat as shown on 637, or, if you are impatient by the limiting size of your oven,

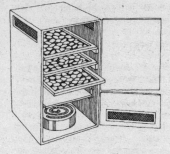

make the larger specially constructed drying cabinet described below. To allow for air circulation in the oven, the overall dimension of the trays should be 3 to 4 inches less than the interior of the oven. To dry in larger quantities, build a cabinet such as shown above, which can be geared to a hot plate, a cooking gas or electric ring or a small chunk-burning stove. Avoid coal- or oil-burning units because their fumes affect flavor. Venting in the drying cabinet is provided by a 2-inch-wide, 12-inch-long screened slot near the top at the sides of the cabinet. In order to allow air intake at the base, the hinged door has a long 2-inch-high slot at the base. Line the cabinet wall and door to the height of the door with aluminum building paper. Diffused heat is achieved by suspending a metal sheet free from the walls on brackets over the heating element as shown. In both oven and cabinet drying, keep the bottom tray 6 to 8 inches from the heat source.

As in all food-processing, drying demands the utmost cleanliness and selectivity so that no imperfect produce introduces spoilage elements. All food should be cut or sliced as evenly and thinly as practical to hasten drying and should be loosely placed on the drying trays in single layers. These trays should have cloth bottoms of mosquito netting, nylon mesh, or even bed sheeting in preference to any metal except stainless steel screening. Other metals may produce off-flavors. If used out of doors, the sides of the trays should be at least 2 inches high so that the covering protecting the food from insects and airborne detritus can be made taut and will not rest on the food. ▶ Any single trays should be elevated on bricks or boards to allow circulation from underneath. If the trays are tiered, they should be shifted periodically so that heat is equalized. In the oven or in a drying cabinet this should occur about every half hour, and the food should also be turned at those intervals.

For sun-drying, special equipment is shown at right, covered with a glass cold frame which intensifies the heat. Be sure to provide screening strips top and bottom for ventilation. The equipment itself should be light enough to be shifted during the day to catch the most sun, and the food on the trays should be turned about every hour. With full sun most foods should dry by this method in about 2 days if the humidity is low. With any of these units it is wise to place a candy or dairy thermometer on the lowest rack to make sure the temperature does not exceed 140°. If new loads of food are put in, it is also wise to place them on the top rack where the heat is apt to be less intense. ▶ Any food dried out of doors must be brought indoors at sundown to protect it from night dews. ▶ No food should be dried out of doors in air-polluted areas.

▶ Testing for dryness is a multi-staged affair. Fruits are considered dried when they produce no moisture when cut and squeezed and are leathery or resilient in texture. If you won-

der how the moist dried fruits you buy are prepared, they contain additives and perhaps sulfur dioxide to protect them from spoilage.

Vegetables are ready when they are brittle and tough and rattle when stirred on the trays. While they are still hot the extent of dryness is hard

to judge, as the vegetables will seem moister than they really are. So in testing remove a few pieces and allow them to cool before making a final judgment. Once the produce has been sun- or heat-dried sufficiently, it must be conditioned. Cool the food on the trays. Have ready enamel or granite ware or a large crock, but ▶ not an aluminum or galvanized metal container. Pour in the contents of the trays. Keep the container covered with a cloth in a warm, dry, airy room. Stir the food once or twice a day for 10 days to 2 weeks. Remove any pieces that seem limp or moist.

At this point oven pasteurization is recommended for all dried fruits and for finely cut, heat-dried, brittle vegetables that may have dried too fast to kill all spoilage elements. Preheat oven to 175°. Put the food on trays, not more than two at a time, loaded not more than 1 inch deep and loosely arranged. Heat in the oven, allowing for the small vegetables about 10 minutes; for fruits, especially oven-dried, about 15 minutes. Cool the pasteurized produce on paper toweling. Place in small labeled and dated paper or plastic bags and then in airtight containers with insect- or rodent-proof lids. Dried fruits keep well about one year, dried vegetables about four months.

To reconstitute dried fruits, see 109. To reconstitute most dried vegetables, cover with cold water until almost restored to their original texture. Use the soaking water to cook the vegetables. ◖ Never soak greens, but cover with boiling water and simmer until tender.

ABOUT DRYING MUSHROOMS

Steam-blanch, 616, mushrooms 3 to 5 minutes to destroy insects or larvae that might damage them during storage. Dry thoroughly on paper towels. Place them on racks, 637, in a densely shady, dry, airy place. If dried out of doors be sure to bring them in at night. When the mushrooms are thoroughly dry, pack in tightly lidded sterile glass jars and store in a cool dark place. To reconstitute, see 255. To use for seasoning, grind dried mushrooms in a nut grinder, 238, or ⏦ blender and store as above.

FREEZING

We are indebted to an Arctic explorer for the following Eskimo recipe for a frozen dinner: "Kill and gut a medium-sized walrus. Net several flocks of small migrating birds and remove one specific small feather from each wing. Store birds whole in interior of walrus. Sew up walrus and freeze. Two years or so later, find the cache—if you can—notify clan of a feast, partially thaw walrus. Slice and serve." Simplicity itself.

Simple, too, are the mechanics of home freezing, a comparatively easy method of food preservation which has been advertised as all things to all cooks. The result is that some frozen-food enthusiasts toss any type of food into the poor freezer and expect fabulous results. Yes, some foods ◗ but not all foods can be preserved by freezing more successfully than in any other way, but ◗ quality produce comes out only if quality produce goes in. There are other important factors, too. Foods chosen must be given ◗ quick and careful preparation. They must be sealed ◗ in moisture- and

vapor-proof wrappings and kept at ◗ constant zero or lower temperatures during storage. Temperatures that fluctuate above and below zero will draw moisture from the food, resulting in loss of quality and nutritive value. Then, of course, the food must be properly thawed and cooked.

Meats, fish, poultry, fruits and pre-cooked foods readily freeze. Vegetables, because of the necessity of blanching, require both more time and more care. But even so, freezing takes a third to half the amount of time and labor involved in canning. And the yields per bushel of produce are about the same, see 619 and 623.

THE FREEZER AND ITS CONTENTS

The economics of keeping a well-stocked freezer presents what we have heard called a "mooty" point. Unless you are a strong-willed planner and dispenser, it may lead to extravagance. When faced with a purely domestic crisis, it is a great temptation to use that choice cut of meat reserved for company, and children love to draw on the seemingly unlimited freezer resources of ice cream and desserts. ◗ It is often only by sharp-eyed scheduling and husbanding of supplies and by raising your own meat and vegetables that you fully realize a freezer's potential for peace of mind and cash savings. ◗ You may also profit, as a quick-witted trader, when markets are glutted with fresh vegetables and fruits or meat and poultry specials. But ◗ avoid bargain frozen foods that have been stored a long time—for they will not have a full complement of vitamins and flavor.

In any case, the freezer is not meant for miserly hoarding. ◗ It should be managed on an overall, continuously shifting plan—a seasonal plan—geared to your family's food needs and preferences. But keep it stocked with favorites, so the family will continue to ask: "What's thawing?"

FILLING THE FREEZER

Space estimates differ, depending on family appetites, but a minimum allowance of 3 cubic feet per person is average if you schedule a turnover every six months.

◗ Neither overload your freezer ◗ nor add, at one time, more than 3 pounds for each cubic foot of freezer space during any 24-hour period. Either procedure will cause the temperature to rise and thus damage the food you are storing. ◗ Until the new packages are frozen, unless the manufacturer directs otherwise, keep them against the freezer plates or the walls of the freezer. ◗ Exceptions are sandwiches and baked items, which, if placed there, attract moisture to themselves. These should be placed on other frozen packages away from the walls.

DEFROSTING THE FREEZER

Your freezer operates most economically if it is located in an area where the temperature is between 50° to 70°. It is hard to specify just how often a manually controlled freezer will need defrosting. The number of times it is opened, how densely it is packed, and how carefully food is wrapped all affect the buildup of condensation. ◗ Defrost whenever there is 1/2 inch of rime on the plates or sides. If frost has not solidified into ice, scraping with a plastic tool is a good method. ◗ Turn off the current first, though. Remove all food from the freezer and refrigerate it immediately or wrap it with layers of newspaper or blankets for insulation. Pans of hot water are sometimes used to hasten defrosting.

No matter how often you have to defrost ◗ be sure to clean up any spillage when it occurs and ◗ to wipe out your freezer at least once a year with a cloth that has been dipped in a solution of 1 tablespoon baking soda to 1 quart of lukewarm water. ◗ Dry the freezer well with either a cloth or a hair dryer. ◗ Be sure the lining is thoroughly dry before you turn the current on again. It is wise to let the freezer run closed for half an hour before returning food to it.

POWER BREAKS

The seriousness of a power break should not be underestimated, because a 25° rise in temperature over a 24-hour period is ruinous to nutritive values. So, if a prolonged break is indicated, call your local dealer or ice cream company for a source of dry ice. This ice has a temperature of 110° below zero F. If placed in the freezer soon after the electricity fails, a 50-pound cake will prevent thawing for 2 or 3 days if the door is immediately closed and not re-opened until 2 or 3 hours after the current is operating. ♦ Handle dry ice with heavy gloves. Do not attempt to chip or cut it, as a stray chip might cause a freeze-burn. In placing the dry ice be sure ♦ a heavy cardboard lies between it and the food. Cover the freezer box with a heavy blanket and pin it so as to expose the motor vents.

Actual thawing, if the box is full and ♦ the freezer is kept closed, is not likely to occur in even 4- to 6-cubic-foot freezers within the first 15 to 20 hours. After 48 hours, the temperature will just reach 40° or 45°—the normal refrigerator range. Food that still retains ice crystals can be refrozen, but meats, poultry and fish registering more than 50° must be cooked and used at once.

ENSURING QUALITY IN THE FREEZING OF FOOD

♦ Quality cannot be created in the freezing process itself. It is some-times lost even though well-fed animals, and fruits and vegetables from rich soils, are used. For example, the keeping qualities of varieties of the same fruit or vegetable differ. Elberta peaches grown in New York are considered tops for freezing, but Elberta peaches grown in Virginia are often reported poor for that purpose. Because new discoveries are being made constantly, it is wise, if you are barging into freezing in a big way, to ♦ consult your county agricultural agent about the best varieties of fruits

and vegetables to grow and to buy from your own neighborhood.

Time and conditions of harvest or slaughter are also factors to reckon with. ♦ Crops are prime when they have sunshine just before maturing. Undue rain before harvest may cause the entire pack to be mediocre. Crops such as ♦ early apples, the first asparagus, etc., keep their flavor best.

♦ The retention of nutritional values and flavors depends on the speed with which food can be processed after harvesting. From then on ♦ it must be kept at such favorable temperatures that microbial and enzymatic activities are held to a minimum. Should they have begun before freezing, the freezing process will not destroy the resultant contamination but only arrest it temporarily. Therefore ♦ you are courting danger to allow perishable frozen foods to thaw for any length of time before cooking. Transfer of frozen food packages from retail store to freezer must be effected with all reasonable speed.

♦ Any frozen foods stored in the ice-cube compartment of the refrigerator should be used within a few days, as the temperature range in this section is between 10° and 25° in most refrigerators, not the required 0° or minus of a freezer. You will find a host of frozen items in the many food shops. Among them are potatoes and other watery foods processed with recently developed machinery that removes harmful excess moisture. But such freeze-dry vacuum-processing is beyond the scope of the home-freezing equipment presently available. So are the freeze-dried foods now popular with backpackers.

Beware of using the freezer for certain foods. ♦ Freezing, for example, will ruin gelatins. ♦ In general, most cooked foods can be frozen, but some do not justify the amount of processing required. Always balance original preparation time against the time it takes to prepare properly for freezing, and omit quick broils, quick-cooking pastas or quick sautés. Freezing techniques, as described later, have settled down into a practice as reliable as canning. But keep in mind that the storage life of frozen food is very decidedly shorter than that for the canned product.

WRAPPING, PACKAGING AND SEALING

Since good results depend so much on the speed with which the fresh foods are prepared and put into the freezer, it is wise to have all filling, wrapping and labeling equipment ready at hand. Use proper funnels for filling cartons, to keep liner edges dry for a perfect seal. Choose only those wrappings that are true freezer-wraps—moistureproof and vapor-proof—to protect the food from drying out and to keep odors from penetrating into the freezer and causing off-flavors in other food. Air left in the containers dries out the food during storage, drawing moisture from the food itself to form a frost in the package—a frost made from the juices and seasoned with the flavors of the food itself. Dehydration or freezer burn can also occur on the surface of the food if the wrapping does not adhere closely enough. ◗ So always exclude as much air as possible from the package.

◗ Liquids and solid foods with juice must be stored not only in leakproof containers but with enough space left for the expansion of the liquid during the freezing process. Allow 1/2 inch in pint and 1 inch in quart cartons. If you use glass, allow 1 inch for a pint and 1 1/2 inches for a quart container with a narrow top opening. If the opening is wide, less headroom is needed. Should you be working with dome lids on glass freezer jars, leave the screw bands on until you are ready to use the food.

We prefer cubical containers, as they conserve a good deal more storage space and stack better than cylindrical ones of the same capacity. Meats and irregularly formed foods are best wrapped in aluminum foil, which should have a weight of .0015 or thicker, needs no sealing, and clings to the contour of the food, helping to exclude air. The pack profits from an overwrap of stockinet, which protects against tearing of the

foil. For economy, old nylon stockings may be used in place of stockinet. Since laminated plastics and papers vary in quality and require the use of tapes adjusted to low temperatures or equally careful sealing with a medium-hot pressing iron, it is often difficult to judge their effectiveness.

◗ All sheet wrappings should be applied with the lock-seal or drug-store wrap above. To make the drug-store or lock-seal wrap, place the food in the center of a piece of paper large enough so that when the ends are brought together, they can be folded as shown on the left above, and, when brought down taut against the food, make an interlocking seam as shown in the center. Turn over the package, so that the seam lies on the table. Pleat-fold one open end, making an extra fold before pressing the folded end against the package. Spin the package around so that the doubly folded end can be braced against your body, as shown on the right. Now very carefully press any excess air from the package. Then fold the remaining open end. Seal the package with ▶ a tape that is formulated for low temperature.

If the object to be wrapped is bulky, you may have to resort to the less protective butcher wrap which follows.

The food is placed diagonally on a large square of paper. One corner is brought over it generously, as shown on the left at the bottom of the page. The adjoining corners are then folded over, as shown in the center, and the entire package folded over in turn, as shown on the right. Keeping the wrapping taut and flat helps exclude excess air.

Be careful, again, to press out excess air before closing polyethylene bags. Twist the bags tightly into a gooseneck and tie with plastic-covered wires or string. These bags remain pliable even at zero temperature and need no overwrap.

Plastic boxes and heavily waxed cartons are good for liquids, but watch for a tight seal. Both may be

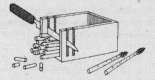

used again. Before reusing, wash the wax cartons with a detergent and cold water to keep the wax firm. ▶ Aluminum foil cartons are especially favored. Be extremely careful to seal them tightly. They chill rapidly and can go from freezer to oven without further handling or loss of contents.

If you are packing vegetables in cartons, size the produce carefully. A device such as the one shown above can be made out of a wooden box. Adjusted to your carton size, it is a great aid for quick, close packing. ▶ Should several servings of meat, cookies or other small items be combined in 1 package, they separate

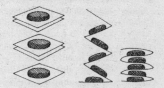

more easily when 2 thicknesses of moisture-proof paper are placed between each 2 units, as shown on the left, or when they are slid into folded foil, as shown on the right above, be-

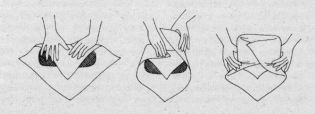

fore the outside wrapping is put on.
◗ Package foods in convenient serving or meal-sized quantities.

LABELING AND DATING

◗ Keep a master record of dates of freezing, as well as poundage on meats and number of portions of other foods. ◗ Labeling and dating the packages themselves, needless to say, are essential. Soft wax or china marking pencils or marking pens do well for cartons. Different colored labels may be slipped between stockinet and other wrappings or under transparent wraps, for quick identification. While many foods keep satisfactorily for months, there are some exceptions, which are noted in detail later, such as fat meats, poultry, prepared doughs and precooked foods. You may find our storage-limit recommendations short compared to others, but we believe you also prefer optimum standards for food flavor and texture to merely mediocre ones.

THAWING AND COOKING FROZEN FOODS

Always thaw frozen foods in their original containers. It is best to thaw them on a refrigerator shelf, with the exception of unbaked doughs, 658. See Index for thawing instructions for individual foods. For emergencies, if the package is absolutely waterproof, it may be immersed in water that is kept cold. This procedure should be adopted only when you are pressed for time, as the result is poor with fragile foods or those with high water content—like strawberries. To thaw food quickly you may use a microwave oven, (I, 116). Use all frozen items immediately after thawing, for growth of bacteria

can occur rapidly in thawed foods left at room temperature, ◗ especially pot pies, TV dinners and foods containing gravies, sauces and stuffings. Prompt preparation after thawing is especially important with blanched products, whose oxygen-resisting enzymes have been destroyed and whose further exposure to air and heat causes rapid adverse changes in quality and nutritional value.

FREEZING FRUITS

Have ready the chilled syrup, 648, and enough ice to wash the fruit in ice-cold water. Choose almost any firm, sound, uniformly sun-ripened fruit. Sort individual pieces carefully and wash well in ice-cold water before removing pits, cores and stems, or paring the fruit if necessary. People who grow their own berries may freeze them successfully without washing—provided they have not been treated with toxic spray. It is safer to wash berries that are not home grown, immersing them briefly but thoroughly in ice-cold water. Drain the fruit well, then spread it out on several thicknesses of paper toweling and cover lightly with additional toweling to absorb as much surface moisture as possible. To avoid crushing or bruising the fruit, use very gentle movements. Large fruits generally pack better if cut into pieces, and less than perfect fruit is best packed crushed or puréed after damaged portions have been removed. Treat fruits that tend to discolor before freezing and during thawing, such as apples, peaches, apricots and pears, with one of the Anti-Browning Solutions, 106, or the solution mixed especially for freezing, opposite. If fruits that tend to discolor are packed in combinations that include citrus fruits, the lemon juice or ascorbic acid may be omitted.

Steam-blanching, 650, is recommended for the following fruits: apple slices and pears, 1 1/2 to 2 minutes; rhubarb, 1 minute; and apricots, 1/2 minute. ♦ Chill the fruit in ice water before packing.

It is not essential to use sugar in freezing fruit, but it is often preferable, see below. Freshly grated unsweetened coconut may be frozen by adding one part sugar to eight parts coconut. Mix it with its own juice, 245, before freezing. Leftover packaged coconut may also be frozen and used as needed. Mashed bananas for banana bread may be frozen in small containers, and frozen slices of banana make easy additions to cereals and desserts, 120. Unsweetened raspberries, blackberries, etc., may be frozen by the **tray freezing** method, see illustrations on 641. Place them unwrapped, in a single layer, on trays in the freezer until solidly frozen. Then later they can be packaged closely, sealed and stored.

Some fruits keep better packaged in dry sugar or in Syrup, 648. Sugar just before packaging and freeze as soon as possible, so the sugar will not draw juices from the fruit. It is sometimes suggested that fruits and berries be served only partially thawed and while still slightly icy, so they do not "weep." While this is a practical approach for garnishes, we so dislike biting into a glassy texture that we suggest that ♦ frozen berries be fully thawed and used for sauces and flavoring, where their taste is superb and their "weeping" not a liability. Thaw fruits on a refrigerator shelf.

ANTI-BROWNING SOLUTION FOR FREEZING

Dissolve 1/2 to 3/4 teaspoon ascorbic acid in a little cold water before adding to 1 quart syrup or 1 quart prepared fruit and use as indicated under packing instructions below. If using lemon juice, which may somewhat alter the flavor of the food, add 1 tablespoon to each quart of syrup.

PACKING FRUITS FOR FREEZING

There are four main ways to freeze and pack fruits. Use the one best suited to your food preferences or dietary needs.

UNSWEETENED DRY PACK

An easy way to freeze the following fruits for pies or jams and preserves, but ♦ not recommended for strawberries. After washing the fruit in ice water where necessary and draining; or peeling, seeding or coring, and conveniently sectioning, place immediately in containers. Shake down to pack closely. Seal and freeze.

*Apples	Elderberries
*Avocados	Loganberries
Blueberries	Melons
Blackberries	Persimmons
Cranberries	Pineapple
Currants	*Plums
*Figs	Prunes
Gooseberries	Raspberries
Grapes	Rhubarb

*Sprinkle the fruit with a solution of dissolved ascorbic acid, see Anti-Browning Solutions, above.

DRY SUGAR PACK

Use this method for quick juicy fruits, washing where necessary, or peeling, coring or seeding, and sectioning. Sprinkle sugar over the fruit on a shallow tray and mix gently until some juice has been drawn out and the sugar is dissolved. Fill containers, shaking to pack closely, and leave 1/2-inch headroom for pints, 3/4-inch for larger containers. Seal and freeze.

For each quart prepared fruit use the amount of sugar indicated

*Apples, 1/2 cup	Loganberries,
*Apricots, 1/2 cup	3/4 cup
*Avocados, 1 cup	Mangoes, 1/2 cup
Blackberries,	*Nectarines,
3/4 cup	2/3 cup
Boysenberries,	*Peaches, 2/3 cup
3/4 cup	*Persimmons,
*Cherries, 3/4 cup	1 cup
Currants, 3/4 cup	*Plums, 1/2 cup
Dewberries,	Raspberries,
3/4 cup	3/4 cup
Gooseberries,	Strawberries,
3/4 cup	3/4 cup

*Before adding sugar, sprinkle the fruit with an Anti-Browning Solution, see 647.

UNSWEETENED WET PACK

Suitable for naturally sweet fruits and berries. After washing and draining the fruit, pack in leakproof containers, and either crush in its own juice or cover with water to which an Anti-Browning Solution, 647, has been added. Allow 1-inch headroom. Seal and freeze.

SYRUP PACK

Whole fruits and those that tend to darken are best packed in syrup, as are fruits intended for desserts and compotes.

◗ Syrups for freezing may be made several days in advance and stored in the refrigerator, to be well chilled when combined with their fruit.

> **For light or 40% syrup, use 1 3/4 cups sugar to 1 pint water**
> **For medium or 50% syrup, use 2 1/2 cups sugar to 1 pint water**
> **A heavier syrup is not recommended**

Some people prefer to combine sugar with corn syrup or honey. If this combination is desired, never use more than 1/4 cup corn syrup to 3/4 cup sugar. Any of these syrups may be made by merely dissolving the sugar and corn syrup in water, but it is preferable to boil the mixture until the sugar is dissolved. Chill well before using.

If using an Anti-Browning Solution, 647, add it to the cold syrup just before packing the fruit.

◗ Be sure the syrup covers the fruit completely. When using syrup with small or sliced fruits or berries, allow about 1 1/2 cups of fruit and 1/3 to 1/2 cup of syrup for a pint container; for halved fruits about 1 1/2 cups of fruit and 3/4 to 1 cup of syrup.

If the fruit tends to rise above the syrup after leaving 1-inch headroom, lightly crush a piece of moisture-proof paper and put it on the top to keep the fruit submerged until the expansion of freezing makes the syrup fill the container. Leave the paper in the container.

> **In the list below, the L stands for light syrup, the M for a medium one. For relative amounts of fruit and syrup, see above.**

*†L	Apples
*†M	Apricots, peeled or unpeeled
L	Blackberries
L	Blueberries

L-M   Boysenberries
*M   Cherries, sweet
M   Cranberries
M   Currants
M   Dewberries
*L   Figs
L   Fruit cocktail
M   Gooseberries
L   Grapefruit
L   Grapes
L   Guavas
L-M   Loganberries
L   Melons
*L   Nectarines
L   Oranges, sections
L-M   Papayas, $1/2$-inch cubes
*L   Peaches
*†L   Pears
L   Pineapples
*L-M   Plums
L-M   Pomegranates
L-M   Prunes
L-M   Raspberries, whole or
        crushed
†L   Rhubarb
M   Strawberries

* Use lemon juice or ascorbic
  acid, see Anti-Browning Solutions, 647.
† Steam-blanch, see 650.

FREEZING FRUIT PURÉES

Fruits such as plums, prunes, avocados, papayas, mangoes, persimmons
and melons keep better in puréed
form if left uncooked. To purée, see
the food mill illustrated on 661.
Applesauce is one of the most delicious of frozen cooked purées, especially if made with early apples.
Cooked purées should be used within
4 months. All may, if necessary, be
packaged without sugar. Otherwise,
allow about 1 cup of sugar per pound
of fruit. Fruit sauces or cobbler fillings made from seedy berries, espe-

cially blackberries, are smoother if
the frozen berries are broken apart
and put unthawed through a meat
grinder. Use a fine blade.

FREEZING FRUIT JUICES

Juices such as apple, raspberry, plum,
cherry and grape, as well as fruit
ciders, freeze most satisfactorily. For
each gallon of cherry or apple juice,
add $1/2$ teaspoon ascorbic acid or
2 teaspoons lemon juice. Peaches for
pressing can be steamed to 150° to
keep color clear without tasting
cooked. Cherries, plums, prunes and
grapes have a better flavor if slightly
cooked, as some of their characteristic flavor is extracted from the skin.
Raspberries are best if the whole
berries are mixed with 1 pound of
sugar to each 10 pounds of fruit and
frozen. Extract the juice when ready
to use. In freezing citrus juices, it is
difficult to retain their vitamin content
without an elaborate vacuum process.
Fruit for jelly and jam may be frozen
unsugared and the juice extracted
later without any cooking. To make
the jelly, proceed as usual, see 663.

FREEZING VEGETABLES

Most vegetables take well to freezing. If they are garden-fresh and
properly processed, their taste, when
served, is hardly distinguishable from
that of fresh produce.
   Choose young, tender vegetables.
Starchy ones such as peas, corn and
lima beans are best when slightly immature. If not prepared and frozen at
once, vegetables, to retain their freshness, must be kept chilled between
harvesting and processing. Wash and
prepare them quickly, as for regular
cooking. If broccoli or cauliflower is
insect-infested, soak $1/2$ hour in a solu-

tion of 2 tablespoons salt to 1 gallon water. Rinse well. In order to blanch them evenly and pack efficiently, sort the vegetables for size. Several handy devices for sizing and cutting are available, and a corn scraper, (I, 315), is a great asset for preparing corn cream-style. Better food values and flavor are retained if vegetables are not shredded or frenched. Green peppers do not need to be blanched before freezing if they are diced after the removal of seeds and membranes. Quick-freeze them on shallow trays before packaging.

It is best to fully cook before freezing such vegetables as pumpkin, squash and sweet potatoes. Mushrooms may be sautéed before freezing by heating 2 cups in 1 tablespoon butter in an uncovered pan about 3 minutes. Cool and freeze immediately. Tomatoes to be served raw do not freeze well, but tomatoes for stewing or seasoning may be scalded 2 minutes to loosen skins, then cored and packaged for the freezer without any additional heating. Cook before serving. Tomato juice is heated to boiling, strained and cooled before freezing. Leave at least 1-inch headroom.

BLANCHING VEGETABLES

Except for the varieties specifically noted below, and those above which we recommend processing fully cooked, all vegetables should be blanched before freezing, for enzymes continue to be active in vegetables even after harvesting and, unless arrested, will bring about changes which lead to nutritional loss and off-flavors. Blanching greatly lessens enzymatic activity and for this reason becomes an essential part of the freezing procedure. There are 2 methods of blanching: boiling and steaming. They may be used more or less interchangeably, although steam-blanching takes 30 seconds to 1 minute longer. However, leafy vegetables like spinach must be boil-blanched to allow quick heat-penetration; and watery ones like squashes and cut sweet corn, which lose flavor badly through leaching, if not completely precooked as recommended, should be steamed. Since blanching is not meant to be a cooking process, but merely a preparatory one, it should be carefully timed. Removal of excess moisture after blanching, and proper chilling before packaging, are two extremely important steps.

♦ To blanch by boiling, allow at least 1 gallon of boiling water to 1 pound of vegetables. Put the vegetables in a wire basket. Submerge them completely in the boiling water, cover and immediately begin to time the blanching, see below. Shake the wire basket several times during this period to allow even penetration of heat. When finished, lift vegetables from boiling water and put at once into a pan of ice water. Chill until the vegetables are cool to the center. Remove, drain and package.

♦ To steam-blanch, bring 2 or 3 inches of water to an active boil in a kettle with a tight lid and a rack. Put the vegetables, not more than a pound at a time, in a wire basket and suspend them above the water. Cover the kettle. When the steam starts to escape under the lid, begin to time for blanching. Shake the basket several times during this period to make sure that all the vegetables are uniformly exposed to the steam. Chill at once to stop further softening of the tissues by heat. If your tap water is 50° or less, hold the vegetables under it. If not, immerse them in ice water. Drain the cooled vegetables well and spread them on several thicknesses of paper toweling. Also cover them with paper toweling to absorb as much of the surface moisture as possible before packaging. Except for greens, which should have a 1-inch head space, the containers should be closely and completely filled, but not stuffed. If frozen vegetables toughen consistently, the water used ♦ may be too hard for good results.

▲ At 500 feet or more above sea level, blanch vegetables 1 minute longer than the time specified in the following chart.

BLANCHING CHART FOR VEGETABLES

VEGETABLE	MINUTES TO BLANCH	MINUTES TO STEAM-BLANCH
†Artichoke, whole	8 to 10	
Asparagus, medium-sized	3	4
Bamboo shoots	7 to 13	
Beans, green or wax	2½	3
Beans, lima, medium-sized	1½	2
Beans, shell	1¾	
Beans, soy and broad, in pod	4	
Bean sprouts	4 to 6	
Beet greens	2½	
Beets, small	Until tender	
Broccoli, split	3 to 4½	3 to 5
Brussels sprouts	3 to 4½	3 to 5
Cabbage, leaf or shredded	1½	2
Carrots, sliced	3	3½
Cauliflower, florets		3
Celery, diced	3	3½
Chard	2½	
Chayote, diced	2	2½
Chinese cabbage, shredded	1½	2
Collards	2½	
Corn to be cut, small ears to large	3 to 7	4 to 8
Corn on cob	6 to 10	7 to 11
Dasheen	2½	3
†Eggplant, 1½-inch slices	4	4½
Kale	2½	
Kohlrabi, diced	1	1¾
†Mushrooms, medium, whole	5	
Mustard greens	2½	
Okra, medium whole	3 to 4	4
Parsnips	2	3
Peas, black-eyed	2	2½
Peas, green	1½ to 2½	2 to 3
Peppers	2	3
†Potatoes, sweet, puréed	Until tender	
Pumpkin, puréed	Until tender	
Rutabaga, diced	2	2½
Spinach	2½	
Spinach, winter, puréed	Until tender	
Turnip greens	2½	
Turnips, diced	2	2½
Vegetables, mixed	Blanch separately; combine after chilling.	

†To preserve natural color, soak for 5 minutes in a solution of 1 teaspoon ascorbic acid and 1 quart water before blanching.

THAWING AND COOKING FROZEN VEGETABLES

Most frozen vegetables, because of previous blanching and a tenderizing process induced by temperature changes during storage, cook in from one-third to one-half the time that fresh vegetables require. Uncooked frozen vegetables may be substituted in recipes calling for fresh vegetables, ♦ but shorten their cooking time. Example: add them to stews for the last minute of cooking. As with fresh vegetables, it is imperative, if flavor and food values are to be retained, not to overcook, especially if you use a pressure pan, see (I, 281).

For table service, cook most vegetables without thawing. Exceptions are broccoli and greens, which profit by partial thawing, and ◗ corn on the cob, which should always be completely thawed, and is delicious if buttered and rewrapped in the aluminum foil in which it was frozen, then baked 20 minutes at 400°. Frozen corn on the cob may also be prepared first by pressure-cooking without previous thawing 1 minute at 15 pounds pressure, cutting off kernels, adding salt and butter and heating 2 minutes in an ovenproof dish under moderate broiler heat.

When cooking unthawed vegetables, break them apart into 4 or 5 chunks, to let the heat penetrate rapidly and evenly. In cooking, use the smallest possible amount of boiling water—¼ cup is enough for most varieties. However, lima beans take almost a cup and soybeans and cauliflower about ½ cup. The vegetables should be ◗ covered immediately with a lid. Once the boiling has begun again ◗ simmer until tender. Because the addition of water in cooking frozen vegetables always to some extent adversely affects flavor, we prefer processing them by steaming or pressure-cooking on a rack over hot water, double-boiler cooking, or baking. This is especially true for corn cut from the cob and for squash.

FREEZING MEATS

Meats, both domestic and game, should be slaughtered, chilled and aged as for canning, 626, after which they may be divided into meal-sized quantities for packaging, see 644.

◗ The reheating of once-thawed and cooked meats does not make for very tasty, nutritious or safe eating. Serve such leftovers cold or heat them in a piquant hot sauce.

The same advice as for all frozen produce applies to the choice of meats: watch quality. Storage at low temperature does not induce enough change to make tough meats tender. If you usually buy quality cuts over the counter, make sure you can trust a different source which sells in quantity.

Beef, lamb and mutton must be properly aged from 5 to 7 days in a chill-room at 34° before being frozen. ◗ Pork and veal should be frozen as soon as they cool, after slaughtering, to forestall the tendency of the fat to turn rancid.

Although some frozen meats may be held over a year, it is a questionable economic or gastronomic procedure. Hold corn-fed beef, lamb and mutton about 6 to 9 months; pork and veal no longer than 8 to 9 months; variety meats 3 to 4 months; and ground meats and stews only 2 to 3 months. ◗ Do not hold meat loaves more than 3 months, as the seasonings deteriorate. Salted or fat meats, such as fresh sausage, smoked or brined hams and bacon, should never be held longer than a month. ◗ Take extra precautions in wrapping smoked meats ◗ to keep the odor from penetrating other foods. Bones, which add flavor to meats during cooking, take up considerable locker space and may also cause wrappings to tear. Even though removal of bones requires both skill and time, it is worth it. Cook bones, thus removed, with meat trimmings to make a concentrated stock, 168. This is valuable for soups and gravies ◗ or for packaging precooked meats, 644. Freeze stock in ice-cube-sized trays, remove and wrap for storage. These concentrates make quick gravy or soup. Game storage depends in part on the type of game and in part on the laws of your state, which may limit holding time. For large game, see directions for meat opposite; for birds, see those for poultry below.

THAWING AND COOKING FROZEN MEATS

Frozen meats may be cooked thawed or unthawed. ♦ But partial or complete thawing helps retain juiciness in thick cuts, and they will cook and brown more evenly. Thin cuts and patties may toughen if left frozen. ♦ Variety meats or meats prepared by breading or dredging must be completely thawed. ♦ Always defrost in the original wrappings on a refrigerator shelf. Allow 5 hours for each pound of thick cuts, less for thinner ones.

♦ Cooking unthawed large cuts of meat takes one and a half times as long as fresh ones. Small, thin cuts take one and a quarter times as long. ♦ Thawed cuts are cooked as for fresh ones.

In broiling unthawed meat, regardless of thickness, place it at least 5 to 6 inches below the heat source. Allow one and one-half times the broiling time. ♦ In any roasting process, use only the constant-heat method, see (I, 553). A meat thermometer is a reassuring aid, see (I, 555).

FREEZING AND THAWING POULTRY

Uncooked broilers, fryers and roasting chickens are most desirable for freezing. For stewers, see Freezing and Thawing Precooked Dishes, 655. If you raise your own, starve the chickens for 24 hours before slaughtering, but give them plenty of water. Bleed them well. Clean and dress, (I, 508),

immediately. Be careful not to tear or bruise the flesh. Before freezing, chill overnight in the refrigerator or in ice until the birds are no longer stiff and the legs and wings can easily be rotated. ♦ Do not age any poultry unless you are fortunate enough to have wild duck or pheasant, which should be aged 2 or 3 days. For details, see directions listed under recipes for each kind of wild fowl. Remove excess cavity fat. Wrap and seal ♦ being careful to expel as much air as possible from the package. One helpful method is to put the bird in a freezer bag and plunge it quickly into a deep pan of cold water—keeping the top of the bag above the surface of the water. Twist the top and fasten.

When preparing several birds, storage space is saved if chickens are halved or disjointed before packaging. Freeze halves, breasts, thighs and drumsticks separately and wrap with double moisture-proof paper between them or store in cartons. Cook the backbones, wings and necks, remove the meat and freeze in the chicken broth. Store young frozen chickens no longer than 9 months, older ones 3 to 4 months. Keep ducks and turkeys 6 to 9 months. A slight discoloration of the bones may occur during storage. It is harmless.

♦ Wrap giblets separately in moisture-proof wrappings and keep frozen only 2 to 3 months.

♦ It is not advisable to freeze stuffed poultry, as frequently the stuffing does not freeze fast enough to avoid spoilage. ♦ Freeze the stuffing separately. Poultry is always best when thawed before cooking, unless used for fricassee, (I, 520). The usual method for a bird weighing less than 5 pounds is to thaw in the original wrappings on the refrigerator shelf, allowing 2 hours per pound. For a faster way, see (I, 507).

Cook immediately after thawing. For detailed information about thawing larger birds, see (I, 507). Although we do not recommend it ◗ unthawed fowl needs about one and one-half times as long to cook as nonfrozen fowl. ◗ Treat thawed birds like fresh ones.

FREEZING, THAWING AND COOKING FISH

Fish, shellfish and frog legs keep most successfully when cleaned and frozen at once. If this is impractical, keep fish under refrigeration from catching to freezing, but in no case over 24 hours. Fish weighing 2 pounds or less, minus viscera, head, tails and fins, are frozen whole. For fish weighing 2 to 4 pounds, filleting is advised, (I, 472). Larger fish are usually cut into steaks, (I, 472), but they too may be frozen whole for stuffing later. Separate fillets or steaks with a double thickness of waterproof paper, 645. Try to use frozen fish within 4 months, and fish heavy in fat, like salmon, within 2 months.

Lobster and crab freeze best if cooked first as for the table but without salt. Remove meat from shells and pack dry meat in airtight containers. Shrimp, minus heads, are best frozen uncooked, as they toughen if frozen afterward. In fact, most shellfish are apt to toughen, cooked or uncooked, if held over 2 months. Oysters, clams and scallops should be shelled, and the liquor saved. Scallops may be washed after shelling, but not the other shellfish. Package all of these in their own liquor to cover and freeze or in a brine using 1 tablespoon salt to 3 cups water. Hold no longer than 3 or 4 months.

Fish and shellfish are often packed commercially in an ice glaze or an ice block to seal from oxygen. While this procedure is not easily adapted to home freezing, it is effective and entirely practical. There are two methods. To freeze in an ice block, place several small cleaned fish, steaks, or fillets in a loaf pan, wax carton or coffee tin, cover with water and freeze. When blocks are solid, remove from pan and wrap in freezer packaging material and store. The second method involves an ice glaze and is especially suitable for whole fish. Simply freeze the fish, cleaned but unwrapped, then dip the frozen fish in water just above the freezing point. Return to freezer, then repeat the dipping until a glaze 1/8 to 1/4 inch thick has formed. Wrap in a moisture-vaporproof material or seal in plastic bag.

Slowly thawed fish loses less juice and is more delicate when cooked than fish quickly thawed. Thaw fish in the original wrappings on a refrigerator shelf and allow about 8 hours per pound. Lobster takes slightly more, scallops, oysters, shellfish and uncooked shrimp slightly less time than given above. Shrimp need not be thawed before cooking, unless it is to be deep-fat-fried. Unthawed fish must be cooked both longer and at much lower temperatures than fresh fish—usually about one and one-quarter times as long.

FREEZING AND THAWING EGGS

Eggs must be removed from the shell before freezing. For short periods, shelled eggs may be frozen individually in an ice-cube tray, then packaged and stored. Usually, however, yolks and whites are stored separately. The whites may be packaged in small vaporproof recipe-sized containers, perhaps in the exact amount for your favorite angel cake. Yolks should be stabilized or they become pasty and hard to mix after freezing. Stabilization is accomplished as follows: If yolks are to be used for unsweetened food, add 1 teaspoon of salt to each pint, if for desserts, add 1 tablespoon of sugar, honey or corn syrup to each pint. Label the yolks accordingly. You will need about 10 whole eggs or 16 whites or 24 yolks for each pint container. To use, ♦ thaw in the refrigerator for 8 to 10 hours.

If you prefer to package whole eggs, stir with 1 1/2 teaspoons sugar or corn syrup or with 1/2 teaspoon salt to each pint, incorporating as little air as possible. In packaging, allow 1/2-inch head space for expansion during freezing. Thaw all eggs before using in recipes. To reconstitute a whole egg, use 3 tablespoons thawed whole eggs. To reconstitute a whole egg from your separately packed whites and yolks, allow 1 1/3 tablespoons of yolk and 2 tablespoons of white.

FREEZING BUTTER, CREAM AND MILK

Unsalted butter stores well, but if salt is added, 3 months should be the limit of storage. ♦ Cream should be pasteurized first, and may be stored 3 to 6 months. When thawed, the uses for thick cream are limited mainly to making frozen desserts and using small amounts in vegetables and casseroles. Its whipping quality will be impaired, its oil rises on contact with coffee, and the texture is unsatisfactory for use with cereals. If you are making ice cream or frozen desserts for the freezer, choose a recipe that calls for heating the cream first. It is not advisable to freeze light or sour cream. ♦ If milk is frozen, use only pasteurized, homogenized milk. Leave 1/2-inch headroom when freezing cream or milk. Store only 1 month. To use, ♦ thaw butter about 3 hours on a

refrigerator shelf and milk or cream about 4 hours.

FREEZING CHEESES

Cheeses of the hard or cheddar type may be stored 6 months. Cream cheese becomes crumbly when frozen but seems to serve well as an ingredient in sandwiches or dips. Dry cottage cheese can be frozen only before the curds are washed free of whey, see 195. It is again washed after thawing, and drained. To thaw, rest cheese about 3 hours on a refrigerator shelf.

FREEZING AND THAWING PRECOOKED DISHES

The precooked frozen meal, for better or for worse, is a reality. If you should go in extensively for this not very enthusiastically endorsed form of cornercutting, you may as well take further advantage of it: labor can be saved by baking several pies, cakes or batches of bread at one session and storing the extras; or by doubling a casserole recipe and freezing half. Prepare school lunches in advance. Frozen sandwiches in the lunchbox will be thawed by lunchtime and will keep other foods cool. We urge you, though, to read about the kinds of products really suitable for freezing, 643, and to remember ♦ to cool the cooked dishes you plan to freeze through and through before you pack them. If you do not cool them sufficiently, the outside edges may freeze hard but the interior may not cool quickly enough to prevent spoilage. ♦ Also, do not try to freeze too much at one time, for overloading your freezer raises the temperature to the detriment of your already stored frozen foods. Be just as careful with packaging cooked foods, 643, as with raw ones. Try to use them within 1 month, and in reheating be sure to thaw properly or reheat slowly.

Main dishes of the creamed type, stews, casseroles, meat pies, rissoles, croquettes and spaghetti sauces are among the most convenient of precooked foods for freezing. Fried foods almost without exception tend to rancidity, toughness and dryness when frozen. No appreciable time is gained by freezing such starchy foods as macaroni, noodles or rice. And potatoes should not be frozen.

Prepare main dishes as usual, following your favorite recipes. But, in all instances, undercook the vegetables involved. Chill precooked foods rapidly over ice water and package closely and carefully, see 643, before freezing. Line casserole dishes with foil before filling, then freeze. When frozen solid, remove the foil-wrapped food, seal tightly and freeze. This releases the casserole until you are ready to use the food, at which time you may remove the foil, return the food to the casserole and heat the dish in the oven.

Stewed meats keep best in heavy sauces. If they are to be used for salads, place them in clear concentrated stock. Chill rapidly to room temperature. Cut in meal-sized portions; package closely and freeze. Hold no longer than 1 month. Thaw in original wrappings on a refrigerator shelf, allowing about as much time as for uncooked meats.

Reheat stews and creamed dishes in a double boiler or in the oven at 350° in a heatproof dish that has been placed in hot water. Stir as little as possible. Allow one and one-half times as long as normal to heat a frozen casserole at the usual temperature. Put frozen meat pies into a 350°–375° oven until brown.

Thaw croquettes or ♦ any breaded food that is to be sautéed or deep fried ♦ uncovered and refrigerated, so that moisture does not form. If the food is already fried, thaw ♦ uncovered and refrigerated, and bake in a 400° oven.

Perhaps the most important thing to consider in precooking frozen foods is not to overcook foods that are to be reheated later. ♦ Also, watch seasonings carefully. Baffling changes take place. Onion, pepper, cloves, garlic and synthetic flavorings tend to become strong or bitter; salt tends to vanish, as do herb flavorings, even the indomitable sage; and curry acquires a musty flavor. Sauces have their own peculiar reactions. Avoid freezing all sauces based on egg. Sauces heavy in fat may develop an off-flavor and have a tendency to separate on reheating, but often recombine with stirring; while those with much milk or cheese tend to curdle. Thickened sauces may need thinning.

A number of vegetables such as squash, boiled and candied sweet potatoes, Harvard beets and creamed celery are best cooked before freezing and good to have on hand. See chart, 651, for these and other suggestions. All such vegetables may be heated in a double boiler or in a 400° oven without thawing.

Corn Pudding, (I, 316) was once a seasonal treat but is now available in frozen form at any time. Prepare the pudding as for immediate use. Put it into aluminum cartons; heat it in a moderate oven at 325° for 10 minutes. Cool over cold water. Cover, seal when thoroughly cool and freeze at once. To serve, heat in a 250° oven until thawed, then bake at 325° for about one hour until golden. If you plan keeping the corn longer than 4 months, merely scrape it, heat, chill and seal it as above. Then when ready to serve it, thaw in a 250° oven until soft, add butter, cream and salt and bake at 325° until golden.

◗ Be careful not to stir air into puréed vegetables. Cool quickly and freeze in ice-cube trays first, then place in bags and seal. If packaging in rigid containers, place a piece of plastic film directly on the purée to prevent oxidative changes.

FREEZING CANAPÉS AND SANDWICHES

Canapés and sandwiches should not be stored longer than a few weeks. Make them up quickly to keep the bread from drying out. For mass production methods, see 64. Be sure to spread all bread well and to make the fillings rather heavy in fats, so that the bread will not become saturated. Or you may prefer to prepare and freeze sandwich spreads for use later with fresh bread. As a corollary, bread for canapés can be cut into fancy shapes, frozen and then thawed slightly just before spreading.
◗ In choosing recipes for fillings, avoid mayonnaise and boiled salad dressings, hard-cooked egg whites, jellies and all crisp salad materials. Garnishes like cress, parsley, tomato and cucumber cannot be frozen, so add these the last moment before serving. Ground meats, poultry, fish, butter, cream and cheddar-type cheese, sieved egg yolk, peanut butter, nut meats, dried fruits and olives are all suitable for freezing.

You may freeze canapés on trays first or wrap them carefully and then freeze them. In either case, keep the different kinds separated from one another and away from the interior walls of the freezer, as this contact makes the bread soggy. Canapés and sandwiches should always be thawed in the wrappings. They take from 1 to 2 hours to thaw on a refrigerator shelf and from 15 to 45 minutes at room temperature—depending on size.

FREEZING SOUPS

To freeze soups, prepare them as for immediate use. Chill them rapidly over ice water. Store in any containers suitable for liquids, 644, allowing head space of $1/2$ inch in pint and 1 inch in quart containers. Concentrated meat or fish stock, the stock simmered until reduced to one-half or one-third its original quantity, see Meat Stock Making, 168, is the most space-saving soup to store. You may freeze them, if you like, in ice-cube trays for additions to gravy and sauces, then put frozen cubes in plastic bags and seal. Another way to freeze liquids is to use a sealed plastic bag inserted in a coffee can with a plastic lid. When the liquid is frozen solid, remove the can. If a soup or chowder calls for potato, it is preferable to add freshly cooked potato just before serving. If you do freeze the potato, undercook it. Fish and meat stock thawed and combined in a ⅄ blender with fresh vegetables make delicate soups in short order. To serve frozen soups, bring them to a boil in a saucepan, unless they are thick or have a cream base, in which case a double boiler is necessary. For cold soups, thaw until liquid and serve while still chilled.

FREEZING SALAD INGREDIENTS

The materials that the word salad brings to mind—fresh crisp greens, tomatoes, cucumbers and aspics—are impossible to freeze, but some of the foods traditionally served with them freeze well and will shorten salad preparation time. For instance, frozen precooked meats, poultry and fish—whole, diced or sliced and covered with concentrated stocks—are welcome ingredients for a salad when thawed and drained. Precooked green beans, evenly sized and unsliced, may be packaged, frozen, and later coated with French dressing. And almost any fruit mixture, excluding pears, may be frozen for use in fruit salads later. If using bananas, freeze slices separately.

FREEZING UNBAKED PASTRY, COOKIES AND DOUGHS

Doughs, batters and unbaked pastry on the whole respond less favorably to freezing than do the finished product. ◗ We do not recommend the freezing of cake doughs and batters. For one thing, the spices and condiments used in their preparation have a disconcerting tendency to "zero out" during the freezing process. For another, all leavens are highly variable under frozen storage, particularly those incorporated into the moister kinds of dough.

Unbaked yeast bread dough is most acceptable when frozen and stored for only a week or ten days. It is made up in the usual way, see 297, kneaded and allowed to rise once until doubled in bulk, then kneaded again and shaped before packaging into loaves not more than 2 inches thick. Thin loaves, of course, will thaw with much greater rapidity than thick ones. Frozen bread dough is a notable exception to the rule that frozen foods are best when slowly thawed. Place the dough in a 250° oven for 45 minutes, then bake it as usual, cool and serve. "Serve soon" would be a timelier suggestion, because thawed and baked bread dough dries out very rapidly. Partially baked breads in the brown-and-serve category may be put in the oven without thawing.

Unbaked dough for yeast rolls should not be held frozen for more than one week. Follow the procedure for frozen dough, above. Grease all roll surfaces; freeze them 2 to 4 hours on trays set away from the interior walls of the freezer, and package within 24 hours after freezing. Or, you may wrap the rolls before freezing, separating them with sheets of moisture-vaporproof material. To serve, remove the rolls from the package, cover with a cloth, put them in a warm place to rise until doubled in bulk—2 to 4 hours—and bake as usual.

Unbaked biscuits may also be frozen on trays or packaged before freezing. They, too, rise well and thaw quickly if rolled thin. Thaw them, wrapped, at room temperature for 1 hour and bake as usual. Pastries heavy in fat, like pies, tarts, filled rings and rich cookies, whether frozen baked or unbaked, come through zero storage rather well; but whenever possible, it is good practice to store all the cookies in the same containers in which they will ultimately be baked. If you want to cut cookies before freezing, put them on trays until hard, see tray freezing, 647. Then package for freezing. But if you want to cut them after freezing, make a roll of the dough and wrap it in moisture-vaporproof material in batch sizes and seal. These uncooked cookie doughs keep about 2 months. Bake cookies in a 350°–375° oven 10 to 12 minutes.

FREEZING BAKED PASTRY, CAKES, COOKIES AND DOUGHS

Doughs previously baked are quicker and easier to freeze than the corresponding raw materials and, generally speaking, yield more satisfactory results. Careful packaging for either category is essential. ♦ Always plan to unfreeze just the amount of baked articles needed, for they dry out rapidly after thawing.

Precooked pastries heavy in fats are the most successful "freezers" of all. Their storage limit is about 3 months. Baked yeast bread and rolls have the longest storage potential—6 months or more—but they do begin to lose flavor after eight weeks. Bake all of these varieties in the usual way and, before packaging, let them cool for 3 hours. If bread is to be used for toast, it is not necessary to thaw it. Otherwise thaw it wrapped, at room temperature, for 2 to 3 hours before serving. Freshen it in a 300° oven for 20 minutes. Should you freeze "boughten" bread, leave it in its original wrapper and slip it into a plastic bag or wrap it in foil as well.

♦ Baked cakes will keep 3 to 4 months unfrosted, but only 2 months if frosted. Filled cakes tend to sogginess, and any filling with an egg base is to be avoided. Actually, it is a better policy to wait and add fillings just before serving. Spice cake should not be stored over 6 weeks, as the flavors change in the freezing process. Use a minimum of spices and omit cloves. If frosted cakes are frozen, use icings with a confectioners' sugar and butter base. Brown sugar icings and those containing egg whites or syrups tend to crystallize and freeze poorly. Boiled frosting becomes sticky on thawing. Do not wrap any iced cakes until the icing has been well firmed by chilling, unwrapped, in the freezer. Place waxed paper over iced portions before putting on the outer wrap and sealing. Protect cakes with an extra carton to avoid crushing. Thaw them, unwrapped, in a covered cake dish at room temperature for 2 hours before serving.

♦ When cookies are baked before freezing, they will keep about 3 months. Bake as usual, cool and package closely, separating each cookie with moisture-vaporproof material. To avoid breakage, store in an extra carton after wrapping. Let the cookies thaw, wrapped, in the refrigerator. ♦ Freshen them with a quick run in a 350° oven.

FREEZING UNBAKED PIES

Use foil pans, or pans you can spare, so your pies can be frozen and baked in the same container. You will get better results with frozen pie crust if it has ♦ a high shortening content. Pie crust may be frozen ready for rolling or be rolled and cut ready to be put in the pan, but ♦ unrolled dough must be handled while it is still chilled so it will remain tender. Freeze unfilled shells in the pan, then remove and stack them in a box before wrapping, or store them wrapped in disposable foil pans. Bake, without thawing, at 425° 12 to 15 minutes. In making complete pies for freezing, brush the inside of the bottom crust with shortening to keep it from becoming soggy. After filling, wipe the top crust also with shortening but do not prick until ready to bake. ♦ Never use water, egg or milk for these glazes.

The best pie fillings for freezing are fresh fruits or mincemeat, and their storage limit is 4 to 6 months. Use pumpkin pie within 6 weeks for best flavor. Fruits like peaches and apricots, which darken on exposure to air, should be treated with ascorbic acid, 647, or scalded in syrup, 619, 2 minutes. Cool before using. The fillings for unbaked pies should have about 1½ times more cornstarch or tapioca than usual, or, if possible, use waxy starches, 214. ♦ Never freeze a cream or custard pie.

Allow at least 1 pint of filling for an 8-inch pie. ♦ Freeze the pie before wrapping if the filling is a wobbly one. Then package closely. Seal and protect against weight of other objects in the freezer until frozen hard.

To bake, remove wrappings, cut vent holes in upper crust and place uncooked pies unthawed on the lowest shelf of a 450° preheated oven 15 to 20 minutes. Reduce heat to 375° until done, about 1 hour in all.

FREEZING BAKED PIES

Please read Freezing Unbaked Pies, above. Use foil pans or containers you are willing to spare, so the ♦ pie can be cooked, stored and reheated in the same pan. Cool after baking, then wrap in sheet wrapping, 644, and seal.

♦ Unfilled baked pie shells are one of the most convenient of all frozen items for filling quickly before serving with creamed foods or fruit fillings. Freeze them unwrapped in the pan, then remove and stack them in a box before wrapping or store them wrapped in disposable foil pans. If you are freezing any precooked fillings with starch, be sure to ♦ cook them very thoroughly and, if possible, use waxy starches, 214.

Thaw a baked pie at room temperature for 2 to 3 hours if it is to be served cold. If it is to be served hot, place it unthawed in a 400° preheated oven 30 to 40 minutes, depending on size.

♦ Never freeze a cream or custard pie, and do not freeze pie meringue. Chiffon pies can be frozen in a baked shell if, before freezing, the filling has at least ¹/₂ cup of whipping cream incorporated into it. ♦ Defrost unwrapped and refrigerated. Garnish with whipped cream before serving, if preferred.

FREEZING DESSERTS

The same principles apply to desserts made in zero storage cabinets as to those which are still-frozen in refrigerators. Whipped cream, whipped egg white or a gelatin base is necessary to prevent the formation of undesirable graininess or crystals. If these stabilizing ingredients are not used, the dessert mixture must be beaten several times during the freezing to break up these crystals. ♦ Such desserts should be used shortly after being frozen and not stored for any length of time.

Churned ice cream is best for freezing when the recipes call for beating the cream. A final beating and refreezing may be necessary if these creams have been stored longer than 3 weeks. For safety, do not store in the freezer longer than 3 months. Remove all frozen desserts from storage 10 to 15 minutes before serving.

Fruit and steamed puddings may be baked, cooled and then frozen. They may be kept in the freezer as long as one year. Thaw at room temperature, or unwrap and place pudding, unthawed, in a steamer or double boiler. Heat to serving temperature.

FREEZING DRIED FRUITS, NUTS AND JELLIES

Dried fruits and nut meats can be successfully frozen whole, chopped or ground for 6 to 7 months. Wrap them in convenient quantities, taking the usual precautions to exclude air from the packages. Jellies and jams, especially raspberry and strawberry, retain for many months the fresh taste and clear color they attain just after preserving.

JELLIES AND PRESERVES

Have you ever tried to raise money for your church or club at a food stand? It's the homemade breads and old-fashioned cooked-down jellies that get snapped up first, for neither of these is likely to be duplicated commercially.

With jams, jellies and preserves, ▶ flavor is largely a matter of keeping sugar content to a minimum. For this reason we do not give recipes thickened with commercial pectin, as their sugar requirement is very high. Store-bought jellies, according to law, must have at least 45% fruit and 55% sugar. The juice is ordinarily extracted by pressure-cooking; and although as much as one-fourth more juice can be secured in this way than by other methods, the natural pectins in the fruit are destroyed by the high heat involved and must be replaced. ▶ These added pectins, in turn, demand a higher percentage of sugar to fruit to make the juices jell. In fact, pectin manufacturers not uncommonly suggest for the homemade product a proportion as high as 60% sugar to 40%

juice or pulp. And they point out as advantages with the use of commercial pectin greater yield, less loss of liquid, and speed of preparation. Only a minute or two of cooking is needed after adding the sugar.

We regard none of these as advantages, or as in any sense comparable with the end product obtained by the open-kettle, cooked-down procedures we advocate, under which fruits low in natural pectins are combined with those having high pectin content, like apples; fruit exceeds sugar, rather than the reverse; and—most important—we wind up with greatly superior flavor.

It has been demonstrated that ▶ cane and beet sugars produce equally good results. But if honey is substituted, there is a distinct and delicious change in flavor. In cooked-down jellies and preserves, honey may replace up to one-half the sugar, but jams and jellies made with honey require longer cooking. If you plan to put up jellies with artificial sweeteners, we suggest you ask your doctor first his opinion of the chemical you propose using; then follow the processor's directions to the letter. You will find the texture of jellies and jams made with such synthetics quite different from—and less interesting than—that of those prepared with sugar or honey.

Jellies, jams, fruit butters, conserves, preserves—just what are the differences among them?

Jelly has great clarity. Two cooking processes are involved. First, the juice alone is extracted from the fruit. Only that portion thin and clear enough to drip through a cloth is cooked with sugar until ◗ sufficiently firm to hold its shape. It is never stiff and never gummy. ◗ **Jams, butters** and **pastes** are purées of progressively increasing density. ◗ **Preserves, marmalades** and **conserves** are bits of fruit cooked to a translucent state in a heavy syrup. These and the jams, all of which need only one cooking, take patience and ◗ careful stirring, so that they reduce without any taint of scorching. For some thicker types, an oven-cooking technique is suggested in the recipes.

Let us come back to the importance of pectins in all jelly and jam making. ◗ With high-pectin fruits such as apples, crab apples, quinces, red currants, gooseberries, plums and cranberries, you need have no worries about jelling. If you should get a syrupy jelly with any of these fruits, either you have used too much sugar or you did not cook the juice long enough after the sugar was added.

Low-pectin fruits—strawberries, blueberries, peaches, apricots, cherries, figs, pears, raspberries, blackberries, grapes and pineapples—or plants such as rhubarb have to be combined either with one of the high-pectin fruits above—or, of course, with commercial pectins.

◗ To determine if fruit juice contains a sufficient amount of pectin to jell, put 1 tablespoon of the cooled fruit juice in a glass. Add the same quantity of grain alcohol and shake gently. The effect of the alcohol is to bring the pectin together in a transparent glob. If a large quantity is present, it will appear in a single mass when poured from the glass. This indicates that equal quantities of sugar and juice should be used. If the pectin does not form a mass, less sugar will be required. If it collects in 2 or 3 masses, use two-thirds to three-fourths as much sugar as juice; if in smaller, even more numerous particles, one-half as much sugar as juice, unless the fruit is very tart.

◗ Get your equipment ready before you begin to cook the jelly or jam. Use a heavy enamel or stainless steel pan with a flat bottom. If you are making jelly, have a bag ready for straining the juice, see Making Juice for Jelly, opposite, and the chapter-heading illustration, 661. ◗ Have ready, too, sterilized jelly glasses. To prepare them, fill glasses or jars three-fourths full of water and place them well apart in a shallow pan partly filled with water. Simmer the water 15 or 20 minutes. Keep the glasses hot until ready to fill. If the lids are placed lightly upon the glasses, they will be sterilized at the same time.

In making jellies and jams, best flavor results if you work with small quantities. ◗ Prepare not more than 6 cups of fruit or juice at a time, preferably only about 4 cups. ◗ If the fruit is one that discolors easily, see Anti-Browning Solutions, 647. Again, to retain flavor, unless fruit is very acid, when sugar can be used cup for cup with fruit ◗ we recommend 3/4 cup sugar to 1 cup fruit or juice. ❊ Jellies and jams may be frozen to advantage, but do not keep them in the refrigerator, as they may "weep." ♦ Store in a cool, dark, dry place. ♦ Discard if they develop mold.

MAKING JUICE FOR JELLY

"Picture-book" jelly takes time. ♦ To prepare juice for jelly by the open-kettle method, wash the fruit well and drain. To accent flavor ♦ add water only if you must. Prick or crush the fruit that forms the bottom layer in the preserving kettle. Less juicy fruits, such as apples and pears, require relatively large amounts of water. Add it to the kettle until you can see it through the top layer of fruit, but ♦ never use enough to float the fruit. Cook over low heat until more moisture is drawn from the fruit and then increase the heat to moderate, continuing to cook ♦ uncovered until the fruit is soft and has begun to lose its color. ♦ Have ready a jelly bag. This should be made of a porous material like unbleached muslin. If well enough sewn, the bag may eventually be suspended; if not, it can be held in a strainer. Wet the bag and wring it out before you pour the jelly into it, as a dry bag can absorb a lot of the precious juice. If you want a sparkling clear and well-flavored jelly ♦ do not squeeze the bag. After using it, rinse the bag in boiling water for subsequent use. See sketch on 661.

If not utilized at once ♦ fruit juice will keep about 6 months and can be made into jelly at your convenience. ❈ You may freeze it, 649, or you may reheat the strained juice, pour it boiling hot into sterilized jars, 614, cover with screw tops and cook in a hot-water bath, 617, at 185° at least 20 minutes. ♦ Seal the jars completely and keep them ♦ stored in a cool dark place.

MAKING JELLY

Measure the strained fruit juice and put it into ♦ a large enamel or stainless steel pan. Simmer the juice, uncovered, about 5 minutes. ♦ Skim off any froth that forms. Measure and add the sugar ♦ stirring until it is dissolved. Because of the addition of the sugar, the boiling point of the mixture will have been raised and the jelly will seem to be boiling at this heat. It should reach 8°F. higher than the boiling point of water in your locality and at this temperature will form a satisfactory jell. For use of a thermometer, see 575.

If you have no jelly thermometer, cook the mix just long enough to bring it to the point of jelling. ♦ Begin to test the juice 10 minutes after the sugar has been added. It is wise to use a timer, illustrated on 661. Place a small amount of jelly in a spoon, cool it slightly and let it drop back into the pan from the side of the spoon.

At first, the drip is light and syrupy. As the syrup thickens, 2 large drops begin to form along the edge of the spoon. ♦ When they come together and fall as a single drop, as shown at the right in 664, the "sheeting stage," 220° to 222°, has been reached. The jelly is then ready to be taken from the heat. The required time for cooking will range from 8 to 30 minutes, depending on the kind of fruit, the amount of sugar and the amount of juice in each pan.

While the juice is cooking, take the jars from the hot water, empty them and reverse them onto a cake cooler. Skim off the foam quickly and pour the jelly into the jars when they are ♦ still hot, but dry. Fill to within 1/2 inch of the top. Cover the jars with 1/8 inch of hot paraffin. If the paraffin becomes very hot, it is apt to pull away from the sides of the jelly glass; so melt the paraffin over hot water in a small metal pitcher as shown in the chapter heading, 661, which can subsequently be covered and stored for the next session. Allow glasses to stand until the paraffin hardens, then cover and store.

If using the jars with a two-piece metal screwdown lid, shown on 613, there is no need to use paraffin. Fill the jars with boiling-hot jelly to within 1/8 inch of the top. Put the rubber on, making sure the top and threads of the jar are clean. Screw the metal band on firmly, then invert the jars for a few seconds to seal completely. Cool the jars in an upright position and store in a cool, dark, dry place.

CURRANT JELLY

▶ Please read about Making Jelly, 663.
Wash:

Red, white or black currants

Drain and place in a stainless steel kettle. It is not necessary to stem currants, and they may be cooked with or without water. If water is used, allow about one-fourth as much water as fruit. Otherwise, crush the bottom layer of currants and pile the rest on top of them. Cook the fruit first over low heat about 5 minutes, then over moderate heat until soft and colorless. Strain through a jelly bag, above. Allow to each cup of juice:

3/4 to 1 cup sugar

Cook only 4 cups of juice at a time.

CURRANT AND RASPBERRY JELLY

▶ Please read about Making Jelly, 663.
Prepare currants as for Currant Jelly, at left.
Crush:

Raspberries

Add from 1 to 1 1/3 cups raspberries for every cup of currants. Cook the fruit until the currants are soft and colorless. Strain the fruit through a jelly bag, 663. Allow to each cup of juice:

3/4 to 1 cup sugar

Cook only 4 cups of juice at a time.

BLACK RASPBERRY AND GOOSEBERRY JELLY

▶ Please read about Making Jelly, 663.
Wash and drain fruit. Place in a saucepan and stew until soft:

4 quarts black raspberries
1/4 cup water

Place in a separate saucepan and stew until soft:

2 quarts gooseberries or about 2 cups sliced green apples with peel and core
1/2 cup water

Combine the fruits and strain through a jelly bag, 663. Allow to each cup of juice:

3/4 to 1 cup sugar

Cook only 4 cups of juice at a time.

APPLE, CRAB APPLE OR QUINCE JELLY

Good in itself, especially if made with tart fruit. Apples, crab apples or quinces, as we have indicated, are also extremely useful in combination with fruits whose pectin content is low, such as blueberries, blackberries, elderberries, raspberries and grapes, whether fresh or frozen. In apples, the greatest amount of pectin lies close to the skin. Apple peelings and cores can be cooked up and strained through a jelly bag for addition to low-pectin juices.

◗ Please read about Making Jelly, 663. Wipe, quarter and remove stems and blossom ends from:

Tart apples, crab apples or quinces

Place in a saucepan. Add water until it can be seen through the top layer of fruit. Cook ◗ uncovered until fruit is soft. Put the juice through a jelly bag, 663. Allow to each cup of juice:

3/4 to 1 cup sugar

Cook only 4 cups at a time.

HERB AND SCENTED JELLIES

◗ Please read about Making Jelly, 663. Prepare:

Apple or Crab Apple Jelly, above

After testing for jelling and before removing the jelly from heat, bruise the leaves and bind together a bunch of one of the following ◗ fresh, unsprayed herbs:

Mint, basil, tarragon, thyme, lemon verbena or rose geranium

Hold the stem ends and pass the leaves through the jelly repeatedly until the desired strength of flavoring is reached. Add a small amount of:

(Vegetable coloring)

PARADISE JELLY

◗ Please read about Making Jelly, 663. Wash and cut into quarters:

3 quarts apples

Peel and cut into quarters:

3 pints quinces

Remove seeds. Place the apples in a pan with:

1 quart cranberries

Barely cover with water. Boil until soft. Follow the same procedure with the quinces. Strain the juices of all the fruits through a jelly bag, 663. Allow to each cup of juice:

1 cup sugar

Cook only 4 cups at a time.

GRAPE JELLY

◗ Please read about Making Jelly, 663. Wash:

Slightly underripe Concord or wild grapes

which are preferable to ripe or overripe grapes because of their tart flavor and higher pectin content. Remove stems. Place crushed fruit in a kettle with a small quantity of water—about 1/2 cup of water to 4 cups of grapes. Add:

1 quartered apple

If you wish to spice the jelly, add at this time:

(1/3 cup vinegar)
(1-inch stick cinnamon)
(1/2 teaspoon whole cloves without heads)

Boil grapes until soft and beginning to lose color. Strain through a jelly bag, 663. Allow to each cup of juice:

3/4 to 1 cup sugar

Cook only 4 cups at a time.

WATERLESS GRAPE OR BERRY JELLY

◗ Please read about Making Jelly, 663. Try this recipe when slightly underripe fruits are available. It is superlative when it works, but everything depends on the condition of the fruit. Wash:

Concord or other slip-skin grapes, or berries

Mash them in a large pot. Cook until soft. Strain the juice. Measure it. Bring juice to a rolling boil. Remove from heat. Add 1½ times more:

Sugar

than you have juice. Stir it over heat until dissolved. Pour the jelly into sterilized glasses and seal. ◗ Should the liquid not jell, nothing but time is lost. Allow 1 apple and ¼ cup water to every 4 cups original fruit used. Cook the apple and water until the apple is soft. Strain off the juice, add it to the unjelled jelly, and recook as for any other jelly.

SEA GRAPE JELLY

◗ Please read about Making Jelly, 663. Wash well:

Sea grapes

Cover with 1½ times as much water as fruit, and cook until the skin and pulp slip from the seeds when pressed. Put the juice through a jelly bag, 663, but do not press. Set this juice aside. Combine the seeds and pulp with an equal amount of water and cook about 15 minutes longer. Drain and combine the juices. Allow to each cup of juice:

1 cup sugar

Cook only 4 cups at a time.

GUAVA JELLY

◗ Please read about Making Jelly, 663. Wash and cut into quarters:

Slightly underripe guavas

Cover with water and boil, then ◗ simmer about ½ hour. Put the juice through a jelly bag, 663, but do not press, as the juice will become bitter. Allow to each cup of juice:

1 cup sugar

Bring again to a boil and add for each cup of juice:

1 teaspoon lime juice

Cook only 4 cups at a time.

PLUM JELLY

Goose plums make delicious jelly or jam.
◗ Please read about Making Jelly, 663. Wash:

Small red plums

Place in a saucepan. Add water until it can be seen through the top layer. Boil plums until soft. Put the pulp through a jelly bag, 663. Allow to each cup of juice:

¾ to 1 cup sugar

Boil only 4 cups at a time.

MAKING JAM

Jam is the easiest type to make—and the most economical—as it needs only one cooking step and utilizes the fruit pulp. Measure the fruit, put it into the pan, crushing the lower layers to provide moisture until more is drawn from the fruit by heat; or, if necessary, add about ½ cup of water. ◗ Simmer the fruit uncovered, until soft, before adding the sugar. ◗ Stir until the sugar is dissolved. ◗ Bring the fruit mixture to a boil and continue to stir, making sure no sticking occurs. ◗ Reduce the heat and cook, uncovered, until the mixture thickens, allowing for additional thickening as it cools. If using a thermometer, shown in the chapter heading, 661, cook to a temperature 9°F. higher than the temperature of boiling water in your locality. To keep the heat diffused, you may even want to use an asbestos pad. Sometimes it takes as long as half an hour for jam to thicken.

RED RED STRAWBERRY JAM

Please read about Making Jam, opposite. Wash, dry well and stem:

> 1 quart ▶ perfect
> strawberries

Put them into a ▶ very deep 10-inch cooking pot, cutting into a few of the berries to release a little juice. Cover with:

> 4 cups sugar

Stir the mixture ▶ very gently with a wooden spoon ▶ over low heat until it has "juiced up." Then raise the heat to moderate and stop stirring. When the whole is a bubbling mass, set your timer for exactly 15 minutes—17 if the berries are very ripe. From this point do not disturb. You may take a wooden spoon and streak it slowly through the bottom to make sure there is no sticking. When the timer rings, tilt the pot. You should see in the liquid at the bottom a tendency to set. Slide the pot off the heat. Allow berries to cool ▶ uncovered. Sprinkle surface with:

> (Juice of ½ lemon)

When cool, stir the berries lightly and place in sterile jars.

BLUEBERRY JAM

If blueberries are picked early in the day and are only half ripe, at the red instead of blue stage, the result is a jam far more flavorful than usual—almost like the one made with Scandinavian lingonberries.

▶ Please read about Making Jam, opposite.

Pick over, wash and measure:

> Blueberries

Put them in a heavy stainless steel pan. Crush the bottom layer. You may add:

> (½ cup water)

Cook over moderate heat, ▶ simmer-

ing until almost tender. Add, for each cup of blueberries:

> ¾ to 1 cup heated sugar

Stir and cook over low heat until a small amount dropped on a plate will stay in place. Place in hot sterilized jars.

SPICED PEAR JAM WITH PINEAPPLE

> **About 2 Quarts**

▶ Please read about Making Jam, opposite.

As it is hard to gauge the acidity of the pear used, taste the jam as it cooks. Add sugar or lemon juice as needed. Peel and core:

> 3 lb. firm Bartlett, Kiefer or
> Seckel pears

Wash well and remove seeds from:

> 1 orange
> 1 lemon

Put the fruit through a grinder, using a coarse blade. Save the juices. Add them to the pulp with:

> 1 cup crushed pineapple
> 4 to 5 cups sugar

Tie in cheesecloth and add:

> 3 or 4 whole cloves
> 6 inches stick cinnamon
> A 1-inch piece ginger

Stir the mixture while heating it. Simmer about 30 minutes. Remove spice bag. Pour jam into sterilized hot glasses.

RASPBERRY, BLACKBERRY, GOOSEBERRY, LOGANBERRY OR ELDERBERRY JAM

▶ Please read about Making Jam, opposite.

Crushing a few berries, combine:

> 4 cups raspberries,
> blackberries, gooseberries,
> elderberries or
> loganberries

with:

3 cups sugar

If the berries are tart, use a scant cup of sugar to 1 cup of fruit. These are not high-pectin fruits, so it is wise to add:

1 to 2 apples, cored and cut into small pieces

Stir and cook over low heat until the sugar is dissolved. ◗ Simmer and stir frequently from the bottom to keep jam from sticking. Cook until a small amount dropped on a plate will stay in place. Pack while hot in hot sterilized jars.

FIVE-FRUITS JAM COCKAIGNE

On the whole, we like food to retain its own native flavor. Our sympathy goes out to the cowboy movie actor who is reported to have said, after his first formal dinner: "I et for two hours and I didn't recognize anything I et, except an olive." However, this composite jam is both mysterious and delicious.

◗ Please read about Making Jam, 666.

Hull and place in kettle, in layers:

Strawberries

pound for pound with:

Sugar

End with a layer of sugar on top. Allow this mixture to stand, covered, 12 hours. , Now bring strawberries quickly to the boiling point and ◗ simmer with as little stirring as possible until the juice thickens, about 15 minutes. As strawberries usually appear a little in advance of the other fruits, these preserves may be placed in sterilized and sealed fruit jars and set aside until the other 4 fruits are available. Stem and seed:

Cherries

Stem:

Currants

Pick over:

Raspberries

Stem and head:

Gooseberries

The first 4 fruits are best used in equal proportions, but gooseberries have so much character that it is well to use a somewhat smaller amount, or their flavor will predominate. Bring the fruits separately or together to the boiling point. Add to each cup of fruit and juice:

¾ cup sugar

◗ Simmer the jam until thick, about 30 minutes. Combine with the strawberry preserves which have been reheated to the boiling point.

QUICK APRICOT PINEAPPLE JAM

Prepare Sauce Cockaigne, 564.
Keep under refrigeration.

ROSE-HIP JAM

Wait to collect the hips until after the first frost. Do not use any which have been sprayed with poisonous insecticides.

◗ Please read about Making Jam, 666.

Place in a heavy stainless steel pan and ◗ simmer until fruit is tender, allowing:

1 cup water

to:

1 lb. rose hips

Rub through a fine sieve. Weigh the pulp. Allow, to each pound of pulp:

1 lb. sugar

◗ Simmer until thick.

APPLE BUTTER

About 5 Pints

For best results use Jonathan, Winesap, Wealthy or other well-flavored cooking varieties.

Wash, remove the stems and quarter:

4 lb. apples

Cook slowly until soft in:

2 cups water, cider or cider vinegar

Put fruit through a fine strainer. Add to each cup of pulp:

1/2 cup white or brown sugar

Add to the strained fruit:

1 teaspoon cinnamon
1/2 teaspoon cloves
1/4 teaspoon allspice
(Grated lemon rind and juice)

Cook the fruit butter over low heat, stirring constantly until the sugar is dissolved. Continue to cook, stirring frequently, until the mixture sheets from a spoon. You can also place a small quantity on a plate. When no rim of liquid separates around the edge of the butter, it is done. Pour into hot sterilized jars.

BAKED APPLE BUTTER

About 5 Quarts

A more convenient method than the above, as stirring is not necessary. Wash and remove cores from:

12 lb. apples: Jonathan, Winesap or McIntosh

Cut them into quarters. Nearly cover with water. Cook gently about 1 1/2 hours. Put the pulp through a fine strainer. Measure it. Allow to each cup of pulp:

1/2 cup sugar

Add to the strained fruit:

Grated rind and juice of 2 lemons
3 teaspoons cinnamon
1 1/2 teaspoons cloves
1/2 teaspoon allspice

Bring these ingredients to the boiling point. Chill. Stir into them:

1 cup port, claret or dry white wine

Place about three-fourths of the purée in a large heat-proof crock. Keep the rest in reserve. Put the crock in a cold oven. Set oven at 300°. Let the apple butter bake until it thickens. As the purée shrinks, fill the crock with reserved apple butter. When the butter is thick, but still moist, put into sterile jars.

PEACH OR APRICOT BUTTER

About 5 Pints

Wash, peel, pit and crush:

4 lb. peaches or apricots

Cook very slowly in their own juice until soft. Stir. Put the fruit through a fine strainer. Add to each cup of pulp:

1/2 to 2/3 cup sugar

Add to the strained fruit:

2 teaspoons cinnamon
1 teaspoon cloves
1/2 teaspoon allspice
(Juice and grated rind of 1 lemon)

Cook as for Apple Butter, above.

DAMSON PLUM BUTTER

Wash and quarter:

Damson plums

Put them in a heat-proof crock, in a pan of boiling water, over direct heat. Cover the whole container and cook until the fruit is soft enough to purée. You may use a food mill shown on 661. To each cup purée allow:

1 cup sugar

Place in a heavy pan and ♦ stir over low heat at least 45 minutes or until the fruit butter is quite stiff. Place in hot sterilized jars.

MAKING PRESERVES AND CONSERVES

These, like jams, need only one cooking and can be made by several methods. The fruit may be placed in a crock or stainless steel pan in layers with equal parts of sugar, ending with the sugar layer on top, and allowed to rest covered 24 hours. The mix is then brought slowly to a boil in a pan and ♦ simmered, uncovered, until the fruit is clear. Alternatively, the fruit may be placed in a very small quantity of water in a heavy stainless or enamel pan with sugar, allowing $1/2$ to $3/4$ cup of sugar per cup of fruit, depending on the sweetness of the fruit. The sugar and fruit are then brought slowly to a boil and ♦ simmered until the fruit is translucent. If using a thermometer, bring syrup to 9°F. higher than the temperature of boiling water in your locality. In either case, should the syrup not be thick enough, the fruit may be drained, put into sterile jars and kept hot while the syrup is simmered, uncovered, to the desired thickness. It is then poured over the fruit. Seal the preserves and store in a dark cool place.

SUNSHINE STRAWBERRY PRESERVES

Like the recipe for Waterless Grape Jelly, 665, this method is risky, but well worth taking the chance if it jells.
Arrange in a large kettle:

2 layers of washed, hulled, perfect strawberries

Sprinkle the layers with an equal amount of:

Sugar

Permit to stand for $1/2$ hour. Heat over low heat until boiling, then ♦ simmer for 15 minutes. Pour the berries onto platters. Cover loosely with a glass or plastic dome, out of the reach of insects. Let the berries stand in the sun 2 or 3 days, until the juice forms a jelly. Turn the berries very gently twice daily. These preserves need not be reheated. Place in hot sterilized glasses and seal.

STRAWBERRY AND PINEAPPLE PRESERVES

♦ Please read about Making Preserves, at left.
Combine:

1 quart hulled berries
4 cups sugar
1 cup canned pineapple
Rind and juice of $1/2$ lemon

♦ Simmer these ingredients about 20 minutes. Stir frequently. When thickened, place in sterile jars.

STRAWBERRY AND RHUBARB PRESERVES

♦ Please read about Making Preserves, at left.
Cut into small pieces:

1 quart rhubarb

Sprinkle over it:

8 cups sugar

Let these ingredients stand 12 hours. Bring quickly to the boiling point. Wash and hull:

2 quarts strawberries

Add to the rhubarb. ♦ Simmer the preserves until thick, about 15 minutes.

CHERRY PRESERVES

♦ Please read about Making Preserves, at left. Wash, stem, seed and place in pot, in layers:

Cherries

pound for pound with:

Sugar

If cherries are very sweet, ³/₄ pound sugar will suffice. End with a layer of sugar on top. Let the cherries stand covered 8 to 10 hours. Then bring this mixture slowly to a boil, stirring frequently. ◗ Simmer until tender—about 20 minutes. If the juice seems too thin, skim off the cherries and place them in sterile jars. Simmer juice until it thickens, then pour over cherries.

PEACH OR APRICOT PRESERVES

◗ Please read about Making Preserves, opposite. Use firm, slightly underripe, well-flavored fruit. Peel and cut into lengthwise slices:

Peaches or apricots

The fruit may be dipped briefly into boiling water to facilitate the removal of skins. Remove the stones. Measure the fruit. Allow to each cup:

  ³/₄ cup sugar
  2 tablespoons water
  1¹/₂ teaspoons lemon juice

Stir this syrup and cook it 5 minutes. Add the fruit. You may omit the water and just pour the sugar over the peaches, letting them stand 2 hours before continuing. ◗ Simmer fruit until transparent. Place in glasses or jars. If the syrup seems too abundant, place the fruit in jars and reduce the syrup until thick. Pour over fruit. Add to the syrup:

  (Lemon juice—about 2 teaspoons to every cup of fruit)

DAMSON, ITALIAN PLUM OR GREENGAGE PRESERVES

◗ Please read about Making Preserves, opposite.
Wash, cut into halves and remove the seeds from:

  Damsons, Italian plums or greengages

Stir into the plums an equal amount of:

  Sugar

The sugar may be moistened with a very little water, or the fruit and sugar may be permitted to stand 12 hours before cooking. Bring the preserves to a boil, then ◗ simmer until the syrup is heavy. Add:

  (2 minced seeded unpeeled oranges)
  (¹/₂ lb. chopped walnuts)

QUINCE PRESERVES

◗ Please read about Making Preserves, opposite.
Scrub:

  Quinces

Slice them into eighths. Core and seed. Pare, reserving fruit, and put the peelings in a pan with just enough water to cover. To each quart of liquid, add:

  1 sliced seeded lemon
  1 sliced seeded orange

◗ Simmer this mixture until the peelings are soft. Strain, reserving only the liquid. Now weigh and add the quince slices. Weigh same quantity:

  Sugar

Bring quince slices to a boil and add the sugar. Bring to a boil again. Then ◗ simmer until the fruit is tender. Place drained fruit in sterile jars. Continue to reduce the syrup until thick. Cover the fruit with the reduced syrup and seal.

HARVEST PRESERVES

◗ Please read about Making Preserves, opposite.
Pare, core, seed and quarter equal parts of:

  Tart apples

Pears
Plums

Prepare as for Quince Preserves, 671.

TOMATO PRESERVES

◗ Please read about Making Preserves, 670.

Scald and skin:

1 lb. tomatoes

Yellow tomatoes may be used with especially fine results. Cover tomatoes with:

An equal amount of sugar

Let stand 12 hours. Drain the juice. Boil it until the syrup falls from a spoon in heavy drops. Add the tomatoes and:

Grated rind and juice of 1 lemon or 2 thinly sliced seeded lemons
2 oz. preserved ginger or 4-inch stick cinnamon

Cook the mixture until thick.

FIG PRESERVES

About 1 Quart

◗ Please read about Making Preserves, 670.

Wash and combine:

1 lb. finely cut unpeeled rhubarb
1/4 lb. chopped stemmed figs
3 tablespoons lemon juice

Cover with:

1 lb. sugar

Let stand 24 hours in a cool place. Bring to a boil in a heavy stainless steel pan and ◗ simmer until thickened.

BAR-LE-DUC OR CURRANT PRESERVES

◗ Please read about Making Preserves, 670.

For use with Bar-le-Duc, 544. If you are a classicist, pierce the bottom of each berry and force the seeds through the opening after washing the berries.

Wash and stem:

Red or white currants

For 1 quart currants, cook to the soft-ball stage, 238°:

1 1/2 cups sugar
1/2 cup honey
1 1/4 cups water

Drop the berries into the boiling syrup. Bring the syrup to the boiling stage again for 1 minute. Pour into sterilized glasses and seal.

GOOSEBERRY PRESERVES

These, being tart, complement a meat course, soft cream cheese or a sweet cake.

◗ Please read about Making Preserves, 670.

Wash.

1 quart gooseberries

Remove stems and blossom ends. Place in heavy saucepan. Add:

1/4 cup water

Place over high heat. Stir. When boiling, add:

3 to 4 cups sugar

◗ Simmer preserves until the berries are clear and the juice thick, about 15 minutes.

KUMQUAT OR CALAMONDIN PRESERVES

About 3 Pints

◗ Please read about Making Preserves, 670.

Weigh:

3 lb. kumquats or calamondins

Separate pulp from skins and reserve it. Cover skins with:

Cold water

Cook until tender. If you do not like the bitter taste, drain several times during this process and replace with fresh water. When tender, drain and slice fine or grind the skins. Meanwhile, cover the pulp with:

3 cups water

and simmer 30 minutes. Strain the pulp and add to the juice:

3 cups water

Discard the pulp. Allow to each cup juice:

³/₄ cup sugar

Heat the juice and ◗ stir in the sugar until dissolved. Add the cut-up skins and cook until syrup jells.

ORANGE MARMALADE

About 4 Jelly Glasses

◗ Please read about Making Preserves, 670.
Fully ripe oranges may still have a greenish peel, but this has nothing to do with their minimum sugar content. Scrub well, cut into quarters and remove the seeds from:

2 large Valencia oranges
2 large or 3 small lemons

Add and simmer for 5 minutes:

3 cups water

Let stand covered for 12 to 18 hours in a cool place. Remove fruit and cut into very small shreds. Return to the water in which it was soaked. Boil 1 hour. Add for each cup of fruit mixture:

1 cup sugar

Boil the marmalade until the juice forms a jelly when tested, 663.

ORANGE, LEMON AND GRAPEFRUIT MARMALADE

About 18 Jelly Glasses

◗ Please read about Making Preserves, 670.
Scrub, cut into halves, remove the seeds and slice into very small pieces:

1 grapefruit
3 oranges
3 lemons

Measure the fruit and juice and add 3 times the amount of water. Soak 12 hours. ◗ Simmer about 20 minutes. Let stand again 12 hours. For every cup of fruit and juice, add:

³/₄ cup sugar

Cook these ingredients in small quantities, about 4 to 6 cups at a time, until they form a jelly when tested, 663.

LIME MARMALADE

About 3 Jelly Glasses

◗ Please read about Making Preserves, 670.
Cut the thin outer rind from:

6 small limes
3 lemons

Prepare as for Orange, Lemon and Grapefruit Marmalade, opposite

TAMARIND MARMALADE

◗ Please read about Making Preserves, 670. Wash:

1 quart tamarinds

Cover with:

1¹/₂ cups water

◗ Simmer until soft. Put through sieve to remove fibers and seeds. Heat the pulp and allow for each cup:

1 cup sugar

◗ Simmer, stirring constantly, until the mixture thickens.

BLUE PLUM CONSERVE

About 20 Jelly Glasses

◗ Please read about Making Conserves, 670.

Peel and chop the thin colored rind of:

2 oranges
1 lemon

Add the juice and seeded, chopped pulp of:

3 oranges
1 lemon

and:

1¼ lb. ground seeded raisins
9 cups sugar

Seed and add:

5 lb. blue plums
4 pared, cubed peaches
(1 teaspoon whole cloves)

If you use the cloves, put them in a cheesecloth bag so you can remove them easily later. Cook the conserve slowly until fairly thick. Stir frequently. Add:

½ lb. chopped walnuts

▶ Simmer the conserve 10 minutes longer.

SWEET CHERRY CONSERVE

About 8 Jelly Glasses

▶ Please read about Making Conserves, 670.

Cut into very thin slices:

2 seeded oranges

Barely cover with water, about ¼ cup. Cook until very tender. Stem, seed and add:

1 quart sweet cherries

Add:

6 tablespoons lemon juice
3½ cups sugar
¾ teaspoon cinnamon
(6 cloves)

▶ Simmer the conserve until thick and clear.

SPICED RHUBARB CONSERVE

About 8 Jelly Glasses

▶ Please read about Making Conserves, 670.

Cut into very thin slices:

1 seeded orange
1 seeded lemon

Tie in a small bag:

1 oz. gingerroot
2 whole cloves

Add the spices, including:

¼ lb. cinnamon candy:
redhots
¼ teaspoon mace

to the fruit with:

½ cup water
¼ cup vinegar

▶ Simmer these ingredients until the fruit is tender. Add and cook, until the conserve is thick:

1½ cups chopped rhubarb
3 cups sugar
(¼ cup white raisins)

TUTTI-FRUTTI COCKAIGNE, BRANDIED OR CROCKED FRUIT

A sort of liquid hope-chest, the contents of which may be served with a meat course or over puddings or ice cream. Be sure that during its preparation ▶ your container is big enough to hold all the ingredients you plan putting into it and, just as important, that ▶ you can store it in a consistently cool place, not above 45°, to prevent runaway fermentation. Place in a sterile stoneware crock or glass jar with a closely fitting lid:

1 quart brandy

Add, as they come into season, five of the following varieties of fruit—perfect and well-drained fruit only:

1 quart strawberries
1 quart seeded cherries
1 quart raspberries
1 quart currants
1 quart gooseberries
1 quart peeled sliced apricots
1 quart peeled sliced peaches
1 quart peeled sliced
pineapple

Avoid apples, as too hard; bananas and pears, as too mushy; blackberries, as too seedy; and seeded grapes, unless skinned, as grape skins become tough. With each addition of fruit, add the same amount of:

Sugar

Stir the tutti-frutti every day with a wooden spoon until the last of the fruit has been added, securing the lid well each time. If you wish to prolong the life of the mixture, for every cup removed, replenish with 1 cup fruit, 1/4 cup sugar and 1/4 cup brandy.

PICKLES AND RELISHES

Peter Piper proved a pretty pampered pepper picker. Less privileged persons—such as you and we—are expected to pick produce unpickled and process it promptly ourselves. Pickling can be accomplished in several ways, some of them a bit lengthy, but none of them difficult. Granted that a considerable number of vitamins and minerals leach away into liquid residue during the pickling process, it remains a piquant and important method of food preservation.

In spite of the fact that our mothers never did it, it is now a recommended practice ♦ to subject pickles and relishes to a boiling-water bath, 617: 15 minutes for pint jars, 20 minutes for quarts.

PICKLING EQUIPMENT

Please read about care of and filling of jars, and other safety factors in Canning Processes, 614. ♦ Because of the acids involved in pickle making, be sure your equipment for brining is stoneware, pottery or glass, and that your pickling kettles are stainless steel or enamel. For stirring and for transferring the pickles, use a long-handled stainless, enamel-covered or slotted wooden spoon or a glass cup. Pack pickles in unflawed sterile glass jars with lids approved for pickling. All equipment should be absolutely clean and grease-free.

ABOUT PICKLING INGREDIENTS

For best results it is ♦ imperative that vegetables and fruit for pickling are in prime condition and are harvested no more than 24 hours in advance. If cucumbers have been held longer, they tend to become hollow during processing. If fruit or vegetables are very firm or slightly unripe ♦ be sure to cook them a little longer so brine can permeate to their centers. This will help keep fruit from floating to the tops of the jars later and will also discourage spoilage.

Black-spined varieties are the usual choice for cucumber pickles.

They may be slightly underripe. ◗ Scrub them well to remove any dirt which might spark subsequent bacterial activity, and trim to retain $1/8$ to $1/4$ inch of stem.

If using garlic as a seasoning, parblanch 2 minutes before adding it to other ingredients, or remove it from the jar before sealing. ◗ Water used should be soft, 166. If you are in a hard-water area, you may want to use distilled water. If the water contains iron or sulfur compounds, the pickles will become dark.

◗ Use only pickling or dairy salt, free from additives which might deter processing, see About Salt, 249. ◗ Vinegar should test 5% to 6% acetic acid. Distilled white vinegar gives the lightest color. Cider-based malt and herb-flavored vinegars, although they yield a richer flavor, will darken pickles. You may want to make up and have ready to use one of the spice vinegars, 179. Homemade wine vinegars of uncertain strength should not be used, as the vinegar will "mother," 178.

Since spices vary so greatly in strength, 258, the amounts given are only approximate. Taste before bottling and dilute with more vinegar if necessary. ◗ Spices should be both fresh and whole. Ground spices darken the pickle; old spices impart a dusty flavor. Tie spices in a cloth bag for easy removal. If left in, they may cloud the liquid. Distillates, like the oils of cinnamon and of clove, are available at drug stores. They give a clearer pickle than steeped condiments, but the flavor is not so lasting.

◗ To make pickles crisp, wash unsprayed grape or cherry leaves and layer them with the cucumbers during the brining process. Discard leaves when making the pickles. Lime and alum are not recommended for crisping. Just a trifle too much alum may make the pickles bitter.

SHORT-BRINE PICKLING

Pickles produced under **long-brine** procedures, 688, require controlled conditions beyond the reach of the home cook. Accordingly, our recipes for homemade pickles are all of the less exacting **short-brine** type. These pickles are soaked in a salt solution only 24 hours or so. This brining period is sufficiently long to draw out moisture, ◗ but not long enough to induce the fermentation needed for adequate keeping. For this reason, an essential further step, after draining off the brine, is to pour over the produce a hot vinegar solution which penetrates the softened vegetable tissue and so preserves it.

In the short-brine process, pack the produce closely in sterile jars, 615, as soon as the brine is drained off and just before the addition of the vinegar. Heat the vinegar solution to the boiling point and fill the jars, leaving $1/4$-inch headroom. Wipe the rims, adjust and seal the lids and process in a boiling-water bath 15 minutes, 617. By this time the interior of the jars should have reached 180°, enough to inhibit destructive enzymes. If a jar shows evidence of leakage or a poor seal, use the contents immediately, or replace the liquid with a fresh boiling pickling solution. Wipe the jars clean, refill them and reprocess 15 minutes in a boiling-water bath. The flavor of almost all pickled produce is improved if it is stored 6 weeks before using them.

Keep an eye on your pickles after you have stored them away in a dark, cool place where they cannot freeze; and if you detect evidences of fermentation, a bulging lid, leakage, or other

signs of spoilage, do not eat or even
taste the product. Destroy it, see 613!

YELLOW CUCUMBER PICKLES

About 14 Quarts

◗ Please read about Pickling Equipment and Ingredients, 676.

The cucumbers used here are simply green ones left on the vine for a spell after ripening. The large, luscious, firm, clear slices of this pickle are served very cold with meat. Pare, cut into strips of about $1^1/2 \times 2^1/2 \times 3/4$ inches, and seed:

    **1 bushel large yellow
       cucumbers**

Soak the strips 12 hours in a:

   10% Brine, 249

Drain, rinse and drain again. Sterilize 14 one-quart jars, 662. Place in each one:

    **A slice of peeled
     horseradish: $1/2 \times 1/3 \times 1/3$
     inches
     A $1/2$-inch piece long hot red
     pepper**
    **4 sprigs seeded dill
       blossoms**
    **1 tablespoon white mustard
       seed**
    2 white peppercorns

Combine:

    3 cups water
    1 cup sugar
   **$1^1/2$ gallons distilled white
       vinegar**

Boil about 5 cups of this pickling solution at a time, enough to cover the bottom of a large saucepan to the depth of $1/2$ inch. Keep several pans going to hasten the process. Immerse in the ◗ boiling vinegar sufficient cucumber strips to cover the bottom of the pan. Let them come to the boiling point. Remove at once to the jars. Do not cook the strips longer, as it will soften them. When a jar is filled with

cucumber strips, cover with boiling mixture. Seal and process 20 minutes in a boiling-water bath, 617, for quarts. Let the pickles ripen at least 6 weeks before serving.

SWEET-SOUR YELLOW CUCUMBER PICKLES OR SENFGURKEN

About 9 Quarts

◗ Please read about Pickling Equipment and Ingredients, 676.
Pare, cut into strips about $1^1/2 \times 2^1/2 \times 3/4$ inches, and seed:

   **12 large yellow cucumbers, see
      above**

Soak them for 12 hours in:

   10% Brine, 249

Drain, rinse and drain again. Have ready 8 or 10 sterilized quart jars, 662. Prepare the following mixture:

    1 gallon pickling vinegar, 677
    8 cups sugar
   $1/4$ cup mustard seed

Place in a cloth bag and add to this solution:

   $3/4$ cup whole mixed spices

◗ Boil about 5 cups of the mixture at a time, enough to cover the bottom of a large stainless steel or enamel pan to a depth of about $1/2$ inch. Place bag of spices in pan. Immerse in the boiling vinegar sufficient cucumber strips to cover the pan bottom. Bring vinegar to boiling point. Remove strips at once. Place them in jars and fill jars with boiling vinegar mixture. Seal and process 20 minutes in a boiling-water bath, 617, for quarts.

SWEET-SOUR SPICED CUCUMBER PICKLES

About 24 Pints

◗ Please read about Pickling Equipment and Ingredients, 676.
These are wonderfully good. Scrub:

20 lb. very small cucumbers

Soak 24 hours in brine made of:

1 cup Pickling Salt, 249
3 quarts water: 12 cups

Remove from brine and add boiling water to cover. Drain quickly in a colander and pack closely while hot in sterilized jars, 662. Cover at once with the following vinegar mixture ▶ just at boiling point:

1 gallon cider vinegar
11 cups sugar

flavored with a spice bag of:

2 oz. whole mixed pickling
spices
1 oz. stick cinnamon
1 teaspoon cloves

Seal jars at once. Process 15 minutes in boiling-water bath, 617, for pints

BREAD AND BUTTER PICKLES

About 12 Pints

▶ Please read about Pickling Equipment and Ingredients, 676.

Wash well:

1 gallon medium-sized
cucumbers: 4 quarts
6 to 12 large peeled onions
or about 3 cups small white
ones
2 green or red peppers, seeds
and membrane removed

Proportions for this recipe may vary, as onion fanciers use the larger amount, and even more, of their beloved vegetable. Cut the unpared cucumbers and the peeled onions into the thinnest slices possible. Shred or chop the peppers. Place vegetables in a bowl. Pour over them:

1/2 cup Pickling Salt, 249

Place in refrigerator 12 hours, covered with weighted lid. Drain vegetables. Rinse in cold water. Drain again thoroughly. A cloth bag similar to a jelly bag is frequently used to let all

the moisture drip from them. Prepare the following syrup:

4 cups mild cider vinegar
4 cups white or brown sugar
1 1/2 teaspoons turmeric or
allspice
2 tablespoons mustard seed
1 1/2 teaspoons celery seed
1/2 teaspoon ground cloves or
1-inch stick cinnamon

Bring these ingredients ▶ just to the boiling point. Add vegetables gradually with very little stirring. Heat to the scalding point but do not let them boil. Pour the pickles into hot sterile jars. Seal and process 15 minutes in a boiling-water bath, 617, for pints.

PICKLED GHERKINS OR CORNICHONS

About 3 Pints

Wash thoroughly:

5 dozen very small French
gherkins or tiny pickling
cucumbers

Dry gherkins and place in glass or enameled bowl. Cover with:

3/4 cup Pickling Salt, 249

Let mixture stand 24 hours. Drain and pack in sterile jars filled to 1 1/4 inches of top. Add to each jar:

5 white peppercorns
1/2 bay leaf
A few sprigs tarragon

Fill jars with boiling:

White wine vinegar
flavored with tarragon

Let jars stand covered overnight, during which period the gherkins will lose their green color. Drain vinegar from jars into an enamel saucepan and add to suit your taste:

Pickling, Salt, 249

Bring vinegar to boiling point. Remove liquid from heat; let cool to lukewarm. Pour it over the gherkins which will regain their color. These little pickles may be further flavored by the addition of:

(**12 or more Pickled Onions, 683**)

Seal jars. Process 15 minutes in a boiling-water bath, 617, for pints.

MUSTARD PICKLE OR CHOW CHOW

About 12 Pints

This formula meets with such enthusiastic approval that we are often tempted to abandon all other mixed pickle recipes.

❯ Please read about Pickling Equipment and Ingredients, 676.

Slice, unpared if tender:

1 quart or more green cucumbers

Cover 12 hours with:

10% Brine, 249

Keep covered until ready to use. Slice to make about 3 quarts of mixed green vegetables:

Green tomatoes, snap beans, green peppers, etc.

Pour over the vegetables to cover:

Boiling salted water: 1 teaspoon salt to 1 quart water

and bring to the boiling point. Drain well and set aside. Peel and slice into a separate bowl:

2 dozen small onions

Break into florets and add:

1 large cauliflower

Slice and add:

2 dozen or more small Pickled Gherkins, 679

Pour over them sufficient boiling salted water to cover. Bring to the boiling point. Drain well and combine all vegetables. Have ready the following mustard sauce prepared in an enamel pan.

Combine and stir until smooth:

1¹/₂ cups flour
6 tablespoons dry mustard
1¹/₂ tablespoons turmeric
2 cups mild cider vinegar

Bring ❯ just to the boiling point:

2 quarts mild cider vinegar
2¹/₂ cups sugar
3 tablespoons celery seed

Slowly add the flour mixture, stirring constantly. When the sauce is smooth and boiling, combine it with the well-drained vegetables. Add if needed:

Salt

Place the pickle in sterile jars and seal. Process 15 minutes in boiling-water bath, 617, for pints.

CURRY SAUCE PICKLE

About 16 Pints

❯ Please read about Pickling Equipment and Ingredients, 676.

Pare, core, seed and chop finely:

12 large green cucumbers

Add:

6 finely chopped large onions
2 finely chopped sweet red peppers, seeds and membrane removed

Sprinkle these ingredients with:

¹/₄ cup Pickling Salt, 249

Let stand refrigerated 3 hours. Drain, rinse, and drain again. Peel and cook until soft:

12 large tomatoes

Combine vegetables and tomatoes. Add to the above and ❯ simmer 30 minutes:

4 teaspoons curry powder
2 teaspoons celery seed
2 tablespoons brown sugar
2 cups cider vinegar

Pack the pickle into sterile jars, seal and process 15 minutes in boiling-water bath, 617, for pints.

OLIVE OIL PICKLE

Approximately 6 Pints

Wash:

24 cucumbers, 3 to 4 inches long

Cut them, unpared, into very thin slices. Sprinkle them with:

½ cup Pickling Salt, 249

Let them stand 3 hours. Drain well. Peel, slice very finely and add:

2 small onions

Combine and add:

1 cup white mustard seed
1 tablespoon celery seed
½ cup olive oil
4 cups vinegar

Mix all the ingredients thoroughly. Place them in sterile jars and seal. Process15 minutes in a boiling-water bath, 617, for pints. The pickle should ripen for 3 weeks.

PICCALILLI

Approximately 10 Pints

◗ Please read about Pickling Equipment and Ingredients, 676.

Cut into very thin slices or dice:

4 quarts small green cucumbers

Seed, remove membranes and slice:

4 medium-sized green peppers

Skin and slice:

4 medium-sized onions

Place these ingredients for 12 hours in:

10% Brine, 249

Drain well. Bring ◗ just to the boiling point:

1 quart cider vinegar
4½ cups sugar

Place in a bag and add:

2½ tablespoons whole mixed spices
½ tablespoon celery seed
½ tablespoon mustard seed

Add the drained vegetables. Bring to the boiling point. Remove spices. Place the pickle in sterile jars, seal and process 15 minutes in boiling-water bath, 617, for pints.

GREEN TOMATO PICKLE OR RELISH

About 12 Pints

Please read about Pickling Equipment and Ingredients, 676.

Wash and cut into thin slices:

1 peck green tomatoes

Peel, cut into thin slices and add:

12 large onions

Sprinkle with

1 cup Pickling Salt, 249

Let stand refrigerated12 hours. Rinse in clear water and drain. Heat to the boiling point:

3 quarts cider vinegar

Seed, remove membranes and add to the vinegar:

12 thinly sliced green peppers
6 diced sweet red peppers

Add:

12 minced cloves garlic
4 lb. brown sugar
2 tablespoons dry mustard
1 tablespoon salt

Add the tomatoes and onions. Tie in a cloth bag and add:

2 tablespoons whole cloves
2 sticks cinnamon: 3 inches each
2 tablespoons powdered ginger
1 tablespoon celery seed

◗ Simmer until tomatoes are transparent, about 1 hour. Stir frequently. Place the pickle in sterile jars and seal. Process 15 minutes in a boiling-water bath, 617, for pints. A fan writes that he puts the finished product in his ⚙ blender for a second or two before bottling his favorite relish.

GREEN TOMATO MOCK MINCEMEAT

About 10 Pints

For a meat-based mincemeat, see 630.
Sprinkle and let stand 1 hour:

1 tablespoon salt

over:

20 small cored and chopped green tomatoes

Drain the tomatoes, cover with boiling water and let stand 5 minutes before draining. Grate the rind and chop the pulp of:

1 orange

Mix the orange and tomatoes in a large saucepan and add:

12 medium pared, chopped apples
1 lb. seeded raisins
1¹/₂ cups chopped suet
3¹/₂ cups firmly packed brown sugar
¹/₂ cup vinegar
2 teaspoons cinnamon
1 teaspoon each cloves and nutmeg
¹/₂ teaspoon ginger

Cook mixture until boiling hot. Pour into hot sterile jars, leaving 1-inch headroom. Process pints 25 minutes at 10 pounds pressure, 616.

TART CORN RELISH

About 6 Pints

◗ Please read about Pickling Equipment and Ingredients, 676. Also please note: this is an unthickened relish—but a succulent one. If you should hanker after it in winter, use 9 cups canned or frozen kernel corn.
Boil 5 minutes:

18 medium-sized ears corn

Cut the kernels from cobs.
Put through a food grinder:

1 head green cabbage
8 peeled white onions

6 green peppers, seeds and membrane removed
6 small hot red peppers

Combine these ingredients with the corn and:

2 teaspoons celery seed
2 teaspoons mustard seed
2 quarts vinegar
¹/₄ cup salt
2 cups sugar
(¹/₃ cup minced pimiento)

Bring ◗ just to the boiling point and simmer the relish for 35 minutes. Place in sterile jars, leaving ¹/₄-inch headroom, seal, and process 15 minutes in boiling-water bath, 617, for pints.

PICKLED DILLED BEANS

4 Pints

◗ Please read about Pickling Equipment and Ingredients, 676.
Pack lengthwise in hot sterile jars, leaving ¹/₄-inch headroom:

2 lb. stemmed tender green beans

To each pint jar add:

¹/₄ teaspoon cayenne pepper
1 clove garlic
1 head dill or 1¹/₂ tablespoons dill seed

Bring to boil:

2¹/₂ cups water
2¹/₂ cups vinegar
¹/₄ cup salt

Pour the mixture over the beans, leaving ¹/₄-inch headroom. Seal the jars and process 15 minutes in a boiling-water bath, 617, for pints.

PICKLED CARROT STICKS

2 Pints

Colorful and tasty as an hors d'oeuvre.
Cook in boiling salted water 10 minutes:

1 lb. peeled, thinly sliced
   carrots

Meanwhile bring to a boil, then simmer 3 minutes:

3/4 cup vinegar
3/4 cup water
1/2 cup sugar
1 teaspoon mixed whole
   pickling spices

Drain the carrots and pack in hot sterilized jars, leaving 1/2-inch headroom. Cover with the hot pickling liquid, seal and process 15 minutes in a boiling-water bath, 617, for pints.

PICKLED ONIONS

♦ Please read about Pickling Equipment and Ingredients, 676.
To peel, cover with boiling water:

4 quarts small white onions

Let the onions stand for 2 minutes. Drain and dip in cold water, then peel. Soak onions refrigerated for 24 hours in:

10% Brine, 249, to cover

Drain and rinse well. Bring ♦ just to the boiling point:

2 quarts white vinegar
2 cups sugar

Add onions and ♦ simmer for 3 minutes. Place at once in sterile jars. Cover with the vinegar. Add to each quart jar:

1/2 inch red hot pepper pod
1/8 bay leaf
(3 cloves without heads)

Seal and process 30 minutes in boiling-water bath, 617.

PICKLED ZUCCHINI

Wash and cut into thin slices:

2 lb. unpeeled small zucchini
2 peeled medium-sized
   onions

Cover the above with cold water and add:

1/4 cup Pickling Salt, 249

Let stand 2 hours, then drain thoroughly. Bring to a boil for 2 minutes:

3 cups cider vinegar
2 cups sugar
1 teaspoon celery seed
2 teaspoons mustard seed
1 teaspoon turmeric

Add the zucchini and onions, remove from heat, and let stand 2 hours. Heat ingredients to the boiling point and cook 5 minutes. Pack in hot jars, leaving 1/8-inch headroom. Seal and process 15 minutes in a boiling-water bath, 617, for pints

PICKLED NASTURTIUM PODS OR SEEDS

Use these as a variation for capers.
After the blossoms fall, pick off the half-ripened:

Nasturtium seed pods

Continue as your crop develops to drop them into a boiled and strained mixture of:

1 quart white wine vinegar
2 teaspoons Pickling
   Salt, 249
1 thinly sliced onion
1/2 teaspoon each allspice,
   mace and celery seed
3 peppercorns

Keep refrigerated and use as desired.

CHILIS PRESERVED IN SHERRY

Make up this combination and use either the chilis or the sherry for flavoring.
Wash well:

Long thin red, yellow or
   green chili peppers

Pack tightly into sterile jars. Cover with:

Dry sherry

Cover and store in a cool dark place.

PICKLED WATERMELON RIND

About 10 Pints

More than acceptable in fruit cakes, if drained and finely chopped.
◗ Please read about Pickling Equipment and Ingredients, 676.

Cut before peeling and remove the green skin and pink flesh from:

**Rind of 1 large
watermelon: about 5 quarts**

Dice the rind into 1-inch cubes. Parblanch it, (I, 106), 3 minutes, until it can be pierced with a fork, ◗ but do not overcook. Drain. Make and bring ◗ just to a boil a syrup of:

**7 cups sugar
2 cups vinegar
¼ teaspoon oil of cloves
½ teaspoon oil of cinnamon**

Pour it over the rind, ◗ just covering it. Let stand overnight. Remove rind. Reboil syrup and pour over rind. Let stand overnight as before. On the third morning, pack the rind in sterile jars. Boil syrup again and pour over rind to overflowing. Seal and process 15 minutes in a boiling-water bath, 617, for pints. The flavor of this pickle may be varied by placing in each jar:

**(A star anise)
(1 to 2 teaspoons chopped
preserved ginger or
Candied Lemon Peel, 604)**

PICKLED DUTCH CHERRIES

◗ Please read about Pickling Equipment and Ingredients, 676. During processing this method needs an even temperature under 80°.

Stem, seed and put into a heavy crock:

Sour cherries

Cover with:

Distilled white vinegar

Let stand 24 hours. Drain. Measure cherries and have ready an equal amount of:

Sugar

Arrange in the crock alternate layers of cherries and sugar. Let stand 1 week, covered and weighted. ◗ Stir well daily. Ladle into sterile jars and process 15 minutes in boiling-water bath, 617, for pints. Store in a cool dark place.

SPICED PEARS

About 3 Pints

◗ Please read about Pickling Equipment and Ingredients, 676.

If you are using Bartlett or similar soft pears, choose rather underripe fruit and prepare as for Brandied Peaches, below. If you are using Kiefer, Seckel or other hard pears, prepare as follows.

Wash, peel and core:

3 lb. pears

Cook them ◗ covered until they begin to soften in:

1½ cups boiling water

Tie in a cloth bag:

**6 cinnamon sticks: 3 inches
long
2 tablespoons whole cloves
2 teaspoons whole ginger**

And ◗ simmer for 5 minutes with:

**2 cups sugar
1 cup white wine vinegar**

Add the partially tenderized pears and the liquid in which they were cooking. Simmer with vinegar syrup 3 minutes. Remove and discard spice bag. Pack fruit into hot sterile jars and cover with the hot syrup. Seal jars and process in boiling-water bath 15 minutes, 617, for pints. Store in a cool dark place.

BRANDIED PEACHES

Select ripe, firm:

Peaches

Weigh them. Rub away fuzz with a coarse towel. Make a thick syrup of equal parts of:

>   **Sugar and water: allow 1 cup sugar and 1 cup water for every lb. of fruit**

Simmer the peaches in the syrup 5 minutes. Drain and place in hot sterile jars. Pour over each jar:

>   **2 to 4 tablespoons brandy**

Pour the syrup over the fruit, filling the jars. Seal and process in boiling-water bath 15 minutes, 617, for pints. Store in a cool dark place 3 months before using. For other liqueur-flavored fruits, see 112 and 674.

INDIAN RELISH OR BASIC CHUTNEY

About 8 Pints

◗ Please read about Pickling Equipment and Ingredients, 676

Put through a food chopper or chop until very fine:

>   **12 green tomatoes**
>   **12 peeled cored tart apples**
>   **3 peeled onions**

Boil:

>   **5 cups vinegar**
>   **5 cups sugar**
>   **1 teaspoon red pepper**
>   **3 teaspoons ginger**
>   **1 teaspoon turmeric**
>   **1 teaspoon salt**

Add the chopped ingredients. ◗ Simmer for 1/2 hour. Pack the relish in sterile jars. Seal and process 15 minutes in boiling-water bath, 617, for pints.

PEACH, MANGO OR KIWI CHUTNEY

12 or 14 Pints

A good way to use up those candied fruits left over from the holiday baking.

◗ Please read about Pickling Equipment and Ingredients, 676.

>   **30 firm peaches**

or use a combination of:

>   **15 peeled tropical mangoes or kiwis and**
>   **8 medium papayas**

Mix with:

>   **3 tablespoons chopped preserved ginger**
>   **3/4 cup chopped citron**
>   **1/4 cup chopped candied lemon peel or 1/2 cup chopped preserved kumquats**

Tie in a bag the following whole spices:

>   **2 cinnamon sticks**
>   **30 whole cloves**
>   **3/4 teaspoon coriander seeds**

Make a syrup of:

>   **6 cups sugar**
>   **4 cups cider vinegar**

When the syrup ◗ just boils, add the chopped fresh and candied fruits and the spice bag. Simmer 5 minutes. Remove spice bag. Put mixture into sterile jars, seal and process 15 minutes in boiling-water bath, 617, for pints.

CURRIED APRICOT CHUTNEY

About 2 Pints

Combine and simmer for 30 minutes:

>   **2 cups water**
>   **2 cups chopped dried apricots: 11-oz. package**
>   **3/4 cup finely chopped onions**
>   **1/4 cup sugar**

In a separate pan, cook for 5 minutes:

>   **1 1/2 cups vinegar**
>   **1 teaspoon ginger**
>   **1 1/2 to 2 teaspoons curry powder**
>   **1 stick cinnamon**
>   **1/2 teaspoon salt**

You may remove the stick of cinnamon before combining the apricot and spiced vinegar mixtures. Stir in:

2 cups white raisins: 10-oz.
package

Place in sterile jars and process 10 minutes in a boiling-water bath, 617, for pints

APPLE OR GREEN TOMATO CHUTNEY

I.   About 3 Pints

◗ Please read about Pickling Equipment and Ingredients, 676.

◗ Simmer at least 2 hours or until the sauce has thickened, stirring frequently:

1 seeded chopped lemon
1 skinned chopped clove garlic
5 cups firm peeled chopped apples or green tomatoes
2¼ cups brown sugar
1½ cups seeded raisins
3 oz. chopped crystallized ginger, or ¼ cup fresh gingerroot
1½ teaspoons salt
¼ teaspoon cayenne
2 cups cider vinegar
(2 chopped red peppers, seeds and membrane removed)

Put the boiling-hot chutney in hot sterile jars and seal. Process 15 minutes in a boiling-water bath, 617, for pints.

II.   About 3 Pints

Similar to the preceding recipe—but with onions and tomatoes added.

Combine and ◗ simmer slowly for 2 hours or until thickened:

2 cups chopped seeded raisins
2 cups chopped slightly underripe green apples
1 cup minced onion
1½ teaspoons salt
6 medium-sized ripe,

skinned, quartered tomatoes
3½ cups brown sugar
1 pint cider vinegar
4 oz. white mustard seed
2 oz. preserved ginger
3 chili peppers

Place hot mixture in hot sterile jars, seal and process 15 minutes in a boiling-water bath, 617, for pints.

CHILI SAUCE

About 8 Pints

◗ Please read about Pickling Equipment and Ingredients, 676.

Wash, peel and quarter:

1 peck ripe tomatoes: 8 quarts

Put through a food grinder:

6 green peppers, seeds and membrane removed
(1 tablespoon dried hot pepper pods)
6 skinned large white onions

Add the tomatoes and:

2 cups brown sugar
3 cups cider vinegar
3 tablespoons coarse salt
1 tablespoon black pepper
1 tablespoon allspice
1 teaspoon ground cloves
1 teaspoon each ginger, cinnamon, nutmeg and celery seed
(2 tablespoons dry mustard)

◗ Simmer these ingredients slowly until very thick, about 3 hours. Stir frequently to prevent scorching. Add salt if needed. Put sauce in ◗ small sterile jars. Seal and process 15 minutes in boiling-water bath, 617, for pints. Store in cool dark place.

TOMATO CATSUP

About 20 Half-Pints

This condiment originated in Malaya, and its name derives from the native word for "taste." No other food so familiar to Americans seems to have so many variations in spelling.

◗ Please read about Pickling Equipment and Ingredients, 676.

Wash and cut into pieces:

1 peck tomatoes: 8 quarts

Add:

8 sliced medium-sized onions

2 long red peppers without seeds or membrane

◗ Simmer these ingredients until soft. Rub through a food mill, see chapter-heading illustration, 676. Add:

3/4 cup brown sugar

Tie in a bag and add:

1 tablespoon each whole allspice, cloves, mace, celery seed and peppercorns

2 inches stick cinnamon

1/2 teaspoon dry mustard

1/2 clove garlic

1 1/2 bay leaves

The spices may be varied. Boil these ingredients quickly, stirring often. ◗ Continue to stir until the quantity is reduced by one-half. Remove the spice bag. Add:

2 cups cider vinegar (Cayenne and coarse salt)

◗ Simmer the catsup for 10 minutes longer. Pour at once into sterile jars, leaving 1/8-inch headroom. Seal and process 15 minutes in a boiling-water bath, 617, for half-pints.

GRAPE CATSUP

About 4 Pints

◗ Please read about Pickling Equipment and Ingredients, 676.

Cover:

5 lb. Concord grapes

with:

1/2 cup water

Bring to a boil. Put the softened grapes through a food mill, colander or sieve and add:

5 cups sugar

2 cups vinegar

1 teaspoon salt

Tie in a bag and add to above:

1/2 cup mixed pickling spices

Simmer and stir until thick. Remove spice bag and pour the grape mixture into hot sterilized jars. Seal and process 15 minutes in a boiling-water bath, 617, for pints.

WALNUT CATSUP

About 3 1/2 Quarts

◗ Please read about Pickling Equipment and Ingredients, 676.

Pick and bruise:

100 immature green English walnuts

still so soft they can be pierced through with a needle. Put them into a crock with:

2 quarts vinegar

6 oz. salt

Cover, mash and stir daily for 8 days. Drain the liquid and put it into an enamel or stainless steel pan with:

4 oz. finely chopped anchovies

12 finely chopped shallots or 1 clove chopped garlic

1/2 cup grated fresh horseradish

1/2 teaspoon each mace, nutmeg, ginger, whole cloves and peppercorns

Cover and bring mixture to a boil, then ◗ simmer gently about 40 minutes. Filter, cool and add:

2 cups Port

Pour into sterile glass bottles. Cork well. Cover the corks with wax. Store in a cool dry place.

PICKLED HORSERADISH

Wash well in hot water:

Horseradish roots

Scrape off the skin. Have ready in a glass or stainless steel bowl a combination of:

2 cups vinegar
1 teaspoon salt

Grate, mince or ⚒ blend the scraped roots and pack in sterile jars. Cover well with the vinegar mixture. Seal and store in refrigerator.

WORCESTERSHIRE SAUCE

About 5 Half-Pints

Put into a jug:

1 quart cider vinegar
6 tablespoons Walnut Catsup, 687
5 tablespoons essence of anchovies, or 2 oz. finely chopped anchovies
1 tablespoons Chili Sauce, 686
A tiny pinch cayenne
1 teaspoon salt
1 tablespoon sugar

Cork and shake 4 times daily for 2 weeks. Strain into sterile bottles. Cork tightly and store in a cool place.

LONG-BRINE AND SOUR PICKLING

If produce is soaked for long enough period at proper temperatures, a mere brine will suffice to preserve it. The salt solution draws from the vegetables soaked in it both moisture and certain natural sugars, and these combine to form an acid bath which "cures" the produce, making it friendly to beneficial ferments and strong enough to resist the organisms that cause spoilage in food. Pickles subjected to the long-brine process

and held at 86° from 2 to 6 weeks turn, after appropriate seasoning, into "dill" types; but see our adaptation below. They may be desalted and further processed in a vinegar solution at 126° for 12 hours to make sour pickles and then in a sugar solution to become sweet-sours.

To learn the details for these long and exacting processes, read "Making Pickles and Relishes at Home" in the U.S.D.A. Home and Garden Bulletin 92.

DILL AND KOSHER DILL PICKLES

About 7 Pints

This procedure bypasses that for long-brined dill pickles. The brine is weaker and the curing more rapid; but the pickles do not keep so well, especially if home-processed. We suggest using a heated brine. Garlic, like all members of the onion family, is very susceptible to bacterial activity, so be sure to remove the garlic cloves before sealing the jars. Wash thoroughly and cut in half lengthwise:

4 lb. cucumbers

Combine and heat to the boiling point:

3 cups white vinegar
3 cups water
¹⁄₃ cup Pickling Salt, 249

If you want to create **Kosher Dills**—without benefit of clergy—add:

12 peeled sliced garlic cloves

When the boiling point is reached ▶ remove the garlic cloves. Pack the cucumbers into hot sterile jars. Add to each jar:

2 tablespoons dill seed
3 peppercorns

Fill the jars to within ¹⁄₂ inch of the top with the hot pickling liquid. Immediately adjust lids. ◗ Be sure to use lids recommended for pickling. Seal and process in boiling-water bath 15 minutes, 617, for pints.

BRINING VEGETABLES

If sufficient salt is used to brine vegetables, no fermentation can take place and no further processing is necessary. This is referred to as *dry salting*. Pack in a crock in very thin layers:

Mushrooms, beans, herbs or other vegetables

well separated with at least $1/2-$ to $3/4$-inch layers of:

Rock salt

Cover the crock tightly and store in a cool dark place. ◗ **Boil the vegetables uncovered 20 minutes before serving.** Stir frequently during this period.

SAUERKRAUT

In brining vegetables with less salt than in the recipe above, it is essential to process them in a boiling-water bath and to observe the cooking period recommended below.

◗ Please read about Pickling Equipment and Ingredients, 676.

A 2-gallon crock holds about 15 pounds of kraut. Choose sound, mature heads of:

Cabbage

Use:

1 lb. salt for 40 lb. cabbage, or 2 teaspoons salt for 1 lb. cabbage

Remove outside leaves, quarter the heads, and cut out cores. Slice the cabbage finely into $1/16$-inch shreds and mix with salt. Pack firmly in stone crocks to within 2 inches of top. Cover with a clean cloth and a plate, or any board except pine. Place a weight on the plate—heavy enough to make the brine come up to the cover and wet the cloth. When fermentation begins, remove the scum daily and place a clean cloth over the cabbage, see the chapter-heading illustration, 613. Wash the plate or board daily, too.

The best quality kraut is made at a temperature below 60° and requires at least a month of fermentation. It may be cured in less time at higher temperatures, but the kraut will not be so good. If sauerkraut turns tan, too much juice has been lost in the fermenting process. When fermentation has ceased, store the kraut in a cool place after sealing by either of the following methods: simply pour a layer of hot paraffin over the surface of the crock; or, for greater effectiveness, ◗ heat kraut to simmering temperature, about 180°; pack firmly in hot jars; add sufficient kraut juice or a weak brine—2 tablespoons salt for 1 quart water—to cover, leaving $1/2$-inch head space, and process in boiling-water bath, 617, 25 minutes for pints, 30 minutes for quarts.

◗ **Boil the sauerkraut, uncovered, 20 minutes before serving, see 613.**

INDEX

"Knowledge," said Dr. Johnson, "is of two kinds. We know a subject as our own, or we know where we can find information on it." Below we put into your hands the second kind of knowledge—a kitchen-door key which will help to open up the first.

If you want information on a certain food, you will find that the initial listing is often an "About," giving characteristics, peculiarities of handling, tests for doneness, storage needs and serving quantities. The titles which follow usually indicate how that particular food may be cooked: Sweetbreads, braised, or Fish, broiled.

In using the Index look for a noun rather than an adjective: Cake, almond, not Almond Cake; unless the modifying term is a foreign one, in which case it will be listed and lead you to an explanation. Foreign terms are frequently translated in an alternate title, thus: Pickled Fish or Escabèche, revealing a process; or, as in Senegalese or Chicken Curry Soup, showing the ingredients mainly responsible for the term. Or the recipe itself will clear your doubts—"à la mode" used with a savory food like beef will describe a stew, whereas with a sweet one, like pie or cake, it will indicate the expected scoop of ice cream. Since cooking terms, both foreign and domestic, are dealt with at the point of use, as described above, we have dispensed with a separate glossary.

Remember, too, that the book as a whole divides into three sections—The Foods We Eat, The Foods We Heat and The Foods We Keep—with Know Your Ingredients at the center of things; and that many "convenience" recipes are grouped under Lunch, Brunch and Supper Dishes. Within chapters, too, initial text or recipes often cover basic methods of preparation, and are followed, as in Fruits, Fish and Vegetables, by alphabetical listings of varieties—from Acerola to Tamarind, Carp to Sea Squab, Artichoke to Zucchini. Under Meats you will find in the Index general comments and processes, with further references to Beef, Veal, Lamb, Pork, Ham, Ground and Variety Meats and Game. In this chapter a further differentiation is made between those cuts cooked by dry heat—often a quick process—and those cooked by moist heat, which, to be effective, is always slower. Note, too, that in the listings below, you can find the illustrations immediately by looking up the *italic* numerals.

As you familiarize yourself with the **Joy**, you will need the Index less and less and will become, in the fullest sense of Dr. Johnson's words, a know-it-all. Meanwhile, happy hunting!